MODERN FINANCIAL
MARKETS AND
INSTITUTIONS

Visit the *Modern Financial Markets and Institutions* Companion Website at **www.pearsoned.co.uk/arnold** to find valuable **student** learning material including:

- Multiple choice questions to help test your understanding
- Links to relevant sites on the World Wide Web
- An online glossary to explain key terms
- Flashcards to help you prepare for exams

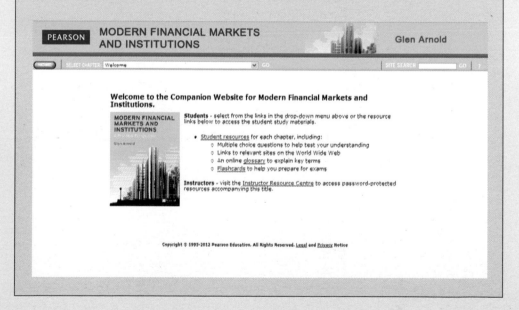

PEARSON

At Pearson, we take learning personally. Our courses and resources are available as books, online and via multi-lingual packages, helping people learn whatever, wherever and however they choose.

We work with leading authors to develop the strongest learning experiences, bringing cutting-edge thinking and best learning practice to a global market. We craft our print and digital resources to do more to help learners not only understand their content, but to see it in action and apply what they learn, whether studying or at work.

Pearson is the world's leading learning company. Our portfolio includes Penguin, Dorling Kindersley, the Financial Times and our educational business, Pearson International. We are also a leading provider of electronic learning programmes and of test development, processing and scoring services to educational institutions, corporations and professional bodies around the world.

Every day our work helps learning flourish, and wherever learning flourishes, so do people.

To learn more please visit us at: **www.pearson.com/uk**

GLEN ARNOLD BSc(Econ), PhD
University of Salford

MODERN FINANCIAL
MARKETS AND
INSTITUTIONS

A Practical Perspective

PEARSON

Harlow, England • London • New York • Boston • San Francisco • Toronto • Sydney • Auckland • Singapore • Hong Kong
Tokyo • Seoul • Taipei • New Delhi • Cape Town • São Paulo • Mexico City • Madrid • Amsterdam • Munich • Paris • Milan

Pearson Education Limited
Edinburgh Gate
Harlow
Essex CM20 2JE
England

and Associated Companies throughout the world

Visit us on the World Wide Web at:
www.pearson.com/uk

First published 2012

© Pearson Education Limited 2012

The right of Glen Arnold to be identified as author of this work has been asserted by him in accordance with the Copyright, Designs and Patents Act 1988.

ISBN: 978-0-273-73035-4

British Library Cataloguing-in-Publication Data
A catalogue record for this book is available from the British Library

Library of Congress Cataloging-in-Publication Data
A catalog record for this book is available from the Library of Congress

10 9 8 7 6 5 4 3 2 1
16 15 14 13 12

Typeset in 10/11.5pt Minion by 30
Printed and bound by Rotolito Lombarda, Italy

To Lesley, my wife, for her loving support and encouragement

Brief contents

Introduction to the book   xvii
Acknowledgements   xxii

1   The value of the financial system   1
2   Banking: retail and corporate   36
3   Investment banking and other banking   75
4   Insurance, pensions and collective investments   116
5   Money markets   167
6   Bond markets   219
7   Central banking   283
8   Equity markets   328
9   Raising share capital   375
10   Futures markets   412
11   Options and swaps   441
12   Foreign exchange markets   480
13   Trade, shipping, commodities and gold   523
14   Hedge funds and private equity   556
15   Regulation of the financial sector   602
16   The financial crisis   645

Appendix   A:1
Glossary   G:1
Index   I:1

Contents

Introduction to the book   xvii
Acknowledgements   xxii

1 The value of the financial system   1
   Learning outcomes   *1*
   The impact of these markets on our lives   2
   Banking   7
   Importance of different financial centres   9
   World without money or financial institutions   12
   Financial markets   20
   Growth in the financial services sector   20
   Debt and equity capital   23
   Primary and secondary markets   24
   Exchange-traded and OTC markets   24
   The financial institutions   24

   Concluding comments   *30*
   Key points and concepts   *31*
   References and further reading   *32*
   Websites   *33*
   Video presentations   *33*
   Case study recommendations   *33*
   Self-review questions   *34*
   Questions and problems   *34*
   Assignments   *35*
   Web-based exercises   *35*

2 Banking: retail and corporate   36
   Learning outcomes   *36*
   What is banking?   37
   Core banking   39
   Lending   40
   Payment mechanisms   46
   Corporate banking   49
   Uncommitted facilities   49
   Committed facilities   49
   Cash management   53
   Guarantees   53
   Overseas trade   53
   Foreign exchange risk management and interest risk management   53
   Other commercial banking services   54

How a bank operates   55
Liquidity management and reserves   57
Asset and liability management   61
Capital adequacy management   61
Income statements   65

Concluding comments   *67*
Key points and concepts   *67*
References and further reading   *71*
Websites   *71*
Video presentations   *71*
Case study recommendations   *71*
Self-review questions   *72*
Questions and problems   *73*
Assignments   *73*
Web-based exercises   *74*

3   Investment banking and other banking   75
    Learning outcomes   *75*
    Investment banking   76
    Global investment banks   81
    Corporate and government assistance   82
    Market activities   86
    International banking   97
    The mutuals   100
    Finance houses   103
    Islamic banking   107

    Concluding comments   *108*
    Key points and concepts   *109*
    References and further reading   *112*
    Websites   *112*
    Video presentations   *112*
    Case study recommendations   *112*
    Self-review questions   *113*
    Questions and problems   *114*
    Assignments   *115*
    Web-based exercises   *115*

4   Insurance, pensions, and collective investments   116
    Learning outcomes   *116*
    Insurance   117
    The London market   124
    Pensions   131
    Pension fund asset holdings   138
    Regulations   140
    Collective investment   142

    Concluding comments   *158*
    Key points and concepts   *158*
    References and further reading   *161*
    Websites   *162*
    Video presentations   *162*
    Case study recommendations   *162*
    Self-review questions   *163*
    Questions and problems   *164*

Assignments 165
Web-based exercises 166

5 Money markets 167

Learning outcomes 167
Interest often comes from discount pricing 168
The markets in short-term money 169
Money market funds 170
Functions of money 171
The time value of money 172
The interbank market 174
Eurocurrency 178
Treasury bills 180
Central banks 187
Commercial paper 187
Credit ratings 190
Repos 192
Local authority/municipal bills 195
Certificate of deposits (CDs) 195
Bills of exchange/banker's acceptances 197
Money market interest rates in the *Financial Times* 200
Comparing interest rates 200

Concluding comments 203
Key points and concepts 204
Appendix 5.1 Converting from a 365-day basis to a 360-day basis 207
Appendix 5.2 Mathematical tools for finance 207
References and further reading 215
Websites 216
Video presentations 216
Case study recommendations 216
Self-review questions 216
Questions and problems 217
Assignments 218
Web-based exercises 218

6 Bond markets 219

Learning outcomes 219
Bonds 221
Government bond markets 222
Government bonds around the world 228
Corporate bonds 232
High-yield (junk) bonds 240
Local authority/municipal bonds 243
Convertible bonds 243
Strip bonds 245
Securitisation 246
Covered bonds 250
Foreign bonds 251
Eurobonds (international bonds) 252
Euro medium-term notes and domestic medium-term notes 255
Islamic bonds (*sukuk*) 257
Valuing bonds 258
Duration 265
Demand and supply curves for bonds 268
The term structure of interest rates 271

Concluding comments   274
Key points and concepts   275
References and further reading   278
Websites   278
Video presentations   279
Case study recommendations   279
Self-review questions   279
Questions and problems   280
Assignments   282
Web-based exercises   282

7   Central banking   283

Learning outcomes   283
Monetary policy   285
How monetary policy impacts the economy   294
Safety and soundness of the financial system   300
Other activities of central banks   316
Bank of England   318
European Central Bank   319
The US Federal Reserve   320

Concluding comments   321
Key points and concepts   321
References and further reading   324
Websites   325
Video presentations   325
Case study recommendations   325
Self-review questions   326
Questions and problems   326
Web-based exercises   327

8   Equity markets   328

Learning outcomes   328
The value of joint stock enterprises/a little history   329
Ordinary shares (equity)   330
Preference shares   332
Some unusual types of shares   333
Stock exchanges around the world   335
The importance of a well-run stock exchange   338
New trading systems   342
The London Stock Exchange   354
How stock exchanges work   359
Share borrowing, lending and shorting   366
The ownership of UK shares   366

Concluding comments   368
Key points and concepts   369
References and further reading   371
Websites   371
Video presentations   372
Case study recommendations   372
Self-review questions   372
Questions and problems   373
Assignments   374
Web-based exercises   374

9   Raising share capital   375

    Learning outcomes   *375*
    Floating on the Main Market of the London Stock Exchange   376
    Post-listing obligations   385
    The Alternative Investment Market (AIM)   387
    PLUS   389
    Understanding the figures in the financial pages   390
    Rights issues   396
    Placings, open offers and clawback   403
    Scrip issues, scrip dividends, splits and consolidation   404
    Share buy-backs and special dividends   404
    Warrants   405

    Concluding comments   *405*
    Key points and concepts   *405*
    References and further reading   *408*
    Websites   *408*
    Video presentations   *409*
    Case study recommendations   *409*
    Self-review questions   *409*
    Questions and problems   *410*
    Assignments   *411*
    Web-based exercises   *411*

10   Futures markets   412

    Learning outcomes   *412*
    What is a derivative?   413
    Forwards   414
    Futures   415
    Settlement   420
    Over-the-counter (OTC) and exchange-traded derivatives   422
    Buying and selling futures   425
    Single stock futures   425
    Short-term interest rate futures   427
    Forward rate agreements (FRAs)   430
    Derivatives users   431

    Concluding comments   *433*
    Key points and concepts   *433*
    References and further reading   *435*
    Websites   *435*
    Video presentations   *435*
    Case study recommendations   *436*
    Self-review questions   *436*
    Questions and problems   *437*
    Assignments   *439*
    Web-based exercises   *440*

11   Options and swaps   441
    Learning outcomes   *441*
    Options   442
    Using share options to reduce risk: hedging   449
    Index options   451
    A comparison of options, futures, forwards and FRAs   453
    Spread betting   453
    Contracts for difference   457

Caps   457
Swaps   459
The relationship between FRAs and swaps   465
Credit default swap (CDS)   467

Concluding comments   471
Key points and concepts   471
Appendix 11.1 Option pricing   473
References and further reading   474
Websites   475
Video presentations   475
Case study recommendations   475
Self-review questions   475
Questions and problems   476
Assignments   479
Web-based exercises   479

12 Foreign exchange markets   480
Learning outcomes   480
The foreign exchange markets   481
FX trading   484
Exchange rates   486
Exchange rate regimes   492
FX volatility and its effects   494
Dealing with exchange rate risk   497
Exchange rate determination   507
Interest rate parity theory   510
Expectations theory   513
The influence of a current account deficit and capital flows   513
Efficiency of FX markets   514

Concluding comments   515
Key points and concepts   515
References and further reading   517
Websites   518
Video presentations   518
Case study recommendations   518
Self-review questions   519
Questions and problems   520
Assignments   522
Web-based exercises   522

13 Trade, shipping, commodities and gold   523
Learning outcomes   523
Trade   524
Shipping   528
Commodities   534
Gold   548

Concluding comments   550
Key points and concepts   551
References and further reading   552
Websites   552
Video presentations   553
Case study recommendations   553
Self-review questions   553
Questions and problems   554

Assignments 554
Web-based exercises 555

14 Hedge funds and private equity 556

Learning outcomes 556
Hedge funds 558
Hedge fund strategies 574
Prime brokerage 578
Private equity 578
Private equity categories 589
Private equity providers 590

Concluding comments 594
Key points and concepts 594
References and further reading 597
Websites 598
Video presentations 598
Case study recommendations 598
Self-review questions 599
Questions and problems 599
Assignments 600
Web-based exercises 600

15 Regulation of the financial sector 602

Learning outcomes 602
Why regulate? 603
The dangers to watch out for in a regulatory system 609
Types of regulation 612
Regulation of UK financial services 615
European Union regulation 631
Global regulation 636
Some gaps in the system? 636

Concluding comments 638
Key points and concepts 638
References and further reading 641
Websites 641
Video presentations 641
Case study recommendations 642
Self-review questions 642
Questions and problems 643
Assignments 644
Web-based exercises 644

16 The financial crisis 645

Learning outcomes 645
The autistic mathematicians and the autistic financial economists 646
Reflexivity 652
Some of the more proximate causes of the crisis 660
The crash 667
Government actions 671

Concluding comments 673
Key points and concepts 674
References and further reading 675
Video presentations 677

Case study recommendations   678
Self-review questions   678
Questions and problems   679

Appendices   A:1

  I Future value of £1 at compound interest   A:2
 II Present value of £1 at compound interest   A:3
III Present value of an annuity of £1 at compound interest   A:4
IV Future value of an annuity of £1 at compound interest   A:5
 V Answers to the mathematical tools exercises in Chapter 5, Appendix 5.2   A:6
VI Answers to end-of-chapter numerical questions   A:7

Glossary   G:1
Index   I:1

Supporting resources

Visit **www.pearsoned.co.uk/arnold** to find valuable online resources

Companion Website for students

- Multiple choice questions to help test your understanding

- Links to relevant sites on the World Wide Web

- An online glossary to explain key terms

- Flashcards to help you prepare for exams

For instructors

- Complete, downloadable Instructor's Manual

- PowerPoint slides that can be downloaded and used for presentations

- Testbank of question material

Also: The Companion Website provides the following features:

- Search tool to help locate specific items of content

- E-mail results and profile tools to send results of quizzes to instructors

- Online help and support to assist with website usage and troubleshooting

For more information please contact your local Pearson Education sales representative or visit **www.pearsoned.co.uk/arnold**

Introduction to the book

Aims of the book

The world of financial markets and institutions is fascinating. In the years following the financial crisis of 2008 it has become clear to everyone that their effective functioning is crucial for the well-being of our societies. If they are badly run then we all suffer. It follows that a wider understanding of the roles they play and their operations is desirable. This book is a contribution to that wider understanding. Despite being an introductory book, building from the assumption of no knowledge of finance, it takes the reader to a high level of competence in a series of easily surmountable steps.

Themes in the book

Practical orientation

There is a heavy emphasis on practical understanding, being pitched at those readers needing a good working knowledge of the financial system rather than those who need high algebra, complex theoretical constructs and public policy prescriptions.

Clear, accessible style

Great care has been taken to explain sometimes difficult topics in an interesting and comprehensible way. An informal language style and an incremental approach lead the reader to a high level of knowledge with as little pain as possible. The large panel of reviewers of the book assisted in the process of developing a text that is, I hope, comprehensive and easy to read.

Real-world relevance

Experience of teaching finance and investment to undergraduates, postgraduates and fund managers in the City has led to the conclusion that, in order to generate enthusiasm and commitment to the subject, it is vital continually to show the relevance of the material to what is going on in the world beyond the textbook. Therefore, this book incorporates vignettes/short case studies as well as plenty of examples of real companies making decisions which draw on the models, concepts and ideas of financial management.

An international perspective

The richly integrated world of modern finance requires that a text of this nature reflects the globalised character of much financial activity. There is a slight bias to the UK financial system (the world's leading financial centre) but also regular reference to international financial markets and institutions. I have been careful to avoid giving a parochial perspective. The financial world has moved on in the last few years with the development of new financial markets and methods of trading, and this is fully reflected in the text.

Real-world case examples

The publishers are part of the Pearson Group, which includes the *Financial Times* and part ownership of *The Economist*. It has been possible to include much more than the usual quantity of real-world case examples in this book by drawing on material from the *Financial Times* and *The Economist*. The aim of these extracts is to bring the subject of finance to life for readers. A typical example is shown in Exhibit 1, which is used to illustrate some of the financial issues explored in the book.

Starting a new internet business requires a lot of money. In 2011 Perform sold shares when it joined the London Stock Exchange to raise a substantial sum to permit it to take its online broadcasting model to a number of new countries. Stock markets not only allow companies to raise money for expansion but also provide an environment for existing shareholders to buy and sell shares among themselves. We look at the workings of share markets in Chapter 8 and at the different ways of raising equity finance in Chapter 9.

Exhibit 1

Perform plans to raise £70m via flotation

by Tim Bradshaw

Perform is set to become the first British digital-media company since Moneysupermarket.com in 2007 to float on London's main market.

The company, which is best known for facilitating an online-only broadcast of an England-Ukraine football match in 2009, provides a variety of online sports content to third parties, mainly video for betting and newspaper sites, as well as running its own services such as Goal.com.

In total, its content reaches 95m unique users a month, generating £64.7m in revenues from advertising, sponsorship and payments from customer sites.

Perform plans to raise £70m to expand internationally, including acquisitions.

Given its compound annual sales growth rate of more than 50 per cent in the past three years, the relative scarcity of London-listed digital media companies and recent valuations from similar groups such as Netflix and Mail.ru, people close to the company believe it could achieve a value upon flotation in excess of £500m.

Perform's business model rests on buying online distribution rights to live and archived content from football leagues, tennis tournaments and other sports groups.

This video is then packaged into a feed and sold to websites, such as Betfair and Bet365, who can use it to encourage in-line betting, where punters place bets in the middle of a live match. Such arrangements,

which provide Perform with a fixed licence-fee revenue, are currently the largest part of its business.

However, Mr Slipper believes advertising and sponsorship is likely to become the main source of revenue, via its YouTube-like ePlayer, which newspapers such as the Daily Mail embed in their sites. Revenue is shared with the publisher.

Credit Suisse, Morgan Stanley and UBS are acting as joint bookrunners.

Source: *Financial Times*, 11 March 2011, p. 20. Reprinted with permission.

Note that Perform employed the investment banks of Credit Suisse, Morgan Stanley and UBS to assist with the transition to a stock market float and to help sell the shares (they acted as joint 'bookrunners' to drum up interest in the shares and get the technicalities right). Perform also plans to acquire other companies with its newly raised money. Investment banks have teams of people to guide companies undertaking these sorts of transactions. Indeed, investment banks undertake a wide variety of advisory work for companies (from helping them to raise debt finance to making use of derivatives) as well as much market trading-related work. Chapter 3 covers investment banking.

The buyers of Perform's shares are likely to be the major investing institutions, including pension funds, insurance companies, as well as unit trusts and mutual funds. These are discussed in Chapter 4.

In both its high-growth phase from a small company and its new form as a publicly listed company, Perform valued the services provided by the major commercial banks, such as transferring money by cheque or electronic transfer, providing interest on cash balances or supplying loans to help growth. Commercial banking is described in Chapter 2.

Then there are the financial institutions supporting businesses by financing equipment on leases or hire purchase. So, Perform may lease its computers, servers and photocopiers, for example. The finance houses providing this sort of service are discussed in Chapter 3.

In years to come Perform may choose to raise more long-term debt finance by selling bonds to investors (Chapter 6) or raise money that is to be repaid over a period of a few days or weeks in the money markets (Chapter 5).

Given that Perform is to expand internationally it will have to face the risk of exchange rates changing and perhaps decide to take mitigating action to reduce those risks (Chapter 12 describes the currency markets). Also, the question arises of whether the company should use derivative financial instruments, such as futures, options and swaps, to reduce its risk exposure to other risks such as that of interest rate changes. (See Chapters 10 and 11 for a description of derivatives and their practical use.)

The financial sector also provides services to oil the wheels of international trade by reducing the risk of granting credit to overseas customers. Chapter 13 covers this as well as the markets in shipping, commodities and gold.

Many internet companies would not exist without the money pumped into them by venture capitalists, who take a high risk by buying shares in young, fast-growing companies. Chapter 14 considers the private equity industry alongside the hedge fund business, which arguably enhances the efficiency of the mechanism for allocating capital to companies.

The book also discusses the need to have ordered, stable and fair markets to encourage funds to flow from savers with money to invest to companies with projects needing funding, thus allowing the building of new factories, offices and websites. Chapter 15 discusses the regulatory systems designed to increase confidence and protect financial market participants, while Chapter 7 explains the role of central banks in ensuring the system as a whole is safe from collapse, as well as in controlling inflation and inspecting individual banks to ensure they are run prudently.

Target readership

The book is aimed at undergraduates of accounting and finance, business/management studies, banking and economics, as well as postgraduate students on MBA/MSc courses in the UK, Europe and the rest of the world.

Those entering the banking, insurance, fund management and other financial services industries should find the book useful.

The practising manager, whether or not they are a specialist in financial decision making, should also find the book useful – not least to understand the language and concepts of business and financial markets.

Students studying for examinations for the professional bodies will benefit from this text. The material is valuable for those working towards a qualification of one of the following organisations:

- Chartered Financial Analyst Institute
- Chartered Institute of Bankers
- UK Society of Investment Professionals
- Association of Corporate Treasurers
- Institute of Chartered Accountants in England and Wales
- Institute of Chartered Accountants of Scotland
- Chartered Institute of Public Finance and Accountancy
- Association of Chartered Certified Accountants
- Chartered Institute of Management Accountants
- Institute of Chartered Secretaries and Administrators

Student learning features

Each chapter has the following elements to help the learning process:

- *Introduction* The intention here is to engage the reader by discussing the importance and relevance of the topic to real businesses and individuals.

- *Learning objectives* This section sets out the expected competencies to be gained by reading the chapter.

- *Worked examples* New techniques are illustrated in the text, with sections which present problems, followed by detailed answers.

- *Mathematical explanations* Students with limited mathematical ability should not be put off by this text. The basics are covered early and in a simple style. New skills are fully explained and illustrated, as and when required.

- *Case studies and articles* Extracts from recent articles from the *Financial Times*, *The Economist* and other sources are used to demonstrate the arguments in the chapter, to add a different dimension to an issue, or merely to show that it is worth taking time to understand the material because this sort of decision is being made in day-to-day business.

- *Key points and concepts* At the end of each chapter there is an outline of the essentials of what has been covered. New concepts, jargon and equations are summarised for easy referral.

- *References and further reading* One of the features of this text is the short commentaries in the lists of articles and books referred to in the body of the chapter, or which are suggested for the interested student who wishes to pursue a topic in greater depth. These allow students to be selective in their follow-up reading. So if, for example, a particular article takes a high-level, algebraic and theoretical approach or is an easy-to-read introduction to the subject, this is highlighted, helping the student to decide whether they should obtain the article.

- *Websites* A list of useful websites is also included.

- *Self-review questions* These short questions are designed to prompt the reader to recall the main elements of the topic. They can act as a revision aid and highlight areas requiring more attention.

- *Essay questions and problems* These vary in the amount of time required, from 5 minutes to 45 minutes or more. They allow the student to demonstrate a thorough understanding of the material presented in the chapter. Some of these questions necessitate the integration of knowledge from previous chapters with the present chapter. The answers to the numerical questions can be found in Appendix VI at the end of the book.

- *Assignments* These are projects which require the reader to investigate real-world practice and relate this to the concepts and techniques learned in the chapter. These assignments can be used both as learning aids and as a way of helping firms or individuals to examine the relationship between current practice and finance theory and frameworks.

- *Web-based assignments* These are designed to encourage searches for up-to-date information from the internet and compilation of material to be presented in a report or essay form to consolidate knowledge gained from the chapter and make the connection with the world of finance as of now.

- *Recommended case studies* A list of case studies relevant to the chapter material is provided. These case studies are drawn from the Harvard Business School website.

At the end of the book there are also the following elements:

- *Appendices* These comprise a future value of £1 table (Appendix I), present value of £1 table (Appendix II), present value of an annuity table (Appendix III), future value of an annuity (Appendix IV), answers to questions in Chapter 5, a review of mathematical tools for finance (Appendix V), and answers to the numerical questions and problems (Appendix VI). Answers to discussion questions, essay and report questions can be found by reading the text.

- *Glossary* There is an extensive glossary of terms, allowing the student quickly to find the meaning of new technical terms or jargon.

Support for students and lecturers

The website dedicated to this book contains a section designed to add value to the student learning process and also includes a section for lecturers who adopt the book. Go to www.pearsoned.co.uk/arnold to access:

Companion Website for students

- Multiple choice questions to help test your understanding
- Links to relevant sites on the World Wide Web
- An online glossary to explain key terms
- Flashcards to help you prepare for exams

For instructors

- Complete, downloadable Instructor's Manual
- PowerPoint slides that can be downloaded and used for presentations
- Testbank of question material

Also: the Companion Website provides the following features:

- Search tool to help locate specific items of content
- E-mail results and profile tools to send results of quizzes to instructors
- Online help and support to assist with website usage and troubleshooting

Acknowledgements

Any work of this kind is a team effort and I would like to thank a number of people who helped to bring this project to fruition over a period of two years.

Susan Henton, my personal assistant, contributed enormously to the content of the book. She searched for data, grappled with complex material and helped to write key sections of the text. The cheerful and willing way she gets on with tasks is a real blessing. They say that you should always hire people smarter than yourself. I have certainly done that with Susan. Her English is much better than mine. She is also getting very good at investment and finance – I'll soon be out of a job!

Rowland Fox read through early draft chapters and made valuable suggestions for improvement.

The team at Pearson Education have been highly professional and very supportive (and patient with me, despite missed deadlines). I would particularly like to thank Kate Brewin, Katie Rowland, Gemma Papageorgiou, Ellen Morgan, Matthew Smith and Carole Drummond.

The academic review panel who made valuable suggestions for improving the text: Ken Hori, Birkbeck, University of London; Hui-Fai Shing, Royal Holloway, University of London; Elena Beccalli, Università Cattolica Milano and London School of Economics.

Publisher's acknowledgements

We are grateful to the following for permission to reproduce copyright material:

Financial Times

Exhibit 1. from Perform plans to raise £70m via flotation, *Financial Times*, 11/03/2011, p. 20 (Tim Bradshaw); Exhibit 1.9 from HK eclipses rivals as the place to list, *Financial Times*, 07/10/2010, p. 3 (Robert Cookson); Exhibit 1.16 from Singh commits India to reform plan, *Financial Times*, 09/11/2009, p. 12 (James Lamont); Exhibit 2.2 from Too early to declare the death of 'universal banking', *Financial Times*, 15/01/2009, p. 20 (Larsen, P. L.); Exhibit 2.5 from Slow but inexorable move to online banking, *Financial Times*, 07/07/2009, p. 18 (Kelleher, E.); Exhibit 2.6 from Syndicated loan sector shows fresh signs of life, *Financial Times*, 17/09/2009, p. 39 (Sakoui, A. and Bullock, N.), Copyright © Financial Times Ltd; Exhibit 2.7 from Liquidity rule change sparks fear of harm to City, *Financial Times*, 06/10/2009, p. 21 (Masters, B. and Jenkins, P.), Copyright © Financial Times Ltd; Exhibit 2.9 from Afghan savers lay siege to Kabul bank, *Financial Times*, 03/09/2010, Copyright © Financial Times Ltd; Exhibit 2.10 from Chinese banks set to increase reserves, *Financial Times*, 03/05/2010, p. 20 (Anderlini, J.), Copyright © Financial Times Ltd; Exhibit 2.11 from Customers feel pinch as lenders pass on the pain and Margins pressured in effort to attract deposits, *Financial Times*, 19/06/2009, p. 19 (Croft, J.), Copyright © Financial Times Ltd; Exhibit 3.1 from Bonuses for performers to rise, *Financial Times*, 05/12/2009 (Megan Murphy and Lina Saigol); Exhibit 3.2 from Pressure rises for formal bank fees enquiry, *Financial Times*, 26/03/2010, p. 6 (Kate Burgess); Exhibit 3.3 from Outsized risk and regulation inhibit entrants, *Financial Times*, 24/03/2010, p. 22 (Patrick Jenkins); Exhibit 3.4 from Conflicts of interest bubble beneath the surface, *Financial Times*, 14/12/2009, p. 21 (Lina Saigol); Exhibit 3.5 from Nomura takeover of Tricorn will see reversal of flight to boutiques, *Financial Times*, 16/12/2009, p. 21 (Lina Saigol); Exhibit 3.6 from Investors angered as costs soar over $750m, *Financial Times*, 02/06/2010, p. 21 (Lina Saigol); Exhibit 3.7 from Advisors set to pitch for share sale of rescued banks, *Financial Times*, 18/07/2009, p. 2 (George Parker and Patrick Jenkins); Exhibit 3.8 from Broking under scrutiny as banks seek fees, *Financial Times*, 08/10/2010, p. 21 (Lina Saigol and Megan Murphy); Exhibit 3.9 from Leaving a lasting Wall Street legacy, *Financial Times*, 28/06/2010, p. 23 (Justin Baer); Exhibit 3.10 from The teams may be no more but the 'flow prop' will be harder to stop, *Financial Times*, 25/01/2010, p. 9 (Patrick Jenkins); Exhibit 3.11 from Goldman looking at an own goal, *Financial Times*, 05/03/2010, p. 21 (Lina Saigol); Exhibit 3.12 from Prop-hostile climate throws up some tough calls for banks, *Financial Times*, 04/08/2010, p. 31 (Megan Murphy and Francesco Guerrera); Exhibit 3.13 from Goldman stung by backlash in China, *Financial Times*, 07/06/2010, p. 19 (Jamil Anderlini); Exhibit 3.16 from Investment strategy about more than faith, *Financial Times*, 21/06/2010, p. 3 (Emmanuelle Smith); Exhibit 4.11 from High net-worth investors keen to sign up as Names, *Financial Times*, 19/01/2009, p. 18 (Ellen Kelleher); Exhibit 4.13 from Lloyd's considers riskier investments, *Financial Times*, 05/04/2010, p. 3 (Steve Johnson); Exhibit 4.16 from Tackling the longevity question, *Financial Times*, 17/12/2009, p. 21 (Paul J. Davies); Exhibit 4.20 from Pensions regain faith in hedge funds, *Financial Times*, 01/02/2010, p. 10 (Sam Jones and Kate Burgess); Exhibit 4.23 from Regulator takes aim as recession hits pensions, *Financial Times*, 24/02/2010, p. 13 (Norma Cohen); Table 4.26 from Unit trust prices, *Financial Times*, 04/03/2011; Exhibit 4.28 from Exchange Traded Fund price in Financial Times, *Financial Times*, 15/07/2010; Exhibit 4.29 from ETFs 'risk causing confusion', *Financial Times*, 12/04/2010 (Chris Flood); Exhibit 4.30 from Investment trust prices in Financial Times, *Financial Times*, 04/03/2011; Exhibit 4.31 from Trust boards accused over independence, *Financial Times*, 21/08/2010, p. 14 (Alice Ross); Exhibit 4.32 from Rainy day funds recast, *Financial Times*, 19/10/2010, p. 12; Exhibit 5.1 from New rules for money funds, *Financial Times*, 14/12/2009, p. 2 (Steve Johnson); Exhibit 5.3 from Little room for Libor to fall further, *Financial Times*, 14/10/2009, p. 38 (David Oakley and Ralph Atkins); Exhibit 5.8 from Life returns to short-term lending market, *Financial Times*, 10/01/2009, p. 25 (Paul J. Davies); Exhibit 5.11 from Run on banks left repo sector highly exposed, *Financial Times*, 11/09/2009, p. 35 (Michael Mackenzie); Table 5.14 from Money market interest rates, *Financial Times*, 16/03/2011; Exhibit 6.3 from Britain draws strong demand for 50-year gilt, *Financial Times*, 24/02/2010, p. 32 (David Oakley); Table 6.4 from Gilts – UK Cash Market, *Financial Times*, 26/03/2011; Table 6.7 from Benchmark Government Bonds, *Financial Times*, 29/03/2011; Exhibit 6.8 from Bonds – High Yield and Emerging Market, *Financial Times*, 29/03/2011; Exhibit 6.9 from Corporate bond issues go local to deliver capital lift, *Financial Times*, 24/03/2010, p. 17 (David Oakley); Exhibit 6.10 from Ratings agency model left largely intact, *Financial Times*, 22/07/2009 (Aline van Duyn and Joanna Chung); Exhibit 6.11 from European high-yield bonds are in demand, *Financial Times*, 14/08/2009, p. 29 (Anousha Sakoui); Exhibit 6.13 from Brakes applied to convertible bond market, *Financial Times*, 06/04/2001, p. 35 (Rebecca Bream); Exhibit 6.14 from It's all a question of the right packaging, *Financial Times*, 25/07/2007, p. 2 (Richard Beales); Exhibit 6.15 from Recent deals signal market's reopening in the same old style, *Financial Times*, 29/10/2009, p. 37 (Jennifer Hughes); Exhibit 6.16 from US bill raises fears for covered bonds, *Financial Times*, 28/03/2011, p. 19 (Jennifer Hughes); Exhibit 6.17 from Philippines set to price $1bn of samurai bonds, *Financial Times*, 16/02/2010, p. 32 (Lindsay Whipp and Roel Landing); Exhibit 6.19 from Autostrade returns to bond market after 40-year gap, *Financial Times*, 13/05/2004, p. 21 (Charles Batchelor and Ivar Simensen); Exhibit 6.25 from www.markets.ft.com/markets/bonds.asp 23 March 2010; Exhibit 7.7 from HK and China act to control inflation, *Financial Times*, 20/11/2010, p. 8 (Justine Lau and Geoff Dyer); Exhibit 7.9 from Bernanke moves closer to formal inflation target, *Financial Times*, 16/10/2010, p. 5 (Robin Harding); Exhibit 7.10 from Bank's U-turn stokes concern over political interference, *Financial Times*, 11/05/2010, p. 8 (Ralph Atkins); Exhibit 7.11 from The Fed is right to turn on the tap, *Financial Times*, 10/11/2010, p. 13 (Martin Wolf); Exhibit 7.12 from Crisis-hit banks flooded Fed with junk, *Financial Times*, 03/12/2010, p. 1 (Francesco Guerrera and Robin Harding); Exhibit 7.13 from Fears grow over banks addicted to ECB funding, *Financial Times*, 14/09/2010, p. 37 (Ralph Atkins and David Oakley); Exhibit 7.15 from Multinationals weigh up Turner proposals, *Financial Times*, 03/11/2009, p. 20 (Brooke Masters); Exhibit 7.19 from Basel III rules behind StanChart capital raising, *Financial Times*, 14/10/2010, p. 21 (Patrick Jenkins); Exhibit 7.20 from Basel rules spark mitigation drives, *Financial Times*, 16/11/2010, p. 21 (Megan Murphy and Brooke Masters); Exhibit 7.21 from Basel: the mouse that did not roar, *Financial Times*, 15/09/2010, p. 13 (Wolf, M.); Exhibit 7.22 from

Trichet lands a 'cunning' blow, *Financial Times*, 03/12/2010, p. 6 (Atkins, R.); Exhibit 7.23 from Inflation rises sees King rebuked, *Financial Times*, 19/05/2010, p. 1 (Giles, C.); Exhibit 8.3 from Facebook signals future IPO with dual-class stock, *Financial Times*, 25/11/2009, p. 21 (Gelles, D. and Waters, R.); Exhibit 8.4 from Lisbon employs 'golden shares' to block Telefonica's bid for Vivo, *Financial Times*, 01/07/2010, p. 15 (Wise, P. , Parker, A. and Mulligan, M.); Exhibit 8.6 from Shenzhen takes over as China's listing hub, *Financial Times*, 19/10/2010, p. 34 (Cookson, R.); Exhibit 8.10 from BATS seen as likely Chi-X suitor, *Financial Times*, 25/08/2010, p. 18 (Grant, J.); Exhibit 8.11 from Europe set for overhaul of rules on share dealing, *Financial Times*, 30/07/2010, p. 31 (Grant, J. and Tait, N.); Exhibit 8.12 from BATS in 'smart order' move, *Financial Times*, 25/01/2010, p. 19 (Grant, J.); Exhibit 8.13 from Multiple venues leave Europe 'open to abuse', *Financial Times*, 07/04/2010, p. 35 (Grant, J.); Exhibit 8.14 from Private investors fail to see benefits of Mifid reform, *Financial Times*, 08/03/2010, p. 8 (Grant, J. and Wilson, J.); Exhibit 8.15 from Algo-trading changes speed of the game on Wall Street, *Financial Times*, 08/05/2010, p. 8 (Grant, J.); Exhibit 8.16 from Flash crash: market reform to be examined, *Financial Times*, 05/10/2010, p. 51 (van Duyn, A. and Demos, T.); Exhibit 8.17 from Call to make 'dark pools' trades public, *Financial Times*, 28/10/2010, p. 33 (Grant, J.); Exhibit 8.18 from Trust in dark pools is dented, *Financial Times*, 26/05/2010 (Grant, J.); Exhibit 8.20 from EM bourses hunt western blue chips, *Financial Times*, 09/08/2010, p. 1 (Johnson, S.); Exhibit 8.25 from LSE hints at building own clearing house, *Financial Times*, 22/05/2010, p. 14 (Grant, J. and Stafford, P.); Exhibit 8.26 from Europe's post-trade dilemma, *Financial Times*, 11/02/2010, p. 34 (Grant, J.); Exhibit 8.27 from Brussels eyes faster times for settlement, *Financial Times*, 25/10/2010, p. 25 (Grant, J. and Tait, N.); Exhibit 8.30 from Rising foreign ownership could be good for the Footsie, *Financial Times*, 10/04/2010, p. 40 (Sakoui, A.); Exhibit 9.2 from India flotation demand set to hit valuations, *Financial Times*, 05/06/2010, p. 16 (Leahy, J.); Exhibit 9.4 from Growing groups turn to incentive fundraising methods, *Financial Times*, 18/12/2009, p. 20 (Blackwell, D.); Exhibit 9.7 from Jupiter surges on market debut, *Financial Times*, 22/06/2010, p. 22 (Johnson, M.); Exhibit 9.8 from http://finance.yahoo.com; Exhibit 9.9 from Photo-Me fined £500,000 by FSA for late disclosure, *Financial Times*, 22/06/2010, p. 19 (Masters, B); Exhibit 9.10 from Tighter rules forcing nomads to run from smaller companies, *Financial Times*, 18/06/2008, p. 21 (Master, B.); Exhibit 9.11 from Micro-caps renew appetite for listings on Plus, *Financial Times*, 06/04/2010, p. 17 (Blackwell, D.); Exhibit 9.12 from London Share Service extracts: Aerospace and Defence, *Financial Times*, 07/03/2011; Exhibit 9.15 from Redrawing the blue-chip index map, *Financial Times*, 01/06/2010 (Jones, A.); Exhibit 9.18 from FTSE Actuaries Share Indices, *Financial Times*, 09/03/2011; Exhibit 9.19 from Knowing your rights is a serious issue, *Financial Times*, 03/02/2010, p. 3 (Burgess, K.); Exhibit 9.20 from Strong response to Lloyds cash call, *Financial Times*, 15/12/2009, p. 20 (Goff, S.); Exhibit 10.1 from Northern Foods passes price rises to customers, *Financial Times*, 10/10/2007, p. 25 (Warwick-Ching, L. and Crooks, E.); Exhibit 10.3 from Leeson hid trading from the outset, *Financial Times*, 18/10/1995, p. 8 (Denton, N.); Exhibit 10.4 from Farmers left short-changed by a margin call squeeze, *Financial Times*, 23/11/2010, p. 35 (Meyer, G. and Farchy, J.); Exhibit 10.5 from Equity index futures table for close of trading on 27th October 2010, www.ft.com; Exhibit 10.7 from Brussels in bid to tame 'wild west' markets, *Financial Times*, 16/09/2010, p. 19 (Tait, N.); Exhibit 10.10 from Interest Rates - Futures, *Financial Times*, 16/12/2010; Exhibit 10.11 from The truth about speculators: they are doing God's work, *Financial Times*, 13/03/2010 (Murphy, P.); Table 11.1 from Call options on AstraZeneca shares, 17 December 2010, *Financial Times*, 18/12/2010; Table 11.6 from Equity Options, *Financial Times*, 18/12/2010; Exhibit 11.10 from Mexico buys $1bn insurance policy against falling oil prices, *Financial Times*, 09/12/2009, p. 19 (Meyer, G. and Blas, J.); Exhibit 11.13 from Homeowners offered tracker protection, *Financial Times*, 03/07/2010, p. 4 (Warwick-Ching, L.); Table 11.15 from Interest Rates - Swaps, *Financial Times*, 17/12/2010; Exhibit 11.17 from Rate rise is music to the ears of 'swappers', *Financial Times*, 30/06/2007, p. 2 (Moore, E.); Exhibit 11.18 from TVA, EIB find winning formula, *Financial Times*, 12/09/1996 (Lapper, R.); Exhibit 11.19 from Milan swaps case puts banks in the hot seat, *Financial Times*, 19/03/2010, p. 35 (Boland, V.); Exhibit 11.23 from Naked truth about the villain of Europe, *Financial Times*, 15/03/2010, p. 3 (Grene, S.); Table 12.6 from *Financial Times*, 13/11/2010; Exhibit 12.9 from Material increase in clothes prices, *Financial Times*, 19/07/2010, p. 4 (Felsted, A.); Exhibit 12.10 from Burberry targets Chinese tourists, *Financial Times*, 20/09/2011, p. 32 (Felsted, A.), Copyright © Financial Times Ltd; Exhibit 12.11 from Australian cattlemen fear loss of exports, *Financial Times*, 15/10/2010, p. 31 (Smith, P.); Exhibit 12.12 from Small fry founder in the wake of surge, *Financial Times*, 10/10/2007, p. 15 (Minder, R.); Table 12.15 from www.ft.com, December 3, 2010; Exhibit 13.7 from Mexico hedges against corn inflation, *Financial Times*, 23/12/2010 (Blas, J.), Copyright © Financial Times Ltd; Exhibit 13.8 from Sugar prices soar to 30 year high, *Financial Times*, 03/11/2010 (Farchy, J.), Copyright © Financial Times Ltd; Exhibit 13.15 from Keeping track of underlying qualities, *Financial Times*, 13/12/2010, p. 4 (Ricketts, D.); Exhibit 13.17 from Buying the metal, not just the contracts, *Financial Times*, 30/11/2010, p. 6 (Farchy, J.), Copyright © Financial Times Ltd; Exhibit 13.18 from Supercycle argument 'remains intact', *Financial Times*, 03/12/2010, p. 1 (Newlands, C.), Copyright © Financial Times Ltd; Exhibit 13.20 from Inflation fears bring on China gold rush, *Financial Times*, 15/12/2010, p. 6 (Hook, L.), Copyright © Financial Times Ltd; Exhibit 14.1 from Industry mulls over alternatives directive, *Financial Times*, 22/11/2010, p. 3 (Sullivan, R.); Exhibit 14.2 from Investing stars lead bumper year for hedge funds, *Financial Times*, 02/03/2011, p. 32 (Mackintosh, J.); Exhibit 14.3 from Hedge funds struggle to justify their star rating, *Financial Times*, 29/08/2010, p. 22 (Mackintosh, J.), Copyright © Financial Times Ltd; Exhibit 14.5 from Hedge funds manage assets of $2,700bn, *Financial Times*, 27/05/2010 (Jones, S.), Copyright © Financial Times Ltd; Exhibit 14.10 from Hedge funds shy away from lower fees, *Financial Times*, 26/02/2010, p. 37 (Jones, S.), Copyright © Financial Times Ltd; Exhibit 14.11 from Hedge fund investors have a great chance to cut fees, *Financial Times*, 06/02/2009, p. 36 (Mackintosh, J.), Copyright © Financial Times Ltd; Exhibit 14.12 from Funds of funds have to work harder, *Financial Times*, 08/01/2009, p. 11 (Gapper, J.), Copyright © Financial Times Ltd; Exhibit 14.13 from US hedge funds are quick to embrace the benefits of Ucits, *Financial Times*, 06/08/2010, p. 29 (Jones, S.), Copyright © Financial Times Ltd; Exhibit 14.14 from BlueCrest Ucits fund to be liquidated, *Financial Times*, 28/10/2010, p. 19 (Jones, S.); Exhibit 14.15 from Marshall Wace eyes ETF listing, *Financial Times*, 18/01/2010, p. 12 (Jones, S.), Copyright © Financial Times Ltd; Exhibit 14.17 from Hedge funds are wary of taking on more risk, *Financial Times*, 24/02/2011, p. 35 (Jones, S.), Copyright © Financial Times Ltd; Exhibit 14.19 from The storms that wept away Meriwether's flagship fund, *Financial Times*, 10/07/2009 (Sender, H.), Copyright © Financial Times Ltd; Exhibit 14.20 from 3i turns profit with Hyva sale, *Financial Times*, 16/12/2010, p. 22 (Arnold, M.); Exhibit 14.27 from Angel funding, *Financial Times*, 01/03/2010, p. 21, Copyright © Financial Times Ltd; Exhibit 14.29 from Buy-out study queries performance, *Financial Times*, 26/07/2010, p. 20 (Arnold, M.), Copyright © Financial Times Ltd; Exhibit 14.32 from Revolving door leaves investors dizzy, *Financial Times*, 02/08/2010, p. 42 (Arnold, M.), Copyright © Financial Times Ltd; Exhibit 15.1 from Oversight of banks costs US far more than EU, *Financial Times*, 24/01/2011, p. 8 (Masters, B.), Copyright © Financial Times Ltd; Exhibit 15.2 from Analyst fined over mis-leading message, *Financial Times*, 14/01/2011, p. 17 (Masters, B.), Copyright © Financial Times Ltd; Exhibit 15.3 from Barclays hit with record fine, *Financial Times*, 19/01/2011, p. 17 (Masters, B. and Goff, S.), Copyright © Financial Times Ltd; Exhibit 15.4 from Regulators increase scrutiny of banks, *Financial Times*, 11/08/2010, p. 13 (Guerrera, F.), Copyright © Financial Times Ltd; Exhibit 15.5 from RBI set to decide on shape of banking, *Financial Times*, 06/01/2011, p. 22 (Lamont, J.), Copyright © Financial Times Ltd; Exhibit 15.6 from The FSA's delays for new businesses spark City fears, *Financial Times*, 11/10/2010, p. 3 (Jones, S.), Copyright © Financial Times Ltd; Exhibit 15.7 from Regulator to soften focus on keeping City's edge, *Financial Times*, 10/06/2009, p. 2 (Davies, P. J. and Masters, B.); Exhibit 15.9 from China starts crackdown on insider trading, *Financial Times*, 25/11/2010, p. 34 (Anderlini, J.), Copyright © Financial Times Ltd; Exhibit 15.10 from FSA sinks talons into Eagle with £2.8m fine, *Financial Times*, 21/05/2010, p. 16 (Masters, B.), Copyright © Financial Times Ltd; Exhibit 15.11 from FSA fines two City brokers for not ringfencing clients' money, *Financial Times*, 08/06/2010, p. 22 (Gray, A.), Copyright © Financial Times Ltd; Exhibit 15.13 from Broker fined for 'market abuse' in FSA commodities crackdown, *Financial Times*, 03/06/2010, p. 17 (Blas, J.), Copyright © Financial Times Ltd; Exhibit 15.14 from Insurance industry says watchdog's fees 'unjustified', *Financial Times*, 12/04/2010, p. 4 (Davies, P. J.), Copyright © Financial Times Ltd; Exhibit 15.15 from FSA's new approach ruffles feathers, *Financial Times*, 20/07/2009, p. 21 (Masters, B.), Copyright © Financial Times Ltd; Exhibit 15.16 from Fund managers to foot Keydata bill, *Financial Times*, 23/01/2011, p. 34 (Ross, A.), Copyright © Financial Times Ltd; Exhibit 15.17 from Insider dealers face sentence in long-running FSA case, *Financial Times*, 02/02/2011, p. 3 (Croft, J. and Masters, B.), Copyright © Financial Times Ltd; Exhibit 15.18

from FSA to probe profit warnings, *Financial Times*, 05/01/2009, p. 1 (Peel, M., Hughes, J. and Pignal, S.), Copyright © Financial Times Ltd; Exhibit 15.19 from RBS fine sets cost on 'cosy and rotten practices', *Financial Times*, 31/03/2010, p. 3 (Peel, M. and Goff, S.), Copyright © Financial Times Ltd; Exhibit 15.20 from Regulator sets sight on pension fund risks, *Financial Times*, 07/12/2010, p. 1 (Cohen, N.), Copyright © Financial Times Ltd; Exhibit 15.21 from Two found guilty in Torex fraud case, *Financial Times*, 20/01/2011, p. 20 (Croft, J. and Stafford, P.); Exhibit 15.22 from EU sets new pay practices in stone, *Financial Times*, 02/07/2010, p. 21 (Masters, B., Murphy, M. and Tait, N.), Copyright © Financial Times Ltd; Exhibit 15.23 from Traders fear threat of political agendas, *Financial Times*, 05/01/2011, p. 6 (Tait, N.), Copyright © Financial Times Ltd.

Figures
Exhibit 1.8 from www.atlapedia.com, Atlapedia is a registered trademark of Latimer Clarke Corporation Pty Ltd.; Exhibit 1.10 from TheCityUK estimates, www.TheCityUK.com; Exhibit 1.12 from *Corporate Financial Management*, 4th edn, Financial Times/Prentice Hall (Glen Arnold 2009) p. 26; Exhibit 1.13 from *Corporate Financial Management*, 4th edn, Financial Times/Prentice Hall (Glen Arnold 2009); Exhibit 1.15 from *BIS and CIA World Factbook*; Exhibit 4.1 from Global premium volume 2009, www.swissre.com, Swiss Re, sigma No 2/2011; Figures 4.14, 14.4, 14.6, 14.7, 14.8, 14.9 from www.TheCityUK.com; Figures 6.2a, 6.2b, 6.2c from Bank for International Settlements; Exhibit 8.1 from www.oldest-share.com, www.oldest-share.com/Private collection; Exhibit 8.29 from Office for National Statistics, Crown Copyright material is reproduced with the permission of the Controller, Office of Public Sector Information (OPSI); Exhibit 10.9 from www.euronext.com, Reproduced with permission of NYSE Euronext; Exhibit 10.12 from http://www.euronext.com/trader, Reproduced with permission of NYSE Euronext; Figures 12.1, 12.2, 12.3, 12.5 from Triennial Central Bank Survey: Report on global foreign exchange market activity in 2010, Bank for International Settlements, www.bis.org; Exhibit 12.9 from www.oanda.com

Maps
Exhibit 6.5 from http://image.guardian.co.uk/sys-files/Guardian/documents/2009/05/22/Credit-rating.pdf, copyright Guardian News & Media Ltd 2009.

Tables
Exhibit 4.4 from www.TheCityUK.com; Exhibit 4.5 from Business Insurance, 6 September 2010, courtesy Insurance Information Institute; Exhibit 4.24 from www.ici.org, source: Investment Company Institute, Washington, DC (2010); Exhibit 4.25 from www.incademy.com; Exhibit s 5.4, 5.5, 5.6 from www.dmo.gov.uk, Crown Copyright material is reproduced with permission under the terms of the Click-Use Licence; Exhibit 6.1 from Fitch Ratings Global Corporate Finance 2010 Transition and Default Study, www.fitchratings.com; Exhibit 10.8 from http://www.futuresindustry.org, reprinted with permission of the Futures Industry Association.; Exhibit 11.11 from FTSE 100 Index Option (European-style), http://www.euronext.com, reproduced with permission of NYSE Euronext; Exhibit 12.19 from www.cmegroup.com; Exhibit 13.20 from Grain Trade Australia, www.graintrade.org

Text
Exhibit 4.17 from 20-year study finds pension funds rational, *Financial Times*, 7 December 2009, p. 6 © David Blake; Exhibit 4.18 from UBS Pension Fund Indicators, TheCityUK Pensions Report 2011, www.TheCityUK.com; Exhibit 7.14 from Banks' survival rates should improve with living wills, *Financial Times*, 10 August 2010, p.30 © Charles Goodhart; Exhibit 12.20 from The Big Mac Index: Why China needs more expensive burgers, *The Economist*, 14 October 2010, © The Economist Newspaper Limited, London; Exhibit 12.21 from How traders have been triumphing over economic theory, *The Economist*, 24/02/2007, p. 88, © The Economist Newspaper Limited, London; Exhibit 15.8 from Bringing back the City's rock-solid reputation, *Financial Times*, 3 November 2009, p. 12, copyright © Peter Spira; Extract on pages 629–30 from The City of London Police Annual Report 2009–10.

In some instances we have been unable to trace the owners of copyright material, and we would appreciate any information that would enable us to do so.

1

The value of the
financial system

LEARNING OUTCOMES

This opening chapter provides an overview of the role of the financial system and briefly describes the main categories of markets, instruments and institutions. By the end of this chapter the reader should be able to:

- outline the character and importance of the main financial markets and instruments;

- explain the key roles played in a modern society by the financial products, markets and institutions;

- describe the relative standing of the major financial centres;

- discuss the changes that have taken place in the way financial services are provided;

- define and illustrate some key financial terms, such as primary market and over-the-counter.

When we switch on the evening news it is not long before there is a report about the financial markets or those institutions that provide financial services. Perhaps it is the Greek or UK governments straining to reduce public expenditure so that they do not have to borrow so much in the bond markets – politicians make pained pronouncements that they do not have any choice because the *markets* are putting so much pressure on them. Perhaps it is an announcement that workers are to receive much lower pensions than first promised because share prices have declined for years. Perhaps a rise in interest rates is hurting business borrowers and young families with mortgages. Or, perhaps, a few home owners in the US cannot repay their debt which, through a chain reaction, leads to the downfall of some mighty banks and threatens worldwide depression.

You do not need me to tell you that financial markets touch the lives of us all, each and every day, from the efficiency of the credit card system to the raising of finance to build a new high-speed rail line. But perhaps you *do* need me to explain how it is that movements in financial markets flow through the system to impact on you. What are the mechanisms at play? What are the different types of financial instruments that people put their money into? What do all the bankers and other financial services workers do with their time?

This chapter explains the importance of the modern financial system by outlining the role of the main markets and institutions. Financial markets and institutions have a major role to play in channelling funds from those with a surplus looking for a return on their money to those in need of investment funds to, say, grow their business or buy a family home. In a well-functioning financial system, funds can flow easily and at low cost from savers to those with a productive use for the money. The increases in wealth we have seen over the past 100 years in most parts of the globe are in no small part due to the development of highly effective financial markets and institutions. Indeed, we can go so far as to say that one of the major reasons that some countries have failed to grow out of poverty is that they have not yet created a properly functioning mechanism for mobilising the savings of their citizens so that they can be used for investment in productive assets such as factories within their country.

The impact of these markets on our lives

We will first look at a number of financial markets and illustrate the impact they have on ordinary people's lives. The markets are:

- the bond markets;
- the share markets;
- the money markets;
- the foreign exchange markets;
- the derivative and commodity markets.

We will also look at the impact of banking.

Bond markets

Companies often need to borrow money so that they can build useful things such as factories and research establishments, for instance stem cell or cancer drug laboratories. One way for them to borrow is to produce a legally binding document, a bond, that states that the company will pay interest for, say, ten years and a capital sum at the end to whoever buys the bond. This is an attractive way for people, pension funds and others to obtain a return on their savings. It is made even more attractive by the fact that the lender does not have to keep their money tied up in the bond for the full ten years, but can sell it to other investors in an active market for bonds. The buyer of the bond may be willing to pay the same as the sum paid by the original owner to obtain the promise of future interest, or they may be willing to pay more or less – much depends on current going rates of return for that type of bond given its risk and anticipated inflation.

Thus a **bond** is merely a document which sets out the borrower's promise to pay sums of money in the future – usually regular interest plus a capital amount upon the maturity of the bond. Many European bond markets are more than three centuries old and during that time they have developed very large and sophisticated sub-markets encompassing government bonds (UK government bonds are called **gilts**, for example), **corporate bonds** (issued by companies), local authority bonds and international bonds, among others.

Exhibit 1.1 shows the rates of interest typical, but relatively safe, corporate bond issuers had to pay over the period 2001–2011. It shows the interest rates payable if the promises to pay regular interest and the capital sum were in euros: the blue line. The green line shows the rate of return if the borrowing (and payments of interest and capital) was done in pounds. Notably, the sterling borrowers paid higher interest rates than the eurozone borrowers – this is mostly because of higher UK inflation expectations at the time of issue than for eurozone countries. The chart also shows the interest rates payable by the Greek government when it sold bonds denominated in euros (the red line). In most years it paid lower interest rates than the typical low-risk euro corporate borrower, but in 2011 we see a dramatic spike in interest rates demanded by lenders to induce them to place their hard-earned savings into Greek government debt. Most Greek companies had to pay more than the government to borrow because they were seen as even more of a risk. This meant that they could not afford to borrow to finance many of the investment projects that they would normally undertake, which contributed to a deep recession and rioting on the streets.

In the UK case, bond investors were very worried in 2008 and 2009 that a high proportion of borrowing companies were going to go bust and as a result they demanded interest rates as high as 10 per cent. Note that these are the rates for the most highly respected (relatively safe) companies; more risky borrowers had to pay much more. As a result of this high cost of finance many plans to build factories, offices, shops, etc. were shelved and thousands of people were made redundant.

Exhibit 1.1	Yields on corporate bonds issued in pounds and euros, and yields on Greek government debt, 2001–2011

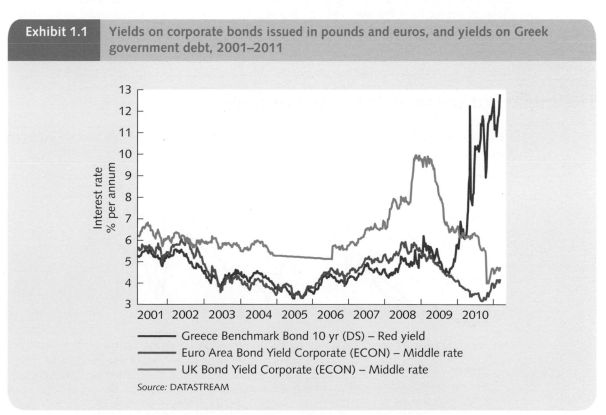

Source: DATASTREAM

Source: Financial Times, 11 March 2011, p. 20. Reprinted with permission.

Equity markets

An important innovation that has allowed much faster growth in people's economic well-being has been the principle of **limited liability** for companies. This means that if you or I buy a share in a company and then the company runs into difficulty and its creditors are chasing after it for payment, those creditors cannot come to us as shareholders and demand what the company owes them. So, if the firm cannot pay, we are not forced into selling our houses, cars, etc. simply because we have supplied share capital to a business to allow it to grow. It is different with sole traders and partnerships where the individuals are liable for the debts of the business.

As a result of limited liability millions of us now own **shares** (also called **equity** and **stock**) in companies and are thereby entitled to receive dividends that might flow from the profits that the firm generates.[1] We are owners of the company and can vote directors on or off the board to try to appoint a team that will act in our best interests. These days most of these shares are not actually held directly by individuals but through various savings schemes, such as pension funds and insurance savings schemes (e.g. endowments linked to mortgages).

All major economies now have share markets, which encourages savers to put money into companies because once the shares have been sold by the company to raise the money it needs, they can then be sold on to other investors in the market should the original investor wish to raise some cash or invest elsewhere. Thus stock exchanges have been important sources of long-term capital for tens of thousands of companies.

Exhibit 1.2 shows that the market value of UK and US shares has been something of a roller-coaster ride over the past 20 years (UK shares are represented by the FTSE 100 index, comprising the largest 100 companies on the market; US shares by the S&P 500 index, representing the largest 500 companies). Market prices shot up in the late 1990s as investors became excited by the new economy shares of the dot.com revolution. When equity markets are booming it can have an effect on people's confidence. They go out and spend more. They invest more in factories, machinery, etc. Thus the economy can get a lift. Conversely, when people feel poorer because

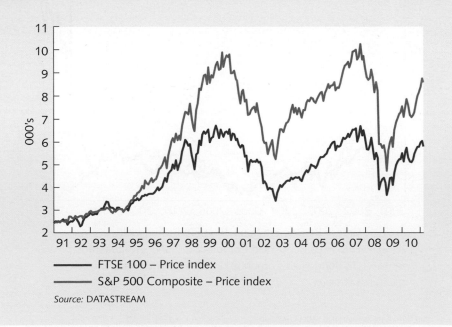

Exhibit 1.2   UK and US share market price movements, 1990–2011 (with the US S&P 500 index rebased to the UK FTSE 100 in 1991)

FTSE 100 – Price index
S&P 500 Composite – Price index

Source: DATASTREAM

---

[1] Dividends are a share of the profits paid out to shareholders.

their investments are down and they are told that their pensions will not have enough value left in them to support them in their old age they become more cautious spenders and investors, resulting in declining demand – as was the case in 2008 and 2011. While stock market movements are not the only causes of economic fluctuations, they are contributors.

Money markets

You and I might, from time to time, need to borrow money for a short while, say on a credit card or via an overdraft. Similarly, large organisations such as companies, governments and banks often need to borrow money for a period of a few days or weeks. They tend not to borrow on credit cards and may find overdrafts inconvenient or relatively expensive. This is where the **money markets** come in – they allow companies, etc. to issue instruments that promise to pay a sum of money after, say, 30 days if the buyer pays an amount now for owning that right. Obviously the amount the lender puts down at the beginning of the 30 days is less than what they collect at the end, thus an effective interest rate is charged. We say that the money markets are **wholesale markets** because they involve large transactions each time – £500,000/€1,000,000 or more. They enable borrowing for less than one year. Banks are particularly active in this market – both as lenders and as borrowers. Large corporations, local government bodies and non-banking financial institutions also lend when they have surplus cash and borrow when short of money.

The largest borrowers in these markets are usually governments. They issue **Treasury bills**, which do not carry an explicit interest but merely promise to pay a sum of money after a period. The most popular length to maturity is three months. The UK government is the biggest issuer in Europe, with billions of pounds worth sold almost every week of the year. The US government also sells a tremendous volume of these instruments, much of which have been bought by the Chinese government as it invests its savings around the world – it is poorly diversified because it has put such a high proportion of its portfolio in US Treasuries.

Exhibit 1.3 shows the interest rates that the UK government had to offer investors to induce them to buy a 91-day promise – that is a promise that in 91 days a fixed amount of money will be paid to the holder of the security. These are rates the government paid for fresh issues in each of the months going back 20 years. Note that even though the bills last for a mere three months, the

Exhibit 1.3 The interest rate the UK government offered investors in its various three-month Treasury bills issued each month 1991–2011

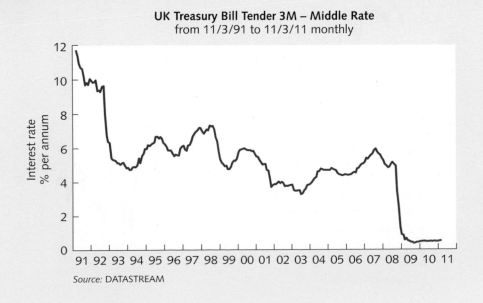

Source: DATASTREAM

interest rates shown are annualised up. So, if an investor receives 0.2 per cent for lending for 91 days, the chart will show a figure of 0.8 per cent. You can see that normally the government pays around 4–6 per cent per year to borrow using three-month loans. In an economy where inflation is around 1.5–3 per cent this allows the lender to the UK government to obtain a real return (above inflation) of around 1–3 per cent. (In the early 1990s the UK had much higher inflation rates.) However, in the wake of the financial crisis the Bank of England significantly reduced interest rates for short-term borrowing for all sorts of instruments and this had a knock-on effect on the interest rate the government had to pay to borrow for three months – it has come all the way down to around 0.5 per cent (around 0.125 per cent for three months). This lowered the borrowing cost for the government, which is just as well given that it borrowed so much.

However, the extremely low interest rates throughout the financial system, including bank account savings rates, produced howls of complaint from savers, who received interest significantly less than inflation. Much of this saving is done through pension funds and so people's pension pots were made smaller.

Foreign exchange markets

Individuals and businesses often need to exchange foreign currency, sometimes purely for pleasure, a holiday say, but mostly for business. For example, a French company building a manufacturing plant in the US exchanges euros for dollars. Today the foreign exchange markets are enormous, with transactions worth $4,000 billion taking place every day. The movements of exchange rates can make a big difference to ordinary people and businesses alike. Consider Manuel, who borrowed €300,000 to buy an apartment in London early in 2006. At that time he could get £1 for every €1.50 – *see* **Exhibit 1.4** – and so he could buy a £200,000 apartment. Unfortunately, in 2009 he needed to sell his apartment to raise cash to support his Spanish business. Not only was Manuel hit by the UK recession, he was doubly unfortunate because at 2009 exchange rates (€1.10 to £1) he could obtain only €220,000, even if he sold the apartment for £200,000. He made an €80,000 loss simply

| Exhibit 1.4 | The exchange rate between euros and UK pounds, 2001–2011 |

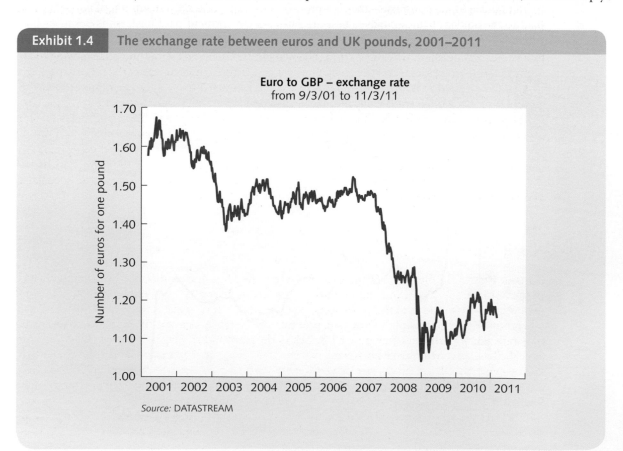

Source: DATASTREAM

because currency rates shifted. As you can see from the chart, they do this quite a lot. The markets and institutions have devised various tools to help individuals like Manuel as well as large organisations such as Unilever reduce the impact of foreign exchange shifts.

Foreign exchange (forex, FX) markets are simply markets in which one currency is exchanged for another. They include the spot market, where currencies are bought and sold for 'immediate' delivery (in reality, one or two days later), and the forward markets, where the deal is agreed now to exchange currencies at some fixed point in the future. Also currency futures and options and other forex derivatives are employed to hedge (manage) risk and to speculate. Chapter 12 is devoted to the FX markets.

Derivative and commodity markets

Imagine you are a cocoa farmer in Ghana. You would like to have certainty on the price you will receive for your cocoa when you harvest it six months from now. An organisation such as Cadbury would also like to know the cost of its cocoa six months from now so that it, like the farmer, can plan ahead and avoid the risk of the spot price at that time being dramatically different from what it is now.

Fortunately financial markets have evolved to help both the farmer and the chocolate maker. Perhaps the farmer could sell a future in cocoa at, say, $3,000 per tonne. A future is a contract to undertake a transaction (e.g. sell cocoa) at a point days, weeks or years from now, at a price agreed now. For example, a future is the right to buy something (e.g. currency, shares, bonds, cocoa, wheat) at some date in the future at an agreed price.

If the farmer sells a future, this guarantees to the farmer that if he delivers the cocoa in six months he will get the price agreed. Perhaps the chocolate maker could also enter the futures markets on one of the organised exchanges to give them certainty over the price that they will pay. Each side is legally obliged to go through with the deals they signed up to – and just to make sure, the exchange requires that each of them leaves money at the exchange so that if the futures price should move against them they will not be tempted to walk away from the deal because if they did they would lose this 'margin' they have at the exchange.

You can see from **Exhibit 1.5** that the futures price of cocoa fluctuates over time and therefore you can understand why buyers and sellers might be concerned about the price moving to an unprofitable level for them and thus why they lock in a futures price in one of the futures markets.

A derivative is a financial instrument whose value is derived from the value of other financial securities or some other underlying asset because it grants a right to undertake a transaction. This *right* becomes a saleable derived financial instrument. Futures have been illustrated, but there are other derivatives. For example, an option gives the purchaser the right, but not the obligation, to buy or sell something at some point in the future, at a price agreed now. The performance of the derivative depends on the behaviour of the underlying asset. Companies can use these markets for the management and transfer of risk. They can be used to reduce risk (hedging) or to speculate. We will look at these possibilities in Chapters 10 and 11.

Banking

A major element in the fabric of the financial system we have not yet discussed is banking. Banks perform many functions, but the main ones are taking deposits, providing loans and allowing people and organisations to make payments to each other. The interest rates bank charge can have a profound effect on people's lives. The rate that the borrower pays is often linked to the bank base rate. Some borrowers may pose a low risk to the bank and so may be charged, say, 2 per cent over the base rate. More risky borrowers pay base rate plus, say, 7 per cent. **Exhibit 1.6** shows that the average base rate set by UK banks over the ten years to 2011 was subject to significant fluctuations. In 2009 the base rate fell to an all-time low rate of 0.5 per cent and so we had remarkably low interest rates charged by the banks. The actions by central banks around the world to lower interest rates had the desired effect, as many families with mortgages or businesses with loans were saved when base rates were pushed down. If base rates had remained at 5 per cent we would have seen much higher house repossession rates, widespread business failure and mass unemployment.

Exhibit 1.5   The futures price of cocoa, March 2009 to March 2011

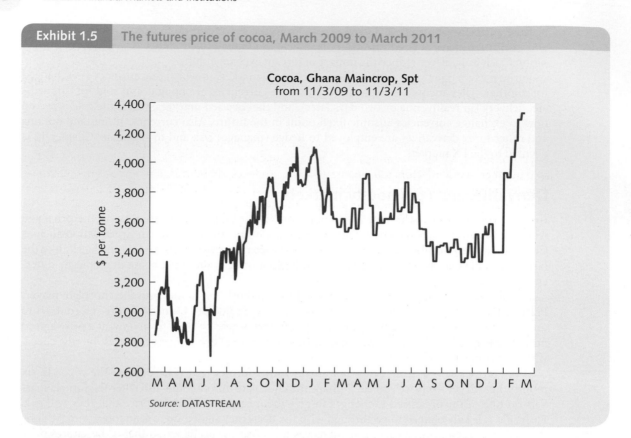

Cocoa, Ghana Maincrop, Spt
from 11/3/09 to 11/3/11

Source: DATASTREAM

Exhibit 1.6   UK bank base rates, 2001–2011

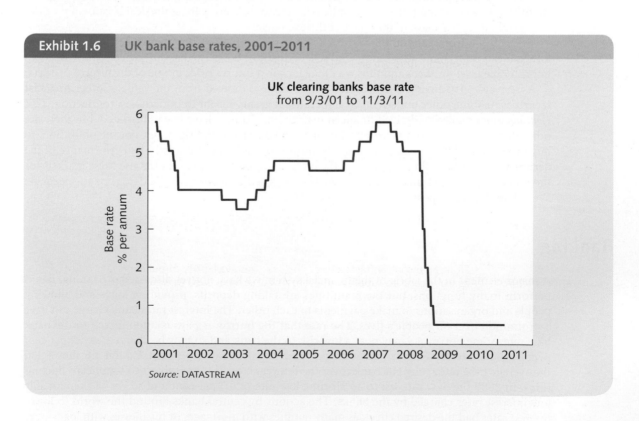

UK clearing banks base rate
from 9/3/01 to 11/3/11

Source: DATASTREAM

Importance of different financial centres

People and institutions involved in financial market activity tend to be concentrated in a few major centres around the world. Every six months the largest 75 financial centres are rated and ranked by drawing on both statistical data and assessments from finance service professionals in an online survey. The results are published in the *Global Financial Centres Report*, sponsored by Qatar Financial Centre Authority and produced by the think-tank Z/Yen Group.

The five groups of factors considered are shown in **Exhibit 1.7**. As you can see, the centres are rated not simply by volume of business (such as share turnover) and other quantitative data but by a number of other factors too. So, for example, evidence about a fair and just business environment is drawn from a corruption perception index and an opacity index. In all, 75 indicators have been used, including office rental rates, airport satisfaction and transport. Around 33,000 financial services professionals (e.g. bankers, asset managers, insurers, lawyers) respond to the online questionnaire in which they are asked to rate on a number of factors those centres with which they are most familiar. To ensure that there is no bias towards their home base, the assessments given on their own centre are excluded from the calculations.

Exhibit 1.7 The five groups of instrumental factors for judging the quality of a financial centre

People
- The availability of skilled personnel, the flexibility of the labour market, business education and the development of 'human capital'.

Business environment
- This is regarded as the most important factor in judging the competitiveness of a financial centre. It covers regulation and tax rates, levels of corruption, economic freedom and the ease of doing business. Fair and just business environment. Government support for the finance sector. Transparency and predictability of regulation.

Market access
- Access to international financial markets. Volume and value of trading in equities and bonds as well as the clustering effect of having many firms involved in the financial services sector together in one centre.

Infrastructure
- IT and transport infrastructure. The cost and availability of buildings and office space. Access to suppliers of professional services such as legal services.

General competitiveness
- The concept that the whole is 'greater than the sum of the parts' considers overall competitiveness levels of cities and how cities are perceived as places to live. Culture and language.

The map in **Exhibit 1.8** shows the ranking of the top 20 financial centres. There is very little difference in the ratings for London and New York. The survey respondents believe that these two centres work together for mutual benefit; a gain for one does not mean a loss for the other. The position of Hong Kong has improved immensely in recent years so that it is now a mere ten points (out of 1,000) behind London. It is one of only a handful of genuine global financial centres. Singapore is expected to join this trio soon. Between them, for example, the top four centres account for 70 per cent of all equity trading.

Exhibit 1.8	The top 20 global financial centres

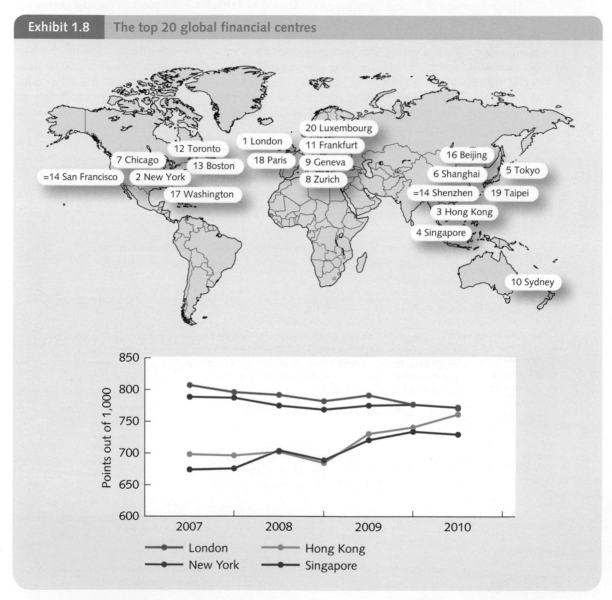

Source: www.atlapedia.com

Remarkably, Shanghai has now entered the top ten. When financial professionals were questioned about which financial centres are likely to become more significant in the next few years, the top five centres mentioned were all Asian – Shenzhen, Shanghai, Singapore, Seoul and Beijing.

Exhibit 1.9 describes the relative importance of Hong Kong and Shanghai as places for companies to raise money from shareholders by issuing shares on these stock markets for the first time. This is called an **initial public offering (IPO)**. The article illustrates the international trend in raising finance these days, with Mongolian, French and Italian companies listing alongside a great number of mainland Chinese firms.

Exhibit 1.9

HK eclipses rivals as the place to list

FT

Robert Cookson

The up-to-$20.5bn initial public offering of AIG's prized Asian business is the talk of the town in Hong Kong, but alongside that juggernaut there are dozens of other companies flocking to list in the city.

So great is the wave of listings that Hong Kong is on track for the second year in a row to eclipse its rivals Shanghai, London, and New York as the world's biggest centre for IPOs.

But as Hong Kong stock prices surge to within striking distance of their 2009 peak, sucking in more and more investors, there are concerns among some fund managers that the market is getting too hot.

So far this year some 53 companies have raised a combined $23.9bn from IPOs in Hong Kong, according to data from Dealogic. That figure dwarfs the $10.7bn raised in New York and $7bn in London.

With AIG alone set to raise at least $13.9bn from the listing of AIA, its Asian business, Hong Kong is now on track to trump its rivals Shanghai and Shenzhen in terms of deal volume in 2010.

"Hong Kong is now firmly established as a major global listing venue – it's the place any issuer has to seriously look at," Mr Lam says.

International companies are being attracted by the prospect of selling shares at higher prices than could be achieved in either their home markets or the traditional capital-raising centres of London or New York.

Prada, the Italian luxury goods company, is considering a possible listing in Hong Kong next year,

following hard on the heels of French perfume house L'Occitane, which raised more than $700m there in April.

On Tuesday, the first Mongolian company to sell shares in Hong Kong completed a $650m offering, pricing its shares in the middle of the target range set by advisers JPMorgan and Citi.

Yet Mongolian Mining Corp and other foreign issuers still make up only a fraction of the deals on the HK stock exchange. Mainland Chinese companies remain the dominant force and are attracting strong – and at times frenzied – demand from both international fund managers and Hong Kong retail investors.

"Investors are risk on," says David Chin, co-head of Asia investment banking at UBS. In particular, companies that would benefit from the rise of the Chinese consumer were "selling like hotcakes", he says.

Boshiwa, a children's clothing retailer likened to Mothercare of the UK, is a good example. The Chinese company, which raised $320m in Hong Kong in September, saw its shares rocket 41 per cent on their trading debut last week. On Wednesday, shares in Boshiwa were trading at a price of 72 times last year's earnings.

"China is clearly rebalancing the economy away from one that is predominantly export and manufacturing-driven towards a more domestic consumption-driven one," said Kester Ng, JPMorgan's co-head of equity capital and derivatives markets for Asia. "Companies that

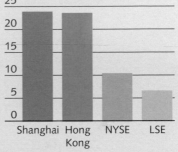

IPOs
Value of new listings, year to date ($bn)

Source: Thomson Reuters Datastream; Dealogic

are linked to the Chinese consumption theme have done really well." This point has not been lost on Chinese companies themselves.

Last week, China Medical System, which makes pharmaceutical products, listed in Hong Kong having raised $129m in an IPO that priced at the top of the target range. On the same day as its Hong Kong debut, it de-listed its shares from London's junior Aim market.

The company is not alone. West China Cement, a cement producer that has long complained that its share were undervalued in London, made the same jump to Hong Kong from Aim in August. And in yet another case, Sihuan Pharmaceutical Holdings, a Chinese drugmaker that de-listed from the Singapore stock exchange last year, seeking to raise up to $700m in a Hong Kong IPO.

Source: Financial Times, 7 October 2010, p. 34. Reprinted with permission.

If we focus on Europe we find that while London dominates, Zurich and Frankfurt are also regarded as global leaders, with rich environments for different types of financial services. Geneva is a specialist in wealth and asset management (running funds invested in shares, etc. for individuals and institutions) but is not a fully diversified centre, lacking a number of financial services. Amsterdam, Dublin and Paris have strong international connections but lack the depth to be global leaders.

If we break down the overall results to specific aspects of financial services then the following are the top five financial centres:

- Asset management (e.g. mutual funds, unit trusts, pension funds):
  - First – London
  - Second – New York
  - Third – Hong Kong
  - Fourth – Singapore

- Banking:
  - First – New York
  - Second – Hong Kong
  - Third – London
  - Fourth – Singapore

- Professional services (e.g. legal, accounting):
  - First – London
  - Second – New York
  - Third – Hong Kong
  - Fourth – Singapore

- Wealth management (advice and investing for wealthy people):
  - First – London
  - Second – Geneva
  - Third – New York
  - Fourth – Toronto

Following the financial crisis of 2008/2009 – caused, as many believe, by the financial sector (especially the banks) – the UK chancellor in his April 2009 budget imposed a 50 per cent super tax on bank bonuses. Some feared that this might cause mass relocation of financial services providers to other centres, such as New York, Zurich, Hong Kong, etc., but many of the governments in these other centres also plan to crack down on bankers and so the UK has not seen an exodus.

In the US financial market activity is split between a number of centres, with New York dominant in equity and bond trading as well as investment banking, Chicago big in derivatives and commodities, and Boston and San Francisco enjoying high reputations for asset management. While the US centres are particularly strong on domestic security issuance – e.g. the largest corporate and government bond market in the world – the US is often outshone by London on international financial services. London, being the dominant centre in the European time-zone centre, has kept its position as a principal centre in international financial markets, as can be seen from **Exhibit 1.10**.

Note that while Hong Kong and Singapore are highly ranked in terms of having the right infrastructure and attractiveness for financial services to grow, as we saw in the Z/Yen survey, they still have a relatively small share of world activity in most categories. Japan, France and Germany have more activity than the Asian centres in a number of segments.

World without money or financial institutions

Let us imagine how financial transactions began in the distant past, when things were much simpler.

Mr Carter needs materials to build his carts, and has a surplus of grain. Mr Carter asks his friend and neighbour Mr Woodcutter to let him have some timber in exchange for grain. Mr Woodcutter agrees and both men are happy.

Exhibit 1.10	Share of world financial market activity

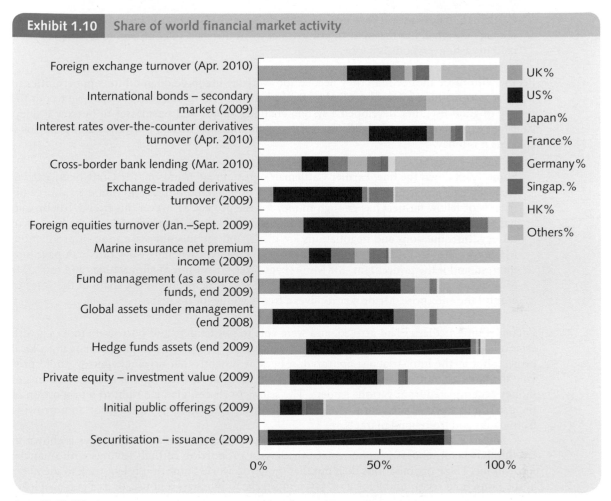

Source: TheCityUK estimates.

Some years down the line, Mr Carter needs some more timber, but does not currently have anything to exchange. Mr Woodcutter says Mr Carter can have the timber now, but when the carts are traded he wants his timber (the principal) back plus some extra (the interest). The nucleus of a financial system is born.

As the world developed and people travelled and traded further afield, this simple barter-based system was insufficient. Money appeared on the scene and has enjoyed a major part in the world's evolution ever since. Money has great appeal because people need something into which all goods and services received can be converted. That something will have to be small and portable, it will have to hold its value over a long period of time and have general acceptability. This will enable people to take the commodities given in exchange for, say, labour and then avoid the necessity of, say, carrying bushels of wheat to market to exchange them for bricks. Instead, money could be paid in exchange for labour and taken to the market to buy bricks. Various things have been used as a **means of exchange**, ranging from cowry shells to cigarettes (in prisons particularly), but the most popular used to be a metal, usually gold or silver. Now it is credit, debit cards and other forms of electronic transfer as well as notes and coins.

However, the advent of money did not provide a total solution.

Take the case of Farmer Cattleman. He wants to build a shed to protect his cows in bad weather but cannot afford it. He gets together with his fellow farmers and they pool their money to build the shed. Each farmer then has the right to use the shed for a set number of cows in proportion to the amount of money put in (they own shares in the enterprise). Farmer

Cattleman, whose idea it was, on whose land the shed is now built and who puts in time to manage the shed, has the right to put extra cows in the shed to compensate for this, or he is paid in cash. Everybody is happy.

People with more money than they needed for everyday life looked round for opportunities to invest it in something safe and profitable. Banks helped to fill this need and were able to put the money to good use; they developed a system enabling people and businesses to borrow money. Constant expansion in the fledgling financial system gradually turned it into the complex global colossus it is today.

Some years down the line, Farmer Cattleman's great, great grandson, Mr Craftsman, a clever chap, invents a machine. He wants to build lots of machines but has no money. None of his friends or fellow farmers has enough money for the project. However, his friend, Mr Broker, has a distant relative, Mr Moneybags, the landowner, in a neighbouring village who has lots of money. Introductions and negotiations are made, and the machines are soon in production. Mr Moneybags lends the money and makes an agreement whereby Mr Craftsman pays him interest, and if the project fails, Mr Moneybags takes possession of all machines and tools. Mr Moneybags also buys shares entitling him to a share of the profits and a share of the votes to control the enterprise. Mr Broker receives a free machine for his help.

Financial intermediaries had arrived, and were able to put lenders and borrowers in touch with each other, for a 'consideration'. One man's surplus money could be put to use financing a local project, but as the industrial age appeared, it became obvious that no single person could provide the large amounts of finance needed; to build a railway, for example, requires vast sums of money accumulated from various lenders. The selling of shares, giving a right to a proportion of the profit and assets of the venture, was found to be a good solution – in addition to borrowing from banks and from bond markets.

A simple way to look at the way money flows between investors and companies is shown in **Exhibit 1.11**. Households generally place the largest proportion of their savings with financial institutions. These organisations then put that money to work. Some of it is lent back to members of the household sector in the form of, say, a mortgage to purchase a house, or as a personal loan. Some of the money is used to buy securities (e.g. bonds, shares) issued by the business sector. The institutions will expect a return on these loans and shares, which flows back in the form of interest and dividends. However, they are often prepared for businesses to retain profit within the firm for further investment in the hope of greater returns in the future. The government sector enters into the financial system in a number of ways. For example, taxes are taken from individuals and businesses; governments usually fail to match their revenues with their expenditure and therefore borrow significant sums from the financial institutions, with a need to return that money with interest. Exhibit 1.11 remains a gross simplification – it has not allowed for overseas financial transactions, for example – but it does demonstrate a crucial role for financial institutions in an advanced market economy.

Primary investors

Typically, the household sector is in financial surplus. This sector contains the savers of society. It is these individuals who become the main providers of funds used for investment in the business sector. **Primary investors** tend to prefer to exchange their cash for financial assets which (a) allow them to get back their money quickly should they need to, with low transaction costs, and (b) have a high degree of certainty over the amount they will receive back. In other words, primary investors like high liquidity and low risk. Lending directly to a firm with a project proposal to build a North Sea oil platform which will not be sold until five years have passed is not a high-liquidity and low-risk investment. However, putting money into a sock under the bed is (if we exclude the possibility of the risk of sock theft).

Exhibit 1.11	The flow of funds and financial intermediation

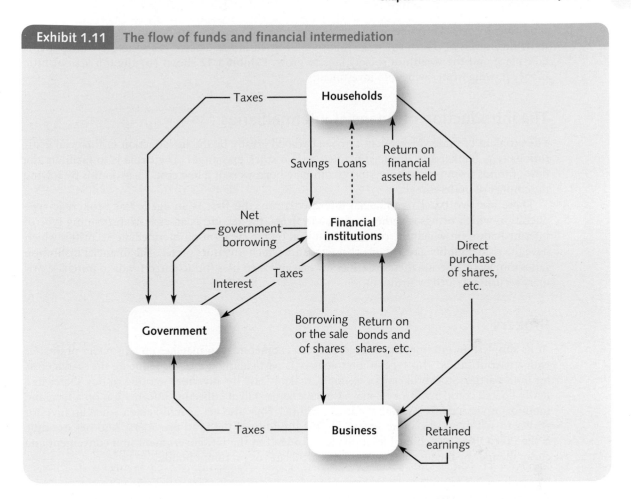

Ultimate borrowers

In our simplified model the **ultimate borrowers** are in the business sector. These firms are trying to maximise the wealth generated by their activities. To do this companies need to invest in capital equipment, in real plant and other assets, often for long periods of time. The firms, in order to serve their social function, need to attract funds for use over many years. Also these funds will be at risk, sometimes very high risk. (Here we are using the term 'borrower' broadly to include all forms of finance, even 'borrowing' by selling shares.)

Conflict of preferences

We have a **conflict of preference** between the primary investors wanting low-cost liquidity and certainty, and the ultimate borrowers wanting long-term risk-bearing capital. A further complicating factor is that savers usually save on a small scale, £100 here or €200 there, whereas businesses are likely to need large sums of money. Imagine some of the problems that would occur in a society which did not have any financial intermediaries. Here, lending and share buying will occur only as a result of direct contact and negotiation between two parties. If there were no organised market where financial securities could be sold on to other investors, the fund provider, once committed, would be trapped in an illiquid investment. Also, the costs that the two parties might incur in searching to find each other in the first place might be considerable. Following contact, a thorough agreement would need to be drawn up to safeguard the investor, and additional expense would be incurred obtaining information to monitor the firm and its progress. In sum, the obstacles to putting saved funds to productive use would lead many to give up and retain their cash. Those who do persevere will demand exceptionally high rates of return from the borrowers to compensate them for poor liquidity, risk, **search costs**, **agreement costs** and monitoring costs. Thus few firms will be able to justify investments because they cannot obtain those high levels of return when the funds are invested in real assets. As a result, few investments take place and the wealth of society fails to grow. **Exhibit 1.12** shows (by the top arrow) little money flowing from saving into investment.

The introduction of financial intermediaries

The problem of under-investment can be alleviated greatly by the introduction of financial institutions (e.g. banks) and financial markets (e.g. a stock exchange). Their role is to facilitate the flow of funds from primary investors to ultimate borrowers at a low cost. They do this by solving the conflict of preferences.

There are two types of financial intermediation: the first is an agency or brokerage-type operation which brings together lenders and firms, the second is an asset-transforming type of intermediation, in which the conflict is resolved by the creation of intermediate securities which have the risk, liquidity and volume characteristics which investors prefer. The financial institution raises money by offering these securities for sale and then uses the acquired funds to purchase primary securities issued by firms.

Brokers

At its simplest an intermediary is a 'go-between', someone who matches up a provider of finance with a user of funds. This type of intermediary is particularly useful for reducing the search costs for both parties. Stockbrokers, for example, make it easy for investors wanting to buy shares in a newly floated company. Brokers may also have some skill at collecting information on a firm and monitoring its activities, saving the investor time. They also act as middlemen when an investor wishes to sell to another, thus enhancing the liquidity of the fund providers. Another example is the Post Office, which enables individuals to lend to the UK government in a convenient and cheap manner by buying National Savings certificates or premium bonds.

Asset transformers

Asset transformation is the creation of an intermediate security with characteristics appealing to the primary investor to attract funds, which are then made available to the ultimate borrower in a form appropriate to them. Intermediaries, by creating a completely new security, the **intermediate security**, increase the opportunities available to savers, encouraging them to invest and thus reducing the cost of finance for the productive sector. The transformation function can act in a number of ways.

- *Risk transformation* For example, instead of an individual lending directly to a business with a great idea, such as digging a tunnel under the English Channel, a bank creates a deposit or current account with relatively low risk for the investor's savings.

  Lending directly to the firm, the saver would demand compensation for the probability of default on the loan and therefore the business would have to pay a very high rate of interest which would inhibit investment.

  The bank acting as an intermediary creates a special kind of security called a bank account agreement. The bank intermediary then uses the funds attracted by the new financial asset to buy a security issued by the tunnel owner (the **primary security**), allowing the tunnel owner to obtain long-term debt capital.

  Because of the extra security that a lender has by holding a bank account as a financial asset rather than by making a loan direct to a firm, the lender is prepared to accept a lower rate of interest and the ultimate borrower obtains funds at a relatively low cost. The bank reduces its risk exposure to any one project by diversifying its loan portfolio among a number of firms. It can also reduce risk by building up expertise in assessing and monitoring firms and their associated risk.

  Another example of risk transformation is when unit or investment companies (see later in this chapter) take savers' funds and spread these over a wide range of company shares.

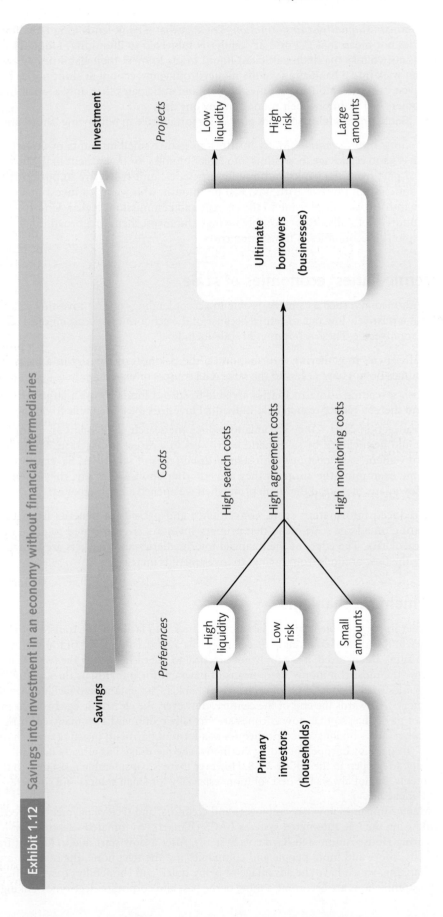

Exhibit 1.12 Savings into investment in an economy without financial intermediaries

- *Maturity (liquidity) transformation* The fact that a bank lends long term for a risky venture does not mean that the primary lender is subjected to illiquidity. Liquidity is not a problem because banks maintain sufficient liquid funds to meet their liabilities when they arise. You can walk into a bank and take the money from your account at short notice because the bank, given its size, exploits economies of scale and anticipates that only a small fraction of its customers will withdraw their money on any one day.

  Banks and building societies play an important role in borrowing 'short' and lending 'long'.

- *Volume transformation* Many institutions gather small amounts of money from numerous savers and repackage these sums into larger bundles for investment in the business sector.

  Apart from the banks and building societies, unit trusts are important here. It is uneconomic for an investor with, say, €50 per month, who wants to invest in shares, to buy small quantities periodically, due to the charges and commissions levied. Unit trusts gather together hundreds of individuals' monthly savings and invest them in a broad range of shares, thereby exploiting economies in transaction costs.

Intermediaries' economies of scale

An intermediary, such as a bank, is able to accept lending to (and investing in shares of) companies at a relatively low rate of return because of the economies of scale enjoyed compared with the primary investor. These economies of scale include:

- Efficiencies in gathering information on the riskiness of lending to a particular firm – individuals do not have access to the same data sources or expert analysis.

- Risk spreading – intermediaries are able to spread funds across a large number of borrowers and thereby reduce overall risk. Individual investors may be unable to do this.

- Transaction costs – they are able to reduce the search, agreement and monitoring costs that would be incurred by savers and borrowers in a direct transaction. Banks, for example, are convenient, safe locations with standardised types of securities. Savers do not have to spend time examining the contract they are entering upon when, say, they open a bank account. How many of us read the small print when we opened a bank account?

The reduced information costs, convenience and passed-on benefits from the economies of operating on a large scale mean that primary investors are motivated to place their savings with intermediaries. The effect of the financial intermediaries and markets are shown in **Exhibit 1.13**, where the flow of funds from savings to investment is increased.

Payment mechanisms

Another important role for financial intermediaries is to facilitate the transfer of money. Over time, money in the form of coins and notes has become a less useful means of transacting business. When larger sums are involved, it is simply not practical to use cash. During the twentieth century cheques became the most commonly used means of payment for individuals throughout the world, while companies used cheques, bills of exchange or bankers' acceptances to facilitate trade payments (*see* Chapter 5). Towards the end of the century, however, the electronic age brought innovation in the field of payments, so that now cheques are virtually redundant – in many countries, supermarkets and other stores no longer accept cheques as a form of payment, insisting on cash or debit or credit cards. In parts of Europe, including Germany, cheque usage has already been phased out and this was due to happen in the UK by 2018. However there is considerable resistance to this, as electronic payments are not always the best solution, especially for small traders and so there was a reprive for the UK cheque.

Many companies now pay employees and creditors, and receive payments, directly through their bank using the UK automated systems BACS (Bankers' Automated Clearing Services) or CHAPS (Clearing House Automated Payments System). After a slow start due to fears of fraud and lack of security, more and more people and companies use the telephone, the internet and smartphones for banking, which have the advantage of being quick and (hopefully) easy. In the financial world, paper transactions are becoming a thing of the past and corporate electronic banking is the norm.

Exhibit 1.13   Savings into investment in an economy with financial intermediaries and financial markets

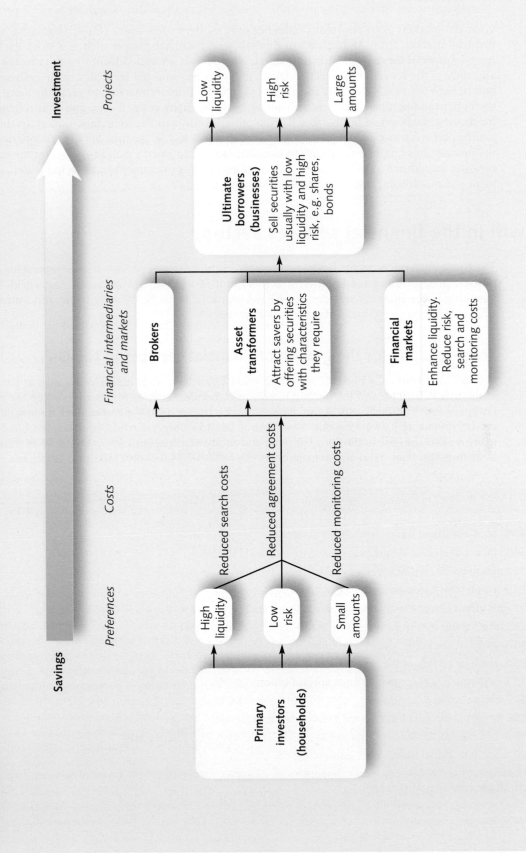

Financial markets

Financial markets exert enormous influence over modern life – every country has some sort of financial market, from Afghanistan to Zimbabwe. A financial market such as a stock exchange has two aspects: there is the primary market, where funds are raised from investors by the firm, and there is the secondary market, in which investors buy and sell securities, such as shares and bonds, between each other. The securities sold into the primary market are generally done so on the understanding that repayment will not be made for many years, if ever, and so it is beneficial for the original buyer to be able to sell on to other investors in the secondary market. In this way the firm achieves its objective of raising finance that will stay in the firm for a lengthy period and the investor has retained the ability to liquidate (turn into cash) a holding by selling to another investor. In addition, a well-regulated exchange encourages investment by reducing search, agreement and monitoring costs – *see* **Exhibit 1.13**.

Growth in the financial services sector

The financial services sector has grown rapidly in the post-war period. It now represents a significant proportion of total economic activity, not just in the UK but across the world. Firms operating in the financial services sector have, arguably, been the most dynamic, innovative and adaptable companies globally over the past 40 years.

Some reasons for the growth of financial services in the UK

London has historically been the most important financial centre, ideally positioned at the heart of the British Empire and the industrialised world. London is open for business when the rest of Europe is active and when the Asian markets are still operating at the end of their trading day and the US is starting its working day. New York is London's biggest rival and overtakes London in many regards, e.g. size of the domestic bond and equity markets, but there is no doubt that London is the foremost financial centre in many areas. *See* **Exhibit 1.14** for some statistical highlights.

Exhibit 1.14	City of London's position in international finance and business services

- o 70% of all eurobond turnover traded in London
- o $450 billion of worldwide premium insurance income in the UK
- o 112 million metal contracts per annum traded in London
- o £3.7 trillion total funds under management in the UK
- o $2.658 trillion pension fund assets under management
- o £38 billion trade surplus generated by the UK financial services sector
- o 43% global share in the 'over-the-counter' derivatives market
- o 95% share of trading in the EU Emissions Trading Scheme
- o 75% of Fortune 500 companies have London offices
- o 249 foreign banks in London
- o 606 foreign companies listed on the London Stock Exchange
- o 18% of cross-border lending arranged in the UK, more than any other country
- o 20% share of global hedge fund assets in the UK
- o Leading western centre for Islamic finance, with 22 banks supplying Islamic financial services, five of which are fully Sharia compliant

Source: www.cityoflondon.gov.uk, 2010.

There are a number of reasons for the growth of the financial services sector in the UK. These include:

- *High income elasticity* As consumers have become increasingly wealthy the demand for financial services has grown by a disproportionate amount. Thus a larger share of national income is devoted to paying this sector fees, etc. to provide services because people desire the benefits offered. Firms have also bought an ever-widening range of financial services from the institutions which have been able to respond quickly to the needs of corporations.

- *International comparative advantage* One of the reasons that London maintains dominance in a number of areas is that it possesses a comparative advantage in providing global financial services. This advantage stems, not least, from the critical mass of collective expertise which it is difficult for rivals to emulate. In some industries, once a cluster of firms and personnel is established, their proximity allows them to be more efficient and learn from each other to improve their skills, deepen knowledge and specialise in tasks. This has happened in Silicon Valley with hi-tech and in the City with financial services. And, of course, London also has the prerequisites of a stable political and trustworthy legal system, no barriers to the flow of money and the English language.

Forty years of innovation

Since the 1970s there has been a remarkably proactive response by the financial sector to changes in the market environment. New financial instruments, techniques of intermediation and markets have been developed with impressive speed. Instruments, which even in the 1990s did not exist, have sprung to prominence to create multi- billion-pound markets, with thousands of employees serving those markets.

There has been a general trend towards deregulation and liberalisation for institutional investors, while recognising that individual investors need protection. Until the mid-1970s there were clearly delineated roles for different types of financial institutions. Banks did banking, insurance firms provided insurance, building societies granted mortgages and so on. There was little competition between the different sectors, and cartel-like arrangements meant that there was only limited competition within each sector. Some effort was made in the 1970s to increase the competitive pressures, particularly for banks. The arrival of large numbers of foreign banks in London helped the process of reform in the UK, but the system remained firmly bound by restrictions, particularly in defining the activities firms could undertake.

The real breakthrough came in the 1980s. The guiding political philosophy of achieving efficiency through competition led to large-scale deregulation of activities and pricing (*see* **Exhibit 1.15**). There was widespread competitive invasion of market segments. Banks became much more active in the mortgage market and set up insurance operations, stockbroking arms, unit trusts and many other services. Building societies, meanwhile, started to invade the banks' territory and offered personal loans, credit cards, cheque accounts. They even went into estate agency, stockbroking and insurance underwriting.

The London Stock Exchange was deregulated in 1986 (in what is known as the **Big Bang**) and this move enabled it to compete more effectively on a global scale and reduce the costs of dealing in shares, particularly for the large institutional investors. The City had become insular and comfortable in its ways, much like a gentlemen's club. Then, in 1986, in the face of serious competition from abroad, it became necessary to make the City more competitive and transparent if it was to continue to service the world's economy as it had done for many years. The introduction of electronic trading, along with the end of fixed-commission trading (an 'accepted rate' to charge rather than one competitively arrived at) and face-to-face dealing, and the sanctioning of foreign ownership of UK brokers successfully pushed the City into the modern era.

The 1970s and early 1980s were periods of volatile interest rates and exchange rates. This resulted in greater uncertainty for businesses. New financial instruments were developed to help manage risk, e.g. derivatives. Many derivatives are traded on LIFFE (the London International Financial Futures and Options Exchange), which has seen volumes rocket since it was opened in 1982. LIFFE, now called NYSE.Liffe, handles around €2 trillion worth of derivatives business every day. Likewise, the volume of swaps, options, futures, etc. traded in the informal over-the-counter market (i.e. not on a regulated exchange) – discussed later in the chapter – has grown exponentially.

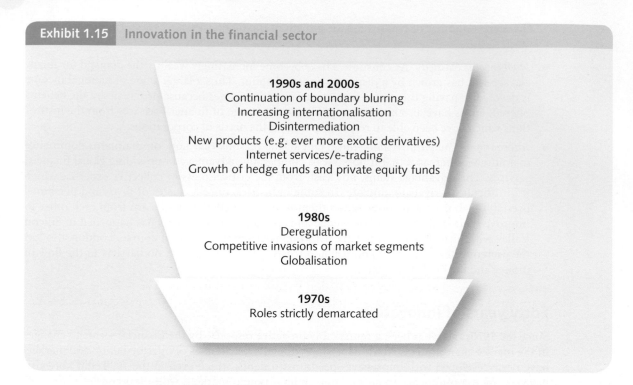

1990s and 2000s
Continuation of boundary blurring
Increasing internationalisation
Disintermediation
New products (e.g. ever more exotic derivatives)
Internet services/e-trading
Growth of hedge funds and private equity funds

1980s
Deregulation
Competitive invasions of market segments
Globalisation

1970s
Roles strictly demarcated

Through the 1980s the trend towards globalisation in financial product trading and services continued apace. Increasingly a worldwide market was established. It became unexceptional for a company to have its shares quoted in New York, London, Frankfurt and Tokyo as well as on its home exchange in Africa. Bond selling and trading became global and currencies were traded 24 hours a day. International banking took on an increasingly high profile, not least because the multinational corporations demanded that their banks provide multifaceted services across the globe, ranging from borrowing in a foreign currency to helping manage cash.

Vast investments have been made in computing and telecommunications systems to cut costs and provide improved services. Automated teller machines (ATMs), banking by telephone and internet, and payment by EFTPOS (electronic funds transfer at point of sale) are now commonplace. A more advanced use of technological innovation is in the global trading of the ever-expanding range of financial instruments. It became possible to sit on a beach in the Caribbean and trade pork belly futures in Chicago, interest rate options in London and shares in Singapore. In the 1990s there was a continuation of the blurring of the boundaries between different types of financial institutions to the point where organisations such as JPMorgan Chase and Barclays are referred to as *financial supermarkets* (or 'universal banks' or 'financial services companies') offering a wide range of services. The irony is that just as this title was being bandied about, the food supermarket giants such as Sainsbury's and Tesco set up banking services, following a path trodden by a number of other non-banking corporations. Marks & Spencer provides credit cards, personal loans and even pensions. Virgin Money sells life insurance, pensions and Individual Savings Accounts (ISAs) over the telephone. The internet has provided a new means of supplying financial services and lowered the barrier to entry into the industry. New banking, stockbroking and insurance services have sprung up. The internet allows people to trade millions of shares at the touch of a button from the comfort of their home, to transfer the proceeds between bank accounts and to search websites for data, company reports, newspaper reports, insurance quotations and so on – all much more cheaply than ever before.

The globalisation of business and investment decisions has continued making national economies increasingly interdependent. Borrowers use the international financial markets to seek the cheapest funds, and investors look in all parts of the globe for the highest returns. Some idea of the extent of global financial flows can be gained by contrasting the *daily* turnover of foreign exchange (approximately US$4 trillion) with the *annual* output of all the goods and services produced by the people in the UK (US$2.15 trillion) – *see* **Exhibit 1.16**. Another effect of tech-

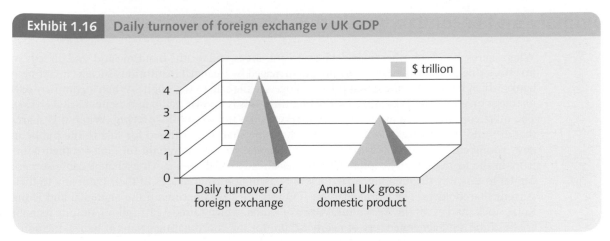

| Exhibit 1.16 | Daily turnover of foreign exchange *v* UK GDP |

Source: BIS and CIA World Factbook.

nological change is the increased mobility of activities within firms. For example, banks have transferred a high proportion of their operations to India, as have insurance companies and other financial firms.

Another feature of recent years has been the development of **disintermediation** – in other words, cutting out the middleman. So, for instance, firms wishing to borrow can bypass the banks and obtain debt finance directly by selling debt securities, such as bonds, in the market. The purchasers can be individuals but are more usually the large savings institutions, such as pension funds, insurance funds and hedge funds. Banks, having lost some interest income from lending to these large firms, have been raising the proportion of their income derived from fees gained by arranging the sale and distribution of these securities as well as *underwriting* their issue (guaranteeing to buy if no one else will). Hedge funds (free from most regulatory control) now account for a high proportion of financial market trading whereas they were barely heard of 15 years ago. Private equity funds, too, which invest in shares and other securities of companies outside a stock exchange, have grown tremendously over the last 20 years.

Debt and equity capital

Companies finance their businesses by raising capital in two main ways. First, they can borrow either by taking out loans or by issuing bonds. The rate of interest that they have to pay is decided by prevailing rates at the time, the standing of the company and the level of risk involved. For example, a stable, well-established firm with a good performance track record would be able to pay interest rates a fraction of a per cent higher than a bank's base rate or slightly above the rate at which very safe banks borrow money (this is the London Interbank Offered Rate (LIBOR), which is discussed in Chapter 5). A new company in a risky industry would have to pay a considerably higher rate. Debt has the advantage of the interest being a tax-deductible expense of running a business. Also, bonds can often be traded in an active secondary market and are therefore liquid investments for investors.

Second, they can raise capital by issuing *shares (equity)* in their company. By buying shares, shareholders own part of the company, and expect returns in the form of dividends paid out from the company's profits and from capital gains made when the shares rise in price. The same criteria apply as for debt: shareholders in well-established, well-performing companies will accept a lower rate of return than shareholders in a new risky venture who demand a higher return to compensate for the extra risk. The return must be commensurate with returns which could be obtained from other securities with the same level of risk. Historically, shares have offered a higher return to investors than government securities over the long run because all equities carry the risk of total loss, so the higher return is needed to encourage investment.

Primary and secondary markets

When shares, bonds or other financial instruments are issued for the first time and sold directly to investors (the primary market), the sales are managed by financial institutions such as investment banks which help decide the initial price and oversee the sale to the public. When a company sells its shares on a regulated exchange for the first time, this is known as the **new issue market** (NIM). The most common issue in the primary market is the **initial public offering**. When it is shares that are sold this is known as a **flotation**, where the shares are offered for sale to the public in new, young companies or well-established companies wishing to obtain funding for their company in the form of equity capital. Companies already listed on a stock exchange can also raise capital in this way through say, a **rights issue** – issuing further shares in their company to their current shareholders. The world's largest IPO was the 2010 floating on the Shanghai and Hong Kong stock markets of the Agricultural Bank of China, which raised $22.1 billion, despite its poor credit rating, and generated fees of nearly $250m for the coordinating group of banks, including Goldman Sachs, Morgan Stanley and Deutsche Bank.

Secondary trading enables the shareholder, bond holder, etc. to liquidate their shares (exchange them for cash) quickly, taking a profit (or loss), while the company's holdings of assets are not diminished because it is not forced to pay the security owners for their shares or bonds. Secondary markets include the stock markets of the world.

Exchange-traded and OTC markets

Exchange trading takes place on the myriad regulated share markets and other security exchanges round the world. There are regulated exchanges in bonds, derivatives, commodities, currencies and other securities. Stock exchanges publish accurate share prices for listed companies and make them available for wide dissemination. The exchanges are funded by a mixture of commission on trades (maybe 10p per deal), admission fees and annual charges for listings, and selling their information to interested parties. All companies listed on stock exchanges have to fulfil a number of statutory requirements and make public their financial reports. These rules are enforced by the exchange and other regulators to reassure investors about the quality of the issuer and the financial instrument.

The **over-the-counter** (OTC) market, also known as the *off-exchange market*, is trade in securities between two parties on a private basis, not on the recognised formal exchanges such as the London Stock Exchange, New York Stock Exchange, etc. The trades can be in shares, bonds, commodities or any other security. A major part of the derivatives market is traded off-exchange, where the flexibility of the OTC market allows the creation of tailor-made derivatives to suit a client's risk situation. Some shares, called unlisted stock, are traded OTC because the company is small and unable to meet stock exchange requirements. OTC trading can be a more risky activity than exchange trading, and there is little transparency in traded prices. For example, bond dealers, who stand ready to buy or sell company bonds in the secondary market, have the benefit of good knowledge about the trades taking place, but their customers (investors) usually do not know what deals were arranged with other customers and so do not know whether the prices they are paying or receiving are fair.

The financial institutions

To help orientate the reader within the financial system and to carry out more jargon busting, a brief outline of the main financial service sectors and markets is given here. Entire chapters are devoted to them later in the book.

The banking sector

Retail and wholesale banking

Put at its simplest, the *retail banks* take (small) deposits from the public which are repackaged and lent to businesses and households. They also provide payment services. They are generally engaged in high-volume and low-value business, which contrasts with *wholesale* banking, which is low volume but each transaction is for a high value (*see* **Exhibit 1.17**). For example, wholesale banks obtain a great deal of the money they use from the sale of financial instruments in values of tens or hundreds of millions of pounds, euros, etc. The distinction between retail and wholesale banks has become blurred over recent years as the large institutions have diversified their operations. The retail banks operate nationwide branch networks and a subset of banks provides a cheque and electronic clearance system – transferring money from one account to another – these are the **clearing banks**. Loans, overdrafts and mortgages are the main forms of retail bank lending. The trend up until 2009 was for retail banks to reduce their reliance on retail deposits and raise more wholesale funds from the financial markets. But this has since been partially reversed as banks found wholesale funding less reliable than obtaining funds to lend from deposits in current or deposit accounts. Northern Rock is an example of a bank that became over-reliant on wholesale funding. When those short-term loans became due for payment in 2008 it found it could not obtain replacement funding. This caused its collapse.

Exhibit 1.17	Comparison between retail and wholesale banking

	Retail banking	Wholesale banking
	High volume	High value
	Low value	Low volume

Investment banks

Investment banks concentrate on dealing with other large organisations, corporations, institutional investors and governments. While they undertake some lending, their main focus is on generating fee and commission income by providing advice and facilitating deals. This sphere is dominated by US, Swiss, UK and German banks – *see* **Exhibit 1.18**.

There are five main areas of activity:

- *Raising external finance for companies* These banks provide advice and arrange finance for corporate clients. Sometimes they provide loans themselves, but often they assist the setting up of a bank syndicate to make a joint loan or make arrangements with other institutions. They will advise and assist a firm issuing a bond. They have expertise in helping firms float their shares on stock exchanges and make rights issues. They may 'underwrite' a bond or share issue (this means that they will buy any part of the issue not taken up by other investors), thus assuring the corporation that it will receive the funds it needs for its investment programme.

- *Broking and dealing* They act as agents for the buying and selling of securities on the financial markets, including shares and bonds. Some also have market-making arms which quote prices at which they are willing to buy or sell from or to, say, a shareholder or a bond holder, thereby assisting the operation of secondary markets. They also trade in the markets on their own account and assist companies with export finance.

Exhibit 1.18   Top investment banks worldwide (2009)

Investment bank	Revenue (in $bn)	Net earnings (in $bn)	Assets under management (in $bn)
Goldman Sachs	45.2	13.4	871
JP Morgan Chase	100.4	11.8	1219
Morgan Stanley	24.74	1.7	779
Citigroup	80.3	−1.6	556
Bank of America	121	6.3	523
Barclays	31.8	10.3	1379
Lazard	1.53	−0.18	98
Credit Suisse	31.05	7.9	384
Deutche Bank	25.3	4.96	181
UBS	24.0	−1.9	159

Source: Balance sheet of respective banks.

- *Fund (asset) management* The investment banks offer services to rich individuals who lack the time or expertise to deal with their own investment strategies. They also manage unit and investment trusts (*see* below and Chapter 4) as well as the portfolios of some pension funds and insurance companies. In addition, corporations often have short-term cash flows which need managing efficiently (treasury management).

- *Assistance in corporate restructuring* Investment banks earn large fees from advising acquirers on mergers and assisting with the merger process. They also gain by helping target firms avoid being taken over too cheaply. Corporate disposal programmes, such as selling off a division, may also need the services of an investment bank.

- *Assisting risk management using derivatives* Risk can be reduced through hedging strategies using futures, options, swaps and the like. However, this is a complex area, with significant room for error and terrible penalties if a mistake is made. The banks may have specialist knowledge to offer in this area.

International banks

There are two main types of international banking:

- *Foreign banking* Transactions (lending/borrowing, etc.) carried out in the domestic currency (e.g. euros in France) with non-residents (e.g. a Japanese company raising money in France).

- *Eurocurrency banking* Transactions in a currency outside the jurisdiction of the country of that currency, e.g. Japanese yen transactions in Canada are outside the control of the Japanese authorities.

The major part of international banking these days is borrowing and lending in foreign currencies. There are about 250 non-UK banks operating in London, the most prominent of which are American, German and Japanese. Their initial function was mainly to provide services for their own nationals, for example for export and import transactions, but nowadays their main emphasis is in the Eurocurrency market and international securities (shares, bonds, etc.) trading. Often funds are held in the UK for the purpose of trading and speculation on the foreign exchange market.

The mutuals

Building societies are mutual organisations owned by their members. They collect funds from millions of savers by enticing them to put their money in interest-bearing accounts. The vast majority of that deposited money is then lent to people wishing to buy a home – in the form of a mortgage. Thus, they take in short-term deposits (although they also borrow on the wholesale financial markets) and they lend money for long periods, usually for 25 years. The number of building societies has declined with a trend to move away from mutual status by the biggest societies and convert to companies with shareholders, offering general banking services.

Many countries have savings banks that, like building societies, do not have outside shareholders but are 'mutually' owned by their members (which generally means customers). There are also savings and loans and cooperative banks constituted along similar lines. Some of these have grown very large and now offer a wide range of services beyond mortgages and the acceptance of deposits.

Finance houses[2]

Finance houses are responsible for the financing of hire purchase agreements and other instalment credit, for example leasing. If you buy a large durable good such as a car or a washing machine you often find that the sales assistant also tries to get you interested in taking the item on credit, so you pay for it over a period of, say, three years. It is usually not the retailer that provides the finance for the credit. The retailer generally works with a finance house which pays the retailer the full purchase price of the good and therefore becomes the owner. You, the customer, get to use the good, but in return you have to make regular payments to the finance house, including interest. Under a hire purchase (HP) agreement, when you have made enough payments you will become the owner. Under leasing the finance house retains ownership. Finance houses also provide factoring services – providing cash to firms in return for the right to receive income from the firms' debtors when they pay up. Most of the large finance houses are subsidiaries of the major conglomerate banks.

Long-term savings institutions

Pension funds

Pension funds are set up to provide pensions for members. For example, the University Superannuation Scheme (USS), to which university lecturers belong, takes 7.5 per cent of working members' salaries each month and puts it into the fund. In addition, the employing organisation pays money into the scheme. When a member retires the USS will pay a pension. Between the time of making a contribution and payment in retirement, which may be decades, the pension trustees oversee the management of the fund. They may place some or all of the fund with specialist investment managers. This is a particularly attractive form of saving because of the generous tax reliefs provided. The long time horizon of the pension business means that large sums are built up and available for investment – for example around £800 billion in the UK funds at the time of writing. Roughly half of this money is invested in UK and overseas shares, with some going to buy bonds and other assets such as money market instruments and property.

Insurance funds

Insurance companies engage in two types of activities:

● *General insurance* This is insurance against specific contingencies such as fire, theft, accident, generally for a one-year period. The money collected in premiums is mostly held in financial assets which are relatively short-term and liquid so that short-term commitments can be met.

---

[2] The term finance house is also used for broadly based financial-service companies carrying out a wide variety of financial activities from share dealing to corporate broking. However, we will confine the term to instalment credit and related services

- *Life assurance* With **term assurance**, your life is assured for a specified period. If you die your beneficiaries get a payout. If you live you get nothing at the end of the period. With **whole-of-life policies**, the insurance company pays a capital sum upon death whenever this occurs. **Endowment policies** are more interesting from a financial systems perspective because they act as a savings vehicle as well as cover against death. The premium will be larger but after a number of years have passed the insurance company pays a substantial sum of money even if you are still alive. The life company has to take the premiums paid over, say, 10 or 25 years and try to invest them wisely to satisfy its commitment to the policy holder. Millions of UK house buyers purchase with an endowment mortgage. They simply pay interest to the lender (e.g. a building society) while also placing premiums into an endowment fund. The hope is that after 25 years or so the value of the accumulated fund will equal or be greater than the inital value of the loan.

  Life assurance companies also provide annuities. Here a policy holder pays an initial lump sum and in return receives regular payments in subsequent years. They have also moved into personal pensions in the UK. Life assurance companies have more than £900 billion under management.

The risk spreaders

These institutions allow small savers a stake in a large diversified portfolio. Thus investors can contribute a small amount each month to an investment fund alongside thousands of other investors and then the pooled fund is professionally managed.

Unit trusts

Unit trusts are 'open-ended' funds, which means that the size of the fund and the number of units depends on the amount of money investors put into the fund. If a fund of 1m units suddenly doubled in size because of an inflow of investor funds it would become a fund of two million units through the creation and selling of more units. The buying and selling prices of the units are determined by the value of the fund. So if a 2m unit fund is invested in £2m worth of shares in the UK stock market the value of each unit will be £1. If over a period the value of the shares rises to £3m, the units will be worth £1.50 each. Unit holders sell units back to the managers of the unit trust if they want to liquidate their holding. The manager would then either sell the units to another investor or sell some of the underlying investments to raise cash to pay the unit holder. The units are usually quoted at two prices depending on whether you are buying (higher) or selling (lower). There is also an ongoing management charge for running the fund.

There is a wide choice of unit trusts specialising in different types of investments ranging from Japanese equities to privatised European companies. Of the £500 billion or so invested in unit trusts and their cousins, open-ended investment companies (OEICs), 50–60 per cent is devoted to shares (one half of which are non-UK) with 20 per cent devoted to bonds. Instruments similar to unit trusts are often called mutual funds in other countries.

Mutual funds

Mutual funds comprise a major portion of the US and Canadian investment market, where the greater part of the population own some mutual fund shares. They are attractive to individual investors because they offer investment diversification and professional fund management. Not many people have the time or expertise to devote to poring over financial statistics in an attempt to pick a good (i.e. profitable) investment. For these people mutual funds provide a satisfactory solution, although they must be aware that past performance is no indicator of future performance and that just because a mutual fund manager has come top of the pile does not mean that he will do the same the following year, and that they will have to pay charges for investing in a fund. Investors can choose the type of investment they prefer, capital growth, income, etc. – and they have the security of knowing that their investment portfolios are safely stored with a custodian, usually a bank.

Investment trusts (investment companies)

Investment trusts differ from unit trusts – they are companies able to issue shares and other securities rather than units. Investors can purchase these securities when the investment company is first launched or purchase shares in the secondary market from other investors. These are known as closed-end funds because the company itself is closed to new investors – if you wished to invest your money you would go to an existing investor (via a broker) to buy shares and not buy from the company. Investment companies usually spread their funds across a range of other companies' shares. They are also more inclined to invest in a broader range of assets than unit trusts – even property, or shares not listed on a stock market. Approximately half of the money devoted to the 400 or so UK investment companies (£80 billion) is put into UK securities, with the remainder placed in overseas securities. The managers of these funds are able to borrow in order to invest. This has the effect of increasing returns to shareholders when things go well. Correspondingly, if the value of the underlying investments falls, the return to shareholders falls even more because of the obligation to meet interest charges.

Open-ended investment companies

Open-ended investment companies are hybrid risk-spreading instruments which allow an investment in an open-ended fund. Designed to be more flexible and transparent than either investment trusts or unit trusts, OEICs have just one price. However, as with unit trusts, OEICs can issue more shares, in line with demand from investors, and they can borrow. Investors may invest in one particular OEIC or in a variety of separate sub-funds under the same management structure.

The risk takers

Private equity funds

These are funds that invest in companies that do not have a stock market trading quote for their shares. The firms are often young and on a rapid growth trajectory, but private equity funds also supply finance to well-established companies. The funds usually buy shares in these companies and occasionally supply debt finance. Frequently the private equity funds are themselves funded by other financial institutions, such as a group of pension funds. Private equity has grown tremendously over the last 20 years to the point where now more than one-fifth of non-government UK workers are employed in a firm financed by private equity.

Hedge funds

Hedge funds gather together investors' money and invest it in a wide variety of financial strategies largely outside the control of the regulators, being created either outside the major financial centres or as private investment partnerships. The investors include wealthy individuals as well as institutions, such as pension funds, insurance funds and banks. Being outside normal regulatory control hedge funds are not confined to investing in particular types of securities or to using particular investment methods. For example, they have far more freedom than unit trusts in 'going short', i.e. selling a security first and then buying it later, hopefully at a lower price. They can also borrow many times the size of the fund to punt on a small movement of currency rates, or share movements, orange juice futures, or whatever they judge will go up (or go down). If the punt (or rather, a series of punts over the year) goes well, the fund managers earn million-pound bonuses (often on the basis of 2 per cent of funds under management fee plus 20 per cent of the profit made for client investors).

Originally, the term 'hedge' made some sense when applied to these funds. They would, through a combination of investments, including derivatives, try to hedge (lower or eliminate) risk while seeking a high absolute return (rather than a return relative to an index). Today the word 'hedge' is misapplied to most of these funds because they generally take aggressive bets on the movements of currencies, equities, interest rates, bonds, etc. around the world. For example, in 2006 one fund, Amaranth, bet on the movement of the price of natural gas and lost US$6 billion in a matter of days. Their activities would not be a concern if they had remained a relatively small part of the investment scene. However, today they command enormous power and billions more are being placed in these funds every week. Already more than £1,300 billion is invested in these funds. Add to that the borrowed money – sometimes ten times the fund's base capital – and you can see why they are to be taken very seriously. Up to 50 per cent of the share trades on a typical day in London or New York is said to be due to hedge funds.

Concluding comments

Financial systems in all their various forms are vital. The growth in financial markets of all types has been exponential in the years following the Second World War. There has been a massive increase in the variety of new and innovative financial instruments available on the markets, as well as a huge increase in the number of markets, along with a trend towards deregulation and globalisation, especially in developing countries. The world of finance is of major importance to countries' economies. In the absence of an effective financial services industry a country will find it difficult or impossible to grow. In the UK, finance is even more important because it is a highly significant factor in exports.

There is an old joke about financial service firms: they just shovel money from one place to another, making sure that some of it sticks to the shovel. The implication is that they contribute little to the well-being of society. Extremists even go so far as to regard these firms as parasites on the 'really productive' parts of the economies. Yet very few people avoid extensive use of financial services. Most have bank accounts, pay insurance premiums and contribute to pension schemes. People do not put their money into a bank account unless they get something in return. Likewise, building societies, insurance companies, pension funds, unit trusts, investment banks and so on can survive only if they offer a service people find beneficial and are willing to pay for. Describing the mobilisation and employment of money in the service of productive investment as pointless or merely 'shovelling it around the system' is as logical as saying that the transport firms which bring goods to the high street do not provide a valuable service because of the absence of a tangible 'thing' created by their activities.

This chapter has tried to convey the importance of financial services to the people of a nation. These arguments are increasingly being accepted. For example, India has recently recognised the centrality of modern financial services to permit fast economic growth – *see* **Exhibit 1.19**.

Exhibit 1.19

Singh commits India to reform plan

By James Lamont in New Delhi

Manmohan Singh, India's prime minister, yesterday sought to override divisions in his ruling coalition by pledging to fulfil a deep financial reform programme in Asia's third largest economy.

The reform agenda includes developing long-term debt markets, a corporate bond market, strong insurance and pension sectors and futures markets. Government disinvestment in state-owned companies would be accelerated.

"These issues will be addressed through gradual but steady progress in financial sector reforms to make the sector more competitive while ensuring an efficient regulatory and oversight system," Mr Singh told the World Economic Forum's meeting in New Delhi.

His comments seek to dispel investor anxiety over previously agreed financial reforms that have not yet been carried out.

"We need to ensure that the financial system can provide the finance needed for our development, and especially for infrastructure development. This opens up a broad agenda for reform," he said.

Some senior bankers consider India's largely state-owned banking system as severely underdeveloped. Kalpana Morparia, the chief executive of banking group JPMorgan in India, described the reach of India's financial system as "appalling", with low numbers of bank account holders and stunted credit extension. She said India has a "long way to go" to reach its goal of 9 per cent economic growth and that it had to take steps to expand its financial sector.

Exhibit 1.19 continued

Mention of insurance and pension reforms was omitted in a budget statement shortly after the election, and senior cabinet ministers have said consensus within the ruling coalition is lacking over the immediate reform agenda.

Mr Singh, who is widely credited for opening up India's economy in 1991 while finance minister, assured foreign investors that he was undeterred from modernising India's economy and making it more welcome to foreign capital. He said the $121bn of foreign direct investment in India over the past eight years was "small", given the size of Asia's third largest economy.

Last week, the government made it mandatory for all profitmaking, listed, state-run firms to float at least a 10 per cent stake for sale to private investors.

Source: Financial Times, 9 November 2009, p. 12. Reprinted with permission.

This chapter has given an introduction to the world of the financial system. Subsequent chapters expand on each sector.

Key points and concepts

- **Money markets** deal in short-term debt securities – wholesale borrowing and lending for less than one year until they mature.

- **Bond markets** handle longer-term debt securities issued by corporations, governments, local authorities and so on. There is usually a secondary market.

- **Equity markets** trade in shares (equities) on a stock market. Firms raise finance by issuing shares. Usually investors can buy/sell in a secondary market.

- **Foreign exchange markets** exchange one currency for another 24 hours a day.

- **Derivatives** are securities derived from an underlying security (currency, shares, commodities, etc.). Their performance depends on the performance of the underlyings.

- **Banking** lies at the heart of the financial system. Its core functions are the taking of deposits, lending and managing payments mechanisms.

- **Financial centres** – London and New York are top. The centres are ranked not just by turnover but by many qualitative factors.

- **Financial institutions and markets** encourage growth and progress by **mobilising savings** and encouraging investment.

- Financial institutions encourage the flow of saving into investment by acting as **brokers** and **asset transformers**, thus alleviating the **conflict of preferences** between the **primary investors** (households) and the **ultimate borrowers** (firms). **Primary investors** are looking for high liquidity and low risk. **Ultimate borrowers** need to attract funds to invest in capital spending, but the funds will be at risk.

- **Asset transformation** is the creation of an intermediate security with characteristics appealing to the primary investor to attract funds, which are then made available to the ultimate borrower in a form appropriate to them. Types of asset transformation are:
  - risk transformation;
  - maturity transformation;
  - volume transformation.

- Intermediaries are able to transform assets and encourage the flow of funds because of their **economies of scale** vis-à-vis the individual investor:
  - efficiencies in gathering information;
  - risk spreading;
  - transaction costs.

- The **secondary markets** in financial securities encourage investment by enabling investor liquidity (being able to sell quickly and cheaply to another investor) while providing the firm with long-term funds.

- The **financial services sector** has grown to be of great economic significance in the UK. Reasons include:

  - high income elasticity;
  - international comparative advantage.

- The financial sector has shown remarkable **dynamism, innovation and adaptability** over the last four decades. Deregulation, new technology, globalisation and the rapid development of new financial products have characterised this sector.

- **Exchange trading** takes place on stock markets, subject to strict regulation.

- **Over-the-counter trading** takes place between two individual parties outside a regulated exchange. Investment can be suited to clients' risk situation.

- **Banking sector:**

  - **retail banks** – high-volume and low-value business;
  - **wholesale banks** – low-volume and high-value business. Mostly fee based;
  - **investment banks** – mostly fee and commission based;
  - **international banks** – mostly Eurocurrency transactions;
  - **building societies** – mutuals, still primarily small deposits aggregated for mortgage lending;
  - **savings banks and cooperative banks** – mutuals run for their members;
  - **finance houses** – hire purchase, leasing, factoring.

- **Long-term savings institutions:**

  - **pension funds** – major investors in financial assets;
  - **insurance funds** – life assurance and endowment policies provide large investment funds.

- **The risk spreaders:**

  - **unit trusts** – trusts which are open-ended investment vehicles issuing units. Allow small investors to invest in diverse range of investments. Size of fund depends on amount invested;
  - **investment trusts** – companies which invest in other companies' financial securities, particularly shares;
  - **mutual funds** – important investment vehicles in the US, offering diversification and professional management;
  - **open-ended investment companies** – a hybrid between unit and investment trusts.

- **The risk takers:**

  - **private equity funds** – invest in companies not quoted on a stock exchange;
  - **hedge funds** – wide variety of investment or speculative strategies largely outside regulators' control.

References and further reading

To keep up to date and reinforce knowledge gained by reading this chapter, I recommend the *Financial Times* and *The Economist*.

Arnold, G. (2012) *Corporate Financial Management*, 5th edn. London: FT Prentice Hall.
  Contains more on many of these markets and instruments from a corporate finance perspective.

Arnold, G. (2010) *The Financial Times Guide to Investing*, 2nd edn. London: FT Prentice Hall.
  Financial markets and instruments explained from an investor's perspective

Global Financial Centres Index (every six months), Z/Yen Group, available at www.zyen.com.
  Provides a summary of professional opinion of leading financial centres.

Vaitilingam, R. (2010) *The Financial Times Guide to using the Financial Pages*, 6th edn. London: Financial Times Prentice Hall.
  Good introductory source of information. Clear and concise.

Websites

Websites for statistics

Association of British Insurers www.abi.org.uk

Association for Financial Markets in Europe www.afme.eu

Bank for International Settlements www.bis.org

Building Societies Association www.bsa.org.uk

CIA World Factbook www.cia.gov

Financial and business information on City of London www.cityoflondon.gov.uk

Chicago Mercantile Exchange www.cmegroup.com

International Monetary Fund www.imf.org

London Stock Exchange www.londonstockexchange.com

Organisation for Economic Co-operation and Development www.oecd.org

World Federation of Exchanges www.world-exchanges.org

World Trade Organization www.wto.org

Websites for information

Alternative Investment Management Association: the hedge fund industry's global, not-for-profit trade association www.aima.org

British Private Equity & Venture Capital Association (BVCA) www.bvca.co.uk

European Central Bank www.ecb.int

The Finance & Leasing Association www.fla.org.uk

Financial Times www.ft.com

Financial Reporting Council: UK accounting regulator www.frc.org.uk

Institute of Financial Services www.ifslearning.ac.uk

Investment Management Association www.investmentfunds.org.uk

National Association of Pension Funds www.napf.co.uk

Securities Industry and Financial Markets Association www.sifma.org

The Banker: provides global financial information www.thebanker.com

Video presentations

Financial services company chief executives and other senior people describe and discuss policy and other aspects of their businesses in interviews, documentaries and webcasts at Cantos.com. (www.cantos.com) – these are free to view.

Case study recommendations

See www.pearsoned.co.uk/arnold for case study synopses.

Also see Harvard University: http://hbsp.harvard.edu/product/cases

● Goldman Sachs: A Bank for All Seasons (A) (2010) Authors: Lena Genello Goldberg and Tiffany Obenchain. Harvard Business School.

● Financial Networks and Informal Banking in China: From Pawnshops to Private Equity (2009) Author: Elizabeth Köll. Harvard Business School.

● Rural Credit Cooperatives in India (2007) Authors: Bidhan Parmar and Wei Li. Darden, University of Virginia. Available from Harvard Business School website.

● The Japanese Financial System: From Postwar to the New Millennium (2001) Author: Ulrike Schaede. Harvard Business School.

● YES BANK: Mainstreaming Development into Indian Banking (2010) Authors: Michael Chu and Namrata Arora. Harvard Business School.

● China's Financial Markets: 2007 (2009) Authors: Li Jin and Bingxing Huo. Harvard Business School.

Self-review questions

1 What is the difference between money markets and bond markets?

2 What are equities and where are they traded?

3 What happens on forex markets?

4 Describe briefly the development of money.

5 Who are primary investors and ultimate borrowers and explain their conflict of preferences.

6 Name some financial intermediaries and explain how they channel household savings into financial investment.

7 What are the types of asset transformation?

8 Explain intermediaries' economies of scale.

9 Distinguish between a primary market and a secondary market.

10 What are the differences between exchange and OTC trading?

11 Briefly distinguish between retail and investment banking.

12 When pension funds and insurance funds invest money, where does the money come from?

13 Distinguish between risk spreading and risk taking, giving examples.

14 What are unit trusts?

15 What are investment trusts?

16 Distinguish between an open-ended scheme and a closed-ended scheme.

17 What are hedge funds?

Questions and problems

1 Describe some of the ways by which financial centres are judged and explain London's position as a leading financial centre.

2 The company you work for needs to raise financing for a big expansion. Describe some of the markets it could make use of to raise finance.

3 Discuss the relationship between economic growth and the development of a financial sector.

4 Why has an increasing share of household savings been channelled through financial intermediaries?

5   Briefly describe the main types of financial institutions and explain their function.

6   You have £30,000 to put into savings. Discuss, with examples, some of the different risk-spreading investment schemes you could invest in.

Assignments

1   Review all the financial services you or your firm purchase. Try to establish a rough estimate of the cost of using each financial intermediary and write a balanced report considering whether you or your firm should continue to pay for that service.

2   Examine the annual report and accounts of three banks and three stockbrokers. Write a report explaining the services they provide to customers and the differences between them.

Web-based exercises

1   Go to the London Stock Exchange website and download statistics on the number of new share issues over the last five years. Write a report, with graphics including a chart showing the amounts of money that were raised for companies, both UK based and overseas.

2   Go to the European Central Bank website to obtain data to allow you to show the volume of bank lending over the last five years. Write a report linking the lending volumes to the pattern of economic growth and other factors impinging on the appetite for borrowing/lending.

Banking: retail and corporate

LEARNING OUTCOMES

By the end of this chapter the reader should be able to:

- contrast the following types of banking: retail, corporate, commercial, investment, universal;

- describe the core elements of banking and the social functions they serve: deposit taking, lending and payments;

- discuss the main types of loans made by banks and the key factors that bankers consider when granting loans;

- outline the range of services offered by banks beyond the core banking functions, such as cash management, insurance, stock broking, providing guarantees and help with overseas trade;

- explain the importance of:

    (a) good liquidity management – ensuring there are sufficient liquid assets to repay obligations falling due to avoid fear of a sudden outflow of cash;

    (b) good asset management skills – banks need to lend money (acquire assets) with the expectation of a low risk of default and in a diversified manner;

    (c) good liability management – finding funds at low cost;

    (d) good capital adequacy management – the buffer of capital provided by shareholders must be at a high enough level to reduce the chance of insolvency problems while balancing the need to make profits by lending;

- identify the main sections of a bank income statement and recognise the main measures that are used to judge a bank's profitability and safety.

We all know from day-to-day experience that banks offer services of great value to us. For example, we open bank accounts to deposit money to keep it somewhere safe, perhaps earning interest. That money once deposited does not sit in a bank vault – at least not most of it – it is lent out to people wanting to, say, buy a house or set up a business. Thus the money is put to good use and economic benefits flow from that. We also appreciate being able to make payments to others through the banking system.

While deposit facilities, lending and payments are the three core functions of banks they have branched out into a wide range of activities, from assisting with overseas trade to advising companies on interest risk management. When we look at the modern investment bank we see a fantastic array of services that our forebears would not have dreamed of, from acting as prime brokers for hedge funds to trading in commodity derivatives in dozens of currencies.

The term bank has been stretched, so we need to be flexible in what we regard as a banking service. In addition to those institutions that have 'bank' in their name, such as Banco Santander or Barclays Bank, this chapter and the next discuss many other institutions that conduct banking activities, such as building societies and savings and loan associations, collectively known as depository institutions or deposit-taking institutions (DTIs).

What is banking?

Banks started out as fairly straightforward businesses, taking in deposits, making loans and providing a payments mechanism. But they grew. They now conduct a much wider range of activities, and it can be difficult to define banking activity in the modern world. **Exhibit 2.1** is my attempt at providing some clarity by grouping the activities into four different types of banking. Some organisations concentrate on providing services in just one, or perhaps two, of the segments, others are universal banks offering a full range of banking. This classification is not perfect – there are many banks that do not neatly fit into these groups and there are other 'banking' activities not listed here – but it does allow us some tractability in understanding what it is that banks do. This classification will be used to structure this chapter and the next.

German, French and Japanese banks tend to be universal banks offering a very wide range of services. The UK is moving much more towards the universal model, but even some of the largest banks such as Lloyds are not heavily committed to investment banking, and there remain many smaller banks that concentrate on commercial banking. The US has thousands of small commercial banks often restricted to operating only in particular states, and a handful of universal banks – although at the time of writing the breadth of their activities was being curtailed by angry politicians and regulators in the wake of the financial crisis, which is largely blamed on investment bankers (*see* Chapter 16 for an explanation of the causes and consequences of the crisis). We frequently find that banks focus on both retail and wholesale commercial banking back home in their domestic markets while focusing on wholesale markets in their international operations. We also find organisations that concentrate exclusively on investment banking, e.g. Goldman Sachs.

Exhibit 2.2 discusses whether the universal banking model is going out of favour in the US. Senior executives weigh up the benefits from economies of scale and the use by different parts of the bank of the capital resources of the organisation against the problems of managing a business that is increasingly complex with cultural difficulties preventing full cooperation across divisions and across borders.

Exhibit 2.1   An overview of the different aspects of banking

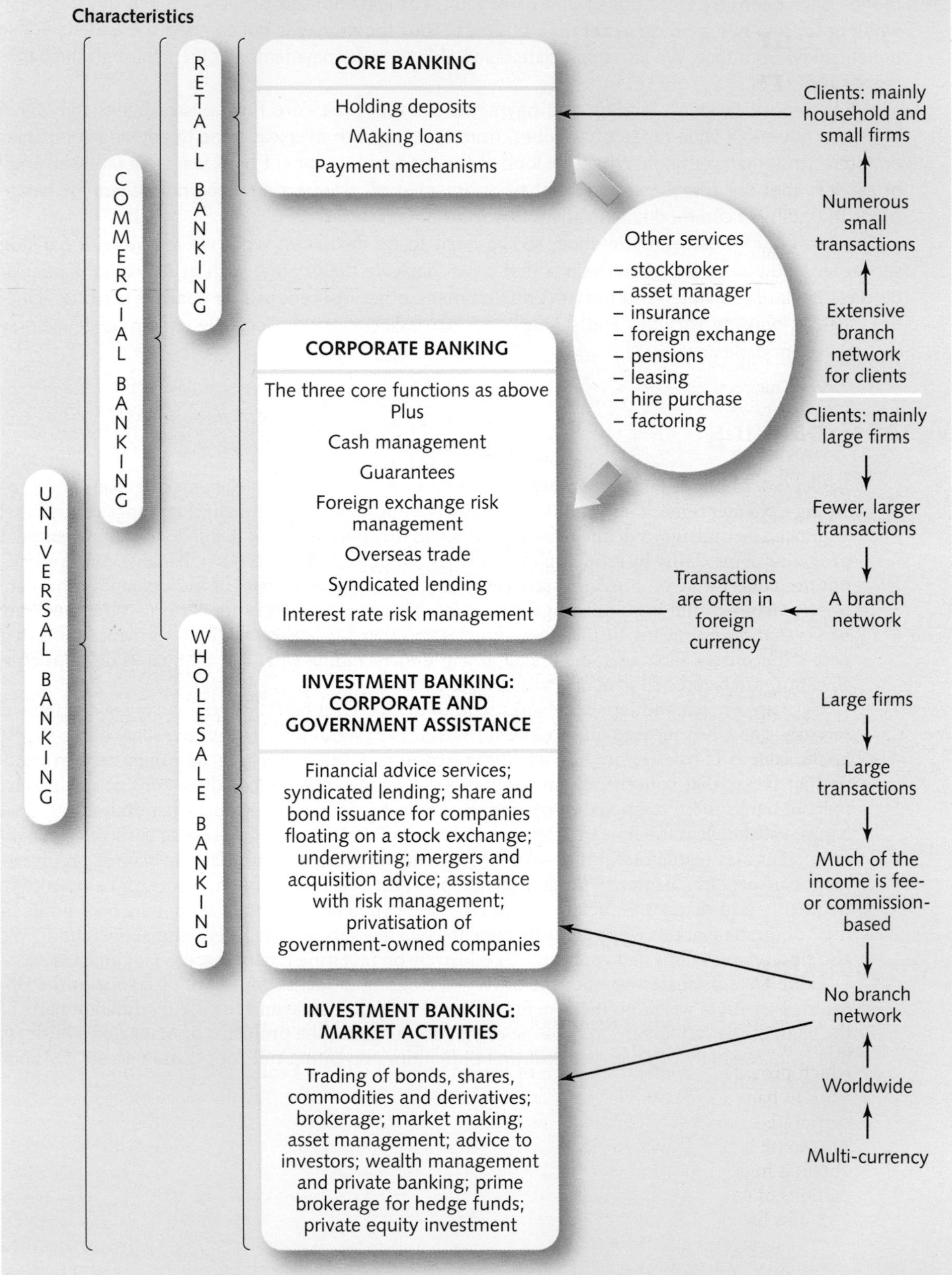

Characteristics

CORE BANKING

Holding deposits
Making loans
Payment mechanisms

Clients: mainly household and small firms

↑

Numerous small transactions

↑

Extensive branch network for clients

Other services

– stockbroker
– asset manager
– insurance
– foreign exchange
– pensions
– leasing
– hire purchase
– factoring

CORPORATE BANKING

The three core functions as above
Plus
Cash management
Guarantees
Foreign exchange risk management
Overseas trade
Syndicated lending
Interest rate risk management

Clients: mainly large firms

↓

Fewer, larger transactions

↓

A branch network

Transactions are often in foreign currency

INVESTMENT BANKING: CORPORATE AND GOVERNMENT ASSISTANCE

Financial advice services; syndicated lending; share and bond issuance for companies floating on a stock exchange; underwriting; mergers and acquisition advice; assistance with risk management; privatisation of government-owned companies

Large firms

↓

Large transactions

↓

Much of the income is fee- or commission-based

↓

No branch network

↑

Worldwide

↑

Multi-currency

INVESTMENT BANKING: MARKET ACTIVITIES

Trading of bonds, shares, commodities and derivatives; brokerage; market making; asset management; advice to investors; wealth management and private banking; prime brokerage for hedge funds; private equity investment

RETAIL BANKING

COMMERCIAL BANKING

UNIVERSAL BANKING

WHOLESALE BANKING

Exhibit 2.2

Too early to declare death of 'universal banking'

FT

Peter Thal Larsen

When Citicorp and Travelers unveiled their ground-breaking merger a decade ago, the deal heralded a new era of consolidation and globalisation in financial services.

However, just because Citigroup is planning to effectively unwind the deal does not mean that all its rivals will be forced to follow suit.

Ever since Citigroup was created, bankers have debated the merits of the so-called global universal bank: the notion that the future of financial services lay with large financial conglomerates that would benefit from economies of scale in information technology and access to capital to serve companies and retail customers around the world.

Over the past 10 years, the Citigroup approach has spawned plenty of imitators.

The merger of Chase with JPMorgan was inspired by a quest for scale, and the perceived benefits of combining commercial and investment banking.

HSBC's drive into the United States also reflected a belief that banks would require genuinely global reach.

More recently, the failed takeover of ABN Amro, the Dutch lender, by Barclays of the United Kingdom was an effort to create an institution that could serve customers from Birmingham to Beijing.

Even before the credit crunch struck, investors were becoming increasingly sceptical about this drive for scale.

The cost benefits of mergers were largely outweighed by increased complexity and the cultural difficulties of integrating and managing large sprawling institutions.

What Citigroup will no longer attempt to do is offer a broad range of financial services products – including insurance, brokerage services and credit cards – under the same umbrella.

"I don't think they're getting away from universal banking," says an executive at a rival lender.

"They're getting away from universal financial services."

There is also the possibility that Citigroup's U-turn represents a failure of execution rather than a failure of strategy.

Even Citigroup bankers admit that, in spite of the bank's prom-

ises to cross-sell a broad range of products to consumers, its various divisions were never properly integrated.

In other words, Citigroup was a financial services conglomerate rather than an unified banking group.

Other universal banks, including JPMorgan Chase and Bank of America, appear to have done a better job at integrating their purchases – although here too the reality often lags behind executives' rhetoric.

Finally, whatever the shortcomings of universal banks, they have survived the current crisis in better shape than some other institutions.

Wall Street's investment banks have been wiped out and many of the smaller institutions that expanded in a single product area – such as specialied mortgage and credit card lenders – have been forced to seek support from larger institutions ... Not withstanding Citigroup's retreat it is still too early to declare the death of universal banking.

Source: Financial Times, 15 January 2009, p. 20. Reprinted with permission

Core banking

At the heart of banking is the acceptance of deposits, the making of loans and enabling customers to make payments. The main source of funds for banks is deposits, as shown in Table 2.1, which provides a crude breakdown of the source of funds for banks. The proportions vary from bank to bank depending on whether the bank is purely retail banking focused or has moved into corporate or investment banking (indeed many investment banks would have no deposits at all). Also some banks deliberately choose to obtain most of their money from deposits whereas others obtain a high proportion from issuing securities on the financial markets in tens or hundreds of millions of pounds, euros, etc., or borrow from other banks in the interbank market.

Banks have to recognise that any money deposited (or lent to them via the issue of a financial market security) will have to be repaid one day; thus deposits and other borrowings are classified as liabilities. If you deposit money in a bank it is an asset for you and part of your wealth because you can withdraw it, but it is an obligation for the bank (when the bank says that you are in credit, it means that you are a creditor – it owes you the money). We will discuss money market borrowing and bank capital later. For now we will concentrate on deposits.

Table 2.1 The typical liabilities of banks – a rough breakdown

	Proportion of assets
Current accounts, also called sight deposits	10–40%
Time deposits, also called savings accounts	10–40%
Money market borrowing (repos, interbank, certificates of deposit[1])	10–40%
Bank capital	8–12%

- *Current account (cheque (check) account or sight account)* An individual can walk into a bank branch and withdraw the money held in their current account at very short notice. Alternatively, they can transfer the money to someone else's account, either using a paper-based method or electronically. These accounts usually pay very low (or no) rates of interest and so are a low-cost source of funds for the bank from that point of view, but the bank will need to spend a considerable amount in processing transfers, monthly statements, providing conveniently located branches, etc. Banks often run current accounts at a loss in order to build up a relationship with a customer so that they can sell them other services.

- *Time or savings deposit accounts* Depositors agree to place money with a bank on the understanding that a set period of notice is required to withdraw cash, ranging from a few days to several months. Alternatively, the customer may place the money in the account for a fixed period. There are usually substantial penalties for early withdrawal and the accounts rarely provide a cheque facility. To compensate for the loss of flexibility to withdraw cash at short notice they offer higher interest rates than current accounts.

Lending

Some bank lending is short term, such as an overdraft, but most of it is long-term lending – certainly longer than the notice periods on most deposit accounts. Banks have developed techniques to screen and monitor borrowers to reduce risk. They also diversify across a range of borrowers. Loans to individuals and to corporations typically account for 50–70 per cent of a commercial bank's assets. Another 10–35 per cent might be lent out to other banks and institutions in the financial markets on a short-term basis, i.e. money market instruments, loans such as interbank lending or repos (*see* Chapter 5). Some is likely to be invested in long-term government bonds, company preference shares or other long-term investments, but this is usually less than 20 per cent. Somewhere between 1 per cent and 10 per cent of the bank's assets may be in the form of buildings, equipment, software or other assets such as gold.

It is possible for banks to lend out most of the money deposited despite a high proportion of deposits being repayable on demand because depositors usually do not all ask for their money back at the same time. However, just in case they need to meet unexpected large outflows, banks hold a fraction of their capital in the form of **liquid reserves**. This is cash (the same as in your wallet or purse) in the vault, at the tills and in ATMs as well as cash deposited at the central bank (banks need bank accounts too), such as the Bank of England, the Federal Reserve in the US or the Bundesbank in Germany. These cash holdings usually account for less than 1 per cent of a bank's assets. Funds kept in a highly liquid form (but not cash) may also include assets that can quickly be turned into cash, such as lending to another bank for 24 hours or 7 days (interbank lending) or government Treasury bills (lending to a government for, say, three or six months), that can be sold to other investors within minutes in a very active secondary market if money is needed.

---

[1] Money market instruments are described in Chapter 5.

Household lending

Consumer loans (personal loans) are often unsecured, meaning that nothing is being used as specifically assigned collateral to be seized by the bank should the borrower fail to pay.[2] In the UK these loans can be up to £25,000 if not secured by collateral and are usually repayable within five years. The interest rate is usually fixed at a constant percentage of the outstanding amount throughout the period. Loans secured on property, such as a house mortgage, are typically repaid over 20–25 years and carry a lower rate of interest than a consumer loan because of the lower risk for the bank. Banks also lend via credit cards – discussed later.

Lending to businesses

For most companies banks remain the main source of externally (i.e. not retained earnings) raised finance. Total bank lending outstanding to the business sector in the UK was more than £500 billion at the time of writing. Spanish companies owed their banks a whopping €900 billion – no wonder they ran into serious trouble in 2011 (they had binge borrowed, much of it to build apartments). While the amounts outstanding were similar to those of Germany, France and Italy (*see* **Exhibit 2.3**), the Spanish have a much smaller economy to support their loans.

Exhibit 2.3	Lending by financial institutions (mostly banks) in selected European countries to businesses and to households – amounts outstanding 2010 (household lending is further broken down to consumer credit and house mortgages) (€ billion)

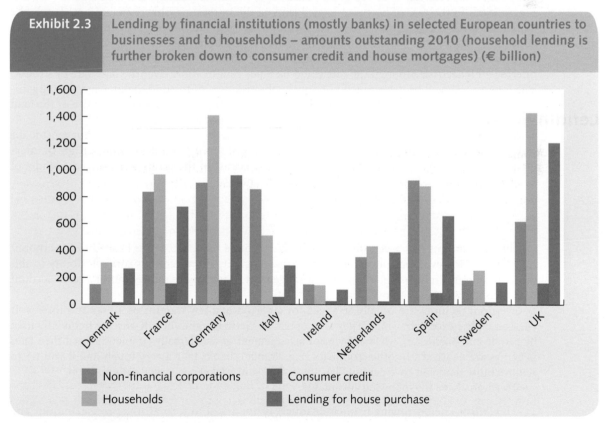

Source: European Central Bank.

Banks make it attractive for companies to borrow from them compared with other forms of borrowing:

● *Administrative and legal costs are low* Because the loan arises from direct negotiation between borrower and lender, this avoids the marketing, arrangement and regulatory expenses involved in, say, a bond issue.

---

[2] The bank will still be able to sue the borrower, who might have to sell assets to repay a loan.

- *Speed* The key provisions of a bank loan can be worked out quickly and the funding facility can be in place within a matter of hours.
- *Flexibility* If the economic circumstances facing the firm should change during the life of the loan, banks are generally better equipped – and more willing – to alter the terms of the lending agreement than bond holders. Negotiating with a single lender in a crisis has distinct advantages. Bank loans are also more flexible in the sense that if the firm does better than originally expected, a bank loan can often be repaid without penalty. Contrast this with many bonds with fixed redemption dates, or hire purchase/leasing arrangements with fixed terms.
- *Availability to small firms* Bank loans are available to firms of almost any size whereas the bond market is for the big players only.

An **arrangement fee** may be payable by the borrower to the bank at the time of the initial lending, say 1 per cent of the loan, but this is subject to negotiation and may be bargained down. The interest rate can be either fixed (same for the whole borrowing period) or floating (variable). If it is floating then the rate will generally be a certain percentage above the bank's **base rate** or **LIBOR**. LIBOR is the London interbank offered rate, that is, the rate of interest charged when a bank lends to a highly reputable and safe bank in London – *see* Chapter 5 for more on this. Because the typical borrowing corporation is not as safe as a high-quality bank, it will pay, say, 1 per cent (also referred to as 100 **basis points, bps**) more than LIBOR if it is in a good bargaining position. In the case of base rate-related lending the interest payable changes immediately the bank announces a change in its base rate. This moves irregularly in response to financial market conditions, which are heavily influenced by the central bank, say the Bank of England in its attempt to control the economy – *see* Chapter 7. For customers in a poorer bargaining position offering a higher-risk proposal the rate could be 5 per cent or more over the base rate or LIBOR. The interest rate will be determined not only by the riskiness of the undertaking and the bargaining strength of the customer but also by the degree of security for the loan and the size of the loan – economies of scale in lending mean that large borrowers pay a lower interest rate.

A generation ago it would have been more normal to negotiate fixed-rate loans, but most loans today are variable rate. If a fixed rate of interest is charged this is generally at a higher rate of interest than the floating rate at the time of arrangement because of the additional risk to the lender of being unable to modify rates as an uncertain future unfolds.

Overdraft

Usually the amount that a depositor can withdraw from a bank account is limited to the amount they put in. However, business and other financial activity often requires some flexibility in this principle and it can be useful to make an arrangement to take more money out of a bank account than it contains – this is an **overdraft**.

Overdraft facilities are usually arranged for a period of a few months or a year and interest is charged on the excess drawings. They are popular in Germany and the UK and are frequently used by people and businesses, whether by prior arrangement or accidentally (if unauthorised then fees/penalties are charged). In other countries (e.g. France), banks take a very tough line if you try to remove more than you have deposited in an account, unless you have prior authorisation.

Overdrafts have the following advantages.

1. *Flexibility* The borrowing firm (individual) is not asked to forecast the precise amount and duration of its borrowing at the outset but has the flexibility to borrow up to a stated limit. Also the borrower is assured that the moment the funds are no longer required they can be quickly and easily repaid without suffering a penalty.

2. *Cheapness* Banks usually charge 2–5 percentage points over base rate (or LIBOR) depending on the creditworthiness, security offered and bargaining position of the borrower. There may also be an arrangement fee of, say, 1 per cent of the facility, but many banks have dropped arrangement fees completely to attract borrowers. These charges may seem high but it must be borne in mind that overdrafts are often loans to smaller and riskier firms which would

otherwise have to pay much more for their funds. Large and well-established borrowers with low financial gearing (low borrowing relative to the amount put in by the business owners) and plenty of collateral can borrow on overdraft at much more advantageous rates. A major saving comes from the fact that the banks charge interest only on the daily outstanding balance. So, if a firm has a large cash inflow one week it can use this to reduce its overdraft, temporarily lowering the interest payable, while retaining the ability to borrow more another week.

A major drawback to an overdraft for the borrower is that the bank retains the right to withdraw the facility at short notice. Thus a heavily indebted firm may receive a letter from the bank insisting that its account be brought to balance within a matter of days. This right lowers the risk to the lender because it can quickly get its money out of a troubled company; this allows it to lower the cost of lending. However, it can be devastating for the borrower and so firms are well advised to think about how they use finance provided by way of an overdraft. It is not usually wise to use the money for an asset which cannot be easily liquidated; for example, it could be problematic if an overdraft is used for a bridge-building project which will take three years to come to fruition.

Term loans

A **term loan** is a business loan with an original maturity of more than one year and a specified schedule of principal and interest payments. These loans are normally for a period of between three and seven years, but the period can range from one to twenty years. It may or may not be secured with collateral and has the advantage over the overdraft of not being repayable at the demand of the bank at short notice (if the borrower sticks to the agreement). The specified terms will include provisions regarding the repayment schedule.

In setting up a term loan the bank can be very flexible with regard to the conditions it sets for the borrower. For example, a proportion of the interest and the principal can be repaid monthly, or annually, and can be varied to correspond with the borrower's cash flows. It is rare for there to be no repayment of the principal during the life of the loan, but it is possible to request that the bulk of the principal is paid in the later years. It could be disastrous, for instance, for a firm engaging in a project which involves large outlays for the next five years followed by cash inflows thereafter to have a bank loan which requires significant interest and principal payments in the near term. If the borrower is to apply the funds to a project which will not generate income for perhaps the first three years, it may be possible to arrange a **grace period** or **repayment holiday** during which only the interest is paid, with the capital being paid off once the project has a sufficiently positive cash flow. Other arrangements can be made to reflect the pattern of cash flow of the firm or project: for example a **'balloon' payment structure** is one when only a small part of the capital is repaid during the main part of the loan period, with the majority repayable as the maturity date approaches. A **'bullet' repayment** arrangement takes this one stage further and provides for all the capital to be repaid at the end of the loan term. Banks generally prefer **self-amortising term loans** with a high proportion of the principal paid off each year. This has the advantage of reducing risk by imposing a programme of debt reduction on the borrowing firm.

Not all term loans are drawn down in a single lump sum at the time of the agreement. In the case of a construction project which needs to keep adding to its borrowing to pay for the different stages of development, an **instalment arrangement** might be required with, say, 25 per cent of the money being made available immediately, 25 per cent at foundation stage and so on. This has the added attraction to the lender of not committing large sums secured against an asset not yet created. From the borrower's point of view a **drawdown arrangement** has an advantage over an overdraft in that the lender is committed to providing the finance if the borrower meets prearranged conditions, whereas with an overdraft the lender can withdraw the arrangement at short notice.

It may be possible for a company to arrange a **mortgage-style repayment schedule** in which monthly payments from the borrower to the lender are constant throughout the term. Indeed, the repayment schedule agreed between bank and borrower is capable of infinite variety – four possibilities are shown in **Exhibit 2.4**.

Exhibit 2.4	Simple examples of loan repayment arrangements

£10,000 borrowed, repayable over four years with interest at 10 per cent p.a. (assuming annual payments, not monthly). Schemes (a) to (d) all pay the equivalent 10 per cent per annum.

(a) Mortgage-style repayment arrangement

Time period (years)	1	2	3	4
Payment (£)	3,155	3,155	3,155	3,154

(b) Interest only paid each year

Time period (years)	1	2	3	4
Payment (£)	1,000	1,000	1,000	11,000

(c) Bullet loan with interest and capital repaid at the end

Time period (years)	1	2	3	4
Payment (£)	0	0	0	14,641

(d) Balloon-style repayment schedule

Time period (years)	1	2	3	4
Payment (£)	0	1,000	6,000	6,831

Security for banks on business lending

When banks are considering the provision of debt finance for a firm they will be concerned about the borrower's competence and honesty. They need to evaluate the proposed project and assess the degree of managerial commitment to its success. The firm will have to explain why the funds are needed and provide detailed cash forecasts covering the period of the loan. Between the bank and the firm stands the classic gulf called asymmetric information in which one party in the negotiation is ignorant of, or cannot observe, some of the information which is essential to the contracting and decision-making process. The bank is unable to assess accurately the ability and determination of the managerial team and will not have a complete understanding of the market environment in which they propose to operate. Companies may overcome bank uncertainty to some degree by providing as much information as possible at the outset and keeping the bank informed of the firm's position as the project progresses.

Bankers encourage the finance director and managing director to consider carefully both the quantity and quality of information flows to the bank. An improved flow of information can lead to a better and more supportive relationship. Firms with significant bank financing requirements to fund growth will be well advised to cultivate and strengthen understanding and rapport with their bank(s). The time to lay the foundations for subsequent borrowing is when the business does not need the money, so that when loans are required there is a reasonable chance of being able to borrow the amount needed on acceptable terms.

There are two types of interaction a company might have with a bank. The first is relationship banking in which there is an understanding on both sides that there will be a long-term relationship in which the company provides information regularly to the bank and the bank can reduce its screening and monitoring costs. Over time, the bank develops special knowledge of the firm and its needs and as a result will be more supportive when the need for borrowing or forbearance in hard times is needed. The other type is transactional banking in which the company shops around for services, looking for the lowest cost for individual tasks. This has the advantage of obtaining cheap individual services but the absence of a long-term relationship can make the firm vulnerable in tough times.

Another way for a bank to reduce its risk is for the firm to offer sufficient collateral for the loan. Collateral provides a means of recovering all or the majority of the bank's investment should the firm fail to repay as promised. If the firm is unable to meet its loan obligations then holders of fixed-charge collateral can seize the specific asset used to back the loan. With a floating charge the legal right to seize assets 'floats' over the general assets of the firm so they can be bought and sold or rented without specific permission from the lender. The charge only crystallises at the point of default on the loan – the assets are frozen within the firm and made available to repay lenders. On liquidation, the proceeds from selling assets will go first to the secured loan holders, including floating-charge bank lenders. Bankers may look at a firm on two levels. First, they might consider a liquidation analysis in which they think about their position in a scenario of business failure. Second, they will look at a firm on the assumption that it is a going concern, where cash flows rather than assets become more important.

Collateral can include stocks (inventories) of unsold goods, debtors and equipment as well as land, buildings and marketable investments such as shares in other companies. In theory, banks often have the right to seize assets or begin proceedings to liquidate; in practice they are reluctant to use these powers because such draconian action can bring adverse publicity. They are careful to create a margin for error in the assignment of sufficient collateral to cover the loan because, in the event of default, assigned assets usually command a much lower price than their value to the company as a going concern. A quick sale at auction produces bargains for the buyers of liquidated assets and usually little for the creditors. Instead of rushing to force a firm to liquidate, banks will often try to reschedule or restructure the finance of the business (e.g. grant a longer period to pay).

Another safety feature applied by banks is the requirement that the borrowing firm abides by a number of **loan covenants** which place restrictions on managerial action until the debt has been repaid in full. Some examples are:

- *Limits on further debt issuance* If lenders provide finance to a firm they do so on certain assumptions concerning the riskiness of the capital structure. They will want to ensure that the loan does not become more risky due to the firm taking on a much greater debt burden relative to its equity base, so they limit the amount and type of further debt issues – particularly debt which is higher ranking ('**senior debt**') for interest payments and for a liquidation payment. **Subordinated debt** – with low ranking on liquidation – is more likely to be acceptable.

- *Dividend level* Lenders are opposed to money being brought into the firm by borrowing at one end while being taken away by shareholders at the other. An excessive withdrawal of shareholder funds may unbalance the financial structure and weaken future cash flows.

- *Limits on the disposal of assets* The retention of certain assets, for example property and land, may be essential to reduce the lender's risk.

- *Financial ratios* A typical covenant here concerns the **interest cover**, for example: 'The annual pre-interest pre-tax profit will remain four times as great as the overall annual interest charge.' Other restrictions might be placed on working capital ratio levels and on the debt to net assets ratio. If these financial ratio limits are breached or interest and capital are not paid on the due date, the bank has a right of termination, in which case it could decide not to make any more funds available or, in extreme cases, insist on the repayment of funds already lent.

While covenants cannot provide completely risk-free lending they can influence the behaviour of the management team so as to reduce the risk of default. The lender's risk can be further reduced by obtaining guarantees from third parties that the loan will be repaid. The guarantor is typically the parent company of the issuer.

Finally, lenders can turn to the directors of the firm to provide additional security. The directors might be asked to sign personal guarantees that the firm will not default. Personal assets (such as homes) may be used as collateral. This erodes the principle of limited liability status and is likely to inhibit risk-taking productive activity. However, for many smaller firms it may be the only way of securing a loan and at least it demonstrates the commitment of the director to the success of the enterprise.[3]

---

[3] Indeed, when the author recently contacted a number of banks to negotiate a loan for a company he controls, the corporate loan officers were all amazed at his cheek in not accepting a personal guarantee clause. 'But we normally get a personal guarantee, it is just standard practice,' they declared. Don't accept this line if you have a strong business plan and strong financial structure.

There are two other factors on the minds of lending officers at banks:

1 *Creditworthiness* This goes beyond examining projected future cash flows and asset backing and considers important factors such as character and talents of the individuals leading the organisation.

2 *The amount that the borrower is prepared to put into the project or activity, relative to that asked from the bank.* If the borrower does not show commitment by putting their own money into a scheme, banks can get nervous and stand-offish.

Payment mechanisms

Banks facilitate payments between people and organisations using either paper or electronic means.

- *Cheque* While still a popular means of settling indebtedness the cheque is increasingly giving way to direct debits, credit and debit cards. Already card transactions outnumber cheques by a large margin in many countries – in the UK, for example, by four to one. A number of banks are hoping to phase out this relatively expensive means of transferring money; the UK had a target date (31 October 2018) for doing away with cheques, but following a public outcry the plan was dropped.

- *Giro* Even before the electronic age people without cheque books could still transfer money to others by using a giro slip which instructs their bank to pay, say, the electricity company. This remains a popular means of payment in Germany, the Netherlands, Austria and Japan. Giro banks were set up in many European countries using their post offices to allow those without a bank account, let alone a cheque book, to make payments. The bill could be paid at the post office counter and the money transferred to the payee. Post offices can be surprisingly big players in the financial system. Indeed, the largest deposit-taking institution in the world is not a bank but the Japanese post office. It holds around £2,000 billion in savings accounts (a quarter of all Japanese household assets) and has bought one-fifth of all the Japanese government bonds in issue – and that is a lot of bonds, given that the Japanese government has outstanding borrowings of 200 per cent of annual gross domestic product.

- *Standing orders and direct debits* These are used for recurring payments. With standing orders the account holder instructs their bank to pay a fixed regular amount to a beneficiary's account. It is only the account holder who can change the order instructions. Direct debits are similar to standing orders except that the supplier of a good or service which is due to paid (e.g. gas or water company) gets the customer to sign the direct debit which allows the supplier to vary the amount and vary the time of payment.

- *Plastic cards* We have got so used to transferring money using plastic that it no longer seems remarkable. A bank card allows us to use ubiquitous ATMs providing a quick way of obtaining cash, checking balances or other services. The debit card (usually the same card as the ATM-enabled card) allows us to make payments by providing the information the retailer needs to set up what is in effect an electronic cheque to credit the retailer's account while debiting our account. They use an EFTPOS (Electronic Funds Transfer at Point of Sale) terminal to initiate the debiting of our accounts. EFTPOS are even more numerous than ATMs. Credit cards allow users to pay for goods, wait for a statement of indebtedness to the credit card company and then decide whether to pay off the whole amount outstanding that month or pay only, say, 5 per cent of the debt owed and borrow the rest until they are in a better position to pay back. They are allowed a fixed maximum borrowing. The credit card company gains income from charging the retailers (usually 1–3 per cent of the transaction value) as well as charging the user interest if they fail to pay off the full amount outstanding each month. The rates on money borrowed this way can be very high. For example, while secured mortgages can be obtained for around 4–6 per cent per year, credit cards typically charge more than 18 per cent. Much of this extra interest is to cover bad debts and fraud. Visa and Mastercard process transactions for the retailer, and card issuer. Thousands of commercial organisations, such as high-street retailers, issue their own versions of credit cards, known as store cards. The retailer usually lacks the infrastructure to process credit cards and so works with a bank or a specialist organisation. American Express and Diners Club cards are different – they are charge cards. Here, the user is expected to pay off the balance every month. Smart cards (electronic purses, chip cards) store information on a microchip. This might be an amount of cash (e-money) loaded onto it using an ATM, personal computer or telephone download. The retailer is able to take money from the customer's card and load it onto their own, ready for paying into their bank account. To purchase goods on the internet, **e-cash** is often used, which is created by setting up an account with a bank which then transfers credits to the user's PC. When the user wants to buy something, cash is taken electronically from the user's PC and transferred to the merchant's computer.

● *Landlines and mobile phones* Telephone banking has been with us for a long time now. Many banks are principally telephone (with internet) based, e.g. First Direct in the UK, but mostly telephone banking is an extra service available for standard branch-based accounts. Not only is telephone banking available 24 hours per day but transactions such as bill paying can be conducted quickly and loans can be arranged. Banks encourage customers to use telephone banking because the cost of undertaking a transaction can be 25–50 per cent that of using the branch. In many parts of Africa (e.g. Kenya), people, many of whom do not have a bank account, are transferring money to each other using mobile phones – for a report on this see http://news.bbc.co.uk/1/hi/8194241.stm. Mobile phone banking, including sophisticated smartphone banking apps, is expected to become very big business over the next decade.

● *Internet* Millions of people now use internet-based accounts, either separate from their normal branch-based account (e.g. Security First Network Bank in the US and Egg in the UK) or as an extra facility attached to their usual account. Transaction costs for banks can be a tenth of those for branch-based activity, so expect to see banks promoting greater use of the internet. **Exhibit 2.5** shows the extent of online banking in the US and the UK.

Clearing systems

After a cheque (or electronic payment) has been written and handed over to the payee there needs to be a system for transferring the money from one bank account to another. This is clearing. Banks within countries came together long ago to work out a way of ensuring accurate and timely settlement of payments. Usually central banks led the process. Those banks linked into the system are referred to as **clearing banks**. These are usually only the large banks with extensive retail banking operations. Smaller banks may make a deal with one of the clearing banks for it to handle its cheque (electronic) clearance. If a cheque or debit card draws money from one account for it to be credited to another person's account at the same bank then the bank will deal with clearing itself. If, however, money needs to be transferred to an account at another bank, the cheque will be put through the central clearing system. This is mostly electronic because the cheque has computer-readable information such as the branch sort code, account number and cheque number displayed – the amount of money is the missing element that needs to be input. Of course, direct debits, standing orders and other regular payments are already inputted into computer systems to permit electronic clearance.

In the UK all clearing is overseen by the UK Payments Council, which acts as controller of various payment services. BACS Ltd (originally the **Bankers' Automated Clearing Services**) clears electronic payment for direct debits and credits, standing orders, salaries, etc. The Cheque and Credit Clearing Company (CCCL) manages the cheque clearing system. CHAPS (Clearing House Automated Payment System) allows money to be electronically transferred the same day (this costs a minimum of £20 but is frequently worth it for large or urgent payments). It is a real-time gross settlement (RTGS) system, meaning that payments are settled individually and continuously through the day rather than waiting until the end of the day (avoiding the risk associated with a bank going bust halfway through the day and not completing the deal). The average payment under CHAPS is more than £2 million, compared with a few hundred under BACS and CCCL. TARGET (Trans-European Automated Real-time Gross Settlement Express Transfer system) – now TARGET2 – is the most important large-value euro system for cross-border transfers within the EU. It too is a real-time settlement system. A large group of US and European banks own an international electronic payments system called SWIFT (Society for Worldwide Interbank Financial Telecommunication), which is a messaging service that sends payment orders between banks and other financial institutions which then settle payments between themselves.

Exhibit 2.5

Slow but inexorable move to cyberspace banking

FT

Ellen Kelleher

The oversupply of Lloyds, Natwest, HSBC and Barclays branches on the high street, not to mention the plethora of building societies, suggests we still prefer chatting with tellers over logging on to the internet to pay bills, check balances and deposit funds.

Yet slowly but surely, the internet is making its mark on the sector as more people over their banking online. Lloyds is to shut up to 400 branches as part of its integration of HBOS. Its rivals are likely to follow suit.

A decade from now, the local branch could well be an endangered species as "cyber-banking" grows ever more popular and more branches close.

"Is there such a need for so many branches? Clearly, there are too many in certain areas," says Ben Yearsley, investment adviser with Hargreaves Lansdown. "The only time I personally go into a bank is to collect foreign currency and to pay in cheques that I occasionally receive, and I can't imagine I am too different to most people."

Since the dotcom boom of a decade ago, high street banks have been pushing their internet businesses, offering incentives to encourage online bill payment and enticing customers with attractive rates.

Crucially, it is the banks' core brands, rather than their internet-only spin-offs, that have been making all the progress.

At the height of the dotcom boom, Abbey launched Cahoot, Halifax brought out Intelligent Finance and the Co-op Bank launched Smile. Yet while these banks have had some success, none has threatened the market position of the sector's leaders.

American banks have been far more successful at persuading their customers to bank online. Just 30 per cent of British adults banked online in the past month while almost half of those in the US did, according to a survey this year by Gartner, the market research group.

But that gap is likely to shrink. About 87 per cent of UK residents with incomes of £15,000 use the internet for browsing, reading newspapers and other activities, Gartner's research indicates.

The move online is likely to be accompanied by a change in the role of the remaining bank branches.

Jason Butler, a planner with Bloomsbury Financial Planning, predicts that large regional centres where advisers offer financial planning and other services will replace the traditional branch networks.

"However, banks need to avoid past mistakes of selling poor value, financial 'rubbish' to their customers," he cautions.

Source: Financial Times, 7 July 2009, p. 18. Reprinted with permission.

Survey of online banking users

Online banking use
% of respondents

■ US   ■ UK

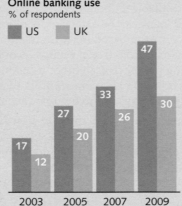

By household income
% of respondents

■ US   ■ UK

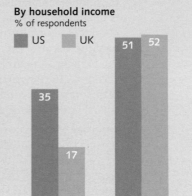

By generation
% of respondents

32 and under

38–44

45–62

63 and older

■ US
■ UK

Reasons given for not banking online
% of respondents*

	US	UK
Prefer other channels	61	58
Security	41	38
Technology	17	18
Access	23	18
None	25	31

Source: Gartner   * Multiple choice

Currently, the European Union is working on a more effective clearing system for cross-border payments because it can be very expensive to transfer money from, say, a Spanish bank account to one in Germany. In the US, high-value payments go through different electronic systems called CHIPS (Clearing House Interbank Payments) and Fedwire; there are a number of systems for small payments clearing.

Corporate banking

There are two categories of bank lending to corporates – uncommitted facilities and committed facilities.

Uncommitted facilities

With an uncommitted facility the bank does not enter an agreement that makes it obliged to provide funds at the borrower's request and the facility can be cancelled and so the borrower may have to repay at short notice. These are usually short-term borrowing arrangements – less than one year. The simplest type is the overdraft, which may be a six-month (or annual) arrangement. There may be an expectation on both sides that the overdraft facility will be renewed – rolled over or revolved – after the six months are up, but the bank has not guaranteed that this will be possible. Indeed, the bank can insist on repayment within the six months.

An uncommitted line of credit is an alternative to an overdraft. The borrower can borrow up to a maximum sum for a period of, say, a month or six months, and can repay and borrow again as needed within that time period. The bank is uncommitted because it merely has to make its best efforts to make the sum available and it has the discretion to remove the facility at short notice. The interest rate is often set as a number of basis points over the interbank lending rate, say one-month LIBOR.

Banks also lend by signing a document that states that the bank will pay a sum of money at a date some time in the future, say in 90 days. The company (the borrower) that requested that the bank draw up the document, called a banker's acceptance, holds it until it needs to borrow. They can do this by selling it at a discount price to the face value (the amount stated to be paid in the future). So, say the acceptance states that €1 million will be paid to the holder on 1st August. It could be sold by the borrower to an investor (perhaps another bank) in the discount market for €980,000 on 15 June. The borrowing company is obliged to reimburse the bank €1 million (and pay fees) on 1 August; on that date the purchaser of the acceptance credit collects €1 million from the bank that signed the acceptance, making a €20,000 return over six weeks. Chapter 5 discusses banker's acceptances.

Committed facilities

A committed facility is one where the lender enters into an obligation to provide funds upon request by the borrower, provided any agreed conditions and covenants in the loan agreement have been and are being met. With many of these forms of borrowing the borrower pays a commitment fee on the undrawn portion of the committed facility. A term loan is one example of a committed facility; here are some others.

Revolving credit

Revolving credit (revolving credit facility, RCF) allows the borrower to both draw down the loan in tranches and to reborrow sums repaid within the term of the facility so long as the committed total limit is not breached, usually for between one and five years. The facility does not require the borrower to make a number of fixed payments to the bank (unlike instalment credit, such as hire purchase). This is usually unsecured lending. The borrower makes payments based only on the amount they've actually used or withdrawn, plus interest. The bank is committing some of its assets to providing the facility to the corporation whether or not, in the end, the borrowing is actually needed (it may be termed a committed line of credit). This uses up some of the bank's loan capacity and therefore it demands fees. Front-end or facility fees are for setting it up and commitment fees on the undrawn amount are for providing the option to the borrower (say 50 basis points or 0.5 per cent) while the commitment remains in place. Of course, the borrower will also be charged interest on the amounts drawn under the facility, usually a number of basis points over an interbank rate.

Project finance

A typical project finance deal is created by an industrial corporation providing some equity capital for a separate legal entity (a 'special purpose vehicle', SPV) to be formed to build and operate a project, for example an oil pipeline, an electricity power plant. The project finance loan is then provided as bank loans or through bond issues direct to the separate entity. The significant feature is that the loan returns are tied to the cash flows and fortunes of a particular project rather than being secured against the parent firm's assets. For most ordinary loans the bank looks at the credit standing of the borrower when deciding terms and conditions. For project finance, while the parent company's (or companies') credit standing is a factor, the main focus is on the financial prospects of the project itself.

To make use of project finance the project needs to be easily identifiable and separable from the rest of the company's activities so that its cash flows and assets can offer the lenders some separate security. Project finance has been used across the globe to finance power plants, roads, ports, sewage facilities, telecommunications networks and much more.

It is a form of finance that has grown rapidly over the last 25 years; globally, about £50 billion is lent in this form per year. A major stimulus has been the development of oil prospects. For the UK, the North Sea provided a number of project finance opportunities. Many of the small companies which developed fields and pipelines would not have been able to participate on the strength of their existing cash flows and balance sheets, but they were able to obtain project finance secured on the oil or fees they would later generate.

There is a spectrum of risk sharing in project finance deals. At one extreme there are projects where the parent firm (or firms) accepts the responsibility of guaranteeing that the lenders will be paid in the event of the project producing insufficient cash flows. This is referred to as recourse finance because the lenders are able to seek the 'help' of the parent. At the other extreme, the lenders accept an agreement whereby, if the project is a failure, they will lose money and have no right of recourse to the parent company; if the project's cash flows are insufficient the lenders have a claim only on the assets of the project itself rather than on the sponsors or developers. Between these two extremes there might be deals whereby the borrower takes the risk until the completion of the construction phase (for example, provides a completion guarantee) and the lender takes on the risk once the project is in the operational phase. Alternatively, the commercial firm may take some risks such as the risk of cost overruns and the lender takes others such as the risk of a government expropriating the project's assets.

The sums and size of projects are usually large and involve a significant degree of complexity and this means high transaction and legal costs. Because of the additional risk to the lenders the interest rates charged tend to be higher than for conventional loans. Whereas a well-known highly creditworthy firm might pay 80 basis points (0.80 per cent) over LIBOR for a 'normal' parent company loan, the project company might have to pay 200 basis points (2 per cent) above LIBOR.

The salient points of project finance are:

1 *Transfer of risk* By making the project a stand-alone investment with its own financing, the parent can gain if it is successful and is somewhat insulated if it is a failure, in that other assets and cash flows may be protected from the effects of project losses. This may lead to a greater willingness to engage in more risky activities, which may benefit both the firm and society. Of course, this benefit is of limited value if there are strong rights of recourse.

2 *Off-balance-sheet financing* The finance is raised on the project's assets and cash flows and therefore is not recorded as debt in the parent company's balance sheet. This sort of off-balance-sheet financing is seen as a useful 'wheeze' or ploy by some managers – for exam-

ple, gearing limits can be bypassed. However, experienced lenders and shareholders are not so easily fooled by accounting tricks.

3   *Political risk* If the project is in a country prone to political instability, with a tendency towards an anti-transnational business attitude and acts of appropriation, a more cautious way of proceeding may be to set up an arm's-length (separate company) relationship with some risk being borne by the banking community, particularly banks in the host country.

4   *Simplified banking relationship* In cases where there are a number of parent companies, it can be easier to arrange finance for a separate project entity than to have to deal with each of the parent companies separately.

5   *Managerial incentives* Managers of projects may be given an equity stake in the project if it is set up as a separate enterprise. This can lead to high rewards for exceptional performance.

Syndicate lending

For large loans a single bank may not be able or willing to lend the whole amount. To do so would be to expose the bank to an unacceptable risk of failure on the part of one of its borrowers. Bankers like to spread their lending to gain the risk-reducing benefits of diversification. They prefer to participate in a number of syndicated loans in which a few banks each contribute a portion of the overall loan. So, for a large multinational company loan of, say, £500 million, a single bank may provide £30 million, with perhaps 100 other banks contributing the remainder. The bank originating the loan will usually manage the syndicate and is called the lead manager (there might be one or more lead banks or 'arranging' banks). This bank (or these banks) may invite a handful of other banks to co-manage the loan and these other banks then persuade other banks to supply much of the funding. That is, they help the process of forming the syndicate group of banks in the general syndication. The managing bank also underwrites much of the loan while inviting other banks to underwrite the rest – that is, guaranteeing to provide the funds if other banks do not step forward.[4]

Syndicated loans are available at short notice, can be provided discreetly (helpful if the money is to finance a merger bid, for example) and are usually cheaper to arrange than a bond issue. While they can be a cheap form of borrowing for large, well-established firms, there will be various fees to pay, from commitment fees to underwriting fees for guaranteeing the availability of the funds and the agent's fee (the agent collects the loan money to transfer it to the borrower and collects interest and other payments from the borrower to transfer them to the syndicate banks, and performs various other administration tasks). The syndicated market is usually really available only for loans of more than £50 million. For around one-third of syndicated loans the credit rating agencies (e.g. Standard & Poor's – *see* Chapter 5) are paid to rate the likelihood of default. The volume of new international syndicated loans now runs into hundreds of billions of pounds per year – *see* **Exhibit 2.6**. (A leveraged loan is one where there is a lot of debt relative to the amount of share capital put in the firm; investment grade means that the credit rating agencies, e.g. Moody's, rank the loan as unlikely to default (a rating of BBB – or above – *see* Chapter 5); M&A is mergers and acquisitions.)

Revolving underwriting facility and note issuance facility

Revolving underwriting facilities (RUF) and note issuance facilities (NIF) were developed as services to large corporations wanting to borrow by selling commercial paper or medium-term notes into the financial markets. The paper and notes are merely legal documents stating that the borrower agrees to pay sum(s) of money in the future, say three month from now. Thus a company could sell for £1.9 million commercial paper that gave the investor the right to receive £2 million in six months. The investor gains £100,000 over six months. (There is more on commercial paper in Chapter 5 and on medium-term notes in Chapter 6.)

---

[4] The term 'mandated lead arranger' or MLA is often used for the managing bank(s). Also 'bookrunner' or 'bookrunner group' indicates those who solicit interest in the loan from lenders and gather offers of support. They gradually 'build a book' – a list of confirmed buyers. They do the syndication.

Exhibit 2.6

Syndicated loan sector shows fresh signs of life

FT

Anousha Sakoui and Nicole Bullock

Global syndicated lending totals $1,150bn so far this year, down 51 per cent on the same period last year, making it the lowest amount at this stage of the year since 1996, says Dealogic. Global investment grade loans so far this year at $886bn stand at less than a third of their $3,000bn peak reached in the full year 2007. Leveraged loans have staged a bigger collapse – so far this year $256bn has been issued globally, against a full year peak of $1,800bn in 2007.

The return of M&A activity could start a fire under the syndicated loan market.

In the US this week, syndication of part of the $4.2bn in financing for Warner Chilcott's purchase of Procter & Gamble's pharmaceutical unit began in earnest.

Mr Douglas at Deloitte says a sign of increased confidence is that some banks are increasing their participation in new loans from an average ticket size of £25m to £50m. Moreover, pricing has come down since the first quarter, tightening up to 100 basis points depending on structure and total leverage.

A leveraged loan is likely to have a total cost of about 450bps over Libor and an investment grade corporate can obtain pricing at about 250bps, according to Mr Douglas. Moreover they are willing to lend for longer.

"Clearly we are a long way from the halcyon days of early 2007 and the syndicated loan markets have shrunk but they will grow from current levels as M&A activity increases," said Mr Douglas.

Source: Financial Times, 17 September 2009, p. 39. Reprinted with permission.

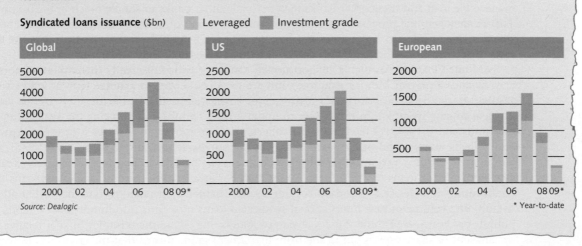

Syndicated loans issuance ($bn)   Leveraged   Investment grade

Source: Dealogic   ** Year-to-date*

The largest corporations often expect to be selling a series of different commercial paper issues over the next five years. Instead of handling each individual issue themselves as the need arises they can go to an *arranging bank*, which will, over the five years, approach a panel of other banks to ask them to purchase the debt. The loan obligation can be in a currency that suits the borrower at the time. The borrower can also select the length of life of the paper (say, 14 days or 105 days) and whether it pays fixed or floating interest rates. If there is a time when it is difficult to sell the paper then the borrower can turn to those banks that have signed up to be underwriters of the RUF or NIF to buy the issue. Underwriters take a fee for guaranteeing that someone will buy the issue. Most of the time they do not have to do anything, but occasionally, often when the market is troubled, they have to step in.

Cash management

Corporations with large day-to-day cash flows soon realise that they need to employ efficient systems to ensure that the potential to earn interest on the cash is not lost while also keeping back enough cash in an easily accessible form to support the business. Banks can help with this. They provide daily information on the firm's cheques that have been paid and account balances so that money can be moved out of no-interest accounts if the balance starts to build up. They can be given the task of automatically redirecting money held in a number of accounts at different banks and branches to a few centralised accounts at one branch. They can also provide software to assist firms in handling money in a variety of currencies and investing it short term.

Guarantees

Banks are sometimes prepared, for a fee, to guarantee that a transaction by a third party will take place or that compensation will be paid if the transaction does not take place. For example, a bank may grant a guarantee to an exporter that an importer will pay for goods supplied. If the importer becomes unable to pay, i.e. does not fulfil its legal obligation, the exporter is protected against that non-compliance as the bank covers those responsibilities and will pay the exporter in a timely manner, as per the agreement.

Overseas trade

Banks provide various services to assist companies when buying and selling across borders. A **letter of credit** is a promise from a bank that an exporter will be paid after shipping goods to an importer. This reassures the exporter and allows an importer to buy even though they may not be well known to the exporter. While a letter of credit is similar to a bank guarantee, it differs in that the bank pays out if the transaction proceeds as planned, while a bank guarantee is to make payment if the transaction does *not* go as planned. With a guarantee the issuing bank waits for the buyer to default before paying out. With a letter of credit the obligation to pay is transferred to the bank, which it will do at the contracted time; even if the importer's finances are perfectly healthy and it could pay from its own resources, the bank will make the payment. Thus the exporter has much greater reassurance of getting paid because a safe bank has taken on the obligation to pay – the risk of bank defaulting (credit risk) is much less than an unknown importer in a distant land. Naturally, the bank will expect its client (the importer) to pay it the amount concerned plus some fees and interest to provide this service.

With **forfaiting** a bank will supply cash to an exporter in return for a right to claim the payments for goods or services supplied to an importer, thus the exporter does not have to wait three months or so to receive cash for the export. The bank advances money and gets that back with interest and fees when the importer eventually pays. There is more on overseas trade in Chapter 13.

Foreign exchange risk management and interest risk management

Companies usually learn through bitter experience that shifts in the exchange rate or in market interest rates can lower profits significantly, sometimes to the point of endangering the firm. There are various risk management tools that a bank can offer a client to mitigate these problems. These usually involve the use of derivatives such as forwards, futures and options. They are considered in Chapters 10, 11 and 12.

Other commercial banking services

Although some banks are state-owned, as in China, or are owned by their customers, e.g. cooperative banks, the majority are run as commercial operations, with the profit motive driving them forward. They are keen on finding new sources of revenue and over the past 30 years or so have done remarkably well in using the competitive advantages they possess, such as knowledge of long-standing customers, trust and presence on the high street, to sell an ever widening range of products and services to individuals and businesses. Customers often find when walking into a branch that the original activities of the bank (e.g. paying in money) are demoted to a corner while staff are encouraged to sell other services to customers. A phrase has been coined to describe the shift to a wide-ranging operation: *financial supermarkets*.

Stockbroking

In many countries, e.g. the UK, most buying and selling of shares and bonds by retail investors (individuals) takes place using independent stockbrokers as agents, rather than the banks. Having said this, the banks have established impressive stockbroking business since they were permitted to enter the industry following the Big Bang of financial reforms in 1986 (*see* Chapter 8). In other countries, e.g. many continental European countries such as Germany and Switzerland, banks have long dominated the buying and selling of financial securities on behalf of investors.

Asset management

Banks often establish their own range of mutual funds, unit trusts or investment trusts (*see* Chapter 4) to offer to investors, allowing them to place their money in a wide range of shares or other securities in a portfolio under professional management. The fees on these funds are usually over 1.5 per cent and they can generate a lot of money for the bank. Alternatively, banks may act as agents for outside fund management groups, receiving a commission for sales made. In Spain, the banks sell *Super Fondos*, in France they provide *SICAVs*, and most of these mutual funds can now be marketed across European borders.

Many commercial banks also have private banking arms to assist wealthy people to manage their money – this is discussed under investment banking (in Chapter 3) – but note that much private banking is conducted by commercial banks without an investment banking subsidiary.

Custody and safety deposits

Share and bond owners often do not want to receive and look after certificates of ownership. The banks provide a service of safekeeping and ensure interest or dividends are claimed. They will also notify the owner of annual general meetings of companies, rights issues and other events. The bank is paid a fee for acting as custodian. As well as the local retail custodianship there is the big league of global custodians (mostly owned by banks) who safeguard the investments of enormous investment funds run by institutional investors – the amounts are measured in billions. In addition to dealing with the technicalities of transfer of ownership of shares and other securities, in a number of countries they collect income, reclaim tax and assist with other aspects of fund administration (*see* Chapter 4 for more on custodianship).

Banks may also provide safety deposit boxes for people to keep items such as jewellery in a vault.

Insurance and pensions

Most banks in continental Europe also own insurance operations or have a close relationship with an insurance company. The French have coined the term bancassurance for the selling of insurance and banking services alongside each other; the Germans have the term Allfinanz. Banks often know their customers well and can tailor insurance offerings to their needs. For example, if a couple with children take out a mortgage with a bank it is an easy sell to point out the need for life insurance to pay off the mortgage should one of the parents die, and for buildings and contents insurance. Banks are also increasingly selling pension savings schemes to their customers. Chapter 4 has more on insurance and pensions.

Foreign exchange

There is a thriving business in exchanging currency for people going on holiday or for business transactions. Traveller's cheques are also available. *See* Chapter 11 for a discussion of the foreign exchange markets with banks at their core.

Asset-based lending

Banks also provide finance for individuals or companies obtaining the use of, say, a car, by leasing it or buying it on hire purchase. Factoring involves the lending of money using a company's trade debtors (what its customers still owe) as security. Asset-based lending is discussed under 'finance houses' in the next chapter.

How a bank operates

The objective of this section is to show how core banking works. The fundamentals are that a bank starts out with some money put in by its owners to pay for buildings, equipment, etc. and to provide a cash buffer of resources should the bank run into difficulties. Shareholders' funds, obtained by the selling of shares in the firm, have the advantage that the shareholders do not have the right to withdraw their money from the company – it is permanent capital (although they may sell the shares to other investors). As well as paying for the initial set-up with premises, etc., shareholders' capital provides a buffer of capital acting as a safety margin against the event of a significant number of the loans granted to borrowers going wrong. The buffer is referred to as capital and loans made are assets of the bank. Deposits (and other loans to the bank) are liabilities.

$$ \text{Total assets} \quad = \quad \text{Total liabilities} \quad + \quad \text{Capital} $$

In addition to capital being raised at the foundation of the business it can be augmented over the years through the bank making profits for its shareholders and deciding to keep it within the business rather than distributing it as dividends. It can also be increased by selling more shares. Exactly how much the buffer of capital should be as a percentage of the assets or liabilities of the bank to provide sufficient safety without being too much of a drag on the bank's profits is a subject of much debate in the financial world. This is especially so in the aftermath of the financial crisis of 2008–2010 when many banks were found to have hardly any buffer at all following the writing off of many loans. (*See* Chapter 7 for a discussion of bank safety rules and Chapter 16 for an outline of the crisis.)

A bank is also likely to be concerned about the possibility of a high proportion of the depositors or other lenders to the bank withdrawing their money on a single day; it thus keeps a proportion of the money it raises in the form of cash (or near cash) rather than lending it all, because it does not want to run out if many depositors insist on transferring their money out of the bank (i.e. the bank faces liquidity risk, running out of liquid assets).

Let us assume for now that a bank, BarcSan, is required by the central bank (its regulator) to hold 8 per cent of the value of its current account deposits in reserves. These are the regulatory required reserves. However, the bank may judge that 8 per cent is not enough and decide to add another 4 per cent of the value of its current account liabilities as **excess reserves**. Reserves consist of both the cash (notes, etc.) that the bank is required to hold in its account with the central bank plus cash (notes, etc.) that it has on its own premises, referred to as **vault cash**. Note that we are referring here to cash reserves and not the capital reserves (the difference between assets and liabilities).

Cash reserves of 12 per cent is unusually high, but useful for illustration. A more normal figure is 1–3 per cent of overall liabilities (not just current account liabilities) held in cash, but another 10 per cent or so might be held in assets that can quickly be converted to cash, such as very short-term loans to other banks, certificates of deposit (*see* Chapter 5) and government Treasury bills; these are termed near-cash. The term for reserves that includes near-cash is 'liquid reserves'.

To understand the working of a bank we will start with a very simple example of a change in the cash held by a bank. Imagine that Mrs Rich deposits £1,000 of cash into her current account at the BarcSan Bank. This has affected the bank's balance sheet. It has an increase of cash (and therefore reserves) of £1,000. This is an asset of the bank. At the same time it has increased its liabilities because the bank owes Mrs Rich £1,000, which she can withdraw at any time. We can illustrate the changes by looking at that part of the balance sheet which deals with this transaction. In the T-account below, the asset (cash) is shown on the left and the increased liability is shown on the right.

BarcSan partial balance sheet

Assets		Liabilities	
Vault cash (part of reserves)	£1,000	Current account	£1,000

Thus BarcSan has increased its reserves because it received a deposit. This increase in reserves could also have come about through Mrs Rich paying in a £1,000 cheque drawn on an account at, say, HSBC. When BarcSan receives the cheque it deposits it at the central bank which then collects £1,000 from HSBC's account with the central bank and transfers it to BarcSan's account at the central bank, increasing its reserves. Remember: cash reserves include both those held at the central bank and these in the bank vault, tills, ATMs, etc.

Given that BarcSan has required reserves at 8 per cent of current account deposits, following the receipt of £1,000 it has increased assets of £80 in required reserves and £920 in excess reserves.

BarcSan partial balance sheet

Assets		Liabilities	
Required reserves	£80	Current account	£1,000
Excess reserves	£920		

These reserves are not paying any interest to BarcSan. What is even more troubling is that the bank is providing an expensive service to Mrs Rich with bank branch convenience, cheque books, statements, etc. This money has to be put to use – at least as much of it as is prudent. One way of making a profit is to lend most of the money. It does this by lending to a business for five-years. Thus the bank borrows on a short-term basis (instant access for Mrs Rich) and lends long (five-year term loan). The bank decides to lend £880 because this would allow it to maintain its required reserve ratio of 8 per cent and its target excess reserve of 4 per cent.

BarcSan partial balance sheet

Assets		Liabilities	
Required reserves	£80	Current account	£1,000
Excess reserves	£40		
Loan	£880		

A bank has to keep enough cash on hand to satisfy current account holders and other customers withdrawing money from their accounts. There may be times when a large volume of cash is withdrawn and the bank has to be ready for that – this is what we refer to as liquidity management. A bank also needs to lend its money (acquire assets) with the expectation of a low risk of default and in a diversified manner – that is, it must have good asset management skills. Third, it must be capable of finding funds at low cost and risk – good liability management. Finally, it must keep its capital at a high enough level to reduce the chance of insolvency problems (assets worth less than liabilities) while balancing the need to make profits by lending – this is capital adequacy management. We will now explore these four tasks for bank managers.

Liquidity management and reserves

Let us look at the (simplified) balance sheet for BarcSan as a whole, all its assets and all its liabilities. We will assume that all deposits are current account deposits and so it keeps 8 per cent of those as required reserves and aims to have a further 4 per cent as excess reserves (either at the central bank or as vault cash). As well as £10 billion in deposits the bank has £900 million in capital accumulated mostly through retaining past profits. It has lent £5.7 billion and bought £3.1 billion of marketable securities such as government bonds and bills.

BarcSan's balance sheet

Assets		Liabilities	
Required reserves	£800m	Deposits	£10,000m
Excess reserves	£1,300m	Bank capital	£900m
Loans	£5,700m		
Securities	£3,100m		

To satisfy its own rule on 12 per cent of current account deposits held as reserves it needs only £1.2 billion, but it currently has £2.1 billion (£800 million + £1,300 million). It has a 'spare' £900 million. If there is a sudden rise in withdrawals from bank accounts as people worry about the bank system collapsing and not being able to repay deposit liabilities (as with Northern Rock in 2007), this will have an impact on BarcSan. If £900 million of cash is withdrawn from BarcSan, its balance changes to:

BarcSan's balance sheet after a sudden withdrawal of £900 million

Assets		Liabilities	
Required reserves	£728m	Deposits	£9,100m
Excess reserves	£472m	Bank capital	£900m
Loans	£5,700m		
Securities	£3,100m		

The bank still has cash reserves above its target because 12 per cent of £9,100 million is £1,092 million[5] whereas the bank has £1,200 million. Because it started with plentiful reserves, the public panic to withdraw funds has not affected the other elements in BarcSan's balance sheet.

Now take a different case, where BarcSan has already lent out any reserves above its prudential level of 12 per cent of deposits.

---

[5] Made up of 8 per cent of £9,100 million = £728 million and 4 per cent of £9,100 million = £364 million.

BarcSan's balance sheet if actual reserves equal target reserves

Assets		Liabilities	
Required reserves	£800m	Deposits	£10,000m
Excess reserves	£400m	Bank capital	£900m
Loans	£6,600m		
Securities	£3,100m		

Now imagine a financial panic. Many depositors rush to the bank's branches to take out their money. In one day £900 million is withdrawn. At the end of the day the balance sheet is looking far from healthy.

BarcSan's balance sheet after £900 million is withdrawn (after the bank just met its reserve target)

Assets		Liabilities	
Required reserves	£300m	Deposits	£9,100m
Excess reserves	£0m	Bank capital	£900m
Loans	£6,600m		
Securities	£3,100m		

Another day like that and it might be wiped out. It is required to hold 8 per cent of £9,100 million as reserves – £728 million – but now has only £300 million. Where is it going to get the shortfall from? There are four possibilities.

1 *Borrowing from the central bank* One of the major duties of a central bank is to act as lender of last resort. It stands ready to lend to banks that lack cash reserves (there is more on this in Chapter 7). However, it will do this at a high price only (high interest rate) to deter banks from calling on it in trivial circumstances. If BarcSan borrows the £428 million shortfall from the central bank to take it back to the regulator's minimum of 8 per cent, its balance sheet now looks like this:

BarcSan's balance sheet if it borrows £428 million from the central bank

Assets		Liabilities	
Required reserves	£728m	Deposits	£9,100m
Excess reserves	£0m	Borrowings from central bank	£428m
Loans	£6,600m	Bank capital	£900m
Securities	£3,100m		

2 *Securities could be sold* Of the securities bought by a bank most are traded in very active markets where it is possible to sell a large quantity without moving the price. Let us assume that the bank sells £428 million of government Treasury bills and bonds to move its reserves back to 8 per cent of deposits.

BarcSan's balance sheet if it sells £428 million of securities

Assets		Liabilities	
Required reserves	£728m	Deposits	£9,100m
Excess reserves	£0m	Bank capital	£900m
Loans	£6,600m		
Securities	£2,672m		

Of course, there are a few more moves that need to be made if the bank wants to reach its target of 12 per cent reserves, but after such a crisis in the financial markets this may take a few years to achieve.

3 *Borrow from other banks and other organisations* There is an active market in interbank loans as well as banks borrowing by selling commercial paper to corporations and other institutions. Perhaps BarcSan could borrow the £428 million it needs here.

BarcSan's balance sheet if it borrows £428 million from the markets

Assets		Liabilities	
Required reserves	£728m	Deposits	£9,100m
Excess reserves	£0m	Borrowed from banks & corporations	£428m
Loans	£6,600m	Bank capital	£900m
Securities	£3,100m		

However, given the cause of the crisis was a system-wide loss of confidence, BarcSan may have difficulty raising money in these markets at this time. This was a problem that beset many banks in 2008. They had grown used to quickly obtaining cash to cover shortfalls from other banks. But in the calamitous loss of confidence following the sub-prime debacle, banks simply stopped lending to each other – those that were caught with insufficient reserves failed or were bailed out by governments. Greek banks experienced a freeze in the interbank loan market in 2011 as potential lenders feared they might not be repaid.

4 *Reducing its loans* Banks receive principal repayments on loans every day as the period of various loan agreements comes to an end, or as portions of loans are repaid during the term of the loan. To raise some money the bank could simply refuse any more loans for a period. I was on the sharp end of this in February 2007 when trying to complete a business property deal. Suddenly Halifax Bank of Scotland refused to lend on what was a pretty safe deal for them. I was nonplussed. What were they playing at? Didn't they know they would lose my company as a customer? Of course, with hindsight we all know that this was the start of the crisis when HBOS was desperately short of cash (it avoided annihilation only by allowing itself to be bought by Lloyds). Another possibility is to sell off some of its loan book to another bank – but the purchasers are unlikely to pay full value, especially in uncertain times. An even more drastic solution is to insist that borrowers repay their loans immediately. This is possible with some types of loans, such as overdrafts, but it results in much resentment and damage to long-term relationships. If BarcSan raised £428 million in one of these ways, its balance sheet would look like this:

BarcSan balance sheet after reducing loans by £428 million

Assets		Liabilities	
Required reserves	£728m	Deposits	£9,100m
Excess reserves	£0m	Bank capital	£900m
Loans	£6,172m		
Securities	£3,100m		

A bank has a trade-off to manage. If it ties up a very high proportion of its money in reserves it loses the opportunity to lend that money to gain a return, but the managers can feel very safe, as they are unlikely to run out of cash. Yet if it goes for maximum interest by lending the vast majority of the money deposited, it could run out of cash. Thus it has to have enough reserves to avoid one or more of the following costly actions for quickly raising money: (a) borrowing from the central bank; (b) selling securities; (c) borrowing from other banks, (d) reducing its loans. Excess reserves provide insurance against incurring liquidity problems due to deposit outflows, but like all insurance it comes at a high price.

The financial regulator in the UK, the Financial Services Authority,[6] announced that once the recession was over, banks would have to hold much higher levels of cash and other liquid assets than they had in the past. The level of liquid assets required can be reduced if the bank has most

---

[6] Responsibility for prudential reserves at banks will pass to the Prudential Regulatory Authority, part of the Bank of England, in 2013.

of its liabilities in long-term instruments. The banks do not like the rule because holding such safe assets lowers profitability, but it reduces the risk to the rest of us having to bail out the banks again – *see* **Exhibit 2.7.**

Exhibit 2.7

Liquidity rule change sparks fear of harm to City

Brooke Masters and Patrick Jenkins

Analysts and financial industry groups have warned that new liquidity rules announced by the FSA could damage bank business models and harm London's competitiveness unless other countries follow suit.

The rules, which will not come into effect until at least the middle of next year, could require UK banks to lift their holdings of high-quality government bonds by £110bn, or roughly one-third, in the first year after they are implemented.

"This puts UK Banks at a massive disadvantage," said Simon Maughan, banks analyst at MF Global. "The risk of banks focusing on capital and liquidity so much is that profitability becomes an afterthought."

The British Bankers Association and others have lobbied hard for the rules to be postponed until an international consensus can develop. The FSA declined to delay publication of its rules, but in a nod to the concerns it has promised they will not take effect until after the recession and will be phased in over time.

That timetable would allow the UK regulator to tweak its rules as other countries move forward with their own plans and as the Basel committee on global bank supervision sets new capital requirements, officials said.

US regulators are working on new liquidity enhancement rules that would look at the ratio of a bank's short-term borrowings to easily sold assets, and Australia announced draft proposals last month, but the FSA is the first to announce specific requirements.

The FSA increased the pressure on other nations to follow its example by saying that it will impose similar rules on the 197

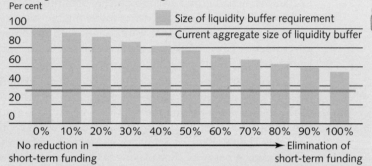

How groups can cut liquidity requirements by reducing their short-term funding
Per cent

branches and subsidiaries of overseas banks that are in the UK, unless their parent group is subject to a regulatory regime with "broad equivalence".

"There are good signs they are moving in the right direction," said Patrick Fell, director of PwC's regulatory capital practice.

Unlike capital requirements, liquidity buffers cannot be boiled down to a simple ratio of a bank's capital to its assets.

Instead banks will have to run a series of stress tests that assume big problems, such as the closure of the foreign exchange markets, a run on deposits, or a reluctance by banks to lend to one another.

Each institution then estimates how much in cash and government bonds it would need to survive and what it could do to mitigate the situation.

The FSA's new liquidity requirements will be based on the results.

The FSA estimates that if it required the UK industry to hold 60 per cent of the doomsday scenario needs, or £110bn in safe, low-yielding treasuries, the annual cost in terms of lost investment income would be roughly £2.2bn.

But Jonathan Pierce, banks analyst at Credit Suisse, said full implementation of the FSA rules would be far more expensive, since it would cut banks' investment income by forcing them to hold 15 per cent of their balance sheet in liquid assets, compared with 5 per cent at the end of last year.

"Applying a 1.5 percentage point negative [impact], that would reduce interest income by around £9.2bn," Mr Pierce said, although he said this was an extreme case that was unlikely to be put into practice.

Banks could cut the amount of government bonds they need to hold by reducing their exposure to risky areas and dependence on short-term funding.

The FSA's announcement yesterday shied away from firm numbers and instead emphasised that the level of bond purchases required would depend on where the FSA sets the liquidity requirements and how much short-term capital banks chose to hold.

Source: Financial Times, 6 October 2009, p. 21. Reprinted with permission.

Asset and liability management

In managing the bank's assets the senior team must balance out the three factors shown in **Exhibit 2.8** to try to maximise shareholder returns in the long run. The highest returns usually come from tying up bank money in long-term loans and securities where it is difficult and/or costly to release the money quickly. Also, higher returns are usually associated with higher risk taking by the bank. However, within those generalisations it makes sense for bank loan officers to search for potential borrowers who are least likely to default and most likely to accept a high interest charge. The skill in asset management comes from assessing who is a good credit risk and who isn't. Banks generally like to take a very low-risk approach and anticipate that only around 1 per cent of their loans will go bad. However, they occasionally engage in riskier prospects. When they do, they charge a higher interest rate to compensate for the expectation that a higher proportion of these loans will default.

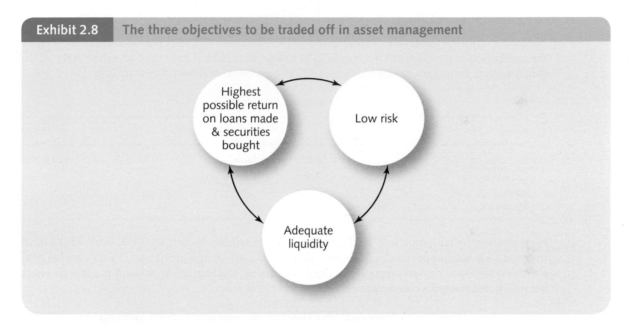

Exhibit 2.8	The three objectives to be traded off in asset management

A crucial aspect of asset management is to be diversified so that no one loan or no one category of loans (say, property related or retail related) or securities dominates the portfolio.

Liability management is focused on the judgements made about the composition of liabilities as well as the adjusting of interest rates offered to lenders to the bank to obtain the target mix of borrowing. Banks are generally advised to be diversified in terms of where they obtain money. Many banks (e.g. Northern Rock) found in 2008 that they had become over-reliant on obtaining funding from the wholesale markets (selling bonds, commercial paper or borrowing from other banks, for example) and not enough of their money came from ordinary depositors with current or time deposits. A balance needs to be struck. Retail depositors tend to be more reliable in leaving their money with a bank, whereas lenders in the wholesale markets move money from place to place quickly if there is any sign of trouble or low rates of return are offered. But wholesale money can allow a bank to grow its balance sheet rapidly, whereas it takes time to attract deposits – all those advertisements, high-street branches, teaser interest rates, etc.

Capital adequacy management

How much capital should the bank hold? In deciding this managers need to trade off the risk of bank failure by not being able to satisfy creditors (depositors, wholesale market lenders, etc.) against the attraction of increasing the return to the bank's owners by having as little capital as possible relative to the asset base. The fear here is of insolvency – an inability to repay obligations over the longer course of events – rather than illiquidity, which is insufficient liquid assets to repay obligations falling due if there is a sudden outflow of cash (e.g. large depositor withdrawals on a particular day, borrowers defaulting, unexpectedly drawing down on lines of credit, or large payments under derivative deals). Another consideration is the minimum capital rules imposed by the regulators to prevent peril to the financial system (discussed in Chapter 7). To understand the difficulty with this trade-off we can compare BarcSan's situation with a less well-capitalised bank, Mercurial.

BarcSan's opening balance sheet

Assets		Liabilities	
Required reserves	£800m	Deposits	£10,000m
Excess reserves	£1,300m	Bank capital	£900m
Loans	£5,700m		
Securities	£3,100m		

BancSan's capital to assets ratio is £900 million/£10,900 million = 8.3 per cent. Mercurial has exactly the same assets as BarcSan, but it has only £400 million in capital. It has raised an extra £500 million from deposits. Its ratio of capital to assets is 3.7 per cent (£400 million/£10,900 million).

Mercurial's balance sheet

Assets		Liabilities	
Required reserves	£800m	Deposits	£10,500m
Excess reserves	£1,300m	Bank capital	£400m
Loans	£5,700m		
Securities	£3,100m		

Now consider what happens if we assume a situation similar to that in 2008. Both banks have invested £500 million in bonds which are backed by US sub-prime mortgages. These now become worthless as house owners stop paying their mortgages. BarcSan can withstand the loss in assets because it maintained a conservative stance on its capital ratio.

BarcSan's balance sheet after £500 million losses on sub-prime mortgages

Assets		Liabilities	
Required reserves	£800m	Deposits	£10,000m
Excess reserves	£1,300m	Bank capital	£400m
Loans	£5,700m		
Securities	£2,600m		

It's capital-to-assets ratio has fallen to a less conservative 3.8 per cent (£400 million/£10,400), but this is a level that still affords some sense of safety for its providers of funds. Mercurial, however, is insolvent. Its assets of £10,400 are less than the amount owed to depositors.

Mercurial's balance sheet after £500 million losses on sub-prime mortgages

Assets		Liabilities	
Required reserves	£800m	Deposits	£10,500m
Excess reserves	£1,300m	Bank capital	−£100m
Loans	£5,700m		
Securities	£2,600m		

One possible course of action is to write to all its depositors to tell them that it cannot repay the full amount that was deposited with the bank. They might panic and rush to the branch to obtain what they are owed in full. The more likely scenario is for the regulator to step in to close or rescue the bank. Occasionally the central bank organises a rescue by a group of other banks – they, too, have an interest in maintaining confidence in the banking system.

In 2009, Royal Bank of Scotland and Lloyds Banking Group, following the sudden destruction of balance sheet reserves when the value of their loans and many securities turned out to be much less than what was shown on the balance sheet, were rescued by the UK government, which injected money into them by buying billions of new shares. This was enough new capital to save them from destruction, but the banks are still clawing their way back to health by holding onto any profits they make to rebuild capital reserves. In 2010, there were liquidity and solvency fears for the Kabul Bank – *see* **Exhibit 2.9**.

Exhibit 2.9

Afghan savers lay siege to Kabul Bank

James Fontanella-Khan and agencies

Crowds of people queued outside Kabul Bank's main branch yesterday seeking to withdraw their deposits as fears grew that the bank was heading for insolvency, **writes James Fontanella-Khan and agencies**.

Two of the bank's executives resigned on Wednesday amid corruption allegations, and media reports claimed the bank was on the verge of a meltdown because of the mismanagement of funds, including giving unrecorded loans to allies of Hamid Karzai, the Afghan president.

"I have $15,000 deposited and now they are telling me they are out of money, and I was able to take only $1,000," Haji Tamim Sohraby, 24, said.

A run on the bank, which is partly owned by Mr Karzai's brother, would have wide political repercussions because it handles the salaries of civil servants, including teachers and soldiers.

Omar Zakhilwal, the finance minister, said, "The government of Afghanistan guarantees every penny...deposited will be paid back if [people] request it."

Additional reporting by Dan Dombey in Kabul

Source: Financial Times, 3 September 2010. Reprinted with permission

Why might banks sail close to the wind in aiming at a very low capital-to-assets ratio?

The motivation to lower the capital-to-assets ratio is to boost the returns to shareholders. To illustrate: imagine both banks make profits after deduction of tax of £150 million per year and we can ignore extraordinary losses such as the sub-prime fiasco. A key measure of profitability is **return on assets (ROA)**.

$$\text{ROA} = \frac{\text{Net profit after tax}}{\text{Total assets}}$$

Given that both firms (in normal conditions) have the same profits and the same assets, we have a ROA of £150 million/£10,900 million = 1.38 per cent.[7] This is a useful measure of bank efficiency in terms of how much profit is generated per pound of assets.

---

[7] This is at the top end of the usual range of ROAs for commercial banks.

However, what shareholders are really interested in is the return for each pound that *they* place in the business. Assuming that the capital figures in the balance sheet are all provided by ordinary shareholders then the return on equity (ROE) is:

$$ROE = \frac{\text{Net profit after tax}}{\text{Equity capital}}$$

$$\text{For BarcSan : ROE} = \frac{£150m}{£900m} = 16.7\%$$

$$\text{For Mercurial: ROE} = \frac{£150m}{£400m} = 37.5\%$$

Mercurial appears to be super-profitable, simply because it obtained such a small proportion of its funds from shareholders. Many conservatively-run banks were quizzed by their shareholders in the mid-noughties on why their returns to equity were low compared with other banks, and 'couldn't they just push up returns with a little less caution on the capital ratio?' Many were tempted to follow the crowd in the good times only to suffer very badly when bank capital levels were exposed as far too daring. You can understand the temptation, and that is why regulation is needed to insist on minimum levels of capital – this is discussed in Chapter 7.

Central banks can use the level of reserves held by banks to control the amount of lending going on in an economy. If the central bank insists that banks hold more in reserves then there is less cash available to offer potential borrowers. China's central bank used this tool in 2010 to try to reduce economic activity and the threat of rising inflation – *see* **Exhibit 2.10**.

Exhibit 2.10

Chinese banks set to increase reserves

Jamil Anderlini in Beijing

China's central bank said yesterday that it will raise the amount banks must hold in reserve for the third time this year, in the latest move by Beijing to cool its booming economy.

The increase comes after regulators ordered China's largest banks to re-examine their loan books and provide estimates of their exposure to uncollateralised loans, especially to provincial governments, according to Chinese bankers and analysts. If bank are unable to find assets to collateralise these loans within the next few months they may be required to downgrade the loans, potentially leading to a spike in non-performing assets on their books, analysts said.

After reporting record profits in the first quarter, Chinese banks are under pressure to rein in lending and restrict loans to certain sectors and industries as Beijing attempts to calm the economy without causing growth to stall.

The biggest concerns for regulators are huge loans to shell companies set up by local governments to supplement their fiscal income, as well as loans to real estate developers and speculators that have helped to inflate a bubble in the property market.

As part of its efforts to reduce lending, the People's Bank of China will raise the reserve requirement ratio for deposit-taking financial institutions by 0.5 percentage points, effective on May 10, bringing the rate to 17 per cent for large Chinese banks and 15 per cent for smaller lenders.

Source: Financial Times, 3 May 2010, p. 20. Reprinted with permission.

Income statements

A bank's income statement is split into two sources of income and three types of operating expense.

Income:

   (a) **Interest income.** This can be interest on loans granted, securities purchased (e.g. a government bond paying interest) or other interest.

   (b) **Non-interest income.** Banks charge for various services, ranging from current account charges to fees on underwriting securities and asset management commission. They may also generate income from trading in the markets.

Operating expenses:

   (a) *Interest expense* Banks pay interest on many deposit accounts and when they borrow in the markets from other banks, corporations or the central bank.

   (b) *Non-interest expense* Buildings, computer systems, salaries, etc.

   (c) *Provisions for loan losses* Banks are required to estimate the likely losses they will make when a proportion of loans default and write this off as an expense even though borrowers have not yet actually defaulted.

In addition, there may be sections of the income statement dealing with gains (or losses) made when the bank sold securities in the financial markets, and 'extraordinary items' which are unusual and infrequent events/transactions producing an extraordinary gain or loss that year.

A key measure of bank performance is the difference between interest earned and interest paid as a percentage of assets. This is the *net interest margin (NIM)*:

$$\text{NIM} = \frac{\text{Interest income} - \text{Interest expense}}{\text{Assets}}$$

A typical NIM is between 1 per cent and 4 per cent. So if a bank is paying 3.5 per cent on average on its deposit accounts and other borrowings, but charges the average borrower 6 per cent, it has a net interest margin of 2.5 per cent. Many NIMs were lowered in 2009 and 2010 as some banks, desperate to attract funds, raised the interest rate on deposit accounts to a figure almost as high as the rate they charged borrowers – they were trying to reduce their dependency on the wholesale market for funds.

Exhibit 2.11 discusses net interest margins for some UK banks. It also discusses another important measure: the loan-to-deposit ratio (amount of loans lent out divided by the amount of funds attracted to bank accounts – these deposits are 'stickier' than funds obtained from the wholesale markets, e.g. from other banks). You can see that the banks are heavily dependent on wholesale finance that has to be repaid within 12 months – this can make them vulnerable to a sudden withdrawal of wholesale funds, as happened in 2008.

Exhibit 2.11

Customers feel pinch as lenders pass on the pain

Jane Croft

According to Mike Trippitt, analyst at Oriel Securities: "What lies ahead of us is the structural impact on banks' profitability of greater liquidity in banks' balance sheets, and the longer maturity of wholesale funding."

The first pressure on net interest margins comes from financial watchdogs' proposed insistence that banks hold higher levels of lower-yielding but safer instruments such as government gilts. The aim is that they have a ready source of liquidity in case markets dry up.

Many banks have increased their holdings of these safer instruments ahead of the new rules. The result is that lower yields are already starting to squeeze net margins – a key measure of profitability – at institutions such as Royal Bank of Scotland and Nationwide, the UK's largest building society.

The building society saw its net interest margin decline to 0.93 per cent in the six months

▶

Exhibit 2.11 continued

to April 2009, from 1.12 per cent in the year to April 2008. It said that holding greater levels of safer investments cut its net interest margin by about 4 basis points.

At RBS, meanwhile, the net interest margin in the first quarter of 2009 fell from 2.05 per cent at the start of the period to 1.73 per cent at the end.

It said that 25 basis points related to the higher cost of term funding and holding a bigger stock of liquid assets.

Stephen Hester, RBS chief executive, recently warned that even though the liquidity proposals might be phased in over a number of years, they could still have a heavy impact. "I think they can cost a lot of money," he told analysts.

He is not alone in this view. Jonathan Pierce, analyst at Credit Suisse, estimates that the banking sector may have to increase its holdings of government bonds to £150bn–£250bn to meet the new liquidity requirements.

Mr Trippitt at Oriel says the cost to the five biggest UK banks of meeting the new requirements would be £4bn.

Second, margins will be squeezed because the new regulations will also require banks to extend the duration of their wholesale funding so it more closely matches the duration of their loans.

The reasoning behind the new rules is straightforward enough.

Loan to deposit ratio
% (Barclays, Lloyds Banking Group, RBS)

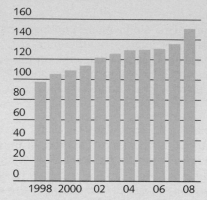

Sources: Credit Suisse; KBW

Funding maturities
£bn (Barclays, Lloyds Banking Group, RBS)*

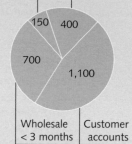

Wholesale 3–12 months   Wholesale >12 months

150   400

700

1,100

Wholesale < 3 months   Customer accounts

*2008 estimate

The "borrow short, lend long" mismatch between 25-year mortgage loans and wholesale funding that needed to be rolled over every three months proved catastrophic when the wholesale markets froze. Watchdogs' insistence on longer maturity funding is intended to prevent this happening again.

But this added security of funding comes at a price. Mr Trippitt believes that lengthening the maturity of wholesale funding to match the asset base would add a further £3bn pressure on the sector as longer term funding is more expensive.

Tim Tookey, finance director at Lloyds Banking Group, said recently that the group's margin had benefited from offering more expensive loans, but that this advantage had been offset "by the impact of falling base rates and higher funding costs as the group continues to extend its wholesale funding maturity profile".

Lloyds has lengthened the maturity of its £442.5bn of wholesale funding so that £63.6bn is now five years or more duration.

Many analysts believe that even when banks have returned to more normal trading patterns after the seismic events of the past couple of years, then return on equity in the sector – which was as high as 20 per cent in the boom years – could fall to 10–15 per cent or even drop down into single figures. It would take more than being able to charge a bit more for home loans to offset such a fall in profitability.

Margins pressured in effort to attract deposits

Jane Croft

Banks are adding to their own margin pressure as they seek to attract retail deposits, to cut their reliance on wholesale funding.

At the height of the boom, banks funded most of the new loans from wholesale funding and this pushed up their loan-to-deposit ratio – a measure of the amount of a bank's loans divided by the amount of its deposits – from 100 per cent a decade ago to about 150 per cent now.

Lloyds Banking Group currently has even higher loan to deposit ratios of 178 per cent.

Some banks have set themselves the aim of achieving a loan-to-deposit ratio of no more than 100 per cent over the next five years. This aim has intensified competition to appeal to savers.

Source: Financial Times, 19 June 2009, p. 19. Reprinted with permission.

Banks (and the financial press) also report the net interest income (NII), which is simply the top half of the NIM ratio, interest income minus interest expense. Of course, this is a measure in absolute amounts of pounds, euros, etc., rather than a percentage.

Another frequently quoted measure is the cost–income ratio (C/I), which measures the bank's efficiency in holding down its costs relative to its income.

$$\frac{\text{Cost}}{\text{Income}} = \frac{\text{Non-interest expenses}}{\text{Net interest income} + \text{Non-interest income}}$$

Concluding comments

Retail and corporate banking is something that most of us take for granted, the services being provided day after day in the background of our lives. It is only when something goes wrong or a service is removed that we fully realise the importance of a healthy and efficient banking system in enriching our lives. If, for example, mortgages or business loans are suddenly difficult to obtain, we quickly feel the effects throughout the economy as the property market and business activity are stifled, house prices fall and people are made redundant. If the payment mechanisms suddenly stopped we would all notice as wages would not get through and goods could not be purchased in the shops; we would have to revert to a much more primitive way of operating.

If banks fail to run themselves in a prudent way and are vulnerable to collapse it is considered wise for governments to spend billions, or even trillions, to prop them up to restore the confidence of bank creditors. If one collapses, the risk to the rest of us might be limited, but if a handful of key players cannot repay their suppliers of funds (depositors, bond holders, etc.) then a domino effect occurs in which the non-payment of an obligation by one bank puts another at risk.

Because of the vital role banks play, governments around the world have taken the risk of dramatically increasing their own borrowings to save the banks. We will be paying for this decision for many years to come as governments cut public spending and raise taxes to reduce their deficits. And yet, despite all this pain, there are few voices which say we should not have saved the banking system. This alone provides a clear illustration of its importance to a modern society: we cannot contemplate living without the banks.

Key points and concepts

- **The three core functions of banks**: taking in deposits, making loans and providing a payments mechanism.

- **Retail banking:** operating the three core functions with an extensive branch network, numerous small transactions on behalf of households and small firms.

- **Corporate banking:** the three core functions plus an array of additional services needed by medium-sized and large firms, e.g. cash management or foreign exchange risk management. There tend to be fewer larger transactions than with retail banking and the transactions are often in an overseas currency.

- **Wholesale banking:** borrowing and lending in large transaction sizes with corporates and other large organisations including other banks. Corporate banking and investment banking tend to be wholesale banking.

- **Commercial banking:** retail and corporate banking.

- **Universal banking:** a very wide range of banking services is offered by one organisation, stretching from retail and corporate banking to investment banking, securities dealing, brokerage, etc.

- **Investment banking:** offering services to clients (generally large organisations, e.g. large corporates or governments) that are usually linked to financial market activities. Fees and/or commission are charged for assistance/advice with matters such as bond or share issues, mergers and risk

▶

management. Investment banks also help with fund management and trade and provide markets in numerous financial instruments. They do not have branch networks and tend to operate worldwide, dealing only in large quantities.

- **Commercial banks generally obtain money from:** current accounts (10–40 per cent of liabilities), time deposits (10–40 per cent), money market borrowing (10–40 per cent) and owners' capital (8–12 per cent).

- An individual can walk into a bank branch and take the money held in their **current account** at very short notice. With time (or savings) deposit accounts depositors agree to place money with a bank on the understanding that a set period of notice is required to withdraw cash. Alternatively, the customer may place the money in the account for a fixed period.

- **Bank assets**: loans to individuals and to corporations typically account for 50–70 per cent of a commercial bank's assets. Another 10–35 per cent might be in money market instruments. Some is likely to be invested in long-term investments – usually below 20 per cent. Up to 10 per cent of the bank's assets may be in the form of buildings, equipment, software or other assets such as gold.

- **Banks make it attractive for companies to borrow** from them compared with other forms of borrowing:
  - administrative and legal costs are low;
  - quick;
  - flexibility. With altering the terms of the lending agreement. If the firm does better than originally expected, a bank loan can often be repaid without penalty;
  - available to small firms.

- **LIBOR** (London Inter-bank Offered Rate) is the rate of interest charged when a bank lends to a highly reputable and safe bank in London.

- A **basis point, bps,** is 100th of 1 per cent.

- **An overdraft** is a permit to overdraw on an account up to a stated limit.

- A **term loan** is a business loan with an original maturity of more than one year and a specified schedule of principal and interest payments.

- **Action to reduce banker's lending risk**:
  - high quality and quantity of *information* flowing from borrower to bank;
  - **collateral**: holders of **fixed charge** collateral can seize the specific asset used to back the loan. With a **floating charge** the legal right to seize assets 'floats' over the general assets of the firm so they can be bought and sold or rented without specific permission from the lender. The charge crystallises only at the point of default on the loan;
  - **loan covenants**;
  - **guarantees from third parties**;
  - **personal guarantees**;
  - **assessment of creditworthiness**;
  - **ensuring that the amount that the borrower is prepared to put into the project is adequate**.

- **Payment mechanisms**:
  - **cheque**;
  - **giro**;
  - **standing orders**;
  - **direct debits**;
  - **debit cards**;
  - **credit cards**;
  - **store cards**;
  - **smart cards (electronic purses, chip cards)**;
  - **e-money, e-cash**;
  - **landlines and mobile phones**;
  - **internet**.

▶

- **Clearing system:** a system for transferring money from one bank account to another conducted by clearing banks.

- **An uncommitted facility**: the bank is not obliged to provide funds at the borrower's request and the facility can be cancelled so the borrower may have to repay at short notice. With an uncommitted line of credit the borrower can borrow up to a maximum sum for a period of, say, six months and can repay and borrow again as needed within that time period.

- **A committed facility**: where the lender enters into an obligation to provide funds upon request by the borrower, provided any agreed conditions and covenants in the loan agreement have been and are being met.
  - **Revolving credit (revolving credit facility RCF)** allows the borrower to both draw down the loan in tranches and to re-borrow sums repaid within the term of the facility so long as the committed total limit is not breached, usually for between one and five years.
  - With a **project finance** loan the loan returns are tied to the cash flows and fortunes of a particular project rather than being secured against the parent firm's assets.
  - **Syndicate loans** are large loans provided by a number of banks, each taking a portion of the overall lending.
  - **Revolving underwriting facilities (RUF) and note issuance facilities (NIF)** allow large corporations to borrow by selling a series of commercial paper issues or notes into the financial markets over a number of years. Underwriters take a fee for guaranteeing that someone will buy the issue.

- **Other bank services for larger corporations:**
  - **Cash management** – banks provide efficient systems to ensure that the potential to earn interest on day-to-day cash held by the business is not lost while also keeping back enough cash in an easily accessible form to support the business.
  - **Guarantee** that a transaction by a third party will take place or that compensation will be paid if the transaction does not take place.
  - A **letter of credit** is a promise from a bank that an exporter will be paid after shipping goods to an importer.
  - With **forfaiting** a bank will supply cash to an exporter in return for a right to claim the payments for goods or services supplied to an importer.
  - Supplying **risk management tools** to cope with foreign exchange and interest rate risk. These usually involve the use of derivatives such as forwards, futures and options.
  - **Stockbroking**.
  - **Asset management** – e.g. share portfolio management.
  - **Custodian** – the banks provide a service of safekeeping and ensuring interest or dividends are claimed on investment portfolios. They will also notify the owner of annual general meetings of companies, rights issues and other events.
  - **Safety deposit boxes**.
  - **Insurance. Bancassurance** is the selling of insurance and banking services alongside each other; the Germans use the term **Allfinanz**.
  - **Foreign exchange**.
  - **Asset-based lending**, e.g. leasing, hire purchase.

- **Permanent capital** of a bank is obtained by the selling of shares in the firm and by shareholders keeping retained earnings within the firm – shareholders do not have the right to withdraw their money from the company below a regulated level of capital.

$$\text{Total assets} \quad = \quad \text{Total liabilities} \quad + \quad \text{Capital}$$

▶

- **Cash reserves** consist of both the cash (notes, etc.) that the bank is required to hold in its account with the central bank plus cash (notes, etc.) that it has on its own premises. **Required reserves** are held because the regulator insists. Additional 'excess reserves' may be held if the bank judges that it needs this extra buffer of cash.

- **Liquidity management:** there may be times when a large volume of cash is withdrawn and the bank has to be ready for that. If this managerial task is performed poorly then there are sources of cash, but these can be costly:
  - **borrowing from the central bank**;
  - **selling securities**;
  - **borrow from other banks and other organisations**;
  - **reduce the loan book**.

- **Asset management:** a bank needs to lend its money (acquire assets) with the expectation of a low risk of default and in a diversified manner.

- **Liability management:** a bank must be capable of finding funds at low cost and with the right mix of borrowing.

- **Capital adequacy management:** a bank needs to keep its capital at a high enough level to reduce the chance of **insolvency** problems (assets becoming worth less than liabilities) while balancing the need to make profits by lending.

- **Return on assets (ROA):**

$$ROA = \frac{Net\ profit\ after\ tax}{Total\ assets}$$

- **Return on equity (ROE):**

$$ROE = \frac{Net\ profit\ after\ tax}{Equity\ capital}$$

- A bank's **income statement** is split into two sources of income and three types of operating expense.
  Income: (i) interest income (ii) non-interest income.
  Operating expenses: (i) interest expense; (ii) non-interest expense; (iii) provisions for loan losses.

- **Net interest margin (NIM):**

$$NIM = \frac{Interest\ income - Interest\ expense}{Assets}$$

- **Loan to deposit ratio:** amount of loans lent out divided by the amount of funds attracted to bank accounts.

- **Net interest income (NII):** interest income minus interest expense.

- **Cost–income ratio (C/I)** measures the bank's efficiency in holding down its costs relative to its income.

$$\frac{Cost}{Income} = \frac{Non\text{-}interest\ expenses}{Net\ interest\ income + Non\text{-}interest\ income}$$

References and further reading

To keep up to date and reinforce knowledge gained by reading this chapter I can recommend the following publications: *Financial Times, The Economist, Corporate Finance Magazine* (London: Euromoney), *Bank of England Quarterly Bulletin* (*www.bankofengland.co.uk/publications/quarterlybulletin/index.htm*) and *Bank for International Settlements Quarterly Review* (www.bis.org).

Casu, B., Girardone, C. and Molyneux, P. (2006) *Introduction to Banking*, 2nd edn. London: FT Prentice Hall.
> A wide-ranging consideration of banking from a UK perspective.

Howells, P. and Bain, K. (2008) *The Economics of Money, Banking and Finance*, 4th edn. London: FT Prentice Hall.
> Provides an interesting run through different banking systems around the world.

Mishkin, F. S. and Eakins, S. G. (2009) *Financial Markets and Institutions*, 6th edn. London: Pearson Prentice Hall.
> Contains a brief, easy-to-follow introduction to the US banking system.

Saunders, A. and Cornett, M. M. (2007) *Financial Markets and Institutions*, 3rd edn. McGraw-Hill.
> A US perspective on banking.

Websites

BACS www.bacs.co.uk
Bank of England www.bankofengland.co.uk
British Bankers Association www.bba.org.uk
CHAPS (Clearing House Automated Payment System) www.chapsco.co.uk
Cheque and Credit Clearing Company (CCCL) www.chequeandcredit.co.uk
CHIPS (Clearing House Interbank Payments) www.chips.org
European Central Bank www.ecb.int
Fedwire www.frbservices.org/fedwire
Financial Services Authority www.fsa.gov.uk
Financial Times www.ft.com
SWIFT (Society for Worldwide Interbank Financial Telecommunication) www.swift.com
UK Payments Council www.paymentscouncil.org.uk
UK Payments Administration www.ukpayments.org.uk

Video presentations

Bank chief executives and other senior people describe and discuss policy and other aspects of banking in interviews, documentaries and webcasts at Cantos.com. (www.cantos.com) – these are free to view.

Case study recommendations

See www.pearsoned.co.uk/arnold for case study synopses.
Also see Harvard University: http://hbsp.harvard.edu/product/cases

- Bank of America: Mobile banking (2010) Authors: Sunil Gupta and Kerry Herman. Harvard Business School. Banking applications for iPhones and tablet computers.
- Developing an App for That: Mobile Application Strategy (Banking) (2010) Authors: Hanna Halaburda, Joshua Gans and Nathaniel Burbank. Harvard Business School. Case study focused on an internal debate of a bank's strategy for mobile banking apps.
- BP Amoco (A): Policy Statement on the Use of Project Finance (2010) Authors: Benjamin C. Esty and Michael Kane. Harvard Business School. Discusses the pros and cons of project finance.
- BP Amoco (B): Financing Development of the Caspian Oil Fields (2010) Authors: Benjamin C. Esty and Michael Kane. Harvard Business School. An interesting project finance case study.

- Why study large projects? (2003) Author: Benjamin C. Esty. Harvard Business School. Provides useful background about project finance in the context of finance theory.
- Poland's A2 Motorway (2008) Authors: Benjamin C. Esty and Michael Kane. Harvard Business School. An interesting project finance case.
- An Overview of Project Finance and Infrastructure Finance – 2009 Update (2010) Authors: Benjamin C. Esty and Aldo Sesia. Harvard Business School. A very useful introduction to project finance.
- Petrolera Zuata, Petrozuata C.A. (2002) Author: Benjamin C. Esty. Harvard Business School. Project finance case.

Self-review questions

1 What are the basic functions of a bank?

2 What are the four different types of banking?

3 What are the two main types of retail bank accounts?

4 Explain four of the types of lending banks offer.

5 What are the advantages to the customer of bank lending compared with other types of lending?

6 What is LIBOR?

7 What is an overdraft?

8 Explain (a) repayment holiday, (b) balloon payment, (c) bullet repayment.

9 What is asymmetric information and what is its significance in the relationship between a bank and a borrower?

10 Explain relationship banking and transactional banking.

11 What is collateral? Give some examples.

12 What are loan covenants? Give some examples.

13 Explain a personal guarantee in the context of banking.

14 Give a brief description of as many payment mechanisms as you can.

15 Explain clearing within the banking system.

16 What is revolving credit?

17 In addition to loans and deposits services, what services do banks provide for corporate customers?

18 Explain cash management.

19 Describe one of the ways in which banks help with overseas trading.

20 For banks, what is (a) asset management, (b) liability management?

21 Describe bank cash reserves.

22 What is the capital-to-assets ratio for a bank and why is it important?

23 Why is a bank's capital level important?

24 For banks, what are (a) ROA, (b) ROE, and what is the significant difference between them?

25 How is a bank's income statement split?

26 What are (a) NIM, (b) NII?

Questions and problems

1 Describe and illustrate, using simplified bank balance sheets, how a bank could find itself with a liquidity crisis and a capital reserve crisis. Describe and explain the actions it can take to move back to more prudent liquidity and capital reserve levels after such a crisis.

2 'Bankers are simply over-paid parasites on the really productive parts of the economy!' Describe and explain the functions of commercial banks and discuss whether you agree with this opinion held by an irate politician.

3 Write an essay distinguishing between the four different types of banking and explain their different functions.

4 Discuss the structure of a bank's source of funds.

5 Compare and contrast (describe and explain the relative advantages and disadvantages) of an overdraft versus a term loan versus project finance versus a syndicated loan.

6 Describe and explain the different ways banks try to mitigate risk in their lending operations.

7 Describe and compare the various types of uncommitted and committed loan facilities provided by banks.

8 Describe, explain and illustrate how a bank could find itself insolvent.

Assignments

1 Collect as much information as you can about the services provided by a bank you know well. Describe those services and discuss the importance to businesses of their provision.

2 Examine the accounts of a number of banks and write a report comparing them on the basis of the key banking ratios and measures.

Web-based exercises

1   Go to www.ukpayments.org.uk. Obtain statistics on payment transactions and write a report on the relative importance of the various payment mechanisms over time.

2   Go to the statistical section of www.bankofengland.co.uk. Obtain statistics on lending to individuals, lending secured on dwellings, consumer credit and a range of other lending to compile a report describing the shifts that have taken place over the last few years.

CHAPTER

3

Investment banking and other banking

LEARNING OUTCOMES

Banking is now a term that covers a surprisingly complex and intellectually rich range of activities. This chapter explains some of that diversity so that the reader might have a sounder grasp of the important functions performed by bankers. By the end of this chapter the reader should be able to:

■ describe the wide variety of activities undertaken by investment bankers;

■ explain the nature and significance of international banking in the modern world;

■ outline the important roles taken on by the banks set up as mutual organisations;

■ discuss the nature of hire purchase, leasing and factoring businesses conducted by finance houses;

■ describe Islamic banking and outline how it differs from conventional banking.

Most of us do not encounter investment banks in our daily lives. Despite them operating in the background, working with companies, governments and other large organisations they are highly influential. The extent of their importance was harshly brought home with the financial crisis of 2008. Even those of us who work in the field of finance had hardly heard of US sub-prime mortgages or the repackaging of these mortgages into bonds issued by investment bankers, let alone the repackaging of the repackaged bonds. And yet all this financial engineering led to a calamity with enormous implications for all of us.

The greedy repackaging of financial claims is to look on the dark side of the role of investment banks; their bread-and-butter jobs are far more down to earth and far more useful. For example, executives go to investment bankers when contemplating a once-in-a-career corporate move, such as buying another company. They lack the knowledge and skill set themselves to be able to cope with the regulations, the raising of finance or the tactics to be employed, so they turn to the specialists at the bank who regularly undertake these tasks for client companies. Another area where executives need specialist help is in raising money by selling bonds or shares. The sums raised can be in the tens or hundreds of millions, and all the details have to be right if investors are to be enticed and the regulators satisfied. Investment bankers also assist companies in managing their risks. For example, they may advise a mining company on the use of derivatives to reduce the risk of commodity prices moving adversely, or interest rates, or currency rates. Then there are their roles in assisting the workings of the financial markets, acting as brokers, market makers and fund managers. The list of people they help is long, despite most of us being unaware of their activities.

The chapter moves on to discuss a number of other types of banking. With increased liberalisation of financial systems, banking has globalised, with foreign banks becoming increasingly important in domestic systems; we thus look at international banking. Then, alongside banks set up as shareholder-owned companies, we have other types of organisation conducting banking-type activities. For example, there are a number of mutually owned (owned by their customers) entities that invite deposits, make loans and participate in the payment system. These include building societies, savings and loans and cooperative banks.

When people or businesses obtain an asset through hire purchase or leasing, the obligations under the agreement are in many ways similar to those of a bank loan. These are certainly considered alternative ways of borrowing money and so can be included under banking. Indeed, most of the large finance houses that operate in these areas are, in fact, subsidiaries of the major banks. Finally, this chapter highlights the differences between conventional banking and Islamic banking.

Investment banking

Investment banks are complex organisations selling a wide range of services as well as trading securities for their own profit. Not all of them are active in the full range discussed below; many are content to specialise in certain services or trading areas. It is important to note that of the services they offer companies and governments, many are regarded as loss-leaders (e.g. analysis of company shares, or even lending by the bank to companies) so that they can engage with potential clients over a long period of time, gain their trust and then offer highly lucrative services when the company makes a major move such as the takeover of another company. Thus, for investment banks to maximise profits they need to be very good at coordinating their various activities so that they can sell a number of different services to a client company or government.

It is people who form relationships rather than organisations, so investment banks need talented employees who can form strong bonds with clients. Such talent is expensive, especially once they have some leverage with their employers because the client executives trust them as individuals, rather than the bank, to help them with, say, a rights issue – there is always the possibility of an investment banker taking his client contact list with him to another employer. This partly explains the high bonus culture at investment banks. Then, on the trading side, the talented individuals who make good bets on the movements of securities, commodities, exchange rates, etc. can also command high bonuses. Investment banks typically put aside around 50 per cent of income for employee compensation (salary + bonuses etc.). Just to give you some idea, the average compensation and benefits for each Goldman Sachs employee in 2010 was $430,000: at the investment bank arm of JP Morgan Chase it was $369,651. *See* **Exhibit 3.1** to gain some idea of more general pay in the sector – these are the rates *after* they made a major contribution to the financial crisis! (VP = vice president of a section, MD = managing director of a section – they tend to have a lot of VPs and MDs.) There are now new rules in the major economies limiting the amount that can be taken as cash to less than 30 per cent of the bonus, with the rest payable over five years or so in shares. This is an attempt to align the interests of the bankers with the long-term interests of their shareholders and wider society. It was felt that they had been focusing on short-term gains and taking high risks to do it so that they could get a large bonus – if it all went wrong then the government would bail them out, they reasoned. And anyway, after a year or two of high bonuses they already had the house in Mayfair and a bulging Swiss bank account.

Exhibit 3.1

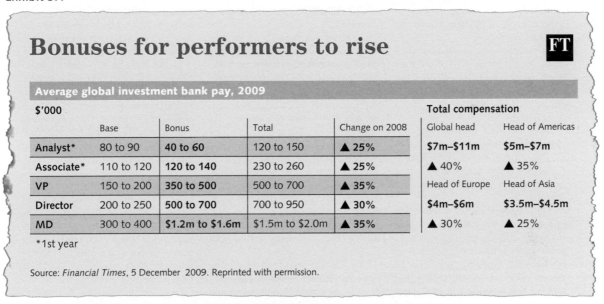

Bonuses for performers to rise   **FT**

Average global investment bank pay, 2009					Total compensation	
$'000						
	Base	Bonus	Total	Change on 2008	Global head	Head of Americas
Analyst*	80 to 90	**40 to 60**	120 to 150	▲ 25%	**$7m–$11m**	**$5m–$7m**
Associate*	110 to 120	**120 to 140**	230 to 260	▲ 25%	▲ 40%	▲ 35%
VP	150 to 200	**350 to 500**	500 to 700	▲ 35%	Head of Europe	Head of Asia
Director	200 to 250	**500 to 700**	700 to 950	▲ 30%	**$4m–$6m**	**$3.5m–$4.5m**
MD	300 to 400	**$1.2m to $1.6m**	$1.5m to $2.0m	▲ 35%	▲ 30%	▲ 25%

*1st year

Source: *Financial Times*, 5 December 2009. Reprinted with permission.

But then there is the question of why investment banks generate such high profits to be able to pay bonuses in the first place. One place to look would be the small number of players in the field with high reputations for handling complex financing and deals – corporate executives are often willing to pay a great deal for what they perceive as the 'best'. On the investing side, when contemplating whether to invest some money, institutions often look for a big-name investment bank's stamp of approval of a firm issuing new securities (e.g. shares) or committing to a merger deal – the big names will refuse to handle an issue of shares or bonds for a company if there is a real risk of the issue upsetting investors by subsequently underperforming. The industry looks very much like an oligopoly in many areas of activity – for some services there may be a choice of only three banks in the world. Lord Myners, who has decades of experience in the City before becoming a government minister, is certainly suspicious – *see* **Exhibit 3.2**.

Exhibit 3.3 discusses the difficulties of introducing more competition into investment banking. Any new entrant that tried to challenge the current leaders would need large amounts of capital to be able to do the deals that clients expect. They would also need to attract the best employees, those capable of inspiring confidence and maintaining a long-term relationship of trust with corporate executives, offering exceptional expertise. They would need to offer the broad range of services that multinational corporate clients now expect. These barriers to entry are considered so strong that they rarely allow a newcomer to seriously attack the market shares of the leaders.

Another place to look for an explanation for the exceptional profits is the extent of the variety of tasks undertaken by the banks – perhaps they gain some special advantage in doing so many different things for other traders, for investors or for companies. So, while helping a company

Exhibit 3.2

Pressure rises for formal bank fees inquiry

Kate Burgess

Political pressure for a formal inquiry into investment banking fees mounted yesterday as Lord Myners, City minister, said there was clear evidence of restricted competition in the market.

"Certain aspects of investment banking in equity underwriting exhibit features of a semi-oligopolistic market," Lord Myners told the Financial Times.

His comments come less than a week after the Office of Fair Trading revealed it was looking at the fees charged by investment banks to decide whether to launch a formal probe.

Lord Myners told an international audience of shareholders at the International Corporate Governance Network yesterday that he welcomed the OFT's focus on this area.

He is understood privately to be encouraging the OFT not to drop the issue. But he also urged investment institutions as the users of investment banking services to launch their own public probe into fees "to test whether . . . vital capital-raising activity is the product of sufficient capital intensity".

He criticised institutional investors for complaining about the rising fees but doing "little or nothing about it themselves – they have, for the most part, acquiesced".

He told the FT: "Here is a real opportunity for investment managers to show they are acting on behalf of their clients and launch an inquiry."

Lord Myners spoke out following shareholder complaints to ministers asking for government reviews. The Association of British Insurers wrote to Lord Mandelson, business secretary, this week calling on him to add his weight to pressure on companies to clamp down on fees paid to banks.

The "enormous" fees paid to investment banks for advising companies on deals might be skewing the outcome of takeovers, the ABI letter warned, and acted as a "deadweight cost" on shareholders that could swallow part of savings derived from mergers and acquisitions.

Lord Myners said yesterday it was clear investment banks had profited from raising margins on trading and intermediating between companies and investors in capital markets.

"The rents attracted for intermediation appear on the face of it to be high for the value added of the risk taken," he said.

He noted that while banks were charging higher fees for assuring companies that a share issue went well, they have reduced their own risks by advising companies to issue shares at a discount and warming up investors to the issue in advance.

Lord Myners said that if shareholders launched their own inquiry into equity underwriting, institutional investors would "head off the charge that some investment managers are unwilling to challenge existing practices or pricing because their relationship with investment banks is too cosy".

Lindsay Tomlinson, chairman of the National Association of Pension Funds, said: "Shareholders are extremely vexed about fees charged by banks for equity issues and mergers and acquisitions, but whether they would set up their own probe is another matter."

Source: *Financial Times*, 26 March 2010, p. 6. Reprinted with permission.

Exhibit 3.3

Outsized risk and regulation inhibit entrants

Patrick Jenkins

In all the furore over bankers' bonuses and bulging bank profits in recent months, one big question seems to have been forgotten: why is it that banks make so much money in the first place? Why does a Goldman Sachs rack up a return on equity of 22 per cent, when a BP makes 17 per cent, or a Pfizer makes 12 per cent – especially

when so many of the now booming banks were at least partly responsible for the financial crisis? Is there a cartel in investment banking, as the UK's Office of Fair Trading last week implied?

The titans of Wall Street and the City of London have long seemed unassailable, that is for sure. The need for vast amounts of capital,

a strong enough brand to attract staff and a compelling enough suite of products and services to draw customers has proved too big an obstacle for all but a tiny clutch of challengers. If Barclays Capital and Deutsche Bank have been winners, their number is dwarfed by the losers. The still-trying category stretches from France

▶

Exhibit 3.3 continued

(Crédit Agricole, Natixis) to Japan (Nomura, Mizuho).

"The barriers to entry have always been pretty high," says Rob Shafir, who heads Credit Suisse in the Americas. "It takes years to build the technology, the human capital, and make the client investment."

But as politicians and regulators have grown increasingly uneasy with the size and scale of established banks – urging for balance sheets to be shrunk and universal banks to be broken up – surely now is the perfect time for new entrants to triumph.

There is certainly space for more players, bankers admit. "In the old days, before the financial crisis, there were 14 or 15 firms," says Colm Kelleher, co-head of Morgan Stanley's investment banking operations. "Now there are seven or eight. So perversely you've ended up with less competition." The investment banking chief of one European bank agrees. "Our industry is too consolidated, it is frightening," he confesses, before adding gleefully: "[Profit] margins in this business are fantastic."

Sure enough, last year was a bumper one for the earnings of investment banks that were not still swamped by the financial crisis. A combination of low interest rates, vanished giants (Lehman and Bear Stearns) and others weakened by toxic asset problems (Citigroup, UBS, Royal Bank of Scotland) left the likes of JPMorgan, Goldman Sachs and BarCap to profit exponentially from inflated margins and booming demand from return-hungry investors.

Yet, according to the consensus views of lawyers, bankers and regulators, no matter how desirable or logical it might be to see stiffer competition, and the break-up of what many see as a global oligopoly, the odds of that happening have ironically widened. It is one of the unintended consequences of the post-crisis world that as regulators seek to make the financial sector

safer, they are also insulating it from fresh competition.

"We'd love to have smarter competitors," says one Wall Street boss. "But every time they ratchet up the regulations, it gets tougher."

Already regulatory authorities around the world have told banks they need to beef up their holdings of liquid funds, and the international architects of bank supervision, the Basel committee, are drawing up tougher rules governing how much capital must underpin riskier activities.

If analysts are right, the ramp-up in regulation will have an effect on banks' return on equity – cutting it from a range of 15–25 per cent to perhaps 5–15 per cent. But it will make breaking into the industry more demanding.

"The structural barriers are certainly higher than they were," says David Weaver, president of Jefferies International. "But it's not only regulatory capital that has got more demanding. If you're a lender, in these markets, you have to step up and provide capital on your balance sheet – the syndication market just isn't there."

That means life has become harder for smaller operators without the appetite to take outsized risks.

Even without tougher regulation, it has proved next to impossible to crack Wall Street without a significant acquisition. Nomura is trying just that – and for the fifth time. Having bought the European and Asian assets of the defunct Lehman Brothers, it is now seeking to build out a US operation to match – so far with limited success.

Even HSBC, which boasts one of the most powerful brands internationally, threw in the towel in 2006 and backed away from John Studzinski's aggressive three-year expansion plan. Executives say it was impossible to compete with rivals that had a greater appetite for risk, particularly when it came to backing transactions with balance-

sheet lending, or to break down their historic relationships with clients.

Hard as the Wall Street challenge is, there have nonetheless been striking changes of market share within the clique. Even banks that have thrived – such as Goldman Sachs – have lost out in some areas. A few years ago Goldman and Morgan Stanley controlled two-thirds of the prime brokerage market – the business of supplying finance and custody to hedge funds. Over the past 18 months, the likes of Credit Suisse and Deutsche Bank have stolen large amounts of that business, as hedge funds concluded, after the failure of Lehman Brothers and Bear Stearns, that they should have relationships with more than just one bank.

There is also plenty of evidence of fresh competition in merger and acquisition advisory work, where virtually the only requirement for starting up in business is a contact book and a decent reputation – hence the profusion of advisory boutiques that spring up every year.

But if a typical company uses three or four advisers on a deal, only one of them would ever be a boutique, mainly because the company is often desperate for the lending capacity that only bulge-bracket banks can provide.

"It's a very, very competitive world out there," says one Wall Street M&A boss. "But there's a finite slice of the pie going to boutiques."

The big hope for those banks outside the bulge bracket is to find profitable niches. HSBC, for example, has retrenched to focus on servicing its core corporate clients, with a bent towards emerging markets.

"If you want to be everywhere in Europe, Asia, the US, it's true that the barriers are very high," agrees Sergio Ermotti, head of investment banking at Italy's Unicredit. "But our focus is on Europe and there we have big opportunities."

Source: *Financial Times*, 24 March 2010, p. 22. Reprinted with permission.

issue bonds they might also act as a market maker in the bond market and provide research to clients. They might also be dealing in that company's shares and acting as a broker for its derivatives trades, while selling its commercial paper, managing its foreign exchange deals and buying commodities for it. They might also be running large investment funds for pension funds and other investors. Like spiders at the centre of information webs, they can detect movements long before others and are in a position to benefit themselves from that superior knowledge. How much of this 'special knowledge' tips over into conflict-of-interest territory (or even insider dealing) is difficult for us to know, but some people suspect that quite a lot of it does – *see* **Exhibit 3.4**.

Exhibit 3.4

Conflicts of interest bubble beneath the surface   **FT**

Lina Saigol

The vexed question of potential conflicts of interest between investment banks and their corporate clients has been laid bare by Citigroup's role in Terra Firma's £4bn acquisition of EMI.

Citigroup not only served as adviser, lender and broker to EMI, but it was also the sole financier to Terra Firma.

"Citi's increasing involvement with EMI in many areas led to inherent conflicts, set Citi up to broker the private equity deal that is at the heart of this action," Terra Firma's lawsuit claims.

However, by their very nature, integrated investment banks are inherently conflicted.

Their aim is to sell companies as many products and services as possible and package them together to maximise a greater "share of wallet".

By providing companies with multiple products and services – from advising on deals and financing them to hedging the related interest rate and currency exposure, and refinancing the debt when the deal closes – a bank can squeeze substantial fees from just one company.

Terra Firma claims, in its lawsuit, that its relationship with Citi was "highly lucrative" for the bank. Citi not only received £92.5m in fees for its multiple capacities on the EMI deal, but also raked in more than £135m between 2000 and 2007 for providing Terra Firma with advice and/or financing in connection with almost 20 transactions worth $57bn (£35bn).

According to the lawsuit, it seems that some EMI executives were worried that Citi was using the same bankers that had previously worked on the renegotiation of EMI's credit facilities and as a result had access to confidential EMI information, to also arrange the debt financing package for Terra Firma's acquisition.

This, Terra Firma argues, suggests that Citigroup had more knowledge about EMI than it did, and would have therefore known what the business was valued. Citi denies this.

Usually, such arrangements do not cause a problem unless a client complains.

In 2006, for example, during Linde's €12bn (£10.8bn) takeover of BOC Group, the UK gases company asked Deutsche to step aside as its broker because of the German banks's multiple roles in the transaction.

Deutsche owned 10 per cent of Linde, was providing it with financing and the bank's chief executive, Josef Ackermann, was also a member of Linde's supervisory board. But when a client is not worried about the thorny issues of potential conflicts, the banks can put all their services into play.

That can even involve a bank co-investing alongside their client in a deal – a strategy Terra Firma should be familiar with.

Four years ago, Citigroup not only provided Terra Firma with the equity, mezzanine debt and advisory service to back the £7bn buy-out of

Viterra, the real estate arm of Eon, but the US bank invested alongside its client in the deal.

This approach – known as the "triple play" in the industry – works until the banks start competing with their clients for an asset.

The more principal money the banks have to invest, the greater the chances of a conflict, which is what happened at the height of the debt boom.

One of the most controversial examples took place in 2006 when Goldman Sachs, having offered to advise airports operator BAA against a hostile bid from Ferrovial, put together its own bidding consortium for the UK airports operator.

The move caused Hank Paulson, Goldman's then chief executive, to publicly reinforce the bank's policy of not investing as a principal in the takeover of a public company without a board recommendation.

The BAA saga also highlighted the challenges banks faced during the recent private equity bidding frenzy of maintaining competitive tension in auctions and keeping potential bidders enthusiastic for as long as possible.

As in any deal, would-be buyers hope to underpay, but it is the job of the sellside bank to bankers running the auctions to get the best deal for the vendors while imposing some discipline on the sale.

One of the favoured tactics of ensuring this is the "dual track" – whereby an asset is sold via

▶

Exhibit 3.4 continued

an auction and prepared for a potential initial public offering at the same time.

This creates pricing tension between the institutional and retail investor base of the company

for sale and the private equity buyers, and usually results in the latter increasing their bids at the last minute.

But while auctions can be an effective way to get the best price

for a business, it is not necessarily a victory to win one.

Source: Financial Times, 14 December 2009, p. 21. Reprinted with permission.

A generation ago we had **merchant banks** operating in the UK and a few other countries, now they have been relabelled as investment banks following the US nomenclature. In modern usage (i.e. US influenced) merchant banking is sometimes used for the subset of investment banking activities concerned with using the bank's capital to facilitate a transaction such as engaging in mergers and acquisitions.

The balance sheet of an investment bank is somewhat different to that of a commercial bank. Investment banks do not (generally) hold retail deposits – unless they are part of a universal bank, of course. Their liabilities come in the form of promises to pay on securities such as bonds or short-term wholesale money market instruments – they would also be using money placed in the company by shareholders (or by partners in a partnership – some investment banks are still partnerships rather than companies). Most of the money lent to investment banks is for repayment at a fixed date in the future and so they are less vulnerable to the risk of unforeseen withdrawals than retail banks, thus they hold little money in a truly liquid form. However, their reliance on wholesale market funding makes them vulnerable to a loss of confidence in the money and bond markets, leading to a lenders' strike – the bank may have to pay off old loans as per the original agreement but not be able to replace the money by borrowing again. This happened a lot in 2008 and 2009.

Instead of holding deposits with the central bank, investment banks tend to place cash at the retail banks or buy money market instruments if they have a temporary surplus of cash.

Global investment banks

Bulge bracket investment banks are those that are regarded as the leaders. They are dominant in key activities such as assisting corporations with bond and equity issuance, underwriting and mergers and acquisition, particularly for larger companies. Goldman Sachs and Morgan Stanley Capital are examples of bulge bracket firms. **Global banks** are those active in a number of countries. The US investment banks became very large in the US between the 1930s and the 1990s because after the Great Depression US banks could become either commercial banks or investment banks but not both.[1] Investment banks were not allowed to take deposits but they were allowed to assist with the issuance of securities, underwriting, securities dealing and other market-related activities. Commercial banks could take deposits and lend but were restricted in their business activities; in particular they were not to engage in underwriting and trading of securities.[2]

Thus, as corporations grew and realised they needed investment banking-type services, they went to the few Wall Street investment banks that dominated the scene. In addition, the US is an economy that is very much oriented to financial markets when it comes to raising finance – much more so than, say, Europe, where bank loans and equity investments by banks into companies are much more normal. Thus, the US developed enormous bond markets (corporate, local authority, government) and enormous equity markets, and at the heart of these markets grew a handful of

---

[1] The Glass-Steagall Act 1933, named after the congressmen who steered it into US law, was repealed in 1999, but following the 2008 crisis new restrictions are coming into place because the commercial banking arms which provide vital services to society were dragged down to near-bankruptcy due to the 'casino-type' activities of the investment banking wings of the universal banks.

[2] Similar restrictions were placed on Italian and Japanese banks.

investment banks. As countries around the world reduced the restrictions inhibiting cross-border banking over the last three decades, the US investment banks became dominant in many other countries, too. They bought up many of the local operators and integrated them into a global operation, leading to more economies of scale and even greater dominance. Having said that, the Americans do not have it all their own way – there are some other large investment banks around, e.g. Barclays of the UK, Union Bank of Switzerland (UBS) and Credit Suisse of Switzerland, Deutsche Bank of Germany, Nomura and Daiwa Securities of Japan.

There are two main types of investment bank today. First, there are the huge, global banks that perform the wide variety of functions described in this chapter. Second, there are much smaller outfits that specialise in particular areas. Thus you might have a boutique investment bank that simply advises companies on financing issues and mergers but does not raise finance for the firm, or underwrite, or engage in securities trading. Rothschild and Lazard are two of the more established names, which, while not exactly boutique, do have fewer potential conflicts of interest as they concentrate on advice and do not undertake secondary market trading or many other aspects of the securities business conducted by the global investment banks. Occasionally boutiques get bought up by the global banks – *see* **Exhibit 3.5** for an example.

Exhibit 3.5

Nomura takeover of Tricorn will see reversal of flight to boutiques

FT

Lina Saigol

Nomura, the Japanese investment bank, is set to buy Tricorn Partners, the London-based corporate finance advisory firm, in a move that will see a reversal of the recent trend for bankers to leave large institutions for smaller, independent boutiques.

Guy Dawson and Justin Dowley, who have run Tricorn since leaving Merrill Lynch seven years ago, will join Nomura as vice-chairmen of Europe, Middle East and Africa investment banking with a mandate to build the Japanese bank's relationships with UK boardrooms.

The acquisition price has not been disclosed but part of the amount that Nomura will pay for Tricorn will depend on earnings that the bankers generate over the next two years.

The acquisition comes during a boom for advisory boutiques which have been able to hire senior bankers on the promise of better pay and healthy dealflow. Mr Dawson and Mr Dowley, whose careers have included the roles of co-heads of European investment banking at Merrill Lynch, have close relationships with several FTSE companies, including Unilever; 3i, Standard Chartered and Travis Perkins.

Nomura has been looking to build its European investment banking franchise following its acquisition of Lehman Brothers' European and Asian M&A and equities business in September last year. That deal triggered the defection of several senior London-based bankers including Michael Tory, who ran UK investment banking.

Mr Dawson and Mr Dowley will also focus on boosting Nomura's roster of corporate broking clients which currently stands at only eight, including four FTSE 100 companies: Tesco, the London Stock Exchange, Legal & General and Invensys.

Source: Financial Times, 16 December 2009, p. 21. Reprinted with permission.

Corporate and government assistance

Advice on financing and raising finance

A corporation reaching the point when it needs to raise capital from outside the firm (i.e. not rely on retained profits) faces a dizzying array of alternative types of finance and ways of raising that finance, from a syndicate bank loan to a bond to selling new shares. Investment banks can advise on the advantages and disadvantages of each and suggest paths to take.

Furthermore, the bank often has the knowledge, contacts and reputation to be able to bring a company needing finance to potential investors. They can help price a new issue of bonds or shares, having awareness of market conditions. They can assist in selling those securities, often roping in a number of other financial institutions to have greater impact in attracting investors. They know the legal and regulatory hurdles that have to be stepped over or manoeuvred around. They will also **underwrite** new security issues – guaranteeing to buy any not purchased by other investors. Just to confuse everybody the Americans commonly refer to the entire process of organising an equity or bond issue on behalf of a firm as 'underwriting', even though true underwriting (the guarantee of a sale) is only a part of it. To confuse even more: the US (and some other countries') investment bankers describe the process of 'underwriting' shares or bonds as meaning that the investment bank purchases the entire issue at an agreed price and then resells it in the market. In the UK and elsewhere the bank does not usually buy and then sell, but merely ensures that it will be sold.

Investment banks help with initial public offerings (IPOs), when a company issues shares on the stock market for the first time. The investment bank will coordinate the whole process, advise on price and try to find buyers for the shares. When underwriting, it usually gets other institutions to take most of the underwriting risk for a fee. Total underwriting fees are typically 6–7 per cent in the US and 3–4 per cent in Europe. There is more on IPOs in Chapter 9.

Investment banks also assist with seasoned equity offerings (SEOs), the issue of new shares for a company already listed or publicly traded on the exchange, also called follow-on offerings. This may be through a rights issue in which the existing shareholders are offered the new shares in proportion to the percentage of the shares issued that each investor already holds, thus an investor that has 4 per cent of the ordinary shares will be offered 4 per cent of the new shares. Again, the investment bank(s) will charge fees for many services, including advice, finding buyers and underwriting. There is a lot more on rights issues and other types of SEOs in Chapter 9.

Corporations are frequently attracted to the idea of raising money by selling a bond; they can often be sold with a lower rate of interest than that charged on a bank loan, and the restrictions placed on managerial action and demand for collateral can be less. Bond issuance, like share issuance, is an infrequent event for the typical firm (or local authority, or some governments) and so the directors are unfamiliar with the rules and regulations, the process and the methods of attracting buyers. Investment banks, for a fee, can help in these areas. Also, investment banks have high reputations among the investing institutions which buy bonds, thus they have more credibility when it comes to selling securities than would a company doing it on its own. Bond sales are usually underwritten by the bank (and sub-underwriters who work with the bank). Chapter 6 is devoted to the bond market.

Companies often need to raise short- and medium-term finance through the issue of financial instruments such as commercial paper and medium-term notes: investment banks stand ready to help them – for a fee, of course. There are also many other types of finance investment banks advise on and assist companies with, including project finance, sale and leaseback (in which the firm sells an asset, say a building and then rents it back so it can continue to use it), preference shares, convertible bonds (*see* Chapter 6).

The origin of many investment (merchant) banks was as providers of services to assist overseas trade in the eighteenth and nineteenth centuries. Importers and exporters have always been nervous about trading with each other. Goods are sent to a foreign country with a different legal system and payment is made months later. This exposes the exporter to all kinds of risk, from the importer simply not paying to running out of money before being paid and currencies moving adversely. One way of reducing risk is for the exporter to get the importer to sign a document guaranteeing that in, say, 90 days it will pay $1m, for example, to the holder of the document. In most cases the exporter does not even have to wait 90 days; it can sell the right to receive $1 millionin a discount market (run by investment banks) and then the purchaser of the bill can collect the $1 million– this is the bill of exchange market, discussed in Chapter 5. The risk for the importer and for the potential purchaser in the discount market can be lessened even more if the guarantor for the payment is a respected bank; thus a bank accepts the bill (for a fee) from the importer. Bank acceptances are also discussed in Chapter 5.

A number of investment banks were given a big boost hundreds of years ago when governments in Europe were keen to borrow money outside their home territory. The banks organised the borrowing. Still today there are dozens of governments faced with poorly developed domestic capital markets which need to raise funds by selling bonds on the international markets, and they often turn to the investment banks to assist with this – thus they issue emerging market bonds.

Here is a point of confusion: in order to distinguish the central activities of financial advice, raising funds for companies and governments, (including underwriting) from the other activities undertaken by the bank, the former are sometimes collectively referred to as 'investment banking' within investment banks. They are also referred to as corporate finance. (In some banks these terms may also encompass mergers, acquisitions and corporate restructuring.) But as you can see below there are many other activities within investment banks than 'investment banking'. I suppose, at least, it separates some of the core elements focused on helping companies (and governments) from the rest.

Mergers, acquisitions, corporate restructuring

Investment banks often have large departments ready to advise companies contemplating the merger or takeover of another firm. This sort of help can be very lucrative for the bank – it would seem that for once-in-a-blue-moon corporate actions like this directors do not look too carefully at the amount they have to pay for what is supposedly the best advice available. Indeed, the M&A departments of the banks do attract some very able people, but the fees seem on the high side for handholding and guidance. But then, they do offer, besides expertise on, say, takeover regulation and tactics, a recognised 'name' respected by investors should the acquiring company need to raise additional finance through a bond issue or a rights issue. The fees for a bundle of services like this can run into tens of millions – *see* **Exhibit 3.6**. For pure advice (without fund raising) the fees for smaller company deals are around 3–4 per cent of the total sale value; for larger deals (billions) they are generally in the range of 0.125–0.5 per cent. When you consider that Goldman Sachs and Morgan Stanley each assist more than $600 billion of M&A each year, even 0.125 per cent fees amount to a large income for advice. And they make a lot more on top by raising finance for the deal makers. Other players in this market usually near the top of the rankings in terms of value of mergers advised on include Credit Suisse, Citigroup, Deutsche Bank, JP Morgan, Lazard, UBS, Barclays and Bank of America Merrill Lynch. In some cases fees are payable by the bidder only if the bid is successful or by the target if there is a successful defence

Exhibit 3.6

Investors angered as costs soar over $750m

Lina Saigol

Prudential risks further enraging its shareholders after incurring costs estimated by bankers of more than $750m (£511m) on its seemingly doomed $35.5bn takeover of AIA.

The British insurer will have to pay AIG a break fee of £153m if it abandons the deal. Bankers said it could also incur costs of about $500m in currency hedging and other financing expenses.

A collapsed deal would also deprive 30 banks of one of the biggest fee-generating opportunities in the City over the past decade at a time when their traditional revenue streams from M&A advisory have dried up.

Estimates from Thomson Reuters and Freeman Consulting suggest the M&A advisory fees and underwriting fees on the planned £14.5bn rights issue would generate about $850m.

That compares with Vodafone's £101bn hostile takeover of Mannesmann in 1999, which produced fees of $283m for the advisers.

More recently, the 16 banks that worked on Royal Bank of Scotland's takeover of ABN Amro took home an estimated $275m in fees.

If Pru's deal succeeds, on the AIA side Citi, Morgan Stanley, Goldman Sachs, Blackstone Group and Deutsche Bank will split about $53m. On the Prudential side, JPMorgan, Credit Suisse, Lazard and Nomura will split about $59m.

The proposed $21.7bn rights offer would generate about $740m in underwriting fees to lead book-runners HSBC, Credit Suisse and JPMorgan Cazenove, to be divided among the 30-bank syndicate.

Banks traditionally pay sub-underwriting fees to institutional investors for their help in guaranteeing to take up all new shares issued, ensuring companies receive their money.

Historically, companies paid 2 per cent in underwriting fees, of which banks kept about a quarter.

The Pru was paying banks between 3.5 and 3.75 per cent for underwriting the rights issue, of which 1.75 to 2 per cent would go to the sub-underwriters.

Source: Financial Times, 2 June 2010.
Reprinted with permission.

Corporate restructuring comes in many forms, from selling off a subsidiary (a divestiture) to assisting a company that has borrowed too much, found itself in difficulties and needs to 'restructure its debt'. This kind of balance sheet restructuring usually means the lenders accepting a reduction in their claim on the firm (e.g. a £100 million loan is reduced to £70 million or the interest that is in arrears is written off), an extension of the time period to pay, the acceptance of shares in the company in return for writing off debt or the replacement of one bunch of debt agreements with others more suited to the company's reduced circumstances.

Investment banks can assist with valuation and procedural matters for bolt-on acquisitions, e.g. the purchase of a subsidiary from another firm. They might also help with organising an alliance or joint venture of firms or represent the interests of one of the firms in an alliance or joint venture.

Sometimes the chief executive of a corporation announces that they are undertaking 'a strategic review' of the company. This is usually code for 'at the right price we might be in favour of someone buying the company, in the meantime we will try to improve matters'. The review is often assisted/conducted by an investment bank, which is likely to receive telephone calls from prospective buyers. Of course, the bankers will have to work out the value of the firm as a revitalised creature and its value to other companies, and will have to polish up their negotiating skills. A confidential memorandum presenting detailed financial information is likely to be prepared for prospective buyers and the bankers may screen enquiries to narrow them down to serious potential owners only.

The corporate finance bankers within investment banks are generally sophisticated, suave communicators who nurture long-term relationships with key executives in the large corporations. These relationship managers tend to spend their time visiting chief executives and chief financial officers of companies, either those that already work with the investment bank or prospective clients. They are not trying to push one particular product onto clients, but give advice on the most suitable from across the bank's full range for the client at that stage of its development – offering the right solution at the right time. The very best relationship managers (often the corporate broker in the UK) put the needs of the client first at all times. Over a period of years they develop a good understanding of the client's business strategy and financing needs. They are then in a position to draw on the various product specialists within the bank to put together a suitable package of services. They are focused on a very distant horizon, often providing financing advice without a fee for many years in the hope that when the time is right for the corporation to launch an IPO, an SEO or a merger bid, it will pay large fees to the bankers it has trusted for so many years. The following is crude stereotyping, but contains enough truth to be interesting: the traders within the banks (see below for trading activities) tend to have a different personality and culture and there can be a degree of suspicion and mutual misunderstanding between them and the corporate bankers. Traders are focused on making money over short time periods. Corporate bankers sometimes characterise the traders as pushy and uncouth. Meanwhile, the traders often fail to understand the corporate bankers' lack of impatience at making money.

Risk management

The treasury departments of large companies have to deal with significant amounts of temporary cash and try to earn a return on this cash for a short period. They also need to manage various risk exposures that the firm has, e.g. the problems that can be caused by shifts in interest rates, commodity prices or foreign exchange rates. Investment banks are able to assist with the investment of temporary cash surpluses and discuss with corporate treasurers the outlook for risk exposures and advise them on how to mitigate the risk.

Lending

With a syndicated loan the investment bank may do more than simply advise and arrange the deal – they might participate as a lender. Investment banks may make other loans available to firms. The fact that most investment banks are part of universal banks is used as a competitive weapon – they can use the big bank's enormous balance sheet to offer low-cost loans to help win investment banking business.

Privatisation

The Thatcher government in the 1980s hit upon the idea of selling off state-owned assets such as Rolls-Royce, British Airways and British Gas. The investment banks assisted in this process, advising and organising the sell-offs, and thus built up a specialised knowledge of privatisation which they were then able to take to other countries as the idea caught on around the globe. The banks have also helped set up public–private partnerships (PPPs) in which governments persuade private firms to build and operate, say, a school or a prison in return for an income flow in subsequent years.

Investment banks are looking forward to helping in the sale of the banks that were rescued by governments around the world and taken into public control – *see* Exhibit 3.7 for an example. Thus investment banks benefit from the aftermath of a crisis they helped to create.

Exhibit 3.7

Advisers set to pitch for share sale of rescued banks

George Parker and Patrick Jenkins

Investment bankers were yesterday invited to pitch for a share of what is likely to be a goldmine in advising on Britain's biggest ever privatisation: the sale of Royal Bank of Scotland and Lloyds Banking Group.

The government might hope to raise at least £100bn from the sale of shares in the two banks, recouping the £70bn the taxpayer spent on rescuing them from collapse and turning a profit.

The sheer size of the privatisation means that UK Financial Investments – which manages the taxpayer shareholding – is expected to feed the shares into the market in tranches over several years.

Yesterday UKFI took the first steps towards assembling a "stable" of investment bank advisers, who

might expect to reap fees running to tens of millions of pounds.

UKFI officials say fees will be "highly competitive" given the scale of the enterprise and the stakes involved for the taxpayer.

The privatisation would dwarf those undertaken by Margaret Thatcher's government in the 1980s, when NM Rothschild earned a reputation as an adviser whose expertise was sought around the world.

Credit Suisse has been one of the closest advisers to the government during the financial crisis. It has played a key role in the design of the government's asset protection scheme, the insurance vehicle that is being put in place to help clean up the toxic assets on the balance sheets of RBS and Lloyds.

Deutsche bank has also been involved in advising on the APS, as have Citigroup and UBS, though UBS's advice mandates with RBS and Lloyds probably preclude it from more government work, on the grounds of conflict of interest.

Much of the advice to the government has been provided for very low fees, in the hope of securing future mandates.

But some bankers believe the UKFI, which stresses its independence from government thinking, could opt instead for an investment bank it has not used before to ensure its advice is not conflicted with that given to the Treasury.

Source: Financial Times, 18 July 2009, p. 2. Reprinted with permission.

Market activities

Alongside great skill in assisting companies with primary market issuance of bonds and shares, investment banks have developed experience and superior capability in secondary market dealing for equities, bonds, money market instruments, derivatives, commodities, currencies, etc. They perform one, two or all three of the following roles in market trading:

- **Broker** Act on behalf of clients to try to secure the best buy or sell deal in the marketplace.
- **Market maker** Quote two prices for a security: the price at which they are willing to buy and a (slightly higher) price at which they are willing to sell the same security. They 'make a market' in an instrument and expect to make numerous purchases and sells during a day, taking an income from the gap between the two prices.

● *Proprietary trading* The bank takes positions in securities in order to try to make a profit for itself rather than for its customers from subsequent favourable movements of prices.

As brokers, investment banks earn commissions on purchases and sales of a wide range of securities. As brokers they do not own the securities but merely act as middlemen, helping buyers and sellers to match up and do a deal. They mainly serve wholesale institutional (e.g. pension funds) and corporate clients rather than individuals, although they may own retail brokerage organisations that serve private investors.

An investment bank may also have a corporate broker arm, which acts on behalf of companies, e.g. providing advice on market conditions, representing the company to the market to generate interest, advising on the rules and regulations applying to stock market-quoted companies. They can also gauge likely demand should a company be interested in selling bonds or shares to investors. Then, during the process of a new issue, they can gauge a suitable price and organise underwriting. They work with the company to maintain a liquid and properly informed market in a client company's shares. They often stand ready to buy and sell the company's shares when market makers and others are refusing to deal. Companies are charged a regular fee by the corporate broker for regular services, but the broker keeps this to a minimum. The idea is to build up a long-term relationship so that the bank might earn a substantial amount should the client need advice and services during a major move such as a rights issue. The corporate broker can also be a bridge linking the client executives to other product providers within the bank. **Exhibit 3.8** describes the tensions between clients and corporate brokers as the investment bank tries to cash in on the relationship in times of corporate activity.

Exhibit 3.8

Broking under scrutiny as banks seek fees

Lina Saigol and Megan Murphy

When Citigroup temporarily cut its ties with BHP Billington in the middle of the Anglo-Australian miner's $39bn (£24.5bn) hostile bid for PotashCorp to work for a rival bidder, it sparked a furious debate in the City about the loyalties of corporate brokers to their clients.

As one of the two corporate brokers to BHP, Citigroup had expected to land a financing and advisory role on the company's biggest takeover attempt yet.

When it did not, the US bank switched allegiance and is now advising Sinochem, the Chinese fertiliser company, on a possible counter-bid for Potash. Bank of America Merrill Lynch, BHP's other broker, is working with Potash on its defence. BHP's lead adviser on the deal is JPMorgan Cazenove, which is not a broker to the company.

Citigroup's swap highlights the pressure banks are under to turn their UK corporate broking relationships into lucrative advisory and financing mandates, and the tensions that can arise as a result.

As companies begin to emerge from the recession with new strategies and management teams, that pressure is set to intensify with banks looking to seize broking market share to win more of the expected advisory work.

Alisdair Gayne, head of corporate broking at Barclays Capital, said: "Some companies were clearly disappointed with the advice given during last year's cash calls and as a result are likely to review their broking relationships."

Corporate broking, a uniquely British business role that involves a bank acting as the main point of contact between companies and their investors, is a fiercely competitive sector, particularly for FTSE 100 clients. However, it is not generally a profitable line of business and its main value for the banks is as a way into more lucrative advisory roles.

It is also one of the hardest businesses to build. Relationships can be sticky, as several US banks discovered before the financial crisis when they went on expensive

poaching sprees to help develop their franchises.

Lehman Brothers, for example, did not have a broking client in the FTSE 100 until 2006 when it replaced ABN Amro Hoare Govett as joint broker to Lloyds.

By the time the bank went bust in 2008, it had only added three other blue-chips to its roster.

"Corporate broking requires long-term investment by banks. It will take time for new entrants to build a client list. Long-term relationships build trust and give the client confidence to use the bank for advice and capital markets execution," said John Woolland, head of corporate broking at UBS.

As global regulators rewrite the industry's rule-book, forcing banks to hold more capital and pare back their riskier activities, corporate broking is seen as an increasingly vital way to boost less capital-intensive businesses, such as mergers and acquisitions advisory work.

BarCap, for example, is on a hiring drive as part of a push

Exhibit 3.8 continued

into broking as it tries to build up its European equities business. However, it does not expect overnight success.

The three dominminant forces in the market, JPMorgan Cazenove, UBS and Bank of America Merrill Lynch, have historically focused on a strategy of critical mass.

The logic is that the more clients they have, the more chances of transactions taking place and the more opportunities to sell other products and boost fees.

Together, those three banks act as either broker or joint broker to 98 FTSE 100 clients.

Some other big institutions, such as Goldman Sachs, have instead chosen to concentrate on large-cap companies, which generate more consistent advisory revenues.

While the bank consistently hovers only in the high single-digits of FTSE 100 clients, for example, it ranks fourth by the overall market capitalisation of its corporate broking customers.

The focus by the bulge bracket on the larger clients has created opportunities for independent brokers, such as Collins Stewart and Evolution Group, to serve smaller companies neglected by the big banks.

Garry Levin, head of corporate finance at Evolution, said: "The economics of the mid-cap independent firms allows them to devote a proportionately greater resource to day-to-day corporate broking services."

As well as calling on their top clients two to three times a week,

| Leading corporate brokers | | |
| Number of clients (includes joint brokerships) | | Equity capital markets deal value |
FTSE100	FTSE 250	(2010 to date)
JPMorgan Cazenove 37	100	$2.9bn
Bank of America Merrill Lynch 32	34	$2.6bn
UBS 29	39	$775m
Morgan Stanley 19	0	$3.2bn
Deutche Bank 18	18	$1.8bn
Citi 16	19	$483m
RBS Hoare Govett 10	37	$1.6bn
Credit Suisse 9	20	$1.5bn
Goldman Sachs 8	0	$851m
Nomura 3	0	$75m

Mr Levin and his team write to all of their clients every evening updating them on trading in their stock and movements among their peers.

However, smaller operators lack the spread of experience and the muscle to handle, for instance, a large cross-border transaction.

Charles Donald, head of corporate broking at Credit Suisse, said: "Companies want the whole package so brokers with a full equities platform will win market share."

At the height of the financial crisis, banks with a strong balance sheet became the first port of call for many companies and financial institutions looking to raise capital.

For years big banks have also been trying to export the corporate broking model to Europe, with limited success.

Bankers had hoped this would finally change in March, when Citigroup was appointed as corporate broker to Deutsche Telekom, but so far no other European corporates have followed suit.

Source: Financial Times, 8 October 2010, p. 21. Reprinted with permission.

Market makers, also known as dealers, fulfil a crucial role in the markets: in those securities in which market makers agree to make a market there will always be someone available who will quote a price at which they will buy or sell – as a purchaser or seller you may not like the price but at least someone is making a trade possible. To take share trading as an example, imagine if you wanted to invest in a small company's shares and there were no market makers. You might hesitate because the shares would fail to have the important quality of **liquidity**, that is the ability to sell the shares quickly at a low transaction cost without moving the price against you. Investors in companies lacking an active secondary market will demand higher rates of return (lower share prices) to compensate for the inability to quickly find a counterparty willing to trade.

We refer to a trading system with market makers at the centre as **a quote-driven system** because client investing firms can obtain firm **bid** and **offer (ask) prices** on a security and the dealers stand ready to trade. A bid price is one that the market maker will buy at (what the client firm could get from selling). An ask or offer price is what the market maker is willing to sell at (what the client firm would have to pay should they want to trade). Naturally, because the market maker is trying to make a profit, the bid price is always lower than the offer price. If the gap becomes too wide, clients will be lured away by better prices offered by competing market makers in that security. The difference between the prices is known as the trader's spread or bid–offer spread. Many of these prices are displayed on electronic systems so that clients can see them displayed on their computer screens throughout the day. Other security bid–offer prices are given to you only if you telephone the market maker and ask for a quote.

Market makers take a considerable risk: they have to hold inventories of shares and other securities to supply those who want to buy. Tying up a lot of money in inventories of shares, bonds, etc. can be very expensive, and there is always the possibility of downward movement in price while they hold millions of pounds or euros in inventory. The degree of risk varies from one security to another and this helps explain the differences in the size of the bid–offer spread. For some securities it is significantly less than 1 per cent of the value, in others it can be 20 per cent or more. The other major factor influencing the spread is the volume of trade that takes place relative to the amount that has to be held in inventory – high volume gives access to a liquid market for the market maker. Thus Marks & Spencer has millions of shares traded every day and so the market maker is not likely to have M&S shares on its hands for long, because they are going out of the door as fast as they are coming in – spreads here can be around one-tenth of 1 per cent. Shares of a small engineering company, meanwhile, might trade in lots of only a few hundred at two- or three-day intervals. Thus the market maker has money tied up for days before selling and is fearful of a price fall between trading days.

We can see how the quote-driven system works through **Exhibit 3.9**. This could apply to markets in a wide variety of securities and instruments, from bonds to commodities, but we will assume that it is company shares. The demand curve shows that as the price declines, the amount demanded to buy from the market maker rises. The supply curve shows rising volume offered by investors with higher prices. The clearing price is 199p – this is where the demand from clients wanting to buy and supply of the securities from those wanting to sell is evenly matched. Naturally, the market makers in this security will be taking a spread around this clearing price so the true price to the buying client might be 199.5p, whereas the price that a seller to the market makers can obtain is only 198.5.

If one of the market makers is currently quoting prices of 200–201p (offering to buy at 200p and sell at 201p) then he will experience a flood of orders from sellers because investors are willing to sell 7,000 shares per hour if offered 200p. However, demand at 201p is a mere 3,000 shares. The market maker will thus end up buying a net 4,000 shares per hour if he takes all the trade. In fact, it is even worse than this for our market maker because the potential buyers can pick up their shares for only 199.5p from other market makers and so he ends up buying 7,000 per hour and not selling any.

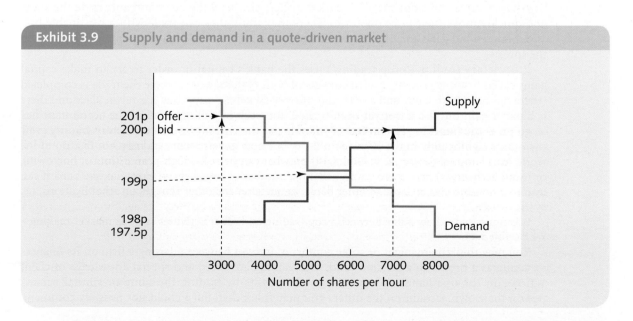

Exhibit 3.9	Supply and demand in a quote-driven market

Even if our market maker is exceptionally optimistic about the market equilibrium price rising significantly above 201p in the next few hours, he is not doing himself any favours by quoting such high prices because he could buy a large number of the shares he wants at a price a lot less than this – there are 5,000 per hour going through other market makers at 199.5p, for example. Thus there is a strong incentive for our market maker to move his prices down towards the intersection of the supply and demand curves.

Now consider a market maker who quotes 198–197.5p. She will experience a flood of buy orders from clients given the prices offered by other market makers in this competitive market. Under the rules governing market makers she is obliged to deal at the prices quoted up to a maximum number of shares (decided by the exchange that controls this particular market). Perhaps this obligation to sell 8,000 shares per hour to clients when she is attracting few (no) clients to sell to her may lead to problems in satisfying demand. She will thus be tempted (unless she has a lot of shares to shift) to move her bid and offer prices to around the market equilibrium price.

A market maker that tries to maintain a large bid–offer spread will fail when there are many market makers for a security. For example, consider the five market makers offering the following prices:

Market maker	Bid price	Offer price
1	198.5p	199.5p
2	197.3p	199.5p
3	197.0p	200.0p
4	198.5p	199.7p
5	198.3p	202.0p

Any potential seller (or broker for the buyer) would look at the various market makers' prices and conclude that they would like to trade with either market maker 1 or 4 at 198.5p. Any buyer of shares would want to trade with 1 or 2. Market maker 4 may be temporarily under stocked with these shares and is content to see inventory build up – he is not going to get many to buy from him at 199.7p when buyers can get away with paying only 199.5p. Market maker 2, meanwhile, will see more sales than purchases – perhaps she has excessive inventory and wishes to allow an outflow for a while.

Of course, for most companies the intersection of the supply and demand curves moves over time. Perhaps the company announces that it has won a large export order at 2pm. Immediately the investors see this news on their computer screens and the demand curve shifts upwards while the supply curve shifts downwards. Market makers also read the news and anticipate the shifts and quickly move their price quotes to where they think they can trade with a reasonable balance between bid deals and offer deals, aiming for a large number of each and making a profit on the spread.

Proprietary trading ('prop trading') uses the bank's capital in order to try to make capital gains called '**trading income**', which consists of both **realised gains**, where the trade is completed (there has been both a buy and a sell), and **unrealised gains** – say a buy has taken place and there is a paper gain but it has not yet been turned into cash by selling, thus all the accountant has to go on is the '**marking to market**' of the value at the current price. Proprietary trading grew in volume significantly in the 20 years to 2010, but now governments and regulators around the world are clamping down (*see* **Exhibit 3.10**) on what can be risky, high-geared (lots of borrowing or using derivatives) bets; there is a fear that if a number of large bets go wrong in one bank it can lead to a domino-like collapse of other banks as one after the other reneges on its obligations, i.e. **systemic risk**.

It is not easy to draw a line between prop trading and other activities such as market making – *see* **Exhibit 3.11**.

You may think there might be some conflict of interest between advising a firm on its finances or acting as a broker to a pension fund, thus gaining advanced and special knowledge of client actions on the one hand, and to try to make profits by trading the same or similar securities on their own account on the other. You may think that, but I could not possibly comment.

Exhibit 3.10

Leaving a lasting Wall Street legacy

Justin Baer

Paul Volcker will leave a lasting imprint on Wall Street after all.

Derided by banks as politically motivated and ineffective to prevent future crises, the former Federal Reserve chairman's "Volcker rule" – much of it, at least – has survived months of lobbying and legislative horsetrading to remain in the landmark financial regulatory reform measure set to land on President Barack Obama's desk this week.

Goldman Sachs, Morgan Stanley and other banks will be forced to dismantle or shed proprietary trading desks that powered profits in the past decade – or nearly led to their demise, depending on the institution.

Regulators will also cap the amount of capital banks can invest alongside clients, prompting the gradual unwinding of funds whose performance has also helped fatten returns.

But it could have been worse. Legislators charged with resolving the differences between the two chambers of Congress softened elements of the Volcker rule.

Banks have been freed to hold on to their hedge fund and private equity arms as well as being allowed to invest some of their capital alongside clients.

They were also offered important restrictions on the proprietary trading ban, including trades made to hedge banks' risks or facilitate clients' needs.

And yet the Volcker rule will still challenge Wall Street in ways the public backlash against pay policies or its behaviour during the crisis had failed to. Designed to discourage banks from taking outsized risks and reaping profits at the expense of clients, the reforms will alter the plans of the industry's stalwarts and crimp future results.

None will face more questions than Goldman, whose trading and risk-taking acumen has come to overshadow its vaunted investment banking arm and now dominates the bank's culture.

Goldman has said its prop-trading activities generate about 10 per cent of its revenue, which totalled $45.2bn last year.

A ban on prop trading could sap 20 cents from Goldman's per-share earnings but a broader definition could cost more, according to Keith Horowitz, an analyst at Citigroup.

Goldman earned $22.13 a share last year.

The Volcker rule has also been weakened to allow banks to invest up

to 3 per cent of tier one capital into in-house hedge funds and private equity. That too should also strike Goldman harder than its peers.

Goldman held about $15.5bn in its own hedge, buy-out and real estate funds as of March, or 23 per cent of its $68.5bn in capital. While the bank will have at least four years to reduce its holdings below 3 per cent, Goldman will need to push billions of dollars into funds or other investments that may not perform as well as its own sponsored vehicles.

Morgan Stanley, whose near-death experience in the financial crisis had already convinced the bank to shift its focus away from prop trading, derives less than 5 per cent of annual revenues from its own accounts. With $23.4bn in revenues last year, it shut down its four credit-trading desks in the wake of a multibillion-dollar loss in 2007 and is considering spinning off its two equity prop arms.

Morgan Stanley had $4.6bn in its own sponsored funds at the end of the first quarter, or 9.2 per cent of the $50.1bn it held in tier one capital.

Source: Financial Times, 28 June 2010, p. 23. Reprinted with permission.

Exhibit 3.11

The teams may be no more but the 'flow prop' will be harder to stop

Patrick Jenkins

From Wall Street to the City of London, "prop" traders – who deal for their bank's own (proprietary) account – are renowned as the widest of wide boys. They are the archetypal buyers of Rolex watches

and red Ferraris, the incarnation of the fat-walleted banker.

Politically, then, they were a logical enough target for Barack Obama's broadside against banks, designed to "protect taxpayers" and

"rein in excesses". The same motivation lay behind the UK's 50 per cent supertax on bank bonuses.

For Mr Obama, though, there was an intellectually compelling justification too. By stopping banks

Exhibit 3.11 continued

from owning hedge funds, private equity and prop trading operations – the kind of "casino banking" that involves betting bank capital to generate quick profits – he is trying to cut risk in the financial sector.

The first two of the three taboos (if Congress backs the president's plan), will be straightforward to implement. But cracking down on prop trading will be far from easy.

Defining it is the core problem. While most banks, in the boom years up to 2007, had vast prop trading teams that would take big bets on anything from the future price of wheat to exchange rates in west Africa, most "dedicated prop" teams were wound down amid the financial crisis. Goldman Sachs, which says it still generates more than 10 per cent of revenues from prop trading, is a big exception.

But the absence of dedicated desks does not mean prop trading no longer exists, however much many banks would like to claim as much. Virtually any trading operation uses so-called "flow prop", whereby a bank piggybanks on the trades it is processing for clients, doing a bit here, a bit there, often hedging a client investment with an opposing risk on the bank's own account.

Such activity, much of it vital to be an effective market-maker for clients, is reckoned to be low-risk – except if a trader gets carried away. Société Générale racked up a loss of nearly €5bn when Jéróme Kerviel did so a couple of years ago.

Bankers and lawyers agree that it will be nightmarish for regulators to separate what is genuinely necessary trading from what is egregious prop. And with many pundits betting that at least some of Europe, notably the UK under any future Conservative administration, will adopt the US blueprint, this is not just an issue for US prop desks. But whether it is through legislative bans or high capital requirements imposed by regulators, prop trading is likely to become much less common within banks.

Banks insist such moves will not eliminate the risk to the system, though, just shift it elsewhere – probably to unregulated hedge funds and low-tax, light-regulation centres such as Hong Kong and Singapore.

Safeguarding banks and their depositors – virtually all of them taxpayers and voters – is a crowd-pleasing move. But in a globalised business, with every kind of financial institution inextricably interlinked, sceptics fear it will do little to make the system safer.

Source: Financial Times, 25 January 2010, p. 9. Reprinted with permission.

The banks themselves protest that they have strong and high Chinese walls that separate the individuals who act as advisers or brokers (and others) from the proprietary traders within the banks – *see* **Exhibit 3.12** for some people's views on conflicts of interest.

Exhibit 3.12

Goldman looking at own goal

FT

Lina Saigol

Sir Alex Ferguson, Manchester United's manager, is not slow to react when a player incurs his wrath. It seems that the club's owners take the same approach with investment banks.

The Glazer family are considering severing ties with Goldman Sachs after Jim O'Neill, the bank's chief economist, was revealed as a member of a consortium looking to buy the football club.

Goldman insists that Mr O'Neill is working in a personal capacity, but his role brings back uncomfortable memories of a clash United had with JPMorgan four years ago

when Malcolm Glazer first bid for the club.

At the time, JPMorgan Cazenove was acting as United's stockbroker while its parent company, JPMorgan, had been arranging £265m of debt for Mr Glazer's bid.

The dual role infuriated Sir Roy Gardner, then chairman of United, who claimed it represented a clear conflict of interest and was hostile in nature.

The row also had wider repercussions. Two months later, Centrica dropped JPMorgan Cazenove as its joint broker. Sir Roy happened to be chief exec-

utive of the UK energy supplier at the time.

In the same year, Roger Carr, who was chairman of Centrica, had his own clash with Goldman Sachs.

Mr Carr was also chairman of Mitchells & Butlers when Goldman made an indicative £4.6bn debt-and-equity offer for the pub group, on behalf of a consortium in which it was one of the largest participants.

Mr Carr described the offer as "hostile and inaproppriate", the bank withdrew from the consortium, and the bid evaporated. Mr Carr's anger struck a chord with Goldman – the bank acted as

▶

Exhibit 3.12 continued

corporate broker to both Centrica and Cadbury, where Mr Carr was also a board member.

Goldman's private equity fund had also been involved in unsolicited approaches to ITV and BAA. Those episodes prompted Hank Paulson, Goldman's then chairman and chief executive, to warn its bankers not to use its principal investment funds in hostile situations.

The potential for conflicts of interest for banks has intensified in recent years in tandem with the rapid development of new financial products. Full-service banks incorporating private equity funds, advisers, traders and asset managers under one roof are likely to run more risks than single-discipline boutiques.

Banks have so-called Chinese Walls, which are supposed to limit the flow of information between different businesses, such as proprietary trading and investment banking.

In reality, these walls are only as sound as the integrity of the banks that erect them.

Source: *Financial Times*, 5 March 2010, p. 21. Reprinted with permission.

Investment banks are adjusting to the new regulatory environment – *see* **Exhibit 3.13**.

Exhibit 3.13

Prop-hostile climate throws up some tough calls for banks

Megan Murphy and Francesco Guerrera

These "prop" desks are now having to live in a new post-crisis world of tougher regulation. Many star traders across Wall Street and the City of London are voting with their feet, decamping for hedge funds in their droves amid a crackdown that will sharply curtail banks' riskier activities. And financial groups are grappling with ways to salvage some of their proprietary operations.

In some cases, such as the recent exit of Pablo Calderini, Deutsche's former head of equity proprietary trading, departures come as institutions look to close "pure" prop desks, which trade exclusively for their own account, rather than clients. Deutsche's investment bank, for example, cut sharply the amount of capital available for equity proprietary trading by 90 per cent in the aftermath of the crisis and closed down its credit proprietary trading desk altogether.

US banks claim not to be in a rush to decide the fate of their own prop desks, noting the new rules give them at least two years to scrap those activities.

However, many are already scrambling behind the scenes to redeploy their best traders, precisely because they don't want them to succumb to the lure of hedge funds and other institutions that will escape the new legislation. Although the importance of prop trading varies between banks, ranging from the 10 per cent or so of Goldman's revenues to less than 2 per cent at Citigroup, all are faced with the same three alternatives.

The first is to shut down prop activities and let traders go. Wall Street executives say banks are unlikely to pursue that option, mainly because they do not want to lose good traders who could be useful elsewhere in the organisation.

However, some admit that they might be forced to take this route if the onset of the legislation prompts a large part of their prop trading workforce to flee for less regulated companies.

The second is to move prop traders to their main "flow" desks dealing with clients' orders. Although superficially attractive, this solution has the potential pitfall that traders who have so far thrived on the "prop" model – being given money by the bank to invest as they please – might not relish, or be any good at, carrying out orders on behalf of customers.

To obviate this problem, banks could opt to move the prop trading desk into their in-house asset management operations and require them to raise third party funds. This alternative has the advantage of placing traders in a set-up that closely resembles the pre-legislation prop desks while enabling the bank to earn fees on their work. In order to succeed, though, this strategy needs prop traders with good track records to persuade investors to park funds.

There is also a fourth more radical, alternative: the complete spin-off or sale of prop trading desks, a move that would lead to a cash windfall for banks but would force them to part company with talented and cash-generating traders.

With such highly-profitable employees leaving almost daily, banks may need to make their minds up sooner rather than later.

Source: *Financial Times*, 4 August 2010, p. 31. Reprinted with permission.

Fixed income, currencies and commodities trading (FICC)

The FICC operations of an investment bank concentrate on sales and trading (e.g. market making) of highly liquid debt securities, swaps (*see* Chapter 11), currencies and commodities on behalf of client firms, rather than on their own account. The top 14 banks generate a combined revenue (income) of around $150 billion from FICC, which accounted for more than half of all revenues in 2009 and early 2010 (admittedly this was a particularly good period for FICC as bid–offer spreads remained high in historical terms following the crisis). The big players in this market are Goldman Sachs, Bank of America, JP Morgan, Deutsche Bank, Citigroup and Barclays (following its acquisition of Lehman's New York operations).

The fixed-income section of a bank specialises in deals in interest-rate securities. This includes the following:

- High-grade (low-risk) corporate bonds: **domestic bonds** (under the laws and regulations of the country where they are issued where the issuer is a local firm), **foreign bonds** (the issuer comes from abroad but the bond is under the jurisdiction of the country of issue) and **international bonds** (or **Eurobonds**), where the bond is issued outside the jurisdiction of the country in whose currency it is denominated. *See* Chapter 6 for a description of bonds.
- **Sovereign bonds** – issued by governments (*see* Chapter 6).
- Credit derivatives such as credit default swaps, which allow investors to buy a kind of insurance against the possibility of a bond failing to pay the agreed interest and/or principal amounts (more in Chapter 11).
- High-yield securities such as high-yield bonds (*see* Chapter 6).
- Bank loans – yes, there is a secondary market in bank loans.
- Local authority/municipal debt.
- Emerging market debt – bonds, etc. issued by governments or corporations in developing markets (some might be economically developed but under-developed with regard to financial markets).
- Distressed debt – borrowers are not meeting their obligations under a debt agreement.
- Mortgage-backed securities and other asset-backed securities – *see* securitisation later in the chapter.
- Interest rate derivatives such as interest rate futures – *see* Chapter 10.
- Money market instruments – *see* Chapter 5.

There are other divisions that deal in currencies and currency derivatives (*see* Chapter 12). There is usually yet another division that specialises in commodities and commodity derivatives (*see* Chapter 13).

In all these FICC areas the bank often acts as a market maker in these products, creator of many of them, as an adviser and broker for clients and as a proprietary trader. How they manage the conflicts of interest inherent in this I cannot tell you – but I can tell you that there are scandals from time to time.

Equities

The equities section of an investment bank helps clients with their investing and trading strategies in shares and equity-linked investments. The more exotic instruments they deal in include:

- futures in shares and futures in market indices (e.g. FTSE 100 index) – *see* Chapter 10;
- equity options giving the right but not the obligation to buy or sell shares at a pre-agreed price some time in the future – *see* Chapter 11;
- warrants on shares (similar to options but issued by the company rather than financial institutions) – *see* Chapter 9;
- preference shares – *see* Chapter 8.

Again, the bank will often act as market maker in these products, creator of many of them, as a broker for clients and as a proprietary trader.

Derivatives

Investment banks not only act as market makers or brokers in the derivative markets but also create new derivatives (*originating*) and market them to clients. Much of the commodity market trading by investment banks is via derivatives such as futures, whereby the buyer enters into a contract to buy or to sell the underlying commodity at a fixed price at a point in the future, say three months hence. They may assist firms trying to hedge in these markets, e.g. an airline trying to fix the future price of its aviation fuel, or they may conduct proprietary trades to make a profit for the bank. Of course, investment banks will also assist with non-derivative commodity trading by helping a client buy for immediate use some quantity of a commodity – **spot trading**.

It has been known for investment bankers to get too enamoured of the fancy derivative strategies they devised for companies and governments. They can be very complex and it can be almost impossible for the client to understand the full implications of the risks they are exposed to. Whether the lack of understanding is to be blamed on the clients or on the lack of effort on the part of the bankers to explain themselves is a moot point. Many Italian local authorities are fuming at the bankers for getting them into a mess with interest rate derivatives. Now Goldman Sachs is heavily criticised in China for selling oil derivatives to state companies – *see* **Exhibit 3.14**.

Exhibit 3.14

Goldman stung by backlash in China   [FT]

By Jamil Anderlini in Beijing

Public criticism of Goldman Sachs has come to China, where the bank has been attacked in the state-controlled media.

Apparently emboldened by congressional inquiries and anger in the west, the media have slated Goldman, arguably the most successful foreign investment bank in China.

"Many people believe Goldman, which goes around the Chinese market slurping gold and sucking silver, may have, using all kinds of deals, created even bigger losses for Chinese companies and investors than it did with its fraudulent actions in the US," the China Youth Daily said last week.

The report followed similar commentary and articles in 21st Century Business Herald and New Century Weekly.

The reports were critical of Goldman for designing and selling oil hedging contracts to state Chinese groups that then lost out when oil prices plunged, contrary to Goldman analysts' predictions, in 2008 and 2009.

Probably the most telling assertion is the complaint that Goldman has been too successful in China, that it has made too much money from underwriting initial public offerings, arranging deals and making its own private equity investments.

Goldman saw a 2007 investment in a pharmaceuticals export company of less than $5m rise to nearly $1bn at the company's IPO.

Source: Financial Times, 7 June 2010, p. 19. Reprinted with permission.

Securitisation (and other structured products)

During the 15 years to the end of 2008 banks (particularly US banks) built an enormous business in rebundling debt. So, say a bank has recently enticed 1,000 households to borrow money from it for house mortgages. It now has the right under the law to receive monthly interest and principal from the households. The traditional thing to do is to hold on to those bank assets until the mortgagees pay off the loan. Banks increasingly thought it better to do something else: 'originate and distribute' debt. Thus once they have the right to the interest, etc., the 1,000 rights on the mortgages are put into a **special purpose vehicle (SPV)** (a separate company), which issues bonds to other investors. The cash raised from selling the bonds goes to the bank so that it can originate another 1,000 mortgages. The investors in the SPV receive regular interest on the long-term bonds that they bought, which is paid for out of the receipts of monthly mortgage payments by 1,000 households.

In theory, the bank makes a nice profit because it gets more for selling the rights than it lent out in the first place. As banks became greedier and keener to originate mortgages and play this game they found they did not have enough of their own money to lend in high volume. They thus turned to the wholesale money markets to raise money. Many of these wholesale loans were only short term – they had to be repaid within days, weeks or months. This was OK if the banks could quickly securitise the newly originated mortgages. But what if everyone suddenly stopped buying securitised bonds? What if you as a bank had borrowed money for 30 days and then lent it out to mortgage holders for 25 years on the expectation of completing the securitisation (or simply expected to take out another 30-day loan when the first expired to tide you through to a securitisation the next month) and then everyone stopped buying securitised bonds or lending to banks wanting to do securitisations because of fears over the banks' solvency? Answer: financial system disaster.

As well as playing a major part in originating their own mortgage loans to people followed by securitisation, investment banks assisted other organisations to carry out securitisation, and they traded in the securitised financial instruments and their derivatives. A major driving motive for the rise in securitisation was to get around the prudential regulations for banks to hold high reserves. The more loans a bank has granted in addition to others that are still residing on the balance sheet, the more it has to hold in capital reserves. As we saw earlier, high capital reserves can lower the return on equity capital. Thus, to raise returns banks took the mortgages off their balance sheets by selling them.

Banks securitise more than simply mortgages, e.g. car loans, credit card debt, student loans and rights to royalties from David Bowie's music. Following the financial crisis of 2008–2010 the securitised market became very small and is no longer a major profit centre for banks. There is more on securitisation in Chapter 6.

The structured finance departments of investment banks have gone beyond simple securitisation. They have developed some weird – and not so wonderful – instruments such as collateralised debt obligations (CDOs): these are discussed further when we consider the financial crisis in Chapter 16.

Asset management

Many investment banks have fund management arms that manage assets on behalf of pension funds, charities or companies. They try to generate high returns relative to risk by selecting investments for the funds. These investments vary widely, from shares and bonds to property and hedge funds.

They also manage the savings of private individuals through the unit trusts, OEICS, mutual funds and investment trusts that they set up and market. As managers they will receive a fee and, possibly, a bonus for exceptional performance. These collective investment vehicles are discussed in the next chapter.

Investment advice

Many investment banks have teams of investment analysts examining the accounts and other data relating to companies quoted on stock markets, so that they can make recommendations on whether or not their shares, bonds or other securities are good value for potential investors. Alongside the analysts there might be private-client representatives talking to individual investors and an *institutional sales force* assisting professional managed funds to find good investments and manage risk. As well as analysing companies they will provide analysis of industries, markets, macroeconomics and currencies worldwide.

Unfortunately, such research may be tainted because analysts within an investment bank are sometimes in contact with the section of the bank that advises the same companies on financing strategy. The corporate finance section may be keen on encouraging the analysts to provide positive research about an issuer of shares or bonds (or a company that they are advising in a merger deal) – if they succumb to this pressure their independence is compromised.

A further pressure comes from the fact that company managers do not like to read that their shares are regarded by an investment bank analyst as being over-valued. If they read such a report then they may retaliate by refusing to speak to analysts from that bank and this can mean that in-depth reports on that company cannot be compiled. Thus we have another incentive for analysts to accentuate the positive and eliminate the negative in their reports. In the US, where this problem seems to be most acute, it can be that there are nine positive reports on companies for every negative one. Despite the availability of many unbiased bankers' analyses, the trend is increasingly for the investing institutions (the buy-side) to employ their own analysts rather than rely on the sell-side analysts who might be assisting the sale of securities.

Wealth management and private banking

Wealth management and private banking (terms that are used interchangeably) are undertaken by a number of banks, some of which are investment banks. It involves services and advice to improve the management of the financial affairs of high-net-worth individuals, including their investments, current deposit accounts (possibly in numerous currencies and jurisdictions), obtaining of loans and tax issues. The definition of a high-net-worth individual varies, but usually means they have more than $1 million in net wealth besides the main home. There are some old and venerable names in this business, such as C. Hoare and Co., and Pictet & Cie, but most of the universal banks also have private banking arms for their wealthier customers.

Prime brokerage for hedge funds

Some investment banks have prime brokerage arms that provide services for hedge funds (discussed in Chapter 14), such as acting as a broker buying and selling blocks of shares, derivatives, etc. (trade execution) for the fund, clearing and settlement of trades, risk management, back-office accounting services, cash management and custodial services. The main source of income for the bank from prime brokerage usually comes in the form of interest charged for lending to the hedge fund, fees for arranging debt supplied by others and income from stock (share) lending to enable the hedge fund to *sell securities short* (i.e. sell without first buying – the buying comes later, hopefully at a lower price than they were sold for). Another role for prime brokers is in helping their hedge fund clients find investors – called a cap-intro (capital introduction) service. Investment banks are often in contact with wealthy family investment offices, private banking offices and institutional investors (end-investors) and so can point them in the direction of those hedge funds for which they are prime brokers. A few investment banks also supply fast electronic trading systems to hedge funds so that they can tap into the markets directly and create automated buy and sell strategies.

Private equity (venture capital) investment

This is finance for new and growing companies that have not gained a quotation on a stock exchange. It can consist of a mixture of debt and equity, and can be an investment for the bank itself or on behalf of clients of the bank. There is more on private equity in Chapter 14.

International banking

International banking means banking business conducted across national borders and/or with foreign currencies. This can be retail or wholesale banking, personal or corporate banking, as well as investment banking. Fifteenth-century Florentine bankers set up subsidiaries in other European countries to help their clients with trade finance and to lend large volumes. The clients were sometimes Italian, but there were many non-Italians who recognised the need to obtain finance and other banking services beyond the confines of their own nation. Nineteenth-century colonialism and globalisation led to a rapid expansion in banking as British, Dutch and Belgian banks established branches in places as far flung as Australia and India, while building a strong presence in the Americas. Towards the end of the nineteenth century banks from many other countries, e.g. Canada and Japan, also developed international activities. The Americans were relatively slow in getting started because they were restrained by law from establishing branches abroad. The rules were relaxed, but the US banks did not respond in any significant way until after the Second World War. Even as late as 1960 only eight US banks had overseas branches. But once they got going they grew rapidly so that now more than 50 US banks have branches abroad and some of these institutions have grown to become the dominant banks in many of the financial centres around the globe.

We need to be clear what we are talking about when we use the term international banking. There are many different levels, different types of services. **Exhibit 3.15** is my attempt at bringing some clarity to this area. **Eurocurrency banking** is very big business – billions every day. This is money deliberately held outside the control of the regulators and governments of the currency. Thus, for example, there is a vast quantity of US dollars held in Eurocurrency accounts in London and other places outside the US which is lent out at Eurocurrency interest rates. There are Euroyen (outside the control of the Japanese), EuroSwiss Francs, etc. This market in international money beyond government control was established long before the creation of the new European currency, the euro. It is important to note that the Eurocurrencies are not confined to European countries; much of the trading takes place in Singapore, the Bahamas and the Cayman Islands. There is much more on Eurocurrencies in Chapter 5.

As large companies established themselves in a number of countries they expected that their home-country bank would expand with them and provide services when they operated abroad. So, a French company operating in the US may need banking services from the US-based branch of its French bank. It might need a loan in dollars to build a factory in Chicago, for instance. Or, when goods are sold in dollars, it needs its bank to exchange them for euros. Of course, the French manufacturer could use a US bank, but companies often prefer to work with their home bank with which they have a long-term relationship, with mutual understanding of customs, culture and practices.

London is the largest cross-border lending financial centre, with an almost 20 per cent share of worldwide activity. It established this position in the days of the British Empire. As well as being at the centre of the English-speaking trading network it pulled in European bankers. The main attraction for the foreign banks coming to London before 1914 was that it allowed them to participate in the London money markets. Here they could invest surplus cash holdings in interest-bearing instruments that were highly liquid. They could not do this on the same scale in their home financial centres. In the 1960s and 1970s there was rapid growth of foreign banks in London due to the take-off of the Euromarkets. US bankers tended to lead here. By the mid-1980s there were more than 400 foreign banks in London. Since then there have been amalgamations and departures of smaller banks so at the time of writing that figure stands at around 250. Having a major presence in London seems to be seen as a requirement to be taken seriously as a player in the banking world. It is at the centre of the world time zones, has great depth and breadth of banking skills and support services (lawyers, accountants, etc.) and is the main Eurocurrency, international bond and foreign exchange trading location.

There are a number of ways in which overseas banking can be organised. A very simple method that does not require the establishment of an office overseas is to employ the services of a **correspondent bank**. Here, a well-established bank in the country is asked to undertake tasks for clients of the foreign bank, such as payment transactions, current accounts, custody services and investing funds in financial markets. They may also introduce banking clients to local business-people. Correspondent banks are paid a fee by the foreign bank.

An operation that requires slightly more commitment to a foreign banking environment is opening a **representative office**. These are often small, rudimentary affairs that assist the parent bank's customers in that country. They might provide information on the country to clients and help them form banking and business relationships in the country. However, they cannot provide core overseas banking business to clients, i.e. no deposits or loans in the overseas country, through the office. Representative offices are also used to entice potential foreign customers, acting as marketing offices for the parent.

An **agency office** is a greater commitment than a representative office. It is usually prohibited from accepting deposits from host-country residents, but can be used to transfer other funds and make loans. It is not subject to the same full regulatory requirement as the host-country banks, such as having insurance for deposits (so depositors can get money back from a government-regulated body if the bank goes bust – *see* Chapter 15).

A **branch** of the parent bank bears its name and legally acts as part of the overall bank. Creditors to the branch have a claim on the organisation as a whole, including the parent's assets. They often provide as full a range of banking services as the banking regulators in the host

Exhibit 3.15	Different types of international banking

International banking

Nationals at home:
Providing deposit and loan facilities as well as trade finance and foreign exchange services to the bank's nationals in the home country. E.g. a UK citizen has a NatWest euro account and borrows in euros

Non-nationals at home:
Providing banking services to non-nationals in the bank's domestic currency in its home base. E.g. NatWest operates a euro account for a German in London, or provides trade finance for an Italian business

Cross-border business:

Eurocurrency/ Eurobanking:
Depositing and lending outside the jurisdiction of the country of the currency – e.g. deposits and loans of dollars in Luxembourg are outside US authorities' control. More on Eurocurrency in Chapter 5

Own nationals in foreign country:
Providing banking services to home citizens and home companies in a foreign country

Multiple currencies and countries:
Providing banking services in a variety of currencies for individuals and companies that come from a wide range of countries

Financial markets dealing:
Banks moving money overseas to invest and borrow for their own account. E.g. trying to make profits for the bank by placing money where it obtains a good return

Functional organisation:
Locating operations to other parts of the globe, e.g. call and IT centres in India servicing European customers

Correspondent banking

Bank remains in home market only.
E.g. many of the banks in London serve customers from all over the world without the need for overseas branches

Multinational banking:
Ownership and control of banking operations outside home market

Current & deposit accounts	Treasury management. Cash management. International payments	Debt & equity financing
Trade finance: letters of credit, forfaiting	Risk management	Foreign exchange

Representative office

Branch

Subsidiary

Purchase of an entire banking group,
e.g. Santander created a UK banking company through the purchase of Alliance and Leicester, Abbey, elements of Bradford & Bingley and RBS's English branches

country allow. Branches are a very common way for banks to expand, but following the 2008 financial crisis with the problems caused by branches not maintaining capital reserves in the host country (e.g. money could be taken back to the parent and if the parent then fails, the depositors (or depositor insurer) may not recover their money), regulators are pushing for less branch banking and more subsidiary banking.

A subsidiary, set up as a separate legal entity in the host country, will be subject to the same regulations as the host country banks. It has its own capital reserves kept within the country and has to follow the same regulatory procedures as the host-country banks. If it runs into trouble, the host-country authorities will expect the parent to pump in more capital, but given the separate company status, the parent may not be obliged to do this and so a subsidiary structure may be safer for the parent. Subsidiaries may be grown from scratch or be formed as a result of an acquisition of a bank(s), as in the case of Santander in the UK, which bought Abbey National in 2004.

The mutuals

There are thousands of financial institutions that perform many bank-type functions but which are member-owned rather than owned by shareholders. These are mutually owned, the members usually being depositors (or depositors plus borrowers together). Profits are either distributed to members or they are ploughed back into the business. They are called by a number of names, including mutuals, thrifts, building societies, cooperative banks, savings and loans, savings banks, people's banks, community banks and credit unions. Even with different labels they generally do much the same type of banking, but there are subtle differences in constitution, target members, borrowing purpose and legal structure from one country to another.

The big advantage they have compared with the corporate banks is that they do not have to pay returns to shareholders which, at least in theory, allows them to offer better rates to savers and borrowers. They also tend to develop a culture of cautious risk taking because they do not have to maximise profits by buying into the latest financial whizz-bang instruments or stretch their capital bases to conduct high levels of lending, thus they are better positioned to survive a financial crisis. However, while most prize conservative banking practices, some have been tempted to take higher risks through overseas expansions, venturing into investment banking and plunging into exotic instruments pools, such as US sub-prime mortgage-based instruments.

A general drawback with many mutuals is that they are vulnerable to going through a poor patch (e.g. a few borrowers failing to repay) because they do not have shareholders to turn to for fresh capital in a crisis, which can result in insolvency. They have to rely on an accumulation of profits and attracting new deposits to rebuild capital, and this can be too slow. Take the years 2008–2010, when European shareholder-owned banks raised more than €100 billion to buttress their capital by selling new shares. The mutuals, meanwhile, had limited options. Their main response was to increase the interest rate on deposits, which resulted in a profits squeeze because they could not raise lending rates to the same extent. This happened at the same time that the regulators were ratcheting up the amount of capital reserves they had to hold. As a result many of them were forced into selling themselves or combining with other mutuals or accepting venture capital money.

There are 4,500 mutuals in Europe alone and with 50 million members the mutually owned financial institutions account for a very substantial share of all the customer deposits in many countries. In France, for example, over 40 per cent of depositors' money goes to cooperatives and the like. In Finland, Austria and the Netherlands the figure is around one-third, and in Germany and the UK it is over 15 per cent. Almost one in five Europeans is a member of a mutual. In Germany alone there are 30 million customers holding more than €1,000 billion.

Origins of the mutuals

People are often vulnerable to the predator-like behaviour of local moneylenders. Early in the nineteenth century, philanthropic Scots, English and Americans recognised the need for institutions that allowed the poor to save in a secure place and to borrow at reasonable interest rates as the need arose. These institutions were designed to avoid dominance by rapacious owners by making them mutually owned. Many Germans set up similar organisations later in the century, to be followed by dozens of others in countries around the world. Mutuals were principally seen as a good way for thrifty, hard-working families to save up to buy a home or to build their business.

We do not have the space to look at the mutuals in every country, so we will examine merely some of the leading economies.

Germany

In Germany, each county or federal state seems to have its own Sparkasse or Landesbank (there are more than 430 Sparkassen and a handful of Landesbanken). In the strictest sense these are often not mutuals because local governments own and control them, but they are established to help the people of a region rather than being run for shareholder benefit. The Sparkasse were founded by local and regional governments to raise finance for infrastructure projects and to make loans to the poor, attracting deposits from households and firms. They opened up the possibility for ordinary people to create long-term, secure and interest-bearing reserves to cope with the adversities of life (illness, age, etc.). They lend over one-fifth of all loans to German households and domestic companies.

Sparkassen are much smaller than the Landesbanken, which were originally established to act as 'central banks' to the savings banks, providing payment clearing and other services and helping them survive rough patches. They carry out some of the international, financial market-orientated banking activities on behalf of the savings banks which are too small to do this.

The Landesbanken are controlled by regional governments (with savings banks having a stake), but depend on funding from markets rather than customer deposits. However, commercial sense often takes second place behind regional politicians' priorities in terms of local jobs, power and prestige. As a result, German bank profitability is one of the lowest in Europe, dragged down by the frequent losses of the Landesbanken. The Landesbanken offer a full range of banking services, including international banking – they are universal banks. They are now much larger than most shareholder-owned banks, e.g. WestLB has more than €250 billion in assets and BayernLB has over €340 billion. All told, they make up about one-sixth of German banking assets and issue about a quarter of corporate loans.

Until 2005 the Landesbanken benefited from state guarantees (creditors to the bank were reassured they would be repaid), which allowed them to borrow cheaply. This they did in abundance and then used the money raised to buy a lot of duff assets, such as US sub-prime mortgage-backed bonds and foreign property. They were prone to over-ambition, poor governance and excessive risk taking. Their adventurousness was to lead to the undoing of many of them in 2009. BayernLB and WestLB, for example, lost billions of euros and had to be bailed out by the government. They still receive state aid. Many commentators see them as market-distorting competitors to the conventional banks due to their special privileges, as well as being unstable. Further, they call for their winding down or privatisation. The EU Commission is furious at the way these inefficient giants are revived time and again by German politicians, thus putting pressure on the rivals not favoured by the government. Thus, Germany has only one world-class bank: Deutsche Bank.

There are also more than 1,100 German credit cooperative banks which are owned by members of a profession or trade. The German coops account for about 13 per cent of lending to households and German companies and 18 per cent of mortgage lending. Bausparkassen accept deposits and provide finance for people wanting to buy a house. They also provide finance to build houses.

Spain

In Spain, there are 17 **cajas** (more properly, cajas de ahoro, often with Caixa in their titles), which account for 40 per cent of the retail assets held by the banking system and more than half of mortgage lending. These local savings banks have their roots in the Catholic church's attempts at providing microfinance (very small deposits and loans) for the poor. But they were described as quasi-mutual because despite some control being in the hands of depositors and employees, they were heavily influenced by regional politicians and their cronies.

During the decade up to 2007 the cajas raised vast amounts of money from the bond markets (mostly by using their rights to receive money from mortgagees as collateral – securitised bonds) and then lent heavily to property developers, other business organisations and politically motivated public works projects. The crash in the Spanish property market has been particularly painful, creating an enormous quantity of bad loans. The global financial crisis then exacerbated the problem. Before the crisis there were 45 cajas, but the weakest were forced to seek protection by merging with stronger ones as the government insisted that they reduce their cost bases, particularly by closing surplus branches. Other post-crisis innovations are the right to sell equity to investors (up to half the caja's equity) and the restricting of the number of elected politicians and public officials on their management and supervisory boards, with the intention of professionalising the management.

The US

In the US, three types of organisation are collectively referred to as 'thrifts': savings and loan associations (S&Ls), savings banks and credit unions. *Savings and loan associations (savings associations)* are primarily focused on lending for real estate and house purchase by families. They have been around for over 180 years and they grew rapidly until the crisis of the early 1980s caused by imprudent lending and the restriction of being tied to lending fixed rate while borrowing floating rate (on deposits) at a time of rising inflation and interest rates. Today 80 per cent or more of the finance they raise comes from savings accounts (most of the rest from the wholesale financial markets), while over 90 per cent of their assets are secured by real estate. There are more than 1,000 S&Ls with over $1.5 trillion of assets.

US savings banks were established by philanthropists in the nineteenth century to encourage the poor to save. While they do lend for house purchase they are not as heavily concentrated on mortgages as the S&Ls. They are permitted to invest in a greater range of assets, so they hold large amounts of government bonds, money market instruments and corporate bonds. There are more than 300 savings banks, mainly concentrated in the northeast of the US (S&Ls are located throughout the country).

Credit unions (CUs) were established on both sides of the Atlantic in the early nineteenth century to help poor people by providing a safe place for their money and allowing them to borrow at reasonable interest rates. They are set up when people have some other association, e.g. church membership or workplace – a 'common bond membership'. The CU member regularly saves money into an account and can then borrow a multiple of the amount as small, fixed-term personal loans (rather than long-term mortgages). CUs are granted tax privileges to encourage the poor to save. Also, employers often help with office space and items such as free electricity. They offer checking (cheque) accounts, savings accounts, credit cards, certificates of deposit and online banking.

Typical loans sizes are $10,000–$15,000, with more than one-third going for car purchase and one-third for house purchase. Most CUs have remained local, but a few are national or international, e.g. Navy Federal Credit Union ($41 billion in assets and 3.4 million members). Multinational corporations often encourage workplace CUs (e.g. Boeing employees). The US has about 8,000 CUs with around 87 million members, accounting for some 10 per cent of consumer deposits and 15 per cent of consumer loans.

United Kingdom

Building societies go back as far as the eighteenth century. They had a very simple function within a town or small region: households (members) saved into them and when they had saved enough they could borrow to purchase a house (if there was a good prospect of them being able to repay). They are not profit maximisers but try to balance the interests of borrowers seeking low interest rates and savers wanting high interest rates.

They dominated the mortgage market until the 1980s, but deregulation led to many new entrants, especially banks. In the last two decades of the twentieth century there was much deregulation so that building societies could offer cheque accounts, unsecured loans, ATMs and lend against commercial assets. In addition, an increasing proportion of their funding has come from the wholesale markets rather than retail members, although this rarely exceeds one-third of liabilities. In 1900 there were over 1,700, but this number has dwindled as a result of building societies combining into larger groups and many larger groups converting themselves into limited companies with shareholders (**demutualisation**) and floating on the London Stock Exchange. Others were bought by banking groups. The reasons for converting to companies include the ability to tap shareholders for funds to support the growth or survival of the business, to allow expansion into new areas such as life insurance and corporate lending, pressure from members to receive a windfall by selling their shares, and empire building by directors.

Of the remaining 49 at the time of writing, Nationwide is the largest with £191 billion of assets. These organisations still account for about one-sixth of UK mortgage lending.

The old building societies now converted to banks generally continued to focus on house lending and so we refer to them as **mortgage banks**. Most of these were bought by universal banks once they floated on the stock market. Thus, Halifax is part of Lloyds (previously part of Halifax Bank of Scotland which was bought by Lloyds in the 2008 crisis), as is Cheltenham and Gloucester. Abbey and Alliance and Leicester are part of Santander.

The UK also has more than 400 credit unions with over 750,000 members with a common bond.[3] They have a history going back to the industrial revolution. Some of the larger ones offer current accounts, debit cards and cash withdrawals from ATMs. Life insurance is often included in membership. The affiliations range from taxi drivers to the Toxteth community. According to the Association of British Credit Unions, over £400 million is saved in UK CUs, and a similar volume of loans.

There is only one UK cooperative bank with 2 per cent of UK bank deposits and 300 branches (including Britannia (a building society) which merged with the Coop in 2009). It offers current accounts, savings accounts, credit cards and loans. Co-operative Insurance offers a variety of insurance products and Co-operative Investments offers products including unit trusts, investment bonds and pensions.

France, the Netherlands and Asia

In France, the savings banks, Caisses d'Epargne, have powers to enter into a wide range of banking activities for retail depositors but not to lend commercial loans. France's biggest retail bank, Crédit Agricole, is a cooperative. It is majority owned by 39 French cooperative retail banks, Caisses Régionales de Crédit Agricole Mutuel. Other mutual/cooperative French banks with large shares of the deposit market are Crédit Mutuel and Banque Populaire.

In the Netherlands, over 40 per cent of all banking deposits are in cooperatives. Rabobank Nederland is an organisation that acts for 143 independent agricultural cooperatives, called Rabobanks. Collectively they form the second biggest banking institution in Holland.

There are tens of thousands of cooperatives in India and in China. Also, Japan has a thriving coop sector.

Finance houses

A **finance house** is an institution which advances credit, usually through factoring, via a hire purchase agreement or a lease. Strictly, these organisations are classified as 'non-bank institutions' but they provide debt finance and they are often owned by the major banks and so are included in this chapter. Typically, they do not take deposits but obtain their funds from the money and bond markets. Some of the largest finance houses are owned by commercial organisations such as General Motors, Ford or General Electric rather than banks.

Factoring

Factoring (or '**invoice finance**') companies provide three services to firms with outstanding **debtors** (also called *trade receivables* – amounts not yet paid by customers), the most important of which is the immediate transfer of cash. This is provided by the factor on the understanding that when invoices are paid by customers the proceeds will go to them. Factoring is increasingly used

---

[3] Worldwide there are 40,000 CUs in 79 countries serving 114 million members.

by companies of all sizes as a way of meeting cash flow needs induced by rising sales and debtor balances. In the UK, about 80 per cent of factoring turnover is handled by the clearing bank subsidiaries, e.g. HSBC Invoice Finance, Lloyds TSB and Royal Bank of Scotland Corporate Banking. However, there are dozens of smaller factoring companies.

1 The provision of finance

At any one time a typical business can have one-fifth or more of its annual turnover outstanding in trade debts: a firm with an annual turnover of £5 million may have a debtor balance of £1million. These large sums create cash difficulties which can pressurise an otherwise healthy business. Factors step in to provide the cash needed to support stock levels, pay suppliers and generally aid more profitable trading and growth. The factor will provide an advanced payment on the security of outstanding invoices. Normally about 80 per cent of the invoice value can be made available to a firm immediately (with some factors this can be as much as 90 per cent). The remaining 20 per cent is transferred from the factor when the customer finally pays up. Naturally the factor will charge a fee and interest on the money advanced. The cost will vary between clients depending on sales volume, the type of industry and the average value of the invoices. The charge for finance is comparable with overdraft rates (1.5–3 per cent over base rate). As on an overdraft, the interest is calculated on the daily outstanding balance of the funds that the borrowing firm has transferred to its business account. Added to this is a service charge that varies between 0.2 per cent and 3 per cent of invoiced sales. This is set at the higher end if there are many small invoices or a lot of customer accounts, or the risk is high.

Exhibit 3.16 shows the stages in a typical factoring transaction. First, goods are delivered to the customer and an invoice is sent. Second, the supplier sells the right to receive the invoice amount to a factor in return for, say, 80 per cent of the face value now. Third, some weeks later the customer pays the sum owing, which goes to the factor. Finally, the factor releases the remaining 20 per cent to the supplier less interest and fees.

Factors frequently reject clients as unsuitable for their services. The factor looks for 'clean and unencumbered debts' so that it can be reasonably certain of receiving invoice payments. It will also want to understand the company's business and to be satisfied with the competence of its management.

This form of finance has some advantages over bank borrowing. The factor does not impose financial ratio covenants or require fixed-asset backing. Also the fear of instant withdrawal of a facility (as with an overdraft) is absent as there is usually a notice period. The disadvantages are the raised cost and the unavailability of factoring to companies with many small-value transactions. Also, some managers say it removes a safety margin: instead of spending frugally while waiting for customers to pay, they may be tempted to splurge the advance.

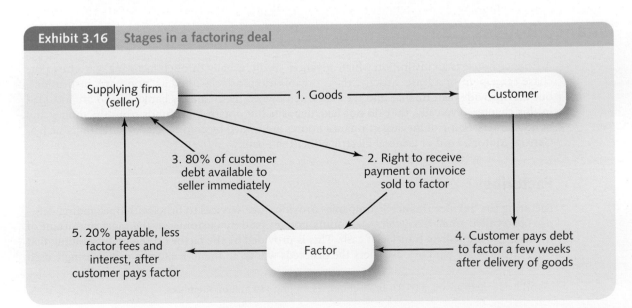

Exhibit 3.16 Stages in a factoring deal

2 Sales ledger administration

Companies, particularly young and fast-growing ones, often do not want the trouble and expense of setting up a sophisticated system for dealing with the collection of outstanding debts. For a fee (0.75–2.5 per cent of turnover) factors will take over the functions of recording credit sales, checking customers' creditworthiness, sending invoices, chasing late payers and ensuring that debts are paid. Factors are experienced professional payment chasers who know all the tricks of the trade (such as 'the cheque is in the post' excuse) and so can obtain payment earlier. With factoring, sales ledger administration and debt collection generally come as part of the package offered by the finance house, unlike with invoice discounting (*see* below).

3 Credit insurance

The third service available from a factor is the provision of insurance against the possibility that a customer does not pay the amount owed. The charge for this service is generally between 0.3 per cent and 0.5 per cent of the value of the invoices.

Invoice discounting

Firms with an annual turnover of less than £10 million typically use factoring (with sales ledger administration), whereas larger firms tend to use **invoice discounting**. Here invoices are pledged to the finance house in return for an immediate payment of up to 90 per cent of the face value. The supplying company guarantees to pay the amount represented on the invoices and is responsible for collecting the debt. The customers are generally totally unaware that the invoices have been discounted. When the due date is reached it is to be hoped that the customer has paid in full. Regardless of whether the customer has paid, the supplying firm is committed to handing over the total invoice amount to the finance house and in return receives the remaining 10 per cent less service fees and interest. Note that even invoice discounting is subject to the specific circumstances of the client agreement and is sometimes made on a non-recourse basis (the selling company does not have to recompense the factoring company if the customer fails to pay).

The finance provider usually advances money under invoice discounting only if the supplier's business is well established and profitable. There must be an effective and professional credit control and sales ledger administration system. Charges are usually lower than for factoring because the sales ledger administration is the responsibility of the supplying company.

Hire purchase

With hire purchase (HP) the finance company buys the equipment that the borrowing firm needs. The equipment (plant, machinery, vehicles, etc.) belongs to the hire purchase company. However, the finance house allows the 'hirer' firm to use the equipment in return for a series of regular payments. These payments are sufficient to cover interest and contribute to paying off the principal. While the monthly instalments are still being made the HP company has the satisfaction and security of being the legal owner and so can take repossession if the hirer defaults on the payments. After all payments have been made the hirer becomes the owner, either automatically or on payment of a modest option-to-purchase fee. Nowadays, consumers buying electrical goods or vehicles have become familiar with sales assistants' attempts to sell an HP agreement also so that the customer pays over an extended period. Sometimes the finance is provided by the same organisation, but more often by a separate finance house.

Some examples of assets that may be acquired on HP are as follows:

- plant and machinery;
- business cars;
- commercial vehicles;
- agricultural equipment;
- hotel equipment;
- medical and dental equipment;

- computers, including software;
- office equipment.

There are clearly some significant advantages of this form of finance, given the fact that hire purchase together with leasing has overtaken bank loans as a source of finance for UK business purchases up to £100,000. The main advantages are as follows:

- *Small initial outlay* The firm does not have to find the full purchase price at the outset. A deposit followed by a series of instalments can be less of a cash flow strain. The funds that the company retains by handing over merely a small deposit can be used elsewhere in the business for productive investment. Set against this are the relatively high interest charges (high relative to the rates a large firm can borrow at but can be relatively low for a small firm) and the additional costs of maintenance and insurance.
- *Easy and quick to arrange* Usually at point of sale, allowing immediate use of the asset.
- *Certainty* This is a medium-term source of finance which cannot be withdrawn provided contractual payments are made, unlike an overdraft. However, the commitment is made for a number of years and it could be costly to terminate the agreement. There are also budgeting advantages to the certainty of a regular cash outflow.
- *HP is often available when other sources of finance are not* For some firms the equity markets are unavailable and banks will no longer lend to them, but HP companies will still provide funds as they have the security of the asset to reassure them.
- *Fixed-rate finance* In most cases the payments are fixed throughout the HP period. While the interest charged will not vary with the general interest rate throughout the life of the agreement, the hirer has to be aware that the HP company will quote an interest rate which is significantly different from the true annual percentage rate.

Leasing

Leasing is similar to HP in that an equipment owner (the lessor) conveys the right to use the equipment in return for regular rental payments by the equipment user (the lessee) over an agreed period of time. The essential difference is that the lessee does not become the owner – the leasing company retains legal title.[4] It is important to distinguish between operating leases and finance leases.

Operating lease

Operating leases commit the lessee to only a short-term contract or one that can be terminated at short notice. These are certainly not expected to last for the entire useful life of the asset and so the finance house has the responsibility of finding an alternative use for the asset when the lessee no longer requires it. Perhaps the asset will be sold in the second-hand market, or it might be leased to another client. Either way the finance house bears the risk of ownership. If the equipment turns out to have become obsolete more quickly than was originally anticipated, it is the lessor that loses out. If the equipment is less reliable than expected, the owner (the finance house) will have to pay for repairs. Usually, with an operating lease, the lessor retains the obligation for repairs, maintenance and insurance.

It is clear why equipment which is subject to rapid obsolescence and frequent breakdown is often leased out on an operating lease. Photocopiers, for example, used by a university department are far better leased so that if they break down the university staff do not have to deal with the problem. In addition, the latest model can be quickly installed in the place of an outdated one.

The most common form of operating lease is contract hire. These leases are often used for a fleet of vehicles. The leasing company takes some responsibility for the management and maintenance of the vehicles and for disposal of the vehicles at the end of the contract hire period (after 12–48 months).

---

[4] However, with many finance leases, after the asset has been leased for the great majority of its useful life (value), the lessee may have the option to purchase it.

Operating leases are also useful if the business involves a short-term project requiring the use of an asset for a limited period. For example, building firms often use equipment supplied under an operating lease (sometimes called *plant hire*). Operating leases are not confined to small items of equipment. There is a growing market in leasing aircraft and ships for periods less than the economic life of the asset, thus making these deals operating leases. Many of Boeing's and Airbus's aircraft go to leasing firms.

Finance lease

Under a finance lease (also called a *capital lease* or a *full payout lease*) the finance provider expects to recover the full cost (or almost the full cost) of the equipment, plus interest, over the period of the lease. With this type of lease the lessee usually has no right of cancellation or termination. Despite the absence of legal ownership the lessee will have to bear the risks and rewards that normally go with ownership: the lessee will usually be responsible for maintenance, insurance and repairs and suffer the frustrations of demand being below expectations or the equipment becoming obsolete more rapidly than anticipated.

Most finance leases contain a primary and a secondary period. It is during the primary period that the lessor receives the capital sum plus interest. In the secondary period the lessee pays a very small, 'nominal' rental payment. If the company does not want to continue using the equipment in the secondary period it may be sold second-hand to an unrelated company.

Advantages of leasing

For companies that become lessees the advantages listed for hire purchase also apply: small initial outlay, certainty, available when other finance sources are not, fixed-rate finance and tax relief. There is an additional advantage of operating leases and that is the transfer of obsolescence risk to the finance provider.

Islamic banking

Under Islamic Sharia law the payment of *riba*[5] (interest) is prohibited and the receiver of finance must not bear all the risk of failure. Also investment in alcohol, tobacco, pornography or gambling is not allowed. However, Islam does encourage entrepreneurial activity and the sharing of risk through equity shares. Thus a bank can create profit-sharing products to offer customers. Depositors can be offered a percentage of the bank's profits rather than a set interest rate. Borrowers repay the bank an amount that is related to the profit produced by the project for which the loan was made. Some examples include:

- *Musharakah* A joint enterprise is established by the bank and borrower. Both contribute capital plus management and labour (although some parties, e.g. banks, contribute little other than capital). Profit (loss) is shared in pre-agreed proportions – there is a prohibition against a fixed lump sum for any party. All partners have unlimited liability. Thus for a house purchase the property is purchased by the bank and clients (perhaps 10 per cent of the purchase price). The customer purchases the bank's share gradually, until he is made sole owner after a specified period, usually 25 years. Over the financing period, the bank's share is rented to the customer.

- *Ijara* Example: a house (or aircraft, say) is bought by the bank and rented to the 'mortgage holder'. The house title may or may not be transferred when the contract ends.

- *Murabaha* Example: a bank buys a house (car, or other property) and sells it to the customer at a fixed price – more than the bank paid – permitting the customer to pay in monthly instalments. When the final instalment is paid the house is transferred to the customer.

More than 600 banks and financial institutions offer services according to Sharia law. They are most heavily concentrated in the Arabian Gulf countries, Malaysia, Pakistan and Iran. But many

---

[5] A strict interpretation of the word *riba* is usury or excessive interest.

conventional banks also offer Sharia products, e.g. HSBC and Lloyds have Islamic mortgages available. Growth has been driven by the rising consciousness in Islamic principles over the last 40 years and the rising wealth of Muslim oil states. What is regarded as compliant with Sharia in one part of the world may not be considered by Islamic scholars to be acceptable in another. Malaysia, for example, tends to be more liberal than Saudi Arabia.

The UK has introduced tax,[6] legislative and regulatory changes to encourage Islamic financial services in the City. This has been successful, attracting over US$10 billion of funds to London, making it one of the top ten centres. Despite its growth, the volume of Islamic finance is still only around 1 per cent of the size of the conventional finance industry. Increasingly, Islamic products are being used by non-Muslims, sometimes due to religious conviction, e.g. Quakers, or because that form of finance has qualities they are looking for – *see* **Exhibit 3.17**.

Exhibit 3.17

Investment strategy about more than faith

Emmanuelle Smith

Despite, or maybe because of the world's economic travails, Islamic finance has continued to stride ahead, as investors seek alternatives to products that have let them down in the recent past.

According to Maris Strategies, assets in Islamic finance rose to $822bn last year, an increase of 29 per cent compared with 2008.

Much of this can be attributed to a growing Muslim population wanting to invest according to the guiding principles of their faith.

But non-Muslims are also attracted to Islamic finance. Gulf African Bank, for example, reported last year that 20 per cent of its customer base was non-Muslim.

Jo Divanna, managing director of Maris Strategies and a leading commentator on the subject, partly attributes this to a conscious effort by companies to widen their appeal by changing terminology.

He says: "Islamic finance is undergoing a rebranding towards western markets by reducing the use of the term Islamic or sharia and focusing instead on the concepts of ethical and green."

"This is not to say they are lowering their standards," he adds, but "simply redefining their image".

Another explanation for the surge of interest is dissatisfaction with conventional finance in the wake of the global financial crisis. So, might the inherently prudent principles of Islamic finance have prevented lending to people who were likely to default, for example?

According to sharia law, the selling of loans is not permitted, nor is interest-bearing debt more generally – all factors that contribute to the crisis.

However, Iqbal Asaria, who teaches an Islamic finance elective at Cass Business School in London, dismisses the argument that the financial crisis could somehow have been averted had Islamic principles been more prevalent.

"The [crisis] was caused by a number of factors, including minimal attention to prudential regulation. These lapses will affect any form of finance – Islamic or conventional."

Mr Divanna agrees, stressing that Islamic finance is not a replacement for conventional finance, but rather than alternative: "There are still risks in lending and facilitating transactions. Islamic finance does not provide safeguards; it merely provides an alternative method of providing services under a unique set of disciplines."

"Sharia-principles are interpretive, so how products work in various parts of the world is different," says Mr Divanna.

"There is a clear difference in attitudes between Muslims in the Gulf, Malaysia, Europe, North Africa and southern Asia," he adds.

Source: *Financial Times*, 21 June 2010, p. 3. Reprinted with permission.

Concluding comments

Evidently, there is much more to modern banking than simply taking deposits, making loans and running a payments mechanism. Banking has branched out into many new areas and taken many different forms. Banks form the bedrock of any sophisticated financial system because the banks lie at the centre of the financial markets, acting as market makers, brokers, advisers, investment

---

[6] For example, stamp duty on a house sale is not paid twice (when the bank buys and when the customer buys from the bank).

managers or traders. They facilitate the functioning of the bond and equity capital markets as well as the foreign exchange, commodities and a host of other markets. Despite the outsized rewards that bankers often receive, few of us would say that they do not, on the whole, provide socially useful services – despite our anger over the financial crisis. However, there are some pockets of activities (e.g. many exotic derivative transactions, securitisations and zero-sum-game proprietary trading) where commentators have questioned whether any real value is created for society, or merely high bonuses for the bankers. But these areas of criticism should not lead us to heap opprobrium on all bankers – the vast majority help us in so many ways.

Key points and concepts

- **Investment banks** – complex organisations offering a wide range of financial services (excluding high-street banking), charging fees and commissions for advice and making arrangements on matters such as mergers, raising of capital for a corporation and risk control.

- They perform some **loss-leading activities** to strengthen relationships with clients for the benefit of future profit making. To **maximise profits** they need to coordinate activities and sell a variety of services to clients.

- **Employees** are often very highly paid because of the amount of business they generate and the influence they have over their clients. Typically, investment banks put aside **50 per cent of income** for paying employees.

- **Some suggested reasons for high investment bank profits:**
  - due to the complexity and size of transactions, there are very few banks able to carry them out therefore there are some elements of oligopolistic power;
  - their reputation for profitable dealing gives them a considerable degree of influence and their advice carries credence and authority;
  - the extent and variety of their dealings give them superior information.

- **Global investment banks** are active in a number of countries. **'Bulge bracket'** is the term used for the leaders, such as Goldman Sachs and JP Morgan, able to handle large deals and a variety of services.

- **'Boutique' investment banks** are smaller investment banks which concentrate on particular areas, usually mergers and acquisitions.

- **Advice on financing and raising finance:**
  - Investment banks have great expertise and knowledge and charge commission on all finance-raising transactions
  - They help with issuing initial public offerings, rights issues, further share issues, bonds, project finance, sale and leaseback, and overseas trade
  - They underwrite new security and equity issues
  - They assist with the issue of bills of exchange and banker's acceptances.

- **Mergers, acquisitions and corporate restructuring:**
  - Investment banks earn very large fees from using their expertise to advise companies
  - **Divestiture** – the selling-off of a subsidiary
  - **Restructure debt** – changing of debt structure (e.g. extending the time to pay) to suit the company's present circumstances
  - **Strategic review** – usually meaning that the company is amenable to a takeover.

- **Relationship manager** – an investment bank employee who builds up a special long-term relationship with a particular company.

- **Risk management** by investment banks is the reducing of risks, particularly on interest rate or foreign currency movements. They also assist companies when they have a temporary surplus of cash and need to invest it well but without undue risk.

- Investment banks can advise on **lending** and obtaining the best loans at favourable rates.

- Investment banks advised the UK government on **privatisation** (the selling-off of state-owned assets).

▶

- Investment banks assist with the setting up of **public–private partnerships (PPPs),** which allow private firms to build and operate a facility (e.g. a prison) in return for an income flow.

- **Brokerage**

  - They act as **corporate brokers** to companies, advising on regulations and all aspects of bond and equity issuance. They may offer services to retail and wholesale investor clients as well, advising on, and facilitating, the buying and selling of securities.

- **Market making** or **dealing**: they facilitate the buying and selling of shares by offering **bid** (buying) and **offer** or **ask** (selling) prices.

  - Market makers operate a **quote-driven** trading system
  - The **bid–offer spread** or **trader's spread** is the margin a market maker makes, the difference between buying and selling prices
  - **Clearing price** is the price of a share where buying and selling demand is matched

- **Proprietary trading** is using an investment bank's capital to make trading profit (**trading income**).

- **'Chinese walls'** is the term used by investment banks to explain how they do not take advantage of inside knowledge because information is not passed from one part of the bank to another.

- **Fixed income, currencies and commodities (FICC)** trading is carried out by investment banks on behalf of clients. It generates large amounts of income trading in a wide variety of bonds, credit and interest rate derivatives, money market instruments and bank loans. Currency and commodity trading is for both spot and derivative deals.

- Investment banks assist their clients in all aspect of **equity trading** as well as acting as market makers or brokers in the **derivative markets**. They also create derivatives and market them to clients.

- **Securitisation** is the bundling together of a group of assets, such as the right to receive interest and principal from mortgages, that can then be sold on and traded, enabling the originator to take on more debt. A **special purpose vehicle (SPV)** is an independent entity containing a bundle of assets.

- **Asset management** (of investment funds) is carried out by investment banks on behalf of charities, pension funds or companies and individuals.

- Investment banks also provide **investment advice. Private-client representatives** give advice to individual investors. An **institutional sales force** gives advice to professional funds.

- Investment banks provide **wealth management** and **private banking** – services and advice to improve the management of the financial affairs of high-net-worth individuals, including their investments, current deposit accounts, obtaining of loans and tax issues.

- Some investment banks offer a **prime brokerage service for hedge funds** – acting as a broker buying and selling blocks of shares (**trade execution**), derivatives, etc. for the fund, clearing and settlement of trades, risk management, back-office accounting services, cash management, custodial services and introductory services.

- Investment banks assist with, and occasionally provide funds for, **private equity (venture capital)** trading in unquoted companies.

- **International banking** is banking business conducted across national borders and/or with foreign currencies.

- **Different types of international banking**

  - For nationals at home
  - For non-nationals at home
  - **Eurocurrency banking** is with money deliberately held outside the control of the regulators and governments of the currency
  - Cross-border
    - For own nationals in foreign country
    - In multiple currencies and countries

▶

- – Financial markets dealing for own account
- – Locating functional operations around the globe.

● **Correspondent banking:** a well-established bank in the country is asked to undertake tasks for clients of the foreign bank.

● **Representative office:** small, rudimentary affairs that assist the parent bank's customers in that country. They might provide information on the country to clients and help them form banking and business relationships in the country. However, they cannot provide core overseas banking business to clients.

● An **agency office** is a greater commitment than a representative office. They are usually prohibited from accepting deposits from host-country residents, but can be used to transfer other funds and make loans. They are not subject to the same full regulatory requirements as the host country banks.

● A **branch** of the parent bank legally acts as part of the overall bank to provide as full a range of banking services as the banking regulators in the host country allow. Branches do not maintain capital reserves in the host country.

● A **subsidiary**, set up as a separate legal entity in the host country, will be subject to the same regulations as the host-country banks. It has its own capital reserves kept within the country and has to follow the same regulatory procedures as the host-country banks.

● Banks run as **mutuals** are member-owned rather than owned by shareholders. The members are usually depositors (or depositors plus borrowers together). Profits are either distributed to members or they are ploughed back into the business. They are called by a number of different names, including mutuals, thrifts, building societies, cooperative banks, savings and loans, savings banks, people's banks, community banks and credit unions.

● Advantages mutuals have over corporate banks:

- – do not have to pay returns to shareholders which, at least in theory, allows them to offer better rates to savers and borrowers;
- – culture of cautious risk taking, thus they are better positioned to survive a financial crisis – but they are not always cautious.

● A general drawback with many mutuals is that they are vulnerable to going through a poor patch because they do not have shareholders to turn to for fresh capital in a crisis.

● **Factoring companies** provide at least three services:

- – providing finance on the security of trade debts;
- – sales ledger administration;
- – credit insurance.

● **Invoice discounting** is the obtaining of money on the security of book debts; usually confidential and with recourse to the supplying firm. The supplying firm manages the sales ledger.

● **Hire purchase** is an agreement to hire goods for a specified period, with an option or an automatic right to purchase the goods at the end for a nominal or zero final payment.

● **Leasing** The legal owner of an asset gives another person or firm (the lessee) the possession of that asset to use in return for specified rental payments. Note that ownership is not transferred to the lessee.

● An **operating lease** commits the lessee to only a short-term contract, less than the useful life of the asset.

● A **finance lease** commits the lessee to a contract for the substantial part of the useful life of the asset.

● **Islamic banking:** under Islamic Sharia law the payment of *riba* (interest) is prohibited and the receiver of finance must not bear all the risk of failure. Also, investment in alcohol, tobacco, pornography or gambling is not allowed. However, Islam does encourage entrepreneurial activity and the sharing of risk through equity shares. Thus a bank can create profit-sharing products to offer customers.

References and further reading

To keep up to date and reinforce knowledge gained by reading this chapter I can recommend the following publications: *Financial Times, The Economist, Bank of England Quarterly Bulletin* and *Bank for International Settlements Quarterly Review* (www.bis.org).

Casu, B., Girardone, C. and Molyneux, P. (2006) *Introduction to Banking*, 2nd edn. London: FT Prentice Hall.
    A wide ranging consideration of banking from a UK perspective

Fleuriet, M. (2008) *Investment Banking Explained*. New York: McGraw-Hill.
    An overview of the role and functioning of investment banks from an insider.

Howells, P. and Bain, K. (2008) *The Economics of Money, Banking and Finance*, 4th edn. London: FT Prentice Hall.
    Provides an interesting run through different banking systems around the world.

Mishkin, F. S. and Eakins, S. G. (2009) *Financial Markets and Institutions*, 6th edn. Harlow: Pearson Prentice Hall.
    Contains a brief, easy-to-follow introduction to the US banking system.

Saunders, A. and Cornett, M. M (2007) *Financial Markets and Institutions*, 3rd edn. New York: McGraw Hill.
    A US perspective on banking.

Websites

Association for Financial Markets in Europe www.afme.eu
Association of British Credit Unions www.abcul.org
Bank of England www.bankofengland.co.uk
Bank for International Settlements www.bis.org
European Association of Cooperative Banks www.eurocoopbanks.coop
British Bankers Association www.bba.org.uk
Building Societies Association www.bsa.org.uk
European Central Bank www.ecb.int
Factors and Discounters Association www.factors.org.uk
Finance and Leasing Association www.fla.org.uk
Financial Services Authority www.fsa.gov.uk
Financial Times www.ft.com
International Capital Markets Association www.icmagroup.org

Video presentations

Bank chief executives and other senior people describe and discuss policy and other aspects of banking in interviews, documentaries and webcasts at Cantos.com. (www.cantos.com) – these are free to view.

Case study recommendations

See www.pearsoned.co.uk/arnold for case study synopses.
Also see Harvard University: http://hbsp.harvard.edu/product/cases

- Public Private Partnership: London Underground (2009) Authors: Arthur McInnes and Frederik Pretorius. Asia Case Research Centre, The University of Hong Kong (available on Harvard website).
- The Credit Suisse/Gerson Lehrman Group Alliance (2010) Authors: Robert G. Eccles and Laura Winig. Harvard Business School.
- Société Générale (A): The Jérôme Kerviel Affair (2010) Author: Francois Brochet. Harvard Business Review.

Self-review questions

1 What is an investment bank?

2 Why are certain individual investment bank employees crucial to the bank's profitability?

3 Give explanations for the high profits that investment banks make.

4 Why might investment bank employees be thought to have knowledge that could create a conflict of interest?

5 Why are investment banks not subject to problems caused by excessive withdrawal of cash by depositors?

6 What are (a) bulge bracket investment banks, (b) global investment banks, (c) boutique investment banks?

7 Explain the underwriting that investment banks carry out.

8 What is (a) an IPO, (b) an SEO?

9 How do investment banks aid overseas trade?

10 Explain corporate financial restructuring and when it might be needed.

11 What is a strategic review and in what circumstances would it be undertaken?

12 What is the importance of relationship managers?

13 What is the difference between a private-client broker and a corporate broker?

14 What is a quote-driven system?

15 What is a bid–offer spread?

16 Explain the significance of proprietary trading.

17 What are Chinese walls?

18 Name as many elements as you can of FICC trading.

19 What is asset management?

20 What is the difference between a private-client representative and an institutional salesman?

21 Describe two types of international banking that do not require staffing overseas offices.

22 Explain the following ways of conducting international banking: correspondent banking, representative office, overseas branches, overseas subsidiary.

23 Describe the difference between a building society and a credit union.

24 What is a Sparkasse, Landesbank and a savings and loan association?

25 What is hire purchase and what are the advantages of this form of finance compared with a bank loan for a corporation?

26 How does hire purchase differ from leasing?

27 Explain the terms 'operating lease' and 'finance lease'.

28 How does Islamic banking differ from conventional banking?

Questions and problems

1 Give an explanation for the supremacy of US investment banks, with examples.

2 Describe and explain how investment banks assist companies wishing to raise finance.

3 Write a description of investment banks' market activities.

4 Explain the function of market makers, how they operate and what risks they face.

5 Discuss the conflicts of interest that are apparent in FICC trading.

6 (a) Using the internet, choose an investment bank and discuss its securitisation policy.
    (b) How did the economic downturn of 2008–2010 affect securitisations?

7 Describe and explain the various ways in which international banking can be conducted.

8 Building societies, mutual savings banks, savings and loans, credit unions and cooperative banks are highly influential in many countries. Describe the nature of these organisations and compare them with shareholder-owned banks.

9 Gordons plc has an annual turnover of £3 million and a pre-tax profit of £400,000. It is not quoted on a stock exchange and the family owning all the shares has no intention of permitting the sale of shares to outsiders or providing more finance themselves. Like many small and medium-sized firms, Gordons has used retained earnings and a rolled-over overdraft facility to finance expansion. This is no longer seen as adequate, especially now that the bank manager is pushing the firm to move to a term loan as its main source of external finance.

    You, as the recently hired finance director, have been in contact with some financial institutions. The Matey hire purchase company is willing to supply the £1 million of additional equipment the firm needs. Gordons will have to pay for this over 25 months at a rate of £50,000 per month with no initial deposit.

    The Helpful Leasing Company is willing to buy the equipment and rent it to Gordons on a finance lease stretching over the four-year useful life of the equipment, with a nominal rent thereafter. The cost of this finance is virtually identical to that for the term loan, that is, 13 per cent annual percentage rate.

Required

Write a report for the board of directors explaining the nature of the four forms of finance which may be used to purchase the new equipment: hire purchase, leasing, bank term loan and overdraft. Point out their relative advantages and disadvantages.

10 A small firm is considering the purchase of a photocopier. This will cost £2,000. An alternative to purchase is to enter into a leasing agreement known as an operating lease, in which the agreement can be terminated with only one month's notice. This will cost £60 per month. The firm is charged interest of 12 per cent on its overdraft.

Required

Consider the advantages and disadvantages of each method of obtaining the use of a photocopier.

11 Explain some of the reasons for the growth in the hire purchase and leasing industry around the world over the past two decades.

12 Explain why a loss-making company is more likely to lease an asset than to buy it.

Assignments

1 Look at a few annual reports and accounts of a non-financial company you know well. Write a report detailing the uses that this company has made of the banking and related services discussed in this chapter.

2 Examine the reports and accounts of six universal banks. Analyse the extent to which their activities are retail, corporate or investment banking, and how they have changed in this regard over the last five years.

Web-based exercises

1 Go to the websites of a number of investment banks and write a report describing their various investment banking activities. Include tables showing the way income from these activities has changed over the past five years.

2 Go to www.fla.org.uk and obtain statistics on leasing and hire purchase. Write a report explaining the different types of asset finance available. Include statistics.

Insurance, pensions and collective investments

LEARNING OUTCOMES

By the end of this chapter the reader should be able to:

■ describe the basic functions of insurance and distinguish between the different types;

■ outline the proportions of insurance fund money that are invested in various assets classes;

■ explain reinsurance, and the insurance markets in London, including Lloyds;

■ describe the different types of pension arrangements, distinguishing funded from unfunded, defined benefit from defined contribution, private from public;

■ explain the roles of pension fund trustees, consultants and managers;

■ discuss the regulation of the pensions industry and the protection of people's pensions;

■ distinguish between open-ended collective investment schemes and closed-ended investment schemes, describing the differences between funds such as unit trusts, mutual funds, investment trusts and exchange-traded funds;

■ explain the importance of sovereign wealth funds in shifting investment funds around the world.

Insurance companies and pension organisations play important roles in the financial system, not only by reducing and transferring risk and in helping us save for our old age but also as substantial holders of financial securities. Because they control enormous funds, their investment decisions can have profound effects on the equity markets, the bond markets and the other places where they apply their money, such as property, private equity and hedge funds.

Another group of organisations that allocates funds to the purchase of securities are the pooled or collective investment funds. These go under various names, from mutual funds and unit trusts to investment trusts and sovereign wealth funds. They help investors to spread their savings across a range of securities under professional management.

Insurance

In the twenty-first century, insurance plays a large and important role in society worldwide. According to Swiss Re, a leading global reinsurer,[1] in 2009 $4,100 billion[2] of insurance premiums were paid. This equates to roughly $600 for every single human being in the world. It is a vast industry, nearly doubling the amount of premiums paid in the past ten years, and impinges on everybody's life. It is an important source of overseas income to the countries which provide it, and plays a vital role in commerce by taking away from companies the risk that they would be forced out of business by, say, a fire on their premises. Instead of being faced by financial ruin, that risk is assumed by the insurance company in return for a carefully calculated premium.

Figures from Swiss Re show that in 2009 the UK had an 8 per cent share of the insurance market, third behind the US and Japan (*see* **Exhibit 4.1**). There was an overall worldwide 2.8 per cent decline in premiums compared with 2008, due mainly to a decline in the number of life insurance premiums, especially in the UK where financial crises and economic turmoil caused a

Exhibit 4.1	Global premium volume (2009)

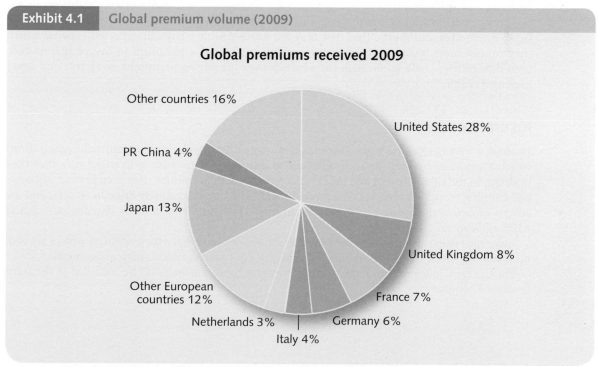

Source: www.swissre.com

---

[1] Reinsurance is when insurers buy insurance for their risks – see later.
[2] http://media.swissre.com/documents/sigma2_2010_stat_appendix_2.pdf

drop in premiums written of more than 21 per cent. Many UK residents use life insurance as a means of saving, and in trying times save less.

There are also offshore tax haven countries which specialise in insurance. The largest of these is Bermuda, a self-governing British overseas territory, where company taxes are significantly lower than in most countries. Thanks to its position as a financial centre where most of the world's large insurance companies have a base, Bermuda has one of the highest per capita GDPs in the world, and is the biggest centre for reinsurance, a specialised form of insurance, where insurance companies insure their insurance business against loss. Bermuda, New York and London make up the three main centres of reinsurance.

History of insurance

Insurance in some form has been in existence since ancient times, when traders faced the risk of financial ruin if their cargoes met with disaster. Traders might contribute to a fund from which those who suffered loss could claim some compensation. As trading developed and increased, rich businessmen would agree to pay for part of any losses in return for a sum of money, and would sign a contract to this effect, *writing* their name *under* the wording of the contract; this is where the term underwriting originates.

The first modern-day insurance companies were fire insurance companies formed after the Great Fire of London in 1666: Hand in Hand (1696), Sun Fire Office (1710) and the Royal Exchange Assurance (1753). During the same period in London, a certain Edward Lloyd's coffee house became a centre for meetings of people with commercial interest in the rapidly expanding shipping industry (see the section on Lloyds of London later in this chapter).

Why do we need insurance?

In life, things go wrong – the car breaks down, the house is flooded, or an ocean tanker goes aground and spills its cargo of oil. In return for a premium, insurance offers customers financial compensation should any of these, or indeed other, things occur. Rather than take the risk upon themselves and maybe find that they are saddled with a large unexpected expense which they cannot meet, people and companies prefer to pay out a premium to insure against risk, even though they could go through the whole of their life paying premiums every year and never making a claim.

Insurance firms

Insurance firms are either normal companies owned by shareholders or mutual organisations which are owned by their policy holders. The insurance firms' task is to make sure that they understand the risks involved and that they receive more in premiums than they pay out in claims and running costs.[3] This has become more difficult with our increasingly litigious society, and the advent of new and expensive-to-replace technology, pollution and modern-day diseases such as AIDS and cancer.

Insurance firms are regulated by domestic legislation, but where they establish offices abroad, these may be subject to less regulation, especially in tax-haven countries such as Bermuda.

For the remainder of the chapter, for brevity insurance mutuals will be included in the term insurance company.

---

[3] Having said this, many insurance firms are not too worried if the claims or running costs are slightly greater than the premiums, if they have use of the float. The **float** is cash that accumulates because policy holders usually pay for insurance up front and there is a time lag before the claims roll in. This float can be invested to earn a return which can more than compensate for an operational loss.

Insurance underwriting

Underwriters work for insurance companies, assessing the risk involved and setting the terms and cost of the premium to be paid. Underwriting is a complex job and has to take into account any number of variables, while coming up with a premium that is both profitable to the insurance company and acceptable (competitive) to its customers. Because of the complexity involved, underwriters usually specialise in one particular type of insurance, such as motor, life, business, etc., so that they can build up their knowledge base and make sound decisions which will make money for their company but also attract custom. A lot of their decisions are based on historical statistics, which help them analyse the risk involved and the likelihood of a claim being made. The greater the number of statistics available, the easier it is to predict risk. It is all a balancing act, and the underwriters' task is to ensure that the balance is weighted in favour of the company.

Asymmetric information

There are various pitfalls which can trap the unwary underwriter or customer into making a bad decision. Asymmetric information is when one party in a negotiation or relationship is not in the same position as the other parties, being ignorant of, or unable to observe, some information which is essential to the contracting and decision-making process. Thus, while insurance companies ask prospective policy holders to give a lot of information when trying to assess the level of risk exposure, the client will always know more than the insurer.

Adverse selection occurs when there is an opportunity or incentive for some firms/individuals to act to take advantage of their informational edge over others. Then the firms/individuals doing that activity will be disproportionately those taking advantage rather than being truly representative of the population as a whole, e.g. the tendency for poorer-than-average risks to continue with insurance. This will raise the cost of insurance for the whole group, including those of less-than-average risk. Thus there is a proclivity for people in dangerous jobs or with high-risk lifestyles to buy insurance, knowing that insurance premiums are based on averages and that they will therefore be at an advantage. Insurance companies and their underwriters try to cover this by limiting the insurance offered or by increasing premiums, but may then find that fewer people subsequently buy insurance cover.

Moral hazard recognises the danger that someone who is insured may be more likely to take risks and be less careful because they are insured – someone might not bother to lock their car 'because it's insured anyway', for instance. Insurers try to minimise this problem by decreasing the amount paid out in a claim, e.g. increasing the excess (the loss that the policy holder bears before the insurer pays out) to be paid if the car is not locked.

The insurance process

Insurance is sold in a variety of ways:

● direct from an insurer at one of their offices, over the phone, or via the internet, which is becoming increasingly popular;

● through an agent who usually works for one insurer;

● through an insurance broker or independent intermediary who is not normally tied to any one particular insurer. Brokers are paid commission on policy sales and are able to search for the most suitable policy;

● through a bank, building society, solicitor, travel agent, mail-order agent or accountant, who will receive commission on sales.

Wherever policies are obtained, the process is the same: a proposal form with relevant questions is completed and sent to the underwriter for assessment of the risk. If information given on proposals is incorrect, the insurance will be invalid.

Types of insurance

Insurance can be split into two types: life (or long-term insurance) and general (or non-life insurance). Both generate significant amounts of money in premiums (*see* **Exhibit 4.2**), with life policies taking the greater share – approximately 60 per cent compared to approximately 40 per cent for general insurance.

Exhibit 4.2	Global premium income 2000–09		
Year	General/non-life insurance $bn	Life/long-term insurance $bn	Totals $bn
2000	927	1,518	2,445
2001	970	1,446	2,416
2002	1,090	1,536	2,626
2003	1,276	1,683	2,959
2004	1,395	1,849	3,244
2005	1,442	2,004	3,446
2006	1,549	2,126	3,675
2007	1,668	2,393	4,061
2008	1,781	2,439	4,220
2009	1,735	2,332	4,067

Source: Swiss Re.

Life/long-term insurance

Life insurance includes a variety of insurance policies to cover people in different ways for loss of life, usually their own.[4] Many life policies allow the insured to add money into the policy amount beyond what is needed for payouts on death, so if the insured is still alive after, say, ten years, a sum of money is received. Thus for many people it is a way of saving, and the insurance companies have to attract customers and compete against other forms of saving.

- **Term assurance,** in return for premiums, covers the policy holder for a set amount of time and will pay out if the policy holder dies within that set time. If the insured survives over the specified period, then no payment is made
- **Whole-of-life** cover is more costly than term assurance because it is guaranteed to pay out when the insured dies as long as the premiums are up to date. The premiums tend to rise as the insured ages to cover the increased likelihood of mortality.
- **Endowment** policies are principally savings vehicles and pay out a set amount at a set future date (or on the earlier death of the insured) in return for premiums paid. They may be '**without profits**', in which case they pay out just the amount set at the start of the policy, or '**with profits**', where the insured receives a bonus each year in the shape of a share of the fund's returns from investments made (if it makes a positive return) and at the maturity of the policy these accrued profits are repaid to the insured. These policies are often linked to mortgages, where the insured pays only the interest on their mortgage and the policy at maturity pays off the mortgage.

---

[4] Long-term insurance applies to permanent illness and disablement as well as death.

- **Annuities** provide a regular income until the death of the insured in return for a lump-sum payment. The insurance company takes the lump sum and invests in the financial markets and elsewhere to make a return.
- Insurance companies may also run **pension schemes** for individuals – see later in the chapter.

General/non-life insurance

This encompasses all other types of insurance. It is usually renewed annually and the premium may be adjusted when required. There are broadly three categories:

- **Property** insurance covers personal and business properties and contents against fire, theft, weather damage, and can also include terrorism, earthquake, domestic appliances and other perils. **Open policies** cover all loss or damage not specifically excluded, while **named peril policies** require the perils covered to be listed.
- **Casualty** insurance includes aviation and marine insurance, car insurance, travel insurance, private medical insurance, pet insurance, accident, sickness or unemployment insurance, critical illness insurance and long-term care insurance.
- **Liability** insurance protects the insured against third-party claims and includes employers' liability, public liability (e.g. a member of the public being hurt by falling masonry from a building site), product liability, pollution liability and commercial fleet liability (e.g. companies that use vehicles as part of their business will have all their vehicles covered by one policy, so that if any of their fleet is involved in an accident, the vehicle and its driver are fully covered by insurance).

What do insurance companies do with the premiums?

All insurance companies take in premiums constantly and they are therefore in possession of a substantial 'pool' or 'float' of ready cash which they are able to invest in various ways – *see* **Exhibit 4.3** for UK insurance companies' investments.

Exhibit 4.3	UK insurance companies' investment holdings				
Year **Type of investment**	**2005** £m	**2006** £m	**2007** £m	**2008** £m	**2009** £m
UK public sector securities	205,121	210,238	212,219	195,673	198,580
Overseas public sector securities	50,925	48,077	57,280	80,596	88,283
UK ordinary stocks and shares	315,365	345,348	343,469	210,824	236,827
Other UK company stocks and shares	157,076	142,426	161,538	153,351	172,375
Overseas ordinary stocks and shares	172,092	186,429	226,939	205,949	244,414
Other overseas company securities	117,428	141,364	144,296	221,220	220,399
Unit trusts	144,615	172,763	199,867	177,029	202,790
Property	95,201	105,293	106,364	103,535	96,924
Cash and other investments	123,966	127,871	147,789	147,836	133,229
TOTAL	1,381,789	1,479,808	1,599,762	1,496,012	1,593,820

Source: ABI.

The distinction between the different types of insurance is important, as the type of business carried out influences the treatment of the premium income. General insurance companies must keep enough in cash or very liquid assets such as money market instruments to be able to pay out on claims whenever they occur. Usually, the amount needed to satisfy claims can be predicted, but in the case of a natural disaster, such as flooding or an earthquake, or in the case of an unusual run of claims, the insurance companies need to be able to pay out large sums of money very quickly. If their underwriters do their job efficiently, their float will grow steadily, and if invested wisely can be a great source of revenue, as well as being a buffer against an excessive number of claims being made.

US investor Warren Buffett is an enthusiastic believer in the advantages of investing in a well-run insurance company, which can then produce a constant stream of 'free' (i.e. free of any interest costs) money, which in turn can generate profits through investments. His company Berkshire Hathaway's float was $17.3 *million* in 1967; by 2011, this float had grown to $66 *billion*. He deliberately bought other insurance companies so that he could apply his investment skills to their floats.

Life insurance companies are able to predict to a far greater extent when they will need to pay out any claims. Their underwriters use sophisticated statistical analysis to work out when claims are likely to need to be met.[5] Therefore they do not require their assets to be readily available and can invest in longer-term investments such as bonds and company shares.

Exhibit 4.4 shows the amount of assets under the control of insurance companies in 2008 in six of the countries pre-eminent in insurance: $15,394 billion for these six countries. The investments they make are crucial to the viability of their companies. They can also have a significant influence on financial markets.

Exhibit 4.4	Invested assets of insurance companies (2008)		
	Life $ billion	Non-life $ billion	Totals $ billion
US	4,896	1,224	6,120
UK	2,347	229	2,576
Japan	2,171	384	2,555
Germany	842	850	1,692
France	1,719	288	2,007
Netherlands	387	57	444
Totals	12,363	3,031	15,394

Source: IFSL (www.thecityUK.com).

If insurance companies fail to do their underwriting or to invest their assets competently, they run the risk of not being able to pay out on claims, but even if they are managed efficiently, they could still suffer from a stretch of bad luck and run out of funds. Insurance companies need several years of profits to make up for a bad year on claims, and each year a number of companies fail when their capital has diminished to the point where it is likely that they will be unable to meet their insurance liabilities. Between 1969 and 1998 in the US insurance companies alone suffered more than 640 insolvencies. Governments worldwide have increased regulations on insurance companies to ensure that they have sufficient financial funding and are run efficiently. In the UK

---

[5] Having said this, they have been stunned in the past decade by increasing longevity – people are living far longer than was predicted in the models of the 1990s.

since 2001 the Financial Services Authority (Financial Conduct Authority from 2013) has overseen all insurance companies, including Lloyds. In the EU, there will be a new directive in 2012, Solvency II, which will aim to implement solvency requirements (keeping a good reserve of capital) that better reflect the risks that companies face and to deliver a supervisory system that is consistent across all member states.

Reinsurance

Reinsurance has evolved as an effective means of coping with the growing number and increasingly complex nature of risks. It is the process by which insurance companies lessen their exposure to risk by transferring the risk to a reinsurer. By transferring all or part of the risk, the insurance company is able to accept more or larger risks from a client. Insurers should only underwrite risk in proportion to the amount of capital they possess, so reinsurance is a way to expand their business without the need to raise further capital.

Reinsurance can be proportional or non-proportional.

- Proportional reinsurance is taken out for part of one particular risk, or part of all risks, and protects the original insurer against legitimate but unforeseeable or extraordinary losses. If a reinsurer takes on 45 per cent of a risk, they receive 45 per cent of the premium and in the event of a claim will pay out 45 per cent of the claim. An insurance company might ask a reinsurer to take on a percentage of all its business, say 20 per cent, and the reinsurer, in return for 20 per cent of all premiums, would assume responsibility for paying out 20 per cent of every claim. The original insurer receives a **ceding commission** as a thank you for providing business to the reinsurer.

- Non-proportional reinsurance is taken out to cover loss **over** a certain amount. For example, if an insurance company insures a shipping company against loss of $5m, it could choose to reinsure any loss in excess of, say, $1m, or $4m.

Reinsurance is often split between a number of reinsurance companies to spread the risk, so that in the event of a large claim being made, no single company stands the whole amount. The ten largest reinsurance companies are shown in **Exhibit 4.5**. They all have offices worldwide and skilful underwriters to undertake this complex task. Most of these companies carry out direct insurance as well.

Exhibit 4.5	Largest global reinsurers (2009)	

	Country	Net premiums $bn
Munich Re Group	Germany	32.8
Swiss Re Group	Switzerland	21.9
Hanover Re Group	Germany	13.3
Berkshire Hathaway	US	12.4
Lloyd's of London	UK	9.5
SCOR	France	8.9
Transatlantic Holdings Inc.	US	4.0
PartnerRe Ltd.	Bermuda	3.9
Everest Re Group Ltd.	Bermuda	3.9
Korean Re	South Korea	2.4

Source: Insurance Information Institute.

The purchase of reinsurance by reinsurance companies is known as **retrocession**. It is entirely possible for a reinsurance company to unknowingly reinsure itself by taking on part of a risk that it has distributed among other reinsurance companies, which in turn redistribute the risk; this is known as **spiralling**.

The London market

The London market is a separate part of the UK insurance and reinsurance business centred in the City of London, and comprises **Lloyd's** and Lloyd's syndicates, **Protection and Indemnity (P & I) Clubs** and members of the **IUA (the International Underwriting Association of London)**. Together they provide international general insurance and reinsurance for complex large commercial risks. It is the only market in which all of the world's 20 largest reinsurance groups are represented. The amount of expertise available from these insurers means that brokers are able to underwrite just about any type of risk. Business is facilitated by their geographical proximity, with every kind of ancillary service providers, such as lawyers and IT, close at hand. The close community of specialist insurers and support service providers means that information spread is rapid and deals can be made quickly.

Exhibit 4.6 shows how the London market was conducted over the ten years from 2000 to 2009 and how it expanded to generate some £24,651 million in premiums.

Exhibit 4.6	The London market premium income						
	Share of London market				**Type of insurance business**		
Year	**Lloyd's £m**	**Insurance companies – IUA members £m**	**P&I Clubs £m**	**Totals £m**	**Marine, Aviation and Transport (MAT) business £m**	**Non-MAT business home and foreign £m**	**Non-marine reinsurance £m**
2000	8,644	8,939	686	18,091	4,312	6,227	7,432
2001	10,446	8,236	955	19,637	4,849	7,107	7,681
2002	12,744	11,037	864	24,645	7,036	8,132	9,477
2003	12,424	10,855	2,064	25,343	7,952	8,300	9,091
2004	11,563	9,365	1,383	22,311	6,234	7,763	8,313
2005	12,102	13,013	1,537	26,652	6,948	8,117	11,587
2006	13,827	8,944	1,535	24,306	7,610	8,280	8,416
2007	13,794	6,722	1,238	21,754	7,546	9,001	5,207
2008	15,689	8,055	907	24,651	8,478	10,306	5,867
2009	19,515	11,519	876	31,910	n/a	n/a	n/a

Source: ABI.

IUA

The International Underwriting Association is the world's largest organisation for international and wholesale insurance and reinsurance companies. It was formed in 1998 by the merger of two separate bodies which previously represented marine and non-marine insurance.

P & I Clubs

Protection and Indemnity (P & I) Clubs (often called Marine P & I Clubs) have been in existence for over 140 years and offer protection and indemnity (insurance) in respect of third-party liabilities and expenses arising from owning or operating ships. They do not cover the actual ships or their cargoes, but do cover third-party risks such as collision, pollution, injury to or loss of life of passengers or crew members, and a long list of others. They are run on a mutual basis (owned by members and not run for profit), although there has recently been a trend towards demutualisation and the provision of insurance cover with fixed premiums.

Lloyd's

Edward Lloyd is believed to have opened his coffee house in Tower Street, London in 1688, and it soon became a meeting place for people with interests in shipping. In 1769 a group of underwriters and brokers moved to other premises, naming them 'New Lloyds Coffee House'. When these premises became too small, the group of 79 each put in £100 and leased and became joint owners of what was henceforth called Lloyd's of London or just Lloyd's. Business, and the expertise of the underwriters and brokers, grew, and in 1871 an Act of Parliament gave Lloyd's authority to acquire property and enact byelaws. Lloyd's had become an established business institution not only in British society but throughout the trading world.

The proficiency and experience of Lloyd's underwriters preserves its position at the forefront of the property and casualty insurance business, and their ability and willingness to undertake unusual risks keeps them in the public eye. Lloyd's is a place where customers, brokers and underwriters meet face to face and discuss requirements. **Exhibit 4.7** gives the percentage breakdown of the insurance cover which they underwrote in 2009. More than half of the business is with North or South Americans; only 20 per cent of business is with UK individuals and organisations. Lloyd's members write insurance in over 80 jurisdictions and write reinsurance in more than 200 countries and territories.

Exhibit 4.7	Lloyd's of London insurance cover (2009)

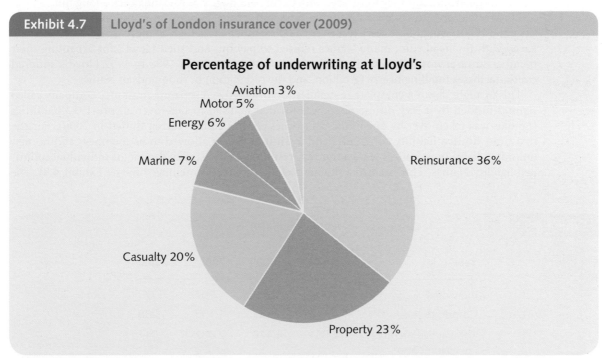

Percentage of underwriting at Lloyd's

Aviation 3%
Motor 5%
Energy 6%
Marine 7%
Reinsurance 36%
Casualty 20%
Property 23%

Source: Lloyd's Annual Report 2009.

Among the more interesting risks that Lloyd's syndicates have underwritten are Father Christmas's beard, the 1981 Derby winner Shergar, which was owned by a syndicate of individuals when it was kidnapped in 1983 (payments were made to horse syndicate members who were insured for theft, but not to those who insured for loss of life), the legs of Betty Grable ($1 million each leg) and Michael Flatley ($47 million!), Ken Dodd's teeth, accidental injury to any of The Beatles, Bruce Springsteen's voice ($6 million), the taste buds of Egon Ronay, the risk that Queen Victoria's first born would be twins, and death from excessive laughter (this cover was taken out in the 1920s when the early comedic films were shown for the first time and had a dramatic effect on their audience).

The structure of Lloyd's

Lloyd's is not an insurance company, it is a society of members – that is, a group of members who trade in insurance via brokers, in an environment run by the **Corporation of Lloyd's**, which is overseen by the **Council of Lloyd's**.

For a long time it was made up of individuals (**Names**) who underwrote particular risks and joined together in syndicates to underwrite an ever larger range of risks of modern life. Syndicates ran (and still run) for one year only, then closed, and other syndicates would be formed, sometimes identical in membership to the one just closed, sometimes with some or all different members. Because claims take some time to become apparent, three years after opening the syndicates accounts are closed, profit taken and any liabilities taken into consideration. However, instead of putting aside reserves of cash to pay for these ongoing liabilities, it became common practice to reinsure them, usually with the same syndicate. In this way, it was possible for losses to accumulate year after year, and it was possible for new members to be liable for losses from years ago. This resulted in meltdown in the late 1980s and 1990s, following a string of natural disasters – the explosion of the Piper Alpha oil rig, the Exxon Valdez oil spill, an earthquake in San Francisco, and Hurricane Hugo – which were combined with US courts awarding huge damages for asbestosis, pollution and health hazards; some of the claims involved all-liability policies and dated back tens of years. For more than 300 years, individual underwriting members had accepted unlimited personal liability for the policies they signed and now they were faced with paying out huge claims dating back a long time.

Lloyd's had gone through a profitable time and a huge expansion in the number of Names since the 1950s, when there were just over 3,000 members, to a high of more than 32,000 in 1988. Faced with financial ruin, many Names refused to pay out and sued Lloyd's for accepting their membership but not fully revealing the historic liabilities. From 1988 to 1992 Lloyd's suffered continual losses totalling nearly £8 billion, and the resignation of thousands of Names.

This brought about a complete reorganisation of Lloyd's. A separate insurance company called *Equitas* funded by a levy on members was formed in 1996 to take over all pre-1992 liabilities (Equitas was taken over by one of the companies controlled by Warren Buffett in 2006). For the first time, limited liability companies and institutions were allowed to be members and no *new* unlimited liability members were admitted, resulting in the steady decline of individual unlimited liability Names. This has had a dramatic effect on Lloyd's membership (*see* **Exhibit 4.8**). The

Exhibit 4.8	Lloyds of London membership 1995–2008			
Year	**1995**	**2000**	**2007**	**2008**
Individual	14,744	3,317	907	773
Corporate	140	853	1,155	1,238
Total active members	14,884	4,170	2,062	2,011
Number of syndicates	170	156	72	81

Source: Lloyds of London.

Central Fund was established, a levy on all premiums, to be used if members are unable to meet claims (now with over £2 billion), underwriting and risk management were improved and syndicates had to produce a business plan which met with the approval of the Corporation of Lloyd's.

Individuals or businesses wishing to invest in Lloyd's must have £350,000 in assets in reserve and about £200,000 in cash that they can place in Lloyd's as back-up for underwriting losses, should they occur. They are then able to buy the right to be a syndicate member and take a share in the syndicate's profit.

Exhibit 4.9 shows where Lloyd's syndicates get their capital from. Clearly, most of it now comes from the worldwide insurance industry rather than from individuals.

Exhibit 4.9	Source of capital for Lloyds

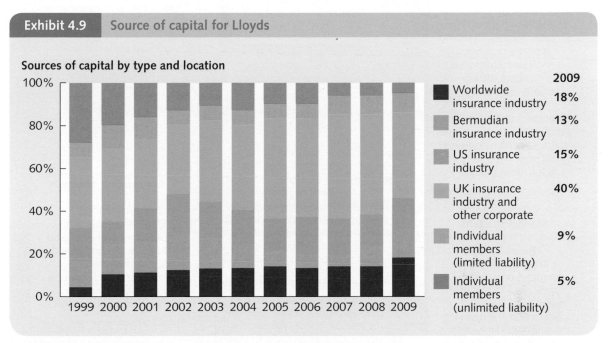

Source: Lloyd's Annual Report 2009.

At the centre of the Lloyd's system are the 80 or so syndicates that accept the insurance risk. Brokers working for the clients needing insurance shop around and negotiate a deal with one or more syndicates. Managing agents are responsible for managing a syndicate and the whole system is supervised by the Corporation of Lloyd's – *see* **Exhibit 4.10**.

Exhibit 4.11 describes the stages a new Name has to go through to underwrite insurance risk.

Money has to be kept in reserve and invested in safe and easily liquidated financial assets to meet the claims of policy holders. Lloyd's tries to be ultra-safe by having three pots of money. The first comes from premiums paid, the second from money supplied by members and the third from a central fund which is topped up by members each year – *see* **Exhibit 4.12**.

The article in **Exhibit 4.13** shows where the money held in each of these three funds was invested and discusses the current debate about the temptation to invest in less liquid and more risky securities to obtain higher returns.

Exhibit 4.10	The players at Lloyds

Members of Lloyds

These are the capital providers that accept the insurance risk via syndicates.
Included are major insurance groups, companies (some listed on stock markets), individuals and limited partnerships. Private members typically support a number of syndicates. Corporate members usually underwrite through a single syndicate. Members choose which syndicate(s) to participate in for the following year (most stick with the same for many years)

Members agents

Advisory and administration services to members.
Help set up limited liability partnerships for non-corporate members (i.e. people).
Arrange investment in a syndicate

Clients seeking insurance

Brokers

Working on behalf of clients

Face-to-face negotiation in the Underwriting Room, One Lime Street

Syndicates

(84 syndicates in 2010)
One or more Lloyds' Members that join together as a group to accept insurance risks.
The specialist underwriters within each syndicate price, underwrite and handle any subsequent claims.
Members receive profits or bear losses in proportion to their share in the syndicate for each underwriting year of account.
Some syndicates specialise in underwriting a certain class of insurance, e.g. aviation.
Many syndicates are now managed and funded by a single corporate group (member)

Corporation of Lloyds

- Oversees market
- Establishes standards
- Sets the level of capital Members must provide to support their proposed underwriting
- Provides services to support market activities

Managing agent

(52 in 2010)
A company set up to manage one or more syndicates on behalf of members. Oversight of underwriting, employing the underwriter, handling day-to-day running of the syndicate's infrastructure and operations.
Managing agents are also located around the world, e.g. there are six firms in Brazil

Source: IFSL (www.thecityUK.com).

Exhibit 4.11

High-net-worth investors keen to sign up as Names

by Ellen Kelleher

Scores of high-net-worth investors are already expressing an interest in signing up as Lloyd's Names to profit from next year's underwriting cycle for the London insurance market.

The way to follow suit is to join one of the three Lloyd's members' agents, Alpha, Argenta or Hampden. These groups set up limited liability underwriting vehicles and represent clients seeking

▶

Exhibit 4.11 continued

to invest in particular syndicates at Lloyd's capacity auctions, held in September.

Members tend to support a variety of syndicates and spread their risk by underwriting different classes of insurance and reinsurance.

The costs of investing in the Lloyd's market remain high, as investors must have at least £350,000 in assets, which is used as collateral, and about £200,000 in cash, which is used to buy the rights to participate in the profits of syndicates.

Another £7,000 to £10,000 is required to start a limited liability partnership (LLP), which must be set up by the end of August to participate in the auctions for the 2010 account.

Prospective members can also purchase an existing LLP.

Members who have set up a limited liability underwriting vehicle must then deposit funds at Lloyd's in November to support their underwriting capacity for the following year.

To write a premium income limit of £1m for the 2010 year, for example, an account would require a £400,000 deposit, in the form of cash, shares or bank guarantees.

Funds deposited are geared by about 2.5 times.

Syndicate capacity bought by members in a particular year is a tradeable asset which can gain or lose capital value and also pay yearly dividends in the form of underwriting profit.

High-net-worth investors are attracted to the market for several reasons.

Losses are now capped, as investors can now only underwrite a group of syndicates through a LLP, which means that the maximum loss they face will be restricted to the capital pledged upfront.

A second benefit is that assets invested in Lloyd's can be used twice to achieve returns. For example, an investor could put up, say, a buy-to-let property or a share portfolio as collateral.

This allows investors to earn a double return on their assets. Also, any losses can be offset against income tax.

Source: Financial Times, 19 January 2009, p. 18. Reprinted with permission.

Exhibit 4.12   The three sources of capital to back up insurance promises at Lloyd's

First: syndicate-level assets ('premium trust fund')	Premiums on policies received by a syndicate are held in its trust fund ready to pay out on claims (over £37bn in 2010)
Second: Members' funds at Lloyd's	Each Member provides capital to support underwriting in case claims exceed premiums. This capital is held in trust as readily saleable assets to meet any Lloyd's insurance liabilities of that Member, but not the liabilities of other Members (over £13bn in 2010)
Third: Central Fund	A further back-up is the Corporation's central assets to meet valid claims that cannot be met by the Member. Members have to pay an annual contribution to maintain it (over £2bn in 2010)

Exhibit 4.13

Lloyd's considers riskier investments

FT

Steve Johnson

Not many investors managed to sail serenely through the financial crisis with scarcely a care in the world, but Lloyd's of London, the 322-year-old insurance market, was among this select band.

The insurance market's conservative investment strategy, heavy in government and corporate bonds, saw it chalk up annual returns of 5.6 per cent in 2007, 2.5 per cent in 2008 and 4 per cent in 2009.

In spite of this, there are signs that the 52 managing agents, the underwriters that manage the 84 syndicates and hold £46bn ($70bn, €52bn) of investable assets, are starting to embrace a little more risk.

The change is being driven by the increasingly paltry returns available on short duration investment-grade debt and the fact that the notoriously cyclical underwriting market appears to be softening, putting pressure on agents to generate returns from the asset side of their balance sheet.

Others see a similar trend. David Osborne, senior consultant at Meridian, the largest consultancy in the Lloyd's market, says: "People are having to re-think their attitude to risk. If they take all the risk off the table and put the money in cash deposits they earn nothing in practice. It's a more difficult set of problems than the insurance market has ever faced before."

Russell Büsst, head of institutional fixed income at Amundi, which manages £2.6bn on behalf of 15 managing agents and 20 syndicates, adds: "The last underwriting cycle was pretty weak and people are trying to make their reserves work harder."

Managing agents have traditionally been highly conservative investors, with the bulk of their assets held in short duration government bonds and investment-trade credit.

These assets, alongside letters of credit provided by banks, still dominate the three layers of

Assets allocation in the Lloyd's market

Premium trust funds (%)

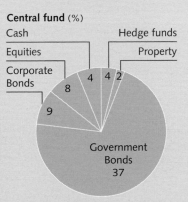

Equities 3
Cash 18
Corporate Bonds 42
Government Bonds 37

Funds at Lloyd's (%)

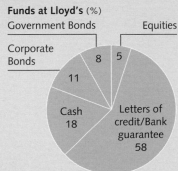

Government Bonds 8
Corporate Bonds 11
Equities 5
Cash 18
Letters of credit/Bank guarantee 58

Central fund (%)

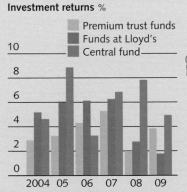

Cash 4
Equities 4
Corporate Bonds 8
Hedge funds
Property 2
9
Government Bonds 37

Investment returns %

Premium trust funds
Funds at Lloyd's
Central fund

2004 05 06 07 08 09

Sources: London Business School; Payden & Rygel Global

capital; members' trust funds, which hold premium income; members' funds at Lloyd's, which holds the capital each syndicate must put up to support its underwriting activity; and the central fund, a mutual fund that provides a backstop for large claims.

However, Robin Creswell, managing principal of Payden & Rygel Global, which manages $5bn for insurance organisations, says some of the larger Lloyd's players had dipped their toes into equities, high yield bonds and hedge funds over the past five years, a lead he expected others to follow.

Hedge funds are more widely held still, despite their relative lack of liquidity, a problem Mr Osborne sees being addressed by the new generation of Ucits hedge funds with a minimum of fortnightly liquidity. "That brings hedge funds

more into the liquidity bracket that managing agents want."

Mr Osborne reports some agents have ventured into property funds in the past six months. However, emerging market debt remains unpopular – many syndicates write political insurance risk, which is closely correlated to the sovereign risk embedded in this aset class.

Luke Savage, finance director of Lloyd's, which manages the central fund, says just 2 per cent of agents' assets are invested in equities, compared to equity exposure of 10–15 per cent for contintental European insurers. "We feel very comfortable having slightly less sparkling performance in return for not putting our members at risk," he says.

Source: Financial Times, 5 April 2010, p. 3. Reprinted with permission.

Pensions

At the end of one's working life, retirement beckons, but how is life financed after retirement? For most people, the answer is some type of pension. While many countries do provide a basic state pension, this usually needs topping up by means of a supplementary pension to give a reasonable quality of life.

There are many types of pension available, but usually the person wishing to have a pension in the future has to begin the process of putting money aside to fund it. This money is put into an organisation which invests it to provide the pensions when required. The total amount invested in these type of schemes is huge. IFSL[6] estimates that global pension assets totalled $31.1 trillion at the end of 2010. Figures for 2009 give a total amount for pension assets of $28.8 trillion. The UK's share of the market is $2.5 trillion, the second largest after the US, whose 63 per cent share dominates the market – *see* **Exhibit 4.14**.

Exhibit 4.14	Global pension assets (2009)

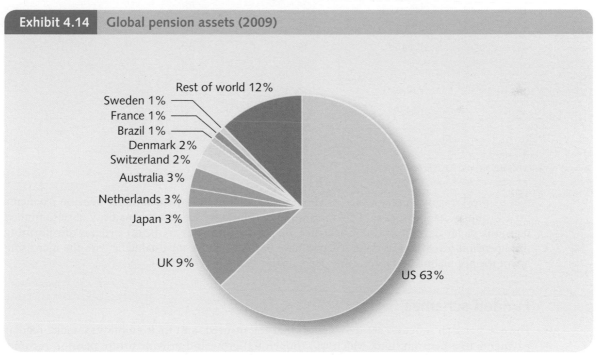

Source: www.TheCityUK.com

In the future, pensions look like being a major problem for many governments. Populations in general are aging as a result of improved health care, disease control and healthier lifestyles. According to figures produced by the United Nations (UN) the percentage of people aged over 65 compared with the working population (aged 15–64) is set to rise considerably – *see* **Exhibit 4.15**. Without action, this is going to cause great difficulties for governments. Many countries are raising the retirement age, with an equivalent delay in pension provision to try to reduce the burden.

Unfunded schemes

In the UK, 3 million workers (such as teachers and civil servants) are members of public **unfunded pension schemes**. These are termed **pay-as-you-go (PAYG)** schemes where the money put aside each month by employees and employers pays the pensions of current pensioners. This means that there is not a pot of accumulated money to pay pensions. If there is a shortfall, it is

---

[6] International Financial Services London, which has now changed its name to TheCityUK.

Exhibit 4.15   Comparative age of population

Population aged over 65 as a percentage of working age population (15–64)

	2010 %	2050 %
Japan	35	74
Italy	31	62
Germany	31	59
France	26	47
UK	25	38
Spain	25	59
Poland	19	52
US	19	35
China	11	38
India	8	20

Source: UN World Population Prospects: The 2008 Revision.

met by the Treasury. Already, there is about £1,000 billion in unfunded future pension payments for UK public- sector workers. Looking around the world we see that the majority of state-funded pensions so far have been PAYG schemes, but many countries are in the process of reforming their pension provisions as these schemes have begun to prove unsustainable with the increasing age of the population and its growing dependency on the state.

Funded schemes

Funded pension schemes are designed so that the insured, and their employers, make regular payments to a pension fund, which will (hopefully) grow and provide future pension income. Many companies and other organisations such as universities already run such schemes for their staff. In the UK, 6 million employees are currently paying into a workplace pension scheme. However, that still leaves 14 million salaried employees not saving into a workplace scheme, and the UK government is keen to ensure that a much higher proportion of employees is part of a funded scheme. Thus, under the Pension Act 2008, UK employers, if they do not currently run a funded pension scheme, will be expected to put the equivalent of a minimum of 1–3 per cent[7] of the employee's salary into a new national pensions savings scheme – known as Nest, the National Employment Savings Trust. The employee will be automatically enrolled, but can opt out and is required to contribute 1–4 per cent[8] of salary, while an additional 1 per cent comes from the government in the form of tax relief. Nest is designed as a low-cost scheme so that even very small companies can contribute to it without having to establish their own schemes.

Increasing longevity and the sharp fall in return on pension fund assets over the past 20 years (especially returns from equities) have caused pension deficits in a considerable number of companies providing a kind of funded pension called defined benefit pensions – see below.

---

[7] Until October 2016 this is 1 per cent; between October 2016 and October 2017 the employer pays 2 per cent; thereafter the contribution is 3 per cent.

[8] Until October 2016 this is 1 per cent; between October 2016 and October 2017 it is 3 per cent; after that the employee will technically pay 5 per cent, with 1 per cent of that being the tax relief.

Companies in the FTSE 100 (the largest companies on the London Stock Exchange) had deficits totalling £41 billion in 2008; this rose to nearly £90 billion in 2009.

The deficit arises when the actual amount of assets expected to be in the pension pot at retirement (with added investment income) is not sufficient to pay out the pensions required.

Defined benefit

A **defined benefit (DB)** pension pays out a fixed amount based upon the number of years worked and the level of final salary or the average level of salary. So, for example, you might be a member of a final salary one-eightieth scheme, which means that the number of years you have been making contributions to the fund is multiplied by $\frac{1}{80}$ and the result is multiplied by your final year's salary (or some average over a number of years). So if you have worked and contributed for 40 years and your final salary is £30,000 you will, under a final salary scheme, be entitled to $\frac{40}{80} \times £30,000 = £15,000$ per year in retirement, and may receive three times that as a lump sum on retiring. Despite the scheme being set up as a separate organisation, the sponsoring employer usually remains responsible for final provision of the pension. To reduce their risk they usually insist on significant contributions from the employee during their working life – 7.5 per cent of salary in the case of members of the Universities Superannuation Scheme, with employing universities putting in another 16 per cent of salary each month.

With pension schemes which were set up to provide pensions before our modern increasing longevity, companies are finding that DB pensions are becoming too costly, especially in combination with recent economic recessions which have caused such an alarming decrease in some pension fund assets that their DB pension schemes are in deficit, i.e. the fund is worth less than the present value of promised benefits. According to an IFSL (TheCityUK) report, 'Pension fund markets 2010', companies in the FTSE100 reported substantial increases in their final salary pension scheme deficits in their end-March accounts, with the aggregate deficit in the region of £96 billion. Some companies (e.g. BT, BBC, Network Rail, IBM, Barclays and BP, among many) are attempting to reduce their DB liabilities by closing the scheme to new employees, taking out insurance (very expensive), transferring them to a different scheme, or offering employees financial incentives to change to another scheme.

Some pension funds are looking for ways to alleviate their predicament (*see* **Exhibit 4.16**) by offloading their pension liabilities to third parties such as insurance companies, but this can be costly.

Exhibit 4.16

Tackling the longevity question

FT

Paul J Davies

Cadbury's deal yesterday to offload £500m of pension fund liabilities to Edmund Truell's Pension Insurance Corp was just the latest in a string of agreements as public and corporate pension schemes tackle their £1,000bn-plus headache.

Trustees across the country are being offered an array of solutions to the expense and volatility of their pension obligations after the recent financial market turmoil added impetus to companies' desire to reduce the risks attached to their schemes.

If the past decade was about the closure of defined benefit pension schemes and the move to defined contribution, the next 10 years are expected to see an ever-greater focus on reducing investment and longevity risks.

JPMorgan and Credit Suisse, Cerberus from private equity, and Swiss Re, Pacific Life Re and Partner Re, have all been moving aggressively into a field that was previously dominated by old-fashioned bulk-annuity deals from Prudential and Legal & General.

What these companies are offering is a troika of options: buy-outs, where a financial company takes over an entire scheme; buy-ins, where a chunk of investment and longevity risks within a scheme are insured by a third-party; and longevity swaps, where a derivative contract takes away only the risk that pensioners live and draw an income much longer than expected. (See box)

Longevity swaps have been the most popular recently, with almost $10bn (£6bn) of deals completed

▶

Exhibit 4.16 continued

Pension scheme options

● Bulk Annuity

The traditional policy offered by large UK insurers. Pension schemes pay a premium and in exchange the insurer writes an annuity that pays the retirement income of a large chunk of a scheme's pensioners who have already retired. Trustees offload all investment, inflation and longevity risks associated with paying income to a group of retirees, insurer gains chunk of assets and a premium

● Buy-outs

A specialist insurer takes over an entire pension scheme. This can only be done for fully funded schemes. The idea grew out of the business of managing the pension schemes of bankrupt companies, but has been applied more to companies still going. Trustees get a replacement sponsor and manager of an entire scheme. Insurer gains all the assets

● Buy-ins

Similar to bulk annuity, Pension schemes purchase an insurance contract that underwrites the risks associated with paying income

to retirees. But these have also been used of offload the liabilities associated with so-called deferred pensioners, usually people who have left a company but have not yet retired. The way to make money here is to offer individuals a cash settlement today in exchange for future pension rights. Trustees offload all investment, inflation and longevity risks associated with paying income to a group of retirees. Insurer gains control over a chunk of assets and a premium

● Longevity swaps

The pure trade. Pension schemes keep assets and so retain investment and inflation risks. The swap counterparty is usually an investment bank, which then lays off most, if not all, of the risk to a reinsurer or into the capital markets. Trustees pay a fixed regular premium to offload the risks that they will have to keep paying out pensions to retirees for longer than planned for. Investment bank and reinsurer pay a floating premium in return, which increases the longer people live

Company pension schemes

Recent market activity
Bulk annuities new business ($bn)

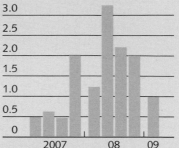

Total liabilities
Defined benefit schemes (£bn)

Pension fund asset allocation
%

Source: Watson Wyatt; IMA; Pension Protection Fund

"We don't like longevity swaps so much, because they need a lot of capital but without much in the way of assets or earnings upfront," says Mr Bloomer.

Source: *Financial Times*, 17 December 2009, p. 21. Reprinted with permission.

since early 2008, mainly by life assurance companies looking to reduce the risks on their own annuity books.

But this summer saw Goldman Sachs complete two such deals directly for corporate schemes at RSA and Babcock.

The popularity of these deals has been driven by affordability at a time when the other options have been too expensive, due to higher premiums to cover the investment risk and lower valuations put on assets that would leave a scheme as part of the deal.

The last big buy-in before the market turmoil was undertaken by Prudential for Cable and Wireless and closed just days ahead of Lehman Brothers' collapse in September 2008.

However, in recent months markets have recovered enough for buy-ins to become more affordable again.

On top of the Cadbury deal with PIC, Goldman Sachs in November completed a £370m buy-in for CDC, the government-owned business that invests in development projects.

In September, Lucida, the Cerberus-backed business run by Jonathan Bloomer, the former Prudential chief executive, completed a £500m buy-in for the Merchant Navy Officers pension fund.

For large insurance groups and for some of the new entrants such as Lucida, the focus is on building up a large pool of assets to manage, which generate profits from the difference between the investment returns and the money paid out to pensioners.

Defined contribution

The **defined contribution (DC)** type of pension is increasingly prevalent. This is a pension where the contributions (from employee and employer) are fixed but the actual pension paid out is linked to the return on the assets of the pension fund and the rate at which the final pension fund is annuitised; at retirement age, an annuity is generally purchased with the accumulated funds to provide the pension.[9] As returns on accumulating money and annuity rates fluctuate with economic and financial volatility, it is entirely possible for the pension to be less (or more) than expected. There is no obligation for the employer to guarantee a level of pension under DC. If the fund underperforms while the employee is still working and saving in the scheme, or administrative costs rise, there will simply be a lower pension. In other words, the risk of poorly performing investments is transferred to the prospective pensioners.

Personal/private pensions

Personal or **private pensions** are not provided by the state. They put the onus of funding a pension solely on the recipient, who pays a regular amount, usually every month, or a lump sum to the pension provider who will invest it on their behalf. These funds are usually run by financial organisations such as insurance companies, building societies or banks. Personal pensions are often the optimal choice for people wishing to organise their own pension, those who are self-employed or whose company does not provide a suitable pension.

Personal pensions are a very tax-efficient way of providing for the long-term future in the UK:

- The contributions qualify for full tax relief. This means that if, say, £2,880 is contributed from taxed earnings, the government then adds back tax (at 20 per cent) to the fund, amounting to £720, meaning that £3,600 is added to your pension pot. Higher-rate taxpayers are able to get additional tax relief.

- Once the money is in the fund it can grow without tax being levied on interest income, or on capital gains. (However, dividend income is taxed.)

- At retirement age 25 per cent of the fund may be taken in cash, tax free.

A pension may be taken while still in employment. There is a wide range of funds, each specialising in a different type of investment – UK or overseas shares, passive/tracker funds or actively managed, corporate bonds and gilts and cash.

A **stakeholder pension (SHP)** is a contract-based pension introduced in 2001 by the UK government. It places limits on charges and allows individuals flexibility around contributions. SHPs are available for an individual to take out on their own, or through an employer in a group scheme (Group SHP). Tax relief rules allow tax to be claimed back on contributions, even for non-taxpayers.

Self-invested personal pension (SIPPs)

Self invested personal pensions are pension plans that allow the contributor to control the type and amount of investments made and have the same tax advantages as personal pension schemes. SIPPs were originally aimed at people with large pension funds (over £200,000) but are now available to anyone with a contribution of £3,600 or more per year. People with multiple pension schemes can bring them all under one SIPP wrapper, resulting in easier management. The downside of SIPPs is that there are likely to be more charges than for a standard personal pension: a set-up fee followed by fixed annual fees, plus charges for each deal. Online SIPP providers can offer a more cost-effective way of managing the plan.

SIPP plans can invest in a wide variety of investments: domestic or international shares, gilts, corporate bonds, unit trusts, OEICs, investment trusts, insurance company funds, exchange-traded derivatives, gold bullion, loans and deposit accounts or even commercial property.

---

[9] Although the UK government is increasingly allowing continued investment rather than forcing pensioners to take out an annuity (which may produce as little as £4,000 per year (until death) for a lump sum of £100,000 drawn from the DC pension pot).

Public pensions

Nearly all countries in the developed world provide some sort of state-funded i.e. public pension for their people. Sometimes these pensions are means-tested (people's incomes and assets are examined to ensure they are poor enough to qualify) and the state will top up the income of the really poor if the pension is insufficient. These pensions are funded by public money, taxes and revenues, and as we have already said, are becoming an increasing burden on government finances. Governments around the world are encouraging people to contribute to private or personal pensions, thus relieving them of an onerous responsibility.

In the UK, a non-earnings-related pension is paid by the state, based on the National Insurance contributions a person has put in over the course of their working life. This is a PAYG scheme, in that the current working generation's payments into the scheme funds current pensioners' income. The UK government, in line with other countries, has plans to increase the pension age to 66 (women 65) in the near future, with a further increase to 70 under discussion, as a way of lowering the amount that has to be raised in taxes to pay these pensions.

Pension fund trustees, consultants and managers

Pension funds create large pools of assets and the task of the funds' controllers is to manage the assets well and generate sufficient income to pay out pension liabilities. The growth in the size of these funds has been quite remarkable and now the amount of assets at their disposal is enormous (more than $30 trillion in 2010), so the managers in charge of the funds are in an incredibly influential position. Indeed, pension funds are now the largest category of investor: they invest in both domestic and international financial markets and can have huge influence on countries' wealth, development and industries.

Because this large 'float' (pension contributions paid in but not yet paid out in pensions) is available, there have been various scandals in the past, where pension fund cash has been used for other purposes (e.g. the Mirror pension fund plundered by Robert Maxwell, who was able to persuade the trustees of the Mirror fund to lend to or invest in other companies controlled by Maxwell, which then failed), or the company has gone bankrupt and thereby left the pensioners with nothing, or the money has been badly invested, leaving insufficient in the pot to pay out pensions. In many cases, if a pension fund collapses, the employee has no redress, unless fraud or other criminal activity can be proved.

Avoiding misappropriation of the money in pension funds is therefore one of the most important tasks for trustees, who control the fund and hire managers to invest the money. Trustees are required to know and understand the various laws relating to pensions and trusts, their funding and the investment of their assets. Their overall objective is to set up their fund as a secure source of funds for retirement benefits and oversee its management.

Consultants are asked to give their professional advice to trustees on the type and amount of investments to be made. They have access to a plethora of historic data from which they can advise on, for instance, the best investment path to take and which investment managers are likely to outperform the stock market. They may also help with the calculations for figuring out the amount needed to be put into the fund each year, taking into account a number of estimates: the estimated return on assets, projected future wage growth (for DB schemes) and future inflation (if the pensions are index-linked, that is rise as inflation goes up).

Managers are tasked with investing and ensuring that the fund returns are satisfactory, but they can sometimes be too cautious or too rash, with disastrous results for the pensioners. As pension funds increased in size, it became apparent that in most cases a single manager could not cope with the volume of investment. This started a trend towards decentralisation – employing multiple managers, each specialising in a particular asset class of investing. Some funds are run only by one or a number of in-house investment fund managers working directly for the fund; others outsource their investment manager functions – this is where the consultants can help in selection. Still others have a mixture, with some of the money managed in-house and some by professional fund managers. *See* **Exhibit 4.17** for a discussion on this ('Alpha' is outperformance in the market after adjusting for increased risk).

Exhibit 4.17

20-year study finds pension funds rational

David Blake

Decentralised investment management is widespread throughout the institutional investment industry and, in particular, the pension fund industry.

Yet, despite the huge economic importance of this practice, very little is known about the economic motivation for decentralising or about how fund performance and risk-taking behaviour are affected by it.

We, at the Pensions Institute, used a proprietary dataset to make a study into decentralisation in investment management in the UK pension fund industry from 1984 to 2004. Over this period, most pension fund sponsors shifted:

a) from employing a single balanced manager, who invested across all asset classes, to specialist managers, who specialise mostly within a single asset class, and

b) from a single manager (either balanced or specialist) to competing multiple managers (balanced, specialist, multi-asset or combinations thereof) within each asset class.

This shift from single balanced managers to multiple specialist managers carries significant decentralisation costs.

Decentralisation involves suboptimal risk-taking at the portfolio level, due to the problem of co-ordinating different managers through incentive contracts. The hiring of multiple managers also increases total fund management fees. We examined whether these shifts have been rational; that is, whether fund sponsors have experienced increased performance to compensate for the suboptimal diversification.

We found that specialist managers did generate superior performance, particularly in respect of stock selection or alpha. By contrast, balanced fund managers failed to display any significant stock-selection or market-timing skills, either in the form of strategic or tactical asset allocation skills. There was also evidence of persistence in performance over time by specialists, especially in UK equities.

We then examined the effects on performance and risk-taking from employing multiple managers. We found mild evidence to support the conjectures that competition between multiple managers produces better performance – but this held only in the case of competing specialist managers in UK equities – and that pension fund sponsors react to the co-ordination problem by controlling risk levels: total pension fund risk (and, in particular, alpha risk) is lower under decentralised investment management.

We found that the switches from balanced to specialist mandates and from single to multiple managers were preceded by poor performance. In the latter case, part of the poor performance was due to the fund becoming too large for a single manager to manage: sponsors properly anticipated diseconomies of scale as funds grew larger and added managers with different strategies before performance deteriorated significantly.

We also studied changes in risk-taking when moving to decentralised management. Here, we found that sponsors appeared to rationally anticipate the difficulty of co-ordinating multiple managers by allocating reduced risk budgets to each manager, which helped to compensate for the suboptimal diversification that results from decentralisation.

Overall, our findings help to explain both the shift from balanced to specialist managers over the sample period – pension funds benefited from superior performance as a result of the shift – and the shift from single to multiple managers – pension funds benefited from risk reduction and from avoiding fund-level diseconomies of scale by employing multiple managers. We interpret these shifts as being rational by pension fund sponsors, despite the greater co-ordination problems and diversification loss.

Finally, we note that, following the end of our sample period in 2004, further specialisation of skills in pension fund management has occurred. For example, there has been the emergence of diversified growth funds which offer investments in such "alternatives" as private equity, hedge funds, commodities, infrastructure, currencies and emerging market debt.

This study can be found at: http://pensions-institute.org/workingpapers/wp0914.pdf

David Blake is director of the Pensions Institute at Cass Business School, London

Source: *Financial Times,* 7 December 2009, p. 6. Reprinted with permission.

Pension fund asset holdings

Pension funds are major purchasers of long-term investments which suit their liabilities well; they need to be able to generate sufficient to be in a position to pay out pension liabilities decades in the future. Until the recent financial crisis, many pension funds held a large proportion of their funds in equities. Since then, equities have been reduced in favour of long-term bonds and fixed-rate instruments, which are thought to give a more secure return (*see* **Exhibit 4.18**). The important factor is to look at the long-term future stability of the fund and invest where this can be best guaranteed.

Exhibit 4.18	**2009 Pension fund asset allocation**		
	Equities %	**Bonds** %	**Other** %
United Kingdom	54	36	10
United States	58	35	7
Japan	36	47	17
Australia	42	19	39
Netherlands	28	47	25

Source: UBS Pension Fund Indicators (TheCityUK Pensions Report 2011).

Figures from annual reports from the BT Pension Scheme (BTPS), the largest pension fund in the UK with assets totalling £34,112 million, show just how wide-ranging its investments are. **Exhibit 4.19** shows how the allocation of their investment assets changes over the years from 2001 to 2009. ('Inflation-linked' means government bonds whose returns go up with higher inflation, 'Other alternatives' includes investments in private equity.)

Exhibit 4.19	**BT pension scheme investment assets 31 December 2001, 2005 and 2009**

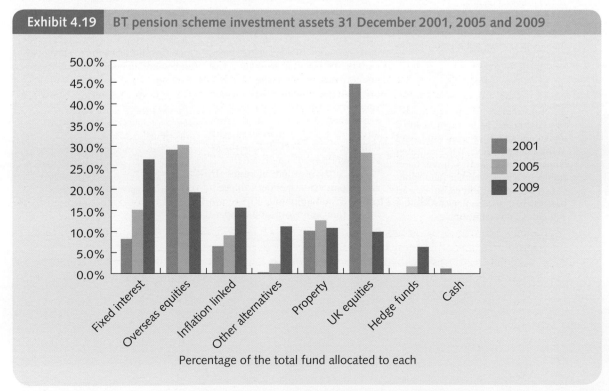

Percentage of the total fund allocated to each

Source: BTPS Annual Report.

Following the financial crisis of 2008, BTPS policy has been to move out of higher-risk UK equities (down to 10 per cent from 29 per cent in 2005) and into 'safer' fixed-rate securities, such as government bonds. It is interesting to see the increase in investment in hedge funds, which were once regarded as highly speculative. Pension funds are trying to recoup their losses through higher-performing investments (*see* **Exhibit 4.20**).

Exhibit 4.20

Pensions regain faith in hedge funds

Sam Jones and Kate Burgess

The number of pension schemes looking to invest money with hedge funds doubled during 2009, according to a leading investment consultancies. Hewitt Associates has seen inquiries from clients to increase sharply as pension fund trustees scrabble to find high-performing investment strategies to help recoup losses suffered in 2008.

"A lot of institutional investors have got over the emotional block that hedge funds are risky products that they should be scared of. Clients are much more comfortable with the asset class," Guy Saintfiet, a senior hedge fund researcher at Hewitt told the Financial Times.

Other consultants – which play a crucial role as intermediaries in guiding pension funds' investments – also report a change in attitudes towards hedge funds. According to Damien Loveday, a senior investment consultant at Towers Watson, pension fund trustees had become more sophisticated. Most UK schemes were now looking to allocate up to 15 per cent of their portfolio to hedge funds, Mr Loveday said.

Pension fund managers are also looking to make allocations directly to hedge fund managers. In the past, institutional investors have preferred exposure via a fund of funds, which pools money and makes diversified investments.

Several of the largest pension funds have already indicated that they are looking to make significant direct allocations to hedge fund managers. The £28bn University Superannuation Scheme – the UK's second largest pension plan – said last Tuesday it expected to invest with as many as 30 managers during the next two years. Its investments will add up to £1.4bn.

In the US, CalPERS, the world's largest pension scheme, said in its end-of-year statement that it had conducted due diligence on 66 hedge funds. Like many of its peers, it has yet to make any investment.

Source: Financial Times, 1 February 2010, p. 4. Reprinted with permission.

BTPS is administered by a board of 11 trustee directors who are jointly responsible for the administration of the scheme. Many of the investment decisions are taken by in-house managers, but a large proportion of the money is placed with outside managers who charge a fee (say, 0.5 per cent of funds under management per year) to invest, e.g. Legal and General Investment Management (LGIM), M&G Asset Management and Blackrock. The managers are answerable to the trustees.

BTPS had a deficit of £7.598 million at the end of 2009 and BT, the operating company, was planning to pay additional contributions into the scheme over the next few years to reduce the deficit. The fact that it has a deficit already is going to be compounded by the way in which the number of pension recipients has grown much larger than the number of contributing members still in work – *see* **Exhibit 4.21**. The drawbacks of a DB scheme that did not collect enough from its workers or the company in decades gone by are clearly shown, as it is simply not possible for current contributions to satisfy historic liabilities, hence the deficit, exacerbated by the financial recession. Many other companies' DB pension funds are in a similar position to BTPS.

BTPS has adjusted its investments to try to improve the asset return. **Exhibit 4.22** shows the 14 largest investments held directly by the scheme at the end of 2009 expressed as a percentage of the total investment assets of the scheme.

Exhibit 4.21   BTPS pension membership 2001, 2005 and 2009

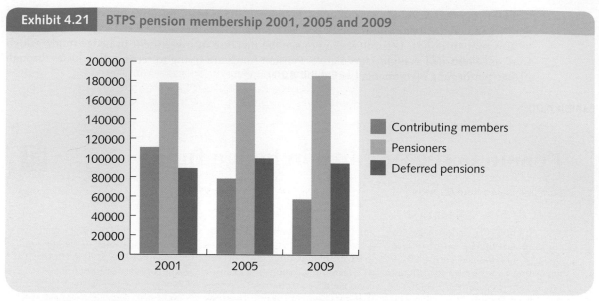

Source: BTPS Annual Reports.

Exhibit 4.22   4.22 BTPS 14 largest investments (2009)

Investment	Asset class	Market value £m	% of total investment assets
LGIM UK Equity Index	Pooled investment vehicles	2,506	7.4
LGIM Europe Large Cap Equity Index	Pooled investment vehicles	1,358	4.0
LGIM North America Equity Index	Pooled investment vehicles	1,297	3.8
LGIM Japan Equity Index	Pooled investment vehicles	981	2.9
UK Treasury 2.5% Index Linked 2020	Index linked	658	1.9
UK Treasury 2.5% Index Linked 2024	Index linked	650	1.9
LGIM Asia Pacific Equity Index	Pooled investment vehicles	575	1.7
UK Treasury 2.5% Index Linked 2016	Index linked	528	1.5
European Equity Managed Fund	Pooled investment vehicles	473	1.4
UK Treasury 1.875% Index Linked 2022	Index linked	334	1.0
UK Treasury 1.25% Index Linked 2027	Index linked	321	0.9
UK Treasury 4.125% Index Linked 2030	Index linked	286	0.8
UK Treasury 1.25% Index Linked 2032	Index linked	275	0.8
Milton Keynes Shopping Centre	Property	264	0.8
Total Fund		12,752	37.4

Source: BTPS Annual Report 2009.

Regulations

In the UK, the **Pensions Regulator** is empowered by the government to regulate work-based pension schemes and has wide-ranging powers to enforce its decisions. Its aim is to protect members' benefits and encourage high standards in running pension schemes. It has powers to compel companies to inject additional money into their pension schemes and to remove trustees should a conflict of interest get in the way of them acting solely for the pension fund members. The regulator also tries to limit the claims made by failed schemes on the Pension Protection Fund (see below). **Exhibit 4.23** describes some of the cases the regulator has dealt with.

In the US, the Department of Labor's Employee Benefits Security Administration (EBSA) and Employee Retirement Income Security Act of 1974 (ERISA) are responsible for overseeing retirement (pension) plans and have established minimum standards for them.

Exhibit 4.23

Regulator takes aim as recession hits pensions

FT

Norma Cohen

Britain's Pensions Regulator will appear tomorrow in a courtroom in Canada, defending its efforts to lay claim to a portion of the assets of Nortel, the telecoms equipment manufacturer that sought protection from creditors last year.

Nortel's UK pension scheme had a shortfall of roughly £1.2bn, and the regulator hopes its claim will help fill the gap.

Such an appearance is unusual for the regulator, which has traditionally kept a low profile.

But in recent months that has changed as the recession, and the resulting increase in deficits, has pushed its caseload up and forced its work into the open as it takes on FTSE 100 stalwarts and multinationals.

The action against Nortel comes just one week after Readers Digest Association announced it would place its UK subsidiary into administration because the regulator failed to grant it immunity from claims for a £125m shortfall in its scheme that would only be partly filled through a corporate restructuring.

The regulator has also been at loggerheads with trustees and executives at BT and British Airways, sponsors of two of the UK's largest schemes, over how they calculate the size of their liabilities. The calculation could have a significant impact on how much cash each employer needs to add to its retirement plan every year.

The moves are at odds with the public stance the regulator has taken in the near five-year period since it opened its doors, in which it presents itself as a facilitator in resolving disputes rather than a participant in them.

David Norgrove, chairman, has said the body's role is to be "a referee, not a judge".

Moreover, he has said that the regulator prefers to threaten to use its powers – such as compelling companies to stump up cash for their scheme or removing trustees whose conflicts of interest are too deep – rather than actually use them. The Pensions Act forbids it from disclosing disputes with companies until formal proceedings begin, leaving much of its work a mystery to the specialists who advise companies and trustees.

But as the financial crisis has deepened and corporate finances have become more strained, the regulator appears to be using its powers more frequently. Indeed, by its own count, it exercised its powers almost as much in the six months to September 30 as in the full year to last March.

Pensions advisers note that the regulator's role is twofold. First, it must protect benefits promised to workers. It does this by ensuring that companies fund their shortfalls over reasonable time frames, with weaker companies urged to fill deficits rapidly.

Second, it must try to limit claims on the Pension Protection Fund, the employer-financed insurance scheme for under-funded plans of insolvent companies.

In light of that dual responsibility, the regulator is taking a tougher line when companies are at higher risk of insolvency.

John Ralfe, an independent pensions adviser, said that few of its efforts are transparent, by law.

Mr Ralfe argues that the regulator could shed more light on its stance by making decisions public, say, a year or two after the dispute occurred. That way, advisers would know more about where the limits are.

But Bob Scott, partner at actuarial consultants Lane Clark & Peacock, said making such decisions public might encourage companies to fund to the minimum they thought the regulator would allow. "Every time the regulator sets a standard, everyone gravitates towards it," he said.

Gary Squires, head of pensions at Zolfo Cooper, a corporate advisory service, said that some of what appears to be a tougher stance is simply the regulator learning about actions that may have been "close to the wind" when they were set a few years earlier but that were not disclosed.

He noted that some employers undertook corporate restructuring that may harm the scheme without asking the regulator's view. "There are companies that find it easier to say 'sorry' than to say 'please'." The regulator is simply trying to make amends.

Source: Financial Times, 24 February 2010, p. 13. Reprinted with permission.

In 2003, the EU issued a Pension Funds Directive with the aim of ensuring a high level of protection for members and beneficiaries of pension funds, and also allowing and encouraging cross-border management of pension schemes. This last aim has found difficulties because of the divergence in each country's fiscal laws and regulations.

In the past, pension funds have been subject to plenty in the way of guidelines and advice, but little in the way of compulsory regulation. However, over the past decade various organisations and governments around the world have introduced regulations aimed at avoiding the reccurrence of pensions fund failures and providing compensation if these failures happen.

Some experts think that pension schemes should be subject to the same stringent rules about solvency that will be applied by the EU to insurance companies by 2012, but that does not solve the problem of present deficits.

Pension protection schemes

In the UK, the Pension Protection Fund (PPF) was established in 2005 to compensate members of DB funds should their company fail and be liquidated, leaving insufficient assets in the pension scheme to cover its pension liabilities. If the scheme has to or will have to pay out more than the contributions put in, then the scheme can be in deficit and be unable to meet its pension liabilities. The PPF pays out up to 90 per cent of what has been promised, up to a maximum of £29,897.42 a year. The cash to finance the PPF comes from a levy imposed on all eligible pension funds.

DC scheme members lose out if fraud or theft occurs and may then be eligible for compensation from the PPF, but they cannot claim compensation for shortfalls in the fund. Their contributions are invested with the hope that they will provide an adequate pension, so although the eventual pension will vary according to the ability (and luck!) of the pension fund managers, their individual fund cannot be in deficit other than through fraud or theft.

Institutional Shareholder Committee

The Institutional Shareholder Committee, founded in 1991, sets out the principles of behaviour for institutional shareholders (such as managers of pension and insurance funds, investment trusts, etc.). It also set standards of behaviour it expects from corporations in which its members hold shares and other securities. The members of the committee are the *Association of British Insurers* (the trade association for the 300 or so British Insurance Companies), the *Association of Investment Companies* (the trade association for the closed-ended investment company industry – *see* later in the chapter), the *Investment Management Association* (representing the UK investment management industry) and the *National Association of Pension Funds* (representing the interests of occupational pension schemes).

In the case of pension funds, it advises that institutional shareholders' primary duty is to the beneficiaries of a pension scheme. It regularly updates its code and encourages managers to behave more like owners and to take an intelligent interest in their investments. If fund managers think that companies such as BP or Shell are not being run properly, they have a duty to intervene rather than sitting quietly and watching as a crisis happens, a duty particularly relevant after the financial recession and company failures of 2008–2009.

The four trade associations listed above keep an eye on corporate management and make recommendations on how institutional investors should vote on issues such as the size of directors' pay. These tend to be widely supported by institutions and often result in the target company changing its decision.

Collective investment

The idea of collective investment (pooled funds) has been around since about 1800. Its concept is simple: money from a group of people is gathered together and put into a range of investments. This reduces the risk of total loss for all contributors by enabling them to invest in a far wider range of investments than they could individually.

Worldwide, collective investments are responsible for vast amounts of funds (*see* **Exhibit 4.24**). According to the Investment Company Institute, the total worldwide assets amount to an astonishing $23 trillion administered by 65,735 funds. About half of these assets and funds are in the US. The UK has more than 2,000 funds responsible for £449,500 million.

Exhibit 4.24	Worldwide mutual (collective) fund assets in millions of dollars

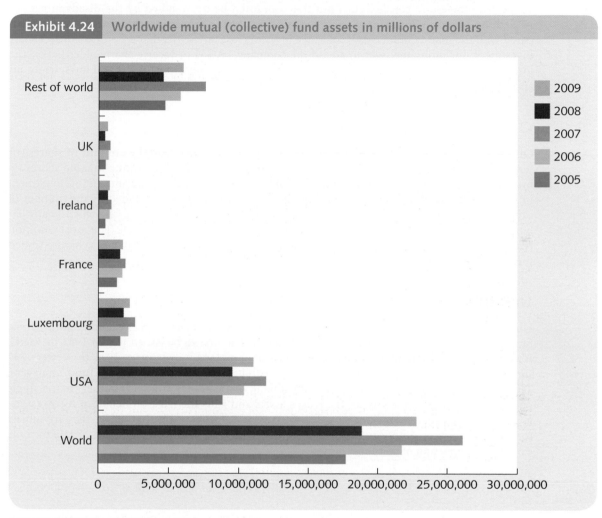

Source: Investment Company Institute, www.ici.org

Collective investment offers some significant advantages to the investor.

● First, a more diverse portfolio can be created. Investors with a relatively small sum to invest, say £3,000, would find it difficult to obtain a broad spread of investments without incurring high transaction costs. If, however, 10,000 people each put £3,000 into a fund there would be £30 million available to invest in a wide range of securities. A large fund like this can buy in large quantities, say £100,000 at a time, thus reducing dealing and administrative costs per pound invested.

● Second, even very small investors can take part in the stock markets and other financial markets. It is possible to gain exposure to the equity, bond or other markets by collective investing for a small amount, e.g. £30 per month.

● Third, professional management removes the demanding tasks of analysing and selecting shares and other securities, going into the marketplace to buy, collecting dividends, etc., by handing over the whole process to professional fund managers.

- Finally, investment can be made into exotic and far-flung markets, South American companies, US hi-tech, Chinese technology, etc. without the risk and the complexities of buying shares direct. Collective funds run by managers familiar with the relevant country or sector can be a good alternative to going it alone.

These advantages are considerable, but they can often be outweighed by the disadvantages of pooled funds, which include high fund-management costs and possible underperformance compared with the market index. Also, collective investors lose any rights that accompany direct share investment, including the right to attend the company's AGM or receive shareholder perks, and lose the fun of selecting their own shares with the attendant emotional highs and lows, triumphs and lessons in humility.

Open-ended investment vehicles

OEIVs are a type of collective fund that does not have restrictions on the amount of shares (or 'units') the fund will issue. If demand is high enough, the fund will continue to issue shares no matter how many investors there are; the size of the fund is dictated by the amount of investment in it. The value of each share is dictated by the net asset value (NAV) divided by the number of existing shares. The NAV is defined as the total value of assets at current market value less any liabilities. Open-ended funds must buy back shares when investors wish to sell. The most common types of OEIVs are unit trusts, open-ended investment companies (OEICs), exchange-traded funds (ETFs) and mutual funds.

Unit trusts

Unit trusts are issued in Australia, Ireland, the Isle of Man, Jersey, New Zealand, South Africa, Singapore and the UK, and sold in units not shares. The first to be issued was in 1931 by M&G. According to the Investment Management Association (IMA), in January 2011 there were 737 funds in the UK managing £220.8 billion – *see* **Exhibit 4.25** for the ten largest fund managers. They are administered by a trustee (usually a bank or insurance company rather than a single person) who is the legal owner of the trust's assets and runs the trust on behalf of its investors, appointing managers and making sure that the trust is run responsibly. In the UK, they are subject to Financial Services Authority (Financial Conduct Authority) regulations, which dictate to some extent the proportion of holdings allowed.

Exhibit 4.25	The managed assets of the ten largest fund providers in the UK	£ billion
1	Fidelity Investments	22.40
2	Threadneedle Investments	12.53
3	Scottish Widows Unit Trusts Managers	11.98
4	Invesco Perpetual	11.70
5	Legal & General Unit Trust Managers Ltd	10.89
6	M&G Group	9.29
7	Schroder Investments Ltd	9.25
8	Halifax Investment Fund Managers Ltd	8.44
9	Gartmore Investment Management Plc	6.61
10	SLTM	6.00

Source: www. incademy.com

The value of the units is determined by the market valuation of the securities owned by the fund. So if, for example, the fund collected together £1 million from hundreds of small investors and issued 1 million units in return, each unit would be worth £1. If the fund managers over the next year invest the pooled fund in shares which increase in value to £1.5 million the value of each unit rises to £1.50.

Unit holders sell units back to the managers of the unit trust if they want to liquidate their holding (turn it into cash). The manager would then either sell the units to other investors or, if that is not possible because of low demand, sell some of the underlying investments to raise cash to redeem the units. Thus, the number of units can change daily, or at least every few days. There is no secondary market trading in unit trusts as all transactions are carried out through the trust managers.

Pricing

The pricing of unit trusts is divided into two parts, the bid price and the offer price. The offer price, the price a new investor has to pay, is calculated by valuing the investments underlying the fund once a day using a method prescribed by the Financial Services Authority (FSA).[10] The bid price, the price a seller receives, is usually set 5–6 per cent below the offer price (for funds invested in shares). The difference between the bid and offer prices is called the spread and pays for two things: first, fund administration, management of the investments, marketing, as well as commission for selling the units; second, the market makers' spreads and brokers' commissions payable by the fund when it buys and sells shares.[11]

Most unit trusts are now priced on a forward basis, which means that the price paid by a buyer of units will be fixed at a future time (often 12 noon) so a buyer may not know the exact price at the time that they send a buy order. Some funds still charge the *historic* price, taking the value from the last valuation.[12]

Quite a high proportion of the initial charge in the bid–offer spread (maybe 4–5 per cent) is commission payable to financial advisers, who recommend investment to individuals. *Fund supermarkets*[13] frequently give a discount on the initial charge. Thus, we have the slightly odd situation where going directly to the fund manager to buy units will result in being charged the full initial fee, whereas buying through an agent may cost 4–5 per cent less.[14]

Charges

There are three charges:

1 Initial charge ('sales' or 'front-end' charge). This is included in the spread between the bid and offer prices. So if the fund has a spread of 6 per cent, it might allocate 5 per cent as an initial charge. Some unit trusts have dropped initial charges to zero – particularly those investing in interest-bearing securities (bonds, etc.) and **tracker funds** (those that do not try to spot shares that will outperform the market, but merely invest in a broad range representative of a stock market index – also called **passive funds**).

2 Annual charges. The annual management fee is typically 1–1.8 per cent. A further charge of about 0.2 per cent covers legal, custody, audit and other administration costs. Over time the annual fees have a larger effect in reducing the value of the investment than the initial charge. Typically, about one-third of the annual fee is paid to the financial adviser who recommended the fund.

3 Exit charges. Some funds make an exit charge instead of an initial charge if the units are sold within, say, the first five years.

---

[10] The market price of the investments currently held plus dealing costs, management expenses and other charges is divided by the number of units in issue to give the maximum offer price that the trust can charge.

[11] Recently unit trusts have been given the option of single pricing, with charges shown separately. Most still have a bid–offer spread.

[12] Some use a mix of historic and forward pricing.

[13] Online or offline organisations that allow investors to invest in a range of unit trusts, investment trusts and OEICs. Investors can select one, two or a dozen funds from different management companies.

[14] The broker, financial adviser or fund supermarket will usually receive 'trail commission' annually (say, 0.5 per cent of the value of your fund holding) for as long as you hold it.

Reading the Financial Times

The *Financial Times* publishes unit trust bid and offer prices every day. An example is shown in **Exhibit 4.26**. The list for Schroders displays both unit trusts and OEICs (discussed below). OEICs have a single price.

Exhibit 4.26 Unit trust prices in the *Financial Times*

FINANCIAL TIMES FRIDAY MARCH 4 2011

Schroders

FT

Schroders   **(UK)**
31 Gresham Street, London EC2V 7QA
Investor Services 0800 718777   Dealing 0800 718788
www.schroder.co.uk
www.ft.com/funds/schroders
Authorised Inv Funds

	Init Notes Chrge	Selling Price	Buying Price	+ or −	Yield
All Maturities Corporate Bond A Inc ♦ 0		55.1		−0.1	5.5
All Maturities Corporate Bond A Acc ♦...0		59.49		−0.12	5.5
All Maturities Corp Bond 1 Acc (Gross) ♦.0 C		179.3		−0.3	5.5
Asian Alpha Plus A Inc ♦.0		69.19		+0.71	0.3
Asian Alpha Plus A Acc ♦ 0		70.29		+0.71	0.3
Asian Income A Inc ♦ 5$^1/_4$		191.1xd	202.9	+1.8	4.7
Asian Income A Acc ♦..5$^1_4$		238.1xd	252.8	+2.1	4.4
Asian Income Maximiser A Inc ♦...0		53.32		+0.47	7.5
Asian Income Maximiser A Acc ♦.0		55.57		+0.49	7.5
Corporate Bond A Inc ♦ 3$^1/_4$		42.48xd	44.36	−0.01	6.1
Corporate Bond A Acc ♦.3$^1/_4$		77.42xd	80.85	−0.01	6.0
Diversified Target Return A Inc ♦..0		54.66		+0.13	0.1
Diversified Target Return A Acc ♦.0		54.88		+0.13	0.1
Diversified Target Return D1 Inc ♦ 0		56.57		+0.14	0.6
Diversified Target Return D1 Acc ♦..0		57.21		+0.14	0.6
European A Inc ♦....5$^1_4$		209.5	221.3	+2.8	0.9
European A Acc ♦....5$^1_4$		247.2	261.1	+3.3	0.9
Euro Alpha Plus A Inc ♦.5$^1_4$		114.1	120.5	+1.9	0.7
Euro Alpha Plus A Acc ♦.5$^1_4$		119.8	126.6	+2	0.6
Euro Smaller Cos A Inc ♦ 5$^1_4$		361.5	383.9	+4.3	0.3
Euro Smaller Cos A Acc ♦..5$^1_4$		380.8	404.4	+4	0.3
Gilt & Fixed Interest A Inc ♦..5$^1_4$ C		56.22xd	59.24	−0.18	4.3
Gilt & Fixed Interest A Acc ♦.5$^1_4$		161.3xd	170	−0.6	4.2
Global Alpha Plus A Inc ♦ 0		54.02		+0.71	0.0
Global Alpha Plus A Acc ♦..0		54.01		+0.71	0.0
Global Climate Change A Inc ♦ 0		58.09xd		+0.39	0.2
		58.07xd		+0.4	0.1

Management company details

Initial charge expressed as a percentage of the amount put into units. "C" indicates a periodic management charge deducted from capital. "E" denotes that an exit charge may be made when investor sells

Selling (bid) and buying (offer) prices expressed in pence. "xd" means ex dividend (a purchaser now would not receive the last announced dividend)

Single price – the buying and selling prices for shares of an OEIC are the same. The price is based on a mid-market valuation of the underlying investments. Managers'/operators' initial charges are shown separately

Price change on previously quoted figure (not all funds update prices daily)

Yield is the income paid by the unit trust in the last 12 months as a percentage of the offer price (after tax for shares, gross for bonds). The yield figures allow for buying expenses

Information about the timing of price quotes/valuation
♦ 1101–1400
▲ 1401–1700
\# 1701–midnight
✠ 0001–1100

Source: Financial Times Friday March 4 2011 (fund prices are also available at www.ft.com/funds. Also Monday's FT includes a supplement, FTFM, carrying extra details).

Buying and selling units

Units can be bought direct from the unit trust management company by filling out an application form. Alternatively, they can be bought through a financial adviser, discount broker or fund supermarket. Because of the uncertainty about the exact purchase price, it is possible to set a *limit* on the price when buying. When it comes to selling all or some units, they can be sold back to the management company, which is obliged to purchase. Payment will be made within five days.

Who looks after the unit holders' interests?

There are four levels of protection for the unit holder:

- *The trustee* These organisations, usually banks or insurance companies, keep an eye on the fund managers to make sure they abide by the terms of the trust deed – for example, sticking to the stated investment objectives, e.g. investing in Japanese shares. Importantly, the trustee holds all the assets of the fund in their name on the unit holder's behalf, so if anything untoward happens to the fund manager the funds are safeguarded. The trustee also oversees the unit price calculation and ensures that the FSA/FCA regulations are obeyed.
- *The FSA (FCA)* Only funds authorised by the FSA/FCA are allowed to advertise in the UK. Unauthorised unit trusts, most of which are established offshore (outside the jurisdiction of the FSA/FCA), are available, but they may carry more risk by virtue of their unregulated status.
- *The ombudsman* Complaints that have not been satisfactorily settled by the management company can be referred to the Financial Ombudsman – *see* Chapter 15.
- *The Financial Services Compensation Scheme* Up to £50,000 is available for a valid claim – for example, when an FSA/FCA-authorised fund becomes insolvent or suffers from poor investment management (*see* Chapter 15 for more on this).

Types of trust available

Unit trusts in the UK offer a wide range of investment choice. UK All Companies funds invest at least 80 per cent of their assets in UK shares. Some funds focus investment in shares paying high dividends (UK Equity Income), others split the funds between equity and bonds (UK Equity and Bond Income), while some invest mostly in government bonds or corporate bonds. Some place the bulk of their money in smaller companies, some in Far East shares. A few trusts invest in commercial property. The possibilities are endless – *see* www.investmentuk.org for a definition of dozens of classes of funds.

Returns

The return on a unit trust consists of two elements: first, income is gained on the underlying investments in the form of interest or dividends; second, the prices of the securities held could rise over time. Some unit trusts pay out all income, after deducting management charges, etc., on set dates (usually twice a year)[15] in cash. **Accumulation units** reinvest the income on behalf of the unit holders and as a result the price of accumulation units tends to rise more rapidly than income units. The *Financial Times* shows listings for prices of **income ('Inc') units** (also called **distribution units**) and accumulation ('Acc') units.

Minimum investment

Some trusts ask for an initial minimum investment of only £250 or so, whereas others insist on at least £1,500. Thereafter, under a savings plan, it may be possible to put in as little as £25. It is often possible to use shares instead of cash as payment for units through a share exchange scheme.

Following the units' progress

A manager's report will be sent every six months detailing the performance of the fund over the half year, the events in the market(s) in which the fund invests, and explaining the

---

[15] Some trusts pay out quarterly or monthly.

manager's investment strategy. It will also comment on future prospects, list the securities held by the fund and display the fund's financial accounts. At least once a year a *statement* is sent showing the number of units held and the latest prices.

The most obvious place to track units is in newspapers such as the *Financial Times*. *Money Management* magazine tracks fund performance over periods of one, two, three, and five years. Many websites, such as fund supermarket websites, carry details of units, e.g. www.citywire.co.uk.

Open-ended investment company

OEICs (pronounced 'oiks') have been around since May 1997 and were introduced as a more flexible and simpler alternative to existing unit trusts. Many unit trusts have turned themselves into OEICs. An OEIC is a company which can be listed on the stock exchange and it issues shares whereas a trust issues units. It is an open-ended diversified collective investment vehicle. OEICs are regulated in a similar way to unit trusts, so investor protection is much the same. Investment in OEICs may be made on a regular basis, or as a lump sum. **Exhibit 4.27** shows the largest OEIC management companies and the total amount invested in their different OEICs.

OEICs have an **authorised corporate director (ACD)** managing the fund and a depositary (usually a large bank) supervising activities to safeguard their assets. The ACD's remit is to invest shareholders' funds in accordance with the fund's objectives. In January 2011, there were 1,672 OEICs in the UK.

Exhibit 4.27	The 20 largest OEIC funds, January 2011

Company	Total OEIC funds under management
Invesco Perpetual	£36,916,825,878
M & G Securities Limited	£27,479,052,205
FIL Investment Management Limited	£23,273,227,135
Threadneedle Investment Services Ltd	£19,557,757,801
Jupiter Unit Trust Managers Limited	£18,457,756,133
Legal & General (Unit Trust) Managers Limited	£18,276,625,165
HBOS Investment Fund Managers Limited	£16,144,077,702
SWIP Fund Management Ltd	£15,435,021,038
Schroder Investment Management Ltd	£14,056,537,098
BlackRock Investment Management (UK) Limited	£13,176,086,674
Capita Financial Managers Limited	£13,129,882,797
First State Investments (UK) Ltd	£11,711,290,564
Henderson Global Investors	£10,990,951,221
St James's Place Unit Trust Group Ltd	£9,812,266,813
BNY Mellon Fund Managers Limited	£9,783,645,249
JP Morgan Asset Management	£9,063,609,405
Investec Asset Management Ltd	£9,057,936,535
Aviva Investors UK Fund Services Limited	£8,576,575,168
Aberdeen Unit Trust Managers Limited	£8,535,431,787
Artemis Fund Managers Ltd	£8,387,985,486

Source: www.investmentuk.org

Compared with unit trusts, OEICs have a simpler pricing system because there is one price for both buyers and sellers. Charges and dealing commissions are shown separately, which makes them more transparent than unit trusts. Some OEICs charge an exit fee. When OEICs are bought or sold, the share price is the value of all the underlying investments (NAV) divided by the number of shares in issue. The price is not based on the supply and demand for its shares (as with investment trusts – see later) and is calculated daily, usually at 12 noon in London.

As an open-ended instrument the fund gets bigger and more shares are created as more people invest. The fund shrinks and shares are cancelled as people withdraw their money.

The OEIC may be a stand-alone fund or may have an 'umbrella' structure, which means that it contains a number of sub-funds, each with a different investment objective, e.g. income or growth. Sub-funds may focus on differing equities, US shares, UK shares, etc. Each sub-fund could have different investors and asset pools. Similarly to unit trusts, OEICs offer income or accumulation shares; income shares offer regular income to investors as the OEIC collects dividends, etc. from investments, while accumulation shares reinvest the income into more shares, so the shareholding increases.

Exchange-traded funds

First introduced in the US in 1990, exchange-traded funds take the idea of tracking a stock market index or sector a stage further. ETFs are set up as companies issuing shares and the money raised is used to buy a range of securities, such as a collection of shares in a particular stock market index or sector, say the FTSE 100 or pharmaceutical shares. Thus, if BP comprises 8 per cent of the total value of the FTSE 100 and the ETF has £100 million to invest, it will buy £8 million of BP shares; if Whitbread is 0.15 per cent of the FTSE 100, the ETF buys £150,000 of Whitbread shares. (Alternatively, many ETFs do not buy the actual shares but gain exposure to the share returns by the purchase of derivatives of the shares.)

They are open-ended funds – the ETF shares are created and cancelled as demand rises or falls. However, they differ from unit trusts and OEICs in that the pricing of ETF shares is left up to the marketplace. ETFs are quoted companies and you can buy and sell their shares at prices subject to change throughout the day (unlike unit trusts and OEICs, where prices are set by a formula once a day). Globally, there are over 2,700 different ETFs listed on more than 40 exchanges with a total value over $1,400 billion. In the US alone over 800 ETFs are traded on the stock markets. They have become so significant there that around 30 per cent of New York Stock Exchange trading is in ETFs.

Despite an ETF's price being set by trading in the stock market they tend to trade at, or near to, the underlying net asset value – the value of the shares in the FTSE 100, for instance. This is different from investment trusts, which frequently trade significantly below net asset value.

With traditional ETFs, newly created ETF shares ('creation units') are delivered to market makers[16] ('authorised participants') in exchange for an entire portfolio of shares matching the index (not for cash). The underlying shares are held by the fund manager, while the new ETF shares are traded by the market maker in the secondary market. To redeem ETF shares the ETF manager delivers underlying shares to the market maker in exchange for ETF shares. ETF managers create new ETF shares only for market makers with at least £1 million to invest, so private investors are excluded at this level. However, private investors can trade in existing ETF shares in the secondary market.

If the price of an ETF share rises above the value of the underlying shares, there will be an arbitrage opportunity for the market maker. Arbitrage means the possibility of simultaneously buying and selling the same or similar securities in two markets and making a risk-free gain, for example buying bananas for £1 in one market and selling them for £1.05 (after costs) in another. In this case the ETF share representing, say, the top 100 UK shares is trading above the price of the 100 shares when sold separately. Market makers, spotting this opportunity, will swap the underlying basket of shares for a **creation unit of ETF shares**, thus realising a profit by then selling the ETF shares into the market. Then the new supply of ETF shares will satisfy the excess demand and ETF prices should fall until they are in line with the underlying NAV.

---

[16] As well as market makers, other institutions receive them.

If the ETF share price falls below the underlying shares' value the market maker will exploit this by having the ETF share redeemed by the ETF manager. The market maker ends up with the more valuable underlying shares and the supply of ETFs in the marketplace has fallen, bringing the price back up to the NAV. The advantage arising from market makers and ETF managers not handing over cash, but instead swapping ETF shares and underlying shares, is that there are no brokerage costs for buying and selling shares. This makes transactions cheap.

Spreads – the difference between market makers' buying and selling prices of ETFs – are generally around 0.05–0.3 per cent (although spreads can widen to 10 per cent or more at times of extreme volatility, for example after 11 September 2001). While there is no initial charge with ETFs, annual management charges range between 0.2 per cent and 0.75 per cent but are typically between 0.3 per cent and 0.5 per cent (these are deducted from dividends). All in all, ETFs are a cheaper way of benefiting from a rising market than unit or investment trusts.

Private investors can purchase ETFs from brokers. Their minimum charge is between £10 and £40 per trade and no stamp duty is payable on purchase (in the UK a stamp duty tax is payable when investors buy shares and other securities). Prices are shown in the Managed Funds section in the *Financial Times* – see **Exhibit 4.28**. The *Financial Times* shows ETFs that track the US market (e.g. MSCI USA index), European shares (e.g. DJEurSTX 50), the UK market (e.g. FTSE 100) and dozens of other markets, from Japanese shares to government bonds. ETFs pay dividends in line with the underlying constituent shares or other income such as interest on bonds, quarterly or semi-annually. This is reflected in the yield (yld) column. Useful websites for ETF investors are iShares (www.ishares.com) and Trustnet (www.trustnet.com/etf).

We have moved a long way from the simple traditional equity ETFs of the 1990s. Nowadays the ETF manager may not purchase all the shares in the index but merely a sample. This is useful for

Exhibit 4.28 Exchange-traded fund price in the *Financial Times*

Exchange Traded Funds   **FT**

	Notes	Price	Chng	52 week High	Low	Yld	Nav	Vol '000s
UBS								
DJEurSTX50A€.......		£23.32	–0.03	£27.71	£20.24	3.5	–	21
DJEurSTX50I€........		£23342.78	–37.04	£27,625.71	£20,895.79	3.8	–	0
FTSE 100SFr..........		£50.82	–0.42	£56.62	£40.59	3.6	–	6
MSCI Can AC$.......		£19.25	–0.04	£20.99	£15.99	0.4	–	1
MSCI EMU€..........		£72.06	–0.23	£84.10	£60.96	2.8	–	37
MSCI EMU VA€.....		£29.37	–0.12	£34.87	£26.53	0.2	–	2
MSCI Eurp A€........		£37.86	+0.06	£41.60	£31.14	0.3	–	5
MSCI Eurp I€.........		£36429.58	–57.81	£41,017.75	£35,336.46	0.4	–	–
MSCI Japan SFr......		£20	+0.04	£21.95	£17.27	1.5	–	28
MSCI Pex Jp$.........		£23.99	–0.10	£27.43	£22.10	0.5	–	3
MSCI USASFr.........		£68.54	–0.17	£75.42	£51.72	1.2	–	1
MSCI USA1$..........		£67312.98	–425.98	£75,868.37	£60,130.02	0.3	–	–
MCSI World SFr.....		£73.61	–0.46	£81.30	£57.69	1.4	–	0

Net asset values and splits analytics supplied by Fundamental Data Ltd as a guide only (www.funddata.com).
See guide to Financial Times Share Service.

Source: Adapted from *Financial Times*, Thursday, July 15 2010. Reprinted with permission.

ETFs invested in, say, Chinese or Vietnamese shares where government restrictions may prevent purchasing all the shares in an index. The exchange-traded concept has been extended beyond equities and bonds to foreign exchange rates, commodities and commodity indices (**exchange-traded commodities, ETCs**). Instead of the provider holding the underlying instrument or commodity, the investment is in swaps or other derivative instruments. The problem with derivative-based ETFs is that there is a risk that the counterparties providing the derivatives may not be able to meet their obligations and then the ETF holder may not have anything tangible backing up the ETF shares. Also, if the ETF provider does not buy the underlying securities but instead relies on derivatives and then goes bust, it could be more complicated for an investor to retrieve their investment.

Derivatives are now used for a lot of share index ETFs – 'synthetic replication' of an index. There is a debate going on in the ETF world as to whether ETFs consisting solely of derivatives are truly ETFs at all. But, regardless of some misgivings, it looks as though volume of synthetic ETFs will overtake that of traditional physical ETFs – *see* **Exhibit 4.29**.

Exhibit 4.29

ETFs 'risk causing confusion'

FT

Chris Flood

Europe's exchange traded funds industry risks creating "confusion, disappointment and disillusion" among investors, according to Deborah Fuhr, global head of ETF research at BlackRock, who said the sector had reached "an important crossroads" after a decade of rapid growth.

Warning that "products which are not even funds are being called ETFs", Ms Fuhr said the industry was at risk of moving away from the traditional virtues of transparency and ease of understanding that had attracted retail and institutional investors.

With ETF assets in Europe forecast to increase by 30 per cent this year, BlackRock said it expected more hedge fund managers to create ETFs by using their own funds as the underlying exposure.

"Hedge funds are noticing the growth and appeal of ETFs which are simple and easy to understand but have powerful distribution networks," said Ms Fuhr.

Although ETFs could provide wider access to hedge funds as an asset class, Ms Fuhr cautioned that these new products would also be

more challenging for investors to understand.

As developers work to include hedge funds, structured products and active funds within ETF wrappers, BlackRock argued this had led to the emergence of funds that did not provide transparency on their underlying portfolios, did not have real time estimates for their net asset value and did not offer daily creation and redemption of their underlying units.

The comments come as the industry this month marks the 10th anniversary of the first ETF launch in Europe, the iShares DJ Stoxx 50, which was listed on the Deutsche Börse.

As of January, assets under management across Europe's ETF industry had risen to $217.9bn across 896 funds, although retail investors only account for 10 to 15 per cent of this market, compared to 40 to 50 per cent in the US.

The emergence of swap-based ETFs since 2005 has been one of the most important developments for European investors, when the advent of Ucits III regulations allowed for wider use of derivatives.

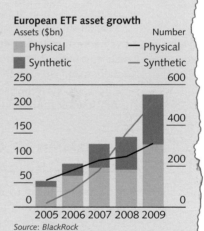

European ETF asset growth

Assets ($bn)   Number

■ Physical   — Physical
■ Synthetic   — Synthetic

Source: BlackRock

BlackRock estimated there were 515 swap-based ETFs with assets of $101.9bn at the end of 2009, compared to 314 physically based ETFs with $125bn of assets.

The first ever ETF, the Toronto 35 Index Participation Fund, was created in March 1990. "Today, there is a growing fan club who cite ETFs as one of the greatest financial innovations of the past two decades," said Ms Fuhr.

Source: Financial Times, 12 April 2010. Reprinted with permission.

Mutual funds

Sometimes the term mutual fund is used as a generic term for collective or pooled investments. However, in the US and Canada the term has the specific meaning in terms of their organisation and legal structure.

Mutual funds began in the US in Boston in 1924 and have become the major part of the US investment market. Around half the households in the US have shares in mutual funds, with over 7,600 mutual funds managing assets totalling over $10.7 trillion in 2010. They are administered by a group of directors appointed by the shareholders, who rely on them to run the fund correctly. The vast majority are open-ended funds, but there are some that are closed-ended.

Investors depend on the expertise of managers to invest and make a profit. Funds fall into three general categories of investment: capital growth, stability of capital or current income. Within these categories is a huge variety of sub-categories, with varying amounts of risk, and investors must choose the type of investment and level of risk. Investors can choose to receive dividends or have them reinvested in the fund.

Mutual funds must comply with the Investment Company Act of 1940 and various other federal rules and regulations, and are monitored by the Securities and Exchange Commission (SEC). The 1940 Act was devised to prevent the unscrupulous, reckless and sometimes fraudulent activities which had been quite common due to the lack of any regulations in the capricious times following their introduction. The Boston funds emerged unscathed through these turbulent times and were a model for future funds.

Securities belonging to the fund must be placed with a custodian (usually one of the major banks) for safekeeping. The value of each mutual share is dependent on the NAV, which in the US is calculated daily at 4pm New York time.

Mutual shares are sold to investors, and the manager of the fund, called the **portfolio manager**, buys investments according to the objective of the fund as set out in the prospectus. As with unit trusts and OEICs, investors can put in a relatively small amount of money and be part of a professionally managed and diversified portfolio.

There are various types of funds, including stock (equity) funds, bond funds, sector funds, money market funds and balanced funds (investing in a mixture of asset types).

Undertakings for Collective Investments in Transferable Securities (UCITS)

For anyone wishing to invest in funds outside their own country, problems occurred because there were no common regulations governing investment funds, and it was difficult, if not impossible, to have any degree of trust in foreign investment companies. There was also a lack of a safety net (e.g. compensation scheme from the industry or government) if the fund turned out to be fraudulently or incompetently run. To counter these problems, the 1985 UCITS directive established **'Undertakings for Collective Investments in Transferable Securities'**, introducing EU-wide rules governing collective investments which could be sold across the EU subject to local tax and marketing laws. So an investor could, with confidence, invest in French, German, Spanish, etc. funds, safe in the knowledge that the funds were subject to statutory regulations.

A subsequent directive in 2002 broadened the range of assets that harmonised funds can invest in and introduced new rules for the supervision of UCITS and a required simplified prospectus, to which firms may add extra information if they wish. The simplified prospectus is designed to be used as a universal marketing tool for UCITS throughout the EU, providing clear information about charges, costs and fund performance that can be easily understood by an average investor.

UCITS III further increased the flexibility of cross-border funds. They can now do many of the things that hedge funds can do, such as use derivatives. The types of funds that choose to go down this route are called Newcits.

Any eligible collective fund (e.g. UK unit trusts or OEICs, but not investment trusts) may apply for UCITS status, enabling them to market their fund throughout the EU.

Closed-ended investment vehicles

These are collective investment vehicles that do not create or redeem shares on a daily basis in response to increases and decreases in demand (in contrast to OEIVs, unit trusts and OEICs, etc.). They are publicly traded companies that have raised their capital through an initial public offering (IPO) and have a fixed number of shares for lengthy periods, as with any other company that issues shares. They are actively managed and often concentrate on a particular sector or industry. The value of their shares fluctuates according to market forces.

Investment trusts (investment companies)

Investment trusts were first launched in London in 1868 to invest in foreign government bonds or fixed-interest stocks. Investment trusts (companies) place the money they raise in assets such as shares, government bonds, corporate bonds and property. Unlike unit trusts, they are set up as companies (they are not trusts at all!) and are subject to company law.[17] If you wish to place your money with an investment trust you do so by buying its shares. Investment trusts are floated on the London Stock Exchange where there is an active secondary market.

An investment trust has a constitution[18] that specifies that its purpose is to invest in specific types of assets. It cannot deviate from this. So it may have been set up to invest in Korean large company shares, US biotechnology shares or whatever, and it is forbidden from switching to a different category of investment. This reassures the investor that money placed with a particular trust to invest in, say, UK large companies won't end up in, say, Russian oil shares. Of course, if you want to take the risk (and possible reward) of investing in Russian oil shares you can probably find an investment trust that specialises in these – there are, after all, over 400 investment trusts quoted in London, with total assets of £80 billion, to choose from.

As a company an investment trust will have a board of directors answerable to shareholders for the trust's actions and performance. With investment trusts being closed-end funds, the amount of money under the directors' control is fixed, which enables them to plan ahead with confidence, unconcerned that tomorrow investors may want to withdraw money from the fund. Investors cannot oblige the trust to buy the shares should they want to sell (in contrast to unit trusts and OEICs). They have to sell to another investor at a price determined by the forces of supply and demand in the secondary market. Purchases and sales are made through stockbrokers in the same way as for any other company share.

The selection of investments for the trust and the general management of the fund may be undertaken by an in-house team of investment managers who are employees of the trust (a *'self-managed'* trust) or the investment management task may be handed over to *external managers*. Most are externally managed. More than 100 investment companies are venture capital trusts (VCTs), which are given tax breaks by the UK government to encourage investment in small businesses not listed on a stock market – *see* Chapter 14.

Discounts and premiums

The biggest factor influencing the share price of an investment trust is the value of the underlying assets owned by the trust. This is expressed as a net asset value per share. In theory, the trust's share price should be pretty close to the value of the assets held, but in practice they frequently sell at a large discount to NAV – only a few sell at a premium to NAV. Discounts of 10–20 per cent are not uncommon; they have even reached 68 per cent. The main factor that drags the price below NAV is the lack of demand for the shares. Here is a typical scenario.

---

[17] Strictly speaking there are 'investment trusts', which are UK registered and managed in the UK, alongside 'offshore investment companies', which are free of some of the UK restrictions, and 'AIM investment companies', which are able to avoid the rule that they must have '25 per cent of shares in public hands' imposed on trusts.

[18] Comprising its memorandum, articles of association and the prospectus on flotation.

In year × there is great interest in, say, eastern European smaller companies so an investment trust is set up and offers its shares (say, 50m) for sale at £1 each. With the money raised, £50 million of eastern European company shares are bought by the trust. For the next year the underlying assets (all those shares in Polish companies, etc.) do no more than maintain their value of £1 per investment trust share and so NAV is constant. Nothing in the fundamentals changes, but the enthusiasm for investing in these up-and-coming nations grows among the UK investing public. Investment trust shareholders who want to sell find that they can do so in the LSE secondary market at above NAV. New buyers are willing to pay £1.08 per share – an 8 per cent premium to the NAV.

However, in the following year a worldwide recession strikes and investors head for safe havens; they pile into bonds and familiar shares at home. The NAV of the trust's shares falls to 60p as prices plummet on the eastern European stock exchanges. What is worse for the investment trust shareholders is that sentiment has become so pessimistic about eastern European companies that they can sell their shares for only 50p. They trade at a discount of 16.67 per cent to NAV (10p/60p).

Discounts may seem to present an excellent opportunity – you can buy assets worth 60p for 50p – but they can be bad for the investor if the discount increases during the time you hold the shares. As you can see from the last column in **Exhibit 4.30**, the discounts can be much larger than the example above. The *Financial Times* publishes the share prices and NAVs of investment trusts (companies) daily.

While much of the discount on a typical investment trust is due to negative sentiment, there are some rational reasons for shares selling below NAV:

- Investors may think trust managers are incompetent and likely to lose more value in the future.
- NAV is calculated after deducting the nominal (stated book) value of the debt and preference shares. In reality, the trust may have to pay back more on the debt and preference shares than this.
- Liquidating the fund incurs costs (e.g. contract cancellations, advisers' fees, stockbrokers' fees) so NAV is not achieved.

Costs

When buying (or selling) investment trust shares, commission will be payable to the stockbroker[19] as usual when buying shares (usually £20–40 for purchases of a few thousand pounds). The trust managers' costs for managing the investments and for administration are charged to the fund, either against annual income or against capital. A typical **total expense ratio (TER)**, including the costs of investment management and administration, directors' fees, audit fees and share registration expenses, is between 1.5 per cent and 1.8 per cent of the fund value (but this excludes performance fees that managers often take). Some voices are saying that investment trusts are not being organised for the benefit of investors as much as they should be – *see* **Exhibit 4.31**.

Borrowing

Investment trusts have the freedom to borrow (unlike unit trusts or OEICs). Borrowing to buy assets is fine if the return on assets over time exceeds the interest charged. However, it is a double-edged sword. The risk associated with gearing up returns becomes all too apparent when asset values fall. Take the case of our trust investing in eastern Europe. If it had sold 50 million shares at £1 each and also borrowed £50 million to buy £100 million of eastern European shares, the NAV would still start at £1 per share (£100 million of assets minus £50 million debt owed, for 50 million shares). If underlying asset values fall by 40 per cent because of the fall in the Warsaw Stock

---

[19] Investment trusts are also sold through financial advisers. The trust may have a savings scheme allowing the investor to buy a few shares each month (starting from as little as £30 per month) or make a lump sum purchase.

Exhibit 4.30

FINANCIAL TIMES FRIDAY MARCH 4 2011

Investment Companies

Notes	Price	Chng	52 week High	Low	Yld	Nav	Dis or Pm(-)
Conventional (Ex Private Equity)							
3i Infra .... †	120.20	+0.30	125.30	104	4.6	112	−7.3
Abf Gd Inc	106.25	–	109	95.50	1.9	111.3	4.5
AbnAsianin †	156.25	+1.88	175	136.25	3.8	157.7	0.9
Wts	37.75	−0.25	51	27.50	–	–	–
AbnAllAsia	301.50	+1	326.25	205.10	0.5	344	12.4
AbnAsian	565	+6.75	670	382	1.5	611.7	7.6
AbnLatAmin	105.75	+1	113	103	0.9	103.1	−2.6
Sub	13.50	–	22.5	12.25	–	–	–
AbnNewDn	819.50	+3.50	940	657.50	1.2	895.1	8.4
AbnNewThai	243.50		−288.50	171.50	2.1293.9		17.2
Sub	54.25	–	87.25	17	–	–	–
AbfSml	664	+3	699.50	490	2.9	764.6	13.2
AbsoluteRet	117.25	+0.38	123.50	110	–	137.5	14.7
AcenciADbt ...	84	–	86.25	70.25	–	100.5	16.4
Acorn	176.75	–	178.50	108	3.2	209.6	15.7
ActiveCap	18.50	–	22.50	13.37	–	24.6	24.8
AdvDvpMk	464	+2.75	515.50	388	–	511.1	9.2
Albany	297	–	288	240	3.5	345.4	16.9
Alliance	362.90	+5.70	381	292.80	2.2422.2		17.9
AltAstsOps	58.20	+2	68.50	44.50	–	80.5	27.4
AltInvStrat	111.25	–	114	99.50	-	130.7	14.9
Altin $	£32.40	+0.43	£34.17	£28.77	−£43.6	25.7	
Anglo&Ovs †	110xd	–	116.50	85.25	2.8	117.7	6.5
Art Alpha .... †	321.25	+6.50	330	225	0.9	325.2	1.2
Sub	79	+1.13	89	50	–	–	–

Price change compared to last trading day

Highest and lowest price in the last 52 weeks

Yield is the dividend in the last 12 months as a percentage of the share price. Dividends are normally paid twice yearly

Net asset value (NAV) in pence per share. The theoretical value of the underlying securities if liquidated immediately

Discount or premium (–); the share price discount from NAV expressed as a percantage of NAV

Source: Adapted from *Financial Times*, 4 March 2011.
Note: the Monday edition of the FT displays the change in price over the week, the actual dividend in pence per share, when dividends are paid, market capitalisation and the date when a shareholder last qualified for the receipt of a dividend (the ex-dividend date).

Exhibit 4.31

Trust boards accused over independence

Alice Ross

Boards of investment trusts have been accused of failing to act in the interests of their shareholders, amid complaints that some are "in the pockets" of fund managers.

Analysts say many investment companies are too small and illiquid for investors to get out, while fund managers are rarely fired for poor performance. Trusts also come

under fire for failing to buy back shares regularly.

Some point the finger at those on the boards of investment trusts, who they accuse of being more

Exhibit 4.31 continued

keen to hold on to their jobs than do what is best for the company. Sitting on an investment trust board may require one day's work a month but can pay more than £20,000 a year – and many board members sit on multiple boards.

"Do turkeys vote for Christmas? That is part of the problem," admits one board member.

Others think board members feel too much loyalty to fund managers. Some fund managers are instrumental in appointing board members and can also brand the investment company with their name, which one board member says "can sway boards" against firing managers.

"Legally the board employs the fund manager but in reality the fund manager employs the board," says Nick Sketch, private client manager at Rensburg Sheppards.

While directors are legally required to avoid a conflict of self-interest, a report from Frostrow Capital says some boards do not clearly demonstrate how potential conflicts are dealt with when a manager is also on the board.

Some board members make an active effort to be proactive, however. Hamish Buchan, who chairs two boards and is a member of four others, says chairmen of boards should contact big shareholders and give them the opportunity to have private meetings with the board once a year.

The Association of Investment Companies also says that putting too much pressure on boards to remove poorly performing fund managers could result in a dismissal at the wrong time.

There are many other options open to boards to improve floundering investment trusts: implementing regular share buy-back schemes to control the discount, request-ing a new fund manager from the same fund management house or simply communicating better with shareholders.

Others think the best thing boards can do is encourage their brokers do get more people interested in a sector that is facing increasing competition from cheaper tracker funds and open-ended fund managers' marketing clout.

Investment trusts have suffered in recent years from the departure of large buyers such as pension funds. The Bank of England pension scheme used to be many brokers' best client but has since sold its holdings.

"The investment trust sector needs to go out and find new clients," says Paul Locke, analyst at Canaccord.

Source: *Financial Times*, 21/22 August 2010, p. 14. Reprinted with permission.

Exchange, the *net* asset value per share falls dramatically from £1 to 20p – an 80 per cent fall – because the assets fall to £60 million, but the debt remains at £50 million:

Value of eastern European shares	£60m
Less debt	–£50m
	£10m

Net asset value per share: £10m/50m = 20p

You can see why trusts that borrow a lot can be very volatile.

Sovereign wealth funds

Sovereign wealth funds (SWFs) are collective funds set up and managed by governments. Thus, a country that has a large flow of income, due to say oil, may establish a fund on behalf of its people so that they can gain a future income from the investment fund after the oil has gone. Given that they now control $3,000–$4,000 billion of investments around the world, their decisions on where to place money can have a significant effect on finance and economics. They used to be buy-and-hold-type investors looking for long-term returns. However, following the financial crisis, many were used as sources of finance to support their domestic economies; this kind of political interference may grow. **Exhibit 4.32** describes a number of SWFs.

Custodians

Custodians are guardians or safe-keepers of securities. The term often refers to custodian banks, whose legal remit is to look after the various assets of investment companies, especially pension funds (and mutual funds in the US), in return for a fee. They safeguard the securities or other assets which the funds own, check on and distribute dividend payments, capital gains and general information relating to the diverse range of assets. One of HSBC's custodianship tasks is to safe-guard gold bullion bars (worth £33 billion in 2010) backing a gold investment fund.

Exhibit 4.32

Wealth of nations   FT

Abu Dhabi

Outside estimates put the value of the opaque Abu Dhabi Investment Authority, the world's biggest sovereign fund, at upwards of $600bn. The portfolio includes quoted equities, fixed income, property, infrastructure and private equity, with global equities the biggest category. The aim is to secure the welfare of the emirate and provide stabilisation funding when necessary. Adia does not seek active management or control. About 60 per cent of the portfolio is in index-replicating assets. It is suing Citigroup over losses on its $7.5bn purchase of shares in the bank in 2007.

Norway

The aim of the Government Pension Fund Global is to manage national petroleum wealth and to meet rising pubic pension liabilities; while also preventing the "Dutch disease" – whereby windfall revenues lead to an overvalued exchange rate that distorts the domestic economy – taking hold. The $510bn fund is split 60/40 between foreign equities and bonds. It takes contrarian views, recently buying Greek government bonds; and ethical views, excluding from the portfolio in August two Israeli companies involved in developing Jewish settlements in occupied Palestinian territory.

Russia

In 2008 the Oil Stabilisation Fund, managing state-controlled energy groups' revenues, was split to recognise its different functions: one managing official reserves; the other, which became the National Welfare Fund SWF, making higher risk investments. The purpose of this SWF is to smooth fluctuations in energy revenues and to fund pensions. But during the financial crisis, when foreign capital fled the country, it sold foreign investments to plug the budget deficit, support the mortgage market and prop up

Top 10 sovereign wealth funds
By assets under management, Sep 2010 ($bn)

SWFs by region
By assets under management 2009 (%)

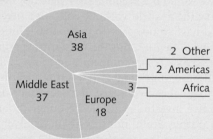

Sources: Sovereign Wealth Fund Institute   * State Aministration of Foreign Exchange

domestic share prices. It is reportedly worth just under $40bn.

Singapore

Temasek – the smaller of the country's two SWFs, with $144bn under management – is one of the rare funds in the sector that aims to engage with the boards and managements of the companies in which it invests. Of its porfolio, 32 per cent is invested in Singapore,

with 46 per cent in the rest of Asia (excluding Japan). It attracted headlines by incurring big losses on the sale of holdings in Bank of America and Barclays but has fully recouped the ground lost in 2008–09. It boasts a total shareholder return of 17 per cent a year since it was set up in 1974.

Source: Financial Times, 19 October 2010, p. 12. Reprinted with permission.

They provide a very necessary protection for investors against any illegal or fraudulent activities of any fund manager, who could be tempted into dishonest behaviour simply by the enormity of the sums involved. The idea is to keep the assets at arm's length from the individuals running the fund.

In the UK, HM Revenue and Customs keeps a list of approved custodians. Domestic custodians look after domestic assets; global custodians oversee assets held in the rest of the world.

Concluding comments

Imagine life without insurance. Would you dare to drive a car? What if you had an accident and were required to replace someone else's car? Or worse, you injured someone so badly that you had to pay out £1 million in compensation? Surely the absence of car insurance alone would cause a reduction in economic output and in the quality of life because we would rarely take the risk of driving. The same logic applies to shipping goods around the world or constructing a building. Ship owners, airlines and builders cannot take the risks of hurting someone, or the risk of a fire or of loss of property from theft or accident, and so would generally refuse to take part in productive activity. We would all be poorer as a result. So clearly, even though the white-collar workers in the insurance industry do not produce a tangible thing that you can see and touch, they do help the rest of society go about pleasurable and business activity.

Imagine a world without pension funds. How fearful would you be as you grew older, not knowing where your income was going to come from? Saving under the mattress is one way to reduce the fear. But wouldn't it be far better to save into a fund that invested that money in industries around the world or in government bonds, producing a nice steady accumulation of wealth? Wouldn't it be better to have the discipline of being a member of a scheme that every month deducts contributions from your salary – that you would barely notice – and places it at arm's length from you, under professional management, and you were forbidden to touch it until you were ready to retire? And even after retirement, you could take only a portion of it each year – imposing another discipline to avoid you over-optimistically spending, or investing in get-rich-quick schemes. Clearly, pension managers, trustees and consultants provide an important service and we would miss them if they were not there.

Imagine a world without collective investment funds. If you wanted to invest in shares you would have to do so as an individual. Not only would the costs be high if you have only a small amount of savings, but the need for expertise would put off many people from even starting the process. As a result companies needing capital to grow would have fewer potential investors and would have to pay higher rates of return on the funds that were provided, reducing their willingness to go ahead with that new factory or develop that new computer program. A world without collective investment would be one with far fewer investment asset choices available to savers – most people would not be any more adventurous than sticking their money in a bank account. At the end of the day they would be poorer and society would be poorer because less risk capital would be employed to create new firms and industries. Clearly, collective investment vehicles under professional management help mobilise savings for productive investment, helping the savers to build their nest-eggs and helping companies to grow.

Key points and concepts

- **Insurance** – in return for a premium, risk is assumed by the insurer.

- **Insurance companies** can be either normal companies or **mutual firms** owned by policy holders.

- **Underwriters** use historical statistics to assess risks and set terms and cost of premiums.

- **Asymmetric information** is when one party in a negotiation or relationship is not in the same position as the other parties, being ignorant of, or unable to observe, some information which is essential to the contracting and decision-making process.

- **Adverse selection** occurs when there is an opportunity or incentive for some firms/individuals to act to take advantage of their informational edge over others. Then the firm/individual doing that activity will be disproportionately those taking advantage rather than being truly representative of the population as a whole, e.g. the tendency for poorer-than-average risks to continue with insurance.

- **Moral hazard** recognises the danger that someone who is insured may be more likely to take risks and be less careful because they are insured.

- **Insurance is sold** in the following ways: direct from insurer; through agent; through broker; through bank, building society, solicitor, travel agent, mail-order agent or accountant.

- **Life/long-term insurance** covers risk of loss of life.

  - **Term assurance** pays out on death within a set time.
  - **Whole of life** is guaranteed to pay out when the insured dies as long as the premiums are up to date.
  - **Endowment policies** pay out at a set future date or on earlier death of the insured.
  - **Annuities** provide regular income until death of the insured.
  - Insurance companies may also run pension schemes.

- **General/non-life insurance** covers risks other than death.

  - **Property insurance** covers all types of property. **Open policies** cover everything not specifically excluded; **named peril policies** cover named risks.
  - **Casualty insurance** covers accidental damage.
  - **Liability insurance** covers third-party damage.

- Premiums go into a **float** used to make investments.

- General insurance companies need a high proportion of liquid investments whereas life insurance companies can invest a higher proportion in longer-term investments.

- **Reinsurance** is when an insurance company insures insurers: **proportional** reinsurance pays out a proportion of a claim; **non-proportional covers** losses over a specified amount.

- **Retrocession:** the purchase of reinsurance by reinsurance companies.

- **Spiralling** is unknowingly reinsuring own risk.

- **Protection and Indemnity (P & I) Clubs** offer protection and indemnity in respect of third-party liabilities and expenses arising from owning or operating ships.

- The **International Underwriting Association** is the world's largest organisation for international and wholesale insurance and reinsurance companies.

- **Lloyd's** is not an insurance company, it is a society of members – that is, a group of members trading in insurance via brokers, in an environment run by the **Corporation of Lloyd's**, which is overseen by the **Council of Lloyd's**. Lloyd's is a meeting place where insurance customers, brokers and underwriters meet face to face and discuss requirements and strike insurance underwriting deals. It concentrates on property and casualty insurance and the underwriters are famed for their ability and willingness to undertake unusual risks. For a long time, it was made up of individuals, **Names,** who underwrote particular risks with unlimited liability and joined together in **syndicates** to underwrite. Now it is dominated by corporate underwriters who still underwrite through syndicates. Syndicates run for one year.

- Public **unfunded pension schemes (pay-as-you-go (PAYG))** is where the money put aside each month by employees and employers pay the pensions of current pensioners. This means that there is not a pot of accumulated money to pay pensions. If there is a shortfall, it is met by the Treasury.

- **Funded pension funds** are designed so that the members, and/or their employers, make regular payments to a pension fund, which will (hopefully) grow and provide future pension income.

- **A pension deficit** arises when the actual amount of assets expected to be in the pension pot at retirement (with added investment income) is not sufficient to pay out the pensions required.

- A **defined benefit (DB) pension** pays out a fixed amount based upon the number of years worked and the level of final salary or the average level of salary.

- A **defined contribution (DC)** is a pension where the contributions (from employee and employer) are fixed but the actual pension paid out is linked to the return on the assets of the pension fund and the rate at which the final pension fund is annuitised; at retirement age, an annuity is generally purchased with the accumulated funds to provide the pension.

- **Personal** or **private pensions** are not provided by the state. They put the onus of funding a pension solely on the recipient, who pays a regular amount, usually every month, or a lump sum to the pension provider who will invest it on their behalf.

- **Self-invested personal pensions** are pension plans that allow the contributor to control the type and amount of investments made.

- Pension funds are run by **trustees** (who control the fund and hire managers to invest the money), **consultants** (who are asked to give their professional advice on the type and amount of investment to be made to trustees) and **managers** (tasked with investing and ensuring that the fund returns are satisfactory).

- Pension schemes are **major investors** in long-term assets, e.g. shares and bonds.

- In the UK, the **Pensions Regulator** is empowered by the government to regulate work-based pension schemes and has wide-ranging powers to enforce its decisions.

- In the UK, the **Pension Protection Fund (PPF)** was established to compensate members of DB pension funds should their company fail leaving insufficient assets in the pension scheme to cover its pension liabilities. Pension protection schemes compensate for failure of DB schemes, or fraud and theft in DC schemes.

- The **Institutional Shareholder Committee** sets out the principles of behaviour for institutional shareholders. It also set standards of behaviour it expects from corporations in which its members hold shares and other securities. The members of the committee are the **Association of British Insurers** (the trade association for the 300 or so British insurance companies), the **Association of Investment Companies** (the trade association for the closed-ended investment company industry), the **Investment Management Association** (representing the UK investment management industry) and the **National Association of Pension Funds** (representing the interests of occupational pension schemes).

- **Collective investment** is pools of money gathered together for investment purposes. Advantages – more diversity in investments; small investors can participate; professional management; investment possible in atypical areas. Disadvantages – poor management leading to poor performance; costs of management; loss of shareholders' perks.

- **Open-ended investment vehicles (OEIVs)** – no restriction on size of fund; shares/units issued or redeemed according to demand.

- **Unit trusts** are investment funds administered as trusts issuing units.

- **Unit trust's trustee** is the legal owner of assets.

- **Value of trust** determined by market valuation of underlying securities.

- Unit trusts have two prices: **offer (buying) price** and **bid (selling)** price. The difference between them is the spread.

- Unit trust prices can be **forward** or **historic**.

- **Charges** – initial, annual and exit.

- Four levels of **protection for unit holder**: trustee; financial regulator; ombudsman; Financial Services Compensation Scheme.

- **Accumulation units** reinvest income within the fund; **income units** pay out a high regular dividend to unit holders.

▶

- **Active management** – manager actively researches and chooses investments.

- **Passive management** – manager tracks market index.

- **Open-ended investment company (OEIC)** – similar to unit trust but formed as a company issuing shares.

- **OEIC size varies** according to number of shares and is valued by market value of assets.

- OEICs run by **authorised corporate directors** with **depositary** safeguarding assets.

- OEICs have **single pricing** scheme with charges added.

- **Exchange-traded funds (ETFs)** are set up as companies issuing shares and the money raised is used to buy a range of securities such as a collection of shares in a particular stock market index or sector.

- **Pricing of ETFs** is dictated by market; prices change constantly.

- Management charges are much lower than for mutual funds, unit trusts and investment trusts.

- Sometimes the term **mutual funds** is used as a generic term for collective or pooled investments. However, in the US and Canada the term has the specific meaning in terms of their organisation and legal structure. The vast majority are open-ended funds, but there are some that are closed-ended funds.

- Mutual funds are run by **shareholder appointed directors**. The manager of the fund, called the **portfolio manager**, buys investments according to the objective of the fund as set out in the prospectus. Assets are placed with a custodian and funds are valued daily.

- **Undertakings for Collective Investments in Transferable Securities** (UCITS) – EU-wide rules governing collective investments which could be sold across the EU subject to local tax and marketing laws, so an investor could, with confidence, invest in French, German, Spanish, etc. funds, safe in the knowledge that the funds were subject to regulation.

- **Closed-ended investment vehicles** – publicly traded companies with a set number of shares. They place the money they raise by selling shares in assets such as shares, government bonds, corporate bonds and property.

- Investment trusts are set up as companies. They have a **constitution** specifying the type of investment.

- Investment trusts are **run by directors** responsible to shareholders.

- Trusts' share prices frequently sell at a large **discount** to net asset value on the secondary market.

- Investment trusts have the **freedom to borrow** (unlike unit trusts or OEICs).

- **Sovereign wealth funds** are collective funds set up and managed by governments.

- **Custodians** are guardians or safe-keepers of securities. Custodians give protection to investors against fraud and dishonesty.

References and further reading

To keep up to date and reinforce knowledge gained by reading this chapter I recommend that you regularly read the *Financial Times* and *The Economist*.

Barclays Equity Gilt Study (2009) Barclays Capital.
   Provides data on the modern ETF market.

Cuthbertson, K. and Nitzsche, D. (2008) *Investments*, 2nd edn. Chichester: John Wiley & Sons.
   Chapter on investment companies.

de Haan, J., Oosterloo, S. and Schoenmaker, D. (2009) *European Financial Markets and Institutions*. Cambridge: Cambridge University Press.
   Good and up-to-date section on institutional investors

Kidwell, D. S., Blackwell, D. W., Whidbee, D. A. and Peterson, R. L. (2008) *Financial Institutions, Markets and Money*, 10th edn. New York: John Wiley & Sons Inc.
   Excellent and thorough analysis of US systems.

Roberts, R. (2008) *The City*, 2nd edn. London: The Economist.
   Easy to read and with useful information. Good section on city scandals.

▶

Saunders, A. and Cornett, M. M. (2007) *Financial Markets and Institutions*, 3rd edn. New York: McGraw-Hill Irwin. Comprehensive information about the US financial system.

Stevenson, D. (2010) *The Financial Times Guide to Exchange Traded Funds and Index Funds*. London: Financial Times Prentice Hall.
An easy to follow introduction for beginners.

Websites

Association of British Insurers www.abi.org.uk
Association of Investment Companies www.theaic.co.uk
Bestinvest, independent financial adviser www.bestinvest.co.uk
Citywire, financial news and advice www.citywire.co.uk
Cofunds, investment advice www.cofunds.co.uk
HM Government Public Services www.direct.gov.uk
Department for Work and Pensions www.dwp.gov.uk
Financial Services Authority www.fsa.gov.uk
Financial Times www.ft.com
Financial Times Stock Exchange www.ftse.com
FundsDirect, fund supermarket www.fundsdirect.co.uk
Hemscott, Share Prices, Stocks, Investing & Company Information www.hemscott.com
Insurance Information Institute www.iii.org
Investment Company Institute www.ici.org
Interactive Investor www.iii.co.uk
Protection and Indemnity Clubs www.igpandi.org
Incademy investor adducation www.incademy.com
UK quoted company announcements www.investegate.co.uk
Investment Management Association www.investmentfunds.org.uk
Investors Chronicle www.investorschronicle.co.uk
International Underwriting Association of London www.iua.co.uk
Lipper (Reuters) www.lipperweb.com
Lloyds of London www.lloyds.com
London Stock Exchange www.londonstockexchange.com
Moneyextra www.moneyextra.com
Morningstar www.morningstar.co.uk
National Association of Pension Funds www.napf.co.uk
OECD www.oecd.org
Independent pensions advice www.pensionsadvisoryservice.org.uk
Standard & Poor's financial services company www.standardandpoors.com
Swiss Re www.swissre.com
TheCityUK (includes IFSL) www.thecityuk.com
Pensions regulator www.thepensionsregulator.gov.uk
Trustnet, financial analysis www.trustnet.com

Video presentations

Bank chief executives and other senior people describe issues connected with financial markets in interviews, documentaries and webcasts at Cantos.com (www.cantos.com) – these are free to view.

Case study recommendations

See www.pearsoned.co.uk/arnold for case study synopses.
Also see Harvard University: http://hbsp.harvard.edu/product/cases

● The U.S. Life Industry (2010) Authors: Robert C. Pozen and MCCall Merchant. Harvard Business School.

- The Chubb Corporation in China (2008) Authors Li Jin, Michael Shih-Ta Chen and Aldo Sesia Jr. Harvard Business School.
- Malcolm Life Enhances its Variable Annuities (2010) Authors: Robert C. Pozen and David J. Pearlman. Harvard Business School.
- Barclays Global Investors and Exchange Traded Funds (2007) Authors: Luis M. Viceira and Alison Berkley Wagonfeld. Harvard Business School.
- Mirae Asset: Korea's Mutual Fund Pioneer (2010) Authors: Mukti Khaire, Michael Shih-Ta Chen and G.A. Donovan. Harvard Business School.
- Barclays Wealth: Reignite WAR or Launch Alphastream? (2010) Authors: Lena G. Goldberg and Elisa Farri. Harvard Business School.
- Pension Policy at The Boots Company PLC (2003) Authors: Luis M. Viceira and Akiko M. Mitsui. Harvard Business School.
- Bill Miller and Value Trust (2005) Authors: Sean D. Carr and Robert F. Bruner. Darden, University of Pennsylvania. Available at Harvard Case Study website.
- Pension Roulette: Have You Bet Too Much on Equities? (2003) Author: G. Bennett Stewart III, Harvard Business Review, June. Available at Harvard Case Study website.
- Fixing the Pension Fund Mix (2004) Author: Robert C. Pozen. Harvard Business Review, March. Available at Harvard Case Study website.

Self-review questions

1 What is the purpose of insurance and why do people pay premiums even though the premiums add up to less than they expect to lose?

2 What are underwriters, and what do they do?

3 How is insurance obtained?

4 Distinguish between the two main types of insurance.

5 Who regulates insurance companies in the UK?

6 What is Solvency II?

7 How has membership of Lloyd's of London altered over the past 20 years?

8 What is a pension?

9 How do defined benefit schemes differ from defined contribution schemes?

10 What is the difference between a public and private pension?

11 What are collective funds?

12 How does a unit trust differ from an investment trust?

13 What is an investment trust and how does it differ from other funds?

14 Define NAV for an investment trust.

15 What are UCITS and what are their advantages?

16   What is an ETF?

17   What are sovereign wealth funds?

Questions and problems

Insurance

1   Explain the following key elements to insurance:

   (a)   asymmetric information;
   (b)   adverse selection;
   (c)   moral hazard;
   (d)   float.

2   Describe and explain the main categories of life insurance and general insurance.

3   Describe and explain reinsurance and its social role.

4   Explain the functioning of Lloyd's of London and discuss its special role in the world insurance market.

5   Describe the difference in the mix of assets in an investment portfolio held by (a) life insurance companies, (b) general insurance companies.

Pensions

1   Distinguish between funded and unfunded pension schemes, and give the advantages and drawbacks of each type of pension.

2   Describe and explain the roles played by trustees, consultants and managers in running defined benefit funded pension schemes.

3   Describe and explain personal pensions.

4   What types of investments do pension funds make and how have the allocations changed over the past ten years?

5   Describe how UK pension funds are regulated.

6   What is the Institutional Shareholder Committee, and what does it do?

Collective investments

1   What are the advantages and disadvantages of collective funds rather than individuals investing on their own?

2   Explain the differences between open- and closed-ended funds, including a description of four types of open-ended investment vehicles.

3   For unit trusts:

   (a)   Describe the make-up of a unit and how the size of the trust is dictated.
   (b)   What charges are made to the unit holders?
   (c)   What type of protection does a unit trust holder have?

4   Compare and contrast an OEIC, an investment trust and an ETF.

5   In the context of collective investments, if a discount on an investment trust is not a price reduction when they are first sold, what is it? Describe the biggest factors influencing the share price of an investment trust.

6   Explain the following for collective investments:

(a) pricing on a forward basis;
(b) open-ended;
(c) initial charge;
(d) accumulation units;
(e) total expense ratio;
(f) premium to NAV.

Assignments

Insurance

1   Consider a family you know well. Describe the different types of insurance they currently pay for. Also describe two types of insurance they could take out but so far have chosen not to. For all the types of insurance discuss the costs and benefits to the family.

2   Examine the reports and accounts of three insurance companies as well as their websites and compile a report describing the different types of insurance they provide explaining the social benefits they provide.

Pensions

1   If you are currently a member of a funded pension scheme, obtain as much information as you can about the deal you have signed up to. In an essay describing the operation of the scheme include a consideration of the tax advantages of the scheme, the management of the fund and the assets that have been bought. (If you are not a member of scheme examine the scheme of someone you know well.)

2   Examine the past five years of annual reports of three leading defined benefit pension schemes, e.g. Universities Superannuation Scheme. To what extent do they use outside managers trying to pick winning shares and other securities? Describe how have they allocated the funds entrusted to them and critically assess their decisions.

3   Mr and Mrs Wright have no company or private pension. They are both aged 47 and in employment. What are their options to provide a pension when they reach retirement age?

Collective investments

1   Obtain the reports and accounts of five leading fund managers who manage unit trusts/OEICs. Also look at their marketing and other material they use to encourage and inform existing and potential investors. Write a report explaining the investment strategies, charges, range of investments and management of the funds.

2   Examine five investment trust companies quoted on the London Stock Exchange. Obtain their accounts and read their stock exchange announcement on financial websites to build up a picture of their operations. Write a report detailing performance, discounts or premiums, management and charges levied on investors.

Web-based exercises

Insurance

Using online insurance companies, get quotes for your life insurance if you are (a) a smoker and (b) a non-smoker. Comment on the results in the context of the usefulness of insurance.

Pensions

Go to the website of Universities Superannuation Scheme (www.uss.co.uk) and, using the annual reports over the past 8 years, write a report on the way the fund is set up, and how its investments have changed.

Collective investments

1   From the Financial Times (www.ft.com), choose a unit trust beginning with the letter D and write a report on its performance over one year and three years.

2   Conduct a web search to find:

    (a)   a UK OEIC prospectus;
    (b)   an ETF prospectus;
    (c)   a mutual fund prospectus; and
    (d)   an investment trust prospectus.

    Write a report on management, purpose and charges. Comment on the relative advantages and disadvantages of these types of funds.

CHAPTER

5

Money markets

LEARNING OUTCOMES

The money markets allow vital connections between those institutions with money to lend for short periods and those needing to borrow. There is not just one market but a wide range, each with its own modes of operating and jargon. By the end of this chapter the reader should:

- ■ have a sound grasp of the usefulness of money markets to the well-being of people around the world;
- ■ be able to describe the functions of money and the components of the rate of return;
- ■ describe the key benchmark interest rates, such as LIBOR, used by financial markets and corporations;
- ■ explain the operation and social value of the following money markets:
  - ■ interbank
  - ■ Eurocurrency
  - ■ Treasury bills
  - ■ commercial paper
  - ■ repurchase agreements
  - ■ local authority issues
  - ■ certificates of deposit
  - ■ bills of exchange and banker's acceptances;
- ■ calculate interest rates on various money market instruments, including conversion to annual rates. Also calculate the price of some money market securities;
- ■ discuss the role of credit rating agencies and the meaning of different ratings, e.g. AAA or A-1+;
- ■ show an understanding of the money markets table in the *Financial Times* and on various websites.

Just as people need to keep control of their finances, making sure that if they do spend more than their income they have a way of tapping into sources of funds by borrowing for short periods (e.g. credit cards or overdraft), so governments, corporations and other organisations have similar requirements. There are times when these organisations are in need of funds for merely a day, a week or the next three months. They thus need a place where they can borrow to make up the shortfall. The money markets fulfil this role. Banks are an alternative source of short-term finance, but in many cases the money markets are cheaper and involve less hassle.

There are other times when organisations have surplus funds and instead of keeping that money as cash or in current accounts at banks, earning little or no interest, they choose to lend it out to other organisations needing short-term funds by purchasing money market instruments from them.

While we, as individuals, borrow to make up shortfalls or lend surpluses (e.g. by putting money in our bank accounts) in tens, hundreds and maybe thousands of pounds or euros, governments and companies borrow or lend in millions of pounds or euros. Thus the money markets are termed a 'wholesale market' rather than a 'retail market'.

In sum the money markets are wholesale financial markets in which lending and borrowing on a short-term basis takes place – that is, usually for less than one year.[1]

Interest often comes from discount pricing

In a literal sense money is not actually traded in these markets, financial instruments are. When manufacturing firms, financial institutions, governments, etc. find themselves in need of short-term funds, they sell an instrument which carries the promise to pay, say, £10 million in 30 days from now. For many of the money market instruments the purchaser of that promise will not pay as much as £10 million because they want to receive an effective interest rate for lending. So they might pay, say, £9.9 million. Thus the security is sold for less than face value. The discount is the difference between face value and purchase price. The yield, the rate of interest gained by the holder, occurs when the instrument reaches maturity and the face value is paid by the issuer to the holder. Note that while most money market securities are issued at a discount, this is not true of all of them. Certificates of deposit and interbank deposits, for example, are issued at their face value and then redeemed at a higher value.

With many of the money market instruments the original purchaser is able to sell the instrument on to another investor before maturity if they want to raise some cash themselves – i.e. there is a secondary market. Thus these securities are said to be negotiable. So, staying with the example, say after 20 days the original lender could sell this promise to pay £10 million in a further 10 days for £9.96 million. Thus a profit can be made by trading the instruments on the secondary market before they reach the redemption date – in this case £60,000.

However, it must be noted that a loss may be incurred by selling in the secondary market. If, say, the original lender can attract buyers only at a price of £9.87 million then it makes a £30,000 loss. This low price may occur if, for instance interest rates on similar financial instruments with ten days to maturity are now yielding a higher rate of return because lenders have become more wary and demand higher rates of return to compensate for higher risk – a lot can change in the financial markets in 20 days. The potential secondary market purchaser would be silly to pay a price higher (receive a lower yield) than the going market rate for this particular issue when there are better deals to be had – i.e. the potential buyer has an opportunity cost (the return on the best alternative use of their investment money) and so the best the original lender can get is £9.87 million, if it has to sell. If it can avoid selling for another ten days then it will receive the full £10 million from the borrower.

The secondary markets in money market instruments are generally very liquid; that is, those organisations lending temporary surpluses to borrowers by buying money market securities are able to get at their capital (turn it into cash) quickly without the risk of reducing the price significantly, and there are low transaction costs in releasing the cash.

---

[1] However, some money market instruments have maturities greater than one year.

The discount and rate of interest (yield) earned is dependent on the risk level and the **maturity** of the instrument. The 'maturity' is the length of time between issue of the instrument (start of borrowing) and the time it is redeemed (money due is paid), or the length of time between when a security is priced or purchased in the secondary market and the date of redemption. The maturity length can vary from overnight (borrowing for just 24 hours) to three months to one year (or more, occasionally). Interest is measured in percentage points, which are further divided into **basis points (bps)**. One basis point equals 1/100 of a percentage point.

Example	Commercial paper

Commercial paper is a very popular way of raising money for large, well-regarded companies. For example, a corporation wishes to borrow £100 million for two months. It issues commercial paper with a face value of £101 million, payable in 60 days' time. A purchaser is prepared to accept the promise of the company to pay out in 60 days and so buys some of the commercial paper, paying £25 million for one-quarter of the total issue at a discount to the face value. In 60 days' time, the purchaser collects £25.25 million from the corporation. It has earned £250,000 in return for lending the corporation £25 million.

The markets in short-term money

Money markets exist all over the world as a means of facilitating business. *Domestic money market* means that the funds are borrowed and lent in the country's home currency and under the authority of the country's regulators. There are also money markets outside the jurisdiction of authorities of the currency they are denominated in – these are the *international* or *Euro money markets*. This is nothing to do with the currency in Europe: they were termed 'Euro markets' long before the euro was dreamed up.

Money markets are used by a wide variety of organisations, from treasury departments of corporations to banks and finance companies (e.g. raising large sums in the money markets to then provide hundreds of loans to people wanting to buy cars on hire-purchase deals). Pension funds and insurance companies maintain a proportion of their investment funds (they lend on the money markets) in liquid, low-risk form to meet unpredictable cash outflows, e.g. following a hurricane. These markets are also used by central banks to influence interest rates charged throughout the economy; for example, changing base rates at banks, which has a great effect on mortgage rates or business loan rates.

In the modern era, rather than having one or a few market locations or buildings in which money market instruments are bought and sold, we have organisations arranging deals over the telephone and then completing them electronically. The process of bringing together buyers and sellers is assisted by the many brokers and dealers who tend to operate from the trading rooms of the big banks and specialist trading houses – they regularly trade money market securities in lots worth tens of millions of pounds, dollars, etc. Some of them act as market makers, maintaining an inventory of securities and advertising prices at which they will sell and, slightly lower, prices at which they will buy. By providing these middle-man services they assist the players in the market to quickly find a counterparty willing to trade, thus enhancing liquidity. They are said to be traders in **STIR** products, that is **short-term interest rate products**.

Some of the trades are simply private deals with legal obligations to be enforced by each side, but some are conducted through a central clearing house, with each party responsible for reporting the deal to the clearing house, which settles the deal by debiting the account of the buyer and crediting the account of the seller. The clearing house then holds the security on behalf of the buyer. The risk of a counterparty reneging on the deal (**counterparty risk**) is reduced by trading through a clearing house.

Case study 5.1	Vodafone

You can get some idea of the importance of money markets to companies from the table below showing figures taken from Vodafone's annual reports. Vodafone keeps a large amount of cash and cash equivalents in reserve: more than £4 billion in 2010. *Cash equivalents* are not quite cash but they are so liquid that they are near-cash (near-money or quasi-money). They are financial assets that can easily be sold to raise cash, or which are due to pay back their capital value in a few days, with low risk regarding the amount of cash they will release. These are mostly money market instruments.

Vodafone keeps this large quantity of money available in this highly liquid and low-risk form so that it can supply its various business units with the cash they need for day-to-day operations or for regular investment projects. Also, it is useful to have readily accessible money to be able to take advantage of investment opportunities as they appear fleetingly (e.g. the purchase of a company). Alternatively, the cash and near cash is there because the company has recently had a major inflow – perhaps it sold a division or has had bumper profits – and it has not yet allocated the money to its final uses, such as paying billions in dividends to shareholders, launching a new product, buying another company or simply paying a tax bill. In the meantime that money may as well be earning Vodafone some interest, so the money that is surplus to the immediate needs of the various business units of Vodafone is gathered together and temporarily lent to other organisations in the money markets.

We will examine the nature of money market funds, repurchase agreements and commercial paper, among a number of other money market instruments, later in the chapter.

Vodafone's money market holdings

Cash and cash equivalents

	2010 £m	2009 £m	2008 £m
Cash at bank and in hand	745	811	451
Money market funds	3,678	3,419	477
Repurchase agreements	–	648	478
Commercial paper	–	–	293
Cash and cash equivalents as presented in the balance sheet	4,423	4,878	1,699

Money market funds

Despite the wholesale nature of the money markets it is possible for private individuals with funds available for lending in thousands of pounds/euros/dollars rather than hundreds of thousands to participate in money market transactions. They can do so via special funds set up to invest in money market instruments by pooling the savings of many people. These money market funds are administered by financial institutions which benefit from economies of scale in investing in a portfolio of money market securities. Savers buy 'shares' in the money market fund. They earn a return, technically a dividend but in effect an interest rate.

Corporations may also deposit money in money market funds to obtain good rates of interest through professional management of the fund. They also value being able to withdraw money from the fund without the need to sell the underlying securities in the secondary markets – in most cases investors in money market funds can gain access to their money within hours: 'same-day' access. It is also possible to put in place a sweep facility so that money is automatically transferred from a bank account (paying little interest), if it exceeds a stated balance, to a money market account (paying more interest) and vice versa – this can be done at the end of each day.

Along with much of the rest of the financial sector money markets went through a crisis in 2008. A money market fund, Reserve Primary Fund, had invested a substantial proportion of its funds in Lehman Brothers short-term debt. When Lehmans went bust the fund was unable to return to investors the amount they had paid into it. This breaking of the buck is a great sin in the money market world – all money market funds are supposed to be incredibly safe. What made it worse was the subsequent freezing-up of credit markets: investors in funds could not withdraw their money at short notice as per the agreement. The market became illiquid because the money market funds could not find buyers for the securities they held and so could not raise cash at the moment when a high proportion of their investors clamoured to withdraw cash. In response, the industry bodies in the US, Europe and elsewhere tightened rules to make sure that there was much more easily accessible cash in the funds – *see* **Exhibit 5.1** for the European response. Note that while the European market is very large at around €400 billion, the US market is even larger, at around $3,800 billion.

Exhibit 5.1

New rules for money funds

FT

Steve Johnson

Europe's €430bn (£388bn, $630bn) triple-A money market fund industry will have to abide by higher standards of maturity, credit quality, liquidity and disclosure under new guidelines due to be unveiled today.

The move follows a series of problems in the supposedly low risk asset class during the credit crisis. A number of "enhanced" European money market funds suffered double-digit losses and the US Treasury felt compelled to prop up its domestic industry after one vehicle, the Reserve Primary Fund, "broke the buck", losing money for investors.

Although triple-A rated European funds avoided these problems the industry body, the Institutional Money Market Funds Association, has still decided to

Assets in triple-A rated Immfa money market funds
By currency type (bn)

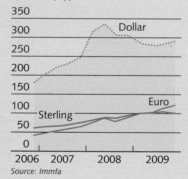

Source: Immfa

tighten its guidelines, which are mandatory for members.

Funds will now have to manage liquidity by ensuring at least 5 per

cent of assets are held in overnight securities and 20 per cent in securities maturing within one week. This is designed to ensure that funds, which all provide daily liquidity to investors, can meet redemption requests even if the secondary market seizes up. "If liquidity disappears in the market place you cannot sell your assets. The only thing you can rely on is natural liquidity", said Nathan Douglas, secretary general of Immfa.

Immfa has also moved to tighten up credit quality by stipulating that the weighted average final maturity of a fund's assets must be no more than 120 days.

Source: Financial Times, FTFM section, 14 December 2009, p. 2. Reprinted with permission.

'Triple-A' means that they have independently been assessed as having a very low risk of defaulting. 'Overnight securities' are those where the lender receives back capital and interest one day after lending. An 'enhanced' fund is one that takes more risk (or invests in lower-liquidity securities) to try to generate a higher return. 'Natural liquidity' means holding securities that pay back their capital in a matter of hours or days rather than the holder relying on selling the securities to other investors in the secondary market.

Functions of money

Before we look at the range of money market instruments and the workings of these markets we need to go right back to basics and discuss what money is and why a rate of return is required.

Money as coinage has been in existence for 3,000 years, evolving from the original barter system, which, as commerce increased, proved to be unduly cumbersome. Under a barter system much time and effort were expended in searching out other individuals interested in a direct trade of one good for another. It soon became apparent that a tool was needed to help make transactions more efficient. People needed something into which all goods and services received could be converted; they needed something small and portable which would hold its value over a long period of time and be universally accepted. Thus people could avoid the necessity of carrying to market the bushels of wheat they had earned by their labour to exchange them for bricks. Instead labour was rewarded by money, which in turn was taken to the market to buy bricks, or any other commodity. Over the years, many varied items have been used as a means of exchange, ranging from cowry shells to cigarettes (in prisons particularly), but gold or silver became the norm. In present times, of course, money is generally represented by paper (bank notes, cheques, etc.), plastic (debit and credit cards) or electronic means.

In any economy, money has three main functions.

- *Means of exchange* As a means of exchange the barter system was inefficient in that it required the buyer and seller to have mutual and simultaneous wants, a *double coincidence of wants*. The invention of tokens or coins and later paper[2] and electronic transfers as a means of exchange has revolutionised the world. It has enabled people and companies from diverse parts of the globe to conduct business with each other safe in the knowledge that each party will receive what they are due in terms of goods or payment. Individuals and corporations are able to trade their goods and services for a universally accepted means of exchange – money.

- *Unit of account* It is important that each unit of coinage represents a particular asset value, is identical to units of the same denomination and that units representing large amounts can be divided into smaller units. In the UK, for example, the unit of account is the pound sterling (£), with 100 sub-units, while in most of Europe the unit of account is the euro (€). To have a standard unit of account is very important for business and personal decisions. Take, for instance, a business with two subsidiaries, operating in different markets – it is very useful to observe their relative performances in terms of a common measuring stick.

- *Store of value* Money has enabled individuals to hold a store of value and not use it straightaway, as would necessarily happen with many of the goods in the barter system, but to keep it until required for future consumption. This money must be capable of being stored and keep its value until retrieved. An individual or corporate body may not want to spend immediately the amount they have earned but save it for later consumption, and its face value must be the same at the later date. However, due to the inflation process, money, because it is unchangeable and retains simply its face value, is not necessarily the best means of storing value. Fine art, antiques, property and interest-paying bank accounts are just some of the myriad ways of storing value which *may* provide protection against inflation.

The time value of money

When people undertake to set aside money for investment, something has to be given up now. For instance, if someone buys shares in a firm or lends to a business, there is a sacrifice of present consumption. One of the incentives to save is the possibility of gaining a higher level of future consumption. Therefore, it is apparent that compensation is required to induce people to make a consumption sacrifice. Compensation will be required for at least three things:

- *Impatience to consume:* individuals generally prefer to have £1.00 today than £1.00 in five years' time. To put this formally: the utility of £1.00 now is greater than £1.00 received five years hence. Individuals are predisposed towards impatience to consume, thus they need an appropriate reward to begin the saving process. The rate of exchange between certain future consumption and certain current consumption is the pure rate of interest – this occurs even in

[2] The Chinese were the first to issue paper bank notes, about 650 AD; the earliest in Europe were issued in Sweden in the seventeenth century.

a world of no inflation and no risk. If you lived in such a world you might be willing to sacrifice £100 of consumption now if you were compensated with £102 to be received in one year. This would mean a pure rate of interest of 2 per cent.

- *Inflation:* the price of time (or the interest rate needed to compensate for impatience to consume) exists even when there is no inflation, simply because people generally prefer consumption now to consumption later. If there is inflation then the providers of finance will have to be compensated for that loss in purchasing power as well as for time.

- *Risk:* the promise of the receipt of a sum of money some years hence generally carries with it an element of risk; the payout may not take place or the amount may be less than expected. Risk simply means that the future return has a variety of possible values. Thus, the issuer of a security, whether it be a share, a bond or a bank account, must be prepared to compensate the investor for impatience to consume, inflation and risk involved, otherwise no one will be willing to buy the security.[3]

Take the case of Mrs Ann Investor who is considering a €1,000 one-year investment and requires compensation for three elements of time value:

1 A return of 2 per cent is required for the pure time value of money.

2 Inflation is anticipated to be 3 per cent over the year. At time zero (t_0) €1,000 buys one basket of goods and services. To buy the same basket of goods and services at time t_1 (one year later), €1,030 is needed. To compensate the investor for impatience to consume and inflation, the investment needs to generate a return of 5.06 per cent, that is:

$$(1 + 0.02)(1 + 0.03) - 1 = 0.0506 = 5.06\%$$

The figure of 5.06 per cent may be regarded here as the **risk-free return (RFR)**, the interest rate which is sufficient to induce investment assuming no uncertainty about cash flows.

Investors tend to view lending to reputable governments through the purchase of bonds or bills as the nearest they are going to get to risk-free investing, because these institutions have an almost unlimited ability to raise income from taxes or to create money and minimal likelihood of default. This applies only if the country has a reputation for good financial management – Greece, Ireland and Portugal had a troublesome 2010 and 2011 when investors doubted the soundness of their governments' finances; they pushed up the interest rates the governments had to pay to allow for the risk of default (non-payment) way beyond the normal RFR accorded a reputable eurozone government, e.g. Germany.

The RFR forms the bedrock for time value of money calculations as the pure time value and the expected inflation rate affect all investments equally. Whether the investment is in property, bonds, shares or a factory, if expected inflation rises from 3 per cent to 5 per cent then the investor's required return on all investments will increase by 2 per cent.

3 Different investment categories carry different degrees of uncertainty about the outcome of the investment. For instance, an investment on the Russian stock market, with its high volatility, may be regarded as more risky than the purchase of a share in BP with its steady growth prospects. Investors require different **risk premiums** on top of the RFR to reflect the perceived level of extra risk. Thus:

required return (time value of money) = RFR + risk premium

---

[3] A further factor (which to some extent could be seen as a form of risk) is that once the lender has committed the funds to a borrower for a set period of time they have to face the risk that at some point they may need the funds. With some investments there are ways of releasing the money – converting the instrument to cash – quickly, at low transaction cost and with certainty over the amount that would be released. This can be achieved by insisting that the borrower repays or from selling the right to receive interest, etc. to another investor in a market. That is, there is high liquidity and therefore low liquidity risk. If lenders/investors do not have access to the possibility of quick, low-cost conversion to cash – high liquidity risk – then they are likely to demand an additional return in compensation.

In the case of Mrs Ann Investor, the risk premium pushes up the total return required to, say, 10 per cent, thus giving full compensation for all three elements of the time value of money.

The interest rates quoted in the financial markets are sufficiently high to compensate for all three elements. A ten-year loan to a reputable government (such as the purchase of a bond) may pay an interest rate of 5 per cent per annum. Some of this is compensation for time preference and a little for risk, but the majority of that interest is likely to be compensation for future inflation. The same applies to the cost of capital for a business; when it issues financial securities, the returns offered include a large element of inflation compensation.

The nominal rate of interest is the rate quoted by lenders and includes the inflation element. The real rate of interest removes inflation.

Real rate of interest = nominal rate of interest − inflation

The interbank market

Originally, the interbank market was defined as the market where banks lend to each other, in both the domestic and international markets. This is a rather strict (old-fashioned) definition, and increasingly, as well as banks being lenders, this group includes large industrial and commercial companies, other financial institutions and international organisations. Thus, the interbank markets exist so that a bank or other large institution which has no immediate demand for its surplus cash can place the money in the interbank market and earn interest on it. In the opposite scenario, if a bank needs to supply a loan to a customer but does not have the necessary money to hand, it can borrow on the interbank market.

There is no secondary trading in the interbank market; the loans are 'non-negotiable' – thus a lender for, say, three months cannot sell the right to receive interest and capital from the borrower to another organisation after, say, 15 days – the lender has to wait until the end of the agreed loan period to recover money. If a bank needs its funds, it simply ceases to deposit money with other banks.

The loans in this market are not secured with collateral. However, the rate of interest is relatively low because those accepting deposits (borrowers) are respectable and safe banks. This interest rate creates the **benchmark** (reference) interest rate known as LIBOR – explained in the next section. Banks with lower respectability and safety will have to pay more than the benchmark rates set by the safest institutions.

Interest rates

In the financial pages of serious newspapers you will find a bewildering variety of interest rates quoted from all over the world. Following is an explanation of some of the terms in common use.

LIBOR

LIBOR or **Libor**, the **London Interbank Offered Rate**, is the most commonly used benchmark rate, in particular the three-month LIBOR rate, which is the interest rate for one bank lending to another (very safe) bank for a fixed three-month period.

Obviously these lending deals are private arrangements between the two banks concerned, but we can get a feel for the rates being charged by surveying the leading banks involved in these markets. This is done every trading day. The official LIBOR rates are calculated by the British Banking Association (BBA) by asking a panel of 16 UK and international banks at what rates they could borrow money as unsecured loans of various maturities.[4] Contributor banks are asked to base their LIBOR submissions on the following question: 'At what rate could you borrow funds, were you to do so by asking for and then accepting interbank offers in a reasonable market size

---

[4] The size of the panel can vary from 8 to 20 banks, but it is usually 16. In February 2011, for instance, the number of contributing banks for US dollar LIBOR increased from 16 to 20.

just prior to 11 am?'[5] The rates from the 16 banks are ranked in order from the highest to the lowest and the arithmetic mean of only the middle two quartiles is taken, i.e. the BBA removes the top four and bottom four rates quoted each day and averages the middle eight rates to calculate LIBOR.

The loans between banks are not just in sterling. London is the leading international financial centre of the world and lending takes place in a variety of currencies. Thus, each day the BBA produces LIBOR interest rates for borrowing in ten currencies with a range of 15 maturities from overnight to 12 months quoted for each currency, producing 150 rates each business day. *See* **Exhibit 5.2** for the LIBOR rates produced on 31 December 2010.

Only the most creditworthy borrowers can borrow at LIBOR; less highly rated borrowers will be able to borrow at LIBOR plus a number of basis points, e.g. LIBOR + 9; so if the three-month LIBOR in US dollars is currently 0.50 per cent, the borrower will pay 9/100 of a percentage point more than this, i.e. 0.59 per cent for three-month borrowing starting today and repayable in three months. These rates are expressed at an annual rate even though the loans may be for only a few days or weeks.

The sterling three-month LIBOR rate has an effect on the rates which are set on a variety of other loans, especially mortgages, to individuals and companies. Because the LIBOR rate is calculated in different currencies, its influence is spread worldwide, and is particularly used in dollar lending outside the US. In all, LIBOR is used to price around $350,000 billion financial products worldwide. **Exhibit 5.3** describes how the interest rates in the LIBOR markets declined dramatically during 2008 to leave rates at extraordinarily low levels during 2009 and 2010.

| **Exhibit 5.2** | LIBOR Rates for 31 December 2010 |

Euro LIBOR	%	Japanese yen LIBOR	%	Australian dollar LIBOR	%	Swedish krona LIBOR	%
Overnight	0.60625	Spot/next	0.10000	Spot/next	4.84500	Spot/next	1.46250
1 week	0.53625	1 week	0.10600	1 week	4.84500	1 week	1.49250
2 weeks	0.58500	2 weeks	0.11500	2 weeks	4.85000	2 weeks	1.53550
1 month	0.71000	1 month	0.12625	1 month	4.85000	1 month	1.54500
2 months	0.81750	2 months	0.15375	2 months	4.89125	2 months	1.78250
3 months	0.93875	3 months	0.18813	3 months	4.95000	3 months	1.91250
4 months	1.00875	4 months	0.24413	4 months	5.00500	4 months	1.94750
5 months	1.09313	5 months	0.30125	5 months	5.05625	5 months	1.97750
6 months	1.18313	6 months	0.34750	6 months	5.13250	6 months	2.01500
7 months	1.23188	7 months	0.39750	7 months	5.19750	7 months	2.06250
8 months	1.28563	8 months	0.44313	8 months	5.28875	8 months	2.11000
9 months	1.33438	9 months	0.48750	9 months	5.37750	9 months	2.17500
10 months	1.38563	10 months	0.51313	10 months	5.47750	10 months	2.22250
11 months	1.42938	11 months	0.53750	11 months	5.57750	11 months	2.26000
12 months	1.47250	12 months	0.56625	12 months	5.67750	12 months	2.31000

[5] From the British Bankers Association: www.bbalibor.com/bbalibor-explained/the-basics. LIBOR is defined as 'the rate at which an individual Contributor Panel bank could borrow funds, were it to do so by asking for and then accepting interbank offers in reasonable market size, just prior to 11.00 London time'.

US dollar LIBOR

	%
Overnight	0.25188
1 week	0.25438
2 weeks	0.25656
1 month	0.26063
2 months	0.28250
3 months	0.30281
4 months	0.34750
5 months	0.40250
6 months	0.45594
7 months	0.50813
8 months	0.55938
9 months	0.61250
10 months	0.66625
11 months	0.72063
12 months	0.78094

Swiss franc LIBOR

	%
Spot/next	0.10333
1 week	0.11000
2 weeks	0.12667
1 month	0.14250
2 months	0.15833
3 months	0.17000
4 months	0.18750
5 months	0.21167
6 months	0.23833
7 months	0.27750
8 months	0.31917
9 months	0.36750
10 months	0.41833
11 months	0.46833
12 months	0.51667

Danish kroner LIBOR

	%
Spot/next	0.82500
1 week	0.80750
2 weeks	0.83425
1 month	0.89350
2 months	1.02725
3 months	1.12125
4 months	1.22450
5 months	1.37450
6 months	1.46425
7 months	1.52100
8 months	1.55750
9 months	1.63000
10 months	1.67250
11 months	1.71250
12 months	1.75250

UK pound LIBOR

	%
Overnight	0.56500
1 week	0.57250
2 weeks	0.57750
1 month	0.59250
2 months	0.64688
3 months	0.75750
4 months	0.84000
5 months	0.94438
6 months	1.05000
7 months	1.12750
8 months	1.21125
9 months	1.29188
10 months	1.37250
11 months	1.44125
12 months	1.50938

Canadian dollar LIBOR

	%
Overnight	0.89500
1 week	0.98500
2 weeks	1.05000
1 month	1.10000
2 months	1.15000
3 months	1.23167
4 months	1.30000
5 months	1.36667
6 months	1.44333
7 months	1.51333
8 months	1.58333
9 months	1.65000
10 months	1.72500
11 months	1.80667
12 months	1.89833

New Zealand dollar LIBOR

	%
Spot/next	3.14000
1 week	3.16750
2 weeks	3.18750
1 month	3.22250
2 months	3.27000
3 months	3.32500
4 months	3.35750
5 months	3.40750
6 months	3.45500
7 months	3.54500
8 months	3.61250
9 months	3.70250
10 months	3.81250
11 months	3.90250
12 months	4.00000

Source: www.bbalibor.com
Note: The percentage rates shown in this table are all expressed as equivalent annual percentages, although the loans can vary from one night to one year.

Exhibit 5.3

Little for room Libor to fall further

David Oakley and Ralph Atkins

The year-long decline in money market rates appears to be over.

London Interbank Offered Rates, or Libor, are at record lows for dollars, euro and sterling, leading many pundits to say that they cannot fall much further. Three-month Libor rates have fallen almost to the levels of base rates in the US and the UK – and below the base rates in the eurozone.

The question now is: at what point will they start rising again?

The reason rates have fallen so fast is that the extraordinary measures taken by the world's central banks since the collapse of Lehman Brothers have left the financial sector awash with liquidity.

It is also a clear sign that confidence has returned to the banking system, with institutions willing to lend to each other.

This is because fears over counter-party risk, which came close to breaking the financial system in the days following Lehman, have receded sharply.

The renewed confidence has even enabled some of the stronger banks to borrow well below Libor, which is fixed every day by the British Bankers Association through a survey of London-based banks.

However, bankers warn that Libor rates could start to rise again, undoing some of the efforts of the central banks, should the global economy show any signs of faltering.

In particular, they say, the failure of banks to increase lending to businesses and consumers, which is critical for economic recovery, could put the money markets under strain.

In short, the money market – the first link in the borrowing chain – may appear to be repaired but, without circulation of funds to consumers and businesses, confidence could start to erode, sending Libor higher.

"Lending rates are very low for banks in the money markets, but they aren't for businesses and consumers," he says. "Many businesses and consumers are also more intent on paying back loans rather than increasing debt in this climate."

It means the economic recovery has reached a critical point, with the markets eagerly watching the money markets for any signs of strain.

Mr Smith says "There is no guarantee that Libor rates can be maintained at the lows, and there is no guarantee that the current extremely loose monetary policy stances will trigger a sustained economic revival."

Source: Financial Times, 14 October 2009, p. 38. Reprinted with permission.

How low can Libor go?

Three - month Libor rates (%)

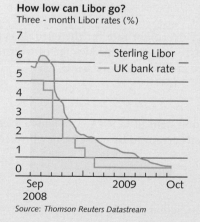

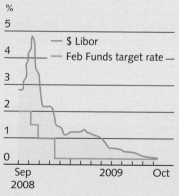

Source: Thomson Reuters Datastream

EURIBOR and some other BORs

Other rates similar to LIBOR which are in common use include **EURIBOR (Euro Interbank Offered Rate)**, which is the rate at which euro interbank term deposits are offered by one prime bank to another prime bank within the eurozone (not London) for periods of one week to one year. It does not cover overnight lending – see EONIA below for that. EURIBOR is calculated as a weighted average of unsecured lending transactions undertaken within the euro area by Eurozone banks.

Many other countries have markets setting rates for lending between domestic banks. **TIBOR (Tokyo Interbank Offered Rate)** is the rate at which Japanese banks lend to each other in Japan. In Singapore we have **SIBOR** and in Hong Kong we have **HIBOR**.

Federal Funds Rate and Prime Rate

In the US, the equivalent to very short-term LIBOR is the **Federal Funds Rate (fed funds)**, the rate at which domestic financial institutions lend to each other for a period of one day. This is strongly influenced by the US central bank, the Federal Reserve. Banks often need to borrow from other banks to maintain a minimum level of reserves at the Federal Reserve. The lending banks are happy to lend because they receive a rate of interest and the money is released the next day (usually). This borrowing is usually unsecured (without collateral) and so is available only to the most creditworthy. The Federal Reserve can influence the fed funds rate by increasing or lowering the level of cash or near-cash reserves the banks have to hold and other market interventions. There is more on the role of the Federal Reserve and the fed funds rate in Chapter 7.

The fed funds interest rate (borrowing in the US) and the overnight US dollar LIBOR rate (borrowing in the UK) are usually very close to each other because they are near-perfect substitutes. If they were not close then a bank could make a nice profit borrowing in one overnight market and depositing the money in another. If the US dollar LIBOR rate is higher, banks needing to borrow will tend to do so in the fed funds market; the increased demand will push up interest rates there, while the absence of demand will encourage lower rates in the US dollar LIBOR market.

The US *prime rate* is the interest rate US banks charge the best corporate customers. It is also used as a benchmark for other loans, e.g. consumer credit loan interest rates are often set as so many basis points above the prime rate.

EONIA

EONIA (Euro OverNight Index Average) is the effective overnight rate for the euro. It is calculated with the help of the **European Central Bank (ECB)** as a weighted average of overnight unsecured lending transactions undertaken within the euro area by Eurozone banks.

EURONIA

EURONIA (Euro Overnight Index Average) is the UK equivalent of EONIA, a weighted average of euro interest rates on unsecured overnight euro deposits arranged by eight money brokers in London.

SONIA

SONIA (Sterling Overnight Interbank Average) tracks the actual sterling overnight rates experienced by market participants (calculated by the wholesale Markets Brokers Association).

Eurocurrency

Eurocurrency has a large part to play in the interbank market as well as other lending/borrowing markets. The terms **Eurocurrency, Eurodollar, Euroyen, Euroswissfrancs**, etc. have nothing to do with the actual euro currency; their name simply means that the currency is deposited and lent outside the jurisdiction of the country that issued the currency. For example, a Japanese bank might make a deposit in yen in a German bank; this would be a Euroyen deposit. An American corporation might pay a Swiss corporation in dollars; these dollars are deposited in a Swiss bank and are Eurodollars.

Today, it is not unusual to find an individual holding a dollar account at a UK bank – a **Eurodeposit account** – which pays interest in dollars linked to general dollar rates. This money can be lent to firms wishing to borrow in Eurodollars prepared to pay interest and capital repayments in dollars. The point is that both the Euroyen deposit and the Eurodollars are outside the control of their country of origin – the regulators have little influence on this market.[6]

Eurocurrency markets came about after the Second World War when substantial amounts of US dollars were deposited in Europe (mainly in London) during the 1950s and 1960s. Countries outside the US were wary about depositing their dollars in US banks, where they would be subject to stringent US regulations. Regulation Q of the US Banking Act of 1933 prohibited banks from paying interest on commercial demand deposits. Additionally, 'Iron Curtain' countries were worried that their dollars could be seized or frozen for political reasons if they were placed where the rule of the US authorities was in force. Countries earning dollars, especially oil-producing countries, looked for banks outside the US where they could deposit their US dollars and earn market rates of interest. US corporations began to expand into Europe and wanted their funds outside the control of the US authorities. So the Eurocurrency market was born, although strictly speaking the term should be *international market*.

The title 'Euro' came about because the modern market was started when the former Soviet Union transferred dollars from New York to a Russian-owned bank in Paris bank at the height of the cold war in 1957. The cable address happened to be EUROBANK. This was long before the currency called the euro was conceived. Nowadays, there is daily **Eurosecurities** business transacted in all of the major financial centres. To add a little precision: 'Eurocurrency' is short-term (less than one year) deposits and loans outside the jurisdiction of the country in whose currency the deposit/loan is denominated. These are term ('time') deposits that may be fixed for just one day (overnight) or for a longer period such as three months. **Eurocredit** is used for the market in medium- and long-term loans in the Euromarkets, with lending rates usually linked to (a few basis points above) the LIBOR rates. Loans longer than six months normally have interest rates that are reset every three or six months depending on the LIBOR rate then prevailing for, say, three-month lending. Thus the interest rate is **floating** rather than **fixed** (constant throughout the lending term). So a corporate borrower with a two-year loan that starts off paying three-month LIBOR plus 150 basis points when three-month LIBOR is 3 per cent pays 4.5 per cent. This is expressed as an annual rate – the borrower will pay only one-quarter of this for three months. If, at the start of the next three months, the three-month LIBOR rate has moved to 3.45 per cent the corporate will pay 4.95 per cent (annual rate) for three months.

The companies which are large enough to use the Eurosecurities markets are able to put themselves at a competitive advantage *vis-à-vis* smaller firms. There are at least four advantages:

● The finance available in these markets can be at a lower cost in both transaction costs and rates of return.

● There are fewer rules and regulations such as needing to obtain official authorisation to issue or needing to queue to issue, leading to speed, innovation and lower costs.

● There may be the ability to hedge foreign currency movements. For example, if a firm has assets denominated in a foreign currency it can be advantageous to also have liabilities in that same currency to reduce the adverse impact of exchange-rate movements (*see* Chapter 12 for hedge currency risk).

● National markets are often not able to provide the same volume of finance. The borrowing needs of some firms are simply too large for their domestic markets to supply. To avoid being hampered in expansion plans, large firms can turn to the international market for finance.

The Eurodollar market has become so deep and broad that it now sets interest rates back in the mother country of the dollar. A very large proportion of US domestic commercial loans and commercial paper interest rates are set at a certain number of basis points above US dollar LIBOR rates determined by banks operating out of London.

---

[6] Just to confuse everybody traders in this market often refer to all types of Eurocurrency, from Eurosterling to Euroyen, as Eurodollars and do not reserve the term for US dollars.

The Eurocurrency market allows countries and corporations to lend and borrow funds world-wide, picking the financial institution which is the most suitable regardless of geographic position. While the world economy is thriving, this works well. However, some spectacular problems were highlighted in 2008. For example, Iceland's financial institutions found themselves in trouble after they found themselves unable to renew loans in the international debt markets.

Treasury bills

Throughout the world, government agencies issue Treasury bills (T-bills or Treasury notes).[7] They are negotiable securities, which means that they can easily be traded in the secondary market and thus easily liquidated to release cash. They can be one of the most risk-free forms of investing (if you are lending to financially stable governments), but pay a lower return for this reason. If a government is short of money because tax revenues are slow to come in, it can issue T-bills to increase funds. T-bills form by far the largest part of the money markets and are generally sold by auction through a national government agency.

UK Treasury bills

In the UK Treasury bills were first issued by the Bank of England in the early 1700s, when there occurred the first concept of money as an amount written on a piece of paper rather than an actual piece of metal with an intrinsic value. They are now issued at weekly tenders by the *Debt Management Office (DMO)* with a face value or par value of £100 and are sold at a discount to par value with a maturity date of one month (28 days), three months (91 days), six months (182 days) or twelve months.[8] They are sold initially by competitive tender to a small group of banks, which can sell them on in turn to other investors. Most holders of Treasury bills are financial institutions. Individuals may hold them, but the minimum purchase amount is £500,000.

Those banks that wish to purchase compete in the weekly tender by placing bids as defined by the yield they will accept. The bids are gathered and different yield prices accepted: the DMO determines what is the highest accepted yield and allocates bills to purchasers bidding below this yield. Purchasers bidding at the accepted yield may not receive the amount they bid for.

The buyer purchases a bill at a discount and may keep it until maturity and receive the par value back. Alternatively, the bill may be sold in an active secondary market to another investor. The T-bill markets are both deep (many buyers and sellers) and liquid, so there is little risk that a holder cannot sell when they want to with low transaction costs. During the time he has held the bill, he has made a *yield* or investment return, the difference between the price paid and the maturity value (or sale price in the secondary market), and this yield is calculated as an annual percentage which can then be compared with other types of investment.

There are two important considerations to take note of when undertaking any calculations associated with T-bills (and other money market securities):

1   In any calculations it is important to be aware of the day count convention. For ease of calculation, some countries/markets use a 30-day month and 360-day year, rather than the actual variable days in a month and a 365-day year, or 366 in a leap year. This can get complicated when the repayment date falls on the 31st of a month. There are various methods for dealing with this. Other markets use the precise number of days until redemption of the instrument and the real number of days in a year. Great care must always be taken to check which day- count convention is being used and to understand terminology, e.g. actual/360, 30/360, actual/actual, actual/365, and so on; it is imperative that an investor knows which convention is being used and how it works. In general the UK still uses the 365-day year in its sterling transactions.

---

[7] In Germany and Austria, a Treasury bill is called a Schatzwechsel; in Russia a Gosudarstvennoe Kratkosrochnoe Obyazatelstvo (GKO); and in France and Canada a Bon de Trésor.
[8] In theory 12-month bills can be issued, but to date none has yet been offered for sale.

2 The difference between **bond equivalent yield** and **discount yield**.

 a The bond equivalent yield, bey (also known as **coupon equivalent rate** or **equivalent bond yield**), is the yield that is quoted in newspapers and it allows comparison of fixed-income securities whose payments are not annual with securities that have annual yields. So a wide variety of debt instrument yield is expressed in the same annual terms, even those that mature in a matter of days, those that have interest paid every three months as well as those with one-yearly interest payment. To calculate the bey:

$$\frac{\text{Discount (that is, Face Value} - \text{Purchase Price)}}{\text{Purchase Price}} \times \frac{\text{Days in Year}}{\text{Days to Maturity}}$$

See Example 1 for a simple use of this idea.

Example 1   Bond equivalent rate

If we need to calculate the yield rate (bond equivalent rate or bey) for a 12-month £100 UK Treasury bill which was sold at a discount of 2 per cent, i.e. at £98, then we recognise that the investment made is £98 and we gain £2 when it is redeemed in one year. Thus we know that the true rate of return is slightly over 2 per cent. Given that there is a full year to maturity (assuming the day-count convention is a 365-day year), we know this is going to be the annual rate:

$$\text{bey} = \frac{\text{Face Value} - \text{Purchase Price}}{\text{Purchase Price}} \times \frac{\text{Days in Year}}{\text{Days to Maturity}} \times 100 = \text{annual rate}$$

$$\text{bey} = \frac{100 - 98}{98} \times \frac{365}{365} \times 100 = 2.04\%$$

(Appendix 5.2 at the end of this chapter runs through the key mathematical tools of finance. If your understanding is a little rusty you might like to read through that now and attempt the exercises.)

 b The discount yield (also known as **discount basis** or **discount rate** or **rate of discount**) is the yield when using the face value as the base rather than the actual amount invested by the buyer. To calculate the discount yield:

$$\frac{\text{Discount (Face Value} - \text{Purchase Price)}}{\text{Face Value}} \times \frac{\text{Days in Year}}{\text{Days to Maturity}}$$

See Example 2.

Example 2   Discount yield

For a T-bill issued at £98 when the face value is £100 and the time to maturity is one year:

$$d = \frac{(\text{Face Value} - \text{Purchase Price})}{\text{Face Value}} \times \frac{\text{Days in Year}}{\text{Days to Maturity}} \times 100 = \text{annual percentage rate}$$

$$d = \frac{(100 - 98)}{100} \times \frac{365}{365} \times 100 = 2\%$$

Just to emphasise: note that the yield rate (bey) is greater than the discount yield rate because the yield is earned on the purchase (discounted) price, not on the face value.

Exhibit 5.4 shows the results from the four sales of Treasury bills which took place weekly during February 2011, on the 4th, 11th, 18th and 25th. Note that the issues occurred at weekly intervals as the UK government borrowed more money or simply replaced maturing debt. The bills must be settled (paid for) and are issued on the next working day (generally the following Monday). The redemption date is the day when the face value of the bill (£100) will be paid to the holder. The nominal amount is the total amount of the face value of the bills offered at the tender (not what was actually paid for them).

Exhibit 5.4	DMO Treasury bill tender results, February 2011

Tender date	Issue date	Redemption date	Nominal amount (£ million)	Bid to cover ratio	Average yield (%)	Average price (£)
1 month						
4 Feb 11	7 Feb 11	7 Mar 11	500	3.35	0.447936%	99.965650
11 Feb 11	14 Feb 11	14 Mar 11	500	4.29	0.448549%	99.965603
18 Feb 11	21 Feb 11	21 Mar 11	500	3.54	0.441919%	99.966111
25 Feb 11	28 Feb 11	28 Mar 11	1,000	2.32	0.462185%	99.964557
3 months						
4 Feb 11	7 Feb 11	9 May 11	1,000	3.30	0.545785%	99.864112
11 Feb 11	14 Feb 11	16 May 11	1,000	3.24	0.531117%	99.867760
18 Feb 11	21 Feb 11	23 May 11	1,000	3.19	0.531527%	99.867658
25 Feb 11	28 Feb 11	31 May 11	1,000	4.51	0.539746%	99.864139
6 months						
4 Feb 11	7 Feb 11	8 Aug 11	1,500	4.54	0.685725%	99.659242
11 Feb 11	14 Feb 11	15 Aug 11	1,500	4.04	0.687697%	99.658265
18 Feb 11	21 Feb 11	22 Aug 11	1,500	4.06	0.694841%	99.654728
25 Feb 11	28 Feb 11	30 Aug 11	1,500	6.25	0.695687%	99.652416

Source: www.dmo.gov.uk

The bid to cover ratio is the ratio of the amount that was actually bid and the amount of T-bills offered; if the number is greater than 1 it shows that there were more bids than the amount on offer. Although extremely rare, it is not unknown for an offer to be undersubscribed[9] – it is a sign of lack of confidence in the government's financial situation and/or indigestion in a market faced with an exceptionally high volume of government borrowing. The average yield is expressed as an annual rate (bond equivalent yield). In this month, Treasury bills yielded a rate as low as 0.4419 per cent per annum, or around 0.0368 per cent per month. The average price is the price paid by purchasers for bills which will pay the holders of the bills £100 in one month, three months or six months.

---

[9] This has happened only twice for UK Treasury bills, both times in 2008, with a six-month bill offered for sale in October and a three-month bill offered for sale in May.

Example 3

If we take the three-month Treasury bill sold at tender on 18 February at a discount price of £99.867658, we can work out the discount (d), yield (bey) and purchase price. Note that the time difference between the date of purchase and redemption is only 91 days in this case and we must express these interest rates in annual terms, so we multiply by 365/91.

Discount yield:

$$d = \frac{(\text{Face Value} - \text{Purchase Price})}{\text{Face Value}} \times \frac{\text{Days in Year}}{\text{Days to Maturity}} \times 100 = \text{annual rate}$$

$$d = \frac{(100 - 99.867658)}{100} \times \frac{365}{91} \times 100 = 0.530822\% \text{ (expressed as an annual rate)}$$

Yield (on the Purchase Price):

$$\text{bey} = \frac{(\text{Face Value} - \text{Purchase Price})}{\text{Purchase Price}} \times \frac{365}{91} \times 100$$

$$\text{bey} = \frac{100 - 99.867658}{99.867658} \times \frac{365}{91} \times 100 = 0.531526\% \text{ (expressed as an annual rate)}$$

Purchase price:

$$\text{Purchase Price} = \text{Face Value} \times \left[1 - \left(\frac{\text{Discount} \times \text{Days to Maturity}}{\text{Days in Year}} \right) \right]$$

$$\text{Purchase Price} = 100 \times \left[1 - \left(\frac{0.00530822 \times 91}{365} \right) \right] = £99.867658$$

The results for the tender of this 18 February bill are shown in **Exhibit 5.5**. From this it can be noted that the actual bids from buyers varied from a yield of 0.51 per cent to a high of 0.548 per cent, with an average of 0.531527 per cent. The bill was over-tendered by a factor of 3.19, i.e. the amount on offer was £1 billion (at face value), and there were actual bids offered totalling £3.1905 billion.

Exhibit 5.5   Results of tender on three-month T-bill

3-month Treasury Bill ISIN code GB00B3K20F10 maturing on 23–May 2011

Lowest accepted yield	0.510000
Average yield	0.531527
Highest accepted yield	0.548000 (About 6.05% allotted)
Average rate of discount (%)	0.530824
Average price per £100 nominal (£)	99.867658
Amount tendered For (£)	3,190,500,000.00
Amount on offer (£)	1,000,000,000.00
Bid to cover ratio	3.19
Amount allocated (£)	999,991,500.00

Source: www.dmo.gov.uk

During the life of the bill, its value fluctuates daily as it is traded between investors – *see* **Exhibit 5.6**, which gives the daily February and March 2011 figures for this particular bill.

Exhibit 5.6	Data for Treasury Bill (named GB00B3K20F10) 22 February to 14 March 2011		
Redemption date	**Close of business date**	**Price (£)**	**Yield (%)**
23 May 2011	22 Feb 2011	99.857277	0.586
23 May 2011	23 Feb 2011	99.860408	0.580
23 May 2011	24 Feb 2011	99.861963	0.580
23 May 2011	25 Feb 2011	99.868675	0.571
23 May 2011	28 Feb 2011	99.872271	0.562
23 May 2011	01 Mar 2011	99.874686	0.559
23 May 2011	02 Mar 2011	99.876369	0.558
23 May 2011	03 Mar 2011	99.876466	0.564
23 May 2011	04 Mar 2011	99.879374	0.572
23 May 2011	07 Mar 2011	99.881184	0.571
23 May 2011	08 Mar 2011	99.882155	0.574
23 May 2011	09 Mar 2011	99.884076	0.572
23 May 2011	10 Mar 2011	99.886078	0.570
23 May 2011	11 Mar 2011	99.892274	0.562
23 May 2011	14 Mar 2011	99.895392	0.554

Source: www.dmo.gov.uk

Note: the price is what a purchaser would pay for the bill on a particular day. The price increases as the days to maturity decrease, and on redemption day, in this case 23 May 2011, the holder will receive the face value of £100. The yield in Exhibit 5.6 is the (annual) return (bey) that a purchaser in the secondary market will achieve between purchase date and maturity date.

Emerging-market Treasury bills

Many emerging-market economies[10] are now able to issue Treasury bills in their own currencies, while others concentrate issuance in one of the major world currencies, especially the US dollar. By borrowing in the US dollar or another international currency the lenders can borrow at lower interest rates because the international lenders are less fearful of a decline in the local currency, but this means that when the country has to redeem the T-bills it faces the risk that the dollar has risen against the local currency and so more local currency than initially thought needs to be paid out to lenders. This problem has caused financial crises in a number of countries over the years, e.g. Mexico in 1995, Russia in 1998 and Brazil in 1999.

US Treasury Bills

In the US, Treasury bills are sold by Treasury Direct (www.treasurydirect.gov), which is part of the US Department of the Treasury. The bills range in maturity from a few days to 52 weeks, with 4-week, 13-week (91 days) and 26-week (182 days) bills being the most common. They are sold at a discount to par value by auction every week, except for the 52-week bills, which are auctioned every four weeks. The auctions are held regularly and the bidders can bid for the bills in two ways (they have to choose one route or the other at the outset):

---

[10] Not yet fully developed economies.

- *Competitive* This is where potential buyers specify the discount rate they are willing to accept. hese bids may be (a) accepted in the full amount the bidder wanted if the discount rate they specified is less than the discount rate set by the auction. This threshold rate is determined by the Treasury, which, when all the bids are gathered in, sets the level of discount that will shift the bill quantity required. Competitive bids are accepted in ascending order until the quantity reaches the amount offered; (b) accepted only partially (the bidder does not receive the full amount of bills bid for) if their bid is the same as the cut-off level that sells the amount of bills the government is trying to sell in that auction; or (c) rejected if the bidder stated a level of discount that is higher than that set at the auction.

or

- *Non-competitive* This is where the buyer agrees to accept the rate or yield which is set at the auction (in other words, the price set by other investors). With a non-competitive bid the buyer is guaranteed to receive the bill to the full amount of bills they wanted. This is a good method for individual investors who are not expert security traders and therefore can avoid calculating bill discount rates.

All bidders, competitive and non-competitive, receive the same discount rate, and therefore the same yield, at the highest accepted bid, and so pay the same amount for their bills.

Individuals may bid and the minimum purchase is $100, unlike in the UK where the minimum bid is £500,000 and individuals may not bid themselves but hold UK Treasury bills only through one of the approved bidders.

Exhibit 5.7 gives the results of US T-bill auctions held during February 2011.

| Exhibit 5.7 | US Treasury bills auctioned February 2011 |

Treasury bills

Auction dates: from: 1 February 2011 to: 28 February 2011
Security terms: All
Sorted by: Auction date in ascending order

Security term	Auction date	Issue date	Maturity date	Discount rate %	Investment rate %	Price per $100
4-Week	02-01-2011	02-03-2011	03-03-2011	0.160	0.162	99.987556
13-Week	02-07-2011	02-10-2011	05-12-2011	0.150	0.152	99.962083
26-Week	02-07-2011	02-10-2011	08-11-2011	0.175	0.178	99.911528
4-Week	02-08-2011	02-10-2011	03-10-2011	0.135	0.137	99.989500
52-Week	02-08-2011	02-10-2011	02-09-2012	0.305	0.310	99.691611
13-Week	02-14-2011	02-17-2011	05-19-2011	0.130	0.132	99.967139
26-Week	02-14-2011	02-17-2011	08-18-2011	0.165	0.167	99.916583
4-Week	02-15-2011	02-17-2011	03-17-2011	0.100	0.101	99.992222
13-Week	02-22-2011	02-24-2011	05-26-2011	0.110	0.112	99.972194
26-Week	02-22-2011	02-24-2011	08-25-2011	0.155	0.157	99.921639
49-Day	02-23-2011	02-25-2011	04-15-2011	0.125	0.127	99.982986
4-Week	02-23-2011	02-24-2011	03-24-2011	0.120	0.122	99.990667
13-Week	02-28-2011	03-03-2011	06-02-2011	0.145	0.147	99.963347
26-Week	02-28-2011	03-03-2011	09-01-2011	0.170	0.173	99.914056

Source: www.treasurydirect.gov

If we take the 26-week T-bill which was auctioned on 22 February 2011 below its par value at $99.921639, we can work out the following figures:

Example 4   US Treasury bill issue

To calculate the **discount yield**, *d*, on the 26-week US T-bill sold on 24 February 2011 at a discount price of $99.921639:

$$d = \frac{(\text{Face Value} - \text{Purchase Price})}{\text{Face Value}} \times \frac{\text{Days in Year}}{\text{Days to Maturity}} \times 100$$

$$d = \frac{(100 - 99.921639)}{100} \times \frac{360}{182} \times 100 = 0.155\%$$

To calculate the purchase price of the same bill:

$$\text{Purchase Price} = \text{Face Value} \times \left[1 - \left(\frac{\text{Discount} \times \text{Days to Maturity}}{\text{Days in Year}} \right) \right]$$

$$\text{Purchase Price} = 100 \times \left[1 - \left(\frac{0.00155 \times 182}{360} \right) \right] = \pounds 99.921639$$

To calculate the actual investment rate of return (bond equivalent yield, bey) from this bill, a 365-day year is used (because a 360-day year would underestimate the return – we use a 366-day year in leap years):

$$\text{bey} = \frac{\text{Face Value} - \text{Purchase Price}}{\text{Purchase Price}} \times \frac{\text{Days in Year}}{\text{Days to Maturity}} \times 100$$

$$\text{bey} = \frac{100 - 99.921639}{99.921639} \times \frac{365}{182} \times 100 = 0.157276\% \text{ per annum}[11]$$

---

[11] To be really precise we need to note that this is not the effective annual rate (EAR) because we have failed to allow for the fact that after half a year we receive $100 (after investing $99.921639) and this can be reinvested for a second six months. Interest can be earned in the second six months on the first six months' interest that has been added to the original capital invested. In other words, the original investment is compounded more than once in the year. To calculate the EAR (if we can assume that in the second six months the interest rate is the same as in the first six months):

$$\left[1 + \frac{0.00157276}{365 \,/\, 182} \right]^{365/182} - 1 \times 100 = 0.157338\%$$

Another example:
You invested for three months and received a 'simple' annual yield of 3 per cent. This is an annual rate that does not allow for compounding over the year, i.e. interest received on interest added after each quarter is ignored. The effective annual rate is:

$$\left[1 + \frac{0.03}{4 \,/\, 1} \right]^{4/1} - 1 \times 100 = 3.0339\%$$

Thus, you receive an extra 0.0339 per cent because after three months you reinvest the maturity amount including interest from the first investment in an identical investment for the remaining nine months. And do the same after six months and nine months. Thus, you receive interest on interest received of 0.0339 per cent. This is, of course, assuming identical investments every three months. While this is unrealistic, at least the EAR provides a gauge of the 'true' annual rate offered on short-term securities.

The inverse relation between bill prices and interest rates

Say you bought a money market instrument with a maturity of six months. Presumably you were willing to pay the price you did because at that price the instrument offers the same rate of return as other instruments with the same level of risk and time to maturity. Now, imagine that two weeks later interest rates on five-and-a-half-month instruments being issued at that time suddenly shoot up (perhaps there has been a loss in confidence throughout the system, or a great increase in the supply of instruments occurs). Now there are securities being issued that offer any buyer a much higher rate of return to maturity than your bill. In the secondary market for your instrument potential buyers are unwilling to pay the price they did only a few days ago because such a high price equals a low discount-from-maturity value and a low effective interest rate. Now that there are alternative investments around that offer much higher interest rates, the discount on your bill will grow larger as the price people are willing to pay falls (people sell yours and buy alternatives), until the rate of return is the same as other instruments in the market.

Thus we see the inverse relation between prices of money market securities in the secondary market and the effective interest rate to maturity: a rise in bill prices means interest rates fall; a fall in bill prices causes interest rates to rise.

Central banks

Central banks are crucial to the working of a number of the money markets. One of the roles of a central bank is to keep the wheels of the financial world moving. They issue money (bank notes and coins), help set the domestic base rate of interest and maintain the stability of the financial system through **open market operations**, i.e. the buying or selling of money market securities to even out the liquidity in the economy. In the UK, the Bank of England sets the key benchmark interest rate for short-term lending by banks, often called the base rate. The European Central Bank based in Frankfurt performs a similar role for short-term euro lending, and in the US the Federal Reserve sets the federal funds rate.

Central banks exert control over their domestic banks, insisting that banks hold a deposit with them. They may deliberately keep banks short of liquidity and thereby reduce the amount of money available, which has the effect of increasing interest rates. Alternatively, they may release more liquidity into the markets, causing interest rates to fall. There is much more on the role of central banks in Chapter 7.

Commercial paper

Commercial paper (CP) is an unsecured short-term instrument of debt, issued primarily by corporations to help with financing their accounts receivable (debtors), inventories (stock) and meeting short-term cash needs, but can also be issued by banks and municipalities. The issue and purchase of commercial paper is one means by which the largest commercial organisations can avoid paying a bank intermediary a middleman fee for linking borrower and lender, e.g. corporations can avoid borrowing through loans from a bank and go direct to the financial market lenders.

Commercial paper promises to the holder a sum of money to be paid in a set number of days – it is a **promissory note**. The lender buys these short-term IOUs (I owe you's) and effectively lends money to the issuer.[12] The buyers include other corporations, insurance companies, pension funds, governments and banks. The investors in commercial paper buy it mostly from dealers, which are usually banks.

Commercial paper has an average maturity of about 40 days; the normal range is 30–90 days, but can be as long as 270 days. Normally these instruments are issued at a discount rather than the borrower being required to pay interest – thus the face value (amount paid on redemp-

---

[12] Originally the promise was written on paper, but today they are more often written electronically (they have been '**dematerialised**').

tion) will be higher than the amount paid for the paper at issuance.[13] The discount rate (and the yield gained by the lender) tends to be higher than for Treasury bills because there is a greater element of risk of default (the borrower may not repay) and because there is less liquidity in the secondary market.

Large corporations with temporary surpluses of cash are able to put that money to use by lending it directly to other commercial firms at a higher rate of effective interest than they might have received by depositing the funds in a bank. This source of finance is in general available only to the most respected corporations with the highest credit ratings (see the next section for a discussion of credit ratings) and is therefore usually issued with no collateral – that is, with no assets pledged by the borrower to be used to pay the obligation should it fail to do so by other means.

The main buyers, such as money market funds, are often restricted to having the bulk of their portfolios invested in those issues regarded by the credit rating agencies as carrying the lowest risk of default. Demand is very limited for lower-rated issues. In some countries using credit rating agencies to rate CP is rare, with the investors buying paper on the basis of the strength of the name of the organisation issuing it – only the largest, most well-known and trusted can issue in these places.

Some companies, such as General Electric, are such frequent issuers of CP that they employ in-house teams to do the selling. Other issuers ask dealers (usually employed by investment banks) either to buy the issue with the expectation of selling it on, or to use 'their best endeavours' to find lenders.

The secondary market in commercial paper is weak or non-existent – while dealers might be found who will buy commercial paper from a lender, it is not easy to complete such deals and can be costly.[14]

Although any one issue of commercial paper is short term, it is possible to use this market as a medium-term source of finance by **rolling over** issues. That is, as one issue matures, another one is launched. A **commercial paper programme** (a **revolving underwriting facility**) can be set up by a bank. In this situation, the bank (or a syndicate of banks) underwrites a specified maximum sum for a period of 5–7 years. The borrower then draws on this every few weeks or months by the issue of commercial paper to other lenders. If there are no bids for the paper the underwriting banks buy the paper at a specified price. A **multi-currency programme** can be arranged in which the issuer can select from a range of currencies when issuing a particular CP under a long-term programme. There is also **extendable commercial paper** – the issuer has a target date for redemption, but is not obligated to do so; it can extend the life of the paper (usually up to a total of 270 days).

Because it is a short-term source of funds it is best to use CP to finance operating expenses or current assets, such as accounts receivable (debtors) or inventories. It would be dangerous to use it to finance fixed assets, such as machinery or land and buildings, because it has to be paid back in a matter of days. While roll-over is often possible, it is by no means guaranteed and many companies have been caught out by relying too much on expecting to roll over.

US commercial paper (USCP)

The largest commercial paper market in the world, by far, is the US, distantly followed by Japan, Canada, France, the UK and other developed economies. Reuters reports that the commercial paper market in the US peaked in August 2007 to a total of $2,200 billion when the credit crisis happened. By mid-February 2011, the total had dropped to $1,041 billion. To put this in perspective, the output of all Americans in one year (gross domestic product) is around $14,000 billion. Of the issuance in February 2011, $355.8 billion was US **asset-backed commercial paper (ABCP)**, i.e.

---

[13] A small amount of commercial paper is issued with interest payments, but this is rare.

[14] One way of investing in commercial paper while obtaining liquidity is to invest via a money market fund: the fund buys a range of CP issues (and other instruments) and so, while it is committed to hold each CP to maturity, because it is well diversified, with many securities maturing every day, it is able to pay out to money market fund investors when they demand it.

commercial paper secured on the collateral of assets such as receivables – for example, the issuer has the right to receive monthly interest from mortgage payers, credit card holders, vehicle loans or some other regular income and uses this cash flow to pay the commercial paper when it becomes due and to provide collateral.[15]

According to US law, because its maturity is less than 270 days, commercial paper does not have to be registered with the Securities and Exchange Commission, the main US financial regulator, and therefore is not subject to the time-consuming and costly registration process required by US federal regulations. The largest US-based financial and other corporate issuers of commercial paper, including both asset-backed and unsecured paper, are General Electric Co and Citigroup Inc followed by Bank of America Corp and Morgan Stanley.

The commercial paper market can be very influential in corporate life. For example, in 2005, Standard & Poor's downgraded the commercial paper of Ford and General Motors, making their commercial paper unattractive to investors and thus increasing the cost of financing to these companies, and reducing the global confidence in both the companies and their products. This contributed to their financial crisis in 2009, when General Motors was forced into bankruptcy.

Eurocommercial paper (Euro-CP)

This is paper which is issued and placed outside the jurisdiction of the country in whose currency it is denominated. So an American corporation might issue commercial paper denominated in Japanese yen outside the control of the Japanese authorities, and this is classified as Eurocommercial paper. The most common denominations are euros, US dollars and GB pounds.

Example 5	Commercial paper

A dealer buys $2 million worth of Eurodollar commercial paper from a borrowing company with a 60-day maturity at a discounted price of $1,994,874. For Eurodollar (and most other Eurocurrency deals) interest is calculated using the 360-day count convention.

The discount yield (using an actual/360 day count) is:

$$d = \frac{(\text{Face Value} - \text{Purchase Price})}{\text{Face Value}} \times \frac{\text{Days in Year}}{\text{Days to Maturity}} \times 100$$

$$d = \frac{(2,000,000 - 1,994,874)}{2,000,000} \times \frac{360}{60} \times 100 = 1.5378\% \text{ per annum}$$

The **yield** (using an actual/365 day count) is:

$$bey = \frac{(\text{Face Value} - \text{Purchase Price})}{\text{Purchase Price}} \times \frac{\text{Days in Year}}{\text{Days to Maturity}} \times 100$$

$$bey = \frac{(2,000,000 - 1,994,874)}{1,994,874} \times \frac{365}{60} \times 100 = 1.5632\% \text{ (annual rate)}$$

---

[15] The issuers of ABCP are usually special entities/companies set up by a bank. These **special-purpose vehicles (SPVs)** or **structured-investment vehicles (SIVs)** or **'conduits'** buy the assets (rights to mortgage interest, etc.) after raising money from issuing commercial paper. Thus they are 'bankruptcy remote' from the parent company that supplied the assets – if they go bust, the parent bank can still survive. Also, they are perceived as less risky for the investors because of the security of the assigned assets, so if the parent goes bust the lenders still have the collateral in the SPV. (At least that was the theory, but many SPVs and their parent banks disappeared or nearly blew up when they could not roll over the ABCP that they were accustomed to doing in 2008.)

Exhibit 5.8 describes how badly the CP market was hit by the loss of confidence in financial institutions in 2008.

Exhibit 5.8

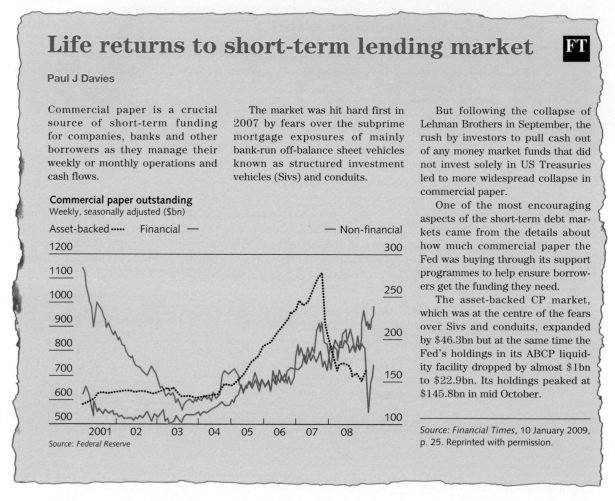

Life returns to short-term lending market   FT

Paul J Davies

Commercial paper is a crucial source of short-term funding for companies, banks and other borrowers as they manage their weekly or monthly operations and cash flows.

The market was hit hard first in 2007 by fears over the subprime mortgage exposures of mainly bank-run off-balance sheet vehicles known as structured investment vehicles (Sivs) and conduits.

But following the collapse of Lehman Brothers in September, the rush by investors to pull cash out of any money market funds that did not invest solely in US Treasuries led to more widespread collapse in commercial paper.

One of the most encouraging aspects of the short-term debt markets came from the details about how much commercial paper the Fed was buying through its support programmes to help ensure borrowers get the funding they need.

The asset-backed CP market, which was at the centre of the fears over Sivs and conduits, expanded by $46.3bn but at the same time the Fed's holdings in its ABCP liquidity facility dropped by almost $1bn to $22.9bn. Its holdings peaked at $145.8bn in mid October.

Commercial paper outstanding
Weekly, seasonally adjusted ($bn)

Asset-backed ·····   Financial —   — Non-financial

Source: Federal Reserve

Source: Financial Times, 10 January 2009, p. 25. Reprinted with permission.

Credit ratings

Firms often pay to have their bonds and short-term borrowing instruments rated by specialist **credit-rating** organisations. The rating given is an evaluation made by the rating agency of the firm's ability to repay its debt and will affect the interest rate on the debt instruments. Standard & Poor's, Moody's and Fitch Ratings are the three most important credit-rating companies. Each uses slightly different terminology for their rating system – *see* **Exhibit 5.9**.

Many government-issued securities have an insignificant risk of default. We would expect that firms in stable industries and with conservative accounting and financing policies and a risk-averse business strategy would have a lower risk of default and therefore a higher credit rating than a firm with greatly fluctuating income and high borrowing.

The highest ratings (AAA for long-term bonds and P-1, A-1+ and F1+ for short-term borrowing) indicate that the capacity to repay interest and principal is extremely strong; the lower ratings (B, Cs and Ds) indicate that there is an increased likelihood of default. Debt rated BB has speculative characteristics, but it is not as likely to default as debt rated CC, which has some protection but there are significant uncertainties and major risks with it. The top part of the table shows the ratings regarded as **investment grade**. This is important because many

Exhibit 5.9 — Credit rating systems

Moody's		Standard & Poor's		Fitch Ratings			
Long term	Short term	Long term	Short term	Long term	Short term		
Aaa	P-1	AAA	A-1+	AAA	F1+	Prime	Investment grade securities
Aa1	P-1	AA+	A-1+	AA+	F1+	High grade	Investment grade securities
Aa2	P-1	AA	A-1+	AA	F1+	High grade	Investment grade securities
Aa3	P-1	AA-	A-1+	AA-	F1+	High grade	Investment grade securities
A1	P-1	A+	A-1	A+	F1	Upper medium grade	Investment grade securities
A2	P-1	A	A-1	A	F1	Upper medium grade	Investment grade securities
A3	P-2	A-	A-2	A-	F2	Upper medium grade	Investment grade securities
Baa1	P-2	BBB+	A-2	BBB+	F2	Lower medium grade	Investment grade securities
Baa2	P-3	BBB	A-3	BBB	F3	Lower medium grade	Investment grade securities
Baa3	P-3	BBB-	A-3	BBB-	F3	Lower medium grade	Investment grade securities
Ba1	Not Prime	BB+	B	BB+	B	Somewhat speculative	Non-investment grade, high-yield or 'junk' securities
Ba2	Not Prime	BB	B	BB	B	Speculative	Non-investment grade, high-yield or 'junk' securities
Ba3	Not Prime	BB-	B	BB-	B	Speculative	Non-investment grade, high-yield or 'junk' securities
B1	Not Prime	B+	B	B+	B	Highly speculative	Non-investment grade, high-yield or 'junk' securities
B2	Not Prime	B	B	B	B	Highly speculative	Non-investment grade, high-yield or 'junk' securities
B3	Not Prime	B-	B	B-	B	Highly speculative	Non-investment grade, high-yield or 'junk' securities
Caa	Not Prime	CCC+	C	CCC	C	Substantial risks	Non-investment grade, high-yield or 'junk' securities
Ca	Not Prime	CCC	C	CCC	C	Extremely speculative	Non-investment grade, high-yield or 'junk' securities
C	Not Prime	CCC-	C	CCC	C	In default with little prospect for discovery	Non-investment grade, high-yield or 'junk' securities
/	Not Prime	D	D	DDD	D	In default	Non-investment grade, high-yield or 'junk' securities
/	Not Prime	D	D	DD	D	In default	Non-investment grade, high-yield or 'junk' securities
/	Not Prime	D	D	D	D	In default	Non-investment grade, high-yield or 'junk' securities

institutional investors are permitted to invest only in investment-grade bonds and short-term instruments. The difference in yield between the different grades in the investment-grade group can be as little as 30 basis points, but this can rise dramatically at times of financial trauma, e.g. in early 2009.

Bonds rated below investment grade are called **high-yield** (or **junk**) **bonds** – discussed in Chapter 6. Short-term securities, such as commercial paper rated B and C, are *not prime*, or *medium or low grade*, or *second-tier* and *third-tier*, and may have limited demand, because of the increased risk. The attraction to lenders of low-grade commercial paper can be enhanced by the issuing company obtaining a line of credit from a bank, under which the bank agrees to make the due payment on the CP should the company be unable to do so.

The rating can be carried out on the firm, but, for bonds and commercial paper, is usually related only to the particular bond or CP. If a loan does not have a rating it could be that the borrower has not paid for one, rather than implying anything more sinister.

The rating and re-rating of bonds and short-term instruments is followed with great interest by borrowers and lenders and can give rise to some heated argument. Credit ratings are of great concern to the borrowing corporation because those with lower ratings tend to have higher costs. Occasionally the ratings agencies disagree over the rating of a loan, in which case it is said to have a split rating.

It has been suggested that during the run-up to the financial crisis of 2008 the credit-rating agencies gave unduly high ratings to loans that were shaky. The agencies were widely regarded as financial watchdogs, and investors have relied on their ratings of public companies and securities to gauge risk and make investment decisions, yet too many of their highly rated investments proved to be risky and speculative.

Repos

A **repo** is a way of borrowing for a few days using a **sale and repurchase agreement** in which securities are sold for cash at an agreed price with a promise to buy back the securities at a specified (higher) price at a future date. The interest on the agreement is the difference between the initial sale price and the agreed buy-back, and because the agreements are usually collateralised (secured) by government-backed securities such as Treasury bills, the interest rate is lower than a typical unsecured loan from a bank. While collateral back-up for the lender is usually provided by the borrower handing over very safe government-issued securities, other very safe securities might be used. If the borrower defaults on its obligations to buy back on maturity, the lender can hold on to or sell the securities.

Repos (RPs) are used very regularly by banks and other financial institutions to borrow money from each other. Companies do use the repo markets, but much less frequently than the banks. This market is also manipulated by central banks to manage their monetary policy – *see* Chapter 7.

The best way to understand the repo market is through an example – *see* Example 6.

Example 6   **A repo using actual data**

A high-street bank needs to borrow £6 million for 14 days. It agrees to sell a portfolio of its financial assets, in this case government bonds, to a lender for £6 million. An agreement is drawn up (a repo) by which the bank agrees to repurchase the portfolio 14 days later for £6,001,219.73. The extra sum of £1,219.73 represents the interest on £6 million over 14 days at an annual rate of 0.53 per cent. The calculation is:

$$\text{Interest} = \text{Selling Price} \times \text{Interest Rate} \times \frac{\text{Days to Maturity}}{\text{Days in Year}}$$

$$\text{Interest} = 6,000,000 \times \frac{0.53}{100} \times \frac{14}{365} = £1,219.73$$

The term for repos is usually between 1 and 14 days, but can be up to a year and occasionally there is no end date – this is called an **open repo**.

A **reverse repo (RRP)** is the lender's side of the transaction, an agreement in which securities are *purchased* with a promise to *sell them back* at an agreed price at a future date. Traders may do this to gain interest. Alternatively, it could be to cover another market transaction. For example, a trading house may need to obtain some Treasury bills or bonds temporarily because it has shorted them – sold them before buying – and needs to find a supply to meet its obligations, so it places a reverse repo order to get an inflow of the securities now. In a transaction, the terms repo and reverse repo are used according to which party initiated the transaction, i.e. if a seller initiates the transaction, it is a repo; if the transaction is initiated by a buyer, it is a reverse repo.

Repos are very useful for banks and other financial institutions which hold large quantities of money market securities such as T-bills. They can gain access to liquidity through the repo for a few days while maintaining a high level of inventory in short-term securities.

Exhibit 5.10 shows the repo rates recorded by the British Banking Association in February 2011.

Exhibit 5.10	Repo rates in February 2011				
	22 Feb.	**23 Feb.**	**24 Feb.**	**25 Feb.**	**28 Feb.**
GBP					
Overnight	0.50167	0.49833	0.49500	0.50000	0.50167
1 week	0.52333	0.52167	0.52000	0.52000	0.52167
2 week	0.53167	0.53000	0.53000	0.53000	0.53333
3 week	0.54167	0.54167	0.53833	0.53833	0.54000
1 month	0.55333	0.55167	0.54833	0.54833	0.55000
2 month	0.59000	0.58500	0.58167	0.57833	0.58333
3 month	0.63333	0.62833	0.63000	0.62000	0.62000
6 month	0.78167	0.78667	0.77833	0.76500	0.76000
9 month	0.89833	0.91167	0.89833	0.86667	0.86667
1 year	1.02167	1.04167	1.00667	0.97167	0.97833

Source: www.bbalibor.com

Example 7	A repo using actual data

A company owning £20 million worth of Treasury bills wishes to raise cash on 28 February 2011 and enters into an agreement to sell the bills and buy them back in one week's time. The agreed buy-back price would be £20 million plus the accrued interest. The annual rate of interest on 28 February for a one-week repo is shown in Exhibit 5.10 as 0.52167 per cent.

$$\text{Buy-back Price} = \text{Selling Price} + \left(\text{Selling Price} \times \text{Interest Rate} \times \frac{\text{Days to Maturity}}{\text{Days in Year}} \right)$$

$$\text{Buy-back Price} = 20,000,000 + \left(20,000,000 \times \frac{0.52167}{100} \times \frac{7}{365} \right) = £20,002,000.9$$

Haircuts

Although the securities bought and sold are generally considered safe collateral for the lender of the cash, there is always the danger that the price of the bills, etc. may fluctuate during the period of the agreement to the detriment of the buyer. Therefore it is common practice to impose a **haircut** on the collateral, where the seller receives the amount of cash secured on the collateral less a margin (the haircut). If the haircut is 0.075 per cent in Example 7, the seller would receive £19,985,000 in return for £20 million worth of securities, and the repo interest is applied only to the lesser amount. The buyer (lender) pays out £19,985,000, but has securities worth £20 million, and receives interest on the amount of cash lent – *see* Example 8.

Example 8   A repo with a haircut

Using the figures from Example 7, the buy-back price can then be calculated:

$$\text{Buy-back Price} = \text{Selling Price} + \left[\left(\text{Selling Price} - \text{Haircut} \right) \times \text{Interest Rate} \times \frac{\text{Days to Maturity}}{\text{Days in Year}} \right]$$

$$\text{Buy-back Price} = 20{,}000{,}000 + \left[\left(20{,}000{,}000 - \left\{ 20{,}000{,}000 \times \frac{0.075}{100} \right\} \right) \times \frac{0.52167}{100} \times \frac{7}{365} \right] = £20{,}001{,}999.4$$

Repo deals are individually negotiated between the two parties and are therefore designed to suit the length of time of borrowing for each of them, thus there is usually little need for redemption before the agreed date. However, if circumstances change and the lender needs the money quickly, it might be possible to arrange an off-setting reverse repo transaction.

Exhibit 5.11 shows how the repo market declined after the collapse of Lehman's. It also points out how dependent the US market is on two banks and how the collateral used in the run-up to the crisis deteriorated.

Exhibit 5.11

Run on banks left repo sector highly exposed

By Michael Mackenzie in New York

FT

The sharp reduction in financial leverage since the collapse of Lehman Brothers is illustrated by the steep decline in the use of repurchase or repo transactions by Wall Street dealers.

In a repo, an investor can borrow cash for a short period from another party, using securities as collateral for the loan. Investors with large portfolios of securities can thus lend these out and earn a return over time.

Federal Reserve data shows that financing volumes of mortgages, US Treasuries and corporate debt by primary dealers has dropped nearly 50 per cent from levels seen before Lehman's demise. Overall repo activity in the US during the first six months of this year has fallen to levels not seen since 2003.

"Everybody now pays more attention to due diligence and looks at their counter party risk a lot more closely," says Scott Skyrm,

senior vice-president at Newedge, a repo broker dealer.

At the centre of the US repo market sits the tri-party model, where a custodian bank, Bank of New York Mellon and JPMorgan helps to administer a repo agreement between two parties. An investor places its money with the custodian bank, which in turn lends it to another institution, and then assets are pledged as collateral for the loan.

Repo market yet to regain pre-Lehman collapse levels in the US and Europe

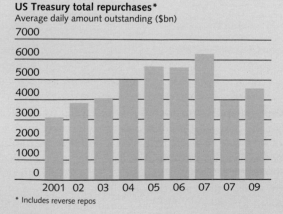

US Treasury total repurchases*
Average daily amount outstanding ($bn)

* Includes reverse repos

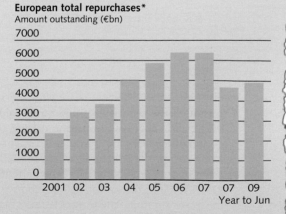

European total repurchases*
Amount outstanding (€bn)

Year to Jun

▶

Exhibit 5.11 continued

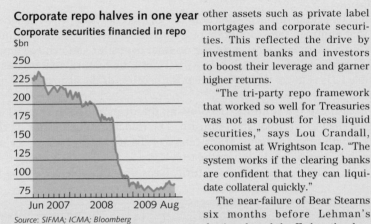

Corporate repo halves in one year
Corporate securities financed in repo
$bn

Source: SIFMA; ICMA; Bloomberg

other assets such as private label mortgages and corporate securities. This reflected the drive by investment banks and investors to boost their leverage and garner higher returns.

"The tri-party repo framework that worked so well for Treasuries was not as robust for less liquid securities," says Lou Crandall, economist at Wrightson Icap. "The system works if the clearing banks are confident that they can liquidate collateral quickly."

The near-failure of Bear Stearns six months before Lehman's demise alerted the Fed to the dangers associated with having two clearing banks supporting the financial system.

Tri-party was very popular with investment banks as it is allowed them to finance their balance sheets with short-term funding.

But as soon as market sentiment turned negative on lower quality or more complex assets,

investors who had funded these repo agreements began to pull their money out. That sparked a run on the investment banks, potentially exposing the clearing banks. This has left regulators and the market with one big fear: if one clearing bank ran into trouble, could the other step forward and support the system? There is also a separate issue, which is that when investors become worried about a particular institution, any move by a clearing bank to tighten standards could spark a bigger run on the borrower in question that ultimately results in bankruptcy or rescue.

"There were a lot of assets that should not have been used as collateral in the repo market to start with. Repo is not a one-size fits-all market," says Joseph Abate, money markets strategist at Barclays Capital.

Source: Financial Times, 11 September 2009, p. 35. Reprinted with permission.

Such a model functions well when liquid assets such as Treasuries are being used, as this type of collateral can easily be sold.

During the credit boom, which peaked in the first half of 2007, the type of collateral being pledged for cash in repo transactions, had steadily migrated away from Treasuries and towards

Local authority/municipal bills

Local authorities issue these short-term instruments to finance capital expenditure and cash flow needs. They are not common in the UK, but widely used in the US, Brazil and Canada where they are issued by many states, cities and local governments. A big attraction in the US is that the interest (but not the capital gain) is generally free of federal (and sometimes state and local) income taxes. They tend to be regarded as safe investments. There is a strong market in local authority bills and bonds in many European countries, notably France, Italy and Germany, where individual federal states issue them regularly. There are also many bill issues by companies close to governments, e.g. the French railway, SNCF, or the German postal service, Deutsche Bundespost.

Certificates of deposit (CDs)

Certificates of deposit are issued by banks when funds are deposited with them by other banks, corporations, individuals or investment companies. The certificates state that a deposit has been made (a time deposit) and that at the maturity date the bank will pay a sum higher than that originally deposited. The maturities can be any length of time between a week and a year (typically 1–4 months)[16] and can be negotiable[17] or non-negotiable. There is a penalty on the saver withdraw-

---

[16] CDs can be issued with a maturity date of two years or longer. The instruments dated for more than one year may pay a variable rate of interest, with the rate altered, say, each year, based on a benchmark rate, e.g. LIBOR. It is possible to find short-term CDs with variable interest rates, e.g. the interest on a six-month CD changes every 30 days depending on the one-month LIBOR rate.

[17] While many CDs can be sold in a highly liquid secondary market to another investor before the maturity date, other CDs are not so liquid, with few potential buyers interested in trading.

ing the money before the maturity date (they are **term securities**). CDs are normally issued in lots ranging from £50,000 to £500,000 in the UK, or $100,000 to $1 million in the US, with similar sized lots in the Eurozone and Japan.

Non-negotiable CDs must be held by the depositor until the CD reaches maturity. The advantage of negotiable CDs is that although they cannot be redeemed at the issuing bank without a penalty, they can be traded in a secondary market, so the original depositor can achieve liquidity but the bank issuing the certificate has a deposit held with it until the maturity date. The rate of interest paid on negotiable CDs is lower than a fixed deposit because of the attraction of high liquidity.

A company with surplus cash can put it into a CD knowing that if its situation changes and it needs extra cash, it can sell the CD (if negotiable) for cash. The tradable value of the CD rises according to the remaining length of its maturity. At the centre of the secondary market is a network of brokers and dealers in CDs, striking deals over the telephone.

CDs are quoted in the trading market on a yield-to-maturity basis – *see* Example 9.

Example 9   CDs

A £75,000 CD is issued on 15 March for two months at 1.04 per cent (expressed as an annual rate, even though the money is deposited for a mere two months). This means that the bank will pay the following at maturity (including accumulated interest):

$$\text{Value at Maturity} = \text{Face Value} + \left(\text{Face Value} \times \frac{\text{Interest}}{100} \times \frac{\text{Days to Maturity}}{\text{Days in year}} \right)$$

$$\text{Value at Maturity} = 75,000 + \left(75,000 \times \frac{1.04}{100} \times \frac{61}{365} \right) = 75,130.36$$

The CD is sold to another investor with 16 days left to maturity. Its present value (at the time of sale) if annual rates of interest on 16-day CDs are 1.04 per cent is:

$$\text{Present Value} = \frac{\text{Value at Maturity}}{1 + \left(\dfrac{\text{Interest}}{100} \times \dfrac{\text{Days to Maturity}}{\text{Days in Year}} \right)}$$

$$\text{Present Value} = \frac{75,130.36}{1 + \left(\dfrac{1.04}{100} \times \dfrac{16}{365} \right)} = 75,096.12$$

Thus, the second holder of the CD will pay £75,096.12 now and receive £75,130.36 from the bank if they hold for another 16 days.

The yield to maturity of this CD held for 16 days is:

$$\text{Yield to Maturity} = \frac{\text{Value at Maturity} - \text{Present Value}}{\text{Present Value}} \times \frac{\text{Days in Year}}{\text{Days to Maturity}} \times 100$$

$$\text{Yield to Maturity expressed as an annual rate} = \frac{75,130.36 - 75,096.12}{75,096.12} \times \frac{365}{16} \times 100 = 1.04\%$$

As well as domestic currency CDs there are **Eurocurrency (Eurodollar) certificates of deposit**. Standard **Eurocurrency deposits** (not CDs) have fixed maturities – say seven days, and you cannot get at that money until the seven days have passed. By issuing Eurodollar CDs banks are able to offer an improvement if those CDs are negotiable, by allowing depositors to sell the CDs to other investors before maturity.

Bills of exchange/banker's acceptances

Bills of exchange and banker's acceptances are instruments that are particularly useful in helping to oil the wheels of international commerce. They enable corporations to obtain credit or to raise money, and also to trade with foreign corporations at low risk of financial inconvenience or loss. An illustration of the problem is provided in Example 10.

Example 10	The international trade problem

Tractors UK has found a firm in South Africa which wishes to buy £2 million worth of its tractors. Tractors UK cannot simply send its tractors to South Africa in the hope that the payment will be sent, nor can the South African firm send money in the hope that the tractors will be sent. The two companies do not know each other well enough to trust that the transaction will be carried out correctly on each side. The solution is to use a bill of exchange or a banker's acceptance, which will provide a legally enforceable promise of payment of £2 million to Tractors UK, which can send the tractors off to South Africa, knowing with a high degree of certainty that payment will be made.

Bills of exchange

Bills of exchange have been used to smooth the progress of overseas trade for a long time. Known to have been used by the Babylonians, Egyptians, Greeks and Romans, the bill of exchange appeared in its present form during the thirteenth century among the Lombards of northern Italy who engaged in widespread foreign trading. These instruments became particularly useful in the burgeoning international trade of the nineteenth and twentieth centuries.

The seller of goods to be exported to a buyer in another country frequently grants the customer a number of months in which to pay. The seller will draw up a bill of exchange (also called a trade bill). This is a legal document showing the indebtedness of the buyer. The bill of exchange is then forwarded to and accepted by the customer, which means that the customer signs a promise to pay the stated amount and currency on the due date. The due date is usually 90 days later, but 30-, 60- or 180-days bills of exchange are not uncommon.

The bill is returned to the seller who then has a choice: either to hold it until maturity, or to sell it at a discount to a bank or discount house. Under the second option the purchaser, called a discounter, will pay a lower amount than the sum to be received in, say, 90 days from the customer. The difference represents the discounter's interest payment.

Bills of exchange are normally used only for transactions greater than £75,000. The effective interest rate charged by the discounter is usually a competitive 150–400 basis points over inter-bank lending rates (for example, LIBOR) depending on the creditworthiness of the seller and the customer. The bank that purchased the bill in the discount market has **recourse** to both of the commercial companies: if the customer does not pay then the seller will be called upon to make good the debt. This overhanging credit risk can sometimes be dealt with by the selling company obtaining credit insurance. Despite the simplification of **Exhibit 5.12**, many bills of exchange do not remain in the hands of the discounter until maturity but are traded in an active secondary market (the money market). Note also that not all bills of exchange are a form of temporary finance. Some are 'sight drafts', that is, payable on demand immediately.

Banker's acceptances

A banker's acceptance, also known as an acceptance credit, is a time draft, which is a document stating the signatory will pay an amount at a future date. Say, for example, that an importer has agreed to buy goods from an exporter with an agreement to pay in three months. The exporter could be instructed to send the document which states that the signatory will pay a sum of money at a set date in the future to the importer's bank. This is 'accepted' by the importer's bank rather than by a customer. (Simultaneously the importer makes a commitment to pay the accepting bank the relevant sum at the maturity date of the bill.)

Exhibit 5.12   Bill of exchange sequence

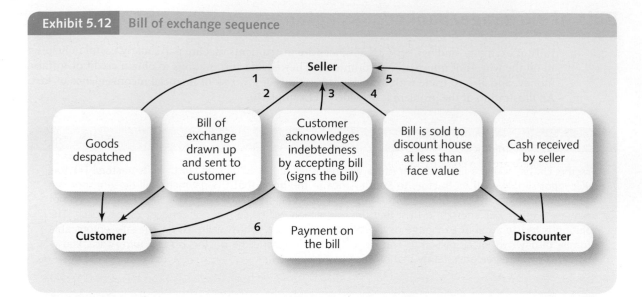

Example 11   Bill of exchange

A customer has accepted a bill of exchange which commits it to pay £300,000 in 90 days. The bill is sold by the supplier immediately to a discount house or bank for £297,000. After 90 days the discounter will realise a profit of £3,000 on a £297,000 asset. To calculate the effective rate of interest:

$$\text{Interest} = \frac{\text{Discount}}{\text{Discounted Price}} \times 100$$

$$\text{Interest} = \frac{3000}{297,000} \times 100 = 1.0101\%$$

To calculate the annual rate of interest, the bond equivalent yield, bey, this equates to:

$$\text{bey} = \frac{\text{Discount}}{\text{Discounted Price}} \times 100 \times \frac{\text{Days in Year}}{\text{Days to Maturity}}$$

$$\text{bey} = \frac{3000}{297,000} \times 100 \times \frac{365}{90} = 4.0965\%$$

Through this arrangement the customer has the benefit of the goods on 90 days' credit, the supplier has made a sale and immediately receives cash from the discount house amounting to 99 per cent of the total due, and the discounter, if it can borrow its funds at less than 1.01 per cent over 90 days, turns in a healthy profit.

This bank commitment to pay the holder of the acceptance credit allows it to be sold with more credibility in the money markets to, say, another bank (a discounter) by the exporter after receiving it from an importing company's bank.

Not all banker's acceptances relate to overseas trade. Many are simply a way of raising money for a firm. The company in need of finance may simply ask its bank to create a banker's acceptance and hand it over. Then the company can sell it in the discount market at a time when it needs to raise some cash.

While banker's acceptances are similar to bills of exchange between a seller and a buyer, they have the advantage that the organisation promising to pay is a reputable bank representing a lower credit risk to any subsequent discounter, thus they normally attract finer discount rates than bills of exchange. The holder of the instrument has two guarantors: first the importer and second the bank.

When the maturity date is reached the company (e.g. importer) pays its bank the value of the bill and the bank pays the ultimate holder of the bill its face value. They are very useful for companies expanding into new markets where their name is not known, and therefore their creditworthiness is also unknown; they can take advantage of the superior creditworthiness of the bank issuing the acceptance, which guarantees that payment will be made.

There are two costs involved:

1   The bank charges acceptance commission for adding its name to the acceptance.

2   The difference between the face value of the acceptance and the discount price, which is the effective interest rate. (Also, dealers take a small cut as they connect firms that want to sell with companies that wish to invest in banker's acceptances.)

These costs are relatively low compared with overdraft costs. However, this facility is available only in hundreds of thousands of pounds, euros, etc. and then only to the most creditworthy of companies. **Exhibit 5.13** summarises the acceptance credit sequence for an export deal.

Exhibit 5.13   Banker's acceptance sequence – for an export deal

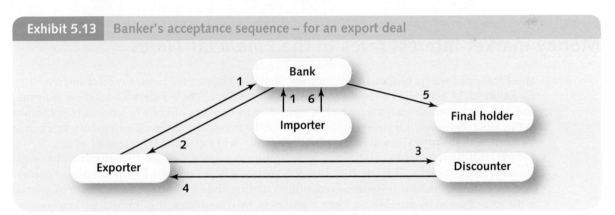

---

1   Banker's acceptance drafted and sent by an exporting company (or its bank) demanding payment for goods sent to an importer's bank. Importer makes arrangements with its bank to help it. Acceptance commission paid to the bank by importer.

2   The bank accepts the promise to pay a sum at a stated future date.

3   The banker's acceptance is sold at a discount.

4   The discounter pays cash for the banker's acceptance.

5   The bank pays the final holder of the banker's acceptance the due sum.

6   The importer pays to the bank the banker's acceptance due sum.

Example 12   The use of a banker's acceptance

A Dutch company buys €3.5 million of goods from a firm in Japan and draws up a document promising to pay for the goods in 60 days' time. The Dutch company asks its bank to accept the document. Once the bank has stamped 'accepted' on the document, it becomes a negotiable (sellable) instrument. The exporter receives the banker's acceptance. After 15 days, the Japanese company decides it needs some extra short-term finance and sells the acceptance at a discount of 0.60 per cent. To calculate how much (the selling price) it receives:

▶

Selling Price = Face Value – (Face Value × Discount Percentage)

$$\text{Selling Price} = 3,500,000 - \left(3,500,000 \times \frac{0.60}{100}\right) = \text{€}3,479,000, \text{ a discount of €21,000}$$

To calculate the annual rate of interest, the bond equivalent yield, bey, which this is costing them:

$$\text{bey} = \frac{\text{Discount}}{\text{Discounted Price}} \times 100 \times \frac{\text{Days in Year}}{\text{Days to Maturity}}$$

$$\text{bey} = \frac{21,000}{3,479,000} \times 100 \times \frac{365}{45} = 4.896\%$$

The exporter has been paid by banker's acceptance immediately the goods are despatched. It can also shield itself from the risk of exchange rates shifting over the next 60 days by discounting the acceptance immediately, receiving euros and then converting these to yen. And, of course, the exporter is not exposed to the credit risk of the importer because it has the guarantee from the importer's bank.

Money market interest rates in the *Financial Times*

The *Financial Times* publishes a table each day showing many of the money market interest rates. *See* **Exhibit 5.14** for a table showing rates for 15 March 2011. The *FT* shows a lot more information at www.ft.com/bonds&rates. The UK three-month Treasury bill rate of interest is not shown in this table. However, it is shown at the bottom of the front page of the *FT* every day – in a box at the bottom of the page you will find the 'UK 3 million' yield expressed as an annual rate.

Special drawing rights (SDRs) are a composite currency designed by the **International Monetary Fund (IMF)**. This currency basket is currently based on four key international currencies, consisting of the euro, Japanese yen, pound sterling and US dollar. The SDR rate of interest is the rate charged by the IMF on loans it makes to IMF members. It is an international reserve asset to supplement its member countries' official reserves when it is felt that, with the increase in world trade, the amount of gold and US dollar reserves does not offer enough security to support this expansion.

Comparing interest rates

Despite money market instruments having maturities of no more than one year it can be seen from the *FT* table in Exhibit 5.14 that they can have remarkably different interest rates depending on the length of time to maturity. For example, on 15 March 2011 a sterling interbank loan for one month cost 0.61313 per cent at an annualised rate whereas a loan of similar default risk (i.e. very low), but lasting for one year, had an annualised interest rate more than double that, at 1.57688 per cent.

These yields to maturity also vary considerably over time – *see* **Exhibits 5.15 and 5.16**, which show comparative interest rates from the UK and the US over a 30-year period. A number of observations can be made about the interest rate on different money market instruments:

- Generally, investors require extra return for longer lending periods, so overnight rates will normally be less than rates on longer-term instruments (although this is not always the case). Notice in Exhibit 5.16 US six-month T-bill rates are generally higher than those for three-month lending.

- The credit rating of the borrowing institution has a strong influence on the rate of interest charged. The rate offered by reputable national governments will usually be lower than the

Exhibit 5.14 Money market interest rates is the *Financial Times*

FINANCIAL TIMES WEDNESDAY MARCH 16 2011

INTEREST RATES – MARKET

Mar 15	Overnight	Change Day	Change Week	Change Month	One month	Three month	Six month	One year
US$ Libor*	0.21150	-0.004	-0.009	-0.022	0.25350	0.30900	0.46000	0.76850
Euro Libor*	0.66875	-0.061	0.215	0.144	0.84750	1.12000	1.43125	1.86500
£ Libor*	0.55688	0.001	0.001	0.001	0.61313	0.80563	1.10750	1.57688
Swiss Fr Libor*	0.08167	–	-0.005	-0.002	0.13667	0.17833	0.24667	0.54500
Yen Libor*	0.49125	0.384	0.386	0.387	0.15875	0.20000	0.34750	0.57125
Canada Libor*	0.96833	-0.003	–	0.008	1.07917	1.20417	1.40000	1.90500
Euro Euribor	–	–	–	–	0.89	1.17	1.47	1.91
Sterling CDs	–	–	–	–	0.66	0.89	1.18	1.56
US$ CDs	–	–	–	–	0.25	0.32	0.45	0.87
Euro CDs	–	–	–	–	0.80	1.05	1.35	1.85
US o'night repo	0.22	0.010	0.020	0.010				
Fed Funds eff	0.14	–	-0.010	-0.010				
US 3m Bills	0.10	0.020	-0.015	-0.015				
SDR int rate	0.43	-0.040	-0.040	0.010				
EONIA	0.72	-0.029	0.271	-0.109				
EURONIA	0.62	-0.057	0.233	-0.136				
SONIA	0.52	0.003	0.000	0.000				
LA 7 Day Notice 0.45–0.40								

Interest rates are quoted for a number of different lengths of time to maturity, from overnight (24 hours) to one year.

The interest rate in the US for a repurchase agreement when the repurchase occurs the next day. The 0.22% interest rate is the annual rate.

Special Drawing Rights of the IMF. The right of interest charged by the IMF on loans made to its members.

Money lent to local authorities for 7 days.

Libor rates in various currencies came from the British Bankers Association (www.bba.org.uk) and are fixed at 11a.m.

Certificates of deposits for deposits of sterling, US dollars and euros (data collected from dealers in this market).

Source: Financial Times, 16 March 2011. Reprinted with permission.

rate offered by a corporation wishing to raise cash by issuing commercial paper, or by a bank issuing certificates of deposit – *see* Exhibits 5.15 and 5.16. However, there are some governments that are required by the financial markets to pay higher interest rates than many international corporates – e.g. Greece, Portugal and Ireland in 2011 paid more than HSBC.

● When expectations about future inflation rise, interest rates rise accordingly, which leads to a decrease in the market price of money market instruments. Conversely, when inflation expectations are lowered, interest rates fall and the market price of the instruments rises. Thus we see that interest rates across the board tend to rise and fall together over time. The high rates of interest offered in the 1980s largely reflected the high inflation of the time.

● Supply and demand – if banks need to borrow large sums of money quickly, they will sell more shorter-term instruments. This will have the effect of increasing market supply of these instruments, and therefore pushing down their price, which in turn will increase the rate of interest, the yield to maturity.

● Money market interest rates with similar terms to maturity stay close together and move up or down with quite a high degree of correlation over time. They are all low risk and all short term, thus there is a reasonable amount of substitutability between them for potential lenders. Thus, if interest rates in, say, the CD market fell significantly below that in, say, the commercial paper market, those banks needing to attract deposits might have difficulty doing so, because potential lenders will put more money in the CP market. The banks will have to raise CD interest rates to attract deposits while the commercial paper borrowers will find they can lower rates – thus some degree of convergence takes place.

● Short-term interest rates can be lowered by central banks intervening in the markets when they judge that the economy is in need of a boost. You can see this sort of action in the figures in the years after the shock of the dot.com bust at the turn of the millennium and following the financial crisis of 2007–2008.

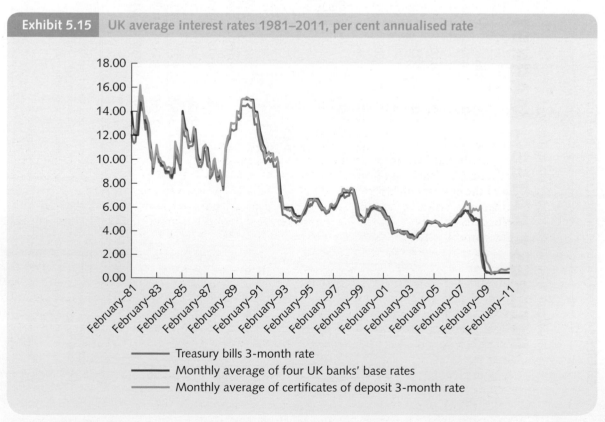

Exhibit 5.15   UK average interest rates 1981–2011, per cent annualised rate

— Treasury bills 3-month rate
— Monthly average of four UK banks' base rates
— Monthly average of certificates of deposit 3-month rate

Source: www.bank of England.co.uk

| Exhibit 5.16 | US average interest rates 1981–2011, per cent annualised |

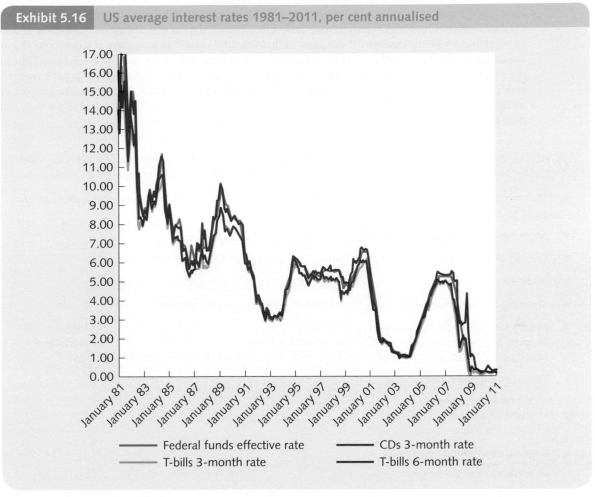

Source: www.federalreserve.gov

Concluding comments

The money markets have grown substantially over the past 30 years to trillions of dollars per year. Their growth has increased the opportunities for governments, corporations, banks and other organisations to lend and borrow. This has greatly assisted the flow of funds in the economy and reduced the cost of obtaining funds at short notice. They have also provided a source of interest for companies and other organisations with cash that can be invested only for short periods.

When making investments with surplus funds, corporations need to recognise they will have to compromise between the three objectives of investment: security, liquidity and yield. To try to achieve more yield will result in less security and/or less liquidity. Usually, for the temporary deployment of short-term surplus funds, low risk (high security) is the top priority because the preservation of capital is necessary so that the firm can meet its daily needs for working capital cash – it needs 'operating cash'. If money is lost then raising alternative funds at short notice to keep day-to-day operations running can be expensive. If the firm has more than enough near-cash to cover any likely short-term requirements then it can consider investing in longer-term instruments with reduced ability to release cash quickly and at low cost – i.e. lower liquidity – to obtain a higher yield.

As with all powerful tools, money markets can be used to destroy wealth as well as to create something positive. An example of the destructive power in the wrong hands came in the mid-2000s when many institutions were over-reliant on regularly rolling over their money market borrowing to finance investment in instruments that would not pay back for many years. Thus, in

2007–2008 banks and other institutions would borrow for, say, 60 days in the commercial paper market to buy long-term bonds whose cash flows depended on the continued monthly mortgage payments being made by thousands of households. When doubts started to emerge about households' ability or willingness to make these payments, knock-on doubts were raised about the so-called securitised bonds secured against the mortgage payments. Money market investors suddenly chose not to buy more instruments as the old ones matured and the banks and other institutions found themselves having to finance the deals. Many could not find the money and then failed. There is more on the financial crisis of 2008 in Chapter 16.

Key points and concepts

- The money markets are **wholesale** financial markets in which lending and **borrowing on a short-term basis** takes place – that is, usually for less than one year.

- Most money market instruments are sold on a **discount basis**.

- Quoted interest rates are usually on an **annualised yield** (bond equivalent yield).

- Many money market instruments are **negotiable** (can be traded in secondary markets).

- Knowing the **day count convention** (e.g. a 360-day year) used is important.

- **Money market funds** are funds set up to invest in money market instruments by pooling the savings of many people or institutions. These **money market funds** are administered by financial institutions which benefit from economies of scale in investing in a portfolio of money market securities.

- **Functions of money are:**
  - a means of exchange;
  - a unit of account;
  - a store of value.

- **Time value of money elements:**
  - impatience to consume;
  - inflation;
  - risk.

- **Required return** (time value of money) = **Risk free return + risk premium**.

- **Real rate of interest = nominal rate of interest – inflation**.

- **Interbank market:** originally defined as the market where banks lend to each other, in both the domestic and international markets. Increasingly, as well as banks being depositors, this group includes large industrial and commercial companies, other financial institutions and international organisations.

- **Interest rates:**
  - May be **floating** (changeable over the life of the loan) or **fixed**.
  - **Three-month LIBOR (London Inter-bank Offered Rate)**, set by the **British Bankers' Association (BBA)** is the most commonly used and important lending rate, only available to very creditworthy borrowers, other borrowers pay LIBOR plus basis points.
  - BBA also sets rates for ten currencies for maturities ranging from overnight to 12 months.
  - **EURIBOR:** rates at which banks in the Eurozone and other countries lend to each other for periods ranging from overnight to up to one year.
  - **Federal Funds rate:** US equivalent to very short-term LIBOR – lending to highly creditworthy banks overnight.
  - **US prime rate** is charged by US banks to the most creditworthy corporate customers.
  - **EONIA:** overnight lending rate for the euro in the Eurozone.
  - **EURONIA:** overnight lending rate for the euro in the UK.
  - **SONIA:** actual average overnight rate for sterling.

▶

● **Eurocurrency (Eurodollars, Euroyen, etc.):** money deposited or lent outside jurisdiction of country of the currency it is issued in, and so not subject to that country's regulations.

   – Nothing to do with the euro.
   – Four advantages for firms compared with domestic borrowing:
     – lower cost of finance;
     – less regulation;
     – able to reduce the impact of exchange rate changes;
     – able to deal in very large amounts.
   – **Eurocredit** market for medium and long-term Eurocurrency securities.

● **Treasury bills** are **negotiable** securities issued, generally at auction at a discount to their par value, by governments needing to borrow. When issued by reputable governments, they are virtually risk-free, but pay low rates of interest. They form the bulk of money market securities.

   – **UK Treasury bills** are issued to an approved list of buyers at competitive weekly tenders by the **Debt Management Office**.

● **Bond equivalent yield (bey),**

$$\frac{\text{Discount (Face Value} - \text{Purchase Price)}}{\text{Purchase Price}} \times \frac{\text{Days in Year}}{\text{Days to Maturity}}$$

● **Discount yield,**

$$\frac{\text{Discount (Face Value} - \text{Purchase Price)}}{\text{Face Value}} \times \frac{\text{Days in Year}}{\text{Days to Maturity}}$$

$$\text{Purchase Price} = \text{Face Value} \times \left[1 - \left(\frac{\text{Discount} \times \text{Days to Maturity}}{\text{Days in Year}} \right) \right]$$

● **US Treasury bills** are sold by the US federal government at a **discount to par** in **competitive** or **non-competitive** auctions. All bidders pay the same amount.

● There is an **inverse relationship between bill prices and interest rates:** if interest rates rise, the purchase price of bills being traded falls, effectively increasing the yield.

● **Central banks** keep the wheels of the financial world moving by issuing bank notes, influencing short-term domestic interest rates and evening-out liquidity in the economy by buying and selling securities.

● **Commercial paper** is an unsecured short-term debt instrument, used mainly by corporations to raise finance:

   – the normal maturity range is between 30 and 90 days and it is issued at a **discount to par**.
   – this facility is available only to corporations with a high credit rating.
   – **commercial paper programme** is a revolving underwriting facility set up by a bank, whereby corporations can draw up to a specified maximum sum for between five and seven years. **Multi-currency programme** allows the issuer to choose the currency of issue.
   – **asset-backed commercial paper:** secured on receivable income or other assets.
   – **Eurocommercial paper (Euro-CP)** is CP issued and placed outside the jurisdiction of the country of its denomination.

● **Credit ratings** are given to CP and other securities by three main **credit ratings agencies, Standard & Poor's, Moody's and Fitch Ratings,** who each use slightly different terminology. A credit rating rates the ability of the CP issuer to repay its debt and influences the rate of interest charged. An **investment** rating is important because institutional investors can often only invest in these grades.

● **Repurchase agreements (repos)** are short-term loans secured by safe securities, which ensures low interest rates. The securities are sold with an agreement to buy them back at a set price on a set date. The term is usually between one and 14 days, but can be up to a year. An **open repo** has no end

▶

date. A **reverse repo** is an agreement to first buy and then sell back securities to a counterparty at a set price on a set date. To calculate the buy back price on a repo:

$$\text{Buy Back Price} = \text{Selling Price} + \left(\text{Selling Price} \times \text{Interest Rate} \times \frac{\text{Days to Maturity}}{\text{Days in Year}} \right)$$

 – a **haircut** protects the buyer from price fluctuations. The seller receives the amount of cash required less a **margin**, the haircut, and pays interest on the principal less the haircut. The calculation is:

$$\text{Buy Back Price} = \text{Selling Price} + \left[\left(\text{Selling Price} - \text{Haircut} \right) \times \text{Interest Rate} \times \frac{\text{Days to Maturity}}{\text{Days in Year}} \right]$$

- **Local authority/municipal bills** are issued to finance some expenditure by local government and associated agencies. They are prevalent in the US (where they are free of some taxes) and Continental Europe.

- **Certificates of deposit (CDs)** are issued by banks when funds are deposited with them. They state that a deposit has been made and that at maturity the bank will pay a (increased) sum to the holder. Their maturity can be up to a year but is typically one to four months.

$$\text{Value of CD at Maturity} = \text{Face Value} + \left(\text{Face Value} \times \frac{\text{Interest}}{100} \times \frac{\text{Days to Maturity}}{\text{Days in Year}} \right)$$

- $$\text{Present Value of a CD} = \frac{\text{Value at Maturity}}{1 + \left(\dfrac{\text{Interest}}{100} \times \dfrac{\text{Days to Maturity}}{\text{Days in Year}} \right)}$$

- $$\text{Yield to Maturity of a CD} = \frac{\text{Value at Maturity} - \text{Present Value}}{\text{Present Value}} \times \frac{\text{Days in Year}}{\text{Days to Maturity}} \times 100$$

- **Bill of exchange**: the acknowledgement of a debt to be paid at a specified time. The legal right to receive this debt can be sold prior to maturity, that is, discounted, and thus can provide a source of finance.

- $$\text{Interest on a discounted bill of exchange} = \frac{\text{Discount}}{\text{Discounted Price}} \times 100$$

- $$\text{Bond equivalent yeild, bey, on a bill of exchange} = \frac{\text{Discount}}{\text{Discounted Price}} \times 100 \times \frac{\text{Days in Year}}{\text{Days to Maturity}}$$

- **Acceptance credit:** a financial institution or other reputable organisation accepts the promise to pay a specified sum in the future to a firm. The firm can pass on this right to a supplier or sell this right, that is discount it, to receive cash from another institution.

$$\text{Selling price of an acceptance credit} = \text{Face Value} - \left(\text{Face Value} \times \text{Discount Percentage} \right)$$

$$\text{Acceptance credit bond equivalent yield, bey} = \frac{\text{Discount}}{\text{Discounted Price}} \times 100 \times \frac{\text{Days in Year}}{\text{Days to Maturity}}$$

Appendix 5.1 Converting from a 365-day basis to a 360-day basis

To compare interest rates calculated with different day-count conventions we need to convert all rates to a common basis. This can be done using the following formula:

$$\text{Interest rate on comparison basis} = \text{interest rate on quoted basis}\left(\frac{\text{number of days in comparison}}{\text{number of days in quoted year}}\right)$$

If you wanted to compare a 5.5 per cent interest quoted on a 365-day year basis with another instrument calculated on the basis of a 360-day year, the calculation would be:

$$\text{Comparison interest rate} = 5.5 \times \left(\frac{360}{365}\right) = 5.42\%$$

So the rate prepared on a 360-day convention is stated at 5.42 per cent, but the effective rate of interest for the year is 5.5 per cent.

The rates prepared on a 360-day basis are lower than those on a 365-day basis.

Appendix 5.2 Mathematical tools for finance

The purpose of this appendix is to explain essential mathematical skills that will be needed for this book. The author has no love of mathematics for its own sake and so only those techniques of direct relevance to the subject matter of this textbook will be covered in this section.

Simple and compound interest

When there are time delays between receipts and payments of financial sums we need to make use of the concepts of simple and compound interest.

Simple interest

Interest is paid only on the original principal. No interest is paid on the accumulated interest payments.

Example 1

Suppose that a sum of £10 is deposited in a bank account that pays 12 per cent per annum. At the end of year 1 the investor has £11.20 in the account. That is:

$$F = P(1+i)$$
$$11.20 = 10(1+0.12)$$

where F = future value, P = present value, i = interest rate.

The initial sum, called the principal, is multiplied by the interest rate to give the annual return. At the end of five years:

$$F = P(1+in)$$

where n = number of years. Thus,

$$16 = 10(1+(0.12 \times 5))$$

Note from the example that the 12 per cent return is a constant amount each year. Interest is not earned on the interest already accumulated from previous years.

Compound interest

The more usual situation in the real world is for interest to be paid on the sum which accumulates – whether or not that sum comes from the principal or from the interest received in previous periods.

Example 2

An investment of £10 is made at an interest rate of 12 per cent with the interest being compounded. In one year the capital will grow by 12 per cent to £11.20. In the second year the capital will grow by 12 per cent, but this time the growth will be on the accumulated value of £11.20 and thus will amount to an extra £1.34. At the end of two years:

$$F = P(1+i)(1+i)$$
$$F = 11.20\,(1+i)$$
$$F = 12.54$$

Alternatively,

$$F = P(1+i)^2$$

Exhibit 5.17 displays the future value of £1 invested at a number of different interest rates and for alternative numbers of years. This is extracted from Appendix I at the end of the book.

| Exhibit 5.17 | The future value of £1 |

		Interest rate (per cent per annum)				
	Year	1	2	5	12	15
	1	1.0100	1.0200	1.0500	1.1200	1.1500
	2	1.0201	1.0404	1.1025	1.2544	1.3225
	3	1.0303	1.0612	1.1576	1.4049	1.5209
	4	1.0406	1.0824	1.2155	1.5735	1.7490
	5	1.0510	1.1041	1.2763	1.7623	2.0114

From the second row of the table in Exhibit 5.17 we can read that £1 invested for two years at 12 per cent amounts to £1.2544. Thus, the investment of £10 provides a future capital sum 1.2544 times the original amount:

£10 × 1.2544 = £12.544

Over five years the result is:

$$F = P(1+i)^n$$
$$17.62 = 10(1 + 0.12)^5$$

The interest on the accumulated interest is therefore the difference between the total arising from simple interest and that from compound interest:

£17.62 − £16.00 = £1.62

Almost all investments pay compound interest and so we will be using compounding throughout the book.

Present values

There are many occasions in financial management when you are given the future sums and need to find out what those future sums are worth in present-value terms today. For example, you wish to know how much you would have to put aside today which will accumulate, with compounded interest, to a defined sum in the future; or you are given the choice between receiving £200 in five years or £100 now and wish to know which is the better option, given anticipated interest rates; or a project gives a return of £1 million in three years for an outlay of £800,000 now and you need to establish whether this is the best use of the £800,000. By the process of discounting, a sum of money to be received in the future is given a monetary value today.

Example 3

If we anticipate the receipt of £17.62 in five years' time we can determine its present value. Rearrangement of the compound formula, and assuming a discount rate of 12 per cent, gives:

$$P = \frac{F}{(1+i)^n} \text{ or } P = F \times \frac{1}{(1+i)^n}$$

$$10 = \frac{17.62}{(1+0.12)^5}$$

Alternatively, discount factors may be used, as shown in **Exhibit 5.18** (this is an extract from Appendix II at the end of the book). The factor needed to discount £1 receivable in five years when the discount rate is 12 per cent is 0.5674.

Therefore the present value of £17.62 is:

$$0.5674 \times £17.62 = £10$$

Exhibit 5.18   The present value of £1

	Interest rate (per cent per annum)				
Year	1	5	10	12	15
1	0.9901	0.9524	0.9091	0.8929	0.8696
2	0.9803	0.9070	0.8264	0.7972	0.7561
3	0.9706	0.8638	0.7513	0.7118	0.6575
4	0.9610	0.8227	0.6830	0.6355	0.5718
5	0.9515	0.7835	0.6209	0.5674	0.4972

Examining the present value table in Exhibit 5.18 you can see that as the discount rate increases, the present value goes down. Also, the further into the future the money is to be received, the less valuable it is in today's terms. Distant cash flows discounted at a high rate have a small present value; for instance, £1,000 receivable in 20 years when the discount rate is 17 per cent has a present value of £43.30. Viewed from another angle, if you invested £43.30 for 20 years it would accumulate to £1,000 if interest compounds at 17 per cent.

Determining the rate of interest

Sometimes you wish to calculate the rate of return that a project is earning. For instance, a savings company may offer to pay you £10,000 in five years if you deposit £8,000 now, when interest rates on accounts elsewhere are offering 6 per cent per annum. In order to make a comparison you need to know the annual rate being offered by the savings company. Thus, we need to find i in the discounting equation.

To be able to calculate i it is necessary to rearrange the compounding formula. Since:

$$F = P(1 + i)^n$$

first, divide both sides by P:

$$F/P = (1 + i)^n$$

(The Ps on the right side cancel out.)

Second, take the root to the power n of both sides and subtract 1 from each side:

$$i = \sqrt[n]{\frac{F}{P}} - 1 \ \text{ or } \ i = \left[\frac{F}{P}\right]^{1/n} - 1$$

Example 4

In the case of a five-year investment requiring an outlay of £10 and having a future value of £17.62 the rate of return is:

$$i = \sqrt[5]{\frac{17.62}{10}} - 1 = 12\%$$

$$i = \left[\frac{17.62}{10}\right]^{1/5} - 1 = 12\%$$

Technical aside

You can use the $\sqrt[x]{y}$, the $\sqrt[y]{x}$ button or a combination of the y^x and $\frac{1}{x}$ buttons depending on the calculator.

Alternatively, use the future value table (Appendix I), an extract of which is shown in Exhibit 5.17. In our example, the return on £1 worth of investment over five years is:

$$\frac{17.62}{10} = 1.762$$

In the body of the future value table look at the year 5 row for a future value of 1.762.
Read off the interest rate of 12 per cent.

An interesting application of this technique outside finance is to use it to put into perspective the pronouncements of politicians. For example, in 1994 John Major made a speech to the Conservative Party conference promising to double national income (the total quantity of goods and services produced) within 25 years. This sounds impressive, but let us see how ambitious this is in terms of an annual percentage increase.

$$i = \sqrt[25]{\frac{F}{P}} - 1$$

F, future income, is double *P*, the present income.

$$i = \sqrt[25]{\frac{2}{1}} - 1 = 0.0281 \ or \ 2.81\%$$

The result is not too bad compared with the previous 20 years. However, performance in the 1950s and 1960s was better and countries in the Far East have annual rates of growth of between 5 per cent and 10 per cent.

The investment period

Rearranging the standard equation so that we can find *n* (the number of years of the investment), we create the following equation:

$$F = P(1 + i)^n$$
$$F / P = (1 + i)^n$$
$$\log(F / P) = \log(1 + i)n$$

$$n = \frac{\log(F / P)}{\log(1 + i)}$$

Example 5

How many years does it take for £10 to grow to £17.62 when the interest rate is 12 per cent?

$$n = \frac{\log(17.62 / 10)}{\log(1 + 0.12)} \text{Therefore } n = 5 \text{ years}$$

An application outside finance: how many years will it take for China to double its real national income if growth rates continue at 10 per cent per annum?
   Answer:

$$n = \frac{\log(2 / 1)}{\log(1 + 0.1)} = 7.3 \text{ years (quadrupling in less than 15 years. At this rate it won't be long before China overtakes the US as the world's biggest economy)}$$

Annuities

Quite often there is not just one payment at the end of a certain number of years, there can be a series of identical payments made over a period of years. For instance:

● bonds usually pay a regular rate of interest;
● individuals can buy, from savings plan companies, the right to receive a number of identical payments over a number of years;
● a business might invest in a project which, it is estimated, will give regular cash inflows over a period of years;
● a typical house mortgage is an annuity.

An annuity is a series of payments or receipts of equal amounts. We are able to calculate the present value of this set of payments.

Example 6

For a regular payment of £10 per year for five years, when the interest rate is 12 per cent, we can calculate the present value of the annuity by three methods.

Method 1

$$P_{an} = \frac{A}{(1+i)} + \frac{A}{(1+i)^2} + \frac{A}{(1+i)^3} + \frac{A}{(1+i)^4} + \frac{A}{(1+i)^5}$$

where A = the periodic receipt.

$$P_{10.5} = \frac{10}{(1.12)} + \frac{10}{(1.12)^2} + \frac{10}{(1.12)^3} + \frac{10}{(1.12)^4} + \frac{10}{(1.12)^5} = £36.05$$

Method 2

Using the derived formula:

$$P_{an} = \frac{1 - 1/(1+i)^n}{i} \times A$$

$$P_{10.5} = \frac{1 - 1/(1+0.12)^5}{0.12} \times 10 = £36.05$$

Method 3

Use the 'present value of an annuity' table. (*See* **Exhibit 5.19**, an extract from the more complete annuity table at the end of the book in Appendix III.) Here we simply look along the year 5 row and 12 per cent column to find the figure of 3.605. This refers to the present value of five annual receipts of £1. So to arrive at £3.605 (or £3.6048 to be even more accurate) someone calculated the present value of £1 received in one year, the present value of £1 received at the end of two years, and so on up to five years. Then these five present values are added together.

For our example we are not anticipating £1 for each future year but £10. Therefore we multiply the annuity factor by £10:

3.605 × £10 = £36.05

Exhibit 5.19	The present value of an annuity of £1 per annum

	Interest rate (per cent per annum)				
Year	1	5	10	12	15
1	0.9901	0.9524	0.9091	0.8929	0.8696
2	1.9704	1.8594	1.7355	1.6901	1.6257
3	2.9410	2.7232	2.4869	2.4018	2.2832
4	3.9020	3.5459	3.1699	3.0373	2.8550
5	4.8535	4.3295	3.7908	3.6048	3.3522

The student is strongly advised against using Method 1. This was presented for conceptual understanding only. For any but the simplest cases, this method can be very time consuming.

Perpetuities

Some contracts run indefinitely and there is no end to a series of identical payments. Perpetuities are rare in the private sector, but certain government securities do not have an end date; that is, the amount paid or the par value when the bond was purchased by the lender will never be repaid, only interest payments are made. For example, the UK government has issued consolidated stocks or war loans which will never be redeemed. Also, in a number of financial valuations it is useful to assume that regular annual payments go on for ever. Perpetuities are annuities which continue indefinitely. The value of a perpetuity is simply the annual amount received divided by the interest rate when the latter is expressed as a decimal.

$$P = \frac{A}{i}$$

If £10 is to be received as an indefinite annual payment then the present value, at a discount rate of 12 per cent, is:

$$P = \frac{10}{0.12} = £83.33$$

It is very important to note that in order to use this formula we are assuming that the first payment arises 365 days after the time at which we are standing (the present time or time zero).

Discounting semi-annually, monthly and daily

Sometimes financial transactions take place on the basis that interest will be calculated more frequently than once a year. For instance, if a bank account paid 12 per cent nominal return per year but credited 6 per cent after half a year, in the second half of the year interest could be earned on the interest credited after the first six months. This will mean that the true annual rate of interest will be greater than 12 per cent.

The greater the frequency with which interest is earned, the higher the future value of the deposit.

Example 7

If you put £10 in a bank account earning 12 per cent per annum then your return after one year is:

$$10(1 + 0.12) = £11.20$$

If the interest is compounded semi-annually (at a nominal annual rate of 12 per cent):

$$10(1 + [0.12 / 2])(1 + [0.12 / 2]) = 10(1 + [0.12 / 2])^2 = £11.236$$

In Example 7 the difference between annual compounding and semi-annual compounding is an extra 3.6p. After six months the bank credits the account with 60p in interest so that in the following six months the investor earns 6 per cent on the £10.60.

If the interest is compounded quarterly:

$$10(1 + [0.12 / 4])^4 = £11.255$$

Daily compounding:

$$10(1 + [0.12 / 365])^{365} = £11.2747$$

Example 8

If £10 is deposited in a bank account that compounds interest quarterly and the nominal return per year is 12 per cent, how much will be in the account after eight years?

$$10(1 + [0.12 / 4])^{4 \times 8} = £25.75$$

Continuous compounding

If the compounding frequency is taken to the limit we say that there is continuous compounding. When the number of compounding periods approaches infinity, the future value is found by $F = Pe^{in}$ where e is the value of the exponential function. This is set as 2.71828 (to five decimal places, as shown on a scientific calculator).

So, the future value of £10 deposited in a bank paying 12 per cent nominal compounded continuously after eight years is:

$$10 \times 2.71828^{0.12 \times 8} = £26.12$$

Converting monthly and daily rates to annual rates

Sometimes you are presented with a monthly or daily rate of interest and wish to know what that is equivalent to in terms of annual percentage rate (APR) (or Effective Annual Rate (EAR)).

If m is the monthly interest or discount rate, then over 12 months:

$$(1 + m)^{12} = 1 + i$$

where i is the annual compound rate.

$$i = (1 + m)^{12} - 1$$

Thus, if a credit card company charges 1.5 per cent per month, the APR is:

$$i = (1 + 0.015)^{12} - 1 = 19.56\%$$

If you want to find the monthly rate when you are given the APR:

$$m = (1 + i)^{1/12} - 1 \text{ or } m = \sqrt[12]{(1 + i)} - 1$$

$$m = (1 + 0.1956)^{1/12} - 1 \times 100 \text{ or } m = \sqrt[12]{(1 + 0.1956)} - 1 = 1.5\%$$

Daily rate:

$$(1 + d)^{365} = 1 + i$$

where d is the daily discount rate.

The following exercises will consolidate the knowledge gained by reading through this appendix (answers are provided at the end of the book in Appendix V).

Mathematical tools exercise

The answers are available in Appendix V.

1   What will a £100 investment be worth in three years' time if the rate of interest is 8 per cent, using: (a) simple interest? (b) annual compound interest?

2 You plan to invest £10,000 in the shares of a company.

(a) If the value of the shares increases by 5 per cent a year, what will be the value of the shares in 20 years?

(b) If the value of the shares increases by 15 per cent a year, what will be the value of the shares in 20 years?

3 How long will it take you to double your money if you invest it at: (a) 5 per cent? (b) 15 per cent?

4 As a winner of a lottery you can choose one of the following prizes:

1 £1 million now.

2 £1.7 million at the end of five years.

3 £135,000 a year for ever, starting in one year.

4 £200,000 for each of the next ten years, starting in one year.

If the time value of money is 9 per cent, which is the most valuable prize?

5 A bank lends a customer £5,000. At the end of ten years he repays this amount plus interest. The amount he repays is £8,950. What is the rate of interest charged by the bank?

6 The Morbid Memorial Garden company will maintain a garden plot around your grave for a payment of £50 now, followed by annual payments, in perpetuity, of £50. How much would you have to put into an account which was to make these payments if the account guaranteed an interest rate of 8 per cent?

7 If the flat (nominal annual) rate of interest is 14 per cent and compounding takes place monthly, what is the effective annual rate of interest (the APR)?

8 What is the present value of £100 to be received in ten years' time when the interest rate (nominal annual) is 12 per cent and (a) annual discounting is used? (b) semi-annual discounting is used?

9 What sum must be invested now to provide an amount of £18,000 at the end of 15 years if interest is to accumulate at 8 per cent for the first ten years and 12 per cent thereafter?

10 How much must be invested now to provide an amount of £10,000 in six years' time assuming interest is compounded quarterly at a nominal annual rate of 8 per cent? What is the effective annual rate?

11 Supersalesman offers you an annuity of £800 per annum for ten years. The price he asks is £4,800. Assuming you could earn 11 per cent on alternative investments, would you buy the annuity?

12 Punter buys a car on hire purchase paying five annual instalments of £1,500, the first being an immediate cash deposit. Assuming an interest rate of 8 per cent is being charged by the hire-purchase company, how much is the current cash price of the car?

References and further reading

To keep up to date and reinforce knowledge gained by reading this chapter I can recommend the following publications: *Financial Times, The Economist, Bank of England Quarterly Bulletin, Bank for International Settlements Quarterly Review* (www.bis.org), and *The Treasurer* (a monthly journal).

Howells, P. and Bains, K. (2008) *The Economics of Money, Banking and Finance: A European text*, 4th edn. Harlow: FT Prentice Hall.

Provides more detail on the European money markets and puts the markets in the context of economic policy.

Saunders, A. and Cornett, M. M. (2007) *Financial Markets and Institutions*, 3rd edn. New York: McGraw-Hill.

Provides more detail on the US market.

Websites

Bank of England www.bankofengland.co.uk
British Bankers Association www.bba.org.uk
British Bankers Association LIBOR website www.bbalibor.com
Federal Reserve in USA www.federalreserve.gov
Financial Times money market pages www.ft.com/bonds&rates
Fitch www.fitchratings.com
Institutional Money Market Funds Association www.immfa.org
International Monetary Fund www.imf.org
Moody's www.moodys.com
Standard & Poor's www.standardandpoors.com
US Treasury www.treasurydirect.gov
Wholesale Market Brokers' Association www.wmba.org.uk

Video presentations

Bank and financial organisation chief executives and other senior people describe and discuss policy and other aspects of their operations in interviews, documentaries and webcasts at Cantos.com. (www.cantos.com) – these are free to view.

Case study recommendations

See www.pearsoned.co.uk/arnold for case study synopses.
Also see Harvard University: http://hbsp.harvard.edu/product/cases

- BlackRock Money Market Management in September 2008 (A) (2010) Authors: Kenneth A. Froot and David Lane. Harvard Business School.
- Note: Credit Rating Agencies (2009) Author: William E. Fruhan, Jr. Harvard Business School.
- The weekend That Changed Wall Street (2009) Authors: Christopher Brandriff and George (Yiorgos) Allayannis. Darden, University of Pennsylvania. Available from Harvard Case Study website.

Self-review questions

1 What are the functions of money?

2 What are the key characteristics of money markets instruments?

3 What are the main money market instruments?

4 What are Treasury bills, and how is a rate of return from them derived?

5 What is the difference between interest paying and zero coupon instruments?

6 What is the difference between rate of interest, discount and yield?

7 Why is the bond equivalent rate important?

8 Why do (a) governments, and (b) companies, use the money markets?

9 How does the UK government sell its Treasury bills?

10 What is Eurocurrency?

11 What is LIBOR?

12 Who issues Treasury bills and how are they sold?

13 What is the day count convention?

14 What is commercial paper and how is its risk assessed?

15 Why does US commercial paper have a maturity of less than 270 days?

16 What are repos?

17 What is the difference between a bill of exchange and a banker's acceptance?

18 What are municipal bills and what are they used for?

19 What are certificates of deposit?

20 What is yield to maturity?

Questions and problems

1 On 1 March 2011 a company raises finance by agreeing a six-month eurodollar loan for $12 million offered at an interest rate of 2.75 per cent. Calculate the cost of the loan in dollars.

    (a) on a 30/360-day count basis   (180 days)
    (b) on a 365-day count, actual/365 basis (183 days)

2 A dealer purchases UK three-month (91 day) Treasury bills with a face value of £500,000 for £498,397. Calculate (a) the discount yield and (b) the bond equivalent yield.

3 You purchase $2,000 worth of six-month US Treasury bills on the secondary market with a quoted yield per annum of 0.44 per cent. The bills have 24 days to maturity. How much would you pay? Use the actual/360-day count convention.

4 A dealer can purchase for $1,574,000 some US commercial paper which has a face value of $1.6m. The paper is 192 days from maturity. Calculate (a) the discount yield and (b) the bond equivalent yield.

5 A bank agrees a repo with another bank. It sells £17 million of Treasury bills and agrees to repurchase them for £17,005,966. Calculate the annualised yield for (a) a maturity of 29 days and (b) a maturity of 136 days. Use a 365-day count.

6 If an interest rate of 3.72 per cent is quoted on a 360-day count convention, what is the bey rate for this?

7 On 17 June you can buy a CD maturing on 10 December with a face value of £6,000,000 with a yield to maturity of 2.68 per cent. You can also purchase for £5,950,000 an identically risky CD with the same time to maturity and the same payment on maturity of £6 million. Provide calculations to show which is your best option.

8 A company arranges a banker's acceptance with 60 days' credit to finance a £5 million expansion. They receive the sum of £4,975,000 after discounting the acceptance. Calculate the annualised bond equivalent yield.

9 The annualised yield on a repo with an initial sale value of £850,000 is 2.61 per cent. The repo has 42 days until maturity. (a) What will be the repurchase price? (b) If the days to maturity are 67, what will be its future purchase price? Use a 365-day count convention throughout.

10 The annualised rate of interest on a seven-day repo with an initial sale value of $3 million is 0.562 per cent. There is a haircut of 0.08 per cent. Assuming a day count convention of actual/360, calculate (a) the amount of the haircut, (b) the amount the seller receives and (c) the buy-back price.

11 Describe the credit rating system and explain what it is used for.

12 Describe and explain the characteristics of the main money market instruments and discuss their advantages and disadvantages from the perspective of a bank needing to raise short-term borrowings.

13 Explain LIBOR and discuss its influence on the commercial world.

14 Explain Eurocurrency and why it came into existence.

Assignments

1 For a company you know well, describe and explain the various money market instruments it makes use of. Consider the costs of these and the advantages brought to the firm by tapping into these sources of finance. Describe the alternative money market instruments that the firm does not currently use. Make recommendations on the company's future use of money market instruments.

2 If you have access to bank data, write a report detailing the types of money market dealings the bank has. Include a consideration of improvements that could be implemented.

Web-based exercises

1 Money market interest rates are available from the Financial Times website www.ft.com/bonds&rates. Compile a list of rates comprising the following and compare the current rates with those over the past five years:

- one-month UK Treasury bills (notes)
- three-month UK Treasury bills
- six-month UK Treasury bills
- Canadian LIBOR overnight rate
- Euro LIBOR overnight rate
- US$ LIBOR overnight rate
- US Fed Funds target rate.

2 (a) Find a recent 'UK Treasury Bill Tender Results' on www.dmo.gov.uk and show the calculations for any issue you choose that link the discount yield, the yield on the purchase price, and the purchase price. Use Example 3 in the chapter as a guide.

   (a) Draw a chart showing the amount of UK Treasury bills issued over the past five years.
   (b) Draw a chart of total stock outstanding of Treasury bills over the past eight years.

3 Find the historic repo rates at www.bbalibor.com and draw a chart for the one-month duration repos going back two years. Write a report explaining how the repo market operates.

Bond markets

LEARNING OUTCOMES

An understanding of the key characteristics of the main categories of bond finance is essential to anyone working in the financial sector or making financing decisions for the commercial firm. At the end of this chapter the reader should be able to:

■ explain the nature and the main types of bonds, their pricing and their valuation;

■ give a considered view of the role of high-yield bonds, convertible bonds, medium-term notes, securitisation and Islamic bonds;

■ demonstrate an understanding of the usefulness of the international bond markets;

■ describe the main elements influencing the demand and supply of bonds;

■ calculate the value of a bond and discuss relative bond price volatility;

■ explain the term structure of interest rates and the reasons for its existence.

The bond markets are concerned with loans for periods of more than one year in contrast with the money markets, where loans are for a few days, weeks or months. The concept of governments, companies and other institutions borrowing funds to invest in long-term capital projects and operations is a straightforward one, yet in the sophisticated capital markets of today with their wide variety of financial instruments and forms of debt, the borrowing and lending decision can be bewildering. Is the domestic bond market or the Eurobond market the better choice? If so, on what terms, fixed- or floating-rate interest, with collateral or unsecured? And what about high-yield bonds or convertibles? The variety of methods of providing long-term finance is infinite. This chapter will outline the major categories and illustrate some of the fundamental issues to be considered by a borrower and a lender.

As you can see from the extract from the annual accounts of the giant drinks company Diageo (**Exhibit 6.1**) a firm may need knowledge and understanding of a great many different debt instruments. The terms loan debentures and medium-term notes, mentioned in the extract, are explained in the chapter.

Exhibit 6.1	Long-term borrowings for Diageo plc

	Repayment date	Currency	Year end interest rates %	2009 £m	2008 £m
Guaranteed bonds 2010	2010	US dollar	4.375	–	376
Guaranteed bonds 2011	2011	US dollar	3.875	301	250
Guaranteed bonds 2012	2012	US dollar	5.125	363	301
Guaranteed bonds 2012	2012	Euro	Floating	641	594
Guaranteed bonds 2013	2013	US dollar	5.2	455	377
Guaranteed bonds 2013	2013	US dollar	5.5	363	301
Guaranteed bonds 2013	2013	Euro	5.5	981	909
Guaranteed bonds 2014	2014	US dollar	7.375	913	–
Guaranteed bonds 2014	2014	Euro	6.625	853	–
Guaranteed bonds 2015	2015	US dollar	5.3	454	376
Guaranteed bonds 2016	2016	US dollar	5.5	363	301
Guaranteed bonds 2017	2017	US dollar	5.75	756	627
Guaranteed bonds 2035	2035	US dollar	7.45	243	201
Guaranteed bonds 2036	2036	US dollar	5.875	361	299
Guaranteed debentures 2011	2011	US dollar	9.0	181	151
Guaranteed debentures 2022	2022	US dollar	8.0	180	149
Medium term notes	2009	US dollar	7.25	–	150
Medium term notes	2018	US dollar	4.85	121	101
Bank and other loans	Various	Various	Various	44	58
Fair value adjustment to borrowings				112	24
Borrowings due after one year				**7,685**	**5,545**

Note: Guaranteed bonds and debentures are those issued by a subsidiary company and guaranteed to be paid by the parent, Diageo.

Source: Fitch Ratings Global Corporate Finance 2010 Transition and Default Study, www.fitchratings.com

Bonds

A **bond** is a long-term contract in which the bond holder lends money to a company, government or some other organisation. In return the company or government, etc. promises to make pre-determined payments (usually regular) in the future which may consist of interest and a capital sum at the end of the bond's life. Basically, bonds may be regarded as merely IOUs with pages of legal clauses expressing the promises made. Most offer both regular interest and a capital sum to be paid on a fixed date in the future, but some do not promise a capital repayment, they just keep paying interest in perpetuity. Others do not offer regular interest, just a lump sum at the end of a period of time. They are the most significant financial instruments in the world today with more than $90,000,000,000,000 ($90 trillion) in issue. They come in all shapes and sizes, from UK government bonds to Chinese company bonds.

The time to maturity for bonds is generally between 5 and 30 years, although a number of firms have issued bonds with a longer maturity date. IBM and Reliance of India have issued 100-year bonds, as have Coca-Cola and Walt Disney (Disney's was known as the 'Sleeping Beauty bond'). There are even some 1,000-year bonds in existence – Canadian Pacific Corporation is paying a dividend of 4 per cent on a 1,000-year bond issued in 1883.

Bonds and equity compared

The advantage of placing your money with an organisation via a bond is that you are *promised* a return. Bond investors are exposed to less risk than share investors because the promise is backed up with a series of legal rights, e.g. the right to receive the annual interest before the equity holders receive any dividend. So in a bad year (e.g. no profits) the bond investors are far more likely to receive a payout than the shareholders. This is usually bolstered with rights to seize company assets if the company reneges on its promise. There is a greater chance of saving the investor's investment if things go very badly for the firm if they are holding its bonds rather than its shares because on liquidation the holders of debt-type financial securities are paid from the proceeds raised by selling off the assets first, before shareholders receive anything.

Offsetting these plus points are the facts that bondholders do not (usually) share in the increase in value created by an extraordinarily successful business and there is an absence of any voting power over the management of the company.

Bonds are often referred to collectively as **fixed-interest securities**. While this is an accurate description for many bonds, others do not offer *regular* interest payments that are *fixed* amounts. Nevertheless, they are all lumped together as fixed-interest to contrast these types of loan instrument with equities (shares) that do not carry a promise of a return.

A wide variety

There are many different types of bonds: government-issued bonds, corporate bonds, high-yield bonds, municipal bonds, convertible bonds, strip bonds, foreign bonds, mortgage/asset-based bonds, covered bonds, Eurobonds and medium-term notes. Bonds with up to five years left until they mature and pay their principal amount are generally known as **shorts,** but the boundary lines are often blurry; **medium-dated** bonds generally have maturities of between 5 and 15 years; **longs** are bonds with maturities of over 15 years. It should be noted that a bond is classified according to the time remaining to maturity, not the maturity when it was issued, so a 30-year bond which has only two years left until it matures is a short.

The value of a bond may fluctuate considerably during its life and this value reflects the changes in the interest rate. A bond issued with a coupon of 5 per cent will see its value drop if the interest rate rises to 10 per cent. To put it simply – if a five-year £100 bond is issued with a coupon of 5 per cent and market interest rates for bonds with similar risk remain at 5 per cent for the five-year life of the bond, its value will remain at £100 throughout its life. If, however, interest rates on alternative equally risky bonds rise to 10 per cent when the bond has three years to maturity, its value then will drop to £87.566 to compensate for the change in interest rate – the method for calculating this is explained later in the chapter.

The size of the bond markets

The volume of bonds issued throughout the world is vast: $91 trillion at the end of 2009 according to the Bank of International Settlements (BIS)[1] – *see* **Exhibits 6.2 (a), (b) and (c)**. There were over $64 trillion (million million) bonds outstanding (not yet redeemed – the capital has not been paid off) in the domestic bond markets of countries.[2] In addition to these domestic bonds there were another $27 trillion of bonds issued outside the domestic markets on the international bond markets. To put these numbers in perspective the annual output (GDP) of the UK for one year is about £1.4 trillion.

Government bond markets

Most governments issue bonds to raise money when their tax receipts are less than their expenditure. We first look at the UK government bond market to get a feel for the workings of these markets, then briefly consider the US, French, German, Japanese and Chinese government bond markets, known as **sovereign bond** markets. Sovereign bonds issued by reputable governments are the most secure in the world. National governments are aware of the need to maintain a high reputation for paying their debts on time. Furthermore, they are able to print more money or to raise taxes, to ensure they have the means to pay (in worst cases).

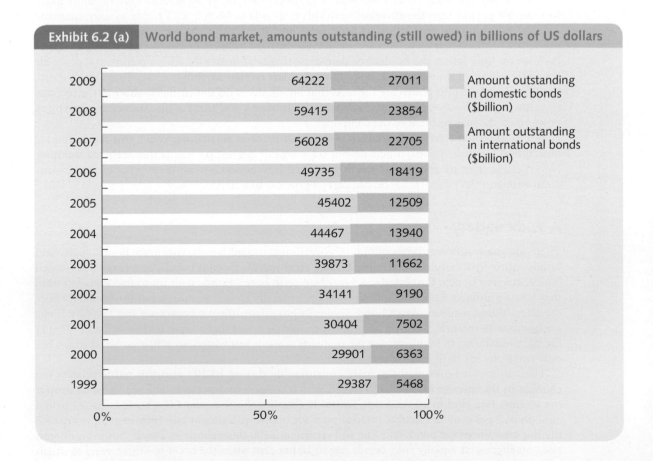

Exhibit 6.2 (a)	World bond market, amounts outstanding (still owed) in billions of US dollars

Year	Amount outstanding in domestic bonds ($billion)	Amount outstanding in international bonds ($billion)
2009	64222	27011
2008	59415	23854
2007	56028	22705
2006	49735	18419
2005	45402	12509
2004	44467	13940
2003	39873	11662
2002	34141	9190
2001	30404	7502
2000	29901	6363
1999	29387	5468

---

[1] The BIS figures include in the figures for domestic bonds a small fraction of money market instruments.
[2] This includes all currencies, even though they are summed in US dollars.

Exhibit 6.2 (b) The total of all issuers worldwide in the domestic markets, plus the four largest domestic markets, amounts outstanding

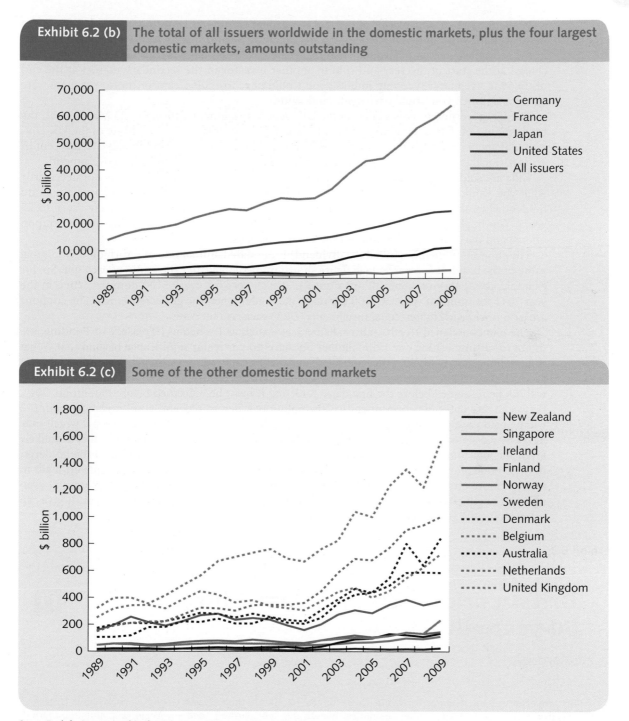

Exhibit 6.2 (c) Some of the other domestic bond markets

Source: Bank for International Settlements.

UK gilts

In most years the British government does not raise enough in taxes to cover its expenditure. It makes up a large part of the difference by selling bonds. These are called gilts because in the old days you would receive a very attractive certificate with gold-leaf edges (**gilt-edged securities**). Buying UK government bonds is one of the safest forms of lending in the world; the risk of the UK government failing to pay is very small – although a few doubts crept in following the high government spending during 2010–2011.

While the risk of non-receipt of interest and capital is minute if you buy and hold gilts to the maturity date, you can lose money buying and selling gilts from year to year (or month to month) in the secondary market before they mature. There have been many occasions when, if you purchased at the start of the year and sold to another investor in the secondary market at the end of the year, even after receiving interest, you would have lost 5 per cent or more. Yet there were many years when you would have made large gains.

The UK government issues gilts via the UK Debt Management Office. On 23 March 2011, the total amount of gilts in issue was £1032.91 billion. This was rising at a rapid rate as the UK government spent around £160 billion more than it raised in taxes – approximately 12 per cent of gross national product, so one in every eight pounds spent was borrowed by the government!

Gilts are sold with a nominal (face or par or maturity) value of £100. This is not necessarily what you would pay. The nominal value signifies what the government will pay *you* (the bond holder) when the bond reaches its maturity or redemption date at the end of, say, 5, 10 or 25 years. You might pay £100, £99, £100.50, or some other sum for it, depending on the coupon offered and the general level of interest rates in the markets.

The coupon (sometimes called the **dividend**) is the stated annual rate of return on the nominal value of the bond. It is a percentage figure shown immediately after the name of each gilt. So, for example, the 'Treasury 4.5pc '42' pays out £4.50 each year for every £100 nominal. Then in the year 2042 the nominal value of £100 is paid to the holder when the gilt is redeemed. The coupons are paid *twice yearly* in two equal instalments (£2.25 each) on set dates.

The names assigned to gilts (also called stocks), such as Exchequer, Treasury or Funding, are useful for distinguishing one from another but have no particular significance beyond that. What is more important is whether they are dated, undated or conversion. *Dated* gilts have a fixed date(s) at which they will be redeemed. Some have a range of dates, e.g. Exchequer 12pc, '13 – '17. This gilt will not be redeemed before the first date, 2013, and it must be redeemed before the second, 2017. Between these dates the government has the option of when to redeem. Until it is redeemed, £12 will be paid each year in coupons. A few *undated* gilts exist, such as War loan 3½ pc, which may never be redeemed. They *can* be redeemed at the discretion of the government, but this is unlikely given the low coupon the government pays – it can go on paying £3.50 per year to the holder(s) of these bonds for ever. Conversion gilts allow the investor to choose whether to convert a gilt to another more attractive one. **Exhibit 6.3** discusses an unusually long dated gilt. Note that even though the gilt pays 4 per cent per year on the nominal value, i.e. it pays £4 per year, it gives an interest rate of 4.569 per cent. Thus we conclude that it was sold for less than £100.

Exhibit 6.3

Britain draws strong demand for 50-year gilt

FT

David Oakley

Britain drew strong demand for an ultra-long bond yesterday in a sign that new issuance of gilts has not been hit by the turbulence surrounding Greece and the peripheral eurozone economies.

The sale of £4.5 billion of the UK's 4 per cent 2060 gilt was placed almost exclusively with domestic investors as pension funds and life insurance companies, needing these bonds to match their liabilities, bought the debt. Order books reached £7.5 billion.

Bankers priced the bonds at the tight end of the range. However, the yield of 4.569 per cent was the highest ever for new 50-year debt, which were first launched in May 2005.

One syndicate banker said: "This shows that the UK has not been affected by worries about Greece and sovereign risk, although there is always strong structural demand from pension funds and insurance companies. This tends to give this part of the curve a strong bid."

Source: Financial Times, 24 February 2010, p. 32. Reprinted with permission.

Prices and returns

The coupons showing on different gilts can have a wide range from 2.5 per cent to 12 per cent. These were (roughly) the rates of interest that the government had to offer at the time of issue. The wide variety reflects how interest rates have fluctuated during the past 80 or more years. These original percentages are not the rates of return offered on the gilt to a buyer in the secondary market today. So, if we take an undated gilt offering a coupon of 2.5 per cent on the nominal value we may find that investors are buying and selling this bond that offers £2.50 per year at a price of £50, not at its nominal value of £100. This gilt offers an investor today a yield of 5 per cent:

$$\frac{£2.50}{£50} \times 100 = 5\%$$

Thus we see some bonds trading above and, as in this case, below the nominal value of £100 in the secondary market. By means of this variation in the price of the bond, investors are able to receive the current going rate of return for that type of investment.

Yield

There are two types of yields on dated gilts. The case of a Treasury 10 pc with five years to maturity currently selling in the secondary market at £120 will serve to illustrate the two different types. From the name of the gilt we glean that it pays a coupon of £10 per year (10 per cent of the nominal value of £100). For £120 investors can buy this gilt from other investors on the secondary market to receive a **current yield** (also known as the **interest yield, flat yield, income yield, simple yield, annual yield** and **running yield**) of 8.33 per cent.

$$\text{Current yield} = \frac{\text{Gross (before tax) interest coupon}}{\text{Market price}} \times 100$$

$$= \frac{£10}{£120} \times 100 = 8.33\%$$

This is not the true rate of return available to the investor because we have failed to take into account the capital loss over the next five years. The investor pays £120 but will receive only the nominal value of £100 at maturity. If this £20 loss is apportioned over the five years it works out at £4 per year. The capital loss as a percentage of what the investor pays (£120) is £4/£120 × 100 = 3.33 per cent per year. This loss to redemption has to be subtracted from the annual interest yield to give an approximation to the **yield to maturity (YTM)** or **redemption yield**. This is also called or **gross redemption yield** ('gross' meaning that it ignores taxation on the bond). We do not know the bond holder's tax status and therefore cannot allow for tax deducted on the interest or capital received on the bond.

Approximation of the yield to maturity: 8.33% − 3.33% = 5%

While this example tries to convey the essence of YTM calculations, it over-simplifies and a compound interest-type calculation is required to get a precise figure – we look at more precise calculations later in the chapter.

The general rules are:

- If a dated gilt is trading at below £100, the purchaser will receive a capital gain between purchase and redemption and so the YTM is greater than the current yield.

- If a dated gilt is selling at more than £100, a capital loss will be made if held to maturity and so the YTM is below the current yield.

Of course, these capital gains and losses are based on the assumption that the investor buys the gilt and then holds it to maturity. In reality many investors sell a few days or months after purchase, in which case they may make capital gains or losses dependent not on what the government pays on maturity but on the market price another investor is prepared to offer. This, in turn, depends on general economic conditions; in particular projected general inflation over the life of the gilt: investors will not buy a gilt offering a 5 per cent redemption yield over five years if future inflation is expected to be 7 per cent per year for that period. Interest rates (particularly for longer-term gilts) are thus strongly influenced by market perceptions of future inflation, which can shift significantly over a year or so.

Bond prices and redemption yields move in opposite directions. Take the case of our five-year gilt purchased for £120 offering a coupon of 10 per cent with a (approximate) redemption yield of 5 per cent. If general interest rates rise to 6 per cent because of an increase in inflation expectations, investors will no longer be interested in buying this gilt for £120 because at this price it yields only 5 per cent. Demand will fall, resulting in a price reduction until the bond yields 6 per cent. A rise in yield goes hand in hand with a fall in price.

Quotes

The gilts market is focused around **gilt-edged market makers (GEMMS)** who are prepared to buy from, or sell gilts to, investors. They quote two prices: the *bid* price is the price at which they will buy, the *offer* price is their selling price. The difference between the bid price and offer price is known as the **dealer's spread**, i.e. their potential profit. The table shown in **Exhibit 6.4** is from a Saturday edition of the *Financial Times*; the week-day editions are not so detailed. More information is available at www.ft.com/bonds&rates.

Note that the current redemption yield shown in the *FT* is relevant only if you are an investor on that particular day paying the price shown. However, if you bought your gilt years ago and expect to hold to maturity you will receive the yield that was obtainable at the time of purchase.

Redemption yields for gilts are quoted daily online by the Debt Management Office at www. dmo.gov.uk. Other sources of information on prices, and on the gilts market generally, include Bloomberg (www.bloomberg.com), Moody's (www.moodys.com), Standard & Poor's (www. standardandpoors.com), Fitch (www.fitchratings.com), J P Morgan (www.adr.com), Bondscape (www.bondscape.net).

Cum-dividend and ex-dividend

Gilts usually pay coupons twice a year. Between payments the interest accrues on a daily basis. If you buy a gilt you are entitled to the accrued interest since the last coupon. You will receive this when the next coupon is paid. That is, you buy the gilt **cum-dividend**.

Gilts (and other bonds) are quoted at **clean prices** – that is, quoted without taking account of the accrued interest. However, the buyer will pay the clean price plus the accrued interest value (called the **dirty price** or **full price** or **invoice price**) and receives all of the next coupon. So, if you buy a gilt four months before the next coupon is due, you would pay the clean price, say £98, plus 60 days' accrued interest (i.e. two months of accrued coupon since the last was paid). The relationship between clean and dirty prices for a bond which pays a coupon every six months is:

$$\text{Dirty price} = \text{Clean price} + \left[\frac{\text{Annual coupon}}{2} \times \frac{\text{Number of days since last coupon}}{\text{Number of days separating coupon payments}} \right]$$

So, if the bond pays an annual coupon of 7 per cent and is currently quoted at a clean price of £101, the dirty price is:

$$\text{Dirty price} = £101 + \left[\frac{£7}{2} \times \frac{60}{182} \right] = £102.15385$$

If you bought just before the coupon is to be paid, the situation is different; there would not be enough time to change the register to make sure that the coupon goes to the new owner. To allow for this problem a gilt switches from being quoted cum-dividend to being **ex-dividend (xd)** a few days before an interest payment. If you bought during the ex-dividend period the person you bought from would receive the accrued interest from the issuer – this would be reflected in the price you pay.

Exhibit 6.4

FINANCIAL TIMES MARCH 26/MARCH 27 2011

GILTS – UK CASH MARKET

Mar 25	Notes Price £	day's wk % Chng	Chng	Red Yield	52 Week High	Low
Shorts (Lives up to Five Years)						
Tr 3.25pc'11	101.77	-0.02	-0.1	0.69	103.91	101.64
Cn 9pc Ln'11	102.47	-0.06	-0.2	0.54	110.58	102.30
Tr 7.75pc '12–15✿	105.61	-0.05	-0.2	0.96	111.75	105.55
Tr 5pc '12	103.91	-0.03	-0.1	0.83	107.59	103.83
Tr 5.25pc '12	105.09	-0.03	-0.1	0.96	108.71	105.03
Tr 9pc '12 ✿	110.69	-0.06	-0.2	1.07	118.08	110.07
Tr 8pc '13	116.43	-0.07	-0.2	1.29	121.52	116.14
Tr 4.5pc '13	106.19	-0.03	-0.1	1.26	109.36	105.84
Tr 2.25pc '14	101.46	-0.05	-0.2	1.74	103.94	99.25
Tr 5pc '14	110.06	-0.07	-0.2	1.96	114.35	109.05
Tr 2.75pc '15	102.11	-0.06	-0.2	2.17	105.44	99.49
Tr 4.75pc '15	110.03	-0.08	-0.3	2.36	115.02	108.49
Tr 8pc '15	124.93	-0.11	-0.3	2.36	131.90	123.34
Tr 2pc '16	97.57	-0.06	-0.2	2.54	100.68	95.68
Five to Ten Years						
Tr 4pc '16	106.71	-0.09	-0.3	2.67	111.51	103.72
Tr 8.75pc '17	134.88	-0.14	-0.3	2.78	142.66	132.55
Ex 12pc '13–17 ✿	127.91	-0.10	-0.3	1.45	134.88	124.18
Tr 5pc '18	111.99	-0.11	-0.3	3.07	117.99	108.39
Tr 3.75pc '19	102.26	-0.11	-0.2	3.44	108.07	97.38
Tr 4.5pc (19)	108.08	-0.12	-0.2	3.33	114.14	103.69
Tr 3.75pc '20	101.21	-0.12	-0.3	3.60	107.49	98.01
Tr 4.75pc '20	109.48	-0.12	-0.3	3.51	116.31	104.75
Ten to Fifteen Years						
Tr 3.75pc '21	100.05	-0.14	-0.4	3.74	100.86	99.70
Tr 8pc '21	137.75	-0.16	-0.3	3.59	147.53	133.08
Tr 5pc '25	110.71	-0.16	-0.5	3.99	118.90	104.76
Over Fifteen Years						
Tr 4.25pc '27	101.07	-0.09	-0.4	4.16	109.11	95.84
Tr 6pc '28	122.98	-0.11	-0.4	4.15	133.11	117.74
Tr 4.75pc '30	106.31	-0.06	-0.4	4.27	115.53	101.24
Tr 4.25pc '32	99.36	-0.06	-0.5	4.30	108.42	94.61
Tr 4.5pc '34	102.29	-0.07	-0.6	4.34	111.90	97.20
Tr 4.25pc '36	98.70	-0.08	-0.6	4.34	108.22	93.16
Tr 4.75pc '38	107.05	-0.08	-0.6	4.31	117.38	101.32
Tr 4.25pc '40	98.63	-0.06	-0.7	4.33	108.31	94.20
Tr 4.5pc '42	103.32	-0.07	-0.7	4.31	113.59	97.46
Tr 4.25pc' 46	99.34	-0.07	-0.8	4.29	109.46	93.31
Tr 4.25pc' 49	99.46	-0.07	-0.8	4.28	110.05	93.19
Tr 4.35pc '55	99.90	-0.07	-0.9	4.26	111.07	93.20
Tr 4pc '60	94.91	-0.07	-1.0	4.25	105.53	88.27
Undated						
Cons 4pc ✿	79.45	-0.06	-1.1	5.03‡	89.71	75.81
War Ln 3.5pc ✿	75.19	-0.07	-1.2	4.66‡	85.81	71.41
Cn 3.5pc '61 Aft ✿	73.46	-0.07	-1.2	4.77‡	83.56	69.91
Tr 3pc '66 Aft ✿	61.80	-0.05	-1.2	4.85‡	70.11	58.87
Cons 2.5pc ✿	52.80	-0.05	-1.2	4.74‡	60.12	50.24
Tr 2.5pc ✿	53.71	-0.05	-1.2	4.66‡	61.29	50.84

	Notes Price £	day's wk % Chng	Chng	Yld (1) (2)	52 Week High	Low
Index-linked						
2.5pc '11 ...... (74.6)	308.73	-0.02	-0.1	– –	-312.05	306.52
2.5pc '13 ...... (89.2)	283.20	+0.13	0.4	– –	-283.31	267.47
2.5pc '16 ...... (81.6)	319.82	+0.13	0.4	-0.48 -0.26	320.16	298.41
1.25pc '17 ..† (193.725)	109.27	-0.03	0.2	-0.14 -0.14	111.13	104.43
2.5pc '20 .... (83.0)	324.71	+0.11	0.2	0.29 0.42	326.47	300.12
1.875pc '22 † (205.65806)	114.69	-0.02	0.0	0.57 0.57	118.05	107.98
2.5pc '24 .... (97.7)	284.65	+0.21	0.1	0.65 0.74	287.46	260.36
1.25pc '27 † (194.06667)	108.09	+0.18	0.0	0.73 0.73	111.97	99.39
4.125pc '30 .... (135.1)	270.55	+0.72	0.2	– –	-274.56	246.91
2pc 35 .... (173.6)	166.98	+0.63	0.1	– –	-169.89	150.03
1.25pc '32 † (217.13226)	110.08	+0.38	0.0	– –	-114.40	101.62
1.125pc '37 † (202.24286)	109.86	+0.50	0.0	– –	-118.48	95.02
0.625pc '40 † (216.52258)	97.39	+0.58	-0.1	– –	-104.52	89.54
0.625pc '42 † (212.46452)	98.25	+0.72	0.1	– –	-103.06	90.35
0.75pc '47 † (207.7667)	103.79	+1.01	0.0	– –	-109.02	94.31
0.5pc '50 ..... † (213.4000)	96.06	+1.15	0.4	– –	-101.10	88.02
1.25pc '55 † (192.2000)	126.22	+1.64	0.7	– –	-134.01	91.98

Prospective real redemption rate on projected inflation of (1) 5% and (2) 3% (b) Figures in parentheses show RPI base for indexing (ie 8 months prior to issue and, for gilts issued since September 2005, 3 months prior to issue) and have been adjusted to reflect rebasing of RPI to 100 in January 1987. Conversion factor 3.945. RPI for Sep 2009: 215.3 and for Apr 2009 211.5.
† For those bonds indicated, with a 3m lag, the "clean" price shown has no inflation adjustment. The yield is calculated using no inflation assumption. ‡ Running yield.

All UK Gilts are Tax free to non-residents on application, xd Ex dividend. Closing mid-prices are shown in pounds per £100 nominal of stock. Weekly percentage changes are calculated on a Friday to Friday basis. Gilt benches and most liquid stocks, are shown in bold type. A full list of Gilts can be found daily on ft.com/bond&rates.

Source: ThompsonReuters

Callout annotations:

Price, price change in day or week. The mid price between the market makers' bid and offer process ('clean' price without accrued interest) is shown for a nominal £100 of stock. Change in mid price from previous day and week

Redemption yield (yield to maturity) in per cent per year (3.99 per cent). Based on price in 2nd column

The real rates of return on the basis of assumed inflation of 5% and 3%

Index linked gilts. The interest and the redemption value rise with the retail price index

Name of gilt and coupon (Treasury 3.25 per cent)

Redemption date (2019): when repayment of the loan will take place

Highest and lowest price over the past year

Note: Monday's FT shows the dates interest will be paid and the dates of the last ex-dividend payment of interest was made

Index-linked gilts

There is a hidden danger with conventional gilts – inflation risk. Say, for example, that you, along with the rest of the gilt-buying community, think that inflation over the next ten years will average 2.5 per cent. As a result you buy ten-year gilts that have a redemption yield of 4.8 per cent, giving a comfortable real income over and above cost-of-living rises. However, two years later inflation starts to take off (oil prices quadruple, or the government goes on a spending spree, or whatever). Now investors reckon that inflation will average 6 per cent over the following eight years. As a result your gilt yield will fail to maintain your capital in real terms.

The government introduced a type of bond that ensures that you receive a return above the inflation rate throughout the entire life of the bond. These are called **index-linked stocks (gilts)**, where the coupon amount, and the nominal value as well, are adjusted or uplifted according to the **Retail Price Index (RPI)**.[3] The deal here is that the gilt initially offers to pay £100 at the end of its term, say ten years away. It also offers to pay a low coupon, say 2 per cent. The key thing about index-linked bonds is that neither the capital sum on maturity nor the coupon stay at these levels unless inflation is zero over the next ten years.

Say inflation is 4 per cent over the first year of the bond's life. The payout on maturity would rise to £104. However, this inflation-linked up-lift happens every year. So, if over the ten years the inflation measure has risen by 60 per cent, the payout on the bond is £160. This means that you can buy just as many goods and services at the end with the capital sum as at the beginning of the bond's life (if you paid £100). (The situation is slightly more complicated than this in that the inflation figures used are those for the three months[4] preceding the relevant coupon dates, but this example illustrates the principle.) Furthermore, the coupon rate also rises through the years if inflation is positive. So after the first year the coupons go up by 4%, $2\% \times (1+0.04) = 2.08\%$, so for every £100 bond, the coupon is £2.08.

Any future rises in inflation lead to further growth in the coupon, so that the last coupon will be 60 per cent larger than the one paid in the first year if inflation over the ten years accumulates to 60 per cent, giving £3.20 per £100 nominal.

A final point on index-linked gilts: because most investors hold them to maturity, secondary trading is thin and dealing spreads are wider than for conventional gilts.

Government bonds around the world

Most countries in the world issue government bonds which are similar in format to UK gilts and are given a credit rating (*see* **Exhibit 6.5**). Some countries are regarded as very safe ('triple-A rated') and so can issue at a low real (after allowing for anticipated inflation) yield. Others, such as Ukraine, are regarded as having more risk and so will have to pay a high-risk premium to entice investors to buy their bonds. Credit ratings are discussed in Chapter 5 and later in this chapter.

As communications have become easy and electronic banking the norm, all bond markets worldwide are interconnected and interest rates have become linked. So, in general, bonds worldwide pay similar rates of interest if they carry the same risk (and inflation is anticipated to be the same). **Exhibit 6.6** shows the interest rates for a few of the bonds of the leading government issuers.

US Treasury notes and bonds

Treasury notes are issued on behalf of the US government by Treasury Direct with a face value of $100 and a coupon payable every six months. They have a maturity of two, three, five, seven or ten years and are sold at monthly auctions, except for ten-year notes which are auctioned quarterly. The auctions are based on the yield amount and can be competitive or non-competitive. At the competitive auctions, only banks, brokers or dealers may bid, up to a maximum of 35 per cent of the total amount on offer, and they are allocated some or all of the requested amount. If they

---

[3] In 2011 there is a plan to issue index-linked gilts which are uplifted for the consumer price index (CPI), a slightly different way of measuring general inflation than the retail price index (RPI).

[4] For index-linked bonds issued before September 2005 the lag is eight months.

Exhibit 6.5   Map of world credit ratings

When investors want to access how risky their investment might be in a particular country in debt they turn for help to one of the big credit rating agencies such as Standards & Poor's (S&P). These companies act like teachers, grading every nation according to the state of their economy, their public finances and the risk of things going wrong in the future. The lower the credit rating, the higher the cost of borrowing

Key

AAA Highest ranking available

A– to AA+

B– to BBB+

C– to CCC+

No data

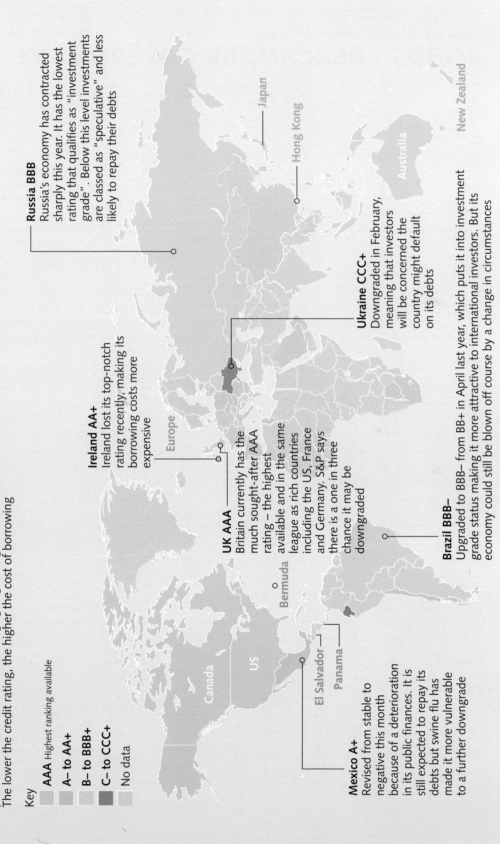

Russia BBB
Russia's economy has contracted sharply this year. It has the lowest rating that qualifies as "investment grade". Below this level investments are classed as "speculative" and less likely to repay their debts

Japan

Hong Kong

Australia

New Zealand

Ukraine CCC+
Downgraded in February, meaning that investors will be concerned the country might default on its debts

Ireland AA+
Ireland lost its top-notch rating recently, making its borrowing costs more expensive

Europe

UK AAA
Britain currently has the much sought-after AAA rating – the highest available and in the same league as rich countries including the US, France and Germany. S&P says there is a one in three chance it may be downgraded

Brazil BBB–
Upgraded to BBB– from BB+ in April last year, which puts it into investment grade status making it more attractive to international investors. But its economy could still be blown off course by a change in circumstances

Bermuda

Canada

US

El Salvador

Panama

Mexico A+
Revised from stable to negative this month because of a deterioration in its public finances. It is still expected to repay its debts but swine flu has made it more vulnerable to a further downgrade

Source: From http://image.guardian.co.uk/sys-files/Guardian/documents/2009/05/22/Credit-rating.pdf. Copyright Guardian News & Media Ltd 2009.

Exhibit 6.6

FINANCIAL TIMES TUESDAY MARCH 29 2011

BONDS – BENCHMARK GOVERNMENT

Mar 28	Red Date	Coupon	Bid Price	Bid Yield	Day chg yield	Wk chg yield	Month chg yld	Year chg yld	
Australia	05/13	6.50	103.10	4.94	0.03	0.15	−0.01	0.01	Redemption date May 2021
	05/21	5.75	101.94	5.50	0.02	0.11	−0.02	−0.23	
Austria	10/13	3.80	104.22	2.08	0.01	0.12	0.20	0.83	
	09/12	3.50	97.86	3.75	0.03	0.16	0.13	0.22	
Belgium	03/13	4.00	103.47	2.20	0.01	0.09	−0.24	1.05	
	09/21	4.25	100.10	4.24	0.01	0.17	−0.05	0.62	Coupon. The amount paid each
Canada	03/13	1.75	99.98	1.76	0.02	0.16	−0.02	0.07	year as a percentage of the nominal
	06/20	3.50	101.72	3.28	0.04	0.11	−0.01	−0.27	value of the bond, 4 per cent
Denmark	11/12	4.00	103.59	1.74	0.01	0.08	0.20	0.14	
	11/19	4.00	104.72	3.36	0.01	0.10	0.15	−0.09	
Finland	09/12	4.25	103.74	1.64	0.01	0.10	0.20	0.42	The yield to redemption based on
	04/20	3.38	99.12	3.49	0.00	0.11	0.14	0.11	the market makers' bid price,
France	01/13	3.75	103.44	1.78	0.01	0.05	0.15	0.87	3.36 per cent
	02/16	2.25	97.22	2.87	0.01	0.13	0.20	0.53	
	10/20	2.50	90.93	3.64	−0.01	0.11	0.11	0.16	
	04/41	4.50	105.37	4.18	−0.01	0.12	0.17	0.07	
Germany	03/13	1.50	99.54	1.74	0.01	0.10	0.20	0.84	
	02/16	2.00	97.29	2.59	0.01	0.13	0.22	0.39	
	01/21	2.50	93.44	3.29	0.00	0.11	0.15	0.14	
	07/40	4.75	116.74	3.79	0.00	0.11	0.19	−0.12	
Greece	05/14	4.50	71.10	17.15	1.28	1.25	3.12	11.95	
	06/20	6.25	65.66	12.78	0.20	0.57	0.92	6.60	
Ireland	04/16	4.60	77.06	10.71	−0.10	0.71	1.70	7.79	
	10/20	5.00	69.75	10.07	0.01	0.48	0.65	5.51	
Italy	06/13	2.00	98.23	2.86	0.07	0.14	0.33	1.56	
	11/15	3.00	96.85	3.79	0.05	0.13	−0.12	1.15	
	03/21	3.75	92.26	4.79	0.04	0.11	−0.06	0.87	
	09/40	5.00	91.97	5.63	0.02	0.11	0.04	0.83	
Japan	04/13	0.20	99.97	0.22	0.00	0.00	−0.03	0.05	
	03/16	0.60	100.58	0.48	0.01	0.00	−0.07	−0.07	
	03/21	1.30	100.51	1.24	0.02	0.03	−0.01	−0.14	
	03/31	2.20	102.31	2.04	0.04	0.02	0.04	−0.10	
Netherlands	01/13	1.75	100.04	1.73	0.00	0.05	0.41	0.79	
	07/21	3.25	97.22	3.58	0.00	0.11	0.24	0.18	
New Zealand	04/13	6.50	105.87	3.50	0.05	0.09	−0.07	−0.35	
	05/21	6.00	102.62	5.66	0.05	0.12	0.11	−0.37	
Norway	05/15	5.00	106.72	3.23	0.03	−0.04	0.13	0.02	
	05/21	3.75	99.53	3.81	0.02	−0.04	0.03	–	
Portugal	09/13	5.45	95.83	7.33	0.28	0.88	1.61	5.62	Bid price. The price that a market
	06/20	4.80	78.80	8.16	0.21	0.57	0.61	3.83	maker will buy from an investor
Spain	04/13	2.30	98.65	2.98	0.04	0.13	−0.26	1.85	should he/she wish to sell. In the
	04/21	5.50	102.54	5.17	−0.01	0.02	−0.24	1.34	case of a UK government bond
Sweden	05/14	6.75	111.52	2.81	0.01	0.08	0.64	1.23	with the unit par value of £100 the
	12/20	5.00	113.20	3.38	0.03	0.10	0.06	0.16	price is £101.71
Switzerland	02/13	4.00	106.10	0.69	−0.01	0.12	0.09	0.22	
	04/21	2.00	100.89	1.90	0.05	0.11	0.02	−0.03	
UK	12/11	3.25	101.71	0.76	0.00	0.06	−0.01	0.08	
	09/15	4.75	109.93	2.38	0.02	0.13	−0.10	−0.39	
	09/20	3.75	101.05	3.62	0.01	0.10	−0.09	−0.42	
	12/40	4.25	98.51	4.34	0.01	0.07	−0.06	−0.28	Yield changes over one day, week,
US	02/13	0.63	99.72	0.77	0.03	0.18	0.05	−0.28	month and year. The yields to
	02/16	2.13	99.64	2.20	0.04	0.26	0.03	−0.39	redemption change (almost) every
	02/21	3.63	101.41	3.46	0.01	0.19	0.03	−0.40	day as the bond price moves with
	02/41	4.75	104.05	4.50	0.00	0.08	−0.02	−0.25	the shifts in demand and supply in the secondary market

London close.
Yields: Local market standard Annualised yield basis. Yields shown for Italy exclude withholding tax at 12.5 per cent payable by non residents.

Source: ThomsonReuters

Source: Financial Times, 29 March 2011, p. 20. Reprinted with permission.

bid at a price higher than that which allows the government to sell all the notes they want to – the cut-off price (or yield) – they will receive all they bid for. For the non-competitive element individuals may also bid and they are guaranteed to receive the amount requested, but they will pay the price that is the outcome of the competitive bid auction. The notes may be traded at any time up to maturity and their yield is quoted in financial publications.

Treasury bonds are auctioned quarterly, have a maturity date of 10–30 years and pay interest twice per year.

Treasury inflation-protected securities (TIPS) are index-linked bonds whose principal value is adjusted according to changes in the Consumer Price Index (CPI). They have maturities of 5, 10 or 30 years and interest is paid twice yearly at a fixed rate on the inflation-adjusted amount. The 5- and 30-year securities are auctioned once a year and the 10-year security is auctioned twice a year.

US government notes and bonds are traded in an active secondary market (in an over-the-counter market rather than on a formal exchange), with dealers posting bid (buying) and ask (selling) prices, and trades conducted over the telephone or by electronic communication. Prices are quoted as a percentage of face value and on a clean basis.

French bonds

The French Treasury, Agence France Trésor (AFT), sells by auction **OATS** (Obligations assimilables du Trésor), which are 7–50-year bonds, mostly fixed rate, but some with floating or index-linked rates, and **BTANS** (Bons du Trésor à intérèts annuels), which are 2–5-year bonds with a fixed rate of interest.

German bonds

In Germany, the German financial agency, Bundesrepublik Deutschland Finanzagentur (BDF), issues at auction 2-, 5-, 10- and 30-year notes and bonds, some of which are index-linked and the minimum bid is €1 million. Two-year Federal Treasury Notes – Bundesschatzanweisungen (Schätze) – five-year Federal Notes – Bundesobligationen (Bobls) – and 10- and 30-year Federal Bonds – Bundesanleihen (Bunds) – are sold via pre-announced auctions by the Bundesbank, the German central bank, on behalf of the BDF.

The yield to maturity offered on German government bonds usually forms the reference or benchmark interest rate for other borrowings in the euro. In other words, it is the lowest rate available, with other interest rates described as so many basis points above, say, the ten-year bund rate.

Japanese bonds

The Japanese Ministry of Finance issues Treasury discount bills and bonds. Japanese government bonds (**JGBs**) with a maturity of 2, 5, 10 and 20 years are auctioned monthly, 30-year bonds are auctioned every other month, and 40-year bonds quarterly. Inflation-indexed linked JGBs are also issued for ten-year maturities. Retail purchasers must purchase a minimum ¥10,000; other purchasers must buy at least ¥50,000 worth of bonds. Many JGBs are traded in the over-the-counter secondary market. A few are traded on the Tokyo Stock Exchange and other exchanges.

Chinese bonds

In 2007, China began dealing in bonds and in 2009 it issued the first bonds denominated in the Chinese renminbi currency. These renminbi sovereign bonds were issued in Hong Kong and available to foreign investors only. China is keen to expand the use of its currency worldwide, hoping to decrease its reliance on the US dollar (China is the largest holder of US Treasury bills and so would be vulnerable if the dollar were to weaken).

Corporate bonds

Corporate bonds offer a higher rate of return than well-represented government bonds but, as you might expect, this comes with a greater degree of risk of failure to pay what was agreed (default). They can be a very useful way for companies to raise money without issuing equity or accepting the conditions of a bank loan.[5] Many corporate bonds are sufficiently negotiable (tradable) that they are *listed* on the London Stock Exchange and other exchanges in Europe, Asia or the Americas, but the majority of trading occurs in the OTC market directly between an investor and a bond dealer. Access to a secondary market means that the investor who originally provided the firm with money does not have to hold on to the bond until the maturity date. However, because so many investors buy and then hold to maturity rather than trade in and out, corporate bonds generally have very thin secondary markets compared with listed shares or money market instruments.

Corporate bonds have generally been the province of investing institutions, such as pension and insurance funds. Private investors tended not to hold them, mainly due to the large amounts of cash involved – the minimum is occasionally £1,000, more often £50,000. The par value of one bond at, say, £50,000, €50,000 or $50,000 is said to have a 50,000 minimum 'lot' or 'piece'. However, in 2010, the London Stock Exchange opened a secondary market trading facility for small investors for a limited range of bonds, where lots are just £100 or £1,000 and the costs of trading are relatively low.

Infinite variation

Corporate bonds come in a variety of forms. The most common is the type with regular (usually semi-annual or annual) fixed coupons and a specified redemption date. These are known as straight, plain vanilla or bullet bonds. Other corporate bonds are a variation on this. Some pay coupons every three months, some do not pay a fixed coupon but one which varies depending on the level of short-term interest rates (floating rate or variable-rate bonds) and some have interest rates linked to the rate of inflation. In fact, the potential for variety and innovation is almost infinite. Bonds issued in the last few years have linked the interest rates paid or the principal payments to a wide variety of economic events, such as a rise in the price of silver, exchange-rate movements, stock market indices, the price of oil, gold, copper – even to the occurrence of an earthquake. These bonds were generally designed to let companies adjust their interest payments to manageable levels in the event of the firm being adversely affected by the changing of some economic variable. For example, a copper mining company, with its interest payments linked to the price of copper, would pay lower interest on its finance if the copper price were to fall. Sampdoria, the Italian football club, issued a €3.5 million bond that paid a higher rate of return if the club won promotion to the 'Serie A' division, 2.5 per cent if it stayed in Serie B, 7 per cent if it moved to Serie A and if the club rose to the top four in Serie A the coupon would rise to 14 per cent.

Debentures and loan stocks

In the UK and a few other countries the most secure type of bond is called a debenture. Debentures are usually secured by either a fixed or a floating charge against the firm's assets. A fixed charge means that specific assets (e.g. buildings, machinery) are used as security, which, in the event of default, can be sold at the insistence of the debenture bond holders and the proceeds used to repay them. Debentures are quite a common way of raising sums of money for capital expenditure – see the debentures issued by Diageo in Exhibit 6.1 for examples. Debentures secured on property may be referred to as mortgage debentures. A floating charge means that the loan is secured by a general charge on all the assets of the corporation (or a class of the firm's assets such as inventory or debtors). In this case the company has a high degree of freedom to use its assets as it wishes, such as sell them or rent them out, until it commits a default which 'crystallises' the floating charge. If this happens a receiver will be appointed with powers to

---

[5] Some so-called 'corporate bonds' are in fact issued by business enterprises owned by the government. Also, the biggest issuers are, in fact, banks rather than non-financial commercial corporations.

dispose of assets and to distribute the proceeds to the creditors. Even though floating-charge debenture holders can force a **liquidation**, fixed-charge debenture holders rank above floating-charge debenture holders in the payout after insolvency.

The terms bond, debenture and **loan stock** are often used interchangeably and the dividing line between debentures and loan stock is a fuzzy one. As a general rule debentures are secured (have the backing of collateral) and loan stock is unsecured, but there are examples that do not fit this classification. If liquidation occurs, the unsecured loan stock holders rank beneath the debenture holders and some other categories of creditors such as the tax authorities.

In the US, Canada and some other countries the definitions are somewhat different and this can be confusing. In these places a debenture is a long-term unsecured bond and so the holders become general creditors who can claim only assets not otherwise pledged. In the US the secured form of bond is referred to as the **mortgage bond** and unsecured shorter-dated issues (less than ten years) are called **notes**.

Trust deeds and covenants

Bond investors are willing to lower the interest they demand if they can be reassured that their money will not be exposed to a high risk. Reassurance is conveyed by placing risk-reducing restrictions on the firm. A **trust deed** (or **bond indenture**) sets out the terms of the contract between bond holders and the company. A **trustee** (if one is appointed) ensures compliance with the contract throughout the life of the bond and has the power to appoint a receiver (to liquidate the firm's assets). If a trustee is not appointed the usual practice is to give each holder an independently exercisable right to take legal action against a delinquent borrower.

The loan agreement will contain a number of **affirmative covenants**. These usually include the requirements to supply regular financial statements, interest and principal payments. The deed may also state the fees due to the lenders and details of what procedures should be followed in the event of a technical default, for example non-payment of interest.

In addition to these basic covenants are the **negative (restrictive) covenants**. These restrict the actions and the rights of the borrower until the debt has been repaid in full. Some examples are:

- *Limits on further debt issuance* If lenders provide finance to a firm they do so on certain assumptions concerning the riskiness of the capital structure. They will want to ensure that the loan does not become more risky due to the firm taking on a much greater debt burden relative to its equity base, so they limit the amount and type of further debt issues – particularly debt which has a higher (**senior**) ranking for interest payments or for a liquidation payment. **Subordinated debt (junior debt)** – with a low ranking on liquidation – is more likely to be acceptable.

- *Dividend level* Lenders are opposed to money being taken into the firm by borrowing at one end, while being taken away by shareholders in dividend payments at the other. An excessive withdrawal of shareholders' funds may unbalance the financial structure and weaken future cash flows.

- *Limits on the disposal of assets* The retention of certain assets, for example property and land, may be essential to reduce the lenders' risk.

- *Financial ratios* A typical covenant here concerns the interest cover, for example: 'The annual profit will remain four times as great as the overall annual interest charge.' Other restrictions might be placed on working capital ratio levels and the debt to net assets ratio.

While negative covenants cannot ensure completely risk-free lending they can influence the behaviour of the managerial team so as to reduce the risk of default. The lenders' risk can be further reduced by obtaining guarantees from third parties (for example **guaranteed loan stock**). The guarantor is typically the parent company of the issuer – *see* the Diageo example in Exhibit 6.1.

Repayments

The principal on many bonds is paid entirely at maturity. However, there are bonds which can be repaid before the final redemption date. A common approach is for the company to issue bonds with a range of dates for redemption; so a bond dated 2018–2022 would allow a company the flexibility to repay the principal over four years. Another way of redeeming bonds is for the issuing firm to buy the outstanding bonds by offering the holder a sum higher than or equal to the amount originally paid. A firm is also able to purchase bonds on the open market.

One way of paying for redemption is to set up a sinking fund that receives regular sums from the firm which will be sufficient, with added interest, to redeem the bonds (the firm may use this to pay off a portion of the bond each year). The sinking fund is overseen by a trustee. The bonds may be purchased in the market either at market prices or at face value. Alternatively, bonds held by investors might be selected randomly and purchased. Because a bond with a sinking fund provision is less risky for the investor, as there is money being set aside, it carries a lower interest rate.

Some bonds are described as 'irredeemable' (or 'perpetual') as they have no fixed redemption date. From the investor's viewpoint they may be irredeemable but the firm has the option to repurchase and can effectively redeem the bonds when it wishes.

Deep discounted bonds

Bonds which are sold at well below the par value are called deep discounted bonds, the most extreme form of which is the zero coupon bond. Because these are sold at a large discount to the nominal value, the investor makes a capital gain by holding the bond instead of receiving coupons. It is easy to calculate the rate of return offered to an investor on this type of bond. For example, if a company issues a bond at a price of £60 which is redeemable at £100 in eight years, the annualised rate of return (r) is:

$$60(1 + r)^8 = 100$$

$$r = \sqrt[8]{\frac{100}{60}} - 1 = 0.066 \text{ or } 6.6\% \text{ per year}$$

These bonds are particularly useful for firms with low cash flows in the near term, for example firms engaged in a major property development that will not mature for many years.

Floating rate notes

A major market has developed over the past three decades called the floating-rate note (FRN) (also called variable-rate notes) market. Two factors have led to the rapid growth in FRN usage. First, the oscillating and unpredictable inflation of the 1970s and 1980s caused many investors to make large real-term losses on fixed-rate bonds as the interest rate fell below the inflation rate. As a result many lenders became reluctant to lend at fixed rates on a long-term basis. This reluctance led to FRNs being cheaper for the issuer because it does not need to offer an interest premium to compensate the investor for being locked into a fixed rate. Second, a number of corporations, especially financial institutions, hold assets which give a return that varies with the short-term interest rate level (for example, bank loans and overdrafts) and so prefer to have a similar floating-rate liability. These instruments pay an interest rate that is linked to a benchmark rate – such as the LIBOR (*see* Chapter 5). The issuer will pay, say, 70 basis points (0.7 of a percentage point) over LIBOR. The coupon might be set for the first six months at the time of issue, after which it is adjusted every six months, so if LIBOR was 3 per cent, the FRN would pay 3.7 per cent for that particular six months.

Credit rating

Firms often pay to have their bonds rated by specialist credit-rating organisations (*see* Chapter 5). The debt rating depends on the likelihood of payments of interest and/or capital not being paid (that is, *default*) and in some cases on the extent to which the lender is protected in the event of a default by the loan issuer (the recoverability of debt).[6] Government bonds from the leading economies have an insignificant risk of default whereas unsecured subordinated corporate loan stock has a much higher risk.

A top rating (AAA) indicates very high quality, where the capacity to repay interest and principal is extremely strong. Single A indicates a strong capacity to pay interest and capital but there is some degree of susceptibility to impairment as economic events unfold. BBB indicates adequate debt service capacity but vulnerability to adverse economic conditions or changing circumstances. B- and C-rated debt has predominantly speculative characteristics. The lowest is D, which indicates the firm is in default. Ratings of BBB− (or Baa3 for Moody's) or above are regarded as 'investment grade' – this is important because many institutional investors are permitted to invest only in investment grade bonds. Bonds rated below investment grade are called high-yield (or junk) bonds.

The agencies consider a wide range of quantitative and qualitative factors in determining the rating for a bond. The quantitative factors include the ratio of assets to liabilities of the company, cash-flow generation and the amount of debt outstanding. The qualitative factors include the competitive position of the company, quality of management and vulnerability to the economic cycle.

The rating and re-rating of bonds is followed with great interest by borrowers and lenders and can give rise to some heated argument. Frequently borrowers complain that their ratings are not judged to be as high as they think they should be, with the result that higher interest rates are payable on their bonds.

The same company can issue bonds with different ratings: one may be raised because it is higher ranking in the capital structure, meaning that if the firm runs into trouble and has difficulty paying its debts the holders of this bond will be paid before the holders of lower-ranking bonds (the subordinated debt). Another difference may be that one bond is secured on specific assets. The ranking order for bonds is:

1 Senior secured debt

2 Senior unsecured debt

3 Senior subordinated debt

4 Subordinated debt

The rating agencies also provide issuer ratings to firms and other organisations, which are assessments of the creditworthiness of the whole entity rather than of a particular bond.

Bond credit ratings are available at www.standardandpoors.com, www.moodys.com and www.fitchratings.com. The *Financial Times* shows credit ratings daily in the tables titled 'Bonds – Global Investment Grade' and 'Bonds – High Yield & Emerging Market' together with yields to redemption and other details – *see* **Exhibits 6.7 and 6.8** (more at www.ftcom/bonds&rates). These give the reader some idea of current market conditions and yield to maturity demanded for bonds of different maturities, currencies and riskiness. The ratings shown are for March 2011 and will not necessarily be applicable in future years because the creditworthiness and the specific debt issue can change significantly in a short period. (In the table S^* = Standard & Poor's, M^* = Moody's and F^* = Fitch.) A key measure in the bond markets is the '**spread**', which is the number of basis points a bond is yielding above a benchmark rate, usually the government bond yield to maturity for that currency and period to redemption.

The so-called 'emerging markets' are, to a large extent, now fully emerged, with many countries such as Brazil and Mexico having fully functioning corporate bond markets drawing on local savings to raise funds for businesses – *see* **Exhibit 6.9**.

---

[6] The rating agencies say that they do not in the strictest sense give an opinion on the likelihood of default, but merely evaluate relative creditworthiness or relative likelihood of default, and because rating scales are relative, default rates fluctuate over time. Thus, a group of middle-rated bonds is expected to be consistent in having a lower rate of default than a group of lower-rated bonds, but it will not, year after year, have a default rate of, say, 2.5 per cent per year.

Exhibit 6.7

FINANCIAL TIMES TUESDAY MARCH 29 2011

BONDS – GLOBAL INVESTMENT GRADE

Mar 28	Red date	Coupon	Ratings S*	Ratings M*	Ratings F*	Bid price	Bid yield	Day's chge yield	Mths's chge yield	Spread vs Govts
US$										
Morgan Stanley	04/12	6.60	A	A2	A	105.51	1.43	–	−0.02	1.19
Household Fin	05/12	7.00	A	A3	AA−	106.01	1.91	–	−0.17	1.66
HBOS Treas UK	06/12	5.50	A+	Aa3	AA−	104.65	1.58	0.04	−0.71	1.30
Bank of America	01/13	4.88	A	A2	A+	104.08	2.62	–	−0.02	1.93
Goldman Sachs	07/13	4.75	A	A1	A+	104.75	2.66	–	−0.03	1.97
Hutchinson 03/33	01/14	6.25	A−	A3	A−	109.45	2.73	0.07	0.06	1.47
Misc Capital	(07/14)	6.13	A−	A3	–	108.16	3.52	–	–	2.31
billionP Paribas	06/15	4.80	AA−	Aa3	A+	103.70	3.84	−0.07	−0.80	1.68
GE Capital	01/16	5.00	AA+	Aa2	–	107.85	3.21	−0.24	−0.29	1.04
Credit Suisse USA	03/16	5.38	A+	Aa1	AA−	109.10	3.35	−0.18	−0.19	0.95
Swire Pacific	04/18	6.25	A−	A3	A	105.98	5.31	–	–	2.50
Goldman Sachs	02/33	6.13	A	A1	A+	101.91	(5.97)	–	−0.02	1.48
Bell South	10/31	6.88	A−	A2	A	113.05	5.78	–	−0.09	1.29
GE Capital	01/39	6.88	AA+	Aa2	–	110.83	6.06	0.06	0.04	1.54
Euro										
HSBC Fin	06/12	3.38	A	A3	AA−	101.41	2.15	0.01	−0.11	1.09
Xstrata Fin CA	06/12	4.88	BBB	Baa2	–	102.90	2.40	0.00	0.24	1.17
Amer Honda Fin	07/13	6.25	A+	A1	–	107.44	2.84	0.01	0.25	1.11
JPMorgan Chase	01/15	5.25	A+	Aa3	AA−	105.85	3.57	0.01	0.20	1.31
GE Cap Euro Fdg	01/18	5.38	AA+	Aa2	–	105.30	4.45	0.01	0.27	1.50
Unicredit	01/20	4.38	(A	Aa3	A)	97.25	4.76	0.01	0.03	1.55
ENEL	05/24	5.25	A−	A2	A	100.12	5.24	0.01	0.18	1.70
Yen										
Citi Group 15	09/12	1.11	A	A3	A+	100.18	0.99	0.01	−0.05	0.81
Deutsche Bahn Fin	12/14	1.65	AA	Aa1	AA	103.64	0.64	0.02	−0.15	0.33
Nomura Sec S 3	03/18	2.28	–	–	–	102.16	1.93	0.02	−0.07	(1.16)
£ Sterling										
(Morgan Stanley)	04/11	7.50	A	A2	A	100.08	4.51	−3.79	2.25	3.66
HSBC Fin	03/12	7.00	A	A3	AA−	104.50	2.34	−0.02	−0.16	1.50
Slough Estates	09/15	6.25	–	–	A−	(105.61)	4.77	−0.03	−0.18	2.40
ASIF III	12/18	(5.00)	A+	A2	A−	96.08	5.56	−0.01	−0.18	2.22

Redemption date: July 2014

Issuer

Credit ratings

Coupon as a percentage of par value

Bond price with par value set at 100

Gross (before deduction of tax) yield to maturity: 5.97 per cent

Spread to the government bond interest rate (in this case Japanese). The extent to which the yield to maturity (bid yield) is greater than that on a government bond of the same length of time to maturity (in this case 1.16 per cent)

Source: Financial Times, 29 March 2011. Reprinted with permission.

Exhibit 6.8

FINANCIAL TIMES TUESDAY MARCH 29 2011

www.ft.com/bonds&rates

BONDS – HIGH YIELD & EMERGING MARKET

Mar 28	Red date	Coupon	S*	Ratings M*	F*	Bid price	Bid yield	Day's chge yield	Mths's chge yield	Spread vs US
High Yield US$										
HSBK Europe	05/13	7.75	B+	Ba3	B+	105.45	5.00	0.09	−57.68	4.19
Kazkommerts Int	04/14	7.88	B	B2	B−	51.00	35.64	28.79	27.34	33.97
Bertin	10/16	10.25	NR	B1	–	111.25	7.70	−0.30	−0.51	5.27
High Yield Euro										
Royal Carib Crs	01/14	5.63	BB	Ba2	–	99.33	5.88	–	0.92	3.91
Kazkommerts Int	02/17	6.88	B	B2	B−	94.84	8.00	0.01	−0.61	5.20
Emerging US$										
Bulgaria	01/15	8.25	BBB	Baa3	BBB−	116.25	3.62	0.06	−0.15	2.34
Peru	02/15	9.88	BBB−	Baa3	BBB−	124.88	2.98	−0.10	−0.09	1.70
Brazil	03/15	7.88	BBB−	Baa3	BBB−	119.19	2.70	−0.08	−0.06	1.42
Mexico	09/16	11.38	BBB	Baa1	BBB	140.38	3.24	0.10	0.01	1.04
Argentina	01/17	11.38	EXCH	EXCH	EXCH	36.50	40.34	–	0.19	38.13
Phillipines	01/19	9.88	BB	Ba3	BB	135.25	4.46	0.01	−0.06	1.60
Brazil	01/20	12.75	BBB−	Baa3	BBB−	161.25	4.30	0.03	0.05	0.85
Colombia	02/20	11.75	BBB−	Ba1	BB+	150.75	4.70	0.00	−0.25	1.24
Russia	03/30	7.50	BBB	Baa1	BBB	116.38	4.72	0.04	−0.14	1.86
Mexico	08/31	8.30	BBB	Baa1	BBB	133.13	5.56	0.00	−0.08	1.06
Indonesia	02/37	6.63	BB	Ba1	BB+	107.00	6.08	0.00	−0.08	1.59
Emerging Euro										
Brazil	02/15	7.38	BBB−	Baa3	BBB−	113.75	3.49	−0.20	−0.26	1.15
Poland	02/16	3.63	A−	A2	A−	99.43	3.75	−0.02	−0.02	1.16
Turkey	03/16	5.00	BB	Ba2	BB+	101.00	4.77	–	0.20	2.16
Mexico	02/20	5.50	BBB	Baa1	BBB	106.50	4.60	–	−0.07	1.40

US$ denominated bonds NY close; all other London close. *S – Standard & Poor's, M – Moody's, F – Fitch.

Source: ThomsonReuters

The change in the yield to maturity over the past day or month

Source: Financial Times, 29 March 2011. Reprinted with permission.

Exhibit 6.9

Corporate bond issues go local to deliver capital lift

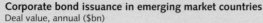

David Oakley

Corporate bond issuance in emerging market currencies has surged to record levels this year, deepening the local sources of capital for companies.

Groups have tapped increasing demand for local currency bonds not only from foreign investors but also a growing number of domestic funds seeking exposure to corporate debt.

This has lowered the cost of borrowing and reduced the risk for companies that foreign fund managers might stop buying their debt in times of crisis.

Emerging market corporate bond issuance has jumped to $68 billion so far this year, up 58 per cent on the same period last year, according to Dealogic.

Local currency corporate bond issuance has made up $49 billion of this, a 29 per cent jump on the same period last year and a 308 per cent increase on the same period three years ago, when these markets were smaller and more immature.

Companies that have tapped the market this year include multinationals such as Vale, the Brazilian iron ore producer, Pemex, the Mexican oil company, TNK-BP, the Russian arm of oil group BP and CNPC, the Chinese energy group.

However, smaller companies are increasingly able to borrow in

Corporate bond issuance in emerging market countries
Deal value, annual ($bn)

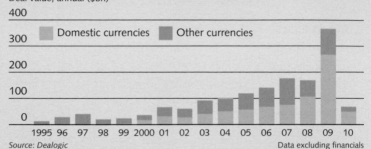

Source: Dealogic   Data excluding financials

the local currency markets, helped by the development of pension fund industries in countries such as Mexico, Brazil, Chile and South Korea. This is because domestic pension funds want assets denominated in their own currencies.

For example, in Mexico, Alsea, the restaurant operator, and Infonavit, the government-backed mortgage lender, have issued bonds recently.

These bonds saw strong demand and traded higher in the secondary market once they were priced, underlining the appetite for this debt.

The local currency corporate bond markets have also been boosted by a lengthening of the average maturity of emerging market government bonds.

This is enabling companies to issue longer-dated debt that gives

them more stability as they can lock in fixed rates, often up to 10 years.

For example, the average maturity of government debt has risen above five years in Mexico, which is now longer than in the US with an average maturity of 4.8 years.

In both Brazil and Turkey, the average maturity of government debt has increased to three years from one and a half years in 2005.

Brett Diment, head of emerging market debt at Aberdeen Asset Managers, said: "In effect, many emerging markets are becoming more like developed markets as they become more sophisticated."

Source: Financial Times, 24 March 2010, p. 17. Reprinted with permission.

A lot of weight is placed on bond ratings by financial institutions and investors, who rely on them for investment actions and can feel aggrieved if the bond ratings fail to live up to expectations. In 2009, the ratings agencies were criticised for not spotting the dangers in a number of bonds which gained their income from thousands of US mortgages (*see* **Exhibit 6.10**).

Bond default rates

Table 6.1 shows the proportion of bonds that have defaulted one, two, three, four, five and ten years after issue over the period 1990–2010. Notice the large differences in default rates between the ratings. After five years only 0.17 per cent of AA bonds defaulted, whereas 11.68 per cent of B bonds defaulted. When examining data on default rates it is important to appreciate that default is a wide-ranging term and could refer to any number of events, from a missed payment to

Exhibit 6.10

Ratings agency model left largely intact

Aline van Duyn and Joanna Chung

Big banks are not the only groups whose income is soaring on the back of commissions and fees from selling and trading the huge amounts of debt being sold by governments, banks and companies.

Credit rating agencies, the biggest of which are Moody's Investors Service and Standard & Poor's, have also seen a surge in revenue, as most debt that is issued – government-backed or not – comes with a credit rating for which the borrower pays a fee.

...The rating agencies remain central to the debt markets and their business models today remain largely intact, in spite of widespread claims that they exacerbated the credit crisis. The criticism centres on the fact that Moody's, S&P and Fitch gave triple A ratings to hundreds of billions of dollars of bonds backed by risky mortgages – but these securities have since been downgraded and are in many cases now worthless.

Ratings continue to be written into the official criteria used by many investors to define what debt they can and cannot buy. They are also still central to risk assessments by regulators. Ironically, some of the biggest investors and borrowers are suing the rating agencies.

The largest pension fund in the US, the California Public Employees' Retirement System (Calpers), has filed a suit against the three leading rating agencies over potential losses of more than $1 billion over what it says are 'wildly inaccurate' triple A ratings. That is just one of many cases. S&P currently faces about 40 separate lawsuits from investors and institutions.

In the past, most lawsuits have failed because rating agencies are protected by the first amendment right to free speech. Their ratings are an 'opinion' and therefore subject to free speech protections.

Whether this will continue to be the case is a key factor in the debate about the future of the industry.

"We are all watching the Calpers suit," says Donald Ross, global strategist at Boyd Watterson Asset Management. "It may be dismissed like many other suits have been on the basis of free speech, but it has the potential to restructure the credit rating business model."

This week's proposed legislation by the US Treasury to reform rating agencies is not widely regarded as fundamentally changing the business of ratings, even though it does put more controls in place.

Already, rating agencies have themselves undertaken reviews aimed at restoring confidence in their ratings, particularly on the structured finance part of the business that includes bonds backed by loans such as mortgages and where most of the controversies have been. This week, a decision by S&P to upgrade bonds backed by commercial mortgages to triple A, just a week after severely cutting them from triple A, highlights the clout of ratings (and the scope to confuse investors).

Michael Barr, the Treasury's assistant secretary for financial institutions, portrayed the proposed legislation as an attempt to ensure that better information is put into the market and to encourage the right incentives for the issuance of ratings.

Other models, including the investor-paid model, also have inherent conflicts of interest that would pose problems, Mr Barr said.

No matter what the reforms, "we are not going to be able to eliminate the need for investors to use their own judgment ... The one thing we want to make clear ... no investor should take as a matter of blind faith what the ratings [agency's] judgment is," Mr Barr said this week.

The SEC, which has created a new group of examiners to oversee

the sector, is looking for ways to reduce reliance on credit ratings. Mary Shapiro, chairman of the SEC, said at a Congressional hearing that new rules would be put forward later this summer.

She said one rule would require issuers to disclose preliminary ratings to get rid of "pernicious" ratings shopping (when a company solicits a preliminary rating from an agency but only pays for and discloses the highest rating it receives); disclose information underlying the ratings; look at sources of revenue disclosure and performance history of ratings over one, five and 10-year periods; and see how the SEC could get investors to do additional due diligence of its own.

"While the administration's proposals are well-intentioned, they are easily criticised as merely cosmetic," says Joseph Grundfest, a law professor at Stanford University. "If you really want change you have to recognise that the industry is dominated by two agencies and the SEC should create a new category of agencies owned by investors."

The status of rating agencies means they have access to information that is not made public, information they do not need to disclose, and this is one reason they are supposed to have better insights into companies and deals than ordinary investors might. It is this special status that some believe should be targeted. "When an opinion has regulatory power, which is what ratings have, it has to come with some accountability," says Arturo Cifuentes, principal with Atacama Partners, a financial advisory firm.

"It is not enough to say it is just an opinion, because it carries more weight than that in the financial system."

Source: Financial Times 22 July 2009. Reprinted with permission.

bankruptcy. For some of these events all is lost from the investor's perspective; for other events a very high percentage, if not all, of the interest and principal is recovered. Hickman (1958) observed that defaulted publicly held and traded bonds tended to sell for 40 cents on the dollar. This average recovery-rate rule of thumb seems to have held over time – in approximate terms – with senior secured bank loans returning more than 60 per cent and subordinated bonds less than 30 per cent.

Table 6.1 Fitch global corporate finance average cumulative default rates 1990–2010

Rating	1 year %	2 years %	3 years %	4 years %	5 years %	10 years %
'AAA'	0	0	0	0	0	0
'AA'	0	0	0	0.08	0.17	0.32
'A'	0.04	0.17	0.37	0.54	0.81	2.12
'BBB'	0.26	0.83	1.48	2.10	2.78	5.13
'BB'	1.12	2.74	4.15	5.23	6.04	12.33
'B'	3.10	7.72	9.93	10.55	11.68	15.21
'CCC to 'C	30.98	41.26	43.22	44.70	45.36	57.89
Investment grade	0.14	0.47	0.84	1.20	1.60	2.95
High yield	3.69	6.91	8.55	9.53	10.43	14.98
All industrials	1.11	2.18	2.83	3.27	3.71	5.37

Source: Fitch Ratings Global Corporate Finance 2010 Transition and Default Study
http://www.fitchratings.com/creditdesk/reports/report_frame.cfm?rpt_id = 606665

High-yield (junk) bonds

High-yield or junk bonds are debt instruments offering a high return with a high risk. They may be either unsecured or secured but rank behind senior loans and bonds. This type of debt generally offers interest rates 2–9 percentage points more than that on senior debt and frequently gives the lenders some right to a share in equity values should the firm perform well. It is a kind of hybrid finance, ranking for payment below straight debt but above equity – it is thus described alternatively as subordinated, intermediate, or low grade. One of the major attractions of this form of finance for the investor is that it often comes with equity warrants or share options attached (see Chapter 11), which can be used to obtain shares in the firm – this is known as an equity kicker. These may be triggered by an event such as the firm joining the stock market.

Bonds with high-risk and high-return characteristics may have started as apparently safe investments but have now become more risky (fallen angels), or they may be bonds issued specifically to provide higher-risk financial instruments for investors. This latter type began its rise to prominence in the US in the 1980s and is now a market with over $100 billion issued per year. The rise of the US junk bond market meant that no business was safe from the threat of takeover, however large – *see* case study 6.1 on Michael Milken.

Issuers of high-yield bonds

High-yield bond finance tends to be used when bank borrowing limits are reached and the firm cannot or will not issue more equity. The finance it provides is cheaper (in terms of required return) than would be available on the equity market and it allows the owners of a business to raise large sums of money without sacrificing voting control. It is a form of finance that permits the firm to move beyond what is normally considered acceptable debt:equity ratios (financial gearing, leverage levels).

High-yield bonds have been employed by firms 'gearing themselves up' to finance merger activity and also for leveraged recapitalisations. For instance, a firm might have run into trouble,

Case study 6.1	The junk bond wizard: Michael Milken

While studying at Wharton Business School in the 1970s Michael Milken came to the belief that the gap in interest rates between safe bonds and high-yield bonds was excessive, given the relative risks. This created an opportunity for financial institutions to make an acceptable return from junk bonds, given their risk level.

At the investment banking firm Drexel Burnham Lambert, Milken was able to persuade a large body of institutional investors to supply finance to the junk bond market as well as provide a service to corporations wishing to grow through the use of junk bonds. Small firms were able to raise billions of dollars to take over large US corporations. Many of these issuers of junk bonds had debt ratios of 90 per cent and above – for every $1 of share capital $9 was borrowed. These gearing levels were concerning for many in the financial markets. It was thought that companies were pushing their luck too far and indeed many did collapse under the weight of their debt.

The market was dealt a particularly severe blow when Michael Milken was convicted, sent to jail and ordered to pay $600 million in fines. Drexel was also convicted, paid $650 million in fines and filed for bankruptcy in 1990.

The junk bond market was in a sorry state in the early 1990s, with high levels of default and few new issues. However, it did not take long for the market to recover.

defaulted and its assets are now under the control of a group of creditors, including bankers and bond holders. One way to allow the business to continue would be to persuade the creditors to accept alternative financial securities in place of their debt securities to bring the leverage (financial gearing) to a reasonable level. They might be prepared to accept a mixture of shares and high-yield bonds. The bonds permit the holders to receive high interest rates in recognition of the riskiness of the firm, and they open up the possibility of an exceptionally high return from warrants or share options should the firm get back to a growth path. The alternative for the lenders may be a return of only a few pence in the pound from the immediate liquidation of the firm's assets.

Junk bond borrowing usually leads to high debt levels, resulting in a high fixed-cost imposition on the firm. This can be a dangerous way of financing expansion and therefore the use of these types of finance has been criticised. Nevertheless, some commentators have praised the way in which high gearing and large annual interest payments have focused the minds of managers and engendered extraordinary performance. Also, without this finance, many takeovers, buyouts and financial restructurings would not take place.

Fast-growing companies also make use of junk bonds. They have been particularly attractive sources for telecommunications and some media businesses which require large investments in the near term but also can offer a relatively stable profits flow in the long term.

Market price movements

Investment-grade bond prices and returns tend to move in line with government bond interest rates, influenced by perceptions of future inflation rather than the risk of default. Junk bond prices (and their yields), meanwhile, are much more related to the prospects for the company's trading fundamentals because the company needs to thrive if it is to cope with the high debt levels and raised interest, and cause the equity kicker to have some value. Thus the factors that affect equity valuation also impact on junk bond valuations. As a result high-yield bonds tend to be more volatile than investment-grade bonds, going up and down depending on expectations concerning the company's survival, strength and profitability.

Comparing US and European high-yield bond markets

The high-yield bond is much more popular in the US than in Europe because of European financial institutions' aversion (constrained by legislation) to such instruments and because of an attachment to bank borrowing as the main way to borrow. The European high-yield bond market is in its infancy. The first high-yield bonds denominated in European currencies were issued as recently as 1997 when Geberit, a Swiss/UK manufacturer, raised DM157.5 million by selling ten-year bonds offering an interest rate which was 423 basis points (4.23 per cent) higher than the interest rate on a ten-year German government bond (bund). Since then there have been hundreds of issues. However, the European high-yield market remains about one-quarter of the size of the US one, although it is growing again after a freeze in 2008 – see **Exhibit 6.11**.

Exhibit 6.11

European high-yield bonds are in demand   FT

Anousha Sakoui

As €10 billion ($14.28 billion) in orders flooded in from investors for Italian car maker Fiat's junk bond last month, even the company's bankers were surprised by the torrent of demand for a €1.25 billion offering of risky debt. Just a few weeks earlier, such a deal might not have been possible.

Indeed, risk aversion levels were so high during the first 18 months of the financial crisis that the European high-yield market was completely closed to new issues.

Yet such has been the change of sentiment in recent weeks that European high-yield bonds have become the best performing fixed income asset class globally – returning almost 50 per cent in 2009, according to Credit Suisse.

So far this year the market has swallowed €6.1 billion of euro-denominated junk bonds, according to Société Générale. The total includes a €2.7 billion bond from Italian telecoms company Wind – the biggest ever unsecured European junk bond – and the Fiat issue. Overall issuance is bigger because it includes other currencies.

Digging down into banks' order books highlights a radical change in the sources of demand for high-yield paper.

With both Wind and Irish bottling company Ardagh Glass, over 70 per cent of orders were from longer term or so-called "real-money" investors, according to analysis by debt information provider Capital Structure. Before the credit crunch, it was typically hedge funds and structured credit investors which accounted for the bulk of demand in Europe.

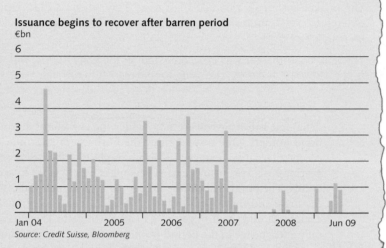

Issuance begins to recover after barren period

€bn

Source: Credit Suisse, Bloomberg

Demand now is driven by pension and insurance funds, suggesting a new pool of long-term liquidity is evolving for riskier European borrowers and one which could be more permanent. The buyers include fund management groups such as Threadneedle – as well as investors that have dedicated high-yield funds such as Bluebay Asset Management.

"European high yield has had a number of false dawns but the expectation is that this time it will be more sustainable," says Dagmar Kent Kershaw, Head of Credit Fund Management at Intermediate Capital Group. "It is fantastic news for a high-yield market which has been starved of product."

Matthew Cestar, co-head of Credit Capital Markets at Credit Suisse, says: "Wind was a seminal deal for Europe, given its multi-billion euro size and complexity. Even in the US, we have only seen a handful of high-yield deals north of a billion dollars. There was some scepticism about whether you

could get a deal away this size, but it was well digested and has rallied because of the scarcity of paper and the quality of the company."

The revival in the high-yield market reflects the strong increase in global risk appetite in recent months as well as a view that default levels may fall short of earlier estimates.

While the US junk bond market has been long established, the European high-yield market has only developed over the past decade. Unlike the US, where borrowers have a long tradition of using bond markets to fund themselves. European companies relied heavily on bank debt in the past.

According to Barclays Capital, the European junk bond market is set to grow from €100 billion currently to €150 billion by the end of 2012. The revival in high yield has also sparked interest in the leveraged loan market, which has rallied 25 per cent this year.

Source: Financial Times, 14 August 2009, p. 29. Reprinted with permission.

Local authority/municipal bonds

Local authority and municipal bonds (Munis) are bonds issued by governments at a subnational level, such as a county, city or state, which pay a fixed rate of interest and are repayable on a specific future date, similar in fact to Treasury bonds.[7] They are a means of raising money to finance developments, buildings or expansion by the local authority. They are riskier than sovereign bonds (the issuers cannot print their own money as governments might) as from time to time cities, etc. do go bust and fail to pay their debts. However, many issuers, particularly in Europe and the US, obtain **bond insurance**, from a private insurance group with a top credit rating, guaranteeing that the bond will be serviced on time. This reduces the interest rate they pay.

General-obligation bonds offer the bond holder a priority claim on the general (usually tax) revenue of the issuer in the event of a default, whereas a holder of **revenue bonds** receives interest and principal repayment from the revenues of a particular project, e.g. the income from a toll bridge.

In the UK, they are out of favour at the moment, although Transport for London issued a 25-year bond in 2006 and there is talk of issuing a 'Brummie' bond (by Birmingham council). In the US and some other countries they are big business – over $2,000 billion in the US. US municipal bonds issued by state and local governments are usually tax exempt, which means that investors do not have to pay federal income tax on the interest they receive. Because of this concession they usually trade at lower yields to maturity than US government bonds. In Japan, over 30 prefectures and cities have issued bonds which in 2007 totalled more than ¥3½ trillion. The German Länder (states) are also large issuers.

Bonds are also issued by counties, school districts, airports, water systems and highways, with the aim of raising finance for specific targets. There are also quasi-state organisations issuing bonds in Europe. In France, Electricité de France, (EdF) and Societé Nationale des Chemins de Fer Français (SNCF, the French railway operator), and in Germany, Deutsche Bahn (DB, the German railway company) are just some of the institutions which have issued bonds.

Convertible bonds

Convertible bonds (or **convertible loan stocks**) carry a rate of interest in the same way as ordinary bonds, but they also give the holder the **right to exchange** the bonds at some stage in the future into ordinary shares according to some prearranged formula.[8] The owner of these bonds is not obliged to exercise this right of conversion and so the bonds may continue until redemption as an interest-bearing instrument. Conversion of these bonds into shares may have the effect of diluting the value of individual shares – there is an increase in the number of shares as more are created, but not necessarily any increase in the profits/value of the company. Usually the **conversion price** is 10–30 per cent greater than the share price at the date of the bond issuance. So, if a £100 bond offered the right to convert to 40 ordinary shares, the conversion price would be £2.50 (that is £100 ÷ 40), which, given the market price of the shares of, say, £2.20, would be a **conversion premium** of 30p divided by £2.20, which equals 13.6 per cent.

Venture Production, a North Sea oil explorer, issued convertible bonds in July 2005. The issue raised £29 million. The bonds were to be redeemed in 2010 if they had not been converted before this and were issued at a par value of £100. The coupon was set at 4.25 per cent and the conversion price was at 474p per share. From this information we can calculate the **conversion ratio**:

$$\text{Conversion ratio} = \frac{\text{Nominal (par) value of bond}}{\text{Conversion price}} = \frac{£100}{£4.74} = 21.1 \text{ shares}$$

Each bond carries the right to convert to 21.1 shares, which is equivalent to paying 474p for each share at the £100 par value of the bond.

---

[7] They are sometimes called semi-sovereigns or sub-sovereigns.
[8] Alternatively they may be convertible into preference shares.

Unusually, in this particular case if the bonds were not converted or redeemed then the holder was to receive 110 per cent of par value rather than simply the par value in October 2010, to give a total yield to maturity of 5.904 per cent. The conversion price was set at a premium of 16 per cent over the ordinary share price at the time of pricing; this was 408p $((474 - 408)/408 = 16$ per cent). At the time of the issue many investors may have looked at the low interest rate on the convertible and said to themselves that although this was greater than the dividend yield on shares (3 per cent) it was less than that on conventional bonds, but offsetting this was the prospect of capital gains made by converting the bonds into shares. If the shares rose to, say, £6, each £100 bond could be converted to 21.1 shares worth 21.1 $£6 = \times £126.6$.

The value of a convertible bond (a type of **equity-linked bond**) rises as the value of ordinary shares increases, but at a lower percentage rate. The value could be analysed as a 'debt portion', which depends on the discounted value of the coupons, and an 'equity portion', where the right to convert is an equity option. If the share price rises above the conversion price, investors may choose to exercise the option to convert if they anticipate that the share price will at least be maintained and the dividend yield is higher than the convertible bond yield. If the share price rise is seen to be temporary, the investor may wish to hold on to the bond. If the share price remains below the conversion price, the value of the convertible will be the same as a straight bond at maturity.

Exhibit 6.12 describes some of the technical terms associated with convertibles.

Exhibit 6.12   Convertible bond technical jargon

Conversion ratio
This gives the number of ordinary shares into which a convertible bond may be converted:

$$\text{Conversion ratio} = \frac{\text{Nominal (par) value of bond}}{\text{Conversion price}}$$

Conversion price
This gives the price of each ordinary share obtainable by exchanging a convertible bond:

$$\text{Conversion price} = \frac{\text{Nominal (par) value of bond}}{\text{Number of shares into which bond may be converted}}$$

Conversion premium
This gives the difference between the conversion price and the market share price, expressed as a percentage:

$$\text{Conversion premium} = \frac{\text{Conversion price} - \text{Market share price}}{\text{Market share price}} \times 100$$

Conversion value
This is the value of a convertible bond if it were converted into ordinary shares at the current share price:

$$\text{Conversion value} = \text{Current share price} \times \text{Conversion ratio}$$

Convertibles with large conversion premiums trade much like ordinary bonds because the option to convert is not a strong feature in their pricing. They offer higher yields and prices are not volatile. Those trading with a small conversion premium have lower yields and the prices are more volatile as they are more closely linked with the share price.

The right to convert may specify a date or several dates over, say, a four-year period, or any time between two dates.

The advantages of convertibles

The advantages of convertible bonds to investors are:

1 Investors are able to wait and see how the share price moves before investing in equity.
2 In the near term there is greater security for their principal compared with equity investment, and the annual coupon is usually higher than the dividend yield.

Raising money by selling convertible bonds has the following advantages to the issuing company:

1 *Lower interest than on a similar debenture* The firm can ask investors to accept a lower interest on these debt instruments because the investor values the conversion right. This was a valuable feature for many dot.com companies when starting out. Amazon and AOL could pay 5–6 per cent on convertibles – less than half what they would have paid on straight bonds.
2 *The interest is tax deductible* Because convertible bonds are a form of debt the coupon payment can be regarded as a cost of the business and can therefore be used to reduce taxable profit.
3 *Self-liquidating* When the share price reaches a level at which conversion is worthwhile the bonds will (normally) be exchanged for shares so the company does not have to find cash to pay off the loan principal – it simply issues more shares. This has obvious cash-flow benefits. However, the disadvantage is that the other equity holders may experience a reduction in earnings per share and dilution of voting rights.
4 *Fewer restrictive covenants* The directors have greater operating and financial flexibility than they would with a secured debenture. Investors accept that a convertible is a hybrid between debt and equity finance and do not tend to ask for high-level security (they are unsecured and subordinated), impose strong operating restrictions on managerial action or insist on strict financial ratio boundaries. Many Silicon Valley companies with little more than a web portal and a brand have used convertibles because of the absence of need to provide a collateral or stick to asset:borrowing ratios.
5 *Underpriced shares* A company which wishes to raise equity finance over the medium term but judges that the stock market is temporarily underpricing its shares may turn to convertible bonds. If the firm performs as the managers expect and the share price rises, the convertible will be exchanged for equity.
6 *Cheap way to issue shares* Graham and Harvey (2001) found that managers favoured convertibles as an inexpensive way to issue 'delayed' equity. Equity is raised at a later date without the high costs of rights issues, etc.
7 *Available finance when straight debt and equity are not available* Some firms locked out of the equity markets (e.g. because of poor recent performance) and the straight debt markets because of high levels of indebtedness may still be able to raise money in the convertible market. Firms use convertible debt 'to attract investors unsure about the riskiness of the company' (Graham and Harvey (2001)).

The bonds sold may give the right to conversion into shares not of the issuers but shares of another company held by the issuer – *see* the cases of Hutchison Whampoa, Telecom Italia and France Telecom in **Exhibit 6.13**. Note that the term 'exchangeable bond' is probably more appropriate in these cases.

Strip bonds

Strips/strip bonds are broken down into their individual cash flows. The dividends or coupons are separated from the bond and are then negotiable zero coupon instruments in their own right with a fixed maturity date and guaranteed payment at maturity. A bond with seven years to run could be stripped into 15 separate zero coupon instruments, the 14 half-yearly dividend payments and the bond itself. As all parts of the bond are now zero coupon, they are traded at a discount to their nominal value.

Exhibit 6.13

Brakes applied to convertible bond market

Rebecca Bream

In January Hong Kong conglomerate Hutchison Whampoa sold $2.65 billion of bonds exchangeable into shares of Vodafone, the UK mobile phone operator. Hutchison had been gradually divesting its stake in the UK group since completing a $3 billion exchangeable bond deal last September.

This was followed at the end of the month by Telecom Italia which sold €2 billion of bonds exchangeable into shares of subsidiaries Telecom Italia Mobile and Internet operator Seat.

In February France Telecom sold €3.3 billion of bonds exchangeable into shares of Orange, completed at the same time as the mobile unit's IPO, and one of the biggest exchangeable bond deals ever sold in Europe.

Source: Financial Times, 6 April 2001, p. 35. Reprinted with permission.

The name 'strips' actually stands for **separate trading of registered interest and principal of securities,** but it is also a good name for its role of separating the coupons from the principal.

The idea of stripping bonds and trading the coupons separately from the bond originated in the 1980s in North America and involved the actual physical cutting of the coupon from its bond. The concept gained in popularity, partly because they can offer investing institutions the maturity profile they need and partly because there can be tax advantages in taking a capital gain rather than interest income. The UK started issuing gilt-edged strips in 1997 and by the mid-2000s most countries in the world of finance allowed stripping of government bonds, with Canada allowing stripping of all bonds, government, municipal and corporate.

To avoid the possibility of losing the actual coupon, which tended to be a small piece of paper, easy to mislay, the stripping is now done electronically and official records are kept. Not all bonds are strippable. In the UK, the DMO lists all the separate parts of the bonds which are able to be stripped, the date on which the stripping commenced and which bonds have been reconstituted. In the US, Treasury Direct gives the same information about US bonds. There are nearly 40 bonds which are strippable, resulting in some 7,000 individual strips. Reconstitution of a stripped bond is possible, where the bond is reassembled once more into a coupon-paying instrument.

Securitisation

In the strange world of modern finance you sometimes need to ask yourself who ends up with your money when you pay your monthly mortgage, or your credit card bill or the instalment payment on your car. In the old days you would have found that it was the organisation you originally borrowed from and whose name is at the top of the monthly statement. Today you cannot be so sure because there is now a thriving market in repackaged debt. In this market, a mortgage lender, for example, collects together a few thousand mortgage 'claims' it has (the right of the lender to receive regular interest and capital from the borrowers); it then sells those claims in a collective package to other institutions, or participants in the market generally. This permits the replacement of long-term assets with cash (improving liquidity and financial gearing), which can then be used to generate more mortgages. It may also allow a profit on the difference between the interest on the mortgages and the interest on the bonds. This can happen if the original mortgages pay, say, 6 per cent and the bonds secured on the flow of payments from the mortgagees pay 5 per cent. The extra 1 per cent (less costs) can enable the originator to sell the bonds for a price in excess of the amount it lent to the mortgagees.

The borrower is often unaware that the mortgage is no longer owned by the original lender and everything appears as it did before, with the mortgage company acting as a collecting agent for the buyer of the mortgages. The mortgage company is usually said to be a seller of **asset-backed** securities (ABS) to other institutions (the 'assets' are the claim on interest and capital) and so this form of finance is often called asset securitisation. These asset-backed securities may be bonds sold into a market with many players. Rather than selling bonds in the mortgage company itself a new company is established, called a special purpose vehicle (SPV) or special purpose entity (SPE). This new entity is then given the right to collect the cash flows from the mortgages. It has to pay the mortgage company for this. To make this payment it sells bonds secured against the assets of the SPV (e.g. mortgage claims). By creating an SPV there is a separation of the credit-worthiness of the assets involved from the general credit worthiness of the mortgage company.

> Asset-backed securitisation involves the pooling and repackaging of relatively small, homogeneous and illiquid financial assets into liquid securities.

The sale of the financial claims can be either 'non-recourse', in which case the buyer of the securities from the mortgage firm or the lender to the SPV (e.g. bond holder) bears the risk of non-payment by the borrowers, or with recourse to the mortgage lender.

Securitisation has even reached the world of rock. Iron Maiden issued a long-dated $30 million asset-backed bond securitised on future earnings from royalties. It followed David Bowie's $55 million bond securitised on the income from his earlier albums and Rod Stewart's $15.4 million securitised loan from Nomura. Tussauds has securitised ticket and merchandise sales, Keele University has securitised the rental income from student accommodation and Arsenal has securitised £260 million future ticket sales at the Emirates Stadium. Loans to Hong Kong taxi drivers have been securitised, as have the cash flows from UK funeral fees.

Securitisation is regarded as beneficial to the financial system because it permits banks and other financial institutions to focus on those aspects of the lending process where they have a competitive edge. Some, for example, have a greater competitive advantage in originating loans than in funding them, so they sell the loans they have created, raising cash to originate more loans. Other motives include the need to change the risk profile of the bank's assets (e.g. reduce its exposure to the housing market) or to reduce the need for reserve capital (if the loans are removed from the asset side of the bank's balance sheet it does not need to retain the same quantity of reserves) – the released reserve capital can then be used in more productive ways.

Securitisation was at the heart of the financial turmoil in 2007 when US sub-prime (poor quality) mortgage borrowers failed to repay in substantial numbers. Mortgage-backed bonds of SPVs plummeted in value, the asset-backed bond market froze and the business model of lending to households expecting to sell bonds backed with a bunch of mortgages (à la Northern Rock) became untenable as no one would buy the securitised bonds.

Exhibit 6.14 describes the securitisation of Dunkin' Donuts' royalties received from its hundreds of franchises around the world – a steady source of income.

Exhibit 6.14

It's all a question of the right packaging   FT

Richard Beales

In a corporate securitisation, assets and related cash flows are carved out from a business into special purpose entities (SPEs) and repackaged. Debt is then raised against the SPEs alone.

'Securitisation isolates a cash flow and insulates it from extraneous events,' says Ted Yarbrough, head of global securitised products at Citigroup.

Depending on the credit quality and the quantum of borrowing, part or all the debt may be highly rated, and there is sometimes a low-rated or unrated subordinated slice of debt as well.

A financing structured this way can achieve higher credit ratings than the business on its own. This partly reflects the structural aspects – for example, the fact that the SPEs

can survive a bankruptcy of the umbrella group – and partly the fact that the securities issued are often 'wrapped', or guaranteed, by highly-rated bond insurers such as Ambac, Figic or MBIA in return for a fee.

This is a complex and costly exercise, but can result in much cheaper debt. Once established, a securitisation can be tapped again later if a business grows.

Exhibit 6.14 continued

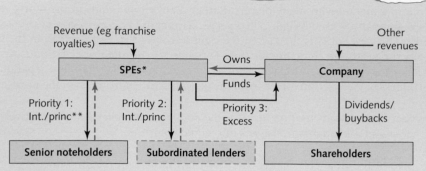

* Special purpose entitles owning franchise agreements, brands etc.
** Often guaranteed by bond insurer in return for additional fee

Sometimes securitisation is best suited to part of a business rather than the whole. When applied to an entire business, as with Dunkin' Brands or Domino's, the new financing typically replaces all traditional debt.

While a securitisation does involve financial constraints, they can be fewer and less onerous than with traditional bank and bond debt. Managers would, for example, have greater flexibility to pay dividends or buy back stock.

This reflects the fact that financiers in a securitisation look only to the specific assets and cash flows held within the SPEs. But Eric Hedman, analyst at Standard & Poor's in New York, notes there can be a trade-off in terms of operational flexibility. 'Prior to the securitisation, Dunkin' was an owner operator. Now, the company is no longer the franchisor, there's an SPE. Any new store agreement is for the benefit of the securitisation.' The company's management also does not have sole discretion over advertising spending, for example.

And the Dunkin' Donuts brand is no longer owned by the company.

'The sign on the wall says 'Copyright DD IP Holder LLC'. That's a bankruptcy-remote SPE set up for the benefit of noteholders [in the securitisation]', Mr Hedman says.

This kind of shift might not suit all managers. But for some executives – particularly those focused on maximising cash returns to shareholders – such considerations can be outweighed by the financial benefits.

Source: Financial Times, 25 July 2007, p. 2. Reprinted with permission.

The really big players in the securitisation market are the US quasi-government bodies of **Fannie Mae**,[9] **Ginnie Mae**[10] and **Freddie Mac**,[11] which buy collections of mortgages from banks and issue bonds backed by the security of these mortgages (**mortgage bonds** or **mortgage-backed securities, MBSs**). They also guarantee that investors will receive timely interest and principal regardless of whether the individual mortgage payers renege. This helps to keep down interest rates in the mortgage market. The US also has a large commercial mortgage-backed securities (CMBS) market where the flows of interest and principal payments come from companies paying off mortgages on commercial property (offices, factories, etc.). Spain (followed by Denmark) is the big player in the euro-denominated ABS market, issuing around half of them.

UK securitisations are often different to those in the rest of the world because the assets backing the securitised bonds are usually changed over the life of the securitisation – *see* **Exhibit 6.15**.

---

[9] A nickname for the Federal National Mortgage Association, FNMA, sponsored by the government but owned by shareholders.

[10] A nickname for the Government National Mortgage Association, GNMA, sponsored by the government but owned by shareholders.

[11] A nickname for the Federal Home Loan Mortgage Corporation, FHLMC, sponsored by the government but owned by shareholders.

Exhibit 6.15

Recent deals signal market's reopening in the same old style

Jennifer Hughes

When Northern Rock decided to wind down its Granite master trust – now to be placed in the lender's "bad bank" rump – industry insiders predicted the death of a structure that had helped the UK dominate the European mortgage-backed market.

The Granite decision, in November 2008, put all bondholders in a queue for repayments that could take years, regardless of the maturity date of the paper they held.

Investors warned that they would demand far simpler structures before venturing near the sector again.

Less than a year later, however, two master-trust-backed deals in the last month have signalled the reopening of the market in the same old style.

They have reignited a debate about how best to structure an instrument considered crucial for boosting economic growth but which represents the very complexity that triggered the crisis.

Policymakers in Europe and the US have called for simpler, more transparent structures. The industry has responded with guidelines and templates for providing more data that many big issuers have agreed to follow.

But the UK, responsible for about half the total European market before the crisis, is a particular challenge because its biggest lenders use a different structure from the rest of the world.

Most mortgage-backed securitisations are based around stand-alone, ring-fenced bundles of loans.

Bonds are backed by the loans in deals known as "pass-throughs" because the mortgage repayments are passed to the bondholders almost as they happen.

This leaves investors with the risk of pre-payment – where the loans are repaid earlier than expected, meaning investors end up with extra cash they must reinvest – or of extension risk, where the bonds mature more slowly than expected.

In the UK, bankers have instead created master trusts – vast pools of mortgages which the lender would periodically top up with new loans and from which it would issue different bonds at different times.

The advantage was that this constant pool allowed the trust to issue the exact bonds investors wanted, such as ones with set maturity dates.

Investors were thereby freed from prepayment and extension risk and left only with credit risk, and the impact of any bad loans would be cushioned by the size of the whole giant mortgage pool.

> The deals have reignited a debate on how to structure an instrument that represents the very complexity that triggered the crisis

---

Master trusts enabled the UK market to expand rapidly.

Investors liked the apparent relative simplicity of the deals. By buying bonds backed by a pool of a known quality, they saved on the effort of analysing each deal in great depth.

But the upshot of the simple front was the complexity that lurked behind the master trust.

"They have got many strong positives but one big negative, and that's the complexity," said one expert, summing up the industry's dilemma.

Because new loans are added to the existing collateral pool when new bonds are issued, the performance statistics of the older loans are diluted by the new loans."

Investors are unhappy at the way the structure leaves them at the mercy of the lender's treasury team, which can decide, under certain circumstances, not to repay the bonds until their legal maturity date.

This is further into the future than the set maturity date and reflects the long-term nature of mortgages.

In effect, this happened with Granite, where Northern Rock decided to no longer support the trust with new mortgages and where it will instead simply pay out on the existing bonds when the underlying mortgages are repaid.

"Everyone is comfortable with credit risk, but it's really also extension risk they've taken. It's not always at the issuer's discretion. They might have to extend if certain things happen."

Investor unhappiness does not appear to have yet held back the market.

Last month's £4 billion ($6.5 billion) deal from Lloyds was snapped up by investors who returned this week to take £3.5 billion of paper offered by Nationwide, a deal even more notable because its Silverstone master trust was to investors.

Bankers expect more deals to follow.

"We've talked to the core investor base and most of them said we want 'master trusts,'" said one banker on the Nationwide transaction.

David Basra, head of debt financing at Citigroup, argues that the UK structure is safer for investors. He helped structure the first master

Exhibit 6.15 continued

trust for Bank of Scotland and has worked on others including Abbey National, Northern Rock, Standard Life and Alliance & Leicester.

"I'd argue that stand-alone pass-through transactions may expose investors to greater credit risk, depending of course on which mortgages back their underlying bonds," he said.

"I think investors may find that they lose more over the cycle on some stand-alone deals because there is a greater chance they'll end up exposed to poorly underwritten risk."

Source: Financial Times, 29 October 2009, p. 37. Reprinted with permission.

Covered bonds

Covered bonds are similar to securitised asset-based bonds in that a specific group of assets (e.g. mortgage receivables) is used to back up the claims of the bond holders – they have the assets acting as collateral. However, there is one crucial difference compared with ABS, which gives an extra layer of protection for investors: these assets and bonds are kept on the balance sheet of the issuing bank, which means that if the pool of assets runs into trouble (as many mortgages did in 2007–2009) investors in the covered bonds can call on the originating bank to pay up – the risk is not transferred. If an underlying loan goes bad (e.g. the mortgagee stops paying) the originating bank has to replace that loan with another. Furthermore, if it is the originating bank that runs into trouble, the investors in the covered bonds have the security of the ring-fenced assets separate from the parent. So long as the issuing institution remains solvent, the cash flows to the covered bond holders is independent of the performance of the assets. Because of their high level of backing, covered bonds are given high credit ratings (AAA) and are therefore a relatively low-cost way for financial institutions to raise money. Typical maturity ranges are 2–10 years. They are common in Europe, where they originated (in Prussia in the eighteenth century), now making up to one-third of bank debt securities. Germany has a particularly large covered bond ('Pfandbriefe') market at around €1,000 billion outstanding. Spain and France have more than €100 billion outstanding. The US market is only just getting going – *see* **Exhibit 6.16**.

Exhibit 6.16

US bill raises fears for covered bonds

Jennifer Hughes

US proposals for a covered bond market risk wrecking the products' centuries-old reputation for boring stability, an industry group has been warned.

European banks are selling record amounts of the bonds, which have their roots in 18th-century Prussia and are backed by pools of loans that remain on a bank's books, unlike the toxic subprime securitisations the financial crisis made infamous.

The securities are considered ultra-safe because banks must replace

dud loans and the pool is ring-fenced for the bondholders in bankruptcy.

A bill launched in the House of Representatives aims to give US products similar bankruptcy protection, considered vital for banks to get the low borrowing costs the bonds deliver in Europe. But the proposals allow for the US bonds to be backed by a far wider range of assets than is common in Europe, where up to four-fifths are based on high-quality mortgages.

Jens Tolckmitt, chief executive of the Association of German

Pfandbrief Banks, said that using other assets, such as student or car loans, could damage the bonds' reputation if those backed by riskier assets attracted different investors who might not hold their nerve, as investors generally did in the crisis. "European-style covered bonds are bought by a very stable investor base that likes seemingly boring products," Mr Tolckmitt said. "If you create something that appeals to hedge funds, those investors may not be there in a crisis."

▶

Exhibit 6.16 continued

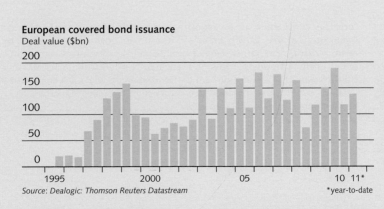

European covered bond issuance
Deal value ($bn)

Source: Dealogic: Thomson Reuters Datastream   *year-to-date

European banks managed to raise funds via covered bonds throughout the crisis even as other markets froze. The bonds remain a lifeline for banks in eurozone countries whose woes have made investors wary of unsecured debt. Last week, Caja Madrid, Banesto and BBVA raised more than €3 billion (£2.6 billion) in covered bonds.

"Will it be possible to safe-guard the quality if you have covered bonds secured by other assets? I'm not sure," Mr Tolckmitt said. "It's wrong to think you name something a covered bond and it will be as well-liked and in demand as European covered bonds."

Canadian and European banks sold more than $30 billion (£19 billion) of covered bonds to US investors in 2010. Market watchers expect that to nearly double this year.

No covered bond has reportedly defaulted, though 19th-century data are sketchy.

Source: Financial Times, 28 March 2011, p. 19. Reprinted with permission.

Foreign bonds

A foreign bond is a bond denominated in the currency of the country where it is issued when the issuer is a non-resident.[12] For example, in Japan bonds issued by non-Japanese companies denominated in yen are foreign bonds. They are known as Samurai bonds and the interest and capital payments will be in yen. Other foreign bonds from around the world issued by non-domestic entities in the domestic market include Yankee bonds (US), Bulldog bonds (UK), Rembrandt bonds (the Netherlands), Matador bonds (Spain), Panda bonds (China), Kangaroo bonds (Australia) and Maple bonds (Canada).

Foreign bonds are regulated by the domestic authority of the country where the bond is issued. These rules can be demanding and an encumbrance to companies needing to act quickly and at low cost. The regulatory authorities have also been criticised for stifling innovation in the financial markets. The growth of the less restricted Eurobond market has put the once dominant foreign bond market in the shade.

Not all foreign bonds are issued by companies – the article in **Exhibit 6.17** discusses the foreign bond issued by the Philippines government in Japan. Note the influence of LIBOR – even for deals in Japan.

Exhibit 6.17

Philippines set to price $1 billion of samurai bonds

The Philippine government is preparing to decide on pricing for up to $1 billion of samurai bonds as early as next week as part of a plan to fund a budget deficit likely to reach a record this year.

The samurai bonds – yen-denominated bonds issued by overseas entities to Japanese institutional investors – will be partially guaranteed by the state-owned Japan Bank for International

▶

[12] A bond denominated in the issuer's local currency and offered to local residents is a domestic bond.

Exhibit 6.17 continued

Cooperation, following its agreement last year to facilitate funding for some emerging economies.

JBIC has already provided such partial guarantees for samurai bonds issued last year by Indonesia, Colombia and Mexico. Indonesia has agreed with JBIC to issue $1.5 billion of samurai bonds this year.

Guarantees from JBIC will help give Japanese institutional inves-tors the confidence to invest in a country whose government's credit rating is below invest-ment grade (Moody's rates the Philippines Ba3) and buy debt with a wider spread than the highest-rated names that tap the samurai market.

The 10-year bonds are likely to have a spread of 85–95 basis points over Libor, a banker said.

That compares with 10-year samurais sold last week by Rabobank of the Netherlands, which is rated triple A by Moody's and Standard & Poor's, sold with a spread of 35bp over Libor.

Source: Financial Times, 16 February 2010, p. 32. Reprinted with permission.

Eurobonds (international bonds)

Let's get one misunderstanding out of the way: Eurobonds are unconnected with the eurozone currency! They were in existence decades before Europe thought of creating the euro; the first Eurobond issue was in 1963 on the Luxembourg stock exchange, with the $15 million issue by Autostrade, the Italian motorway company. The term 'Euro' in Eurobond does not even mean European.

So what are they then? External bonds is a simple way of describing them. More precisely, Eurobonds are bonds sold outside the jurisdiction of the country of the currency in which the bond is denominated. So, for example, the UK financial regulators have little influence over Eurobonds issued in Luxembourg and denominated in sterling (known as Eurosterling bonds), even though the transactions (for example interest and capital payments) are in sterling. The Autostrade issue, although denominated in US dollars, was not subject to US regulations because it was issued outside the US. Bonds issued in US dollars (Eurodollar bonds) in Paris are outside the jurisdiction of the US authorities.

Eurobonds are medium- to long-term instruments with standard maturities of three, five, seven and ten years, but there are long maturities of 15–30 years driven by pension fund and insurance fund demand for long-dated assets. They are not subject to the rules and regulations which are imposed on foreign bonds, such as the requirement to issue a detailed prospectus.[13] More importantly, they are not subject to an interest-withholding tax. In many countries the majority of domestic bonds are subject to a withholding tax by which basic rate income tax is deducted before the investor receives interest. Interest on Eurobonds is paid gross without any tax deducted – which has attractions to investors keen on delaying, avoiding or evading tax.

Moreover, Eurobonds are bearer bonds, which means that the holders do not have to disclose their identity – all that is required to receive interest and capital is for the holder to have pos-session of the bond. Such anonymity makes it possible for holders to avoid paying tax in their own country. In contrast, domestic bonds are usually registered, which means that companies and governments are able to identify the owners. Despite the absence of official regulation, the International Capital Market Association (ICMA), a self-regulatory body, imposes some restric-tions, rules and standardised procedures on Eurobond issue and trading.

Eurobonds are distinct from euro bonds, which are bonds denominated in euros and issued in the Eurozone countries. Increasingly, people differentiate between the two by calling the old-style Eurobonds 'international bonds', leaving the title 'euro' for the currency introduced in 1999. Of course, there have been euro-denominated bonds issued outside the jurisdiction of the authorities in the euro area; these are Euroeurobonds.

---

[13] Although new EU rules mean that a prospectus is required if the bond is marketed to retail (non-professional) investors.

The development of the Eurobond (international bond) market

In the 1960s many countries (e.g. USSR), companies and individuals held surplus dollars outside the US and were reluctant to hold these funds in American banks under US jurisdiction. Also, stringent US tax laws were off-putting, as was the tough regulatory environment in the US domestic financial markets, making it more expensive for foreign institutions to borrow dollars in the US. These factors encouraged investors and borrowers alike to undertake transactions in dollars outside the US. London's strength as a financial centre, the UK authorities' more relaxed attitude to business and its position in the global time zones made it a natural leader in the Euro markets.

The market grew modestly through the 1970s and then at a rapid rate in the 1980s. By then the Eurodollar bonds had been joined by bonds denominated in a wide variety of currencies. The market was stimulated not only by the tax and anonymity benefits, which brought a lower cost of finance than for the domestic bonds, but also by the increasing demand from transnational companies and governments needing large sums in alternative currencies and with the potential for innovatory characteristics. It was further boosted by the recycling of dollars from the oil-exporting countries.

In 1979 less than $20 billion worth of bonds were issued in a variety of currencies. The rate of new issuance has grown 100-fold to around $2,000 billion a year, with a total amount outstanding (bonds issued but not yet repaid) in 2009 of over $26,000 billion – *see* **Exhibit 6.18**. Corporations account for a relatively small proportion of the international bond market. The biggest issuers are the banks. Issues by governments ('sovereign issues') and state agencies in the public sector account for less than one-tenth of issues. Other issuers are international agencies such as the World Bank, the International Bank for Reconstruction and Development and the European Investment Bank. The two dominant currencies of issue are the US dollar and the euro, with the euro generally more popular than the dollar. Even though the majority of Eurobond trading takes place through London, sterling is not one of the main currencies, and what is more, it tends to be large US and other foreign banks located in London which dominate the market.

Exhibit 6.18   International bond and notes outstanding and recent issues

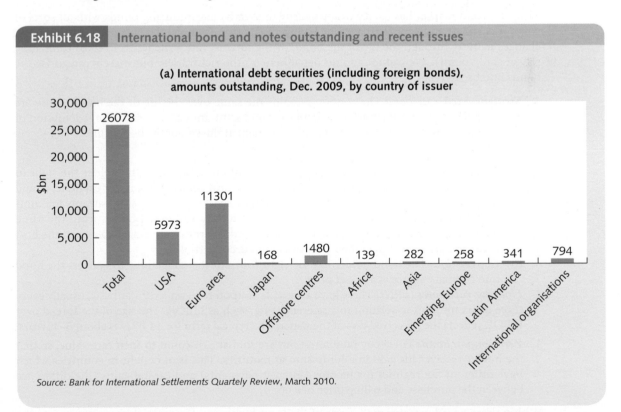

(a) International debt securities (including foreign bonds), amounts outstanding, Dec. 2009, by country of issuer

Source: Bank for International Settlements Quartely Review, March 2010.

Exhibit 6.18   Continued

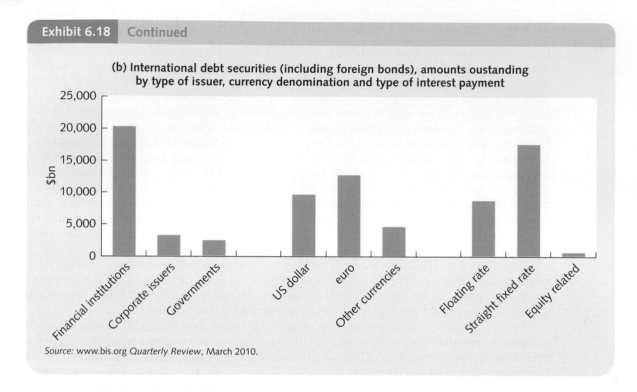

(b) International debt securities (including foreign bonds), amounts oustanding by type of issuer, currency denomination and type of interest payment

Source: www.bis.org *Quarterly Review*, March 2010.

Types of Eurobonds

The Eurobond market has been extraordinarily innovative in producing bonds with all sorts of coupon payment and capital repayment arrangements (for example, the currency of the coupon changes halfway through the life of the bond, or the interest rate switches from fixed to floating rate at some point). We cannot go into detail here on the rich variety but merely categorise the bonds into broad types.

1   *Straight fixed-rate bond* The coupon remains the same over the life of the bond. These are usually paid annually, in contrast to domestic bond semi-annual coupons. The redemption of these bonds is usually made with a 'bullet' repayment at the end of the bond's life.

2   *Equity related* These take two forms:

   (a) *Bonds with warrants attached* Warrants are options which give the holder the right to buy some other asset at a given price in the future. An equity warrant, for example, would give the right, but not the obligation, to purchase shares. There are also warrants for commodities such as gold or oil, and for the right to buy additional bonds from the same issuer at the same price and yield as the host bond. Warrants are detachable from the host bond and are securities in their own right, unlike convertibles.

   (b) *Convertibles* The bond holder has the right (but not the obligation) to convert the bond into ordinary shares at a preset price.

3   *Floating-rate notes (FRNs)* These have a variable coupon reset on a regular basis, usually every three or six months, in relation to a reference rate, such as LIBOR. The size of the spread over LIBOR reflects the perceived risk of the issuer. The typical term for an FRN is about 5–12years.

4   *Zero coupon bonds* These pay no interest but are sold at a discount to their face value, so that the holder receives his gain in a lump sum at maturity. This is of benefit in countries which have different tax regimes for income (interest payments) and capital gains (the difference between the purchase and selling price of a bond).

Within these broad categories all kinds of '**bells and whistles**' (features) can be attached to the bonds, for example **reverse floaters** – the coupon declines as LIBOR rises; **capped bonds** – the interest rate cannot rise above a certain level. Many bonds have **call-back features** under which the issuer has the right, but not the obligation, to buy the bond back after a period of time has elapsed, say five years, at a price specified when the bond was issued. This might be at the par value but is usually slightly higher. This is obviously not something bond holders favour, especially when the bond price has risen significantly above the par value. Because there are real disadvantages for investors, bonds with call features offer higher interest rates. Issuers like call features because a significant price rise for the bond implies that current market interest rates are considerably less than the coupon rate on the bond. They can buy back and issue new bonds at a lower yield. Also, some bonds place tight covenant restrictions on the firm so it is useful to be able to buy them back and issue less restrictive bonds in their place. Finally, exercising the call may permit the corporate to adjust its financial leverage by reducing its debt. Call features are often not operative for the first seven years of a long-dated bond.

A 'put' feature gives the bond holder the right, but not the obligation, to sell the bond back to the issuer (usually at par value) on designated dates. It may be a valuable right if interest rates have risen, depressing the price of the bond in the market below what could be achieved by selling to the issuer. The mere existence of the right generally ensures that the price remains above par value. This extra advantage for the holder has to be paid for – usually achieved by the issuer offering a lower yield.

The majority of Eurobonds (more than 80 per cent) are rated AAA or AA, although some are issued rated below BBB-. Denominations are usually $1,000, $5,000 or $50,000 (or similar large sums in the currency of issue – known as 1,000, 5,000 or 50,000 lots or pieces).

Issuing Eurobonds

With Eurobonds, and other large bond issues, a bank (lead manager or **book runner** or **lead underwriter**), or group of banks acting for the issuer, invites a large number of other banks or other investors to buy some of the bonds. The managing group of banks may enlist a number of smaller institutions to use their extensive contacts to sell the bonds (the selling group or syndicate).[14] Eurobonds are traded on the secondary market through intermediaries acting as market makers. Most Eurobonds are listed on the London, Dublin or Luxembourg stock exchanges, but the market is primarily an over-the-counter one, that is, most transactions take place outside a recognised exchange. Most deals are conducted using the telephone, computers, telex and fax, but there are a number of electronic platforms for trading Eurobonds. The extent to which electronic platforms will replace telephone dealing is as yet unclear. It is not possible to go to a central source for price information. Most issues rarely trade. Those that do are generally private transactions between investor and bond dealer and there is no obligation to inform the public about the deal. The prices and yield on some Eurobonds are shown in Exhibits 6.7 and 6.8 on pages 236–7.

Exhibit 6.19 presents the advantages and drawbacks of Eurobonds.

Exhibit 6.20 describes the first Eurobond from 40 years ago by Autostrade, a company that continues to make use of this financial market.

Euro medium-term notes and domestic medium-term notes

By issuing a medium-term note (MTN) a company promises to pay the holders a certain sum on the maturity date, and in many cases a coupon interest in the meantime. These instruments are typically unsecured and may carry floating or fixed interest rates. Medium-term notes have been sold with a maturity of as little as nine months and as great as 30 years, so the term is a little deceiving. They can be denominated in the domestic currency of the borrower (MTN) or in a foreign currency (Euro MTN). MTNs normally pay an interest rate above LIBOR, usually varying between 0.2 per cent and 3 per cent over LIBOR.

---

[14] In some cases the issuer pays the investment bank(s) a fee to underwrite the bonds on a 'firm commitment' basis, which means that if any of the bonds are not bought by funds, etc. then the underwriter will end up holding them. In other cases the bonds are underwritten on a 'best efforts' basis: the issuer accepts that they may receive less than they anticipated as the investment bank does not guarantee sales.

Exhibit 6.19   Advantages and drawbacks of Eurobonds as a source of finance for corporations

Advantage	*Drawback*
1 Large loans for long periods are available.	**1** Only for the largest companies – minimum realistic issue size is about £50m.
2 Often cheaper than domestic bonds. The finance provider receives the interest without tax deduction and retains anonymity and therefore supplies cheaper finance. Economies of scale also reduce costs.	**2** Because interest and capital are paid in a foreign currency there is a risk that exchange rate movements mean more of the home currency is required to buy the foreign currency than was anticipated.
3 Ability to hedge interest rate and exchange rate risk, e.g. a Canadian corporation buying assets in Europe (such as a company) may finance the asset by taking on a Eurobond liability in euros, thus reducing variability in net value when expressed in Canadian dollars when the C\$/€ exchange rate moves.	**3** The secondary market can be illiquid.
4 The bonds are usually unsecured. The limitations placed on management are less than those for a secured bond.	
5 The lower level of regulation allows greater innovation and tailor-made financial instruments.	
6 Issuance procedures are simple and bonds can be issued with speed, allowing borrowers to take advantage of an opportunity (e.g. raising money for a corporate purchase) in a timely way	
7 Being outside the control of governments they cannot be frozen in an international dispute.	

Exhibit 6.20

Autostrade returns to bond market after 40-year gap   **FT**

By Charles Batchelor and Ivar Simensen

Autostrade, the Italian motorway operator that launched the Eurobond market in 1963, is to return to the bond market this month after a gap of more than 40 years.

The company yesterday revealed plans for a bond issue worth up to €6.5 billion (£4.5 billion) to pay off bank loans and finance a 10-year investment programme. It would be by far the largest corporate bond offering in Europe this year – ahead of issues by Britain's Network Rail and Telecom Italia.

'We go to the market once every 40 years,' joked Luca Bettonte, who was born in the year the market started and has been finance director of Autostrade since November.

'This will give us a financial structure more adapted to the needs of the group,' he added.

Autostrade is expected to issue bonds in both euros and sterling following roadshows in continental Europe, the UK and US.

It was in July 1963 that the motorway group issued a \$15m (£9m), 15-year bond, creating a market that was to wrest control of non-US bond issues from the American investment banks and cement London's position as an international financial centre.

European banks had been relegated to an underwriting role by the

▶

Exhibit 6.20 continued

US banks that managed these issues – and hence earned much lower fees.

Siegmund Warburg founder of SG Warburg – now part of UBS the Swiss bank group – led negotiations with regulators in the UK and elsewhere to issue bonds that soaked up the large offshore dollar pool created by recurrent US balance of payments deficits.

The fledgling market received a crucial boost just 2½ weeks after the Autostrade issue when President John F. Kennedy announced an interest equalisation tax.

The president's aim was to improve the US balance of payments but the result was to increase the cost of US borrowing by European issuers.

The Eurobond market has gone from strength to strength, gaining further impetus from the creation of the euro in 1999 and euro-denominated issues last year overtook international dollar-denominated bonds.

The funds raised 40 years ago were intended for Finsider, the nationalised Italian steel manufacturer. Autostrade – then also state-owned – had a more favourable tax position and so was used as a channel for the funds.

Now a publicly listed company, Autostrade is 62 per cent owned by Schema Ventotto, a holding company in which the Benetton family has a 60 per cent stake.

The new issue will be managed by Barclays Capital, Caylon, Goldman Sachs, Invercaixa Valores, Mediobanca and UBM.

Source: Financial Times, 13 May 2004, p. 21. Reprinted with permission.

An **MTN programme** stretching over many years can be set up with one set of legal documents. Then, numerous notes can be issued under the programme in future years. A programme allows greater certainty that the firm will be able to issue an MTN when it needs the finance and allows issuers to bypass the costly and time-consuming documentation associated with each stand-alone note/bond. The programme can allow for notes of various qualities, maturities, currencies or type of interest (fixed or floating). Over the years the market can be tapped at short notice in the most suitable form at that time, e.g. US dollars rather than pounds, or redemption in three years rather than in two. It is possible to sell in small denominations, e.g. $5 million and on a continuous basis, regularly dripping notes into the market. The banks organising the MTN programme charge a **commitment fee** (around 10–15 basis points) for keeping open the option to borrow under an MTN programme, even if the company chooses not to do so in the end. Management fees will also be payable to the syndication of banks organising the MTN facility.

The success of an MTN programme depends on the efficiency of the lead manager and the flexibility of the issuer to match market appetite for lending in particular currencies or maturities with the issuer's demands for funds. The annual cost of running an MTN programme, excluding credit-rating agency fees, can be around £100,000. The cost of setting up an MTN programme is high compared with the cost of a single bond issue (and more expensive than most bank debt, except for the very best AAA- AA- and some A-rated companies). Many companies set one up because they believe that the initial expense is outweighed by the flexibility and cost savings that a programme can provide over time. Diageo's outstanding MTNs are shown at the start of the chapter.

Islamic bonds (*sukuk*)

Sukuk (the plural form of the Arabic word *Sakk* from which the word cheque is derived) are bonds which conform to Shari'ah (Sharia) law, which forbids interest income, or *riba*. There was always a question mark over the ability of modern financing to comply with Islamic (Shari'ah) law, which not only prohibits the charging or paying of interest but insists that real assets underlie all financial transactions. Ways have been found to participate in the financial world while still keeping to Shari'ah law, although certain Islamic scholars oppose some of the instruments created.

Whereas conventional bonds are promises to pay interest and principal, *sukuk* represent part *ownership* of tangible assets, businesses or investments, so the returns are generated by some sort of share of the gain (or loss) made and the risk is shared. Money alone should not create a profit and finance should serve the real economy, not just the financial one. They are administered through an SPV which issues *sukuk* certificates. These certificates entitle the holder to a rental income or a profit share from the certificate. *Sukuk* may be issued on existing as well as other specific assets that may become available at a future date.

From inception in 1975, when the Islamic Development Bank and the Dubai Islamic Bank (the first commercial Islamic bank) were established to operate in strict accordance with Shari'ah law, Islamic banking has made significant progress worldwide, and it was estimated in 2011 that there were over $100 billion of *sukuk* outstanding (and more than $1,000 billion of Islamic finance, including bank sources).

There is some confusion over whether investors can always seize the underlying assets in the event of default on a *sukuk*, or whether the assets are merely placed in a *sukuk* structure to comply with Shari'ah law. Lawyers and bankers say that the latter is the case, with most *sukuk* being, in reality, unsecured instruments. They differentiate between 'asset-backed' and 'asset-based' *sukuk*:

- **Asset-backed**: there is a true sale between the originator and the SPV that issues the *sukuk*, and *sukuk* holders do not have recourse to the originator. The value of the assets owned by the SPV, and therefore the *sukuk* holders, may vary over time. The majority of *sukuk* issues are not asset backed.

- **Asset-based**: these are closer to conventional debt in that the *sukuk* holders have recourse to the originator if there is a payment shortfall.

Tesco and Toyota have both issued ringgit *sukuk* in Malaysia. In a further development in November 2009, General Electric (GE) became the first large western corporation to expand its investor base into this arena with the issuance of its $500 million *sukuk*. The assets underlying this *sukuk* are GE's interests in aircraft and rental payments from aircraft leasing.

Valuing bonds

Bonds, particularly those which are traded in secondary markets such as the London Stock Exchange, are priced according to supply and demand. The main influences on the price of a bond will be the general level of interest rates for securities of that risk level and maturity and the length of time to maturity. As a bond comes closer to its maturity date, its market value comes closer to its nominal value; this is known as the **pull to par**, **pull to maturity** or **pull to redemption**. If the coupon rate of interest on the par value is less than the current market interest rate the bond will trade at less than the par value.

Take the case of an irredeemable bond with an annual coupon of 8 per cent. This financial asset offers to any potential purchaser a regular €80 per year for ever (i.e. 8 per cent of the par value of €1,000). When the bond was issued, general interest rates for this risk class may well have been 8 per cent and so the bond may have been sold at €1,000. However, interest rates change over time. Suppose that the current rate of interest is now 10 per cent. Investors will no longer be willing to pay €1,000 for an instrument that yields only €80 per year. The current market value of the bond will fall to €800 (€80/0.10) because this is the maximum amount needed to pay for similar bonds given the current interest rate of 10 per cent. We say that the bond is trading at a **discount** to its maturity value because it is trading below €1,000. If the coupon is more than the current market interest rate, the market price of the bond will be greater than the nominal (par) value. Thus, if market rates are 6 per cent, the irredeemable bond will be priced at €1,333.33 (€80/0.06). We say it is trading at a **premium** to its maturity value, i.e. at more than €1,000.[15] Again, notice the inverse relationship between the price of a bond and the rate of return offered on it.

The formula relating the price of an irredeemable bond, the coupon and the market rate of interest is:

$$P_D = \frac{C}{k_D}$$

where P_D = price of bond

C = nominal annual income (the coupon rate × nominal (par) value of the bond)

k_D = market discount rate, annual return required on bonds of similar risk and characteristics

---

[15] The ratio of the current bond price to its maturity (nominal) value, i.e. whether it is at a discount or premium, is known as the par value relation.

Also:

$$V_D = \frac{I}{k_D}$$

where V_D = total market value of all of the bonds of this type
 I = total annual nominal interest of all the bonds of this type

We may wish to establish the market rate of interest represented by the market price of the bond. For example, if an irredeemable bond offers an annual coupon of 9.5 per cent and is currently trading at £87.50, with the next coupon due in one year, the rate of return is:

$$k_D = \frac{C}{P_D} = \frac{9.5}{87.5} \times 100 = 10.86\%$$

Redeemable bonds

A purchaser of a redeemable bond buys two types of income promise: first the coupon, second the redemption payment. The amount that an investor will pay depends on the amount these income flows are worth when discounted at the rate of return required on that risk class of debt. The relationships are expressed in the following formulae:

$$P_D = \frac{C_1}{1 + k_D} + \frac{C_2}{(1 + k_D)^2} + \frac{C_3}{(1 + k_D)^3} + \frac{C_4}{(1 + k_D)^4} + \dots + \frac{C_n}{(1 + k_D)^n} + \frac{R_n}{(1 + k_D)^n}$$

and:

$$V_D = \frac{I_1}{1 + k_D} + \frac{I_2}{(1 + k_D)^2} + \frac{I_3}{(1 + k_D)^3} + \frac{I_4}{(1 + k_D)^4} + \dots + \frac{I_n}{(1 + k_D)^n} + \frac{R^*_n}{(1 + k_D)^n}$$

where C_1, C_2, C_3 and C_4 = nominal interest per bond in years 1, 2, 3 and 4 up to n years
 $I_1, I_2, I_3,$ and I_4 = total nominal interest in years 1, 2, 3 and 4 up to n years
 R_n and R^*_n = redemption value of a single bond, and total redemption value of all bonds in issue in year n, the redemption or maturity date

The worked example of Blackaby illustrates the valuation of a bond when the market redemption yield is given.

Worked example 6.1   **Blackaby plc**

Blackaby plc issued a bond with a par value of £100 in September 2011, redeemable in September 2017 at par. The coupon is 8 per cent payable annually in September. The facts available from this are:

- the bond might have a par value of £100 but this may not be what investors will pay for it;
- the annual cash payment will be £8 (8 per cent of par);
- in September 2017, £100 will be handed over to the bond holder (in the absence of default).

Question 1
What is the price investors will pay for this bond at the time of issue if the market rate of interest for a security in this risk class is 7 per cent?

▶

Answer

$$P_D = \frac{8}{1+0.07} + \frac{8}{(1+0.07)^2} + \frac{8}{(1+0.07)^3} + \dots + \frac{8}{(1+0.07)^6} + \frac{100}{(1+0.07)^6}$$

£8 annuity for 6 years @ 7 per cent = 4.7665 × 8	=	38.132
plus $\dfrac{100}{(1+0.07)^6}$	=	66.634
	$P_D =$	£104.766

Question 2

What is the bond's value in the secondary market in September 2014 if market interest rates rise by 200 basis points (i.e. for this risk class they are 9 per cent) between 2011 and 2014? (Assume the next coupon payment is in one year.)

Answer

£8 annuity for 3 years @ 9 per cent = 2.5313 × 8	=	20.25
plus $\dfrac{100}{(1+0.09)^3}$	=	77.22
	$P_D =$	£97.47

Again, note that as interest rates rise, the price of bonds falls.

If we need to calculate the rate of return demanded by investors from a particular bond when we know the market price and coupon amounts, we can compute the internal rate of return (IRR).[16]

For example, Bluebird plc issued a bond many years ago which is due for redemption at par of £100 in three years. The annual coupon is 6 per cent (next one payable in one year) and the market price is £91. The rate of return now offered in the market by this bond is found by solving for k_D:

$$P_D = \frac{C_1}{1+k_D} + \frac{C_2}{(1+k_D)^2} + \frac{C_3}{(1+k_D)^3} + \frac{R_3}{(1+k_D)^3}$$

$$91 = \frac{6}{1+k_D} + \frac{6}{(1+k_D)^2} + \frac{106}{(1+k_D)^3}$$

We solve this problem through iteration, i.e. trial and error. Here we do this by trying one interest rate after another on paper, but there are computer programs and financial calculators which go through much the same procedure, only faster – learning the slow way helps understanding! First we will try 9 per cent, as this seems roughly right given the capital gain of around 3 per cent per year over the three years plus the 6 per cent coupon.

At an interest rate (k_D) of 9 per cent, the right side of the equation amounts to £92.41. This is more than £91, so we conclude that we are not discounting the cash flows on the right side of the equation by a rate of return sufficiently high. At an interest rate of 10 per cent the right-hand side of the equation amounts to £90.05. This is less than the £91 we are aiming at, so the internal rate of return lies somewhere between 9 per cent and 10 per cent. We can be more precise using linear interpolation:

---

[16] If you would like a refresher on IRR and other discounted cash-flow calculations, consult Chapter 2 of Arnold, G. (2012) *Corporate Financial Management*, Harlow: Pearson Education.

Interest rate	9%	?	10%
Value of discounted cash flows	£92.41	£91	£90.05

We are trying to find the value of the '?', where the cash flows on the right side are discounted at just the right rate to equal the amount paid for the bond on the left (£91).

$$k_D = 9\% + \frac{92.41 - 91}{92.41 - 90.05} \times (10 - 9) = 9.6\%$$

Thus, the cash flows offered on this bond represent an average annual rate of return of 9.6 per cent on a £91 investment if the bond is held to maturity and the coupon payments are reinvested at 9.6 per cent before then. This is the yield to maturity or YTM discussed in the next section.

An Excel spreadsheet version of this calculation is available at www.pearson.com/arnold.

The two types of yield

The **current yield**,[17] discussed earlier in the chapter, is the gross (before tax) interest amount divided by the current market price of the bond expressed as a percentage:

$$\frac{\text{Gross interest (coupon)}}{\text{Market price}} \times 100$$

Thus, for a holder of Bluebird's bonds the current yield is:

$$\frac{£6}{£91} \times 100 = 6.59\%$$

This is a gross yield. The after-tax yield will be influenced by the investor's tax position.

Net interest yield = Gross yield$(1 - T)$,

where T = the tax rate applicable to the bond holder

At a time when interest rates are higher than 6.59 per cent it is obvious that any potential purchaser of Bluebird bonds in the market will be looking for a return other than from the coupon. That additional return comes in the form of a capital gain over three years of £100 − £91 = £9. A rough estimate of this annual gain is (9/91) ÷ 3 = 3.3 per cent per year. When this is added to the current yield we have an approximation to the second type of yield, the **yield to maturity** (also called the **redemption yield**). The yield to maturity of a bond is the discount rate such that the present value of all the cash inflows from the bond (interest plus principal) is equal to the bond's current market price. The rough estimate of 9.89 per cent (6.59 per cent + 3.3 per cent) has not taken into account the precise timing of the investor's income flows. When this is adjusted for, the yield to maturity is 9.6 per cent – the internal rate of return calculated above. Thus, the yield to maturity includes both coupon payments and the capital gain or loss on maturity.

In the *Financial Times*' bond tables (e.g. Exhibit 6.7 on page 236) the column headed **bid yield** is the yield to maturity given the current bid price (traders quote bid and offer prices; the bid is the price at which market makers will buy from investors, the offer price is what an investor would pay to buy). It is important to note that many investors sell their bonds before the redemption date. The price received depends on market conditions. If general interest rates have risen over the holding period, the bond will be worth less than if market interest rates remained constant, which will have a depressing effect on the rate of return received even though coupons may have been paid during the time the bonds were owned.

---

[17] Also known as the interest yield, flat yield, income yield, simple yield, annual yield and running yield.

For example, if an investor bought Bluebird bonds at £91 and sold them one year later when the rate of return on two-year bonds of this risk level in the market is 10 per cent, instead of receiving the original 9.6 per cent yield to maturity they will achieve a rate of return of only 8.86 per cent over the year of holding, viz:

$$\text{Market value of bond after 1 year} = \frac{6}{1+0.1} + \frac{106}{(1+0.1)^2} = 93.06$$

$$\text{Thus, the return to our investor is: } 91 = \frac{93.06 + 6}{1+r} \qquad r = 8.86\%$$

Semi-annual interest

The example of Bluebird is based on the assumption of annual interest payments. This makes initial understanding easier and reflects the reality for many types of bond, particularly internationally traded bonds. However, many companies and governments around the world issue domestic bonds with semi-annual interest payments. The rate of return calculation on these bonds is slightly more complicated.

For example, Redwing has an 11 per cent bond outstanding which pays interest semi-annually. It will be redeemed in two years at €100 and has a current market price of €96, with the next interest payment due in six months. The yield to maturity on this bond is calculated as follows:

Cash flows

Point in time (years)	0.5	1	1.5	2
Cash flow	€5.5	€5.5	€5.5	€5.5 + £100

The nominal interest rate over a six-month period is 5.5 per cent (11%/2):

$$96 = \frac{5.50}{1+\dfrac{k_D}{2}} + \frac{5.50}{\left(1+\dfrac{k_D}{2}\right)^2} + \frac{5.50}{\left(1+\dfrac{k_D}{2}\right)^3} + \frac{5.50}{\left(1+\dfrac{k_D}{2}\right)^4} + \frac{100}{\left(1+\dfrac{k_D}{2}\right)^4}$$

At a rate of 6 per cent for $k_D/2$ the right-hand side equals:

$$5.50 \times \text{4-period annuity @ 6 per cent} = 5.50 \times 3.4651 = 19.058$$

$$\text{plus } \frac{100}{(1+0.06)^4} = \underline{79.209}$$

$$€98.267$$

At a rate of 7 per cent for $k_D/2$ the right-hand side equals:

$$5.50 \times \text{4-period annuity @ 7 per cent} = 5.50 \times 3.3872 = 18.630$$

$$\text{plus } \frac{100}{(1+0.07)^4} = \underline{76.290}$$

$$€94.920$$

The IRR of the cash flow equals: $6\% + \dfrac{98.267 - 96}{98.267 - 94.92} \times (7 - 6) = 6.68\%$

The IRR needs to be converted from a half-yearly cash flow basis to an annual basis:

$$(1+0.0668)^2 - 1 = 0.1381 \text{ or } 13.81\%$$

Yield to maturity versus rate of return

It is important to understand the difference between yield to maturity and rate of return that an individual investor in a bond receives if they sell before the maturity date. Assume that Tom has just bought four bonds. The maturity dates are one year from now, five years from now, ten years from now and twenty years from now. For the sake of simplicity assume that all the bonds are trading in the secondary market at €1,000, which is also their par values to be paid at maturity, and that they each offer a yield to maturity of 6 per cent (annual coupons are €60).

Tom is planning to sell the bonds in a year from now. The question is, what rate of return will he receive if between now and then the yield to maturity investors demand in the secondary market on these bonds rises from 6 per cent to 10 per cent? (Again, assume for the sake of simplicity that the yield to maturity of 10 per cent is the same regardless of whether the bond has a short or a long time until maturity – there is a 'flat yield curve' as discussed later.)

In the case of the one-year bond Tom does not have to sell in the secondary market; the issuer redeems the bond at its par value of €1,000. Tom also receives the coupon of €60, so the rate of return he gains is 6 per cent. This is the same as the yield to maturity when he bought.

There is a general rule for bonds: the yield to maturity and the rate of return are equal only when the time to maturity is the same as the holding period. We can illustrate this with the five-ten- and twenty-year bonds.

For the five-year bond:

Rate of return over the one-year holding period, $r = \dfrac{C + P_{t+1} - P_t}{P_t} \times 100$

where, C $\quad$ = coupon

$\quad$ P_{t+1} = price of bond after one year

$\quad$ P_t $\quad$ = price of bond at the start.

Thus, there is an interest element (C) plus a capital gain or loss $((P_{t+1} - P_t)/P_t)$ element to the rate of return.

To calculate P_{t+1}:

P_{t+1} = four annual coupons discounted to time t+1 (€60 × annuity factor for four years at 10%) plus the redemption amount discounted back to t+1.

€60 × 3.1699	=	190.19
$\dfrac{1000}{(1+0.1)^4}$	=	683.01
P_{t+1}	=	873.20

Rate of return, $r = \dfrac{60 + 873.20 - 1000}{1000} \times 100 = -6.7\%$

So, while the yield to maturity at time t was 6 per cent, the rate of return over the one-year holding period was –6.7 per cent because of the large capital loss on the bond.

It is even worse for the ten-year and twenty-year bonds. If yields to maturity rise from 6 per cent to 10 per cent over the holding year then these bonds can be sold for only €769.64 and €665.40 at time t+1:

Ten-year bond:

Rate of return, $r = \dfrac{C + P_{t+1} - P_t}{P_t} \times 100$

P_{t+1} with 9 annual coupons, 10 per cent discount rate:

€60 × 5.759	=	345.54
$\dfrac{1000}{(1+0.1)^9}$	=	424.10
P_{t+1}	=	€769.64

Rate of return, $r = \dfrac{60 + 769.64 - 1000}{1000} \times 100 = -17\%$

Twenty-year bond:

Rate of return, $r = \dfrac{C + P_{t+1} - P_t}{P_t} \times 100$

P_{t+1} with 19 annual coupons, 10 per cent discount rate:

€60 × 8.3649	=	501.89
$\dfrac{€1000}{(1+0.1)^{19}}$	=	163.51
P_{t+1}	=	€665.40

Rate of return, $r = \dfrac{60 + 665.4 - 1000}{1000} \times 100 = 27.5\%$

Table 6.2 Summary table for Tom's bonds

Years to maturity when first purchased	Initial yield to maturity	Price at time t €	Price at time t+1 €	Capital loss	Rate of return
1	6%	1,000	1,000.00	0.0	6.0%
5	6%	1,000	873.20	−126.80	−6.7%
10	6%	1,000	769.64	−230.36	−17.0%
20	6%	1,000	665.40	−334.60	−27.5%

Of course, if each of the bonds is held until maturity, Tom will receive a 6 per cent rate of return. Also, perhaps we are forgetting the potential upside: if yields to maturity for these bonds in the secondary market fall during the year, Tom makes a capital gain if he sells. Again, we have an illustration of the inverse relationship between the price of a bond and the yield to maturity. We also have the (when first encountered) counter-intuitive result that a rise in interest rates results in a poor bond investment – Tom will not be happy with the return on his bonds.

Volatility of bond returns

The Tom example also demonstrates how volatility changes with time to maturity. The most volatile bond is the one stretching for 20 years – its price is very sensitive to market interest rates. We say there is a large amount of **interest rate risk.** The degree of price change is much smaller for the five-year bond and non-existent for the one-year bond (although there would be some impact of market interest rate changes if the one-year bond was sold in a few months rather than after the whole year is out).

Rates of returns and prices for long-term bonds are more volatile than they are for short-term bonds (holding all other factors constant).

This means that if the investor has a time horizon of only a year or two, long-term bonds may be seen as risky investments – even if they have very low default risk, they have high interest rate risk.

It is not uncommon for long-term bonds to lose 5 per cent of their value in a year, even if they are reputable government bonds – *see* **Exhibit 6.21**.

Exhibit 6.21	Annual real gilt returns, 1900–2010 (%)

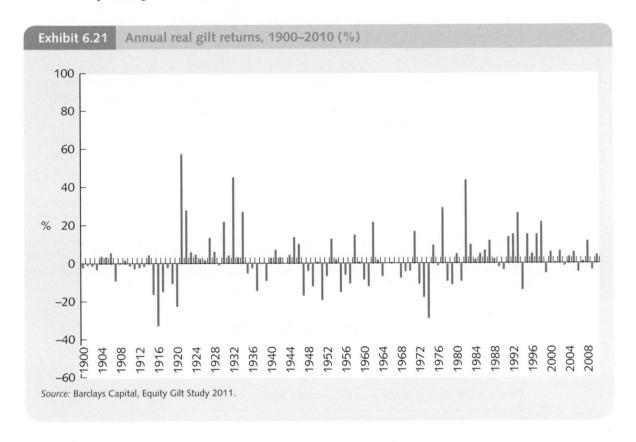

Source: Barclays Capital, Equity Gilt Study 2011.

Duration

The duration[18] of a bond can give us a guide on the amount of interest rate risk it is carrying relative to other bonds. The duration metric is a summary measure of how far into the future is the average date of the cash flows to be received, when the cash flows are weighted by their size after they have been discounted. In other words:

> The duration of a bond is the weighted average maturity of all payments (coupons plus principal) to be received from owning a bond, where the weights are the discounted present values of the payments.

So, for zero coupon bonds the effective duration is the same as its actual term to maturity – the 'average' maturity time is the same as the final payout (the only cash flow received). So, a three-year zero coupon bond has a duration of three years. For coupon-paying bonds the duration is shorter than the stated term to maturity because as the years go by the investor receives income from the bond which pushes the weighted average maturity of income flows more towards the start date than is the case on a zero coupon bond.

A three-year coupon-paying bond offering £7 per year (with the first in one year from now) and £100 on maturity can be seen as having cash flows equal to the following three zero coupon bonds:

> A one-year zero coupon bond paying £7 in one year
> A two-year zero coupon bond paying £7 in two years
> A three-year zero coupon bond paying £107 in three years

---

[18] Often referred to as Macaulay's duration after Frederick Macaulay, who formulated it in the 1930s.

If the present yields to maturity for bonds of this risk class are also 7 per cent then the duration can be calculated – *see* Table 6.3.

Table 6.3 Calculating duration on a three-year 7 per cent coupon bond

Period	Coupon and principal (zero coupon bonds)	Present value (PV) if discounted at 7% (the current market YTM)	Weights (% of total present value)	Weighted maturity (Period × weights ÷100). In years
1	£7	£6.54	£6.54 ÷ £100 = 6.54%	1 × 0.0654 = 0.0654
2	£7	£6.11	£6.12 ÷ £100 = 6.11%	2 × 0.0611 = 0.1224
3	£107	£87.34	£87.34 ÷ £100 = 87.34%	3 × 0.8734 = 2.6202
			100.00%	
Total present value		£100.00	DURATION	2.8078 years

As we might expect, the duration of 2.8078 years is almost as much as the time to maturity, but it is lowered from full three years because some of the income is received before the end of three years. This three-year 7 per cent coupon bond has the same duration as a 2.8078-year zero coupon bond also yielding 7 per cent.

Duration if the term to maturity is lengthened

If we now look at a four-year bond offering £7 per year when the yield to maturity is 7 per cent we expect to find its duration greater than that on the three-year bond – *see* Table 6.4.

Table 6.4 Calculating duration on a four-year 7 per cent coupon bond

Period	Coupon and principal (zero coupon bonds)	Present value (PV) if discounted at 7%	Weights (% of total present value)	Weighted maturity (Period × weights ÷100). In years
1	£7	£6.54	£6.54 ÷ £100 = 6.54%	1 × 0.0654 = 0.0654
2	£7	£6.11	£6.11 ÷ £100 = 6.11%	2 × 0.0611 = 0.1222
3	£7	£5.71	£5.71 ÷ 100 = 5.71%	3 × 0.0571 = 0.1713
4	£107	£81.63	£81.63 ÷ £100 = 81.63%	4 × 0.8163 = 3.2652
			100.00%	
Total present value		£100.00	DURATION	3.6241 years

This illustrates a general rule:

Holding other factors constant, the longer the term to maturity of a bond, the longer its duration.

Duration and changes in yield to maturity

The time to maturity of a bond is not enough on its own to tell you what its volatility level is. Thus, all four-year bonds do not have the same duration (say, 3.6241 years). This can be illustrated using the four-year bond example again, keeping everything the same except that the yield to maturity is now 10 per cent. Thus, we discount the future cash flows at the higher discount rate of 10 per cent, not 7 per cent – *see* Table 6.5.

Table 6.5 Calculating duration on a four-year 7 per cent coupon bond when the yield to maturity is 10 per cent

Period	Coupon and principal (zero coupon bonds)	Present value (PV) if discounted at 10%	Weights (% of total present value)	Weighted maturity (Period × weights ÷100). In years
1	£7	£6.36	£6.36 ÷ £90.49 = 7.03%	1 × 0.0703 = 0.0703
2	£7	£5.79	£5.79 ÷ £90.49 = 6.40%	2 × 0.0640 = 0.1280
3	£7	£5.26	£5.26÷£90.49 = 5.81%	3 × 0.0581 = 0.1743
4	£107	£73.08	£73.08 ÷ £90.49 = 80.76%	4 × 0.8076 = 3.2304
			100.00%	
Total present value		£90.49	DURATION	3.603 years

With the interest rate at 10 per cent duration has fallen from 3.6241 years to 3.603 years. This is because at the higher interest rate the more distant cash flows are discounted more heavily and thus contribute a lower overall proportion of the overall discounted cash flows – the nearer-term cash flows gain relative weight as the duration reduces.

This illustrates another rule:

If interest rates rise, the duration falls (keeping everything else constant).

Duration if coupons increase

If we take two bonds, both with the same the yield to maturity but one has higher coupons, then the duration will be lower on that bond, resulting in a bond with less volatility or interest rate risk. To illustrate we can go back to example of the four-year bond above with a yield to maturity of 7 per cent (Table 6.4). We can compare its duration with that for another bond with the same yield to maturity but with the following pattern of cash flows:

Current market price = £144.03
Four annual coupons of £20
Par (nominal) value to be redeemed in four years = £100

Table 6.6 Calculating duration on a four-year 20 per cent coupon bond when the yield to maturity remains at 7 per cent

Period	Coupon and principal (zero coupon bonds)	Present value (PV) if discounted at 7%	Weights (% of total present value)	Weighted maturity (Period × weights ÷100). In years
1	£20	£18.69	£18.69 ÷ £144.03 = 12.98%	1 × 0.1298 = 0.1298
2	£20	£17.47	£17.47 ÷ £144.03 = 12.13%	2 × 0.1213 = 0.2426
3	£20	£16.32	£16.32÷£144.03 = 11.33%	3 × 0.1133 = 0.3399
4	£120	£91.55	£91.55 ÷ £144.03 = 63.56%	4 × 0.6356 = 2.5424
			100.00%	
Total present value		£144.03	DURATION	3.2547 years

The bond with £20 coupons has a shorter duration, at 3.2547 years, than the bond with the £7 coupon, at 3.6241 years, despite the yield to maturity and time to maturity remaining the same. Thus we come to another rule:

The higher the coupon rate on the bond, the shorter the bond's duration.

Using duration as a guide to interest rate risk

As duration increases, the percentage change in the market value of a bond increases for a given change in interest rates, i.e. interest rate risk rises with duration. Thus, we can use duration as a measure of interest rate risk. It is not a perfect measure, but it does provide a good approximation (when interest rate changes are small) of the extent to which the price of a bond will change if yields to maturity rise or fall – as expressed in the following formula:

$$\text{Percentage change in bond price from one period to the next} \approx -\text{Duration} \times \frac{\text{change in YTM}}{1 + \text{YTM}}$$

For example, if an investor is holding the four-year bond yielding 7 per cent at time t in Table 6.4 with a duration of 3.6241 years, you could ask how much would the price of the bond change if interest rates (YTM) rose by 1 per cent?

Answer:

Change in interest rate = 0.01
Current YTM   = 0.07

$$\text{Change in bond price} \approx -3.6241 \times \frac{0.01}{1 + 0.07} = -0.0339 = -3.39\%$$

Thus, for a 1 per cent change in market interest rates this bond's price moves by roughly 3.39 per cent.[19] We can compare this degree of sensitivity to interest rate changes with other bonds. Let us take the four-year bond in Table 6.6 offering 20 per cent coupons for a YTM of 7 per cent. It has a duration of 3.2547 years.

$$\text{Change in bond price} \approx -3.2547 \times \frac{0.01}{1 + 0.07} = -0.0304 = -3.04\%$$

Clearly, this bond carries less interest rate risk than the 7 per cent coupon bond, as its price changes by only 3.04 per cent when yields change by 1 per cent. The lower duration and therefore lower interest rate risk, but same yield to maturity, on the 20 per cent coupon bond may induce an investor to switch investment funds from the more risky bond (7 per cent coupon) to this less risky one.

Demand and supply curves for bonds

The prices of bonds in the market respond in the same way as other assets to shifts in demand and supply. Here we look at the main influences causing those shifts. First, we need to draw the distinction between a movement along a curve and a shift in the entire curve – see **Exhibit 6.22**.

A movement along a demand curve means that investors are responding to price changes (which, of course, relate directly to YTM). For each given price they demand a particular quantity – as prices rise, demand falls. For movements along the supply curve, issuers supply more bonds if the price rises – meaning that the YTM is falling. Equilibrium is reached where the supply and demand curves intersect.

There are some factors that shift the entire curve. Thus, for every given price there is a new quantity demanded or supplied – see **Exhibits 6.23 and 6.24** for the main factors.

If we move the focus from bonds taken as a group to particular bonds or a class of bonds then we have some other factors influencing demand: (a) the interest rate offered on other bonds, and (b) a change in perception on the risk of the bond defaulting relative to other bonds. The YTM being offered on other bonds also affects the supply curve for a *particular* bond or a class of bonds.

---

[19] Note that this formula can be used only for small changes in yield to maturity of one percentage point or less, and even then it is only an approximation.

| Exhibit 6.22 | Supply curve, demand curve and equilibrium price for bonds |

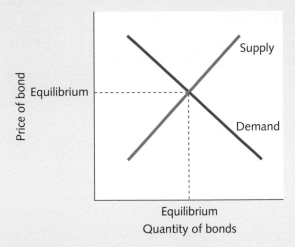

| Exhibit 6.23 | The main factors that shift the demand curve for bonds |

Expected inflation
A rise in inflation expectations reduces the expected real return on bonds, so demand will fall

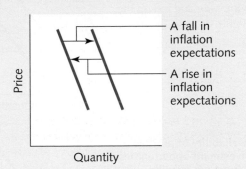

A fall in inflation expectations

A rise in inflation expectations

Riskiness of bonds relative to other assets
If the perception of the risk of investing in bonds relative to other assets rises then demand will fall

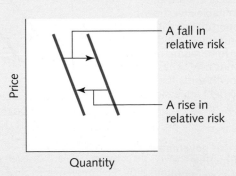

A fall in relative risk

A rise in relative risk

Wealth
If the economy is in an expansion phase, demand may rise as people have more to invest. Recession may reduce demand

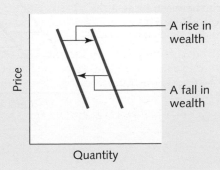

A rise in wealth

A fall in wealth

▶

Exhibit 6.23   Continued

Liquidity of bonds relative to other assets
If it becomes easier, cheaper and quicker to sell bonds, then this will increase demand

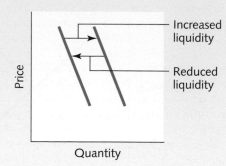

Exhibit 6.24   The main factors that shift the supply curve for bonds

Expected inflation
Higher inflation lowers the real cost of borrowing and moves the supply curve to the right

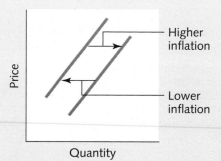

Availability of profitable investment opportunities
If there are plentiful profitable investment opportunities within companies, the demand for fund raising by selling bonds rises. Thus, economic growth shifts the curve to the right, recession shifts it to the left

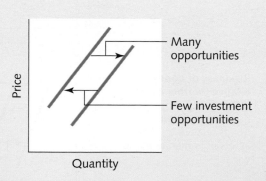

Size of government borrowing
If a government has a large gap between taxes and expenditure it may increase the supply of bonds

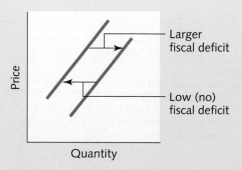

The term structure of interest rates

It is not safe to assume that the yield to maturity on a bond remains the same regardless of the length of time of the loan. So, if the interest rate on a three-year bond is 7 per cent per year it may or may not be 7 per cent on a five-year bond of the same risk class. Lenders in the financial markets demand different interest rates on loans of differing lengths of time to maturity – that is, there is a term structure of the interest rates. Four of these relationships are shown in **Exhibit 6.25** for lending to the UK, Eurozone, Japanese and US governments.[20] Note that default (and liquidity) risk remains constant along one of the lines; the reason for the different rates is the time to maturity of the bonds. Thus, a two-year US government bond has to offer about 1 per cent whereas a ten-year bond offered by the same borrower gives about 3.7 per cent. Note that the yield curve for the eurozone is only for the most creditworthy governments which have adopted the euro (e.g. Germany). Less safe governments had to pay a lot more in 2010 as investors worried whether they would default.

| Exhibit 6.25 | Yield curves for the UK, US, Eurozone and Japanese government bills and bonds |

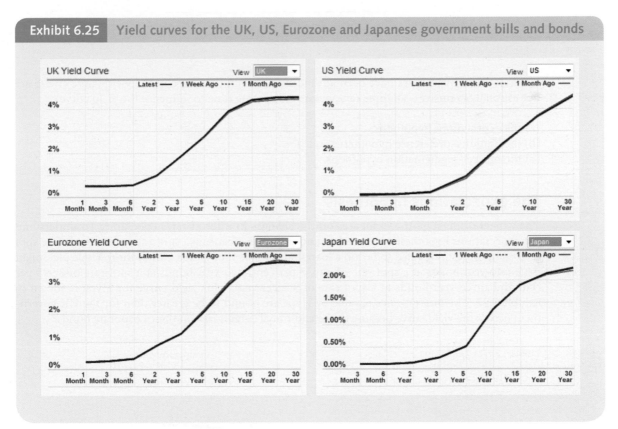

Source: www.markets.ft.com/markets/bonds.asp, 23 March 2010.

An upward-sloping yield curve occurs in most years, but 2010 demonstrated an extreme upward slope because governments and central banks around the world forced down short-term interest rates to try to reflate their economies. Occasionally we have a situation where short-term interest rates (lending for, say, one year) exceed those of long-term interest rates (say, a 20-year bond). A downward-sloping term structure (yield curve inversion) and a flat yield curve are shown in **Exhibit 6.26**.

---

[20] Using the benchmark yield curves as examples of the term structure of interest rates may offend theoretical purity (because we should be using zero coupon bonds rather than those with coupons which have to be reinvested before the redemption date), but they are handy approximate measures and help illustrate this section.

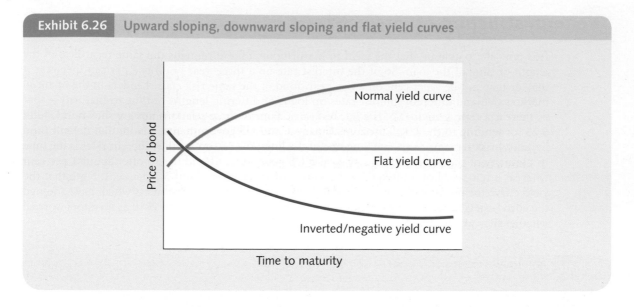

Exhibit 6.26 Upward sloping, downward sloping and flat yield curves

Three main hypotheses have been advanced to explain the shape of the yield curve (these are not mutually exclusive – all three can operate at the same time to influence the yield curve):

(a) the expectations hypothesis;
(b) the liquidity-preference hypothesis; and
(c) the market-segmentation hypothesis.

The expectations hypothesis

The **expectations hypothesis** focuses on the changes in interest rates over time. To understand the expectations hypothesis you need to know what is meant by a **spot rate of interest**. The spot rate is an interest rate fixed today on a loan that is made today. So a corporation, Hype plc, might issue one-year bonds at a spot rate of, say, 8 per cent, two-year bonds at a spot rate of 8.995 per cent and three-year bonds at a spot rate of 9.5 per cent. This yield curve for Hype is shown in **Exhibit 6.27**. The interest rates payable by Hype are bound to be greater than for the UK government across the yield curve because of the additional default risk on these corporate bonds.

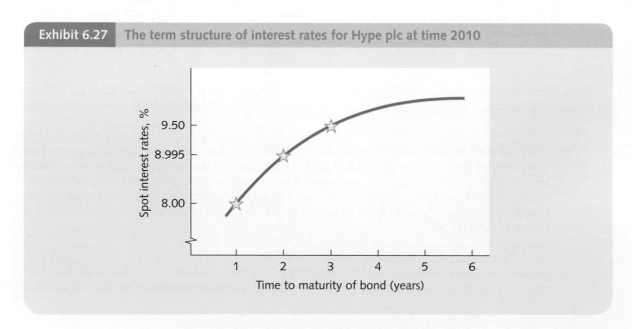

Exhibit 6.27 The term structure of interest rates for Hype plc at time 2010

Spot rates change over time. The market may have allowed Hype to issue one-year bonds yielding 8 per cent at a point in time in 2010, but a year later (time 2011) the one-year spot rate may have changed to become 10 per cent. If investors expect that one-year spot rates will become 10 per cent at time 2011 they will have a theoretical limit on the yield that they require from a two-year bond when viewed from time 2010. Imagine that an investor (lender) wishes to lend £1,000 for a two-year period and is contemplating two alternative approaches:

1 Buy a one-year bond at a spot rate of 8 per cent; after one year has passed the bond will come to maturity. The released funds can then be invested in another one-year bond at a spot rate of 10 per cent, expected to be the going rate for bonds of this risk class at time 2011.

2 Buy a two-year bond at the spot rate at time 2010.

Under the first option the lender will have a sum of £1,188 at the end of two years:

$$£1,000 \ (1 + 0.08) = £1,080$$
$$\text{followed by } £1,080 \ (1 + 0.1) = £1,188$$

Given the anticipated change in one-year spot rates to 10 per cent the investor will buy the two-year bond only if it gives the same average annual yield over two years as the first option of a series of one-year bonds. The annual interest required will be:

$$£1,000 \ (1 + k)^2 = £1,188$$

$$k = \sqrt{(1,188 \, / \, 1,000)} - 1 = 0.08995 \text{ or } 8.995 \text{ per cent}$$

Thus, it is the expectation of spot interest rates changing which determines the shape of the yield curve according to the expectations hypothesis.

Now consider a downward-sloping yield curve where the spot rate on a one-year instrument is 11 per cent and the expectation is that one-year spot rates will fall to 8 per cent the following year. An investor considering a two-year investment will obtain an annual yield of 9.49 per cent by investing in a series of one-year bonds, viz:

$$£1,000(1.08)(1.11) = £1,198.80$$

$$k = \sqrt{(1198.8 \, / \, 1,000)} - 1 = 0.0949 \text{ or } 9.49 \text{ per cent per year}$$

$$\text{or} \sqrt{(1.08)(1.11)} - 1 = 0.0949$$

With this expectation for movements in one-year spot rates, lenders will demand an annual rate of return of 9.49 per cent from two-year bonds of the same risk class.

Thus, in circumstances where short-term spot interest rates are expected to fall, the yield curve will be downward sloping.

Worked example 6.2   Spot rates

If the present spot rate for a one-year bond is 5 per cent and for a two-year bond 6.5 per cent, what is the expected one-year spot rate in a year's time?*

Answer

If the two-year rate is set to equal the rate on a series of one-year spot rates then:

$$(1 + 0.05)(1 + x) = (1 + 0.065)^2$$

$$x = \frac{(1 + 0.065)^2}{1 + 0.05} - 1 = 0.0802 \text{ or } 8.02 \text{ per cent}$$

*In the financial markets it is possible to agree now to lend money in one year's time for, say, a year (or two years or six months, etc.) at a rate of interest agreed at the outset. This is a 'forward'.

The liquidity-preference hypothesis

The expectations hypothesis does not adequately explain why the most common shape of the yield curve is upward sloping. The liquidity-preference hypothesis (liquidity premium theory) helps explain the upward slope by pointing out that investors require an extra return for lending on a long-term basis. Lenders demand a premium return on long-term bonds compared with short-term instruments because of greater interest rate risk and the risk of misjudging future interest rates. Putting your money into a ten-year bond on the anticipation of particular levels of interest rates exposes you to the possibility that rates will rise above the rate offered on the bond at some point in its long life. Thus, if five years later interest rates double, say because of a rise in inflation expectations, the market price of the bond will fall substantially, leaving the holder with a large capital loss. By investing in a series of one-year bonds, however, the investor can take advantage of rising interest rates as they occur. The ten-year bond locks in a fixed rate for the full ten years if held to maturity. Investors prefer short-term bonds so that they can benefit from rising rates and so will accept a lower return on short-dated instruments. The liquidity-preference theory focuses on a different type of risk attaching to long-dated debt instruments other than default risk – a risk related to uncertainty over future interest rates. A suggested reinforcing factor to the upward slope is that borrowers usually prefer long-term debt because of the fear of having to repay short-term debt at inappropriate moments. Thus, borrowers increase the supply of long-term debt instruments, adding to the tendency for long-term rates to be higher than short-term rates.

Note that the word liquidity in the title is incorrectly used, but it has stuck so we still use it. Liquidity refers to the speed and ease of the sale of an asset. In the case of long-term bonds (especially government bonds), sale in the secondary market is often as quick and easy as for short-term bonds. The premium for long bonds is compensation for the extra risk of capital loss; 'term premium' might be a better title for the hypothesis.

The market-segmentation hypothesis

The market-segmentation hypothesis argues that the debt market is not one homogeneous whole, that there are, in fact, a number of sub-markets defined by maturity range. The yield curve is therefore created (or at least influenced) by the supply and demand conditions in each of these sub-markets. For example, banks tend to be active in the short-term end of the market and pension funds to be buyers in the long-dated segment.

If banks need to borrow large quantities quickly they will sell some of their short-term instruments, increasing the supply on the market, pushing down the price and raising the yield. Meanwhile pension funds may be flush with cash and may buy large quantities of 20-year bonds, helping to temporarily move yields downwards at the long end of the market. At other times banks, pension funds and the buying and selling pressures of a multitude of other financial institutions will influence the supply and demand position in the opposite direction. The point is that the players in the different parts of the yield curve tend to be different. This hypothesis helps to explain the often lumpy or humped yield curve.

A final thought on the term structure of interest rates

It is sometimes thought that in circumstances of a steeply rising yield curve it would be advantageous to borrow short term rather than long term. However, this can be a dangerous strategy because long-term debt may be trading at a higher rate of interest because of the expected rise in spot short-term rates and so when the borrower comes to refinance in, say, a year's time, the short-term interest rate is much higher than the long-term rate and this high rate has to be paid out of the second year's cash flows, which may not be convenient.

Concluding comments

Governments and companies around the world have learned of the enormous power of the bond markets. James Carville, President Clinton's political adviser, once said: 'I used to think that if there was reincarnation, I wanted to come back as the president or the pope or as a .400 baseball hitter. But now I would like to come back as the bond market. You can intimidate everybody.'

He had experienced the great difficulties politicians often have in going against the logic of bond investors. President Clinton tried to increase the gap between what the US government spends and what it raises in taxes. The administration expected to fill the gap by borrowing in the bond markets. But investors started to sell bonds, raising the yields as they worried about all the additional borrowing and the risk of higher inflation in the economy. The president was forced to abandon the strategy and instead balance the government budget.

In 2011 many governments were desperately dependent on the availability of money in the bond markets to allow them to spend one-third or more than they raised in taxes. If there was any hint of a government not being able to repay because it had over-borrowed or that inflation was about to take off, investors refused to continue supplying new bond finance or pushed up the yields they required. This had a very sobering, indeed intimidating, effect on the politicians.

The bond markets had a major role to play in the run-up to the financial crisis in 2008, with securitised bonds and derivatives of securitised bonds at the heart of the matter. Then, in the recovery, companies queued up to sell new bonds to raise cash as they fought to survive the economic downturn. Without the bond markets being willing to supply those funds, some of our leading companies would have met their demise; after all, the banks were not willing/able to lend and equity investors were scared.

These are just a few examples that clearly demonstrate the value of developing an understanding of these markets and appreciation of the tremendous power of the collective will of the participants. I hope this chapter has provided a base for continued learning about the markets and their influences on all our lives.

Key points and concepts

- A **bond** is a long-term contract in which the bond holders lend money to a company, government or some other issuing organisation. A straight 'vanilla' bond pays regular interest plus the capital on the redemption date.

- Bond investors in corporate bonds are exposed to less **risk** than share investors because they have the right to receive the annual interest before the equity holders receive any dividend and often have rights to seize company assets if the company reneges. But the bond holders do not (usually) share in the increase in **value created** by an extraordinarily successful business and there is an absence of any **voting power** over the management of the company.

- **Gilts** are UK government bonds, issued via the UK **Debt Management Office (DMO)** and are normally sold with a **nominal (face** or **par** or **maturity)** value of £100.

- Bond prices and redemption yields move in opposite directions.

- **Gilt-edged market makers (GEMMS)** are prepared to buy from, or sell gilts to, investors. The **bid** price is the price at which they will buy, the **offer** price is their selling price.

- If you buy a bond **cum-dividend y**ou will receive the next coupon paid.

- Bonds are quoted at **clean prices**, without taking account of the accrued interest. A buyer will pay the clean price plus the accrued interest value (called the **dirty price** or **full price** or **invoice price**) and receives all of the next coupon.

- $\text{Dirty price} = \text{Clean price} + \dfrac{\text{Annual coupon}}{2} \times \dfrac{\text{Number of days since last coupon}}{\text{Number of days separating coupon payments}}$

- If you buy during the **ex-dividend** period the person you bought from will receive the accrued interest from the issuer.

- **Index-linked stocks (gilts):** the coupon amount, and the nominal value, are adjusted or **uplifted** according to inflation.

▶

- **US Treasury notes** are issued on behalf of the US government by Treasury Direct with a face value of $100 and a coupon payable every six months and maturities of 2, 3, 5, 7 or 10 years. US **Treasury bonds** are auctioned quarterly, have a maturity date of 10 to 30 years and pay interest twice per year. US **Treasury Inflation-Protected Securities (TIPS)** are index-linked bonds whose principal value is adjusted according to changes in the **Consumer Price Index (CPI).**

- Corporate bonds generally offer a higher rate of return than government bonds with more risk. The majority of trading occurs in the **over-the-counter (OTC)** market in thin secondary markets.

   - **Straight, plain vanilla** or **bullet** bonds: regular (usually semi-annual or annual) fixed coupons and a specified redemption date.
   - Debentures are generally more secure than **loan stock** (in the UK and some other countries).
   - A **trust deed (or bond indenture)** has **affirmative covenants** outlining the nature of the bond contract and **negative** (restrictive) **covenants** impose constraints on managerial action to reduce risk for the lenders.
   - A **floating rate note (FRN) (variable rate note/bond)** is a bond with an interest rate which varies as a benchmark interest rate changes (e.g. LIBOR).
   - A **credit rating** depends on (a), the likelihood of payments of interest and/or capital not being paid (i.e. default); and (b), the extent to which the lender is protected in the event of a default.
   - **High-yield bonds** are forms of debt offering a high return with a high risk.

- **Local authority and municipal bonds ('Munis')** are bonds issued by governments at a sub-national level, such as a county, city or state, which pay a fixed rate of interest and are repayable on a specific future date.

- **Convertible bonds** are issued as debt instruments but they also give the holder the right to exchange the bonds at some time in the future into ordinary shares according to some prearranged formula. Advantages for corporate issuers are:

   - lower interest than on debentures;
   - interest is tax deductible;
   - they are self liquidating;
   - there are few negative covenants;
   - shares might be temporarily underpriced;
   - it is a cheap way to issue shares;
   - they are an available form of finance when straight debt and equity are not.

- **Strips** are bonds which are broken down into their individual cash flows. The dividends or coupons are separated from the bond and are then negotiable zero coupon instruments in their own right with a fixed maturity date.

- **Asset backed securitisation** involves the pooling and repackaging of relatively small, homogeneous and illiquid financial assets into liquid securities.

- **Covered bonds** are similar to securitised asset-backed bonds in that a group of assets (e.g. mortgage receivables) are used to back up the claims of the bond holders, but these assets and bonds are kept on the balance sheet of the issuing bank, thus investors can call on the originating bank to pay up.

- A **foreign bond** is a bond denominated in the currency of the country where it is issued, when the issuer is a non-resident.

- **Eurobonds** are bonds sold outside the jurisdiction of the country of the currency in which the bond is denominated. They are bearer bonds not subject to withholding tax.

- **Call back features**: the issuer has the right, but not the obligation, to buy the bond back after a period of time has elapsed, say five years, at a price specified when the bond was issued.

- A **'Put' feature** gives the bondholder the right, but not the obligation, to sell the bond back to the issuer (usually at par value) on designated dates.

- **Medium-term notes (MTNs).** A note (contract) under which a company promises to pay the holders a certain sum on the maturity date, and in many cases a coupon interest in the meantime. Typically

▶

unsecured, carrying floating or fixed interest rates, and sold with a maturity of as little as nine months and as great as 30 years. An **MTN programme** stretching over many years can be set up with one set of legal documents. Then, numerous notes can be issued under the programme in future years.

● *Sukuk* **bonds** are bonds conforming to Shari'ah law, which forbids interest income, or *riba*, and insists that real assets underlie all financial transactions. *Sukuk* represent part *ownership* of tangible assets, businesses or investments, so the returns are generated by some sort of share of the gain (or loss) made and the risk is shared.

  – A bond is **priced** according to general market interest rates for risk class and maturity: Irredeemable:

$$P_D = \frac{C}{k_D} \quad \text{and:} \quad V_D = \frac{I}{k_D}$$

  Redeemable:

$$P_D = \frac{C_1}{1+k_D} + \frac{C_2}{(1+k_D)^2} + \frac{C_3}{(1+k_D)^3} + \frac{C_4}{(1+k_D)^4} + \dots + \frac{C_n}{(1+k_D)^n} + \frac{R_n}{(1+k_D)^n}$$

  and:

$$V_D = \frac{I_1}{1+k_D} + \frac{I_2}{(1+k_D)^2} + \frac{I_3}{(1+k_D)^3} + \frac{I_4}{(1+k_D)^4} + \dots + \frac{I_n}{(1+k_D)^n} + \frac{R^*_n}{(1+k_D)^n}$$

  – The **current (interest) yield** on a bond is:

$$\frac{\text{Gross interest (coupon)}}{\text{Market price}} \times 100$$

  – The **yield to maturity** includes both annual coupon returns and capital gains or losses on maturity. It is the discount rate such that the present value of all the cash inflows from the bond (interest plus principal) is equal to the bond's current market price.

● **Interest rate risk** is the extent to which the price of a bond changes when general market yields change for that risk class of bonds. The volatility of long dated bond tends to be greater than short dated ones.

● **The duration of a bond** is the weighted average maturity of all payments (coupons plus principal) to be received from owning a bond, where the weights are the discounted present values of the payments.

● Percentage change in bond price from one period to the next $\approx -\text{Duration} \times \dfrac{\text{Change in YTM}}{1+\text{YTM}}$

● Factors that **shift the demand curve** for bonds: expected inflation, riskiness of bonds relative to other assets, wealth, liquidity of bonds relative to other assets.

● The main factors that **shift the supply curve** for bonds: expected inflation, availability of profitable investment opportunities, size of government borrowing.

● The **term structure of interest rates** describes the manner in which the same default risk class of debt securities provides different rates of return depending on the length of time to maturity. There are three hypotheses relating to the term structure of interest rates:

  – the expectations hypothesis;
  – the liquidity-preference hypothesis;
  – the market-segmentation hypothesis.

References and further reading

To keep up to date and reinforce knowledge gained by reading this chapter I can recommend the following publications: *Financial Times, The Economist, Bank of England Quarterly Bulletin, Bank for International Settlements Quarterly Review* (www.bis.org), *The Treasurer* (a monthly journal).

Blake, D. (2000) *Financial Market Analysis*, 2nd edn. Chichester: John Wiley & Sons.
> A technical and detailed examination of long-term debt markets.

Chisholm, A .M. (2009) *An Introduction to International Capital Markets*, 2nd edn. Chichester: J. Wiley and Sons.
> Containing four well-written and accessible chapters detailing the bond markets around the world – particularly good on bond valuation and duration calculations.

Debt Management Office, *Quarterly Review*.

Eiteman, D. K., Stonehill, A. I. and Moffett, M. H. (2009) *Multinational Business Finance*, 12th edn. Reading, MA: Addison Wesley.
> Some useful, easy-to-follow material on international debt markets.

Fabozzi, F. J. (2009) *Bond Markets, Analysis and Strategies*, 7th edn. Harlow: Financial Times Prentice Hall.
> A detailed yet accessible description of bonds with a US bond market focus.

Graham, J. R. and Harvey, C. R. (2001) 'The theory and practice of corporate finance: evidence from the field', *Journal of Financial Economics*, Vol. 60, Issues 2–3, May, pp. 187–243.
> US survey of corporate use of debt.

Hickman, B. G. (1958) 'Corporate bond quality and investor experience', *National Bureau of Economic Research*, 14, Princeton, NJ.
> Early research into the returns and default rates on bonds.

Hicks, J. R. (1946) *Value and Capital: An Inquiry into some Fundamental Principles of Economic Theory*, 2nd edn. Oxford: Oxford University Press.
> Liquidity-preference hypothesis to explain the term structure of interest rates.

Howells, P. and Bain, K. (2008) *The Economics of Money, Banking and Finance*, 4th edn. London: Financial Times Prentice Hall.

Lutz, F. A. and Lutz, V. C. (1951) *The Theory of Investment in the Firm*. Princeton, NJ: Princeton University Press.
> Expectations hypothesis of the term structure of interest rates.

Saunders, A. and Cornett, M. M. (2007) *Financial Markets and Institutions*, 3rd edn. Boston: McGraw-Hill.
> Contains much more on the US bond markets and on mathematical calculations associated with bond pricing, YTM, etc.

Veronesi, P. (2010) *Fixed Income Securities: Valuation, Risk and Risk Management*. New Jersey: John Wiley and Sons.
> A much more detailed look at the bond markets, with a focus on the US.

Websites

Association of Corporate Treasurers www.treasurers.org
Bank of England www.bankofengland.co.uk
Bank for International Settlements www.bis.org
Bloomberg www.bloomberg.com,
Bondscape www.bondscape.net
Economist www.economist.com
Financial Times www.ft.com/bonds&rates
Fitch www.fitchratings.com
International Capital Market Association www.icmagroup.org
International Capital Markets Association – bond prices pages www.BondMarketPrices.com
Investor Chronicle bond prices, yield etc. www.investorchronicle.co.uk/bonds
JP Morgan www.adr.com
Moody's www.moodys.com
Standard & Poor's www.standardandpoors.com

Video presentations

Financial organisation and corporate chief executives and other senior people describe and discuss policy and other aspects of their operations in interviews, documentaries and webcasts at Cantos.com. (www.cantos.com) – these are free to view.

Case study recommendations

See www.pearsoned.co.uk/arnold for case study synopses.
Also see Harvard University: http://hbsp.harvard.edu/product/cases

- Washington Mutual's Covered Bonds (2009) Authors: Daniel B. Bergstresser, Robin Greenwood and James Quinn. Harvard Business School.
- Note: Credit Rating Agencies (2009) Author: William E. Fruhan, Jr. Harvard Business School.
- Standard & Poor's Sovereign Credit Ratings: Scales and Process (2005) Authors: Rawi Abdelal and Christopher M. Bruner. Harvard Business School.
- Note on Duration and Convexity (2004) Authors: George Chacko, Peter Hecht, Vincent Dessain and Aders Sjöman. Harvard Business School.
- Walt Disney Company's Sleeping Beauty Bonds – Duration Analysis (2000) Author: Carliss Y. Baldwin. Harvard Business School.
- Yield Curve Basics (2006) Author: Frank Warnock. Darden, University of Pennsylvania. Available at Harvard case study website.
- Rockwood Specialities: High-yield Debt Issue (2004) Authors: Kevin (Sungam) Kim and Susan Chaplinsky. Darden, University of Pennsylvania. Available at Harvard case study website.
- Parex Banka: Issuing a 200 Million Bond (2007) Authors: Jordan Mitchell and Basil Kalymon. Richard Ivey School of Business. The University of Western Ontario. Available at Harvard case study website.
- Cypress Semiconductor: 1.25 per cent Convertible Notes (2008) Author: Robert M. Conroy. Darden, University of Pennsylvania. Available at Harvard case study website.
- Tata Steel Limited: Convertible Alternative Reference Securities (2008) Authors: Vasant Sivaraman and Adithya Anand. Richard Ivey School of Business. The University of Western Ontario. Available at Harvard case study website.
- Lyons Document Storage Corporation: Bond Accounting (2010) Author: William J. Bruns. Harvard Business School.

Self-review questions

1 Explain the following (related to bonds):

   (a) Par value.
   (b) Trustee.
   (c) Debenture.
   (d) Zero coupon bond.
   (e) Floating-rate note.

2 The inexperienced finance trainee at Mugs-R-Us plc says that he can save the company money on its forthcoming issue of ten-year bonds. 'The rate of return required for bonds of this risk class in the financial markets is 10 per cent and yet I overheard our investment banking adviser say, "We could issue a bond at a coupon of only 9 per cent." I reckon we could save the company a large sum on the £100 million issue.' Do you agree with the trainee's logic?

3 Is securitisation something to do with anti-criminal precautions? If not, explain what it is and why firms do it.

4 Why does convertible debt carry a lower coupon than straight debt?

5 What are the differences between a domestic bond, a Eurobond and a foreign bond?

6 What is the credit rating on a bond and what factors determine it?

7 Why do bond issuers accept restrictive covenants?

8 What are high-yield bonds? What is their role in financing firms?

9 What is a bearer bond?

10 What is a debenture?

11 What is the difference between a fixed-rate and a floating-rate bond?

Questions and problems

1 Imagine that the market yield to maturity for three-year bonds in a particular risk class is 12 per cent. You buy a bond in that risk class which offers an annual coupon of 10 per cent for the next three years, with the first payment in one year. The bond will be redeemed at par (£100) in three years.

   (a) How much would you pay for the bond?
   (b) If you paid £105 what yield to maturity would you obtain?

2 A €100 bond with two years to maturity and an annual coupon of 9 per cent is available. (The next coupon is payable in one year.)

   (a) If the market requires a yield to maturity of 9 per cent for a bond of this risk class what will be its market price?
   (b) If the market price is €98, what yield to maturity does it offer?
   (c) If the required yield to maturity on this type of bond changes to 7 per cent, what will the market price change to?

3 (a) If a government sold a 10-year bond with a par value of £100 and an (annual) coupon of 9 per cent, what price can be charged if investors require a 9.5 per cent yield to maturity on such bonds?
   (b) If yields to maturity on bonds of this risk class fall to 8.5 per cent, what could the bonds be sold for?
   (c) If it were sold for £105, what yield to maturity is the bond offering?
   (d) What is the flat yield on this bond if it is selling at £105?

4 The price of a bond issued by C & M plc is 85.50 per cent of par value. The bond will pay an annual 8.5 per cent coupon until maturity (the next coupon will be paid in one year). The bond matures in seven years.

   (a) What will be the market price of the bond if yields to maturity for this risk class fall to 7.5 per cent?
   (b) What will be the market price of the bond if yields to maturity for this risk class rise to 18 per cent?

5 A zero coupon bond with a par value of $100 matures in five years.

   (a) What is the price of the bond if the yield to maturity is 5 per cent?
   (b) What is the price of the bond if the yield to maturity is 10 per cent?

6 Bond 1 has an annual coupon rate of 6 per cent and Bond 2 has an annual coupon of 12 per cent. Both bonds mature in one year and have a par value of €100. If the yield to maturity on bonds of this risk class is 10 per cent at what price will the bonds sell? Assume that the next coupons are due in one year's time.

7 You are considering three alternative investments in bonds. The bonds have different times to maturity, but carry the same default risk. You would like to gain an impression of the extent of price volatility for each given alternative change in future interest rates. The investments are:

(i) a two-year bond with an annual coupon of 6 per cent, par value of £100 and the next coupon payment in one year. The present yield to maturity on this bond is 6.5 per cent.
(ii) a ten-year bond with an annual coupon of 6 per cent, a par value of £100 and the next coupon payable in one year. The present yield to maturity on this bond is 7.2 per cent.
(iii) a 20-year bond with an annual coupon of 6 per cent, a par value of £100 and the next coupon due in one year. The present yield to maturity on this bond is 7.7 per cent.

(a) Draw an approximate yield curve.
(b) Calculate the market price of each of the bonds.
(c) Calculate the market price of the bonds on the assumption that yields to maturity rise by 200 basis points for all bonds.
(d) Now calculate the market price of the bonds on the assumption that yields to maturity fall by 200 basis points to 4.5 per cent, 5.2 per cent and 5.7 per cent respectively.
(e) Which bond price is the most volatile in circumstances of changing yields to maturity?
(f) Explain the liquidity-preference theory of the term structure of yields to maturity.

8 What are the factors that explain the difference in yields to maturity between long-term and short-term bonds?

9 Find the present yield to maturity on government securities with maturities of one year, five years and ten years in the *Financial Times*. How has the yield curve changed since 2010 as shown in the chapter? What might account for this shift?

10 If the yield to maturity on a two-year zero coupon bond is 13 per cent and the yield to maturity on a one-year zero coupon bond is 10 per cent, what is the expected spot rate of one-year bonds in one year's time assuming the expectations hypothesis is applicable?

11 If the yield to maturity on a one-year bond is 8 per cent and the expected spot rate on a one-year bond, beginning in one year's time, is 7 per cent, what will be the yield to maturity on a two-year bond under the expectations hypothesis of the term structure of interest rates?

12 In 2011 the term structure of interest rates for UK government securities was upward sloping whereas in other years it is downward sloping. Explain how these curves come about with reference to the expectations, liquidity and market-segmentation hypotheses.

13 'Convertibles are great because they offer a lower return than straight debt and we just dish out shares rather than have to find cash to redeem the bonds' – executive at Myopic plc. Comment on this statement as though you were a shareholder in Myopic.

14 Lummer plc has issued £60 million 15-year 8.5 per cent coupon bonds with a par value of £100. Each bond is convertible into 40 shares of Lummer ordinary shares, which are currently trading at £1.90.

(a) What is the conversion price?
(b) What is the conversion premium?
(c) What is the conversion value of the bond?

15 Explain the following terms and their relevance to debt-finance decision makers:

    (a) Negative covenant.
    (b) Conversion premium.
    (c) Collateral.
    (d) Strip bonds.
    (e) *Sukuk.*

16 Flying High plc plans to expand rapidly over the next five years and is considering the following forms of finance to support that expansion.

    (a) A five-year £10 million floating-rate term loan from MidBarc Bank plc at an initial annual interest rate of 9 per cent.
    (b) A five-year Eurodollar bond fixed at 8 per cent per year with a nominal value of US$15 million. The current exchange rate is €1.50 to £1.
    (c) A £10 million convertible bond offering a yield to redemption of 6 per cent and a conversion premium of 15 per cent.

As the financial adviser to the board you have been asked to explain each of these forms of finance and point out the relative advantages and drawbacks. Do this in report form.

17 'We avoid debt finance because of the unacceptable constraint placed on managerial actions.' Explain what this executive means and suggest forms of long-term borrowing which have few constraints.

Assignments

1 Review the bonds issued by a company familiar to you. Consider the merits and drawbacks of these relative to alternative types of bonds that might have been issued.

2 Write a report for an investing institution explaining how it might alter the risk on a bond portfolio by selecting particular types of bonds or shifting the average time to maturity of the bonds in the portfolio.

Web-based exercises

1 Go to www.ft.com/bonds&rates and obtain the yields to maturity on a range of international bonds denominated in dollars. Place on the x-axis of a graph credit ratings and on the y-axis the yields to maturity for bonds to be redeemed between 5 and 20 years hence. Comment on the results.

2 From www.ft.com/bonds&rates obtain yields to maturity on eurozone government bonds. Draw a graph showing yield curves for each government bond market and comment on the spreads over the rates payable by the German government.

3 Visit the websites of Standard & Poor's (www.standardandpoors.com), Moody's (www.moodys.com) and Fitch (www.fitchratings.com) and compile a list of the major factors they examine to form an opinion on the appropriate credit rating for a bond.

Central banking

LEARNING OUTCOMES

A modern society could not function efficiently without the services provided by a central bank. They not only improve the well-being of the banking sector but, through their oversight of the entire financial system, make life better for all of us. By the end of this chapter you should be able to:

■ explain the conduct of monetary policy through the system of reserve requirements combined with open market operations and discount rate changes;

■ make clear the ways in which monetary policy impacts various aspect of the nation's economy;

■ discuss the advantages and disadvantages of maintaining a central bank independent of political influence;

■ describe the rationale and importance of deposit insurance, the lender of last resort function and the measures to control the banks judged too big to fail;

■ explain the main regulatory variables that a central bank examines when judging a bank's safety and soundness (using the CAMELS system);

■ explain the issues of bank liquidity and solvency risk, and describe the ways in which the regulators have tried to reduce these, including the Basel Accords;

■ outline the central bank's role in the following:

- banker to the national government and management of national debt;
- the issue of currency;
- smooth functioning of payment systems;
- currency reserve control;
- coordination with international bodies;

■ describe how the following central banks work: Bank of England, European Central Bank and the US Federal Reserve System.

If interest rates are held at a level that is too low then inflation will start to take off. This can be disruptive to businesses in addition to destroying people's savings. It is especially problematic if inflation is high and fluctuating. Then unpredictability makes planning very difficult. However, if interest rates are set at an excessively high level this will inhibit business activity, cause people to put off buying houses and reduce spending in the shops, leading to a recession, with massive job losses. Clearly a society needs an organisation whose task it is to select the appropriate interest rate for the economic conditions it faces: neither too high nor too low. That organisation is the central bank.

Banks are organisations that have high levels of borrowing. That is, the deposits put into them plus the money borrowed from the wholesale financial markets is many times the amount put in by shareholders. Most of the money raised from depositors, wholesale lenders and shareholders is lent out. There are two constant dangers in this. One is that a large proportion of depositors or other lenders insist on withdrawing their cash in the immediate future when the assets that the bank holds (e.g. business loans) cannot be liquidated quickly to satisfy these demands. The second is that the assets of the bank decline while the liabilities remain the same or increase, resulting eventually in insolvency as assets are no longer greater than liabilities. Central banks are usually the regulators that investigate whether banks are being properly managed so that neither liquidity risk nor solvency risk is high.

In addition to the crucial functions of monetary policy (interest rate and money supply) and bank supervision for safety and soundness, central banks help a society in a number of other ways. For example, they usually manage, or at least oversee, the payment systems such as cheque clearing. They also help establish special schemes to guarantee that a depositor will receive at least a minimum sum should the bank become insolvent. This helps create confidence in the banking system. The alternative of regular bank runs in which nervous depositors queue to take their money from a bank before it runs out of cash can lead to human misery and loss of economic output. Another useful service to bolster confidence in the system is that of lender of last resort – if the usual sources of funds for a bank (e.g. depositors, other banks or wholesale money markets) are no longer forthcoming with money, then the central bank will stand ready to supply funds to see the bank over a difficult period. Central banks act as bankers for the government and may assist with management of the government's debt. They may also hold a nation's reserves of gold and foreign currency, and take some part in managing the currency's exchange rate.

Note that this chapter describes the wide variety of responsibilities that a nation *may* choose to allocate to the purview of the central bank. However, many countries decide to establish alternative organisations to undertake some of the tasks described here while leaving the central bank to concentrate on a few of them.

Monetary policy

Central banks are given the task of managing the amount of money in an economy and the interest rates in that economy. That is, they conduct **monetary policy**. Getting monetary policy right is crucial to the well-being of a society. If there is too much money relative to the output of goods and services, with interest rates held too low, then inflation will take off. The resulting uncertainty about future price levels is likely to inhibit economic growth, or, at the very least, penalise those who are not protected against inflation. If monetary policy is too tight, with too little money in the economy and interest rates too high, then production will be lower than it otherwise could be and the greater unemployment will cause misery.

To understand how a central bank controls money supply and interest rates you need to appreciate that it acts as banker to the banks (including other depository institutions, e.g. building societies). As well as accepting deposits from them it has special powers because it can insist that each bank leaves a certain proportion of the amount it has received as deposits from its customers (households, small businesses, etc.) at the central bank. If a bank's reserves at the central bank fall below the minimum required then it has to top this up. Furthermore, banks and other depository institutions like to maintain an additional buffer beyond the **required reserves**[1] at the central bank.

---

[1] Called banks' operational deposits with the Bank of England.

This extra safety margin of money is called **excess reserves**. This is an amount that makes the bank feel comfortable about the prospect of a sudden outflow of cash – say dozens of large depositors withdraw billions over a period of a week (there is more on the need for reserves in Chapter 2). The target amount of the excess reserves may, in fact, be largely dictated by the banking regulator (which is usually the central bank) and may be strongly influenced by international agreements on the appropriate amounts, e.g. Basel III – see 'Bank supervision' later in this chapter.

Thus the central bank has a liability – it accepted deposits from banks. Another liability of a central bank is what you see written on notes (or coins) that you have in your wallet or purse: the central bank 'promise to pay the bearer on demand the sum of ...' or some similarly worded promise.[2] Thus a typical commercial bank will hold some of its assets in the form of reserves either at the central bank or in the form of vault cash in hand. As well as the money held in the banks an economy will have **currency in circulation**, that is outside of banks. The combination of the two is the monetary base:

| **Monetary base** | = | currency in circulation | + | reserves |
| **Reserves** | = | required reserves | + | vault cash (excess reserves) |

It is changes in these accounts that determine the size of a nation's money supply (everything else being held constant). If there is an increase either in the currency in circulation or in reserves there will be an increase in the money supply. An increase in reserves, either cash deposited by a bank at the central bank or vault cash, leads to an increase in the level of deposits and thus contributes to the money supply. Central banks conduct monetary policy by changing the country's monetary base.

Typically, a central bank might insist that, say, 10 per cent of the amount deposited by customers be held as the **required reserve ratio** (reserves as a percentage of deposits). The reserve accounts held by banks at the central bank are used to settle accounts between depository institutions when cheques and electronic payments are cleared. A bank may also hold, say, another 5–10 per cent of the amount deposited by customers as excess reserves. It is important to note that the sole supplier of reserves – notes and coins and balances at the central bank as liabilities of the central bank – is the central bank.

The monetary base described above is often referred to as M0, which is a very extreme form of **narrow money**, i.e. defining what money is in a very narrow way. Banks can use this base to create **broad money**, which is a multiple of the monetary base. The definitions of broad money vary from country to country, but generally include money that is held in the form of a current (checking) account or deposit account, and some money market instruments. These broad money aggregates often have names such as M3 or M4. You can see why it is difficult to define money because banks can 'create money'. This is illustrated through **Exhibit 7.1**.

Exhibit 7.1	Money creation – the credit multiplier

Assume that all banks in a monetary system are required to keep 20 per cent of deposits as reserves. Bank A has $100 million of deposits from customers. Because it is sticking to the reserve requirement (required by both the central bank and its own prudential reserves policy) it lends out only $80 million and keeps $20 million as cash or in its account with the central bank (assume no vault cash for simplicity).

Bank A's opening balance sheet

Assets		Liabilities	
Reserves	$20m	Deposits	$100m
Loans	$80m		

---

[2] A long time ago you might have been able to take along your currency notes to the central bank and receive gold or silver in exchange. Today if you take along, say, a £20 note you will receive only other notes in return, say four £5 notes. Because these notes (and coins) are generally accepted as a medium of exchange and store of value, they can function as money.

Exhibit 7.1   Continued

Now if deposits in Bank A are increased by $5 million the position changes. Deposits rise to $105 million and reserves rise to $25 million as the additional $5 million is initially held as reserves at the central bank.

Bank A. An increase in deposits – intermediate period

Assets		Liabilities	
Reserves	$25m	Deposits	$105m
Loans	$80m		

This means that the reserve ratio has risen to $25m ÷ $105m = 23.8 per cent. The bank earns no or little interest from reserves, so it will wish to reduce it back to 20 per cent by lending out the extra. The next balance sheet shows the amount of lending that leaves a 20 per cent reserve ratio, $84 million.

Bank A. Lending out just enough to attain minimum reserve ratio

Assets		Liabilities	
Reserves	$21m	Deposits	$105m
Loans	$84m		

Now let us bring in more banks. In lending an additional $4 million Bank A will have an impact on the rest of the banking system. If the $4 million is lent to a company and, initially at least, that company deposits the money in Bank B, then at the central bank, Bank A's account will be debited (reserves go down) and Bank B's account will be credited (reserves increase). Bank B will lend out 80 per cent of the amount, or $3.2 million keeping $800,000 in reserves to maintain its 20 per cent ratio of reserves to deposits. The $3.2 million lent finds its way to Bank C, which again holds 20 per cent as reserves and lends the rest, and so on. At each stage 80 per cent of the deposit is lent out, increasing the deposits of other banks, encouraging them to lend.

The effect on the banking system of an injection of $5m of money, under a reserve ratio of 20%

	Change in deposits, $m	Change in loans, $m	Change in reserves, $m
Bank A	5.00	4.00	1.00
Bank B	4.00	3.20	0.80
Bank C	3.20	2.56	0.64
Bank D	2.56	2.05	0.51
Bank E	2.05	1.64	0.41
Bank F	....	....	....
Bank G	....	....	....
Total of all banks	25	20	5

The credit multiplier is a reciprocal of the reserve ratio, which in this case = 1 ÷ 0.20 = 5. Following an injection of $5 million into the financial system the whole process ends when an additional $25 million of deposits has been created; equilibrium has been reached again. (The model is a simplification for illustrative purposes. In reality, there might be leakages from the system due to money flowing abroad, or people holding cash or buying government bonds rather than placing it in bank deposits.)

Remember: the creator of the monetary base is the central bank because it has a monopoly on the issuance of currency. If it has control over this then it can strongly influence the broader money supply (including deposits at banks) through the reserves requirements. So, once the system has settled down from the injection of a new deposit, it will be fairly stable – little money creation or removal.

Let us think about where the initial deposit put into Bank A might have come from. If it came from a customer who withdrew it from another bank, the example is null and void because while Bank A benefits from the $5 million deposit, the other bank, Bank X, sees a reduction in its reserves at the central bank by an equal amount. It can now lend less than it could before because it has to rebuild its reserves. Thus the stimulus effect of Bank A's deposit is exactly offset by the removal of money from the system by Bank X. If, however, the $5 million came from the central bank purchasing Treasury bills from an investor who then put the newly created cash received into his account with Bank A, we have new money coming into the system and we can expect something like the credit multiplier effect shown above. The central bank is the only player here who can create money out of thin air and pump it into the system if the system is at equilibrium.

Thus, despite commercial banks' ability to create money on the way to equilibrium, there is a limit to the amount that the system as a whole can go up to because for every dollar, pound, euro, etc. created there has to be a fraction held as a cash reserve. It is the central bank that controls the total volume of monetary base (reserves at the central bank plus cash in circulation and at deposit-taking institutions) and so the broader aggregates of money have an upper limit. Small changes in the monetary base can have a large impact on the amount of broad money in the system and so we often refer to the monetary base as **high-powered money**. It is the monetary base that central banks target to influence money supply, interest rates, inflation and economic output.

Central banks have three major tools they use to increase or decrease the money supply and interest rates:

- open market operations;
- discount rate changes;
- reserve requirement ratio changes.

Open market operations

This is the most important tool of monetary policy in most countries today. **Open market operations** means the buying and selling of government securities (Treasury bills and bonds) in the normal trading markets on a day-to-day basis. In purchasing government securities the central bank creates money to hand it over to those selling. It issues currency notes or it writes a cheque in the name of the owner. When the cheque is drawn on, the central bank just creates an amount of credit for itself to satisfy the buyer – money from thin air. When the central bank sells government securities, the purchasers draw on their money in the banking system which leads to a lowering of reserves.

To illustrate the creation of money by a central bank we can take Bank A's balance sheet from Exhibit 7.1. The starting position is:

Bank A. Lending out just enough to attain minimum reserve ratio

Assets		Liabilities	
Reserves	$21m	Deposits	$105m
Loans	$84m		

The central bank wants to inject money into the financial system and lower interest rates. It offers to buy billions of dollars of government securities. One of the customers of Bank A sells $6 million of securities to the central bank. The central bank sends money to the customer of Bank A who deposits the newly created money (an electronic record rather than cash) in Bank A.[3] Bank A adds this $6 million to its reserve account at the central bank. Now Bank A's balance sheet looks like this.

---

[3] In many financial systems there is a select group of security dealers (often a wing of the major commercial and investment banks) with whom the central bank buys and sells government securities. It is these security dealers' deposit accounts that are credited and debited.

Bank A balance sheet after an injection of $6m

Assets		Liabilities	
Reserves	$27m	Deposits	$111m
Loans	$84m		

Bank A has a very high reserve level relative to its deposits, $27m ÷ $111m = 24.3 per cent. The managers will want to employ the surplus money above that needed to maintain the target reserve ratio (20 per cent) to earn higher interest by lending it, thus new money flows into the financial system. If the central bank wanted to drain money from the system through open market operations it would sell government securities to investors, which reduces the amount held by banks in their reserve accounts at the central bank or reduces vault cash. This would curb lending and raise interest rates.

Central banks tend to use Treasury securities to conduct open market operations because the secondary market in these securities is very liquid and a large volume of these securities held by dealers and investors, meaning that the market can absorb a large number of buy and sell transactions. The main method used is a repurchase agreement – a repo – in which the central bank purchases securities with a prior agreement to sell them back to the counterparty after, say, 24 hours, 7 days or 14 days. The difference between the buying and selling price provides the effective interest rate. If the central bank wanted to drain money it would engage in a reverse repo (there is more on repos in Chapter 5).

Repos and reverse repos are, by their nature, temporary interventions because the opposite transaction takes place on maturity, a few days after the first buy or sell. There are times when the central bank wants to effect a more permanent change in the money supply. Then it can go for an outright transaction, a purchase or a sale, that is not destined to be reversed in a few days.

What you need to bear in mind is that every day banks trade surplus reserves with each other. Banks always have an incentive to lend – even if only for 24 hours – if they find themselves with too many reserves. Each day there will be dozens of other banks that find themselves temporarily below the reserve level they need and so they willingly borrow in the interbank market.

The supply and demand of reserves

The main target for central banks is usually the overnight (24-hour) interest rate on loans of reserves from one bank to another. In the US this is the federal funds rate in the Eurozone it is the overnight repo rate in euros, and in the UK it is the overnight sterling repo rate. Switzerland opts for the Swiss franc LIBOR target rate.

The demand curve for reserves falls as interest rates rise. That is, the quantity of reserves demanded by banks (holding all else constant) reduces if banks have a higher opportunity cost of keeping money in the form of reserves. They would rather lend it out to achieve higher interest rates. This becomes more and more of a lost opportunity as rates in the short-term interest rate markets rise. Bankers increasingly start to think that they can economise on the vault cash buffer if interest rates are high and so lend these out more at the overnight repo rate, say. Thus, the demand curve for reserves, D, slopes downwards in **Exhibit 7.2**.

The central bank usually has a continuous programme of lending and so there is a large quantity of money borrowed by the banks from the central bank at any one time. It is through the adjustment to the amount of lent reserves outstanding that the central bank controls interest rates. The supply curve for reserves, S, shown in blue, is the amount of reserves borrowed from the central bank supplied through its open market operations – fixed at that point in time. Equilibrium occurs where the demand for reserves equals the quantity supplied. This occurs at an interest rate of A, providing the short-term interest rate in the market.

Now imagine that the central bank wishes to increase the supply of money and lower interest rates. It does this by increasing its purchases of government securities, providing a greater quantity of reserves. This pushes the supply curve in **Exhibit 7.3** from S1 to S2 and moves the equilibrium interest rate from A to B. Obviously, if the central bank reduced its reserves outstanding to the banking system by selling additional securities, the supply curve would move to the left and interest rates would rise.

Exhibit 7.2 The demand and supply of reserves

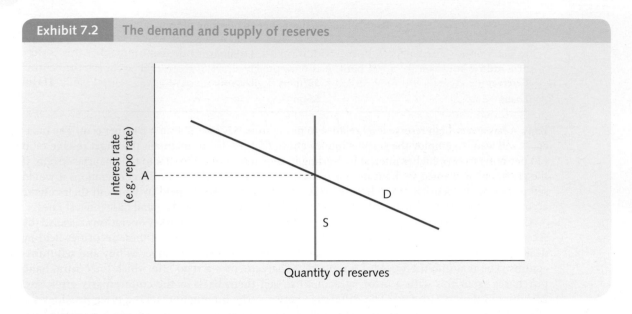

Exhibit 7.3 An open market increase in the supply of reserves

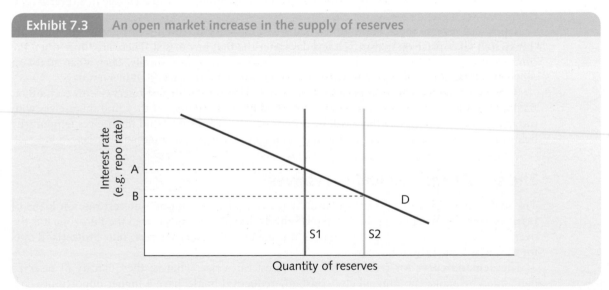

So far we have discussed **dynamic open market operations**, that is, where the central bank takes the initiative to change the level of reserves and the monetary base within a reasonably static banking environment. However, many times the environment is not static because there are a number of factors changing demand for borrowed reserves e.g. greater or lesser banker confidence in the economy and thus the potential for low-risk lending. Thus, it intervenes – a **defensive open market operation** – to offset the other factors influencing reserves.

When the central bank wants to change short-term interest rates it can often do so merely by announcing its new target rate and threatening to undertake open market operations to achieve it rather than actually intervening. The money market participants know that if they do not immediately move to the new rate they will find difficulties. For example, if the central bank shifts to target an interest rate lower than previously (i.e. it will lend on the repo market at a new lower rate) then anyone wanting to borrow will be foolish to borrow at a higher rate. Conversely, if the central bank announces a new higher target rate, anyone wanting to lend will be foolish to accept a lower rate than the central bank's target, because it stands ready to trade at its stated rate.

Discount rate changes

There is an option for banks to borrow additional reserves from the central bank – this is **discount window borrowing**.[4] So, if Bank A is temporarily short of reserves it could ask the central bank to simply create additional reserves and add them to its account at the central bank. There is thus an increase in reserves in the financial system and an increase in the money supply. Furthermore, Bank A could borrow from the central bank's discount window even if it was not short of reserves. It could then lend the money to businesses and individuals or lend the additional reserves to other banks in the money markets (e.g. repo).

Discount loans have to be repaid. When they are, the total amount of reserves, the monetary base and the money supply will fall.

So, why are banks not continually borrowing from the discount window? Well, there's a catch. The central bank tends to charge an interest rate on discount window borrowing that is significantly higher (usually around 100 basis points) than banks can borrow in the money markets. If this interest premium falls then an increasing number of banks will borrow at the discount rate. If the premium rises then few banks will borrow this way. Thus banks rein in their lending to customers for fear of having to borrow themselves at punitive interest rates. The discount rate acts as a back-stop for the open market target interest rate. The money market rate will not rise above the discount rate, so long as the central bank remains willing to supply unlimited funds at the discount rate.

If we introduce the possibility of large volumes of supply of money (reserves) from the central bank at a high interest rate then we have the upside-down L-shaped supply curve shown in **Exhibit 7.4**. If the demand curve D1 is the relevant demand schedule then the horizontal portion of the curve – banks borrowing from the central bank at the discount rate – does not come into play. Banks will continue to borrow and lend in the money markets but not from the central bank, and the equilibrium interest rate remains at A. This is the case most of the time: changes in the discount rate have no direct effect on the market interest rate.

Exhibit 7.4	Discount rate lending availability changes the supply curve

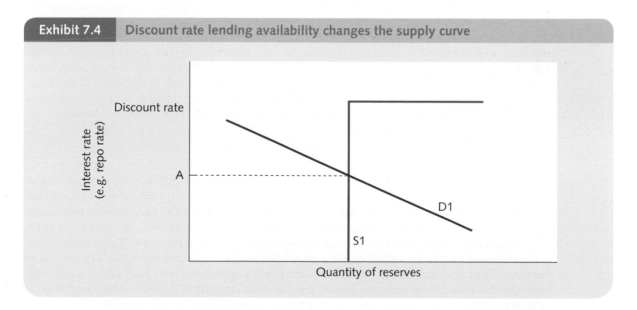

Now consider the case where there has been a shock to the system and banks increase their demand for reserves all the way along the curve – the demand curve has shifted to the right, from D1 to D2. Indeed, it has shifted so much that banks now borrow from the central bank at the discount rate to top up their reserves – *see* demand curve D2 intersecting the supply curve at the discount rate at point M in **Exhibit 7.5**. Now, if the central bank moves the discount rate up or

[4] The European Central Bank offers loans at the '**marginal lending rate**' rather than the discount rate, in its '**marginal lending facility**'. In the UK the discount window is often referred to as '**standing facilities**'.

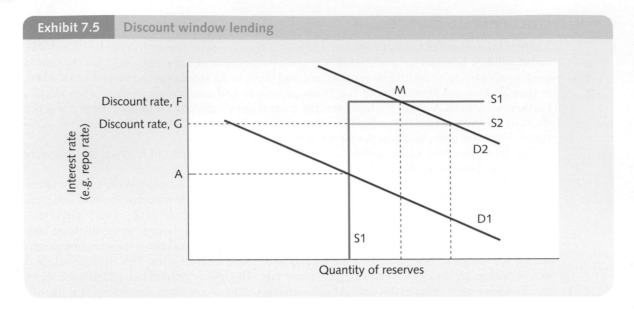

Exhibit 7.5 Discount window lending

down, the point of intersection with the demand curve shifts and thus the market interest rates change. If the central bank wanted lower interest rates, it could move the discount rate from, say, F to G, leading to increased borrowing from the central bank and an increased money supply.

A few decades ago adjusting the discount rate was the main way in which many central banks effected monetary policy, but the problem with this approach became increasingly apparent. It is difficult to predict the quantity of discount rate borrowing that will occur if the discount rate is raised or lowered, and so it is difficult to accurately change the money supply. Today changes in the discount rate are used to signal to the market that the central bank would like to see higher or lower interest rates: a raising indicates that tighter monetary conditions are required with higher interest rates throughout; lowering it indicates that looser, more expansionary monetary conditions are seen as necessary. Discount rate borrowing is used by generally sound banks in normal market conditions on a short-term basis, typically overnight, at a rate above the normal open market target rate. But, given the higher interest rate, it is used sparingly. Companies in real trouble, unable to borrow in the money markets and experiencing severe liquidity problems, may have to pay an even higher interest rate than the discount rate to borrow from the central bank.

Reserve requirement ratio changes

The power to change the reserve requirement ratio is a further tool used by central banks to control a nation's money supply. A decrease in the reserve requirement ratio means that banks do not need to hold as much money at the central bank or in vault cash and so they are able to lend out a greater percentage of their deposits, thus increasing the supply of money. The new loans result in consumption or investment in the economy, which raises inflows into other banks in the financial system and the credit multiplier effect takes hold, as illustrated in Exhibit 7.1. The process of borrowing and depositing in the banking system continues until deposits have grown sufficiently such that the new reserve amounts permit just the right amount of deposits – the target reserve ratio is reached.

Exhibit 7.6 shows that when the required reserve ratio is raised, the quantity of reserves demanded by banks increases for any given interest rate – the demand curve shifts from D1 to D2. This results in a new equilibrium being formed at the higher interest rate of C.

Conversely, a decrease in the required ratio leads to a decrease in the quantity of reserves demanded by banks, allowing more to be lent out, e.g. via repos, resulting in falling interest rates.

The main drawback to using changes in the reserve ratio is that it is difficult to make many frequent small adjustments because to do so would be disruptive to the banking system (a sudden rise can cause liquidity problems for banks with low excess reserves). Open market operations, however, can be used every day to cope with fluctuations in monetary conditions.

| Exhibit 7.6 | A change in required reserves shifts the demand curve |

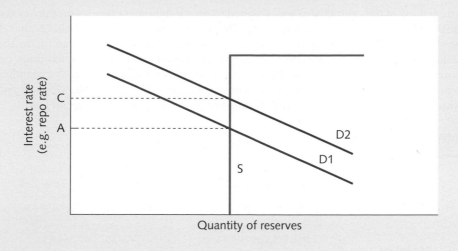

Exhibit 7.7 discusses the raising of reserves in China to bear down on inflation.

Exhibit 7.7

HK and China act to control inflation   **FT**

By Justine Lau in Hong Kong and Geoff Dyer in Beijing

Beijing and Hong Kong have unveiled a raft of measures to curb rising prices as both governments struggle to curb inflationary pressures and real estate speculation in their fast-growing economies.

The Chinese central bank on Friday raised capital reserve requirements for its banks for the fifth time this year in order to "appropriately control" credit and liquidity.

Meanwhile, the Hong Kong government signifcantly raised the stamp duty on residential prop-

erty transactions to damp property speculation.

The People's Bank of China said the proportion of deposits to be set aside by banks should increase by 50 basis points to 18.5 per cent for large banks, the highest level ever.

In an effort to tackle spiralling property prices in Hong Kong – partly because of an influx of money from mainland China – the government raised the stamp duty on properties resold within six months to a hefty 15 per cent.

Seperately, the Hong Kong Monetary Authority, the territory's de facto central bank, announced an increase in the down payment for properties worth more than HK$12m (US$1.5m) to 50 per cent, up from 40 per cent. It also increased the deposit requirement on any properties not occupied by owners or held by a company to 50 per cent.

Source: Financial Times, 20 November 2010, p. 8. Reprinted with permission.

Averaging reserves

The leading central banks usually do not require that reserves are a fixed percentage of deposits every day. Instead they insist on the average reserve ratio over a month being above a particular level. Thus, banks are permitted to go below the designated ratio for a number of days in the month, but will have to make up for this on other days. This allows a bank more flexibility because there are bound to be days when there is a large outflow (e.g. when millions of people pay their tax bills), which can be followed by a gradual rebuilding of reserves by borrowing from other financial institutions (or the central bank) over the following week or so.

How monetary policy impacts the economy

The actions of the central bank are designed to have a significant impact on the key economic variables. These relationships are shown in **Exhibit 7.8**. If the central bank believes that the economy needs to expand at a faster rate (while not unleashing high inflation), it can follow the pink route (selecting the most appropriate monetary tool). Lower interest rates encourage consumers to borrow and businesses to invest. If, however, it looks as though it is already expanding too fast to achieve the required inflation rate, the central bank can rein it in by following the purple route in which interest rates rise, money supply falls and people and businesses spend less.

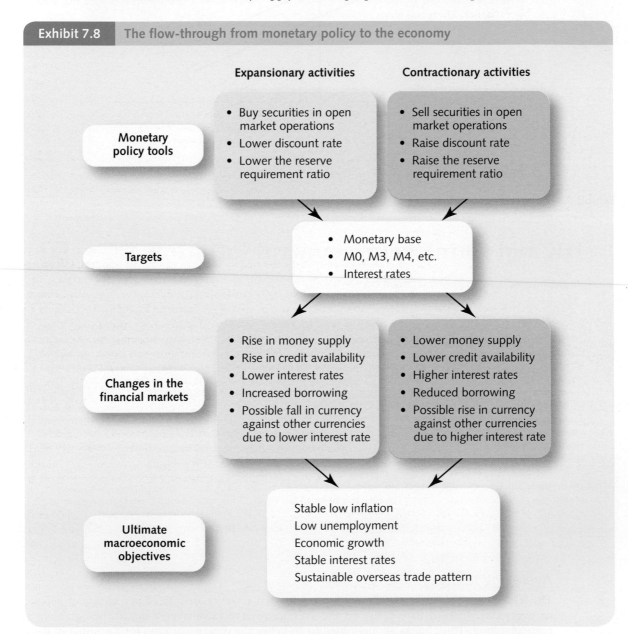

Exhibit 7.8   The flow-through from monetary policy to the economy

We have not yet discussed the impact of interest rate changes on the exchange rate. This is a complicated area, but generally the rule is: if interest rates are falling relative to those in foreign countries, the currency drops relative to those other currencies because international investors, looking for high returns, place their money elsewhere by selling the assets in the currency with the low interest rate and buying another currency to invest in that country. However, this superficially neat relationship is complicated by numerous other factors, not least anticipated inflation rates – there is more on exchange rate determination in Chapter 12. A fall in relative value of a currency is likely to make it easier for exporters to sell abroad as their products become relatively cheaper compared with foreign goods.

Some central banks have a specific goal for inflation. For example, the European Central Bank has a stated aim of a rate below, but close to, 2 per cent over the medium term, whereas the Bank of England is required to achieve 2 per cent, but anything within the 1–3 per cent range is regarded as acceptable in the short run, so long as there is a plan to move to nearer 2 per cent. Those central banks that have a specific target as well as those that do not, other than 'low and stable inflation', also take into account the impact of their actions on the other major macroeconomic variables. There are a number of other elements they consider:

- *High employment and steady economic growth* Not only does unemployment often cause pain to those families affected by it, but the economy wastes resources in idleness, lowering long-term well-being. Having said that, it makes sense to allow some unemployment as people are happily searching for the right position for them. So, while they are searching they are classified as unemployed. Many people who have taken time out to attend college, raise a family or go travelling may re-enter the jobs market but not find an appropriate job quickly and so they are classified as unemployed. Matching people to suitable posts does not happen instantaneously, thus there will always be some amount of **frictional unemployment**.

  Another type is **structural unemployment**. This is where the skills people have do not match what the market needs or the location of people does not match the needs of employers. For example, in the 1980s millions of coal miners were made redundant and found it difficult to obtain new positions when their skill-set and the location of their family homes were not suited to the newer industries.

  If the central bank tries to stimulate the economy through lower interest rates to such an extent that frictional and structural unemployment is reduced below its natural rate, inflation is likely to rise as output fails to keep up with the new quantities of money flooding the economy. Thus, we tolerate, even welcome, some unemployment. The best that policy makers can hope for is that the economy reaches its **natural rate of unemployment**, i.e. a level of **non-accelerating inflation rate of unemployment** (NAIRU). To achieve long-run reductions in unemployment below the current NAIRU policy makers need to work on the supply-side efficiency of the economy, e.g. raise skill levels, create a more pro-business, pro-innovation environment and culture, lower labour market rigidities inhibiting corporations from hiring and people from moving, lower taxes to encourage investment by firms. The difficulty for our economic leaders is estimating the level of NAIRU. Is it at 4 per cent unemployment or 6 per cent? If a better job-finding service were launched, would NAIRU decline significantly? It is these issues that economists, central bankers and politicians debate.

- *Interest rate stability* People and businesses are harmed by volatility in interest rates because of the additional uncertainty it introduces to their decision making, resulting in forward-planning problems. Thus house purchase decisions, factory investment decisions or bond market purchase decisions are made more hesitantly in a fluctuating interest rate economy, leading to lower economic output.

- *Stability of the financial system* We discussed the main roles of the financial system players in Chapter 1, particularly the channelling of savings into productive use. These mechanisms can be disrupted if financial crises are permitted to occur. Just ask the Icelanders, Greeks and the Irish if they value the stability of the financial system. Instability can cause economic output drops, high unemployment, asset price crashes (e.g. houses) and austerity measures cutting wages and pensions. While monetary policy is one tool to promote stability, there are many more measures that the central bank (or other designated regulators) can take. These are discussed later in the chapter.

- *Stability in the foreign exchange markets* The economies of the nation states are increasingly integrated into the world economy with ever larger volumes of imports, exports and overseas investment. The value of a currency relative to others can have profound effects on the producers in that economy. For example, a rise in the currency may make exporting more difficult. Also, fluctuations in the currency make planning difficult. Thus central banks are cognisant of the impact of interest rate changes on the level and stability of the exchange rate.

Over a run of years the goal of price stability does not conflict with the other goals. For example, higher inflation does not produce lower unemployment so there is no long-term trade-off between these two goals. There might be a trade-off in the short run. So, lowering interest rates may encourage consumer spending, house purchase and corporate investment, and the taking on of more workers. But once the economy has reached its productive capacity limit, additional demand from the lower rates is likely to push up wages and prices, rather than output. The alarmed authorities then need to take firm action (e.g. much higher interest rates) to squeeze demand out of the economy, causing painfully higher levels of unemployment. All in all, it is better if price stability at a low inflation rate is pursued from year to year, rather than having to make corrections after explosions or slumps in demand. Stability promotes economic growth.

Having said this, it is important to avoid focusing excessively on inflation in the short term and thereby forcing economic growth to fluctuate too much. For example, for a number of months in 2010 and 2011 UK inflation was above the 3 per cent limit. Mervyn King, the Governor of the BoE, explained that it would be wrong to raise interest rates to counteract this, because he believed that the high inflation rate was merely temporary and to raise rates while the UK economy was in recession could be very damaging. He thus temporarily prioritised growth over immediate inflation, while keeping a watchful stance on anticipated inflation a year or so down the line.

Many financial systems have a hierarchy of objectives whereby price stability is set as the primary objective. Then, so long as that is achieved, the other objectives can be aimed at. The US is going through a debate about its goals at the time of writing. The Federal Reserve is supposed to balance out high growth, maximum employment and stable prices, but policy makers are considering a switch to a hierarchy with inflation prioritised – *see* **Exhibit 7.9**.

Exhibit 7.9

Bernanke moves closer to formal inflation target

FT

Robin Harding

Ben Bernanke's road to an explicit inflation objective for the Federal Reserve has been a long one and he has still not reached the end of it.

Yesterday, however, the Fed chairman took another big step towards setting a numerical target for the US central bank by putting his interpretation of the Fed's inflation mandate into a speech. "FOMC [Federal Open Market Committee] participants generally judge the mandate-consistent inflation rate to be about 2 per cent or a bit below," Mr Bernanke said.

That does not sound dramatic but it is of vital importance because the Fed is moving towards another round of quantitative easing – the

policy of expanding its balance sheet by buying assets to push down long-term interest rates – in order to deal with a sluggish economic recovery that has left US unemployment stuck at 9.6 per cent.

Focusing on a 2 per cent inflation goal tells the world how the Fed will justify another round of quantitative easing and how it will control its size. Mr Bernanke's speech implies that the Fed will buy assets until it is on track to hit its inflation goal.

The number is important for another reason as well: it should help to persuade the public that inflation will return to 2 per cent in the future. That should encourage people to borrow at current low

interest rates and deter any expectations that could be self-fulfilling, of a spiral into deflation.

Mr Bernanke has been pressing for a clear inflation goal since he became Fed chairman in 2006. At his confirmation hearings in 2005, Mr Bernanke extolled the benefits of inflation targets. Most central banks around the world, such as the Bank of England and the European Central Bank, have some kind of numerical inflation goal.

Additional reporting by Chris Giles in London and Edward Luce in Boston

Source: Financial Times, 16/17 October 2010, p. 5. Reprinted with permission.

The independence of central banks

An important question for a government to decide is the degree of freedom it gives its central bank to conduct monetary policy. Is it to be conducted by the central bank's own experts or should elected politicians have the ultimate say on whether interest rates should rise or fall?

There are two types of independence:

- *Instrument independence* The central bank can decide when and how to use monetary policy instruments without political interference.

- *Goal independence* The central bank decides the goals of monetary policy.

Instrument independence is common, but goal independence is rare. The US central bank, the Fed, has both types of independence – politicians do not control the Board of Governors nor the purse strings of the Fed (although they can influence the appointment of some board members). The European Central Bank has an extraordinary degree of independence. The member country governments of the Eurosystem are not permitted to instruct the ECB. The Maastricht Treaty, which established the monetary union, states that the long-term goal of the ECB is price stability, but does not specify what that means, leaving it up to the Executive Board members to decide the target inflation rate. And, of course, the ECB has control over the tools it uses. Furthermore, whereas the US system can be changed by new legislation (if the politicians change the law they can establish control over the Fed), this is more difficult in the Eurozone, because the Eurosystem's charter can be altered only by a revision of the Maastricht Treaty, which requires consent of *all* the signatory countries. In 1997, the Bank of England was given a high degree of instrument independence to decide when and how to raise or lower interest rates (prior to that the Chancellor of the Exchequer had ultimate control). However, the government can in extreme economic circumstances overrule the Bank for a limited period. The inflation goal is still established by the Chancellor.

The advantages of independence

- *Political control can lead to higher inflation* It is argued that politicians often have a short-term perspective driven by the need to impress voters before the next election. This may mean sacrificing a stable price level to achieve immediate improvements in unemployment, growth or house mortgage rates. The populace, also often short-sighted, sees the immediate improvement, but does not grasp the long-term damage wrought when inflation takes off in the low interest rate environment. It is only a year or so later that they suffer the effects of economic instability and the need to bring down inflation. A politically insulated central bank is more likely to take decisions which are beneficial over the long run, even if they cause a little pain now. Thus, instead of politically motivated booms just before elections and busts after them, we see a more stable pattern of growth and inflation.

- *Reduced temptation to support government spending* The central bank regularly buys and sells bonds and Treasury bills previously issued by the government to influence the interest rates banks are charging each other when borrowing to top up their reserves. It is another step to start buying government instruments direct when the government wishes to expand its spending. In buying them the central bank will create new money which the government will put into the economy when it buys new bridges, for instance, or pays out more in social security. This can be dangerously inflationary. It is what Zimbabwe did in the 2000s – resulting in inflation of millions of percent per year.

- *Politicians lack expertise* Central bank employees have much more skill in this area than the average politician, or even the above-average politician.

The disadvantages of independence

- *Undemocratic* The central bank makes important decisions that affect everyone and yet it is in the control of people who are not accountable at the ballot box. Politicians control fiscal policy (government spending and taxation); perhaps they should also control monetary policy so that the two can be better coordinated. But would such consolidating of the levers of economic power really bring about a better result?

- **Central banks fail from time to time** In the early 1930s central banks failed to put money into the financial system at crucial moments. They also failed to analyse and act upon the build-up to the 2008 crisis, in particular the excessive borrowing and rise in asset (e.g. house) prices. Are these failures of independence? Were there wiser political voices outside the central bank anticipating problems and calling for robust countervailing action? I can't speak of the 1930s politicians, but my memory of 2006 and 2007 is not peppered with smart politicians' warnings of doom.

Some academic research has investigated the correlation between independence and inflation performance and concluded that more independence leads to lower inflation without lower real economic performance (unemployment or output).[5]

Political independence is so highly prized by Eurozone policy makers that there was a storm in 2010 when the ECB was persuaded to purchase European government bonds to help the financial rescue of Greece in May and to try to avoid one in Portugal and Spain in December. Even though this did not put more money into the financial system because the ECB sold other securities to offset the potential monetary boost, it was seen as bestowing a favour on a few countries by propping up their bond markets – *see* **Exhibit 7.10**.

Exhibit 7.10

Bank's U-turn stokes concern over political interference   FT

By **Ralph Atkins** in Frankfurt

The European Central Bank rode to the eurozone's rescue yesterday after executing one of the sharpest policy U-turns in its 12 year history, but in the process raising concerns about its politicisation in the wake of Europe's financial crises.

Purchases of eurozone government bonds on an undisclosed scale – a step regarded as unthinkable until recently – began just hours after the ECB's 3.15am announcement of a package of measures to shore-up the eurozone's stability.

The controversial step provoked rare public dissent within the ECB's decision-making government council. Axel Weber, Germany's Bundesbank president and known ECB "hawk", criticised the move "even in this exceptional situation", in an interview due to be published today in a German newspaper.

The ECB also said it was stepping up the provision of emergency liquidity to banks by reintroducing unlimited offers of three and six month funds, and teaming up

with the US Federal Reserve and other central banks to provide extra dollar liquidity.

The action threw into reverse the ECB's "exit strategy", by which it had been undoing gradually the exceptional measures it had taken since the collapse of Lehman Brothers in September 2008.

As such, they were a clear show of force by the eurozone's monetary guardian. But the package was controversial because it took the ECB significantly closer, if not beyond, the boundary separating fiscal and monetary policy in Europe's monetary union – creating risks to the central bank's independence.

"The more you are part of the game, the harder it is to be independent," said Jörg Krämer, chief economist at Commerzbank in Frankfurt.

Speaking in Basel, Jean-Claude Trichet, the ECB president, said that despite Mr Weber's objections, the ECB's governing council had approved the bond purchases by

an "overwhelming majority" and he denied the ECB had succumbed to political interference.

The ECB had delayed its decisions until after European Union finance ministers had reached agreement, in the early hours of yesterday, on separate emergency funding facilities. The co-ordinated approach almost certainly boosted the impact of yesterday's moves. But the delay could have added to last week's financial market volatility.

By intervening in the public and private debt markets, the ECB has now moved closer to the large-scale outright asset purchase schemes launched by the US Fed and UK Bank of England. But there are also big differences. The ECB's "securities markets programme" is aimed at easing tensions in financial markets and is not a "quantitative easing" programme to boost economic growth or inflation.

The ECB's refusal to give details on the programme's scale were part of efforts to stress its techni-

▶

---

[5] See references at the end of the chapter

Exhibit 7.10 continued

cal nature, and yesterday's market reaction suggested it could have a big impact even with modest purchases. Asset purchases will also be "neutralised" with the liquidity injected into financial system reabsorbed elsewhere by the ECB, perhaps into fixed-term deposits, to reduce inflation risks.

That strictly monetary focus of the programme could have helped Mr Trichet persuade other "hawks" on the governing council to agree to the plan. However, they might also have been persuaded by the sheer scale of the crisis in the eurozone, such as the surge in the financial market nervousness on Friday.

Source: *Financial Times*, 11 May 2010, p. 8. Reprinted with permission.

Quantitative easing

In extreme circumstances a central bank may find that interest rates have been reduced to the lowest level they could go and yet still economic activity does not pick up. People are so shocked by the crisis – increased chance of unemployment, lower house prices, lower business profits – that they cut their consumption and investment regardless of being able to borrow at very low interest rates. This happened in 2009 and 2010. Annualised short-term interest rates in Eurozone countries were less than 1 per cent, in the UK they were 0.5 per cent and in the US they were between 0 per cent and 0.25 per cent. Clearly, low short-term interest rates were not enough to get the economy moving, even with the additional boost of government deficit spending to the extent that up to one-eighth of all spending was from government borrowing.

In response another policy tool was devised: **quantitative easing**. This involves the central bank electronically creating money ('printing money') which is then used to buy assets from investors in the market. Thus pension funds, insurance companies, non-financial firms, etc. can sell assets, mostly long-term government bonds (but can include mortgage-backed securities and corporate bonds), and their bank accounts are credited with newly created money. This raises bank reserves, allowing more lending in the economy. Furthermore, the increased demand for government bonds raises their prices and lowers interest rates along the yield curve. In the UK the BoE bought £200 billion of such assets during 2009 and 2010. The Fed bought $1,750 billion bonds (mostly mortgage-backed and government), then ran a second round (called QE2) in 2010–2011 of $600 billion. There is much discussion about the effectiveness and dangers of quantitative easing – *see* **Exhibit 7.11**.

Exhibit 7.11

The Fed is right to turn on the tap

FT

Martin Wolf

The sky is falling, scream the hysterics: the Federal Reserve is pouring forth dollars in such quantities that they will soon be worthless. Nothing could be further from the truth. As in Japan, the policy known as "quantitative easing" is far more likely to prove ineffective than lethal. It is a leaky hose, not a monetary Noah's Flood.

So what is the Fed doing? Why is it doing it? Why are the criticisms ludicrous? What should the Fed be doing, instead?

The answer to the first is clear. As the Fed stated on November 3, "to promote a stronger pace of economic recovery and to help ensure that inflation, over time, is at levels consistent with its mandate, the [federal open market] committee decided today to expand its holdings of securities. The committee will maintain its existing policy of reinvesting principle payments from its securities holdings. In addition, the committee intends to purchase a further $600bn of longer-term

Treasury securities by the end of the second quarter of 2011, a pace of about $75bn per month."

Ben Bernanke, the Fed chairman, gave the rationale in a speech last month. He pointed out that US unemployment is far above any reasonable estimate of equilibrium. Moreover, prospective economic growth makes it unlikely that this will change over the course of 2011. This is bad enough, but what makes it worse is that underlying inflation has fallen close to

▶

Exhibit 7.11 continued

1 per cent, in spite of the expansion of the Fed's balance sheet, over which so many tears were shed. Expectations of inflation were well anchored, he added, but that might change once deflation gripped. Given the slack, that might not be far away.

The Fed, added the chairman, has a dual mandate, to foster maximum unemployment and price stability. Doing nothing would be incompatible with this obligation. The only question is what is to be done. The answer is the proposed purchases of Treasury bonds. This simply extends classic open market operations up the yield curve. It would also only expand the Fed's balance sheet by about a quarter, or around 4 per cent of gross domestic product. Is the US really on the same road as the Weimar Republic? In a word, no.

It is hardly a surprise that Wolfgang Schäuble, finance minister of Germany, thinks differently. He describes the US growth model as in "deep crisis", adding that "it's not right when the Americans accuse China of manipulating exchange rates and then push the dollar exchange rate lower by opening up the flood gates". Presumably, he believes that, in a proper world, the US would be forced to allow the deflationary route imposed upon Greece and Ireland instead. This is not going to happen. Nor should it.

Boiled down, the criticisms of the Fed come down to two: its policies are leading to hyperinflation; and they are "beggar my neighbour", in consequence, if not intention.

The first of these criticisms is not just wrong, but weird. The essence of the contemporary monetary system is creation of money, out of nothing, by private banks' often foolish lending. Why is such privatisation of a public function right and proper, but action by the central bank, to meet pressing public need, a road to catastrophe? When banks will not lend and the broad money supply is barely growing, that is just what it should be doing.

The hysterics then add that it is impossible to shrink the Fed's balance sheet fast enough to prevent excessive monetary expansion. That is also nonsense. If the economy took off, nothing would be easier. Indeed, the Fed explained precisely what it would do in its monetary report to Congress last July. If the worst came to the worst, it could just raise reserve requirements.

Now turn to the argument that the Fed is deliberately weakening the dollar. Any moderately aware person knows that the Fed's mandate does not include the external value of the dollar. Those governments that have piled up an extra $6,800bn in foreign reserves since January 2000, much of it in dollars, are consenting adults. Not only did no one ask China, the foremost example, to add the huge sum of $2,400bn to its reserves, but many strongly asked it not to do so.

It is also simply false to argue that the weakening dollar is due to Fed policies alone. Indeed, anyone with half a brain should realise that the US can no longer combine a large trade deficit with a manageable fiscal position. Those who want their US bonds to stay sound should welcome anything that helps the US expand domestic demand and rebalance its external position. Current US monetary policies are, contrary to Mr Schäuble's views, simply the yang to the yin of east Asian mercantilism.

More fundamentally, market forces, not monetary policy, are pushing global rebalancing, as the private sector tries to put its money where it sees the opportunities. The Fed's monetary policies merely add a twist. Instead of all the futile bleating, what was needed was a co-ordinated appreciation of the currencies of the emerging economies. The fault here does not lie with the US. I sympathise strongly with a Brazil or a South Africa, but not with China.

The sky is not falling. But this does not mean the Fed's policies are the best possible. It is probable that any impact on the yields on medium-term bonds will have a modest economic effect. It would be far better if the Fed could shift inflation expectations upwards, by issuing a commitment to offset a prolonged period of below-target inflation with one of above-target inflation. A decision to monetise additional government spending might be an even more effective tool. Equally necessary is a plan to accelerate the restructuring of the overhang of excessive debt. But, in the absence of co-operation with the newly elected Congress, what the Fed is doing is, alas, about the most we can do now expect, though it should have dared to do more. Meanwhile "sound" people will shriek that the sky is falling only to be surprised that it is not. We have seen this play before – in Japan in the 1990s. Japan fell into chronic deflation, instead.

Source: *Financial Times*, 10 November 2010, p. 13. Reprinted with permission.

Safety and soundness of the financial system

The collapse of many banks into insolvency in 2008 is a reminder of the vulnerability of these institutions. The mere fear of a bank collapse can lead to recession/depression as a damaging wave of lowered confidence in financial institutions sweeps through economies. A hundred years ago banks would fail on a regular basis, but today we have a number of mechanisms to reassure people and businesses that their money is safe within the banking system. Some of these mechanisms were found wanting in the recent financial crisis and so policy makers are currently looking for fixes for these. Nevertheless, the modern system is generally far safer than it was 100 years ago.

Depositor insurance

Bank runs occur when depositors fear that because a bank holds in cash or near-cash only a fraction of the total deposits, if, say, 20 per cent of depositors want to take their money in cash the bank would not be able to pay and could be declared bust. Most of the time people are sanguine about this problem because they know that on a typical day the amount of net withdrawals (i.e. money taken from the bank minus money put into accounts at that bank) is a minuscule proportion of total deposits. This all relies on psychology: people have to have a great deal of confidence that the bank will be able to pay out when they want their money back. The trouble arises when something disturbs that confidence. In the film *It's a Wonderful Life* George (James Stewart) loses $8,000 of the bank's money. News that the bank might be in trouble leaks out and people queue up to demand their cash. The bank cannot pay everyone immediately despite there being plenty of value in the bank in the form of house mortgages. The story was repeated in 2007 in the UK (without Clarence, the Angel!) when news spread that Northern Rock, a building society turned bank, might be unable to repay depositors. Panicked depositors queued around the block in towns and cities up and down the country to take out their money.

Losing one bank to a run, caused either by rational or irrational fear and rumour, is bad enough, but the problem stretches further than that because the bank subject to a run is likely to have lent other banks money or have other interbank transactions outstanding, e.g. it might be due to pay large sums on a number of derivatives deals. Once it feels under pressure from its depositors it might withdraw money it holds with other banks to raise some cash, causing one or two of them to have liquidity problems. They might then collapse, leading to yet more banks (which have lent to these banks or hold deposits from these banks) coming under pressure. And so a domino effect might flow through the banking system.

One way to reduce the risk of bank runs (and to make the system fairer for the innocent depositors) is for the government or some regulatory body to step in and say they will guarantee that depositors will be repaid even if the bank cannot do so. In the case of Northern Rock the UK government had to step in and guarantee all deposits without a limit on how much it would pay out to any one depositor. This was an extreme situation; normally a limit is set. Thus, in the European scheme the limit is €100,000 per depositor. It is thought that people with large deposits are sophisticated enough to look after themselves, to be able to assess the bank's true financial status, and so should avoid high-risk banks, or at least demand a premium return for the additional risk. This policy does have a drawback though. In the autumn of 2010 corporations transferred billions of euros from their deposits in Irish banks because they were afraid the whole system was about to collapse and they saw the €100,000 of insurance as peanuts in comparison with their deposits. To some extent this fear became self-fulfilling as Irish banks lost cash and could not replace it other than through borrowing more from the ECB (see lender of last resort function below). Eventually the Irish financial system had to be rescued by the International Monetary Fund, European countries and the ECB.

In the US, the insurer of deposits is not the Fed but the **Federal Deposit and Insurance Corporation (FDIC)**, which pays out up to $250,000 per depositor. In the UK, until the Northern Rock crisis the **Financial Services Compensation Scheme** (outside of BoE) paid £30,000 in full and 90 per cent of the next £20,000. Because many depositors held more than £30,000 they knew that they were not fully covered and so rushed to withdraw their money from Northern Rock. Today the Scheme pays out full compensation up to the maximum of £85,000, which covers the vast majority of depositors.

Lender of last resort

Another safety net for banks and their depositors is the **lender of last resort** function of the central bank: to prevent a bank failure leading on to other bank failures the central bank will step in to provide reserves when no one else will lend to the banks. Following the September 11 2001 World Trade Center attack many cheques were stuck on grounded aircraft and so a number of banks missed an inflow of money for a few days, thus their reserves declined. Furthermore, bank customers increased their demand for cash. The Federal Reserve kept the banking system going by adding $38 billion through repurchase agreements to the banks that needed money to restore their reserve levels. It also increased its discount window lending by 200-fold to $45 billion. The terrorists did not bring down the financial system.

In 2008, the sub-prime crisis produced fear among the banks. They did not know the extent of another bank's exposure to the sub-prime mortgage instrument risk. In response they held onto cash and refused to lend it to other banks. The ECB and the Fed therefore provided very large volumes of short-term funds to the banks so that they could maintain reserve levels and not run out of cash.

Note that the lender of last resort function is not there all the time – it is for when the central bank governors judge there to be an emergency. Also, not every bank will be bailed out – many will be left to fail depending on the route they took to get to a poor liquidity or solvency position (was it fecklessness or bad luck, for example) or whether the bank's failure will cause systemic collapse of the banking industry.

It is necessary to have both the lender of last resort role and deposit insurance schemes because insurance tends to cover only about 1 per cent of the outstanding deposits – there are many financial deals, usually between banks, which dwarf retail deposits. These financial and corporate institutions need reassurance that the central bank will not permit a failure due to a bank running short of reserves – a liquidity crisis.

In the recent financial crisis central banks found many ways to lend to the banks. In the UK, for example, the BoE introduced the Special Liquidity Scheme in 2008 which allowed banks to exchange, for up to three years, bonds backed by mortgage payments (securitised bonds) for UK Treasury bills. These could then be sold when the bank needed extra reserves. The BoE also relaxed the rules on the type of securities that can be used as collateral in repos, i.e. beyond government securities. The Fed bought $1.25 trillion of mortgage-backed securities in 2009 to keep the mortgage market going – no one else would buy. It also allowed banks to draw down overnight loans from the Fed using some pretty risky securities as collateral (the Fed normally insists on US government bills and bonds as collateral) – *see* **Exhibit 7.12.**

Exhibit 7.12

Crisis-hit banks flooded Fed with junk

By Francesco Guerrera in New York and Robin Harding in Washington

Banks flooded the Federal Reserve with billions of dollars in "junk bonds" and other low-grade collateral in exchange for much-needed liquidity during the crisis, as the financial sector struggled under a crippling credit crunch, new data show.

More than 36 per cent of the cumulative collateral pledged to the US central bank in return for overnight funding under Primary Dealer Credit Facility was equities or bonds ranked below investment grade. A further 17 per cent was unrated credit or loans, according to a Financial Times analysis of Fed data released this week.

Only 1 per cent of the collateral was Treasury bonds which are normally used in transactions between banks and the monetary authorities.

The Fed created the PDCF in March 2008 after the demise of Bear Stearns to ease investment banks' liquidity problems. At the time, it

allowed banks to pledge only investment grade-rated collateral.

But after the failure of talks to save Lehman paved the way for its bankruptcy, the Fed broadened the collateral requirements to include any asset that can be used in the tri-party repo system.

Investment banks responded by using their inventory of equities and other low-grade securities to borrow from the Fed. The Fed protected itself by imposing larger "haircuts" on riskier securities and emphasises that all of its emergency lending was paid back in full with interest.

Within a day of easing the collateral requirements, Credit Suisse had borrowed $1bn from the PDCF, using it for the first of only two times, against a collateral portfolio that was made up of 91 per cent equity.

Credit Suisse declined to comment but people familiar with the situation said the two deals were

tests to check whether the system was working.

By the following Monday, 41 per cent off all collateral pledged against PDCF borrowing by several banks was equity, and another 11 per cent was subinvestment grade bonds. At its peak – on September 29 2008 – the Fed had exposure to $86bn of equity and subinvestment grade debt as PDCF collateral.

Morgan Stanley and Merrill Lynch were among the largest pledgers of low-grade collateral in the turbulent weeks that followed the collapse of Lehman Brothers in September 2008.

Morgan Stanley and Merrill declined to comment, but people close to the situation stressed that the loans had been repaid in full and that the collateral met the Fed's requirements.

Source: Financial Times, 3 December 2010, p. 1. Reprinted with permission.

The European Central Bank also felt obliged to help banks unable to borrow in the financial markets. But by 2010 it was worried that some banks were addicted to obtaining money from the ECB and totally unable to obtain it commercially – *see* **Exhibit 7.13**.

Exhibit 7.13

Fears grow over banks addicted to ECB funding

FT

Ralph Atkins and David Oakley

In November last year, Jean-Claude Trichet, European Central Bank president, had a blunt message for bankers and politicians.

Addressing the annual European banking congress in Frankfurt's palatial 19th century Alte Oper building, he warned that emergency measures were all very well, "but if their use is prolonged, they can lead to dependence and even addiction".

Ten months later, evidence is growing that "addiction" by banks in eurozone countries such as Portugal, Ireland and Greece to ECB liquidity support remains high, and may even have increased.

That is in spite of the improvement in the global economic climate and the boost to confidence in the eurozone financial system that July's bank "stress test" results were supposed to bring.

"In some countries, ECB funding remains critical to the stability of the financial system" says Nick Matthews, European economist at Royal Bank of Scotland.

After the collapse of Lehman Brothers in late 2008, the ECB started matching in full eurozone banks' demand for liquidity for periods of up to a year. At times, as a result of the emergency strategy – called "enhanced credit support" by the ECB – the total amount lent soared as high as €900bn ($1,158bn).

Much of the borrowing reflected the paralysis in the financial markets: banks could only borrow from the ECB. But there was also opportunistic borrowing. In June last year the central bank lent €442bn in 12-month liquidity, the highest amount ever injected into the financial system in a single ECB

operation, as banks bid heavily for funds that they could use to earn higher returns elsewhere. Since June this year, when that €442bn was repaid, ECB figures show overall lending has fallen gradually. With market interest rates lower than the 1 per cent charged by the ECB, the attractiveness of its liquidity has fallen.

But some banks have been unable to shake the habit. The ECB does not give figures on lending by country. Instead analysts have compiled their own geographical breakdown using data issued by national centre banks in the 16 eurozone countries. These show steep falls recently in countries such as Germany and Austria, but stabilisation at high levels, or even increases in the "peripherals" – Spain, Portugal, Greece and Ireland.

In August, the amount borrowed by Greek banks crept up to €96bn, more than twice as much as a year earlier. Portugal held steady at about €50bn.

Even national data do not show clearly what exactly is happening. Ireland's high figure almost certainly reflects use of ECB liquidity by subsidiaries of foreign banks based in the country. Spain's figures look high – but much less so relative to the size of its economy or banking system. Elsewhere, it is unclear whether the problems are general or focused on a just a few banks.

It is apparent, however, that at least some banks have become locked in a cycle of dependency – and no coincidence that they are mainly in those eurozone countries where worries about spiralling public debt also have been greatest. Weaknesses in banking systems have

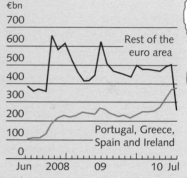

Dependence growing on borrowing from the ECB
€bn

intensified worries about the eventual cost to taxpayers of the financial crisis. In turn, the bleak economic prospects of countries facing a severe fiscal crunch and a loss of competitiveness relative to Germany have reinforced concerns about those countries' banking systems

The ECB, although urging fiscal discipline and the strengthening of bank systems, does not expect the cycle to be broken soon.

Earlier this month, Mr Trichet announced that the ECB would continue to match in full banks' demand for liquidity for periods of three months or less until at least the start of 2011. Inter-dealer brokers say in the peripheral countries there is little lending beyond one-week between banks in private markets because of continuing worries over counterparty risk.

"The addiction of many European banks, particularly those in the periphery, to the ECB for lending will be hard to break," says Padhraic Garvety, global head of developed markets rates strategy at ING.

Exhibit 7.13 continued

"Private markets remain severely stressed with banks not prepared to risk lending to many institutions, which mean these institutions will have to borrow from the ECB."

In a Financial Times interview last week Mr Trichet argued "enhanced credit support" was being phased out, noting that the ECB was no longer providing six-month and 12-month liquidity. As a result, whether it likes it or not, the ECB is being forced by the weaknesses of the eurozone "periphery" to maintain a policy of unlimited liquidity that is having similar effects on the economy as "quantitative easing" in the US or UK.

"Despite the differences in philosophy between the US Federal Reserve and the ECB, the final impact of both their strategies is to put a lid on long term interest rates – and that helps the economy," says Gilles Moec, European economist at Deutsche Bank.

So far, the ECB sees no inflationary dangers, but that could change. The eurozone economic recovery in the first half of this year surpassed expectations, and appears not to have slowed dramatically in the third quarter.

Source: Financial Times, 14 September 2010, p. 37. Reprinted with permission.

An extreme form of support for a bank is for the government to nationalise it, as happened with Northern Rock in 2008 and Anglo Irish Bank in 2009. While not fully nationalised, more than 80 per cent of Royal Bank of Scotland's shares and 43 per cent of Lloyds Bank shares are now owned by the UK taxpayer.

Too big to fail

The danger with having a lender of last resort facility available to banks is that it might encourage banks to take high risks. If their bets are successful then the managers and their shareholders reap the reward; if they fail they are bailed out by the central bank or government. This is a moral hazard problem – encouraging bad behaviour. The problem for the rest of society is not too great when it comes to small banks, whose failure would not cause knock-on failures of other banks or financial institutions. The authorities often let these go bust and impose pain on the managers (lose jobs), shareholders (lose all value in their shares) and bond holders (bonds become worthless), to encourage other banks to believe that they will not be saved regardless of incompetence or recklessness. The problem arises with the large banks, which have numerous interbank and other borrowings and derivative transactions which could pose a threat to the entire system should they fail – because if they go then many of their counterparties might lose so much in the fallout (liquidity-wise or solvency-wise) that they fail too. These are the banks that pose a systemic risk. Rather than size being the relevant criterion, we should really focus on degree of importance and significance of the bank, dubbed 'too important to fail'. The phrase 'too big to fail' has stuck with the media, but increasingly policy makers are using Sifi – systemically important financial institutions.

The regulators frequently face a difficult decision. For example, in 2008 Bear Stearns was saved because it was seen as necessary to step in and save the bank. Then along comes the failing Lehman Brothers asking for help. Rightly or wrongly the authorities felt that Lehman could be allowed to go without money from the central bank or government being pumped in to save it. Many now believe this was an error, that Lehman posed a very high systemic risk which went unrecognised until it was too late (more on this story in Chapter 16).

Governments and regulators are grappling with the problem of having so many banks that are too big to fail. Should we break them up into smaller units so that each individual unit can go bust without any systemic/domino effect? Should we tax them more because of the costs they impose on society? Should we impose very high capital reserve ratios and liquidity reserve ratios (and make them even higher for the most risky activities) to reduce the likelihood of liquidation? Should we introduce **living wills**, whereby banks have to report regularly to the authorities on how they would put into effect an orderly winding down of the business as well as how they would plan for recovery in a crisis?[6] – *see* **Exhibit 7.14**.

---

[6] A resolution regime would need to be established and authority to control a bank's demise be given to a resolution agency. This might involve forcing holders of bank bonds to accept losses alongside shareholders.

Exhibit 7.14

Banks' survival rates should improve with living wills   FT

By Charles Goodhart

In the aftermath of the financial crisis, there has been much concern about the massive bail-out costs. We believe that the authorities, under the exceptional circumstances in late 2008, had no choice but to support the financial system.

But, if anything, the handling of the current financial crisis has reinforced too big to fail doctrine. So how can one reduce moral hazard and reduce expectations of future bail-outs?

We propose the use of living wills to curtail too-big-to-fail, perhaps even thereby allowing systemically important banks, such as Citigroup, Goldman Sachs or Barclays, to fail or, at least, to be unwound. The aim is to put in place, ex ante, conditions that would allow a wider range of options beyond having the whole bank rescued.

In the recent banking crisis, the authorities, almost without exception, acted purely on the basis of narrow national interest

Living wills can play a vital role in the post-crisis world. Take the definition of a systemically important financial intermediary (SIFI). The need for special treatment of such SIFIs plays, for example, a central role in the recently enacted Dodd-Frank financial reform act in the US. But we do not know how to distinguish between a SIFI and an intermediary that is not a SIFI, and we suspect that the distinction between what is systemic, and what is not, will be fluid, varying over time depending on conditions. The fuzzy outlines of the definition of "systemic" are likely to force upon regulatory authorities more discre-

tionary decisions than either they, or the regulated, will find comfortable.

What we do know, however, is that the set of systemic financial intermediaries overlaps the set of cross-border financial intermediaries. So, a need to resolve a systemic financial institution in difficulties will imply an equivalent requirement for handling cross-border problems. Yet, when there was a need for such resolution in the recent crisis – for example, Lehman, RBS, Fortis and the Icelandic banks – the authorities, almost without exception, acted purely on the basis of narrow national interest. This gross incompatability, between the (global) cross-border reality and national regulatory/legal attempts to respond, represents a glaring weakness in the world's financial system. It should not be allowed to persist. So how do we proceed to reconcile the global, cross-border reality of SIFIs with the inevitable national focus of regulation? Perhaps the most important new instrument in the global armoury for this purpose will be the requirement for cross-border SIFIs to complete a living will.

What are the key elements of such living wills? First, there should be discussions between the senior management of a bank and its supervisors about requiring a cross-border SIFI to simplify its often opaque structure, particularly to facilitate it being wound down in a really serious crisis. But before that stage may be reached, the living will will also require the bank to make contingent funding and de-risking plans to recover. Next, if that should fail, credible resolution plans should be drawn up to keep a bank alive, if needed. In the case of international banks, these plans could include a burden sharing mechanism for central banks (liquidity support) and ministries

of finance (capital support). The burden sharing should be agreed on an institution by institution basis. Third, a bankruptcy scenario might help to bring possible shortcomings in deposit guarantee schemes and inconsistencies between insolvency regimes to the forefront of attention before the event pressurising the authorities (including lawmakers) to tackle such inconsistencies occurs.

Countries should dig into the legal nitty-gritty and design a common and credible cross-border insolvency regime

But we believe that living wills, though an essential future component of a satisfactory global financial system, will not be enough by themselves. In addition, there needs to be a common insolvency framework, should (parts of) an institution need to be put into liquidation. A major barrier, at present, is the patchwork of different legal structures, controlling such insolvencies, in all such countries. The insolvency procedure for international banks is currently a nightmare for depositors, creditors, and shareholders, but a paradise for insolvency lawyers.

Could we not take this opportunity to devise, introduce and enact identical laws in all major countries? There are precedents; the acceptance in the law of many countries of the close-out netting clauses of an International Swaps and Derivatives Association master agreement for settling outstanding derivative contracts in the event of one of the parties' failure to make a payment or bankruptcy is one.

▶

Exhibit 7.14 continued

Even so, countries should dig into the legal nitty-gritty and design a common and credible cross-border insolvency regime for systemic banks, that is if countries really want to curtail the current too big –

or, too complex – to fail practice.

Charles Goodhart is emeritus professor of banking and finance at the London School of Economics. This piece was co-authored by Dirk Schoenmaker,

dean of the Duisenberg School of Finance in Amsterdam

Source: *Financial Times*, 10 August 2010, p. 30. Reprinted with permission.

The too big to fail problem is particularly acute with an international bank made up of branches (where capital and liquid assets are kept in a single country) rather than a collection of self-sufficient subsidiaries – *see* **Exhibit 7.15**.

Exhibit 7.15

Multinationals weigh up Turner proposals

Brooke Masters

Large multinational banks that organise themselves as a constellation of self-sufficient subsidiaries could be candidates for lower capital requirements than those that operate as fully integrated global groups, Lord Turner, chairman of the UK Financial Services Authority, said yesterday.

Lord Turner's proposal, discussed at a UK forum on how to deal with banks that are seen as "too big to fail", could offer significant competitive advantages to banks such as Santander, owner of the Abbey National in the UK, and to a lesser extent Standard Chartered.

By contrast, banks that rely on integrated treasury functions with complex reporting and legal lines that cross national borders are likely to face higher capital require-

ments to counteract what are seen as the greater risks they pose. Such banks could well include Barclays, the global investment banks and, to a lesser extent, HSBC.

"There may be a trade-off here between greater internal separation and higher levels of whole group capital," Lord Turner said.

Traditionally, UK regulators have allowed the branches and subsidiaries of large multinational banks to use capital and liquidity held at the group level to satisfy national requirements.

But the financial crisis revealed the problems with this approach. The collapse of Lehman Brothers left its UK subsidiary with insufficient capital to even pay daily bills. And when the Icelandic banks collapsed, the UK government had to step in to protect UK depositors

who had money in branches and subsidiaries in this country.

The FSA has already begun pressuring non-UK banks to hold more capital and liquid assets in the UK as part of its tighter supervision of banks in the wake of the crisis. And regulators around the world have begun talking about higher overall capital requirements for systemically important groups.

Antonio Horta-Osorio, chief executive of Abbey National, conceded the stand-alone subsidiary structure was "more expensive" but argued it had advantages. "It creates a solid liquidity and capital base and makes sure there is appropriate burden-sharing ... This acts as a firewall to prevent contagion."

Source: *Financial Times*, 3 November 2009, p. 20. Reprinted with permission.

Bank supervision

It is important that an authority investigates and approves the appointment of those who operate banks and continues monitoring and surveillance to ensure they are operated well. This is **bank supervision** or **prudential supervision**. Banks can be powerful money-grabbing tools in the hands of crooks. They can also be a temptation to over-ambitious entrepreneurs who may see a large pot of (depositors') money that could be used to invest in speculative ventures. Thus, the authorities (often central banks) license or charter all banks (and other deposit-taking institutions) to ensure that they are run by fit and proper persons. In this way any proposal for a new bank is scrutinised, as are the controllers of the bank. The regulator then requires regular reports and makes regular visits to the banks to ensure that there is compliance with the safety rules. This usually includes aspects shown in **Exhibit 7.16**.

The central bank may also consider whether consumers are sufficiently well protected against unfair selling, bad advice, poor quality products, as well as discrimination (e.g. racial). It may also look at whether the bank's electronic systems are safe against cyber attack, e.g. criminals hacking into accounts and stealing money.

If, on examination, a bank performs badly on any of the CAMELS factors, the regulator will order it to correct its behaviour. In extreme cases the bank will be closed.

It is not always the case that the central bank acts as the main supervisor of banks. In the UK, the Financial Services Authority is the primary bank supervisor until 2013 when responsibility (apart from consumer protection aspects) will be handed over to the BoE.

Capital and liquidity adequacy

Banks know that they would be foolish to lend out all the money they take as deposits. It makes sense to have self-imposed rules on what proportion to keep in cash and what proportion to keep in short-term securities (e.g. money market instruments) that could fairly quickly be turned into cash. However, banks are foolish from time to time and are tempted away from the rational path and therefore need externally imposed rules to prevent them from stepping over the line that takes them into imprudent territory. Holding cash and short-term lending is usually less profitable than long-term lending and so ambitious bankers, looking to boost profits, sometimes transfer more of their resources to long-term lending, leaving only a small buffer of cash or near-cash to meet immediate extraordinary cash outflows should, say, large numbers of depositors insist on a return of their money. In other words, they take excessively high liquidity risk.

The other major risk is solvency risk. This is less to do with running out of cash in the immediate future and more to do with allowing the capital base of the bank to diminish to such an extent that the assets of the bank (loans to customers, etc.) are barely greater than the liabilities (e.g. deposits). In such a situation it would not take too many bad debt write-offs as customers go bust, for example, for the bank to find that it cannot repay all its depositors and other creditors. Other events that could reduce assets below liabilities include a collapse in value of the bank's complex securities holdings, fraud, or the failure of a subsidiary.

Thus, it is possible for a bank to look good on a liquidity perspective – plenty of cash in the vault – but nevertheless its liabilities exceed its assets. Conversely, a bank could have plenty of capital, as assets greatly exceed liabilities, but run out of cash in the short term due to a large outflow over a matter of days. Obviously lowering both liquidity risk and solvency risk is important to the well-being of the financial system.

I remember an impassioned debate in 2008 as one bank after another called on their central banks for funds. The managers would declare that the only issue facing them was a short-term decline in cash balances: they had grown used to drawing loans from the money market on a daily basis and suddenly these were now closed. At first the central banks agreed and supplied the needed cash. There were sceptical voices in the press saying that the loss of bank assets, as households found they could not repay their mortgages and as corporate loans turned sour (particularly those lent to property developers), meant that the buffer of capital was diminishing by the day, to the point where many banks were headed towards negative equity territory. We witnessed a rapid morphing from a liquidity crisis into a bank solvency crisis. As the economy spiralled downwards it became plain for all to see that there was going to be such a volume of loan impairments and financial instrument counterparty defaults that banks desperately needed more equity capital injected into them to widen the gap between assets and liabilities to a safe level.

A safe reserve level

The questions regulators have grappled with for many decades are: what is a safe level for capital reserves? And what is a safe level for liquidity reserves? If we look at capital reserves first we can start our thinking by recognising that some assets held by a bank have little or no risk of default. Obviously, as cash has no risk of default there is no need to keep a capital buffer for this asset. Some types of loans made by banks, e.g. lending to the German, UK or US governments, have some degree

Exhibit 7.16   The CAMELS method of bank inspection

		Examples of questions considered
C	**Capital adequacy**	Does it have sufficient equity capital for the amount of lending it is doing? Are management prepared to obtain additional capital?
A	**Asset quality**	Are the assets held too risky? Is there good diversification? Are there sound processes/systems for controlling risk (e.g. staff are abiding by prudent policies and have limits of the risk exposure they can create)? Is there sufficient provision for bad debts? (The bank examiner can force a write-off)
M	**Management**	is the quality of its management good? Honest and competent at identifying, measuring, monitoring and controlling risk? Are there adequate controls and internal information flows? Good controls to prevent fraud?
E	**Earnings**	Are earnings stable at a reasonably high level? Is the source of earnings high quality?
L	**Liquidity**	Does the bank hold sufficient reserves? Are there plenty of assets that can be converted to cash quickly without serious loss of value? Does the bank have good access to money market loans?
S	**Sensitivity to market risk**	Are management processes good for coping with interest rate risk, exchange rate risk, equity market risk and commodity risk? Is the bank particulary sensitive to these risks?

of risk of default but this is very small. Lending to a manufacturer, however, usually has a fairly high level of default. It is clear that we need different amounts of capital depending on the asset category. Thus, the total of all unsecured corporate loans a bank holds might need to be backed up with, say, 8 per cent of the balance sheet value composed of capital, whereas the loans to local government lending needs to be backed up with only, say, 1.6 per cent of the value in the form of capital.

This line of thought is leading us to the concept of risk-weighted assets. Thus, if the 'normal' capital proportion put aside is 8 per cent for loans such as unsecured corporate debt, this is given a weighting of 100 per cent, i.e. it is not reduced from the full 8 per cent. So a £10 million loan needs the bank to have £800,000 of capital – of course, the bank will also source money from depositors, etc. to lend the £10 million. A total of £10 billion of loans needs £800 million. The weight for mortgages might be only 50 per cent, which means that if the bank holds £5 billion of mortgages it has to back that with capital of £200 million (0.08 × 0.50 × £5bn). The holding of government bills issued by a developing country as bank assets might require only 20 per cent of the full capital safety reserve – the risk weighting is 20 per cent. Thus, a collection of £3 billion of bills will require £3bn × 0.20 × 0.08 = £48 million

Another way of looking at this is to first reduce the asset values by their risk weighting and then take 8 per cent of the risk-weighted value – *see* **Exhibit 7.17**.

Exhibit 7.17 A bank's capital risk weighting

Assets	Full balance sheet value £m	Risk weighting %	Risk weighted value £m
Cash	100	0	0
T-bills	3,000	20	600
Mortgages	5,000	50	2,500
Unsecured loans	10,000	100	10,000
Total	**18,100**		**13,100**

Total capital required: £13,100m × 0.08 = £1,048 million Thus, bank assets must exceed bank liabilities by £1,048 million to withstand the possibility of a substantial proportion becoming bad loans.

Basel I

Capital reserve levels are not just national affairs because banking is international. The 'banker to the central banks' is the Bank for International Settlements, based in Basel, Switzerland. The central bankers gathered together in the 1980s to discuss setting minimum solvency standards applicable to any bank from a member country of the Basel committee. Now the 'Basel rules' have been adopted in more than 100 countries.

To understand the Basel rules you need to first deal with a point of difficulty I have so far skipped over: defining what we mean by capital. The Basel I committee split capital into two: tier 1 and tier 2.

Tier 1:

● Equity capital placed in the bank by shareholders when they purchase shares.
● Additional equity capital created from retained profits over the years.
● Non-cumulative perpetual preference shares. Because they do not form a liability payable should the bank have a bad run of luck – they do not have to be redeemed, nor do dividends have to be paid – they can act as a buffer against a drop in asset values.
● Minority interests in subsidiaries whose accounts are consolidated in the group accounts (less goodwill and other intangible assets).

One half of capital had to be tier 1 (4 per cent of risk-weighted assets), but the other 4 per cent could be tier 2. Tier 2 consisted of various balance sheet elements that might also act as a (less effective) buffer, such as cumulative perpetual preference shares, revaluation reserves and subordinated debt that did not have to repaid for at least five years (being subordinated, on liquidation, depositors and other creditors would be paid first).

Banks regarded as being undercapitalised under the Basel rules might have been seized by national authorities in the worst case. However, it was more likely that the country's regulator insisted will insist on guiding them back to health, which could include rights issues to raise more equity capital, asset sales, subsidiary sales and the sacking of executives.

Basel II

In the late 1990s regulators and bankers concluded that the Basel I rules were too simplistic because they took broad categories of loan and insisted that the same risk weight apply to each. Thus, when any bank from an Organisation for Economic Cooperation and Development (OECD) country borrowed, the lending was regarded as having the same risk weighting (i.e. 20 per cent) as for all other OECD banks, regardless of whether it was a US bank or from a more risky country. The risk weighting for this type of loan was much lower than lending to multinational corporations whose loans were often given a 100 per cent weight, yet most observers would agree that many multinationals are safer borrowers than some banks in some OECD countries. Another bone of contention was that Basel I did not properly differentiate between a loan to a company with a AAA credit rating and one to a company with a much lower rating – they all carried the same weight. This led to a form of **regulatory arbitrage** in which, within a category (same risk weight), banks mostly could be tempted to lend to the riskiest clients because this paid the highest interest without requiring any more capital than a low-risk low-interest-rate loan.

Basel II was launched in the mid-2000s and made much greater use of credit ratings of both government debt and corporate debt to decide weightings. Thus, AAA or AA debt would get a zero weighting, whereas grades of B- or less would get a 150 per cent weighting. It went further and recognised that a high proportion of bank assets did not have credit ratings and so banks were permitted to use 'internal ratings' devised from their own models to risk-weight assets (subject to monitoring by their national central banks). Also, Basel II took account of market risk (the risk that financial market assets, such as securitised bonds, can decrease in price on the markets) and operational risk (the way the bank is run can lead to calamity, e.g. a rogue trader destroys the bank, or there are other operational dangers, e.g. another 9/11 attack could damage a bank's access to finance). Banks were required to disclose some other risks, such as concentration risk (too many eggs in one basket) and liquidity risk.

Also, there are a number of off-balance-sheet assets (and liabilities) for which capital needs to be assigned. Thus, the holding of positions in derivatives, or positions in the foreign exchange market or commodity market, or commercial letters of credit and bank guarantees creates the possibility of loss and so could erode capital. Under Basel II these items were risk-weighted and added to the on-balance-sheet assets.

Unfortunately, Basel II was not a success. Surprise, surprise, once the banks were able to use their own valuation and risk models to influence the regulatory capital level, the amount they held fell. Well, you see, bankers were so smart that they had diversified away much of the risk, or they had bought insurance so that if a loan went bad the insurer paid up. Lower risk, therefore lower risk weighting. Perfect. Except they forgot to account for the possibility of asset returns all going down together (so much for diversification) or for the insurers/derivative counterparties going bust and not paying out.

Basel III

Basel II was rapidly overtaken by events: the financial crisis revealed that many banks had not been cautious enough in setting their capital and liquidity reserves. The regulatory framework simply did not work. The rules were complicated, carefully calculated from detailed formulae, but as with so much in finance, the answers were precisely wrong rather than roughly right. Only five days before Lehman's went bust it had a tier 1 capital ratio of 11 per cent. There was far too much optimism, far too much faith in the reported market value of assets, and far too little recognition of the possibility that the new-fangled financial instruments can lose value overnight and that, when they do so, many banks experience knock-on effects and they all collapse together in an enmeshed mass. Banks had moved so far away from simple deposit taking and lending into weird and dangerous securities that it was difficult for the regulators to keep up. Banks would deliberately structure an obligation so that it could be granted a low risk weighting, even though the bankers knew that the real exposure was high. For example, if you took a group of mortgages that had a risk weighting of 50 per cent and converted it into securitised bonds with a AAA rating, you could sell them to other investors, taking them off the balance sheet. You could then replace the asset by buying other banks' AAA-rated mortgage-backed bonds and you no longer needed to hold much capital reserve for them. Risk just seemed to disappear from the system. There is more on the crisis in Chapter 16.

At the time of writing Basel III is being designed and rolled out. This is much tougher. First, the definition of what can be called capital has been narrowed to exclude virtually everything other than money put in by bank shareholders or kept in the bank on behalf of shareholders from retained earnings. This is called **core tier 1** and leaves out preference shares, unsecured bonds, etc. Second, instead of tier 1 being 4 per cent of risk-weighted assets and tier 2 being 4 per cent of risk-weighted assets we have the requirement that tier 2 capital be completely left out of the picture and that core tier 1 be effectively raised to 7 per cent, from the previous typical level of 2 per cent. The picture is a little more complicated than that – as shown in **Exhibit 7.18**.

Exhibit 7.18	Basel III core tier 1 capital to be held by banks as a percentage of risk-weighted assets

'Minimum'

4.5%

Simply to operate as a bank this is required (up from 2% under Basel II)

'Conservation buffer'

2.5%

Any bank that wants to pay a dividend or bonuses to staff must have 4.5% plus 2.5%

'Countercyclical buffer'

0 – 2.5%

National regulators may impose this extra requirement in boom times to counter the effects of a bubble

'Systemic groups' buffer'

1 – 2%

(estimated, still in discussion)

The systemically important financial institutions (super-sized or key players) that pose a global risk have to hold more

Those undertaking risky activities, especially trading financial instruments such as securitised bonds in the market, face much higher capital requirements under Basel III. The capital reserve levels shown in Exhibit 7.18 are to be required in normal times. In a financial crisis regulators expect the buffer to be partially used up – thus it might fall to the minimum 4.5 per cent level.

These new rules are to be phased in over the period until the end of 2018. For 2013–2015 the minimum (simply to operate as a bank) is to be gradually raised to 4.5 per cent of risk-weighted assets. In the four years after 2015 the conservation buffer will be phased in on top of the minimum until the full 7 per cent is reached. This seems a leisurely timetable, but many central banks have already signalled that they expect their banks to achieve the targets much faster than this – see **Exhibit 7.19**.

Exhibit 7.19

Basel III rules behind StanChart capital raising

FT

Patrick Jenkins

Surprise was the general response of analysts and investors after Standard Chartered unveiled its £3.3bn rights issue.

Why would a bank with strong capital ratios and solid profitability raise fresh capital, when so many other banks with weaker ratios and profitability have insisted they will not tap shareholders?

StanChart is only the second group, after Deutsche Bank, to launch a rights issue following disclosure of the new, tougher Basel III rules on bank capital published last month.

To an extent, there is a bank-specific explanation, given that StanChart's focus on emerging markets gives it strong growth momentum, in contrast with the contraction mode many banks are in following the financial crisis.

"How do we simultaneously take advantage of growth opportunities and meet the new capital requirements?" said Peter Sands, chief executive. "This is the right thing to do. The logic of it all makes sense. Investors understand it."

They might understand it, but they were still surprised. Many had expected StanChart, like most banks, to build up retained earnings over the coming years, and gradually come into line with the new Basel III requirements, which will be phased in by 2019.

Those rules in essence say that a bank's core tier one capital ratio – which measures equity and other core capital as a proportion of risk-weighed assets – should be 7 per cent, with an as-yet undefined top-up, expected to be up to 2 per cent, for big, systemically important banks.

> "This is the right thing to do. The logic of it makes sense. Investors understand it."

By raising a fresh £3.3bn, StanChart will take its existing 9 per cent ratio to about 11 per cent, although changes in the way the ratio is calculated – narrowing the definition of core capital and increasing the risk weightings on some assets – will cut that back to about 10 per cent.

Mr Sands would not say where he wanted the ratio to be, but one person close to the bank said: "In future you will want to operate at 11 or 12 per cent."

Retained earnings should allow the bank to reach that level within a couple of years, bankers said.

Moving to such an inflated level of capital is not just a matter of wanting to maintain a margin of error above the Basel minimum. "For StanChart, which has big operations in Singapore and Hong Kong, the unwritten regulatory rule in those jurisdictions is that the ratio will be at 11 per cent or more," said one adviser. "A lot of regional peers already have higher levels of capital."

That is important in a world where local regulators are demanding more of a focus on local levels of capital and liquidity.

Bank's capital positions

	Market capitalisation (latest)	Core tier one capital ratio % (at Jun 30 2010)	Equity capital raised Since start of banking crisis*
HSBC	£118.7bn	9.9	£13.2bn
Santander	€78.9bn	8.6	€7.2bn
Lloyds Banking Group	£49.4bn	9.0	£35.3bn
Standard Chartered	£39.1bn	9.0	£5.2bn Including £3.3bn announced Oct13
Barclays	£35.2bn	10.0	£4.0bn
Royal Bank of Scotland	£27.6bn	10.5	£32.8bn

* Includes right issues, placements and open offers
Source: Thomson Reuters Datastream; Dealogic

▶

Exhibit 7.19 continued

After the collapse of Lehman Brothers two years ago, and the squabble between countries, particularly the UK and US over the bank's assets, regulators are insistent that multinational groups must not hoard all their eggs in one central basket.

Analysts at Credit Suisse said on Wednesday that StanChart's previous level of capital, though relatively robust, would have been insufficient to maintain the level of growth evident in the first half of the year, when risk-weighted assets expanded by an annualised 18 per cent, and at the same time hoard capital to build up capital ratios.

The peculiarities of StanChart's business focus, and its relatively cautious financial management, limited the read-across for the likelihood of capital raising by other banks, analysts said.

HSBC, the closest parallel, is more strongly capitalised already, with an existing core tier one ratio of close to 10 per cent, and less marked asset growth.

But banks' share prices on Wednesday looked like a proxy for the market's view of their relative strength.

Analysts highlighted capital weaknesses at French banks, particularly Crédit Agricole, but also Société Générale, whose shares were among the biggest fallers among European banks. Among UK peers, Barclays was the weak performer, although its management is known to believe there is no need to raise fresh equity and is planning instead to boost capital with retained profits.

"So far," said one investment banker who has worked on a recent rights issue, "everybody has been saying 'we don't need any money, we don't need any money, we don't need any money.' I'm curious to see what impact the StanChart rights issue has on those views."

Source: Financial Times, 14 October 2010, p. 21. Reprinted with permission.

Some countries have already been explicit in stating that they will go further than the Basel committee recommendations. Switzerland, with bank assets many times greater than national GDP, is insisting that UBS and Credit Suisse expand the conservation buffer from 2.5 per cent to 8.5 per cent. However, three percentage points of that may be in the form of a new type of capital called **contingent convertible (CoCos)** instruments. These behave like bonds, paying a coupon, but convert to equity if a bank's capital ratio falls below a predetermined level. The Swiss are also insisting on a 6 per cent systemic groups' buffer, rather than 1–2 per cent. That is a total of 19 per cent of risk-weighted assets as a capital buffer! At least it does not intend to add a counter-cyclical buffer as well.[7] UK regulators have signalled that UK banks will also be subject to higher capital ratios than under Basel II – the current expectation is that 10 per cent will be the minimum core tier 1 ratio.

The Basel III rules are already resulting in shifts in banks' balance sheets – *see* **Exhibit 7.20.**

Exhibit 7.20

Basel rules spark mitigation drives   **FT**

Megan Murphy and **Brooke Masters**

With global reforms set to force banks to hold more capital against riskier kinds of financial assets, the world's biggest investment banks have begun to embrace a new buzzword: mitigation.

The Basel III rules endorsed by the Group of 20 leading economies last week may be squeezing banks on multiple fronts. But one of the most difficult changes to gauge is how the rules will inflate banks' risk-weighted assets, and whether lenders can trim balance sheets without hurting their bottom lines.

Over the third-quarter results season, most leading banks disclosed projections of how the new rules would increase their RWAs, with estimates ranging from a 60–70 per cent uplift at some of the big Swiss banks, to 20–30 per cent at JPMorgan Chase, and as much as 80 per cent at "pureplay" investment banks such as Morgan Stanley.

But by mitigating – selling off or otherwise reducing the amount of riskier assets held – most banks also believe that they can limit

▶

---

[7] Switzerland, as a small country, has to be very careful because the assets of its banks are many times annual GDP. A slip by them could bankrupt the entire nation, as happened to Iceland.

Exhibit 7.20 continued

the impact of the reforms without significantly harming earnings.

Some of the easiest ways for banks to reduce their RWAs is to shut down or limit their exposure to business lines that will attract a higher risk weighting, such as so-called correlation trading, structured credit and asset securitisation.

Steering derivatives trading through centrally cleared exchanges, rather than over the counter trading, can also have a big impact.

McKinsey, the global consultancy, says that the rule-changes will also force banks to spend far more on calculating and tracking risk. The average mid-sized European bank, for example, will spend between €45m and €70m simply on IT and people to comply with the new regulations.

Financial institutions will almost certainly try to substitute similar but lower-risk products wherever possible, the consultancy says.

Bankers may well try to shift short-term corporate lending from receivables financing to factoring, which has a lower risk-weighting and therefore requires less capital, the report says. They may also try to convince large corporate borrowers to shift from loans to bonds because the latter generate fees without adding to the stock of assets that must be supported by capital.

McKinsey also argues that banks can cut their requirements by using more sophisticated measures of risk and new systems to allocate liquidity based on potential profits.

Source: Financial Times, 16 November 2010, p. 21. Reprinted with permission.

Basel III on liquidity risk

Basel III also deals with liquidity – the ability to pay out cash on deposit withdrawals and other outflows of cash while satisfying loan commitments and other obligations. Liquidity management consists of two parts:

- *Asset management* Making sure there is enough cash and near-cash available at any one time.
- *Liability management* Obtaining liquid resources quickly and avoiding excessive outflows of cash to repay creditors in the near term. For example, the bank maintains access to the money markets and obtains additional funds for liquidity by borrowing there if required – it needs to offer only a slightly higher interest rate than others to obtain billions almost instantly. That is the theory at least, but we now have less faith in this method than bankers did before 2008 because all of a sudden no one was lending in these markets. The other aspect of liability management is not to have a high proportion of liabilities maturing in the next few months or years. Thus, long-term bond issues are to be favoured with a spread of maturities over many years.

The Basel III rules insist that banks maintain a high '**liquidity coverage ratio**', that is enough cash and near-cash to survive a 30-day market crisis on the same scale as the Lehman-induced crisis – a complete freeze in the money markets so the bank cannot access borrowed cash. However, because many banks lobbied their governments hard saying that they could not reach this level of liquidity quickly without significantly reducing lending the implementation of this new rule has been delayed until 2015. Until then it is 'observational', regulator-speak for monitoring, as banks work their way up to the standard to see if there are serious unintended consequences. No politician wanted to take the slightest chance of reduced lending at a time when we were trying to recover from recession.

The other liquidity risk-reducing measure is known as the '**net stable funding rule**'. It seeks to reduce banks' dependence on short-term funding. Another Northern Rock fiasco is what the regulators are trying to avoid: it borrowed on the short-term money market to lend long-term for mortgages, and then the short-term market froze. The new rule will not apply until 2018 because of the current weakness of the banks in some countries.

The current direction of travel is much more focused on macro-prudential regulation than previously, that is, trying to reduce systemic risks rather than assuming that a sound system can be built by focusing only on supervising individual banks (micro-prudential regulation). One aspect of this is to prevent bubbles building up in the financial system (e.g. irrational optimism about the increasing value of a group of assets, e.g. houses). Hence the extra capital added in boom times (a counter-cyclical regulatory capital regime). Another aspect is to prevent contagion across the system: measures here include high capital ratios for all banks at all times and inspections to ensure limited exposure to any one counterparty bank going bust. However, central banks will have a difficult time explaining to lenders, borrowers and politicians that we should have greater constraints on bank lending when times are good. Politicians are likely to ask, why is the central bank slowing things down when clearly we are not in a bubble (they never see them beforehand), merely booming as a result of the brilliant and beneficent policies that have led us to a new era of faster growth?

There are many sceptical voices concerned that the capital requirements under Basel III still leave the taxpayer vulnerable to picking up the pieces after another banking crisis – *see* **Exhibit 7.21**.

Exhibit 7.21

Basel: the mouse that did not roar

FT

Martin Wolf

To celebrate the second anniversary of the fall of Lehman, the mountain of Basel has laboured mightily and brought forth a mouse. Needless to say, the banking industry will insist the mouse is a tiger about to gobble up the world economy. Such special pleading – of which this pampered industry is a master – should be ignored: withdrawing incentives for reckless behaviour is not a cost to society; it is costly to the beneficiaries. The latter must not be confused with the former. The world needs a smaller and safer banking industry. The defect of the new rules is that they will fail to deliver this.

Am I being too harsh? "Global banking regulators ... sealed a deal to ... triple the size of the capital reserves that the world's banks must hold against losses," says the FT. This sounds tough, but only if one fails to realise that tripling almost nothing does not give one very much.

The new package sets a risk-weighted capital ratio of 4.5 per cent, more than double the current 2 per cent level, plus a new buffer of 2.5 per cent. Banks whose capital falls within the buffer zone will face restrictions on paying dividends and discretionary bonuses. So the rule sets an effective floor of 7 per cent. But the new standards are also to be implemented fully by 2019, by when the world will probably have seen another financial crisis or two.

This amount of equity is far below levels markets would impose if investors did not continue to expect governments to bail out creditors in a crisis, as historical

Long-run capital ratios for UK and US banks (%)

*Two separate studies

Size of the UK banking system
Banking sector assets as a % of GDP

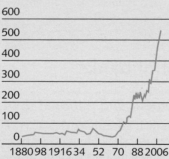

Forecast impact of higher capital standards on growth
Effect of a 1% point rise in the target capital ratio on GDP (Average of national central bank models, % deviation from baseline)

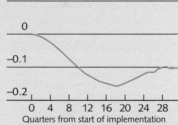

Quarters from start of implementation

Return on equity in UK financial sector (%)

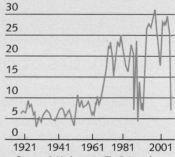

Sources: Second chart from BIS, all others from Halcane, Brennan & Madoures in 'The Future of Finance' (LSE 2010)

experience shows (see chart). It would not take much of a disaster to bring such leveraged entities close enough to insolvency to panic uninsured creditors. These new ratios are also very much the children of Basel II, the previous regulatory regime: they rely on what should by now be discredited risk-weightings.

We cannot assess the costs of regulation without recognising a

few facts: first, both the economy and the financial system have just survived a near death experience; second, the costs of the crisis include millions of unemployed and tens of trillions of dollars in lost output, as the Bank of England's Andy Haldane has argued; third, governments rescued the financial system by socialising its risks; finally, the financial industry is the only one with limitless access to the

Exhibit 7.21 continued

public purse and is, as a result, by far the most subsidised in the world.

It is necessary to go back to first principles in assessing the alleged costs of higher capital (and liquidity) requirements.

First, it is untrue that equity is expensive, as another excellent paper by Anat R. Admati of Stanford University and others argues, once we allow for the fact that more equity reduces the risk to creditors and to taxpayers, as we should. Less equity means higher returns, but also higher risk (see chart).

Second, to the extent that creditors bear the costs of failure, more equity means cheaper debt. Thus, if debt were truly unsubsidised, changing the ratio of equity to debt should not affect the costs of funding the balance sheet.

Third, to the extent that taxpayers bear the risk, more equity offsets this implicit subsidy. The public at large has zero interest – in fact, a negative interest – in subsidising risk-taking by banks, in general. For this reason, the subsidy it offers by providing free insurance must be offset by imposing higher capital requirements.

Fourth, the public has an interest in imposing higher equity requirements than any individual

bank would, in its own interest, wish to bear. Banks create systemic risk endogenously. That cost must be internalised by the decision makers. More risk-bearing capacity is one way of doing so.

Finally, to the extent that the public wants a specific form of risk-taking subsidised – lending to small and medium-sized enterprise, for example – it should do so directly. To subsidise the banking system as a whole, to persuade it to undertake what is but a small part of its activity, is grotesquely inefficient.

The conclusion, then, is that equity requirements need to be very much higher, perhaps as high as 20 or 30 per cent, without the risk-weighting. It would then be possible to dispense with the various forms of contingent capital that are far more likely to exacerbate panic in a crisis than assuage it. It is only because we have become used to these extraordinarily fragile structures that this demand seems so outrageous.

This is not to deny two huge problems.

One is that any such transition will be like taking drugs from an addict. The simplest way to minimise the costs would be for governments to underwrite the

additional capital and then, over time, sell what they take up into the market. Even so, the aggregate balance sheets of the aggregate banking system probably need to shrink. Such deleveraging almost certainly means a longer period of large fiscal deficits than almost anybody now imagines.

The other is that there is tremendous potential for regulatory arbitrage, with risks shifted elsewhere in the system. Such risks can easily collapse back on to the banking system. Thus higher capital requirements for banks will only work if regulators are able to identify the emergence of systemic risks elsewhere.

The regulators are trying to make the existing financial system less unsafe, incrementally. That is better than nothing. But it will not create a safe system. The world cannot afford another such crisis for at least a generation. By these standards what is emerging is simply insufficient. This mouse will never roar loudly enough.

martin.wolf@ft.com

Source: *Financial Times*, 15 September 2010, p. 13. Reprinted with permission.

Other activities of central banks

Banker to the government and national debt management

Central banks usually act as their government's banker. They hold the government's bank account and provide services such as deposit holding. As taxes go in, the account balance rises, but as the government pays private contractors, its account at the central bank will be debited, while the commercial banker to the contractor will see an uplift in its central bank account.

It may also administer the national debt, raising money by selling Treasury bills and bonds. Increasingly this task is undertaken by a separate organisation; in the UK by the Debt Management Office. National debt is the cumulative outstanding borrowings of a government. This can amount to a very large sum of money. Japan's national debt is over 200 per cent of annual GDP, for example. For the UK the figure is over 80 per cent, while Italy and Belgium are already over 100 per cent.

In normal circumstances the central bank will not lend to the government by buying its bonds, but extreme situations have seen a relaxation of that policy – *see* **Exhibit 7.22**.

Exhibit 7.22

Trichet lands a 'cunning' blow   FT

Ralph Atkins

Like a boxer wanting more power for his punch, the European Central Bank is trying a new tactic to combat the eurozone crisis: moving to catch financial markets unawares.

Jean-Claude Trichet, the ECB president, disappointed some investors on Thursday by not announcing a dramatic increase in the bank's bond purchases.

But while he spoke, the euro's monetary guardian was stepping up its intervention in government debt markets to levels not seen since the programme was launched in May.

The feint brought some immediate success in reversing the surge in borrowing costs seen by countries such as Portugal and Spain. But it also kept the main thrust of the ECB's strategy for tackling the crisis on track.

As before, the euro's monetary guardian was not embarking on quantitative easing to stimulate the economy in the manner of the US Federal Reserve, said Mr Trichet. The ECB's aim was to correct malfunctioning markets, not ride to the rescue of struggling eurozone countries.

It would continue to offset any inflationary risks by withdrawing from the financial system the same amount of liquidity as it spend on bonds.

Spending would be "commensurate" with the extent to which the

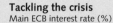

Tackling the crisis
Main ECB interest rate (%)

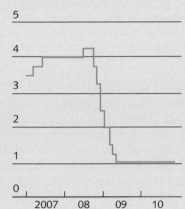

Source: Thomson Reuters Datastream; Bloomberg

ECB believed markets were malfunctioning, he said. Tensions were currently "acute". There was no limit to the eventual size of the programme.

"It is pretty cunning because there is a sense that they are not going to commit anything – but they are alert, and if things deteriorate they will act," said Giles Moec, European economist at Deutsche Bank. "For those who position themselves for a continuation of the European debacle, there is a risk."

The calculations behind Mr Trichet's low-key comments were probably also political. The tactics had been approved by an "over-

whelming majority" of the 22-strong governing council in Frankfurt on Thursday, he said. This suggested that Axel Weber, the Bundesbank chief, had maintained his opposition to the programme – although he may have been joined by fewer colleagues than when it was originally agreed. Mr Weber says that buying government bonds muddles fiscal and monetary policies, creating inflation risks and incentives for irresponsible government behaviour.

Source: *Financial Times*, 3 December 2010, p. 6. Reprinted with permission.

Currency issue

Central banks control the issue of bank notes and often control the issue of coins.[8] Notes are issued to commercial banks as they demand them, but in return their reserves at the central bank are surrendered. It is important that the central bank has a monopoly over deciding the size of the issue because excess amounts can result in high inflation, while too little can inhibit the economy. In the past, if the economy grew in nominal terms by 6 per cent the central bank would generally issue a further 6 per cent of notes to keep up with the needs of commerce. However, in recent times this relationship has become more complicated as we increasingly use electronic funds transfer rather than cash.

---

[8] In the UK, for example, coins are produced by another organisation, the Royal Mint.

In addition to increasing the volume of notes the central bank stands ready to replace banknotes that are wearing out.

Smooth functioning of the payments system

A central bank may run some or all of the payment systems in an economy, such as cheque clearing and for electronic transactions. Those systems it does not run it may oversee as a regulator.

Currency reserve control

Countries find it prudent to hold a reserve of gold and foreign currencies at their central banks. This can be useful as rainy day money and for intervening in the foreign exchange markets, e.g. using the foreign currency to buy the home currency, thereby increasing demand for it and raising its exchange rate. Even countries that permit a floating exchange rate (*see* Chapter 12) may want to smooth out sharp day-to-day fluctuations.

Coordination with other central banks and international bodies

We have already discussed one form of international cooperation (on solvency and liquidity rules) under the auspices of the BIS at Basel. The BIS also acts as a kind of banker to the central banks. It helps in the transfer of money from one central bank to another and keeps a proportion of the central banks' reserves. Central banks also work with the International Monetary Fund. For example, they worked together on the bail-out of the Irish government in 2010/2011. Another international economic and financial point of discussion and coordination is the regular G20 meetings – gatherings of finance ministers, presidents and prime ministers of the 20 leading economies. Central bankers have a significant input in terms of preparing for the meetings and then may help with the process of implementing agreements.

Bank of England

The Bank of England is more than 300 years old. Despite its name it is the central bank for the whole of the UK. Originally it was mainly used as the government's bank which raised borrowed money for its master. In Victorian times it was granted a monopoly on the issue of new banknotes and was used to rescue individual banks and the banking system. It also managed the nation's foreign currency and gold reserves.

It is managed by the Court of Directors, which consists of a governor, two deputy governors and nine non-executive directors. Governors are appointed for five years and directors for three years.

The BoE is responsible for the overall stability of the banking system as a whole, which will involve:

- stability of the monetary system. Setting interest rates and dealing with day-to-day fluctuations in liquidity;
- payment systems oversight and strengthening to reduce systemic risk;
- macro-prudential regulation of the financial system as whole;
- authorisation and micro-prudential supervision of banks and other deposit-taking institutions (from 2013);
- note issuance;
- lender of last resort in selected instances – some banks will be allowed to fail;
- managing the UK's gold and currency reserves and intervening in the foreign exchange markets.

Monetary policy is decided by the **Monetary Policy Committee (MPC)**, which consists of the Governor, his two deputies, the Bank's chief economist and director for markets and four outside experts. These experts are drawn from the academic community as well as the world of business (particularly banks). Also, they can and have been non-UK citizens, with expertise being the overriding consideration. The MPC meets each month to decide on the short-term interest rate target. The BoE staff then engage in open market operations in the money market to move the market rates to the desired target. If the inflation rate falls below 1 per cent or rises above 3 per cent then the Governor has to write a letter to the Chancellor of the Exchequer explaining why – *see* **Exhibit 7.23**.

Exhibit 7.23

Inflation rise sees King rebuked

By Chris Giles

Mervyn King came under attack from economists yesterday after the Bank of England governor was forced to write to the chancellor to explain another unexpected rise in the rate of inflation.

Annual inflation, measured by the consumer price index, rose to 3.7 per cent in April – up 0.3 percentage points from March and close to double the Bank of England's 2 per cent target.

On the retail price inflation measure, the annual rise in the cost of living jumped from 4.4 per cent in March to 5.3 per cent in April.

In a letter to George Osbourne, chancellor, Mr King again played down concerns, insisting that it was highly likely that the rise in inflation was temporary. He argued that it was caused by one-off factors of sterling weakness, high oil process and January's rise in value added tax.

But his soothing letter was met with increasing concern among economists that the Bank was too relaxed about its over-optimistic inflation forecasts.

Mr King's letter did betray some greater doubt about the temporary nature of the high inflation, unlike his letter in February, which did not suggest there was any chance of it persisting. "If the current period of above-target inflation causes inflation expectations to move up, that may lead to some persistence in the current high levels of inflation," the governor wrote.

In his response to the governor, Mr Osbourne urged the Bank to "remain vigilant towards any upside risks to inflation, including the risks to inflation expectations, of any prolonged period of above-target inflation".

Source: *Financial Times*, 19 May 2010, p. 1. Reprinted with permission

European Central Bank

The ECB, given responsibility for monetary policy in 1999, is part of the European System of Central Banks (ESCB) (Eurosystem). The National Central Banks (NCBs) were not discarded but remain important parts of the regulatory system. The ECB and the ESCB control monetary policy for those countries that are members of the European Monetary Union, the Eurozone. The governors of each of the 17 NCBs each have a vote on the Governing Council which makes decisions on monetary policy. Each of the NCBs became independent from both the European Commission and the governments of the individual states when the ESCB was established, if they were not already independent.

The ECB, based in Frankfurt, has an executive board consisting of the president, the vice-president and four other members, who are appointed by a committee of heads of state for eight years. These six people are also voting members of the Governing Council. The Governing Council of 23 meets each month to decide monetary policy and announces the target short-term interest (repo) rate (the target financing rate).

Monetary operations are not centralised at the ECB, but are conducted by the individual NCBs. In open market operations (called main refinancing operations (MRO)), banks and other credit institutions submit bids to borrow and the central banks decide which bids to accept – the unattractively priced offers will not be accepted. This is usually in the repo market or secured loans market. For discount lending (marginal lending facility) the national central banks will lend, against collateral, overnight loans at, say, 75 or 100 basis points over the target financing rate, thus providing a ceiling rate in the markets. Banks may also deposit money with the ECB and receive interest, say 75 or 100 basis points below the target financing rate (deposit facility).

The ECB insists that banks hold a sum equivalent to 2 per cent of the amount held in cheque accounts and other short-term deposits in reserve accounts at the national central bank (interest is paid on this money at a low rate, currently 0.25 per cent).[9]

As well as monetary policy, including the issuance of banknotes, the ECB is responsible for the conduct of foreign exchange operations and holds and manages the official reserves (gold and currency) of the Eurozone countries. It also promotes the smooth working of payment systems. Prudential supervision of financial institutions is a responsibility of the NCBs, as are payment mechanisms and the stability of their national financial systems.

The US Federal Reserve

The Americans have a heightened fear of centralised power and as a consequence emphasise the need for checks and balances in society. One manifestation of their mistrust was the failure of the nineteenth-century experiments with establishing central banks because the public mistrusted such a nationwide system, especially if it could be manipulated by Wall Street money men. Thus for much of the nineteenth and the early part of the twentieth century there was no central bank to act as lender of last resort should banks' reserves get uncomfortably low. As a result there were regular runs on banks and hundreds of bank collapses. The 1907 crisis brought so many bank failures and massive losses to depositors that a consensus was finally reached to create a central bank, which was established in 1913.

However, the Federal Reserve is unlike other central banks because it was structured in such a way as to disperse power to the regions of the country and to disperse power among a number of individuals so that neither Wall Street nor politicians could manipulate it. There are 12 Federal Reserve banks, one for each region of the country. These are overseen by directors who are mostly drawn from the private-sector banks and corporates in that region, so that they reflect the American citizenry. These regional Federal Reserve banks supervise the financial institutions in their area. (The New York one is the busiest on this score, with so many universal banks to watch over.) They also make discount rate loans to banks in their area; issue new currency; clear cheques; supervise the safety and soundness of banks in their area with regard to applications for a bank to expand or merge and investigate and report on local business conditions.

In addition to the 12 regional Federal Reserve banks there is a Board of Governors of the Federal Reserve System based in Washington, which has seven members called governors (usually economists), including the chairman, at the time of writing Ben Bernanke. These are appointed by the president of the United States and confirmed by the Senate, but for terms much longer than those of the President or members of congress at 14 years, to reduce the chance of political control of a governor.

Monetary policy through the use of open market operations is decided by the **Federal Open Market Committee (FOMC)** whose voting members include the seven governors of the Federal Reserve Board plus the presidents of the New York Fed and four other regional Feds.[10] Thus, there is input from the regions. Note that the Board has the majority of the votes. The FOMC meets about every six weeks to decide the general stance on open market operations (setting the target federal funds rate, which is the interest rate banks charge each other to lend their balances at the Federal Reserve overnight), but the actual day-to-day interventions in the money markets are conducted by the trading desk at the Federal Reserve Bank of New York. The manager of this desk reports back to the FOMC members daily.

The Board sets reserve requirements and shares the responsibility with the regional reserve banks for discount rate policy. The Fed now pays interest on reserves. The Board plays a key role in ensuring the smooth functioning and continued development of the nation's payments system. The Board approves bank mergers and applications for new activities, regulates the permissible

---

[9] These are the items that count for the 2 per cent reserve requirement: overnight deposits, deposits with agreed maturity or period of notice up to two years, debt securities issued with maturity up to two years, money market paper.

[10] The 12 presidents of the regional Feds rotate as voting members. All 12 presidents attend the meetings; it is just that seven of them participate in discussions but do not have a vote.

activities of domestic and foreign banks in the US. However, the safety and soundness of the US financial system is entrusted to a number of different government agencies alongside the Fed.

The chairman and his team have some other duties:

- advising the nation's president on economic policy;
- representing the country in international negotiations on economic matters.

Concluding comments

In 2010 and 2011 countries all over Europe leaned heavily on the expertise and power of their central banks to bail them out of deep economic difficulties. Their banks were in crisis as the financial markets lost faith in the ability of them or their governments to repay money borrowed through bonds. The European Central Bank and the national central banks of the Eurozone had two years previously slashed interest rates to historic lows and in so doing probably saved the continent from a 1930s-style Depression. This was still not enough to restore the banking system to health and so a raft of additional measures was implemented by the central banks, including raising the deposit insurance limit to reassure depositors and acting as lender of last resort to a number of banks (the Irish banks, for example, borrowed €130 billion from the ECB when no one else would lend). In the UK, we had a massive quantitative easing programme to lower long-term interest rates and boost bank reserves to encourage lending. While these emergency measures were effective in keeping the patient alive, thought was also given to the long-term health of the financial system. Thus we had the Basel tightening of the capital and liquidity reserve ratios.

For most people the technical-sounding tools used by central bankers seem arcane and boring when we hear about them on the evening news. Yet if it wasn't for the vigilance and forward planning of these organisations we would have suffered a much worse fate as a result of the financial crisis. The financial world would have become a wasteland as bank after bank fell, and many important functions such as the mobilisation of savings for productive use would have taken decades to recover. It is vital that we continue to develop ways of strengthening the financial system through better regulation, rules on reserves and controlling the power of over-mighty universal banks. Clearly, the regime central banks put in place prior to 2008 was inadequate – we must do better in the future, for all our sakes.

Key points and concepts

- **Monetary policy:** managing the amount of money in an economy and the interest rates in that economy.

- **Required reserves:** a bank's reserves of cash that a central bank insists are deposited with it.

- **Excess reserves:** additional reserves held by a commercial bank above those held at the central bank.

- **Monetary base** =   currency in circulation   +   reserves

- **Reserves**   =   required reserves   +   vault cash (excess reserves)

- **Required reserve ratio:** reserves as a percentage of deposits.

- The **credit multiplier** occurs when there is an increase (decrease) in the quantity of reserves in the banking system. The increase (decrease) produces a multiple effect on the amount of money in the economy. It is the reciprocal of the reserve ratio.

- Central banks have three main **tools** they use **to increase or decrease the money supply and interest rates:**

  - **Open market operations**: the buying and selling of government securities (Treasury bills and bonds) in the normal trading markets on a day to day basis. In purchasing government securities the central bank creates money to hand it over to those selling. It issues currency notes or it writes a cheque in the name of the owner. When the cheque is drawn on, the central bank just creates an amount of credit for itself to satisfy the buyer.

▶

- **Discount rate changes**: a bank that is temporarily short of reserves could ask the central bank to simply create additional reserves and add them to its account at the central bank. It will pay interest at a significantly higher rate (usually 100 basis points more) than the normal overnight rate.
- **Reserve requirement ratio changes**: a decrease in the reserve requirement ratio means that banks do not need to hold as much money at the central bank and/or in vault cash, and so they are able to lend out a greater percentage of their deposits, thus increasing the supply of money.

● Some central banks have **a specific goal for inflation**. For example, the European Central Bank, ECB, has a stated aim of a rate below, but close to, 2 per cent over the medium term.

● **Other potential goals of the central bank are**:

- **high employment and steady economic growth** – the best that policymakers can hope for is that the economy reaches its **natural rate of unemployment**, i.e. a level of **non-accelerating inflation rate of unemployment, NAIRU.** There will usually be **frictional unemployment (**matching people to suitable posts does not happen instantaneously) **and some structural unemployment** (where the skills people have do not match what the market needs or the location of people does not match the needs of employers);
- **interest rate stability**;
- **stability of the financial system**;
- **stability in the foreign exchange markets.**

● Over a run of years the goal of **price stability does not conflict with the other goals**. But there might be a trade-off in the short run.

● There are two types of **central bank independence**. These are:

- **instrument independence** – the central bank can decide when and how to use monetary policy instruments without political interference;
- **goal independence** – the central bank decides the goals of monetary policy.

● **Advantages of central bank independence are**:

- political control can lead to higher inflation;
- there is reduced temptation to support government spending;
- politicians lack expertise.

● **The disadvantages of independence are**:

- the situation is undemocratic;
- central banks fail from time to time.

● **Quantitative easing:** the central bank electronically creates money ('printing money') which is then used to buy assets from investors in the market. It can raise bank reserves and lower interest rates along the yield curve.

● **Depositor insurance:** the government or some regulatory body steps in and says they will guarantee that depositors will be repaid even if the bank cannot do so – a limit is usually set.

● **Lender of last resort**: to prevent a bank failure leading on to other bank failures the central bank will step in to provide reserves when no one else will lend to the banks.

● **Too big to fail**: large banks, which have numerous interbank and other borrowings and derivative transactions, could pose a threat to the entire system should they fail. These are the banks that pose a **systemic risk**. Increasingly policymakers are using the phrase **'Sifi, systemically important financial institutions'.** Partial solutions include breaking banks into smaller units, taxing them more because of the costs they impose on society, imposing very high capital reserve ratios and liquidity reserve ratios, introducing **living wills** (banks have to report regularly to the authorities on how they would put into effect an orderly winding down of the business as well as how they would plan for recovery in a crisis).

● **Bank supervision** or **prudential supervision:** an authority investigates and approves the appointment of those who operate banks and continues monitoring and surveillance to ensure they are operated well.

▶

- **The CAMELS method of bank inspection:**

  - Capital adequacy;
  - Asset quality;
  - Management;
  - Earnings;
  - Liquidity;
  - Sensitivity to market risk.

- **Liquidity risk:** the ability to pay out cash on deposit withdrawals and other outflows of cash while satisfying loan commitments and other obligations. Liquidity management consists of two parts. These are:

  - **asset management** – making sure there is enough cash and near-cash available at any one time;
  - **liability management** – obtaining liquid resources quickly and avoiding excessive outflows of cash to repay creditors in the near-term – e.g. access to the money markets, and not having a high proportion of liabilities maturing in the next few months or years.

- **Solvency risk:** allowing the capital base of the bank to diminish to such an extent that the assets of the bank (loans to customers, etc.) are barely greater than the liabilities (e.g. deposits).

- **Risk-weighted assets:** some bank assets are reduced to, say, 50 per cent or 20 per cent of their balance sheet value for the purposes of calculating the value of their assets to then apply the required capital reserve ratio of, say, 7 per cent.

- **Basel I:** set minimum solvency standards applicable to any bank from a member country of the Basel committee.

- **Basel II:** made much greater use of credit ratings to decide weightings. Banks were permitted to use 'internal ratings' devised from their own models to risk-weight assets. Took account of market risk, operational risk, concentration risk and liquidity risk. Off-balance-sheet assets (and liabilities) need capital to be assigned.

- **Basel III:** capital is narrowly defined as **core tier 1** and leaves out preference shares, unsecured bonds, etc. Capital is to be held by banks as a percentage of risk-weighted assets: 4.5 per cent minimum; an additional 2.5 per cent if the bank wants to pay dividends or bonuses, an additional 0–2.5 per cent as a counter-cyclical buffer and another 1–2 per cent as a systemic groups' risk buffer.

- **Contingent convertible ('CoCos'):** they behave like bonds, paying a coupon, but convert to equity if a bank's capital ratio falls below a predetermined level.

- **Basel III on liquidity risk:** (a) banks maintain a high '**liquidity coverage ratio'**, that is enough cash and near cash to survive a 30-day market crisis, (b) the '**net stable funding rule'** seeks to reduce banks' dependence on short-term funding.

- **Macro-prudential regulation:** trying to reduce systemic risks rather than assuming that a sound system can be built by focusing only on supervising individual banks (**micro-prudential regulation**).

- **Counter-cyclical regulatory capital regime:** extra capital added to banks' balance sheets in boom times.

- **Other activities of central banks are:**

  - as banker to the government, and national debt management;
  - currency issuing;
  - the smooth functioning of the payments system;
  - currency reserve control;
  - coordination with other central banks and international bodies.

- **Bank of England activities are:**

  - the stability of the monetary system. Setting interest rates and dealing with day to day fluctuations in liquidity;

▶

- payment systems oversight and strengthening to reduce systemic risk;
- macro-prudential regulation of the financial system as a whole;
- authorisation and micro-prudential supervision of banks and other deposit-taking institutions (from 2013);
- note issuance;
- lender of last resort in selected instances;
- managing the UK's gold and currency reserves and intervening in the foreign exchange markets;
- monetary policy, which is decided by the **Monetary Policy Committee (MPC)**.

- **European Central Bank, ECB**; part of the **European System of Central Banks, ESCB (Eurosystem)**. The ECB and the ESCB control monetary policy for those countries that are members of the **European Monetary Union**, the Eurozone.

 - The governors of each of the 17 National Central Banks each have a vote on the **Governing Council** which makes decisions on monetary policy. Also on the Governing Council are six Executive board members of the ECB.

- In the US there are 12 **Federal Reserve** banks, one for each region of the country, which supervise the financial institutions in their area: they make discount rate loans to banks in their area; issue new currency; clear cheques; supervise the safety and soundness of banks in their area with regard to applications for a bank to expand or merge; and investigate and report on local business conditions.

- The **Board of Governors of the Federal Reserve System** based in Washington has seven members which are all on the **Federal Open Market Committee (FOMC)** which decides open market operations. The FOMC also includes the presidents of the New York Fed and four other regional Feds. The Board sets reserve requirements and shares the responsibility with the regional Reserve Banks for discount rate policy.

References and further reading

To keep up to date and reinforce knowledge gained by reading this chapter I can recommend the following publications: *Financial Times*, *The Economist*, *Bank of England Quarterly Bulletin* and *Bank for International Settlements Quarterly Review* (www.bis.org).

Alesina, A. and Summers, L. H. (1993) 'Central bank independence and macroeconomic performance: some comparative evidence', *Journal of Money, Credit and Banking*, Vol. 25, No. 2, May.
 Finding: central bank independence promotes price stability.

Alpanda, S. and Honig, A. (2010) 'Political monetary cycles and a *de facto* ranking of central bank independence', *Journal of International Money and Finance*, Vol. 29, pp. 1003–1023.
 Finding: independent central banks withstand political pressure to stimulate the economy before elections.

Brumm, H. J. (2006) 'The effect of central bank independence on inflation in developing countries', *Economic Letters*, Vol. 90, pp. 189–193.
 Finding: greater central banking independence correlates with lower inflation.

Casu, B., Girardone, C. and Molyneux, P. (2012) *Introduction to Banking*, 2nd edn. Harlow: Pearson Education.
 Some more detail on central banking is provided in an accessible approach.

Congdon, T. (2009) 'Central banking in a free society', Institute for Economic Affairs, www.iea.org.uk.
 A monograph providing an overview of the function of central banking and advancing some radical ideas for improvement.

Davies, H. and Green, D. (2010) Banking on the Future: The Fall and Rise of Central Banking. Princeton, NJ: Princeton University Press.
 An insider's look into how central banks have evolved and why they are critical to the functioning of market economies. The book asks whether, in light of the recent economic fallout, the central banking model needs radical reform.

De Jong, E. (2002) 'Why are price stability and statutory independence of central banks negatively correlated? The role of culture', *European Journal of Political Economy*, Vol. 18, pp. 675–694.

Inequality appears to explain the relationship between central bank independence and inflation.

Grunwald, M. (2009) 'Person of the year: Ben Bernanke', *Time*, Vol. 174, No. 25/26, pp. 20–44.

In addition to a profile of the Federal Reserve Chairman there is an easy-to-follow guide on the workings of the Fed.

Jácome, J. I. and Vázquez, F. (2008) 'Is there any link between legal central bank independence and inflation? Evidence from Latin America and the Caribbean', *European Journal of Political Economy*, Vol. 24, pp. 788–801.

Higher independence and lower inflation is the relationship.

Klomp, J. and De Haan, J. (2008) 'Central bank independence and financial instability', *Journal of Financial Stability*, Vol. 5, Issue 4, pp. 321–338.

Independence seems to assist financial stability.

Mishkin, F. (2009) *Economics of Money, Banking and Financial Markets*, 9th edn. Harlow: Pearson Education.

A very well-respected textbook on the subject – US based.

Siklos, P. L. (2008) 'No single definition of central bank independence is right for all countries', *European Journal of Political Economy*, Vol. 24, pp. 802–816.

'We do find strong evidence that several core elements of ... CBI (central bank independence) do reduce inflation'.

Websites

Bank of England www.bankofengland.co.uk
Bank for International Settlements www.bis.org
Banque de France (France's central bank) www.banque-france.fr
Banque Nationale de Belgique (Belgium's central bank) www.nbb.be
Central Bank of Ireland www.centralbank.ie
Danmarks Nationalbank (Denmark's central bank) www.nationalbanken.dk
De Nederlandsche Bank (Netherland's central bank) www.dnb.nl
Deutsche Bundesbank (Germany's central bank) www.bundesbank.de
European Central Bank www.ecb.int
Federal Reserve Bank www.federalreserve.gov
Norway's Central Bank www.norges-bank.no
Suomen Pankki (Finland's central bank) www.suomenpankki.fi
Sveriges Riksbank (Sweden's central bank) www.riksbank.com

Video presentations

Bank chief executives and other senior people describe and discuss policy and other aspects of banking in interviews, documentaries and webcasts at Cantos.com. (www.cantos.com) – these are free to view.

Case study recommendations

See www.pearsoned.co.uk/arnold for case study synopses.
Also see Harvard University: http://hbsp.harvard.edu/product/cases

- Bank Failure in Jamaica (2006) Author: Jenifer Daley. Richard Ivey School of Business, University of Western Ontario. Available on Harvard Case Study website.
- Basel III: An Evaluation of New Banking Regulations (2010) Authors: David Blaylock and David Conklin. Richard Ivey School of Business, University of Western Ontario. Available on Harvard Case Study website.

Self-review questions

1 What do you understand by the term monetary policy?

2 Describe the two types (or levels) of independence for a central bank.

3 Explain monetary base, required reserves and excess reserves.

4 Define open market operations by a central bank.

5 What are the inflation targets for the central banks in the US, UK and the Eurozone countries?

6 What is quantitative easing?

7 What is meant by a bank being too big to fail?

8 What is (a) frictional unemployment, (b) structural unemployment, (c) NAIRU?

9 Explain (a) depositor insurance, (b) lender of last resort, (c) systemically important financial institution.

10 What is macro-prudential and micro-prudential supervision of banks?

Questions and problems

1 Describe and illustrate the credit multiplier.

2 Describe and explain the way in which central banks use open market operations, discount lending and changing the bank reserve requirement levels to influence the economy.

3 'The safety and soundness of the financial system relies to a large extent on the action of the central banks.' Explain this statement and illustrate the ways in which central banks improve safety and soundness.

4 Argue the case for and against the political independence of central banks.

5 'I think there should be no back-up to prevent a bank from failing or to protect depositors if it does fail. Let the market decide these things. People should be careful about where they deposit their money. Riskier institutions will have to offer greater rates of return. We do not need a nanny state.' Explain your reasons for agreeing or disagreeing with these statements.

6 The CAMELS system is a popular list for regulators. Explain what it is and its importance.

7 Describe and explain the importance of the following in the context of central banking:

   (a) banker to the national government;
   (b) issue of currency;
   (c) functioning of payment systems;
   (d) lender of last resort.

8 The Basel Accords have had a great impact on the banking industry. Describe these and explain their significance to the ordinary person.

9 Compare and contrast structures and decision-making powers of the Federal Reserve, the European System of Central Banks and the Bank of England.

10 Use supply and demand curves to illustrate how a central bank conducts monetary policy using open market operations, a discount window and altering reserve levels.

Web-based exercises

1 Visit the websites of the European Central Bank, the Federal Reserve and the Bank of England and gather statistics on inflation rates and short-term interest rates over the past ten years. Write a report explaining how monetary policy is implemented in these three economic areas and comment on the relative success of these central banks in achieving their declared goals.

2 Explore the dozen or so websites listed above to gather evidence on the monetary policy tools that these central banks have used over the past five years. Write a report describing the methods that have been employed. Include tables of popularity of method.

Equity markets

LEARNING OUTCOMES

This chapter is designed to help you understand the main features of equity capital and the markets on which shares are traded. By the end of it the reader should be able to:

■ compare and contrast equity and debt capital, as well as explain the features of preference shares;

■ discuss the role and functioning of stock markets;

■ describe and explain the recent innovations leading to more equity trading taking place outside the main exchanges;

■ explain the different markets available to companies on the London Stock Exchange and the way in which shares are traded there;

■ outline the trends in the ownership of UK shares over the past 50 years.

Society needs people who are willing to take the risk of total failure of a business enterprise. Banks are not willing to accept that risk. They strike deals with companies whereby even if the profits are low or a loss is made they are still paid interest and capital. Also, they usually require collateral so that if the business plan turns out to be a dud the bank can recoup its money by selling off property or other assets (or, at least most of their money most of the time). Holders of other forms of debt capital, such as bonds, take similar low-risk/low-return deals.

Imagine if debt were the only form of capital available for businesses to grow. Very few would be established because it would be rare for managers to come across an investment project (e.g. new product-line factory) that offered the lenders the security they need. I can think of only one company that is virtually completely financed by debt. This is the water company for Wales. It can get away without many shares (equity) because there is so little uncertainty regarding its future income. It is regulated and the bills it charges to customers are highly predictable for years to come and so it can offer its lenders high security, not just from its cash flow but also from the land, reservoirs, etc. that it owns.

Now consider a company producing TV programmes. Could it finance itself entirely with debt? No, because if £100 million was put in by lenders to invest in ten TV serials there would be nothing for them to fall back on should half of its shows be poorly received by viewers, or even if one-tenth was poorly received. They might be willing to lend, say, £40 million if the other £60 million came from investors who were willing to accept the risk of total loss. Then the lenders would know that their money was likely to be reasonably safe (assuming that they had faith in the track record of the executives in charge and the historical statistics suggested that only two or three programmes were likely to be commercial flops). Naturally, the risk takers providing this £60 million of capital would want a high reward for exposing their hard-earned savings. They would also want some say over who the directors of the company were and the power to vote down major moves proposed by the managers. They would also require regular information on progress. These holders of shares (equities) in the success or failure of the enterprise act as shock-absorbers so that other parties contributing to a firm, from suppliers and creditors to bankers and leasing companies, do not have to bear the shock of a surprise recession, a loss of market share to competitors or a badly made TV series.

Another attractive feature of share capital for building businesses is that it does not have a date at which it will be redeemed by the company. Thus the managers (and creditors) know that the capital will be available for the very long term, that the shareholders cannot turn around one day and demand their money back. However, this causes a problem for investors because they may want to sell their shares a year a two down the line. While many shareholders are willing to accept that their companies are too small to join a stock market or that the disadvantages of doing so outweigh the advantages, a minority of companies have decided to float their shares on an exchange. This brings many benefits in addition to permitting shareholders to sell (or buy more) when they want to, including facilitating mergers and the raising of more equity finance.

After discussing the different types of long-term capital available to a company this chapter describes stock exchanges around the world and their importance. Challenges to the old established exchanges such as new share-trading facilities set up in the last five years, or high-frequency trading and dark pools of liquidity are also explored. We then look at the London Stock Exchange in more detail, comparing it to the other major exchanges. Also, the ways in which shares are traded are discussed, including the role of clearing houses and settlement systems.

The value of joint stock enterprises/a little history

Although it is thought that Roman *publicani* (state contractors) carried out some active trading in parts of their businesses, it was in seventeenth-century Europe that the first shares were issued and traded, and the first stock exchange was founded in Amsterdam. These shares were in the Vereinigte Oostindische Compagnie (the Dutch East India Company). The oldest VOC share still in existence was issued on 27 September 1606 (*see* **Exhibit 8.1**).

| Exhibit 8.1 | World's oldest surviving share certificate |

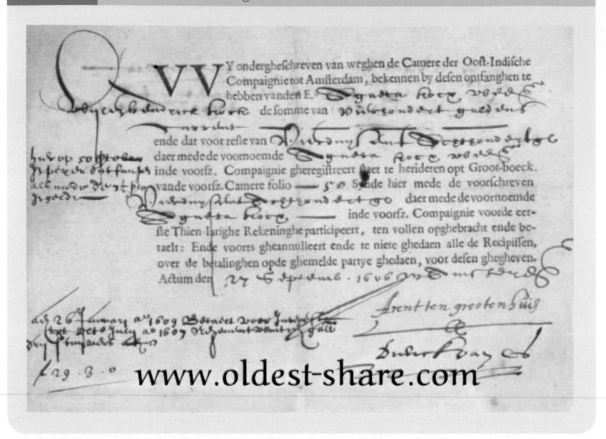

Source: From www.oldest-share.com, www.oldest-shares.com/Private collection.

The opening of routes to the east saw a huge surge in spice trading, with groups of merchants pooling their resources to finance voyages in the hope of significant profits. This collective investing – buying shares in a trading company – lessened their exposure to risk and there were plenty of wealthy individuals eager to purchase the shares.

In the UK, trading in securities began in 1698 when a John Castaing based at Jonathan's Coffee-house published a list of share and commodity prices called 'The Course of the Exchange and other things'. A club, formed at Jonathan's in 1801 to deal in shares and made up of subscribing members, was called the Stock Exchange.

Shares enabled companies to expand to take advantage of the industrial age by attracting investors to buy equity in the companies in return for a share in the profits. As the sums needed to finance this expansion grew ever larger, financing by means of equities proved to be a satisfactory solution.

Ordinary shares (equity)

Ordinary shares represent the equity capital of the firm and are a means of raising long-term finance to run the business. The holders of these securities share in the (hopefully) rising prosperity of a company. These investors, as owners of the firm, have the right to exercise some control over the company. They can vote at shareholder meetings to determine such crucial matters as the composition of the team of directors. They can also vote on major strategic and policy issues such as the type of activities that the firm might engage in, or the decision to merge with another firm. These ordinary shareholders have a claim to a share of the company's profits in the form of dividend payments, and in a worst-case scenario, a right to share in the proceeds of a liquidation sale of the firm's assets, albeit after all other creditors such as banks, tax authorities, trade creditors etc. have been paid.

Limited liability means that investors are liable for the company's debts only up to the amount they invested. It was in the nineteenth century that the idea of limited liability emerged. It encouraged investors to put their savings into shareholdings without the risk that if the company failed investors would be liable for all company liabilities, at a time when many investment opportunities carried great risk, for example railway building in Europe or the Americas.

To exercise effective control over the firm the shareholders need information; and while management are reluctant to put large amounts of commercially sensitive information which might be useful to competitors into the public domain, they are required to make available to each shareholder a copy of the annual report.

To regain invested funds an equity investor must either sell the shares to another investor (or in rare circumstances to the company – in many countries firms are now allowed to repurchase their own shares, a share buy-back, under strict conditions) or force the company into liquidation, in which case all assets are sold and the proceeds distributed.

Annual, semi-annual or quarterly dividend payments are paid at the discretion of the directors, and individual shareholders are often effectively powerless to influence the income from a share – not only because of the risk attached to the trading profits which generate the resources for a dividend, but also because of the relative power of directors in a firm with a disparate or divided shareholder body. If a shareholder owns 100 shares of a company with millions of shares in issue, there is little likelihood of this person exerting any influence at all; institutional shareholders who often own very large numbers of shares are able to bring more pressure to bear.

Contrasting equity and debt finance

Debt is another means of raising finance, but it is very different from equity finance. Usually the lenders to the firm have no official control; they are unable to vote at general meetings and therefore cannot choose directors and determine major strategic issues. However, there are circumstances in which lenders have significant influence. For instance, they may insist that the company does not exceed certain liquidity or solvency ratio levels (not too much debt), or they may take a charge over a particular building as security for a loan, thus restricting the directors' freedom of action over the use and disposal of that building. Debt finance also contrasts with equity finance in that it usually requires regular cash outlays in the form of interest and the repayment of the capital sum, whereas equity finance is not compelled to make any dividend payments. The firm will be obliged to maintain the repayment schedule through good years and bad or face the possibility of action being taken by the lender to recover its money by forcing the firm to sell assets or liquidate. With equity finance, in bad times dividend payments can be suspended to aid cash flow.

The attraction of holding shares is that if the company does well there are no limits to the size of the claim equity shareholders have on profit. There have been numerous instances of investors placing modest sums into the shares of young firms and finding themselves millionaires. For example, if you had bought $1,000 worth of shares in Google in 1999, your holding would now be worth millions.

The attraction of share issuing for companies is that, unlike a loan, share finance does not have to be repaid, which can be helpful if the company is short of cash. Offsetting this are some disadvantages: issuing shares is a costly business (share investors require higher rates of return and the transaction costs of the issue process can be high – *see* next chapter on the costs of share issuance); issuing shares to external investors may mean loss of ultimate control of the company by the current dominant shareholders.

There is some lack of clarity as to the distinction between stocks and shares. Shares are equities in companies. Stocks are financial instruments that pay interest (e.g. bonds). However, in the US shares are also called '**common stocks**' and the shareholders are usually referred to as the **stockholders**. So when some people use the term 'stocks' they could be referring to either bonds or shares.

Preference shares

Preference shares usually offer their owners a fixed rate of dividend each year. However, if the firm has insufficient profits the amount paid may be reduced, sometimes to zero. Thus, there is no guarantee that an annual income will be received, unlike with debt capital. The dividend on preference shares is paid before anything is paid out to ordinary shareholders – indeed, after the preference dividend obligation has been met there may be nothing left for ordinary shareholders. Preference shares are attractive to some investors because they offer a regular income at a higher rate of return than that available on fixed-interest securities, e.g. bonds. However, this higher return also comes with higher risk, as the preference dividend ranks after bond interest and upon liquidation preference holders are further back in the queue as recipients of the proceeds of asset sell-offs.

Preference shares are part of shareholders' funds but are not equity share capital. The holders are not usually able to benefit from any extraordinarily good performance of the firm – any profits above expectations go to the ordinary shareholders. Also preference shares usually carry no voting rights, except if the dividend is in arrears or in the case of liquidation. Many preference share prices and other data are listed in the financial pages of newspapers.

Advantages to the firm of preference share capital

- *Dividend 'optional'* Preference dividends can be omitted for one or more years, giving directors more flexibility and a greater chance of surviving a downturn in trading.

- *Influence over management* Preference shares are an additional source of capital which, because they do not have voting rights, do not dilute the influence of the ordinary shareholders. Thus it is possible to raise shareholder capital and retain voting control.

- *Extraordinary profits* Preference shareholders receive a set return and do not share in extraordinary profits (unless the preference shares are 'participating' – see below).

- *Financial gearing considerations* There are limits to safe levels of borrowing. If a firm is unable to raise finance by borrowing, preference shares are an alternative source of financing, if shareholders are unwilling to provide more equity risk capital. They can be an alternative, though less effective, shock-absorber to selling more ordinary shares.

Disadvantages to the firm of preference share capital

- *High cost of capital* The higher risk attached to the annual returns and capital cause preference shareholders to demand a higher level of return than debt holders.

- *Dividends are not tax deductible* Tax is payable on the firm's profit before the deduction of the preference dividend (as it is for ordinary share dividends). In contrast, interest has to be paid whether or not a profit is made. This cost is regarded as a legitmate expense reducing taxable profit – see **Exhibit 8.2**. Both firms have raised £1m, but Company A sold bonds yielding 8 per cent, Company B sold preference shares offering a dividend yield of 8 per cent.

Types of preference shares

There are a number of variations on the theme of preference shares. Here are some additional features:

- *Cumulative* If dividends are missed in any year the right to receive a dividend is carried forward. These prior-year dividends have to be paid before any payout to ordinary shareholders.

- *Participating* As well as the fixed payment, the dividend may be increased if the company has high profits. (Usually the additional payment is a proportion of any ordinary dividend declared.)

- *Redeemable* These have a finite life, at the end of which the initial capital investment will be repaid.

Exhibit 8.2	The effect of the tax deductibility of interest and the non-tax deductibility of preference share dividends

	Company A Raised £1m by selling bonds yielding 8%	Company B Raised £1m by issuing preference shares with 8% yield
Profits before tax, dividends and interest	200,000	200,000
Interest payable on bonds	(80,000)	0
Taxable profit	120,000	200,000
Tax payable @ 30% of taxable profit	(36,000)	(60,000)
Profit after tax	84,000	140,000
Preference dividend	(0)	(80,000)
Available for ordinary shareholders	84,000	60,000

Company A has a lower tax bill because its bond interest is used to reduce taxable profit, resulting in an extra £24,000 (£84,000–£60,000) available for ordinary shareholders.

- **Irredeemables** These have no fixed redemption date.
- *Convertibles* These can be converted at the holder's request into ordinary shares at specific dates and on pre-set terms (for example, one ordinary share for every two preference shares). These shares often carry a lower dividend yield since there is the attraction of a potentially large capital gain.
- *Variable rate* A variable dividend is paid. The rate may be linked to general interest rates, e.g. LIBOR, or to some other variable factor.

Some unusual types of shares

In addition to ordinary shares and preference shares there are other, more unusual, types of shares.

Non-voting shares or reduced voting shares are sometimes issued by family-controlled firms which need additional equity finance but wish to avoid the diluting effects of an ordinary share issue. These shares are often called 'A' shares or 'B' shares (or N/V) and usually get the same dividends and the same share of assets in a liquidation as voting shares. The issue of non-voting or reduced voting shares is contentious, with many in the financial markets saying that everyone who puts equity into a company should have a vote on how that money is spent: the 'one share one vote' principle. However, investors can buy 'non-voters' for less than 'voters' and thereby gain a higher dividend yield. Also, without the possibility of issuing non-voting shares, many companies would simply prefer to forgo expansion. Around one-third of Europe's largest businesses fail to observe the 'one share one vote' principle. In the US the Ford family owns a mere 3.75 per cent of the shares. However, when the motor company joined the NYSE in 1956 the family's shares were converted into a special class that guaranteed 40 per cent of the voting power, no matter how many ordinary shares are in issue. When Google floated in 2004 Larry Page and Sergey Brin, the founders, held 'B' shares each with ten times as many votes per share as the 'A' shares issued to other investors. In the UK, there are relatively few companies with reduced voting rights compared with continental Europe. Dual-class is a US share (stock) issue where the shares issued have different degrees of voting rights. **Exhibit 8.3** discusses Facebook's dual-class stock issue.

Deferred ordinary shares rank lower than ordinary shares for an agreed rate of dividend, so in a poor year the ordinary holders might get their payment while deferred ordinary holders receive nothing.

Exhibit 8.3

Facebook signals future IPO with dual-class stock

By David Gelles and Richard Waters in San Francisco

Facebook has followed Google's lead and introduced a dual-class stock structure, the clearest sign yet that the world's most popular social networking site is preparing for an eventual public offering.

In doing so, Mark Zuckerberg, the company's 25-year-old chief executive, looks to be cementing his long-term grip on the site he founded.

Dual-class stock structures are controversial because they give certain shareholders much stronger voting rights than others.

"Dual-class stock is an anathema to institutional investors," said Charles Elson, professor of corporate governance at the University of Delaware.

"Ultimately, shareholders lose. If something were to go wrong, there's absolutely nothing they can do about it."

The use of separate classes of shares to protect the voting control of a narrow group of investors has traditionally been used in the US only in the media business.

Facebook confirmed the plan in a statement, saying that "existing shareholders wanted to maintain control over voting on certain issues to help ensure the company can continue to focus on the long-term to build a great business."

Mr Zuckerberg said that he plans to take the company public eventually. But yesterday Facebook said an IPO was not imminent.

Source: Financial Times, 25 November 2009, p. 21. Reprinted with permission.

Golden shares are shares with extraordinary special powers, for example the right to block a takeover or to restrict the influence of minority shareholders. Governments hold golden shares in some of the biggest companies in the UK and Europe (Royal Mail Group, Rolls-Royce, National Air Traffic Control, BAE Systems, BAA and Eurostar in the UK, VW and Portugal Teleco). However, European law states that golden shares are contrary to the EU principle of the free movement of capital and as such are illegal – *see* **Exhibit 8.4**. Their numbers have dwindled.

Exhibit 8.4

Lisbon employs 'golden shares' to block Telefónica's bid for Vivo

By Peter Wise in Lisbon, Andrew Parker in New York and Mark Mulligan in Madrid

Lisbon has used special veto rights to override shareholders and block Telefónica's €7.15bn (£5.8bn) bid to buy Portugal Telecom out of Vivo, their Brazilian mobile phone joint venture.

The use by the Portuguese government of its "golden shares" to overrule 74 per cent of shareholders who voted in favour of the offer was a surprise new twist to the acrimonious bid battle between the two Iberian operators. The government owns 500 golden shares in Portugal Telecom, which give the state spe-

cial veto rights over important company decisions.

But the intervention is expected to be challenged by the European Commission and by Telefónica, which had raised its bid by 10 per cent to €7.15bn hours before Portugal Telecom shareholders met to vote on it.

According to shareholders attending the closed meeting, members of the Portugal Telecom board had asked the government not to interfere. The board called an emergency meeting yesterday.

Shareholders including Banco Espírito Santo and Ongoing rejected Telefónica's previous bids of €5.17bn and €6.5bn but voted in favour of the new offer.

However, José Sócrates, Portugal's centre-left prime minister, said Telefónica's offer did not reflect the value of Vivo to Portugal Telecom. The government was "acting in the interest of the country", he said.

The legality of the state's rights in the company is being challenged in the European Court of Justice,

▶

Exhibit 8.4 continued

which is expected to issue a ruling on July 8 finding the golden shares structure invalid.

Zeinal Bava, Portugal Telecom's chief executive, had previously said the bid for Vivo was not a case where the golden shares could be used. But he said yesterday the decision of the chairman of the meeting to accept the use of the government veto took precedence over "whatever the board may or may not think".'

Source: Financial Times, 1 July 2010, p. 15. Reprinted with permission.

Stock exchanges around the world

What is a stock market?

Stock markets are places where governments and industries can raise long-term capital and investors can buy and sell various types of financial instruments. Stock exchanges[1] grew in response to the demand for funds to finance investment and (especially in the early days) ventures in overseas trade. Until the Napoleonic Wars the Dutch capital markets were pre-eminent, raising funds for investment abroad and loans for governments and businesses, and developing a thriving secondary market in which investors could sell their financial securities to other investors. This transferability of ownership of financial assets was an important breakthrough for the development of sophisticated financial systems. It offered the investor liquidity, which encouraged the flow of funds to firms, while leaving the capital in the business venture untouched.

Much early industrialisation was financed by individuals or partnerships, but as the capital requirements became larger it was clear that joint-stock enterprises were needed, in which the money of numerous investors was brought together to give joint ownership with the promise of a share of profits. Canal corporations, docks companies, manufacturing enterprises, railways, mining, brewing and insurance companies were added to the list of firms with shares and bonds traded on the stock exchanges of Europe, the US and a few places in Asia in the nineteenth century.

Growth of stock markets

Since the nineteenth century stock markets have prospered and expanded globally. New markets have appeared in developing countries, to join and rival the traditional stock markets. **Exhibit 8.5** details the relative size of stock markets around the world according to the total market capitalisation (number of shares multiplied by share price) of the companies traded on them.

The world has changed dramatically in the last 30 years. Liberalisation and the accelerating wave of privatisation pushed stock markets to the forefront of developing countries' tools of economic progress. The strong ideological opposition to capitalism has been replaced with stock markets in Moscow, Warsaw and Sofia. Even countries which still espouse communism, such as China and Vietnam, now have thriving and increasingly influential stock exchanges designed to facilitate the mobilisation of capital and its employment in productive endeavour, with – horror of horrors to some hard-line communists – a return going to the capital providers.

China has two thriving stock exchanges, in Shanghai and Shenzhen, with over 2,000 companies listed. There are now tens of millions of Chinese investors who can only be properly described as 'capitalists' given that they put at risk their savings on the expectations of a reward on their capital. **Exhibit 8.6** describes the rivalry between China's two main markets.

---

[1] Stock exchange and stock market will be used interchangeably. Bourse is an alternative word used particularly in Continental Europe.

Exhibit 8.5	Relative sizes of global stock markets by market capitalisation

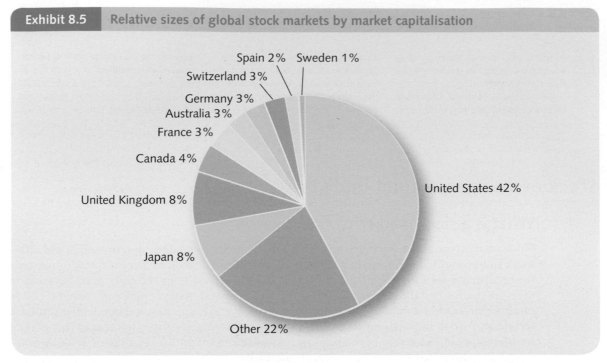

Source: Credit Suisse Global Investment Returns Yearbook 2011.

Exhibit 8.6

Shenzhen takes over as China's listing hub   FT

Robert Cookson

For years, Shanghai has been the undisputed king of China's equity markets, vitalised by a steady stream of initial public offerings from the country's biggest and best state-owned enterprises.

But this year Shanghai has been outgunned by Shenzhen, its less glamorous rival in the south of China, due to an extraordinary boom there in IPOs by smaller, private companies.

The Shenzhen Stock Exchange has seen 246 companies raise a record $33.6bn by new listings this year, triple last year's total and much more than the $24.1bn raised in Shanghai.

Most of the companies listing in Shenhzen are small and medium-sized groups owned by private entrepreneurs, as opposed to the state-owned behemoths that typically gravitate to Shanghai.

IPOs in China
Amount raised ($bn)

Number

Sources: Dealogic

*Includes listings on
ChiNext from 2009

"Chinese policymakers have seen the central importance to the country's future of allowing private companies greater access to private flows of equity capital," says Mr Fuhrman.

▶

Exhibit 8.6 continued

The China Securities Regulatory Commission, which controls stock market listings in the country, appears to have sharply accelerated approvals of IPOs in Shenzhen this year. Market participants say the CSRC has also become less involved in decisions about size, timing, and pricing of share sales.

Shenzhen's IPO boom represents a substantial fresh source of capital for smaller private companies, which have typically been starved of funds by a state-owned banking system that has preferred to lend to other organs of the government.

The bourse is also an increasingly attractive place for private equity groups to make lucrative exits from their investments in China.

Goldman Sachs made a near 200-fold profit on the bank's original $5m investment in Hepalink, a pharmaceutical company, when the drugmaker listed in Shenzhen in April.

Chinese investors, who are restricted from investing abroad, remain hungry for fast-growing domestic companies – even as valuations double the average found in foreign markets.

"What is certainly out there in abundance – and what's desperate for capital – is the private and quasi-private sector," says Mr Howie. "Their time has come."'

Source: *Financial Times*, 19 October 2010, p. 34. Reprinted with permission.

Importance of stock exchanges

Today the important contribution of stock exchanges to economic well-being is recognised from Uzbekistan to Uruguay. There are now more than 100 countries with exchanges and many of these countries have more than one exchange. Many exchanges have been amalgamated with larger ones: the London Stock Exchange merged with the Borsa Italiana in 2007; the NYSE merged in 2006 with the Euronext group, itself a merger of the Paris, Amsterdam, Brussels and Lisbon exchanges, in 2008 with the American Stock Exchange, and in 2011 it was attempting to merge with the Deutsche Börse; the US market NASDAQ merged in 2007 with OMX, the Scandanavian and Baltic group of exchanges (Stockholm, Helsinki, Copenhagen and Iceland, and Estonia, Latvia, Lithuania and Armenia) and also with the Boston and Philadelphia exchanges, with the result that NASDAQ OMX is the largest US electronic exchange, listing over 2,800 companies in the US and another 800 in Europe. In addition to actual mergers, many stock exchanges have holdings in other exchanges or have mutual trading agreements. For instance, the Tokyo Stock Exchange has a 4.9 per cent shareholding in the Singapore exchange.

Exhibit 8.7 focuses on the share trading aspect of 20 of these markets, but most markets usually also trade bonds and other securities. Note the size and importance now of markets outside Europe and North America.

A comparison of the major markets

Until quite recently the LSE was the leading stock exchange in the world for trading shares in overseas companies and one of the biggest for the trading of domestic company shares. However, the electronic revolution and mergers have dramatically increased the market in foreign equity trading in the US, and NYSE Euronext and NASDAQ OMX now head the field in both foreign and domestic trading (*see* **Exhibits 8.8** and **8.9**). Looking only at domestic (home-grown companies') equity, China's domestic trading has shown a huge increase as it opens itself to capitalism.

More mergers and alliances between exchanges are bound to follow, not least because the major financial institutions that operate across the globe desire a seamless, less costly way of trading shares over borders. The ultimate ambition for some visionaries is a single highly liquid equity market allowing investors to trade and companies to raise capital, wherever it suits them, or at least to do so within a continent such as Europe. Ideally, there would be no distortions in share price, costs of trading or regulation as investors cross from one country to another. Whether it is necessary to merge all together Europe's disparate stock exchanges to achieve frictionless pan-European trading is a matter that is hotly debated. Some argue that the absence of a single securities market damages the EU's competitive position *vis-à-vis* the huge, streamlined and

Exhibit 8.7	The world's 20 largest stock exchanges at the end of 2010, ranked according to domestic market capitalisation of equities

End of 2010	Domestic equities market capitalisation* $ million	Total share trading in year $ million	Number of listed companies		
			Total	Domestic	Foreign
NYSE Euronext (US element only)	13,394,082	17,795,600	2,317	1,799	518
NASDAQ OMX (US element only)	3,889,370	12,659,198	2,778	2,480	298
Tokyo SE Group	3,827,774	3,787,952	2,293	2,281	12
London SE Group	3,613,064	2,741,325	2,966	2,362	604
NYSE Euronext (Europe)	2,930,072	2,018,077	1,135	983	152
Shanghai SE	2,716,470	4,496,194	894	894	NA
Hong Kong Exchanges	2,711,316	1,496,433	1,413	1,396	17
TSX (TMX) Group (Canada)	2,170,433	1,368,954	3,741	3,654	87
Bombay SE	1,631,830	258,696	5,034	5,034	NA
National Stock Exchange India	1,596,625	801,017	1,552	1,551	1
BM&FBOVESPA (Brazil)	1,545,566	868,813	381	373	8
Australian SE	1,454,491	1,062,650	1,999	1,913	86
Deutsche Börse	1,429,719	1,628,496	765	690	75
Shenzhen SE	1,311,370	3,572,529	1,169	1,169	0
SIX Swiss Exchange	1,229,357	788,361	296	246	50
BME Spanish Exchanges	1,171,625	1,360,910	3,345	3,310	35
Korea Exchange	1,091,911	1,607,247	1,798	1,781	17
NASDAQ OMX Nordic Exchange (European element)	1,042,154	750,279	778	752	26
MICEX (Russia)	949,149	408,078	250	249	1
Johannesburg SE	925,007	340,025	397	352	45

* The total value, at market prices, of all issued shares of companies quoted on the stock market.

Source: World Federation of Exchanges: www.worldexchanges.org.

highly liquid US capital markets, which have now become a major force in non-domestic trading. Furthermore, they say, it prevents European companies and investors from enjoying the full benefits of the euro.

The importance of a well-run stock exchange

A well-run stock exchange has a number of characteristics. It is one where a '**fair game**' takes place; that is, where it is not possible for some investors and fund raisers to benefit at the expense of other participants – all players are on a level playing field. It is a market which is well regulated to avoid abuses, negligence and fraud in order to reassure investors who put their savings at risk. It is also one in which it is reasonably cheap to carry out transactions. In addition, a large number of buyers and sellers are likely to be needed for the efficient price setting of shares and to

Exhibit 8.8 | Value of equity trading in foreign companies on stock exchanges in year

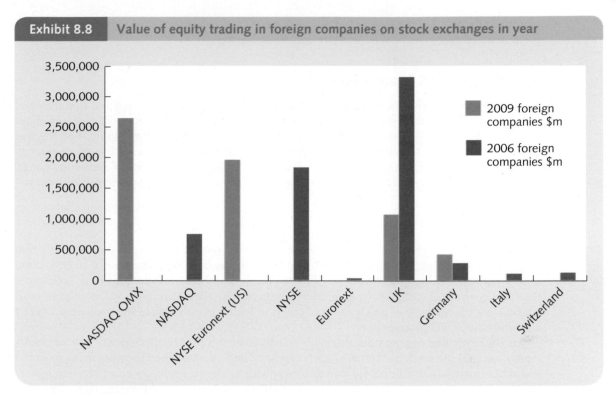

Source: World Federation of Exchanges.

Exhibit 8.9 | Value of equity trading in domestic companies on stock exchanges in year

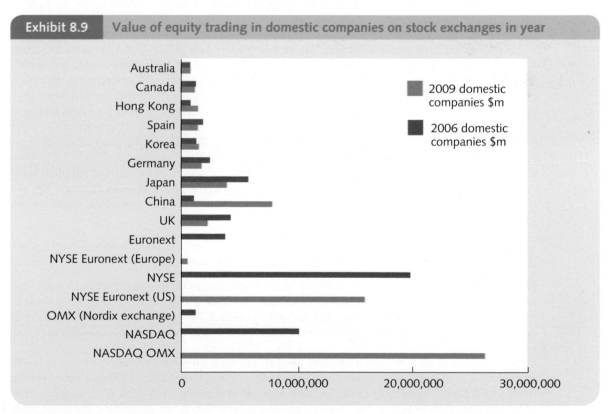

Source: World Federation of Exchanges.

provide sufficient liquidity, allowing the investor to sell at any time without altering the market price. There are six main benefits of a well-run stock exchange.

1 Firms can find funds and grow

Because investors in financial securities with a stock market quotation are assured that they are, generally, able to sell their shares quickly, cheaply and with a reasonable degree of certainty about the price, they are willing to supply funds to firms at a lower cost than they would if selling was slow, or expensive, or the sale price was subject to much uncertainty. Thus stock markets encourage investment by mobilising savings. As well as stimulating the investment of domestic savings, stock markets can be useful for attracting foreign savings and for aiding the privatisation process.

2 Allocation of capital

One of the key economic problems for a nation is finding a mechanism for deciding what mixture of goods and services to produce. An extreme solution has been tried and shown to be lacking in sophistication – that of a totalitarian directed economy where bureaucratic diktat determines the exact quantity of each line of commodity produced. The alternative method favoured in most nations (for the majority of goods and services) is to let the market decide what will be produced and which firms will produce it.

An efficiently functioning stock market is able to assist this process through the flow of investment capital. If the stock market was poorly regulated and operated then the mispricing of shares and other financial securities could lead to society's scarce capital resources being put into sectors which are inappropriate given the objective of maximising economic well-being. If, for instance, the market priced the shares of a badly managed company in a declining industrial sector at a high level then that firm would find it relatively easy to sell shares and raise funds for further investment in its business or to take over other firms. This would deprive companies with better prospects and with a greater potential contribution to make to society of essential finance.

To take an extreme example: imagine the year is 1910 and on the stock market are some firms which manufacture horse-drawn carriages. There are also one or two young companies which have taken up the risky challenge of producing motor cars. Analysts will examine the prospects of the two types of enterprise before deciding which firms will get a warm reception when they ask for more capital in a sale of shares. The unfavoured firms will find their share prices falling as investors sell their shares and will be unable to attract more savers' money. One way for the older firm to stay in business would be to shift resources within the firm to the production of those commodities for which consumer demand is on a rising trend.

More recently there has been a dramatic shift in finance resources as markets supplied hundreds of billions to high-technology industries, such as mobile phone chip technology, e.g. the Cambridge-based company ARM plc, which designs and licenses 95 per cent of the world's chips for mobiles, or Skype in internet telephony.

3 For shareholders

Shareholders benefit from the availability of a speedy, cheap secondary market if they want to sell. Not only do shareholders like to know that they can sell shares when they want to, they may simply want to know the value of their holdings even if they have no intention of selling at present. By contrast, an unquoted firm's shareholders often find it very difficult to assess the value of their holding.

Founders of firms may be particularly keen to obtain a quotation for their firms. This will enable them to diversify their assets by selling a proportion of their holdings. Also, venture capital firms which fund unquoted firms during their rapid growth phase often press the management to aim for a quotation to permit the venture capitalist to have the option of realising the gains made on the original investment, or simply to boost the value of their holding by making it more liquid.

4 Status and publicity

The public profile of a firm can be enhanced by being quoted on an exchange. Banks and other financial institutions generally have more confidence in a quoted firm and therefore are more likely to provide funds at a lower cost. Their confidence is raised because the company's activities are now subject to detailed scrutiny. The publicity surrounding the process of gaining a quotation may have a positive impact on the image of the firm in the eyes of customers, suppliers and employees and so may lead to a beneficial effect on their day-to-day business.

5 Mergers

Mergers can be facilitated better by a quotation. This is especially true if the payments offered to the target firm's shareholders for their holdings are shares in the acquiring firm. A quoted share has a value defined by the market, whereas shares in unquoted firms are difficult to assess.

The stock exchange also assists what is called 'the **market in managerial control**'. This is a mechanism in which teams of managers are seen as competing for control of corporate assets. Or, to put it more simply, mergers through the stock market permit the displacement of inefficient management with a more successful team. Thus, according to this line of reasoning, assets will be used more productively and society will be better off. This market in managerial control is not as effective as is sometimes claimed (it tends to be over-emphasised by acquiring managers).

6 Improves corporate behaviour

If a firm's shares are traded on an exchange, the directors may be encouraged to behave in a manner conducive to shareholders' interests. This is achieved through a number of pressure points. For example, to obtain a quotation on a reputable exchange, companies are required to disclose a far greater range and depth of information than is required by accounting standards or the Companies Act. This information is then disseminated widely and can become the focus of much public and press comment. Before a company is admitted to an exchange the authorities insist on being assured that the management team are sufficiently competent and, if necessary, additional directors are appointed to supplement the board's range of knowledge and skills. Investment analysts also ask for regular briefings from senior managers and continuously monitor the performance of firms. For a quoted company, directors are required to consult shareholders on important decisions, such as mergers. They also have to be very careful to release price-sensitive information in a timely and orderly fashion and they are strictly forbidden to use inside information to make a profit by buying or selling the firm's shares.

Tasks for stock exchanges

Traditionally, exchanges perform the following tasks in order to play their valuable role in a modern society:

- supervision of trading to ensure fairness and efficiency;
- the authorisation of market participants such as brokers and market makers;
- creation of an environment in which prices are formed efficiently and without distortion (**price discovery** or **price formation**). This requires not only regulation of a high order and low transaction costs but also a liquid market in which there are many buyers and sellers, permitting investors to enter or exit quickly without moving the price;
- organisation of the **settlement** of transactions (after the deal has been struck the buyer must pay for the shares and the shares must be transferred to the new owners);
- the regulation of the admission of companies to the exchange and the regulation of companies on the exchange;
- the dissemination of information, e.g. trading data, prices and company announcements. Investors are more willing to trade if prompt and complete information about trades, companies and prices is available.

In recent years the need for stock exchanges to carry out all these activities has been called into question. If we take the case of the LSE, the settlement of transactions was long ago handed over to CREST (discussed later in this chapter). Also the responsibility for authorising the listing of companies was transferred to the UK Listing Authority arm of the Financial Services Authority (the principal UK regulator). The LSE's Regulatory News Service (which distributes important company announcements and other price-sensitive news) has to compete with other distribution platforms outside the LSE's control as listed companies are now able to choose between competing providers of news dissemination platforms (there are currently eight regulatory information services).

New trading systems

Multilateral trading facilities (MTFs)

Traditional stock exchanges had virtual monopoly positions for the trading of shares and other securities in their home countries. They had little incentive to cut fees or to improve their trading technology. This resulted in the main users, institutional investment funds, banks, brokers and hedge funds, becoming frustrated with the raw deal they were getting.

Starting in the US in the early 2000s they determined that the national stock exchanges could do with some competition, so they got together, chipped in a few million for start-up costs and created new trading platforms. These were equipped with nimbler technology and required far fewer staff than the traditional exchanges. They had narrower differences between the price to buy (bid) and the price to sell (offer) a share, lower execution (transaction) costs and the time between sending an order and the order being complete was much faster than the traditional exchanges. Not only did the institutions now have a cheaper way of trading shares but they could also use the presence of the new trading platforms to force the old exchanges to change their ways.

The Americans called these platforms electronic communications networks (ECNs). They are also known as multilateral trading facilities (a term more favoured in Europe) and they have certainly had an effect. As recently as 2003 about 80 per cent of the trading volume in the shares listed on the NYSE was handled by the NYSE itself. Today, less than one-quarter of the trades go through the NYSE; the rest are traded through a number of MTFs including BATS, Direct Edge and ArcaEx (and 'dark pools' – see later). NYSE is not alone; NASDAQ has lost a lot of trade to the new venues as well.

A major breakthrough in Europe occurred in November 2007, with the introduction of the EU's Markets in Financial Instruments Directive (Mifid), which aims to provide a 'harmonised regulatory regime for investment services across the 30 member states of the European Economic Area. The main objectives of the Directive are to increase competition and consumer protection in investment services'. Following this Directive, brokers acting on behalf of share (and other security) buyers and sellers must now demonstrate that they are achieving the keenest price and using the most efficient, cost-effective trading venues.[2] This encouraged the establishment of cheaper and faster electronic trading platforms to challenge the old ones. And, of course, European institutional investors were just as keen as their US counterparts to have alternatives to the national exchanges.

These traditional stock markets have lost a lot of trade to the new generation of European MTFs (such as BATS Europe, Chi-X and Turquoise). These trade the shares from companies quoted on a variety of national exchanges across Europe, and they are far less strictly regulated than stock markets. As recently as 2007 shares in the FTSE100 index were traded largely through the LSE. Today there are 20 alternative trading platforms, five of which are MTFs (the others are 'dark pools'). MTFs have taken around one-third of continental European share trading and about half of trading in large UK companies' shares, causing a drop in volume of trading at the LSE and other traditional stock exchanges. Japan has joined the movement. It now has five new competing trading venues

---

[2] 'Best execution', a requirement of Mifid, of a trade means demonstrating that the broker obtained the best price, low cost of execution, speed and the likelihood of settlement of the trade going well.

outside the Tokyo Stock Exchange (TSE), but they are not (yet) taking much market share as the TSE's fees are not considered expensive and it offers a fast trading service.

BATS, one of the largest MTFs, was founded in 2005 as an e-trading exchange and quickly took a sizeable share of the US equity trading market. It has now has expanded into Europe and has further expansion plans. It already turns over more shares than either Euronext (Europe) or Deutsche Börse – *see* **Exhibit 8.10**.

Exhibit 8.10

BATS seen as likely Chi-X suitor   **FT**

Jeremy Grant

Alasdair Haynes, chief executive of Chi-X Europe, has a habit when he is speaking at industry conferences of describing his business as "an exchange".

Technically, he is wrong. Chi-X was launched in 2007 as a "multilateral trading facility" (MTF) – regulatory jargon for a type of share trading platform that emerged in the wake of the enactment by Brussels of Markets in Financial Instruments Directive (Mifid).

"According to the Oxford dictionary and Websters that's what we are," Mr Haynes insists. "We're a meeting place of buyers and sellers." But in one important way

Chi-X deserves to be ranked alongside the likes of bourses such as the London Stock Exchange and Deutsche Börse. After only three years in existence, it handles more share trading than the German bourse, and more than the LSE's UK markets division.

Small wonder that Chi-X has now started to attract interest from potential buyers. An as-yet unnamed party wrote to Mr Haynes last weekend expressing interest in the business.

Speculation is centred on Nasdaq OMX and Deutsche Börse, which both lack a substantial pan-European presence. But another

name on observers' lips is Chi-X's main rival: BATS Global Markets, parent of BATS Europe.

Like Chi-X, BATS Europe was set up as an MTF to take advantage of Mifid, which broke the national monopolies of Europe's established exchanges and allowed upstart platforms such as Chi-X to emerge.

Most were backed by banks and brokers that were the biggest providers of orders to the exchanges.

Now, however, the economics of running an MTF are tougher than in 2007, before the financial crisis. Volumes in Europe are anaemic, meaning it will be harder for them

Shareholders of both Chi-X Europe and BATS

Bank of America/ Merrill Lynch
Citigroup
Credit Suisse
Getco
Morgan Stanley

Chi-X Europe only shareholders

BNP Paribas
Citadel
Fortis
Goldman Sachs
Instinet (Nomura)
Optiver
Société Générale
UBS

BATS only shareholders

Dave Cummings
Deutsche Bank
JPMorgan
Lehman Estate
Lime Brokerage
Wedbush

Sources: Thomson Reuters; FT research

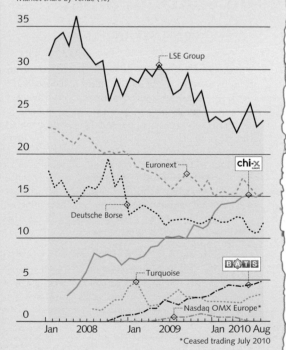

European share trading volumes
Market share by venue (%)

*Ceased trading July 2010

Exhibit 8.10 continued

to reach profitability (although Mr Haynes says Chi-X has been operationally profitable in the seven consecutive months up to July).

Step one in consolidation of the MTF's took place this year when the LSE bought Turquoise, another bank-backed venture that launched after Chi-X.

Some suggest the next step might involve the shareholders of BATS and Chi-X coming to an arrangement. After all, they share five of the same shareholders: Getco, the Chicago-based market-making firm: Citi; Credit Suisse; Bank of America/Merrill Lynch; and Morgan Stanley.

With volumes low, it is questionable whether all shareholders would want to stay committed to two platforms with the ongoing investment in technology and post-trade arrangements that this involves.

Source: Financial Times, 25 August 2010, p. 18. Reprinted with permission.

The proliferation of trading venues means that prices are increasingly being set for shares in a number of different places. In 2007, Rolls-Royce's shares were publically traded in one place; now it is bought and sold on 14 platforms. This raises the difficulty of maintaining the quality of high transparency in trades required to promote trust in the market process. While the prices on the different platforms track one another, only those traders with very sophisticated systems for seeing the trades going through each of the 14 venues can know what is going on and whether there are opportunities to buy or sell quickly when discrepancies in prices make it worthwhile. This benefits linked-up traders who can act fast, but this is at the expense of ordinary investors. The splitting of trading between so many platforms has also led to concern that the important quality of liquidity is being lost. In response the EU and country regulators have listened to the voices calling for a 'consolidated tape' which would list all the bid and offer prices from all venues, throughout Europe at least – *see* **Exhibit 8.11**.

Exhibit 8.11

Europe set for overhaul of rules on share dealing

FT

Jeremy Grant and **Nikki Tait**

For the past three years in Europe, traders have watched as the share dealing landscape has changed beyond recognition.

Thanks to reforms passed by the European Commission, competitors have emerged for national exchanges, while new rivals have proliferated, creating a spaghetti junction of trading venues, spewing out market data and prices.

Yesterday, however, regulators fired their first salvo in attempting to bring more order to the markets.

The Committee of European Securities Regulators kicked off the biggest overhaul of the region's securities regulations in years, calling for a wide range of reforms to bolster transparency of Europe's increasingly fragmented equities and over-the-counter derivatives markets.

Among its top recommendations was a call for the establishment of a central point where prices for shares traded across multiple venues can easily be seen – a so-called "consolidated tape".

Europe's share markets were revolutionised in 2007 with the passage by Brussels of the Markets in Financial Instruments Directive (Mifid).

That kicked off competition between exchanges and allowed the emergence of competing venues.

While the proliferation of trading venues has brought down transaction costs, an unintended consequence is that there is no publicly-available central system for gathering such post-trade data, as there is in industries like insurance, where consumers can check price comparison websites.

Three years ago, shares in the FTSE 100 were largely traded on the London Stock Exchange. Now they are available on 21 venues, including the LSE, a rival platform called Chi-X, and off-exchange venues known as "dark pools", where large orders are matched in private.

"Fragmentation of transparency information, if not addressed properly, raises concerns because it could undermine the overarching transparency objective in Mifid, and may

▶

Exhibit 8.11 continued

Recommendations by the Committee of European Securities Regulators

Market data

Create a single point of access to post-trade market data, in a so-called 'consolidated tape.' Regulators to impose a publicly-run solution if that does not happen within about two years

Force down the cost of post-trade data by insisting that exchanges and other venues make available pre- and post-trade data separately. Currently they are bundled together, meaning data in Europe can cost up to 10 times more than in the US

Trading venues

Upstart trading venues – known as 'multilateral trading facilities' – that have been competing with national exchanges to be brought in line with the way established exchanges are regulated

Banks that operate trade matching facilities known as 'crossing networks', where large orders are done out of the public eye, to be required to publish the number, value and volume of transactions

Trading behaviour

Electronic messages used by traders to convey information to certain market participants about buying and selling interest in a share – known as 'indications of interest, or 'IOIs' – to be treated as normal orders and made public to the whole market

On 'high-frequency' trading, where rapid-fire computer algorithms can make thousands of trades in seconds, CESR did not recommend any action, saying "further work" was needed

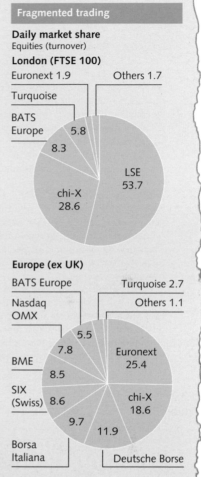

Fragmented trading

Daily market share
Equities (turnover)
London (FTSE 100)
Euronext 1.9   Others 1.7
Turquoise
BATS Europe 5.8
8.3
LSE 53.7
chi-X 28.6

Europe (ex UK)
BATS Europe   Turquoise 2.7
Nasdaq OMX   Others 1.1
5.5
7.8   Euronext 25.4
BME
8.5
SIX (Swiss) 8.6   chi-X 18.6
9.7   11.9
Borsa Italiana   Deutsche Borse

Sources: Thomson Reuters

result in less transparent markets," CESR said in its report yesterday.

It did not limit its recommendations to equities. The Paris-based body, which co-ordinates activities of EU securities regulators, recommended ways to bring transparency to derivatives data and called for the same reporting rules applying to equities to also apply to exchange-traded funds.

It also suggested new rules to tighten up on dark pools operated by banks and advocated clamping down on sending electronic messages into the market to test buying and selling interest.

Yet there is urgency to address issues such as lack of transparency in market data.

Regulators on both sides of the Atlantic are already concerned that the unfettered growth of competition is damaging investor trust in market structures.

Source: *Financial Times*, 30 July 2010, p. 31. Reprinted with permission.

The MTFs themselves have responded to the need for their customers to have access to a number of trading venues at the same time. They have introduced 'smart order routing' that directs a trade to the platform that offers the best price, even if that is not on their facility – *see* **Exhibit 8.12**.

Serious concerns have been raised about the lower level of regulation on MTFs. Regulators require the main national markets to employ a team of people to survey trades every day to ensure that the market is not being abused. MTFs are not required to do this. Xavier Rolet, CEO of the LSE at the time of writing, and other traditional stock exchange chiefs have complained of an 'uneven playing field' because they have to bear the costly regulatory burden (according to Mr Rolet, the LSE has 150 regulatory staff compared with Chi-X's five and it pays about €5 million p.a. in regulatory fees compared with Chi-X's £125,000). **Exhibit 8.13** describes the dangers of fragmentation.

Exhibit 8.12

BATS in 'smart order' move

By Jeremy Grant in London

BATS Europe, one of five share dealing venues battling Europe's established bourses, is set to offer traders a new service that seeks out where their orders are most likely to find a match on both the region's multiple "dark pools" or standard trading platforms.

The move makes US-based BATS, the second of the region's small trading venues to offer such a "smart order routing" service after Nasdaq OMX Europe, a rival platform owned by Nasdaq OMX, the transatlantic exchange.

Smart order routing is a service commonly offered by brokers and banks as a way of encouraging investors to place more orders with them.

Smart order routing has grown in popularity in Europe as the number of trading venues has proliferated in the wake of the Markets in Financial Instruments Directive, which broke exchanges' monopolies in 2007.

It uses technology that scans multiple pools of liquidity, identifying where the best price for a particular share is likely to be found. It also helps ascertain where large orders can easily be done, and can split orders into smaller sizes and seek the best venues for them to be matched, often within a matter of seconds.

The BATS move shows that the lines are blurring between the role of brokers in seeking out the best deals for investors and exchanges and trading platforms, traditionally only recipients of orders from brokers. It also shows that the platforms to which orders are routed by such technology are themselves offering the same service as a way to attract more orders.

That is because complete orders – made up of thousands of shares – are often not filled completely at any given venue. Any exchange or trading platform that is able to find matches for any unfilled orders by "order routing" them away to other venues – even rival ones – are seen as offering a valuable service.

Like Nasdaq OMX Europe, BATS Europe will charge a fee for its smart order routing service.

Source: Financial Times, 25 January 2010, p. 19. Reprinted with permission.

Exhibit 8.13

Multiple venues leave Europe 'open to abuse'

Jeremy Grant

"Layering", "spoofing" and "painting the tape" are just some of the underhand practices that crop up from time to time in equity markets.

But regulators could soon be using these terms much more frequently in the wake of fresh warnings about the potential for market abuse in Europe.

A group of consulting groups in Britain has published a study showing that the fragmentation of trading venues as a result of the Markets in Financial Instruments Directive (Mifid) has left Europe open to abuse by traders wanting to manipulate the markets.

They contend that the fragmentation of trading across multiple venues – exchanges, newer platforms and dark pools – means that regulators cannot spot fraud as easily – and may be missing it completely.

That will come as unwelcome news to the architects of Mifid in Brussels who devised it as a way of spurring competition, allowing the emergence of "multilateral trading facilities" and lowering trading costs for investors.

It is also likely to fuel a row between exchanges and their smaller rivals over who is better at keeping tabs on market abuse.

The consulting groups behind the Alliance of Independent Advisors to Financial Markets, or Avenues, argue that the function of ensuring markets are fair – such as the surveillance of bids and offers and executed trades – is "now almost impossible to undertake comprehensively".

It says the potential for abuse has been heightened by the fact that a Market Abuse Directive passed by the European Commission came into force two years before Mifid in 2007, when no MTFs existed and when most trading was done on national exchanges.

Yet with the advent of Mifid, as much as half of trading in some big name stocks takes place away from exchanges, so surveillance staff only see a fraction of activity in many stocks. Last month, the London Stock Exchange's share of trading in FTSE 100 stocks dipped below 50 per cent for the first time.

"No single exchange now sees all the activity on any given stock for which they are responsible. MTFs do not invest in comparable

▶

Exhibit 8.13 continued

surveillance infrastructures and internal broker-dealer 'crossing networks' [dark pools] are in effect unregulated in Market Abuse Directive terms," Avenues says.

Similar concerns have been raised in the US, where equity markets are fragmented between the New York Stock Exchange, Nasdaq and smaller platforms such as BATS and Direct Edge.

Rick Ketchum, chief executive of the Financial Industry Regulatory Authority, which regulates US brokerage firms, recently acknowledged that "the decline of the primary market concept, where there was a single price discovery market whose on-site regulator saw 90-plus per cent of the trading activity, has obviously become a reality".

Mats Wilhelmsson, chief operating officer at Scila, a Swedish seller of market surveillance systems – and a former head of surveillance at the Swedish markets regulator – agrees with Avenues' conclusions. He says that "some types of market manipulation are much easier to execute in the post-Mifid environment because of [market] fragmentation".

He singles out "front-running", where a broker, knowing a client has a large buy or sell order, will carry out a buy or sell order of its own first, to take advantage of the price movement that the broker knows the client order is likely to have once it is placed in the market.

Joost van der Does de Willebois, chairman of Euronext Amsterdam, the Dutch segment of NYSE Euronext, says Euronext has long been required by regulators to maintain a "market integrity unit" of surveillance staff to monitor markets – not a requirement for MTFs. "We would argue that Mifid has created an unlevel playing field for which we have good evidence. It all

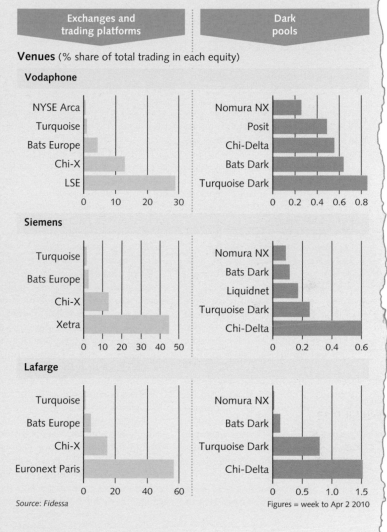

Source: Fidessa

Figures = week to Apr 2 2010

comes down to cost, they compete on lower costs," he says.

Brian Taylor, managing director of BTA Consulting, a member of Avenues, argues that industry and regulators should come together to create a "utility" to carry out surveillance across Europe, involving all venues and not just exchanges.

Regulators in Brussels are set to review the market abuse directive

later this year. Maria Velentza, head of the securities markets unit in the European Commission's directorate-general for the internal market and services, which is reviewing Mifid, says Brussels will study the issue.

"We are going to fix this."'

Source: *Financial Times*, 7 April 2010, p. 35. Reprinted with permission.

The main idea of introducing Mifid was to lower the cost of trading equities. But many professional asset managers are frustrated by the unintended consequences. While the cost of using platforms themselves has fallen between 20 per cent and 80 per cent (the old exchanges have lowered their charges significantly), there have been increases in complexity and in technology needed to access the new venues. Individual investors, too, are not terribly impressed with the changes that have taken place – *see* **Exhibit 8.14**.

Exhibit 8.14

Private investors fail to see benefits of Mifid reform

Jeremy Grant and James Wilson

Among hundreds of investors who flocked to a fair in Frankfurt last week – listening to pitches for opportunities from exchange-traded funds to Canadian gold mines – it was difficult to find anyone who believed that the "Mifid" [Markets in Financial Instruments Directive] had helped them.

Mifid was enacted by the European Commission in 2007. It was designed to cut the cost of dealing in company shares across Europe, heralding an era where private, or "retail" investors, would place more of their savings into traded financial instruments, relieving the burden of pension provision on stricken European government budgets.

But for retail investors at the German fair such as Kirsten Meyer-Witting, a consultant who trades shares for herself, the supposed benefits of Mifid have yet to materialise. She says: "Things have got cheaper but not necessary because of Mifid. I would not be able to say what difference it has made."

An association representing more than 29 investor groups across Europe goes further. Guillaume Prache, managing director of the European Federation of Investors (EFI), says brokerage fees have come down for large institutions trading shares, such as banks but not for retail investors.

He says brokers serving retail investors often fail to show prices across all the available venues, usually only showing prices on the national exchange – as before Mifid.

Partly that is a problem of education: many retail brokers simply are not aware of the range of trading venues in a post-Mifid world. Niki Beattie, managing director of The Market Structure Practice, a consultancy, says: "I don't think the individual investor has benefitted from Mifid. Regulators and the Commission need to do a better job of educating investors."

In addition, many small and medium-sized brokers cannot afford to build the data feed connections so that prices can be shown widely. Mr Prache says: "If you go to your broker screen you often get only the regulated [exchange] market information for any given share. That's obviously one failure of Mifid."

Markus Kienle, a representative of the SdK, an organisation representing small investors, says: "When you look at the results of the advice people are getting you would get the impression that Mifid has not brought very much.

"Organisational models don't help to improve the quality of advice. I think transparency is as bad as it was before." However, Marco Tüngler, managing director of the DSW, a big association representing German private investors, argues that Mifid has benefited retail investors, including helping them see fees set by bank brokers laid out more explicitly than before. "It has taken people a couple of years to get used to it but there is pressure on price now and customers are more ready to negotiate with their bank. They are more independent," he says.

Source: Financial Times, 8 March 2010, p. 8. Reprinted with permission.

Trading speed

Nowadays most share dealing is done using linked computer systems in trading rooms set miles apart rather than telephone or face-to-face deals. Computer programs source the best buying and selling prices and execute the deals virtually instantaneously. Also, traders can link up to the markets without needing to ask a broker to execute a trade. **Exhibit 8.15** shows some benefits of electronic (e-) trading.

Electronic trading has gone further as some investors demand very fast dealing times. This has led to the development of **high-frequency trading (HFT)**, which usually uses computer programmed algorithms to buy or sell quickly. The blisteringly fast trading speed gives a millisecond advantage to the HF trader, enabling them to be the first to buy or sell shares, futures, options or other derivatives of shares. This is the key to the success of HFT: super-computers which can process massive volumes of information and make decisions based on that information. They respond when particular conditions occur, say, sell or buy when a certain share price hits a certain level, without the need for humans to punch in orders to keyboards. The drive for speed has led to traders placing their computer servers within exchanges' data centres so as to reduce the physical distance between systems – after all, a microsecond can make all the difference. The old exchanges have had to respond. For example, the LSE has installed what it describes as the quick-

Exhibit 8.15	Benefits of e-trading

Liquidity is increased (there are more buyers and sellers) because companies can trade with each other regardless of location

Competition is increased because e-trading removes barriers and encourages globalisation: traders can trade anywhere by just pressing a button, no need to go through brokers or exchanges

Transparency can be increased; it is often much easier to find out security prices when the details are circulating the world electronically

Transaction cost are reduced to dealers and investors

The spread (difference between buying and selling prices) is reduced

Retail as well as institutional investors can take advantage of these benefits

est share trading system in the world on its Turquoise platform[3] which trades European equities in 124 microseconds, 2,000 times faster than the blink of a human eye. This is the time taken from the moment when a client inputs an order to the exchange and a message comes back to the client that the deal is done.

HFT now accounts for more than half of all equity trading in the US and one-third in Europe, and is causing concern in some quarters about the behaviour of the traders, especially those who rely on computer programmed responses. There is a worry that markets are becoming a playground for a few specialist traders rather than places that help economic activity by, say, raising capital for businesses. There is also the well-justified fear that programs might all send the same 'sell' signal at the same time, causing a crash by automatically selling shares. **Exhibit 8.16** discusses some of the worries.

Exhibit 8.16

'Algo-trading' changes speed of the game on Wall Street

By Jeremy Grant in London

"Guys this is probably the craziest I've seen it down here ever!" That was the strangled cry of a trader in the futures trading pits of Chicago on Thursday afternoon when the stock market plunged a stomach-churning 9 per cent.

But the roller-coaster ride was not caused by traders shouting at each other. It was, instead, driven by computers. For today's stock markets are over-whelmingly governed by mathematical algorithms programmed to jump in and out of the markets almost at the speed of

▶

[3] A 51 per cent stake in Turquoise was purchased by the LSE in 2010. It offers trading in more than 2,000 European shares.

Exhibit 8.16 continued

light, in a frenzied search for trades that yield a quick profit.

To proponents of "algorithmic trading", this has made markets more efficient and opened up new opportunities. No longer are we so reliant on a wink and a nod in a trading pit. Rapid advances in technology have helped suck in new market participants, boosting the amount of liquidity for the investing public.

But "algo-trading", and the rise of so-called "high-frequency" traders that often use it, is so pervasive that some suspect it may be hard to see how ordinary investors can be expected to trust market structures in which they have placed their faith for decades. Instead, they seem to serve the interests of short-term traders using the latest computer wizardry.

More than half the US equity markets involve the use of a form of algorithmic or high-frequency trading. That is a hugh increase since the 1987 stock market crash, where programme trades were blamed for exacerbating falls.

Moreover, trading takes place not only on the main exchanges – the New York Stock Exchange and Nasdaq – but on a plethora of other platforms, including "dark pools" and systems operated by brokers themselves. Less than 35 per cent of trading in NYSE-listed shares actually takes place on the New York Stock Exchange these days.

The speed of trades is mind-boggling. Last month Algo Technologies, a US company, unveiled a system that can handle a trade in 16 microseconds.

Stock exchanges are courting "algo" traders, eager to attract business away from rival platforms. For most ordinary investors the idea of an exchange is still the neo-classical facade of the mighty NYSE on Wall Street.

But in reality, most shares change hands in vast data centres. One of them, the size of three football fields, opened for business this week in Basildon, UK, built by NYSE Euronext, owner of the New York exchange.

Yet amid the technological revolution, it is unclear whether exchanges and brokers have the risk management systems to guard against algos running wild, perhaps traggered by erroneous or "fat finger" trades.

Something else worries observers. The trader in Chicago shouting himself hoarse was quoting prices in S&P index futures, not ordinary shares, which often trade in a direct relationship with equities. That means a problem in the equity markets quickly becomes a problem elsewhere – raising the spectre of a systemic hit to the financial system.

As Wall Street digests the turmoil, the Securities and Exchange Commission is engaged in the most far-reaching study of how technology has changed the way markets work.

It wants to figure out whether ordinary investors have been put at a disadvantage by the technological revolution.

Source: Financial Times, 8 May 2010, p. 8. Reprinted with permission.

The trigger for the large market decline on 6 May 2010 (mentioned in Exhibit 8.16) was a trade put on by a conventional asset manager (using futures in a share market index), but the problem was greatly exaggerated by algorithmic-based HFT – *see* **Exhibit 8.17** (a '*fat finger trade*' is where a trader accidentally presses the wrong button on a computer keyboard and buys, say, 20 million shares instead of 2 million). The defenders of HFT counter the critics by saying that it benefits markets by providing liquidity and narrower bid–offer spreads because the HF traders arbitrage away price differences across multiple platforms.

Exhibit 8.17

Flash crash: market reform to be examined

Aline van Duyn and Telis Demos

The high-frequency trading firms that have come to dominate daily trading in US equity markets may feel entitled to a little slack.

After suffering a good deal of political heat over May's "flash crash" on Wall Street, it turns out that a large order by a traditional

investor was the trigger for the wild market swings.

A report by the Securities and Exchange Commission and the Commmodity Futures Trading Commission concluded on Friday that the May 6 sell-out was sparked by a rapidly executed $4.1bn sale

of stock-index futures by a single institutional investor, who was hedging against the risk of a market downturn.

The order was placed via a computer-based order execution programme so quickly – in just 20 minutes – that it triggered wild

▶

Exhibit 8.17 continued

automated selling by other traders, including the high-frequency traders (HFTs).

The decision to sell on "autopilot" into markets that were already jittery over concerns on possible European sovereign-debt default was unusual.

Regulators have not explained why the seller, identified by a person familiar with the matter as money manager Waddell & Reed, demanded that the trade be executed so quickly, especially as previous similar trades and been placed over a five-hour time frame. The sell order was for e-Mini S&P 500 futures.

"The report seems to conclude that the spark that got the whole thing started was a trade by a plain-vanilla asset manager, and that could take some of the pressure off the high-frequency trading community," says Justin Schack, director of market structure analysis at Rosenblatt Securities. The automation of trading has led to a surge in volumes driven by high-speed computer programmes. Around a dozen HFTs dominate volumes in equity markets – both cash shares and futures – on many days.

The rapid growth of such trading has led smaller investors to complain that they are at a disadvantage.

The fragmented structure of equity market, where trades are conducted across some 50 venues ranging from the New York Stock Exchange to "dark pools", had already attracted the attention of regulators.

Since the flash crash, political pressure to take action to curb the influence of the HFTs has increased, even though it was not clear whether such trading was the reason for the market swings.

The report, however, does show that there is a difference between the volume of shares changing hands, and the actual underlying demand – or liquidity – for shares. HFTs make razor-thin margins on each trade, and only make money if they do many of them.

"HFTs began to quickly buy and then resell contracts to each other – generating a "hot-potato" volume effect as the same positions were rapidly passed back and forth," says the flash crash report.

Over the course of just 14 seconds, the report says 27,000 contracts of e-Mini S&P 500 futures were traded, around half by HFTs. On a net basis, however, only 200 additional contracts were bought in those seconds.

One widely held assumption about the way markets operate is that the high levels of trading activity means liquidity – when large positions can be bought or sold without affecting the price significantly. The report's findings appear to undermine that.

"Just as there's a difference in tennis or ping pong between the rally before the point and the point itself, in markets, there's a difference between a position going back and forth between market makers and a position actually bought by a fundamental buyer who will hold it overnight," said Gary Gensler, chairman of the CFTC, on Monday.

Mr Gensler said that a committee will consider the report and make recommendations to both the CFTC and the SEC, in particular in three areas.

First, the committee should look more closely at how investors place orders. It should examine whether customers such as Waddell & Reed and the brokers executing orders for the customers should be subject to trading limits or have an obligation for orderly execution.

The second question would be whether there should be more visibility on the full extent of orders.

The third would be whether there should be further "market pauses" – such as the circuit breakers introduced by regulators after the flash crash that can give investors and traders time to rethink their strategies in periods of market turbulence.

The debate about the dominance of high-speed trading is unlikely to end soon. Lawmakers are waiting for the next moves from regulators – and the outcome of November's congressional elections – but aides say they believe legislation will be needed and that the current circuit breaker proposals are likely to be inadequate in preventing a future spiral of selling.

Paul Kanjorski, chairman of the House financial services sub-committee on capital markets, said after the report that regulators needed to review and revise equity market rules. "While automated, high-frequency trading may provide our markets with some benefits, it can also carry the potential for serious harm and market mischief," he said.

Patrick Armstrong, a New York Stock Exchange trader and head of the Alliance of Floor Brokers, an advocacy group, says that regulators are not "pointing the finger hard enough" at the HFT players in the market.

"The world is starting to wake up to the realities of speed versus price, and I just don't understand why we need to continue to get faster," he says.

Additional reporting by Michael Mackenzie and Tom Braithwaite

Source: Financial Times, 5 October 2010, p. 39. Reprinted with permission.

Dark pools

If you are an institutional trader and you want to sell a large block of shares in a company, you have a problem. With the main exchanges you are usually required to advertise up-front the number of shares you wish to sell together with a price you are willing to accept. So, if the usual size of trade in your chosen share is between 1,000 and 10,000 and you suddenly come along and offer 200,000 shares, your inputting of that information on the exchange's dealing system is going to have an effect on the market price. Other traders instantly become aware that you are trying to shift an extraordinarily large volume and will lower the prices at which they are willing to buy to take advantage of your need. Similarly, there is a problem when you wish to buy a large block of shares in a company – the market moves against you.

The main solution to this problem is for you to break down the order into much smaller pieces. With modern computers you can instruct the exchange's system to display an order to sell, say, 5,000, and then as soon as that has been sold the system automatically posts another order for, say 4,000, and then 6,000 when that has sold, and so on until you have sold the full 200,000. You have not spooked the market and have hopefully got decent prices. Because electronic trading, with its greater ability to split large orders, has largely replaced older methods (pit trading and market maker-based trading – see later in the chapter and in Chapter 3), the typical US order size of the 1990s has fallen from 1,400 shares or $40,000 to only 300 shares and $6,000 on the NYSE or NASDAQ. In the UK, average order sizes have fallen 90 per cent to around £8,000 on the LSE, and similar falls occurred in other markets such as Deutsche Börse and Hong Kong.

The solution of splitting large orders on the regulated exchanges has helped but it does not work perfectly because experienced traders often recognise who is dealing and start to see a pattern emerging: they can see the displayed prices before the deal goes through, and they can see you adding orders regularly. To try to resolve this, since 2004 the large institutions, such as banks, have set up a number of new trading venues, called **dark pools**, where large orders can be placed anonymously without the need to advertise the price or size to the wider market *before* a trade is agreed. It is still a requirement that completed deals are announced to all market users, but this is not as immediate as on the regulated exchanges (although regulators are calling for a speeding up). There are distinct advantages in not forewarning the mass of traders that a large body of shares is seeking a new home or someone is looking to bulk-buy shares. Even when a trade is published, there is no way of ascertaining whether it was a full or part trade that was executed, nor any way for investors to know what buyers and sellers are still around.

The US has over 40 dark pools in operation, with about half that number in Europe. A typical large order in a dark pool can be as large as 55,000 shares. Dark pools have taken about 8–10 per cent of share trading in the US, about 5 per cent of those in Europe and a growing proportion in Asia.

The **lit pools** on the normal national exchanges, where prices, bid-offer spreads and offered sizes are visible to every member of the public, contribute to transparency and the price discovery process – *see* later in this chapter. The problem with the proliferation of trading venues and dispersed order flow is the fragmentation of trading in a company's shares resulting in poorer liquidity on any one platform. Market regulators are trying to improve matters – *see* **Exhibit 8.18**.

Exhibit 8.18

Call to make 'dark pools' trades public

By **Jeremy Grant** in Amsterdam

Share trading that takes place in "dark pools" should be revealed to the public and regulators should "take steps to support the use" of "transparent" orders over "dark" trades, according to the global umbrella body for national securities watchdogs.

The International Organisation of Securities Commissions (Iosco) on Wednesday published six "draft principles" to "address regulatory concerns" over dark pools, on which public consultation ends in January.

The call is the clearest sign yet of a possible regulatory clampdown on dark pools, which match trades in private with prices only revealed after a trade is done. Many are the modern, electronic equivalent of old telephone-brokered markets.

Growth of dark pools is being fuelled by "high-frequency" trading, which has sliced orders into ever smaller sizes on stock exchanges and other platforms.

That is causing asset managers and other institutions to direct larger trades towards dark pools to minimise the risk of prices moving against them.

But dark pools have generated controversy, with regulators scrutinising them amid questions over their transparency and whether too much pricing of shares takes place

▶

Exhibit 8.18 continued

away from mainstream, or "lit", markets such as exchanges.

About 10 per cent of US shares are traded in dark pools, about half of that in Europe and a growing proportion in Asia.

Dark pools are run by independent operators or by banks – which call them "crossing networks" – or sometimes by exchanges themselves.

Iosco said that its principles were designed to "minimise the adverse impact of the increased use of dark pools and dark orders in transparent markets on the price discovery process".

It said that a technical committee studying dark pools had "focused on a number of areas that had been identified as pos-

sibly having adverse effects on the market", such as "transparency and price discovery, market fragmentatation, knowledge of trading intentions, fair access; and the ability to assess actual trading volume in dark pools".

Source: Financial Times, 28 October 2010, p. 33. Reprinted with permission.

Exhibit 8.19 discusses the level of suspicion concerning dark pools and high-frequency traders.

Exhibit 8.19

Trust in dark pools is dented

FT

Jeremy Grant

If there was ever a business in need of a new name, it is "dark pools".

This week, the role of these trading facilities is once again under the microscope after revelations that rapid electronic traders – possibly "high-frequency" traders (HFTs) – sniffed out what was going on in two leading European dark pools and profited from the information they found.

At all times, the priority is not to reveal who you are or to reveal at what price you want to trade. That is market sensitive information that can be used by rivals, jeopardising your trade, and explains why prices are not made public until matches are found.

Yet last week it emerged that slivers of information had leaked out of two dark pools, one operated by Chi-X and BATs, operators of two of the "multilateral trading facilities" (MTFs).

The information – contained in certain data feeds – gave enough clues to anyone who was interested about what orders certain large – although unnamed – participants had sitting in those pools. Traders could then place trades on the public exchanges – on which

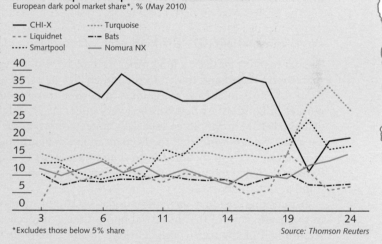

Trust in European dark pools was shaken last week
European dark pool market share*, % (May 2010)
*Excludes those below 5% share
Source: Thomson Reuters

dark pools often base their bid-offer spreads – in the hope of profiting, trading experts say.

Within a few minutes of the discovery, volumes on Chi-Delta – the Chi-X platform – and on the BATS platform plunged as so-called "buyside" participants called their brokers with instructions to pull their orders, fearful their orders were being exploited.

By contrast volumes shot up on rivals like Turquoise where data feeds did not reveal such information.

Trust in market structures has already been badly shaken this month, following the "flash crash" on Wall Street, when computerised trading exacerbated a hugh fall in stocks.

But the latest development in dark pools shows trust is in equally short supply in an increasingly important corner of the region's equity markets.

The sudden withdrawal of trades from the two platforms also raises questions over the role of high-

Exhibit 8.19 continued

frequency trading in dark pools. Hitherto such traders, who seek to profit from minute changes in prices between trading venues, were assumed to operate only on exchanges and MTFs. But some suspect that they may be picking off trades in dark pools without the original poster of the order knowing.

Joe Saluzzi, co-head of equity trading at Themis Trading, a US securities firm, says participants have to ask whether some HFTs are actually "predatory" in dark pools, by taking advantage of information they are not supposed to have. "People are going to say they thought they were able to trade, cloaked and anonymously, but now I am supporting a multi-million dollar industry called high-frequency trading," he says.

Themis believes the problem lies in the data feeds provided by trading venues. "Information in these feeds allows high-frequency trading firms to track when an investor changes price on his order, how much stock the investor is buying or selling in accumulation, as well as the ascertaining of hidden order flow."

Chi-Delta and BATS have changed their data feeds so that such so-called "information leakage" has stopped.

Asset managers and others using dark pools can protect themselves against predatory trading by stipulating that their orders can only interact with other orders if those orders are of a certain minimum size.

Rob McGrath, head of trading, Americas at Schroders, says his firm can protect itself "pretty well". But he says "in the past the exchanges had first look at your orders; now the high-frequency traders are using technology to find similar information".

Source: *Financial Times*, 26 May 2010. Reprinted with permission.

The London Stock Exchange

We will now concentrate on describing UK markets, although the principal features tend to be found in all stock exchanges.

A short history of the LSE

Capital markets go back a long time. In the late Middle Ages securities very much like modern shares were issued and traded in the Italian city states, as were government bonds. The demand from investors in British companies to be able to buy and sell shares led to the creation of a market in London. At first this was very informal – holders of financial securities (e.g. shares) would meet at known places, especially coffee-houses, in the ancient part of London known as the City (the *'Square Mile'* that the Romans built a wall around, just to the north-west of the Tower of London). Early in the nineteenth century the Stock Exchange developed a set of rules and procedures designed to enable investors to buy and sell shares with ease and to minimise the risk of fraud or unfairness.

Astonishing as it may seem given today's push for mergers of a number of national exchanges, in the heady days of the industrial boom times – especially the expansion in railways – in the second half of the nineteenth century, 15 stock markets were formed in England (Liverpool, Manchester, Huddersfield, Nottingham, Leicester, Bradford, Oldham, Hull, Bristol, Birmingham, Leeds, Newcastle, York, Halifax and Sheffield), five in Scotland (Glasgow, Edinburgh, Aberdeen, Dundee and Greenock) and three in Wales (Cardiff, Swansea and Newport). The boom times did not last, however, and survival for many of these exchanges was brief. Some continued on until the 1970s but either merged with the LSE or faded away. Modern communications meant that share trading could be conducted hundreds of miles from the company's base or the shareholders, and London amassed more and more trade, killing off the regional exchanges. There is, however, a move towards bringing back local stock exchanges to give local companies access to equity finance. Investbx was formed in 2007 in Birmingham with the aim of helping small to medium businesses raise capital for growth, although it has yet to take off.

'Big Bang'

Before the 'Big Bang' in 1986, brokers and other market service providers organised share and other security trading such that there was little competition, commission rates were kept high and trading was done on a face-to-face basis. It became clear in the 1970s and 1980s that the LSE was losing trade to overseas stock markets. For the LSE to remain competitive in the modern world, changes had to happen.

'Big Bang' is the term used for a collection of reforms that resulted in fixed broker commissions disappearing, foreign competitors being allowed to own member firms (market makers or brokers), and the screen-based computer system of trading replacing floor-based face-to-face trading.

The market makers and brokers quickly passed into the hands of large financial conglomerates. Commission fell sharply for large orders (from 0.4 per cent to around 0.2 per cent of the value traded). However, private clients (investors buying small quantities of shares on their own account) saw an initial slight rise in commission because this sector had previously been subsidised by the fees charged to the institutions. Brokers started to specialise. Some would offer the traditional service of advice and dealing, whereas others would offer a no-frills dealing-only service. This 'execution-only' service is now very cheap.

Recent moves

After centuries of being an organisation owned and run by its members, in 2001 the LSE became a public limited company with its shares traded on a secondary market. It has come a long way from its clubby days. In 2004 the Stock Exchange moved from its historic site in Old Broad Street to Paternoster Square near St Paul's Cathedral. The exchange toyed with the idea of moving out of the City but decided that its identity was tied too closely to the Square Mile to move outside, and the proximity of other professionals in the same area was too convenient.

Variety of securities traded

The LSE is a marketplace for many other types of financial securities besides shares – *see* Exhibit 8.20.

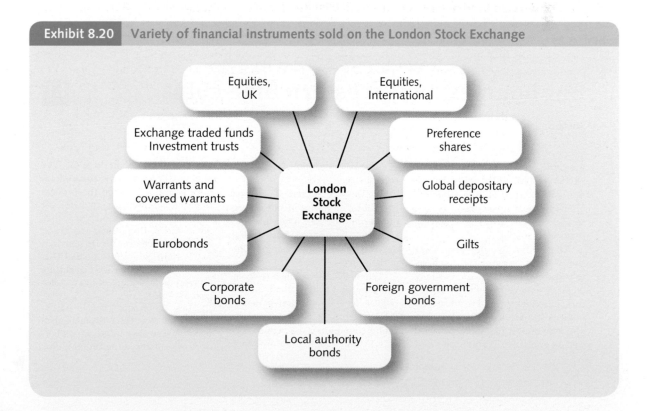

Exhibit 8.20   Variety of financial instruments sold on the London Stock Exchange

There are four types of fixed-interest securities traded in London: government bonds, local authority bonds, corporate bonds and Eurobonds. As well as long-term bonds the LSE trades medium-term notes and specialised types of bond such as those that are convertible into shares. Specialist securities, such as warrants and covered warrants, are normally bought and traded by a few investors who are particularly knowledgeable in investment matters (warrants are a type of derivative security and are discussed in Chapter 9).

Depositary receipts

There has been a rapid development of a market in depositary receipts. These are certificates that can be bought and sold, and represent evidence of ownership of a company's shares held by a depository. Their purpose is to allow investments in foreign companies without the rigmarole of going through all necessary checks and regulations. Thus, an Indian company's shares could be packaged in, say, groups of five by a depository (usually a bank) which then sells a certificate representing a bundle of shares. The depositary receipt can be denominated in a currency other than the corporation's domestic currency and dividends can be received in the currency of the depositary receipt (say, pounds) rather than the currency of the original shares (say, rupees). These are attractive securities for sophisticated international investors because they may be more liquid and more easily traded than the underlying shares.

The investment bank J.P. Morgan created the first American Depositary Receipt (ADR) in 1927 and today is the world's largest ADR depository. The non-American ones are usually referred to as Global Depositary Receipts (GDRs). They may be used to avoid settlement (see later), foreign exchange and foreign ownership (government restrictions on investment by foreigners) difficulties which may exist in the company's home market. From the company's point of view depositary receipts are attractive because they allow a market in the company's shares (even though they are wrapped up in a depositary receipt), permitting fund raising and the other benefits of a quotation on a regulated global capital market without the company needing to jump the regulatory hurdles necessary to place its shares directly on an exchange for them to be traded.

DRs have been very useful as a means for companies in emerging countries (such as Kazakhstan, Brazil or India) to raise capital from the developed world's exchanges. However, emerging nations have developed to such an extent that they now have wealthy investors looking to invest in the developed world – *see* **Exhibit 8.21**.

Exhibit 8.21

EM bourses hunt western blue chips

Steve Johnson

A swathe of emerging market stock exchanges are lining up to launch depositary receipt programmes, allowing local investors to access foreign companies without leaving their home market.

The move would also ease the way for western companies to raise capital from increasingly wealthy emerging market investors, mirroring a trend that has seen emerging market companies raise almost $200bn (£125bn, €151bn) by launching American and (European-listed) global depository receipts since 2005.

In May, Standard Chartered, the UK-headquartered but emerging market-focused bank, blazed a trail by listing the first Indian depository receipt – raising $500m in the process.

Telefónica, the Spanish telecoms company, and Dufry Group, a Swiss retailer, have listed Brazilian depositary receipts, while a number of Indian companies have launched DRs in Singapore. Anthony Moro, head of emerging markets for BNY Mellon's depositary receipts operation, said he expected the process to accelerate, with five to 10 "super regional exchanges", such as Dubai, South Africa, Hong Kong and Brazil, emerging as centres for DR activity.

"We are calling it alphabet DRs and it's a topic that we are getting an incredible amount of interest in," said Mr Moro.

"It's a concept that is catching on because the DR mechanism make it very easy to go across borders. It makes something global

▶

Exhibit 8.21 continued

look like something local. Investors will always prefer to invest in their home market if they can."

Claudine Gallagher, global head of depository receipts at JPMorgan, added: "I definitely think it's a trend. Taiwan, Japan, Russia and Hong Kong have all passed regulations to allow DRs in their markets. Markets like Brazil, Singapore and Taiwan have grown up. They have breadth and depth. The local investor base is savvy enough now and interested in having foreign diversification."

Ms Gallagher said she expected to see DR issuance on the Hong Kong market "in the next six to nine months".

Standard Chartered and rival HSBC have said they intend to issue DRs on the Shanghai exchange if and when Chinese regulations allow.

Depositary receipt programmes, which share the same pot of liquidity with the primary listing, also have an advantage over multiple stock listings, which create fragmented pools of liquidity.

However, Mr Moro said companies would only list DRs in countries in which they had an established footprint, given the compliance costs of operating sponsored programmes.

Mr Dagg said most companies seeking to raise capital were still looking at London and New York, rather than emerging markets.

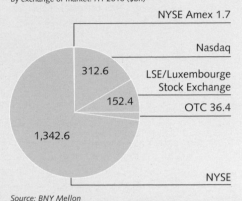

Depositary receipt trading volumes
By exchange or market. H1 2010 ($bn)

NYSE Amex 1.7
Nasdaq
LSE/Luxembourge Stock Exchange
OTC 36.4
NYSE

312.6
152.4
1,342.6

Source: BNY Mellon

Source: Financial Times, 9 August 2010. Reprinted with permission.

The LSE primary market

Through its primary market in listed securities, the LSE has succeeded in encouraging large sums of money to flow annually to firms wanting to invest and grow. On its different markets, it has quoted (at 28 February 2011) 2,650 companies with a total market value of £4,153,960 million. The vast majority of these companies raised funds by selling shares, bonds or other financial instruments through the LSE either when they first floated or by issuing further shares in subsequent years (e.g. through a rights issue – *see* Chapter 9). There are 1,178 companies on the Exchange's market for smaller and younger companies, the Alternative Investment Market (AIM), which started in 1995. These companies, too, have raised precious funds to allow growth. The Main Market (MM) includes 318 listings for companies registered outside the UK, and 86 listings for TechMARK companies, which specialise in innovative technology and healthcare – *see* **Exhibit 8.22**. Within the Main Market there are additional small markets for specialist funds (**SFM** – specialist investment funds such as hedge funds, private equity funds, and certain emerging market and specialist property funds, seeking admission to a public market in London, can use this market to target institutional, professional and highly knowledgeable investors) and professional securities (**PSM** – this is where depositary receipts are quoted and traded).

Newly listed UK firms on the LSE raised new capital by selling £6,998 million of shares in 2010. Another £12.3 billion was raised by already listed firms selling shares through further issues of equity and by selling sterling bonds, convertibles and preference shares. In addition, listed companies sold £184.4 billion of Eurobonds to investors. Over on the more lightly regulated AIM market £3,550 million was raised – *see* **Exhibit 8.23**. At the same time as raising fresh capital, companies transfer money the other way by, for example, redeeming bonds, paying interest on debt or dividends on shares. Nevertheless, it is clear that large sums are raised for companies through the primary market. Each year there is great interest and excitement inside dozens of companies as they prepare for flotation. Since 1999, there have been almost 900 new admissions on the MM and over 2,000 on the AIM; these issues have raised billions for the companies involved.

The requirements for joining the MM are stringent. The listing particulars should give a complete picture of the company: its trading history, financial record, management and business prospects. It should (normally) have at least a three-year trading history and has to make at least 25 per cent of its

Exhibit 8.22   All companies on the London Stock Exchange, 28 February 2011

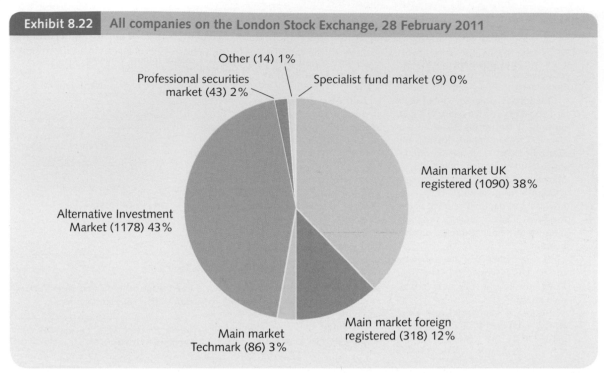

Other (14) 1%

Professional securities
market (43) 2%

Specialist fund market (9) 0%

Main market UK
registered (1090) 38%

Alternative Investment
Market (1178) 43%

Main market foreign
registered (318) 12%

Main market
Techmark (86) 3%

Source: London Stock Exchange.

Exhibit 8.23   Money raised by UK companies on the Main Market and money raised on the Alternative Investment Market (including international companies on AIM) 1999–2010

| | Main Market | | | | | | AIM | |
| | New companies issuing shares | | Other issues of shares and other securities | | Eurobonds | | | |
	No. of companies	£m raised	No. of issues	£m raised	No. of issues	£m raised	No. of new companies joining AIM	£m raised on AIM, including international and further issues
1999	106	5,353	893	9,917	1,022	85,515	102	1,076
2000	172	11,399	895	13,979	1,012	100,556	277	2,965
2001	113	6,922	866	14,824	935	83,342	177	1,600
2002	59	5,082	763	11,696	815	86,657	160	1,486
2003	32	2,445	618	4,920	1,096	118,755	162	2,443
2004	58	3,610	690	8,862	1,170	127,508	355	4,667
2005	86	6,078	772	8,099	1,099	148,309	519	8,791
2006	82	9,088	665	14,445	1,500	216,495	462	13,058
2007	73	7,613	479	8,995	2,025	165,925	282	10,116
2008	53	3,110	402	51,666	2,101	432,445	114	3,496
2009	17	458	378	73,907	1,858	254,571	36	2,988
2010	57	6,998	390	12,360	2,096	184,465	102	3,550

Source: London Stock Exchange factsheets.

ordinary shares publicly available (there is more on the requirements in Chapter 9). Given the costs associated with gaining a listing (often much more than £500,000), it may be surprising to find that the total value of the ordinary shares of the majority of quoted companies is less than £250 million – *see* **Exhibit 8.24**. The average market capitalisation of Aim companies is less than £25 million.

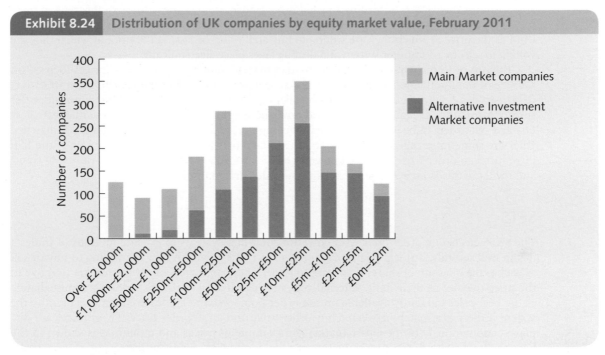

Exhibit 8.24 Distribution of UK companies by equity market value, February 2011

Source: London Stock Exchange factsheets.

The secondary markets

There is a huge amount of shareholder-to-shareholder trading. In a typical month, more than 12 million bargains (trades between buyers and sellers) are struck between investors in shares on the LSE, worth over £200 billion. The size of bargains varies enormously, from £500 trades by private investors to hundreds of millions by the major funds.

The secondary market turnover exceeds the primary market sales. Indeed, the amount raised in the primary equity market in a *year* is about the same as the value of shares that trade hands *daily* in the secondary market. This high level of activity ensures a liquid market, enabling shares to change ownership speedily, at low cost and without large movements in price – one of the main objectives of a well-run exchange.

How stock exchanges work

Types of trading

Traditionally, shares were traded between two traders, face to face. A few stock exchanges around the world still have a place where buyers and sellers (or at least their representatives) meet to trade. For example, the NYSE continues to make some use of a large trading floor with thousands of face-to-face deals taking place every working day (**open outcry trading**). This is the traditional image of a stock market, and if television reporters have a story about what is going on in the world's security markets, they often show an image of traders rushing around, talking quickly amid a flurry of small slips of paper on the NYSE trading floor. Most trading now, however, is done silently in front of banks of computers, with deals being completed in nano-seconds. The stress levels for those dealing remain as high, if not higher, than ever, as now a slight mistake with a finger on a keyboard can cause mayhem.

Quote-driven trading was how most stock exchanges were operated. With this type of approach, market makers give a price at which they would buy (lower price) or sell (higher price), and make their profits on the margins between buying and selling. Traditionally, they operated in 'trading pits' and used an 'open outcry' system of trading, i.e. shouting and using hand signals to make trades, much like you might see with bookmakers at a small horse race meeting. They were able to adjust their prices according to what other traders were doing. Although this type of trading still takes place, it has been superseded by electronic trading. Market makers input their prices ('bid' is the price at which they are willing to buy and 'offer' or 'ask' is the price at which they are willing to sell) to a computer system and dealing takes place electronically.

Criticism of trading systems based on market makers quoting bid and offer prices focused on the size of the middleman's (the market maker's) margin and led to the development of order-driven trading, where buyers trade with sellers at a single price so that there is no bid–offer spread. Most stock exchanges in the world now operate this type of system. These markets allow buy and sell orders to be entered on a central computer, and investors are automatically matched (they are sometimes called matched-bargain systems or order book trading). In 1997, the LSE introduced an order-driven service known as SETS (Stock Exchange Electronic Trading System) and I will use this as an example to explain how order-driven trading works.

SETS

The SETS electronic order book uses powerful computer systems to execute millions of trades a day in milliseconds. Traders (via brokers) enter the prices at which they are willing to buy or sell as well as the quantity of shares they want to trade. They can then wait for the market to move to the price they set as their limit. Alternatively, they can instruct brokers to transact immediately at the best price currently available on the order book system. Trades are then executed by the system if there is a match between a buy order price and a sell order price. These prices are displayed anonymously to the entire market. An example of prices and quantities is shown in the lower half of **Exhibit 8.25** – a reproduction of a SETS screen as seen by brokers.

The buy orders are shown on the left and the sell orders on the right. So, at the bottom of the screen, we can observe for Lloyd's GRP's shares someone (or more than one person) has entered that they are willing to buy 100,000 shares at a maximum price of 69.92p (bottom line on screen). Someone else has entered that they would like to sell 6,930 shares at a minimum price of 70.53p. Clearly the computer cannot match these two orders and neither of these two investors will be able to trade. They will either have to adjust their limit prices or wait until the market moves in their favour.

As we travel up the screen we observe a closing of the gap between the prices buyers are willing to pay and the offering price of sellers. On the seventh line from the bottom we see that buyers want 28,169 shares at 70.13p whereas sellers are prepared to accept 70.23p for 5,054 shares. Now we are getting much closer to a match. Indeed, if we look above the yellow strip we can see the price where buyers and sellers were last matched – the 'last traded price' is 70.18p. These screens are available to market participants at all times and so they are able to judge where to pitch their price limits. For example, if I was a buyer of 5,000 shares entering the market I would not be inclined to offer more than 70.20p given the current state of supply and demand. However, if I was a seller of 5,000 shares I would recognise that the price offered would not have to fall below 70.17p to attract buyers. If, however, I was a buyer of 130,000 shares rather than just 5,000 I would have two options: I could set a maximum price of 70.20p in which case I would transact for 87,116 immediately but would leave the other 42,884 unfilled order in the market hoping for a general market price decline; alternatively, I could set my limit at 70.44p in which case I could transact with those investors prepared to sell at 70.20p, 70.23p, 70.43p and 70.44p. The unfilled orders of the sellers at 70.44p (130,000–118,170) are carried forward on SETS.

Supporters of the older quote-driven system say that a major problem with the order-driven system is that there may be few or no shares offered at prices close to a market clearing rate and so little trade can take place. In other words, the market can be very illiquid. There may indeed be times when no sellers are posting sensible prices and other times when buyers are scarce. This is when the quote-driven system may be more liquid because market makers who make a book in a company's shares must continuously offer prices and are obliged to trade at the price shown. By way of counter-criticism, it is alleged there have been times when it has been difficult to contact

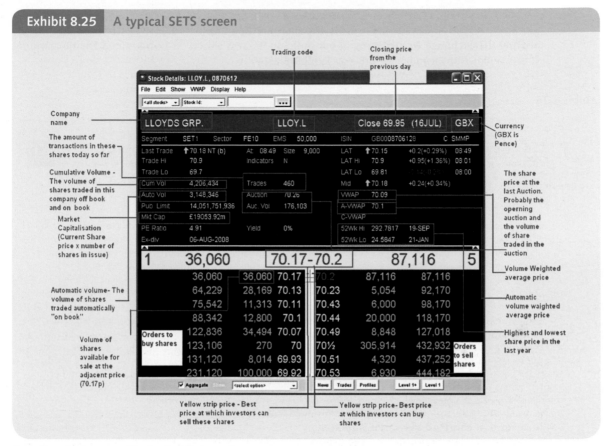

Source: Reproduced courtesy of London Stock Exchange plc.

market makers to trade at their displayed prices, even though in theory they are obliged to make themselves available to quote and trade at bid and offer prices throughout the trading day. To improve trading liquidity on SETS, in 2007 the system was modified so that market makers can now post prices on it. Thus it offers a continuous order book with automatic execution, but also has market makers providing continuous bid and offer prices for many shares. It is thought that by having the two systems combined there will be tighter bid–offer spreads, greater transparency of trades and improved liquidity.

Clearing and settlement

When a trade has been completed and reported to the exchange it is necessary to **clear** the trade. That is, the exchange ensures that all reports of the trade are reconciled to make sure all parties are in agreement as to the number and the price of shares traded. The exchange also checks that the buyer and seller have the cash and securities to do the deal. Also the company registrar is notified of the change in ownership. Later the transfer of ownership from seller to buyer has to take place; this is called **settlement**. These days clearing frequently does not just mean checking that a buyer and a seller agree on the deal; the clearing house also acts as a '**central counterparty**' which acts as a buyer to every seller and as a seller to every buyer. This eliminates the risk of failure to complete a deal by guaranteeing that shares will be delivered against payment and vice versa. **Clearing houses** and central counterparties (CCPs in Europe, Central Counterparty Clearing (CCCs) in the US) provide an invaluable service – they execute and guarantee every aspect of the transaction. Instead of having to wait for cheque clearance, or documents to be signed and arrive by post, traders set up accounts with clearing houses and CCPs so that transactions can be carried out immediately, with the CCP absorbing any loss should either default. With a CCP investors can also 'net' their trades, so that if one part of the investing institution has bought 1 million shares while another has sold 1.5 million the trades are paired so that settlement is for only 500,000 shares.

The LSE's Italian partner already operates its own clearing house, Cassa di Compensazione e Garanzia (CC&G), but for most of its UK share trading LSE uses LCH.Clearnet. At the time of writing the exchange was thinking about building its own clearer in London and then expanding it into a pan-European operation – *see* **Exhibit 8.26**.

Exhibit 8.26

LSE hints at building own clearing house

By **Jeremy Grant** and **Phillip Stafford**

The London Stock Exchange signalled yesterday a big shift in how the clearing business operates in the City of London by saying it was "reviewing" its long-standing relationship with LCH.Clearnet, the clearing house.

The move makes it more likely that the LSE will build its own clearer in London. The 210-year-old bourse is one of the last big exchanges yet to fall into line with a global trend towards exchange ownership of post-trade businesses, especially in derivatives.

Ownership of a clearing house helps generate extra revenues in the form of clearing fees on top of the trading fees already charged by exchanges. It has become increasingly important strategically to exchanges as they vie for business in equities and derivatives.

A clearing house stands between a buyer and seller in a trade, stepping in to complete the transaction in case either party defaults.

The LSE has long lacked its own clearing house, relying instead on LCH.Clearnet, the product of a merger in 2003 of the London Clearing House and Clearnet, former clearer for the Paris bourse.

Xavier Rolet, LSE chief executive, said the lack of "in-house capabilities" in the post-trade business and "dependency on certain not-always-ideal external suppliers" had prevented the London bourse from "innovating successfully".

The Frenchman, who arrived at the helm of the LSE a year ago, has made building a bigger derivatives and post-trade business a priority as the exchange reduces its reliance on share trading, where it faces fierce competition from Chi-X Europe, BATS Europe and others.

Source: Financial Times, 22 May 2010, p. 14. Reprinted with permission.

The European clearing and settlement system compares badly with the US one, being more expensive, which is not helped by the fact that most clearing in Europe is done by organisations owned by the exchanges where the trade took place – *see* **Exhibit 8.27**. The article also discusses the dangers to the financial system caused by the promises made to buyers and sellers by the CCP – they still have to buy from the seller even if the buyer reneges on the deal and so in a major downturn in the market they could end up holding assets that are plummeting in value.

Exhibit 8.27

Europe's post-trade dilemma

By **Jeremy Grant**

Competition between trading venues in Europe is so brutal that the fees charged by exchanges and their smaller rivals – such as Chi-X Europe – are at rock-bottom levels.

Yet while this is obviously good for traders, the overall cost of trad-ing on European equities markets is still stubbornly high – up to eight times as expensive as in the US, according to many estimates.

The reason lies in the "plumb-ing" that sits underneath most exchange trading: the unglamorous post-trade services of clearing and settlement that ensure that trades are completed and that cash and assets change hands at the end of the trading cycle.

Europe has multiple post-trade providers, with no fewer than

►

Exhibit 8.27 continued

seven clearing houses and 17 "central securities depositories", which handle settlement. By contrast, the US has one, quasi-utility clearer for cash equities in the Depository Trust & Clearing Corporation.

Clearers in Europe started to compete with each other with the advent of Mifid – the markets in financial instruments directive – which allowed competition at the trading level.

But full competition, and further downward pressure on fees, has not happened and clearing houses have largely stuck to servicing the exchanges with which they have long relationships. Clearers owned outright by exchanges – such as Eurex Clearing, owned by Deutsche Börse – overwhelmingly clear for their parent.

This lack of competition has kept trading costs high, deterring traders.

Brad Hunt, managing director of electronic trading at Goldman Sachs in London, says: "Fragmented clearing in Europe is inefficient on many levels and this conspires to keep costs for end-investors in European markets stubbornly high."

The European Commission had hoped to change this by insisting that clearers create links with each other to give traders a choice where their trades are sent for clearing.

But the process, known as interoperability, has ground to a halt in recent months. In the wake of the crisis, regulators are no longer as focused on engendering competition; they fear interoperability will create risks in the financial system.

Regulators are studying whether two-way or three-way linkages between clearers – as interoperability would create – could trigger a domino effect if one clearer were to default.

For interoperability to work, Xavier Rolet, chief executive of the London Stock Exchange, says, a way must be found to harmonise standards across Europe when it comes to clearing houses' regulatory capital and risk management policies. Currently, such policies differ between clearing houses.

Clearers should be regulated by central banks, which would be their "lenders of last resort", says Mr Rolet. At present, they are mostly regulated by financial market watchdogs.

Source: Financial Times, 11 February 2010, p. 34. Reprinted with permission.

For the LSE, as in most of Europe, share settlement is T+3, which means that shares are transferred to new owners three days after the trade takes place, but there is pressure to move to T+2 – *see* **Exhibit 8.28**.

To facilitate settlement a company called Euroclear UK & Ireland uses the **CREST** system and acts as a **central securities depository (CSD)** for the UK and Ireland. CREST enables dematerialisation by keeping an electronic register of the shares, a record of shares traded on stock markets and provides an electronic means of settlement and registration. This system is cheaper and

Exhibit 8.28

Brussels eyes faster times for settlement

By Jeremy Grant in London and Nikki Tait in Brussels

European regulators are considering ways to cut the time it takes for securities to be processed after trades are done in a bid to reduce risks to the system in the event of defaults and other large financial failures.

Reducing the so-called "settlement cycle" would be one of the biggest moves taken by regulators in the wake of the 2008 financial crisis.

Settlement is the post-trade process that ensures securities are exchanged for cash, completing a

transaction such as the trading of stocks and shares.

Currently settlement in most of Europe takes place three days after the trade is made, in a system known as "T+3". Germany uses T+2.

Reducing the cycle by a day would cut by a third the time it takes for a deal to be finalised – and thus reduce the scope for failures such as defaults while transactions work their way through settlement and custody processes. It would also make it easier for the region

to handle corporate actions such as rights issues and takeover bids.

The idea of reducing the settlement cycle was identified before the financial crisis as a way of harmonising pan-European post-trade structures to make the region's capital markets more efficient.

But the issue has received fresh impetus since the collapse of Lehman Brothers, whose default raised alarm over counterparty risk.

Source: Financial Times, 25 October 2010, p. 25. Reprinted with permission.

quicker than the old one which used paper – ownership is now transferred with a few strokes of a keyboard. The volume of this trading is huge, around 1.3 million transactions daily in over 16,000 securities, with a value in excess of £1.4 trillion. Under the CREST system shares are usually held in the name of a nominee company rather than in the name of the actual purchaser. Brokers and investment managers run these nominee accounts. Thus, when an investor trades, their broker holds their shares electronically in their (the broker's) nominee account and arranges settlement through their membership of the CREST system. This increases the speed of transactions enormously. There might be dozens of investors with shares held by a particular nominee company. The nominee company appears as the registered owner of the shares as far as the company (say Sainsbury or BT) is concerned. Despite this, the beneficial owners receive all dividends and any sale proceeds. Some investors oppose the CREST system because under such a system they do not automatically receive annual reports and other documentation, such as an invitation to the annual general meeting. They also potentially lose the right to vote (after all, the company does not know who the beneficial owners are). Those investors who take their ownership of a part of a company seriously can insist on remaining outside of CREST. In this way they receive share certificates and are treated as the real owners of the business. This is more expensive when share dealing, but that is not a great concern for investors who trade infrequently.

There is a compromise position: personal membership of CREST. The investor is then both the legal owner and the beneficial owner of the shares, and also benefits from rapid (and cheap) electronic share settlement. The owner will be sent all company communications and retain voting rights. However, this is more expensive than the normal CREST accounts.

SETSqx

Trading on SETS is for companies whose trading is liquid, i.e. large companies with a high proportion of the shares held by a wide range of investors (a large free float) so there are plenty of shares traded each day. There are other means of trading for less frequently traded shares. SETSqx (Stock Exchange Electronic Trading Service – quotes and crosses) trades in MM and AIM shares which are less liquid and not traded on SETS. SETSqx combines order-book technology (similar to the SETS method of trading) with the best of the LSE's existing quote-driven trading. On SETSqx a single market maker's quote can be displayed if a market maker is interested in quoting a price. (Ideally, the exchange would like many market makers' quoting prices so that competition encourages keener prices for share owners.)

An investor wanting to trade with a market maker can do so in the normal way, but also can connect, usually via brokers, to the electronic system and put onto the system's screen display an order for shares stating a price at which they would like to trade, either to sell or to buy – particularly useful if there are no market makers in that share. If someone else on the system likes the displayed price they can phone the originator and a deal is done.

This may still leave some orders for trades unexecuted (i.e. no one phones up and trades at the advertised price). To cope with this, or to trade shares anonymously, throughout the day there are auctions in which investors make bids and the system matches up buyers and sellers. Now all MM shares trade on either SETS or SETSqx.

Quote-driven trading

The LSE's **Stock Exchange Automated Quotation (SEAQ)** system deals mainly in smaller, less liquid companies not on its MM. It is the LSE's quote-driven service that allows market makers to quote prices in AIM securities (those AIM securities not traded on SETS or SETSqx) as well as a number of fixed-interest securities. It lists over 800 companies on its electronic notice board where market makers display prices at which they are willing to buy or sell.

The SEAQ computer gathers together the bid-offer quotes from all the market makers that make a market in that particular share. These competing quotations are then available to brokers and other financial institutions linked up to the SEAQ system.

Exhibit 8.29 goes through the stage in buying or selling on the LSE's SEAQ system. What happens when you, as an investor, telephone your broker to buy shares is this: when you mentioned the company name the broker immediately punched into their computer the company code. So within a second of your mentioning your interest in the company the broker has on their screen all the prices that different market makers are willing to pay as well as all the prices at which they are willing to sell the shares. It can be confusing and time consuming for the broker to look at all the prices to find the best current rates. Fortunately they do not have to do this as the screen displays a 'yellow strip' above the market makers' prices, which provides the identity of the market makers offering the best bid and offer prices (these are called touch prices). It is the price in the yellow strip that the broker will immediately report to you over the telephone. So, you might be told 105–109. If you were happy with 109p you would then instruct your broker to buy, say, 1,000 shares.

Exhibit 8.29	The SEAQ quote-driven system

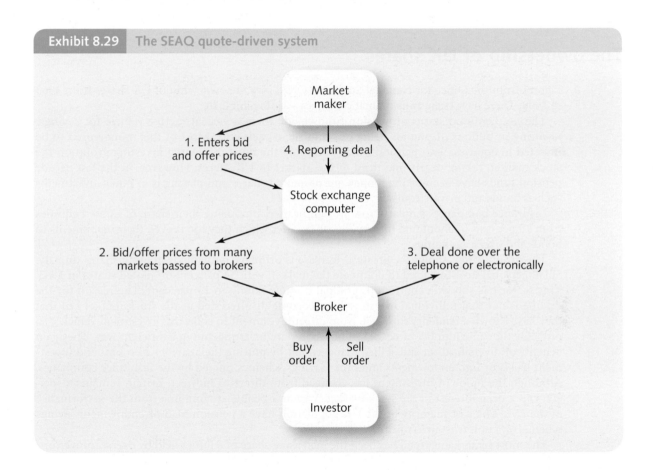

The market makers are obliged to deal (up to a certain number of shares) at the price quoted, but they have the freedom to adjust prices after deals are completed. Transactions may be completed by the broker speaking to the market maker on the telephone, but an increasing number of trades are completed electronically. All trades are reported to the central electronic computer exchange and are disseminated to market participants (usually within three minutes) so that they are aware of the price at which recent trades were completed.

The underlying logic of the quote-driven system is that through the competitive actions of numerous market makers, investors are able to buy or sell at any time at the best price. A problem arises for some very small or infrequently traded firms. Market makers are reluctant to commit capital to holding shares in such firms and so for some there may be only one market maker's quote, for others there may be none. These shares have a better trading environment on SETSqx.

Share borrowing, lending and shorting

If a share price is expected to fall, a trader can borrow shares (paying commission to the lender) for, say, a month, sell them immediately at the market price and hope to buy the requisite number of shares in a month's time at the expected lower price. This practice is known as shorting, or going short, selling shares before buying them. If the unexpected happens and the share price rises, the trader will make a loss on his shorted shares. The opposite of going short is going long, where a dealer buys securities and holds on to them.

Brokers, sometimes acting on behalf of institutions, lend some of the securities in their care to satisfy trading needs, taking commission from the deals. The lenders get equivalent securities back at the end of the loan term and the borrowers get a chance to trade without the injection of fresh capital.

The ownership of UK shares

Figures from the Office for National Statistics (ONS) give the ownership of UK shares from 1963 to 2008. There have been some dramatic changes – *see* **Exhibit 8.30**.

The tax-favoured status of pension funds made them a very attractive vehicle for savings, resulting in billions of pounds being put into them each year. Most of this money used to be invested in equities, with pension funds becoming the most influential investing group on the stock market, taking nearly one-third of the market in UK shares. However, in the last decade pension funds have been taking money out of quoted shares and placing it in other investments such as bonds and private equity.

Insurance companies similarly rose in significance, increasing their share of quoted equities from 10 per cent to about one-fifth by the 1990s, after which they too moved their investments to bonds and overseas equities.

The group which shows the greatest decrease is ordinary individuals holding shares directly. Small personal investors used to dominate the market, with 54 per cent of quoted shares in 1963. This sector has shown a continuous gradual decline, falling to 13 per cent. The reason for the decline is not that individual investors have become disinterested in the stock market but that they have shown a tendency to switch from direct investment to collective investment vehicles, so probably the same number of people (if not more) are investing, but in a different way. They gain benefits of diversification and skilled management by putting their savings into unit and investment trusts or into endowments and other savings schemes offered by the insurance companies. Although the mode of investment has changed from direct to indirect, Britain remains a society with a deep interest in the stock market. Very few people are immune from the performance of the LSE. The vast majority of the UK population have a pension plan or endowment savings scheme, or a unit trust investment.

The most remarkable trend has been the increasing share of equities held by overseas investors: only 7 per cent in 1963, but over 40 per cent in 2008. This increase partly reflects international mergers where the new company is listed in the UK, and foreign companies sometimes floating their UK subsidiaries but holding on to a large shareholding. It also reflects an increasing tendency of investors to buy shares in overseas markets. **Exhibit 8.31** discusses the increasing influence of overseas investors in the UK stock market. The rising internationalisation of share ownership is not just manifest in the UK. For each of the following countries more than 30 per cent of the domestic company shares is owned by overseas organisations: the Netherlands, Switzerland, Greece, Portugal, Poland, France, Norway, Sweden, Spain, Austria and Denmark. The higher level of international institutional ownership is changing companies, bringing more stringent corporate governance to orientate the companies more in shareholders' favour, an increase in transparency, including more open reporting on company performance, and more manager engagement with shareholders.

Also note the rise in the 'other' category over the last decade. This is largely due to the rising importance of hedge funds and venture capital companies.

| Exhibit 8.30 | Percentage ownership of UK shares 1963–2008 |

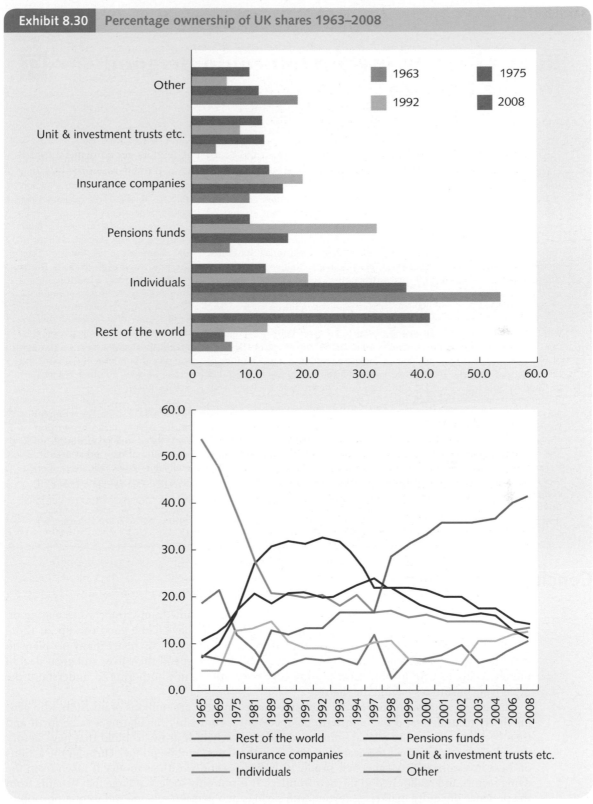

Source: ONS.

Exhibit 8.31

Rising foreign ownership could be good for the Footsie

Anousha Sakoui

One clear trend in the UK equity market in recent years has been the falling proportion of UK shares held by domestic investors, and the rising number held by international investors.

The latest data show UK investors now hold less than 60 per cent of the UK stock market, whereas foreign ownership is at 41.5 per cent, a record high.

At the current rate, the majority of UK plc will be in foreign hands within a decade. That is an event that will inevitability prompt a bout of national soul-searching, in much the same way that the recent sale of Cadbury to Kraft of the US did. But does it matter to the performance of the stock market who owns UK shares? Possibly. There is some anecdotal evidence that UK funds are more reluctant sellers of the UK shares than international investors, who have a greater number of companies they can reinvest their funds in. But selling by UK investors seems for the moment to be

more than matched by purchases by international investors.

Long-term holders of UK shares, such as pension funds and insurance groups, now own around 26 per cent of the UK equity market, according to the latest data from the Office of National Statistics. This is a big change from 1998, when they owned 43.3 per cent.

Last year's survey by the National Association of Pension Funds was particularly telling. Some 14 per cent of pension schemes do not invest in UK equities at all and less than one fifth of the industry's total assets are in UK equities, down from 21.1 per cent in 2008.

Meanwhile, according to the ONS, foreign ownership of UK shares reached 41.5 per cent at the end of 2008. James Agnew, chairman of corporate broking at Deutsche Bank, estimates European investor holdings have been constant since 2000 at around 18 per cent, while US investors have

increased their holdings from around 9 per cent to 16 per cent and the rest of the world's ownership has doubled from around 4 per cent to 8 per cent.

Some foreign investors have emerged as the largest holders of UK shares over this period. They include sovereign wealth funds such as Norway's national pension fund and the Government of Singapore Investment Corporation. This trend of increasing foreign interest in UK shares is expected to continue. That can be seen through the recent purchase of Cadbury and it can be seen in other recent corporate moves.

One key attraction for foreign investors is that UK companies derive a very large proportion of their sales and profits from international markets. Many FTSE 100 companies have high levels of exposure to emerging markets growth.

Source: Financial Times, 10/11 April 2010, p. 40. Reprinted with permission.

Concluding comments

Equity markets are often portrayed as casinos. News reports show frantic traders speculating on where prices are going next, becoming euphoric if the shares have had a good run up, or thoroughly depressed if the market is down. Indeed, it is fair to say that there are many people who treat the equity markets as places to make a quick buck, who spend their lives and great deal of money trying to gain a short-term trading edge over others, not bothering to understand the underlying businesses behind the shares.

This image is unfortunate because alongside the speculators are millions of investors who genuinely try to understand the long-term prospects for a company, calculating a value for it and then deciding whether to allocate money to the firm to help it grow, to build that new factory to make recently invented medical instruments or that latest mobile phone. Through the actions of these investors society gains new products, industries and wealth as money is taken from the dying sectors and reallocated to the new frontiers. It is not only society at large that benefits from the presence of equity markets – anyone with savings in a pension scheme will want a portion of that money placed in shares with prospects of high rates of return over the next few decades.

To meet these societal needs stock markets have evolved through their history, never more so than in the last decade. Where before we had national stock markets in the financial centres of each country, today we have many markets combining to form international groups such as NYSE

Euronext. To provide some competition for the national monopolies we have seen the growth of alternative trading platforms such as multilateral trading facilities and dark pools. At the same time technological innovation has changed the method of trading shares so that it is now very much built around sophisticated computer systems that can handle millions of transactions in a day, and can complete thousands of trades in less than the time it takes to blink. We have also seen the amazing growth of stock markets in Asia, to the point where they are a serious challenge to the old centres of equity finance in Europe and North America. Indeed, it is a fairly safe prediction to say that many Asian markets will come to be at least as great as London and New York in the next few years. This makes sense: every society needs equity investors to assist growth through the mobilisation of savings into productive use; and every investor would prefer to have the liquidity that is offered by stock markets than have the difficulty of finding a buyer should they need to sell.

Key points and concepts

- **Shares** were first issued as a way of raising large amounts of risk capital for a venture from numerous investors, each being offered a share of profits.

- **Ordinary shares** represent part ownership of a company. There is no obligation to pay a dividend or redeem shares.

- **Limited liability** restricts the amount of responsibility that a shareholder has for a company's debts.

- **The rights of ordinary shareholders:** (1) to exercise some control over the company (2) a claim to a share of the company's profits in the form of dividend payments, and in a worst-case scenario, a right to share in the proceeds of a liquidation sale of the firm's assets (3) to receive information about the company's progress.

- **Dividend** payments, annual or semi-annual, are paid at the discretion of directors but these decisions are approved by shareholders.

- **Debt finance** is an alternative means of raising finance for company, but requires obligatory repayments at regular intervals. Lower rates of return are offered on debt than on equity. Debt does not carry rights of control over the firm.

- **Preference shares: advantages to a company of preference shares are:**
  - the dividend may be omitted;
  - less influence over management because they have no voting rights (normally);
  - no increase in dividend if a company makes good profits;
  - alternative source of finance if more borrowing is unavailable.

- **Disadvantages to a company of preference shares are:**
  - rate of return is higher than for debt;
  - preference share dividends are not tax deductible.

- **Types of preference shares are:**
  - **cumulative** – if dividend payments are missed they are carried forward;
  - **participating** – extra payments if company has high profits;
  - **redeemable** – they have a finite life;
  - **convertible** – they may be converted into ordinary shares;
  - **variable rate** – variable dividend is paid.

- **Other types of shares are:**
  - **non-voting/reduced voting** – issued when current shareholders do not wish to dilute their influence by issuing ordinary voting shares;
  - **deferred** – in a poor year holders receive no dividend;
  - **golden** – they have extraordinary powers.

▶

- **Stock exchanges** – where governments, industries and investors can buy and sell shares and other financial instruments, thus contributing to the economic well-being of a country by encouraging the mobilisation of savings.

- **Stock exchanges** have merged to form large conglomerates.

- **A well-run stock exchange**:

  - a 'fair game' takes place;
  - it is well regulated to avoid abuses, negligence and fraud;
  - it is reasonably cheap to carry out transactions;
  - there is a large number of buyers and sellers.

- **Benefits of a well-run exchange:**

  - firms can find funds and grow;
  - allocation of society's scarce capital;
  - shareholders benefit from the availability of a speedy, cheap secondary market if they want to sell;
  - enhances the status and publicity of companies;
  - mergers can be facilitated better by a quotation;
  - improves corporate behaviour.

- **Tasks for stock exchanges**

  - supervision of trading to ensure fairness and efficiency;
  - the authorisation of market participants such as brokers and market makers;
  - creation of an environment in which prices are formed efficiently and without distortion;
  - organisation of the settlement of transactions;
  - the regulation of the admission of companies to the exchange and the regulation of companies on the exchange;
  - the dissemination of information.

- **Mifid** (Markets in Financial Instruments Directive) aims to harmonise European trading, encourage competition and protect the consumer.

- **MTFs (Multilateral Trading Facilities)** bring together buyers and sellers of financial instruments and are less regulated than the stock exchanges. Their trading platforms are electronic trading facilities carrying out trading quickly and sometimes without human intervention.

- **Algorithmic trading** is trading carried out by computers using algorithms.

- **HFT (high-frequency trading)** is blisteringly quick electronic trading which gives its users milli-seconds' advantage.

- **Dark pools** are anonymous trading systems designed to negate problems of openly trading large blocks of shares.

- **Big Bang** happened in 1986 and revolutionised the London Stock Exchange. It meant:

  - the end of fixed broker commission;
  - foreign competition being allowed;
  - face-to-face trading was replaced by computer trading.

- **London Stock Exchange** used to be the leading stock exchange for international shares; now huge growth in the US and developing countries is rivalling the LSE.

- **Depositary receipts** are negotiable certificates proving ownership of foreign shares and provide an easy means of trading in foreign shares.

- **Order-driven trading** is used by most stock exchanges around the world; buy and sell orders are entered on to the central computer and automatically matched; problems can occur if there is poor liquidity.

- **SETS** (Stock Exchange Electronic Trading System) carries out the LSE's electronic order book trading.

▶

- **Clearing** ensures that all reports of the trade are reconciled to make sure all parties are in agreement as to the number and the price of shares traded. The exchange also checks that the buyer and seller have the cash and securities to do the deal. Also the company registrar is notified of the change in ownership. Usually the clearing houses also act as a **'central counterparty',** which is a buyer to every seller and as a seller to every buyer.

- **Settlement:** the transfer of ownership from seller to buyer takes place. **CREST,** the UK settlement company, holds shares in nominee accounts enabling trading to be done instantaneously, and keeps a register of all shares and trading.

- **SETSqx (Stock Exchange Electronic Trading Service – quotes and crosses)** trades in less liquid MM and AIM shares through a system that combines market makers' quotes, direct posting and agreement of trades and daily auctions.

- **Quote-driven trading** involves market makers making prices in shares and trading with other market makers on behalf of investors.

- **SEAQ (**Stock Exchange Automated Quotation) is the LSE's quote-driven system dealing in companies not on the MM.

- **Shorting,** or **going short:** a trader can borrow shares and sell them immediately at the market price, hoping to buy the requisite amount of shares at a lower price at a later date to replace the borrowed shares and thus make a profit.

- **Ownership of UK shares –**

  - Pension and insurance funds own a substantial proportion, but in the past decade the proportion has dropped as they invested overseas and in bonds.
  - There has been a large decrease in individual shareholders caused by investors putting money into collective investment instead.
  - There has been a big increase in foreign investment in UK and European shares.

References and further reading

Credit Suisse Global investment Returns Yearbook.
An annual publication discussing returns on shares and other financial assets for leading exchanges over 110 years. Downloadable from the internet for free.

Economist magazine.
Regular reading will provide an excellent foundation for understanding equity markets.

Financial Times.
An important source of information on events in the equity markets.

Kidwell, D. S., Blackwell, D. W., Whidbee, D. A. and Peterson, R. L. (2008) *Financial Institutions, Markets and*

Money, 10th edn. New York: John Wiley & Sons Inc.
A US perspective.

Saunders, A. and Cornett, M. M. (2007) *Financial Markets and Institutions,* 3rd edn. Boston: McGraw-Hill Irwin.
Information about US financial system.

Vaitilingam, R. (2010) *The Financial Times Guide to using the Financial Pages,* 6th edn. London: Financial Times Prentice Hall.
Good introductory source of information. Clear and concise.

Websites

ADVFN. Financial data www.advfn.com
Aite Group. Independent research and advice www.aitegroup.com
Euroclear www.euroclear.com
Federation of European Securities Exchanges www.fese.eu

Financial Services Authority www.fsa.gov.uk
United Kingdom Listing Authority www.fsa.gov.uk/Pages/Doing/UKLA
Financial Times www.ft.com
FTSE Group. Stock market indices and information www.ftse.com
Hemscott. Share prices and financial data www.hemscott.com
Interactive Investor www.iii.co.uk
Investegate. Company information www.investegate.co.uk
Investors Chronicle, weekly stock market analysis www.investorschronicle.com
LCH.Clearnet. Clearing house www.lchclearnet.com
Intelligent Financial Systems. Information of trading in Europes markets www.liquidmetrix.com
London Stock Exchange www.londonstockexchange.com
New York Stock Exchange www.nyse.com
Office for National Statistics www.ons.gov.uk
Wall Street Journal www.wsj.com
Yahoo Finance. Financial data www.yahoofinance.com
World Federation of Exchanges www.world-exchanges.org

Video presentations

Chief executives and other senior people describe and discuss policy including the benefits of stock markets in interviews, documentaries and webcasts at Cantos.com. (www.cantos.com) – these are free to view.

Case study recommendations

See www.pearsoned.co.uk/arnold for case study synopses.
Also see Harvard University: http://hbsp.harvard.edu/product/cases

- CalPERS' Emerging Equity Markets Principles (2009) Authors: Robert G. Eccles and Aldo Sesia. Harvard Business School.
- Microstrategy, Incorporated: Pipe (2003) Authors: Richard Crawford and Susan Chaplinsky. Darden, University of Pennsylvania. Available at Harvard website.
- Freeport-McMoRan: Financing an Acquisition (2009) Author: David Stowell. Kellogg School of Management. Available at Harvard website.
- Note on Depositary Receipts (2004) Author: Walter Kuemmerle. Harvard Business School.
- Cross-Border Listings and Depositary Receipts (2004) Author: Mithir Desai. Harvard Business School.

Self-review questions

1 What is equity capital? Explain the advantages to the firm of raising capital this way. What are the disadvantages?

2 What is debt finance, and how does it differ from equity finance?

3 What is a preference share and why might a company favour this form of finance?

4 What would be the characteristics of a cumulative redeemable participating convertible preference share?

5 Why are non-voting shares disliked by the investing institutions?

6 What other types of ordinary shares are there?

7 What are the main advantages and disadvantages of raising finance through selling (a) ordinary shares, and (b) preference shares?

8 What is a stock market?

9 Explain the concept of limited liability.

10 Describe the global growth of stock markets.

11 Why are stock markets important and what do they trade in?

12 What was the importance of the Big Bang?

13 How has the London Stock Exchange kept its position as one of the leading markets?

14 How has the relative importance of the NYSE and LSE changed?

15 What is Mifid and what were its aims?

16 What are multilateral trading platforms?

17 What is the significance of high frequency trading?

18 Describe the function of a dark pool.

19 Why are depositary receipts useful?

20 Explain the difference between primary and secondary markets.

21 How has the ownership of UK shares changed over the past 50 years?

22 Explain why finance has been 'globalised' over the past 20 years.

23 What are the characteristics of, and who benefits from, a well-run exchange?

24 What securities, other than shares, are traded on the London Stock Exchange?

25 Why is a healthy secondary market good for the primary share market?

26 Explain the acronyms AIM, SETS, MTF and HFT.

27 What is CREST?

Questions and problems

1 You have been asked by the prospective directors of a shortly to be established business what is meant by ordinary shares, preference shares and debt capital. Further, you have been asked to provide a brief explanation of their relative advantages and disadvantages as sources of funds to expand the business. Write an essay to assist these managers.

2 Describe and explain the difference between order-driven and quote-driven trading.

3   Describe the changes that have taken place in share trading venues over the past decade.

4   'Stock markets are merely casinos allowing speculators to get rich while doing nothing for ordinary people like you and me'. Write an essay explaining why you agree or disagree with this statement.

5   Describe the shifts in UK share ownership over the past 60 years. Suggest some reasons for the changes.

6   Describe what a badly run stock exchange would be like and explain how society would be poorer as a result.

7   Many countries are encouraging small investors to buy quoted shares. Why might they be doing this? Write an essay to include a discussion of the societal benefits of a stock exchange.

8   Discuss some of the consequences you believe might follow from the shift in UK share ownership over the past 30 years.

9   Frame-up plc is considering a flotation on the Main Market of the London Stock Exchange. The managing director has asked you to produce a 1,000-word report explaining the advantages of such a move.

Assignments

1   Analyse a company you know well in the following way. If it is already quoted on a stock market try to discover the cost of being there and write a report weighing up the advantages and disadvantages of maintaining a quotation. If its shares are not quoted on a market write a report weighing up the advantages and disadvantages of joining a market given its circumstances.

2   Examine a company you know well to discover the extent to which it obtains its finance from ordinary shares, preference shares or debt capital. Write a report and explain the merits and problems with each of these forms of finance and recommend action on the balance of finance if you think it is needed.

Web-based exercises

1   Go to the statistical section of the website of the London Stock Exchange, www.londonstockexchange.com. Compile a report describing the money raised on the market from investors in the primary market in each of the past twelve months. Describe the benefits these companies might gain.

2   Go to the website of the World Federation of Exchanges, www.world-exchanges.org, and write a report using the statistical data detailing the growth of the largest 40 stock exchanges in terms of market capitalisation of domestic and overseas companies, the number of listed companies and the value of share trading over the past few years. Consider the exchanges' relative positions.

Raising share capital

LEARNING OUTCOMES

Much of what financial markets and institutions do is related to raising finance for companies. This chapter will help orientate you in the world of equity finance raising for stock market quoted companies. By the end of the chapter you should be able to:

■ explain the processes involved in a company joining a stock market to have its shares traded in a regulated market for the first time. This includes describing the role of various financial advisers and institutions;

■ outline the main ongoing regulations for a company quoted on the London Stock Exchange, including disclosure of price-sensitive information, reporting profits and other accounts, restrictions on directors and the corporate governance regulations;

■ demonstrate understanding of the figures presented in the financial pages for shares and share indices;

■ run through the main considerations for rights issues, placings, open offers, vendor placings, scrip issues, share splits, warrants, share buy-backs and special dividends.

Many institutions assist a company in floating its shares on a stock market for the first time, as well as help a company to raise additional equity finance in the years following the initial public offering. This chapter describes their various roles, from investment bankers acting as sponsors to corporate brokers, registrars and lawyers. It also explains the regulations for stock market quoted companies, such as the need to make public all price-sensitive information or the restrictions placed on directors.

It is important that a student of finance be able to read and interpret the data shown in the financial pages of newspapers, particularly the *Financial Times*. To help in this area the chapter has reproductions of the equity tables in the *FT*, together with explanations of what the entries mean.

Throughout this chapter there is focus on the UK, but the key principles are in place in all major financial centres.

Floating on the Main Market of the London Stock Exchange

Once a company reaches a certain size, it has the possibility of floating on a stock market, 'going public', through a 'new issue' of shares also called an initial public offering (IPO). To become a listed company is a major step for a firm, and the substantial sums of money involved can lead to a new, accelerated phase of business growth. While this opens up fresh possibilities of investment finance from outside investors it also brings the disadvantage for current shareholders of giving away some influence and control as well as incurring some significant costs. Many, if not most, companies are content to grow without the aid of stock markets. For example, J.C. Bamford (JCB), which manufactures earth-moving machines, has built a large, export award-winning company, without needing to bring in outside shareholders, and remains a private company.

The legal implications of obtaining a quotation as a listed company are enormous. Companies wishing to be listed on the Main Market have to sign a **listing agreement** that commits directors to certain standards of behaviour and levels of reporting to shareholders. The United Kingdom Listing Authority (UKLA), part of the Financial Services Authority, rigorously enforces a set of demanding rules.

Joining the MM of the LSE involves two stages. The securities (usually shares) have to be: (a) admitted to the Official List by the UKLA (hence the term 'listed' company) and also (b) admitted by the Exchange for trading.

Going public can wrack up huge costs – *see* **Exhibit 9.1**. The cost as a proportion of the amount raised varies but is usually at least 5 per cent and can be as high as one-third – many of the costs are fixed so if only a small number of new shares are issued the percentage costs are high.

Exhibit 9.1	Typical floating costs for a company issuing £20 million of shares in an IPO on the Main Market of the London Stock Exchange

	£
Financial advisers	200,000–400,000
Underwriters	400,000–1,000,000
Legal expenses	200,000–400,000
Accounting	100,000–300,000
Listing fees	< 20,000
Printing, public relations, etc.	< 100,000
Total costs	1,020,000–2,220,000

Source: Financial Times, 5 June 2010, p. 6. Reprinted with permission.

Many firms consider the stresses and the costs worthwhile because listing brings numerous advantages besides raising fresh finance, including providing shareholders with a dynamic, transparent and liquid secondary market for trading shares, a raising of the company's status and visibility, and the possibility of mergers with other firms.

All companies obtaining a full MM listing must ensure that at least 25 per cent of their share capital is in public hands, so that the shares are capable of being traded actively on the market.[1] The Indian markets adopted the same 25 per cent rule in 2010 – *see* **Exhibit 9.2**.

Exhibit 9.2

India flotation demand set to hit valuations

FT

By **Joe Leahy** in Mumbai

The Indian government yesterday ordered listed companies to ensure that at least 25 per cent of their shares are publicly held within three years in a move that could hit the valuations of hundreds of businesses.

The measure, which increases the minimum public float from 10 per cent, could lead to shares worth Rs2,500bn ($53bn) being sold over the next three years – more than the total that Indian companies have raised from equity issues in the past decade.

Leading companies that are expected to be forced to begin shedding stakes include Wipro, the third-largest outsourcing group.

"A dispersed shareholding structure is essential ... to provide liquidity to the investors and to discover fair prices," the Indian finance ministry said in a statement.

Corporate governance activists have long argued that the low compulsory public float made it easier for the controlling shareholders of India's companies to manipulate

stocks by buying and selling small volumes of shares.

Under the rules, the government said those listed companies that presently have less than 25 per cent of their stock in public hands must sell an additional 5 per cent of their shares a year until they reach the target.

Source: Financial Times, 5 June 2010, p. 16. Reprinted with permission.

United Kingdom Listing Authority (UKLA)

The UKLA is responsible for approval of the prospectuses and admission to the Official List (most of these companies are on the Main Market of the LSE, although PLUS markets – *see* later – may also admit Official List companies). The UKLA maintains details of all listed companies and updates its list daily with additions, cancellations, suspensions and restorations. It also rigorously enforces a set of demanding rules regarding the conduct of the company and its officials in the years following the listing.

The UKLA usually insists that a company has a track record (in the form of accounting figures) stretching back at least three years. However, this requirement has been relaxed for scientific research-based companies and companies undertaking major capital projects. In the case of scientific research-based companies there is the requirement that they have been conducting their activity for three years even if no revenue was produced. Some major project companies, for example Eurotunnel, have been allowed to join the market despite an absence of a trading activity or a profit record. Companies can be admitted to the techMARK, part of the Official List, with only one year of accounts.

---

[1] 'In public hands' means a free float, that is, the shares are not held by those closest to the company, such as directors, founding family or dominant shareholder, who may be unlikely to sell their shares. Occasionally a company is admitted with a free float of less than 25 per cent. For example, Eurasian Natural Resources had a free float of only 21.3 per cent when it joined the MM in 2008. The company successfully argued that it was large enough for its shares to have liquid trading in spite of the smaller free float.

The first step in floating a company is to apply to the UKLA to be put on the Official List. The listing fee is £225, plus an annual fee, based on the market capitalisation of the company, of at least £3,700 rising to more than £1 million for capitalisation over £25,000 million.

Financial advisers

The sponsor

Experts are required to guide firms through the complexities of an official listing. The key adviser in a flotation is the **sponsor**. This may be an investment bank, stockbroker or other professional adviser, but must be on the UKLA's approved list of sponsors. Directors, particularly of small companies, often first seek advice from their existing professional advisers, for example accountants and lawyers. Sponsors have to be chosen with care as the relationship is likely to be one which continues long after the flotation. For large or particularly complex issues investment banks are employed, although experienced stockbrokers have been used. The UKLA requires sponsors to certify that a company has complied with all the regulatory requirements and to ensure that all necessary documentation is filed on time.

The sponsor (sometimes called the **issuing house**) will first examine the company and the aspirations of the management team to assess whether flotation is an appropriate corporate objective by taking into account its structure, strategy and capital needs. The sponsor will also comment on the composition of the board and the calibre of the directors. The sponsor may even recommend supplementation with additional directors if the existing team does not come up to the quality expected. Sponsors can be quite forceful in this because they do not want to damage their reputation by bringing a poorly managed company to market. The sponsor will draw up a timetable, which can be lengthy – sometimes the planning period for a successful flotation may extend over two years. Another important function is to help draft the prospectus and provide input to the marketing strategy. Throughout the process of flotation there will be many other professional advisers involved and it is vital that their activities mesh into a coherent whole. It is the sponsor's responsibility to coordinate the activities of all the other professional advisers.

The corporate broker

When a **corporate broker** is employed as a sponsor the two roles can be combined. If the sponsor is, say, an investment bank, the UKLA requires that a broker is also appointed. However, most investment banks also have corporate broking arms and so can take on both roles. Brokers play a vital role in advising on share market conditions and the likely demand from investors for the company's shares. They also represent the company to investors to try to generate interest. When debating issues such as the method of share issue to be employed, the marketing strategy, the size of the issue, the timing or the pricing of the shares, the company may value the market knowledge the broker has to offer.

Underwriters

Shortly before the flotation the sponsor will have the task of advising on the best price to ask for the shares, and, at the time of flotation, the sponsor will usually underwrite the issue. Most new issues are underwritten because the correct pricing of a new issue of shares is extremely difficult. If the price is set too high, demand will be less than supply and not all the shares will be taken up. The company is usually keen to know that it will receive the expected money from the issue so that it can plan ahead. To make sure it sells the shares it buys a kind of insurance called **underwriting**. In return for a fee the underwriter guarantees to buy the proportion of the issue not taken up by the market. An investment bank sponsoring the issue will usually charge a fee of 2–4 per cent of the issue proceeds and then pays part of that fee, say 1.25–3.0 per cent of the issue proceeds, to sub-underwriters (usually large financial institutions such as pension funds and banks), which each agree to buy a certain number of shares if called on to do so. In most cases the underwriters do not have to purchase any shares because the general public are keen to take them up. However, occasionally they receive a shock and have to buy large quantities.

Legal expenses

All legal requirements in the flotation preparation and in the information displayed in the prospectus must be observed. Lawyers prepare the 'verification' questions which are used to confirm that every statement in the prospectus can be justified as fact. Directors bear the ultimate responsibility for the truthfulness of the documents. Examples of other legal issues are directors' contracts, changes to the articles of association, re-registering the company as a public limited company (rather than a limited company which is not able to offer its shares to the wider public), underwriting agreements and share option schemes.

Accounting

The reporting accountant in a flotation has to be different from the company's existing auditors, but can be a separate team in the same firm.

The accountant will be asked by the sponsor to prepare a detailed report on the firm's financial controls, track record, financing and forecasts (the 'long form' report). Not all of this information will be included in the prospectus but it does serve to reassure the sponsor that the company is suitable for flotation. Accountants may also have a role in tax planning from both the company's viewpoint and that of its shareholders. They also investigate working capital requirements. The UKLA insists that companies show that they have enough working capital for current needs and for at least the next 12 months.

Registrars

The record on the ownership of shares is maintained by registrars as shares are bought and sold. Registrars keep the company's register and issue share certificates. There are about two dozen major registrars linked up to CREST through which they are required to electronically adjust their records of ownership of company shares within two hours of a trade taking place.

Listing fees

Listing fees are charged by stock markets for admission to listing, followed by annual charges, graduated according to the size of the company. *See* **Exhibit 9.3** for LSE fees.

Exhibit 9.3	London Stock Exchange listing fees 2011	
Main Market admission fees		**£**
Minimum (under £5m capitalisation)		6,708
Maximum (over £500m capitalisation)		388,173
Main Market annual fees		**UK**
Minimum (under £50m capitalisation)		4,410
Maximum (over £500m capitalisation)		43,470
		International
Minimum (under £25m capitalisation)		6,773
Maximum (over £1,025m capitalisation)		21,634
AIM admission fees		
Minimum (under £5m capitalisation)		6,720
Maximum (over £250m capitalisation)		75,810
AIM annual fee		5,350

Source: London Stock Exchange.

Printing, advertising, public relations, etc.

Public relations and advertising companies are used to influence investors and persuade them to buy the shares. Although the shares are underwritten, and therefore there is a guarantee that they will all be sold, albeit maybe at a lower price than the offer price, it is a huge relief to all concerned if the public response is favourable and the shares are sold to investors. It demonstrates public confidence in the company and shows that the listing was justified, and the sponsors can gauge investor appetite accurately.

Prospectus

To create a stable market and encourage investors to place their money with companies the UKLA tries to minimise the risk of investing by ensuring that the firms which obtain a quotation abide by high standards; this includes producing a well-crafted prospectus. The **prospectus ('listing particulars')** is designed to inform potential shareholders about the company. This may contain far more information about the firm than it has previously dared to put into the public domain. The prospectus acts as a marketing tool as the firm attempts to persuade investors to apply for shares.

The content and accuracy of this vital document are the responsibility of the directors. Contained within it must be three years of audited accounts, details of indebtedness and a statement as to the adequacy of working capital. Statements by experts are often required: valuers may be needed to confirm the current value of property, engineers may be needed to state the viability of processes or machinery and accountants may be needed to comment on the profit figures. All major contracts entered into in the past two years will have to be detailed and a description of the risks facing the firm provided. Any persons with a shareholding of more than 3 per cent have to be named. A mass of operational data is also required, ranging from an analysis of sales by geographical area and type of activity, to information on research and development and significant investments in other companies.

Methods of issue

The sponsor will look at the motives for wanting a quotation, at the amount of money that is to be raised, at the history and reputation of the firm, and will then advise on the best method of issuing the shares. There are various methods, ranging from a full-scale offer for sale to a relatively simple introduction. The final choice often rests on the costs of issue, which can vary considerably. Here are the main options:

- *Offer for sale* The company sponsor offers shares to the public by inviting subscriptions from institutional and individual investors. Sometimes newspapers carry a notice and an application form. However, most investors will need to contact the sponsor or the broker to obtain an application form. Publications such as *Investors Chronicle* show the telephone numbers to call for each company floating. Also details of forthcoming flotations are available at www.london-stockexchange.com and www.hemscott.com. Normally the shares are offered at a fixed price determined by the company's directors and their financial advisers. A variation of this method is an **offer for sale by tender**. Here investors are invited to state a price at which they are willing to buy (above a minimum reserve price). The sponsor gathers the applications and then selects a price which will dispose of all the shares – the strike price. Investors bidding a price above this will be allocated shares at the strike price – not at the price of their bid. Those who bid below the strike price will not receive any shares. This method is useful in situations where it is very difficult to value a company, for instance where there is no comparable company already listed or where the level of demand may be difficult to assess.

- *Introductions* These do not raise any new money for the company. If the company's shares are already quoted on another stock exchange or there is a wide spread of shareholders, with more than 25 per cent of the shares in public hands, the Exchange permits a company to be 'introduced' to the market. This method may allow companies trading on AIM to move up to the Main Market or foreign corporations to gain a London listing. This is the cheapest method of flotation since there are no underwriting costs and relatively small advertising expenditures.

● *Placing* In a placing, shares are offered to the public but the term 'public' is narrowly defined. Instead of engaging in advertising to the population at large, the sponsor or broker handling the issue sells the shares to institutions it is in contact with, such as pension and insurance funds. The costs of this method are considerably lower than those of an offer for sale. There are lower publicity costs and legal costs. A drawback of this method is that the spread of shareholders is going to be more limited. To alleviate this problem the Stock Exchange insists on a large number of placees holding shares after the new issue. A generation ago the most frequently used method of new issue was the offer for sale. This ensured a wide spread of share ownership and thus a more liquid secondary market. It also permitted all investors to participate in new issues. Placings were permitted only for small offerings (< £15m) when the costs of an offer for sale would have been prohibitive. Today any size of new issue can be placed. As this method is much cheaper and easier than an offer for sale, companies have naturally switched to placings so there are now few offers for sale. Placings are normally carried out by sponsors and brokers, but, as **Exhibit 9.4** shows, companies can do their own.

Exhibit 9.4

Growing groups turn to inventive fundraising methods

FT

David Blackwell

Futuragene earlier this month carried out what could be described as a DIY placing. The company, a specialist in plant cell modification, did not involve its broker in the sales process.

"We found the investors," says Stanley Hirsch, chief executive, of himself and chairman Mark Pritchard. "We had the contacts and were able to move more rapidly – and we incurred no broker fees. As a result, the gross proceeds are almost completely net proceeds."

The board considered a general offer to existing shareholders through a rights or other pre-emptive issue to be inappropriate because of "the significant additional costs that would be incurred and the delay that would be caused by the production and approval of a prospectus".

Instead the company placed 6m shares at 50p each with several new shareholders raising £3m. The placing brought in a substantial new shareholder – Hartford Growth (Trading) Fund, which now has a 5 per cent stake. The shares closed yesterday up $^3/_4$p at $70^3/_4$p.

Source: Financial Times, 18 December 2009, p. 20. Reprinted with permission.

● *Intermediaries offer* A method which is often combined with a placing is an intermediaries offer. Here the shares are offered for sale to financial institutions such as stockbrokers. Clients of these intermediaries can then apply to buy shares from them.

● *Reverse takeover* Sometimes a larger unquoted company makes a deal with a smaller quoted company whereby the smaller company 'takes over' the larger firm by swapping newly created shares in itself for the shares in the unquoted firm currently held by its owners. Because the quoted firm creates and issues more new shares itself than it had to start with, the unquoted firm's shareholders end up with the majority of the shares in the newly merged entity. They therefore now control a quoted company. The only task remaining is to decide on a name for the company – frequently the name of the previously unquoted company is chosen. A reverse takeover is a way for a company to gain a listing/quotation without the hassle of an official new issue.

● *Book-building* Selling new issues of shares through book-building is a popular technique in the US and is starting to catch on in Europe. Under this method the financial advisers to an issue contact major institutional investors to get from them bids for the shares over a period of 8–10 working days. The investors' orders are sorted according to price, quantity and other factors such as 'firmness' of bid (e.g. a 'strike bid' means the investor will buy a given number of shares within the initial price range, leaving it to others to set the price; a 'limit bid' means the investor would buy a particular quantity at a particular price). This data may then be used to establish a price for the issue and the allocation of shares.

Exhibit 9.5 shows share prices for five well-known companies since they floated on the Main Market. Each has been assisted by being on the London Stock Exchange but their performances are something of a mixed bag, with Burberry's share price zooming away, easyJet's going nowhere and Debenhams' declining. Burberry has experienced a surge in demand for its products worldwide (and thus its shares) as its fashion brand has caught on in many countries, particularly in Asia. easyJet has a constant battle in the highly competitive short-haul travel market and so has struggled to give a decent return to its shareholders. Debenhams was sold by private equity companies at a price thought to be too high, made worse by the recession. Halfords has developed a reputation for good management and so has ridden out the recession well, giving shareholders a good return. William Hill has suffered from the proliferation of competitors such as betting exchanges and online gambling.

Exhibit 9.5	Share price performances of some recent flotations

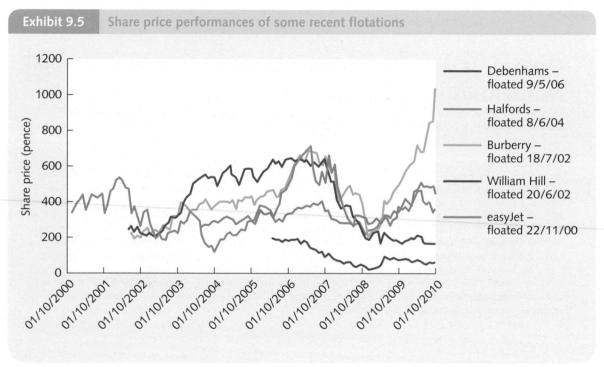

Source: Yahoo Finance.

Case study 9.1	A flotation: Ocado

This case study will help explain the timetable for an IPO in the UK. The key date in an IPO is **'impact day'** when the full prospectus is published and the price is announced in a fixed-price offer for sale or in a placing. In this example all the timings will be relative to impact day – which is 20 July 2010.

Pre-launch publicity: 1–2 years before impact day

The company was formed in 2000 by Tim Steiner, Jason Gissing and Jonathan Faiman, all of them former Goldman Sachs employees. A partnership with the up-market grocer Waitrose was formed, giving Ocado exclusive rights to deliver internet-ordered Waitrose goods using a central warehouse and a fleet of trucks. It had raised £350 million from a range of investors including Procter & Gamble and Jörn Rausing, the Tetra Pak billionaire. The former investment bankers running the company were well aware of the need to drum up investment interest in the company long before the actual flotation, thus they would often give interviews to the press, glossing over the absence of profits and directing attention to the long-term potential of online grocery sales.

Preparation to float: several weeks before impact day

In April 2010, three months before the float and nine years after Ocado started to operate as an unquoted company, Goldman Sachs International, J.P. Morgan Cazenove and UBS were appointed as joint sponsors, joint global-coordinators and joint bookrunners. Immediately, the talk was 'a possible £1 billion float this summer' despite the business never having produced a profit. If it achieved £1 billion the three founders would have shares worth £160 million. It had beefed up its board of directors in the previous month, announcing the appointment of David Grigson, former finance director of Reuters, and Ruth Anderson, former vice-chairman of KPMG in the UK, as non-executive directors. Michael Grade, a well-respected City figure, joined as chairman.

Ocado signed up a further five banks in the 'junior syndicate' – Barclays Capital, Lloyds, HSBC, Numis and Jefferies – to work alongside the sponsors on the IPO in an effort to really give the sale of the shares a push (they all have contacts and clients who might be persuaded to buy).

The sponsors and other advisers then worked on details such as drawing up an accountant's report, the price and method of issue, and organising underwriting. Between six weeks and one week before impact day the sponsors were required to show all the documents to the UKLA for approval.

In June, Ocado said that when the flotation happened about 500,000 of its customers would be given the opportunity to buy shares alongside the major buyers, the institutional funds. Retail investors were expected to buy only £20–£50 million shares; the main offering was in a placing following a book-building process, where the shares are offered to institutional investors.

The company planned to raise around £200 million by selling *new shares* equivalent to about one-fifth of the total shares already in issue. In addition, the original backers of Ocado (particularly John Lewis pension fund with a 26.5 per cent stake and Steiner and Gissing) wanted to sell 155 million shares in the float, which worried many potential investors: why did the original investors want to get out if this company had such potential? And why was it so highly valued relative to, say, Tesco? And why did Steiner get £651,000 annually in salary and other benefits from a business that had never made a profit? *Investors Chronicle* commented:

> This offer is not so much cash-and-carry as cash-in-and-scarper, with holders John Lewis and book-runner UBS planning to dump £200 million of shares. The management team of former Goldman Sachs bankers are also entitled to offload shares worth as much as £19 million between them. (9 July 2010)

In the first week of July the sponsors were still confident that they could sell £200 million of new shares. They published the pathfinder prospectus on Tuesday 7 July and began a two week **roadshow** in which they went around both Europe and the US giving presentations to institutional investors to entice them to buy. The price range they talked about (no final decision yet) was 200–275p, valuing the company at around £1 billion. The conversations at the roadshow would tell the sponsor how realistic this was.

Ocado floated its shares at a time when the stock market was experiencing an uncertain period. Other companies intending to float, such as Fairfield Energy (an off-shore oil company), Madame Tussauds (the waxworks museum) and New Look (a fashion chain), decided to postpone their listings and wait for better economic conditions.

Impact day

Tuesday 20 July: the full prospectus was published and the price was announced at 180p, which was a long way short of its initial hoped-for price of 275p. Despite the best efforts of company officials, sponsors and supporters, there was insufficient interest in the shares at the suggested price range of between 200p and 275p. To ensure sufficient take-up of its offering it was forced to slash the price of its IPO to 180p. This reduction in price enabled the flotation to take place successfully. Steiner refused to sell any of his shares at this 'too cheap' price.

Following impact day investors applied to buy and send in payments. The company made its formal application for listing and admission to the Exchange.

Admission to the Exchange

For an offer for sale there might be two weeks or so between impact day and admission to the Exchange and dealing starting. However, with an issue like Ocado using a book-building process and placing of shares with institutions the timetable can be cut short. It was trading on the MM on 21 July. Its retail customers largely shunned the issue after reading the sceptical reports in the press and comments from professional analysts. At the lower price there were enough institutions willing to buy the shares so they raised the required £200 million. But around half of the IPO shares were taken up by existing investors, which included Fidelity, and regulatory filings showed only one major new investor. The existing shareholders ended up selling only £155 million of their shares.

On the first day of trading the shares fell to 164p and they continued to fall for the next few months – *see* Exhibit 9.6.

Exhibit 9.6   Ocado's share prices in the first few weeks after flotation

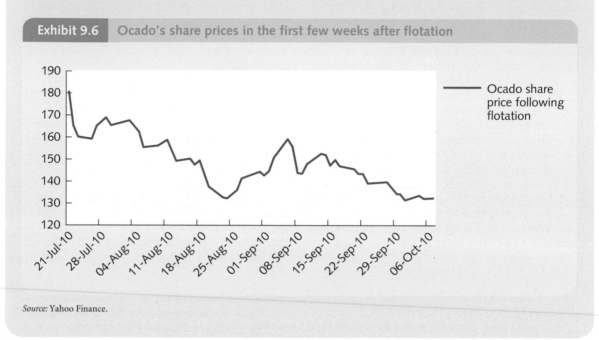

Source: Yahoo Finance.

By way of contrast, Jupiter, a fund management company, performed very well following its flotation on 21 June 2010. Although it floated at a price near the bottom of its stated range, it had a 2.5 times coverage of its order book (there were 2.5 more investors wishing to buy than shares available) – *see* Exhibits 9.7 and 9.8.

Exhibit 9.7

Jupiter surges on market debut

By **Miles Johnson**

Shares in Jupiter Fund Management surged 15 per cent on their first day of trading.

Jupiter, a private equity-backed fund manager led by Edward Bonham Carter, yesterday formally returned to the public markets for the first time since 1995 after selling £220m of shares last week.

Shares in the asset manager jumped from 165p to 190$\frac{1}{2}$p, adding £116m to its market value in the biggest first-day rise for a main market London listing since December 2007, according to Dealogic.

Companies and their advisers can be criticised for "leaving money on the table" when a listing jumps on the first day of trading.

Jupiter had sold the shares at a price of 165p, near the bottom of its 150p-to-210p stated range, but had covered its order book 2.5 times, people close to the listing said.

It had enough investor demand to sell its shares at a higher price, but had chosen a lower price to achieve "a high quality book", these people said.

Source: Financial Times, 22 June 2010, p. 22. Reprinted with permission.

Exhibit 9.8   Jupiter's share price following flotation

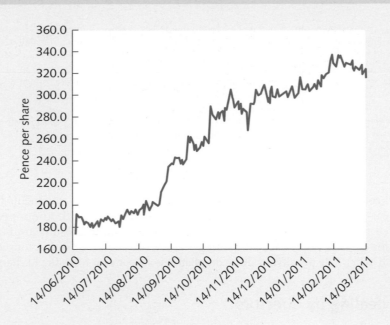

Source: Yahoo Finance.

Post-listing obligations

The UKLA insists on certain 'continuing obligations' designed to protect or enlighten shareholders. One of these is that all price-sensitive information is given to the market as soon as possible and that there is 'full and accurate disclosure' to all investors at the same time. Information is price sensitive if it might influence the share price or the trading in the shares. Investors need to be sure that they are not disadvantaged by market distortions caused by some participants having the benefit of superior information. Public announcements will be required in a number of instances, for example: the development of major new products; the signing of major contracts; details of an acquisition; a sale of large assets; a change in directors or a decision to pay a dividend. The website www.investegate.co.uk shows all major announcements made by companies going back many years. The FSA hands out fines to companies which do not comply with the rules – *see* **Exhibit 9.9**.

Exhibit 9.9

Photo-Me fined £500,000 by FSA for late disclosure

By **Brooke Masters**

Photo-Me International, the photo booth operator, has been fined £500,000 for failing to tell the market promptly that its effort to win a significant new contract had hit hurdles and that sales of minilabs were falling behind expectations.

The fine is the largest handed down by the Financial Services Authority for failure to disclose market-moving inside information quickly enough.

The City regulator said in its final notice that the failure created a false market in Photo-Me shares for 44 days in early 2007.

The fine is part of a string of enforcement actions carried out by a newly aggressive FSA, which also announced yesterday that it had fined Vantage Capital, the inter-dealer broker, a record £700,000 for allowing an unapproved person to perform a key leadership function for four years.

Margaret Cole, the FSA's enforcement director, said the

▶

Exhibit 9.9 continued

Photo-Me action "demonstrates our commitment to enforcing the UK listing regime and ensuring clean, efficient and orderly markets".

Over the past two years, Woolworths, Wolfson Microelectronics and Entertainment Rights have all paid fines for failing to update the markets.

The FSA found that in late 2006, Photo-Me had led the market to believe it would win large sales contracts and "strong minilab sales". But the company then waited too long to announce it faced new competition for a contract with a US supermarket chain, and a director failed to open an e-mail with disappointing January sales information.

When Photo-Me finally issued a profit warning in March 2007, its shares dropped 24 per cent.

Source: *Financial Times*, 22 June 2010, p. 19. Reprinted with permission.

Listed companies are also required to provide detailed financial statements within six months of the year-end. Firms usually choose to make **preliminary profit announcements** based on unaudited results for the year a few weeks before the audited results are published. **Interim reports** for the first half of each accounting year are also required (within four months of the end of the half-year). The penalty for non-compliance is suspension from the Exchange.

Share dealing by directors

There are strict rules concerning the buying and selling of the company's shares by its own directors once it is on the stock exchange. The Criminal Justice Act 1993 and the **Model Code for Director Dealings** have to be followed. Directors are prevented from dealing for a minimum period (normally two months) prior to an announcement of regularly recurring information such as annual results. They are also forbidden to deal before the announcement of matters of an exceptional nature involving unpublished information which is potentially price sensitive. These rules apply to any employee in possession of such information. When directors do buy or sell shares in their company they are required to disclose these dealings publicly. Most (free) financial websites (e.g. www.advfn.com or www.iii.co.uk) show all major announcements made by companies going back many years, including director purchases and sales.

UK Corporate Governance Code

There is a considerable range of legislation and other regulatory pressures designed to encourage directors to act in shareholders' interests. In the UK, the Companies Acts require certain minimum standards of behaviour, as does the LSE. For example, directors are forbidden to use their position to profit at the expense of shareholders. There is the back-up of the financial industry regulator, the FSA/FCA, and the Financial Reporting Council (FRC, an accounting body).

Following a number of financial scandals, guidelines of best practice in corporate governance were issued by the Cadbury, Greenbury, Hampel, Higgs and Smith committees, now consolidated in the **UK Corporate Governance Code**, which is backed by the FSA/FCA, the LSE and the FRC.

Under the code, directors of companies listed on the MM are required to state in the accounts how the principles of the code have been applied.[2] If the principles have not been followed they have to state why. The principles include:

- The board should include a balance of executive and non-executive directors (and in particular independent non-executive directors[3]) such that no individual or small group of individuals can dominate the board's decision taking. For large companies (the largest 350 on

---

[2] Overseas companies listed on the Main Market are required to disclose the significant ways in which their corporate governance practices differ from those set out in the code.

[3] The board should determine whether the director is independent in character and judgement and whether there are relationships or circumstances which are likely to affect, or could appear to affect, the director's judgement. To be independent the non-executive directors generally should not, for example, be a customer, former employee, supplier, or friend of the founding family or the chief executive.

the LSE) at least half the board, excluding the chairman, should comprise non-executive directors determined by the board to be independent. The independent non-executive directors can act as a powerful counterweight to the executive directors. These directors are not full-time and not concerned with day-to-day management. They may be able to take a broader view than executive directors, who may become excessively focused on detail. The experienced individuals who become non-executive directors are not expected to be dependent on the director's fee for income and can therefore afford to be independently minded. They are expected to 'constructively challenge and help develop proposals on strategy . . . scrutinise the performance of management in meeting agreed goals and objectives and monitor the reporting of performance.'[4]

● There should be a balance of power on the board such that no one individual can dominate and impose their will. The running of the board of directors (by a chairman) should be a separate responsibility conducted by a person who is not also responsible for running the business, i.e. the chief executive officer (CEO) or managing director (MD) (this is frequently ignored in practice, which is permitted if a written justification is presented to shareholders).

● There should be transparency on directors' remuneration requiring a remuneration committee consisting exclusively of non-executive directors, independent of management. No director should be involved in deciding his or her remuneration. A significant proportion of remuneration should be linked to corporate and individual performance.

● The procedure for the appointment of board directors should be formal (nomination committee), objective (based on merit) and transparent (information on the terms and conditions made available). Directors are to retire by rotation at least every three years – they may be re-elected.

● The audit committee (responsible for validating financial figures, e.g. by appointing effective external auditors) should consist exclusively of independent non-executive directors, otherwise the committee would not be able to act as a check and balance to the executive directors.

● Directors are required to communicate with shareholders, e.g. to use the annual general meeting to explain the company's performance and encourage discussion.

The 'comply or explain' approach is in contrast to many other systems of regulation of corporate governance around the world – these are often strict rule-based systems with lawyers to the fore (e.g. Sarbanes–Oxley regulations in the US). 'The flexibility it offers [the 'comply or explain' approach] has been widely welcomed both by company boards and by investors. It is for shareholders and others to evaluate the company's statement. While it is expected that companies will comply with the Code's provisions most of the time, it is recognised that departure from the provisions of the Code may be justified in particular circumstances' (FSA, 2003, pp. 1–2). Furthermore, some of the provisions do not apply to companies smaller than the largest 350 listed on the London Stock Exchange. However, failure to comply or explain properly will result in suspension from the stock exchange.

The Alternative Investment Market (AIM)

There is a long-recognised need for equity capital by small, young companies which are unable to afford the costs of full listing. Many stock exchanges have alternative equity markets that set less stringent rules and regulations for joining or remaining quoted (often called 'second-tier markets').

Lightly regulated markets have a continuing dilemma. If the regulation is too lax, scandals of fraud or incompetence will arise, damaging the image and credibility of the market and thus reducing the flow of investor funds to companies. (This happened to the German market for small companies, Neuer Markt, which had to close in 2002 because of the loss in investor confidence.) If the market is too tightly regulated, with more company investigations, more information disclosure and a requirement for longer trading track records prior to flotation, the associated costs and inconvenience will deter many companies from seeking a quotation.

[4] Financial Services Authority (2003) The Combined Code on Corporate Governance, p. 4. The latest version is available at www.frc.org.uk/corporate/ukcgcode.cfm

In the UK, there are many small young companies needing to raise equity capital but which are excluded from the MM because of the huge cost of obtaining and maintaining a listing. The AIM sets less stringent rules, regulations and costs for joining or remaining quoted.

The driving philosophy behind the AIM is to offer young and developing companies access to new sources of finance, while providing investors with the opportunity to buy and sell shares in a trading environment which is run, regulated and marketed by the LSE. Efforts are made to keep the costs down and make the rules as simple as possible. In contrast to the MM, there is no requirement for AIM companies to have been in business for a minimum three-year period or for a set proportion of their shares to be in public hands – if they wish to sell only 1 per cent or 5 per cent of the shares to outsiders, that is OK. They do not have to ensure that 25 per cent of the shares are in public hands. However, investors have some degree of reassurance about the quality of companies coming to the market. These firms have to appoint, and retain at all times, a **nominated adviser** and nominated broker. The nominated adviser, the **nomad,** is selected by the company from a Stock Exchange approved register, and must have demonstrated to the Exchange that they have sufficient experience and qualifications to act as a 'quality controller', confirming to the LSE that the company has complied with the rules. Unlike with MM companies there is no pre-vetting of admission documents by the UKLA or the Exchange, as a lot of weight is placed on the nomad's investigations and informed opinion about the company.

Nominated brokers have an important role to play in bringing together buyers and sellers of shares. Investors in the company are reassured that at least one broker is ready to help shareholders to trade. The adviser and broker are to be retained throughout the company's life on the AIM. They have high reputations and it is regarded as a very bad sign if either of them abruptly refuses further association with a firm.

AIM companies are also expected to comply with strict rules regarding the publication of price-sensitive information and the quality of annual and interim reports. Upon flotation, an **AIM admission document** is required. This is similar to a prospectus required for companies floating on the MM, but is not as comprehensive and therefore has a lower cost. The LSE charges companies an annual fee to maintain a quotation on AIM. If to this is added the cost of financial advisers and of management time spent communicating with institutions and investors, the annual cost of being quoted on AIM runs into tens of thousands of pounds. This can be a deterrent for many companies. The cost of an initial offering of shares runs into hundreds of thousands of pounds. The cost of joining AIM is around £100,000–£200,000, but if additional money is raised by selling new shares the organisation and underwriting costs push this up over £500,000 in many cases. Nominated advisers argue that their policing role on behalf of the LSE means they have to incur much higher investigatory costs than was envisaged when AIM was first established, thus they have higher ongoing as well as initial costs.

However, there are cost savings compared with the MM. As well as the flotation prospectus being less detailed and therefore cheaper, the annual expense of managing a quotation is less. For example, AIM companies are not bound by the Listing Rules administered by the UKLA but instead are subject to the AIM rules, written and administered by the LSE. AIM companies do not have to disclose as much information as companies on the Official List. Price-sensitive information will have to be published, but normally this will require only an electronic message from the adviser to the Exchange rather than a circular to shareholders.

Recently the LSE has tightened the rules on the quality assurance provided by nominated advisers, but this has raised costs for companies – *see* **Exhibit 9.10**.

Offsetting the cost advantages AIM has over the Official List is the fact that the higher level of regulation and related enhanced image, prestige and security of Official List companies means that equity capital can usually be raised at a lower required rate of return (the shares can be sold for more per unit of projected profit). However, as Exhibit 9.10 illustrates, AIM has pretty high standards of regulation anyway.

The AIM is not just a stepping-stone for companies planning to graduate to the Official List; it has many attractive features in its own right. Indeed, many Official List companies have moved to AIM in recent years.

Exhibit 9.10

Tighter rules forcing nomads to run from smaller companies

Brooke Masters

Fewer firms are serving as nominated advisers (nomads) to companies traded on London's junior market and many of those that remain are charging more for their services in the wake of last year's publication of the first-ever AIM rulebook and the first fines levied against a nomad.

The total number of nomads has fallen from 85 last February, when the rulebook was published, to 71. Some of the reduction is due to consolidation and tougher economic times, but the tighter rules helped drive away firms because they felt they could not make money while performing the record keeping and services required. Annual fees for ongoing nomad service to a £50m company now run between £50,000 and £75,000 a year, double the fees charged by some firms last year.

Andrew Monk, chief executive of nomad Blue Oar, said: "It is now more responsibility to look after an AIM company than a fully listed company and they're more likely to be riskier because they are a smaller company. You have to charge more."

In a system invented by AIM, nomads serve as gate-keepers for London's junior market and are responsible for making sure the companies they advise adhere to the Stock Exchange's principles. The system is often lauded as more flexible and less costly for fledgling companies, but it has harsh critics who say it attracts companies with lower corporate governance standards.

While defending its approach, the London Stock Exchange has noticeably tightened up its rules and doubled the number of people assigned to AIM's regulatory and enforcement staff. The rulebook also ratcheted up the pressure on nomads by spelling out specific actions they could, and should, take. That has forced some to do more and others to improve their record keeping.

Nick Bayley, LSE's head of trading services, said: "It's harder now for a nominated adviser to argue it acted with due skill and care, if it has failed without good reason to do the things expected under the new nomad rules."

Some nomads welcome the more explicit standards, arguing they will reassure investors.

"Liquidity is key to making the market a success and part of liquidity is getting investors to trust the advisers to regulate what is going on," said Nick Stagg, chief executive of Landsbanki Securities (UK).

Source: Adapted from *Financial Times*, 18 June 2008, p. 21.

PLUS

PLUS is a stock exchange based in London and is used by companies that do not want to pay the costs of a flotation on one of the markets run by the LSE. Companies quoted on PLUS provide a service to their shareholders, allowing them to buy and sell shares at reasonable cost. It also allows the company to gain access to capital, for example by selling more shares in a rights issue, without submitting to the rigour and expense of a quotation on the LSE. The downside is that trading in PLUS-quoted shares can be illiquid (not many buyers or sellers); bid–offer spreads vary widely with 30 per cent to 50 per cent not uncommon.

PLUS (originally called Ofex) was set up by the broker J. P. Jenkins in 1995 and is owned by PLUS-Markets group (www.plusmarketsgroup.com). Joining fees range from a minimum of £15,000 to £100,000 for the largest companies, and annual fees are between £5,665 and £50,500. In addition there are Corporate Adviser's fees of around £20,000, plus an annual retainer. If new money is to be raised there will be additional advisery and other costs. PLUS companies are generally small and often brand new, but there are also some long-established and well-known firms, such as Thwaites and Adnams.

Many companies gain a quotation on PLUS without raising fresh capital simply to allow a market price to be set and current shareholders to trade. If no money is raised, no formal admission document or prospectus is required, but the Corporate Adviser (to be retained by the company at all times) will insist that good accounting systems are in place with annual audited accounts and semi-annual accounts. The Corporate Adviser will also ensure that the company has at least one non-executive director and adequate working capital. In 2010 there were more than 200 companies with a combined market capitalisation of around £2 billion quoted on the PLUS exchange.

In addition to the 200 or so shares that are listed on the PLUS-quoted system, PLUS Market provides a trading platform for all UK listed shares, plus some European shares and some unlisted shares. PLUS itself is listed on the AIM market of the LSE, having raised £26 million for the expansion of its trading and quotation services in 2006.

Exhibit 9.11 discusses the floating of some companies on PLUS in 2010.

Exhibit 9.11

Micro-caps renew appetite for listings on Plus

David Blackwell

Two companies raised money on joining Plus Markets at the end of last month, ending a dearth of initial public offerings on the third-tier market.

Climate Human Capital, a recruitment company specialising in the "green" sector, arrived on the market last Tuesday after raising £750,000 gross through a placing at 50p a share. At Thursday's closing price of 55p, the company had a market valuation of £1.7m.

If followed a week after Global Brands Licensing raised £1m through a placing at 1p a share. Shares in the company, which plans to create a Marilyn Monroe clothing range, closed on Thursday at $3^{1}/_{4}$p, giving it a market capitalisation of £22.8m.

There are also another half a dozen companies waiting to be introduced to Plus, signalling a renewed appetite among micro-caps for a quote. Bioventix, which is developing anti-bodies for both commercial and research purposes, will join the market tomorrow.

Among others waiting in the wings is In House Group, a property company and refugee from Aim, which cancelled trading in its shares a month after Beaumont Cornish, its nominated adviser, resigned in December.

Climate Human Capital has been brought to market by WH Ireland, which has been a Plus adviser for 10 years but which represents only four companies on the market. The last company introduced by WH Ireland was China Meihua, a bio-technology company in which no shares have been traded since its arrival in August.

Katy Mitchell of WH Ireland said China Meihua had taken the quote in order to raise its profile and prove its corporate governance. Ms Mitchell said that Plus was working hard to improve its appeal to small companies at a time when it was difficult to raise funds.

Michael Brennan, chief executive of Climate Human Capital, said the company was too small to go

to Aim. But joining Plus would give it "a certain profile" and help to attract investors, as well as allowing it to offer incentives to staff through share schemes.

The company raised its money from wealthy individuals and has enough to develop the company over the next 12 months. "If we do need to raise more, we can do so through existing investors," he said.

He claimed the company was the world's first quoted recruitment specialist centred on the "green" sector. It would be headhunting for activities as diverse as wind farms and non-governmental organisations.

After costs of about £200,000, the net proceeds of the flotation were £550,000. "It is expensive – but we don't need to raise an enormous amount," he said. "We had to get what we needed to get the company going. Now we will grow it in an organic fashion."

Source: Financial Times, 6 April 2010, p. 17. Reprinted with permission.

Understanding the figures in the financial pages

The financial pages of the broadsheet newspapers, particularly the *Financial Times,* provide some important statistics on company share price performance and valuation ratios. **Exhibit 9.12** shows extracts from two issues of the *Financial Times.* The information provided in the Monday edition is different from that provided on the other days of the week. (There is more discussion on these ratios in Arnold, G. (2010) *The Financial Times Guide to Investing,* Harlow: Prentice Hall.)

Exhibit 9.12 London Share Service extracts: Aerospace and Defence

WEDNESDAY MARCH 9 2011

Notes	Price	Chng	52 Week High	Low	Vol 000's	P/E	Yld
Aerospace & Defence							
AvonRub....	232.50	–	252.50	75.50	11	15.3	0.6
BAE Sys.....q	327.70	+2.60	389.90	288.10	11,785	1	5.3
Chemring....	£33.54	+0.29	£37.11	£25.51	100	18.6	1.8
Cobham.....q	235.30	+5.60	278.60	188.60	7,330	17.5	2.5
Hampson...†	37.25	+0.25	69	18	223	19	2.4
Meggitt.....q	352.40	-1.90	388.90	255.70	9,292	17.4	2.6
RollsRyc.....	600.50	+0.50	674.50	318.93	10,614	21	2.4
Senior....	139	-4	161.40	89	4,994	12.3	2.2
UltraElc.....q	£16.79	-0.10	£19.03	£14.70	656	17.4	2.1
UMECO.....†	481	-12	512.50	318	7	15.5	3.7

MONDAY MARCH 7 2011   FT

Notes	Price	Wks% Chg	Div	Div Cov	Mcap £m	Last xd
Aerospace & Defence						
AvonRub....	232	+2.0	1.50	10.2	71.3	1'08
BAE Sys.....q	324.30	-1.0	17.50	18.4	11,057.4	20.10
Chemring....	£33.01	+0.3	59	3.4	1,168.0	14.7
Cobham.....q	224.30	-1.7	6	2.2	2,589.6	13.10
Hampson...†	37	+1.4	0.90	2.2	103.3	8.9
Meggitt.....q	353.60	+4.6	9.20	2.2	2,715.2	11.8
RollsRyc.....	604	-1.3	14.40	2.0	11,307.9	27.10
Senior....	142.20	-7.5	3.12	3.6	570.1	27.10
UltraElc.....q	£16.97	-5.1	34.60	2.8	1,166.2	18.8
UMECO.....†	488.50	+3.4	17.75	1.7	235.2	12.1

Market price: This is the mid-price (midway between the best buying and selling prices) quoted at 4.30 p.m. on the previous day.

Change in closing price on Tuesday compared with previous trading day.

The highest and lowest prices during the previous 52 weeks.

Dividend yield: The dividend divided by the current share price expressed as a percentage:

$$\frac{\text{dividend per share}}{\text{current share price}} \times 100$$

Volume of trade in those shares that day.

Price/earnings ratio (PER): Share price divided by the company's earnings (profits after tax) per share in the latest twelve-month period. A much examined and talked about measure:

$$PER = \frac{\text{share price}}{\text{earnings per share}}$$

Share price change over the previous week.

The dividend paid in the company's last full year – it is the cash payment in pence per share (after deduction of 10% tax for UK firms).

Dividend cover: Profit after tax divided by the dividend payment, or earnings per share divided by dividend per share:

$$\text{Dividend cover} = \frac{\text{earnings per share}}{\text{dividend per share}}$$

Ex-dividend date is the last date on which the share went ex-dividend (new buyers of the shares will not receive the recently announced dividend after this date, 12th January in this case.

Market capitalisation is calculated by multiplying the number of shares issued by their market price.

Source: Financial Times, 7 and 9 March 2011. Reprinted with permission.

Indices

Information on individual companies in isolation is less useful than information set in the context of the firm's peer group, or in comparison with quoted companies generally. For example, if Tesco's shares fall by 1 per cent on a particular day, an investor might be keen to learn whether the market as a whole rose or fell on that day, and by how much. An index measures the relative value of a group of shares and publishes the data for comparison purposes.

The oldest index is the Dow Jones Industrial Average (DJIA), which began in 1896 with 12 stocks (only one of which, General Electric, is still on the index) valued at 40.74. The number of companies was increased to 30 in 1928 valued at 239, since when the number of stocks has remained the same, but the index is now valued at over 10,000 – *see* **Exhibit 9.13**.

| **Exhibit 9.13** | Dow Jones Industrial Average 1928–2011 |

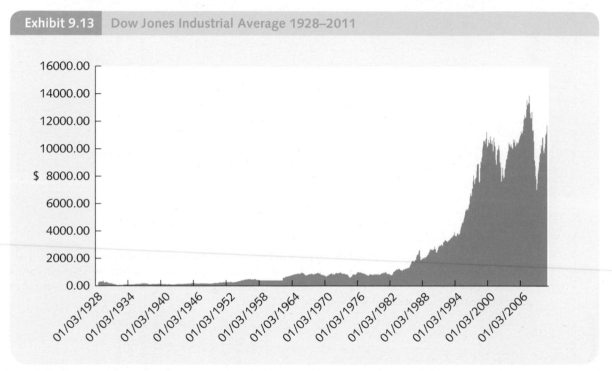

Source: Yahoo Finance.

The companies on the Dow represent the largest and best-known US companies (*see* **Exhibit 9.14**) and the DJIA is one of the few indices to be weighted by the share price, so higher priced shares are given more weight – they may be smaller companies in terms of market capitalisation than others in the index but their percentage share price changes have more effect on the index. In recent years the S&P500 (Standard & Poor's 500) index has been given more attention than the DJIA because it more accurately represents the US market given that it contains 500 companies (and is market capitalisation weighted – see below).

Most indices are capitalisation weighted. To calculate these indices each component share is weighted by the size of the company; by its market capitalisation. Thus, a 2 per cent movement in the share price of a large company has a greater effect on an index than a 2 per cent change in a small company's share price.

The oldest UK index is the FTSE All Share index, formed in 1962 with a base value of 100, comprising all companies on the London Stock Exchange above a certain size and liquidity. Since then the FTSE (a joint venture of the *Financial Times* and the London *Stock Exchange*) has produced an increasing number of indices, the most famous of which is the FTSE 100, the 'Footsie', which began in 1984 with a base value of 1000. It is an index of the 100 most highly capitalised UK-based 'blue chip' companies, which generally have a market capitalisation over £2 billion (large and relatively safe companies are referred to as 'blue chips'). Twenty-one of the original companies are still on the list, and its performance is closely watched by investors throughout the

Exhibit 9.14   Dow Jones Industrial Average companies 2011

The DJIA 2011

3M Company	Intel Corporation
Alcoa Inc.	International Business Machines
American Express Company	Johnson & Johnson
AT&T Inc.	JP Morgan Chase & Co.
Bank of America Corporation	Kraft Foods Inc.
Boeing Company	McDonald's Corporation
Caterpillar, Inc.	Merck & Company, Inc.
Chevron Corporation	Microsoft Corporation
Cisco Systems, Inc.	Pfizer, Inc.
Coca-Cola Company	Procter & Gamble Company
E.I. du Pont de Nemours and Co.	The Travelers Companies, Inc.
Exxon Mobil Corporation	United Technologies Corporation
General Electric Company	Verizon Communications Inc.
Hewlett-Packard Company	Wal-Mart Stores, Inc.
Home Depot, Inc.	Walt Disney Company

Source: Yahoo Finance.

world. It reflects the global economic climate because the turnover of these London-quoted companies is largely derived from outside the UK. It is calculated every 15 seconds so changes can be observed throughout the day. Every quarter, the 100 companies are reviewed to make sure their place in the FTSE 100 is warranted – *see* **Exhibit 9.15**.

Exhibit 9.15

Redrawing the blue-chip index map   **FT**

The next FTSE 100 shake-up will give it an increasingly international look, writes **Adam Jones**

The FTSE 100 is poised for a fresh bout of internationalisation that will make it even less of a weathervane for the British economy.

Next week's quarterly review of the UK's most famous share index is almost certain to lead to the inclusion of Essar Energy, the Indian power, oil and gas group that floated in London in April.

Companies with a chance of entering with Essar include African Barrick Gold, a spin-off from Barrick Gold of Canada, which is the largest gold producer in Tanzania, and Petropavlosk, the Russian gold miner formerly known as Peter Hambro Mining.

Meanwhile, candidates for possible relegation in the June 9 review include Thomas Cook and the London Stock Exchange, according to Winterflood Securities.

Broadly speaking, the FTSE 100 is a roll-call of the top 100 UK-listed companies by market capitalisation, although some other criteria apply.

Miners have led the charge. The likes of the Kazakhstan-focused Kazakhmys, Vedanta Resources (operates in India, Zambia and Australia) and Fresnillo (based in Mexico) now stand shoulder to shoulder with UK-centric blue chips such as Marks & Spencer. David Hobbs, a director of FTSE, the body that compiles the index, says it is wrong to view their arrival as a rupture with the past, however.

"The FTSE 100 has never been and was never intended to be a representation of the UK economy," he says, pointing out that constituent companies have always drawn much of their turnover from overseas.

Corporate nationality can be hard to pin down in any case. British Airways for instance, will be part

▶

Exhibit 9.15 continued

of a new company incorporated in Spain after it merges with Iberia.

Mr Hobbs and his colleagues recently had to decide if shares in this new entity could still be part of the FTSE 100. They provisionally decided that it could because of 'investor perception" and a likely London bias to post-merger trading.

A thumbs-down from FTSE, which is owned by the Financial Times Group and the LSE, would have been a blow to BA as there is still an international marketing cachet to being a part of the FTSE 100.

"It's a recognition," says Anil Agarwal, the controlling shareholder and executive chairman of Vedanta, which listed in London in 2003 and entered the FTSE 100 in 2006.

Membership of the index also means that some institutional investors are obliged to hold a company's shares. This can be controversial, given that the newcomers are sometimes deemed to be riskier bets.

Richard Lambert, director-general of the Confederation of British Industry, thinks the influx from overseas had not left UK-focused businesses starved of capital, however.

'UK plcs raised an enormous amount of equity last year," he says.

Many international companies are drawn to listing in London because of the depth of the pool of investors. An extra attraction for foreign businesses is the relatively flexible approach to corporate governance.

In the case of the miners, immigration has also become self-reinforcing. As the more mining groups listed, the more the City deepened its sector-specific expertise – such as specialist analysts and bankers – which in turn pulled in more businesses.

Some overseas-focused FTSE 100 members may have only a token UK office. But they have still been a substantial source of fees to local bankers, lawyers, accountants, public relations firms and company secretarial services.

Shallow local roots can also deepen into a substantial presence, as proved by SABMiller. The brewer, then South African Breweries, listed on the London Stock Exchange in 1999.

It now employs about 30–40 at its London head office and about 480 in the UK overall. But Graham Mackay, chief executive, recalls a very different set-up initially: "When we first came to list it was three of us and a filing cabinet."

FTSE 100			2010	

10 largest companies by market capitalisation (£bn) May 28

Royal Dutch Shell	HSBC	BP	Vodafone	GlaxoSmithKline
111.9	109.9	93.0	73.0	60.1

Rio Tinto	BHP Billiton	AstraZeneca	British American Tobacco	Lloyds Banking Group
48.7	42.2	41.8	40.8	38.0

1984

10 largest companies by market capitalisation at launch of index (£bn)

British Petroleum	Shell Transport & Trading	GEC	ICI	Marks and Spencer
7.4	6.3	4.9	3.9	2.8

BAT Industries	Glaxo	BTR	Beecham	Grand Metropolitan
2.6	2.6	2.2	2.2	2.0

Mining sector has grown . . .

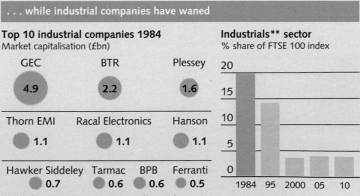

Basic materials* sector
% share of FTSE 100 index

(bar chart: 1984, 95, 2000, 05, 10; y-axis 0 to 20)

Top 10 miners 2010
Market capitalisation (£bn)

Rio Tinto	BHP Billiton	Anglo American
48.7	42.2	35.1

Xstrata	ENRC	Antofagasta
29.8	12.9	8.8

Fresnillo	Kazakhmys	Vedanta	Randgold
6.5	6.3	5.3	5.4

Market capitalisations are for London listings (Shell includes A and B shares)

* includes mining and chemicals

. . . while industrial companies have waned

Top 10 industrial companies 1984
Market capitalisation (£bn)

GEC	BTR	Plessey
4.9	2.2	1.6

Thorn EMI	Racal Electronics	Hanson
1.1	1.1	1.1

Hawker Siddeley	Tarmac	BPB	Ferranti
0.7	0.6	0.6	0.5

** includes engineering, construction and materials
Sources: Thomson Reuters Datastream; FT research

Industrials sector**
% share of FTSE 100 index

(bar chart: 1984, 95, 2000, 05, 10; y-axis 0 to 20)

Interactive graphic: www. ft.com/ftse100

Source: Financial Times, 1 June 2010. Reprinted with permission.

The FTSE 100 rose significantly in its first 16 years, but has done poorly since 2000 – it has not even matched inflation (*see* **Exhibit 9.16**).

Exhibit 9.16   Performance of FTSE 100 from its inception to 2011

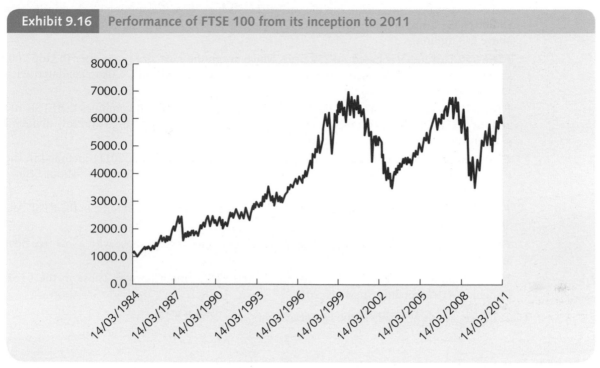

Source: Yahoo Finance.

The FTSE manages thousands of different indices and has offices all over the world. Furthermore, there are many other agencies calculating indices, the most important of which are shown in **Exhibit 9.17**.

Exhibit 9.17   Important stock market indices

UK Indices	Non-UK indices	
FTSE 100	NASDAQ Comp	US
FTSE 250	Dow Jones	US
FTSE 350	S&P 500	US
FTSE All-Share	FTSE MIB	Italy
FTSE AIM All-Share	Xetra DAX	Germany
FTSE SmallCap	D J Eurostoxx 50	Eurozone
FTSE All-Small	CAC 40	France
	AEX	Netherlands
	BEL20	Belgium
	PSI General	Portugal
	Nikkei 225	Tokyo
	Hang Seng	Hong Kong
	ASX All Ordinaries	Australia
	FTSEurofirst100	Europe
	FTSE All World	World

Source: London Stock Exchange.

FTSE All-Share This index is the most representative in that it reflects the average movements of over 600 shares comprising 98–99 per cent of the value of the London market. This index is broken down into a number of industrial and commercial sectors, so that investors and companies can use sector-specific yardsticks, such as those for mining or chemicals – *see* **Exhibit 9.18**. Companies in the FTSE All-Share index have market capitalisations (roughly) above £40 million.

FTSE 250 This index is based on 250 firms which are in the next size range after the top 100. Capitalisations are generally between £300 million and £2 billion . (Also calculated with investment trusts removed.)

FTSE 350 This index is based on the largest 350 quoted companies. It combines the FTSE 100 and the FTSE 250. This cohort of shares is also split into two to give high and low dividend yield groups. A second 350 index excludes investment trusts.

FTSE SmallCap This index covers companies (268 of them in March 2011) included in the FTSE All-Share but excluded from the FTSE 350, with a market capitalisation of about £40m–£300 million.

FTSE Fledgling This includes companies listed on the MM but too small to be in the FTSE All-Share index.

FTSE AIM All-Share This is an index of all AIM companies (except those with a low free float and low liquidity).

FTSE All-Small This combines companies in the FTSE SmallCap with those in the FTSE Fledgling (419 companies in March 2011).

These indices are shown daily in the *Financial Times* – *see* **Exhibit 9.18**.

Rights issues

In addition to, or as an alternative to, floating on a stock market, which usually involves raising finance by selling shares to a new group of shareholders, a company may raise finance by making a rights issue, in which existing shareholders are invited to pay for new shares in proportion to their present holdings.

This is a very popular method of raising new funds, especially if the company does not want or is unable to finance through borrowing. It is easy and relatively cheap (compared with new issues). Directors are not required to seek the prior consent of shareholders, and the London Stock Exchange will intervene in larger issues only (to adjust the timing so that the market does not suffer from too many issues in one period).

Pre-emption rights

The UK has particularly strong traditions and laws concerning pre-emption rights. These require that a company raising new equity capital by selling shares must first offer those shares to the existing shareholders. The owners of the company are entitled to subscribe for the new shares in proportion to their existing holding, which enables them to maintain the influence of their existing percentage ownership of the company – the only difference is that each slice of the company cake is bigger because it is part of a larger financial asset. The importance of pre-emption rights across Europe and much of the rest of the world is discussed in **Exhibit 9.19**.

Rights issues are usually offered at a significantly discounted price from the market value of the current shares – typically 10–20 per cent. Shareholders can either buy these shares themselves or sell the 'right' to buy them to another investor. For further reassurance that the firm will raise the anticipated finance, rights issues are usually underwritten by financial institutions (the financial institution guarantees to buy any shares not sold).

Exhibit 9.18

FTSE ACTUARIES SHARE INDICES

Produced in conjunction with the Faculty and Institute of Actuaries

FT

UK SERIES
www.ft.com/equities

	£ Stlg Mar 8	Day's chge%	Euro index	£ Stlg Mar 7	£ Stlg Mar 4	Year ago	Div yield%	Cover	P/E ratio	Xd adj	Total Return
FTSE 100 (100)	5974.8	–	5408.1	5973.8	5990.4	5602.3	3.01	2.37	14.00	32.59	3924.54
FTSE 250 (250)	11743.5	–	10629.7	11747.9	11723.0	9774.7	2.31	2.41	17.90	24.17	7143.68
FTSE 250 ex Inv Co (204)	12402.2	-0.1	11225.9	12413.1	12388.9	10208.7	2.44	2.46	16.62	24.93	7665.73
FTSE 350 (350)	3170.0	–	2869.4	3169.7	3176.5	2927.8	2.92	2.38	14.42	15.87	4222.95
FTSE 350 ex Inv Co (303)	3156.5	–	2857.1	3156.4	3163.4	2917.3	2.95	2.38	14.25	15.98	2162.52
FTSE 350 Higher Yield (110)	3155.7	+0.4	2856.5	3141.8	3138.2	3024.8	4.12	1.60	15.13	23.15	4071.69
FTSE 350 Lower Yield (240)	2883.1	-0.4	2609.6	2894.7	2909.8	2590.1	1.77	4.10	13.80	8.00	2741.62
FTSE SmallCap (268)	3276.1	–	2965.41	3274.61	3273.90	2867.76	2.58	1.69	22.99	8.89	3954.33
FTSE SmallCap ex Inv Co (162)	2698.4	-0.1	2442.43	2699.92	2696.75	2376.58	3.08	1.77	18.30	7.23	3397.77
FTSE All-Share (618)	3103.1	–	2808.83	3102.82	3109.26	2862.26	2.91	2.36	14.55	15.36	4186.55
FTSE All-Share ex Inv Co (465)	3081.8	–	2789.51	3081.73	3088.41	2846.09	2.95	2.37	14.30	15.49	2147.55
FTSE All-Share ex Multinationals (552)	909.9	+0.2	682.61	907.80	909.08	793.70	2.88	2.53	13.72	1.95	1325.22
FTSE Fledgling (151)	4990.9	+0.2	4517.57	4979.65	4972.27	4117.95	3.20	‡	‡	14.46	7954.60
FTSE Fledgling ex Inv Co (98)	6006.1	+0.2	5436.46	5997.02	5980.75	4795.23	4.01	‡	‡	11.93	9342.29
FTSE All-Small (419)	2262.8	+0.1	2048.17	2261.36	2260.61	1969.18	2.64	1.29	29.42	6.18	3507.82
FTSE All-Small ex Inv Co (260)	2002.9	–	1812.98	2003.74	2001.11	1747.00	3.17	1.24	25.39	5.24	3198.30
FTSE AIM All-Share (816)	932.8	-0.2	844.3	934.8	938.2	689.6	0.57	‡	‡	0.44	956.62

Exhibit 9.18 continued

FTSE Sector Indices	£ Stlg Mar 8	Day's chge%	Euro index	£ Stlg Mar 7	£ Stlg Mar 4	Year ago	Div yield%	Cover	P/E ratio	Xd adj	Total Return
Oil & Gas (24)	**9285.1**	**-1.0**	**8404.44**	**9374.82**	**9353.19**	**8867.70**	**2.35**	**1.11**	**38.43**	**67.05**	**6409.60**
Oil & Gas Producers (17)	8767.9	-1.0	7936.32	8853.42	8834.25	8470.77	2.39	1.06	39.54	65.81	6246.17
Oil Equipment Services (5)	25541.6	-0.8	23119.19	25742.70	25606.06	16980.25	1.20	3.76	22.20		16292.26
Basic Materials (32)	**8020.4**	**-1.5**	**7259.74**	**8139.26**	**8243.07**	**7028.43**	**1.44**	**7.84**	**8.82**	**21.54**	**6741.35**
Chemicals (7)	7514.9	-0.3	6802.19	7535.09	7483.62	5277.02	1.84	2.64	20.66	12.67	5786.24
Forestry & Paper (1)	6711.3	+0.4	6074.76	6681.88	6670.13	5169.20	2.95	3.29	10.28		5941.49
Industrial Metals & Mining (3)	8684.5	-1.2	7860.87	8792.26	8884.20	6883.29	0.40	8.56	28.97		7016.18
Mining (21)	25213.2	-1.5	22821.90	25604.44	25955.39	22307.92	1.42	8.21	8.56	69.95	11020.33
Industrials (113)	**3128.1**	**-0.1**	**2831.42**	**3130.30**	**3125.21**	**2614.53**	**2.51**	**2.26**	**17.59**	**1.40**	**2731.29**
Construction & Materials (10)	4211.8	-0.5	3812.35	4231.77	4198.49	3553.57	3.90	1.78	14.37	7.22	3574.30
Aerospace & Defence (10)	3417.4	+0.4	3093.26	3404.47	3401.39	3464.66	3.46	1.93	14.96	0.35	3141.43
General Industrials (6)	2663.3	–	2410.67	2664.36	2649.78	1918.92	2.62	2.45	15.56	1.96	2454.89
Electronic & Electrical Equipment (12)	3772.4	-0.2	3414.59	3779.81	3739.39	1971.17	1.90	2.38	22.09	7.71	2984.38
Industrial Engineering (13)	7017.0	-0.8	6351.53	7076.73	7068.91	4714.92	2.30	2.50	17.46	4.45	7270.98
Industrial Transportation (9)	3301.3	+0.1	2988.22	3298.13	3239.66	2975.34	3.79	1.59	16.55		2299.60
Support Services (53)	4412.1	-0.1	3993.67	4415.97	4419.49	3723.17	1.97	2.56	19.77	1.21	3921.26
Consumer Goods (35)	**10300.1**	**+0.6**	**9323.20**	**10234.76**	**10265.96**	**9851.07**	**3.50**	**2.09**	**13.69**	**89.20**	**6228.62**
Automobiles & Parts (1)	4997.7	+1.3	4523.74	4933.02	4909.05	2895.57	2.40	3.99	10.46		4023.86
Beverages (4)	9257.1	+0.7	8379.10	9191.86	9169.35	8352.27	2.75	1.87	19.42	64.14	5589.28

Source: Financial Times, 9 March 2011. Reprinted with permission.

Exhibit 9.19

Knowing your rights is a serious issue

Kate Burgess

Ask shareholders which rights they treasure most highly and many say it is their right to pre-emption, which protects their holdings from being diluted by new share issues.

Many countries impose rules on share issues, forcing companies to tell existing shareholders of their plans or give existing shareholders the right of first refusal of new shares.

Last year 1,012 companies across the world raised $196.3bn via rights issues, according to Dealogic, the data provider. Three-quarters of this sum was raised in Europe.

Just over 100 UK companies raised $65.2bn in 2009 and 245 continental European companies $82.8bn, says Dealogic. This accounts for about two-thirds of all cash calls in the region.

But few shareholders elsewhere take these rights more seriously than those in the UK, where protections have developed over centuries to stop managers transferring wealth from the owners of companies to new investors.

Market historians have found references to rights issues in the UK in 1719 and they were going strong by 1900 and pre-emption is now enshrined in UK company law.

The UK system stands out in two ways. UK investors' rights are separately valued and even shareholders who do not take up their entitlements to new shares are paid something for their rights.

Second, the system is designed to treat all shareholders equally. The Association of British Insurers, which is responsible for the government-backed guidelines on rights issues, distinguishes between rights issues found in many parts of the world and fully pre-emptive rights issues in the UK, which give existing shareholders first refusal of new shares.

The UK imposes some of the toughest constraints on companies raising funds. There are, for example, restrictions on how deeply new issues are discounted as well as a 5 per cent limit on "disapplication" – the amount of shares a company can sell without talking to shareholders.

Evidence of just how jealousy British shareholders guard their rights to participate equally in share issues came last year with the brouhaha over Rio Tinto's attempt to raise $19.5bn via a deal with Chinalco.

Investors were furious at the deal, which would have doubled the Chinese state-owned aluminium company's stake in Rio to 18 per cent at what investors said was an over-generous price. Rio was forced instead to opt for a $15.2bn rights issue and a joint venture with rival BHP Billiton.

As Legal & General Investment Management – the UK's largest investor – stiffly reminded the board at the time: "Shareholder pre-emption rights are paramount".

"Pre-emption is an article of faith in the UK," says Daniel Epstein, a partner at law firm Allen & Overy.

It contrasts sharply with the US, where pre-emption was restricted by state legislation in 1930 and does not feature in the company law of Delaware, where most US companies are incorporated.

In the US, managements can sell what they want to the highest bidder and investors have limited protection from their actions.

Elsewhere round the world from Canada to Egypt and Australia, some form of pre-emption exists but the procedures and levels of protection differ.

In Egypt, say lawyers, companies can fulfil their obligations to investors by informing them of an issue in a local newspaper. Investors do not have tradeable rights. "There is an enti-tlement understood as a right but there is no mechanism for monetising it," says Mr Epstein.

Even in Europe, pre-emption varies. The concept has been enshrined in European law since the 1970s. But as Paul Myners, now City minister, said in a 2004 government-sponsored report, the provisions in the 2nd Company Law Directive "are relatively permissive and hence there is some variation between the regimes in different Member states".

In the UK, regulators and shareholders argue that tight rules on pre-emption give investors confidence, which helps companies to raise capital at a lower cost, compared with share issues elsewhere.

Placing shares in the US costs an average of 5 per cent or more, compared with 3 or 4 per cent in the UK.

US bankers say they charge more because the market includes more private investors with small holdings – marketing to a diverse shareholder base costs more than to big investment groups based in one or two cities.

That said, the UK's rights issue process has not gone unchallenged. US bankers have long complained that the system is protracted and the requirement to send out wads of documents ahead of a shareholder vote and then give investors time to trade their rights introduces risk.

The pre-emption concept is gaining ground in other jurisdictions. In Japan, pre-emption rights issues were almost unknown. But as struggling companies last year found they needed to raise equity in more flexible ways, calls for share issues that protect shareholder rights have gained support, from the Tokyo stock exchange, among others.

Source: *Financial Times*, 3 February 2010, p. 3. Reprinted with permission.

An example

Take the case of the imaginary listed company Swell plc with 100 million shares in issue. It wants to raise £25 million for expansion but does not want to borrow the money. Its existing shares are quoted on the stock market at 120p, so the new rights shares will have to be issued at a lower price to appeal to shareholders because there is a risk of the market price falling in the period between the announcement and the purchasing of new shares. The offer must remain open for shareholders to get their applications in for at least two weeks (ten working days).

Swell has decided to issue 25 million shares at 100p each, raising the required £25 million, thus the ratio of new shares to old is 25:100, a 'one-for-four' rights issue. Each shareholder will be offered one new share for every four already held. The discount on these new shares is 20p or 16.7 per cent.

If the market price before the issue is 120p, valuing the entire company at £120 million and another £25 million is pumped into the company by selling 25 million shares at £1, it logically follows that the market price after the rights issue cannot remain at 120p (assuming all else equal). A company that was previously valued at £120 million which then adds £25 million of value to itself (in the form of cash) should be worth £145 million. This company now has 125 million shares, therefore each share is worth £1.16 (i.e. £145 million divided by 125 million shares).

An alternative way of calculating the **ex-rights price** is as follows:

Ex-rights price		
Four existing shares at a price of 120p		480p
One new share for cash at 100p	+	100p
Value of five shares	=	580p
Value of one share ex-rights 580p/5		**116p**

Shareholders have experienced a decline in the price of their old shares from 120p to 116p. A fall of this magnitude necessarily follows from the introduction of new shares at a discounted price. However, the loss is exactly offset by the gain in share value on the new rights issue shares, which were issued at 100p but have a market price of 116p. This can be illustrated through the example of Sid, who owned 100 shares worth £120 prior to the rights announcement. Sid loses £4 on the old shares – their value is now £116. However, he makes a gain of £4 on the new shares:

Cost of rights shares (25 × £1)	£25
Ex-rights value (25 × £1.16)	£29
Gain	£4

When the press talks glibly of a rights offer being 'very attractively priced for shareholders', they are generally talking nonsense. Whatever the size of the discount, the same value will be removed from the old shares to leave the shareholder no worse or better off. Logically, value cannot be handed over to the shareholders from the size of the discount decision. Shareholders own all the company's shares before and after the rights issue – they can't hand value to themselves without also taking value from themselves. Of course, if the prospects for the company's profits rise because it can now make capital expenditures, leading to dominant market positions, then the value of shares will rise – for both the old and the new shares. But this is value creation that has nothing to do with the level of the discount.

What if a shareholder does not want to take up the rights?

As owners of the firm all shareholders must be treated in the same way. To make sure that shareholders do not lose out because they are unwilling or unable to buy more shares the law requires that shareholders have a third choice, other than to buy or not buy the new shares. This is to sell the rights on to someone else on the stock market (selling the rights nil paid). Indeed, so deeply enshrined are pre-emption rights that even if the shareholder does nothing the company will sell his rights to the new shares on his behalf and send the proceeds to him. Thus, the shareholder is compensated for the fact that their shareholding has been diluted by the increased number of shares in issue.

Take the case of the impoverished Sid, who is unable to find the necessary £25. He could sell the rights to subscribe for the shares to another investor and not have to go through the process of taking up any of the shares himself. Thus, Sid would benefit to the extent of 16p per share or a total of £4 (if the market price stays constant), which adequately compensates for the loss on the 100 shares he holds. But the extent of his control over the company has been reduced – his percentage share of the votes has decreased.

The value of a right on one old share in Swell is this theoretical market value of a share ex-rights less the subscription price divided by the number of old shares required to purchase one new share:

$$\frac{116p - 100p}{4} = 4p$$

In the case of the Lloyds issue (*see* **Exhibit 9.20**) those shareholders who did not take up the new shares received 18.5p for each share declined.

Exhibit 9.20

Strong response to Lloyds cash call

By Sharlene Goff

Lloyds Banking Group has announced strong demand for its £13.5bn rights issue, with 95 per cent of investors taking up their new shares.

The bank said it had received acceptances for 34.7m shares, leaving a "rump" of 1.7m. The shares were placed in the market yesterday at a price of 55.5p a share, a premium of 18.5p to the 37p issue price.

The take-up was at the high end of analysts' expectations, particularly given that Lloyds has about 2.8m small shareholders, one of the largest bases of private investors in the UK.

Investors were offered 1.34 new shares for each existing one they owned at 37p per share. Lloyds,

43 per cent-owned by the government, has raised a total of £23.5bn, £1bn more than thought, as it launched a larger-than-expected debt swap of £10bn in addition to the rights issue.

Eric Daniels, chief executive, yesterday thanked shareholders for "their considerable support" for the capital raising. "Our focus remains on delivering on our plans to become the UK's leading financial services company, which we believe will result in significant benefits for all our shareholders," he said.

Lloyds' share price fell 1p – or 1.9 per cent – yesterday to close at 55.2p. The shares have fallen about 5 per cent since the rights issue was announced last month.

Shareholders who did not take up their rights will receive a cheque for 18.5p a share, the difference between the issue price and the placement price of the unwanted shares.

Lloyds said investors who did accept the new shares would receive formal share certificates by December 29.

A number of institutional investors divided the "rump" of remaining shares. Bank of America Merrill Lynch and UBS were lead underwriters on the rights issue.

Source: Financial Times, 15 December 2009, p. 20. Reprinted with permission.

Ex-rights and cum-rights

Old shares bought in the stock market which are designated **cum-rights** carry with them to the new owner the right to subscribe for the new shares in the rights issue. After a cut-off date the shares go **ex-rights**, which means that any purchaser of old shares will not have the right to the new shares; that right remains with the former shareholder.

Discounts

It does not matter greatly whether Swell raises £25 million on a one-for-four basis at 100p or on a one-for-three basis at 75p per share, or on some other basis (*see* **Exhibit 9.21**).

Exhibit 9.21	Comparison of different rights bases

Rights basis	Number of new shares (m)	Price of new shares (p)	Total raised (£m)
1 for 4	25	100	25
1 for 3	33.3	75	25
1 for 2	50	50	25
1 for 1	100	25	25

Whatever the basis of the rights issue, the company will receive £25 million and shareholders will see the price of their old shares decrease, but this will be exactly offset by the value of the rights on the new shares. However, the ex-rights price changes according to the basis of the rights issue – *see* **Exhibit 9.22**.

Exhibit 9.22	Ex-rights prices for different rights issue bases

Original shares		New shares				Total			Ex-rights price	
4 shares @ 120p	480p	1 share @ 100p	+	100p	Value of 5 shares	=	580p	Value of 1 share (580/5)		116p
3 shares @ 120p	360p	1 share @ 75p	+	75p	Value of 4 shares	=	435p	Value of 1 share (435/4)		108.75p
2 shares @ 120p	240p	1 share @ 50p	+	50p	Value of 3 shares	=	290p	Value of 1 share 290/3)		96.67p
1 share @ 120p	120p	1 share @ 25p	+	25p	Value of 2 shares	=	145p	Value of 1 share (145/2)		72.5p

If Swell chose the one-for-one basis this would be regarded as a deep-discounted rights issue. With an issue of this sort there is only a minute probability that the market price will fall below the rights offer price and therefore there is almost complete certainty that the offer will be taken up. It seems reasonable to suggest that the underwriting service provided by the institutions is largely redundant here and that the firm can make a significant saving. Yet a large majority of all rights issues are underwritten, usually involving between 100 and 400 sub-underwriters, with fees for all the professionals involved.

Placings, open offers and clawback

Some companies argue that the lengthy procedures and expense associated with rights issues (e.g. the time and trouble it takes to get a prospectus prepared and approved by the UKLA) frustrate directors' efforts to take advantage of opportunities in a timely fashion. Firms in the US have much more freedom to bypass pre-emption rights. They are able to sell blocks of shares to securities houses for distribution elsewhere in the market. This is fast and has low transaction costs. If this were permitted in the UK there would be a concern for existing shareholders: they could experience a dilution of their voting power and/or the shares could be sold at such a low price that a portion of the firm is handed over to new shareholders too cheaply. The UK authorities have produced a compromise, under which firms must obtain shareholders' approval through a special resolution (a majority of 75 per cent of those voting) at the company's annual general meeting, or at an extraordinary general meeting to waive the pre-emption right. Even then the shares must not be sold to outside investors at more than a 5 per cent or 10 per cent discount to the share price. While the maximum discount for MM companies under the listing rules is 10 per cent, the Association of British Insurers' guidelines are for a maximum of 5 per cent. This is an important condition. It does not make any difference to existing shareholders if new shares are offered at a deep discount to the market price as long as they are offered to them. If external investors get a discount there is a transfer of value from the current shareholders to the new.

In placings, new shares of companies already listed are sold directly to a narrow group of external investors. The institutions, as existing shareholders, have produced guidelines to prevent abuse, which normally allow a placing of only a small proportion of the company's capital (a maximum of 5 per cent in a single year, and no more than 7.5 per cent is to be added to the company's equity capital over a rolling three-year period) in the absence of a clawback.[5] Under clawback, existing shareholders have the right to reclaim the shares as though they were entitled to them under a rights issue. They can buy them at the price they were offered to the external investors. With a clawback the issue becomes an 'open offer'. Under an open offer companies can increase their share capital by between 15 per cent and 18 per cent. Beyond that the investors (e.g. Association of British Insurers) prefer a rights issue. The major difference compared with a rights issue is that if they do not exercise this clawback right they receive no compensation for any reduction in the price of their existing shares – there are no nil-paid rights to sell.

Vendor placing

If a company wishes to pay for an asset such as a subsidiary of another firm or an entire company with newly issued shares, but the vendor does not want to hold the shares, the purchaser could arrange for the new shares to be bought by institutional investors for cash. In this way the buyer gets the asset, the vendor (e.g. shareholders in the target company in a merger or takeover) receive cash and the institutional investor makes an investment. There is usually a clawback arrangement for a vendor placing (if the issue is more than 10 per cent of market capitalisation of the acquirer). Again, the price discount can be no more than 5 per cent or 10 per cent of the current share price.

Bought deal

Instead of selling shares to investors, companies are sometimes able to make an arrangement with a securities house whereby it buys all the shares being offered for cash. The securities house then sells the shares on to investors included in its distribution network, hoping to make a profit on the deal. Securities houses often compete to buy a package of shares from the company, with the highest bidder winning. The securities houses take the risk of being unable to sell the shares for at least the amount that they paid. Bought deals are limited by the 5 per cent or 10 per cent pre-emption rules.

---

[5] Companies can ask to go beyond these limits if they give appropriate justification, but this is rare. Placings are usually structured so that a prospectus is not required, so this saves money. They can also be completed in a matter of days rather than weeks or months for rights issues.

Scrip issues, scrip dividends, splits and consolidation

Scrip issues do not raise new money: a company simply gives all shareholders more shares in proportion to their existing holdings. The value of each shareholding does not change because the share price drops in proportion to the additional shares. They are also known as capitalisation issues or bonus issues. The purpose is to make shares more attractive by bringing down the price. British investors are thought to consider a share price of £10 and above as less attractive than one in single figures. So a company with shares trading at £15 on the market might distribute two 'free' shares for every one held – a two-for-one scrip issue. Since the amount of money in the firm and its economic potential are constant, the share price will theoretically fall to £5. Scrip issues are often regarded as indicating confidence in future earnings increases. If this new optimism is expressed in the share price it may not fall as much as theory would suggest. However, many people are sceptical about the benefits of scrips, especially in light of the transaction costs.

A number of companies have an annual scrip issue while maintaining a constant dividend per share, effectively raising the level of profit distribution. For example, if a company pays a regular dividend of 20p per share but also has a one-for-ten scrip, the annual income will go up by 10 per cent. (A holder of 10 shares who previously received 200p now receives 220p on a holding of 11 shares.)

Scrip dividends are slightly different: shareholders are offered a choice between receiving a cash dividend and receiving additional shares. This is more like a rights issue because the shareholders are making a cash sacrifice if they accept the scrip shares. Shareholders are able to add to their holding without paying a stockbroker's commission. Companies are able to raise additional equity capital without the expense of a rights issue.

A 'share split' (stock split) means that the nominal value of each share is reduced in proportion to the increase in the number of shares, so the total book value of shares remains the same. So, for example, a company may have 1 million shares in issue with a nominal value of 50p each. It issues a further 1 million shares to existing shareholders with the nominal value of each share reducing to 25p, but total nominal value remains at £500,000. Of course, the share price will halve – assuming all else is constant.

If the share price goes too low, say 15p, companies may decide to pursue consolidation of shares. This is the opposite of a split: the number of shares is reduced and the nominal value of each remaining share rises. If the nominal (par) value is 5p the company could consolidate on the basis of five shares for one. A 25p nominal share would replace five 5p nominal shares and the new share would then trade in the market at $5 \times 15p = 75p$ (or slightly more if investors are more attracted to shares within a 'normal' price range).

Share buy-backs and special dividends

Occasionally directors conclude that the company has too much equity capital and that it would be appropriate to hand back some of the cash to shareholders. It could be that the company is able to generate higher returns on each remaining share by borrowing more to reduce the number of shares by self-purchase. It could be that the directors think the shares are undervalued, and by reducing the quantity on the market the price will rise. It could be that the directors are aware of the tendency of companies to squander surplus cash on value-destroying mergers, and they want to avoid the temptation.

Buy-backs may also be a useful alternative when the company is unsure about the sustainability of a possible increase in the normal cash dividend. A stable policy may be pursued on dividends, and then shares are repurchased as and when surplus cash is available. This two-track approach avoids sending an over-optimistic signal about future growth through changing underlying dividend levels.

It is necessary for companies to ask shareholders' permission to buy back shares. Many companies now regularly vote at AGMs to allow buy-backs of up to 10 per cent of share capital in the following 12 months. The directors then have the freedom to choose when, and if, they will buy in shares.

A second possible approach to returning surplus funds is to pay a special dividend. This is the same as the normal dividend, but bigger and paid on a one-off basis.

Warrants

Warrants give the holder the right to subscribe for a specified number of shares at a fixed price during or at the end of a specified time period. If a company has shares currently trading at £3 it might choose to sell warrants, each of which grants the holder the right to buy a share in the company at, say, £4 over the next five years. If by the fifth year the share price has risen to £6 the warrant holders could exercise their rights and then sell the shares immediately, gaining £2 per share, which is likely to be a considerable return on the original warrant price of a few pence. Warrants are frequently attached to bonds, and make the bond more attractive because the investor benefits from a relatively safe (but low) income on the bond if the firm performs in a mediocre fashion, but if the firm does very well and the share price rises significantly the investor will participate in some of the extra returns through the 'sweetener' or 'equity kicker' provided by the warrant.

There is no requirement for investors to hold warrants until exercised or they expire. There is an active secondary market on the London Stock Exchange.

Concluding comments

Raising money for a company by selling shares is a complicated business. There are so many factors to be properly coordinated. There are numerous legal issues, regulations to be observed, the marketing of the shares to potential investors and the underwriting process to organise, to name but a few. It may seem that the financial institutions guiding firms earn outlandish fees, but it must be admitted that they do provide considerable social benefit.

Key points and concepts

- London Stock Exchange's **Main Market** is the most heavily regulated UK exchange.

- The **Alternative Investment Market (AIM)** is the lightly regulated exchange designed for small, young companies.

- **PLUS** provides a share trading facility for companies, less costly than the LSE.

- **Go public** means to issue and trade shares on a stock market for the first time.

- Joining the Main Market of the LSE involves two stages. The securities (usually shares) have to be: (a) admitted to the Official List by the UKLA; and also (b) admitted by the Exchange for trading.

- **UKLA** (UK Listing Authority) is part of the Financial Services Authority/Financial Conduct Authority and maintains the **Official List** of companies eligible to be traded on the most highly regulated exchanges.

- **Cost of floating on the Main Market** is high, between £1m and £2m for a company issuing £20m shares.

- **All companies** wishing to list on MM must ensure that at least 25 per cent of share capital is in public hands, and must have at least three years of accounting figures (except for TechMARK companies, and companies undertaking exceptional activities).

- **Financial expenses involved in flotation:**

  - **Sponsor:** must be approved by UKLA; may be individual or a bank; guides a company through the process.

▶

- **Corporate broker:** may be same as sponsor; advises on price, demand and marketing.
- **Underwriter:** guarantees to buy shares if they are not sold.
- **Legal advisers:** fulfill legal requirements.
- **Accounting advisers:** prepare detailed report on a company's finances and advise on tax implications.
- **Registrars** maintain records of these companies and are linked to **CREST**.
- **Listing fees:** set by the MM or AIM; vary according to the size of a company.
- **Printing, advertising, public relations:** to encourage investment.
- **Prospectus:** detailed document designed to attract investment.

- **Different types of flotation are:**

  - **offer for sale**: shares offered to general market, at a fixed price or by tender.
  - **introduction:** no new money is raised.
  - **placing**: shares are placed with institutional investors.
  - **intermediaries offer:** shares are offered for sale to financial institutions such as stockbrokers. Clients of these intermediaries can then apply to buy shares from them.
  - **reverse takeover:** a larger unquoted company makes a deal with a smaller quoted company whereby the smaller company 'takes over' the larger firm by swapping newly created shares in itself for the shares in the unquoted firm currently held by its owners.
  - **book-building:** financial advisers to an issue contact major institutional investors to get from them bids for the shares over a period.

- **Stages in a flotation are:**

  - pre-launch publicity;
  - deciding technicalities, e.g. method, price, underwriting;
  - pathfinder prospectus; advisers and company executives usually undertake a roadshow to sell the shares;
  - launch of public offer – prospectus and price on impact day;
  - close of offer;
  - allotment of shares;
  - announcement of price and first trading.

- **Post-listing obligations are:**

  - **disclosure** of price-sensitive information;
  - **regular financial reports**;
  - **limits on director share dealing**;
  - **UK Corporate Governance Code to be observed**.

- **To float on AIM** the companies do not have to allow a free float of 25 per cent of the shares, nor have a three-year trading history. There are lower joining costs and ongoing costs than for Main Market.

- **Nomad** (nominated adviser) must be appointed by companies wishing to become quoted on AIM. **Nomad** must be on approved register; acts as quality controller of company.

- **Nominated broker** advises on share market and brings together buyers and sellers of shares.

- **To float on AIM** companies must meet LSE rules and provide admission document.

- **Admission and annual fees:** charged by all exchanges; charges are less on AIM than on MM.

- **The higher level of regulation and related enhanced image, prestige and security of Official List** companies means that equity capital can usually be raised at a lower required rate of return.

- **Analyst's ratios:**

  - **PER** (price-earnings ratio) is share price divided by earnings per share:

  $$\frac{\text{Share price}}{\text{Earnings per share}}$$

- **Dividend yield:**

$$\frac{\text{Dividend per share}}{\text{Share price}} \times 100$$

- **Dividend cover:**

$$\frac{\text{Earnings per share}}{\text{Dividend per share}}$$

- **Market capitalisation:** is the number of shares in issue multiplied by the share price.

- **Ex-dividend date** is the date after which new buyers will not receive recent dividend.

- **Indices** give the relative performance information of a chosen group of shares.

- **DJIA** (Dow Jones Industrial Average) is the oldest share index and is weighted by share price.

- **S&P 500** represents the US market better than the DJIA because it contains 500 US shares and is market capitalisation weighted.

- **Most indices** are weighted by market capitalisation.

- **FTSE All-Share** is the oldest UK index, and tracks the vast majority (by value) of the London market. **FTSE 100** (the Footsie) is the most famous UK index, tracking performance of the UK's biggest 100 listed companies.

- A **rights issue** invites existing shareholders to invest in additional shares. It raises cash for a company without resorting to further debt.

- A **rights issue offer** must be open for at least two weeks.

- **Pre-emption rights:** further share issues must be offered to existing shareholders first; shareholders can sell this right if they do not take it up.

- **Cum-rights:** the new owner of shares has the right to subscribe to the rights issue.

- **Ex-rights:** after the cut-off date, the purchaser of old shares will not receive the right to purchase new rights issue shares.

- **The theoretical ex-rights price** is a weighted average of the price of the existing shares and the new shares.

- The **nil paid rights** can be sold instead of buying new shares.

- **Value of a right on a new share:**

Theoretical market value of share ex-rights – Subscription price.

- **Value of a right on an old share:**

$$\frac{\text{Theoretical market value of share ex-rights} - \text{Subscription price}}{\text{Number of old shares required to purchase one new share}}$$

- **The pre-emption right** can be bypassed in the UK under strict conditions.

- **Placings:** new shares from companies already listed are placed with institutional investors; they are limited to being no more than 5 per cent of share capital in a year, and 7.5 per cent over three years.

- **Clawback:** existing shareholders can buy new issues of shares at the offered price in an **open offer**, but do not receive compensation if they do not take up the offer.

- **Vendor placing:** when shareholders in a company are offered shares in the acquirer as part of a deal but do not wish to hold the shares. The acquirer's shares are bought by an institutional investor and the vendors receive the cash.

- **Bought deal** is when all of a new issue is sold to an institutional investor, who can then (hopefully) sell the shares on at a profit.

▶

- **Scrip issue** is a further issue of shares given to existing shareholders in proportion to their current shareholdings; the idea is to reduce the price of each share. Scrip issues may be issued annually to shareholders and indicate confidence in future earnings.

- **Scrip dividends** are issued to shareholders instead of a cash dividend.

- **Splits** reduce the nominal value of each share in proportion to the increase in the number of shares; the book value of the company remains the same.

- **Share buy-back** is a way of returning money to shareholders and possibly increasing dividends per share as there will be fewer shares over which to spread the payout.

- **Special dividend** is a one-off dividend returning funds to shareholders.

- **Warrants** give the warrant holder the right to buy shares at a fixed price on or before a specified point in time in the future.

References and further reading

Arnold, G. (2010) *The Financial Times Guide to Investing*, 2nd edn. London: Financial Times Prentice Hall.
    More on financial ratios and measures.

Economist magazine.
    Regular reading will provide an excellent foundation for understanding equity markets.

Financial Times.
    An important source of information on events in the equity markets.

Kidwell, D. S., Blackwell, D. W., Whidbee, D. A. and Peterson, R. L. (2008) *Financial Institutions, Markets and Money*, 10th edn. New York: John Wiley & Sons Inc.
    A US perspective.

London Stock Exchange website publications contain easy-to-read guides to floating a company and other matters.

Saunders, A. and Cornett, M. M. (2007) *Financial Markets and Institutions*, 3rd edn. Boston: McGraw-Hill Irwin.
    Information about US financial system.

Vaitilingam, R. (2010) *The Financial Times Guide to Using the Financial Pages*, 6th edn. London: Financial Times Prentice Hall.
    Good introductory source of information. Clear and concise.

Websites

ADVFN. Financial data www.advfn.com
Aite Group. Independent research and advice www.aitegroup.com
The Economist www.economist.com
Euronext www.euronext.com
Federation of European Securities Exchanges www.fese.eu
Financial Services Authority www.fsa.gov.uk
Financial Times www.ft.com
UK Listing Authority www.fsa.gov.uk/Pages/Doing/UKLA
FTSE Group. Stock market indices and information www.ftse.com
Financial Reporting Council, UK Corporate Governance Code www.frc.org.uk/corporate/ukcgcode.cfm
Hemscott. Share prices and financial data www.hemscott.com
Interactive Investor www.iii.co.uk
Investegate. Company information www.investegate.co.uk
Investors Chronicle, weekly stock market analysis www.investorschronicle.com
Intelligent Financial Sustems www.liquidmetrix.com
London Stock Exchange www.londonstockexchange.com
New York Stock Exchange www.nyse.com

Office for National Statistics www.ons.gov.uk

PLUS exchange www.plusmarketsgroup.com

Wall Street Journal www.wsj.com

Yahoo Finance. Financial data www.yahoofinance.com

Video presentations

Chief executives and other senior people describe and discuss policy and aspects of raising equity capital in interviews, documentaries and webcasts at Cantos.com. (www.cantos.com) – these are free to view.

Case study recommendations

See www.pearsoned.co.uk/arnold for case study synopses.

Also see Harvard University: http://hbsp.harvard.edu/product/cases

- Rosneft's Initial Public Offering (A) (2007) Authors: Lena Chua Booth, Michael H. Moffett and Frank Tuzzolino. Thunderbird School of Global Management. Available at Harvard Case Study Website.
- Is a Share Buyback Right for Your Company? (2001) Author: Justin Pettit. Harvard Business Review, April. Available at Harvard Case Study Website.
- Case Technology Limited: A Chinese IPO in Singapore (2005) Authors: Nigel Goodwin and Larry Wynant. Nanyang Business School Singapore. Available at Harvard Case Study Website.
- Bertelsmann: The Ownership Question (2006) Authors: Frederic A. Neumann and Josep Tàpies. IESE Business School. Available at Harvard Case Study Website.
- Warburg Pincus and *emgs*: The IPO Decision (A) (2008) Authors: Felda Hardymon and Ann Leamon. Harvard Business School.
- Granite Apparel: Funding an Expansion (2010) Authors: Ken Mark, James E. Hatch and Larry Wynant. Richard Ivey School of Business. Available at Harvard Case Study Website.
- Note on IPO Share Allocation (2010) Authors: Claire Megat Raffaelli, Mark Leslie and Michael E. Marks. Stanford Graduate School of Business. Available at Harvard Case Study Website.
- TRX, Inc.: Initial Public Offering (2008) Authors: Susan Chaplinsky, Kensai Morita and Xing Zeng. Darden, University of Pennsylvania.

Self-review questions

1 What equity markets can companies list their shares on in the UK?

2 Why is listing on a stock market important for a company?

3 What are the differences in criteria for a company gaining an AIM quotation rather than a Main Market listing?

4 What is a nomad?

5 What is PLUS?

6 What are (a) PER (b) dividend yield (c) dividend cover (d) market capitalisation?

7 What is a stock index?

8 Describe two different methods for calculating indices.

9   What is the Footsie?

10   What does floating a company mean?

11   Explain why a company might decide to float on the stock market.

12   How do companies qualify for a flotation on the Main Market of the LSE?

13   Why are most flotations underwritten?

14   What is the UKLA and what does it do?

15   What are registrars?

16   Describe the functions of (a) a sponsor (b) a corporate broker during an initial public offering.

17   What responsibilities does a company/directors have after it has listed?

18   What is a rights issue?

19   Explain a pre-emption right.

20   What do the terms cum-rights and ex-rights mean?

21   What is (a) a scrip (b) a warrant (c) a split?

22   What are (a) buy-backs (b) special dividends?

Questions and problems

1   Discuss the differences between floating on the Main Market and the Alternative Investment Market, noting the relative advantages and disadvantages.

2   Describe with examples what a stock index is and its importance.

3   Describe in detail the process for a new company to obtain a listing, detailing the different processes, expenses and advisers.

4   Describe, compare and contrast rights issues and other share issues for a company already listed on a stock market.

5   Bluelamp plc has grown from a company with £10,000 turnover to one with a £17 million turnover and £1.8 million profit in the past five years. The existing owners have put all their financial resources into the firm to enable it to grow. The directors wish to take advantage of a very exciting market opportunity but would need to find £20 million of new equity capital as the balance sheet is already over-geared (i.e. has high debt). The options being discussed, in a rather uninformed way, are flotation on the Main Market of the London Stock Exchange or a flotation on the Alternative Investment Market. Write a report to enlighten the board on the merits and disadvantages of each of these possibilities.

6   Checkers plc is considering a flotation on the Main Market of the London Stock Exchange. Outline a timetable of events likely to be encountered which will assist management planning.

7   Discuss the merits and problems of the pre-emption right for UK companies.

8 Explain why failure to carry through a plan to raise capital by floating on the London Stock Exchange Main Market might be highly disruptive to a firm.

9 There are a number of different methods of floating a company on the new issue market of the London Stock Exchange Main Market (e.g. offer for sale). Describe these and comment on the ability of small investors to buy newly issued shares.

10 Mahogany plc has an ordinary share price of £3 and is quoted on the Alternative Investment Market. It intends to raise £20 million through a one-for-three rights issue priced at £2.

(a) What will the ex-rights price be?
(b) How many old ordinary shares were in circulation prior to the rights issue?
(c) Patrick owns 9,000 shares and is unable to find the cash necessary to buy the rights shares. Reassure) Patrick that he will not lose value. How much might he receive from the company?
(d) What is the value of a right on one old share?
(e) What do the terms cum-rights and ex-rights mean?
(f) Advise Mahogany on the virtues of a deep-discounted rights issue.

11 Write an essay advocating the case for flotation on a recognised investment exchange.

12 The shareholders of Yellowhammer plc are to offer a one-for-four rights issue at £1.50 when its shares are trading at £1.90. What is the theoretical ex-rights price and the value of a right per old share?

13 Explain the function of a prospectus in a new share issue.

14 If par values are not something to do with golf, public to private is not something to do with sexual modesty and a pathfinder prospectus is not something to do with scouting, what are they? Explain the context in which these terms are used.

Assignments

1 Consider the equity base of your company, or one you are familiar with. Write a report outlining the options available should the firm need to raise further equity funds. Also consider if preference share capital should be employed.

2 Obtain newspaper articles discussing the run up to the flotation of a company and during the subsequent few months. Also obtain the flotation prospectus of the company. Write a case study that includes a discussion of the procedures leading to the float, the timetable, the advisers, the regulations and director restrictions.

Web-based exercises

1 From the London Stock Exchange website, choose a company which listed on the Main Market in 2008, and write a report on its progress to date. Examine the company announcements over the past few years and then comment on the extent and nature of its directors' 'continuing obligations'.

2 Go to the New York Stock Exchange website, www.nyse.com, and Euronext's, www.euronext.com, and read about the requirements and processes for companies wishing to join NYSE or Euronext in Europe. Write a report contrasting the requirements and processes with those for companies wishing to join the LSE.

Futures markets

LEARNING OUTCOMES

This chapter describes those types of derivatives where the counterparty accepts a commitment to buy (or sell) a quantity of the underlying at a point in the future. They do not permit the option to decide at a later date whether or not to go ahead with the transaction. (Options, giving a right but not an obligation, are dealt with in the next chapter.) At the end of this chapter the reader should be able to:

■ explain the nature of forwards and their advantages over futures;

■ describe a variety of futures markets, including equity futures, interest rate futures and single stock futures, and illustrate their use in hedging and speculating;

■ outline the nature and potential use of forward rate agreements;

■ compare exchange-traded markets with over-the-counter markets.

Derivatives – forwards, futures, options, swaps, etc. – are the subject of this and the next two chapters. Derivative instruments have become increasingly important financial instruments over the past 30 years. These powerful tools can be exploited either to reduce risk or to go in search of high returns. Naturally, exceptionally high returns come with exceptionally high risk. So traders and corporate managers using derivatives for this purpose need to understand the risks to which they are exposing their company. Many fortunes have been lost by managers/traders mesmerised by the potential for riches while failing to take the time to fully understand the instruments they were buying. They jumped in, unaware of, or ignoring, the potential for enormous loss. These three chapters describe the main types of derivative and show how they can be used for controlling risk (hedging) and for revving-up returns (speculating).

What is a derivative?

A **derivative instrument** is an asset whose performance is based on (derived from) the behaviour of the value of an underlying asset (usually referred to simply as the 'underlying'). The most common **underlyings** include commodities (for example, tea or pork bellies), shares, bonds, share indices, currencies and interest rates. Derivatives are contracts which give the right, and sometimes the obligation, to buy or sell a quantity of the underlying, or benefit in another way from a rise or fall in the value of the underlying. It is the legal *right* that becomes an asset, with its own value, and it is the right that is purchased or sold.

The derivatives markets have received an enormous amount of attention from the press in recent years. This is hardly surprising as spectacular losses have been made and a number of companies brought to the point of collapse through the employment of derivative instruments. Some examples of the unfortunate use of derivatives include:

● Procter & Gamble, which lost $102 million speculating on the movements of future interest rates in 1994.

● Barings, Britain's oldest merchant bank, which lost over £800 million on the Nikkei Index (the Japanese share index) contracts on the Singapore and Osaka derivatives exchanges, leading to the bank's demise in 1995.

● Long-Term Capital Management (LTCM), which attempted to exploit the 'mispricing' of financial instruments by making use of option pricing theory. In 1998 the firm collapsed and the Federal Reserve Bank of New York cajoled 14 banks and brokerage houses to put up $3.6 billion to save LTCM and thereby prevent a financial system breakdown.

● Financial institutions that were destroyed in 2008 because they bought derivatives whose values depended on US mortgage borrowers continuing to pay their mortgages. When a proportion could not pay their debts, the derivatives (of asset-backed bonds) became either very difficult or impossible to value. The uncertainty surrounding the value of these derivatives was a trigger for the financial crisis and the subsequent recession. There was financial distress for hundreds of financial institutions that had no connection with the US mortgage market or the related derivatives.

● Société Générale, which lost €4.9 billion in 2008 when a trader placed bets on the future movements of equity markets using derivatives (up to €50 billion was gambled at one time).

In many of the financial scandals derivatives have been used (or misused) to speculate rather than to reduce risk. This chapter examines both of these applications of derivatives but places particular emphasis on the hedging (risk-mitigating) facility they provide. These are powerful tools and managers can abuse that power either through ignorance or through deliberate acceptance of greater risk in the anticipation of greater reward. However, there is nothing inherently wrong with the tools themselves. If employed properly they can be remarkably effective at limiting risk.

A long history

Derivative instruments have been employed for more than 2,000 years. Olive growers in ancient Greece unwilling to accept the risk of a low price for their crop when harvested months later would enter into forward agreements whereby a price was agreed for delivery at a specific time. This reduced uncertainty for both the grower and the purchaser of the olives. In the Middle Ages forward contracts were traded in a kind of secondary market, particularly for wheat in Europe. A futures market was established in Osaka's rice market in Japan in the seventeenth century. Tulip bulb options were traded in seventeenth-century Amsterdam.

Commodity futures trading really began to take off in the nineteenth century with the Chicago Board of Trade regulating the trading of grains and other futures and options, and the London Metal Exchange dominating metal trading.

So derivatives are not new. What is different today is the size and importance of the derivatives markets. The last quarter of the twentieth century witnessed an explosive growth in volumes of trade, variety of derivatives products, and the number and range of users and uses. In the 30 years to 2010 the face value of outstanding derivatives contracts rose dramatically to stand at about US$600 trillion (US$600,000,000,000,000). Compare that with a UK annual GDP of around £1.4 trillion.

Forwards

Imagine you are responsible for purchasing potatoes to make crisps (chips) for your firm, a snack food producer. In the free market for potatoes the price rises or falls depending on the balance between buyers and sellers. These movements can be dramatic. Obviously, you would like to acquire potatoes at a price which was as low as possible, while the potato producer wishes to sell for a price that is as high as possible. However, both parties may have a similar interest in reducing the uncertainty of price. This will assist both to plan production and budget effectively. One way in which this could be done is to reach an agreement with the producer(s) to purchase a quantity of potatoes at a price agreed today to be delivered and paid for at a specified time in the future. Crisp producers buy up to 80 per cent of their potatoes up to two years forward. Once the forward agreements have been signed and sealed the crisp manufacturer may later be somewhat regretful if the spot price (price for immediate delivery) subsequently falls below the price agreed months earlier. Unlike option contracts, forwards commit both parties to complete the deal. However, the manufacturer is obviously content to live with this potential for regret in order to remove the risk associated with such an important raw material.

> A **forward contract** is an agreement between two parties to undertake an exchange at an agreed future date at a price agreed now.

The party buying at the future date is said to be taking a *long position*. The counterparty which will deliver at the future date is said to be taking a *short position*.

There are forward markets in a wide range of commodities but the most important forward markets today are for foreign exchange, in which hundreds of billions of dollars worth of currency are traded every working day – this will be considered in Chapter 12.

Forward contracts are tailor-made to meet the requirements of the parties. This gives flexibility on the amounts and delivery dates. Forwards are not traded on an exchange but are over-the-counter instruments – private agreements outside the regulation of an exchange. This makes them different from futures, which are standardised contracts traded on exchanges. A forward agreement exposes the counterparties to the risk of default – the failure by the other to deliver on the agreement. The risk grows in proportion to the extent by which the spot price diverges from the forward price and the incentive to renege increases. A forward has the advantage over futures of being more available for long-term maturities, say arranging a purchase or sale three years from now, whereas most futures on regulated exchanges are limited to delivery dates within the next 12 months.

Forward contracts are difficult to cancel, as agreement from each counterparty is needed. Also, to close the contract early may result in a penalty being charged. Despite these drawbacks forward markets continue to flourish, an example of which can be seen in **Exhibit 10.1**.

Exhibit 10.1

Northern Foods passes price rises to customers

by Lucy Warwick-Ching and Ed Crooks

Customers will be hit by higher food prices as Northern Foods, maker of Fox's biscuits and Goodfellas's pizza, prepares to pass on £40m of rising commodity costs to customers, including the big supermarkets.

Stefan Barden, chief executive, said that in the last three months short supplies and high demand had pushed up the prices of cereals, dairy products, cocoa and fats. Poor harvests have also hit vegetable prices.

These cost increases are expected to add £32m–£40m to Northern Foods' £400m raw material bill, an increase of 8–10 per cent. However, Mr Barden said that, thanks to long-term contracts, forward buying and hedging, the increase this year would only be between 4–5 per cent, resulting in an extra £16m–£20m.

Source: Financial Times, 10 October 2007, p. 25. Reprinted with permission.

Futures

Futures contracts are in many ways similar to forward contracts. They are agreements between two parties to undertake a transaction at an agreed price on a specified future date. However, they differ from forwards in some important respects. Futures contracts are exchange-based instruments traded on a regulated exchange. The buyer and the seller of a contract do not transact with each other directly. The **clearing house** becomes the formal **counterparty** to every transaction. This reduces the risk of non-compliance with the contract significantly for the buyer or seller of a future, as it is highly unlikely that the clearing house will be unable to fulfil its obligation.

In contrast to buying options, which give you the choice to walk away from the deal, with futures you are committed and are unable to back away. This is a very important difference. In purchasing an option the maximum you can lose is the premium paid whereas you can lose multiples of the amount you employ in taking a futures position.

A simple example will demonstrate this. Imagine a farmer wishes to lock in a price for his wheat, which will be harvested in six months. You agree to purchase the wheat from the farmer six months hence at a price of £60 per tonne. You are hoping that by the time the wheat is delivered the price has risen and you can sell at a profit. The farmer is worried that all he has from you is the promise to pay £60 per tonne in six months, and if the market price falls you will walk away from the deal. To reassure him you are asked to put money into what the farmer calls a *margin account*. He asks and you agree to deposit £6 for each tonne you have agreed to buy. If you fail to complete the bargain the farmer will be able to draw on the money from the margin account and then sell the wheat as it is harvested at the going rate for immediate ('spot') delivery. So, as far as the farmer is concerned, the price of wheat for delivery at harvest time could fall to £54 and he is still going to get £60 for each tonne: £6 from what you paid into the margin account and £54 from selling at the spot price.

But what if the price falls below £54? The farmer is exposed to risk – something he had tried to avoid by entering a futures deal. It is for this reason that the farmer asks you to top up your margin account on a daily basis so that there is always a buffer. He sets a *maintenance margin* level of £6 per tonne. This means you have to maintain at least £6 per tonne in the margin account. So, if the day after you buy the future, the harvest time price in the futures market falls to £57 you have only £3 per tonne left in the margin account as a buffer for the farmer. You agreed to buy at £60 but the going rate is only £57. To bring the margin account up to a £6 buffer you will be required to put in another £3 per tonne. If the price the next day falls to £50 you will be required to put up another £7 per tonne. You agreed to buy at £60, with the market price at £50 you have put a total of £6 + £3 + £7 = £16 into the margin account. By putting in top-ups as the price moves against you, you will always ensure there is at least £6 per tonne, providing security for the farmer. Even if you go bankrupt or simply renege on the deal he will receive at least £60 per tonne, either from the spot market or from a combination of a lower market price plus money from the margin account. As the price fell to £50 you have a £10 per tonne incentive to walk away from the deal except for the fact that you have put £16 into an account that the farmer can draw on should you be so stupid or unfortunate. If the price is £50 per tonne at expiry of the contract and you have put £16 in the margin account you are entitled to the spare £6 per tonne of margin.

It is in the margin account that we have the source of multiple losses in the futures markets. Say your life savings amount to £10 and you are convinced there will be a drought and shortage of wheat following the next harvest. In your view the price will rise to £95 per tonne. So, to cash in on your forecast you agree to buy a future for one tonne of wheat. You have agreed with the farmer that in six months you will pay £60 for the wheat, which you expect to then sell for £95. (The farmer is obviously less convinced than you that prices are destined to rise.)

To gain this right (and obligation) to buy at £60 you need only have £6 for the **initial margin**. The other £4 might be useful to meet day-to-day **margin calls** should the wheat price fall from £60 (temporarily, in your view). If the price does rise to £95 you will make a £35 profit, having laid out only £6 (plus some other cash temporarily). This is a very high return of 583 per cent over six months. But what if the price at harvest time is £40? You have agreed to pay £60, therefore the loss of £20 wipes out your savings and you are made bankrupt. You lose over three times your initial margin. That is the downside to the gearing effect of futures.

The above example demonstrates the essential features of futures market trading, but in reality participants in the market do not transact directly with each other, but go through a regulated exchange. Your opposite number, called a counterparty, is not a farmer but an organisation that acts as counterparty to all futures traders, buyers or sellers, called the central counterparty at the clearing house.

In the example we have assumed that the maintenance margin level is set at the same level as the initial margin. In reality it is often set at 70–80 per cent of the initial margin level.

An exchange provides standardised legal agreements traded in highly liquid markets. The contracts cannot be tailor-made, e.g. for 77 tonnes of wheat or coffee delivered in 37 days from now. The fact that the agreements are standardised allows a wide market appeal because buyers and sellers know what is being traded: the contracts are for a specific quality of the underlying, in specific amounts with specific delivery dates. For example, for sugar traded on NYSE Liffe one contract is for a specified grade of sugar and each contract is for a standard 50 tonnes with fixed delivery days in late August, October, December, March and May (Chapter 13 explores the commodities markets).

It is important to remember that it is the contracts themselves that are a form of security bought and sold in the market. Thus, a December future priced at $282.5 per tonne is a derivative of sugar and is not the same thing as sugar. To buy this future is to enter into an agreement with rights and obligations. It is these that are being bought and sold and not the commodity. When exercise of the contract takes place then the physical amount of sugar is bought or sold.[1] However, as with most derivatives, usually futures positions are cancelled by an offsetting transaction before exercise.

Marking to market and margins

With the clearing house being the formal counterparty for every buyer or seller of a futures contract, an enormous potential for credit risk is imposed on the organisation given the volume of futures traded and the size of the underlying they represent. (NYSE Liffe, for example, has an average daily volume of around 5 million contracts worth hundreds of billions of pounds/dollars.) If only a small fraction of market participants fail to deliver, this could run into hundreds of millions of pounds/dollars. To protect itself the clearing house operates a margining system by which the futures buyer or seller has to provide, usually in cash, an initial margin. The amount required depends on the futures market, the level of volatility of the underlying and the potential for default; however, it is likely to be in the region of 0.1–15 per cent of the value of the underlying. The initial margin is not a 'down payment' for the underlying: the funds do not flow to a buyer or seller of the underlying but stay with the clearing house. It is merely a way of guaranteeing that the buyer or seller will pay up should the price of the underlying move against them. It is refunded when the futures position is closed (if the market has not moved adversely).

---

[1] Note that some futures contracts have cash delivery rather than physical delivery – *see* later.

The clearing house also operates a system of daily **marking to market**. At the end of every trading day the counterparty's profits or losses created as a result of that day's price change are calculated. Any counterparty that made a loss has his/her member's margin account debited. The following morning the losing counterparty must inject more cash to cover the loss if the amount in the account has fallen below a threshold level (the maintenance margin). An inability to pay a daily loss causes default and the contract is closed, thus protecting the clearing house from the possibility that the counterparty might accumulate further daily losses without providing cash to cover them. The margin account of the counterparty that makes a daily gain is credited. This may be withdrawn the next day. The daily credits and debits to members' margin accounts are known as the **variation margin.**

Worked example 10.1   Margins

Imagine a buyer and seller of a future on Monday with an underlying value of £50,000 are each required to provide an initial margin of 10 per cent, or £5,000. The buyer will make profits if the price rises while the seller will make profits if the price falls. In **Exhibit 10.2** it is assumed that counterparties have to keep all of the initial margin permanently as a buffer.[2] (In reality this may be relaxed by an exchange.)

At the end of Tuesday the buyer of the contract has £1,000 debited from their member's account. This will have to be paid over the following day or the exchange will automatically close the member's position and crystallise the loss. If the buyer does provide the variation margin and the position is kept open until Friday, the account will have an accumulated credit of £5,000. The buyer has the right to buy at £50,000 but can sell at £55,000. If the buyer and the seller closed their positions on Friday the buyer would be entitled to receive the initial margin plus the accumulated profit, £5,000 + £5,000 = £10,000, whereas the seller would receive nothing (£5,000 initial margin minus losses of £5,000).

Exhibit 10.2   Example of initial margin, variation margin and marking to market

£	Monday	Tuesday	Wednesday	Thursday	Friday
			Day		
Value of future (based on daily closing price)	50,000	49,000	44,000	50,000	55,000
Buyers' position					
Initial margin	5,000				
Variation margin (+ credited) (− debited)	0	−1,000	−5,000	+ 6,000	+ 5,000
Accumulated profit (loss)	0	−1,000	−6,000	0	+ 5,000
Sellers' position					
Initial margin	5,000				
Variation margin (+ credited) (− debited)	0	+ 1,000	+ 5,000	−6,000	−5,000
Accumulated profit (loss)	0	+ 1,000	+ 6,000	0	−5,000

This example illustrates the effect of leverage in futures contracts. The initial margin payments are small relative to the value of the underlying. When the underlying changes by a small percentage the effect is magnified for the future, and large percentage gains and losses are made on the amount committed to the transaction:

---

[2] Initial margin is the same as maintenance margin in this case.

$$\text{Underlying change (Monday–Friday)} \frac{55{,}000 - 50{,}000}{50{,}000} \times 100 = 10\%$$

$$\text{Percentage return to buyer of future} \frac{5{,}000}{5{,}000} \times 100 = 100\%$$

$$\text{Percentage return to seller of future} \frac{-5{,}000}{5{,}000} \times 100 = -100\%$$

To lose all the money committed to a financial transaction may seem disappointing but it is as nothing compared with the losses that can be made on futures. It is possible to lose a multiple of the amount set down as an initial margin. For example, if the future rose to £70,000 the seller would have to provide a £20,000 variation margin – four times the amount committed in the first place. Clearly, playing the futures market can seriously damage your wealth. This was proved with a vengeance by Nick Leeson of Barings Bank. He bought futures in the Nikkei 225 Index – the main Japanese share index – in both the Osaka and the Singapore derivative exchanges. He was betting that the market would rise as he committed the bank to buying the index at a particular price. When the index fell, margin payments had to be made. Leeson took a double-or-quits attitude: 'I mean a lot of futures traders when the market is against them will double up'.[3] He continued to buy futures. To generate some cash, to make variation margin payments, he wrote combinations of call and put options ('straddles') for which counterparties paid premiums – *see* Chapter 11. This compounded the problem when the Nikkei 225 Index continued to fall in 1994. The put options became an increasingly expensive commitment to bear – counterparties had the right to sell the index to Barings at a price much higher than the prevailing price. More than £800m was lost (*see* **Exhibit 10.3**).

Exhibit 10.3

Leeson hid trading from the outset

Mr Nick Leeson opened 88888, the account in which he hid his unauthorised trading, just two days after Barings began trading on Simex at the start of July 1992.

The Singapore inspectors, who have had access to Simex data not made available to the Bank of England, show that Mr Leeson's secret futures and options positions grew slowly at first.

After losing S$10.7m (£4.8m) between July and October 1992, Mr Leeson brought the balance on the hidden 88888 account back close to zero in July 1993. This tallies with his own account, given in a television interview, of the relief he felt when he made back his losses in mid-1993.

But it appears that the main method by which Mr Leeson recovered his losses, initially made on futures positions, was by selling options in a way which stored up trouble. When the market moved against him and his futures lost money, he tended to write 'straddles', a combination of options.

These produced an immediate premium which reduced the deficit in the 88888 account. But the options, on the Nikkei index of Japanese stocks, exposed Mr Leeson to a movement in the market in either direction.

They produced an initial profit, with a counterbalancing risk of loss on expiry of the options contracts. It was a highly risky form of borrowing.

From the timing of Mr Leeson's trading, it appears that the sale of these 'straddles' was an attempt to plug the hole left by punts on the market which had gone awry.

For example, in November 1993, Mr Leeson's futures losses had mounted to S$4.2bn from S$788m the previous month. This coincided with Mr Leeson's most intense bout of options trading, which lifted the value of the options portfolio to a surplus of S$478m the following month.

But their value collapsed after the Kobe earthquake, which triggered a sharp increase in the volatility of the Japanese stock market. In any case, Mr Leeson's profits on options in 1994 were not sufficient to offset his other losses.

Source: Nicholas Denton, *Financial Times*, 18 October 1995, p. 8. Reprinted with permission.

---

[3] Nick Leeson in an interview with David Frost reported in the *Financial Times*, 11 September 1995.

When markets are volatile the exchanges increase the size of the margins they require. In 2010 this, together with rising commodity prices, had a significant impact on farmers. As they tried to hedge the positions of their future crop sales in a market where prices moved up and down rapidly (but mostly up) the exchanges demanded more and more cash as margin. Farmers lose from price decreases in the cash market and so each year need to take a short position in the futures market, i.e. sell first and buy later to close their position. Thus, if prices fall they make a profit on the futures, offsetting the loss on the actual crop when sold in the cash market. The main problem in 2010 was that the price of the futures of many commodities soared (*see* chart in **Exhibit 10.4**). The exchanges both insisted on more variation margin simply because the futures position deteriorated for those with short futures positions and because the exchange increased the percentages for initial and maintenance margin because of the greater volatility.

Exhibit 10.4

Farmers left short-changed by a margin call squeeze

FT

Gregory Meyer and Jack Farchy

Times could not be better for US cotton farmers. Demand from mills is strong, this year's crop is a bumper one and prices have been stratospheric.

But farmers belonging to Calcot, a cotton marketing co-operative in California, have not been reaping all the gains, at least not yet. The co-op this autumn told members final payments for their cotton would be delayed until next year because it is locked up as collateral for crop hedging deals.

Companies that own or produce physical commodities often sell futures contracts to protect their financial positions. When prices rise, however, the derivatives positions fall increasingly into the red, leading brokers to demand more collateral to ensure the companies' losses are not borne by the exchange.

With commodities markets experiencing share swings – prices have been soaring and plunging in the space of days or even hours in recent weeks – exchanges are demanding larger amounts of collateral from participants holding futures positions. Quite simply, the lengthy bull run in commodities means it is becoming ever more expensive to trade them.

Indeed, the so-called "margin calls" are eating into the cash flows of everyone trading futures contracts, from farming co-ops like Calcot to the world's biggest trading houses, banks and hedge funds.

"The current futures market situation has put tremendous pressure on our financial resources to meet margin calls," The Calcot president has told members.

Glencore, the world's largest commodity trader, and Bunge, one of the top agricultural traders, have reported working capital outflows in their third quarter results, in part

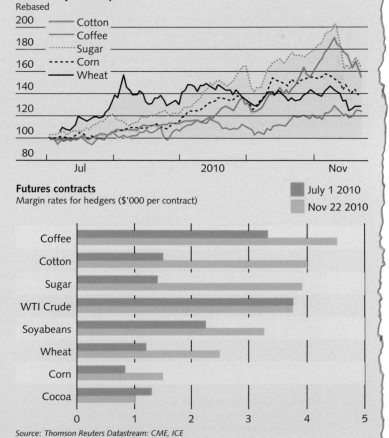

Commodity futures prices
Rebased

Legend: Cotton, Coffee, Sugar, Corn, Wheat

Futures contracts
Margin rates for hedgers ($'000 per contract)

July 1 2010 / Nov 22 2010

Categories: Coffee, Cotton, Sugar, WTI Crude, Soyabeans, Wheat, Corn, Cocoa

Source: Thomson Reuters Datastream; CME, ICE

Exhibit 10.4 continued

as a result of higher margin calls. The higher capital requirements are driving fundamental shifts in commodity trading. Privately-held and publicity-shy traders such as Glencore, Trafigura and Louis Dreyfus are dipping their toes into the capital markets for the first time. Some smaller traders are struggling just to stay in business.

"As the commodity business becomes more capital intensive, I think there is some sort of Darwinian process that will take place," says Ricardo Leiman, chief executive of Noble, a Hong Kong-based trading house. "The amounts of capital are quite demanding."

The effects of higher margin requirements have been particularly brutal in the agricultural sector, where prices for cotton, sugar, wheat and corn have all experienced violent swings. Cotton, for example, has doubled in price in just four months, before falling 22 per cent in less than two weeks.

"We've seen stress in cotton and in coffee and in sugar – just look at what prices have done in the last three to six months and you'll see where the stress is," says Michael Vellucci, with Brown Brothers Harriman, a privately-held bank in New York.

Each significant move upwards means more margin for those who have taken short positions in the market. In ICE cotton, a market move of one cent requires an additional $500 in margin per 50,000-pound contract. Since July 1, cotton has risen more than 39 cents, meaning an additional $19,500 in margin per contract.

The issue is not so much one of solvency since, barring an unexpected disaster such as crop failure, the trader or producer owns the underlying commodity as well as the short position on the futures market – the very nature of hedging price risk.

But for the duration of the hedge, the demands for margin can have a sizeable impact on a company's liquidity, or availability of cash, especially for those whose exposure is not spread across commodities and global markets. Forced liquidation of short futures positions, moreover, can give markets a further upward push.

As volatility rises, banks rate commodity trading as a riskier activity, requiring them to hold more capital or scale back the size of their positions. Likewise, as exchanges raise the "initial margin", or the amount of capital required to open a futures position, investors such as hedge funds who regularly take short-term bets are being forced to reconsider how they are allocating their funds to commodities.

Banks and industry executives say they now prepare for price spikes, either by arranging credit lines or reducing inventory. Mr Leiman of Noble says: "If we expect prices to sky-rocket on a certain commodity, we obviously don't want to pile up on inventories on that which will have a detrimental impact on the balance sheet." Others are employing more sophisticated tactics. Some merchants with short positions in the futures markets are buying options that would profit from a spike in prices in an attempt to neutralise the impact of extreme volatility.

Bankers are also coming up with ways to limit the effects of bigger margin calls. They are offering, for a fee, to meet the liquidity risks associated with futures positions on behalf of corporate clients, via an "exchange of futures for swaps". Some are providing a simple hedge by buying the physical commodity directly from producers or trading companies at a set price, circumventing the futures market.

These efforts appear to be paying off. So far there have been no reports of merchants going under, as some did after a sudden spike in cotton prices in March 2008. "People are better prepared now," one commodities banker says.

But with prices expected to continue to see-saw, many believe an industry shake-out is all but inevitable. Mr Vellucci says: "It is far from easy. At a certain point people run out of capital."

Source: Financial Times, 23 November 2010, p. 35. Reprinted with permission.

Settlement

Historically the futures markets developed on the basis of the ***physical delivery*** of the underlying. So if you had contracted to buy 40,000 lb. of lean hogs you would receive the meat as settlement.[4] However, in most futures markets today (including that for lean hogs) only a small proportion of contracts result in physical delivery. The majority are closed out before the expiry of the contract and all that changes hands is cash, either as a profit or as a loss. Speculators certainly do not want to end up with five tonnes of coffee or 15,000 pounds of orange juice and so will ***reverse their trade*** before the contract expires; for example, if they originally bought a contract for 50 tonnes of white sugar they later sell a contract for 50 tonnes of white sugar.

Hedgers, say confectionery manufacturers, may sometimes take delivery from the exchange but in most cases will have established purchasing channels for sugar, cocoa, etc. In these cases they

---

[4] If a seller of a future which is about to expire wishes to deliver the underlying (say Cocoa, Coffee or Zinc) it gives the exchange notice of intention to deliver a few days before the expiry of the futures contract. Then the underlying is transported to a delivery point at the seller's expense – the exchange usually maintains warehouses. The buyer who wishes to take physical delivery notifies the exchange when the contract expires. The exchange will decide which buyers may take away which warehoused underlying.

'may use the futures markets not as a way of obtaining goods but as a way of offsetting the risk of the prices of goods moving adversely. So a confectionery manufacturer may still plan to buy, say, sugar, at the spot price from its longstanding supplier in six months and simultaneously, to hedge the risk of the price rising, will buy six-month futures in sugar. This position will then be closed before expiry. If the price of the underlying has risen the manufacturer pays more to the supplier but has a compensating gain on the future. If the price falls the supplier is paid less and so a gain is made here, but, under a perfect hedge, the future has lost an equal value.

As the futures markets developed it became clear that most participants did not want the complications of physical delivery and this led to the development of futures contracts where **cash settlement** takes place. This permitted a wider range of futures contracts to be created. Futures contracts based on intangible commodities such as a share index or a rate of interest are now extremely important financial instruments. With these no physical delivery takes place and if the contract is held to the maturity date one party will hand over cash to the other (via the clearing house system).

Equity index futures

Equity index futures are an example of a cash settlement market. The underlyings here are collections of shares, for example 225 Japanese shares for the Nikkei 225. Hedgers and speculators do not want 225 different shares to be delivered say one month from now. They are quite content to receive or hand over the profit or loss made by buying and then selling (or the other way around) a future of the index.

The equity index futures table (**Exhibit 10.5**) from FT.com shows futures in indices from stock markets around the world for 27th October 2010. These are notional futures contracts. If not closed out before expiry (by the holder of a future doing the reverse transaction to their first – so if they

Exhibit 10.5. Equity index futures table from www.ft.com for close of trading on 27 October 2010

EQUITY INDEX FUTURES   **FT**

Oct 27		Open	Sett	Change	High	Low	Est.vol.	Open int.
DJIA	Dec	11049.00	11072.00	−52.00	11085.00	10970.00	1	5,787
DJ Euro Stoxx‡	Dec	2838.00	2822.00	−26.00	2856.00	2811.00	1,249.363	2,021,455
S&P 500	Dec	1178.70	1178.80	−4.00	1178.90	1178.20	7	323,869
Mini S&P 500	Dec	1178.50	1178.75	−4.00	1179.00	1178.00	3,099	2,686,156
Nasdaq 100	Dec	–	2123.75	+7.75	–	2124.00	–	24,833
Mini Nasdaq	Dec	2123.50	2123.75	+7.75	2124.75	2123.50	53	452,922
CAC 40	Nov	3824.50	3796.50	−36.00	3850.50	3789.50	136,995	363,897
DAX	Dec	6613.00	6580.00	−53.00	6639.00	6562.50	145,073	179,479
AEX	Nov	339.20	336.95	−2.70	339.90	336.50	27,861	89,753
MIB 30	Dec	21200.00	21191.00	−99.00	21470.00	21130.00	18,590	41,712
IBEX 35	Nov	10660.00	10618.50	−100.00	10785.00	10605.00	12,388	37,044
SMI	Dec	6465.00	6482.00	−1.00	6520.00	6445.00	31,658	141,841
FTSE 100	Dec	5699.00	5634.50	−59.50	5699.50	5612.50	105,727	608,833
Hang Seng	Oct	23553.00	23109.00	−508.00	23711.00	23096.00	120,632	41,937
Nikkei 225†	Dec	9380.00	9410.00	+50.00	9400.00	9350.00	8,056	305,035
Topix	Dec	816.00	817.50	+1.50	818.00	815.50	372	389,021
KOSPI 200	Dec	248.20	246.50	−2.00	249.35	245.85	429,047	97,317

North American Latest. Contracts shown are among the 25 most traded based on estimates of average volumes in 2004. CBOT volume, high & low for pit & electronic trading at settlement. Previous day's Open Interest. †Osaka contract. ‡Eurex contract.

Source: Financial Times, www.ft.com. 27 October 2010.

bought the future first, selling will close the position) they are settled in cash based on the average level of the relevant index (say, the FTSE 100) between stated times on the last day of the contract.

Exhibit 10.5 is very much a cut-down version of the futures available to traders. As well as the November and December delivery futures shown NYSE Liffe also offers traders the possibility of buying or selling futures that 'deliver' in March, June and September. Delivery dates are the third Friday of the month.

The table shows the first price traded at the beginning of the current day (Open), the settlement price (usually the last traded price) used to mark margin accounts to market, the change from the previous day's settlement price, the highest and lowest prices during the day's settlement price, the number of contracts traded that day (Est. vol.) and the total number of open contracts (these are trading contracts opened over the last few months that have not yet been closed by an equal and opposite futures transaction).

Each point on the UK's FTSE 100 share index future is worth £10, by convention. So if the future rises from 5634.50 to 5684.50 and you bought a future at 5634.50 you have made $50 \times £10$ = £500 if you were to now sell at 5684.50.

Worked example 10.2   Hedging with a share index future

It is 27 October 2010 and the FT 100 is at 5646. A fund manager wishes to hedge a £13 million fund against a decline in the market. A December FTSE 100 future is available at 5634.50 – see Exhibit 10.5. The investor retains the shares in the portfolio and *sells* 231 index futures contracts. Each futures contract is worth £56,345 (5634.5 points × £10). So 231 contracts are needed to cover £13 million (£13,000,000/(£10 × 5634.5) = 231).[5]

Outcome in December

For the sake of argument assume that the index falls by 10 per cent from 5646 to 5081, leaving the portfolio value at £11,700,000 (assuming the portfolio moves exactly in line with the FT 100 index). The closing of the futures position offsets this £1,300,000 loss by buying 231 futures at 5081 to close the position producing a profit[6] of:

Able to sell at 5634.5 × 231 × £10 =	£13,015,695
Able to buy at 5081 × 231 × £10 =	−£11,737,110
	£1,278,585

These contracts are cash settled so £1,278,585 will be paid. Furthermore, the investor receives back the margin laid down, less broker's fees.

Note that this was not a perfect hedge as more than £13 million was covered by the derivative (and the 10 per cent fall was from 5646 not 5634.50).

Over-the-counter (OTC) and exchange-traded derivatives

An OTC derivative is a tailor-made, individual arrangement between counterparties, usually a company and its bank. Standardised contracts (exchange-traded derivatives) are available on dozens of derivative exchanges around the world, for example the CME Group (includes Chicago Board of Trade, CBOT, the old Chicago Mercantile Exchange and the New York Mercantile Exchange, NYMEX), NYSE Liffe, and the Eurex in Germany and Switzerland. **Exhibit 10.6** compares OTC and exchange-traded derivatives.

---

[5] Technically 230.72 contracts are needed but we cannot deal in a fraction of a contract so we need to round up or down.
[6] Assuming that the futures price is equal to the spot price of the FTSE 100. This would occur close to the expiry date of the future.

Exhibit 10.6   OTC and exchange-traded derivatives

OTC derivative

Advantages

- Contracts can be tailor-made, which allows perfect hedging and permits hedges of more unusual underlyings. It also permits contracts of very long maturities.
- Companies with a longstanding relationship with a bank can often arrange derivative deals with it, without the need to find any specific margin or deposit. The bank is willing to accept the counterparty risk of its customer reneging on the deal because it regards this possibility as very low risk, given its longstanding knowledge of the firm.

Disadvantages

- It might be difficult to find a counterparty willing to take the opposite position for a very specific contract that suits you, e.g. to buy 250 tonnes of orange juice exactly 290 days from now. Even if the counterparty can be found the deal might be at a disadvantageous price to you because of the limited choice of counterparties you have available.
- There is a risk that the counterparty will fail to honour the transaction, therefore close attention is paid to the creditworthiness of participants – those with less than high quality reputations may not be able to transact in OTC derivatives (unless secured by a great deal of collateral). Some OTC derivative markets now have a central organisation that is counterparty to both the long holder and the short holder, but central counterparties in the OTC markets are still the exception rather than the rule (although government and regulators are pressing for more involvement of central counterparties following the financial crisis during which many traders were left exposed when their counterparties disappeared through insolvency).
- Low level of market regulation with resultant loss of transparency (e.g. what deals have taken place?) and price dissemination (private deals are not usually made public).
- Often difficult to reverse a hedge once the agreement has been made. It is sometimes difficult to find a counterparty willing to do exactly the opposite transaction to your first position. Even if you found one, you then have two counterparty risks, and often the maturity dates of the two contracts do not exactly match, leaving some unhedged exposure.
- Higher transaction costs. Because they are tailor-made both sides need to scrutinise the deal (e.g. using expensive lawyers) and monitor counterparties subsequently. This extra cost is not worth it for small deals and so forward contracts are usually counted in millions of pounds, euros, etc., whereas futures are usually in tens or hundreds of thousands.
- Transaction may not be settled promptly at the agreed time – whereas the clearing house on an exchange will insist on prompt settlement.

Exchange-traded derivative

Advantages

- Counterparty risk is reduced because the clearing house is counterparty.
- High regulation encourages transparency and openness on the price of recent trades.
- Liquidity is usually much higher than for OTC – large orders can be cleared quickly due to high daily volume of trade.
- Positions can be reversed by closing quickly – an equal and opposite transaction is completed in minutes.

Disadvantages

- Standardisation may be restrictive, e.g. standardised terms for quality of underlying, quantity, delivery dates. Small companies, with say a £100,000 share portfolio to hedge or a €400,000 loan to hedge, find the standard quantities cumbersome (short term interest rates can be hedged – see later. For euros this is in €1m multiples only).
- The limited trading hours and margin requirements may be inconvenient.

In the wake of the financial crisis governments and regulators are trying to move as much of the derivatives trades as possible away from opaque OTC markets where there is counterparty risk to exchanges, or at least electronic trading platforms, where they will be processed through clearing houses with central counterparty functions. Also there will be more open reporting of trades – at least to regulators – *see* **Exhibit 10.7**.

Exhibit 10.7

Brussels in bid to tame 'wild west' markets

By **Nikki Tait** in Brussels

Tough rules to clamp down on the use of privately traded derivatives and speculation in shares have been unveiled by the European Commission in a bid to tame what it has called the "wild west" of financial markets.

The proposed rules aim to bring more transparency to the often-opaque world of so-called over-the-counter derivatives – financial instruments traded off-exchange between two parties.

"No financial market can afford to remain a wild west territory. The absence of any regulatory framework for OTC derivatives contributed to the financial crisis and the tremendous consequences," Michel Barnier, European Union internal market commissioner, said on Wednesday. "Today, we are pro-posing rules which will bring more transparency and responsibility to derivatives markets – so we know who is doing what and who owes what to whom."

The proposals follow agreement by G20 leaders last year to stand-ardise derivatives trading and move them on to exchanges or electronic trading platforms where appropri-ate. The proposals will closely align the EU with the new regime which is coming into force in the US.

The rules will require standard OTC derivatives to be processed through clearing houses – a move aimed at reducing systemic risk arising from a default of one party in an OTC deal. They will also require OTC contracts – the bilat-eral agreements between buyers and sellers – to be reported to "trade repositories" or data banks, and for this information to be avail-able to regulators.

There will be exemptions from the clearing obligation for non-financial information – such as manufacturing companies – who are using OTC derivatives to hedge busi-ness risks. But Brussels also plans to make it more expensive for firms to deal in non-cleared contracts, by requiring them to hold more capital against these – although that meas-ure will be introduced in separate legislation shortly.

The rules being proposed by the Commission will need approval both from EU member states and the European parliament. The aim is to have them in force by mid to late 2012.

Source: Financial Times, 16 September 2010, p. 19. Reprinted with permission.

There is intense competition between the 35 leading derivative exchanges around the world. They regularly design new types of futures to try to attract trade. Recent innovations include futures in house prices and in carbon (trade in the permission to emit carbon is now big busi-ness). **Exhibit 10.8** shows the largest derivatives exchanges.

Exhibit 10.8   The ten largest derivative exchanges – measured by volume traded (number of contracts)

Ranked by number of contracts traded and/or cleared

Rank	Exchange	Jan.–Jun. 2009	Jan.–Jun. 2010	% change
1	Korea Exchange	1,464,666,838	1,781,536,153	21.6%
2	CME Group (includes CBOT and Nymex)	1,283,607,627	1,571,345,534	22.4%
3	Eurex (includes ISE)	1,405,987,678	1,485,540,933	5.7%
4	NYSE Euronext (includes all EU and US markets)	847,659,175	1,210,532,100	42.8%
5	National Stock Exchange of India	397,729,690	783,897,711	97.1%
6	BM&FBovespa	424,295,918	727,962,093	71.6%
7	Chicago Board Options Exchange (includes CFE)	570,283,325	611,323,954	7.2%
8	Nasdaq OMX Group (includes all EU and US markets)	405,462,144	507,953,470	25.3%
9	Shanghai Futures Exchange	151,544,472	300,419,287	98.2%
10	Russian Trading Systems Stock Exchange	200,344,367	280,759,882	40.1%

Note: NYSE Euronext encompasses NYSE Liffe.
Source: http://www.futuresindustry.org

Buying and selling futures

A trader in futures must deal through a registered broker (a futures commission merchant). NYSE Liffe provide a list of designated brokers (these follow rules and codes of conduct imposed by the regulators and the exchange). Gone are the days of open pit trading and those brightly coloured jackets in the UK. Trades are now conducted over a computer system on Liffe (LIFFE CONNECT™) or similar systems at other exchanges such as the Intercontinental Exchange (ICE) in the US. You can place a price limit for your trade – the maximum you are willing to pay if you are buying or a minimum if you are selling. Alternatively you can make an at-the-market order, to be executed immediately at the price determined by current supply and demand conditions. The buyer of a contract is said to be in a long position – they agree to receive the underlying. The seller who agrees to deliver the underlying is said to be in a short position.

If the amount in the trader's account falls below the maintenance margin the trader will receive a demand to inject additional money. This may happen every day so the trader cannot buy/sell a future and then go on holiday for a month (unless they leave plenty of cash with the broker to meet margin calls). Prices are set by competing market makers on LIFFE CONNECT™. Real-time market prices are available on the Internet, as well as historical prices (*www.liffe-data.com*).

Trading costs include brokerage commissions, market maker's spread, taxes and fees imposed by the exchange.

Single stock futures

As well as being able to buy or sell futures on commodities or entire share indices, you can trade futures in a particular company's shares. You can agree to buy 100 or 1,000 shares (one future contract)[7] in, say, Royal Dutch Shell two or three months from now at a price that is agreed now (maximum of six months ahead). **Exhibit 10.9** shows one of the stock futures traded on NYSE Liffe on 14 December 2010.

Suppose you want to speculate that Royal Dutch Shell will fall in price between 14 December 2010 (now) and the third Friday[8] in February 2011 (the delivery date for the February futures shown in Exhibit 10.9). You could sell, say, 1,000 contracts (100,000 shares for delivery in February) at a price of €24.289 (the ask price of €24.326 is what you can deal at with the market maker if you were going long – buying. The market maker in these futures makes a spread profit of €24.326–€24.289 if he fulfils both a buy and a sell order for one futures contract). Imagine now that the February futures price falls to €20 in late February; you could close your position by buying 1,000 futures. Your profit would be:

Sold 100,000 shares at €24.289	€2,428,900
Bought 100,000 shares at €20	€2,000,000
	€428,900

(less dealing costs). You could have made this profit by putting down a margin of only about €150,000,[9] thus almost quadrupling your money in a few weeks.

On the other hand, if the March futures rose to €27 and you closed your position for fear of the price rising further, then the loss of €2,428,900 – €2,700,000 = –€271,100 would wipe out your initial margin and you would be required to provide a further €121,100. If single stock futures are held to the delivery date then they are usually settled in cash rather than by the delivery of shares (i.e. if you have made a gain you receive it in cash). However, a few are settled with physically delivered shares. The *Financial Times* no longer carries single stock futures data, but the Euronext (part of NYSE Liffe) website covers dozens of companies.

---

[7] Usually euro-denominated contracts are for a lot size of 100 whereas sterling-denominated companies have a lot size of 1,000.

[8] Many derivatives, including many stock futures, have delivery dates as the third Friday of the month, but some have the third Wednesday of the month or some other standard date.

[9] Initial margin varies depending on the volatility of the share, but it is generally in the range of 5–20 per cent of overall contract value.

Exhibit 10.9 Single stock (share) futures on NYSE Liffe – Royal Dutch Shell 'A' share priced in euros

Codes and classification

| Code | RD | Market | NYSE Liffe London | Vol. | 212 | 14/12/10 |
| | | Currency | € | O.I. | | 13/12/10 |

Underlying

Name	ROYAL DUTCH SHELLA	ISIN	GB00B03MLX29		Market	Euronext Amsterdam	
Currency	€	Best bid	24.58	14/12/10 16:14	Best ask	24.585	14/12/10 16:14
Time	CET	Last	24.58	14/12/10 16:14	Last change %	0.57	
Volume	3,664,714	High	24.605		Low	24.38	

Prices – 14/12/10

Delivery	Time (CET)	Last	Vol	Day volume	Bid	Ask	%+/−	Settl.
DEC 10	–	–	–	–	24.548	24.582	–	24.441
JAN 11	–	–	–	–	24.576	24.613	–	24.458
FEB 11	–	–	–	–	24.289	24.326	–	24.265
MAR 11	–	–	–	–	–	–	–	24.285

Vol – (Volume) is the number of contracts traded in the most recent transaction.

Day's Volume – Number of trades that have taken place so far in the trading day. This figure updates as the day progresses and more trades take place.

% + /– Percentage price of last trade compared to yesterday's settlement price.

Settl – The previous day's settlement price.

O.I. – (Open Interest) is the outstanding long and short positions of the previous trading day updated in the morning each day

Source: http://www.euronext.com

Worked example 10.3　　An example of single stock future use

Suppose you hold 30,000 Vodafone shares with a current market price of 126p. You bought these for 76p and therefore your capital gain is 50p per share, or £15,000. You are convinced the market is due for a fall. To protect yourself you could sell the Vodafone shares. However, this will result in capital gain tax.

An alternative is to sell 30 stock futures in Vodafone at 126.50p while holding onto the shares. If the market does fall you are protected on the downside. The gain made on the stock futures offsets the loss on the underlying shares. So, if the underlying and the future price falls to 95p the loss on the shares, £9,300, is offset by the gain on the stock futures.

Sold for 126.50p	= £37,950
Bought for 95p	= £28,500
	£ 9,450

This stock futures gain can be taken over into another tax year to use the capital allowance. So, in effect, you have delayed capital gain realisation, thereby legitimately avoiding tax while locking in your gain during the market fall.

Short-term interest rate futures

Trillions of pounds, dollars and euros of trading takes place every year in the short-term interest rate futures markets. These are notional fixed-term deposits, usually for three-month periods starting at a specific time in the future. The buyer of one contract is buying the (theoretical) right to deposit money at a particular rate of interest for three months.

So if the current time is December you could arrange a futures contract for you to 'deposit' and 'receive interest' on, say £1 million, with the deposit starting next June and ending in September. The rate of interest you will 'receive' over the three summer months is agreed in December. (This is a notional receipt of interest, as these contracts are cash settled rather than actual deposits being made and interest received – *see* below for an example.) So you now own the right to deposit £1 million and receive × per cent interest for three months (at least in notional terms).

Short-term interest rate futures will be illustrated using the three-month sterling market, that is, deposits of pounds receiving notional interest for three months starting at some point in the future. Note, however, that there are many other three-month deposits you could make. For example, you could 'deposit' euros for three months, the interest rate on which is calculated with reference to 'Euribor 3m', which is the interest rate highly rated banks pay to other banks for three-month deposits of the currency of the Eurozone countries, the euro. Other three-month deposits are often for money held outside the jurisdiction of the currency's country of origin (i.e. 'Euro' currencies, in the sense of being international money and *not* the new currency in the Eurozone) and include Swiss francs deposited in London (Euroswiss), Eurodollars and Euroyens – *see* **Exhibit 10.10**. (Eurocurrency is discussed in Chapter 5.)

The unit of trading for a three-month sterling time deposit is £500,000. Cash delivery by closing out the futures position is the means of settlement, so the buyer would not actually require the seller of the future to accept the £500,000 on deposit for three months at the interest rate indicated by the futures price. Although the term 'delivery' no longer has significance for the underlying it does define the date and time of the expiry of the contract. This occurs in late September, December, March and June and the nearest two consecutive months. (*See* www.euronext.com for precise definitions and delivery dates.)

Short-term interest contracts are quoted on an index basis rather than on the basis of the interest rate itself. The price is defined as:

$$P = 100 - i$$
where:
P = price index
i = the future interest rate in percentage terms.

Thus, on 15 December 2010 the settlement price for a June three-month sterling future was 98.99, which implies an interest rate of $100 - 98.99 = 1.01$ per cent for the period June to September – *see* Exhibit 10.10. Similarly, the September quote would imply an interest rate of $100 - 98.80 = 1.20$ per cent for the three months September to December 2011.

In both cases the implied interest rate refers to a rate applicable for a notional deposit of £500,000 for three months on expiry of the contract – the June futures contract expires in June (i.e. the right to 'deposit' in June through to September expires in June) and the September future expires in September. The 1.01 per cent rate for three-month money starting from June 2011 is the *annual* rate of interest even though the deal is for a deposit of only one-quarter of a year.

The price of 98.99 is not a price in the usual sense – it does not mean £98.99. It is used to maintain the standard inverse relationship between prices and interest rates. For example, if traders in this market one week later, on 22 December 2010, adjusted supply and demand conditions because they expect generally raised inflation and raised interest rates by the middle of 2011, they would push up the interest rates for three-month deposits starting in June 2011 to, say, 2.0 per cent. Then the price of the future would fall to 98.00. Thus, a rise in interest rates for a three-month deposit of money results in a fall in the price of the contract – analogous to the inverse relationship between interest rates offered on long-term bonds and the price of those bonds.

In relation to short-term interest rate futures it is this inverse change in capital value when interest rates change that it is crucial to grasp. Understanding this is more important than trying to envisage deposits of £500,000 being placed some time in the future.

Exhibit 10.10

INTEREST RATES – FUTURES

Dec 15	Open	Sett	Change	High	Low	Est. vol	Open int
Euribor 3m* FEB1	0.00	98.92	+0.02	0.00	0.00	–	1,541
Euribor 3m* MAY1	0.00	98.89	+0.01	0.00	0.00	–	–
Euribor 3m* SEP1	98.55	98.58	+0.02	98.59	98.54	84.866	344.932
Euribor 3m* DEC1	98.36	98.40	+0.02	98.41	98.35	93.157	348.739
Euroswiss 3m,* MAR1	99.80	99.79	–0.01	99.81	99.79	15.071	93.965
Euroswiss 3m*JUN1	99.72	99.71	–0.01	99.73	99.69	12.090	96.865
Euroswiss 3m*SEP1	99.61	99.61	–	99.62	99.57	10.122	61.921
Sterling 3m* JAN1	0.00	99.19	–	0.00	0.00	–	–
Sterling 3m* MAR1	99.15	99.15	–	99.16	99.13	49.997	280.688
Sterling 3m*JUN1	98.97	98.99	+0.01	99.00	98.95	58.162	238.445
Sterling 3m*SEP1	98.80	98.80	–	98.81	98.76	64.444	217.596
Eurodollar 3m† FEB1	99.625	99.63	–	99.625	99.595	2.671	15.390
Eurodollar 3m†MAY1	0.000	99.49	–	0.000	99.450	–	–
Eurodollar 3m†SEP1	99.270	99.29	–	99.305	99.245	207.871	904.643
Eurodollar 3m†DEC1	99.090	99.11	–	99.140	99.070	230.140	746.097
Fed Fnds 30d‡Dec	0.000	99.83	–	0.000	0.000	–	98.298
Fed Fnds 30d‡JAN1	0.000	99.83	–	0.000	0.000	–	64.748
Fed Fnds 30d‡FEB1	0.000	99.82	–	0.000	0.000	–	56.037
Euroyen 3m‡‡FEB1	0.000	99.665	–0.005	0.000	0.000	–	–
Euroyen 3m‡‡JUN1	99.615	99.615	–	99.620	99.600	12.978	369.635
Euroyen 3m‡‡SEP1	99.585	99.590	–	99.590	99.560	27.089	224.875
Euroyen 3m‡‡DEC1	99.550	99.555	–0.010	99.560	99.525	15.011	162.893

Contracts are based on volumes traded in 2004   Sources: *NYSE LIFFE. †CME. ‡‡TIFFE

Source: *Financial Times*, 16 December 2010. Reprinted with permission

---

Worked example 10.4   Hedging three-month deposits

An example of these derivatives in use may help with gaining an understanding of their hedging qualities. Imagine the treasurer of a large company anticipates the receipt of £100m in late September 2011, slightly more than ten months hence. She expects that the money will be needed for production purposes in January 2012 but for the three months following late September it can be placed on deposit. There is a risk that interest rates will fall between now (December 2010) and September 2011 from their present level of 1.20 per cent per annum for three-month deposits starting in late September. (The sterling 3m September future in Exhibit 10.10 shows a price of 98.80, indicating an interest rate of 1.20 per cent.)

The treasurer does not want to take a passive approach and simply wait for the inflow of money and deposit it at whatever rate is then prevailing without taking some steps to ensure a good return. To achieve certainty in September 2011 she buys, in December 2010, September 2011 expiry three-month sterling interest rate futures at a price of 98.80. Each future has a notional value of £500,000 and therefore she has to buy 200 to hedge the £100 million inflow.

Suppose in September 2011 that three-month interest rates have fallen to 0.95 per cent. Following the actual receipt of the £100 million the treasurer can place it on deposit and receive a return over the next three months of £100m × 0.0 095 × $\frac{3}{12}$ = £237,500. This is significantly less than if September 2011 three-month deposit interest rates had remained at 1.20 per cent throughout the ten-month waiting period.

Return at 1.20 per cent (£100m × 0.012 × $\frac{3}{12}$)	=	£300,000
Return at 0.95 per cent (£100m × 0.0095 × $\frac{3}{12}$)	=	£237,500
Loss		£62,500

However, the treasurer's caution pays off because the futures have risen in value as the interest rates have fallen.

The 200 futures contracts were bought at 98.80. With interest rates at 0.95 per cent for three-month deposits starting in September the futures in September have a value of 100 − 0.95 = 99.05. The treasurer in September can close the futures position by selling the futures for 99.05. Thus, a purchase was made in December 2010 at 98.80 and a sale in September 2011 at 99.05, therefore the gain that is made amounts to 99.05 − 98.80 = 0.25.

This is where a **tick** needs to be introduced. A tick is the minimum price movement on a future. On a three-month sterling interest rate contract a tick is a movement of 0.01 per cent on a trading unit of £500,000.

One-hundredth of 1 per cent of £500,000 is equal to £50, but this is not the value of one tick. A further complication is that the price of a future is based on annual interest rates whereas the contract is for three months. Therefore £50/4 = £12.50 is the value of a tick movement in a three-month sterling interest rate futures contract. In this case we have a gain of 25 ticks with an overall value of 25 × £12.50 = £312.50 per contract, or £62,500 for 200 contracts. The profit on the futures exactly offsets the loss of anticipated interest when the £100m is put on deposit for three months in September.

Note that the deal struck in December was not to enter into a contract to actually deposit £100m with the counterparty on the NYSE Liffe market. The £100m is deposited in September with any one of hundreds of banks with no connection to the futures contract that the treasurer entered into. The actual deposit and the notional deposit (on NYSE Liffe) are two separate transactions. However, the transactions are cleverly arranged so that the value movements on these two exactly offset each other. All that is received from NYSE Liffe is the tick difference, based on the price change between the buying and selling prices of the futures contracts – no interest is received.

Worked example 10.5   **Hedging a loan**

In December 2010 Holwell plc plans to borrow £5 million for three months at a later date. This will begin in June 2011. Worried that short-term interest rates will rise, Holwell hedges by *selling* ten three-month sterling interest rate futures contracts with June expiry. The price of each futures contract is 98.99, so Holwell has locked into an annual interest rate of 1.01 per cent or 0.2525 per cent for three months. The cost of borrowing is therefore:

£5m × 0.002525 = £12,625

Suppose that interest rates rise to annual rates of 1.6 per cent, or 0.4 per cent per quarter. The cost of borrowing for Holwell will be:

£5m × 0.004 = £20,000

However, Holwell is able to *buy* ten futures contracts to close the position on the exchange. Each contract has fallen in value from 98.99 to 98.40; this is 59 ticks. The profit credited to Holwell's margin account on NYSE Liffe will now stand at:

Bought at 98.40, sold at 98.99:
59 ticks × £12.50 × 10 contracts = £7,375

▶

Holwell pays interest to its lender for the three months June to September at 1.6 per cent annual rate. The extra interest is an additional £7,375 (£20,000 – £12,625) compared with the rate in the market for June to September when Holwell was looking at the issue back in December. However, the derivative profit offsets the extra interest cost on the loan Holwell takes out in June.

Note that if interest rates fall Holwell will gain by being charged lower interest on the actual loan, but this will be offset by the loss of the futures. Holwell sacrifices the benefits of potential favourable movements in rates to reduce risk.

Forward rate agreements (FRAs)

FRAs are useful devices for hedging future interest rate risk. They are agreements about the future level of interest rates. The rate of interest at some point in the future is compared with the level agreed when the FRA was established and compensation is paid by one party to the other based on the difference.

For example, a company needs to borrow £6 million in six months' time for a period of a year. It arranges this with Bank X at a variable rate of interest. The current rate of interest is 7 per cent. (For the sake of argument assume that this is the LIBOR rate for borrowing starting in six months and lasting one year, and that this company can borrow at LIBOR.) The company is concerned that by the time the loan is drawn down interest rates will be higher than 7 per cent, increasing the cost of borrowing.

The company enters into a separate agreement with another bank (Y) – an FRA. It 'purchases' an FRA at an interest rate of 7 per cent. This is to take effect six months from now and relates to a 12-month loan. Bank Y will not lend any money to the company but it has committed itself to paying compensation should interest rates (LIBOR) rise above 7 per cent.

Suppose that in six months spot one-year interest rates are 8.5 per cent. The company will be obliged to pay Bank X this rate: £6 million × 0.085 = £510,000; this is £90,000 more than if the interest rates were 7 per cent.[10] However, the FRA with Bank Y entitles the company to claim compensation equal to the difference between the rate agreed in the FRA and the spot rate. This is (0.085 – 0.07) × £6m = £90,000. So any increase in interest cost above 7 per cent is exactly matched by a compensating payment provided by the counterparty to the FRA. However, if rates fall below 7 per cent the company makes payments to Bank Y. For example, if the spot rate in six months is 5 per cent the company benefits because of the lower rate charged by Bank X, but suffers an equal offsetting compensation payment to Bank Y of (0.07 – 0.05) × £6m = £120,000. The company has generated certainty over the effective interest cost of borrowing in the future. Whichever way the interest rates move it will pay £420,000.

This example is a gross simplification. In reality FRAs are generally agreed for three-month periods. So this company could have four separate FRAs for the year. It would agree different rates for each three-month period. If three-month LIBOR turns out to be higher than the agreed rate, Bank Y will pay the difference to the company. If it is lower the company pays Bank Y the difference.

The 'sale' of an FRA by a company protects it against a fall in interest rates. For example, if £10 million is expected to be available for putting into a one-year bank deposit in three months from now the company could lock into a rate now by selling an FRA to a bank. Suppose the agreed rate is 6.5 per cent and the spot rate in three months is 6 per cent, then the depositor will receive 6 per cent from the bank into which the money is placed plus ½ per cent from the FRA counterparty bank.

The examples above are described as 6 against 18 (or 6 × 18) and 3 against 15 (or 3 × 15). The first is a 12-month contract starting in six months, the second is a 12-month contract starting in three months. Typically sums of £5m–£100 million are hedged in single deals in this market. Companies do not need to have an underlying lending or borrowing transaction – they could enter into an FRA in isolation and make or receive compensating payments only.

---

[10] All figures are slightly simplified because we are ignoring the fact that the compensation is received in six months whereas interest to Bank X is payable in 18 months.

Banks enter FRAs between themselves as well as transacting with corporates. FRAs can be arranged in highly liquid markets in all the major currencies – the market has so much activity that the rates offered are displayed on computer screens by banks and brokers. Deals are agreed either over the telephone or over a dealing system such as Reuters.

Derivatives users

There are three types of user of the derivatives markets: hedgers, speculators and arbitrageurs.

Hedgers

To hedge is to enter into transactions which protect a business or assets against changes in some underlying. The instruments bought as a hedge tend to have the opposite-value movements to the underlying. Financial and commodity markets are used to transfer risk from an individual or corporation to another more willing and/or able to bear that risk.

Consider a firm which discovers a rich deposit of platinum in Kenya. The management are afraid to develop the site because they are uncertain about the revenues that will actually be realised. Some of the sources of uncertainty are that: (a) the price of platinum could fall, (b) the floating-rate loan taken out to develop the site could become expensive if interest rates rise and (c) the value of the currencies could move adversely. The senior managers have more or less decided that they will apply the firm's funds to a less risky venture. A recent graduate steps forward and suggests that this would be a pity, saying: 'The company is passing up a great opportunity, and Kenya and the world economy will be poorer as a result. Besides, the company does not have to bear all of these risks given the sophistication of modern financial markets. The risks can be hedged, to limit the downside. For example, the platinum could be sold on the forwards or the futures market, which will provide a firm price. The interest-rate risk can be reduced by using an FRA or the interest futures markets. Other possibilities here include a 'cap' or a swap arrangement into a fixed-rate loan (these are discussed in the next chapter). The currency risk can be controlled by using currency forwards or options (discussed in Chapter 12).' The board decide to press ahead with development of the mine and thus show that derivatives can be used to promote economic well-being by transferring risk.

Speculators

Speculators take a position in financial instruments and other assets with a view to obtaining a profit on changes in price. Speculators accept high risk in anticipation of high reward. The gearing effect of derivatives makes speculation in these instruments particularly profitable, or particularly ruinous. Speculators are also attracted to derivatives markets because they are often more liquid than the underlying markets. In addition the speculator is able to sell before buying (to 'short' the market) in order to profit from a fall. More complex trading strategies are also possible.

The term speculator in popular parlance is often used in a somewhat critical fashion. This is generally unwarranted. Speculators are needed by financial markets to help create trading liquidity. Many people argue that prices are more, not less, likely to be stable as a result of speculative activity. Usually speculators have dissimilar views regarding future market movements and this provides two-way liquidity which allows other market participants, such as hedgers, to carry out a transaction quickly without moving the price. Imagine if only hedgers with an underlying were permitted to buy or sell derivatives. Very few trades would take place each day. If a firm wished to make a large hedge this would be noticed in the market and the price of the derivative would be greatly affected. Speculators also provide a kind of insurance for hedgers – they accept risk in return for a premium.

Speculators are also quick to spot new opportunities and to shift capital to new areas of economic output. For example, if a speculator foresees a massive rise in the demand for cobalt because of its use in mobile phones they will start to buy futures in the commodity, pushing up the price. This will alert the mining companies to go in search of more cobalt deposits around the world and pump money into those countries that have it, such as the Congo. The speculator has to examine the underlying economic messages emanating from the world economy and respond to them in a truthful manner – dumping the currency of a badly run country or selling bond derivatives in banks, for example. Those on the receiving end of those messages often resent having the truth revealed when they have tried to conceal it for so long and hoped to go on doing so. **Exhibit 10.11** discusses the populist anti-speculator rhetoric as well as pointing out the value of speculators.

Exhibit 10.11

The truth about speculators: they are doing God's work

Paul Murphy

"Speculators" are in the frame. Every day, it seems, a politician or senior official from somewhere across Europe spits out the dirty word "speculators" and then proceeds to demand immediate action, retribution, or both.

There's never much detail in these attacks. No need for it. Speculation is bad, right? And if there is any detail, such as discussion of those dreaded credit default swaps, there's usually some mix-up about who's doing the buying or selling or shorting or snorting or whatever people do these days with mutated derivatives.

No matter. Speculation is evil since speculators produce nothing of tangible value. Parasite Capital, LP. Case closed.

The populist rhetoric goes down well. Understandably, the people of Europe, staring austerity in the face, want someone to blame – and the notion that somebody, somewhere is benefitting from their misery makes the blood of ordinary mortals boil. So the claptrap works. Good politicians are seen to be bringing the bad guys to heel, albeit belatedly.

The trouble is that speculation is to financial markets what claptrap is to the political system: absolutely crucial. Populist bombast grabs the attention of the electorate, it gets a politician known and, ultimately, ensures they get elected. Similarly, speculators, faceless or otherwise, make markets more efficient by providing the liquidity which makes trades possible and, ultimately, produce more accurate prices. They help us allocate capital as efficiently as we can.

How is it that our political elite does not know this? Have Europe's leaders forgotten that we live in a market economy?

Clearly, there's a need for an educational refresher on the matter.

Ms Merkel et al might like to start with an 80 year-old tome – Phillip Carret's classic from 1930, *The Art of Speculation* (reprinted 1997).

Yes, the contents page alone might bring on a coronary in Athens, Berlin or Paris ("The speculator increases profits by borrowing money ... Short selling is essential to an orderly market ... The short seller does not injure the long trader"), but Carret's prose is as elegant and instructive today as it was eight decades ago. A taste:

"Those who decry stock market speculation usually have stock market gambling in mind. The speculators are those who use brains as well as ink in writing the order slips for their brokers. They perform a service of substantial value to society."

"Just as water always seeks its level, answering the pull of gravity, so in the securities markets prices are always seeking a level of values. Speculation is the agency by which the adjustment is made. Has a new industry arisen, filling a new demand, adding new wealth to society, requiring new capital in generous value? The alert speculator discovers it, buys the securities, advertises its prosperity to the investing public, provides it with a new credit base."

"In this fashion the speculator is the advance agent of the investor, seeking always to bring market prices into line with investment values, opening new reservoirs of capital to the growing enterprise, shutting off the supply from enterprises which have not profitably used that which they already possessed."

Carret teaches that speculators and speculation touch all parts of our lives – from high street retailers offering a new line of fashion to the hedge fund denizens of London's Mayfair or Greenwich, Connecticut, taking a dim view on the stresses affecting European monetary union. Indeed, even the most conservative self-declared "investor" is always part-speculator.

More from his instruction manual: "In fact, speculation is inseparable from investment. The investor must assume some degree of speculative risk; the intelligent investor will seek a certain measure of speculative profit. If he has the time, the temperament, the ability, the investor may go a step further and seek speculative profit in preference to dividend and interest income from his capital."

"In doing so he is performing a valuable service to the investor, acting as his advance agent in seeking the most profitable channels of investment, increasing the marketability of investment holdings, helping to support the financial machinery which is designed primarily for the service of the investor."

Carret, we should note, was no market spiv. But he did take

Exhibit 10.11 continued

the risk of setting up one of America's first mutual funds, the Fidelity Investment Trust, which later became better known as the Pioneer Trust. He died 12 years ago at the age of 101.

His teachings are as relevant now as ever. Greece, Italy, the UK and others under supposed "speculative attack" are in that position because there is a view that they are "falling upon evil days".

"Advance agents" are telling us that there are problems with too much public debt in the western world, and simply legislating or regulating those agents out of the way is not going to fix things.

What Carret is pointing out is that speculators tell us the truth about what is happening or is likely to happen soon. For a number of European governments, the truth is a little too much to bear right now.

The writer is editor of FT Alphaville

Source: Financial Times, 13/14 March 2010. Reprinted with permission.

Arbitrageurs

The act of **arbitrage** is to exploit price differences on the same instrument or similar assets. The arbitrageur buys at the lower price and immediately resells at the higher price. So, for example, Nick Leeson claimed that he was arbitraging Nikkei 225 Index futures. The same future is traded in both Osaka and Singapore. Theoretically the price should be identical on both markets, but in reality this is not always the case and it is possible simultaneously to buy the future in one market and sell the future in the other and thereby make a risk-free profit. An arbitrageur waits for these opportunities to exploit a market inefficiency. The problem for Barings Bank was that Nick Leeson obtained funds to put down as margin payments on arbitrage trades but then bought futures in both markets – surreptitiously switching from an arbitrage activity to a highly risky, speculative activity. True arbitrageurs help to ensure pricing efficiency – their acts of buying or selling tend to reduce pricing anomalies.

Concluding comments

From a small base in the 1970s derivatives have grown to be of enormous importance. Almost all medium and large industrial and commercial firms use derivatives, usually to manage risk, but occasionally to speculate and arbitrage. Banks are usually at the centre of derivatives trading, dealing on behalf of clients, as market makers or trading on their own account. Other financial institutions are increasingly employing these instruments to lay off risk or to speculate. They can be used across the globe, and traded night and day.

The trend suggests that derivatives will continue their relentless rise in significance. They can no longer be dismissed as peripheral to the workings of the financial and economic systems. The implications for investors, corporate institutions, financial institutions, regulators and governments are going to be profound. These are incredibly powerful tools, and, like all powerful tools, they can be used for good or ill. Ignorance of the nature of the risks being transferred, combined with greed, has already led to some very unfortunate consequences. However, on a day-to-day basis, and away from the newspaper headlines, the ability of firms to quietly tap the markets and hedge risk encourages wealth creation and promotes general economic well-being.

Key points and concepts

- **A derivative instrument** is an asset whose performance is based on the behaviour of an underlying asset (the underlying).

- **A forward contract** is an agreement between two parties to undertake an exchange at an agreed future date at a price agreed now. Forwards are tailor-made, over-the-counter agreements, allowing flexibility.

▶

- The party buying at the future date is said to be taking a *long position*. The counterparty which will deliver at the future date is said to be taking a *short position*.

- **Futures** are agreements between two parties to undertake a transaction at an agreed price on a specified future date. They are exchange-traded instruments with a clearing house acting as counterparty to every transaction standardised as to:
  - quality of underlying;
  - quantity of underlying;
  - legal agreement details;
  - delivery dates;
  - trading times;
  - margins.

- For futures, **initial margin** (0.1 per cent to 15 per cent) is required from each buyer or seller. Each day profits or losses are established through **marking to market**, and **variation margin** is payable by the holder of the loss-making future who loses to avoid going below the **maintenance margin** level.

- The majority of futures contracts are **closed** (by undertaking an equal and opposite transaction) **before expiry** and so **cash losses or profits** are made rather than settlement by delivery of the underlying. Some futures are **settled by cash** only – there is no **physical delivery**.

- **Equity index futures** are a cash settlement market in which the underlyings are notional collections of shares.

- **Over-the-counter (OTC)** derivatives are tailor-made and available on a wide range of underlyings. They allow perfect hedging and there is the possibility of a bank counterparty not requiring margin or deposit. However, they suffer from counterparty risk, low regulation, poor transparency and poor price dissemination, frequent inability to reverse a hedge and higher transaction costs.

- **Exchange-traded** derivatives have lower credit (counterparty) risk, greater regulation, higher liquidity and greater ability to reverse positions than OTC derivatives. However, standardisation can be restrictive.

- A trader in futures must deal through a **registered broker**. Trades are now conducted over a computer system on Liffe **(LIFFE CONNECT™)**. You can place a **price limit** for your trade or make an **at-the-market order**, to be executed immediately at the price determined by current supply and demand conditions.

- **Single stock futures** have as their underlying 100 or 1,000 shares in a single company quoted on a stock market, e.g. BP shares. You can go long or short on the future which will be dated up to six months from the current time.

- **Short-term interest-rate futures** can be used to hedge against rises and falls in interest rates at some point in the future. The price for a £500,000 notional three-month contract is expressed as an index: $P = 100 - i$
  As interest rates rise the value of the index falls.

- **Forward rate agreements** (FRAs) are arrangements whereby one party pays the other should interest rates at some point in the future differ from an agreed rate.

- **Hedgers** enter into transactions to protect a business or assets against changes in some underlying.

- **Speculators** accept high risk by taking a position in financial instruments and other assets with a view to obtaining a profit on changes in value.

- **Arbitrageurs** exploit price differences on the same or similar assets.

References and further reading

Andersen, T. J. (2006) *Global Derivatives: A Strategic Management Perspective*. Harlow: FT Prentice Hall.
Describes the use of derivatives from a corporate perspective. Easy to read and takes the reader from an introductory level to an intermediate level.

Bank of England Quarterly Bulletins.
An important and easily digestible source of up-to-date information.

Chisholm, A. M. (2009) *An Introduction to International Capital Markets*. 2nd edn. Chichester: John Wiley.
Deals with a number of more technical aspects clearly.

Choudhry, M., Joannas, D., Landuyt, G. Periera, R. and Pienaar, R. (2010) *Capital Market Instruments: Analysis and Valuation*, 3rd edn. Basingstoke: Palgrave Macmillan.
A textbook-style book written by practitioners. Some basic material but mostly higher level with plenty of mathematics.

The Economist.
Valuable reading for anyone interested in finance (and world affairs, politics, economics, science, etc.).

Financial Times.
An important source for understanding the latest developments in this dynamic market.

Headley, J. S. and Tufano, P. (2001) 'Why manage risk?' Harvard Business School Note. Available from Harvard Business Online – www.hbr.org/case_studies
A short easy-to-read description of why companies hedge risk.

Hull, J. C. (2010) *Fundamentals of futures and options markets*. 7th edn. Pearson Education.
A relatively easy to follow description but also contains some high level material.

McDonald, R. L. (2006) *Derivatives Markets*, 2nd edn. Harlow: Pearson/Addison Wesley.
A more technical/theoretical approach. US focused.

Miller, M. H. (1997) *Merton Miller on Derivatives*. New York: Wiley.
An accessible (no maths) account of the advantages and disadvantages of derivatives to companies, society and the financial system.

Taylor, F. (2011) *Mastering Derivatives Markets*, 4th edn. London: FT Prentice Hall.
A good introduction to derivative instruments and markets.

Vaitilingam, R. (2011) *The Financial Times Guide to Using the Financial Pages*, 6th edn. London: FT Prentice Hall.
Explains the tables displayed by the *Financial Times* and provides some background about the instruments – for the beginner.

Websites

CNN Financial News www.money.cnn.com
Prices on Liffe www.nyxdata.com
Bloomberg www.bloomberg.com
CME group www.cmegroup.com
Reuters www.reuters.com
Wall Street Journal www.wsj.com
Financial Times www.ft.com
Futures and Options World www.fow.com
London International Financial Futures and Options Exchange (NYSE Liffe) www.euronext.com
Chicago Board Options Exchange www.cboe.com
Intercontinental Exchange www.theice.com
Eurex, the European Derivative Exchange www.eurexchange.com
International Swaps and Derivatives Association www.isda.org
Futures Industry Association http://www.futuresindustry.org/

Video presentations

Chief executives and other senior people describe and discuss policy and other aspects of derivative use in interviews, documentaries and webcasts at Cantos.com. (www.cantos.com) – these are free to view.

Case study recommendations

See www.pearsoned.co.uk/arnold for case study synopses.
Also see Harvard University: http://hbsp.harvard.edu/product/cases

- Introduction to Derivatives (2008) Authors: Jaclyn Grimshaw, Walid Busaba and Zeigham Khokher. Richard Ivey School of Business, The University of Western Ontario. Available at Harvard Case Study website.
- The Dojima Rice Market and the Origins of Futures Trading (2010) Authors: David Moss and Eugene Kintgen. Harvard Business School.
- Hedging with Forwards and Futures (2009) Author: Robert M. Conroy. Darden, University of Pennsylvania. Available at Harvard Case Study website.
- Forwards and Futures (2008) Author: Robert M. Conroy. Darden, University of Pennsylvania. Available at Harvard Case Study website.
- Extracting Information from the Futures and Forward Markets: The Relation between Spot Prices, Forward Prices, and Expected Future Spot Prices. (2001) Author: Lisa K. Mulbroek. Harvard Business School.
- Euronext.liffe and the Over-the-Counter Derivatives Market (2006) Author: Estelle Cantillon. Harvard Business School.

Self-review questions

1 What are derivatives and why do they have value?

2 Why can vast sums be made or lost in a short space of time speculating with derivatives?

3 Distinguish between delivery of the underlying and cash settlement.

4 Explain the advantages of entering into a forward contract.

5 How do futures differ from forwards?

6 Describe the following:

- clearing house;
- initial margin;
- marking to market;
- variation margin.

7 Describe a single stock future.

8 Explain forward rate agreements.

9 Distinguish between a hedger, a speculator and an arbitrageur.

10 Why do the over-the-counter markets in derivatives and the exchange-based derivatives markets coexist?

Questions and problems

1   Adam, a speculator, is convinced that the stock market will fall significantly in the forthcoming months. The current market index (14 August) level is 4997 (FTSE 100). He is investigating a strategy to exploit this market fall: sell five FTSE 100 Index futures on NYSE Liffe with a December expiry, current price 5086.

Extracts from the Financial Times

FTSE 100 Index Futures (LIFFE) £10 per full index point		
	Open	Sett. Price
September	5069	5020
December	5128	5086

Assume: no transaction costs.

Required

For the derivative

   (a) What would the profit (loss) be if the index rose to 5500 in December under the strategy?
   (b) What would the profit (loss) be if the index fell to 4500 in December under the strategy?

2   A manager controlling a broadly based portfolio of UK large shares wishes to hedge against a possible fall in the market. It is October and the portfolio stands at £30m with the FTSE 100 Index at 5020. The March futures price is 5035 (£10 per index point).

Required

   (a) Describe a way in which the manager could hedge against a falling market. Show the number of derivatives.
   (b) What are the profits/losses if the FTSE 100 Index moves to 4000 or 6000 in March?
   (c) Draw a profit/loss diagram for the strategy. Show the value of the underlying portfolio at different index levels, the value of the derivative and the combined value of the underlying and the derivative.

3   A buyer of a futures contract in Imaginationum with an underlying value of £400,000 on 1 August is required to deliver an initial margin of 5 per cent to the clearing house. This margin must be maintained as each day the counterparties in the futures are marked to market.

Required

   (a) Display a table showing the variation margin required to be paid by this buyer and the accumulated profit/loss balance on her margin account in the eight days following the purchase of the future. (Assume that the maintenance margin is the same as the initial margin.)

Day	1	2	3	4	5	6	7	8
Value of Imaginationum (£000s)	390	410	370	450	420	400	360	410

(b) Explain what is meant by 'gearing returns' with reference to this example.
(c) Compare forwards and futures markets and explain the coexistence of these two.

4   A corporate treasurer expects to receive £20 million in late September, six months hence. The money will be needed for expansion purposes the following December. However, in the intervening three months it can be deposited to earn interest. The treasurer is concerned that interest rates will fall from the present level of 8 per cent over the next six months, resulting in a poorer return on the deposited money.

A forward rate agreement (FRA) is available at 8 per cent.
Three-month sterling interest futures starting in late September are available, priced at 92.00.

Assume: No transaction costs and that a perfect hedge is possible.

Required

(a) Describe two hedging transactions that the treasurer could employ.
(b) Show the profit/loss on the underlying and the derivative under each strategy if market interest rates fall to 7 per cent, and if they rise to 9 per cent.

5   Three-month sterling interest-rate futures are quoted as follows on 30 August:

£500,000, points of 100% Settlement price	
September	91.50
December	91.70
March	91.90

Red Wheel plc expects to need to borrow £15 million at floating rate in late December for three months and is concerned that interest rates will rise between August and December.

Assume: no transaction costs.

Required

(a) Show a hedging strategy that Red Wheel could employ to reduce uncertainty.
(b) What is the effective rate of interest payable by Red Wheel after taking account of the derivative transaction if three-month spot rates are 10 per cent in December? Show the gain on the derivative.
(c) What is the effective rate of interest after taking account of the derivative transaction if three-month spot rates are 7 per cent in December? Show the loss on the derivative.
(d) Compare short-term interest-rate futures and FRAs as alternative hedging techniques for a situation such as Red Wheel's.

6   Speculators, hedgers and arbitrageurs are all desirable participants in the derivatives markets. Explain the role of each.

7 The bid and offer prices for single stock futures in Akzo Nobel are shown in **Exhibit 10.12**.

Exhibit 10.12 Single stock future prices for Akzo Nobel on 7 January 2011

AKZO NOBEL NV

Codes and Classification

Code	AKZ	Market	NYSE Liffe London	Vol.	-	07/01/11
		Currency	€	O.I.	81,030	06/01/11

Underlying

Name	AKZO NOBEL	ISIN	NL0000009132		Market	Euronext Amsterdam
Currency	€	Best bid	45.645	07/01/11 17:39	Best ask	45.66 07/01/11 17:39
Time	CET	Last	45.66	07/01/11 17:37	Last change %	-0.52
Volume	1,096,514	High	45.89		Low	45.09

Prices

Delivery	Time (CET)	Last	Vol	Day Volume	Bid Size	Ask	Ask Size	%+/-	Open	High	Low	Settl.	O.I.
JAN 11	–	–	–	–	–	–	–	–	–	–	–	45.909	10
FEB 11	–	–	–	–	–	–	–	–	–	–	–	45.937	10
MAR 11	–	–	–	–	–	–	–	–	–	–	–	45.96	81,010
JUN 11	–	–	–	–	–	–	–	–	–	–	–	45.377	

Source: http://www.euronext.com/trader

Each future is for 100 shares and is cash settled. Prices quoted by market makers are in euros per share. Shares are selling on the spot market for €45.65.

You own 50,000 shares in Akzo Nobel, but you are not sure about the company's prospects. On the one hand as Europe emerges from recession, demand for Akzo Nobel's products will rise, leading to good share returns. On the other, Europe could have a second downturn and so Akzo Nobel's shares will plummet. You estimate that the uncertainty will be lifted by 11 March 2011.

(a) Describe a hedging strategy you could employ to reduce price uncertainty between now (7 January 2011) and 11 March 2011.
(b) Show the gain/losses on underlying and derivative transaction if the share price on 11 March is €50.
(c) Show the gain/losses on underlying and derivative transaction if the share price on 11 March is €40.

Assignments

1 Obtain the annual report and accounts of ten leading companies in your country. Write a report describing the use of futures, forwards and forward rate agreements by these companies and explaining the benefits they gain from using the derivative markets.

2   Investigate the extent of futures, forwards and FRAs use by the treasury department of a firm you know well. Explain the purpose of their use and consider alternative instruments than those they have used in the past.

Web-based exercises

1   Go to www.euronext.com to obtain information on the variety of stock index futures, commodity futures and stock futures. Draw up tables showing the specifications in terms of unit of trading, delivery months, minimum price movement (tick size), delivery day and any other factors that are relevant to understanding the operation of these markets. Write a report detailing the possible hedges that a large corporation might use these markets for (include numerical illustrations).

2   Go to www.ft.com to obtain the latest data for three-month sterling, Eurodollar and Euribor three-month interest rate futures. Now imagine that you are a consultant to a multinational corporation that has the following expected transactions over the next year:

(a) Receipt of US$10m in seven months from now. This is to be held on deposit for three months until it is used by the Venezuelan subsidiary. The managers want to lock in the interest rate for the period they hold the dollars.

(b) Borrowing of £20 million and €50 million starting in nine months from now. The borrowing (from the company's UK bank) is at variable rate depending on interest rates reigning at the time. The directors want to hedge against a rise in interest rates over the next nine months.

Required: advise the directors on the hedges they could put in place in the interest rate futures market. In this process explain and illustrate the transactions, the gains and losses on the underlying and interest rate futures position for some possible interest rates six and nine months hence.

Options and swaps

LEARNING OUTCOMES

There are many practical uses of the derivatives discussed in this chapter, and this is where our emphasis lies, on the practical rather than the theoretical and mathematical. By the end of the chapter you should be able to:

- explain the nature of options and illustrate the use of individual share options and share index options;

- describe the way in which spread betting and contracts for difference deals work;

- outline the advantages of using caps and floors;

- discuss the use of interest rate swaps, and their relationship with forward rate agreements;

- show the value of the credit default swaps markets for those faced with credit risk.

The last chapter showed how derivatives can be used to fix a future outcome. So, if you are currently vulnerable to rises in interest rates, for example, you can arrange an offsetting future agreement that has the opposite value movements to your current exposure. If interest rates rise you lose on the underlying but gain an equal amount on the future. If they fall you gain by paying less on the underlying but lose an equal amount on the future.

The problem with futures, forwards and FRAs is that they do not allow you to benefit from a favourable movement in the underlying. Options, on the other hand, do. With an option you can choose at a later date whether or not you would like to proceed with the deal or not. If you let it lapse after a favourable movement in the underlying you can gain that benefit without suffering an equal loss on the derivative.

The other major category examined in this chapter is swaps. These allow you to exchange a series of future cash payment obligations. For example, your company could have a loan agreement whereby it pays a series of interest amounts based on whatever six-month LIBOR is at the time, through a period of seven years. Obviously, the concern you have is that LIBOR might jump to a much higher level at some point in the seven years, which might jeopardise the firm. One solution is to agree with a counterparty to pay it fixed interest rate obligations if it agrees to pay you LIBOR every six months. This can reduce risk for both.

Credit default swaps, invented only in the 1990s, allow you to pass on the risk of a borrower defaulting on a debt deal to other participants in the financial markets, in return for a fee (premium). These are instruments that can be used to reduce risk or to speculate.

As well as options, swaps and credit default swaps this chapter examines caps, which permit a limit to be set on interest paid, and floors, which can be used to set a minimum interest to be received. And then there are spread bets and contracts for difference which allow the purchaser to gain from a rise or fall in the price of an underlying without ever owning it. These are very popular with small investors as well as large corporations engaged in takeovers, or simply for hedging and speculating.

Options

An **option** is a contract giving one party the right, but not the obligation, to buy or sell a financial instrument, commodity or some other underlying asset at a given price, at or before a specified date. The purchaser of the option can either exercise the right or let it lapse – the choice is theirs.

A very simple option would be where a firm pays the owner of land a non-returnable **premium** (say £10,000) for an option to buy the land at an agreed price because the firm is considering the development of a retail park within the next five years. The property developer may pay a number of option premiums to owners of land in different parts of the country. If planning permission is eventually granted on a particular plot the option to purchase may be **exercised**. In other words the developer pays the price agreed with the farmer at the time that the option contract was arranged, say £1 million, to purchase the land. Options on other plots may be **allowed to lapse** and will have no value. By using an option the property developer has 'kept the options open' with regard to which site to buy and develop and, indeed, whether to enter the retail park business at all.

Options can also be traded. Perhaps the option to buy could be sold to another company keener to develop a particular site than the original option purchaser. It may be sold for much more than the original £10,000 option premium, even before planning permission has been granted.

Once planning permission has been granted the greenfield site may be worth £1.5 million. If there is an option to buy at £1 million the option right has an **intrinsic value** of £500,000, representing a 4,900 per cent return on £10,000. From this we can see the gearing effect of options: very large sums can be gained in a short period of time for a small initial cash outlay.

Share options

Share options have been traded for centuries but their use expanded dramatically with the creation of traded option markets in Chicago, Amsterdam and, in 1978, the London Traded Options Market. In 1992 this became part of the London International Financial Futures and Options

Exchange (LIFFE). Euronext bought LIFFE in 2002, which later combined with the New York Stock Exchange, so LIFFE is now called NYSE Liffe.

A **share call option** gives the purchaser a right, but not the obligation, to *buy* a fixed number of shares at a specified price at some time in the future. In the case of traded options on NYSE Liffe, one option contract relates to a quantity of 1,000 shares. The seller of the option, who receives the premium, is referred to as the **writer**. The writer of a call option is obligated to sell the agreed quantity of shares at the agreed price sometime in the future. **American-style options** can be exercised by the buyer at any time up to the expiry date, whereas **European-style options** can be exercised only on a predetermined future date. Just to confuse everybody, the distinction has nothing to do with geography: most options traded in Europe are American-style options.

Call option holder (call option buyer)

Now let us examine the call options available on an underlying share – AstraZeneca on 17 December 2010. There are a number of options available for this share, many of which are not reported in the table presented in the *Financial Times*.[1] A section of this table is reproduced as **Exhibit 11.1**. These are American-style options.

Exhibit 11.1	Call options on AstraZeneca shares, 17 December 2010		
	Call option prices (premiums) pence		
Exercise price	**December**	**January**	**February**
2900p	41	94.5	101.5
3000p	–	41	52.5
Share price on 17 December 2010 = 2941p			

Source: *Financial Times*, 18/19 December 2010. Reprinted with permission.

So, what do the figures mean? If you wished to obtain the right to buy 1,000 shares on or before late January 2011,[2] at an **exercise price** of 3000p, you would pay a premium of £410 (1,000 × 41p). If you wished to keep your option to purchase open for another month you could select the February call. But this right to insist that the writer sells the shares at the fixed price of 3000p on or before a date in late February will cost another £115 (the total premium payable on one option contract = £525). This extra £115 represents additional *time* value. Time value arises because of the potential for the market price of the underlying to change in a way that creates intrinsic value.

The intrinsic value of an option is the payoff that would be received if the underlying were at its current level when the option expires. In this case, there is currently (17 December 2010) no intrinsic value because the right to buy is at 3000p whereas the share price is 2941p. However, if you look at a call option with an exercise price of 2900p then the right to buy at 2900p has intrinsic value because if you purchased at 2900p by exercising the option, thereby obtaining 1,000 shares, you could immediately sell at 2941p in the share market: intrinsic value = 41p per share, or £410 for 1,000 shares. The longer the time over which the option is exercisable, the greater the chance that the price will move to give intrinsic value – this explains the higher premiums on more distant expiry options. Time value is the amount by which the option premium exceeds the intrinsic value.

[1] The Saturday paper version presents a traded option table. For the other days of the week you need to go to www.ft.com, or the original source, www.euronext.com.
[2] The expiry date is the third Wednesday of the expiry month.

The two exercise price (also called **strike price**) levels presented in Exhibit 11.1 illustrate an **in-the-money option** (the 2900 call option) and an **out-of-the-money option** (the 3000 call option). The underlying share price is above the strike price of 2900 and so this call option has an intrinsic value of 41p and is therefore in-the-money. The right to buy at 3000p is out-of-the-money because the share price is below the option exercise price and therefore has no intrinsic value. The holder of a 3000p option would not exercise this right to buy at 3000p because the shares can be bought on the stock exchange for 2941p. (It is sometimes possible to buy an **at-the-money option**, which is one where the market share price is equal to the option exercise price.)

To emphasise the key points: the option premiums vary in proportion to the length of time over which the option is exercisable (e.g. they are higher for a February option than for a January option). Also, call options with lower exercise prices will have higher premiums.

An illustration

Suppose that you are confident that AstraZeneca shares are going to rise significantly over the next two months to 3200p and you purchase a February 2900 call at 101.5 pence.[3] The cost of this right to purchase 1,000 shares is £1015 (101.5p × 1,000 shares). If the share rises as expected then you could exercise the right to purchase the shares for a total of £29,000 and then sell these in the market for £32,000. A profit of £3,000 less £1015 = £1,985 is made before transaction costs (the brokers' fees, etc. would be in the region of £20–£50). This represents a massive 196 per cent rise before costs (£1,985/£1015).

However, the future is uncertain and the share price may not rise as expected. Let us consider two other possibilities. First, the share price may remain at 2941p throughout the life of the option. Second, the stock market may have a severe downturn and AstraZeneca shares may fall to 2700p. These possibilities are shown in **Exhibit 11.2**.

Exhibit 11.2	Profits and losses on the AstraZeneca February 2900 call following purchase on 17 December 2010

	Assumed share prices in February at expiry date		
	3200p	2941p	2700p
Cost of purchasing shares by exercising the option	£29,000	£29,000	£29,000
Value of shares bought	£32,000	£29,410	£27,000
Profit from exercise of option and sale of shares in the market	£3,000	£410	Not exercised
Less option premium paid	£1015	£1015	£1015
Profit (loss) before transaction costs	£1,985	–£605	–£1015
Percentage return over 2 months	196%	–60%	–100%

In the case of a standstill in the share price the option gradually loses its time value over the three months until, at expiry, only the intrinsic value of 41p per share remains. The fall in the share price to 2700p illustrates one of the advantages of purchasing options over some other derivatives: the holder has a right to abandon the option and is not forced to buy the underlying share at the option exercise price – this saves £2,000. It would have added insult to injury to have to buy at £29,000 and sell at £27,000 after having already lost £1015 on the premium for the purchase of the option. A comparison of **Exhibits 11.3 and 11.4** shows the extent to which the purchase of an

---

[3] For this exercise we will assume that the option is held to expiry and not traded before then. However, in many cases this option will be sold on to another trader long before the expiry date approaches (at a profit or loss).

option gears up the return from share price movements: a wider dispersion of returns is experienced. On 17 December 2010, 1,000 shares could be bought for £29,410. If the market value rose to £32,000, an 8.8 per cent return would be made, compared with a 196 per cent return if options are bought. We would all like the higher positive return on the option than the lower one available on the underlying – but would we all accept the downside risk associated with this option? Consider the following possibilities:

● If share price remains at 2941p:
  ● Return if shares are bought: 0%.
  ● Return if one 2900 February call option is bought: –60 per cent (paid £1015 for the option which declines to its intrinsic value of only £410[4]).
● If share price falls to 2700p:
  ● Return if shares are bought: –8.2%.
  ● Return if one 2900 February call option is bought: –100 per cent (the option is worth nothing).

Exhibit 11.3	Profit and loss if 1,000 shares in AstraZeneca are bought on 17 December 2010 at £29.41

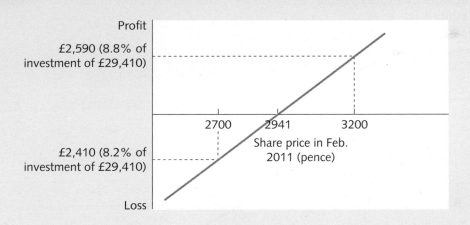

Exhibit 11.4	Profit and loss if one 2900 February call option contract (for 1,000 shares) in AstraZeneca bought on 17 December 2010 and held to maturity

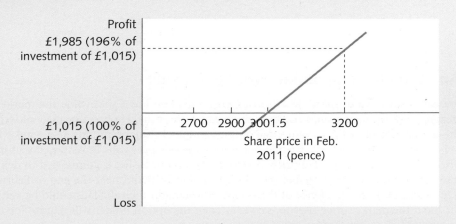

---

[4] £410 is the intrinsic value at expiry (2941–2900p) × 1,000 = £410.

The holder of the call option will not exercise unless the share price is at least 2900p: at a lower price it will be cheaper to buy the 1,000 shares on the stock market. Break-even does not occur until a price of 3001.5p because of the need to cover the cost of the premium (2900p + 101.5p). However, at higher prices the option value increases, penny for penny, with the share price. Also the downside risk is limited to the size of the option premium.

Call option writers

The returns position for the writer of a call option in AstraZeneca can also be presented in a diagram (*see* **Exhibit 11.5**). With all these examples note that there is an assumption that the position is held to expiry.

If the market price is less than the exercise price (2900p) in February the option will not be exercised and the call writer profits to the extent of the option premium (101.5p per share). A market price greater than the exercise price will result in the option being exercised and the writer will be forced to deliver 1,000 shares for a price of 2900p. This may mean buying shares on the stock market to supply to the option holder. As the share price rises this becomes increasingly onerous and losses mount. Note that in the sophisticated traded option markets of today very few option positions are held to expiry. In most cases the option holder sells the option in the market to make a cash profit or loss. Option writers often cancel out their exposure before expiry – for example they could purchase an option to buy the same quantity of shares at the same price and expiry date.

Exhibit 11.5	Profit and loss to a call option writer of one 2900 February call option contract (for 1,000 shares) in AstraZeneca on 17 December 2010

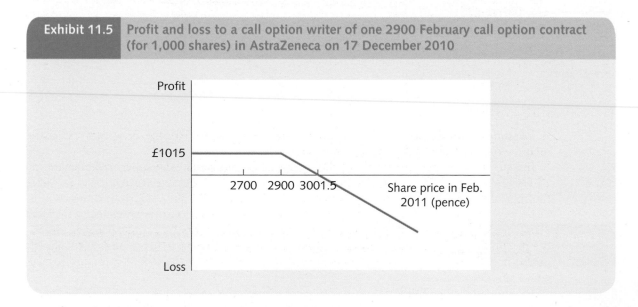

An example of an option-writing strategy

Joe has a portfolio of shares worth £100,000 and is confident that while the market will go up steadily over time it will not rise over the next few months. He has a strategy of writing out-of-the-money (i.e. no intrinsic value) call options and pocketing premiums on a regular basis. Today (17 December 2010) Joe has written one option on February calls in AstraZeneca for an exercise price of 2900p (current share price 2941p). In other words, Joe is committed to delivering (selling) 1,000 shares at any time between 17 December 2010 and near the end of February 2011 for a price of £29 at the insistence of the person who bought the call. This could be very unpleasant for Joe if the market price rises to, say, £33. Then the option holder will require Joe to sell shares worth £33,000 to him/her for only £29,000.

However, Joe is prepared to take this risk for two reasons. First he receives the premium of 101.5p per share up front – this is 3.5 per cent of each share's value. This £1015 will cushion any feeling of future regret at his actions. Second, Joe holds 1,000 AstraZeneca shares in his portfolio and so would not need to go into the market to buy the shares to then sell them to the option holder if the price did rise significantly. Joe has written a covered call option – so called because he has backing in the form of the underlying shares. Joe loses out only if the share price on the day the option is exercised is greater than the strike price (£29) plus the premium (£1.015). He is prepared to risk losing some of the potential upside (above 2900p + 101.5p = 3001.5) to gain the premium. He also reduces his loss on the downside: if the shares in his portfolio fall he has the premium as a cushion.

Some speculators engage in uncovered (naked) option writing. It is possible to lose a multiple of your current resources if you write many option contracts and the price moves against you. Imagine that Joe had only £20,000 in savings and entered the options market by writing 40 AstraZeneca February 2011 2900 calls receiving a premium of £1.015 × 40 × 1,000 = £40,600.[5] If the price moves to £33 Joe has to buy shares for £33 and then sell them to the option holders for £29, a loss of £4 per share: £4 × 40 × 1,000 = £160,000. Despite receiving the premiums Joe has wiped out his savings.

Liffe share options

The *Financial Times* lists more than 50 companies' shares in which options are traded – *see* **Exhibit 11.6,** which shows some option prices for 17 December 2010, including that of AstraZeneca. This table is a cut down version of the data available at www.euronext.com, where over 250 company options are traded through the day. Also a wider variety of strike prices is shown at www.euronext.com than the *Financial Times* can accommodate.

Put options

A put option gives the holder the right, but not the obligation, to sell a specific quantity of shares on or before a specified date at a fixed exercise price.

Imagine you are pessimistic about the prospects for Sainsbury, the supermarket chain, on 17 December 2010. You could purchase, for a premium of 12.75p per share (£127.5 in total), the right to sell 1,000 shares in or before late February 2011 at 370p (*see* Exhibit 11.6). If a fall in price subsequently takes place, to, say, 340p, you can insist on exercising the right to sell at 370p. The writer of the put option is obliged to purchase shares at 370p while being aware that the put holder is able to buy shares at 340p on the stock exchange. The option holder makes a profit of 370 − 340 − 12.75 = 17.25p per share (£172.50), a 135 per cent return (before costs of £20–£40).

For the put option holder, if the market price exceeds the exercise price, it will not be wise to exercise as shares can be sold for a higher price on the Stock Exchange. Therefore the maximum loss, equal to the premium paid, is incurred. The option writer gains the premium if the share price remains above the exercise price, but may incur a large loss if the market price falls significantly (*see* **Exhibits 11.7 and 11.8**).

As with calls, in most cases the option holder would take profits by selling the option on to another investor via NYSE Liffe rather than waiting to exercise at expiry.

---

[5] This is simplified. In reality Joe would have to provide a margin of cash or shares to reassure the clearing house that he could pay up if the market moved against him. So it could be that all of the premium received would be tied up in margin held by the clearing house (the role of a clearing house is explained in Chapter 10).

Exhibit 11.6

FINANCIAL TIMES DECEMBER 18/DECEMBER 19 2010

EQUITY OPTIONS

FT

Option	Strike	Calls Dec	Calls Jan	Calls Feb	Puts Dec	Puts Jan	Puts Feb
AstraZeneca (*2941)	2900	41	94.5	101.5	–	48	135
	3000	–	41	52.5	59	97.5	203
Aviva (*385.900)	380	6	13.75	19	–	7.25	12.25
	390	–	8.25	15.5	4	12	17
BAE Systems (*325)	320	5	12.25	16	–	7	10.25
	330	–	7	10.5	5	11.75	14.5
Barclays (*259.75)	250	9.75	16	20.75	–	5.75	10.5
	260	–	10.25	15.25	0.25	10.25	15
BG Group (*1324.5)	1300	24.5	50.5	69	–	26.5	44
	1350	–	26	45	25.5	52	70
BHP Billiton (*2500)	2400	100	149	188.5	–	48	87.5
	2500	0.5	87.5	132.5	0.5	88.5	130
BP (*467.150)	460	7.25	16.75	22	–	9.25	16.25
	470	–	11.25	16.75	2.75	13.75	21.25
BR Airways (*270.200)	260	10.25	15.5	21.75	–	8.25	12.75
	270	0.25	11.75	15.75	–	10.75	16.75
BAT (*2455)	2400	55	81	104.5	–	26	46
	2500	–	28	49	45	72	92
BT Group (*182.400)	180	2.5	4.75	7.75	–	4.75	7.75
	185	–	2.75	5.5	2.5	7.75	10.25
Diageo (*1180)	1150	30	43	55	–	13	24
	1200	–	16	27.75	20	36	47
GlaxoSmKl (*1265.5)	1250	15.5	35	47	–	18.5	40
	1300	–	12	22	34.5	44.5	69
HSBC (*655.5)	640	15.5	24.75	32.5	–	9.245	16.5
	660	–	13.25	20.75	4.5	17.75	25.25
Kingfisher (*255.400)	250	5.5	10	13.5	–	4.5	7.75
	260	–	4.5	8	4.5	9	12.5

Option	Strike	Calls Dec	Calls Jan	Calls Feb	Puts Dec	Puts Jan	Puts Feb
Lan Sec Gp (*657)	640	17	27.5	33.25	–	8.25	14
	660	–	15.25	21.25	3	16.5	22.5
Legal & Gen (*99.200)	98	1.25	4	5.5	–	2.5	4.5
	100	–	2.75	4.5	0.75	3.5	5.25
Lloyds Bkg (*66.5)	64	2.5	4.25	5.5	–	2	2.75
	68	–	2	3.25	1.5	3.5	4.75
Man Group (*294)	290	4	13	17.75	–	8.5	13.5
	300	–	8	13	6	14.25	19
Marks & S (*375.400)	370	5.5	13.5	18	–	8.25	12
	380	–	8.75	12.5	4.5	13	16.75
Morrison (Wm) (*264.600)	260	4.5	8	10.5	–	3.5	5.5
	270	–	3	5.25	5.5	8.5	10
Rio Tinto (*4418)	4400	18	174.5	258.5	–	156	238.5
	4600	–	91	166.5	182	269	346
Royal Blk Scot (*37.820)	36	1.75	3.25	4	–	1.25	2
	38	–	2	2.75	0.25	2	2.75
Royal Dutch Shell 'B' (*2069.5)	2000	69.5	85	100	–	14.5	40.5
	2100	–	26	42.5	30.5	54.5	89.5
ITV (*72,100)	69	4					
	72	–		7			1.75
RSA Ins Grp (*124.100)	120	4	5.25	6.5	1	3	4
	125	–	2	3.25	3		
Sainsbury (*372.100)	370	12	11.25	15.25	8	8.75	12.75
	380	–	7	11		14.5	18.5
Std Chartd (*1734)	1638	96					
	1734						
Tesco (*433.400)	430	3.5	10.75	15	–	7.25	11.25
	440	–	5.75	9.75	6.75	12.5	16.25
Vodafone (*170.050)	165	5	7	8.75	–	2	3.75
	170	–	3.75	5.75	–	3.75	5.75

Option	Strike	Calls Dec	Calls Jan/Mar	Calls Feb/Jun	Puts Dec	Puts Jan/Mar	Puts Feb/Jun
Xstrata (*1449.5)	1400	49.5	91	122	–	41	70.5
	1450	–	62.5	94	0.5	6.2	93.5
3i Group (*328.5)	320	8.5	17.75	26	–	9.75	17
	330				1.5		
Carnival (*2764)	2700	64			1.5		
	2800	–	113	174	36	151.5	215
Compass (*579)	560	19	31	41	1	21	32.5
	580	5.75	14.25		–	11.75	
Experian (*813.5)	800	13.5	37.75	53.5	6.5	29.5	43.25
	820					75	107
Impl Tobacco (*1941)	1900	41	71.5	98.5	9	75	107
	1950				9	53	89
IntCont Hotels (*1234)	1200	34	86.5	110	16		
	1250	5					
Intl Power (*435)	430	5	13.5	20.5	5	18.5	29
	440						
Lon Stk Exchg (*823)	820	4	26	42.5			
	840	3	32	49.75	17	47.75	60.75
Natl Grid (*522)	540	12	25.25		12.5		
	560		14	21.75	8	21.25	42.75
Next (*1985)	1950	35	97.5	137	15	110	180.5
	2000						
Pearson (*1017)	1000	17	49	60.25	33	29.5	57.75
	1050						
Reckitt Brckisr Gp (*3577)	3500	77	118	168.5	23	180.5	235
	3600						

Option	Strike	Calls Dec	Calls Mar	Calls Jun	Puts Dec	Puts Mar	Puts Jun
Reed Elsevier (*528)	520	8	25.5	32.5	–	16.75	33.25
	540	–			12		
Rentokil Init (*97.850)	96	1.75	6.75	9	–	4.25	5.75
	100	–	4.75	7.25	2.25	6.25	8.25
Rolls-Royce (*630)	620	10	25.25	35.75	–	10	50.5
	640	–			10	34.25	
SAB Miller (*2243.5)	2200	43.5	115	166.5	–	70.5	109
	2300	–		113.5	56.5		159
Sage (*275.800)	270	5.75	14.25	–	–	11.75	–
	280	–	9	13.25	4.25	17.5	23.75
Scot & Sfn Energy (*1185)	1150	35	52	–	6.5	31	–
	1200	–	24.5	40.5	15	58	73.5
Shire (*1530)	1500	30	86	117	9	56	84.5
	1550	–			20		
Sm & Nephew (*655.5)	640	15.5	42.75	53.25	16	26	40.25
	660	–			4.5		
Standard Life (*210)	205	5	9.75	12.25	5	14	18.5
	210	–					
Unilever (*1972)	1950	22	55.5	84.5	5.25	99	138
	2000	–			28		
Utd Utilities (*585.5)	580	5.5	23	–	17	16	–
	600	–	13.75	22.75	14.5	27	46.25
Whitbread (*1805)	1800	5	81.5	116.5	8	75.5	127.5
	1850	–			45		
Wolseley (*1959)	1950	9	78.5	129.5	15	128.5	169.5
	2000	–			41		
WPP (*783)	780	3	29.25	47	33	44.25	66.75
	800	–			17		

*Underlying security price. Premiums shown are based on settlement prices. Source: Euronext.liffe December 17 Total contracts, Equity & Index options: 1,417,589 Calls: 124,243 Puts: 116,159

Exhibit 11.7	Put option holder profit profile for one Sainsbury 370 February 2011 put option contract (for 1,000 shares) bought on 17 December 2010

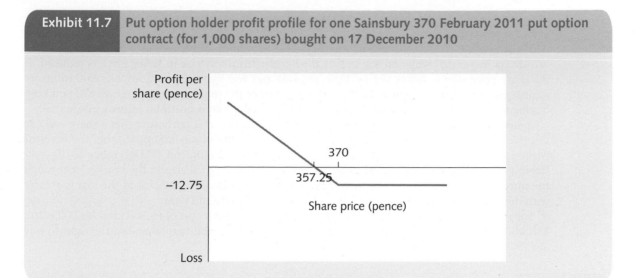

Exhibit 11.8	Put option *writer* profit profile for one Sainsbury 370 February 2011 put option contract (for 1,000 shares) sold on 17 December 2010

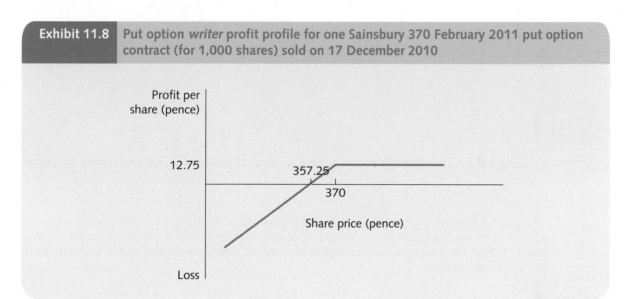

Using share options to reduce risk: hedging

Hedging with options is especially attractive because they can give protection against unfavourable movements in the underlying while permitting the possibility of benefiting from favourable movements. Suppose you hold 1,000 shares in Sainsbury on 17 December 2010. Your shareholding is worth £3,721 (see price in brackets underneath 'Sainsbury' in Exhibit 11.6). There are rumours flying around the market that the company may become the target of a takeover bid. If this materialises the share price will rocket; if it does not the market will be disappointed and the price will fall dramatically. What are you to do? One way to avoid the downside risk is to sell the shares. The problem is that you may regret this action if the bid does subsequently occur and you have forgone the opportunity of a large profit. An alternative approach is to retain the shares and buy a put option. This will rise in value as the share price falls. If the share price rises you gain from your underlying share holding.

Assume a 370 February put is purchased for a premium of £127.5 (*see* Exhibit 11.6). If the share price falls to 300p in late February you lose on your underlying shares by £721 ((372.1p − 300p) × 1,000). However, the put option will have an intrinsic value of £700 ((370p − 300p) × 1,000), thus reducing the loss and limiting the downside risk. Below 370p, for every 1p lost in a share price, 1p is gained on the put option, so the maximum loss is £148.5 (£21 intrinsic value + £127.5 option premium).

Thus, hedging reduces the dispersion of possible outcomes. There is a floor below which losses cannot be increased, while on the upside the benefit from any rise in share price is reduced. If the share price stands still at 372.1p, however, you may feel that the premium you paid to insure against an adverse movement at 12.75p or 3.4 per cent of the share price was excessive. If you keep buying this type of 'insurance' through the year it can reduce your portfolio returns substantially.

A simpler example of risk reduction occurs when an investor is fairly sure that a share will rise in price but is not so confident as to discount the possibility of a fall. Suppose that the investor wished to buy 10,000 shares in Diageo, currently priced at 1180p (on 17 December 2010) – *see* Exhibit 11.6. This can be achieved either by a direct purchase of shares in the market or through the purchase of an option. If the share price does fall significantly, the size of the loss is greater with the share purchase – the option loss is limited to the premium paid.

Suppose that ten February 1150 call options are purchased at a cost of £5,500 (55p × 1,000 × 10). Exhibit 11.9 shows that the option is less risky because of the ability to abandon the right to buy at 1150p.

Exhibit 11.9   Losses on alternative buying strategies

Diageo share price falls to:	Loss on 10,000 shares	Loss on 10 call options
1150	£3,000	£5,500
1100	£8,000	£5,500
1050	£13,000	£5,500
1000	£18,000	£5,500
950	£23,000	£5,500

Mexico wanted certainty over the amount it would gain by selling $13 billion of its oil on the international market in 2010, so it bought a put option – see Exhibit 11.10. Even though the cost was $1 billion the government thought it well worth it, especially after it gained so much on its put options in 2009.

Exhibit 11.10

Mexico buys \$1bn insurance policy against falling oil prices

By **Gregory Meyer** in New York and **Javier Blas** in London

Mexico has taken out a $1bn (£614m) insurance policy against oil prices falling next year, a clear signal that commodities producers remain wary of the threat of a double-dip recession.

The world's sixth-largest oil producer said yesterday that it had hedged all its net oil exports – 230m barrels – for 2010 by buying

protection against oil price falling below $57 a barrel.

"We want this as an insurance policy," said Agustin Carstens, Mexico's finance minister. "If we don't collect any resources from this transaction, it's OK with us." That would mean the oil price had remained above $57 a barrel, he added.

The move follows a successful hedging strategy at $70 this year which netted Mexico more than $5bn on the back of low prices between January and June.

Although that figure is lower than expectations because of recent high oil prices, it still represents more than 7 per cent of Mexican government revenues this year.

▶

Exhibit 11.10 continued

Barclays Capital, Deutsche Bank, Goldman Sachs and Morgan Stanley arranged this year's hedge. Bankers said Barclays Capital was leading next year's.

Mr Carstens, joined by senior executives from the banks, said Mexico's hedging showed that derivatives, "when used responsibly", could be "very useful". Mexico bought put options – contracts that give the holder the right to sell oil at a predetermined price.

His view contrasts sharply with recent comments by senior Chinese officials, who criticised some of the same banks for selling derivatives products, including oil hedges, to state companies. Many had heavy losses.

Mexico has based its budget next year on an oil price of about $59 a barrel.

Olivier Jakob, of the Swiss-based consultancy Petromatrix, said there was potential for a drop

in oil prices in 2010 unless demand recovered meaningfully. "The fundamental supply and demand picture looks weak, but the weakness of the US dollar and financial flows are supporting oil prices right now," he explained.

Source: Financial Times, 9 December 2009, p. 19. Reprinted with permission.

Index options

Options on whole share indices can be purchased: for example, Standard & Poor's 500 (US), FTSE 100 (UK), CAC 40 (France), XETRA Dax (Germany). Large investors usually have a varied portfolio of shares so, rather than hedging individual shareholdings with options, they may hedge through options on the entire index of shares. Also speculators can take a position on the future movement of the market as a whole.

A major difference between index options and share options is that the former are cash settled – so for the FTSE 100 option, there is no delivery of 100 different shares on the expiry day. Rather, a cash difference representing the price change changes hands.

Exhibit 11.11 shows the January expiry options for the FTSE 100 Index on 20 December 2010. The date of the download was 20 December and the FTSE 100 at that time was at 5,902. By convention (so everyone knows where they stand) the index is regarded as a price and each one-point movement on the index represents £10. So if you purchased one contract in January expiry 5,875 calls ('C') you would pay an option premium of 110 index points × £10 = £1,100.[6] The different calls and put strike prices are shown in the middle column of the table, with the call prices to the left and the put prices to the right.

Imagine that the following day, 21 December 2010, the FTSE 100 moved from its level on 20 December 2010 of 5,902 to 5,940 and the option price on the 5,875 January call moved to 150 index points (65 points of intrinsic value and 85 points of time value). To convert this into money you could sell the option at £10 per point per contract (150 × £10 = £1,500). In 24 hours your £1,100 has gone up to £1,500, a 36 per cent rise. Large gains can be made when the market moves in your favour. If it moves against you, large percentage losses will occur in just a few hours.

Note that there are many additional option expiry dates stretching months into the future other than the January one shown in Exhibit 11.11. In fact, there are eight months available: 'Nearest eight of March, June, September, December plus such additional months that the nearest four calendar months are always available for trading' (www.euronext.com).

Hedging against a decline in the market using index options

An investor with an £1,175,000 broadly spread portfolio of shares is concerned that the market may fall over the next two months. One strategy to lower risk is to purchase put options on the share index. If the market does fall, losses on the portfolio will be offset by gains on the value of the index put option.

---

[6] Notice that market makers have a bid/ask (offer) spread. So if you want to buy the 5875 call option you would pay 110 points or £1100 as a premium, but if you wanted to sell the option to the market maker you would receive 107 points or £1070.

Exhibit 11.11 FTSE 100 index option for January delivery options, £10 per index point

FTSE 100 INDEX OPTION (EUROPEAN-STYLE)
Codes and classification

| Code | ESX | Market | NYSE Liffe London | Vol. | 13,456 | 20/12/10 |
| Exercise type | European | Currency | £ | O.I. | 1,836,756 | 17/12/10 |

Underlying

Name	London FTSE 100	ISIN	GB0001383545	Market	LSE	
Currency	£					
Time	CET	Last	5,901.89 20/12/10 15:30	Last change %	0.51	
		High	5,913.83	Low	5,865.51	

January 2011 prices – 20/12/10

| | | | | | Calls | | | | | | | | | | Puts | | | | | |
Settl.	Day volume	Vol	Time (CET)	Last	Bid	Ask	AQ Bid	AQ Ask	C	Strike	P	AQ Bid	AQ Ask	Bid	Ask	Last	Time (CET)	Vol	Day volume	Settl.
124.50	–	–	–	–	140.00	142.50	139.50	143.50	C	5,825	P	60.50	64.00	61.00	63.50	77.50	09:23	21	21	85.00
109.50	63	5	12:05	124.00	123.00	126.00	123.00	127.00	C	5,850	P	69.00	72.50	69.50	71.50	71.00	12:05	5	40	95.00
95.50	3	3	11:27	97.00	107.00	110.00	107.00	111.00	C	5,875	P	77.50	81.00	78.50	80.50	97.00	09:59	10	10	106.00
82.50	51	1	13:34	100.00	92.50	95.00	92.50	96.00	C	5,900	P	88.00	91.50	88.50	91.00	89.00	13:52	1	28	118.00
70.50	12	9	12:56	80.50	79.00	81.50	78.50	82.00	C	5,925	P	98.50	102.50	100.00	102.00	102.00	12:56	9	12	131.00

Note: Settlement price is for the trading day 17/12/2010

Vol – (Volume) is the number of contracts traded in the most recent transaction.
Day's Volume – Number of trades that have taken place so far in the trading day. This figure updates as the day progresses and more trades take place.
% + /- Percentage price of last trade compared to yesterday's settlement price.
Settl – The previous day's settlement price.
O.I. – (Open Interest) is the outstanding long and short positions of the previous trading day updated in the morning each day

Note: The columns titled 'Bid' and 'Ask' (without the 'AQ') show the actual prices of the bid–offer spreads quoted by dealers. The four columns titled either 'AQ Bid' or 'AQ Ask' show the AutoQuote bid–offer spreads for both types of option (Calls and Puts). The NYSE Liffe web site provides a system ('AutoQuote', hence AQ) that **predicts** bid-offer spreads for those options. The AQ predicted bids and offers are frequently inaccurate. We need to concentrate on the Bid and Ask columns set by real market makers.

Source: http://www.euronext.com

First the investor has to calculate the number of option contracts needed to hedge the underlying. With the index at 5,902 on 20 December 2010 and each point of that index settled at £10, one contract has a value of 5,902 × £10 = £59,020. To cover an £1,175,000 portfolio (£1,175,000 ÷ £59,020 = 19.9) twenty contracts are needed (investors can trade in whole contracts only). The investor opts to buy 20 January 5,850 puts for 71.50 points per contract[7] – *see* Exhibit 11.11. The premium payable is:

71.50 points × £10 × 20 = £14,300

---

[7] This is not a **perfect hedge** as there is an element of the underlying risk without offsetting derivative cover.

This amounts to a 1.2 per cent 'insurance premium' (£14,300/£1,175,000) against a downturn in the market.

Consider what happens if the market does fall by a large amount, say 15 per cent, between 20 December and the third Friday in January (when the option matures). The index falls from 5,902 to 5,016, and the loss on the portfolio is

£1,175,000 × 0.15 = £176,250

If the portfolio is unhedged, the investor suffers from a market fall. However, in this case the put options gain in value as the index falls because they carry the right to sell at 5,850. If the investor closed the option position by buying at a level of 5,016, with the right to sell at 5,850, a 834-point difference, a gain is made :

Gain on options (5,850 − 5,016) × 20 × £10 =	£166,800
Less option premium paid	£14,300
	£152,500

A substantial proportion of the fall in portfolio value is compensated for through the use of the put derivative.

Aunt Agathas and options

Millions of ordinary small investors (Aunt Agathas in the City jargon) have their money applied to the derivatives markets even though they may remain blissfully unaware that such 'exotic' transactions are being conducted on their behalf. Take the case of equity-linked bonds. Investors nervous of investing in the stock market for fear of downward swings are promised a guarantee that they will receive at least the return of their original capital, even if the stock market falls. If it rises they will receive a return linked to the rise (say the capital gain element – excluding dividends). The bulk of the capital invested in these equity-linked bonds may be placed in safe fixed-interest investments, with the stock-market-linked return created through the use of options and other derivatives. Following derivative disasters there is always some discussion over the wisdom of using such highly geared instruments. However, the financial services industry easily defends itself by pointing out the risk-reducing possibilities of these products if properly managed.

A comparison of options, futures, forwards and FRAs

We have covered a great deal of ground in the field of derivatives. It is time to summarise the main advantages and disadvantages of the derivatives discussed so far – *see* **Exhibit 11.12.**

Spread betting

You can bet on the future movements of shares (and other securities) in a similar way to betting on horses. If the share moves the way you said it would, you gain. However, unlike with horses, if it moves against you the loss can be a multiple of the amount you first put down – you lose money for every 1p adverse movement in a share price. So, if you bet that Marks & Spencer's share price will rise, and you punt £10 for every penny rise, if M&S increases by 30p you win £300. However, if M&S falls 30p you have to hand over £300. This is the basic principle, but the actual operation is slightly more complicated. If you believe that the price is destined to rise you will contact (by telephone, or using the internet) one of the **spread betting** companies. They will quote you two prices (the **spread**), say, 348p–352p, for M&S. The first is called the **'bid' price** and is the relevant price if you are *selling*. The second is the **'offer' price** and is the relevant price if you are *buying*.

Exhibit 11.12	A comparison of options, futures, forwards and forward rate agreements

Options	Futures	Forwards and FRAs
Advantages		
Downside risk is limited but the buyer is able to participate in favourable movements in the underlying.	Can create certainty: specific rates are locked in.	Can create certainty: specific rates are locked in.
Available on or off exchanges. Exchange regulation and clearing house reduce counterparty default risk for those options traded on exchanges.	Exchange trading only. Exchange regulation and clearing house reduce counterparty default risk.	Tailor-made, off-exchange. Not standardised as to size, duration and terms. Good for companies with non-standard risk exposures.
	No premium is payable. (However margin payments are required.)	No margins or premiums payable.[8] (Occasionally a good faith performance margin is required by one or more parties in a forward. Also credit limits may be imposed.)
For many options there are highly liquid markets resulting in keen option premium pricing and ability to reverse a position quickly at low cost. For others trading is thin and so premiums payable may become distorted and offsetting transactions costly and difficult.	Very liquid markets. Able to reverse transactions quickly and cheaply.	
Disadvantages		
Premium payable reduces returns when market movements are advantageous.	No right to let the contract lapse. Benefits from favourable movements in underlying are forgone.	No right to let the contract lapse. Benefits from favourable movements in underlying are forgone.
	In a hedge position if the underlying transaction does not materialise the future position owner can experience a switch from a covered to an uncovered position, the potential loss is unlimited.	In a hedge position if the underlying transaction does not materialise the forward/FRA position owner can experience a switch from a covered to an uncovered position, the potential loss is unlimited.
Margin required when writing options.	Many exchange restrictions – on size of contract, duration (e.g. only certain months of the year), trading times (e.g. when NYSE Liffe is open).	Greater risk of counterparty default – not exchange traded therefore counterparty is not the clearing house. However, this may change for many OTC derivatives.
		Generally the minimum contract size is for millions rather than a few thousand (as on the futures or options markets).
	Margin calls require daily work for 'back office'.	More difficult to liquidate position (than with exchange-traded instruments) by creating an offsetting transaction that cancels position.

[8] Regulators around the world are currently moving toward insisting that over-the-counter derivatives be cleared through a formal system with a central counterparty (a clearing house) reducing risk for each participant. This will mean that margin payments will be required.

Given your optimism about M&S, the relevant price is 352p. You agree to bet £10 per 1p rise in the price. You 'buy' at 352p. Now imagine that you were correct and the spread on M&S moves to 375p–379p. You can close your position by telephoning the spread dealer and *'selling' to close*. The relevant price for you (betting on a rise) on the close is the lower of the two quoted: 375p. So you have made a gain of 23p (375p–352p), which translates into £230 given a bet of £10 per penny.

If you had been pessimistic about M&S when the spread quote was at 348p–352p you would have bet by 'selling' at 348p. A movement up to 375p–379p would result in a loss of 31p (379p –348p), £310 at £10 per penny. However, if the spread quote moves to 320p–324p the gain is 348p less 324p=24p (or £240 if you bet £10 per penny move).

You can see how the spread betting company can make money from the spread: you sell and buy at the least advantageous price on the spread. Presumably there are other investors doing the opposite, if you are 'buying' at 352p they are 'selling' at 348p. The spread betting company's books are balanced but a 4p gain is made.[9] The size of these spreads varies depending on volume of trade and degree of competition between spread betting firms, but they are larger than the market makers' spreads on the underlying shares.

Money up-front

The bookmaker (spread betting company) will require you to demonstrate that you are able to pay should the bet go against you. When you lay a bet you will be asked for a sum of money called the **notional trading requirement** or 'margin', or 'deposit'.[10] This will obviously be a larger sum if you are betting £10 per penny (point) rather than £5 per penny (point) movement in the underlying share (or index), or if the share (or index) is particularly volatile.

Furthermore, if the bet starts to go against you and the position is held open over a number of days you will be asked to top up the funds deposited with the spread betting company through margin calls. Naturally, these will be returned to you if there are moves in your favour.

Imagine you placed an 'up bet' on Vodafone when the spread quote is 103p–104p. You therefore 'buy' at 104p, betting £100 per penny movement. The maximum possible loss occurs when Vodafone goes to zero: 104p loss at £100 per penny is equal to £10,400. The spread betting company requires 10 per cent of this maximum loss (in this particular case), so you deposit £1,040.[11] If the Vodafone spread falls by 5p to 98p–99p the next day, your account will be debited £500 (5 × £100=£500). The spread betting company then asks you to top up your account by paying an additional margin of £500. For the next two weeks Vodafone oscillates greatly. On some days your account is credited, on others you are asked for more margin through 'cash calls'. After 14 days you close your position by telephoning the spread betting company and telling the dealer that you would like to sell Vodafone 'to close'. It is important to make it clear that you are not selling Vodafone 'to open' as that means a fresh separate bet on Vodafone falling.

The spread quoted is 108p–109p. You have gained £400 (sold at 108p and bought at 104p, i.e. a 4p rise at £100 per penny). This is a good return on an initial cash injection of £1,040 (plus a few cash calls during the two weeks). However, the potential risk of it all going wrong was also very high.

An alternative to betting and then being subject to a series of cash calls is to place a 'stop-loss' at the time of the bet. Under a stop-loss the spread betting company closes your position for you if the underlying share moves to the stated stop-loss price. At the time that you place the bet you hand over margin to the spread betting company equal to the maximum loss that could occur should the stop-loss be triggered. For example, if you make an up bet on Pearson when the spread quote is 780p–800p at £10 per penny and you set a stop-loss at 640p (i.e. 20 per cent below the bet level) the maximum loss if the stop-loss is triggered is 160 × £10=£1,600, so you will be asked to

---

[9] If the spread betting company's books are not balanced it may hedge its own position by using futures, or the cash market or contracts for difference (*see* below). They can also make money from lending money to traders.

[10] Some companies offer credit facilities – useful if you want to leave funds in a high interest account – but you will have to provide reassurance on the liquidity and amount of your funds.

[11] The notional trading requirement (margin) can be as low as 3 per cent for bets on a share index and 5 per cent for individual share bets, but is more usually 20 per cent. However, in the volatile market of 2009 margins of 40 per cent for small company shares were not unusual.

provide £1,600 of margin. This cash may already be in a special account opened when you registered with the spread betting company, or could be transferred by debit card over the telephone.

There are two types of stop-loss order. A 'standard' stop-loss is one where the company will *try* to close your position, but if the market is falling like a stone it may not be able to close it before the market price has zoomed past the stop-loss limit. With a 'guaranteed' ('controlled risk') stop-loss the spread betting company will close at the agreed stop-loss price even if the market price has moved beyond this before they were able to act. To have a guarantee you will have to pay a wider spread at the time that the bet is placed. A standard stop-loss does not require a wider spread.

Types of bet

There are three types of share or index bet. An intraday (cash or spot) bet is one that starts and is closed in the same trading day. A futures-based bet is one on the price of shares (index) on the next quarter day or the one after that (quarter days are in late March, June, September and December). So in the above Vodafone example the spread quotes would have been based on the future price for a Vodafone share on the next quarter day.[12] This price is made by the spread betting company but cannot deviate too far from prices in the market place (otherwise arbitrageurs will be given an invitation to make money risk-free by doing opposite transactions in the market and with spread betting companies).

Traditionally, futures-based betting was the way to spread a bet over a few days or weeks. However, spread betting companies have now introduced rolling cash spread betting (rolling daily bets). The spread better 'rolls' their position overnight to the next day.

Uses of spread betting

Spread betting can be used as a kind of insurance. For example, when you hold the underlying shares and you think it possible that the price will fall substantially in the short term, but a potential capital gains tax causes you to hesitate in selling the underlying shares, you could place a bet such that you gain if the share price falls. You will stabilise your position: if the share falls your portfolio declines but you win (an equal amount) on the bet; if the share rises you gain on the portfolio but lose on the bet. You can then select the time when you sell the shares – it might be good to wait a few months until the next tax year when you can use your annual capital gains tax allowance.

Spread betting can also be used to take highly leveraged positions where a small movement in the underlying leads to a large percentage gain on the amount initially committed to the bet – as in the Vodafone example.

Finally, spread betting allows you to gain from share (index) falls. You are restricted from shorting shares – selling shares you don't own in anticipation of closing your position by buying the same quantity at a lower price later – in the stock market, but spread betting makes this easy, at least for movements over a few months.

Further points

- In addition to spread betting on shares and share indices, you can spread-bet commodities, bonds, interest rates, currencies, futures, options, house prices and even the outcomes of sporting events.
- Most spread betting companies quote about 400 companies online, but will give you quotes on many more (smaller ones) if you phone.
- The spreads are at the discretion of the spread betting firm – when you ask for prices do not reveal whether you are a potential buyer or a seller.
- Even when the equity markets are closed spread bets can be made.

[12] If you want to roll over any quarterly contracts you need to contact the spread betting firm shortly before the expiry date to leave a rollover instruction. The company will close the current trade and then set up a new trade in the same underlying. You will have to pay a spread, but in arranged rollovers this is much less than normal (usually one-half).

Contracts for difference

Trading in contracts for difference (CFDs) is very similar to spread betting. However, with CFDs there is no settlement date – your open position can continue until you choose to close it (or it is closed for you because you have failed to provide margin).

In a CFD contract the buyer and seller agree to pay, in cash, at the closing of the contract, the difference between the opening and closing price of the underlying shares, multiplied by the number of shares in the contract.[13]

For example, imagine that you have a deposit account with a CFD broker. You have placed £20,000 in this account. You are pessimistic about Vodafone's shares and ask for a price quote from the broker.[14] She replies with: '102 bid and 103 offer.' You agree to sell CFDs for 160,000 shares in Vodafone at a price of 102p. Note that with the amount of cash you have (£20,000) you would not be able to purchase this many shares. It is because the CFD brokers permit trading on margins of around 10–20 per cent that you can leverage up the use of the £20,000. If we assume that the CFD broker requires 10 per cent as margin then just over £16,000 of the deposit money will now be held as margin (and not simply as a deposit), leaving you with just under £4,000 as *free equity*. It is good to have some free equity as you might have to meet margin calls if the price starts to move against you. If the shares now fall to 92 bid and 93 offer you will be showing a gain on your margin account of 102p – 93p = 9p per share, or £14,400. If you close your position your deposit account will then contain the original £20,000 plus £14,400.

On the other hand if Vodafone's share price moves to 113p–114p you lose and the CFD broker will require additional margin. If you close your position at this point your loss will be 114p – 102p = 12p per share or $0.12 \times 160{,}000 = £19{,}200$.

Additional points

- Some brokers quote a narrower spread, but then charge up to 0.25 per cent of the trade value on both the opening and closing transactions.

- Stop-losses can be set up, freeing you from monitoring the market every minute to avoid big losses, as your position is automatically closed if the market goes against you.

- When you sell a CFD as your opening position any dividend due during your period of ownership will be taken from your margin account. Those with a buy ('long') position will receive a payment equivalent to the net dividend.

- If you take a long position (buy) the CFD trader will charge you interest during the period of holding the CFD (typically LIBOR plus 2–3 per cent). If you are a long-term holder CFDs are expensive – buy the underlying. If you sell (go short), interest will be added to your account (typically 2–3 per cent below LIBOR).

- The right to vote at AGMs, etc. is usually not conferred to the CFD holder (although the CFD provider may facilitate the clients wishes, e.g. voting on a merger, in some cases).

- CFDs are available on most shares, right down to market capitalisations of £10 million.

- You must carefully monitor your position on a day-to-day basis if you do not have a stop-loss, as you may have to meet margin calls and/or close out positions.

Caps

An **interest rate cap** is a contract that gives the purchaser the right effectively to set a maximum level for interest rates payable. Compensation is paid to the purchaser of a cap if interest rates rise above an agreed level. This is a hedging technique used to cover interest rate risk on longer-term borrowing (usually 2–5 years). Under these arrangements a company borrowing money can benefit from interest rate falls but can place a limit to the amount paid in interest should interest rates rise.

---

[13] The underlying can also be an equity index, a commodity, bonds or exchange rates.
[14] A high proportion of CFD trade is now conducted online rather than over the telephone.

Worked example 11.1   Interest rate cap

Oakham plc wishes to borrow £20 million for five years. It arranges this with Bank A at a variable rate based on LIBOR plus 1.5 per cent. The interest rate is reset every quarter based on three-month LIBOR. Currently this stands at an annual rate of 3 per cent. The firm is concerned that over a five-year period the interest rate could rise to a dangerous extent.

Oakham buys an interest rate cap set at LIBOR of 4.5 per cent from Bank B. For the sake of argument we will assume that this costs 2.3 per cent of the principal amount, or £20m × 0.023 = £460,000 payable immediately to the cap seller. If over the subsequent five years LIBOR rises above 4.5 per cent in any three-month period Oakham will receive sufficient compensation from the cap seller to offset exactly any extra interest above 4.5 per cent. So if for the whole of the third year LIBOR rose to 5.5 per cent Oakham would pay interest at 5.5 per cent plus 1.5 per cent to bank A but would also receive 1 per cent compensation from the cap seller (a quarter every three months), thus capping the interest payable. If interest rates fall, Oakham benefits by paying Bank A less.

The premium (£460,000) payable up front covers the buyer for the entire five years, with no further payment due.

Caps are usually arranged for amounts of £5 million or more, but can be for underlyings of only $1 million – but when they are this low it may be difficult to obtain competing cost quotes from the banks. It is up to the client to select the strike rate and whether the rollover frequency (when LIBOR is compared with the strike) will be, say, three months or six months. They are available in all the main currencies.

The size of the cap premium[15] depends on the difference between current interest rates and the level at which the cap becomes effective; the length of time covered; and the expected volatility of interest rates. The cap seller does not need to assess the creditworthiness of the purchaser because it receives payment of the premium in advance. Thus, a cap is particularly suitable for highly geared firms, such as leveraged buyouts.

Floors and collars

Buyers of interest rate caps are sometimes keen to reduce the large cash payment at the outset. They can do this by simultaneously selling a floor, which results in a counterparty paying a premium. With a floor, if the interest rate falls below an agreed level, the seller (the floor writer) makes compensatory payments to the floor buyer. These payments are determined by the difference between the prevailing rates and the floor rate.

Returning to Oakham, the treasurer could buy a cap set at 4.5 per cent LIBOR for a premium of £460,000 and sell a floor at 2 per cent LIBOR receiving, say, £200,000. In any three-month period over the five-year life of the loan, if LIBOR rose above 4.5 per cent the cap seller would pay compensation to Oakham; if LIBOR fell below 2 per cent Oakham would save on the amount paid to Bank A but will have to make payments to the floor buyer, thus restricting the benefits from falls in LIBOR. Oakham, for a net premium of £260,000, has ensured that its effective interest payments will not diverge from the range 2 per cent + 1.5 per cent = 3.5 per cent at the lower end, to 4.5 per cent + 1.5 per cent = 6 per cent at the upper end.

The combination of selling a floor at a low strike rate and buying a cap at a higher strike rate is called a collar.

Exhibit 11.13 describes a cap for mortgage holders. (Trackers are mortgages that go up and down with bank base rates. SVR = the lender's standard variable rate, which is also a floating rate of interest.)

---

[15] The word 'premium' gives a clue as to the underlying nature of these instruments: they are a series of options for the buyer to decide at, say three-monthly, intervals whether to exercise the option to insist that the difference between the agreed fixed rate of interest and the current LIBOR will be paid over. Thus on each three-month roll-over day throughout the five years the cap holder will compare the strike on his cap (4.5 per cent for Oakham) with the three-month LIBOR fixing that morning (see Chapter 5) and exercise the cover if it makes sense to do so.

Exhibit 11.13

Homeowners offered tracker protection FT

Lucy Warwick-Ching

Wealthy homeowners could find it easier to hedge their loans against future interest rate rises following the launch of a new insurance product, designed for borrowers with larger mortgages.

John Charcol, the mortgage adviser, launched The Interest Rate Protector this week, an interest rate capping product backed by a high street bank, which protects residential and buy-to-let borrowers from rising rates.

While there are already a few products on the market designed to help borrowers protect themselves against rate jumps – including one from Marketguard and a product on offer by Savills Private Finance – mortgage brokers said the new deal would boost competition in the market and provide more protection for borrowers.

"While interest rates have been low for many months, there is only one way they can move, which is upwards," said Melanie Bien, director of mortgage broker Private Finance. "What nobody knows is when. With this uncertainty, it is understandable why those on cheap

tracker mortgages want to enjoy low rates for as long as possible, perhaps with some protection built in, in the form of a cap."

Charcol's product is aimed at borrowers who are not on fixed rate deals – who make up roughly 50 per cent of the market – and more specifically those on cheap lifetime trackers or SVRs.

The cost of buying the cap varies daily with market conditions. The minimum cover that can be purchased is £500,000 and the unit cost falls as the loan size increases. For example, a five-year cap for £500,000 of cover costs around of £17,500 for a cap at 3 per cent Bank of England base rate, £14,000 for a cap at 4 per cent and £12,000 for a cap at 5 per cent. Cover for a £1m mortgage would be around £30,000, £23,000 and £19,000 respectively.

If the bank rate rises above the chosen cap level, then Charcol makes monthly payments to cover the difference between that level and bank rate either until the end of the insured term or until the bank rate falls back below the chosen level.

"Unless you're the proud owner of a crystal ball, knowing what the future for interest rates looks like is all but impossible," says Ray Boulger at John Charcol. "Thus many borrowers face a challenging judgement call if they decide they want some protection. Those paying under 1 per cent – as some on the cheapest lifetime trackers are – would see their rate at least quadruple if they moved to a five or 10-year fixed rate."

The deal could also appeal to buy-to-let investors who are stuck on trackers and standard variable rate mortgages because of high gearing and/or inadequate rental income to meet lenders' current criteria.

But some brokers said that while the capped product gives protection, the fees are a lot to pay upfront. 'The concept is good and it is great to see innovation in this market," says David Hollingworth at London and Country Mortgages. "But the premium is quite high so it is unlikely to be an option for the mass market."

Source: Financial Times, 3/4 July 2010. Reprinted with permission.

Swaps

A swap is an exchange of cash payment obligations. An interest-rate swap is where one company arranges with a counterparty to exchange interest-rate payments. For example, the first company may be paying fixed-rate interest but prefers to pay floating rates. The second company may be paying floating rates of interest, which go up and down with LIBOR, but would benefit from a switch to a fixed obligation. Imagine that firm S has a £200m ten-year loan paying a fixed rate of interest of 8 per cent, and firm T has a £200 million ten-year loan on which interest is reset every six months with reference to LIBOR, at LIBOR plus 2 per cent. Under a swap arrangement S would agree to pay T's floating-rate interest on each due date over the next ten years, and T would be obligated to pay S's 8 per cent interest.

One motive for entering into a swap arrangement is to reduce or eliminate exposure to rises in interest rates. Over the short run, futures, options and FRAs could be used to hedge interest-rate exposure. However, for longer-term loans (more than two years) swaps are usually more suitable because they can run for the entire lifetime of the loan. So if a treasurer of a company with a large floating-rate loan forecasts that interest rates will rise over the next four years, they could arrange to swap interest payments with a fixed-rate interest payer for those four years.

Another reason for using swaps is to take advantage of market imperfections. Sometimes the interest-rate risk premium charged in the fixed-rate borrowing market differs from that in the floating-rate market for a particular borrower. See worked example 11.2.

Worked example 11.2   Swaps

Take the two companies, Cat plc and Dog plc, both of which want to borrow £150m for eight years. Cat would like to borrow on a fixed-rate basis because this would better match its asset position. Dog prefers to borrow at floating rates because of optimism about future interest-rate falls. The treasurers of each firm have obtained quotations from banks operating in the markets for both fixed- and floating-rate eight-year debt. Cat could obtain fixed-rate borrowing at 10 per cent and floating rate at LIBOR +2 per cent. Dog is able to borrow at 8 per cent fixed and LIBOR +1 per cent floating:

	Fixed	Floating
Cat can borrow at	10%	LIBOR + 2%
Dog can borrow at	8%	LIBOR + 1%

In the absence of a swap market Cat would probably borrow at 10 per cent and Dog would pay LIBOR + 1 per cent. However, with a swap arrangement both firms can achieve lower interest rates.

Notice that because of Dog's higher credit rating it can borrow at a lower rate than Cat in both the fixed- and the floating-rate market – it has an absolute advantage in both. However the risk premium charged in the two markets is not consistent. Cat has to pay an extra 1 per cent in the floating-rate market, but an extra 2 per cent in the fixed-rate market. Cat has an absolute disadvantage for both, but has a comparative advantage in the floating-rate market.

To achieve lower interest rates each firm should borrow in the market where it has comparative advantage and then swap interest obligations. So Cat borrows floating-rate funds, paying LIBOR +2 per cent, and Dog borrows fixed-rate debt, paying 8 per cent.

Then they agree to swap interest payments at rates which lead to benefits for both firms in terms of: (a) achieving the most appropriate interest pattern (fixed or floating), and (b) the interest rate that is payable, which is lower than if Cat had borrowed at fixed and Dog had borrowed at floating rates. *One* way of achieving this is to arrange the swap on the following basis:

- Cat pays to Dog fixed interest of 9.5 per cent;
- Dog pays to Cat LIBOR +2 per cent.

This is illustrated in **Exhibit 11.14.**

Exhibit 11.14   An interest rate swap

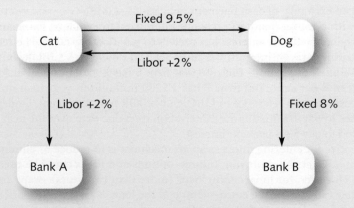

Now let us examine the position for each firm.

Cat pays LIBOR +2 per cent to a bank but also receives LIBOR +2 per cent from Dog and so these two cancel out. Cat also pays 9.5 per cent fixed to Dog. This is 50 basis points (0.5 per cent) lower than if Cat had borrowed at fixed rate directly from the bank. On £150m this is worth £750,000 per year.

Cat:
Pays	LIBOR +2%
Receives	LIBOR +2%
Pays	Fixed 9.5%
Net payment	Fixed 9.5%

Dog takes on the obligation of paying a bank fixed interest at 8 per cent while receiving 9.5 per cent fixed from Cat on the regular payment days. The net effect is 1.5 per cent receivable less the Libor +2 per cent payment to Cat – a floating-rate liability of Libor +0.5 per cent.

Dog:
Pays	Fixed 8%
Receives	Fixed 9.5%
Pays	LIBOR +2%
Net payment	LIBOR +0.5%

Again there is a saving of 50 basis points or £750,000 per year.[16] The net annual £1.5m saving is before transaction costs.

Prior to the widespread development of a highly liquid swap market each counterparty incurred considerable expense in making the contracts watertight. Even then, the risk of one of the counterparties failing to fulfil its obligations was a potential problem. Today intermediaries (for example, banks) take counterparty positions in swaps and this reduces risk and avoids the necessity for one corporation to search for another with a corresponding swap preference. The intermediary generally finds an opposite counterparty for the swap at a later date. Furthermore, standardised contracts reduce the time and effort needed to arrange a swap and have permitted the development of a thriving secondary market, and this has assisted liquidity. This more developed approach, with a bank intermediary offering rates to swap fixed to floating, or floating to fixed is illustrated in worked example 11.3.

Worked example 11.3   Swaps with an intermediary bank

Paris Expori, a French property developer, has agreed to buy and develop a shopping centre in the heart of England. It will need to borrow £80m to do this for a period of six years. The company treasurer has contacted a number of banks to enquire what they would charge if a term loan was granted by them. The quotes are for both floating (LIBOR related) rates and fixed rates. She has also looked into the possibilities of issuing a floating rate bond with the interest re-fixed to LIBOR at six-month intervals and the issuance of a fixed interest rate bond. She has concluded that all the fixed rates offered are excessively high – each quote is over 5.5 per cent. The best floating rate offer is a reasonable LIBOR +200 basis points, but the board of directors insist that, because the company already has too much exposure to a rise in interest rates, such a large loan should not add to the company's exposure.

The Treasurer's solution is to borrow £80m at floating rate and then contact one of banks offering swap rates to swap into a fixed rate. The date is 16 December 2010 and an idea of the swap rates available are shown in the *Financial Times* table displayed in Exhibit 11.15 – in reality you need to contact brokers and individual banks.

▶

---

[16] Under a swap arrangement the principal amount (in this case £150m) is usually never swapped and Cat retains the obligation to pay the principal to bank A. Neither of the banks is involved in the swap and may not be aware that it has taken place. The swap focuses entirely in the three-monthly or six-monthly interest payments.

Exhibit 11.15

INTEREST RATES – SWAPS   FT

Dec 16	Euro-€ Bid	Ask	£ Stlg Bid	Ask	SwFr Bid	Ask	US $ Bid	Ask	Yen Bid	Ask
1 year	1.39	1.44	0.97	1.00	0.30	0.36	0.53	0.56	0.33	0.39
2 year	1.73	1.78	1.60	1.64	0.56	0.64	0.93	0.96	0.40	0.46
3 year	2.07	2.12	2.04	2.08	0.88	0.96	1.42	1.45	0.47	0.53
4 year	2.38	2.43	2.42	2.47	1.20	1.28	1.92	1.95	0.56	0.62
5 year	2.65	2.70	2.75	2.80	1.48	1.56	2.38	2.41	0.67	0.73
6 year	2.86	2.91	3.03	3.08	1.71	1.79	2.76	2.79	0.81	0.87
7 year	3.04	3.09	3.26	3.31	1.90	1.98	3.07	3.10	0.95	1.01
8 year	3.18	3.23	3.46	3.51	2.05	2.13	3.31	3.34	1.08	1.14
9 year	3.30	3.35	3.61	3.66	2.18	2.26	3.51	3.54	1.21	1.27
10 year	3.40	3.45	3.74	3.79	2.28	2.36	3.67	3.70	1.32	1.38
12 year	3.58	3.63	3.91	3.98	2.43	2.53	3.90	3.93	1.52	1.60
15 year	3.75	3.80	4.07	4.16	2.55	2.65	4.11	4.14	1.75	1.83
20 year	3.80	3.85	4.12	4.25	2.54	2.64	4.26	4.29	1.97	2.05
25 year	3.71	3.76	4.12	4.25	2.48	2.58	4.33	4.36	2.04	2.12
30 year	3.59	3.64	4.08	4.21	2.43	2.53	4.36	4.39	2.06	2.14

Bid and ask rates as of close of London business. US $ is quoted annual money actual/360 basis against 3 month Libor. £ and Yen quoted on a semi-annual/365 basis against 6 month Libor. Euro/Swiss Franc quoted on annual bond 30/360 basis against 6 month Euribor/Libor with exception of the 1 year rate which is quoted against 3 month Euribor/Libor.

Source: ICAP plc.

Source: Financial Times, 17 December 2010. Reprinted with permission.

For this illustration we are most interested in the pound sterling columns (£ Stlg). Two prices are given for each contract period. The ask rate is the interest you would pay under the swap if you were to pay fixed rate and receive the LIBOR rate set for each of the six months over the term of the agreement with the bank doing swap. The bid rate is the fixed rate you would receive from the bank in return for you paying LIBOR to it. The banks in these markets expect to conclude numerous deals both paying fixed and receiving fixed rates, and they make a few basis points of profit between the two.

Paris Expori must ensure that any deal it makes with a bank in the swap market matches the underlying floating rate loan transaction it has concluded with another bank – e.g. length of time to maturity, dates of resetting interest rates ('rollover dates'). The deal it wants to make in the swap market is to pay fixed rate and receive floating rate. Looking along the six-year row we see that the fixed rate payable is 3.08 per cent per annum if Paris Expori is a top ranking company. However, it is not regarded as a counterparty as safe as one of these banks and so it will have to pay slightly more, say 3.15 per cent. This rate will be paid semi-annually – roughly one-half of 3.15 per cent for six months. In return Paris Expori will receive six-month LIBOR, which will be reset for each six-month period depending on market rates at the time.

Thus, on each of the six-monthly rollover dates the LIBOR rate of interest will be deducted from the agreed fixed rate of 3.15 and the difference paid by one party to the other. For example, if six months after the agreement starts LIBOR is set at 1.00 per cent (expressed as an annual rate) at the 11 a.m. London fixing, Paris Expori owes 3.15 per cent to the bank (which needs adjusting down for the six-month period) while the bank owes Paris Expori 1.00 per cent (halve that for the six months). Rather than make two payments, only the difference changes hands: 2.15 per cent (half that for six months) – *see* **Exhibit 11.16**.

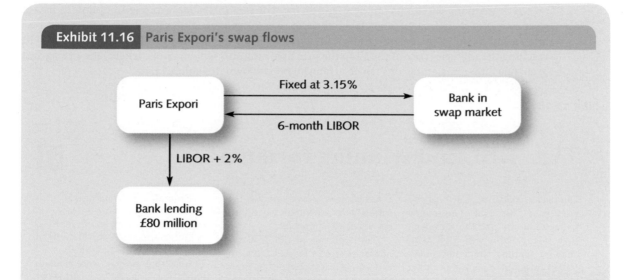

Exhibit 11.16 Paris Expori's swap flows

Paris Expori — Fixed at 3.15% → Bank in swap market

Bank in swap market — 6-month LIBOR → Paris Expori

Paris Expori → LIBOR + 2% → Bank lending £80 million

Paris Expori is now receiving LIBOR to offset the payment of LIBOR it makes to the bank that lent it £80 million. However, it has to pay 200 basis points more than this to the lending bank as well as the fixed rate of 3.15 per cent per annum, thus it has fixed its interest at 5.15 per cent for the six year life of the loan. This is better than the 5.5 per cent offered as a direct fixed rate loan to the company.

A practical use of a swap arrangement by an individual is shown in Exhibit 11.17. The mortgage holder starts by paying base rate plus 1 per cent to the mortgage company (5.5% + 1%) but agrees a swap whereby he pays 6.2 fixed rate and receives base rate.

Exhibit 11.17

Rate rise is music to the ears of 'swappers'

Unlike many home owners, those who have taken out interest rate swaps will be hoping that the Bank of England raises interest rates sooner rather than later.

One client of Stonehenge, which advises wealthy families, recently arranged an interest rate swap on his £5m mortgage for three years. Due to the size of the loan he had to take out a variable mortgage at a rate of 6.5 per cent. Convinced that interest rates will increase significantly over the next three years he was concerned that his variable rate left him vulnerable to the possibility of large and changeable repayments.

He decided to take out a swap, which effectively takes the cost of his mortgage to 7.2 per cent. This meant taking out a 3 year swap priced at 6.2 per cent, 0.7 of a percentage point above base rates of current base rates of 5.5 per cent.

If base rates go above his swap rate of 6.2 per cent, the bank will pay him the difference between his fixed rate and the interest rate, effectively insuring him against further interest rate hikes. If base rates stay below this level he pays out the difference.

The benefits come if the Bank of England raises rates higher. If rates rise to 6.5 per cent, say, his variable mortgage would jump to 7.5 per cent and each year he would need to pay £375,000. While rising interest rates will push up his variable rate, they will also push up the amount he receives back from his bank on his swap.

In this case he would get back the difference between his swap rate of 6.2 per cent and the interest rate of 6.5 per cent. He can then use this 0.3 per cent payment of 7.5 per cent, keeping his payments at a fixed rate of 7.2 per cent.

But by using an interest rate swap, he has ensured that his payments never exceed 7.2 per cent – or £360,000 per year.

Source: Elaine Moore, *Financial Times*, 30 June 2007, Money, p. 2. Reprinted with permission.

There are many variations on the swaps theme. For example, a swaption is an option to have a swap at a later date. In a currency swap the two parties exchange interest obligations (or receipts) and (usually) the principal amount for an agreed period, between two different currencies. On reaching the maturity date of the swap the principal amounts will be re-exchanged at a pre-agreed exchange rate. An example of such an arrangement is shown in **Exhibit 11.18**.

Exhibit 11.18

TVA, EIB find winning formula   FT

The back-to-back swap deal priced yesterday for the Tennessee Valley Authority and the European Investment Bank will give both cheaper funding than they could obtain through conventional bond issuance.

TVA, the US government-owned power utility, is issuing a 10-year DM1.5bn eurobond with a Frankfurt listing, while EIB is raising $1bn with a 10-year issue in the US market. The issuers will swap the proceeds.

Speaking in London yesterday, the treasurers of both organisations said the arrangement – now relatively unusual in the swaps market – had allowed them to reduce borrowing costs, although they did not specify by what amount.

Two elements of the deal were important in this respect. First, the EIB has a much stronger comparative advantage over TVA in funding in dollars than it does in D-Marks. Lehman Brothers, co-bookrunner on both deals, said the EIB priced its 10-year dollar paper at 17 basis points over Treasuries, about 6 to 7 points lower than TVA could have done.

In the German market EIB enjoys a smaller advantage; it could raise funds at about 4 basis points less than the 17 points over bonds achieved by TVA.

Second, by swapping the proceeds on a back-to-back basis rather than through counterparties, bid/offer spreads were eliminated and transaction costs reduced.

Resulting savings were pooled, providing benefits for both borrowers.

Both also diversified their funding sources. Lehman said some 65 per cent of the TVA bonds were placed in Europe, 20 per cent in Asia, and 15 per cent in the US. About half the EIB issue was placed in the US, 35 per cent in Europe, and 15 per cent in Asia.

Source: Richard Lapper, Capital Markets Editor, *Financial Times*, 12 September 1996. Reprinted with permission.

Banks have been accused of confusing clients in swap deals, resulting in large perceived losses and court cases – *see* **Exhibit 11.19**

Exhibit 11.19

Milan swaps case puts banks in the hot seat   FT

Vincent Boland

If any European country was going to be a test bed for the raging global debate on the use of complex derivatives, it was Italy.

Not only is the country, at the sovereign level, one of the eurozone's most indebted nations (with a debt-to-GDP ratio that the Italian finance ministry estimates will be 116.9 per cent this year) it also has heavily indebted local authorities, where the ticking time bombs are really located.

This week one of those time bombs erupted. A judge in Milan on Wednesday levelled charges of fraud against four international banks – Deutsche Bank, Germany's Depfa, UBS, and JPMorgan – and ordered 11 bankers and two former municipal employees to stand trial for their roles in a complex and controversial €1.7bn ($2.3bn) bond issue that the city claims has hurt it financially.

Alfredo Robledo, the Milan chief prosecutor, sounded almost tentative in his summing up of the seriousness of the case against the banks when the judge's ruling was issued.

"It is [at] a delicate stage," he said of the investigation process he has been spearheading for the past three years into the circumstances of the bond issue and an accompanying swaps transaction that is at the centre of the fraud allegations.

It suggests a level of defiance, or brinkmanship, among all the parties involved: on the part of the city,

Exhibit 11.19 continued

that its accusation that it has been hurt to the tune of at least €56m, and possibly more, can be proven; and on the part of the banks that no fraud was committed and that the case is baseless.

The four banks insisted on Wednesday that their employees did nothing wrong. JPMorgan said they acted "with the highest degree of professionalism and entirely appropriately", a sentiment echoed by the others.

The two former municipal officials are Giorgio Porta, a former general manager of the office of the mayor of Milan, and Mauro Mauri, a financial adviser to the city. Both men deny any wrong-doing. Gabriele Albertini, the former Milan mayor who was in office when the bond issue was launched, says he has "the highest trust" in the two men. He also defends the decision to restructure the city's debt profile, of which the bond issue and the

swaps agreement that accompanied it were part, arguing that it saved the city €198m over four years.

The transaction, on the face of it, was a fairly straightforward one. The city hired the four banks to underwrite a €1.7bn issue of 30-year bonds at a fixed rate of interest. Simultaneously, it entered into a swaps agreement with the banks that enabled it to exchange the fixed rate for a floating rate, in the belief that it would be able to take advantage of falling interest rates over a period of time.

Eurozone interest rates went against the city almost from the start. When it issued the bonds the European Central Bank's variable rate tender interest rate was 2 per cent. It climbed to 4 per cent by the middle of 2007, around the time that Mr Robledo began his investigation, and is now 4.25 per cent.

There are two main charges against the banks and the indi-

viduals. The first is that the banks misrepresented to the city the financial benefits of the debt restructuring exercise, of which the bond issue and the swaps agreement were part.

The second is that the banks were not transparent in explaining the terms and conditions of the swaps agreement, and that the city incurred €56m of hidden costs as a result of it, on top of the fees – which by some estimates are around €50m – the city paid for the deal.

Other Italian municipalities are watching the Milan case closely because they, too, are sitting on possible derivatives time bombs.

The Bank of Italy estimates that local authorities may be exposed to about €1bn of losses on these derivatives contracts.

Source: Financial Times, 19 March 2010, p. 35. Reprinted with permission.

The relationship between FRAs and swaps

If a corporation buys (or sells) a sequence of LIBOR-based FRAs stretching over, say, two years, in which each of the three-month periods making up that two years is covered by an FRA then we have an arrangement similar to a two-year swap. The company has made a series of commitments to pay or receive differences between the FRA agreed rate and the prevailing spot rate at three-month intervals. For example, Colston plc has a loan for £100 million. This is a floating-rate liability. Interest is set at three-month LIBOR every three months over its two-year life. So, every three months, whatever the rate that London banks are charging for three-month loans to each other is to be charged to Colston.

Thus the company is vulnerable to interest rate rises. The current time is June 20x1 and spot LIBOR rate is set at 5.09 per cent. This is the annualised rate that Colston will pay for the next three months (it will pay one-quarter of this for three-month borrowing). To lock in a rate for the next rollover date, i.e. in September, the company could buy (in June) an FRA set at LIBOR for the three months starting in September and ending in December (a 3 × 6 forward rate agreement). This FRA is priced at 5.71 per cent. The amount covered can be exactly £100 million because FRA arrangements are flexible to suit the client, being an over-the-counter market. The £100 million is known as the notional amount.

The FRA buyer (Colston) has technically agreed to deliver to the FRA seller 5.71 per cent (*see* **Exhibit 11.20**). In return the FRA seller will pay Colston whatever is the spot rate for LIBOR in September. Of course, it would be inefficient to have these two payments made when only one payment (the difference between the two rates) is needed. So, if LIBOR is 5.71 per cent in September no payment is made by either side. However, if LIBOR in September resets at 6.2 per cent Colston will receive a settlement cash flow of 0.49 per cent, or 49 basis points, on £100 million for the three-month period. Thus a payment of £122,500 is received (£100m × 0.0049 × 3/12) from the FRA seller.[17]

---

[17] This is the amount payable in December for the September FRA. If the agreement is for payment to be made in September the amount will be reduced (discounted) at the annualised rate of 6.2 per cent.

Exhibit 11.20   FRA arrangements

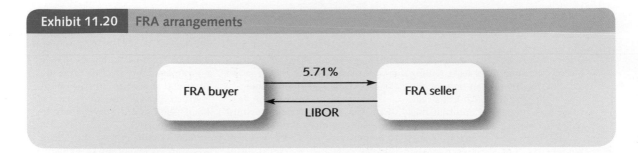

If, however, the spot LIBOR in September is 5.5 per cent, Colston will pay a settlement cash flow of 21 basis points: £100m × 0.0021 × 3/12=£52,500.

FRAs are priced at-the-money, i.e. the current rate in the market for future LIBOR. In the case of Colston in June this is 5.71 per cent for September three-month FRA. The participants in this market consider that the market rate has zero initial value to both parties. However, as rates change the contract gains value for one or other of the contractors.

Colston has locked in the interest rate it will pay for the three months September to December, but what about the other months of the two-year loan commitment? It could enter a series of FRAs for each of the remaining rollover dates. The rates that would be set are shown in Exhibit 11.21.

Exhibit 11.21   FRA prices for the next two years

Time	Libor rate quoted in June 20x1 for three-month periods starting at various dates over next two years
June 20x1 (Spot)	5.09
Sept. 20x1	5.71
Dec. 20x1	6.05
Mar. 20x2	6.42
June 20x2	6.70
Sept. 20x2	6.98
Dec. 20x2	7.06
Mar. 20x3	7.18

By executing seven FRAs at these rates Colston would pay its lender 5.09 per cent (annualised rate) for the first three months. Thereafter, regardless of how LIBOR moves the effective cost of the loan is 5.71 per cent for the second three months, 6.05 per cent for the third, and so on. Each one of these FRA deals is like a mini swap, with Colston committed to delivering the rate shown in the exhibit and the FRA seller committed to delivering LIBOR to Colston. Or, rather, net payments on the difference between the FRA rate and LIBOR are made. Exhibit 11.22 illustrates for the first four payments.

Using FRAs in this way Colston knows how much it has to pay out over the next two years and so is not vulnerable to unexpected changes in LIBOR. But note that the interest rates are different from one three-month period to another. An alternative open to Colston is to buy a contract with the same rate payable in each of the eight quarters. This rate would be an approximate average of the FRA rates stretching over the two years. This is called a swap. A rough average of the eight LIBOR rates payable in Exhibit 11.21 is 6.39 per cent. The interest rate swap arrangement is

Exhibit 11.22

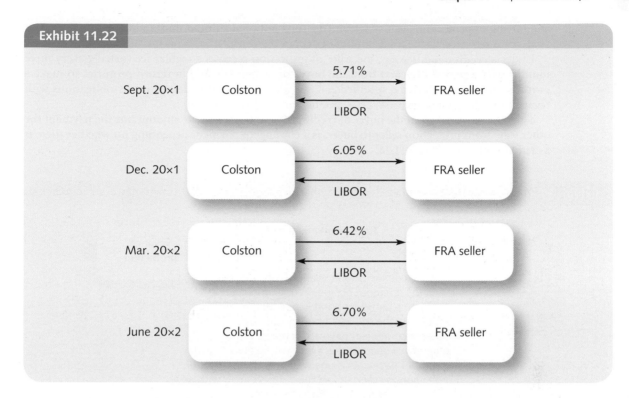

shown in **Exhibit 11.23**. For each three-month period Colston pays the counterparty the swap rate (6.39 per cent) and receives LIBOR. If interest rates rise above 6.39 per cent Colston would benefit from the swap arrangement because it receives payments from the swap counterparty, which amount to the difference between 6.39 per cent and LIBOR. This enables Colston to accept any increase in LIBOR with equanimity, as the effective cost of the loan is constant at 6.39 per cent (plus 200 bp) regardless of how much is paid to the lender.

Exhibit 11.23   Colston's payouts and receipts under a swap

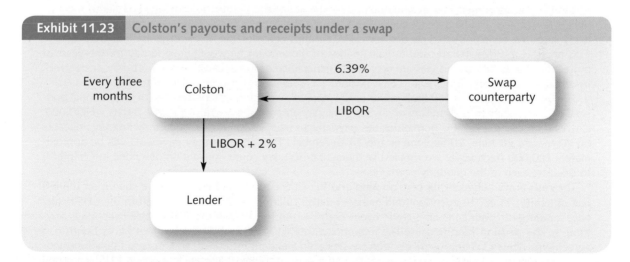

Credit default swap (CDS)

Until the early 1990s once a lender to a company had assumed the risk of loss through default or a similar 'credit event' (failure of the borrower to abide by the agreement) there was little that they could do except wait to see if the borrower paid all the interest and principal on time, as agreed at the outset. In other words, the lender retained all the credit risk and could not pass any of it on to others more willing to bear it. Today, however, we have an enormous market in the selling and buying of protection against default (the total notional amount outstanding on credit default swap contracts exceeds the total amount of debt in the world!).

Under a credit default swap, the seller of protection receives a regular fee (usually every three months over a period of years) from the buyer of protection, and in return promises to make a payoff should the underlying specified reference entity (e.g. BP) default on its obligations with regard to a reference obligation, i.e. a specific bond or loan.

Thus the payment from the buyer of credit protection is a regular amount but the payment the other way, from protection seller to buyer, is a contingent payment depending on whether there is a credit event – *see* Exhibit 11.24.

Exhibit 11.24

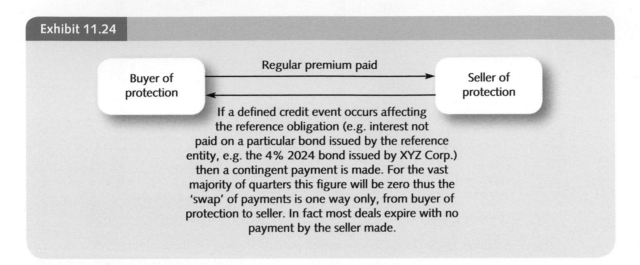

Worked example 11.4   **Credit default swap**

A pension fund manager has bought £20 million (nominal value) of bonds from a software company, Appsoft. He is concerned that at some point over the life of the bonds the company will fail to meet its obligations – there will be a credit event. Even though this is unlikely the manager needs to make absolutely sure that he is protected on the downside. He thus consults one of the organisations that provide CDS prices (e.g. www.markit.com) to gain an idea of the amount he would have to pay for the years of protection. The prices on this website only give a general indication because they report only deals struck by one dealer sometime the previous day. To obtain a more precise cost he will need to contact dealers.

The quote he is given is 160 basis points as the 'spread' expressed as a percentage of the notional principal per year. Thus for £20 million of cover he will pay an annual amount of £20m × 0.016 = £320,000. However, in this market it is normal for this payment to be split up into four quarterly amounts payable on 20 March, 20 June, 20 September and 20 December. Thus the quarterly payments will be approximately £80,000 (technically we should use the actual/360 day count convention described in Chapter 5 to calculate each of the quarterly payments).

The cash flows between the pension fund and the CDS dealer (market maker) are shown on the left half of Exhibit 11.25. The pension fund manager makes quarterly payments and in return the CDS dealer pays an amount contingent on a credit event occurring. In most cases the CDS dealer never pays anything to the pension fund because the reference entity (Appsoft in this case) abides by its bond/loan agreements. Thus CDS arrangements are very similar to standard insurance, and, in fact, many insurance companies have entered this market as protection sellers. The major difference between CDS protection and standard insurance is that with insurance you have to own the asset and suffer the loss to receive a payout.[18] With a CDS you can buy the 'protection' and receive a payout from the dealer regardless of

---

[18] To take out insurance you have to have an insurable interest (the insured party can suffer a loss if the asset is damaged etc). This was introduced to prevent the phenomenon of people insuring an asset or another person and then destroying/murdering.

whether you own the asset. So another fund may never own bonds in Appsoft, but can speculate in the CDS market; for example, make regular quarterly payments to the dealer in the hope that Appsoft commits a default and the dealer is forced to make a large payout.

The right side of Exhibit 11.25 shows the payments between the dealer and a hedge fund manager who will take on the credit event risk in return for a quarterly payment. Thus the dealer ends up both buying protection and selling protection. But notice that he has made a margin between the two. Protection is sold for 160 basis points and bought for 155 basis points.

Exhibit 11.25   Credit default swap arrangement: five-year Appsoft with 155/160 bid/offer

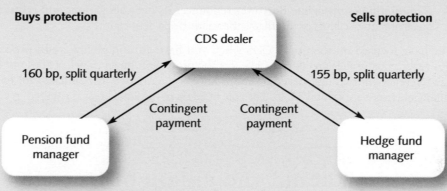

Reference entity: Appsoft
Reference obligation: 7% 2020 subordinated bonds
Calculation amount: £20 million

Settlement and credit events

Most CDSs are physically settled which means that when a credit event occurs the protection buyer will deliver debt assets of the reference entity to the protection seller. In return the protection seller pays their par value (£20 million in the case Appsoft). The bonds or loans delivered do not have to be the specified reference obligation, but they cannot be subordinated (higher risk) to it – Appsoft might have issued some other bonds which the pension fund manager chooses to deliver instead of the bond acting as the reference obligation. Once the settlement process is triggered the CDS quarterly premiums paid by the protection buyer cease.

A minority of CDSs are cash settled, that is a credit event triggers a cash payment. To figure out how much is to be paid we first need to find the recovery value on the debt, that is the current market value of the instrument now that it has defaulted. A default does not usually result in the debt becoming completely worthless; a typical recovery rate on a defaulted bond is around 40 per cent of its par value, but this varies tremendously. For some defaulted bonds there may be an active secondary market which will fix the current price, for others it is necessary to conduct an auction process in which dealers submit prices at which they would buy and sell the reference entity's debt obligations. In the case of Lehman Brothers October 2008 auction, the price was set at 8.625 through billions of dollars worth of actual trades, which means that dealers were still willing to pay 8.625 per cent of the par value of Lehman's bonds to hold them even though they were in default. The protection sellers therefore had to make up the remainder of the par value as a cash payment to the CDS holders, i.e. 91.375 per cent of the par value was paid out. When Metro-Goldwyn-Mayer defaulted in 2009 the bonds were valued at 58.5 per cent of par and so 41.5 per cent was paid out.

So far we have skipped over what we mean by a credit event. The following are the main categories:

- *Insolvency of the entity.*
- *Failure to pay* Principal and/or interest not paid.
- *Debt restructuring* When companies have difficulty paying their debt they negotiate with their lenders to vary the terms of their debt in their favour, e.g. an extension of maturity, interest deferral, principal forgiveness, swapping debt for shares in the firm, resulting in a poorer deal for the lenders. These restructurings are often defined as defaults, but some CDS agreements specifically exclude this type of event due to the lack of clarity on whether a particular restructuring is really a default.
- *Obligation acceleration* At least one obligation under the debt deal has become payable before its normal maturity date – this may be due to the reference entity defaulting on another debt triggering an early payment.
- *Repudiation/moratorium* Borrower renounces its debt obligations and refuses to pay, e.g. a government disclaims or disaffirms the validity of a debt claim.

We have focused on the use of CDS when you have an underlying credit exposure to hedge. However, most trades are 'naked CDS', i.e. the protection buyer or seller does not hold a debt in the reference entity. These naked positions have been criticised by politicians for exacerbating the financial crisis – *see* **Exhibit 11.26**. The role of CDSs in the 2008 crisis is covered in Chapter 16.

Exhibit 11.26

Naked truth about the villain of Europe   FT

Sophia Grene

Credit default swaps are the scapegoat du jour of politicos looking to blame evil capitalists for recent economic disasters.

They do make a good scapegoat – hard to understand, lacking transparency, seemingly motivated (on the part at least of naked CDS traders) by a desire to profit by others' misfortune.

And talk of large amounts of money – trillions of notional dollars – can be bandied about, which is always impressive.

A credit default swap is an agreement between two parties: one promises a stream of payments to the other, in return for which, the second party will pay out the value of an underlying credit if the credit's original issuer defaults.

This sounds like a fairly straightforward insurance contract – but because it is a swap, it is not technically insurance and therefore there is no requirement for the buyer of the CDS to own the underlying credit or have "insurable interest" in such a credit.

This is what is known as a "naked CDS" and politicians in Europe are currently suggesting such trades should be banned, claiming they exacerbated Greece's recent financial crisis.

But not all users of CDS are hedge funds or investment banks trying to push on-the-edge companies or countries over the cliff. Some would even question whether those malevolent players exist.

"I don't get the impression that any hedge fund is big enough or bad enough to bully a company or economy into default," says Thomas Ross, who manages credit funds for Henderson Global Investors.

And Luke Spajic, head of pan-European credit and asset backed securities portfolio management at Pimco, adds: "It's not like investors pick on healthy companies or economies."

So why might an asset manager use a naked CDS? A simple example might be a bond fund manager who owns a number of corporate credits in the widget-making sector.

If a major widget-maker were to default, the value of the fund's investments would fall, even if it did not hold any of that company's paper.

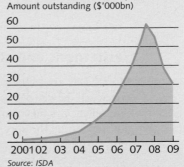

Global credit default swaps
Amount outstanding ($'000bn)

Source: ISDA

In order to hedge against such a risk, it might take out a CDS on the widget maker at risk of defaulting.

Given that the CDS are often more liquid than the bonds they refer to, many asset managers use them, rather than the underlying bonds, to gain exposure to a particular credit or to hedge a risk they do not want in the portfolio.

"We were pretty early adopters of CDS," says Mitesh Shah, deputy head of fixed income at Henderson. "On our central dealing desk, it's now about two-thirds CDS, one third physical."

▶

Exhibit 11.26 continued

Working with CDS rather than bonds requires a great deal of attention to processing these contracts, which are still all over-the-counter rather than exchange traded, as well as a focus on risk management, but the efficiencies are worth it, he says.

The fact that CDS are not traded on exchange, or even (yet) through any central clearing houses, makes it hard to get a handle on the value of CDS outstanding. It also means that there is no single source of data.

To complicate matters, brokers writing CDS will usually lay off the risk by taking on an opposite contract elsewhere, so in many cases notional volumes include contrasts that could be offset.

While the total of outstanding notional CDS contracts was $31,220bn (£20,768bn, €22,846bn) in the middle of 2009, the net was just $393bn of protection bought.

Many commentators are calling for CDS to be traded on exchange, making it easier to see at a glance what is going on in the currently murky market. That is a long way off for the moment.

A more realistic aim is to standardise most contracts and make sure they are traded through central clearing houses.

This would have the advantage not only of greater transparency but also limit the counterparty risk inherent in a swap contract, since the clearing house would bear the risk in case either side of a contract goes bust.

Bringing CDS on exchange or standardising the contracts is a long way short of banning naked CDS, though. While there is general support in the asset management community for the former, which would improve liquidity and trans-

parency, nobody seems to think banning naked CDS trades would be helpful.

Although it might have some of the intended consequences, by damping rapid increases in spreads (the premium paid for insuring against the default of a credit likely to go bust), this would be offset by problems elsewhere.

"It might move volatility out of the credit affected – but it would probably increase the correlation with other asset classes," says Mr Spajic.

"It might prevent the wide speculative moves we've seen [in CDS spreads], but it would accelerate the pace of dumping cash bonds. It would be just like the old days before CDS"

Source: Financial Times, 15 March 2010, p. 3. Reprinted with permission.

Concluding comments

In the hands of the ill-informed and the reckless derivatives can be very dangerous financial instruments. This was proved with a vengeance by the banking sector in 2008 when it became apparent that many people were given power to gain derivative exposure without anyone in the organisation really understanding the nature of the risks they were taking on. They had seen other bankers gain large bonuses and wanted some of the action for themselves, whether or not they understood the potential for things to go wrong. And after all, the mathematicians in the bank said that their models told them that it was very unlikely there would be a serious problem. They had collected data for the prior three years or so and the statistics showed that rarely does the market move so dramatically that a serious loss is incurred. The data said that hardly anyone defaults on sub-prime mortgages, for example. The problem is that mathematicians usually lack the wider and longer-term perspective of someone who has studied financial markets and really understands the nature of the risks when humans are involved.

Hopefully, this chapter has helped you down the road of knowledge, so that you will not repeat the mistakes of others.

Key points and concepts

- **An option** is a contract giving one party the right, but not the obligation, to buy (call option) or sell (put option) a financial instrument, commodity or some other underlying asset, at a given price, at or before a specified date.

- The **writer of a call option** is obligated to sell the agreed quantity of the underlying at some time in the future at the insistence of the option purchaser (holder). A **writer of a put** is obligated to buy.

- **American-style options** can be exercised at any time up to the expiry date whereas **European-style options** can only be exercised on a predetermined future date.

▶

- **Intrinsic value** on an option: the payoff that would be received if the underlying is at its current level when the option expires.

- An **out-of-the-money option** is one that has no intrinsic value.

- An **in-the-money option** has intrinsic value.

- **Time value** arises because of the potential for the market price of the underlying, over the time to expiry of the option, to change in a way that creates intrinsic value.

- **Share options** can be used for hedging or speculating on shares.

- **Index options** whose underlying is a share index are cash settled.

- With a **spread betting up-bet on a share** the hedger or speculator agrees to a payoff of an amount (say £10) for every one pence rise in the share price of a particular company. If it should decline the hedger or speculator pays the spread betting company the same amount for every pence fall. Similar arrangements are available for commodities, bonds, interest rates, currencies, futures, options, house prices and the outcomes of sporting events. A down-bet gains if values fall.

- With a **contract for difference, CFD,** the buyer and seller agree to pay, in cash, at the closing of the contract, the difference between the opening and closing price of the underlying shares or other underlying, multiplied by the number of shares (or other underlying) in the contract.

- An **interest rate cap** is a contract that gives the purchaser the right effectively to set a maximum level for interest rates payable. Compensation is paid to the purchaser of a cap if interest rates rise above an agreed level.

- With an **interest rate floor**, if the interest rate falls below an agreed level, the seller (the **floor writer**) makes compensatory payments to the floor buyer.

- The combination of selling a floor at a low strike rate and buying a cap at a higher strike rate is called a **collar.**

- A **swap** is an exchange of cash payment obligations. An **interest-rate swap** is where one company arranges with a counterparty to exchange interest-rate payments.

- **Motives for entering into a swap arrangement**: (a) to reduce or eliminate exposure to rises in interest rates; (b) to take advantage of market imperfections in the fixed and floating rate bond/loan markets.

- **Intermediaries** (for example, banks) **take counterparty positions in swaps** and this reduces risk and avoids the necessity for one corporation to search for another with a corresponding swap preference.

- A **swaption** is an option to have a swap at a later date.

- In a **currency swap** the two parties exchange interest obligations (or receipts) and (usually) the principal amount for an agreed period, between two different currencies. On reaching the maturity date of the swap the principal amounts will be re-exchanged at a pre-agreed exchange rate.

- Under a **credit default swap, CDS,** the seller of protection receives a regular fee from the buyer of protection, and in return promises to make a payoff should the underlying specified **reference entity** default on its obligations with regard to a **reference obligation.**

- Most CDSs are **physically settled:** when a credit event occurs the protection buyer will deliver debt assets of the reference entity to the protection seller in return for the cash payout.

- A minority of CDSs are **cash settled**: the recovery value on the debt is found and the protection seller pays the difference between that and the par value of the reference obligation.

Appendix 11.1 Option pricing

This appendix describes the factors that influence the market value of a call option on a share. The principles apply to the pricing of other options. The complex mathematics associated with option pricing will be avoided because of their unsuitability for an introductory text. Interested readers are referred to the references and further reading list later in this chapter.

Notation to be used:

C = value of call option
S = current market price of share
X = future exercise price
r_f = risk-free interest rate (per annum)
t = time to expiry (in years)
s = standard deviation of the share price
e = mathematical fixed constant: 2.718 . . .

The factors affecting option value

1 *Options have a minimum value of zero*

   $C \geq 0$

   Even if the share price falls significantly below the exercise price of the option the worst that can happen to the option holder is that the option becomes worth nothing – no further loss is created.

2 *The market value of an option will be greater than the intrinsic value at any time prior to expiry*
   This is because there is a chance that if the option is not exercised immediately it will become more valuable due to the movement of the underlying – it will become (or will move deeper) in-the-money. *An option has time value* that increases, the longer the time to expiry.

   Market value = Intrinsic value + Time value

3 *Intrinsic value (S − X) rises as share price increases or exercise price falls* However this simple relationship needs to be made a little more sophisticated because S − X is based on the assumption of immediate exercise when the option is about to expire. However if the option is not about to expire there is some value in not having to pay the exercise price until the future exercise date. (Instead of buying the share a call option could be purchased and the remainder invested in a risk-free asset until the exercise date.) So intrinsic value is given a boost by discounting the exercise price by the risk-free rate of return:

   $$\text{Intrinsic value} = S - \frac{X}{\left(1+r_f\right)^t}$$

4 *The higher the risk-free rate of return the higher will be intrinsic value,* because the money saved by buying an option rather than the underlying security can be invested in a riskless rate of return until the option expires.

5 *The maximum value of an option is the price of the share*

   $C \leq S$

6 *A major influence boosting the time value is the volatility of the underlying share price* A share which has a stable, placid history is less likely to have a significant upward shift in value during the option's lifetime than one which has been highly variable. In option pricing models this factor is measured by the variance (σ^2) or standard deviation (σ) of the share price.

Black and Scholes' option pricing model

Black and Scholes' option pricing model (BSOPM) was published in 1973 and is still widely employed today despite the more recent modifications to the original model and the development of different option-pricing models. The BSOPM is as follows:

$$C = SN(d_1) - Xe^{-r_f t}N(d_2)$$

where:

N(.) = cumulative normal distribution function of d_1 and d_2

$$d_1 = \frac{\ln(S/X) + \left(r_f + \sigma^2/2\right)t}{\sigma\sqrt{t}}$$

In = natural log

$$d_2 = d_1 - \sigma\sqrt{t}$$

References and further reading

Andersen, T. J. (2006) *Global Derivatives: A Strategic Management Perspective.* Harlow: FT Prentice Hall.
    Describes the use of derivatives from a corporate perspective. Easy to read and takes the reader from an introductory level to an intermediate level.

Baltazar, M. (2008) *The Beginner's Guide to Financial Spread Betting*, 2nd edn. Petersfield: Harriman House.
    A simple introductory guide.

Bank of England Quarterly Bulletins.
    An important and easily digestible source of up-to-date information.

Black, F. and Scholes, M. (1973) 'The pricing of options and corporate liabilities', *Journal of Political Economy*, May/June, pp. 637–659.
    The first useful option pricing model – complex mathematics.

Chisholm, A. M. (2009) *An Introduction to International Capital Markets*, 2nd edn. Chichester: John Wiley.
    Deals with a number of more technical aspects clearly

Choudhry, M., Joannas, D., Landuyt, G., Periera, R. and Pienaar, R. (2010) *Capital Market Instruments: Analysis and Valuation*, 3rd edn. Basingstoke: Palgrave Macmillan.
    A textbook-style book written by practitioners. Some basic material but mostly higher level with plenty of mathematics.

The Economist
    Valuable reading for anyone interested in finance (and world affairs, politics, economics, science etc.)

Financial Times
    An important source for understanding the latest developments in this dynamic market.

Headley, J. S. and Tufano, P. (2001) 'Why manage risk?' Harvard Business School Note. Available from Harvard Business Online.
    A short, easy-to-read description of why companies hedge risk.

Hull, J. C. (2010) *Fundamentals of Futures and Options Markets*, 7th edn. Harlow: Pearson Education.
    A relatively easy-to-follow description but also contains some high level material.

McDonald, R. L. (2006) *Derivatives Markets*, 2nd edn. Harlow: Pearson/Addison Wesley.
    A more technical/theoretical approach. US focused.

Miller, M. H. (1997) *Merton Miller on Derivatives.* New York: Wiley.
    An accessible (no maths) account of the advantages and disadvantages of derivatives to companies, society and the financial system.

Taylor, F. (2011) *Mastering Derivatives Markets*, 4th edn. London: FT Prentice Hall.
    A good introduction to derivative instruments and markets.

Vaitilingam, R. (2011) *The Financial Times Guide to Using the Financial Pages*, 6th edn. London: FT Prentice Hall.
    Explains the tables displayed by the *Financial Times* and provides some background about the instruments – for the beginner.

Websites

ADVFN www.advfn.com
CNN Financial News www.money.cnn.com
Prices on LIFFE www.nyxdata.com
Bloomberg www.bloomberg.com
CME group www.cmegroup.com
Reuters www.reuters.com
Wall Street Journal www.wsj.com
Financial Times www.ft.com
Futures and Options World www.fow.com
London International Financial Futures and Options Exchange (NYSE Liffe) www.euronext.com
Chicago Board Options Exchange www.cboe.com
Intercontinental Exchange www.theice.com
Eurex, the European Derivative Exchange www.eurexchange.com
International Swaps and Derivatives Association www.isda.org
Futures Industry Association http://www.futuresindustry.org/
Markit Financial Information Services www.markit.com

Video presentations

Chief executives and other senior people describe and discuss policy and other aspects of risk management in interviews, documentaries and webcasts at Cantos.com. (www.cantos.com) – these are free to view.

Case study recommendations

See www.pearsoned.co.uk/arnold for case study synopses.
Also see Harvard University: http://hbsp.harvard.edu/product/cases

- An overview of Credit Derivatives (1999) Authors: Stephen Lynagh and Sanjiv R. Das. Harvard Business School.
- First American Bank: Credit Default Swaps. (2002) Authors: Eli Peter Strick and George Chacko. Harvard Business School.
- Nextel Partners: Put Option (2009) Authors: Timothy Luehrman and Douglas C Scott. Harvard Business School.
- Introduction to Credit Default Swaps (2010) Authors: Muhammad Fuad Farooqi, Walid Busaba and Zeigham Khokher. Richard Ivey School of Business, University of Western Ontario. Available at Harvard Case Study website.
- Options on Stock Indexes, Currencies and Futures (2008) Author: Robert M. Conroy. Darden, University of Pennsylvania. Available at Harvard Case Study website.

Self-review questions

1   Describe the following:

- traded option;
- call option;
- put option;
- in-the-money option;
- out-of-the-money option;
- intrinsic value;

- time value;
- index option;
- option writer.

2 Compare the hedging characteristics of options and futures.

3 Describe an index option.

4 What is spread betting?

5 Illustrate a use of the contracts for difference market.

6 Describe an interest rate cap.

7 How might the sale of an interest rate floor reduce the cost of hedging against a rise in interest rates?

8 Describe an interest swap.

9 What is a currency swap?

10 Explain credit default swaps.

Questions and problems

1 You hold 20,000 shares in ABC plc which are currently priced at 500p. ABC has developed a revolutionary flying machine. If trials prove successful the share price will rise significantly. If the government bans the use of the machine, following a trial failure, the share price will collapse.

Required

(a) Explain and illustrate how you could use the traded options market to hedge your position.
   Further information
   Current time: 30 January.
   Traded option quotes on ABC plc on 30 January:

		Calls			Puts		
	Option	March	June	Sept.	March	June	Sept.
ABC plc	450	62	88	99	11	19	27
	500	30	50	70	30	42	57
	550	9	20	33	70	85	93

(b) What is meant by intrinsic value, time value, in-the-money, at-the-money and out-of-the-money? Use the above table to illustrate.

2   Palm's share price stands at £4.80. You purchase one March 500p put on Palm's shares for 52p. What is your profit or loss on the option if you hold the option to maturity under each of the following share prices?

(a) 550p
(b) 448p
(c) 420p

3   What is the intrinsic and time value on each of the following options given a share price of 732p?

Exercise price	Calls	Puts
	Feb.	Feb.
700	55½	17½
750	28	40

Which options are in-the-money and which are out-of-the-money?

4   On 14 August British Biotech traded options were quoted on NYSE Liffe as follows:

			Calls			Puts	
	Option	Sept.	Dec.	March	Sept.	Dec.	March
British Biotech	160	30½	40	53	7½	16½	23½
(177½)	180	20½	31	45½	16½	27	34½

Assume: No transaction costs.

Required

(a) Imagine you write a December 180 put on 14 August. Draw a graph showing your profit and loss at share prices ranging from 100p to 250p.
(b) Add to the graph the profit or loss on the purchase of 1,000 shares in British Biotech held until late December at share prices between 100p and 250p. (Current share price = 177.5p)
(c) Show the profit or loss of the combination of (a) and (b) on the graph.

5   (a) Black plc has a £50 million ten-year floating-rate loan from Bank A at LIBOR + 150 basis points. The treasurer is worried that interest rates will rise to a level that will put the firm in a dangerous position. White plc is willing to swap its fixed-interest commitment for the next ten years. White currently pays 9 per cent to Bank B. Libor is currently 8 per cent. Show the interest-rate payment flows in a diagram under a swap arrangement in which each firm pays the other's interest payments.
(b) What are the drawbacks of this swap arrangement for Black?
(c) Black can buy a ten-year interest-rate cap set at a Libor of 8.5 per cent. This will cost 4 per cent of the amount covered. Show the annual payment flows if in the fourth year Libor rises to 10 per cent.
(d) Describe a 'floor' and show how it can be used to alleviate the cost of a cap.

6   'The derivatives markets destroy wealth rather than help create it; they should be made illegal.' Explain your reasons for agreeing or disagreeing with this speaker.

7   Invent examples to demonstrate the different hedging qualities of options, futures and forwards.

8 Describe what is meant by a swap agreement and explain why some of the arrangements are entered into.

9 Describe the credit default market and illustrate its use for lenders exposed to credit risk.

10 Shares in the oil company, Georgia plc, are currently priced at 560p–561p by market makers. News is coming through about the failure to find oil in a field it has been exploring for the past year. You do not hold any shares in Georgia but you are convinced that the share price will fall significantly when the failure is finally confirmed on the last test well.

A spread betting company is offering the following spread on Georgia's shares: 555p–565p. The notional trading margin required is 10 per cent.

A contracts for difference company is quoting prices on Georgia of '556p bid and 566p offer'. It requires a margin of 10 per cent.

You have £20,000 to set aside for either a spread bet deal or a CFD deal in Georgia's shares, of which £12,000 is to be used as initial margin. The remaining £8,000 will be held in reserve in case of margin calls.

Required:

(a) Use the case of Georgia to describe and illustrate spread betting and contracts for difference.
(b) What profits/losses will be made on the spread bet if the spread bet prices move to 640p–650p? What is that as a percentage of initial notional trading margin?
(c) What profits/losses will be made on the spread bet if the spread bet prices move to 480p–490p? What is that as a percentage of initial notional trading margin?
(d) What profits/losses will be made on the contract for difference if the contract for difference prices move to 620p–630p? What is that as a percentage of initial margin?
(e) What profits/losses will be made on the contract for difference if the contract for difference prices move to 475p–485p? What is that as a percentage of initial margin?

11 Attik Inc. will shortly embark on a major project which will require $100 million of borrowing for five years. The Corporate Treasurer has obtained a number of quotes from potential lenders of the $100 million. The best fixed interest rate deal is at a rate of 8 per cent per year. The best floating rate deal is at LIBOR plus 2.5 per cent. The directors have stated a preference for floating rate borrowing for this project to better balance the overall borrowing profile of the firm.

Battik Inc. also needs to borrow $100 million for five years. The best offers it has had from lenders is for it to pay 7 per cent per annum for fixed rate debt and to pay LIBOR plus 1.2 per cent for floating rate debt. It would like to borrow fixed rate debt given the likely pattern of its future cash flows.

Describe a possible swap arrangement that will improve on the position for each firm compared with what they would pay if they simply borrowed in their preferred market (fixed or floating).

12 Describe and explain the similarities and differences between a series of forward rate agreements covering a three-year period and a swap for the same period. Include a discussion of how the rates charged in each market will be linked.

13 The current interest swap rates quoted by dealers are shown in the table:

	Euro-€ %		£ Stlg.%	
	Bid	Offer	Bid	Offer
1 year	2.70	2.75	3.50	3.55
2 years	3.10	3.15	3.67	3.72
3 years	3.78	3.83	4.01	4.06
4 years	4.20	4.25	4.56	4.61
5 years	4.32	4.37	4.78	4.83

Your firm currently has a €400 million five-year floating rate loan obligation paying 230 basis points over LIBOR. Currently, euro three-month LIBOR stands at 2.60 per cent.
It also has a four-year £230 million fixed rate loan at 6.2 per cent per annum.

It would suit its cash flows and risk profile better if the euro loan was swapped into a fixed rate obligation and the sterling obligation was swapped into a floating rate obligation. Describe how the company could achieve these objectives using the prices quoted in the table which have been obtained from swap market intermediaries.
Note: the rates in the table are for AAA rated banks; your firm will have to pay 20 basis points over these rates given its greater counterparty risk.

14 Your financial institution has lent €500 million to the State of Italy. Italy already has national debt amounting to more than 110 per cent of its annual GDP, and this concerns you greatly – it might default. The €500 million was lent through the purchase of a bond with a 5 per cent coupon maturing in five years (the reference obligation).

You have asked credit default swap market participants the spread you would have to pay to receive a payout of par value should Italy default on this reference obligation. Answer: 212 basis points.

Use this information to describe, explain and illustrate how credit default swaps can be used to reduce risk for your firm.

Assignments

1 Describe as many uses of options by a firm you know well as you can. These can include exchange-traded options, currency options, index options and other OTC options.

2 Investigate the extent of derivatives use by the treasury department of a firm you know well. Explain the purpose of derivatives use and consider alternative instruments to those used in the past.

Web-based exercises

1 Visit the website www.markit.com and download the prices of the credit default swap spreads for a number of bonds issued by countries and companies. Also visit www.standardandpoors.com to obtain credit ratings for the same bonds. Analyse the relationship between credit rating and size of the credit default spread, and present in a report.

2 Go to the traded option section of www.ft.com and download the prices of an in-the-money option for each day for a period of one month prior to expiry. Draw a graph of the underlying share price, intrinsic value and time value over that month.

Foreign exchange markets

LEARNING OUTCOMES

The currency markets have an enormous impact on businesses and on individuals. These are often indirect effects, e.g. redundancies arising through loss of international competitiveness. This chapter sheds light on the nature of the FX markets and on the impact of FX shifts and discusses ways of reducing the risk. By the end of it the reader should be able to:

■ explain the role and importance of the foreign exchange markets;

■ outline the operation of the FX markets;

■ contrast various fixed exchange rate regimes with floating or managed floating;

■ describe hedging techniques to reduce the risk associated with transactions entered into in another currency;

■ consider methods of dealing with the risk that assets, income and liabilities denominated in another currency, when translated into home-currency terms, are distorted;

■ describe techniques for reducing the impact of foreign exchange changes on the competitive position of the firm;

■ outline the theories that attempt to explain the reasons for currency rate changes.

Foreign exchange (forex or FX) markets developed thousands of years ago in response to the growth of international trade. To begin with, universal stores of value (such as gold or a set weight (e.g. shekel of barley) were used, and a trader would receive from his customer an amount in gold or barley equivalent to the value of the goods in his own country. The UK currency, the pound sterling, was originally a pound weight of sterling silver, giving traders the ability to price their goods in a foreign country in terms of the weight of silver. As currency usage increased, traders from one country selling their wares in another country had to develop a less cumbersome method of working out how much they should receive for their goods and so direct exchanges of currency became more prevalent.

Today most of that trading is carried out by the FX departments of major banks. The amount traded on the foreign exchange markets is a colossal amount around $4,000 billion per day. Actual import and export trading forms a tiny percentage of this figure. According to the United Nations Conference on Trade and Development world exports are more than $16,000 billion per year, equating to a mere $44 billion per day, about 1 per cent of the amount traded on the FX markets. The vast amount remaining is made up of currency trading, by banks, governments, institutions, companies and individuals.

This chapter looks at the foreign exchange markets from a number of angles. First, there is a description of the different types of FX markets, from simple spot 'immediate' delivery of one currency for another (immediate means within two days), to forwards which allow exchange of currency at a future date. Then we examine the way in which FX prices are quoted, with a particular emphasis on understanding the tables in the *Financial Times*. It has not always been the case that the main currencies have been allowed to float against each other determined by market forces. In the past rates of exchange were usually set by government in a variety of interventionist regimes. We look at some of these alternatives to floating. Another important angle is the impact of shifts in FX rates on people and businesses. Significant sums can be lost and firms can go out of business if they fail to manage the risk. We discuss some of the techniques used, which helps to illustrate a number of the instruments available in the FX markets. Finally, we ask how the level of exchange rate is determined: What are the major influences?

The foreign exchange markets

On the most basic level, foreign exchange markets are (hugely liquid) markets in which one currency is exchanged for another, at a rate usually determined by market supply and demand. For example, if there is a lot of demand from the UK for US dollars, then the buying actions of market players will lead to pressure for the price of each US dollar to rise and conversely the price of each UK pound will fall (less demand and greater supply).

FX trading takes place round the globe 24 hours a day. It is largely OTC trading where the trades are carried out between two parties directly without going through a regulated exchange. The huge amounts of trading makes a significant impact on international flows of capital. Of the global total of $3.98 trillion estimated in 2010 (*see* **Exhibit 12.1**), over one-third is through London.

We can see from the Exhibit 12.1 that there are many different FX markets. In other words, there are many different types of foreign exchange deals available:

- *Spot transaction* A single outright transaction involving the exchange of two currencies at a rate agreed on the date of the contract for value or delivery (cash settlement) within two business days.[1]

- *Forward* A transaction involving the exchange of two currencies at a rate agreed on the date of the contract for value or delivery (cash settlement) at some time in the future (more than two business days later). These contracts are negotiated and agreed between the two parties without going through a regulated exchange. Later in the chapter we look at the use of forward markets by corporations to fix the exchange rate for a transaction they will undertake months, or even years, from now. This brings a high degree of certainty about the rate of exchange at which they will be able to transact.

---

[1] Non-working days do not count, so a Friday deal is settled on the following Tuesday. There are also some exceptions, e.g. the US dollar/Canadian dollar deals are settled the next day.

Exhibit 12.1   Global daily FX turnover in April 2010

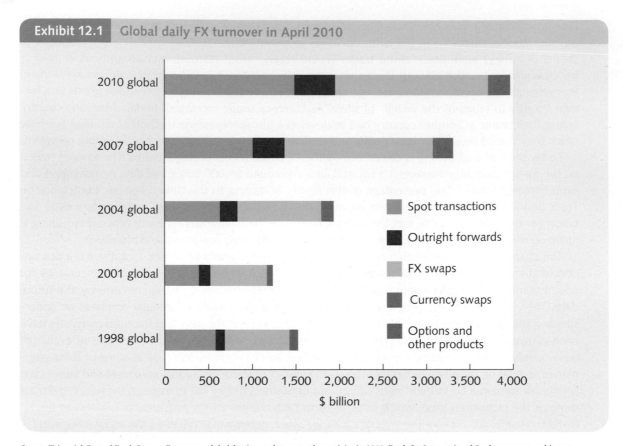

Source: Triennial Central Bank Survey: Report on global foreign exchange market activity in 2010. Bank for International Settlements, www.bis.org

- *Foreign exchange swap (FX swap)* A single deal with two parts to it. First, there is the actual exchange of two currencies on a specific date at a rate agreed at the time of the conclusion of the contract – this is usually a spot exchange but it can be a forward. Second, there is a reverse exchange of the same two currencies at a date further in the future at a rate agreed at the time of the contract. The rates of exchange are usually different in the two parts. These FX swaps take place all the time between professional players based in banks as they try to balance out their currency positions and reduce their risk exposure. They usually cover a period of no more than one week. As Exhibit 12.1 shows, these arrangements make up the largest element in the FX markets, but they are of little significance to non-bank players.

- *Currency swap* A contract which commits two counterparties to exchange streams of interest payments in different currencies for an agreed period of time and usually to exchange principal amounts in different currencies at a pre-agreed exchange rate at maturity. These are the swaps discussed in Chapter 11 being linked to long-term loans with interest payments to be made – they should not be confused with FX swaps. A currency swaption is an option to enter into a currency swap contract.

- *Currency option* An option contract that gives the right but not the obligation to buy or sell a currency at a specified exchange rate during a specified period.

- *Future* Foreign currency futures are exchange-traded transactions to completion exchange of currency at a future date, with standard contract sizes and maturity dates – for example, £62,500 for next November at an agreed rate.

Although over one-third of all FX trading takes place in London (*see* **Exhibit 12.2**), with London carrying out twice as much trade as its nearest rival, the US, the actual currency that dominates is the US dollar, which acts as a counterparty in over 85 per cent of all trading on one side of the trade – *see* **Exhibit 12.3**. The currencies most commonly traded are USD, the US dollar ($), EUR, the euro (€), JPY, the Japanese yen (¥), GBP, the UK pound (£), AUD, the Australian dollar (A$), CAD, the Canadian dollar (C$) and CHF, the Swiss franc (SFr).

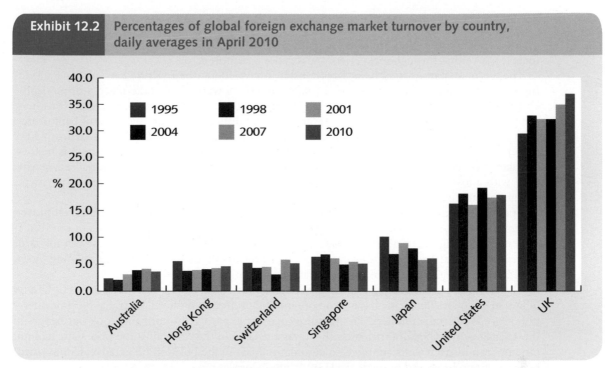

Source: Triennial Central Bank Survey: Report on global foreign exchange market activity in 2010. Bank for International Settlements, www.bis.org

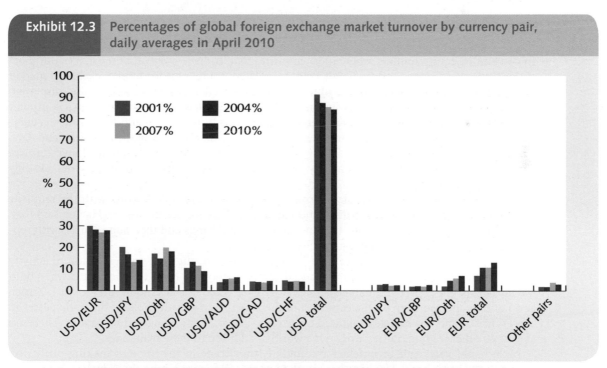

Source: Triennial Central Bank Survey: Report on global foreign exchange market activity in 2010. Bank for International Settlements, www.bis.org

The US dollar has become the currency that is accepted and used worldwide. This is partly due to the legacy left from the Bretton Woods agreement (see later in the chapter for details on this), but mostly to do with the size, strength and stability of the US economy.

FX mistakes

There are many cases of calamitous FX trading, where one counterparty in the trading has made major losses either through inexperience, arrogance or simple error.

The German state-owned bank Kreditanstalt für Wiederaufbau (KfW) carried out FX trading like most other banks and many of its transactions were set to take place automatically. During the weekend of 13/14 September 2008 the world became aware that Lehman Brothers, the US-based investment bank, was in severe financial difficulty and on the brink of bankruptcy. On the morning of 15 September an automatic payment of €319 million was sent from KfW to Lehman. This was the KfW side of a €/USD currency swap. What happened next is history: Lehman Brothers filed for bankruptcy and the return part of the trade never materialised, leaving KfW with a loss of €319 million. No one at KfW had thought to check the automatic payments system for any relating to Lehman.

In 2002, US currency trader John Rusnak racked up losses of $691 million for his employer, Baltimore-based Allfirst Bank, a subsidiary of Allied Irish Banks (AIB), seemingly not out of dishonesty but trying to cover up bad trades. Rusnak made losses in 1997 on Japanese yen forwards and spent the next few years using ever more ingenious methods to hide his accumulating losses, until February 2002 when suspicions arose and investigations began.

The Hong Kong-based steel and mining conglomerate Citic Pacific was hit by losses of US$1.9 billion in October 2008. Citic has an iron ore mining project in Western Australia. For this operation it needs Australian dollars. To minimise currency exposure the company took out hedges in the A$ against the US$; unfortunately there was a decline in the A$ against the US$. Citic had not put any stop losses into its contracts to automatically close the position on an adverse movement below a certain level, and so made the US$1.9 billion loss.

FX trading

In contrast to equity trading, where most countries tend to have one (or, at most, a handful of) major trading exchanges and trading is tightly regulated, trading on the foreign exchange market does not have a focal position where all trading is supervised and data is collected and displayed. The trading is carried out in numerous locations, wherever a trader is and can access a computer screen or a mobile phone screen. Many trading platforms now offer an app for the new generation of mobile phones and tablet computers giving traders full access to all their facilities and data, enabling them to download data and carry out trading wherever they are. Individual investors can also take advantage of this new technology, giving them access to data that was once available only to professional traders.

Some of the trades are on regulated exchanges but most are not. Anyone with the requisite knowledge can take part in FX trading, and regulation is lax for the most part. Having said that, the vast majority of trading is done by major international banks and their subsidiaries, with reputations to lose so there is a high degree of self-regulation.

Trading is constant, taking place on a 24-hour basis, with the high concentration of activity moving with the sun from one major financial centre to another. Most trading occurs when both the European and New York markets are open – this is when it is afternoon in Frankfurt, Zurich and London and morning on the east coast of the Americas. Later the bulk of the trade passes to San Francisco and Los Angeles, followed by Sydney, Tokyo, Hong Kong and Singapore. There are at least 40 other trading centres around the world in addition to these main ones.

Most banks carry out proprietary trading, i.e. they trade in the hope of making profits on behalf of the bank itself. The banks are in the process of concentrating their dealers in three or four regional hubs. These typically include London as well as New York and a site in Asia, where Tokyo, Hong Kong and Singapore are keen to establish their dominance. According to a survey by the magazine *Euromoney*, FX trading carried out by banks is highly concentrated, with over 77 per cent carried out by only ten banks (*see* **Exhibit 12.4**), with Deutsche Bank having held top spot for the past six years to 2009.

When a non-bank organisation needs an FX deal it mostly trades with a bank, but there are exchanges for some types of dealing. The main difference between FX trading via banks and

Exhibit 12.4	2009 FX trading by banks

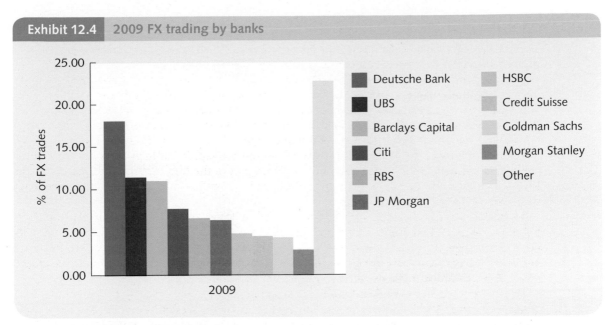

Source: www.euromoney.com

FX trading carried out on exchanges such as the Chicago Mercantile Exchange (CME) is that exchange trading tends to deal in standard amounts and maturities. The amounts and maturities of these contracts are fixed and inflexible, so they may be less suitable for company use, where the company might need to hedge specific amounts for a specific time, and would therefore be better served using the flexibility offered by a bank. Dealing through an exchange facilitates clearing and settlement and exchange-traded currency instruments are liquid and tradable.

The buyers and sellers of foreign currencies are:

- commercial companies with export or import interests;
- international banks and commercial banks carrying our proprietary trading;
- dealers trading and acting as market makers in currency (usually the big banks);
- brokers buying and selling currencies on behalf of a client, e.g. a client bank or commercial firm;
- governments needing foreign currency for overseas trade or to pay for activities abroad;
- speculators or arbitrageurs taking advantage of perceived FX pricing anomalies;
- tourists or investors (e.g. in property or shares) needing to pay in foreign currency;
- fund managers investing abroad (pensions, insurance companies, etc.);
- central banks (smoothing out fluctuations or managing the rate to a desired level).

There are various ways in which deals are done. First, there is the traditional approach of the two dealers talking on the telephone and agreeing to trade. One of the dealers here may be a non-bank customer such as a manufacturing firm. If the customer approaches the bank without going through an intermediary these are 'customer direct trades'. However, a broker will frequently act on behalf of a customer to deal with banks in the FX markets – if conducted over the telephone these are 'voice broker' trades. The trades between banks, referred to as 'inter-dealer direct trades', can be either via direct telephone communication or direct electronic dealing systems – these electronic deals are shown separately as the largest segment in **Exhibit 12.5**. Increasingly deals are conducted over electronic dealing systems. Banks are the main users of these systems, but there are special systems set up for customers. Some of these are run by a single bank as a 'proprietary platform'. Others are managed by a group of banks – multibank dealing systems. Examples of multibank systems include FXAll, Currenex, FXConnect, Globalink and eSpeed.

The electronic platforms have allowed smaller banks to access the best prices and provide them with the opportunity to deal alongside the large banks on an even basis because of the transparency

Exhibit 12.5	Foreign exchange market turnover by execution method, 2010

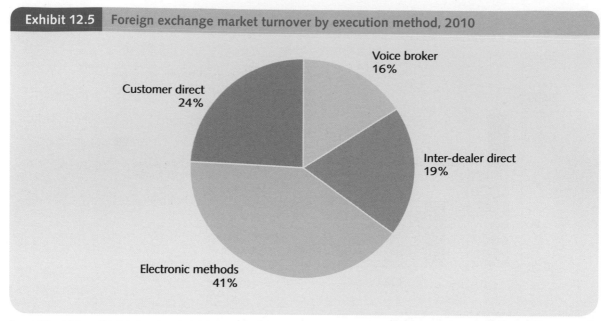

Source: Triennial Central Bank Survey: Report on global foreign exchange market activity in 2010. Bank for International Settlements, www.bis.org

of the systems. Rapid price dissemination from electronic systems has, to a great extent, 'levelled the playing field', whereas in the old days only the large banks could 'see' the market prices through their telephone contacts.

Exchange rates

We now look more closely at exchange rates. We start with some terms used in FX markets. First, we provide a definition of an exchange rate:

> An exchange rate is the price of one currency (**the base currency**) expressed in terms of another (**the secondary, counter or quote currency**).

Therefore if the exchange rate between the US dollar and the pound is US$1.60 = £1.00 this means that £1.00 will cost US$1.60. Taking the reciprocal, US$1.00 will cost 62.50 pence. The standardised forms of expression are:

US$/£ : 1.60   or   US$1.60/£   or   USD1.60/£

Exchange rates are expressed in terms of the number of units of the first currency per single unit of the second currency. Most currencies are quoted to four decimal places and the smallest variation used in trading is a pip which is one ten-thousandth of one unit of currency (e.g. $1), or 0.0001. So for the US$/£ exchange rate on 16 November 2010 the rate was quoted in the *Financial Times* as:

US$1.5988/£

However, this is still not accurate enough because currency exchange rates are not generally expressed in terms of a single 'middle rate' as above, but are given as a rate at which you can buy the first currency (bid rate) and a rate at which you can sell the first currency (offer rate). This is called the spread and it enables market makers (traders) to make a profit on buying and selling currencies. In the case of the US$/£ exchange rate the market rates on 16 November 2010 were:

US$1.5988/£ 'middle rate'

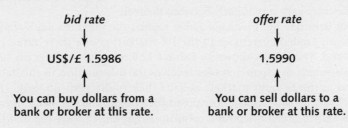

So if you wished to purchase US$1 million the cost would be:

$$\frac{\$1,000,000}{1.5986} = £625,547$$

However, if you wished to sell US$1 million you would receive:

$$\frac{\$1,000,000}{1.5990} = £625,391$$

The foreign exchange dealers are transacting with numerous buyers and sellers every day and they make a profit on the difference between the bid price and offer price (the bid/offer spread). In the above example if a dealer sold US$1 million and bought US$1 million with a bid/offer spread of 0.04 of a cent, a profit of £625,547 – £625,391 = £156 is made.

Worked example 12.1   Forex

The basic elements of forex are so important for the rest of the chapter that it is worthwhile to pause and consolidate understanding of the quoted rates through some exercises.

Answer the following questions on the basis that the euro/US$ (EUR/USD) exchange rate is 1.3605–1.3609, that is, US$1.3605/€ or US$1.3609/€ depending on whether you are buying or selling euros.

1 What is the cost of buying €200,000?
2 How much would it cost to purchase US$4m?
3 How many dollars would be received from selling €800,000?
4 How many euros would be received from selling US$240,000?

Answers

1 €200,000 × 1.3609 = $272,180

2 $\dfrac{\$4,000,000}{1.3605} = €2,940,096$

3 €800,000 × 1.3605 = $1,088,400

4 $\dfrac{\$240,000}{1.3609} = €176,354$

Sources of information

Information on currency exchange rates is easily available in newspapers such as the *Financial Times*, or on websites such as Reuters, Yahoo Finance or any of the other numerous financial websites. Rates may vary very slightly between them all.

Tuesday to Saturday the *Financial Times* reports the previous day's trading in over 50 of the most commonly traded currencies in the FX market, giving their value relative to the dollar, euro and pound. The figures shown in **Exhibit 12.6** relate to dealings on 12 November 2010. Of course, by the time a newspaper reader receives the information in this table the rates may well have changed as the 24-hour markets execute their trades continuously. However, www.ft.com and other websites provide much more up-to-the-minute and detailed information.

The prices shown under the pound columns in Exhibit 12.6 are the middle price of the foreign currency in terms of £1 in London at 4pm the previous afternoon. So, for instance, the mid-price of £1 for immediate delivery is 1.6338 Australian dollars. For the US dollar columns the prices for the pound and euro are the number of dollars per currency unit, either per pound or per euro. However, for other currencies the rate shown is the number of units of the other currency per US$1 – for example, 1.0098 Canadian dollars per US dollar. For the euro columns the rate shown is the number of units of the other currency per euro – for example the spot mid-rate against the pound is 84.84 pence per euro.

On Mondays the *FT* publishes a much more comprehensive list of exchange rates for over 200 countries, again with their relative values against the dollar, euro and pound.

While the most common currencies often have forward rates quoted, there are many currencies for which forward quotes are difficult to obtain. The so-called exotic currencies generally do not have forward rates quoted by dealers. These are currencies for which there is little trading demand to support international business, etc. On the other hand, spot markets exist for most of the world's currencies.

The first forward price (middle price) is given as the 'One month' rate. Looking at the sterling and US$ rates you could commit yourself to the sale of a quantity of dollars for delivery in one month at a rate that is fixed at about US$1.6148 per pound. In this case you will need fewer US dollars to buy £1 in one month's time compared with the spot rate of exchange, therefore the dollar is at a premium on the one-month forward rate.

The forward rate for one month shows a different relationship with the spot rate for the euro against the pound. Here more euros are required (€1.1788) to purchase a pound in one month's time compared with an 'immediate' spot purchase (€1.1787), therefore the euro on one-month forward delivery is at a discount to the pound. We look at the relationships between spot and forward rates later in the chapter (interest rate parity theory).

The *Financial Times* table lists quotations up to one year for the four strongest currencies, the dollar, euro, yen and pound, but, as this is an over-the-counter market, it is possible to go as far forward in time as required – provided a counterparty can be found. Use of forward exchange rates is widespread. For example, airline companies expecting to purchase planes many years hence may use the distant forward market to purchase the foreign currency they need to pay the manufacturer so that they know with certainty the quantity of their home currency they are required to find when the planes are delivered.

The table in Exhibit 12.6 displays standard periods of time for forward rates, one month, three months and one year. These are instantly available and are frequently traded. However, forward rates are not confined to these particular days in the future. It is possible to obtain rates for any day in the future, say, 74 or 36 days hence for any amount of currency, but these would require a specific quotation from a bank.

The Special Drawing Rights (SDRs) of the International Monetary Fund (IMF) shown at the bottom of the table are artificial currencies made up from baskets of fixed amounts of four currencies, the pound sterling, the US dollar, the yen and the euro.

Exhibit 12.6 Currency rates from the FT 13/14 November 2010

CURRENCY RATES

www.ft.com/currencydata

Nov 12	Currency	DOLLAR Closing Mid	DOLLAR Day's Change	EURO Closing Mid	EURO Day's Change	POUND Closing Mid	POUND Day's Change
Argentina	(Peso)	3.9613	0.0007	5.4280	0.0141	6.3981	0.0008
Australia	(A$)	1.0115	0.0091	1.3861	0.0158	1.6338	0.0145
Bahrain	(Dinar)	0.3771	–	0.5167	0.0013	0.6090	0.0000
Bolivia	(Boliviano)	7.0200	–	9.6192	0.0231	11.3384	–0.0007
Brazil	(R$)	1.7181	–0.0009	2.3542	0.0044	2.7750	–0.0016
Canada	(C$)	1.0098	0.0049	1.3836	0.0100	1.6309	0.0078
Chile	(Peso)	481.650	0.8000	659.981	2.6830	777.937	1.2440
China	(Yuan)	6.6370	0.0113	9.0944	0.0373	10.7198	0.0176
Colombia	(Peso)	1863.85	7.2000	2553.94	15.9923	3010.40	11.4427
Costa Rica	(Colon)	513.490	–3.6200	703.610	–3.2538	829.365	–5.8985
Czech Rep.	(Koruna)	17.9551	–0.0668	24.6030	–0.0320	29.0003	–0.1096
Denmark	(DKr)	5.4395	–0.0134	7.4534	–0.0004	8.7855	–0.0222
Egypt	(Egypt £)	5.7510	–0.0017	7.8803	0.0166	9.2888	–0.0034
Estonia	(Kroon)	11.4188	–0.0275	15.6466	–	18.4431	–0.0456
Hong Kong	(HK$)	7.7511	0.0006	10.6210	0.0263	12.5192	0.0001
Hungary	(Forint)	201.894	–0.4911	276.645	–0.0050	326.089	–0.8134
India	(Rs)	44.7425	0.4275	61.3084	0.7320	72.2659	0.6860
Indonesia	(Rupiah)	8924.50	26.5000	12228.8	65.6752	14414.4	41.9120
Iran	(Rial)	10405.0	–	14257.5	34.3365	16805.6	–1.0405
Israel	(Shk)	3.6745	0.0193	5.0350	0.0385	5.9349	0.0308
Japan	(Y)	82.3700	–0.1100	112.868	0.1214	133.040	–0.1859
One Month		82.3520	–0.0015	112.810	–0.0004	132.982	–0.0016
Three Month		82.2971	–0.0039	112.646	–0.0066	132.821	–0.0049
One Year		81.8845	–0.0045	111.650	0.0023	131.680	–0.0400
Kenya	(Shilling)	80.5000	0.1000	110.305	0.4023	130.020	0.1534
Kuwait	(Dinar)	0.2807	–0.0001	0.3846	0.0008	0.4534	–0.0002
Malaysia	(M$)	3.1145	0.0230	4.2677	0.0418	5.0304	0.0369
Mexico	(New Peso)	12.2567	–0.0242	16.7934	0.0074	19.7948	–0.0404
New Zealand	(NZ$)	1.2910	0.0079	1.7690	0.0150	2.0852	0.0126
Nigeria	(Naira)	150.700	0.1500	206.497	0.7024	243.403	0.2272
Norway	(NKr)	5.9486	0.0166	8.1511	0.0423	9.6079	0.0261
Pakistan	(Rupee)	85.6650	0.2700	117.383	0.6518	138.362	0.4275
Peru	(New Sol)	2.8025	0.0020	3.8401	0.0120	4.5265	0.0030
Philippines	(Peso)	43.7200	–0.1550	59.9074	–0.0675	70.6144	–0.2548

	Currency	DOLLAR Closing Mid	DOLLAR Day's Change	EURO Closing Mid	EURO Day's Change	POUND Closing Mid	POUND Day's Change
Poland	(Zloty)	2.8656	–0.0101	3.9265	–0.0044	4.6283	–0.0166
Romania	(New Leu)	3.1343	–0.0011	4.2948	0.0088	5.0624	–0.0021
Russia	(Rouble)	30.7913	0.1698	42.1917	0.3337	49.7325	0.2712
Saudi Arabia	(SR)	3.7498	–0.0005	5.1381	0.0117	6.0565	–0.0011
Singapore	(S$)	1.2957	0.0065	1.7754	0.0132	2.0927	0.0104
South Africa	(R)	6.9363	0.0025	9.5044	0.0263	11.2031	0.0033
South Korea	(Won)	1127.85	20.1500	1545.44	31.2660	1821.65	32.4345
Sweden	(SKr)	6.8300	0.0042	9.3588	0.0282	11.0315	0.0060
Switzerland	(SFr)	0.9771	0.0040	1.3389	0.0086	1.5781	0.0062
Taiwan	(T$)	30.2105	0.1685	41.3960	0.3300	48.7945	0.2691
Thailand	(Bt)	29.7750	0.1500	40.7992	0.3033	48.0911	0.2393
Tunisia	(Dinar)	1.4118	–0.0015	1.9346	0.0027	2.2803	–0.0025
Turkey	(Lira)	1.4343	0.0012	1.9653	0.0064	2.3166	0.0018
U A E	(Dirham)	3.6727	0.0000	5.0325	0.0121	5.9320	–0.0004
UK (0.6191)*	(£)	1.6152	–0.0001	0.8484	0.0021	–	–
One Month		1.6148	0.000	0.8483	0.0000	–	–
Three Month		1.6139	–	0.8481	–	–	–
One Year		1.6081	–0.0004	0.8479	–0.0008	–	–
Ukraine	(Hrywnja)	7.9515	–0.0020	10.8956	0.0235	12.8429	–0.0040
Uruguay	(Peso)	19.8000	–	27.1310	0.0654	31.9800	–0.0020
USA	($)	–	–	1.3703	0.0033	1.6152	–0.0001
One Month		–		1.3699	0.0000	1.6148	0.0000
Three Month		–		1.3688	0.0000	1.6139	–0.0001
One Year		–		1.3635	0.0001	1.6081	0.0000
Venezuela †	(Bolivar Fuerte)	4.2947		5.8848	0.0142	6.9365	–0.0004
Vietnam	(Dong)	19495.0		26713.0	64.3335	31487.4	–1.9495
Euro (0.7298)*	(Euro)	1.3703	0.0033	–	–	1.1787	–0.0030
One Month		1.3699	0.0000	–		1.1788	–
Three Month		1.3688	0.0000	–		1.1791	0.0000
One Year		1.3635	0.001	–		1.1794	0.0004
SDR		0.6398	–0.0007	0.8767	0.0012	1.0334	–0.0011

Rates are derived from WM/Reuters at 4pm (London time). * The closing mid-point rates for the Euro and £ against the $ are shown in brackets. The other figures in the dollar column of both the Euro and Sterling rows are in the reciprocal form in line with market convention. † New Venezuelan Bolivar Fuerte introduced on Jan 1st 2008. Currency redenominated by 1000. Some values are rounded by the F.T. The exchange rates printed in this table are also available on the internet at **http://www.FT.com/marketsdata**

Euro Locking Rates: Austrian Schilling 13.7603. Belgium/Luxembourg Franc 40.3399. Cyprus 0.585274. Finnish Markka 5.94572. French Franc 6.55957. German Mark 1.95583. Greek Drachma 340.75. Irish Punt 0.787564. Italian Lira 1936.27. Malta 0.4293. Netherlands Guilder 2.20371. Portuguese Escudo 200.482. Slovenia Tolar 239.64. Spanish Peseta 166.386.

Source: Financial Times, 13/14 November 2010. Reprinted with permission.

Worked example 12.2   Covering in the forward market

Suppose that on 12 November 2010 a UK exporter sells goods to a customer in France invoiced at €5,000,000. Payment is due three months later. With the spot rate of exchange at €1.1787/£ (see Exhibit 12.6) the exporter, in deciding to sell the goods, has in mind a sales price of:

$$\frac{€5,000,000}{1.1787} = £4,241,961$$

The UK firm bases its decision on the profitability of the deal on this amount expressed in pounds.

However, the rate of exchange may vary between November and February: the size and direction of the move is uncertain. If the pound strengthens against the euro and the rate is then €1.40/£, the UK exporter will make a currency loss by waiting three months and exchanging the euro received into sterling at spot rates in February. The exporter will receive only £3,571,429

$$\frac{€5,000,000}{1.40} = £3,571,429 \quad \text{causing a loss of} \quad \begin{array}{r} £4,241,961 \\ -£3,571,429 \\ \hline £670,532 \end{array}$$

If sterling weakens to €1.10/£ a currency gain is made. The pounds received in February if euro are exchanged at this spot rate will be:

$$\frac{€5,000,000}{1.10} = £4,545,455 \quad \text{and the currency gain will be} \quad \begin{array}{r} £4,545,455 \\ -£4,241,961 \\ \hline £303,494 \end{array}$$

Rather than run the risk of a possible loss on the currency side of the deal the exporter may decide to cover in the forward market. Under this arrangement the exporter promises to sell €5m against the pound in three months (the agreement is made on 12 November for delivery of currency in February). The forward rate available (ignoring any market makers' spreads and transaction costs) on 12 November is €1.1791/£. This forward contract means that the exporter will receive £4,240,522 in February

$$\frac{€5,000,000}{1.1791} = £4,240,522$$

regardless of the way in which the spot exchange rate moves over the three months.

In February the transactions in Exhibit 12.7 take place.

Exhibit 12.7   Example of the forward market

From the outset (in November) the exporter knew the amount to be received in February (assuming away counterparty risk). It might, with hindsight, have been better not to use the forward market but to exchange the euro in February at a spot rate of say €1.1000/£. This would have resulted in a larger income for the firm. But in November when the export took place there was uncertainty about what the spot rate would be in February. If the exporter had waited to exchange the currency until February and the spot rate in February had turned out to be €1.4000/£ the exporter would have made less.

Covering in the forward market is a form of insurance which leads to greater certainty – and certainty has a value. For many companies it is vital that they have this certainty about income and expenditure; they cannot afford to leave things and hope they will turn out satisfactorily.

Settlement

The vast sums of money traded every working day across the world mean that banks are exposed to the risk that they may irrevocably pay over currency to a counterparty before they receive another currency in return because settlement systems are operating in different time zones. A bank could fail after receiving one leg of its foreign exchange trades but before paying the other leg – this is called Herstatt risk after Bankhaus Herstatt, a German bank, which failed in 1974 with $620 million of unsettled trades (where one side of the trade has paid but the other side has not). In this case the crisis was due to the time difference between Europe and the US; Bankhaus Herstatt received its dollar payments in Frankfurt, but ceased trading before the reciprocal payment could be made in New York. Its failure caused panic and gridlock in the FX markets, which took weeks to unravel.

Following this disaster, the major banks formed a new means of settlement, Continuous Linked Settlement, which began operating in 2002. The new entity, CLS Bank, is owned by banking members who trade in the FX markets. The whole point of CLS is PvP (payment versus payment), simultaneous settlement of both legs of trading, thereby eliminating Herstatt risk, but also incurring charges (the charges are small in relation to the sums involved, £0.07 for every £1 million of trading value). CLS claim to match payments within 38 minutes, and if a trade is not matched, it is returned to its originator, so there is no possibility of one party to the trade suffering loss due to the other party's failure to settle. Even though matching takes place in minutes spot transactions will be settled (currency actually transferred) two days later.

Settlement is offered in seventeen currencies and nearly 10,000 banks, financial institutions and investment funds use the service, with up to 1 million trades settled daily.

Over 50 per cent of global FX trading uses multi-lateral netting, where the nett value only of trades is settled. For example if a bank sold $1 billion, but also bought $900 million, the settlement is for only $100 million. This reduces the forex risk element.

CME in Chicago offers guaranteed clearing and settlement through its own clearing service CME ClearPort, and claims never to have had any defaults in 100 years of trading.

Cross exchange rates

The major currencies of the world, US dollar, euro, pound and Swiss franc are easily exchangeable directly into other currencies. Some currency pairs are traded much less frequently and so the market is thin and illiquid, which usually means costly. For example, the Philippines peso and the United Arab Emirates dirham would see little trade and so a company exporting from the Philippines to UAE receiving dirhams would have difficulty obtaining quotation for a good rate of exchange. The traditional way of dealing with this was to exchange the dirhams into one of the major currencies, usually the US dollar, and then to exchange the dollars for pesos. Thus most currency rates are quoted in terms of the US dollar primarily, rather than against the 170 other currencies in the world – it simply becomes too cumbersome to quote all the possible two-currency rates and so the rate against the US dollar is set as the benchmark. Of course, today a single bank will be able to offer a service of quoting both the dirham:dollar and the peso:dollar rates, in which case it is not necessary to bother with the exchange to and from dollars, but merely to quote the rates and, if the client likes them, for the bank to transact dirhams for pesos.

> A **cross-rate** is the exchange rate of two currencies that are normally expressed in terms of a third currency, usually the US dollar.

Thus the Philippines peso and the UAE dirham are both cross currencies because they are normally quoted against the dollar. Tables of cross-rates are produced which show the exchange rate between these lesser used currencies. At first glance you see what appears to be a direct rate of exchange, say dirhams for pesos, but for most of these the rates are derived from prices against the US dollar. For example, if the exchange rates are four dirhams for one US dollar, and 60 pesos to one dollar then the cross-rate of dirhams to pesos is as shown in Exhibit 12.8. Four dirhams equal 60 pesos, therefore one dirham can be exchanged for 15 pesos.

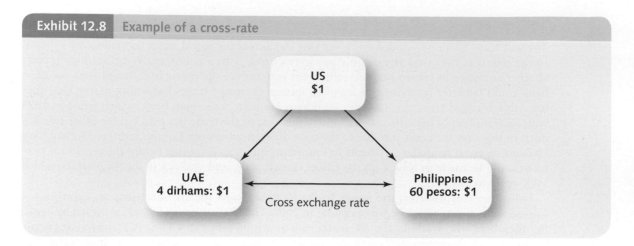

Exhibit 12.8 Example of a cross-rate

Exchange rate regimes

Fixed FX regimes

Fixed exchange rate regimes require the participating countries to keep their currencies held at a constant rate or within a certain percentage of an agreed rate. Any deviation from the agreed percentage must be managed and brought back into line by the domestic central bank buying or selling its own currency. If there are significant changes to domestic economic circumstances, then a currency may be devalued or revalued, with the agreement of the participating countries.

Gold standard

Towards the end of the nineteenth century, trading countries adopted the **gold standard**, where their currency was fixed at a set price in gold. This encouraged stability in currencies relative to other currencies. It also prevented inflation, as economies could only grow their money supply in correlation to their supply of gold; it discouraged governments from overspending by issuing more banknotes than their reserves of gold warranted.

The gold standard enabled traders dealing overseas to exchange the income received in foreign currency for a set amount of gold and the amount of gold had a set value in their home currency, thus exchange rates were effectively fixed. People were entitled to exchange banknotes for actual gold, and banks issued banknotes based on the amount of gold held in their vaults.

The turmoil faced by the world as a result of the First World War and then the economic crises of the 1920s and 1930s caused the gold standard to be discontinued. Governments needed to issue banknotes in excess of their gold reserves to stabilise their economies, having in many cases used much of their gold to finance warfare. A central bank's promise on its banknotes came to be based more on the country's credibility and economic standing rather than its actual physical holding of gold.

Various attempts were made to revive the gold standard, but it became increasingly difficult for any government to hold sufficient gold to guarantee all its banknotes in issue, while also altering money supply to make economic adjustments for its future stability and prosperity. A major drawback for reviving the gold standard is the limited supply of gold in the world and the physical impossibility of countries possessing gold reserves to cover their issue of currency, stifling any possibility of expansion. To give an idea of the numbers involved: the World Bank estimates that all countries' gold reserves in 2010 were about 30 tonnes, valued at a little over £600 billion. In the UK alone, public spending in 2010 was a similar amount.

Bretton Woods

After the economic chaos following the First World War the UK and US determined to try to prevent similar problems after the Second World War. To promote post-war economic and financial stability, delegates from all 44 allied countries gathered at the **Bretton Woods** conference (named after the New Hampshire town where it took place) in 1944. The negotiations resulted in an exchange rate system whereby the currencies were fixed to the US dollar, which in turn was fixed to the price of gold at $35 per ounce of gold. At this time, the US was the major industrial nation in the world, and also held the most reserves of gold. This agreement kept the US at the forefront of the modern world and promoted the ever-present hegemony of the US dollar as the major currency of the world.

The participating countries had to keep within a band of 1 per cent of the fixed value and central banks would buy or sell the dollar against their own currency to keep within the limits. Leading the UK delegation was John Maynard Keynes, the world-renowned economist, who was instrumental in the planning of the other major achievements to come out of the conference, the World Bank and the International Monetary Fund through which exchange rate stability was ensured.

The Bretton Woods agreement lasted for nearly 30 years until the 1970s when inflation, the cost of the Vietnam war and US welfare reforms forced the US to cancel the dollar's convertibility to gold. The US had started to export higher inflation to the rest of the world and there was an excess supply of US dollars in the world, more and more of which other countries tried to convert into gold at the agreed rate. Faced with drained gold reserves, in 1971 the US president Richard Nixon suspended the Bretton Woods agreement and allowed the US dollar to float against other currencies.

Since then, most currencies have floated against other currencies, with central banks intervening when necessary to buy and sell their own currency to keep its value

European Exchange Rate Mechanism

Following the collapse of the Bretton Woods agreement, some European countries made various attempts to establish fixed rates between their currencies to encourage trade.

The Maastricht Treaty in 1992 aimed to stabilise economic conditions and promote integration between European countries. It created the Economic and Monetary Union (EMU), which eventually led to the adoption of the euro in 1999 as the universal currency for most EU members. In the lead up to the EMU, the currencies of participating countries were subject to the Exchange Rate Mechanism (ERM), which kept each currency between strict limits.

Fixing exchange rates between European countries or adopting the euro had mixed blessings. While the stability of the currency helps in forward planning, the UK and Italy were forced out of the ERM in 1992 because the changing economic circumstances in their countries meant that the pound and the lira were set at an excessively high rate of exchange, stifling economic recovery.[2] In more recent years a common interest rate in the Eurozone countries has meant an awkwardly low interest rate environment for Ireland, Greece and Spain, which resulted in unsustainable property booms and wage rises followed by busts.

Pegs and bands

There are quite a few countries which keep their currency pegged to the US dollar. They include the Hong Kong dollar, pegged to the US dollar since 1998, and a number of emerging nations. While the HK$ is fixed to the US dollar it moves in line with that currency as it fluctuates against other currencies, so it is not fixed against other currencies. It is thought that the dollar is stable (relative to some developing countries, anyway), and so keeping pegged to the dollar helps to maintain a currency's own stability. It also helps to prevent the home currency rising against the dollar which may make exporting more difficult.

Floating FX regimes

Most major countries now adopt a floating FX regime, where the exchange rate for their currency is governed by supply and demand. This allows countries to keep control of their monetary policy, and it has been noted that floating rates are predisposed towards equilibrium, that is the supply and demand even each other out.

Some floating regimes do not have official limits for the movements of their currencies but nevertheless governments sometimes intervene to prevent their currency moving too far in a

---

[2] Technically the ERM allowed some floating of exchange rates, but within narrow bands.

certain direction. These are known as **managed floats or dirty floats**. The low rate of the Chinese yuan against the US dollar has caused great frustration in many countries, despite it being managed to gradually appreciate (very slowly). Exporters from other countries argue that the Chinese government is keeping the yuan artificially low to boost its exporters.

FX volatility and its effects

You might wonder what is the significance of fluctuating FX rates. If you go on holiday to Europe, you might get more or less euro for your pound or dollar than last year – usually a fairly minor boost or inconvenience. But for companies trading millions, billions or trillions internationally, even small differences in exchange rates can have major consequences.

If a UK firm holds dollars or assets denominated in dollars and the value of the dollar rises against the pound, then the dollars and dollar assets are worth more in pounds and an FX profit is made. Conversely, should the pound rise relative to the dollar, dollars and dollar assets are worth less compared to the pound and an FX loss will be incurred. These potential gains or losses can be very large.

For example, as shown on **Exhibit 12.9**, between December 2007 and February 2009 the dollar appreciated by just over a third against the pound, so anyone who sold pounds for dollars in December 2007 and kept them would have made a 33 per cent profit on changing them back into pounds. If the money had also been put to work earning interest more could have been realised.

Exhibit 12.9	The exchange rate rates of the US dollar and GB pound

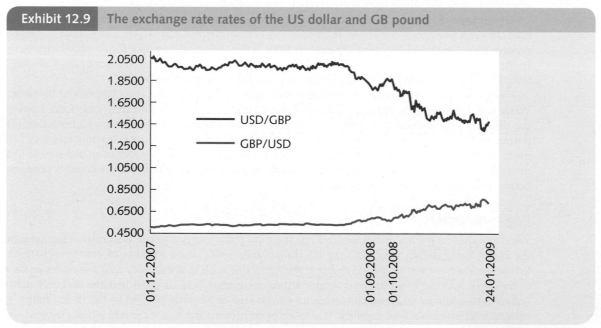

Source: www.oanda.com

Shifts in the value of foreign exchange can impact on various aspects of trading activities. Fluctuating FX rates may wipe out profits from a project, an export deal or a portfolio investment (for example a pension fund buying foreign shares). One of the problems caused by exchange rate fluctuations can be illustrated by worked example 12.3.

Worked example 12.3

On 24 July 2008 two UK companies, GBX and GBA, agreed to purchase $10,000 of goods from US company USY. GBX paid the $10,000 in July 2008 but GBA paid in January 2009, expecting to exchange pounds for dollars then.

At the time of purchase, the goods would have cost £5,012 if the pounds were exchanged at the prevailing spot rate. However, due to GBP/USD rates changing, when 24 January came, company GBA had to pay £7,283 to obtain $10,000, so GBA made a substantial FX loss compared with if it had obtained the dollars in July 2008 – *see* **Exhibit 12.10**.

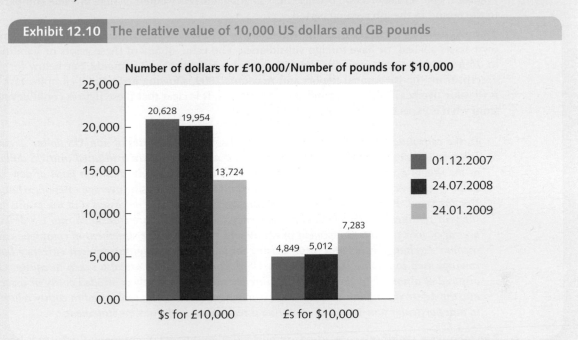

Exhibit 12.10   The relative value of 10,000 US dollars and GB pounds

UK clothing companies found that their imported goods were more costly mostly because of a shift in the pound's exchange rate – *see* **Exhibit 12.11**.

Exhibit 12.11

Material increase in clothes prices   **FT**

by Andrea Felsted

Verdict, a retail research group, forecasts clothing inflation of 4.4 per cent this year, the highest level since 1986.

The forecast will be bad news for consumers, who have become used to ever cheaper garments and are set to see their incomes squeezed by austerity measures. It will also heighten fears over inflation, which remains stubbornly high.

"Despite the additional pressures on the consumer, prices can't defy gravity forever and, ultimately, over the next few years the only way will be up," says Neil Saunders, consulting director at Verdict.

British consumers have enjoyed a decade of deflation as value retailers such as Primark and supermarkets have whittled away prices, while China's emergence as a manufacturing base brought the cheap clothing that has reshaped the high street. But this era is coming to an end, as the weakness of sterling makes garments purchased with dollars from suppliers in Asia more expensive.

Last year, British retailers were able to offset higher costs from currency weakness by striking competitive deals with Chinese suppliers keen to keep factories running amid a dearth of US orders. Lower commodity prices also fed through to better terms from suppliers.

But Chinese factories are now winning more orders, while the country's wage costs are rising as Chinese workers strive for better terms and conditions. Suppliers' leeway to offer deals has been clipped by their own costs rising. Cotton has gained about 50 per cent in the past year, and is trading close to its highest level in 14 years.

Shipping costs have also escalated, while British retailers are experiencing a "double whammy" according to Luca Solca, analyst at Sanford C. Bernstein, from the weakness of sterling – reflecting Britain's overstretched balance sheet – and a rising renminbi.

Source: Financial Times, 19 July 2010, p. 4. Reprinted with permission.

Apart from the problems fluctuating exchange rates cause for importers there are at least four other major issues:

- **Income to be received from abroad** For example, if a UK firm has exported goods to Canada on six months' credit terms, payable in Canadian dollars (C$), it is uncertain how many pounds it will actually receive because the Canadian currency could change in value compared to the pound in the intervening period.

- **The valuation of foreign assets and liabilities** In today's globalised marketplace many firms own assets abroad, or have foreign subsidiaries. The value of any of these assets or liabilities in domestic currency terms can change simply because of FX movements. See below for an excerpt from the BP Annual Report and Accounts 2009, showing just what a complex task it is to value overseas subsidiaries and their operations. It is clear that these figures could deviate from what is expected due to currency fluctuations.

  > In the consolidated financial statements, the assets and liabilities of non-US dollar ... currency subsidiaries, jointly controlled entities and associates, ... are translated into US dollars at the rate of exchange ruling at the balance sheet date. The results and cash flows of non-US dollar ... currency subsidiaries ... are translated into US dollars using average rates of exchange [for the year]. Exchange adjustments arising when the opening net assets and the profits for the year retained by non-US dollar ... currency subsidiaries ... are translated into US dollars are taken to a separate component of equity and reported in the statement of comprehensive income. Exchange gains and losses arising on long-term intragroup foreign currency borrowings used to finance the group's non-US dollar investments are also taken to equity. On disposal of a non-US dollar functional currency subsidiary, jointly controlled entity or associate, the deferred cumulative amount of exchange gains and losses recognized in equity relating to that particular non-US dollar operation is reclassified to the income statement.

- **The long-term viability of operations in particular countries** UK company Burberry is benefitting from the weakness of sterling to gain custom from Chinese consumers – *see* Exhibit 12.12. Thus we see that the long-term future returns of subsidiaries located in some countries can be enhanced by a favourable FX change. On the other hand, firms can be destroyed if they are operating in the wrong currency at the wrong time.

- **The acceptability, or otherwise, of an overseas investment project** When evaluating the value-creating potential of major new investments a firm must be aware that the likely future currency changes can have a significant effect on estimated value generated from the venture.

Exhibit 12.12

Burberry targets Chinese tourists

FT

By Andrea Felsted

Burberry is targeting the spending power of Chinese consumers in the world's big luxury markets, as more Chinese travel overseas.

While Burberry is expanding in China – particularly focusing on the affluent male consumer – Angela Ahrendts, chief executive, said the Chinese tourist was another important source of business.

"Over 30 per cent of our business in the UK today is to a Chinese consumer. They are free to travel there now and as a company we think not just [about] the Chinese market but how we cater to the Chinese consumer, with multiple dialects, in the top 10 flagship markets in the world," she said.

"They have read about them, dreamed about them, and now they are going to London, Paris, New York and Los Angeles."

Stacey Cartwright, chief financial officer, said that when it came to the UK, sales to Chinese consumers were being boosted by the weakness of sterling which increased their spending power. She estimated that Burberry goods were 40 per cent cheaper in the UK than China, primarily because of taxes and duties.

Source: Financial Times, 20 September 2010. Reprinted with permission.

How, then, do companies deal with all this volatility? There are various ways of vitiating the risk of currency fluctuations.

Dealing with exchange rate risk

For firms which operate in international trade, there are three forms of exposure to risk, transaction risk, translation risk and economic risk.

Transaction risk

Transaction risk is the risk that transactions already entered into, or for which the firm is likely to have a commitment in a foreign currency, will have a variable value in the home currency because of exchange-rate movements.

This type of risk is primarily associated with imports or exports. If a company imports or exports goods on credit the amount it will pay out or receive in home-currency terms is subject to uncertainty.

Transaction risk also arises when firms invest abroad, say, opening a new office or manufacturing plant. If the costs of construction are paid for over a period the firm may be exchanging the home currency for the foreign currency to make the payments. The amounts of the home currency required are uncertain if the exchange rate is subject to rate shifts. Also the cash inflows back to the parent are subject to exchange rate risk.

In addition, when companies borrow in a foreign currency, committing themselves to regular interest and principal payments in that currency, they are exposed to FX risk.

Translation risk

Translation risk arises because financial data denominated in one currency are then expressed in terms of another currency. Between two accounting dates the figures can be affected by exchange-rate movements, greatly distorting comparability. The financial statements of overseas business units are usually translated into the home currency in order that they might be consolidated with the group's financial statements. Income, expenses, assets and liabilities have to be re-expressed in terms of the home currency. Note that this is purely a paper-based exercise; it is translation and not the conversion of real money from one currency to another. If exchange rates were stable, comparing subsidiary performance and asset position would be straightforward. However, if exchange rates move significantly the results can be severely distorted.

There are two elements to translation risk:

1 ***The balance sheet effect*** Assets and liabilities denominated in a foreign currency can fluctuate in value in home-currency terms with FX-market changes. For example, if a UK company acquires A$1 million of assets in Australia when the rate of exchange is A$1.6/£ this can go into the UK group's accounts at a value of £625,000. If, over the course of the next year, the Australian dollar falls against sterling to A$1.8/£, when the consolidated accounts are drawn up and the asset is translated at the current exchange rate at the end of the year it is valued at only £555,556, a 'paper loss' of £69,444. And yet the asset has not changed in value in A$ terms one jot. These 'losses' are normally dealt with through balance sheet reserves.

2 ***The profit and loss account effect*** Currency changes can have an adverse impact on the group's profits because of the translation of foreign subsidiaries' profits. This often occurs even though the subsidiaries' managers are performing well and increasing profit in terms of the currency in which they operate.

Economic risk

A company's economic value may decline as a result of FX movements causing a loss in competitive strength. The worth of a company is the discounted cash flows payable to the owners.

It is possible that a shift in exchange rates can reduce the cash flows of foreign subsidiaries and home-based production far into the future (and not just affect the near future cash flows as in transaction exposure). In Australia, the strength of the home currency may well lead to a fall in their cattle export trade and so curtail the foreign income received – *see* Exhibit 12.13.

Exhibit 12.13

Australian cattlemen fear loss of exports   FT

Peter Smith

The 680 cattle on display at the livestock sale yards in Wodonga, an agricultural centre in south-eastern Australia, are making their final appearance before being prodded on to trucks and taken to the slaughterhouse.

After much slicing and dicing, cattle parts will emerge in chilled or frozen packages to be sent around the world. The Japanese take the premium cuts, the Koreans want the short ribs, and the Americans mix lean Australian beef with their corn-fed cattle for hamburger patties.

"Big, fat cows are making A\$1,200," says Ross Trethowan, a livestock and wheat farmer who runs a 1,600-hectare property.

But the fifth-generation farmer also knows his livelihood is tied to the world's commodity and currency markets. And the Australian cattle industry – alongside tourism, mining and manufacturing – is likely to be one of the hardest hit by the country's strengthening currency.

Mr Trethowan is fearful about any erosion in his competitiveness due to the Australian dollar's strength. The currency on Thursday hit a new high of US\$0.998, its highest level against the greenback since it was floated 27 years ago, and market observers believe parity is only days away.

'It keeps the price of [imported] fuel and fertiliser down, but it will damage us if it stays that strong," says Mr Trethowan. "We are still a long way behind the eight ball after those tough years of drought, so we can't afford to take a big hit."

Robert Reid, another farmer selling cattle at the auction, reckons the higher Australian dollar is already hitting the market just as greater numbers of cattle are coming up for sale.

Cattle prices have fallen by roughly 5 per cent in the past week alone, he says, and he blames that fall on the Australian dollar's rise.

"I would prefer it to be closer to US\$0.80. That's the right value," he says.

Australia is the world's second biggest beef exporter behind Brazil and nearly two-thirds of its beef production is destined for international markets.

However, Australia's beef export sales fell from A\$5.1bn to A\$4.2bn in the year to June, according to Meat & Livestock Australia, an industry body.

The drop of 18 per cent reflects the higher dollar, lower volumes of cattle being sold and weak economic conditions in top export markets such as Japan, according to Tim McRae, economist for Meat & Livestock Australia.

Mr McRae says the weak US dollar means that US producers have replaced those from South America as the big threat to Australian exporters.

"The two markets where Aussie and US beef exporters are slugging it out are Japan and South Korea, and we have seen a big increase in both markets by US exporters this year," he says.

"If the dollar stays high, it will make it that much harder to sell Aussie beef," Mr McRae said.

18%
Decline in Australian beef exports in the year to June

Andrew Broad, president of the state of Victoria's farmers' federation, says Australian producers are

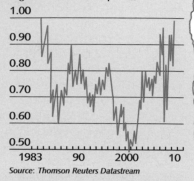

High and lows of the Australian dollar
Against US dollar (US\$ per A\$)

Source: Thomson Reuters Datastream

disadvantaged when countries keep their currencies artificially low.

"Farmers are seeing a better return after the end of the financial crisis and after the good season, but it's not as good as it could be because of the currency," Mr Broad said.

"We already have high interest rates in Australia which are putting a brake on the agricultural sector, but the Australian dollar is putting on another brake," Mr Broad says.

John McPhee, owner of the Wodonga abattoirs, agrees that the stronger dollar has affected his business "quite dramatically".

"If you lock in sales at a US dollar rate and then the Australian dollar goes in the other direction, you are still committed to supply.

"But what it means is you will get a lot less for it than you thought."

Mr McPhee says he had to adjust to deal with the market. "You have to sell your meat, cover the price of the dollar you are paying with the bank, and then move on," he said.

Source: *Financial Times*, 15 October 2010 p. 7. Reprinted with permission.

There are two ways in which competitive position can be undermined by FX changes:

- **Directly** If your firm's home currency strengthens then foreign competitors are able to gain sales and profits at your expense because your products are more expensive in the eyes of customers both abroad and at home, or you have reduced margins.

- **Indirectly** Even if your home currency does not move adversely vis-à-vis your customer's currency you can lose competitive position. For example suppose a South African firm is selling into Hong Kong and its main competitor is a New Zealand firm. If the New Zealand dollar weakens against the Hong Kong dollar the South African firm has lost some competitive position.

  Another indirect effect occurs even for firms which are entirely domestically oriented. For example, the cafés and shops surrounding a large export-oriented manufacturing plant may be severely affected by the closure of the factory due to an adverse forex movement.

Economic risk can badly damage a business – *see* **Exhibit 12.14**.

Exhibit 12.14

Small fry flounder in the wake of surge

Raphael Minder

Hank Morrison, whose Philippine company makes model aircraft, says he could be out of business within six months if the Filipino peso continues to rally against the US dollar.

'With the way the peso is going, it's become almost impossible,' he says. 'I'm not only operating at a loss but in effect the more I make the more I lose.'

As an emergency step, Mr Morrison has decided to halve his production of model aircraft, 95 per cent of which end up in America on the shelves of collectors or indus-

try buyers such as Boeing. That is bad news both for Mr Morrison's 60 Filipino employees and for Philippine exports.

Source: Financial Times, 10 October 2007, p. 15. Reprinted with permission.

Transaction risk strategies

The following section illustrates a number of strategies available to deal with transaction risk by focusing on the alternatives open to an exporter selling goods on credit. By going through these options we see the practical use of the financial markets for companies.

We will use the example of a UK company exporting £1 million of goods to a Canadian firm when the spot rate of exchange is C$1.60/£. The Canadian firm is given three months to pay, and naturally the spot rate in three months is unknown at the time of the shipment of goods. What can the firm do?

Invoice the customer in the home currency

One easy way to bypass exchange-rate risk is to insist that all foreign customers pay in your currency and your firm pays for all imports in your home currency. In the case of this example the Canadian importer will be required to send £1 million in three months, and the FX markets are not involved, except for the obtaining of £1 million by the Canadian company. However, the exchange-rate risk has not gone away, it has just been passed on to the customer.

Do nothing

Under this policy the UK firm invoices the Canadian firm for C$1.6 million, waits three months and then exchanges into sterling at whatever spot rate is available then. Perhaps an exchange-rate gain will be made, perhaps a loss will be made. Many firms adopt this policy and take a 'win some, lose some' attitude. Given the fees and other transaction costs of some hedging strategies this can make sense.

There are two considerations here. The first is the degree of risk aversion to higher cash flow variability, coupled with the sensitivity of shareholders to reported fluctuations of earnings due to foreign exchange gains and losses. The second, which is related to the first point, is the size of the transaction. If £1 million is a large proportion of annual turnover, and greater than profit, then the company may be more worried about FX risk.

Netting

Multinational companies often have subsidiaries in different countries selling to other members of the group. Netting is where the subsidiaries settle intra-organisational currency debts for the *net* amount owed in a currency rather than the *gross* amount. For example, if a UK parent owned a subsidiary in Canada and sold C$1.6 million of goods to the subsidiary on credit while the Canadian subsidiary is owed C$1.2 million by the UK company, instead of transferring a total of C$2.8 million the intra-group transfer is the net amount of C$400,000, so lessening the amount subject to currency risk – *see* Exhibit 12.15.

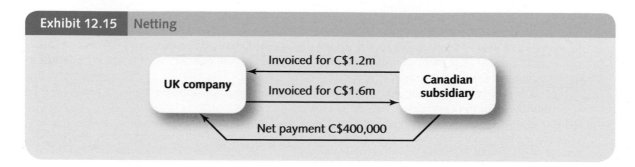

Exhibit 12.15   Netting

Invoiced for C$1.2m

UK company

Invoiced for C$1.6m

Canadian subsidiary

Net payment C$400,000

Matching

Netting only applies to transfers within a group of companies. Matching can be used for both intra-group transactions and those involving third parties. The company matches the inflows and outflows in different currencies caused by trade, etc., so that it is only necessary to deal on the FX markets for the unmatched portion of the total transactions. CLS settlement enables matching between members.

So if, say, the Canadian importer is not a group company and the UK firm also imported a raw material from another Canadian company to the value of C$1.4 million it is necessary only to hedge the balance of C$200,000 (*see* Exhibit 12.16).

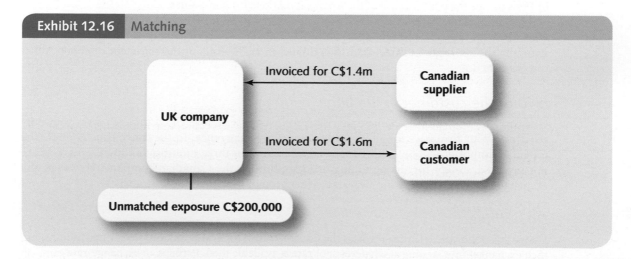

Exhibit 12.16   Matching

Invoiced for C$1.4m

Canadian supplier

UK company

Invoiced for C$1.6m

Canadian customer

Unmatched exposure C$200,000

Naturally, to net and match properly, the timing of the expected receipts and payments would have to be the same.

Forward market hedge

Although other forms of exchange rate risk management are available, forward cover represents the most frequently employed method of hedging. A contract is agreed to exchange two currencies at a fixed time in the future at a predetermined rate. The risk of FX variation is removed for the company taking out the contract.

So if the three-month forward rate is C$1.65/£ the UK exporter could lock in the receipt of £969,697 in three months by selling forward C$1.6 million.

$$\frac{C\$1,600,000}{1.65} = £969,697$$

No foreign exchange-rate risk now exists because the dollars to be received from the importer are matched by the funds to be exchanged for sterling. There is still a risk of the importer not paying, at all or on time, and the risk of the counterparty in the FX market not fulfilling its obligations.

Money market hedge

Money market hedging involves borrowing in the money markets. For example, the exporter could, at the time of the export, borrow in Canadian dollars on the money markets for a three-month period. The amount borrowed, plus three months' interest, will be equal to the amount to be received from the importer (C$1.6m).

If the interest rate charged over three months is, 8 per cent annualised, 2 per cent for three months, then the appropriate size of the loan is:

$$C\$ = C\$?(1 + 0.02) \quad C\$? = \frac{C\$1,600,000}{1.02} = C\$1,568,627$$

Thus the exporter has created a liability (borrowed funds) which matches the asset (debt owed by Canadian firm).

The borrowed dollars are then converted to sterling on the spot market for the exporter to receive £980,392 immediately:

$$\frac{C\$1,568,627}{1.6} = £980,392$$

The exporter has removed FX risk because it now holds cash in sterling three months before the debt was originally due, taking a small loss of £19,608, but this could be offset by three months' interest.

Three months later C$1.6 million is received from the importer and this exactly matches the outstanding debt:

Amount borrowed + Interest = Debt owed at end of period

$$C\$1,568,627 + (C\$1,568,627 \times 0.02) = £1.6m$$

The five steps in the money market hedge are as shown in Exhibit 12.17.

An importer could also use a money market hedge. A Swiss company importing Japanese cars for payment in yen in three months could borrow in Swiss francs now and convert the funds at the spot rate into yen. This money is deposited to earn interest, with the result that after three months the principal plus interest equals the invoice amount.

Futures hedge

A foreign currency futures contract is an agreement to exchange a specific amount of a currency for another at a fixed future date for a predetermined price. Futures are similar to forwards in many ways. They are, however, standardised contracts traded on regulated exchanges. Forwards can be tailor-made in a wide range of currencies with variable amounts of currency and delivery

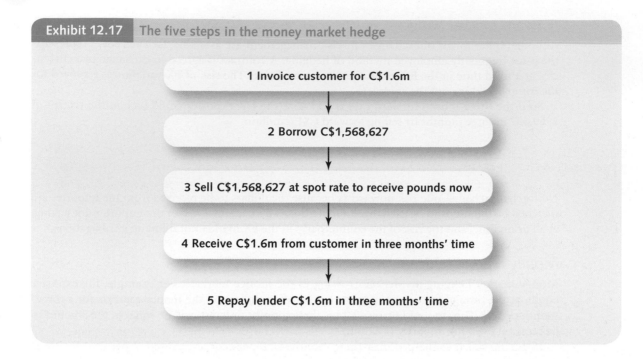

Exhibit 12.17 The five steps in the money market hedge

1 Invoice customer for C$1.6m

2 Borrow C$1,568,627

3 Sell C$1,568,627 at spot rate to receive pounds now

4 Receive C$1.6m from customer in three months' time

5 Repay lender C$1.6m in three months' time

dates, whereas futures are only available in a limited range of currencies and for a few specific forward time periods – *see* Chapter 10.

The vast majority of futures market trading in currencies is through the Chicago Mercantile Exchange (CME) and ICE Futures US, formerly NYBOT, the New York Board of Trade, which is now part of the Intercontinental Exchange group. The CME, for example, deals in 49 futures and 32 options contracts on 20 currencies.

A single futures contract is for a fixed amount of currency. For example, the sterling contract is for £62,500. It is not possible to buy or sell a smaller amount than this, nor to transact in quantities other than whole-number multiples of this. To buy a sterling futures contract is to make a commitment to deliver a quantity of US dollars and receive in return £62,500. One contract for euros is for €125,000.

On 3 December 2010 the CME and NYBOT quoted contracts (shown at www.ft.com) for delivery in December 2010 and February and March 2011 – *see* **Exhibit 12.18**. For example, the March contract for euros and US$ was priced at 1.3369 at the end of the trading day (the 'Open' column indicates the rate at the start of trading on 3 December, the 'Sett' column indicates closing prices.) This means that if you *buy* one contract you are committed to deliver US$1.3369 for every euro of the €125,000 you will receive in late March,[3] that is US$167,113. If you *sold* one contract at 1.3369 you would deliver €125,000 and receive US$167,113.

A firm hedging with currency futures will usually attempt to have a futures position that has an equal and opposite profit profile to the underlying transaction. Frequently the futures position will be closed before delivery is due, to give a cash profit or loss to offset the spot market profit or loss (for more details on futures *see* Chapter 10) – although physical delivery of the currency is possible.

To illustrate, if a US firm exports €125,000 worth of goods to a German firm on 3 December 2010 on four months' credit for payment in late March and the current spot exchange rate is US$1.3154/€ there is a foreign exchange risk. If the March future is trading at a price of US$1.3369 per euro the exporter's position could be hedged by *selling* one euro futures contract on CME.

---

[3] On the third Wednesday of the delivery month.

Exhibit 12.18 Currency Futures table from www.ft.com, 3 December 2010

Dec 3		Open	Sett	Change	High	Low	Est. vol	Open int
£-Sterling*	DEC0	0.8485	0.8495	0.0021	0.8512	0.8484	7	4,220
£-Yen*	DEC0	110.6100	110.8850	0.0900	110.61	110.61	570	6,580
$-Can $†	DEC0	0.9966	0.9954	-0.0008	0.9997	0.9918	97,966	94,410
$-Euro €†	DEC0	1.3213	1.3378	0.0176	1.3402	1.3192	381,834	186,909
$-Euro €†	MAR1	1.3206	1.3369	0.0175	1.3392	1.3185	16,376	16,868
$-Sw Franc †	DEC0	1.0075	1.0229	0.0167	1.0258	1.0050	52,251	41,331
$-Yen †	DEC0	1.1926	1.2061	0.0147	1.2118	1.1924	153,736	122,850
$-Yen †	MAR1	1.1943	1.2074	0.0147	1.2130	1.1940	5,987	5,379
$-Sterling †	MAR1	1.5588	1.5730	0.0163	1.5755	1.5572	5,166	3,084
$-Aust $ †	DEC0	0.9758	0.9897	0.0146	0.9911	0.9730	111,619	102,532
$-Mex Peso †	FEB1	–	80575	-275.00	–	–	–	1

Sources: *NYBOT; Sterling €100,000 and Yen: €100,000. †CME: Australian $: A$100,000, Canadian $: C$100,000, Euro: €125,000; Mexican Peso: 500,000, Swiss Franc: SFr125,000; Yen: ¥12,5m ($ per ¥100); Sterling: £62,500. CME volume, high & low for pit & electronic trading at settlement. Contracts shown are based on the volumes traded in 2004.

If in March the euro falls against the dollar to US$1.10/€ the calculation is:

Value of €125,000 received from customer when converted to dollars at spot in March (€125,000 × 1.10)	US$137,500
Amount if exchange rate was constant at US$1.3154/€	US$164,425
Forex loss	–US$26,925

However, an offsetting gain is made on the futures contract:

Sold at US$1.3369/€ (€125,000 × 1.3369)	US$167,112.50
Bought in March to close position at US$1.10/€ (€125,000 × 1.10)	US$137,500.00
Forex loss	+US$29,612.50

Alternatively the exporter could simply deliver the €125,000 received from the importer to CME in return for US$167,112.50

In the above example a perfect hedge was not achieved because the gain on the futures contract did not exactly equate to the loss on the underlying position (i.e. the euros to be received from the German customer). Perfect hedging is frequently unobtainable with futures because of their standardised nature which limits the amount (multiples of €125,000, for example) and timing (the underlying transaction takes place on a date where there is no future).

Currency option hedge

The final possible course of action to reduce FX transaction risk to be discussed in this chapter is to make use of the currency option market.

A currency option is a contract giving the buyer (that is, the holder) the right, but not the obligation, to buy or sell a specific amount of currency at a specific exchange rate (the strike price), on or before a specified future date.

A call option gives the right to buy a particular currency

A put option gives the right to sell a particular currency

The option writer (usually a bank) guarantees, if the option buyer chooses to exercise the right, to exchange the currency at the predetermined rate. Because the writer is accepting risk the buyer must pay a premium to the writer – normally within two business days of the option purchase. (For more details on options *see* Chapter 11.)

Exhibit 12.19 shows the currency options premiums for the currency rates between the pound GBP and the US dollar USD. This data is taken from the website of the Chicago Mercantile Exchange (CME) on 29 December 2010 as trading is taking place.

Exhibit 12.19 GBP/USD option for March 2011 as quoted in December 2010

Type				
American Options ▼				
Expiration				
MAR 2011 ▼				

Strike price	Type	Last	Change	Prior Settle
15200	CALL	0.0407 a	+0.0038	0.0369
15200	PUT	0.0180 b	−0.0028	0.0208
15300	CALL	0.0341 a	+0.0032	0.0309
15300	PUT	0.0215 b	−0.0033	0.0248
15400	CALL	0.0283 a	+0.0028	0.0255
15400	PUT	0.0257 b	−0.0037	0.0294
15500	CALL	0.0232 a	+0.0024	0.0208
15500	PUT	0.0305 b	−0.0042	0.0347
15600	CALL	0.0188 b	+0.0021	0.0167
15600	PUT	0.0360 b	−0.0046	0.0406

Note: a and b refer to the price being at or below (a) or at or above (b) the previous price.
Source: www.cme.com

For the GBP/USD call options the purchaser has the right but not the obligation to purchase pounds for dollars. Potential call option buyers have a number of possible rates of exchange open to them. The exhibit shows strike prices of $1.5200/£ to $1.5600/£ in the first column. The premiums payable, shown in the third column, are quoted as US dollars per pound. One contract is for £62,500, and only whole numbers of contracts on the exchange may be purchased. If you purchased a 15200 call option for expiry in March you would pay a premium of 4.07 US cents per UK pound (the total premium payable would be $0.0407 × 62,500 = $2,543.75) giving you the right to buy pounds with dollars in March at a rate of $1.52/£. Note that a less favourable exchange rate, e.g. 15600($1.56/£) commands a lower premium, only 1.88 cents per pound in the contract.

The purchase of a put option gives you the right but not the obligation to sell pounds and receive dollars. Again the quantity of a contract is £62,500.

The crucial advantage an option has over a forward is the absence of an obligation to buy or sell. It is the option buyer's decision whether to insist on exchange at the strike rate or to let the option lapse.

With forwards, if the exchange rate happens to move in your favour after you are committed to a forward contract you cannot take any advantage of that movement. We saw above that if the forward rate was C$1.65/£ the exporter would receive £969,697 in three months. If the spot exchange rate had moved to, say, C$1.5/£ over the three months the exporter would have liked to abandon the agreement to sell the dollars at C$1.65/£, but is unable to do so because of the legal commitment. With an option there is always the possibility of abandoning the deal and exchanging at spot. When the Canadian firm pays the exporter would receive an income of:

$$\frac{C\$1,600,000}{1.5} = £1,066,667$$

This is an extra £96,970.

An option permits:

- hedging against unfavourable currency movement;
- profit from favourable currency movement.

Worked example 12.4   Currency option contract

Now, imagine that the UK exporting firm, when the goods are delivered to the Canadian firm, hedges by buying a three-month sterling call option giving the right but not the obligation to deliver Canadian dollars to a bank in exchange for pounds with a strike price of C\$1.65/£. A premium will need to be paid up front. Assume this is 2 per cent of the amount covered, that is, a non-refundable $0.02 \times C\$1,600,000 = C\$32,000$ is payable two business days after the option deal is struck.

Three months later

The dollars are delivered by the importer on the due date. Should the option at C\$1.65/£ be exercised? Let us consider two scenarios.

Scenario 1

The dollar has strengthened against the pound to C\$1.5/£. If the company exercises the right to exchange at C\$1.65/£ the UK firm will receive:

$$\frac{C\$1,600,000}{1.65} = £969,697$$

If the company lets the option lapse – 'abandons it' – and exchanges the dollars in the spot market, the amount received will be:

$$\frac{C\$1,600,000}{1.5} = £1,066,667$$

an extra £96,970.

Clearly, in this case the best course of action would be to abandon the option, and exchange at the spot rate.

Scenario 2

Now assume that the dollar has weakened against sterling to C\$1.8/£. If the treasurer contacts the bank (the option writer) to confirm that the exporter wishes to exercise the C\$1.65/£ option the treasurer will arrange delivery of C\$1,600,000 to the bank and will receive £969,697 in return:

$$\frac{C\$1,600,000}{1.65} = £969,697$$

If the option is abandoned and the C\$1.6 million is sold in the spot FX market, the amount received will be:

$$\frac{C\$1,600,000}{1.8} = £888,889$$

a loss of £80,808. This is unattractive and so the option will be exercised.

With the option, the worst that could happen is that the exporter receives £969,697 less the premium. However, the upside potential is unconstrained.

Option contracts are generally for sums greater than US$1,000,000 on the OTC market (direct deals with banks) whereas one contract on the CME is, for example, for £62,500. The drawback with exchange-based derivatives is the smaller range of currencies available and the inability to tailor-make a hedging position.

Managing translation risk

The effect of translation risk on the balance sheet can be lessened by matching the currency of assets and liabilities. For example, Graft plc has decided to go ahead with a US$190 million project in the US. One way of financing this is to borrow £100 million and exchange this for dollars at the current exchange rate of US$1.9/£. Thus, at the beginning of the year the additional entries into the consolidated accounts are as shown in worked example 12.5.

Worked example 12.5   Translation risk

Opening balance sheet

Liabilities		Assets	
Loan	£100m	US assets	£100m

The US$190 million of US assets are translated at US$1.9/£ so all figures are expressed in the parent company's currency.

Now imagine that over the course of the next year the dollar depreciates against sterling to US$2.30/£. In the consolidated group accounts there is still a £100 million loan but the asset bought with that loan, while still worth US$190 million,[4] is valued at only £82.61 million when translated into sterling. In the parent company's currency terms, £17.39 million needs to be written off:

Year-end balance sheet

Liabilities		Assets	
Loan	£100.00m	US assets	£82.61m
Forex loss	−£17.39m		

Alternatively Graft plc could finance its dollar assets by obtaining a dollar loan. Thus, when the dollar depreciates, both the asset value and the liability value in translated sterling terms become less.

Opening balance sheet

Liabilities		Assets	
Loan	£100m	US assets	£100m

If forex rates move to US$2.30/£:

Year-end balance sheet

Liabilities		Assets	
Loan	£82.61m	US assets	£82.61m

There is no currency loss to deal with.

---

[4] Assuming, for the sake of simplicity, no diminution of asset value in dollar terms.

One constraint on the solution set out in worked example 12.5 is that some governments insist that a proportion of assets acquired within their countries is financed by the parent firm. Another constraint is that the financial markets in some countries are insufficiently developed to permit large-scale borrowing.

Managing economic risk

Economic exposure is concerned with the long-term effects of forex movements on a firm's ability to compete and add value. These effects are very difficult to estimate in advance, given their long-term nature, and therefore the hedging techniques described for transaction risk are of limited use. The forwards markets may be used to a certain extent, but these only extend for a short period for most currencies. Also the matching principle could be employed, whereby overseas assets are matched as far as possible by overseas liabilities.

The main method of insulating the firm from economic risk is to position the company in such a way as to maintain maximum flexibility – to be able to react to changes in FX rates which may be causing damage to the firm. Firms which are internationally diversified may have a greater degree of flexibility than those based in one or two markets. For example, a company with production facilities in numerous countries can shift output to those plants where the exchange rate change has been favourable. The international car assemblers have an advantage here over the purely domestic producer.

Forex changes can impact on the costs of raw materials and other inputs. By maintaining flexibility in sourcing supplies a firm could achieve a competitive advantage by deliberately planning its affairs so that it can switch suppliers quickly and cheaply.

An aware multinational could allow for forex changes when deciding in which countries to launch an advertising campaign. For example, it may be pointless increasing marketing spend in a country whose currency has depreciated rapidly recently, making the domestically-produced competing product relatively cheap.

Exchange rate determination

A number of factors influence the rate of exchange between currencies. This section briefly considers some of them.

Purchasing power parity theory

The theory of **purchasing power parity (PPP)** is based on the idea that a basket of traded goods should cost the same regardless of the currency in which it is sold. For example, if a basket of traded goods sold for £10,000 in the UK and an identical 'basket' sold for US$15,000 in the USA then the rate of exchange should be US$1.50/£. Imagine what would happen if this were not the case; say, for example, the rate of exchange was US$3.00/£. Now British consumers can buy a basket of traded goods in the US market for half the price they would pay in the UK market (£5,000 can now be exchanged for US$15,000). Naturally the demand for dollars would rise as UK consumers rushed out of sterling to buy dollars. This would cause the FX rates to change – the dollar would rise in value until the purchasing power of each currency was brought to an equilibrium, that is, where there is no incentive to exchange currencies to take advantage of lower prices abroad because of a misaligned exchange rate.

The definition of PPP is:

Exchange rates are in equilibrium when their domestic purchasing powers at that rate of exchange are equal.

So, for example:

Price of a basket of goods in UK in sterling	×	US$/£ exchange rate	=	Price of a basket of goods in USA in dollars
£10,000	×	1.50	=	US$15,000

The PPP theory becomes more interesting if relationships over a period of time are examined. Inflation in each country will affect the price of a basket of goods in domestic currency terms. This in turn will influence the exchange rate between currencies with different domestic inflation rates.

Let us suppose that sterling and the US dollar are at PPP equilibrium at the start of the year with rates at US$1.50/£. Then over the year the inflation rate in the UK is 15 per cent so the same basket costs £11,500 at the end of the year. If during the same period US prices rise by 3 per cent the US domestic cost of a basket will be US$15,450. If the exchange rate remains at US$1.50/£ there will be a disequilibrium and PPP is not achieved. A UK consumer is faced with a choice of either buying £11,500 of UK-produced goods or exchanging £11,500 into dollars and buying US goods. The consumer's £11,500 will buy US$17,250 at US$1.50/£. This is more than one basket; therefore the best option is to buy goods in the US. The buying pressure on the dollar will shift exchange rates to a new equilibrium in which a basket costs the same price in both countries. To find this new equilibrium exchange rate we could use the following formula:

$$\frac{1 + I_{US}}{1 + I_{UK}} = \frac{US\$/£_1}{US\$/£_0}$$

where: I_{US} = US inflation rate;
I_{UK} = UK inflation rate;
$US\$/£_1$ = the spot rate of exchange at the end of the period;
$US\$/£_0$ = the spot rate of exchange at the beginning of the period.

$$\frac{1 + 0.03}{1 + 0.15} = \frac{US\$/£_1}{1.50}$$

$$US\$/£_1 = \frac{1 + 0.03}{1 + 0.15} \times 1.50 = 1.3435$$

The US dollar appreciates against the pound by 10.43 per cent because inflation is lower in the US over the period.

At this new exchange rate a basket of goods costing US$15,450 in the US has a sterling cost of 15,450/1.3435 = £11,500 and thus PPP is maintained.

The pure PPP concludes that the country with the higher inflation rate will be subject to a depreciation of its currency, and the extent of that depreciation is proportional to the relative difference in the two countries' inflation rates. However, the theory is most valid for countries which are both geographically and demographically close. The PPP theory has some serious problems when applied in practice:

- **It applies only to goods freely traded internationally at no cost of trade** Many goods and services do not enter international trade and so their relative prices are not taken into account in the determination of currency rates. Medical services, haircuts, building and live entertainment, to name but a few, are rarely imported; therefore they are not subject to PPP. The theory also has limited applicability to goods with a high transportation cost relative to their value, for example road stone or cement. The PPP disequilibrium would have to be very large to make it worthwhile importing products of this kind. There may also be barriers inhibiting trade, for example regulations, tariffs, quotas, cultural resistance.

- **It works in the long run, but that may be years away** Customers may be slow to recognise the incentive to purchase from another country when there is a PPP disequilibrium. There is usually some inertia due to buying habits that have become routine. Furthermore, governments may manage exchange rates for a considerable period, thus defying the forces pressing toward PPP. In addition, in the short term there are other elements at play such as balance of payments disequilibria, capital transactions (purchase of assets such as factories, businesses or shares by foreigners) and speculation.

The evidence is that relative inflation is one influence on exchange rates, but it is not the only factor. There have been large deviations from PPP for substantial periods.

The OECD uses its resources to produce continuously updated statistics indicating what the exchange should be for a representative basket of goods to cost 100 units of domestic currency. Another set of statistics and a far simpler indicator of currency discrepancies is the 'Big Mac Index', initiated by *The Economist*, which compares the price of a Big Mac in different countries – see **Exhibit 12.20**.

Exhibit 12.20

The Big Mac index

Why China needs more expensive burgers

The Economist, 14 October 2010

A WEAK currency, despite its appeal to exporters and politicians, is no free lunch. But it can provide a cheap one. In China, for example, a McDonald's Big Mac costs just 14.5 yuan on average in Beijing and Shenzhen, the equivalent of $2.18 at market exchange rates. In America, in contrast, the same burger averages $3.71.

That makes China's yuan one of the most undervalued currencies in the Big Mac index, our gratifyingly simple guide to currency misalignments, updated this week (see chart). The index is based on the idea of purchasing-power parity, which says that a currency's price should reflect the amount of goods and services it can buy. Since 14.5 yuan can buy as much burger as $3.71, a yuan should be worth $0.26 on the foreign-exchange market. In fact, it cost $0.15, suggesting that it is undervalued by about 40%. The tensions caused by such misalignments prompted Brazil's finance minister, Guido Mantega, to complain last month that his country was a potential casualty of a 'currency war'. Perhaps it was something he ate. In Brazil a Big Mac costs the equivalent of $5.26, implying that the real is now overvalued by 42%. The index also suggests that the euro is overvalued by about 29%. And the Swiss, who avoid most wars, are in the thick of this one. Their franc is the most expensive currency on our list. The Japanese are so far the only rich country to intervene directly in the markets to weaken their currency. But according to burgernomics, the yen is only 5 per cent overvalued, not much of a *casus belli*. If a currency war is in the offing, America's congressmen seem increasingly determined to arm themselves. A bill passed by the House of Representatives last month would treat undervalued currencies as an illegal export subsidy and allow American firms to request countervailing tariffs. The size of those tariffs would reflect the scale of the undervaluation.

How does the bill propose to calculate this misalignment? It relies not on Big Macs, but on the less digestible methods favoured by the IMF. The fund uses three related approaches. First, it calculates the

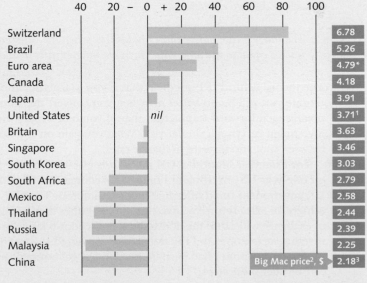

Bunfight
Big Mac index, local-currency under(-)/over(+) valuation against the dollar, %

Country	Big Mac price[2], $
Switzerland	6.78
Brazil	5.26
Euro area	4.79*
Canada	4.18
Japan	3.91
United States	3.71[1]
Britain	3.63
Singapore	3.46
South Korea	3.03
South Africa	2.79
Mexico	2.58
Thailand	2.44
Russia	2.39
Malaysia	2.25
China	2.18[3]

Source: McDonald's; The Economist

*Weighted average of member countries [1]Average of four cities [2]At market exchange rate (Oct 13th) [3]Average of two cities

real exchange rate that would steadily bring a country's current-account balance (equivalent to the trade balance plus a few other things) into line with a 'norm' based on the country's growth, income per person, demography and budget balance.

The fund's second approach ignores current-account balances and instead calculates a direct statistical relationship between the real exchange rate and things like a country's terms of trade (the price of its exports compared with its imports), its productivity and its foreign assets and liabilities. The strength of Brazil's currency, for example, may partly reflect the high price of exports such as soyabeans.

Third, the fund also calculates the exchange rate that would stabilise the country's foreign assets and liabilities at a reasonable level. If, for example, a country runs sizeable trade surpluses, resulting in a rapid build-up of foreign assets, it probably has an undervalued exchange rate.

The IMF has typically assessed its members' policies one at a time. But the fund's managing director, Dominique Strauss-Kahn, now proposes to assess its biggest members all at once to make sure their macroeconomic strategies do not work at cross-purposes. He is keen to identify the ways in which a country's policies, including its exchange-rate policies, 'spill over' to its neighbours.

Those spillovers depend on the size of the economy as much as the scale of any misalignments. But the biggest economies are also the hardest to bully. The fund's last annual report on the Chinese economy, in July, included the government's rebuttal of every criticism the fund offered. In a decorous compromise the report concluded that the yuan was 'substantially' undervalued but refrained from quantifying the size of the problem.

Big revaluations of the kind required to satisfy the fund or equalise the price of burgers are unlikely. A recent study of the Big Mac index by Kenneth Clements, Yihui Lan and Shi Pei Seah of the University of Western Australia showed that misalignments are remarkably persistent. As a result, the raw index did a poor job of predicting exchange rates: undervalued currencies remain too cheap and overvalued currencies remain too pricey.

But since this bias is systematic, it can be identified and removed. Once that is done, the three economists show that a reconstituted index is good at predicting real exchange rates over horizons of a year or more. Since *The Economist* costs just $6.99 (a little less than two burgers) on the news-stand, the index provides decent value for money for would-be currency speculators, the authors conclude. The Big Mac index may itself be undervalued.

Interest rate parity theory

While PPP is concerned with differences in spot rates at different points in time and relating these to inflation rates, the interest rate parity (IRP) theory concerns the relationship between spot rates and forward rates, and links differences between these to the nominal interest rates available in each of the two currencies.

The interest rate parity theory holds true when the difference between spot and forward exchange rates is equal to the differential between interest rates available in the two currencies.

The theory behind IRP predicts that if you place your money in a currency with a high interest rate you will be no better off when you convert the sum back into your home currency via a prearranged forward transaction than if you had simply invested in a domestic interest-bearing investment carrying a similar risk. What you gain on the extra interest you lose on the difference between spot and forward exchange rates.

For example, suppose a UK investor is attracted by the 8 per cent interest rate being offered on one-year US government bonds. This compares well with the similarly very low risk one-year UK government bond offering 6 per cent interest. The IRP theory says that this investor will not achieve an extra return by investing abroad rather than at home because the one-year forward rate of exchange will cause the US$ to be at a discount relative to the present spot rate. Thus, when the investment matures and the dollars are converted to sterling the investor will have achieved the same as if the money had been invested in UK government bonds.

Consider these steps:

1   *Beginning of year*

Exchange £1 million for US$1.5 million at the spot rate of US$1.5/£.
Buy US$1.5 million government bonds yielding 8 per cent.
Arrange a one-year forward transaction at US$1.5283/£ to sell dollars.

2   *End of year*

Exchange US$1.62 million (US$1.5 million × 1.08 to include added interest) with the bank which agreed the forward exchange at the beginning of the year at the rate 1.5283 to produce $1.62m ÷ 1.5283 = £1.06 million. This is equal to the amount that would have been received by investing in UK government bonds, 6 per cent over the year. The differential between the spot and forward rates exactly offsets the difference in interest rates.

The formula which links together the spot, forward and interest rate differences is:

$$\frac{1 + r_{US}}{1 + r_{UK}} = \frac{US\$/£_F}{US\$/£_S}$$

where: r_{US} = interest rate available in the USA;
r_{UK} = interest rate available in the UK (for the same risk);
$US\$/£_F$ = the forward exchange rate;
$US\$/£_S$ = the spot exchange rate.

To test this relationship consider the case where both the spot rate and the forward rate are at US$1.50/£. Here the investor can prearrange to convert the dollar investment back into sterling through a forward agreement and obtain an extra 2 per cent by investing in the US. However, the investor will not be alone in recognising this remarkable opportunity. Companies, forex dealers and fund managers will turn to this type of trading. They would sell UK bonds, buy dollars spot, buy US bonds and sell dollars forward. This would quickly lead us away from disequilibrium as the pressure of these transactions would lower UK bond prices and therefore raise interest rates, cause a rise in the value of the spot dollar against sterling, a rise in the price of US bonds and therefore a fall in interest rates being offered and a fall in the dollar forward rate. These adjustments will eliminate the investment return differences and re-establish IRP equilibrium.

The IRP insists that the relationship between exchange and interest rates is as follows:

● *High nominal interest rate currency* Currency trades at a discount on the forward rate compared with spot rate.

● *Low nominal interest rate currency* Currency trades at a premium on the forward rate compared with spot rate.

The IRP theory *generally* holds true in practice. However, there are deviations caused by factors such as taxation (which alters the rate of return earned on investments), or government controls on capital flows, controls on currency trading and intervention in foreign exchange markets interfering with the attainment of equilibrium through arbitrage.

The article in **Exhibit 12.21** describes two types of IRP.

Exhibit 12.21

Carry on speculating

How traders have been triumphing over economic theory

No comment on the financial markets these days is complete without mention of the 'carry trade', the borrowing or selling of currencies with low interest rates and the purchase of currencies with high rates. The trade is often blamed for the weakness of the Japanese yen and the unexpected enthusiasm of investors for the New Zealand and Australian dollars.

But why does the carry trade work? In theory, it shouldn't – or not for as long as it has. Foreign-exchange markets operate under a state of 'covered interest parity'. In other words, the difference between two countries' interest rates is exactly reflected in the gap between the spot, or current, exchange rate and the forward market. High-interest-rate currencies are at a discount in the forward market; low-rate currencies at a premium.

▶

If that were not so, it would be possible for a Japanese investor to sell yen, buy dollars, invest those dollars at high American interest rates for 12 months and simultaneously sell the dollars forward for yen to lock in a profit in a year's time. The potential for arbitrage means such profits cannot be earned.

However, economic theory also suggests that 'uncovered interest parity' should operate. Countries that offer high interest rates should be compensating investors for the risk that their currency will depreciate. In other words, the forward rate should be a good guess of the likely future spot rate.

In the real world, uncovered interest parity has not applied over the past 25 years or so. A recent academic study* has shown that high-rate currencies have tended to appreciate and low-rate currencies to depreciate, the reverse of theory. Carry-trade strategies would have brought substantial profits, not far short of stockmarket returns, although dealing costs would have limited the size of the bets traders could make.

Academics have struggled for some time to explain this discrepancy. One possibility is that investors demand a risk premium, separate from the better interest rate, to compensate them for investing in a foreign currency. As this risk premium varies, it might overwhelm the effects of interest-rate changes. For example, American investors might worry about the credibility of the Bank of Japan, but Japanese investors may regard the dollar as a 'safe haven'. This would drive the dollar up and the yen down.

However, according to Andrew Scott, of the London Business School, it has been a struggle to find risk premiums that are large enough to explain exchange-rate volatility. So academics have been looking at the structure of foreign-exchange markets, to see if behavioural factors might be at work.

One obvious possibility is that the actions of carry traders are self-fulfilling; when they borrow the yen and buy the dollar, they drive the former down and the latter up. If other investors follow 'momentum' strategies – jumping on the bandwagon of existing trends – this would tend to push up currencies with high interest rates.

Financial jaywalking

Such a strategy has its dangers. It has been likened to 'picking up nickels in front of steamrollers': you have a long run of small gains but eventually get squashed. In the currency markets, this would mean a steady series of profits from the interest-rate premium that are all wiped out by a large, sudden shift in exchange rates: think of the pound's exit from the European exchange-rate mechanism in 1992. The foreign-exchange markets have been remarkably calm since the Asian crisis of 1998 (when the yen rose sharply, hitting many carry traders). So a whole generation of investors may have grown up in a state of blissful innocence, unaware that their carry strategy has severe dangers.

Inflation may provide an alternative explanation. The theory of purchasing-power parity (PPP) implies that high-inflation currencies should depreciate, relative to harder monies. In other words, while nominal exchange rates might vary, real rates should be pretty constant. And over the very long term, this seems to happen. A study by the London Business School†, with ABN Amro, a Dutch bank, found that real exchange rates in 17 countries moved by less than an average of 0.2 per cent a year over the period 1900–2006.

Other things being equal (such as roughly similar real interest rates across countries) nominal interest rates should be higher in countries with higher inflation rates. So this should give support to uncovered-interest parity and deter the carry trade. Clearly, though, PPP has not been a useful guide over the past ten years, as the deflation-prone yen has declined against the dollar.

Perhaps the success of the carry trade reflects biases built up in an earlier era, during the inflationary 1970s and 1980s. Currencies prone to inflation back then, such as sterling and the dollar, have had to pay higher interest rates to compensate investors for their reputation. In fact, because inflation has declined, investors in Britain and America have been overcompensated for the risks – a windfall gain that has been exploited by followers of the carry trade. However, it is hard to believe that this effect could have lasted for as long as it has. So the reasons for the success of the carry trade remain a bit of a mystery.

What does seem plain, however, is that the carry trade tends to break down when markets become more turbulent. In such conditions, those who borrowed yen to borrow to buy other assets (such as emerging-market shares) might face a double blow as the yen rose while asset prices fell. If the turbulence were sufficiently large, many years' worth of profits from the carry trade might be wiped out. A steamroller could yet restore the reputation of economic theory.

* 'The Returns to Currency Speculation', by Craig Burnside, Martin Eichenbaum, Isaac Kleschelski and Sergio Rebelo, www.nber.org/papers/w12489

† Global Investment Returns Yearbook 2007

Source: The Economist, 24 February 2007, p. 88. Reprinted with permission. © The Economist Newspaper Limited 2007.

Expectations theory

The expectations theory states that the current forward exchange rate is an unbiased predictor of the spot rate at that point in the future.

Note that the theory does not say that the forward rate predicts precisely what spot rates will be in the future; it is merely an unbiased predictor or provides the statistical expectation. The forward rate will frequently underestimate the actual future spot rate. However, it will also frequently overestimate the actual future spot rate. On (a statistical) average, however, it predicts the future spot rate because it neither consistently under- nor consistently over-estimates.

Traders in foreign currency nudge the market towards the fulfilment of the expectations theory. If a trader takes a view that the forward rate is lower than the expected future spot price there is an incentive to buy forward. Then when the forward matures and the trader's view on the spot rate turns out to be correct the trader is able to buy at a low price and immediately sell at spot to make a profit. The buying pressure on the forward raises the price until equilibrium occurs, in which the forward price equals the market consensus view on the future spot price, which is an unbiased predictor.

The general conclusions from empirical studies investigating the truthfulness of the expectations theory is that for the more widely traded currencies it generally works well. However, there may be numerous periods when relative interest rates (under IRP theory) are the dominant influence. The forward rate can be taken to be unbiased as a predictor of the future spot rate, that is, it has an equal chance of being below or of being above the actual spot rate. However, it is a poor predictor – sometimes it is wide of the mark in one direction and sometimes wide of the mark in the other.

This knowledge may be useful to companies contemplating whether to hedge through using forward rates, with the attendant transaction costs, on a regular basis or whether to adopt a 'do nothing' policy, accepting that sometimes one loses on forex and sometimes one wins. For a firm with numerous transactions, the future spot rate will average the same as the forward rate, and so the 'do nothing' policy may be the cheaper and more attractive option.

The influence of a current account deficit and capital flows

Another influence on exchange rate movements is the presence or otherwise of an unsustainable balance of payments. If an economy is importing more goods and services than it is exporting it is said to have a current-account deficit. The exchange rate will move (in theory) so as to achieve current-account balance. So, an overvalued exchange rate makes exporting difficult and encourages home consumers to buy goods produced in other countries. If the exchange rate then declines exporters can sell more abroad and consumers are more likely to purchase the domestically produced version of a product as it becomes cheaper relative to imported goods. The trade deficit is eventually eliminated through this mechanism. The Fundamental Equilibrium Exchange Rate (FEER) is the exchange rate that results in a sustainable current-account balance. Any movement away from the FEER is a disequilibrium that sets in train forces that tend to bring the exchange rate back to equilibrium. That is the theory. In reality, there are many factors other than the trade balance causing forex rates to move.

Only around 1 per cent of all FX transactions are related to imports and exports of goods and services. Exchange rates can diverge from FEER for many years if foreign investors are willing to continue to finance a current-account deficit. They do this by buying assets (bonds, shares, companies, property, etc.) in the country with the negative balance of payments. The main influence on these capital transfers of money (and therefore demand for the deficit country's currency) is investors' expectations regarding the returns available on financial assets. If investors believe that the economy with a current-account deficit nevertheless offers good future returns on the bond market or the equity market, say, they will still bid up the value of its currency as they buy it to invest.

In the period 2000–2004 the US ran a very large current-account deficit and yet the currency did not fall in value. Foreign investors thought that the returns offered on US financial assets, particularly shares, were attractive and so continued to support the dollar as they pumped money into the economy. While the American people went on a spending spree (with expenditure higher than take-home pay), in the process buying mountains of foreign-produced goods, money flowed in as financial assets were bought, thus allowing the dollar to remain high. In the later stages of this unsustainable deficit the major buyers of US assets were Asian central banks, as countries such as China and Japan bought US Treasury bills and bonds to inject demand for dollars so that their exporters did not suffer from a rising currency against the dollar. Of course, it was widely recognised that the dollar could plummet should overseas investors ever start to believe that the US economic miracle is over (or that it was not really a productivity miracle after all) if they were to sell US financial assets, sell the dollar and move funds to somewhere else in the world offering more exciting (or safer) returns. This is what started to happen in 2004–2007. But it was halted by the financial crisis. The US was seen as a 'safe haven', and so investors around the world bought dollars to invest in US assets. Ironic, really, as it was the US mortgage market and Wall Street she-nanigans that caused the crisis.

Efficiency of FX markets

Whether the forex markets are efficient at pricing spot and forward currency rates is hotly debated. If they are efficient then speculators on average should not be able to make abnormal returns by using information to take positions. In an efficient market the best prediction of tomorrow's price is the price today, because prices move in a random walk fashion, depending on the arrival of new information. Prices adjust quickly to new information, but it is impossible to state in advance the direction of future movements because, by its nature, news is unpredictable (it might be 'bad' or it might be 'good').

If the market is efficient, any type of forecasting is a pointless exercise because any information used to predict the future will have already been processed by the market participants and be reflected in the price.

There are three levels of market efficiency:

- **Weak form** Historic prices and volume information is fully reflected in current prices, and therefore a trader cannot make abnormal profits by observing past price changes and trying to predict the future.

- **Semi-strong form** All publicly available information is fully reflected in prices, therefore abnormal profits are not available by acting on information once it is made public.

- **Strong form** Public and private (that is, available to insiders, for example those working for a central bank) information is reflected in prices.

Much empirical research has been conducted into currency market efficiency and the overall conclusion, such as it is, is that the question remains open. Some strategies, on some occasions, have produced handsome profits. On the other hand, many studies show a high degree of efficiency with little opportunity for abnormal reward. Most of the studies examine the major trading currencies of the world – perhaps there is more potential for the discovery of inefficiency in the more exotic currencies. Central bank intervention in foreign exchange markets also seems to be a cause of inefficiency.

Trying to outwit the market can be exciting, but it can also be dangerous. Alan Greenspan, former chairman of the US Federal Reserve, said: 'To my knowledge no model projecting movements in exchange rates is superior to tossing a coin.'[5]

---

[5] Quoted in Samuel Brittan, 'The dollar needs benign neglect', *Financial Times*, 30 January 2004, p. 21.

Concluding comments

Where would we be without the ability to exchange currency so that we can buy goods and services from abroad and foreigners can buy from our country? Also, imagine how limiting it would be if we could not obtain currency to buy assets in other countries whether that be a factory, shares in companies, government bonds or merely an apartment. Life would be less rich, in more senses than one. The benefits from cross-border transactions are obvious to all of us. But perhaps the risks of exchange rate change is less obvious. Hopefully this chapter has stimulated thought on the risks and provided insight into the main techniques used to mitigate them. The FX markets, institutions and instruments provide tools we need to make life better.

Key points and concepts

- An **exchange rate** is the price of one currency expressed in terms of another.

- The **foreign exchange market** grew dramatically over the last quarter of the twentieth century. About US$4,000 billion is now traded each day on average. Most of this trading is between banks rather than for underlying (for example, import/export) reasons.

- **Spot transaction**: single outright transaction involving the exchange of two currencies at a rate agreed on the date of the contract for value or delivery (cash settlement) within two business days.

- **Forward**: transaction involving the exchange of two currencies at a rate agreed on the date of the contract for value or delivery (cash settlement) at some time in the future (more than two business days later).

- **Foreign exchange swap (FX swap)**: a single deal with two parts to it. First, there is the actual exchange of two currencies on a specific date at a rate agreed at the time of the conclusion of the contract – this is usually a spot exchange. Second, there is a reverse exchange of the same two currencies at a date further in the future at a rate agreed at the time of the contract. The rates of exchange are usually different in the two parts.

- **Currency swap**: contract which commits two counterparties to exchange streams of interest payments in different currencies for an agreed period of time and usually to exchange principal amounts in different currencies at a pre-agreed exchange rate at maturity. A **currency swaption**: option to enter into a currency swap contract.

- **Currency option:** an option contract that gives the right but not the obligation to buy or sell a currency with another currency at a specified exchange rate during a specified period.

- **Future:** foreign currency futures are exchange traded forward transactions with standard contract sizes and maturity dates.

- **Trading** on the foreign exchange market does not have a focal position where all trading is supervised and data are collected and displayed; it is carried out in numerous locations, mostly over the counter.

- **Customer direct trades:** the customer (non-bank) approaches the bank without going through an intermediary.

- **Voice broker trades**: a broker acts on behalf of a customer to deal with banks in the FX markets over the telephone (brokers can also access electronic trading platforms).

- **Inter-dealer direct trades:** trades between banks. These can be either via direct telephone communication or direct electronic dealing systems.

- **Electronic dealing systems**: banks are the main users of these systems, but there are special systems set up for customers. Some of these are run by a single bank as a **'proprietary platform'**. Others are managed by a group of banks, **'multibank dealing systems'**.

- **Exchange rates are quoted** with a bid rate (the rate at which you can buy) and an offer rate (the rate at which you can sell).

▶

- Most currencies are quoted to four decimal places and the smallest variation used in trading is a **pip** which is one ten thousandth of 1 unit of currency (e.g. $1).

- A bank could fail after receiving one leg of its foreign exchange trades but before paying the other leg – this is called **Herstatt risk. Continuous Linked Settlement** allows **PvP, payment versus payment**, simultaneous settlement of both legs of trading, thereby eliminating Herstatt risk.

- A **cross-rate** is the exchange rate of two currencies that are normally expressed in terms of a third currency, usually the US dollar.

- **Fixed exchange rate regimes** require the participating countries to keep their currencies held at a constant rate or within a certain percentage of an agreed rate.

- **Gold standard:** currencies were fixed at a set price in gold.

- **Bretton Woods:** an exchange rate system whereby the currencies were fixed to the US dollar, which in turn was fixed to the price of gold at $35 per ounce of gold.

- **Currency peg:** one currency is pegged (fixed) to, say, the US dollar. It moves in line with that currency as it fluctuates against other currencies, so it is not fixed against other currencies.

- **Floating FX regime:** the exchange rate for a currency is governed by supply and demand.

- **Managed floats or dirty floats:** no official limits for the movements of their currencies but nevertheless governments sometimes intervene to prevent their currency moving too far in a certain direction.

- **Forex shifts can affect:**
  - income received from abroad;
  - amounts paid for imports;
  - the valuation of foreign assets and liabilities;
  - the long-term viability of foreign operations;
  - the acceptability of an overseas project.

- **Transaction risk** is the risk that transactions already entered into, or for which the firm is likely to have a commitment, in a foreign currency, will have a variable value in the home currency.

- **Translation risk** arises because financial data denominated in one currency then expressed in terms of another are affected by exchange rate movements.

- **Economic risk:** Forex movements cause a decline in economic value because of a loss of competitive strength.

- **Transaction risk strategies:**
  - invoice customer in home currency;
  - do nothing;
  - netting;
  - matching;
  - forward market hedge;
  - money market hedge;
  - futures hedge;
  - currency option hedge.

- One way of **managing translation risk** is to try to match foreign assets and liabilities.

- The **management of economic exposure** requires the maintenance of flexibility with regard to manufacturing (for example, location of sources of supply), marketing (for example, advertising campaign, pricing) and finance (currency).

- The **purchasing power parity (PPP) theory** states that exchange rates are in equilibrium when their domestic purchasing powers at that rate are equal. In an inflationary environment the relationship between two countries' inflation rates and the spot exchange rates between two points in time is (with the US and the UK as examples):

▶

$$\frac{1 + I_{US}}{1 + I_{UK}} = \frac{US\$/£_1}{US\$/£_0}$$

- The **interest rate parity (IRP) theory** holds true when the difference between spot and forward exchange rates is equal to the differential between the interest rates available in the two currencies. Using the US and the UK currencies as examples:

$$\frac{1 + r_{US}}{1 + r_{UK}} = \frac{US\$/£_F}{US\$/£_S}$$

- The **expectations theory** states that the current forward exchange rate is an unbiased predictor of the spot rate at that point in the future.

- The **Fundamental Equilibrium Exchange Rate** (FEER) is the exchange rate that results in a sustainable current account balance.

- **Flows of money for investment** in financial assets across national borders can be an important influence on forex rates.

- The currency markets are generally **efficient,** but there is evidence suggesting pockets of inefficiency.

References and further reading

To keep up to date and reinforce knowledge gained by reading this chapter I can recommend the following publications: *Financial Times, The Economist, Bank of England Quarterly Bulletin, Bank for International Settlements Quarterly Review* (www.bis.org), and *The Treasurer* (a monthly journal).

Bank for International Settlements (2010) Triennial Central Bank Survey Report on global foreign exchange market activity in 2010 www.bis.org.

An excellent source of data and comment.

Buckley, A. (2003) *Multinational Finance*, 5th edn. London: FT Prentice Hall.

There is much more in this book than in this chapter on FX risk and other aspects of companies dealing overseas.

Burnside, C., Eichenbaum, M., Kleschelski, I. and Rebelo, S. (2006) 'The Returns to Currency Speculation', NBER Working Paper No. 12489 (www.nber.org/papers/w12489).

'Currencies that are at a forward premium tend to depreciate. This 'forward-premium puzzle' represents an egregious deviation from uncovered interest parity.'

Desai, M. A. (2004) 'Foreign exchange markets and transactions', Harvard Business School note. (Available at Harvard Business School website.)

A very easy-to-follow introduction to the basics of forex markets.

Eiteman, D. K, Stonehill, A. I and Moffett, M. H. (2007) *Multinational Business Finance*, 11th edn. Reading, MA: Pearson/Addison Wesley.

A good introduction to many financial aspects of running a multinational business. Easy to read. Useful case studies.

Fox, R. and Madura, J. (2007) *International Financial Management*. London: Thompson.

A well-written, easy-to-follow introduction to FX markets.

Taylor, F. (2011) *Mastering Derivatives Markets*, 4th edn, Harlow: FT Prentice Hall.

Contains a useful chapter on currency options and swaps.

Pilbeam, K. (2010) *Finance and Financial Markets*, 3rd edn. London: Palgrave.

Contains an accessible chapter with more on the economic theories of exchange rate determination (PPP, IRP theories, etc.).

Vaitilingam, R. (2011) *The Financial Times Guide to Using the Financial Pages*, 6th edn. London: FT Prentice Hall.

A helpful guide to the way in which the *Financial Times* reports on the forex markets, among others.

Websites

UK Forex Foreign Exchange Services www.ukforex.co.uk
Bank for International Settlements www.bis.org
The Financial Times www.FT.com
ADVFN. Provider of FX data www.advfn.com
Bank of England www.bankofengland.co.uk
Currenex www.currenex.com
European Central Bank www.ecb.int
Liffe www.nyseliffeus.com
Liffe www.euronext.com
FXConnect www.fxconnect.com
ICE www.theice.com
International Monetary Fund www.imf.org
Chicago Mercantile Exchange www.cmegroup.com
FXAll www.fxall.com
Yahoo finance uk.finance.yahoo.com
State Street Global Markets www.globallink.com
Reuters uk.reuters.com
OANDA. FX market maker and data provider www.oanda.com
World Trade Organisation www.wto.org
Organisation for Economic Co-operation and Development www.oecd.org
CLS group (Continuous linked settlement) www.cls-group.com

Video presentations

Bank and financial organisation chief executives and other senior people describe and discuss policy and other aspects of their operations in interviews, documentaries and webcasts at Cantos.com (www.cantos.com) – these are free to view.

Case study recommendations

See www.pearsoned.co.uk/arnold for case study synopses.
Also see Harvard University: http://hbsp.harvard.edu/product/cases

- Samoa Tala (2008) Authors: Joshua Coval, Bhagwan Chowdhry and Konark Saxena. Harvard Business School.
- Managing Foreign Exchange Risk: Acquiring Nusantara Comunications Inc. (2008) Author: Sergio Rebelo. Kellogg School of Management. Available at Harvard Case Study website.
- Managing Foreign Exchange Risks (1986) Authors: William R. Reed, E. Richard Brownlee II, Leslie E. Grayson, Robert M. Conroy and Brent D. Wilson. Darden University of Virginia. Available at Harvard Case Study website.
- Futures on the Mexican Peso (1996) Authors: Kenneth A. Froot, Matthew McBrady and Mark S. Seasholes. Harvard Business School.
- Jaguar plc. (1984) Authors: Timothy A. Luehrman and William T. Schiano (1990). Harvard Business School.
- Dozier Industries (2002) Author: Bruce McKern. Stanford Graduate School of Business (available on Harvard website).
- Hedging Currency risks at AIFS (2005) Authors: Mihir A. Desai, Vincent Dessain and Anders Sjôman. Harvard Business School.
- Foreign exchange hedging strategies at General Motors: Transactional and translational exposures (2005) Authors: Mihir A Desai and Mark F. Veblen. Harvard Business School.

Self-review questions

1 Describe the difference between the spot and forward currency markets.

2 Explain through a simple example how the forward market can be used to hedge against a currency risk.

3 Define the following in relation to foreign exchange:

   (a) transaction risk;
   (b) translation risk;
   (c) economic risk.

4 What are the advantages and disadvantages of responding to foreign exchange risk by: (a) invoicing in your currency; (b) doing nothing?

5 Draw out the difference between netting and matching by describing both.

6 What is a money market hedge?

7 How does a currency future differ from a currency forward?

8 Compare hedging using forwards with hedging using options.

9 Describe how you would manage translation and economic risk.

10 Explain the purchasing power parity (PPP) theory of exchange-rate determination.

11 Describe the relationship between spot rates and forward rates under the interest rate parity (IRP) theory.

12 What is the expectations theory?

13 Compare a fixed exchange rate regime with a floating exchange rate regime.

14 What is a gold standard for foreign exchange?

15 What is the main effect of the Bretton Woods agreement on FX rates?

16 What is an FX swap, and how does it differ from a currency swap?

17 What are the following when referring to the foreign exchange markets?

   (a) a pip;
   (b) a peg;
   (c) a dirty float;
   (d) Herstatt risk.

Questions and problems

1 Answer the following given that the rate of exchange between the Japanese yen and sterling is quoted at £/¥188.869–189.131:

   (a) How many pounds will a company obtain if it sold ¥1m?
   (b) What is the cost of £500,000?
   (c) How many yen would be received from selling £1m?
   (d) What is the cost of buying ¥100,000?

2 On 1 April an Australian exporter sells A$10 million of coal to a New Zealand company. The importer is sent an invoice for NZ$11 million payable in six months. The spot rate of exchange between the Australian and New Zealand dollars is NZ$1.1/A$.

   Required

   (a) If the spot rate of exchange six months later is NZ$1.2/A$ what exchange rate gain or loss will be made by the Australian exporter?
   (b) If the spot rate of exchange six months later is NZ$1.05/A$ what exchange rate gain or loss will be made by the Australian exporter?
   (c) A six-month forward is available at NZ$1.09/A$. Show how risk can be reduced using the forward.
   (d) Discuss the relative merits of using forwards and options to hedge forex risk.

3 Describe the main types of risk facing an organisation which has dealings in a foreign currency. Can all these risks be hedged, and should all these risks be hedged at all times?

4 (a) A UK company exports machine parts to South Africa on three months' credit. The invoice totals R150 million and the current spot rate is R7.46/£. Exchange rates have been volatile in recent months and the directors are concerned that forex rates might move so as to make the export deal unprofitable. They are considering three hedge strategies:

   (i)   forward market hedge;
   (ii) money market hedge;
   (iii) option hedge.

   Other information:

   ● three-month forward rate: R7.5/£;
   ● interest payable for three months' borrowing in rand: 2.5 per cent for the three months (not an annual rate);
   ● a three-month American-style rand put, sterling call option is available for R150 million with a strike price of R7.5/£ for a premium payable now of £400,000 on the over-the-counter market.

   Required

   Show how the hedging strategies might work. Use the following assumed spot rates at the end of three months in order to illustrate the nature of each of the hedges:

   R7.00/£.
   R8.00/£.

   (b) Explain why it may not always make sense for a company to hedge forex risk.

5 Describe how foreign exchange changes can undermine the competitive position of the firm. Suggest some measures to reduce this risk.

6 Describe the main types of exchange rate regimes, including fixed, gold standard, Bretton Woods system, pegged, floating and dirty floating.

7 (a) A basket of goods sells for SFr2,000 in Switzerland when the same basket of goods sells for £1,000 in the UK. The current exchange rate is SFr2.0/£. Over the forthcoming year inflation in Switzerland is estimated to be 2 per cent and in the UK, 4 per cent. If the purchasing power parity theory holds true what will the exchange rate be at the end of the year?

(b) What factors prevent the PPP always holding true in the short run?

8 (a) The rate of interest available on a one-year government bond in Canada is 5 per cent. A similar-risk one-year bond in Australia yields 7 per cent. The current spot rate of exchange is C$1.02/A$. What will be the one-year forward rate if the market obeys the interest rate parity theory?

(b) Describe the expectation theory of foreign exchange.

9 Lozenge plc has taken delivery of 50,000 electronic devices from a Malaysian company. The seller is in a strong bargaining position and has priced the devices in Malaysian dollars at M$12 each. It has granted Lozenge three months' credit.

The Malaysian interest rate is 3 per cent per quarter.

Lozenge has all its money tied up in its operations but could borrow in sterling at 3 per cent per quarter (three months) if necessary.

Forex rates	Malaysian dollar/£
Spot	5.4165
Three-month forward	5.425

A three-month sterling put, Malaysian dollar call currency option with a strike price of M$5.425/£ for M$600,000 is available for a premium of M$15,000.

Required

Discuss and illustrate three hedging strategies available to Lozenge. Weigh up the advantages and disadvantages of each strategy. Show all calculations.

10 The spot rate between the euro and the US dollar is €1.77/US$ and the expected annual rates of inflation are expected to be 2 per cent and 5 per cent respectively.

(a) If the purchasing power parity theory holds, what will the spot rate of exchange be in one year?

(b) If the interest rates available on government bonds are 6 per cent in the Eurozone and 9 per cent in the US, and the interest rate parity theory holds, what is the current one-year forward rate?

11 The spot rate of exchange is Won1,507/£ between Korea and the UK. The one-month forward rate is Won1,450/£. A UK company has exported goods to Korea invoiced in Won to the value of Won1,507 million on one month's credit.

To borrow in Won for one month will cost 0.5 per cent, whereas to borrow in sterling for one month will cost 0.6 per cent of the amount borrowed.

Required

(a) Show how the forward market can be used to hedge.

(b) Show how the money market can be used to hedge.

12 Describe and explain Herstatt risk and the advantages of Continuous Linked Settlement.

Assignments

1   Examine a recent import or export deal at a company you know well. Write a report detailing the extent of exposure to transaction risk prior to any hedge activity. Describe the risk-reducing steps taken, if any, and critically compare alternative strategies.

2   Write a report for a company you know well, describing the extent to which it is exposed to transaction, translation and economic risk. Consider ways of coping with these risks and recommend a plan of action.

Web-based exercises

1   Go to www.cmegroup.com and download current price tables for currency options for the US dollar against the pound and the US dollar against the euro, with expiry dates up to six months from now.

   (a) calculate the intrinsic value of each option for every strike price shown;
   (b) calculate the time value for each option for every strike price shown;
   (c) invent a US corporation with foreign currency risk exposure in pounds and in euros in order to illustrate the usefulness of the options markets to hedge risk. Describe and explain the positions that the corporation would take and the outcomes on the underlying at various rates of exchange at expiry and the outcomes on the derivatives at various rates of exchange at expiry.

2   Go to www.ft.com and download the most recent currency futures table. Now expand the table by going to the original sources of the information (the exchanges) to show futures with additional expiry dates. Create examples using the data you have collected to demonstrate how the futures markets can be used to both speculate and hedge a corporation's FX exposure. Invent numbers for the underlying exposure and the outcomes at a variety of possible exchange rates in the months ahead.

13

Trade, shipping, commodities and gold

LEARNING OUTCOMES

The financial services described in this chapter have been operating for centuries because they have satisfied such obvious needs for safe and efficient trading venues, finance to oil the wheels of trade and risk reducing tools to encourage buyers and sellers to come together. By the end of this chapter the reader should be able to:

■ explain the techniques developed to reduce risk for companies buying or selling overseas, including documentary letters of credit, bills of exchange, banker's acceptances, forfaiting, factoring, insurance and export credit guarantees;

■ describe the role and importance of the Baltic Exchange in bringing shipowners and cargo owners together;

■ discuss marine insurance, Lloyd's Register group and shipping finance;

■ describe the commodity exchanges, their role and functioning;

■ explain how gold is traded in London.

The trading of goods and services across national boundaries has many obvious advantages for producer and customer alike. However, this trade can be inhibited if there is insufficient finance or the risk to the seller of failure to pay is high. One way of lowering that risk is to insist that the buyer pays for the goods before they are delivered. However, little international trade can be carried out on this basis because of the raised risk to the importer of not receiving the goods or receiving lower quality goods – they simply will not accept this condition. Many financial innovations have been introduced to reduce risk for both the exporter and the importer. The first part of this chapter examines them.

Ships are usually not owned by the same organisations that own the goods which are to be transported across oceans. We therefore need some mechanism to connect shipowners and those with freight to be carried. They both need a place where they can make a deal – agree how many thousands of dollars per day to transport cargo. The financial markets assist here in both facilitating deal-making and in reducing risk for both shipowners and charterers.

Producers of foods, metals, plastics, oil and other commodities need an organised market structure in which they can, with reassurance of being paid, sell their materials either for immediate 'spot' delivery, or agree a price now for delivery in a few months from now. The buyers of these vital resources also value being able to purchase through well-regulated exchanges, where risk of non-compliance with agreements is reduced. Another risk is that of adverse market price movements over a period of time, e.g. the price of copper rises for a manufacturer. The modern financial markets facilitate hedging against market risks of this kind.

Finally, this chapter looks at the trading of a special commodity, gold. Some of the demand for gold derives from its industrial uses, but the majority is due to human affection for a metal that never rusts or tarnishes and is in short supply. We look at the operation of the world's leading trading centre in London.

Trade

International trade consists of the import and export of goods and services using various means of transport and transfer. Figures from the United Nations Conference on Trade and Development (UNCTAD) show the amazing growth in world trade exports and imports over the past 30 years – much faster than growth in the output of goods and services worldwide – see **Exhibit 13.1**.

Despite the contraction in 2009 compared with 2008 due to the recession, exports still totalled nearly $16 trillion. Note the slight difference in exports and imports – the world seems to have a trade deficit with itself! There is a black hole in the statistics, which has not been adequately explained.

For this trade to be carried out efficiently, a huge infrastructure is needed, including legal services (cross-border trading requires efficient processing of the necessary documentation), accounting, financing, transportation, as well as risk mitigation. One of the most important issues is the transfer of money overseas safely and securely, and in a way that is fair and as risk-free as possible to both sides. For companies exporting goods, how and when they receive payments for their goods is of paramount importance.

Payment for exports

Exhibit 13.2 describes two extreme approaches to payments for exports. The following tools help to reduce risk for both the importer and exporter.

1 Documentary letters of credit

These are issued by financial institutions, normally banks. In return for reassurance (evidence) that all the documents needed for the goods to be exported and imported, documents showing actual shipment of the goods ('bills of lading' – see below) and official licences, etc. are present and correct, the exporter receives full payment from the importer's bank. Obviously, the importer needs to make the arrangement with its bank beforehand and will later reimburse the bank the sum transferred to the exporter. Thus, once shipment has occurred exporters are able to receive

| Exhibit 13.1 | Exports and imports of merchandise and services, 1980–2009 |

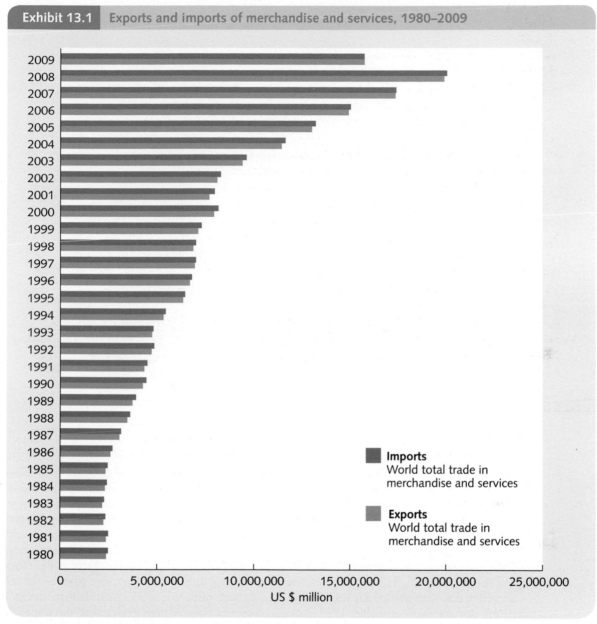

Source: www.unctad.org

payment for their goods in their own country from a bank,[1] even before the goods arrive at their destination. It is an important stipulation that the exporter will receive payment from the importer's bank regardless of the ability of the buyer to pay, thus the importer's bank has substituted its credit standing for that of the importer.

The importer has reassurance that payment will not have been made unless the exporter has complied with the terms and conditions of the contract to the satisfaction of its bank, and so can expect to receive the goods when they are required. The importer's bank normally arranges for a bank in the exporter's home country to transfer the money to the exporter. Thus, for a fee(s) and interest banks have made arrangements so that neither the importer nor the exporter need accept high risk with regard to payment. However, the risk to the importer of receiving goods from the exporter of lower quality than those stated in the documents remains.

---

[1] In some cases cash may not be received. Instead a promise to pay at a fixed future date is received from the bank.

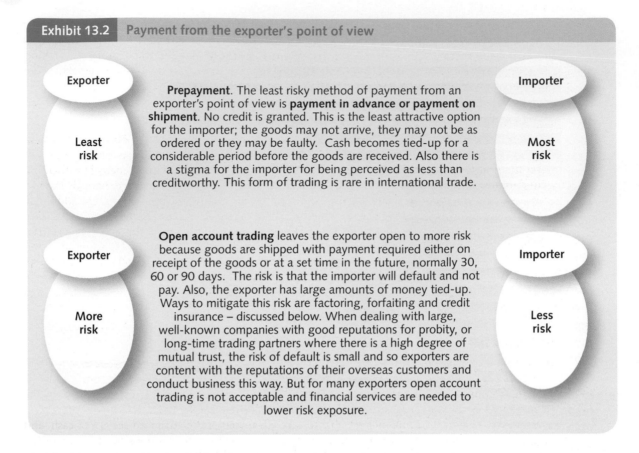

Exporter   Importer

Least risk   Most risk

Prepayment. The least risky method of payment from an exporter's point of view is **payment in advance or payment on shipment**. No credit is granted. This is the least attractive option for the importer; the goods may not arrive, they may not be as ordered or they may be faulty. Cash becomes tied-up for a considerable period before the goods are received. Also there is a stigma for the importer for being perceived as less than creditworthy. This form of trading is rare in international trade.

Exporter   Importer

More risk   Less risk

Open account trading leaves the exporter open to more risk because goods are shipped with payment required either on receipt of the goods or at a set time in the future, normally 30, 60 or 90 days. The risk is that the importer will default and not pay. Also, the exporter has large amounts of money tied-up. Ways to mitigate this risk are factoring, forfaiting and credit insurance – discussed below. When dealing with large, well-known companies with good reputations for probity, or long-time trading partners where there is a high degree of mutual trust, the risk of default is small and so exporters are content with the reputations of their overseas customers and conduct business this way. But for many exporters open account trading is not acceptable and financial services are needed to lower risk exposure.

2 Bills of exchange and banker's acceptances

Bills of exchange and banker's acceptances were explained in Chapter 5. They are legal documents detailing the amount owing with a promise to pay on the due date. Bills of exchange are drawn up by the exporter (more usually its bank) and then signed by the importer which commits it to paying a sum of money on the due date which may be immediate (a sight draft) or say 90 days later (a time draft).

Bills of exchange do not provide as much protection for the exporter as documentary letters of credit because it is the importer that is providing the promise to pay rather than a bank. Once signed the bill is returned to the exporter, who may hold on until expiry to receive payment or sell in an active discount market for slightly less than its face value if it is a negotiable instrument – some are not saleable/negotiable. The bill of exchange provides written evidence of the importer accepting an obligation to pay in a standard form and so the exporter's risk is reduced compared with open account trading. It is further reduced because the exporter can (usually) sell the bill and receive cash quickly.

To provide greater security for an exporter a similar document to pay a sum of money in the future may be drawn up, but this time the importer asks its bank to sign and accept the obligation. This is a banker's acceptance, or more properly in this context, a **trade acceptance**. These banker's acceptances (banker's drafts) are usually highly marketable so they too can be sold at a discount before the stated redemption date. Bills of exchange and banker's acceptances usually require shipping documentation to be provided. This consists of the exporter supplying a **bill of lading** (a document issued by a carrier to an exporter or its bank confirming that the goods have been received by the carrier, that the carrier accepts responsibility to deliver the goods to the importer and evidence of ownership of the goods), insurance certificates and commercial invoices. The documents are passed to the importer, which enables it to claim ownership after it has paid (accepting a time draft/bill that is payable immediately) or it has provided a bill of exchange or banker's acceptance for payment at a later date.

Documents are usually handled by both the exporter's and importer's banks on their behalf to provide both professionalism and reassurance to the other side. The risk to the importer of receiving goods from the exporter of lower quality than those stated in the documents remains. Trading using bills of exchange and banker's acceptances is more expensive than prepayment or open account trading, but less expensive than documentary letters of credit.

3 Forfaiting

If an exporter holds a series of promissory notes (indicating acceptance of an obligation to pay in the future) from the importer guaranteeing that it will pay amounts at say six-monthly intervals over the next four years then this series of rights can be sold to a forfaiting company at a discount. The forfaiter then assumes responsibility for collecting the debts as they fall due. Because the forfaiter pays for the notes straightaway the exporter now has finance for production. For additional safety the promissory notes are usually guaranteed by the importer's bank. The forfaiter may keep the notes until payment is due, or they may sell them on in the financial markets. The exporter receives guaranteed payment for their goods less the fee/discount charged by the forfaiting company. The importer obtains extended credit. Forfaiting deals are large transactions of a value in excess of £250,000 and are non-recourse, i.e. the exporter will not be called on by the forfaiter to make up the difference should an importer or its bank fail to pay. Forfaiters are usually part of large banks.

4 Factoring

Factoring was dealt with in Chapter 3. In return for a fee, factors agree to collect customer credit payments that are due to a company. The company receives immediately say 80 per cent of its outstanding trade debtor balance from the factor, with the remainder handed over when the factor receives full payment of the debt from the importer. Factors charge fees and interest on outstanding balances. Companies are able to take advantage of the advanced receipt of cash, and the risk of non-payment is negated because the factor usually takes on the risk of failure of the importer to pay. A disadvantage may be that the factor could adopt aggressive tactics to get paid by the importer which may damage relationships with a customer. Factors work with other factors in relevant countries who help with assessing the importer's creditworthiness and the handling of the collection of payments.

5 Insurance and guarantees

While there can be no absolute guarantee that trading will proceed smoothly, there are checks and arrangements that trading companies can make to ensure that trading transactions are as well-organised and legally watertight as possible. An exporting company will perform checks on the creditworthiness of their customers, looking into their financial history for any evidence of problems and making sure that they are a *bona fide* trading company in their own country. Furthermore, international shipments are generally insured because of the vulnerability of the goods to damage or complete loss should say a ship sink or a container be lost overboard. Marine insurance, which will cover fire, collision, sinking, etc., is discussed later in the chapter and in Chapter 4.

Many countries operate government-backed export credit guarantee schemes which provide insurance for exporters so that they will not suffer loss if their overseas customer defaults or if for any other reason the exporter or its bank is not paid. The fee charged to the exporter is related to the risk involved. The guarantee is often so well respected in the financial markets that when it is in place banks and others become willing to lend for an export transaction where they might otherwise have declined. Banks are often offered a guarantee of 100 per cent repayment, which means that they will reduce the interest rate charged on finance to exporters.

Political risk can occur if the government of the importing country changes rules and regulations (e.g. expropriation of assets, restrictions on remittances of profits back home, price controls) or becomes unstable (e.g. civil unrest, war) or if the domestic currency is prone to excess fluctuation. The export credit guarantee schemes usually provide insurance against political risk.

Foreign exchange risk

An important consideration for any company operating across borders is the risk that currency exchange rates might move adversely. The risk that shifts in exchange rates could turn a profitable transaction into a loss can be dealt with by hedging in the financial markets. Thus, a UK company expecting to receive 20 miilion Mexican pesos in 3 months' time can alleviate the uncertainty of what that will be worth in pounds by arranging a financial transaction which will hedge against FX fluctuations. Various types of FX hedging are explained in Chapter 12.

Shipping

A broad definition of shipping includes all types of transport overseas, whether by air, sea, railway or road. However, we will concentrate here on ocean-going ships. Air transport, although potentially much quicker, is expensive, and limited in the weight or category it can carry – it is simply not economic to move oil or iron ore by air, for example. Rail and road transport works better over short distance routes connected by land, but much of modern trade is over thousands of miles and so sea transport is usually cheaper. Ships can be adapted to carry any commodity. **Exhibit 13.3** shows the types of various sea-going vessels and the weight they carry. Advances in technology, particularly in the field of refrigeration, have led to the increase in the amount of container ships in use, from a mere 10,290 tonnes in 1980 to nearly 17 times that amount 30 years later in 2010.

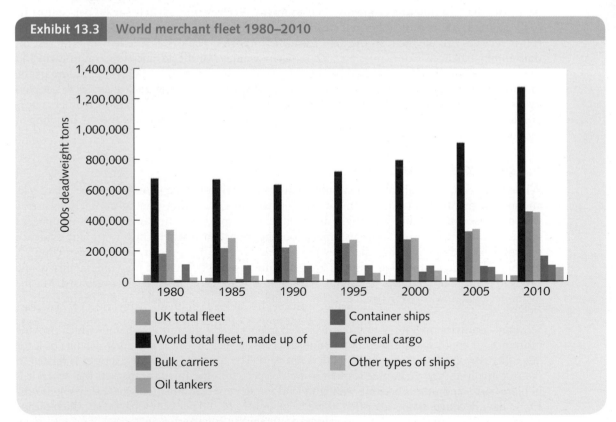

Exhibit 13.3   World merchant fleet 1980–2010

Source: www.unctad.org

London has historically been the centre of the shipping world. Although the UK merchant fleet no longer dominates the seas (UK registered vessels account for less than 3 per cent of world shipping – *see* Exhibit 13.3), the UK has built on this history of maritime trading, and retains its place as a centre for ship trading (buying and selling second hand ships), ship chartering (agreements to carry goods between destinations) and insurance. It is also where airfreight and available aircraft capacity is matched with potential users.

Growth of trade and shipping

Early trade and shipping on a global basis were difficult and dangerous, particularly when venturing on the routes around the southern tips of Africa or South America. Two canals made shipping distances shorter (and therefore quicker) and safer – *see* **Exhibit 13.4**. The Suez canal was opened in 1869 and linked the Mediterranean area to east Africa and the near and far east, drastically cutting journey time and expense. The Panama canal opened in 1914, cutting nearly two thirds off the route from one side of America to the other.

Exhibit 13.4   The Suez and Panama canals

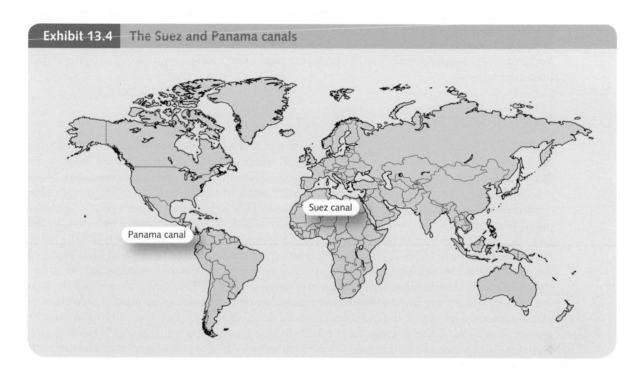

As trade increased, ships became ever larger. There are ships today (supertankers) as large as 550,000 tonnes. These have outgrown both the Suez or Panama canals, and are often unable to dock at any port, having to be loaded or unloaded at sea. Having said that, the majority of vessels in use are designed specifically to be able to traverse the canals; they are bulk carriers, transporting unpackaged goods such as wheat, coal or iron ore, oil tankers supplying the world's ever-increasing need for oil and container ships carrying thousands of different items from computers to toys.

The Baltic Exchange

Shipping companies developed in seventeenth century Europe, particularly in Holland (helped by the Dutch East India Company and other traders) and the UK (helped by the Hudson Bay Company, still in existence today but now a Canadian company, and the East India Company). UK shipping deals would be agreed in the coffee houses of London, where merchants and sea captains would gather.

The Virginia and Baltick coffee house, named after the two most widely used maritime trade routes, was the original home of the Baltic Exchange. It was a meeting place for merchants and shipowners. In 1823 it became a regulated market for ship and freight, owned and operated by a group of members who were subject to strict admission procedures to ensure probity. Today the Baltic

Exchange is a private (i.e. unlisted) limited company acting on behalf of its 550 plus members to encourage free-flowing trade by coordinating the activities of shipowners, shipbrokers and ship charterers. Its members organise the global chartering of ships for the transport of bulk raw materials to manufacturers, the buying and selling of merchant ships and the resolving of disputes.

Of the 550 members, some are chartering agents representing merchants who need to find a ship to move their cargoes. Owner brokers represent the shipowners. Some of the members are the merchants and shipowners themselves. Where they go after they have delivered their current cargo is decided at the Baltic, with dealings done largely via computers and telephones. To a remarkable extent, ship chartering is a last minute business because no one can be absolutely sure that the ship will not be delayed on its current voyage through, say, bad weather. Thus as a ship approaches its current destination back in London the Baltic brokers will be trying to carry out orders sent by owners based in say Rio or Accra to secure its next journey, going from the port that it will arrive at in a few days. They will contact brokers at the Baltic Exchange who represent clients needing to shift goods from that port. About one-third to one-half of all world ship chartering goes through the Baltic Exchange.[2] It also handles one-half of the international trade of second hand vessels. Other leading ship broking centres include New York, Oslo, Hamburg, Rotterdam, Paris and Brussels, but the deals here tend to be focused on national shipping rather than international.

Baltic indices

Industries and traders worldwide take a great interest in the information on freight and shipping rates (cost of transporting from port A to port B) which is published and updated daily by the Baltic Exchange. In 1985 the Baltic Freight Index (BFI) was launched, giving an assessment, based on information from ship brokers worldwide, of the cost of freight transport. The initial index combined information on 13 trade routes – *see* **Exhibit 13.5**. Now there are four main indices produced from more than 40 daily route assessments, the Baltic Exchange Capesize Index (BCI); the Baltic Exchange Panamax Index (BPI); the Baltic Exchange Supramax Index (BSI); and the Baltic Exchange Handysize Index (BHSI). The important Baltic Exchange Dry Index (BDI) replaced the BFI in 2001. It is calculated by taking information from raw materials transported via 20 key shipping routes on the other four indices and summarising it. The BDI is closely watched, as the cost of transporting raw commodities to manufacturers provides an important indication of global economic activity. A rise indicates increased demand for shipping, thus hinting at broader economic growth. A rise in cargo rates results in margin and profit increases for the shipping industry. Falls, which can be dramatic (75 per cent or more in a matter of weeks) can be devastating for shipowners.

Forward Freight Agreements (FFAs)

At the same time as the BFI was set up, trading in derivatives of future freight rates was instigated, where standard contracts could be bought or sold. The most common type of trade is Forward Freight Agreements. FFAs allow shipowners, charterers and traders to protect themselves against the inherent volatility of freight rates by taking an offsetting position in a forward contract, the price of which is based on a freight index. FFAs give the contract owner the right to buy or sell the price of freight for transport starting at future dates. They are based on one of the Baltic indices composed of a shipping route for tankers or an index comprising a basket of routes for dry bulk contracts. (Forwards and futures are discussed in Chapter 10.)

For example, on 1 April a shipowner charters out his 75,000 deadweight tonnage, dwt, Panamax ship in the spot market on a 91-day contract at $20,000 per day. He thinks that freight rates will drop in the near future and wants to lock in the rate at which he can charter out his ship after the current contract expires.

---

[2] Half of tanker chartering and between one-third and two-fifths of dry bulk chartering.

Exhibit 13.5	Baltic Freight Index 1985			
Route	**Vessel size**	**Cargo**	**Route description**	**Weightings**
1	55,000	Light Grain	US Gulf to ARA	20%
2	52,000	HSS	US Gulf to S Japan	20%
3	52,000	HSS	US Pacific coast to S Japan	15%
4	21,000	HSS	US Gulf to Venezuela	5%
5	20,000	Barley	Antwerp to Red Sea	5%
6	120,000	Coal	Hampton Roads to S Japan	5%
7	65,000	Coal	Hampton Roads to ARA	5%
8	110,000	Coal	Queensland to Rotterdam	5%
9	55,000	Coke	Vancouver to Rotterdam	5%
10	90,000	Iron Ore	Monrovia to Rotterdam	5%
11	20,000	Sugar	Recife (Brazil) to US East Coast	5%
12	20,000	Potash	Hamburg to west coast India	2½%
13	14,000	Phosphates	Aqaba to west coast India	2½%

Source: www.balticexchange.com

Note: ARA – Amsterdam-Rotterdam-Antwerp; HSS – heavy grain Sorghums and Soyas; weighting – percentage proportion of journeys on each route.

To do this he *sells* a 60-day Panamax forward contract for $18,000 per day dated for 1 July. On 1 July the ship owner receives back his ship and then contracts it for freight for 60 days for $17,000 per day – the prevailing rate. He has less income from the freight contract than he expected (because forward rates for July to September shipping quoted back in April indicated $18,000 per day). However, he can now close his FFA position by buying back a 60-day Panamax forward contract for $17,000.

Sold FFA	$18,000 × 60 days	$1,080,000
Bought FFA	$17,000 × 60 days	$1,020,000
Gain on the future position		$60,000

This offsets the decreased income on the underlying freight deal.

All traders have to be registered with a clearing house and trades are marked to market daily, i.e. any deficit occurring has to be deposited by the trader, reducing the exposure to risk. FFAs are OTC contracts made between two parties. Freight rates are volatile, as can be seen from **Exhibit 13.6** which shows BDI trading figures from 1993 to 2009. The cost of hiring a ship fell to a tenth of previous levels in the recession of 2008–2009.

Marine insurance

Marine insurance began in London hundreds of years ago, when groups of merchants would underwrite a particular cargo against loss or damage. Lloyd's of London, described in Chapter 4, is one of the leading marine insurers. Ships' hulls and cargoes are insured. In addition shipowners take out third-party liability against a variety of risks. Allied to marine insurance are the group of legal firms specialising in marine law. These firms need to be able to offer advice in many countries of the world, and in differing legal jurisdictions.

Exhibit 13.6	BDI trading report 1985–2009

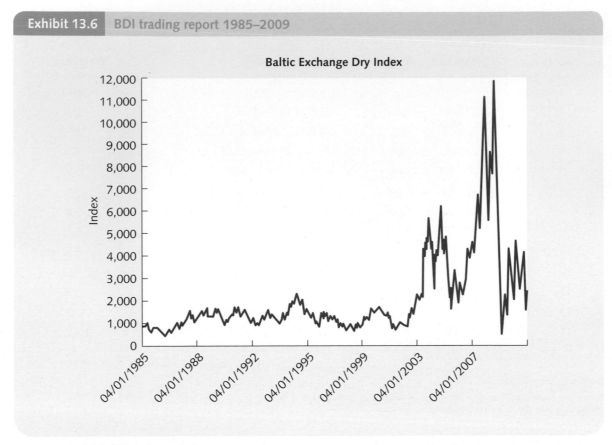

Source: Copyright © 2010 Baltic Exchange Inormation Services Ltd.

Lloyd's Register

Edward Lloyd, the founder of the Lloyd's of London insurance company, was also responsible for a comprehensive list of shipping. Beginning in 1764, and still very much in existence, the Lloyd's Register lists all merchant vessels in the world, giving a detailed list of information on the ships themselves and related information – *see* **Exhibit 13.7**. Lloyd's Register involves classification of ships, setting standards for the quality and reliability in their design, building and operating. The Register is an independent body, and carries out inspections for various countries and offers advice to shipping participants about risks associated with specific ships. It also provides independent safety, integrity and operational performance assessments in other transport sectors and in energy production industries. For example, it provides quality assurance and certification for offshore structures and installations such as power stations and railway infrastructure.

The Register also publishes lists of shipowners, shipbuilders, casualties, wrecks, off-shore units and a host of other information relating to shipping.

Shipping finance

Shipping finance involves enormous sums of money lent by banks to owners, secured on the ship itself, and, if the ship has a secured time charter (i.e. is chartered for a specific length of time), sometimes secured on the charter. Most financing, no matter where the ship was built, or registered, or the owners are domiciled, is usually carried out in US dollars, which became the international currency of choice for most of the world after the Second World War. The main providers of finance for the shipping industry include international commercial banks, investment banks and smaller boutique banks, which act as arrangers or introducers of capital. At any one time global bank lending for ship finance is generally between $300 billion and $400 billion outstanding. The leading lenders are German and Norwegian banks, each with about 30 per cent market shares, followed by UK banks with 13 per cent.

Exhibit 13.7	Information required on ships in Lloyd's Register

Place of build
Type of ship
Rig (for sailing vessels)
Classification
Shipbuilder (since 1859)
Former names (where known)
Survey dates
Date of build
Official number (since 1872)
Navigational aid
Call sign/signal letters (since 1874)
Cargo facilities
Destined voyage (1764 to 1873)
Speed (since 1966)
Manager
Port of registry and flag
Dimensions (draught since 1764, all since 1863)
Machinery (since 1874)
Shipowner
Master/captain's name: until 1921 for steamers, 1764–1947 for sailing vessels
Signal letters/call signs indexed to ship name
Dry and wet docks from 1884
Index of compound names from 1890 to 1940 (then in vol. II of the *Register*)
Changes of name until 1940 (then in vol. II of *Register*)
Lloyd's Register staff and committees (loose from 1972)
Maps from 1984
Marine associations from 1892
Marine enginebuilders and boilermakers
Marine insurance companies
Masters and mates supplement 1850–52
Ports gazetteer from 1984
Scale for Anchor sizes 1845
Shipbreakers
Shipbuilders and existing ships built by them from 1886
Shipowners 1876 to 1955
Statistics of collisions and casualties 1845–9
Statistical tables
Steamers arranged by flag and tonnage until 1939
Fast steamers and motorships
Subscribers to the Register
Telegraphic addresses from 1886
Telex numbers of shipowners
Warships from 1886 to 1939, revised: 14 April 2010
Weight of water per cubic foot in various places from 1895

Source: www.lr.org

Things have changed from the time when each seafaring country had its own merchant navy. Shipping has developed into an international industry, with many ships registered under flags of convenience, i.e. registered in countries where restrictions are lax regarding the nationality of the owners and crews. So a Korean-built Panamanian-registered ship owned by a Norwegian shipping company and crewed by Filipinos could be financed through the London office of an American bank. Many financing deals are carried out in London regardless of where the ship or its owners are based. Because of its concentration of expertise in terms of legal, arbitration, insurance, ship broking, financing and shipping derivatives London remains the major shipping centre of the world. English law has become the favoured choice for shipping contracts.

Commodities

Commodities are physical goods which can be stored (i.e they are not immediately perishable), can be accurately measured and are generally fungible (they are interchangeable), thus one tonne of sugar is very much like another tonne of sugar (of the same grade). They can be soft (affected by the climate) or hard such as copper or silver.

Prices of commodities are generally fixed by supply and demand, and can change dramatically, especially the soft commodities which are affected by weather conditions. If the corn or coffee bean harvests are poor, supply will be lowered, resulting in a high price worldwide. If there is an oversupply due to an exceptionally good harvest, then the opposite happens, and the price of corn or coffee will fall – *see* **Exhibits 13.8 and 13.9**.

Large companies relying on their supplies of raw products will hedge the cost of their supplies by taking out forward, futures or option contracts as we see in the case of Mexico in Exhibit 13.8 (derivatives are discussed in Chapters 10 and 11). These contracts enable companies to even out the cost of their supplies.

Commodity exchanges

Commodities are traded in various ways. For some, like furs and tea, the buyers need to be able to observe the quality of the produce and so these are traded through auctions after the potential buyers have conducted an examination. Others, such as nuts, fibres and spices are traded in sale rooms face to face, often through agents representing the buyers or sellers. However, many com-

Exhibit 13.8

Mexico hedges against corn inflation

FT

By **Javier Blas** in London

Mexico has taken the unusual step of insuring itself against the effect of rising corn prices on tortilla, a food staple for millions in the country, in the latest sign of growing concern about food inflation in emerging countries.

Rising food inflation has become a big headache in countries from Mexico to China and India as bad weather has ruined crops, forcing prices up.

Food accounts for up to half of all household spending in emerging countries, compared to just 10 to 15 per cent in Europe and the US.

The move by Mexico, disclosed by its economic minister, came as the quoted price of corn in Chicago hit a two-year high on the back of a smaller-than-expected harvest in the US, which accounts for more than half of the world's exports.

Bruno Ferrari told local media on Wednesday the government had

bought futures contracts to fix the cost of corn. "The prices are guaranteed," he said. "The supply is also guaranteed ... until the third quarter of the next year." A government official confirmed his comments.

Mexican tortilla makers threatened last week to raise prices by 50 per cent to offset the impact of higher corn and natural gas costs. That has prompted fears of a repeat of the tortilla riots of 2007, when protesters demonstrated against rising food prices.

Richard Feltes, grain analyst at brokerage R.J. O'Brien, said it was the first time he could recall a country had disclosed it was buying futures.

"There had been rumours in the past about other countries, including China, but it has never been confirmed," he said.

Traders expect corn and other agricultural commodities to surge

higher in early 2011 due to low inventories and concerns about the size of the crop in Latin America. Brazil and Argentina, which produce the bulk of the southern hemisphere's exportable surplus of food, have had little rain.

Corn prices rose on Wednesday to $6.08\frac{3}{4}$ a bushel, up 46 per cent from January and the highest level since mid-2008. The US Department of Agriculture has warned the country's corn stocks will fall to their lowest in 15 years by the middle of next year.

"There is a better than 50–50 chance that the corn market will take out the all-time high of $7.65 a bushel set in June 2008," Mr Feltes said.

Source: Financial Times, 23 December 2010. Reprinted with permission.

Exhibit 13.9

Sugar prices soar to 30-year high   FT

By **Jack Farchy**

The price of sugar has jumped to a 30-year high as the Brazilian harvest has tailed off sharply, hardening expectations of a shortage.

Traders believe that prices could soar over the coming months as the market faces a supply shortfall driven by smaller-than-forecast crops in important growing countries from Brazil to Russia and western Europe.

At the same time, inventories are at their lowest levels in decades. "All buyers we see are buying on a hand-to-mouth basis," said Peter de Klerk of Czarnikow, the London sugar merchant.

That has pushed prices up sharply, with raw sugar futures in New York soaring 135 per cent from a low of 13 cents in May.

On Tuesday ICE March sugar rose 4 per cent to a peak of 30.64 cents a pound, surpassing the level reached in February and rising

to their highest point since 1980, when prices jumped to nearly 45 cents.

The dramatic rise in sugar prices is causing headaches for policymakers. While sugar is widely available in the west and its price is rarely considered, it is an essential source of cheap calories in emerging economies, where surging sugar prices are driving food inflation.

On Tuesday India's central bank raised benchmark interest rates for the sixth time this year in an attempt to curb inflation.

New Delhi has emerged as a crucial factor in the sugar market, as India's harvest is expected to be large, but the government is still debating how much sugar to allow the country's industry to export. Traders expect India to authorise exports of 1m–2m tonnes starting in December. Anything less, or even a delay to the decision, could

send prices spiralling higher, traders warn.

"They need to start selling additional volumes by mid-December, otherwise the hole in the market is getting wider," said Mr de Klerk.

The latest move up in prices was triggered by a spell of dry weather in Brazil, which dominates the global sugar trade with about half of world exports.

Unica, the country's cane industry association, said last week that production was down 30 per cent in the first half of October from 2009, while Kingsman, a consultancy in Lausanne, has downgraded its forecast for the Brazilian crop by 2.3 per cent. "If Brazil is going to have a lower harvest it makes it that much harder to fill the deficit," said Jonathan Kingsman.

Source: Financial Times, 3 November 2010. Reprinted with permission.

modities can be of a standardised quality, e.g. tin or lead of a specific grade and purity, and so can be traded without visual inspection because the exchange itself specifies and enforces the quality.

The first formal exchange was the Chicago Board of Trade (CBOT), which began trading standardised contracts in 1865 in grain futures. Chicago was at the centre of the railroad expansion, and was therefore the ideal place for grain to be delivered, traded and distributed. To help farmers and their customers, standards were set for the weight and quality of the grain, which was stored centrally. Farmers and traders began to commit to selling and buying in the future. A farmer might agree to sell a set quantity of grain for a set price at a future date. However, this could lead to some degree of regret for either the future buyer or seller at the future date, depending on the market price then. But at least each side can create some certainty – *see* **Exhibit 13.10** for an example.

As contracts became more commonly used, the derivative contract became a tradable instrument. Traders who thought that a bushel would fall in price might sell a contract for the same number of bushels. They could then later buy a contract even if they had no gain to close the position. Conversely if they thought the price would rise, they would buy a future, hold on to the contract and sell the derivative at a later date. A profit can be taken by buying and selling a derivative without ever receiving the underlying commodity. This type of trading became commonplace, and created the high liquidity we see in commodity derivatives. Now over 95 per cent of commodity trading is in the derivative market, and most of the contracts to take delivery of a commodity are never actually executed, being off-set before delivery is due. There is no limit to the number of contracts on offer. There may be 15,000 tonnes of tin actually on the market, but there may well be 400,000 plus tonnes of tin derivatives. Buyers of contracts are said to be taking a long position; sellers are said to be going short.

Exhibit 13.10	Effect of price changes on grain contract

**Contract agreed in March
for delivery in July**

	Quantity	Price		Total
	1,000 bushels	$250 per bushel		$250,000

The farmer and dealer agree and execute the contract

**Good worldwide harvest in
July, market price = $235**
More grain, lower price

	1,000 bushels	$235 per bushel		$235,000

*The contract protects the farmer from the $15,000 drop in price, but the dealer has some cause to regret
the futures contract – but at least he had certainty*

**Bad worldwide harvest in
July, market price = $274**
Less grain, higher price

	1,000 bushels	$274 per bushel		$274,000

The farmer does not benefit from the price rise, and the dealer gains $24,000, but both had certainty.

Standardisation

The essence of commodity trading is **standardisation**; sellers, producers and traders must be able to rely on the amount and quality of what is traded without having to undertake a physical inspection. Tight regulations govern modern commodity trading, and each commodity must comply with exact specifications. CBOT (Chicago Board of Trade) is now part of the CME Group (originally Chicago Mercantile Exchange) the largest commodity trading centre in the world. The other main exchanges for commodity trading are NYSE Liffe, the leading soft commodities exchange in Europe, ICE Futures (US and Europe) part of Intercontinental Exchange (ICE), the New York Mercantile Exchange (NYMEX) and commodity Exchange (COMEX) both now part of the CME Group, the London Metal Exchange (LME), the Singapore Exchange (SGX) and the Australian Securities Exchange (ASX). **Exhibit 13.11** gives a list (by no means exhaustive) of commonly traded commodities and the quantities in which they are traded. Additionally there will be specific standards that the commodities will have to meet.

Exhibit 13.11	Commonly traded commodities

Commodity	Main trading on	Size of contract
Agricultural products		
Corn	CBOT	5000 bushels
Corn	NYSE Liffe	50 tons
Oats	CBOT	5000 bushels
Rough rice	CBOT	2000 cwt
Soybeans	CBOT	5000 bushels
Rapeseed	NYSE Liffe	50 tons
Soybean meal	CBOT	100 short tons

▶

Commodity	Main trading on	Size of contract
Soybean oil	CBOT	60,000 lb
Wheat	CBOT	5000 bushels
Cocoa	ICE Futures US	10 tons
Coffee C	ICE Futures US	37,500 lb
Cotton no.2	ICE Futures US	50,000 lb
Sugar no.11	ICE Futures US	112,000 lb
Sugar no.14	ICE Futures US	112,000 lb

Livestock and meat

Commodity	Main trading on	Size of contract
Lean hogs	CME	40,000 lb (20 tons)
Live cattle	CME	40,000 lb (20 tons)
Feeder cattle	CME	50,000 lb (25 tons)

Energy

Commodity	Main trading on	Size of contract
WTI crude oil	NYMEX, ICE	1000 bbl (42,000 U.S. gal)
Brent crude	ICE Futures Europe	1000 bbl (42,000 U.S. gal)
Ethanol	CBOT	29,000 U.S. gal
Natural gas	NYMEX	10,000 mmBTU
Heating oil	NYMEX	1000 bbl (42,000 U.S. gal)
Gulf coast gasoline	NYMEX	1000 bbl (42,000 U.S. gal)
Propane	NYMEX	1000 bbl (42,000 U.S. gal)

Precious metals

Commodity	Main trading on	Size of contract
Gold	COMEX	troy ounce
Platinum	NYMEX	troy ounce
Palladium	NYMEX	troy ounce
Silver	COMEX	troy ounce

Industrial metals

Commodity	Main trading on	Size of contract
Copper	LME	25 Metric Tonnes
Lead	LME	25 Metric Tonnes
Zinc	LME	25 Metric Tonnes
Tin	LME	25 Metric Tonnes
Aluminium	LME	25 Metric Tonnes
Aluminium alloy	LME	20 Metric Tonnes
Nickel	LME	6 Metric Tonnes
Cobalt	LME	1 Metric Tonnes
Molybdenum	LME	6 Metric Tonnes

Commodity	Main trading on	Size of contract
Other		
Rubber	SGX	1 kg
Palm oil	Bursa Malaysia (BMD)	1000 kg
Wool	ASX	2500 kg
Polypropylene	LME	1000 kg

Source: various exchanges.

Some commodities are traded mainly in the locality of their production, such as wool in Australia. To give an idea of the complexity of commodity trading, **Exhibit 13.12** gives the different types of wool that are traded. Wool is not just wool!

Exhibit 13.12	Wool contracts

Fine Wool Futures (19 micron)

Greasy Wool Futures (21 micron)

Greasy Wool Options (21 micron)

Broad Wool Futures (23 micron)

China Type Futures (19.5 micron)

China Type Futures (21.0 micron)

China Type Futures (22.6 micron)

Source: www.asx.com.au

The London Metal Exchange (LME)

The LME, located in the heart of the City, trades hard commodities in 'rings' between 11.40 am and 5.00 pm – it deals in non-ferrous metals plus plastic. Each commodity is allocated a five-minute ring session in turn. Thus, steel is traded between 11.40 am and 11.45 am, aluminium alloy is next at 11.45 am to 11.50. It offers futures and options in these for delivery in only a matter of days or up to 27 months hence (aluminium is exceptional with 123 months ahead contracts available).

Dealers sit in an assigned seat in a circle and bid verbally for a trade – an open 'outcry' system. There are currently 12 ring dealing members and all business which is required to be dealt 'across the floor' must be passed through one of these members. The ring system concentrates liquidity which ensures both transparency of pricing, and more representative prices than may be obtained through the other means of trading LME has. The ring sessions set official prices for non-ferrous metals and steel.

While the ring offers the greatest liquidity it suffers from the drawback that it is available for only a part of the 24-hour working day. To partially fill this gap the LME also trades through a computer system called **LMEselect**, which operates between 01:00 and 19:00 (London Time). On top of that it offers 24-hour telephone trading, called **inter-office trading**. Potential traders can see an indicative price on a screen. If they like the price they can contact a broker and then complete a deal there and then. The price actually offered by the broker in a telephone call will not necessarily be identical to the indicative prices – much depends on the size of the deal, the state of the market, and the client's credit standing and relationship with the broker.

All LME prices are quoted in US dollars, but the LME permits contracts in sterling, Japanese yen and euros and provides official exchange rates from US Dollars for each of them. Because of the high level of activity on this market – it trades around $30 billion of contract per day – the prices 'discovered' at the LME are recognised and relied upon by industry throughout the world.

Members of the exchange are required to deliver physical metal on the date specified in the contract unless the contract has been 'squared' by a buyer later selling an identical contract. Most trades are neutralised by both a buy position and a sell position, and no physical delivery is necessary. To obtain physical delivery the buyer will need to present a warrant at one of LME's registered warehouses. There are more than 600 of these located in the US, Europe and Asia. All contracts are cleared through LCH-Clearnet, which acts as a central counterparty to all contracts.

NYSE Liffe

NYSE Liffe operates commodity trading in Europe in the commodities shown in **Figure 13.13**.

Exhibit 13.13	Commodities traded on Euronext

Cocoa Futures	Rapeseed Futures
Cocoa Options	Rapeseed Options
Robusta Coffee Futures (no. 409)	
Robusta Coffee Options	
Corn Futures	White Sugar Futures
Corn Options	White Sugar Options
Malting Barley Futures	Feed Wheat Futures
Malting Barley Options	Feed Wheat Options
Milling Wheat Options	Milling Wheat Futures
Skimmed Milk Powder Futures	

Source: www.euronext.com

To give some indication of just how detailed the specifications are for commodities to meet the quality parameters **Exhibit 13.14** gives details of a NYSE Liffe futures contract for skimmed milk powder.

Derivative trading in commodities

While commodity derivative trading (options and futures) has increased tremendously in volume, it remains only a small percentage of all derivatives trading, which is dominated by interest rate and foreign exchange trading, as can be seen in the figures from Bank for International Settlements for derivative trading in **Exhibit 13.15**.

Exhibit 13.14 NYSE Liffe skimmed milk powder futures contract

Skimmed Milk Powder Futures

Unit of trading	Twenty-four tonnes
Origins tenderable	Skimmed milk powder from any EU origin
Quality	*Physical and chemical analysis:*
	Fat 1.25% maximum
	Protein 34.0% (non-fat dry matter) minimum
	Ash 8.2% maximum
	Moisture 4.0%, maximum
	Scorched Particles Disc B maximum
	Titratable acidity 0.15%, maximum
	Solubility index 1.0 ml maximum
	WPN index 1.51– 5.99 mg/g - medium heat
	Microbiological analysis:
	Standard plate count 10.000/g, maximum
	E-coli negative in 1g
	Salmonella negative in 25g
	Yeast and mould 100/g, maximum
	Inhibitors negative
Delivery months	January, March, May, July, September, November such that six delivery months are available for trading
Price basis	Euros per metric tonne. Delivered free onto Buyer's transport in accordance with Incoterm FCA at a delivery point that is within a 150 km radius of Antwerp, Hamburg or Rotterdam
Minimum price movement (tick size and value)	50 euro cents per tonne (€12)
Last trading day	The last business day prior to the tender day
Notice day/Tender day	The sixth business day preceding the first business day of the delivery period for that delivery month
Trading hours	10:45 to 18:30 (Paris time)
Full contract specification and related documentation	Skimmed Milk Powder Futures & Options
Last update	12/10/2010

Source: www.euronext.com

| Exhibit 13.15 | Derivative trading by notional amounts outstanding |

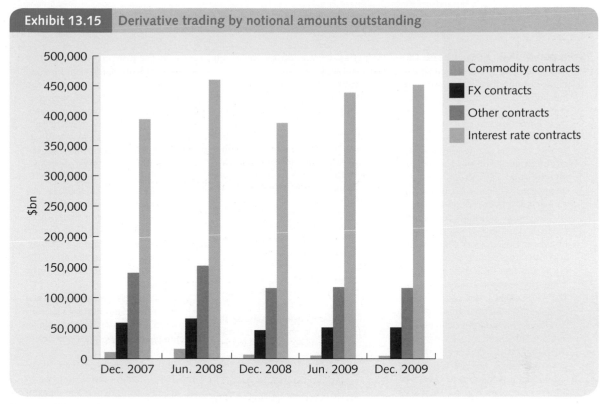

Source: www.bis.org

Commodity indices

Commodity indices are another way to trade in commodities. A **commodity index** is nominally made up of a group of commodities linked together to form a theoretical basket of futures contracts. The Dow Jones, founder of the earliest stock index and now 90 per cent owned by the CME, calculates 23 commodity indices based on 19 commodities (aluminium, coffee, copper, corn, cotton, crude oil, gold, heating oil, lean hogs, live cattle, natural gas, nickel, silver, soybean oil, soybeans, sugar, unleaded gasoline, wheat and zinc), with a bewildering variety of sub-indices based on an individual commodity and different future delivery dates. The formation and calculation of the indices is far from easy. How many commodities to include? What happens when a future expires? What weights to attach to each commodity? These are difficult judgements – *see* **Exhibit 13.16**.

Exhibit 13.16

Keeping track of underlying qualities

By David Ricketts

Investing via indices is one of the most common routes investors take to gain access to commodities. But understanding how commodities indices work in practice, and the subtle differences that exist between them, may not be so straightforward.

Even defining what constitutes "the market" can be a significant challenge for commodities indices and that can ultimately lead to variations between different providers, says Simon Fox, an investment consultant at Mercer.

"The concept of a market index in commodities does not exist in the same way it does with equities and bonds," says Mr Fox.

"Even the well-known commodities indices are really just commodity trading strategies.

Exhibit 13.16 continued

Indices also have to explain why their particular mix of underlying commodities represents the market and they all reach different conclusions."

Commodities indices are made up of a basket of futures contracts across various commodity sectors, although variations in the weightings to each sector from one index to another will have an impact on an investor's overall exposure.

The most popular commodity index is the S&P Goldman Sachs Commodity Index (S&P GSCI), which currently has about $75bn tracking it and has its largest weighting in energy – about 70 per cent. The S&P GCSI Light Index has an energy weighting at about half this figure.

Other commodities indices vary in their allocations to energy. The Dow Jones UBS Commodity Index, the second most popular commodity index, has a weighting to energy of 33 per cent (Dow Jones UBS places a cap on any sector weighting at 33 per cent), while the Rogers index has an energy weighting of 45 per cent.

Most of the main indices re-weight their allocations to sectors on an annual basis, although Thomson Reuters/Jefferies Commodities Research Bureau Index does this on a monthly basis.

The number of underlying commodities is also a differentiating factor between the indices on offer, and investors can expect wide variations in returns, and the diversification benefits, from each as a result.

The Deutsche Bank Liquid Commodities Indices has six underlying commodities, for example, while the Thomson Reuters/Jefferies Commodities Research Bureau Index has 19.

Meanwhile, the Rogers index has the largest range with 36 underlying commodities, including lumber, azuki beans, wool, rubber and silk.

But it is the use of futures that imposes one of the main constraints on investors, mainly the inability of being fully able to benefit from underlying market movements, or spot returns.

"Some of the commodities indices have come under criticism because investors believed they would get exposure to spot prices, but the indices do not track these," says Dimitris Melas, executive director of research at MSCI.

"If an investor saw the price of oil double and assumed the index in which they invested with would also double, they would be very disappointed."

To enable investors to gain exposure to commodities via equities, MSCI launched its Commodity Producers Indices in 2008. Mr Melas says these are essentially equity indices that allow investors to access sectors and companies active in the commodities space, such as energy or agricultural organisations.

Another feature of commodities indices is the process of "rolling" futures contracts. When they expire, and where exactly along the yield curve new futures contracts are purchased, can also have an impact on returns.

"Depending on the shape of the curve, it [the return] can be positive or negative," says Bharat Manium, managing director, commodity investor structuring at Barclays Capital.

"What you are doing is buying one asset and selling another asset. If the price at which you buy and sell are the same, you have no returns from that process. If the price at which you are buying is higher than the one you are selling, then you will have a negative return."

Mercer's Mr Fox says "rolling" futures can leave investors exposed to other potential drags on investment performance.

He says: "Where indices are highly transparent and they have a lot of money following them, there is a risk that other market participants can take advantage of that, for example over the rolling of the contract. This can erode the returns for investors."

Others believe investors gaining exposure to commodities via indices should consider whether banks or independent organisations are in control of them.

"In many cases it can make sense for commodities indices to be offered by independent organisations, as you do not have the potential conflict of interest having a trading desk alongside those who are calculating the index," says Mr Melas.

It is a claim, unsurprisingly, that banks are reluctant to support.

"From our perspective, the group that publishes and calculates indices is separate from sales and trading," says Barclays Capital's Mr Manium.

"They are also active not only in commodities indices, but in all the asset classes. Over 1,000 different commodity indices are published daily by this team."

Source: Financial Times, 13 December 2010. Reprinted with permission.

Many companies round the world operate commodity indices. The S&P GSCI commodity index consists of 24 commodities – *see* **Exhibit 13.17**. The weights in the index for each commodity are shown.

Exchange-traded funds (ETFs)

In addition to trading directly in a commodity it is possible to buy tradable shares in exchange traded funds which then hold either the commodity or a derivative of it. Then the ETF investors can benefit from a rise in the underlying commodity through selling ETF shares at a later date without the hassle of dealing in the commodity itself. Alternatively, the hedger or speculator can

Exhibit 13.17	S&P GSCI commodity index		
Wheat (Chicago)	4.05%	Oil (#2 heating)	4.54%
Wheat (Kansas)	0.86%	Oil (RBOB)	4.56%
Corn	3.99%	Oil (Brent crude)	13.14%
Soybeans	2.77%	Oil (Gasoil)	4.78%
Coffee 'C'	0.78%	Natural Gas	5.32%
Sugar #11	1.92%	Aluminum (high gd. prim)	2.37%
Cocoa	0.36%	Copper – Grade A	2.81%
Cotton #2	0.96%	Standard Lead	0.40%
Lean hogs	1.54%	Primary Nickel	0.65%
Cattle (Live)	3.01%	Zinc (special high grade)	0.55%
Cattle (Feeder)	0.56%	Gold	2.86%
Oil (WTI crude)	36.91%	Silver	0.31%

Source: www.standardandpoors.com

buy an ETF share that is designed to rise in value as the underlying commodity falls. Managers run the ETF, buying and selling the underlying and/or derivatives of it. ETFs that invest in commodities are often termed **exchange-traded commodities (ETCs)**.

ETFs were explained in Chapter 4, so we will not go into much detail here. Most are invested in derivatives of commodities rather than holding tonnes of zinc or barrels of oil, etc. However, there are some new ETFs on the market that hold actual physical commodities. Precious metal ETFs have been popular, and there are now funds trading in other metals, and actually holding the metal in a warehouse – *see* **Exhibit 13.18**.

Exhibit 13.18

Buying the metal, not just the contracts   **FT**

Jack Farchy

Commodity investment is getting physical. A host of companies are working on products that give investors physical exposure to copper, aluminium and other base metals, spurred on by the success of similar investment vehicles in precious metal markets.

The new products – exchange-traded funds (ETFs) that hold physical metal – are set to open the markets to mainstream investors for the first time. But, if successful, they could also revolutionise the fundamental drivers of the markets by allowing investors to hoard metal. "There is no question that

ETFs will create a new category of physical demand for the market," says Mike Frawley, global head of metals at Newedge, a brokerage.

The building momentum behind the launch of the new products comes as base metals prices have risen sharply from the depths of the financial crisis, buoyed by resurgent demand from China and other emerging economies.

For metals such as copper and tin, with demand already outstripping supply, a fresh source of demand from investors could send prices soaring from current record levels.

Bankers say the drive for physical base metal ETFs comes from investors seeking exposure to a "hard asset" amid ever-increasing concerns about the debasement of paper currencies. Equally, and especially in the US, the products are being requested by equity fund managers, who have limited ability to gain exposure to base metals via the US equities markets.

The first movers are JPMorgan and BlackRock iShares, which have separately begun the process of launching physical copper ETFs in the US. Elsewhere, ETF Securities, a London-based ETF specialist, has

▶

Exhibit 13.18 continued

announced its intention to launch ETFs in all the base metals traded on the London Stock Exchange. And Credit Suisse and Glencore, the world's largest commodity trading house, have applied to launch a physical aluminium investment product in Switzerland.

The main drawback from an investor's point of view is likely to be relatively high costs. Jean Bourlot, head of commodities at UBS, says: "Storage and insurance costs for base metals – aluminium in particular – are much higher than precious metals, which may be seen as a deterrent."

Neither JPMorgan nor BlackRock has provided details of the costs for their proposed copper ETFs, but bankers say they are aiming significantly to undershoot the annual fees traditionally charged by hedge fund managers – 2 per cent a year plus 20 per cent of profits. Specialists believe that with annual charges of about 1.5 per cent, the ETFs could gain traction among investors.

On the flip side, what may be expensive for investors is likely to be a boon for banks and brokers. JPMorgan, through its Henry Bath subsidiary, will reap handsome warehousing fees and Goldman Sachs, through its Metro subsidiary, is to provide the warehousing service for the BlackRock product. Moreover, dealers will have a new opportunity to arbitrage between the market price of metal and the price of the ETF shares.

Source: Financial Times, 30 November 2010, p. 6. Reprinted with permission.

Speculative bubbles

Commodities are prone to speculative bubbles, often stimulated by a perceived shortage or surplus, or by being in fashion or going out of fashion. One of the most spectacular bubbles happened in seventeenth-century Holland and involved tulip bulbs.

Tulips were brought over to Europe from Turkey at the end of the sixteenth century and became very popular in Holland with a resulting increase in price. Propagating tulips was widespread and certain rarer varieties with attractive markings on their petals commanded high prices. As the tulip fad expanded and almost everyone in Holland decided they had to have a tulip bulb, demand increased and prices rose ever higher. Tulips were physically sold when they could be lifted from the ground, between June and September. After that, they needed to be planted to grow and flower in April.

The spot market for tulips took place when the bulbs were available for sale; at other times of the year, a futures market developed, where people would agree to pay a certain price for a tulip bulb when it became available; this contract to buy a bulb could be traded and traders made and lost vast sums of money trading in tulip bulb futures.

Such was the craze for tulips that people were paying the equivalent of thousands of pounds for a single bulb and using all their money and savings, and many ordinary people and traders made considerable profits out of trading bulbs. It seemed that tulipmania could go on for ever and the price of tulip bulbs would continue to increase.

However, the mania could not continue. At some point in 1637 the bottom fell out of the tulip market. It is thought that either a buyer failed to complete a purchase, or some prudent people decided to sell their bulbs. Panic set in. All of a sudden people who had paid large sums of money for bulbs found themselves in possession of bulbs worth one-hundredth of their purchase price; contracts were worthless and many people lost fortunes.

While more recent bubbles have not been quite as extreme as tulipmania, it is very easy for a commodity to become disproportionately popular for no good reason only for its value to fall back leaving participants in the bubble licking their wounds – *see* **Exhibit 13.19** for a discussion about the possibility of a commodity bubble.

Agricultural commodities

Agricultural commodities include a variety of raw unprocessed food stuffs which are transported in bulk. There are strict guidelines and standards for each commodity, and these can be very complex. For example, in Australia, for wheat alone there are thirty different standards, and they all have to comply with a long list of quality requirements. **Exhibit 13.20** lists the quality parameters for one of these varieties of wheat, APH1 (Australian Prime Hard 1). Other types of agricultural commodities are subject to similar quality parameters, and domestic government bodies carry out regular and thorough checks to ensure the parameters are kept.

Exhibit 13.19

Supercycle argument 'remains intact'

Chris Newlands

Talk to anyone in the know about commodities and it will not take long for the conversation to shift to one of how the sector is in the throes of a "supercycle".

Perhaps five years ago – before the credit crisis took hold – they might have talked with more exuberance as to how commodity prices were set to remain high for an extended period of time because of factors such as China's insatiable appetite for raw materials, but today the chatter is still fervent.

And there appears to be good reason. The price of gold and copper has hit record levels this year, the share price of BHP Billiton, the world's biggest mining company, has topped all-time highs, while the Reuters-Jefferies CRB index last month rose to a two-year record above 300 points.

"I believe the supercycle argument remains intact," says Simon James, funding partner of Gore Browne Investment Management who believes both emerging and developed economies have big plans to invest in their infrastructure.

George Cheveley, co-portfolio manager of Investec's Enhanced Natural Resources fund, adds: "With emerging markets, led by China, in the midst of the commodity-intensive phase of their economic growth and the western world needing to repair and renew infrastructure, we expect demand growth for commodities to substantially exceed the rates seen in the 20 years from 1974–1994 and remain strong for at least another 10."

Figures from Barclays Capital show that between 2000 and 2009. China, Brazil, India and the Middle East's share of global coal demand grew from 36 per cent to 55 per cent, while their combined demand for soyabeans rose from 33 per cent to 44 per cent.

China's share of global copper demand (38 per cent), meanwhile, is now almost twice that of the US.

Obviously, the supercycle argument lost ground in 2008, when commodity prices fell sharply back to earth after considerable increases, but that has not halted investors' interest in the asset class.

Amrita Sen, a commodities analyst at Barclays Capital, says there has been "unprecedented" interest in commodity investments over the past couple of years. Investor funds, she says, "have flowed into commodities at the fastest-ever rates as the sector has moved to the top of the list of investors' favoured alternative investment exposures".

Pension funds have been particularly interested buyers, although the signs are they are not as fixated as they once were. The $130bn retirement fund for Canada's Quebec region, Caisse de Dépôt et Placement du Quebec, for example, closed its commodities portfolio entirely at the start of the year, while a June survey conducted by sister FT publication NRPN of 23 Nordic pension funds found almost a quarter intended to reduce their exposure to commodities before the end of this year.

Statistics from the UK's National Association of Pension Funds paints a similar picture. In 2007, figures showed 4 per cent of schemes invested in commodities, rising to 8 per cent in 2008. Last year, however, that fell back to 5 per cent.

The fear is that perhaps commodity prices are reaching bubble territory and that investor demand could be a contributory factor.

"To me ... [this] is not what long-term investors look for," Roland Lescure, chief investment officer for the Caisse de Dépôt et Placement du Quebec, told the press as explanation of his scheme's commodities exit.

Gore Browne's Mr James recognises those fears: "The most important contributors towards the development of a bubble in commodities are in place – cheap money and a scarcity of investment opportunities," he says. "Commodities are difficult to value, but there is a distinct sense of euphoria in a number of industrial metals and agricultural crops, and in gold."

His is somewhat a lone voice, however, with many quick to counter this view. Pioneer's Peter Konigbauer, for example, who is senior portfolio manager of the firm's Commodity Alpha fund, says: "We don't see a bubble in commodity prices. Energy prices are a long way off previous levels and we still believe in fundamentally higher prices in the future. Energy demand is picking up worldwide and the outlook is bullish."

Barclays Capital's Ms Sen agrees: "Investment activity in commodities has attracted a lot of attention with a particular focus on the institutional inflows linked to commodity indices.

"Unfortunately, much of the analysis and comment is ill-founded and confusing as we do not see commodity prices as being in a bubble, nor do we see the involvement of institutional investors as being a cause of price rises."

It is very clear, she continues, that institutional and retail holdings of commodity futures are extremely small and "nowhere near big enough" to distort the relationship between prices and market fundamentals.

"Given that institutional investors rebalance portfolios to achieve a desired allocation across assets, they are generally a stabilising influence [because in order] to achieve their desired balance they tend to sell after prices have risen and buy after prices have fallen." In other words, she says, "they do exactly the reverse of what participants in a bubble do."

Bob Greer, real return product manager at Pimco, advocates Ms Sen's viewpoint. "Hedge fund money might increase volatility as it flows in and out of specific

▶

Exhibit 13.19 continued

commodities – but not so with index money, which is more stable."

The pull of commodities for investors has been well-documented. In addition to the growth prospects, the notion is commodities are a natural hedge against event risks because they behave differently to other financial assets and often perform well in periods of rising inflation, political uncertainty and climate change – events that tend to have a negative impact on equities and bonds.

The argument is also said to hold true for the different commodity assets themselves.

"Whilst commodity prices correlate to some extent over short periods, especially when currency or demand are the most influential driver, over longer periods commodity prices do not generally correlate with each other because most have completely different supply fundamentals," says Mr Cheveley.

This, he says, means "it is not true that commodities in general are heading for bubble territory" and is "unlikely ever to be true".

To illustrate his point he cites the fact that cotton and silver prices have risen more than 60 per cent

year-to-date, while US natural gas prices are down 36.5 per cent and zinc is 17 per cent lower.

"For those commodities, however, that have risen strongly this year, in all cases the rises are supported by fundamental tightness and thus it would seem at least premature, and probably just plain wrong, to say they are heading into bubble territory," he says.

Source: Financial Times, 13 December 2010. p. 1. Reprinted with permission.

Exhibit 13.20 Quality parameters for Australian wheat

Quality parameter	APH1
Basic quality parameters	
Varietal restrictions	Yes
Protein min. (%)	14.0
Protein max. (%)	n/a
Moisture max. (%)	12.5
Test weight min. (kg/hl)	74.0
Unmillable material	
Above screen max. (% by weight)	0.6
Screenings (below screen) max. (% by weight)	5.0
Defective grains (% by count, 300 grain sample; unless otherwise stated)	
Sprouted max. (% by count)	nil
Falling number min. (seconds)	350
Stained, including staining due to moist plant material max. (% by count)	5.0
Pink stained max. (% by count)	2.0
Field fungi max. (count per half litre)	10
Dry green or sappy max. (% by count)	1.0
Frost damaged max. (% by count)	1.0
Heat damaged, bin burnt, storage mould affected or rotted max. (entire load)	nil
All smuts except loose smut max. (entire load)	nil
Takeall affected max. (% by count)	1.0
Insect damaged max. (% count)	1.0
Over-dried damaged max. (% count)	nil
Vitreous kernels min. (% by count)	n/a

▶

Quality parameter	APH1
Foreign seed contaminants max. (count total per half litre; unless otherwise stated)	
Type 1 max. (individual seeds per half litre)	8
Type 2 max. (entire load)	nil
Type 3a max. (seeds in total per half litre)	2
Type 3b max. (seeds in total per half litre)	4
Type 3c max. (seeds in total per half litre)	8
Type 4 max. (seeds in total per half litre)	20
Type 5 max. (seeds in total per half litre)	40
Type 6 max. (seeds in total per half litre)	10
Type 7a max. (seeds in total per half litre)	1
Type 7b max. (seeds in total per half litre)	50
Small foreign seeds max. (% by weight)	0.6
Other contaminants max. (count per half litre; unless otherwise stated)	
Picking compounds max. (entire load)	nil
Chemicals not approved for wheat max. (entire load)	nil
Ryegrass ergot max. (length in cm per half litre)	2.0
Cereal ergot mass (count per half litre)	1
Stored grain insects and pea weevil – live max. (entire load)	nil
Insects – large max. live or dead (count per half litre)	3
Insects – small max. live or dead (count per half litre)	10
Earcockle max. (count per half litre)	10
Snails max. live or dead (count per half litre)	1
Loose smut max. (count per half litre)	3
Sand max. (count per half litre)	20
Earth max. (count per half litre)	1
Objectionable material max. (entire load)	nil
Other non-objectionable material max. (% by weight)	0.1
Bread wheat max. (% by count; 300 grain sample)	n/a

Source: Grain Trade Australia, www.graintrade.org.au

Clearing

Exchanges ensure that all reports of a trade are reconciled to make sure all parties are in agreement as to the quantity and prices transacted. There are also checks to reassure that the buyer and seller have the cash and the underlying to do the deal. In many cases the exchange subcontracts this clearing function to a specialist organisation. LCH.Clearnet, a merger between the London Clearing House and the European-based Clearnet, is one of the major global clearing houses, with offices worldwide. It operates by also assuming the counterparty risk in every deal between its members; that is it acts as the buyer to every seller, and the seller to every buyer. Members pay a margin on each deal, the amount of which is assessed according to the risk involved. If a member fails, the margin is used to fulfil their obligations. LCH.Clearnet is Europe's main commodity clearing house for OTC and exchange traded commodities, operating for, among others, the LME, NYSE Liffe and the London Bullion Market Association (LBMA), which trades in gold, silver and other precious metals. Some exchanges such as CME have their own clearing system.

Carbon trading

Carbon trading is a new type of commodity trading, which trades in carbon emissions. It is a strange concept, where traders deal in an intangible substance with a non-existent delivery. It came about as a partial solution to the problem of global warming, which the majority of scientists say is caused by the amount of carbon emitted by our increasingly industrialised world. The Kyoto treaty dictated in February 2005 that a group of industrialised countries (Australia, New Zealand, Canada, Japan and most of Europe) must reduce total greenhouse gas emissions (most importantly carbon). However, not all countries signed the treaty, notably the US, the single biggest user and emitter of carbon gases. Despite this the European Union countries have set tough targets for carbon reduction before 2020.

Carbon is traded in a 'cap-and-trade' system. With cap-and-trade, companies are set a limit to the amount of carbon that they emit. If they emit over the required amount of carbon emissions, they are encouraged to reduce them by more efficient and less energy-greedy methods of production, or if this is not possible they are able to trade carbon reduction with another company. Instead of reducing their own emissions, which could be costly and have negative effects on productivity, they are able to pay some other company in another part of the world to reduce its emissions, which the other company is able to do more cheaply and at no cost to its own production levels. Thus we have a market in carbon emission.

Carbon is traded in metric tonnes of CO_2 (carbon dioxide). More than 90 per cent of trade takes place in London. Standardised contracts are traded on exchanges, with OTC trading also prevalent. Trading in 2009 was over $120 billion, and most experts expect the figure to increase substantially in the future.

Gold

Gold is used in a host of manufacturing processes. It is the only yellow metal and the only one that never rusts or tarnishes; it is indestructible and non-reactive. It can be alloyed with other metals to give it different properties. It has high conductivity, making it an essential component of many electrical and electronic devices. Its non-reactive behaviour makes it useful in various medical procedures.

From time immemorial gold was minted into coins, and was an easily tradable commodity, always being regarded as a store of value and a sign of wealth. In times of crisis, investment in gold is seen as a safe option because of the perceived value derived from its scarcity – *see* **Exhibit 13.21**.

Exhibit 13.21

Inflation fears bring on China gold rush

Leslie Hook

At Beijing's largest gold shop, the queues to buy bullion mini bars have turned into scrums as customers jostle for one of the country's hottest commodities.

The phone behind the bullion counter rings off the hook as a frantic sales clerk tries to answer buyers' questions. The electronic chart displayed behind him says it all: the price of gold is rising and

Chinese investors, worried about inflation, want in on the trend.

"We were thinking about giving our daughter Rmb10,000 ($1,500) in cash for her wedding," says an elderly couple. "But then we thought gold might be better value."

Others are shopping for themselves. "I've been buying gold for about six years as an investment," says a young man in his early 30s

who works for a power company. Like many gold shoppers, he is reluctant to give his name or talk about his finances, but discloses his purchase of a 100g mini bar.

For more than 50 years, the state controlled China's gold market and domestic gold prices. However, today the shiny yellow metal has re-emerged as a popular hedge against inflation. November's inflation data

▶

Exhibit 13.21 continued

revealed prices had risen 5.1 per cent from a year ago, the sharpest increase since July 2008.

Low interest rates mean that returns on bank deposits are often negative in real terms, and there are few other options for storing cash. Real estate investment has been curtailed because of government fears of a bubble. Chinese stock exchanges have slumped after a crackdown on insider trading.

The lack of a viable alternative makes gold bars and products popular investment options.

According to the World Gold Council, Chinese retail demand for the precious metal jumped 70 per cent to 153.2 tonnes in the 12 months to September, compared with the same period a year ago. Demand for gold jewellery, by contrast, was up just 8 per cent in China during that same period, to 373.6 tonnes.

China's bullion bullishness is having a big effect on global gold markets. China's imports jumped to 209 tonnes during the first 10 months of this year – a fivefold increase from the previous year, says the Shanghai Gold Exchange. China, already the world's largest gold miner, is now the second-largest consumer behind India.

"People don't want to put their money in a bank," explains Zhu Yan'an, a store official. "The growth in gold bar sales has been really pronounced."

At a nearby Bank of China branch, the duty manager says apologetically that he has only one gold bar left in stock "Last week an Indian buyer came and bought all of our 1oz, 2oz and 5oz bars," he explains. "I haven't been able to get any new supplies yet."

Gold-linked investment products, or "paper gold", are also multiplying. The government recently approved its first fund to invest in overseas gold-backed exchange-traded funds. Hong-Kong's bullion exchange has just announced a gold contract denominated in renminbi.

"I buy gold because it's fun," says Lu Feng, a 26-year-old paper company manager who has just spent Rmb18,500 on gold coins engraved with pandas. He proudly displays the shiny 10-coin set to friends. The friends, however, settle for silver.

The rising price seems to be fuelling the gold mania in what is, for now, a self-sustaining cycle. "The more the price goes up, the more people buy," says Liu Hui, who sells the precious metal at a shop near Beijing's silk market.

On the counter in front of her, Mao Zedong gazes out serenely from an engraved 100g mini bar, complete with one of his poems inscribed on the back

Source: Financial Times 15 December 2010. Reprinted with permission.

The total supply of gold in the world is estimated by the World Gold Council to be 165,000 tonnes, the total ever mined – 95 per cent of this has been mined since the California Gold Rush in the nineteenth century. The scarcity of gold is apparent when you realise that this whole total of gold would fit into a box measuring 20 cubic metres and this scarcity is what pushes up the price of gold. Unlike many commodities, more gold cannot be easily manufactured or obtained.

Gold is quoted in US$ per troy ounce (equal to 31.103 grams) and is held by some nations to guarantee their paper money. The World Bank issues figures detailing gold reserves held by countries – *see* **Exhibit 13.22**. The total amount held by all countries is estimated to be 30,462.8 metric tonnes, and valued at the London price in early 2011 of $1400 per troy ounce gives a total value of more than $1 trillion.

The London Bullion Market Association (LBMA) is the premier global market for trading and clearing gold and silver, which is an OTC market. Gold and silver are generally traded in bars; as with all commodities, there are strict specifications for each bar, and they are all hall-marked to guarantee their purity and identify their provenance. Despite the unit of trading being a troy ounce the minimum traded for clients are generally 1,000 ounces of gold and 50,000 ounces of silver. The unit of delivery for gold is a gold bar of generally close to 400 ounces or 12.5 kilograms. The unit of delivery for silver is a silver bar with weight between 750 and 1,100 ounces, although bars between 500 and 1,250 ounces will be accepted.

Market-making members of the LBMA provide continuous two-way bid and offer quotations in gold and silver for spot and forwards. Business is generally conducted via telephone or over electronic dealing systems. For example, in making a gold price, the dealer may quote $1,220–1,221, where $1,220 represents the bid price the dealer will pay for gold and $1,221, the offer price at which the dealer sells gold. In addition to the two-way bid and offer market available from market makers during the London trading day there are 'Fixings'. With this clients place orders with the dealing rooms of fixing members, who net all orders before communicating the net interest to their representative at the fixing. The gold or silver price is then adjusted up and down until sell and buy orders are matched, at which point the price is declared 'fixed' and all orders are

Exhibit 13.22	World official gold holdings, June 2010		
		Tonnes	% of reserves
1	United States	8,133.5	72.8%
2	Germany	3,406.8	68.1%
3	International Monetary Fund	2,966.8	not available
4	Italy	2,451.8	67.0%
5	France	2,435.4	65.6%
6	China	1,054.1	1.6%
7	Switzerland	1,040.1	24.1%
8	Japan	765.1	2.8%
9	Russia	668.6	5.5%
10	Netherlands	612.5	55.2%
11	India	557.7	7.5%
12	European Central Bank	501.4	27.1%
13	Taiwan	423.6	4.3%
14	Portugal	382.5	82.2%
15	Venezuela	363.9	47.6%
16	Saudi Arabia	322.9	2.8%
17	United Kingdom	310.3	16.6%
18	Lebanon	286.8	26.1%
19	Spain	281.6	37.1%
20	Austria	280.0	56.1%

Source: World Gold Council.

executed on the basis of that price. The spread between buying and selling prices is narrower in the fixings than at other times.

Silver fixing is carried out by telephone conference between the three members of London Silver Fixing: the Bank of Nova Scotia – ScotiaMocatta – HSBC and Deutsche Bank AG London. Silver is fixed each working day at 12 pm. Gold fixing is carried out in a similar way between the five members of London Gold Fixing, the Bank of Nova Scotia, ScotiaMocatta, HSBC, Deutsche Bank AG London, Société Générale and Barclays Capital. Gold Fixings are held twice each working day at 10.30 am and 3 pm.

Concluding comments

Trade, shipping and commodities for centuries have helped countries to grow and prosper. They are a vital part of life. In every country in the world, domestic goods are supplemented and sometimes supplanted by foreign imports. The financial markets and institutions assist the flow of goods and services around the world by providing finance, trading venues and ways of reducing risk. Regulation and standardisation have enabled commodities to be imported and exported with confidence. Because there are global standards for most commodities participants know exactly what they are buying or selling. Trading in commodities can be a highly speculative, risky undertaking, open to climatic, political, economic or terrorist influences, but it is vital for producers and customers that the market be available for trade and for hedging.

Key points and concepts

- **International trade** consists of the import and export of goods and services using various means of transport and transfer.

- **Infrastructure** needed to facilitate trade: legal, accounting, financing, transportation, and risk mitigation.

- Ways of transferring payment

  - **Payment in advance:** best for exporters, risky for importers.
  - **Open account trading:** best for importers, risky for exporters.
  - **Documentary letters of credit:** in return for reassurance (evidence) that all the documents needed for the goods to be exported and imported, documents showing actual shipment of the goods, official licences, etc., are present and correct, the exporter receives full payment from the importer's bank.
  - **Bills of exchange:** drawn up by the exporter (more usually its bank) and then signed by the importer which commits it to paying a sum of money on the due date which may be immediate (a sight draft) or, say, 90 days later (a time draft). **Banker's acceptances** commit the signatory bank to make the future payment. A **bill of lading** is normally needed for documentary letters of credit, bills of exchange and banker's acceptances: a document issued by a carrier to an exporter or its bank confirming that the goods have been received by the carrier, that the carrier accepts responsibility to deliver the goods to the importer and evidence of ownership of the goods.

- **Forfaiting:** an exporter holding a series of promissory notes from the importer guaranteeing that it will pay amounts at, say, intervals over a number of years can sell this series of rights to a forfaiting company at a discount.

- **Factoring** charges a fee to collect trade debt owed to a company. The company receives immediately, say, 80 per cent of its outstanding debt from the factor, with the remainder handed over less fees when the factor receives full payment of the debt from the importer.

- **Insurance and guarantees**

  - Companies need to check out their customers.
  - International shipments are generally insured because of the vulnerability of the goods to damage or complete loss.
  - **Export guarantee schemes:** government-based agencies provide insurance against customer defaulting or if for any other reason the exporter or its bank is not paid.
  - **Political risk:** can occur if the government of the importing country changes rules and regulations or becomes unstable or if the domestic currency is prone to excess fluctuation.

- London is a historic centre for shipping deals and many commodities.

- **Shipping transactions were first formalised on an exchange** in the UK in London coffee houses during the seventeenth century. The **Baltic Exchange** is the leading centre for ship trading (buying and selling second-hand ships) and ship chartering (agreements to carry goods between destinations). It is also where airfreight and available aircraft capacity is matched with potential users.

- The Baltic Exchange developed **indices** giving indications of the cost of shipping. The **Baltic Exchange Dry Index , BDI,** is an important indicator of the cost of shipping rates on key routes.

- **Forward Freight Agreements (FFAs)** allow shipowners, charterers and traders to protect themselves against the volatility of freight rates by taking an offsetting position in a forward, the price of which is based on a freight index. FFAs gives the contract owner the right to buy or sell the price of freight for transport starting at future dates. They are based on one of the Baltic indices composed of a shipping route for tankers or an index comprising a basket of routes for dry bulk contracts.

- **Marine insurance** is a very important market in London.

- **Lloyd's Register** is a worldwide register of ships and shipping details.

- **Shipping finance is** mainly carried out in dollars via London-based financial institutions. The main providers of finance for the shipping industry include international commercial banks, investment banks and smaller boutique banks, which act as arrangers or introducers of capital.

- **Commodities** are physical goods which can be stored (not immediately perishable), can be accurately measured and are generally fungible. They can be soft (affected by the climate) or hard, such as copper or silver.

- **Commodities are traded in various ways:** through **auctions** after the potential buyers have conducted an examination; **in sale rooms** face to face, often through agents representing the buyers or sellers. However, many commodities can be of a standardised quality, e.g. tin or lead, and so can be traded without visual inspection because the **exchange** itself specifies and enforces the quality.

- **Over 95 per cent** of commodity trading is in derivatives.

- **All commodities** must comply with strict standards and guidelines.

- **Commodity indices** enable derivative trading in groups of commodities. They are very difficult to construct with intellectual consistency.

- London is the centre for **metal trading. The London Metal Exchange, LME,** oversees trading of non-ferrous metals in a ring, by computer and by telephone. It has 600 licensed warehouses around the world to take physical delivery. Most trades are neutralised by both a buy position and a sell position.

- **ETFs** are funds trading in baskets of commodities. Investors can buy shares in ETFs to gain exposure to commodity price moves. ETFs that invest in commodities are often termed **exchange-traded commodities, ETCs.**

- Commodities can be prone to **speculative bubbles.**

- **Agricultural commodities** are raw unprocessed foodstuffs which must comply with strict standards.

- **Carbon trading** is trading in carbon dioxide emissions.

- The London Bullion Market Association (LBMA) is the premier global market for trading and clearing gold and silver, which is an over-the-counter (OTC) market.

References and further reading

Branch, A. E. (2007) *Elements of Shipping*, 8th edn. Oxford: Routledge.

Comprehensive book on shipping.

Buckley, A. (2003) *Multinational Finance*, 5th edn. London: FT Prentice Hall.

There is much more in this book on financing overseas trade.

Garner, C. (2010) *A Trader's First Book on Commodities*. Upper Saddle River, NJ: FT Press.

A simple guide to commodity markets from a trader's/speculator's perspective.

Madura, J. and Fox, R. (2007) *International Financial Management*. London: Thomson.

Contains a useful chapter on financing international trade written in an introductory clear style.

Stevenson, D. (2010) *The Financial Times Guide to Exchange Traded Funds*. Harlow: FT Prentice Hall.

Contains an easy-to-follow chapter on exchange-traded commodities.

Websites

Australian Securities Exchange www.asx.com.au

The Baltic Exchange www.balticexchange.com

CME Group, CBOT, NYMEX COMEX www.cmegroup.com

Euronext www.euronext.com
World Gold Council www.gold.org
London Gold Fixing www.goldfixing.com
Grain Trade Australia www.graintrade.org.au
International Monetary Fund www.imf.org
London Bullion Market Association www.lbma.org.uk
London Metal Exchange www.lme.com
Lloyd's Register Group www.lr.org
London Silver Fixing www.silverfixing.com
Standard & Poors www.standardandpoors.com
Intercontinental Exchange, NYBOT www.theice.com
United Nations Conference on Trade and Development www.unctad.org
The World Bank www.worldbank.org

Video presentations

Chief executives and other senior people describe and discuss commodities, trading and shipping, in interviews, documentaries and webcasts at Cantos.com. (www.cantos.com) – these are free to view.

Case study recommendations

See www.pearsoned.co.uk/arnold for case study synopses.
Also see Harvard University: http://hbsp.harvard.edu/product/cases

- Aristotle Onassis and the Greek Shipping Industry (2008) Authors: Geoffrey Jones and Paul Gomopoulos. Harvard Business School.
- Cargill (A) (2007) Authors: Ray A. Goldberg and José Miguel Porraz. Harvard Business School.
- Exporting to Ghana (2004) Authors: Ken Mark and David Sharp. Richard Ivey School of Business, University of Western Ontario. Available at Harvard Case Study website.

Self-review questions

1 What is international trade?

2 What types of financial services are useful to encourage international trade?

3 What is forfaiting?

4 What is factoring?

5 What is the Baltic Exchange and why is it important?

6 What is an FFA and where can it be traded?

7 What is marine insurance?

8 What is Lloyd's Register?

9 Why are ship purchases carried out in dollars?

10 What is a flag of convenience?

11 What are commodities and what is the difference between hard and soft commodities?

12 What is an exchange-traded fund for commodities, an ETC?

13 How do producers and suppliers reduce volatility in income using the commodity markets?

14 What would a holder of a commodity future contract due for delivery in one month do if the actual goods are not required after all?

15 Why are commodities standardised on exchanges?

16 What is a commodity index?

17 What is a speculative commodity bubble?

18 What does the London Metal Exchange do?

19 What is the LBMA?

20 How is gold traded in London?

Questions and problems

1 What are the different methods by which trading companies can pay for imported goods, and what are the advantages and disadvantages of each method? Include a description of the role of financial institutions in reducing risk for importers and exporters.

2 Who are the members of the Baltic Exchange? Describe and explain the advantages to society of the activities of the Baltic Exchange.

3 Describe the Lloyd's Register and explain its significance and importance.

4 Describe and explain the role of commodity exchanges in promoting economic growth.

5 Describe the market for gold in London.

Assignments

1 Consider a company you know well that engages in trade internationally. Describe the ways in which it uses financial tools to reduce the risk associated with making or receiving payments such as documentary letters of credit, bills of exchange, forfaiting or factoring. Also consider insurance for overseas trading.

2 For a company you know well that charters ships to transport its goods, investigate and then write a report on the stages in the process of reaching a deal with shipowners.

3 If your company purchases (or sells) commodities that are traded on international markets, investigate and describe in a report the processes it goes through to obtain (sell) them. Also evaluate alternative sources of supply and the role that regulated exchanges might have in reducing the risk associated with your firm's procurement of commodities.

Web-based exercises

1   Go to the Baltic Exchange website and write a report on the trends in its freight indices over the past 10 years. Describe the components of the indices and comment on their value for those needing to hedge future freight rates.

2   From the CME Group website, write a report on soybean contracts, and make a chart of recent prices. Comment on the volatility of the prices. Illustrate how this market might be used by a farmer and a food manufacturer to hedge future prices.

3   Using the internet, write a report on the purpose of carbon trading and how the market operates.

4   Download the gold fixing prices for the past 30 years. Write a report on any pattern you observe between the price of gold and economic upheavals.

Hedge funds and private equity

LEARNING OUTCOMES

By the end of this chapter, the reader should have a clear understanding of hedge funds and private equity and be able to:

- explain what hedge funds are and who are the participants;

- explain the different types of hedge fund;

- describe the fee structure of hedge funds;

- discuss the strategies used by hedge funds;

- explain the function of prime brokers;

- describe private equity and how it is carried out;

- understand the function of business angels;

- distinguish the different types of private equity;

- explain exit strategies.

Hedge funds and private equity – what comes into your head when you see those words? Here are some words people often associate with them – greed, excess, vultures, asset strippers. These opinions are not helped by the eye-catching headlines about the huge amounts made by some of these funds. John Paulson, whose fund made $4 billion in 2007 betting against the US housing market, is reported to have made $5 billion in 2010.

Both hedge funds and private equity aim to spot financial situations where there is a market inefficiency (irrational pricing) and use investment to gain advantage. Where they see things out of balance, hedge funds have the freedom to invest where normal investment managers cannot, notably by using short selling. Private equity comes to the rescue of many companies who would otherwise be unable to make progress through lack of funding. In both cases the motivation is not altruistic; hedge funds and private equity exist to make profit for investors.

Over the past 30 years, there has been a huge growth in the amount of investment in hedge funds and private equity. Private investors and investment institutions (e.g. pension funds) seeking a profitable home for their funds have found that these two types of investment can offer good rates of returns. However, there are worries about the lack of information concerning the use to which their money is put. There are also worries that these types of funds can be very illiquid investments unsuitable for many investors (their money can be locked-in for months or years), and that besides investment risk clients can have undue exposure to risks such as fraud. The industry is in a state of flux at the moment, with the EU and the US attempting to bring in new regulations designed to promote greater transparency, liquidity and safeguards for investors – *see* **Exhibit 14.1**.

Exhibit 14.1

Industry mulls over alternatives directive

Ruth Sullivan

In the past few weeks hedge fund groups and private equity companies have been digesting tough new Pan-European regulations from last month's long-awaited directive for the alternative asset management industry.

After more than 18 months of wrangling over the text between European Union officials and the industry, some of the more severe restrictions have been softened, but just how workable is the Alternative Investment Fund Managers Directive?

"It is a lot better than the original [document]. What initially looked like a death sentence [for the industry] has not happened," says Andrew Baker, chief executive of Aima, the hedge fund association.

But Aima would not have voted in favour of the directive had it had the opportunity to do so, he adds.

Simon Horner, public affairs manager at the British Private Equity and Venture Capital Association, agrees. While he believes "on balance the directive is viable", it is nevertheless "a compromise and not ideal".

Much will depend on the next stage when the detail of the framework will be fleshed out by the European Commission and Esma, the European securities and markets regulator, which opens its door to business in January.

"The devil will be in the detail. We are not out of the deep water yet," says Jarkko Syyrila, deputy director general at Efama, the European asset management body.

Although Brussels has opted for a lighter touch than initially envisaged some sticking points remain. One of the biggest concerns is how the regulation will affect depositaries, the safe-keepers of funds' assets. First-draft proposals to make depositaries, such as banks, liable for all asset losses were regarded as draconian but have since been softened.

The issue of liability and compensation for lost assets came into the spotlight two years ago when investors saw their money disappear from funds of hedge funds invested in the Ponzi scam run by US fraudster Bernard Madoff.

Although the new regime aims to target hedge fund groups and private equity companies – in part regarded by some as having contributed to the financial crisis – other types of companies such as investment trusts are also caught in the directive's broad sweep.

New rules against asset stripping by private equity companies, through limiting the selling of assets for the first two years after an acquisition, are also causing the industry concern. The industry fears the limitation would discourage investment.

From 2013, when the directive has to be adopted into national

▶

Exhibit 14.1 continued

laws, approved fund managers will be allowed to market their funds across the EU rather than relying on the current method of seeking approval on an individual country basis, known as private placement.

Efama believes private placement has its advantages. "We still think individual member states know what is best for their countries but private placement will go," says Mr Syyrila, referring to the plan to phase out this option.

He is concerned that the pan-European marketing rights or EU passports – which after much negotiation will be extended to managers and funds outside the region from 2015 – will be a "full passport" but also one where the "hurdle is not too high. If you put too much [regulatory] onus on managers they might walk away," he adds.

Source: *Financial Times*, 22 November 2010. Reprinted with permission.

Hedge funds seek inefficiencies or discrepancies in financial market prices and take advantage of them; private equity provides financing for unquoted companies in need of it. Both provide perfectly legitimate solutions for problems, but the manner in which they do this, and the fact that their actions can precipitate events (such as a run from sub-prime mortgages or a particular currency), are the cause of major concern. However, the concern seems to be something of a moral problem. It cannot be a bad thing for inefficiencies in financial markets to be brought to public attention, or financing to be made available to companies, but is it right that huge profits should be made this way? That seems to be the crux of the criticism directed at both hedge funds and private equity.

Hedge funds

To the man in the street, there is a certain mystique about hedge funds. What are they? What do they do? How do they make money? The first half of this chapter seeks to demystify and explain them. Probably the one detail that everyone thinks they know about hedge funds is that they make money, lots of money, and indeed some of them do – *see* **Exhibit 14.2**.

Exhibit 14.2

Investing stars lead bumper year for hedge funds

James Mackintosh

To the outside world, hedge funds often look much like investment banks on speed: far bigger bonuses, far bigger risks and far bigger profits.

The latest figures seem to confirm that prejudice. In the second half of last year, the current top 100 funds made $70bn for their clients, and – assuming they took only the standard 20 per cent cut – fees for themselves of about $17.5bn.

The top 10 hedge funds, measured by all-time dollar returns, made profits for their investors of $28bn, equivalent to the profits of

six of the largest banks. Paulson & Co, which employs about 120 people, made $5.8bn for clients in six months, more than the net income of Goldman Sachs, which employs about 32,500.

The data calculated by LCH Investments, an investor in hedge funds managed by the Edmond de Rothschild group, may help to explain why Wall Street banks fought so hard to stop the Dodd-Frank rules banning them from hedge fund activity – a battle they ultimately lost.

The exit of the banks from proprietary trading, a kind of internal hedge fund, should help to boost hedge fund returns by reducing competition, many managers and investors believe. Indeed the winding down of many prop desks last year ahead of the rules, led by Goldman, may already have supported returns.

Nagi Kawabani, chief executive of London and Geneva-based Brevan Howard, the only non-US hedge fund to make the top 10 list, says: "It's a plus because there's

▶

Exhibit 14.2 continued

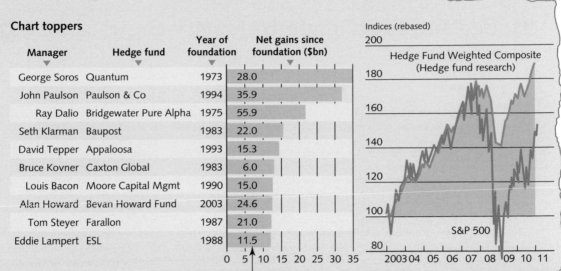

Chart toppers

Manager	Hedge fund	Year of foundation	Net gains since foundation ($bn)
George Soros	Quantum	1973	28.0
John Paulson	Paulson & Co	1994	35.9
Ray Dalio	Bridgewater Pure Alpha	1975	55.9
Seth Klarman	Baupost	1983	22.0
David Tepper	Appaloosa	1993	15.3
Bruce Kovner	Caxton Global	1983	6.0
Louis Bacon	Moore Capital Mgmt	1990	15.0
Alan Howard	Bevan Howard Fund	2003	24.6
Tom Steyer	Farallon	1987	21.0
Eddie Lampert	ESL	1988	11.5

(figures in bars) assets under management in strategy, $bn

Indices (rebased) — Hedge Fund Weighted Composite (Hedge fund research) — S&P 500

Source: LCH Investments; Bloomberg: Thomson Reuters Datastream

less capital chasing the same trades we chase, but it may affect liquidity [in markets]."

But he cautions that the boost may be temporary. "It is not like the banks pulling out means their guys have suddenly gone off and started to paint. They will reappear somewhere else."

Future returns, then, will come down to the success of the traditional hedge fund pitch: skill and the ability to spend more on research and technology.

The best funds on the LCH rankings are those that manage to produce good returns even after expanding. The table is dominated by managers who have become investing legends and whose moves are closely followed by would-be imitators.

George Soros, whose Quantum fund has made $35bn after fees for investors since it was set up in 1973, is ranked as the man who has done most for clients in dollar terms. He is closely followed by John Paulson who entered history books by making the most money for investors – and himself – in a single year in 2007 with his bet against subprime. After that comes Bridgewater's Pure Alpha, run by Ray Dalio, whose research is some of the most sought-after on Wall Street. The words of Seth Klarman, founder of Baupost, next on the list, are widely sought after, with copies of his out-of-print book *Margin of Safety* selling for upwards of $1,000.

In the past six months only one fund fell out of the top 10, Steven Cohen's SAC Capital, as the much larger San Francisco-based Farallon Capital Management pushed past it with strong returns, continuing its recovery from a terrible time during the credit crunch. One widely respected fund, Renaissance Technologies' Medallion, is not included as no data is available since it took the decision to reject external clients a few years ago.

But not all of the all-time top 10 did well last year. Brevan told clients recently that all three of its big ideas failed and it was basically flat on the year (an "aberration", says Mr Kawkabani).

The mass of smaller funds continued to underperform the leaders in the second half of last year. While the top 100 funds made $70bn on assets under management of $746bn, the 7,000 or so other funds, which run more than twice as much money, only managed to make $59bn for investors.

Source: Financial Times, 2 March 2011, p. 32. Reprinted with permission.

But there are many sceptical voices when it comes to whether the average hedge fund produces a high return – *see* **Exhibit 14.3** for an interesting discussion of hedge fund performance.

What are hedge funds?

The origin of hedge funds goes back to 1949, when Alfred Winslow Jones, an investment manager from New York, came up with an innovative investment strategy; he took both short and long positions in shares. He sold shares he did not own by borrowing the shares (e.g. from a broker, for a fee) expecting them to fall in price so that he could buy them for less when he needed to return them to the broker and so make a profit (**short position**). At the same time, he bought shares he expected to rise in price (**long position**).

Exhibit 14.3

Hedge funds struggle to justify their star rating

FT

James Mackintosh

If it looks like a cow, and moos like a cow, chances are the animal could make a tasty dish – but isn't venison. Investors should take note. Hedge funds, the most expensive item on the investment menu, have been producing returns almost identical to portfolios from the cheap burger joints of the advisory business, made up of 60 per cent equities and 40 per cent bonds.

No wonder hedge funds are worried. Bankers report increasing concern among these latter-day masters of the universe over how they will pay the fat bonuses their traders demand this year. Some high-profile managers have given up altogether.

"Absolute return", the ability to make money whatever the weather, is proving elusive. Hedge funds need to demonstrate to the pension funds and endowments that have become their biggest clients that they can at least earn returns that are independent of shares and bonds – the holy grail of institutional investors, who care about correlation more than returns.

Unfortunately for them, their similarity to the simple equity/bond portfolio seems to be increasing – undermining the industry even more than the insight a few years ago that hedge funds could be replicated with complex computer codes.

Furthermore, research shows that investors do far worse from hedge funds than standard measures suggest. Ilia Dichev at Emory

University in Atlanta and Gwen Yu at Harvard found that investors miss all the hedge fund outperformance by overtrading. Put simply, they buy funds that have already gone up and subsequently do less well, and sell funds that have gone down and subsequently recover. The pair conclude that actual investors in the "star" funds, which seem on paper to have the best returns, really earn 8–9 percentage points less.

Investors got another unwelcome reminder this month of the worst danger of investing in hedge funds: the risk that they cannot withdraw.

Hundreds of the largest investors in the sector were expecting final resolution of one of the most egregious uses of hedge funds' ability to restrict withdrawals.

Not surprisingly, some investors are unhappy with the situation. Hopefully they will learn the lesson: investments that make returns by investing in hard-to-sell assets are, well, hard to sell.

This links back into performance. During the boom years for hedge funds, huge numbers of funds boosted returns with private equity, over-the-counter derivatives and other hard-to-trade assets. Managers appeared smarter than they really were, because they were taking a risk they did not recognise.

Both absolute and uncorrelated returns, it turns out, are hard to earn without risk. And few managers want to take any sort of risk at the moment, leaving them making

returns more similar to the markets. Leverage is close to its lowest ever, after volatile trading repeatedly outfoxed managers. Simple strategies reliant on stockpicking skill have also been hurt by high levels of correlation between stocks.

Hedge funds still hold an allure, both for investors and, thanks to their secrecy, the media.

Put together the lack of uncorrelated returns, unjustifiably high fees, the past failure of investors to pick the funds that will perform in future and the danger of not being able to get one's money back, and hedge funds sound a lot less appealing.

As one big investor in the sector puts it: "If you can't generate alternative low or non-correlated returns, there is little point in the asset class."

Better, perhaps, to conclude that there is no asset class. Some hedge funds are truly uncorrelated, reliant on lawsuits, exotic derivatives, computer programs or the brilliance of their founders for returns. Others are little more than overpriced mutual funds. Investors need to accept that not everyone can get their money into the new hedge funds able to deliver what they want. Until then, investors are paying Cipriani prices for what too frequently turns out to be a cheeseburger and fries.

Source: Financial Times, 28/29 August 2010, p. 22. Reprinted with permission.

If a share he expected to rise did actually rise in price he made money. If the share prices of those he had shorted did actually fall he made money on them also. Even if the entire market fell he would make money, so long as the shorted shares fell more than the long position shares. If the entire market rose he made money overall, so long as the long position shares rose more than the short position shares.[1]

---

[1] Of course, this neat symmetry works only if the amount of short exposure to general market movements is the same as the long exposure, i.e. the position is 'market neutral' – *see* later in the chapter. If there is not a balance between the long exposure and the short exposure to overall market movements we have a 'relative value strategy'.

The definition of Jones' hedge fund then is a fund which aims to achieve a good **absolute return,** to preserve the principal for investors, whether the market rises or falls. Standard conventional investment funds tend to be long only – buying assets such as shares in the hope that prices will rise. They seek to make a **relative return,** relative to the performance of a particular index or market. So, if their fund decreases in value by 20 per cent they receive a pat on the back if the market index against which they are measured went down by say 22 per cent over the same period. The type of fund Jones ran, by contrast, takes a **market neutral** strategy, aiming to make an acceptable return regardless of whether the market fluctuates up or down.

Jones' strategy was largely unknown until 1966, when *Fortune* magazine published an article describing his 'hedge fund' and how it had outperformed all other funds by a huge amount, even with the performance fee of 20 per cent taken into account (Jones charged clients 20 per cent of the profit he made for them). This led to the formation of numerous hedge funds and a massive expansion in the amount of hedge fund investment, with investors enthusiastically handing over their money to participate in the exceptional returns which hedge fund managers promised and sometimes delivered. Now hedge funds have grown so large that it is thought they account for well over 50 per cent of all trading on the London Stock Exchange and other world markets. TheCityUK estimate that there are nearly 9,500 hedge funds managing assets of $1,700 billion – *see* **Exhibit 14.4**. Another estimate, based on data from custodians and administrators, puts the figure of hedge funds assets under management at $2,700 billion – *see* **Exhibit 14.5**. Note that lack of any central registry leads to a lack of accurate data.

Exhibit 14.4	Number and assets of global hedge funds

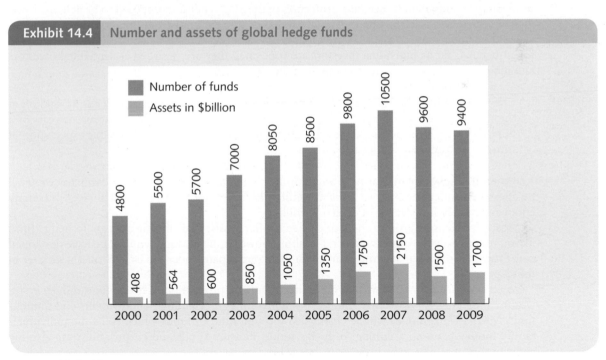

Source: www.TheCityUK.com

Who invests?

Most conventional fund managers are not only limited to a restricted list of investible assets but are subject to tough supervision by regulators. In comparison, hedge funds are for the most part lightly regulated and taxed, free to invest in a wide variety of markets and instruments. This freedom to range more widely than conventional funds was first fully appreciated by wealthy Americans, who, as individuals or through family trusts, placed large sums in the hands of hedge fund managers. Conventional investment funds are registered with the US regulator, the Securities and Exchange Commission, which imposes risk-reducing restrictions on the fund if it is to be allowed to accept money from ordinary savers. To prevent the need for registration and

Exhibit 14.5

Hedge funds manage assets of $2,700bn

By **Sam Jones**

The global hedge fund industry has more then $2,700bn of assets under management according to a survey of custodians and administrators released today – a figure that would make the industry far larger than most market participants have previously estimated.

The $2,700bn estimate, calculated for a HFM Week survey, is a more accurate figure than those traditionally reported as indicative of the size of the hedge fund industry. And, unlike some other surveys, the estimates ignore any leverage in funds, keeping figures lower.

Most estimates – which put the total size of hedge fund assets under management between $1,700bn and $2,000bn – rely on information provided by individual managers.

Source: Financial Times, 27 May 2010.
Reprinted with permission.

thus scrutiny and regulation by the SEC, small US hedge funds keep the number of investors to 99 or fewer accredited investors. Accredited investors are those who are thought wealthy enough or professional enough not to need the protection of the SEC. They are supposed to be able to largely look after themselves in the financial jungle, to have sufficient knowledge and experience in financial and business matters that they are capable of evaluating the merits and risks of a hedge fund investment. As far as individual investors are concerned they are regarded as accredited investors and therefore hedge funds can accept their money if:

> They have individual net worth, or joint net worth with a spouse, that exceeds $1 million at the time of purchase, or income exceeding $200,000 in each of the two most recent years or a joint income with a spouse exceeding $300,000 for those years, and a reasonable expectation of the same income level in the current year.

An accredited investor may also be an institution such as a bank, insurance company or small business investment company. If the accredited investor is a trust or a charity, e.g. university endowment, then its assets must exceed $5 million.[2]

Most jurisdictions around the world have similar restrictions limiting access to hedge fund investment to only the professional and wealthy. However, hedge funds in Europe have developed new products recently that allow small investors to participate under the UCITS rules – *see* later in the chapter.

As you can see from **Exhibit 14.6** the source of a large proportion of hedge fund money is still wealthy individuals and wealthy families, often investing through their endowments and foundations. Much of this money will be channelled through fund of funds which splits the individual/family money between a number of hedge funds. Pension funds and corporations are also big contributors of money to be invested by hedge fund managers.

Gates and lock-ups

Money invested in hedge funds is often locked up for a period (which could be two years or more) during which time the funds are not available for withdrawal by the ultimate investors. Funds may also be gated; a limit is placed on the amount that can be withdrawn from the fund at any one time. A common gate is a 25 per cent limit in any one quarter of a year. Gates and

---

[2] An alternative way of gaining SEC exemption is for the hedge fund to obtain investment funds only from qualified purchasers. This type of fund can have up to 499 investors. Qualified purchasers are:
- individuals with a net worth > $5million;
- institutional investors with a net worth > $25 million.

Exhibit 14.6   Global hedge funds, percentage share of source of capital

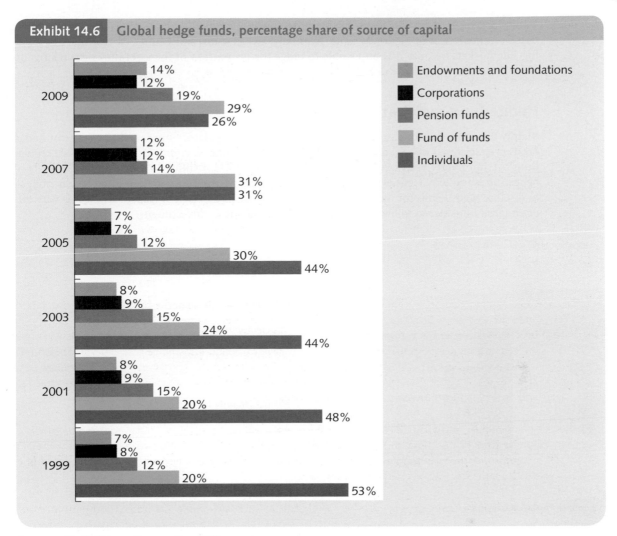

Legend:
- Endowments and foundations
- Corporations
- Pension funds
- Fund of funds
- Individuals

2009
- 14%
- 12%
- 19%
- 29%
- 26%

2007
- 12%
- 12%
- 14%
- 31%
- 31%

2005
- 7%
- 7%
- 12%
- 30%
- 44%

2003
- 8%
- 9%
- 15%
- 24%
- 44%

2001
- 8%
- 9%
- 15%
- 20%
- 48%

1999
- 7%
- 8%
- 12%
- 20%
- 53%

Source: www.TheCityUK.com, Hennessee Group LLC.

lock-ups are devices to prevent the manager having to liquidate funds at a time when prices are not favourable for redemption, and to prevent a run on funds. For example, if the manager has invested in a number of corporate bonds currently in a distressed state (e.g. coupon payments have been missed or covenants breached) because the issuing firms are struggling, he may be justified in refusing to repay hedge fund investors on demand. To do so would mean selling the distressed bonds before the benefits of the new arrangements (e.g. additional financial support) he is making with the distressed firms have worked through to make a profit. Alternatively, the fund might have invested in very illiquid assets such as property loans that cannot be liquidated quickly to reimburse the fund's investors at short notice.

Side pocket

A **side pocket** enables a fund manager to separate a difficult to value or illiquid investment from all other investments. An investor who withdraws from the fund cannot redeem any investment which has been placed in a side pocket, until and unless the fund manager decides to liquidate it. This is because of the danger of putting a false value on these assets. If an investor could ask the manager to guess at the value and receive a payout based on that, this would be unfair to the remaining investors if the guess was over-optimistic and it turned out that the value when actually sold is much less. Side pockets restrictions were used a lot in 2008 when Lehman Brothers collapsed. Many hedge fund assets became impossible to sell and extremely difficult to value. It would have been unfair to allow some investors to withdraw holdings in hedge funds at that point based on theoretical or historical value. Naturally, any new investor's funds do not share in existing side pockets because it is impossible to judge the proportion of the asset they own relative to older investors.

Hedge fund registration

Mainly to reduce tax for investors, but also to lower the regulatory burden, 60 per cent of hedge funds are registered in offshore tax havens and the remainder in countries or states where regulations are not overly restrictive, such as Delaware in the US. **Exhibit 14.7** shows the domicile of hedge funds for 2009. This explains part of the mystique; hedge funds are often not legally obliged to disclose their details for public consumption. Because of this lack of transparency, it is very difficult for an outsider to know the value of a hedge fund and its investments.

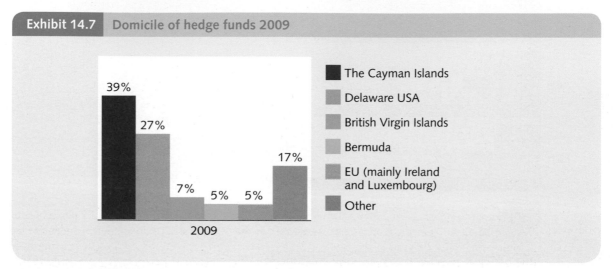

| Exhibit 14.7 | Domicile of hedge funds 2009 |

Source: www.TheCityUK.com

Fund managers

The quality of fund managers is crucially important to the success of a hedge fund. They usually have free rein to invest in whatever they choose, and most have a substantial personal investment in their fund. While being permitted to use idiosyncratic schemes for investing, prior to raising money from investors they usually state to investors the types of strategies they will be employing, e.g. investing in shares both long and short, or investing in distressed debt.

There is much discussion about a fund manager's alpha. Alpha is the return achieved above the return expected given the risk class of investment that he engages in – the 'risk-adjusted return'. The simplified way of estimating this is to judge the managers performance by how many percentage points over the average benchmark return on an index such as the S&P 500 he has achieved. A manager who consistently produces good alpha is thought to possess good investing skill and is in great demand.

Hedge funds are managed by investment companies which will generally be onshore companies registered and regulated by their domestic laws. For example, there are many managers based on the US East Coast in towns such as New York and the Gold Coast area of Connecticut, despite the funds themselves being registered in say the British Virgin Islands. They value being close to major financial centres from which they can draw talent. This also allows them to be close to their investors. These managers, either a single manager or a management team, perform the investment and administration of the funds. Sometimes they are part of large investment companies, sometimes they are run by a single manager.

Most UK hedge funds are incorporated in places like the Cayman Islands and so outside any UK regulations; however, these funds are usually managed by UK-domiciled managers – usually with offices in Mayfair. The *managers* based in the UK are subject to FSA regulations.

According to TheCityUK (*see* **Exhibit 14.8**), New York is the leading centre for hedge fund managers, with 41 per cent, followed by London with 20 per cent managing three-quarters of European hedge fund investments. These two locations, with their strong pools of professionals of every calling, are ideal providers of all professional, financial and managerial services to both hedge funds and other investment entities.

Exhibit 14.8	Percentage share of total hedge fund assets by location of manager

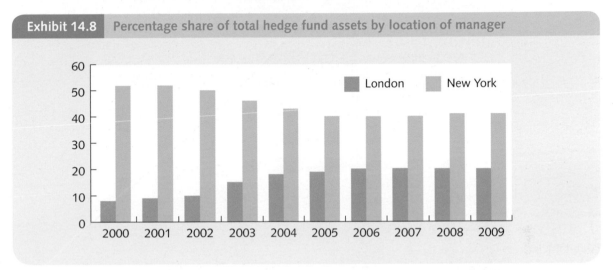

Source: www.TheCityUK.com estimates.

In return for their efforts, managers charge annual fees, generally between 1 and 2 per cent, but this can be up to 5 per cent, of the net asset value of the fund, plus a performance or incentive fee of generally 20 per cent, although this can be as much as 50 per cent, of any profits.[3] Commonly this is '2 and 20', that is a 2 per cent annual fee plus a 20 per cent performance fee. Taking, for example, J.P. Morgan, administering a fund of $50.4 billion (*see* **Exhibit 14.9**), even a 1 per cent management fee would be $504 million, plus a performance fee.

Hedge fund managers are often reported to be earning vast amounts of money and it is easy to see how this can happen. Performance fees are not paid in most other forms of investment, where it is usual to charge just an annual fee. Many other investment vehicles are banned from offering performance fees. The idea behind a performance fee is to encourage the managers to stretch themselves to make a billionormal profits, but this can also encourage them to take undue risks, as there is no mechanism in place for them to share losses as well as profits, and even if losses are made they still earn their management fee. Occasionally there may be a clawback scheme, where fees can be claimed back in the event of underperformance in years following good years with high fees paid to managers – *see* **Exhibit 14.10**.

There are two commonly (but far from universally) used checks on performance fees:

- *High water marks (loss carryforward provision)* Where a fund's performance has dropped, the manager does not receive a performance fee until the fund reaches its previous position. For example, if a fund is launched with $1 billion which rises to £1.2 billion in the first year due to good investment choices, the managers might take 20 per cent of the gain ($40 million) as a fee. If in the next year it drops to $1.1 billion, the managers will not receive a performance fee. If in the third year the fund rises to $1.3 billion, the performance fee applies only to the return above the previous high point ($1.2 billion) and so only 20 per cent of $100 million is paid rather than the full return for that year of $1.3–1.1 billion.

---

[3] Management fees are generally paid monthly or quarterly.

Exhibit 14.9 The ten largest hedge funds, January 2010

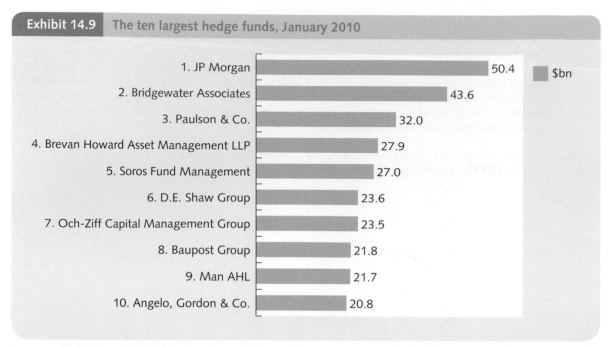

	$bn
1. JP Morgan	50.4
2. Bridgewater Associates	43.6
3. Paulson & Co.	32.0
4. Brevan Howard Asset Management LLP	27.9
5. Soros Fund Management	27.0
6. D.E. Shaw Group	23.6
7. Och-Ziff Capital Management Group	23.5
8. Baupost Group	21.8
9. Man AHL	21.7
10. Angelo, Gordon & Co.	20.8

Source: www.TheCityUK.com, Hedgefund Intelligence.

Exhibit 14.10

Hedge funds shy away from lower fees

By **Sam Jones** in **London**

Just one in 10 hedge fund managers expects to see the fees they charge investors fall in spite of recent under-performance that has seen income reduced, according to a Credit Suisse survey.

The industry suffered its heaviest outflows ever in 2008–09 but hedge funds still balk at the idea of cutting the standard "two and 20" fee structure, 2 per cent of assets and 20 per cent of returns, that they charge clients, the poll found.

But the survey, which took in responses from nearly a third of the $1,700bn global hedge fund industry, found that managers are open to negotiation.

Two-thirds of respondents said they were willing to bargain on fees if investors consented to longer lock-up periods and such deals have already begun to take place.

MSD Capital, the manager of Michael Dell's $10bn fortune, recently launched a new distressed debt fund open to outside investors that carries a three-year lock-up but with the promise that fees cannot be withdrawn from the fund for that period as well.

Theleme Partners, launched this year by Patrick Degorce, a former partner at activist fund TCI, charges a proportional management fee that decreases as assets under management increase.

For institutional investors in particular, such structures are likely to be particularly attractive.

Calpers, the largest pension fund in the world, which has more than $5.9bn allocated to hedge funds, announced a review of its hedge fund relationships last year and has been placing pressure on managers to reform the way they charge, according to the fund with which it invests.

Meanwhile in the UK, Hermes BPK, which manages hedge fund investments on behalf of the BT pension scheme, has also been pushing for change and is itself to allow its own clients to claw back the fees it charges in the event of under-performance.

Such fee negotiations are all part of a longer due diligence period in which investors research hedge funds, according to Credit Suisse.

The bank's survey also found that the average time spent by investors conducting due diligence has risen from 5.8 to 7.5 months.

While 41 per cent of funds of funds – the largest single class of hedge fund investor – previously spent three months or less conducting their due diligence, now just 9 per cent do, highlighting the particular pressure they have come under to demonstrate greater rigour in the wake of the Madoff scandal.

Hedge funds are also looking to meet the needs of investors keen for so-called managed accounts, which are segregated portfolios tailored to the specific needs of the account holder.

Source: Financial Times, 26 February 2010, p. 37. Reprinted with permission.

- *Hurdle rates* Performance fees will be triggered only once the fund has achieved a minimum annualised performance. The hurdle might be set as the yield on a government treasury bill, LIBOR or a fixed percentage, say 5 per cent per year. When the hurdle rate is surpassed the manager may either be entitled to a performance fee as a percentage of the entire annualised return or just a share of the return above the hurdle rate.

Some funds charge investors for withdrawing money from a fund (redemption fee, withdrawal fee or surrender charge). This may apply only to the first year of the investment or to a specific proportion of the investment the investor made. This is to discourage disinvestment when the fund might be engaged in illiquid or complex investing strategies.

Exhibit 14.11 gives a good description of fees.

Exhibit 14.11

Hedge funds investors have a great chance to cut fees

James Macintosh

Walk around London's Mayfair or New York's Midtown at the moment and – if you can avoid tripping over unemployed bankers – you can listen in on plenty of conversations about kicking hedge funds while they are down.

This is not about punishing flashy fund managers for their worst-ever year, although there is no shortage of *schadenfreude*. Rather, investors are riled about fees, the famed "2 and 20" – 2 per cent a year and 20 per cent of profits – the standard hedge fund charges.

It is now commonly accepted that fees will fall, as hedge funds' demands for capital exceeds supply from investors, and market forces work their magic. In fact, fees are already falling at many funds, something Bentley dealers and yacht brokers should be watching closely.

But investors are not just worked up about hedgies creaming off too much money. They are also becoming increasingly vocal about the structure of fees.

Changes being demanded include hurdle rates, or minimum returns before performance fees are paid; clawbacks of performance fees if good years are followed by losses; greater transparency; information about who other investors are; and even the right to trade their hedge fund holdings in the secondary markets.

About time too. Hedge fund fees are outrageous, not because of their size – although sensible investors should worry about this – but because they fail to do their job properly.

One of the key differences between hedge funds and mainstream funds is that hedge fund managers are supposed to have their interests aligned with those of investors, thanks to the performance fee.

But there are four areas where the fee structure is broken. The first is the ability to make money from doing virtually nothing. Consider a $1bn hedge fund, charging 2+20 which made 5 per cent in 2007 – possible with risk-free government bonds. This would earn the manager a $30m fee, with $20m of profits left to give to investors. The manager could sit on a beach all year and still collect his bonus.

The second problem is connected: even a very successful hedge fund may pay most of its outperformance, "alpha" in the jargon, in fees.

Calculations by actuaries Watson Wyatt show that even where a fund appears to be making money, the scale of fees it takes can be extortionate because so much of many hedge funds' returns comes from being long equities.

It considers a typical long-short equity hedge fund charging 1.5+20,

with full exposure to the market and a 30 per cent short position.

If such a fund managed to outperform by 5 percentage points on both long and short positions – a very strong performance if sustained – it would cream off 65 per cent of the "alpha", the value added by the fund, in fees.

These problems are easily fixed by imposing a hurdle rate: performance fees are not earned until the manager has exceeded a base level of profit.

The third problem is the lack of risk for hedge fund managers. If they do well, they get fat fees. If they do badly the next year, they don't have to repay anything – encouraging wild risk taking in the hope of getting rich.

Hedge funds have recognised this problem for their own staff, who are typically paid bonuses based on their own performance. Big names such as Tudor Investment Corp and Brevan Howard impose "clawbacks', holding back part of bonuses until later years and withdrawing them if money is lost.

But none has yet accepted a clawback provision for their fees. They should.

The final problem is the incentive for big funds just to produce moderate performance to hold on to assets. Annual fees are designed to finance the hedge fund manager's

Exhibit 14.11 continued

business, with performance fees paying bonuses. As funds grow, though, the annual fee becomes a big source of profit in itself, suggesting it should be lowered as assets expand.

Consider John Paulson, founder of Paulson & Co in New York. He offers a bargain in hedge fund land: fees of 1+20, against the norm of 2+20. But with $35bn under management, that now gives his firm a steady income of $350m a year, without doing anything.

Mr Paulson has, commendably, ignored such issues, making profits last year and producing eye-wateringly good returns in 2007 thanks to his prediction of the sub-prime crisis.

Fixing these problems is difficult, because investors have different priorities, as a survey of its clients by Albourne Partners, which advises investors with £200bn in hedge funds, showed.

Not all of the above problems apply to every fund, but with thousands of investors clamouring for different fee structures, hedge funds have an incentive to sit tight and change nothing.

Investors should get together, work out what they want and set a new standard for funds to comply with, to ensure they take advantage of what could be a brief period of negotiating power.

Source: *Financial Times*, 6 February 2009. Reprinted with permission.

Hedge funds may restrict the flow of additional money to the fund to an amount that can be sensibly managed, and even close the funds to new investors. When these vehicles grow too large, the sheer volume of funds available can make it very difficult to place investments, and the scale of operations can result in loss of flexibility in selecting investment assets.

Fund of hedge funds

A **fund of hedge funds** is a fund which invests in other hedge funds, thereby spreading the risk, so if one hedge fund in the fund is doing badly, the others will compensate for this. A fund of hedge funds manager is expected to make a good, varied choice in hedge funds for investment, with the aim of producing far better than average returns. They are supposed to investigate the funds thoroughly to ensure that they are run with high integrity, efficiency and wisdom. This seems a good idea for investors, but the downside is that there are two lots of annual fees and performance fees to be paid out, usually on a 1 and 10 basis to the fund of hedge funds manager, plus 2 and 20 to the fund manager. Unfortunately, not all fund of hedge funds managers have been successful (see **Exhibit 14.12**); some have been too complacent.

Exhibit 14.12

Funds of funds have to work harder

John Gapper

"For Monica and Walter Noel, their hilltop retreat in Mustique is all about the mix – of family, friends, great times and a sexy global design style," declared Town & Country in 2005 about the founder of the hedge fund group, Fairfield Greenwich, his Swiss-Brazilian wife and their five photogenic daughters.

It was a fairy tale existence, in more ways then one. The Noels' millions it turns out, were largely derived from Bernie Madoff's alleged $50bn (€36bn, £33bn) Ponzi scheme. The fees to investors on Fairfield's biggest hedge fund, the Madoff-managed Fairfield Sentry, produced two-thirds of Fairfield's $250m revenues, and $200m profits, in 2007.

Those figures, disclosed by The New York Times, illustrated just what a nice business the funds-of-funds industry had become. That profit of $200m was mostly distributed to Fairfield's 21 partners, including four of Mr Noel's sons-in-law.

The Noels did not know the family business was supported by fraud but that is not exactly a justification since Fairfield, like other funds of funds and European private banks that entrusted their investors' money to Mr Madoff, were paid above all to keep it safe.

Exhibit 14.12 continued

Now the funds-of-funds industry, which hardly existed two decades ago but today handles 45 percent of all hedge fund assets, has moved from hilltop retreat to dog house.

Fairfield Greenwich, which had $7.5bn invested with Mr Madoff, faces at least one class action lawsuit from enraged investors. In legal terms, it may have a defence, since a US court ruled in another case that a hedge fund advisory group was not liable for failing to spot a Ponzi scheme.

Still, Madoff-linked groups such as Farifield Greenwich, Tremont Capital and Union Bancaire Privée clearly failed to perform their lucrative jobs well enough. That rounds off a bad year for funds of funds, which have performed even worse than hedge funds and now look ridiculous.

Warren Buffett always thought they did. The Sage of Omaha has a thing against "helpers", such as hedge funds, that take investors' money in fees while performing not much better than a low-cost index fund.

That applies especially to funds of funds, which exist to carry out due diligence for investors who do not have the time or resources to do it themselves, and put their money in a selection of hedge funds. For that, they charge 1 per cent plus 10 per cent of any investment profits.

Mr Buffett thinks this is money for old rope, a view it is hard to dispute in the case of the Madoff brokers. He has made a $1m bet with Protégé Partners, a New York fund manager, that an S&P 500 index fund will outperform five funds of funds, after fees, over 10 years.

Fraud aside, there are problems with the investment pitch that funds of funds make. Many sold the idea that they had access to the best hedge fund managers, who had closed funds to new investors.

Whatever the truth of that in the past, the industry cannot afford to be stand-offish now. "The days of managers who never opened the doors to new investors are gone," says Chris Jones, chief investment officer of Key Asset Management, a fund of funds.

I still believe there is a role for the good funds of funds, simply on numerical grounds. The hedge fund industry is so fragmented – with about 7,500 single manger funds and perhaps 2,000 funds of funds – that none but the very largest institutions can do all the work.

Fraud is a real risk in the hedge fund world, filled with fancy promises and demands for secrecy, and the investors are ill-equipped to root it out themselves.

Two decades ago, hedge funds obtained most of their funds directly from individuals and family trusts. Now, there are many more funds to deal with and institutional money is steadily encroaching.

But funds of funds need to work harder and show that they actually contribute something valuable. The lack of safeguards on Mr Madoff's operations was breathtaking – a tiny auditor, no separate custody assets or clearing of trades and so on.

Source: Financial Times, 8 January 2009, p. 11. Reprinted with permission.

Listed funds

While the majority of hedge funds are not listed and benefit from a lax regulatory regime, there are some which list on stock markets, and so make themselves available for the retail investor, who is normally priced out of the hedge fund market. Being listed means that the shares are liquid (investors can easily sell or buy the shares on the stock market) and dealings have to be transparent (holdings of the fund have to be detailed in the annual report). Traditional hedge funds are illiquid and opaque. For example, the hedge fund run by Brevan Howard requires an initial investment of $20m; however, its BH Global Fund listed on the London Stock Exchange, offering investment in six of Brevan Howard's hedge funds, is available for £10.89 per share.

UCITS

The aim of the UCITS regulation, launched by the European Union in 1985, was to allow collective investment schemes to operate freely throughout the EU on the authority of a single member state. The regulating country supervises these funds closely, restricting what they can do, but once approved in that country it can advertise itself to investors in other EU countries. The investors may be individuals or institutions. A requirement is for UCIT funds to be highly liquid permitting investors to be able to sell their investment at short notice; therefore the securities held by the fund must be readily tradable. They also have to be transparent (public disclosure of risks assumed and significant positions), and the portfolios must be well diversified. Also, the amount of leverage (borrowing, etc.) that can be used to gain exposure to underlying investments is constrained.

Historically, the UCITS structure was used merely for long only strategies, e.g. for long-term equity investment by unit trusts. The UCITS III update of 2001 allowed UCITS compliant funds to use derivatives and opened the way for hedge fund strategies to be used. With proposed new legislation in the EU and the US threatening to curtail and regulate normal hedge funds, many of them have decided to register their funds as onshore UCITS compliant funds, which opens up for them the lucrative retail non-professional market – *see* **Exhibit 14.13**. Hedge fund-style vehicles available within the UCITS III framework have been dubbed 'newcits'. Some of the hedge fund strategies are suitable for UCITS because they can be liquidated fairly quickly, such as equity long-short. But others, those that involve complex and illiquid strategies, are simply unsuitable.

Exhibit 14.13

US hedge funds are quick to embrace the benefits of Ucits   **FT**

Sam Jones

On a Monaco rooftop in June, the sun glittering over the Mediterranean as it dipped below the Cap d'Ail, about 200 hedge fund managers, many from the US, glugged champagne after a day discussing something rather less bubbly: "undertakings for collective investments in transferable securities".

Ucits, though, are the biggest thing in the hedge fund industry. Ostensibly a variety of European mutual fund, tightly regulated by EU laws, they have become the toast of London's Mayfair and now New York.

Thanks to the tweaks in the EU laws that created Ucits, hedge fund managers have discovered ways to repackage their strategies in Ucits funds. In doing so, they have accessed retail and institutional investors who had been shut out of the high-octane hedge fund work. According to consultancy Eurekahedge, there are nearly $100bn of Ucits-compliant hedge fund investments in about 980 funds open to retail investors, a number that has leapt in the past 18 months from almost nothing.

"Ucits hedge funds now account for 7 per cent of the total hedge fund universe of $1,500bn but have attracted 20 per cent of the net inflows into the industry year-to-date," according to Alexander Mearns, chief executive of Eurekahedge.

Hitherto, almost all Ucits start-ups have been European. But, as the accents in Monaco at the GAIM hedge fund conference this June attested, there are signs that is changing.

The attraction for US managers – as for European – is twofold. First, Ucits funds are to be exempt from the forthcoming AIFM directive, and EU law that threatens to freeze US managers out of Europe. Second, Ucits are a way for hedge funds to tap a vast institutional investor base.

"There are a lot of European countries where it is very difficult for investors to put money into offshore hedge funds," according to Emmanuel Roman, co-chief executive of GLG Partners. "The bylaws of lots of companies in Germany and France prevent it." Ucits are familiar and saleable.

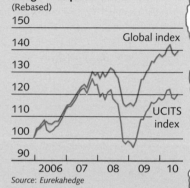

Hedge fund performance
(Rebased)

Global index

UCITS index

2006 07 08 09 10
Source: Eurekahedge

But there are problems. Ucits have to be highly liquid and transparent. They have investment limits. Mr Roman says: "There are some products for which it works

Evolution of a European strategy

When European legislators created the Ucits fund designation in 1986, hedge funds were very far from their minds, **writes Sam Jones in London**.

The law was intended to harmonise long-only fund managment products throughout the EU.

Ucits are required by law to be transparent and highly liquid, with diversified portfolios in readily-traded securities. Ucits funds cannot invest more than 10 per cent of their assets in commodities, for example.

Recent changes to EU law meant that Ucits funds could use derivatives, however, opening them up to hedge fund strategies for which being able to go short an instru-

ment is fundamental. While for liquid strategies such as equity long/short, managed futures, or even merger arbitrage, the leap into Ucits is achievable with relative ease, many worry that more complex unsuitable strategies are being shoehorned into Ucits in an effort to gather assets.

Investors, they say, could end up buying into products that are far riskier than they believe.

Critics say that Ucits funds are often imperfect – sometimes poor – replicas of the genuine offshore hedge funds they share names with and can underperform not least because of even higher fees than the typical hedge fund.

▶

Exhibit 14.13 continued

and some for which it doesn't: distressed, fixed income arbitrage, for example. The way I think about it is to imagine how the fund would fare if all the money had to come out in two weeks."

Paul Graham at UK fund manager Gartmore agrees. "What we do on the equity long/short hedge fund sides is extremely portable into the Ucits framework."

There is an added danger in trying to attract institutional investors into what was designed as a retail product, Mr Graham says. "They are not aligned with Mr Smith and Mrs Jones in Manchester or Cardiff, who have very different objectives to institutional investors. When they redeem their much larger investments, they can move prices." Were that to happen, small investors could get crushed.

Source: Financial Times, 6 August 2010, p. 29. Reprinted with permission.

In a 2011 survey conducted by Deutsche Bank 55 per cent of hedge fund investors said they preferred to allocate money to onshore UCITS hedge fund vehicles rather than offshore funds. Indeed, over the 2011–2012 period it is anticipated that more than $400 billion will flow into UCITS hedge funds, more than for traditional offshore hedge funds.

While the lure of being able to invest in a (expected-to-be) lucrative hedge fund has attracted considerable investment, results have not always been as expected, see **Exhibit 14.14**. It is reported that hedge fund UCITS vehicles returned just 4.1 per cent in 2010 far below the average gain for standard offshore hedge funds of about 10 per cent.[4]

Exhibit 14.14

BlueCrest Ucits fund set to be liquidated   **FT**

By **Sam Jones**

BlueCrest Capital, Europe's third-largest hedge fund, is to liquidate a $630m (£399m) fund that it launched last year.

The BlueCrest BlueTrend Ucits fund was an onshore version of the firm's successful computer-driven $9bn BlueTrend fund.

The move is one of the first setbacks in the recent growth of Ucits-compliant hedge funds vehicles. Ucits funds, which are regulated by European law, have historically been used exclusively by long-only asset managers.

Critics have long held that hedge fund Ucits products are not always suitable for those to whom they are marketed and are imperfect replicas of the strategies on which they are based.

As well as having exacting transparency and liquidity requirements, Ucits funds are restricted by European law as to which instruments they can invest in – an impediment that is understood to be behind BlueCrest's decisions to wind up its fund.

According to a letter sent out to shareholders on Wednesday, the BlueTrend Ucits fund was failing accurately to track the performance of the offshore BlueTrend parent fund. "It is anticipated, based on analysis by the investment manager, BlueCrest Capital Management, that this tracking error may increase further in the economic conditions," said the letter.

Demand for the product has been high since it launched, thanks in part to the success of the fund on which it is based, BlueTrend.

BlueTrend has been one of the strongest performing hedge funds to emerge from the credit crisis, having returned 43 per cent in 2008. The BlueTrend Ucits fund was launched in 2009.

Source: Financial Times, 28 October 2010, p. 12. Reprinted with permission.

Another way for retail investors to dabble in hedge funds is to invest in a hedge fund ETF (*see* Chapter 4). ETFs are normally a fairly cheap way of investing (typically 0.15–0.50 per cent of assets each year go as fees). However, hedge fund ETFs incur all the costly hedge fund fees and do

---

[4] Absolute Hedge statistics reported in Jones, S. (2011) 'Investors back onshore hedge funds', *Financial Times*, 8 February 2011, p. 32.

not always offer good returns. Marshall Wace launched a hedge fund ETF to mirror their top six hedge funds, on 1 March 2010 at an initial price of 1002p – *see* **Exhibit 14.15**.

Exhibit 14.15

Marshall Wace eyes ETF listing

By **Sam Jones** in New York

Marshall Wace, one of Europe's largest hedge funds, will today unveil plans to launch a publicly listed exchange-traded fund to track its flagship Tops fund strategy in an effort to rebuild assets after large redemptions in 2009.

The move marks a rekindling of a trend popular among top-tier hedge funds at the height of the boom to list versions of their restricted, proprietary strategies on stock exchanges.

The Marshall Wace vehicle, expected to raise $500m (£307m), will be structured as an ETF, the first such structure of its kind, and unlike a closed-ended listing will be able to grow in size according to investor demand.

The fund, to be named Marshall Wace Tops Global Alpha, will be listed on both the London and Frankfurt exchanges and will track an index designed to mirror the holdings of the six existing Marshall Wace Tops funds, proprietary hedge fund strategies currently only available to institutions and wealthy individuals.

Although the cost of running the Marshall Wace ETF itself for investors will remain small at 0.25 per cent annually, the underlying structure it tracks will still carry a 1.5 per cent annual charge and 20 per cent performance fee as is germane to hedge fund strategies.

The Tops (trade optimised portfolio system) strategy was conceived in 2001 by the then 21-year-old Anthony Clake and Ian Wace, the co-founder of the firm, and has courted praise and criticism in equal measure.

The system works by taking buy and sell recommendations from hundreds of brokers daily.

The recommendations are processed by a computer algorithm to sort out good ideas from bad ones.

Trades – and with them, healthy commissions – are routed via the brokers that submitted the best tips.

Critics have said the system leads to preferential advice from brokerages and potential market abuses, but the Financial Services Authority, the UK's market regulator, concluded the opposite in 2006.

In 2009, the six Tops funds returned between 6 per cent and 26 per cent, according to a person familiar with the situation.

On average, the funds have returned 10.9 per cent each year.

Source: Financial Times, 18 January 2010, p. 12. Reprinted with permission.

Hedge fund indices

Some hedge funds have performed better than average, but many others are less than impressive being broadly similar to any other investment returns. There is a problem in judging performance because of a general lack of reliable and independently verifiable information about hedge funds, making it difficult to track returns. Nevertheless there are a number of hedge fund indices. The compilers of these are faced with great difficulties, not least that the underlying investments are often obscure instruments that lack a daily price setting in a liquid market, and so until the investment is sold (which may be years away) we cannot judge the performance.

Also, there are dozens, if not hundreds, of different strategies/types of assets bought and sold by hedge funds. This heterogeneity means that it is difficult to compare like with like – even within one asset class, say bonds, different fund managers will concentrate on bonds in different countries, credit-quality bands or issuer type. There is also the problem that each year hundreds of funds are launched and hundreds disappear, so it is difficult to figure out which fund performances to include in an index.

Fund participation (sending the information to an index creator) is voluntary which is likely to lead to self-selection bias because those that are doing well are more likely to volunteer to be included. There is also survivorship bias because those that have gone bust or folded through lack of interest due to poor performance may not be included in the index.[5] End-of-life reporting bias

[5] Burton Malkiel and Atanu Saha (2005) found that 'live' funds tended to return over 8 percentage points more than 'dead' funds.

occurs when a hedge fund is declining rapidly and stops reporting its performance to the index providers. Thus losses go unreported. Backfill bias occurs when a fund only starts reporting its performance when the strategy proves successful. The index compiler may then allow the successful managers to 'backfill' its historic data once the fund is ready (presumably after it has had a good run). This introduces a positive bias given that those that are never successful do not go into the index.[6]

Some hedge fund index compilers are more rigorous than others. Hedge Fund Research, for example, insists that it eliminates survivorship bias by including all dead funds. Backfill bias is dealt with by only including performances after admission to the index.

Leverage

One major concern with hedge funds is the amount of leverage they use. Leverage gives the opportunity to invest greater sums than the amount of investors' capital. Leverage can be achieved by borrowing to invest or by entering into a financial transaction where the fund only has to come up with, say, 5 per cent or 10 per cent of the underlying exposure as a margin or deposit. It allows for greater profits, but if things go awry, it also gives the possibility of unlimited losses – *see* **Exhibit 14.16**. Here the hedge fund has exposure to the returns on 100,000 shares currently priced at £4. This is long position; benefiting from rises. The fund has put down only 10 per cent of the underlying value, £40,000, to gain exposure to the price moves on £400,000 of shares. This can be achieved in a variety of ways, most likely to be through derivatives.

Exhibit 14.16	The significance of leverage				
Share price	£4.00	£4.50	£5.00	£3.50	£3.00
Gain long exposure to 100,000 shares @ £4	£400,000	£450,000	£500,000	£350,000	£300,000
10% margin (leverage of 10:1)	–£40,000	–£40,000	–£40,000	–£40,000	–£40,000
Gain/loss		£50,000	£100,000	–£50,000	–£100,000
Gain/loss as a % of initial margin		$\frac{£50,000}{£40,000}$ $=125\%$	$\frac{£100,000}{£40,000}$ $=250\%$	$\frac{-£50,000}{£40,000}$ $=-125\%$	$\frac{-£100,000}{£40,000}$ $=-250\%$

The problem with leverage was evidenced in a spectacular fashion in 1998, with the collapse of the hedge fund Long Term Capital Management. With two Nobel-prize winning economists in its team, LTCM used a strategy called fixed income arbitrage, betting on minute differences in government bond prices and the expectation that these differences would converge. Because the differences were so small, it needed to use a huge amount of leverage to make a significant profit. Disaster struck when the Russian government defaulted on its bonds, causing bond prices in general to diverge considerably. LTCM had assets of $4 billion, but leverage of nearly $130 billion (a ratio of over 30 to 1). It owed vast sums to other financial institutions. If it failed to pay its

[6] Burton Malkiel and Atanu Saha (2005) found that backfill returns were, on average, 5 percentage points more than contemporaneously reported returns between 1994 and 2003.

debts they might become insolvent. With such enormous potential losses, which could damage the economy, the Fed persuaded a group of banks to bail LTCM out. A more normal leverage ratio is around 2.5, meaning that for every £1 obtained from investors the manager gains exposure to the price movements on £2.50 of assets – *see* **Exhibit 14.17**. Note how wide the differences in leverage are for the different strategies.

Exhibit 14.17

Hedge funds are wary of taking on more risk

Sam Jones

FT

In spite of a growing appetite for risk and a sense of a once-in-a-generation set of market opportunities, hedge fund managers continue to be wary in their use of leverage.

The days of "picking up nickels in front of a steamroller" – the metaphor by which high-octane, high-borrowing, hedge fund strategies used to be known – are still a distant thing of the past, even with individual blowups such as those of Platinum Grove, JWM Partners and Peloton Partners in recent memory.

By and large, hedge funds have access to more leverage than they need or are wary of taking on too much risk, following a volatile year in 2010.

On the one hand, bullish managers in the current environment have an abundance or market opportunities, while on the other, bearish managers remain fearful of another eurozone crisis.

While in 2009 the average hedge fund manager returned 24.57 per cent, 2010 saw an average return of just 10.58 per cent, according to Hedge Fund Research. Poor performance last year was almost entirely down to a choppy and unpredictable market that caught out bulls early on and then burned bears at the end. Anyone whose positions were levered suffered all

the more. Even notable bulls such as John Paulson were forced to retrench mid-year in response to macro-economic shocks. Last July the Paulson & Co Recovery fund told investors it has reduced its net exposure – a measure of directional bias – from 140 per cent to 107 per cent.

According to data from Credit Suisse, made available to its hedge fund clients last week, the average hedge fund started 2010 with leverage of about 2.53 times and ended the year with leverage of about 2.52 times, rising to as much as 2.68 in March.

In other words, for every $1 of client money a hedge fund had at the beginning of the year, the bank on average lent out a further $1.53 to the fund on top.

The level has since risen to 2.65 times, says Credit Suisse – following growing confidence in December and a sense that an equity-led market rally would continue through this year.

The bank's figures may actually overstate the amount of leverage funds use, he says. "The actual number is likely to be lower since... cash balances are not captured. Leverage for the average equity long short manager is more likely to be around 140–160 per cent," he said.

Different hedge fund strategies have continued to use leverage to markedly different degrees.

Relative value specialists – which trade on pricing anomalies in fixed-income securities – are the only players that have significantly decreased their use of leverage in January, but their use of it remains well above the industry norm at 6.49 times and is inherent to the success of the strategy itself.

Other quantitative strategies, such as equity statistical arbitrage, have also continued to use high leverage. The average statistical arbitrage fund levers anywhere between 10 and 20 times, according to market participants.

In almost all cases, however, supply of leverage continues to outstrip demand.

"Broadly speaking the capacity to borrow has been greater than our requirements," says Pat Trew, chief risk officer at the $9bn multi-strategy London manager CQS. "There is a disparity between the amount of leverage offered and the amount utilised. We haven't' really seen a material increase in our funds' leverage over the past nine months."

Source: Financial Times, 24 February 2011, p. 35. Reprinted with permission.

Hedge fund strategies

While it not possible to know exactly how many hedge funds there are (TheCityUK estimates there to be about 9,400 in 2010, Hedge Fund Intelligence collects data from 13,000), or to give a total amount invested, we can explain their most common strategies. Jones' original strategy was revised and a whole host of strategies emerged, all with one aim in mind: to make profit no matter what the state of world markets or economies, to make an absolute return. Some managers use analytical tools, some use financial modelling; all seek alpha. The range of hedge fund strategies changes over time as managers try to think up new schemes to exploit supposed superior information or analytical technique. The common themes linking them are that hedge funds are able to follow strategies that are often forbidden to traditional fund managers, managers are greatly incentivised by the fee structure, there is light regulation and a fundamental lack of transparency. Beyond that it is difficult to categorise the strategies as many of them overlap or comprise a mixture of strategies.

Here we have space to provide only a brief description of some of the strategies.

- *Arbitrage* is taking advantage of small discrepancies in the prices of the same financial instrument or similar securities by simultaneously selling the overpriced security and buying the underpriced security. So, for example, identical shares could be selling in a number of different stock markets, and because of differences in local supply and demand are selling at, say, one-tenth of 1 per cent difference in two of them. An arbitrageur will buy shares in the lowest priced arena and simultaneously sell them in the higher priced market, making an immediate profit. These acts will help to close the gap because the increased buying demand in the low priced market will raise prices there, and the additional supply in the high priced market will lower prices there. Arbitrage goes hand in hand with leverage; the price disparity is usually very small and so leverage is needed for the financial gain to be worthwhile. For example, if the discrepancy is one-tenth of 1 per cent on an instrument priced at £2.35, then to make £2,350 an investment of £2,350,000 must be made. If it is possible to borrow 90 per cent of a £23.5 million position, then the profit would be £23,500 if prices move according to plan, but huge losses can occur if price movements are unfavourable. If you borrow 90 per cent of the £23.5 million and the prices move the wrong way, you still owe £21.15m!

- *Long/short strategy (relative value)* involves buying one type of financial instrument long and selling another instrument short to exploit pricing anomalies between related (but not identical) assets that are mispriced relative to each other. Equity long/short (Jones' original strategy) has been successful for some hedge funds. Managers may divide the funds with a bias one particular way, e.g. 30 per cent of the fund can be exposed to short positions and 70 per cent long, or any particular ratio they choose. If leverage is used, a fund could be 30 per cent short and 100 per cent long, with the total of 130 per cent indicating leverage of 30 per cent. If the fund has a high exposure to short positions and a relative low exposure to longs (dedicated short bias) and then the market acts against their expectations a great deal of money can be lost. Exhibit 14.18 shows that because a share price could conceivably rise to any height short positions can lose multiples of the amount first committed.

Exhibit 14.18	The implications of short selling

Sell short 100,000 shares @ £3.00 per share. Exposure = £300,000, gained with £60,000 of capital

If the share price moves to	£0.00	£2.50	£3.50	£6.00	£20.00
Buy 100,000 shares to close the position	£0	£250,000	£350,000	£600,000	£2m
Gain/loss	Maximum possible Gain £300,000	Gain £50,000	Loss £50,000	Loss £300,000	Loss £1.7m

Many funds apply long/short to two different stock market indices (and their derivatives) rather than individual shares. The long/short principle is also used for many other instruments, from bonds to derivatives.

- *Market-neutral* strategies are those that try to provide a return regardless of the overall market movement because the short position exposure is as great as the long position. The trader has no net exposure to broad market moves. They can be equity long/short, but are usually positions in other investments (often derivatives) where there is a price discrepancy to be exploited. The underlying strategy relies on the hope (not always fulfilled in the time that the hedge fund can maintain its position) that these prices will converge to a fair value.

- *Fixed-income relative value/fixed-income arbitrage* evolved from classical arbitrage, but instead of identical securities the two securities bought and sold are merely similar. This is not the traditional 'riskless arbitrage' where you are bound to make a profit buying and selling the same security; in contrast this approach is based on a theory of a 'normal' price relationship between two assets that are somewhat substitutes for each other. Hedge fund managers become convinced that the difference in price between two similar assets (say, AAA-rated bonds issued by Tesco and Sainsbury) is unreasonably wide (perhaps much greater than the historical norm, or fundamental analysis indicates a mispricing) or narrow and that they will revert to 'true relative value.' He/she sells short the relatively overpriced security and buys the underpriced security. Once prices have reverted to true value, the trade can be liquidated at a profit. However, these are risky strategies because the market can be perverse and push prices even further away from true value for many years. Another strategy is to benefit from small price differentials in fixed income securities such as two issues of US government bonds, say a 30-year bond and one that has 29 years to run. Because of the resources needed in terms of capital, professional ability and technological infrastructure, fixed income arbitrage tends to be used by larger hedge funds. Long Term Capital Management and Relative Value Opportunity II suffered using this strategy – *see* **Exhibit 14.19**.

Exhibit 14.19

The storms that swept away Meriwether's flagship fund

FT

Henny Sender

John Meriwether's decision to shutter his flagship Relative Value Opportunity II hedge fund, even as many other groups with a similar approach are flourishing, underscores how conditions in the hedge fund world have changed.

It is the second time Mr Meriwether has called it quits. In 1998, the implosion of Mr Meriwether's Long-Term Capital Management led to fears for the stability of Wall Street.

Mr Meriwether's approach for his latest fund was a relative value strategy that sought to identify small price discrepancies across a range of securities, whether currencies or fixed income, for the leading economies and to take positions on the expectation that those anomalies would disappear.

But because the price moves can be so slight, the strategy relies on much borrowed money to produce adequate profits at the best of times.

Mr Meriwether, and other hedge fund managers, found that the desks of the Wall Street firms that financed them were no longer willing to do so, forcing them to sell securities in a market where demand vanished.

"To try to take advantage of relative mispricings turned out to be a crappy business," said one consultant, a former colleague of Mr Meriwether's.

"Whenever liquidity becomes an issue, you are exposed."

Those familiar with Mr Meriwether's portfolio said that as a value investor he was slow to cut his losses, and added to positions as securities became cheaper.

For example, some relative value funds, including Mr Meriwether's JWM Partners, bought a kind of Japanese government bond that was inflation protected, then accumulated more and more as the bonds dropped in value, and were left with big losses.

"You learn a certain trading style and it can be tough to change," the consultant said.

The Relative Value Fixed Income Convertible Arbitrage Index, the most comparable measure to the strategy employed by Mr

▶

Exhibit 14.19 continued

Meriwether's fund, was among the most disastrous strategies last year, down almost 34 per cent, according to Chicago-based Hedge Fund Research.

Yet in this year's first half, the index gained almost 30 per cent.

Analysts say those hedge funds that have survived have done so by changing their style and adopting an approach which requires moving quickly to cut losses rather than doubling up as prices fall.

"The funds that have done well are those that have actually stopped doing traditional relative value trades and put on directional trades instead," said a managing director at a firm investing in a variety of hedge funds on behalf of institutions and wealthy families in New York.

"Traditional relative value is dead."

The manager cited MKP and Cura as examples of funds that had made a transition from leveraged relative value trading

Source: Financial Times, 10 July 2009. Reprinted with permission.

- *Convertible bond (warrant) arbitrage* This is taking a long position in convertible bonds or warrants while hedging with a short position, typically by shorting shares in the same company. Convertible bonds and warrants are priced as a function of the share price; their value is derived from the price of the shares because they grant the right to convert to or purchase shares at a fixed price sometime in the future. However, occasionally they are not priced efficiently due to illiquidity in the convertible and warrant markets, because of uncertainty over the rights on the convertible and because of analyst neglect in these markets compared with the equity markets – the right to convert or purchase shares becomes underpriced. This is a form of risk 'arbitrage' and not the traditional risk-free arbitrage; the market can move prices even further away from the rational level for a long time.

- *Event-driven* strategies take advantage of special situations. For example, distressed securities investing is when hedge fund managers buy shares or debt belonging to companies which are experiencing serious financial problems and could be facing bankruptcy. They often believe that other investors have overreacted to the troubles and pushed market prices too low. Having investigated thoroughly, they think that a recovery of some value is possible. Other investors, particularly creditors, may lack the flexibility and patience of the hedge fund to hold onto distressed assets, e.g. pension funds are often forbidden from holding sub-investment grade bonds, banks may be desperate to remove loans no longer paying interest from their balance sheets. The other creditors may not have the time or the special knowledge to assist a company through a reorganisation of its finances, which can take several years – they would rather sell now, even at a low price.

- *Merger arbitrage* is another event-driven strategy. Often the shares of the target company will rise when the intention for one company to acquire the other is made public. Shares in the acquiring company often fall because of the tendency to over-pay and reduce shareholder value. Despite the price movements the share price of the target typically remains below the acquisition price. This is usually because of doubts in the market that the merger will be completed – the potential acquirer could just walk away, the target managers put up a good defence or a monopolies inquiry is launched. Or it may be because the market is underestimating the potential for a second bid or rival offer for the target. So some funds take a long position in the target and a short position in the acquirer. If the acquirer has offered shares in itself in return for the shares in the target when the offer is accepted the hedge fund exchanges its shares in the target for shares in the acquirer. These shares offset the earlier short position in the acquirer. A risk of this strategy is the possibility of the merger failing to go ahead (e.g. the monopoly regulator prevents it) and therefore the target's shares fall significantly while the acquirer's might rise.

- *Activist strategy* The hedge fund buys a portion of the shares in a company and uses the ownership to press for improvement in returns to shareholders. The hedge fund manager engages with the company's board and management. They may rally other shareholders to insist on one or more management actions: divestment; breaking up the group and selling off divisions; share buy-backs; raised dividends; mergers with other firms; or even sale of the entire business or liquidation.

- *Global macro* Funds profit (and lose) from bets taken against countries, currencies, global economic dislocations in interest rates and other macroeconomic variables. Using leverage, they typically take concentrated positions in any type of financial instrument (equity, currency, commodity, interest rates, etc.), trying to ensure that the downside would not be catastrophic, but the upside has unlimited potential. They try to anticipate global macroeconomic events anywhere in the world. Returns can be spectacular, such as when George Soros' Quantum fund took a major position against the value of the UK pound, anticipating that the pound would devalue in 1992. Soros was proved right and governments were forced to devalue and withdraw from the European Exchange Rate Mechanism. He placed the equivalent of $10 billion in currencies other than sterling. When it devalued, his investments in those other currencies went up when translated back into sterling. Soros is thought to have made $1 billion from the dealings and became known as the man who broke the Bank of England. Soros saw a situation that was out of balance and which could not be maintained. Global macro positions may be 'directional' – betting on a rise in interest rates or a currency for example – or relative value – the pairing of two similar assets on a long and short position, looking for a current difference to change, e.g. the interest rate on US ten-year Treasuries to move relative to the interest rate on German Bunds.

- *Fundamental growth* Investing in companies they think have more earnings growth and capital appreciation potential than the average company.

- *Fundamental value* Investing in undervalued companies currently out of favour with the generality of investors.

- *Multi strategy* Funds use the same pool of investment to invest in different strategies. The idea is that diversification makes for more consistent returns, but the downside is that it also prevents full exploitation of a successful strategy.

Prime brokerage

Prime broker services are mainly supplied by investment banks. They are an essential requirement for hedge funds as they provide the means for the funds to carry out their business, without getting tangled up in regulations. The banks stand ready to act as a broker, buying and selling securities; lend securities (for short selling); offer a central facility to enable clearing and settlement of trades; settlement is netted. Many prime brokers offer custody services, where securities can be safely stored. The many funds that depend on leverage to generate adequate returns given the tiny amounts involved in arbitrage could not function without prime brokers arranging the leverage.

Prime brokers may charge annual fees for some services offered, but their major revenue comes from the spreads on financing and stock arrangements, commission on trading and settlement fees. With the prime broker taking care of all these administrative tasks, fund managers can concentrate on their main function, making profitable investments for their clients.

Prime brokerage services are also discussed in Chapter 3.

Private equity

We have looked at some of the details of raising money on the Stock Exchange in Chapters 8 and 9, but in the commercial world there are millions of companies which are not quoted on any stock exchange. We now consider a few of the ways in which equity capital is generated for these unquoted firms.

Private equity is medium- to long-term finance invested in companies not quoted on any stock exchange to profit from their growth. It enables companies which are unable to access further funding from current shareholders or banks to obtain the required funding from other investors. It is not easy to distinguish between private equity and venture capital. Some use the term private equity to define all unquoted company equity investment, others confine 'private equity' to investment in companies already well established, and apply 'venture capital' to investment in companies at an early stage of development with high growth potential.

Private equity/venture capital in its modern form began after the Second World War when a French immigrant, Georges Doriot, founded the American Research and Development Corporation (ARD) in 1946. ARD invested in and provided capital for new businesses, helping the economy regenerate after the Second World War. A gap was created because large, long-established and respectable companies listed on stock exchanges were more cautious in backing innovative projects which could lead to large potential losses, and equity and bond investors tended to concentrate their money on stock exchange quoted companies.

Private equity funds

Private equity usually takes the form of a fund which then invests in a group of companies. Many investments result in total loss and so private equity investment in a single company can be a huge risk. The diversity of private equity funds gives greater opportunities for good overall returns, even if a high proportion of the investee companies turn out bad performances.

The private equity managers that run these funds, looking for and evaluating investment opportunities in companies, are known as the **general partners** (GPs). While other investors in the funds are called **limited partners** (LPs); these can be institutions or individuals. The GPs select companies which are deemed suitable for investment using finance provided by their limited partners, and sometimes loans and bank borrowings. Both the GPs and the LPs can make spectacular returns. Take the case of 3i's investment in Hyva (*see* **Exhibit 14.20**). The private equity fund bought the company for around €125 million and five years later sold it for €525 million.

Exhibit 14.20

3i turns profit with Hyva sale

FT

By **Martin Arnold**

The private equity group 3i has realised one of its most profitable deals by selling Hyva, the leading make of hydraulic pumps for waste and tipper trucks, for €525m to Unitas Capital, the Hong Kong-based buy-out group.

The sale of Hyva, which is Dutch-based but makes 60 per cent of its revenues in Asia, has been hailed by Michael Queen, 3i chief executive, as proof that 3i can make big returns by buying European companies and expanding them in emerging markets.

"This is a rare opportunity to buy a company that has significant market-leading position in three of the four Bric economies:

China, India and Brazil," said John Lewis, a partner at Unitas Capital, the former Asian buy-out arm of JPMorgan.

Unitas, which has about $4bn (£2.6bn) under management, saw off competition for Hyva from Chongqing Machinery & Electric, the Chinese state-controlled industrial group, and buy-out rivals Nordic Capital, Permira and Bain Capital.

3i bought Hyva for €125m in 2004, investing €30.7m of equity and raising debt from ABN Amro. When 3i recapitalised the company in late 2006, it was repaid €25m and it increased its stake by buying out another shareholder the following year.

The Dutch-based hydraulic company has more than trebled revenues and earnings before interest, tax, depreciation and amortisation under 3i's ownership to a forecast of €490m (£417m) and €65 respectively this year.

A decisive factor in Unitas winning the deal was its ability to raise about €250m of debt from Asian-based lenders, including Standard Chartered, Nomura, Goldman Sachs and Bank of America Merrill Lynch.

3i has sold companies worth more than €2.5bn this year.

Source: Financial Times, 16 December 2010, p. 22. Reprinted with permission.

The GPs are paid management fees (usually 1–2.5 per cent) and a share (usually about 20 per cent) in the eventual capital gain, known as the **carried interest (the carry)**. The fees cover all the management expenses of administering the private equity company or fund, and provide an income for GPs during lean times when the fund has not sold profitable investments. Limited partners may include pension or insurance funds, wealthy individuals or families, or sovereign wealth funds. **Exhibit 14.21** shows the sources of funding for UK funds from 2007 to 2009. It also

| Exhibit 14.21 | Source of private equity funds 2007–2009 |

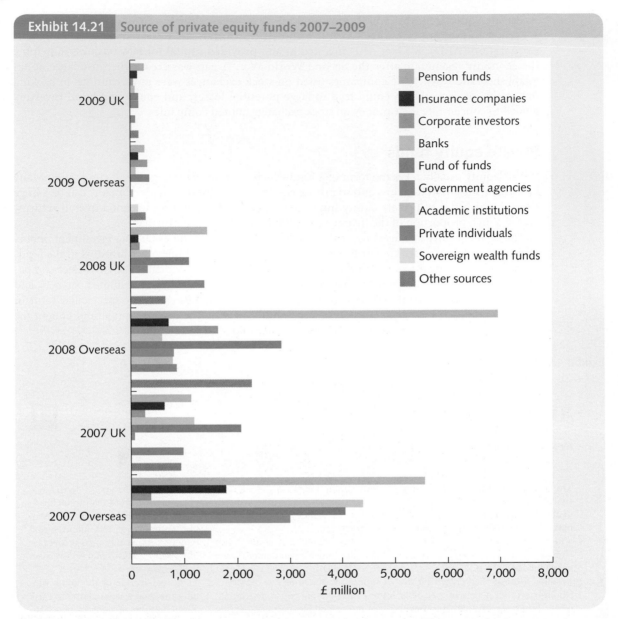

Source: bvca.co.uk

shows the dramatic decrease in funding caused by the financial crisis of 2008–2009. Limited partners allow their funds to be used by the GPs in return for a future capital gain, thus gaining a return which is taxed less heavily than salaried income. When the investee company is sold, or the private equity fund closed, the LPs share the remaining 80 per cent of the carried interest.

The size of the private equity and venture capital industry

In the UK, the British Private Equity & Venture Capital Association (BVCA), formed over 25 years ago, is the voice of the private equity and venture capital industry. It has more than 470 members managing more than £32 billion of funds between them. In 2010, BVCA members invested a total of £20,447 million, £12,210 million overseas and £8,237 million in the UK. While this sounds a lot, it is less than the amount invested in previous years – *see* **Exhibit 14.22**.

The European Private Equity & Venture Capital Association (EVCA) has been performing a similar task in Europe for about the same length of time. Its report shows a similar decrease in its figures for 2009, and some recovery in 2010 at €42.6 billion – *see* **Exhibit 14.23**.

Exhibit 14.22   Global investment activity of BVCA members

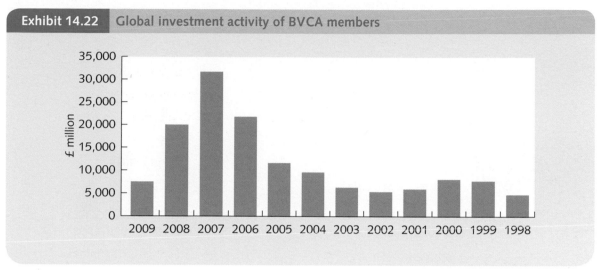

Source: www.bvca.co.uk

Exhibit 14.23   Annual European private equity investment

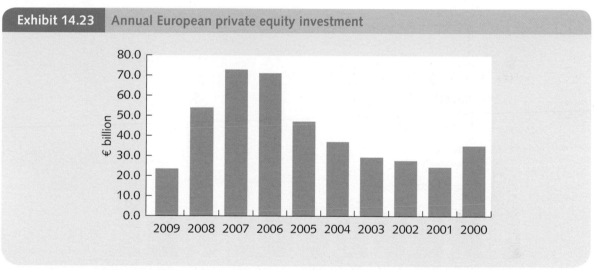

Source: www.evca.eu.

In the US, the National Venture Capital Association (NVCA), represents the US venture capital industry. Its report (**Exhibit 14.24**) shows a decrease for 2009, but not as dramatic as the UK and European decreases (the figure for 2010 is €23.2 billion). It is interesting to see on the chart the results of the dot.com bubble of the late 1990s and 2000, when venture capital poured into internet start-ups at every level. Like the tulipmania mentioned in Chapter 13, the internet craze seemed ever expanding and ever profitable, until 2000, when over $100 billion of venture capital was invested. In March 2000, the NASDAQ collapsed. This was the place that so many companies backed by private equity and venture capital had initial public offerings, turning themselves into stock market quoted companies. Most of these plummeted in value in 2000, trillions of dollars of value were lost and the venture capital industry shrank as investors became afraid of backing speculative ventures.

The effect of the financial crisis of 2008 is also apparent in **Exhibit 14.25**. Notice that in the years 2005 to 2009 the private equity funds raised hundreds of billions more than they actually invested. Thus, today we have many funds with large stockpiles of cash looking for an investment home. Many managers are waiting like vultures to pick up companies cheap in the aftermath of the recession. The US has the biggest share of the private equity market with 36 per cent of investments, and the UK is the next largest with 13 per cent of all global investments.

Exhibit 14.24   US venture capital investments

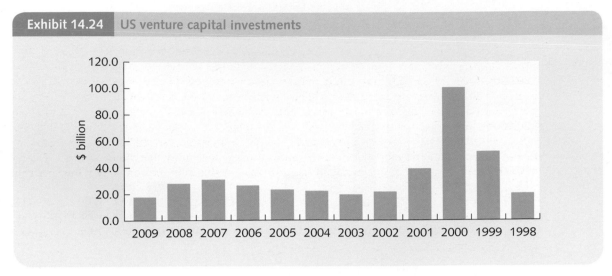

Source: www.nvca.org

Exhibit 14.25   Global private equity market

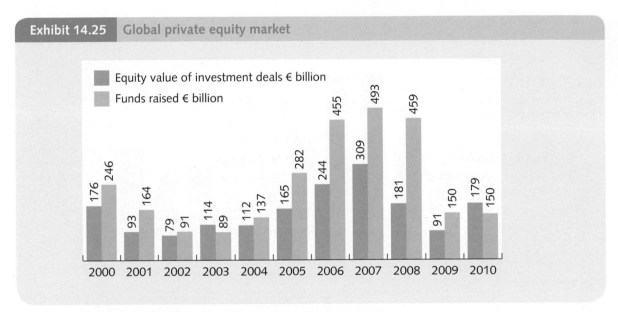

Source: TheCityUK estimates based on PEREP_Analytics, Thomson Reuters, EVCA, PwC, AVCJ data.

Why is private equity needed?

While more mature companies can turn to the stock market to raise debt or equity capital and small companies can usually rely on retained earnings, capital injections from the founder family and bank borrowing for growth, in between these lie **financing gaps**; intermediate businesses which are too large or too fast growing to ask the individual shareholders (family and friends) for more funds or to obtain sufficient bank finance, but are not yet ready to launch on the stock market. Also there are many small start-up businesses with great ideas who simply lack wealthy family and friends able to put up the large amounts of equity capital needed to get going in the first place. Private equity may also provide funding for under-performing companies or those in financial difficulties which would prosper given adequate funds. Thus, for all these reasons companies frustrated in their plans to exploit market opportunities due to a lack of available funds have welcomed the rapid development of the private equity industry over the past 40 years to fill these gaps in financing.

The costs and inconveniences of being listed on a stock market mean that many managers and shareholders prefer to obtain additional funds from private equity funds – even those that are perfectly capable of raising money on stock markets deliberately stay away from them. Private equity funds can be more long-term focused than stock market investors, allowing higher near-term investment in, say, research and development or marketing even at the expense of this year's or next year's earnings per share figures. The corporate managers also avoid the hassle of regular time-consuming meetings with institutional shareholders, so they are freer to get on with the job of creating long-term wealth for shareholders. They might also welcome the technical/managerial expertise and contacts that many private equity funds can draw on – many funds specialise in par-ticular industries and develop a deep talent pool. Also, private equity shareholders are more likely to be in favour of granting directors and senior managers shares in the company if they perform well. This can make them very wealthy.

It is estimated by the BVCA that there are 10,000 UK companies with 3m employees (one in six of the non-government workforce) financed by private equity money, so it is clear that private equity investment is crucial to the UK economy. **Exhibit 14.26** provides a list of some well-known UK companies which are backed by private equity.

Exhibit 14.26	Well-known UK companies backed by private equity

Agent Provocateur	New Look
Alliance Boots	Odeon & UCI Cinemas
Autonomy	Phones4U
Birds Eye Iglo	Pizza Express/Zizzi/Ask – Gondola Group
Cambridge Silicon Radio	Plastic Logic
CenterParcs	Poundland
Earls Court & Olympia	Pret A Manger
Findus Group (Foodvest)	The AA/Saga
Fitness First	Travelex
Jimmy Choo	Travelodge
Merlin Entertainments Group	UCI Cinemas/Odeon Cinemas
Moto	Weetabix
National Car Parks	West Cornwall Pasty Co.

Source: bvca.co.uk

Business angels (informal venture capitalists)

Business angels are wealthy individuals who provide their own money to be used as capital in new business ventures. They generally have substantial business and entrepreneurial experience, and usually invest between £10,000 and £250,000 primarily in start-up, early-stage or expand-ing firms. About three-quarters of business angel investments are for sums of less than £100,000 and the average investment is £25,000–30,000. The majority of investments are in the form of equity finance but they do purchase debt instruments and preference shares. The companies they invest in will be years away from obtaining a quotation or being advanced enough for a sale to other companies or investors, so in becoming a business angel the investor accepts that it may be difficult to dispose of their shares, even if the company is progressing well. They also accept a high degree of risk of complete failure – which happens in about one in three cases. They usu-ally do not have a controlling shareholding and they are willing to invest at an earlier stage than most formal venture capitalists – *see* **Exhibit 14.27**. They often dislike the term business angel,

Exhibit 14.27

Angel funding

FT

Technology start-up companies say they are increasingly turning to angel investors and their own resources as venture capital groups become increasingly reluctant to provide funding.

Kate Jillings, co-founder of BusinessBecause.com, a news and networking site for business schools, sold her flat to fund the business after deciding that it was not even worth trying to get VC investment.

"We had to weigh up whether to invest time in the business and growing the revenues or whether we chased investors." Ms Jillings says.

"We decided it was more sensible to fight for revenue than fight for funding. We initially funded it through our savings and debt. We got to the point where we had put so much of ourselves in the business, we didn't want to spend two months on the investor merry go round."

World on a Hanger and Empora.com, two UK-based fashion websites, on the other hand, have found that angel investors are often stepping into the gap left by VCs. Highly professional "super angels" – usually formerly successful entrepreneurs who are investing their gains back into the market – are becoming increasingly prominent in the market.

Empora.com, for example, raised money from Alexander Straub, the internet entrepreneur and investor. Robin Klein, Doug Richard of television's *Dragon's Den* fame and the Samver brothers in Germany are among the many others active on the angel scene.

"Risk aversion among VCs has grown. But for riskier deals there are now more internet savvy angels than ever to fill the gap," says Ari Helgason, co-founder of World on a Hanger.

Source: Financial Times, 1 March 2010, p. 21. Reprinted with permission.

preferring the title **informal venture capitalist**. They are generally looking for entrepreneurial companies which have high aspirations and potential for growth.

A typical business angel makes one or two investments in a three-year period, often in an investment syndicate (with an **archangel**, an experienced angel investor, coordinating the group). They generally invest in companies within a reasonable travelling distance from their homes because most like to be 'hands-on' investors, playing a significant role in strategy and management – on average angels allocate ten hours a week to their investments. Most angels take a seat on the board and are actively involved. On the other hand, there are many who have infrequent contact with their companies. Business angels are patient investors willing to hold their investment for at least a five-year period.

How business angels work

The main way in which firms and angels find each other is through friends and business associates, although there are a number of formal networks. *See* British Venture Capital Association at www.bvca.co.uk for a list of networks. **Angel network** events are organised where entrepreneurs can make a pitch to potential investors, who, if they like what they hear in response to their questions, may put in tens of thousands of pounds. The popular *Dragon's Den* programme produced by the BBC is an example of business angels at work. Entrepreneurs put forward their ideas to the 'Dragons', and if they are thought to be a good investment money from the Dragons will be invested. Prior to the event, the TV producers will arrange screening of the business opportunities to avoid time wasting by total no-hopers. Similar screening is generally carried out before an angel network event.

To be a member of a network, investors are expected either to earn at least £100,000 per year or to have a net worth of at least £250,000 (excluding main residence). If an investor has a specialist skill to offer, for example they are an experienced company director or chartered accountant, membership may be permitted despite a lower income or net worth.

Entrepreneurs need to be aware that obtaining money from informal venture capitalists is no easy task – the rejection rate runs at over 90 per cent; but if rejected the determined entrepreneur has many other angel networks to try. Returns on business angel investments are mostly negative. However, they can be spectacular; the angels who put €2 million into Skype multiplied their money by 350 times when the company was sold to eBay for €2.1 billion in 2005.

Venture capital

The business ideas backed by venture capitalists are usually new, innovative, often high-tech and usually very risky, brought to them by entrepreneurs. With little or no trading track record or financial history, new companies usually find obtaining finance for growth and expansion difficult, and this is where venture capital may be the solution. Venture capital is a medium- to long-term investment and can consist of a package of debt and equity finance. Many of the investments are into little more than a management team with a good idea – which may not have started selling a product or even developed a prototype. It is believed, as a rule of thumb in the venture capital industry, that out of ten investments two will fail completely, two will perform excellently and the remaining six will range from poor to very good.

Venture capital funds

Venture capital funds are intermediaries who channel money from institutions or individuals into investment in private companies. Their aim is to help a number of companies grow in the expectation that in the future a company can be sold or floated on a stock exchange for a considerable profit. As with private equity, venture capital fund managers are the GPs who actively participate in and manage the venture capital investment fund. The LPs, such as pension funds or individuals, provide the capital for the venture capitalist to invest.

As we discussed in Chapter 8, high risk goes with high return. Venture capitalists therefore expect to get a return of between five and ten times their initial equity investment in about 5–7 years. This means that the firms receiving equity finance are expected to produce annual returns of at least 26 per cent. Alongside the usual drawbacks of equity capital from the investors' viewpoint (last in the queue for income and on liquidation, etc.), investors in small unquoted companies also suffer from a lack of liquidity because the shares are not quoted on a public exchange.

Types of support

Private equity and venture capital offer support to a wide range of companies at varying stages in their development.

Seedcorn

A form of venture capital providing financing to allow the development of a business concept. Development may also involve expenditure on the production of prototypes and additional research. Usually involves angel investor funding rather than venture funds.

Start-up

Also referred to as venture capital, a product or idea is further developed and/or initial marketing is carried out. The companies involved are very young and have not yet sold their product commercially. Usually involves angel investor funding rather than venture funds.

Other early-stage

Again, often referred to as venture capital, funds are provided for initial commercial manufacturing and sales. Many companies at this stage will remain unprofitable. Usually involves angel investor funding rather than venture funds.

Expansion (development or growth)

Companies at this stage are on to a fast-growth track and need extra financial support to fund increased production capacity, working capital and for the further development of the product or market. The company may be large enough to accept substantial investment from venture funds – if not then angel investment is more likely.

Management buyout (MBO)

The acquisition of a company or part of a company by an existing management team. A team of managers buy a whole business, a subsidiary or a section from their employers, so that they own and run it for themselves. Companies are often willing to sell to these teams, if the business is under-performing or does not fit with the strategic core business. The MBO team has limited funds and so calls on private equity to provide the bulk of the finance.

Management buy-in (MBI)

The acquisition of a company or part of a company by a new management team from outside the company. The new team of managers usually have insufficient finance to complete the deal and so partner with a private equity fund that usually buys the majority of the shares

Leveraged buyout (LBO)

The buyout of an existing company, with the capital raised (and therefore the capital structure for the company afterwards) being between 60 and 90 per cent debt finance. One advantage of this is that interest on debt is tax deductible, and therefore less company tax is paid. The major disadvantage is the risk of insolvency with so much debt to be serviced. Private equity groups usually provide the bulk of the equity and perhaps some of the debt or preference share capital with the rest coming from banks or the financial markets.

Secondary purchase

A private equity backed company is sold to another private equity fund. This is one of the exit strategies, where the first private equity fund can make a capital gain by selling its equity in the company to another private equity fund

Public-to-private (PTP)

The management of a company currently quoted on a stock exchange may return it to unquoted status with the assistance of private equity finance to buy the shares, giving it the advantage of lower costs, less regulation and official and public scrutiny.

Private equity firms are less keen on financing seedcorn, start-ups and other early-stage companies than expansions, MBOs, MBIs and PTPs. This is largely due to the very high risk associated with early-stage ventures and the disproportionate time and costs of financing smaller deals. To make it worthwhile for a private equity or venture capital organisation to consider a company, the investment must be at least £250,000 – the average investment is about £5 million – and it is difficult to find funding for investments of less than £2 million. Business angels are the solution for lesser funding requirements.

Because of the greater risks associated with the youngest companies, the private equity or venture capital funds may require returns of the order of 50–80 per cent per annum. For well-established companies with a proven product and battle-hardened and respected management the returns required may drop to the high 20s. These returns may seem exorbitant, especially to the managers set the task of achieving them, but they have to be viewed in the light of the fact that many private equity or venture capital investments will turn out to be failures and so, taken overall, the performance of the funds is significantly less than these figures suggest. In fact, the BVCA, which represents 'every major source of venture capital in the UK', reports that returns on funds are not excessively high – *see* **Exhibit 14.28**.

Exhibit 14.28	Returns on UK private equity funds

Internal rates of return (IRR) to investors since inception of the fund from 1996 to December 2009, net of costs and fees. 470 UK-managed funds are included

	Percent per annum
Venture capital funds	−2.2
Small management buyouts	17.3
Mid management buyouts	14.0
Large management buyouts	19.2
Total	16.1
Comparators' returns over 10 years to Dec. 2009	
UK listed shares (FT All-share)	1.8
Overseas equity	1.9
UK bonds	5.5
Overseas bonds	7.3
Property	6.2

Note: Excluding private equity investment trusts and Venture Capital Trusts.

Source: 2009 Performance Measurement Survey, BVCA, PricewaterhouseCoopers and Capital Dynamics – http://admin.bvca.co.uk//library/documents

The situation is similar globally – *see* **Exhibit 14.29**.

Exhibit 14.29

Buy-out study queries performance

Martin Arnold

Private equity has been attacked before. Trade unions have branded buy-out bosses as asset-strippers and job-cutters. Politicians have rebuked them for dodging tax. But now the industry is being criticised at its core: financial performance.

The main theme of today's report from the Centre for the Study of Financial Innovation, a London think-tank, is to ask why supposedly sophisticated investors, including pension funds, keep putting money into an asset class that underperforms.

As evidence for this underperformance, it cites a 2005 paper by Steven Kaplan, of the University of Chicago and Antoinette Schoar of the Massachusetts Institute of Technology, which found that net of fees the average buy-out fund underperformed the S&P 500 between 1980 and 2001.

Given that private equity is an illiquid asset class, locking up investors' money for as long as 10 years, and is more risky, because of the extra debt used in many leveraged buy-outs, this underperformance is a serious indictment.

Backing up these claims, the report's author, Peter Morris, a

Exhibit 14.29 continued

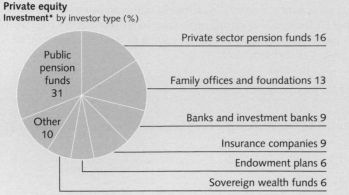

Private equity
Investment* by investor type (%)

Private sector pension funds 16

Public pension funds 31

Family offices and foundations 13

Banks and investment banks 9

Other 10

Insurance companies 9

Endowment plans 6

Sovereign wealth funds 6

* Excluding fund of funds and assets managers

Equity returns (as at Dec 2009)

	Apollo	Blackstone	KKR
Assets under management ($bn)	34	24.8	38.8
Gross return (%)	39	30.7	25.8
Net return (%)	26	22.6	19.2
Implied all – annual cost (%)	13	8.1	6.6

Source: Preqin, CSFI

The winners and the losers

Losers

• Gala Coral, the betting and bingo group, was taken over by its lenders this year triggering almost £700m of losses for Permira, Candover and Cinven.

• Cerberus bought an 80 per cent stake in Chrysler for $7.4bn in 2007 but it suffered considerable losses after the US carmaker filed for bankruptcy last year.

Winners

• MEMC Electronics materials, the chipmaker, was bought by TPG for six dollar notes sent by mail and then sold a few years later for about $2bn.

• The Carlyle Group paid slightly less than £50m for Firth Rixson, the 160-year-old Sheffield engineering company, in 2002 and sold it for £945m in 2007.

---

former Morgan Stanley banker, cites an analysis of 542 recent buy-out deals in the portfolio of Yale University's endowment, which after stripping out the impact of extra debt, underperformed the stock market by 40 per cent.

The credit crisis has caused some big buy-out deals to implode. Terra Firma has written down to zero the equity it invested in a £4.2bn ($6.5bn) buy-out of EMI, while struggling to stop lender Citigroup taking control of the music group.

Mr Morris also criticises the standard used to measure most private equity performance: the internal rate of return. He argues that because it tracks performance over the life of a fund but does not take into account the timing of when money flows into and back out of different deals, the IRR sometimes inflates returns.

To explain why investors continue to put money into an underperforming asset class, Mr Morris says: "One possibility is that some investors may simply not understand."

Alternatively he says private equity could be a way for pension

funds to "roll the dice" by doing riskier debt-funded deals, but to do it "under the table" by outsourcing it to a buy-out group that can take the blame if things go awry.

He also attacks the fee structure of private equity which is based on a fee of 2 per cent of funds raised and a 20 per cent cut of profits made.

Citing a study by Andrew Metrick, of the Yale School of Management, and Ayako Yusado, of the University of California, he says that two-thirds of private equity managers' income comes from fixed fees and only a third from per-formance-related pay.

"The risk is all taken by the investors and, beyond them, by the taxpayers who underwrite the world's financial system," he says. "But a disproportionate share of the upside goes to the managers, in the form of fees and profit share."

Yet private equity's support-ers point to other studies showing it outperforms the stock market. Research published last month by the HEC School of Management and the London Business School found that 20 funds of funds managed by Pantheon had achieved average

annual returns of 19.6 per cent, beating comparable public markets.

"I do think private equity deserves some credit for its use of debt and for its market selection," says Simon Walker, chief executive of the British Private Equity and Venture Capital Association.

"[The CSFI report] is unbal-anced and it is a beat-up. I'm not saying it is worthless. But we'd love to have a serious discussion on it."

The report concludes by calling for private equity fees to reward only the alpha they generate, not the benefits of extra debt or rising stock markets. It also says that private equity groups should disclose more information on their performance and activities to "allow outsiders to hold them accountable".

"Complexity and opacity are usually not signs of brilliance but evidence of rent-seeking," it says, warning that the behaviour of sup-posedly sophisticated investors may need as much scrutiny as that of banks.

Source: Financial Times, 26 July 2010, p. 20. Reprinted with permission.

Venture capital funds are rarely looking for a controlling shareholding in a company and are often content with a 20 or 30 per cent share. However, MBI/MBO/LBO funds usually take most of the shares of a company because the management team can only afford a small proportion of the shares. The fund may also provide money by purchasing convertible preference shares which gives it rights to convert to ordinary shares – this will boost its equity holding and increase the return if the firm performs well. It may also insist, in an initial investment agreement, on some widespread powers. For instance, the company may need to gain the private equity/venture capitalist's approval for the issue of further securities, and there may be a veto over the acquisition of other companies.

Even though their equity holding is generally less than 50 per cent the venture capital funds frequently have special rights to appoint a number of directors. If specific negative events happen, such as a poor performance, they may have the right to appoint most of the board of directors and therefore take effective control. More than once the founding entrepreneur has been aggrieved to find themselves removed from power. (Despite the loss of power, they often have a large shareholding in what has grown to be a multi-million-pound company.) They are often sufficiently upset to refer to the fund which separated them from their creation as 'vulture capitalist'. But this is to focus on the dark side. When everything goes well, we have, as they say in the business jargon, 'a win-win-win situation': the company receives vital capital to grow fast, the venture capitalist receives a high return and society gains new products and economic progress.

Many of the UK's most noteworthy companies were helped by the venture capital industry, as we saw in **Exhibit 14.26**, and US companies such as Google, Apple, Starbucks and Sun Microsystems also developed through venture capital in the US.

Private equity categories

As you have gathered by now, as share investment outside stock markets has grown it has become differentiated. The main categories are shown in **Exhibit 14.30**. with private equity as the umbrella term covering the various activities. In this more differentiated setting the term venture capital is generally confined to describing the building of companies from the ground floor, or at least from a very low base.

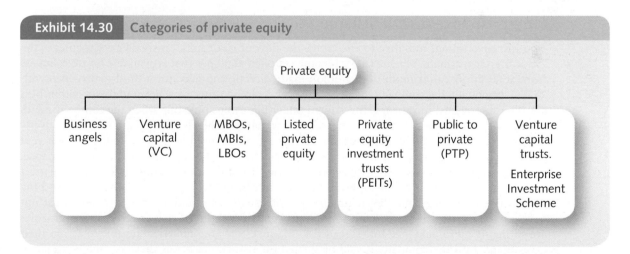

| Exhibit 14.30 | Categories of private equity |

Management buyouts and buy-ins of established businesses (already off the ground floor) have become a specialist task, with a number of dedicated funds. Many of these funds are formed as private partnerships by wealthy individuals, a high proportion of funds are American owned.

Small investors can buy shares in **listed private equity (LPEQ)** funds which are companies investing in unquoted companies but which have their own shares quoted on a stock exchange. There are about 80 investable listed private equity companies in Europe, with a total market capitalisation of €45 billion, of which €12 billion are London-listed companies (see www.lpeq. com). They come in two varieties: first, those that are straightforward listed companies, and those that are listed as investment trusts. An example of the first type is Conversus Capital, which is listed on Euronext-Amsterdam. It has $2.5 billion in assets under management, and a portfolio of over 1,800 unquoted companies in North America, Europe and Asia.

Private equity investment trusts (PEITs) are the second type of LPEQs. They are stock market quoted investment trusts with a focus on investing their shareholders' money in more risky unquoted developing companies. The disadvantage of listed private equity companies is the absence of special tax concessions compared with Venture Capital Trusts and Enterprise Investment Schemes – *see* below. However, investors are able to exit their investments easily by dealing on the stock market.

Venture capital trusts

It is important to distinguish between venture capital funds and venture capital trusts (VCTs) which are investment vehicles with important tax breaks designed to encourage investment in small and fast-growing companies. VCTs are companies whose shares are traded on the London Stock Exchange. The tax breaks for investors putting money into VCTs include an immediate relief on their current year's income at 30 per cent (by putting £10,000 into a VCT an investor will pay £3,000 less tax on income, so the effective cost is only £7,000). Any returns (income and capital gains) on a VCT are exempt from tax. Investors can place up to £200,000 each per year into VCTs. These benefits are only available to investors buying new VCT shares who hold the investment for five years. The VCT managers can only invest in companies with gross assets less than £15 million and the maximum amount a VCT is allowed to put into each unquoted company's shares is limited to £1 million per year. 'Unquoted' for VCT means not listed on the main list of the London Stock Exchange but can include AIM and PLUS companies. A maximum of 15 per cent of the VCT fund can be invested in any one company. Up to half of the fund's investment in qualifying companies can be in the form of loans. These trusts offer investors a way of investing in a broad spread of small firms with high potential, but with greater uncertainty, in a tax-efficient manner. But beware, many of the funds that have been in operation for a few years have shown low returns due to a combination of poor investment selection and high management charges.

Enterprise Investment Scheme

Another government initiative to encourage the flow of risk capital to smaller companies is the Enterprise Investment Scheme (EIS). Income tax relief at 30 per cent is available for investments from £500 up to a maximum of £1 million made directly (no need for a fund manager as with VCTs) into qualifying company shares. There is also capital gains tax relief, and losses within EISs are allowable against income tax. Investment under EIS means investing when the company issues shares, not the purchase of shares in the secondary market. The tax benefits are lost if the investments are held for less than three years. Investors are not allowed to hold more than 30 per cent of the shares in any EIS company. Certain trading activities which are excluded, such as finance, property and agriculture (HMRC gives the definitive list of these exclusions). The company must have fewer than 250 full-time employees. It must not be quoted on LSE's Main Market and the most it can raise under the EIS in any one year is usually £10 million. The company must not have gross assets worth more than £15 million. Funds which invest in a range of EIS companies are springing up to help investors spread risk. EIS investors are unlikely to be able to regain their investment until the company is sold or floated on a stock market as there is usually no share trading for many years.

Private equity providers

There are a number of different types of private equity providers, although the boundaries are increasingly blurred as a number of funds now raise money from a variety of sources. The independents can be firms, funds or investment trusts, either quoted or private, which have raised their capital from more than one source. The main sources are pension and insurance funds, but banks, corporate investors, sovereign wealth funds and private individuals also put money into these private equity or venture capital funds. **Captives** are funds managed on behalf of a parent institution (banks, pension funds, etc.). **Semi-captives** invest funds on behalf of a parent and also manage independently raised funds.

How an independent private equity fund is established and managed

Many private equity funds are established as limited liability partnerships (LLP),[7] raising capital from a group of investors. It is usually stated at the outset that it will be run down after 10 or 12 years and the value in the LLP will be distributed to members. The project is touted to potential investors (e.g. pension funds), often by the investor relations team or by using external placement agents. The investment strategy is set out, e.g. a focus on bio-technology or internet companies. The general partners will state a minimum to be raised to reach **'first close'**. When this is achieved the fund comes into existence. There may be a series of 'closes' beyond the minimum to create a much larger fund. The **'final close'** is the end of the capital-raising phase.

The investment phase now begins. The GPs are given discretion to invest the money; they are usually given a period of up to five years to do so. They are likely to limit exposure to any one investment to less than 10 per cent of the fund. They might arrange to borrow money to complete individual deals. For the larger investments, particularly MBOs and MBIs, the private equity fund may provide only a fraction of the total funds required. Thus, in a £50 million buyout the LLP might supply (individually or in a syndicate with other private equity funds), say, £15 million in the form of share capital (ordinary and preference shares). Another £20 million may come from a group of banks in the form of debt finance. The remainder may be supplied as mezzanine debt – high-return high-risk debt which usually has some rights to share in equity values should the company perform.

Occasionally the LPs are given the opportunity to both participate in an investment via the private equity fund and to invest directly. This is called **co-investing**.

The fund usually holds on to the investments for three, five or more years to allow it to improve and grow. When the company is in a thriving state they are likely to sell to realise a return on their investment. This is called an **exit** – the various types of exits are discussed in the next section.

The performance-related return (carried interest) due to the GPs is generally based on the performance of the entire fund rather than on individual deals – although some do give deal-by-deal carried interest. In the first five years the managers are likely to be most dependent on the management fee of 1–2.5 per cent of funds under management rather than carried interest. In the period after five years they are likely to be most motivated by the carried interest on the maturing investments. The various stages are set out in **Exhibit 14.31**.

Exits

The exit is when private equity and venture capital investors reap their rewards; this is their goal towards which all efforts have been expended. Before the expiry of the fund (say after ten years) moves will be made to sell the investments. Hopefully the companies within the fund will have prospered or been reorganised enough to make it an attractive proposition for resale or listing on a stock exchange.

Only when the investee company is sold do the private equity or venture capital partners receive any return on their investment, except for the GPs who receive annual fees.

---

[7] A partnership in which some or all of the partners have limited liability. Thus the partner is protected from being liable for the misconduct or incompetence of other partners. In the absence of fraud or wrongful trading a partner cannot lose more than the amount invested. As a 'corporate body' it has a life independent of any individual member and so does not have to be dissolved on the death or leaving of a partner.

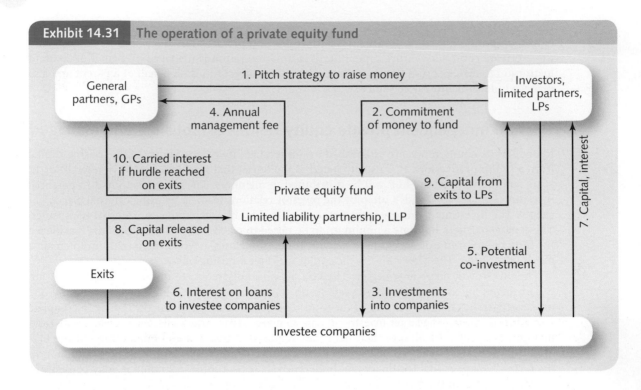

Exhibit 14.31   The operation of a private equity fund

The exit options are:

Repurchase

The company has prospered and the existing management is in a position to purchase the equity in the company, often accompanied by a general recapitalisation of the firm – more debt taken on.

Secondary/Tertiary/Quaternary buyouts

The equity is sold to another private equity group. This may then be sold on to a third buyer (tertiary buyout) and on occasions, a fourth (quaternary buyout) – *see* **Exhibit 14.32**.

Trade sale

The equity is sold to or merged with another company – usually one in the same industry – and a capital gain (loss) is realised for investors.

Going public

The equity is floated on a stock market (*see* Chapter 9) and a capital gain is realised for investors.

Liquidation

The worst exit strategy – the company goes bust and everyone makes a loss.

Exhibit 14.32

Revolving door leaves investors dizzy

Martin Arnold

What do French retailer Picard Surgelés, the US provider of healthcare cost management services Multiplan and the UK chain of betting shops Gala Coral have in common?

They are all companies in the hands of their third or fourth consecutive private equity owners, as the trend for buy-out groups to sell assets to each other leaves come companies stuck in the revolving door of "pass-the-parcel" deals.

Picard Surgelés was sold for €1.5bn ($2bn) last week to Lion Capital, which became the third private equity owner of France's leading frozen-food chain after earlier buy-outs by BC Partners and candover.

In a similar vein, Multiplan was sold last month for $3.1bn, making BC Partners and Silver Lake Partners the new owners following on from Carlyle and initially General Atlantic.

Going one step further, a consortium of distressed debt investors led by Apollo Management and Cerberus recently took over Gala Coral, making them its fourth set of private equity owners.

What is it about these companies that means they keep passing between private equity owners rather than being floated on to the stock market or sold to a bigger trade buyer? And what do investors think about the spread of pass-the-parcel deals?

"We didn't IPO the company [Picard] now because it comes off two years of flat earnings, but it is definitely IPO-able in short order," says André François-Poncet, head of BC Partners' office in Paris.

Even some firms that usually steer clear of pass-the-parcel deals are starting to do some.

Kohlberg Kravis Roberts recently bought UK pet accessory chain Pets at Home and Nordic healthcare group Ambea from rival buy-out groups.

"There is a lot of new stuff here at Pets at Home that can be done, without taking away from the great stuff they've already been doing," says John Pfeffer, head of KKR's retail industry team in Europe.

As examples he cites further improved sourcing of products, expansion of own-label brands, bolstering of online sales and better use of space in stores.

"We can draw on our deep retail experience, having done more than $57bn of retail deals," he said.

There are well-known cases of tertiary buy-outs hitting the wall, such as Gala Coral, which was taken over by its lenders last month, triggering £700m ($1bn) losses for its buy-out owners, and Simmons, the US mattress maker that filed for bankruptcy in 2009.

However, some companies have thrived after a tertiary buy-out, such as Merlin Entertainment, operator of the London Eye, Madame Tussauds and Legoland theme parks, and Jimmy Choo, the maker of diamante-encrusted stilettos.

Towerbrook bought Jimmy Choo for £185m three years ago, becoming the third successive private equity owner of the company that has risen from a one-man backstreet atelier to shoemaker for the stars in little more than a decade.

John Harley, Ernst & Young's global head of private equity, says: "You need to look at the entrepreneur behind these companies, as often they want to keep driving the company forward and choose another private equity owner rather than an IPO."

Source: Financial Times, 2 August 2010, p. 42. Reprinted with permission.

Global private equity secondary buy-out volumes

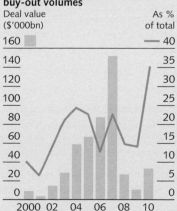

European deal pricing

Price to earnings multiple for all European deals above €100m

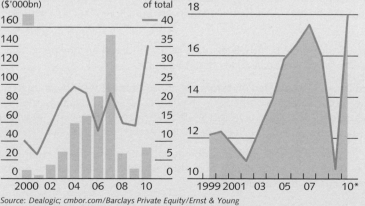

Average deal structures for MBOs/MBIs above €100m (€bn)

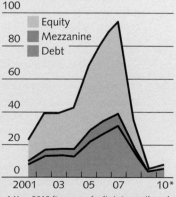

Source: Dealogic; cmbor.com/Barclays Private Equity/Ernst & Young

* Year 2010 figures are for first six months only

Concluding comments

Hedge funds and private equity have come in for more than their fair share of sensational headlines. However, the bulk of all their business consists of perfectly acceptable financial transactions. The problem with hedge funds is that they appear to be making more money for people who are wealthy already and it is difficult to see the benefits they bring to the general public. John Paulson made over $4 billion for his fund by betting that mortgage lending in the US had reached unsustainable levels and would have to fall. His predictions were right: mortgage lending was spiralling out of control and reaching bubble proportions and millions of people suffered as the housing market contracted. The bubble had to burst, and we welcome a view different to the complacent consensus. Perhaps we should pay more attention to the signals sent to the market by people like John Paulson that investors were generally being too optimistic about US mortgages. Should a fund manager be criticised because he made correct predictions? But is it right that so much profit should be made? Paulson, and many other individuals who have made significant amounts of money out of financial markets, such as Warren Buffett and George Soros, have shown truly philanthropic conduct and donated billions of dollars to various charities.

Paulson and Soros certainly showed the ability to generate alpha in their investments, but alpha appears to have been becoming rarer for two related reasons. First, the sheer volume of trading may be reducing the chance of finding market anomalies that are a source of hedge fund performance. Second, the remuneration model is attracting more managers, which may dilute the talent available in the industry. It is harder to find a different path when there are so many participants.

Just as there will always be people with good business ideas but not the means to put them into production, so there will always exist people with spare money looking for an interesting investment outside the stock market and able to face the risk of a total loss of their investment. In a nutshell, that is private equity.

Private equity has come in for a considerable amount of criticism over the treatment of some investee companies. In certain cases, when private equity became involved, the reorganisation initiated major asset sales ('asset stripping' according to the critics), sacking workers and curtailing expensive research and development, which may have resulted in raised short-term profits and the increasing attractiveness of the company to other buyers, but critics feel that these actions are damaging to long-term economic stability and prosperity.

But bear in mind that without private equity many companies that now thrive as household names would not have got off the ground. Companies such as Google, Skype and CenterParcs have brought great pleasure as well as wealth. These are usually high-risk ventures and we need skilful fund managers to continue to make profits for their investors and receive suitable recompense for their efforts and risk taking.

Key points and concepts

- A **hedge fund** is a collective investment vehicle that operates relatively free from regulation allowing it to take steps in managing a portfolio that other fund managers are unable to take, e.g. borrowing to invest, shorting securities.

- Hedge funds originated in the US, and were based on **absolute return**, rather than striving to achieve a return relative to a market index as conventional funds tend to aim for.

- US hedge funds are permitted to sell to **accredited investors**, i.e. those thought wealthy enough or professional enough not to need the protection of the SEC. They are capable of evaluating the merits and risks of a hedge fund investment – individual investors must have net worth, or joint net worth with a spouse, that exceeds $1m at the time of purchase, or income exceeding $200,000.

- Money invested in hedge funds is often **locked up** for a period during which time the funds are not available for withdrawal by the ultimate investors. Funds may also be **gated**; a limit is placed on the amount that can be withdrawn from the fund at any one time.

- A **side pocket** enables a fund manager to separate a difficult to value or illiquid investment from all other investments.

▶

- Many hedge funds register **offshore** (e.g Cayman Islands) where regulations and tax are lighter.

- Hedge funds are generally **opaque,** not obliged to disclose any dealings except to investors.

- **Alpha** is the return achieved above the return expected given the risk class of investment that a fund manager engages in – the 'risk-adjusted return'.

- Hedge funds are managed by investment companies which are usually registered **onshore.**

- **Typical hedge fund management fees** are 1–5 per cent **annual fee,** 15–50 per cent **performance fee.** The most common is **2 per cent plus 20 per cent.**

- **High water marks (loss carryforward provision):** where a fund's performance has dropped, the manager does not receive a performance fee until the fund reaches its previous position.

- **Hurdle rates:** performance fees will only be triggered once the fund has achieved a minimum annualised performance.

- **Fund of hedge funds** – a manager invests in a range of hedge funds; two lots of fees are charged. Advantages are of diversification and a manager who investigates the quality of hedge funds.

- **Listed hedge funds** trade on stock markets and so are available to retail investors.

- **UCITS (Undertakings for Collective Investment in Transferable Securities)** regulation allows collective investment schemes to operate freely throughout the EU on the authority of a single member state. A requirement is for UCITs funds to be highly liquid, therefore the securities held by the fund must be readily tradeable. They also have to be transparent and the portfolios must be well diversified. The amount of leverage that can be used is constrained. UCITs compliant funds can use derivatives and other hedge fund strategies.

- **Hedge fund ETFs** are more costly than normal ETFs.

- **Hedge fund indices** aim to replicate hedge fund performance. But there are difficulties: a general lack of reliable and independently verifiable information; the underlying investments are often obscure instruments that lack a daily price setting in a liquid market; there are hundreds of different strategies/types of assets bought and sold by hedge funds, therefore it is difficult to compare like with like; each year hundreds of funds are launched and hundreds disappear, so it is difficult to figure out which fund performances to include in an index; fund participation in an index is voluntary (self-selection bias); there is survivorship bias because those that have gone bust or folded through lack of interest due to poor performance will not report to the index compiler. There is also end-of-life bias and backfill bias.

- **Leverage** is used by many hedge funds, especially those using arbitrage strategies. Leverage can be achieved by borrowing to invest or by entering into a financial transaction where the fund only has to come up with, say, 5 per cent or 10 per cent of the underlying exposure as a margin or deposit.

- **Hedge fund strategies** –

  - **Arbitrage** is taking advantage of small discrepancies in the prices of the same financial instrument or similar securities by simultaneously selling the overpriced security and buying the underpriced security.
  - **Long/short strategy (relative value)** involves buying one type of financial instrument long and selling another instrument short to exploit pricing anomalies between related (but not identical) assets that are mispriced relative to each other.
  - **Market neutral** strategies are those that provide a return regardless of the overall market movement because the short position exposure is as great as the long position.
  - **Fixed income relative value/Fixed income arbitrage** evolved from classical arbitrage, but instead of identical securities the two securities bought and sold are merely similar.
  - **Convertible bond (warrant) arbitrage.** This is taking a long position in convertible bonds or warrants while hedging with a short position, typically by shorting shares in the same company.
  - **Event driven** strategies take advantage of special situations. For example, **distressed securities investing** is when hedge fund managers buy shares or debt belonging to companies which are experiencing serious financial problems and could be facing bankruptcy.

▶

- **Merger arbitrage:** funds take a long position in the target and a short position in the acquirer.
  - **Activist strategy:** the hedge fund buys a portion of the shares in a company and uses the ownership to press for improvement in returns to shareholders.
  - **Global macro.** Funds profit (and lose) from bets taken against countries, currencies, global economic dislocations in interest rates and other macroeconomic variables.
  - **Fundamental growth:** investing in companies funds consider to have more earnings growth and capital appreciation potential than the average company.
  - **Fundamental value:** investing in undervalued companies currently out of favour with most investors.
  - **Multi strategy:** funds use the same pool of investment to invest in different strategies.

- **Prime brokers** facilitate financial transactions for hedge fund managers including lending and custody.

- **Private equity** provides medium to long-term finance for **unquoted companies.**

- **Venture capital** often refers to investment in start-up or young companies.

- **Private equity funds** invest in a diverse group of companies.

- **General partners** carry out the administration of funds. GPs' aim is to find a company suitable for investment, and eventually make a profitable sale. They earn fees which pay all administration costs, and if the venture is successful a share in the eventual gain (**carried interest**), usually 20 per cent of the
gain made.

- **Limited partners** are the individuals and institutions which invest in the funds.

- **Financing gap** occurs in established businesses not ready to float, but unable to raise more shareholder funds.

- **Business angels/informal venture capitalists** – wealthy individuals willing to invest their own money and often experience and time. Average investment: £25,000 to £30,000.

- **Angel networks** enable entrepreneurs to try to attract investment from members of clubs of business angels. A member of the network needs substantial assets, perhaps £250,000, or to earn £100,000 p.a.

- Angels generally like to play a significant role in strategy and management. Most take a seat on the board. They are patient investors willing to hold their investment for at least a five-year period.

- Private equity and venture capital investments are illiquid (not easily tradeable), and are last in the queue in the event of liquidation.

- Types of support are:
  - **seedcorn** financing, to allow the development of a business concept;
  - **start-up** finances further development and marketing of project;
  - **other early stage** finances manufacturing and sales;
  - **expansion,** more finance needed for growth;
  - **management buyout,** an existing team takes over a business or section;
  - **management buy-in,** an external group of managers takes over all or part of a company;
  - **leveraged buyout,** is the buying out of a company using substantial amounts of borrowed funds;
  - **secondary purchase,** a company backed by private equity is sold to another private equity fund;
  - **public-to-private,** a company uses private equity finance to purchase its shares and returns to unquoted status.

- Private equity categories are –
  - **business angels;**
  - **venture capital;**
  - **management buyouts, buy-ins and leveraged buyouts;**
  - **listed private equity,** which enables retail investors to invest and trade in private equity funds.
  - **private equity investment trusts (PEITs),** stock market quoted investment trusts with a focus on investing their shareholders' money in more risky unquoted developing companies.

▶

- **public to private:** a company quoted on a stock market returns to unquoted status.
- **Venture Capital Trusts,** investment vehicles with important tax breaks designed to encourage investment in small and fast-growing companies. VCTs are companies whose shares are traded on the London Stock Exchange.
- **Enterprise Investment Scheme,** a government initiative to encourage the flow of risk capital to smaller companies by offering investors who invest in them tax breaks.

- Private equity providers are –

  - **independents:** public or private companies, funds or trusts which have raised funding from more than one source;
  - **captives;** funds managed on behalf of a parent institution;
  - **semi-captives,** which manage funds on behalf of a parent and raise independent funds.

- **Exit** is where investors realise profits:

  - **repurchase:** the company has prospered and repurchases its shares from the private equity fund.
  - **secondary/tertiary/quaternary buyouts:** the company is sold on to another fund.
  - **trade sale:** the company is sold or merged with another company.
  - **going public:** the company is floated and its shares are sold on the stock market.
  - **liquidation:** the company fails.

References and further reading

To keep up to date and reinforce knowledge gained by reading this chapter I can recommend the *Financial Times* and *The Economist*.

Coggan, P. (2010) *Guide to Hedge Funds*, 2nd edn. London: The Economist.
   Good basic guide.

Connor, G. and Lasarte, T. (2004) 'An Introduction to Hedge Fund Strategies' Working Paper. International Asset Management and The London School of Economics and Political Science.
   An excellent discussion of hedge fund strategies (www.iam.uk.com/press/lse-publications/An-Introduction-to-Hedge-Fund-Strategies.pdf).

Demaria, C. (2010) *Introduction to Private Equity*. Chichester: John Wiley & Sons.
   A comprehensive easy-to-follow description of the private equity industry with a European slant.

Dichev, I. D. and Yu, G. (2011) 'Higher risk, lower returns: What hedge fund investors really earn', *Journal of Financial Economics*.
   They find that the real alpha of hedge fund investors is close to zero and lower than that on the S&P500.
   The underlying hedge funds on average perform above the risk-adjusted return, but hedge fund investors tend to switch their money to the wrong funds at the wrong time.

Griffin, J. and Xu, J. (2009) 'How smart are the smart guys? A unique view from hedge fund stock holdings', *The Review of Financial Studies*, Vol. 22, pp. 2531–2570.
   Hedge funds do not create alpha (a return in excess of the risk-adjusted rate).

Haislip, A. (2011) *Essentials of Venture Capital*. Hoboken, NJ: John Wiley & Sons.
   An easy to read introduction to venture capital, most reference to US.

Kidwell, D., Blackwell, D., Whidbee, D., and Peterson, R. (2008) *Financial Institutions, Markets, and Money*, 10th edn. Hoboken, NJ: John Wiley & Sons.
   US based introduction to hedge funds.

Lerner, J., Hardymon, F. and Leamon, A. (2009) *Venture Capital and Private Equity: A Casebook*, 4th edn. Hoboken, NJ: John Wiley & Sons.
   This collection of (mostly Harvard) case studies provides thorough insight into the US venture capital and private equity industry with detailed examples.

Malkiel, B. G. and Saha, A. (2005) 'Hedge funds: risk and return', *Financial Analysts Journal*, Vol. 61, No. 6, pp. 80–88.
   An examination of hedge fund returns, highlighting positive biases in published indices. Also hedge funds are more risky than is commonly supposed.

Metrick, A. and Yasuda, A. (2007) *Venture Capital and the Finance of Innovation*. 2nd edn. Hoboken, NJ: John Wiley & Sons.
   A useful introduction at the beginning, but becomes quite theoretical and technical later on.

Naik, N. Y., Ramadorai, T. and Stromqvist, M. (2007) 'Capacity constraints and hedge fund strategy returns', *European Financial Management*, Vol. 13, pp. 239–256.
   Hedge funds have achieved a positive alpha, but it has declined over time.

Websites

3i www.3i.com
Alternative Investment Management Association www.aima.org
Angel Investment Network www.angelinvestmentnetwork.co.uk
The British Business Angels Association www.bbaa.org.uk
Beer and Partners www.beerandpartners.com
The Department for Business, Innovation and Skills www.bis.gov.uk
British Private Equity & Venture Capital Association www.bvca.co.uk
Cavendish Management Resources www.cmrworld.com
The Development Capital Exchange www.dcxworld.com
European Fund and Asset Management Association www.efama.org
European Investment Fund www.eif.org
Equity Ventures Ltd www.equityventures.co.uk
European Private Equity & Venture Capital Association www.evca.eu
Gateway 2 investment www.g2i.org
HedgeFund Intelligence. Provider of hedge fund news and data www.hedgefundintelligence.com
Hennessee Group. US hedge fund advice and statistics www.hennesseegroup.com
Her Majesty's Revenue and Customs (VCTs and Enterprise investment schemes) www.hmrc.gov.uk
Hotbed (unquoted investments) www.hotbed.uk.com
TheCityUK http://www.thecityuk.com/
Listed Private Equity (incorporates www.ipeit.com) www.lpeq.com
National Venture Capital Association www.nvca.org
Yahoo Finance uk.finance.yahoo.com
Venture Giant www.venturegiant.com

Video presentations

Fund managers and other senior people describe and discuss policy and other aspects of hedge funds and private equity in interviews, documentaries and webcasts at Cantos.com. (www.cantos.com) – these are free to view.

Case study recommendations

See www.pearsoned.co.uk/arnold for case study synopses.
Also see Harvard University: http://hbsp.harvard.edu/product/cases

- The Children's Investment Fund, 2005 (2006) Authors: Randolph B. Cohen and Joshua B. Sandbulte. Harvard Business School.
- Ithmar Capital (2010) Authors: Josh Lerner and Ann Leamon. Harvard Business School.
- Ligand Pharmaceuticals Incorporated (2009) Authors: Nabil N. El-hage, Michael Gorzynski. Harvard Business School.
- The Hedge Fund Industry (2010) Author: William E. Fruhan Jr. Harvard Business School.
- GlobeOp: Enabling Hedge Funds, 2000-2003 (A) (2008) Authors: Victoria Chang, Glenn Carroll and David Modest. Stanford Graduate School of Business.
- GlobeOp (B): Organising for Hedge Fund Growth, 2000 to 2008 (2009) Authors: Victoria Chang and Glenn Carroll. Stanford Graduate School of Business.
- How Venture Capitalists Evaluate Potential Venture Opportunities (2004) Authors: Michael J. Roberts and L. Barley. Harvard Business School.
- 3i Group plc. (2003) Authors: Josh Lerner, Felda Hardymon and Ann Leamon. Harvard Business School.

Self-review questions

1 What is a hedge fund?

2 What was the first strategy for a hedge fund initiated by the founder of the industry?

3 What does absolute return mean?

4 What is a relative return?

5 Describe market neutral strategy.

6 Why might a hedge fund refuse an investor's money?

7 Why are hedge funds registered offshore, and where are the most common domiciles?

8 What are (a) gates (b) lock-ups (c) side pockets?

9 What is alpha?

10 Who manages hedge funds?

11 What does 2 and 20 mean?

12 What are (a) clawback (b) high water mark (c) hurdle rate?

13 Describe a fund of hedge funds.

14 Describe situations where an investor in a hedge fund might not be able to withdraw their funds.

15 What are listed funds?

16 What is private equity?

17 For private equity, describe (a) general partner (b) limited partner.

18 What is a business angel network?

19 What are (a) independents (b) captives (c) semi-captives?

20 What is an exit strategy for a private equity fund?

Questions and problems

1 Why is it difficult to assess hedge fund data? Explain why it might matter.

2 What differentiates a hedge fund manager from other financial managers?

3 Describe in detail the fee structure used by hedge funds.

4 Explain the relevance of UCITS to the hedge fund industry.

5 What is arbitrage (risk free or otherwise) and describe ways in which it can be used by hedge funds.

6 Describe and explain as many hedge fund strategies as you can.

7 Describe what prime brokers do for hedge funds.

8 Where does private equity investment come from?

9 Discuss why many firms choose to accept private equity funding rather than join a stock market.

10 Describe the nature of business angel investing and explain the benefits angels bring to a firm.

11 List, describe and contrast the different types of private equity.

12 If business angels are not connected with divine intervention in business matters, seedcorn capital is not something to do with growing food and a captured fund is not theft, what are they and how might they assist a company.

13 What is (a) a VCT (b) the EIS (c) UCITS?

14 Describe the different ways in which private equity investors can hope to realise a profit.

Assignments

1 Choose a hedge fund that you have read about, and find its performance from the internet. Compare its performance with:

    (a) a share index for European shares;
    (b) an S&P tracker fund.

2 Imagine you had £2,500,000 to invest in a hedge fund or in private equity. After describing them, explain the relative advantages and disadvantages of the following types of investing:

    (a) Hedge fund using various arbitrage strategies.
    (b) Hedge fund using event-driven strategies.
    (c) Hedge fund using global macro strategies.
    (d) Business angel investing.
    (e) Venture capital fund concentrating on early stage businesses.

Web-based exercises

1 Search the internet for recent articles on hedge funds. Write an essay focusing on the following:

    (a) the performance of various types of hedge funds over the past five years;
    (b) a description of the four hedge fund investing strategies that have produced the highest returns over this period.

2 Using the internet, find examples of private equity funding a business three to five years ago that has now been exited. Write a report/case study describing the capital structure and the progress of the firm and the private equity fund.

3   Go to the websites of the British Private Equity & Venture Capital Association (www.bvca.co.uk), the National Venture Capital Association (www.nvca.org) and the European Private Equity & Venture Capital Association (www.evca.eu) to download statistics on amounts raised and amounts invested over the past five years. Using the commentaries on the websites as well as the data, write an essay explaining the main developments in the industry over this time.

Regulation of the financial sector

LEARNING OUTCOMES

By the end of this chapter the reader should be able to:

■ discuss the market failings that lead to the need for financial industry regulation;

■ weigh up the arguments for and against tighter regulation, explaining the dangers that come with extensive regulation;

■ outline the core elements of financial regulation;

■ describe the UK regulatory system;

■ discuss the European Union financial regulatory structure and some attempts at global coordination.

Customers of financial services firms place a great deal of trust in the managers when they hand over their money or follow their advice. Naturally, in most cases clients do not understand in any great detail where their money goes. They accept a promise that it will be returned to them, or at least that, if it is put at risk in order to generate a return, the managers will be careful, thoughtful and skilled in applying their savings to investment.

The lack of customer control and lack of customer information once the money is handed over leaves investors, depositors, insurance purchasers, etc. exposed to a number of human failings. There is the danger of incompetence that either through ignorance or laziness financial service providers waste the client's money, possibly losing it all. There is also the danger of outright fraud and other criminal acts that siphon money from the innocent to the crooked.

The financial service industry recognised long ago that it is in its own best interest to establish minimum standards of behaviour. If the users of financial services fear that malpractice is prevalent they will not allow their funds to flow through the system and the financial sector will shrink. These minimum standards need some sort of enforcement mechanism beyond a gentleman's agreement that all participants will behave ethically. Crooks and incompetents would love to join an industry where the majority of providers act with probity, because they can free-ride on the industry's reputation. Thus we need regulation. This may be provided by the industry itself with the back-up of statutory laws or could be provided by the government in some form.

This chapter first explains why, despite its high cost, we have regulation, and then discusses the dangers that arise in a regulated system. The main tasks and activities required of regulators is outlined followed by an examination of one of the most sophisticated regulatory structures in the world, the UK's. We then look at the additional regulatory rules imposed at the European Union level and at the global level.

Some people draw a distinction between regulation and supervision:

Regulation The process of rule making and legislation creating the supervisory system. The rules may come from the laws of the land or from the stipulations of the regulatory agency.

Supervision Monitoring the position and behaviour of individual firms, and enforcing the regulations if required.

For our purposes we will assume that the word regulation covers supervision as well.

Why regulate?

Financial regulation is expensive. It cost hundreds of millions, even billions, to pay for regulators to carry out their tasks in a modern economy. There are further billions to be paid by the banks, insurance companies and other financial service firms in compliance costs, i.e. putting in place systems and training to ensure that staff behave according to the rules. These additional costs are likely to be passed on to clients. Then there are the potential losses because new organisations that are keen to provide a financial service are put off entering the industry by the costs and time of obtaining a license from the regulator and the subsequent monitoring – perhaps society loses much innovatory and competitive fizz as a result. **Exhibit 15.1** gives us some idea of the costs.

So, given the costs, a fundamental question is: why do we bother with regulation? This section presents some ideas to answer that question.

Asymmetric information

Asymmetric information is one of the forms of market failure in financial services in which the market participants will drive the industry to a sub-optimal outcome if left to their own devices. The other two reasons for intervention, also forms of market failure – contagion and monopoly/oligopoly – are discussed later.

Exhibit 15.1

Oversight of banks costs US far more than EU

By **Brooke Masters** in London

The US spends more than six times as much to supervise banks and other credit institutions as the European Union, research has found.

The various federal and state agencies that supervise banks in the US spent $4.4bn on 18,000 frontline employees in 2009–10, while the 27 EU nations spent $2.2bn on 10,000 employees, according to analysis by the Oliver Wyman consultancy.

The US spend $1m per $1bn of banking revenues, compared with $150,000 in the EU.

The costs cover day-to-day supervision of the system for safety and soundness as well as consumer protection and conduct issues.

There are several reasons for the differences. The US has many more very small banks and spends correspondingly more on them. It also has about 10,500 institutions to safeguard, while the EU has 6,500. The two spend roughly the same per bank, at $150,000.

The US also has more overlap between its state and federal agencies.

Source: Financial Times, 24 January 2011, p. 8. Reprinted with permission.

Asymmetric information *occurs when one party in a negotiation or relationship is not in the same position as other parties, being ignorant of, or unable to observe, some information which is essential to the contracting and decision-making process.*

Managers and other employees of financial service companies have an information set that is often superior to that of the clients. This can lead to exploitation; for example, buyers of a financial product are unable to assess the true risk and return. Thus a large part of regulation is about ensuring that consumers receive relevant information about products in an understandable way.

Asymmetric information manifests itself in a number of ways:

● reducing safety and soundness for the consumer or a financial market counterparty;

● producing conflicts of interest within financial service firms which can be deleterious to the interests of consumers or counterparties;

● facilitating bad behaviour such as fraud;

● hiding and tolerating incompetence.

We will now look at each of these in turn.

Safety and soundness

Consumers are frequently unable to assess the safety and soundness of a financial institution or the products it provides. They simply do not have the time or the expertise to evaluate whether the organisation is taking too much risk with their money. An example here is the flood of money that went into Icelandic Banks in the mid-2000s. Large numbers of savers from all over Europe were attracted by the high interest rates offered on deposit accounts. Little did they know that the accumulated bank deposits were lent out to high risk ventures with only small amounts being retained as a safety buffer. The managers of these banks were tempted by the higher interest rates they could charge on the more risky lending, producing large short term (apparent) profits and therefore large bonuses. Regulators are supposed to conduct prudential bank regulation (discussed in Chapters 2 and 7) to protect consumers from unsound bank policies and actions. They clearly failed in the case of the Icelandic banks, so after their collapse the authorities (governments in this case) were forced to guarantee all deposits, which is an expensive way to protect depositors. They are now much keener on ensuring banks are managed for safety and soundness.

A large part of the bank regulator's role is to ensure that banks have enough capital buffer (surplus of assets over liabilities) to be able to cover their obligations, even allowing for a large potential diminution of asset value due to, say, loan defaults. They are also concerned that a bank keeps back a sizeable amount of cash and other liquid resources to be able to meet short-term liquidity outflows. Capital reserves and liquidity reserves were discussed in detail in Chapters 2 and 7 and so, despite this being a very important element in financial regulation, we will not discuss it any further here. Another element of safety and soundness for banks is that they do not have too many eggs in one (or a few) basket, say an excessive proportion of lending to one sector (e.g. property developers) – called **concentration risk**.

Buyers of insurance are usually unable to assess the likelihood of the insurance company becoming insolvent, and therefore unable to meet obligations to policy holders. The soundness of insurance firms is of great importance, not only to those with car and house insurance but also to the tens of millions of people who now save vast amounts through insurance products, from endowment mortgages and insurance bonds to personal pensions and retirement annuities.

Other questions in this area are: How sound is the stock broker who holds your shares in one of its accounts? How safely managed is your company pension fund, or your investment trust, or unit trust? Is your venture capital trust money being applied recklessly to absurdly risky ventures without adequate diversification?

Safety and soundness concerns arise not only in the relationship between financial service providers and consumers but also in the trading that takes place between financial intermediaries, for example, interbank lending and borrowing, trading in the foreign exchange market or derivatives trading all involve a degree of counterparty risk.

Conflicts of interest

Conflicts of interest arise when a person or institution has a number of objectives (interests) and is free to choose which receives the most emphasis, when one of them might have the potential to corrupt the motivation to act. The choice made may not be one that would suit the consumer because it might be tainted by the self-interest of the financial service provider. But the consumer is unable to see the extent of the bias due to asymmetric information. Take, for example, an independent financial advisor who is supposed to advise a client on the best home for their savings but who is tempted by the large commission paid by a unit trust company to push the client into their product.

When conflict of interest scandals come to light it diminishes the trust that potential investors have in the system. And so the financial markets do not channel as much saving into productive investment opportunities as they would in the absence of conflicted objectives. Thus, society as well as investors lose because of the reduced flow and increased cost of funds. Regulation that provides reassurance that conflicts of interest are minimised can thus add to the wealth of society.

Conflicts of interest can lead to the misuse of information, the providing of false information, the providing of biased or selective information, or the concealing of information.

- *Misuse* An example of the misuse of information is **spinning** by an investment bank organising an initial public offering of a company's shares that it thinks will rise substantially. It allocates blocks of shares to a few select clients such as directors of companies that may give the bank a mandate to assist in raising capital (e.g. an IPO) in the future. These selected executives will make a killing in the week or two following the flotation. They will then repay the investment bank by directing their company to pay fat fees for a new bond or equity issue. This might be a lot more expensive for the company than if it shopped around for an arranger of funding. Thus the cost of capital raising is inflated and bankers take home large bonuses. Another example would be where an executive of a manufacturing firm is in possession of information that, when it is released to the market, will lead to a significant rise in the company's share price. In the meantime he buys shares in the firm expecting to profit from his insider knowledge.

- *False* An example of false information dissemination can arise when auditing firms also supply a client company with management consulting services (e.g. advice on tax, management systems, strategy). The latter services can result in fees that are many times what they receive from the audit. Client companies may pressure auditors by threatening to move their consulting custom to another firm if they do not see things their way. In accounting much judgement is required about issues such as the value of a non-current asset or the likelihood of a customer debt being paid. There is therefore wriggle-room for putting a positive gloss on profits and balance sheet strength. This can easily tip over into false information in the sense of, while being within the letter of the accounting rules, it breaks the spirit. A similar conflict was said to have occurred when credit rating agencies were accused of being too generous in rating the chance of default of bonds issued by many banks and special purpose vehicles set up to receive interest from US sub-prime mortgages in securitisation deals in the mid-2000s (*see* Chapter 6). The issuing company pays for the rating but the consumers of that information are the bond investors, hence the conflict of interest. The rating agencies were accused of trying to attract future rating mandates by being less than unbiased. They defended themselves vigorously saying that they cannot afford to be seen as anything other than impartial and objective if their ratings are to be taking seriously. They stand to lose their entire business franchise if they cannot be relied upon by bond buyers. Thus they have a high degree of self-policing. If bond-buyer faith in the rating agencies did ever seriously decline there would be a danger of a much reduced flow of funds to companies and therefore lower wealth in society. **Exhibit 15.2** describes the consequences flowing from an analyst providing false information.

- *Biased* An example of biased information arises in a badly organised investment bank which while issuing research reports and advising investors on good bond purchases also arranges a bond issue by a client company. A great deal of effort goes into understanding the company when arranging a bond issue, and the information generated may be useful to the research team supplying analysis to investors. However, the issuing firm would like to sell the bonds at

Exhibit 15.2

Analyst fined over misleading message   FT

By Brooke Masters

A former MF Global analyst has been fined £50,000 for sending clients and colleagues a "misleading and inaccurate" instant message that appeared to contain inside information about a UK-listed company.

The Financial Services Authority said trading in shares of Enterprise Inns more than trebled and the price rose more than 4 per cent in the two hours after Christopher Gower sent his message, entitled "Hot off the press" to 14 clients and a message group of 60 colleagues.

The case is the first FSA enforcement action to stem from an instant message and reflects growing concern among regulators about rumour-mongering and loose treatment of potential inside information by financial professionals.

Margaret Cole, FSA head of enforcement, said: "There is no excuse for a senior retail analyst to be so careless with messages that could have such an impact on the market. Gower's dissemination of inaccurate information contributed to a large increase in the volume

of shares traded and a disorderly market in ETI shares."

Mr Gower's solicitor declined to comment, as did MF Global.

The FSA said Mr Gower's message on May 7 2008, which cited a meeting he had with the chief executive of Punch Taverns, gave the impression inaccurately he was passing on inside information about Enterprise's efforts to win permission to convert to a real estate investment trust.

But the regulator stopped short of charging Mr Gower with market abuse, saying that his conduct was "careless" and failed to meet market standards.

Angele Hayes, partner at Mayer Brown, the law firm, said: "This case emphasises the scrupulous care analysts need to take when they make informal communications about companies they are following... [and] shows that the 'broker's banter' defence will not assist if analysts are caught gilding the lily."

The FSA brought a similar case in 2006 against Sean Pignatelli, a

Credit Suisse equity salesman. He was fined £20,000 for passing on what appeared to be inside information about US-listed Boston Scientific.

In 2008, the regulator warned in a newsletter that it was concerned about the spread of rumours and urged regulated firms to set out their policies about passing on information and do more training of their staff. It warned last year about leaks.

US regulators are also cracking down on rumours. The Securities and Exchange Commission in 2008 charged a Wall Street trader with spreading false stories about a company that he was selling short.

Paul Glass, a lawyer with Taylor Wessing, said: "This case is a reminder that the FSA isn't just interested in insider dealing... Any disclosure of misleading information by an approved person which affects the market is likely to be investigated."

Source: Financial Times, 14 January 2011, p. 17. Reprinted with permission.

as high a price as possible and so would like the researchers to be optimistic. If the fee received for organising the bond is sufficiently large then the investment bank may (if not properly controlled) select the information it releases to boost the potential sales level. These banks are supposed to have high 'Chinese walls' separating different departments to prevent these conflicts of interest, but it is surprising how positive many of them are about the equity or debt securities of their client companies (it is difficult to find negative comment).

- **Concealment** An example of the concealment of information is when a bank has a loan outstanding to a company that it suspects is running into serious financial difficulties. Bank officers have access to this information but the bond issue department is nevertheless encouraged to sell bonds in the company without telling investors about the company's likelihood of distress. The loan is paid off and the bank earns a fee for selling the bonds.

Many conflicts of interest are not exploited even in the absence of regulation because the incentive to do so is not sufficiently high. Also, financial firms often live and die by their reputations. Any conflict that became visible would be punished as other financial organisations and clients shunned the firm. Having said that, we still need regulation because these constraints may not work on particular individuals with immediate bonuses to puff-up, or when the firm itself is excessively focused on short-term profits rather than long-term reputation.

Fraud

Financial markets present opportunities to make large profits over short periods of time; this is especially the case if a trusted professional lacks moral fibre. While the majority of people in the financial sector are honourable and of high integrity, such a honey pot is bound to attract greedy knaves who are clever enough to dream up a range of chicanery.

Incompetence

Consumers often receive poor service due to incompetence. This may be bad advice because of the inattention or ignorance of a financial adviser – *see* **Exhibit 15.3** for an example. There may be incompetence in managing a client's funds or their business interests. In financial services incompetence can continue undetected for years. For example, in the handling of pension fund money, the manager will render the service of investing to supply pensions decades after the savers have injected funds into the scheme. It may only be after retirement that it is revealed whether it will meet the financial needs of the retirees.

Exhibit 15.3

Barclays hit with record fine

FT

By **Brooke Masters** and **Sharlene Goff** in London

Barclay will pay a record £7.7m fine and up to £59m in compensation for failing to provide adequate investment advice to more than 12,000 of its customers, many of whom were retirees who suffered losses in the financial crisis.

The fine is the largest imposed by the Financial Services Authority for a case involving retail investors and the sixth largest in the regulators history.

The FSA said Barclays had failed to ensure that two Aviva funds were suitable for clients who invested

nearly £700m in them between 2006 and 2008. Many were seeking additional income and Barclays staff failed adequately to explain the risks involved, the regulator said.

More than 1,700 of the investors in Aviva's Global Balanced Income Fund and the Global Cautious Income Fund have already complained and received £17m in compensation. The FSA said Barclays may have to pay up to £42m more.

The bank plans to write to all clients who have not already com-

plained and compensate them for their losses. "We are serious in our apologies to these customers. This is not something we want to ever happen again," said Paul McNamara, Barclays managing director of insurance and investments.

The FSA said Barclays also failed promptly to rectify the situation after it identified unsuitable sales in 2008. "Thousands of investors, many of whom were seeking to invest their retirement savings, have suffered... Given Barclays' position as one of the UK's major

▶

Exhibit 15.3 continued

retail banks we view these breaches as particularly serious and fully deserving of what is a very substantial fine," said Margaret Cole, FSA enforcement director.

Aviva was urged to improve its documentation but is not facing an enforcement case, people familiar with the issue said.

Consumer groups said tougher enforcement was needed. "This is yet another example of banks giving poor financial advice to their customers," said Peter Vicary-Smith, chief executive of Which?, the consumer organisation. "We believe the fine imposed by the FSA is far too lenient. If we're going to deter financial institutions from failing their customers, then fines need to be much higher."

The financial crisis has led regulators around the world to focus more closely on whether retail investors are being sold suitable products and adequately warned about risks.

Source: Financial Times, 19 January 2011, p. 17. Reprinted with permission.

Contagion

In some financial sectors, say banking, the failure of a company may lead to the failure of others leading to instability in the whole system. This is called contagion risk. As we have seen following the collapse of Lehman Brothers in 2008 contagion can have very serious consequences for the economic health of a nation as well as for consumers of financial products. If a domino effect takes hold, where one bank's failure (or perceived likely failure) to meet its obligations to other banks or clients, leads to more bank collapses and further losses it can ruin the entire system, possibly taking us down into a 1930s-style depression. Economists would describe this as an example of an 'externality' in which the social cost of failure exceeds the private cost.

The damage caused by spreading contagion is so bad that it is well worth the effort to ensure individual banks are unlikely to collapse by regulating the amount of capital and liquid assets they hold. It is also worth insisting that they write and continuously update 'living wills' so that they can be revived or closed down in an orderly way without fatally wounding other banks should they run into trouble. (Living wills are discussed in Chapter 7.) It is also advisable to insist that none is either too big to fail (i.e. the government cannot contemplate letting it go into bankruptcy) or 'too big to save', where no government can raise enough money to save it. **Exhibit 15.4** describes the US regulator's tightening of scrutiny to reduce contagion risk, which stretches to insurers and hedge funds.

Exhibit 15.4

Regulators increase scrutiny of US banks

By Francesco Guerrera in New York

US regulators have increased their scrutiny of the country's largest banks in recent months, digging deeper into riskier activities and pushing institutions to conduct more rigorous "stress tests" of their financial health.

Wall Street executives say that since the end of the financial crisis examiners from the Federal Reserve, the main banking watchdog, have become tougher and more detailed in their policing of large financial institutions.

"They are all over us," said a senior Wall Street banker. "They want to see a lot more detail and are demanding a lot more information."

The tighter oversight is part of the authorities' effort to reduce the chances of another financial crisis as devastating as the last one by closing regulatory gaps that allowed banks to take on huge risks and unsustainable amounts of debt.

The overhaul of US financial rules that became law last month gives the Fed sweeping powers to oversee a wide range of companies – from banks to insurers and hedge funds – whose failure would endanger the financial system.

Regulators such as the Fed and the Securities and Exchange Commission have been criticised for failing to curtail the excesses that led to the implosions of Lehman Brothers, AIG and Bear Stearns and forced the government to inject funds into Morgan Stanley, Goldman Sachs, Citigroup and Bank of America.

▶

Exhibit 15.4 continued

The New York Fed, which oversees most large financial groups, declined to comment on its scrutiny but executives said the tougher policing centred on the severity of internal stress tests and more detailed probes of banks' profits.

Federal examiners have asked banks for more details on the profitability of different businesses, such as trading, capital markets and investment banking, rather than focusing on group-wide balance sheets as in the past, bankers said.

Corporate executives often complain about the costs and complexity of regulations but several top bankers said that the post-crisis changes have been among the toughest in recent times.

The deeper analysis indicates authorities now recognise that before the crisis rising bank profits were often coupled with an increase in hidden risks. For example, regulators paid little attention to the increase in the amount of mortgage-backed securities on banks' books partly because their performance was good and their risks were not clearly visible on balance sheets.

Bankers say regulators are also putting pressure on them to be more pessimistic in stress tests aimed at measuring banks' ability to respond to economic shocks.

Institutions had been taking the collapse in housing prices and the economic slow-down of the recent crisis as their most extreme case but the authorities wanted them to use even more dramatic assumptions, they added.

Stricter oversight in the US is part of an overhaul of global financial rules that could force institutions to significantly alter their business models. The Fed's new stand is similar to the approach adopted by the UK's Financial Services Authority.

Source: Financial Times, 11 August 2010, p. 13. Reprinted with permission.

Monopoly/oligopoly

Many markets will, if left to their own devices, tend towards a structure where one or a few firms exert undue market power over product pricing. Consumers need protection against monopolistic/oligopolistic exploitation.

There are many forces encouraging movement towards monopoly in financial services apart from the desire to control prices. Economies of scale are such that it makes sense for many banks and other institutions to become very large. Banks with branches in every town and with capabilities to serve multinational firms in every country have an advantage in attracting customers. With stock exchanges, liquidity in share trading may be lowered if there is more than one national exchange. There are also network effects: a single payments system linking the major banks makes more sense than a number of competing systems because each participant needs to make as many connections within the network as possible.

Where natural monopoly makes sense there is even more need to regulate to avoid abuse by over-charging. Where the benefit of lowering the cost of production by reducing the industry structure to a single firm or a handful of suppliers is roughly balanced by the social loss from ceding pricing power to the producers, there is a case for regulators to insist on a certain minimum number of players or maximum market shares for any one provider.

The dangers to watch out for in a regulatory system

Moral hazard

The mere presence of regulation can cause moral hazard, which is:

The presence of a safety net encourages adverse behaviour (e.g. carelessness).

Thus regulation can be counterproductive, in that, if consumers believe that they will be bailed out by the government if thing go wrong they will be tempted to take higher risk. Why not place your money in a deposit account offering an unrealistically high interest rate? The bank may go bust but your deposit is safe. Why not pay into a savings scheme offered by an insurance company offering a guarantee of doubling your money over four years? If the company fails you can insist on the government/regulatory fund making good on the promise. In this way irresponsible, badly managed and crooked banks and other financial institutions survive, drawing society's scarce resources away from more productive investment.

Agency capture

Agency capture occurs when those that are supposed to be regulated take some control of the regulatory process. Then the regulation is modified to suit the interests of the producers rather than the consumers. For example, under Basel II (*see* Chapter 7) the large banks managed to persuade the regulators that it would be sensible for capital requirements to be set in the mould of the banks' own internal risk models. Many people say that the banks were too influential in lowering capital limits, manipulating the rules on risk-weighting assets and in using their own models. This helped to precipitate the 2008 crisis as banks were found to have taken too much risk.

The regulated firms usually have far more financial interest in the activities of regulators than consumers; and so they apply themselves to persuading their overseers to relax their constraints. In many cases the people working in the regulatory organisation are paid significantly less than the financial service high flyers, and they can sometimes be intimidated or outsmarted. Furthermore, many of the more senior regulators have come from the industry they are now regulating and therefore share many of their attitudes and values. Also, they may expect to return to work in the industry following their stint as policemen; they may thus avoid offending potential future employers.

Excessive compliance cost

The cost to regulated firms of adhering to the rules will usually result in raised fees, lower return or some other penalty for consumers because the institution is likely to pass the additional burden through to clients.

Stifling innovation and growth

The requirements to be licensed and the additional costs of subsequent compliance can impose such a bureaucratic load that few or no firms dare to enter the industry. Thus, inefficient monopolies are sustained and oligopolies with implicit cartel-type arrangements persist in over-charging consumers because they are not challenged by new entrants.

The poor level of innovation and competition in Indian's banking system is of great concern to the government that has for so long promoted state-owned banks as the way forward – *see* **Exhibit 15.5.** But India has to be careful about allowing industrial conglomerates to take control of banks and then use the money within for their own purposes.

Exhibit 15.5

RBI set to decide on shape of banking

James Lamont

The Reserve Bank of India is on the cusp of a critical decision about the future of Indian Banking.

Guidelines expected to be published by the end of this month will indicate whether big corporations can snap up highly desirable new banking licences on offer as India seeks to modernise its financial system.

After five months of consultation, central bank officials say opinion is divided over whether big corporations, such as Reliance Industries, the Tata Group or Bharti, should be permitted to own banks, as well as how much the initial capitalisation of a new bank should be. The RBI must also decide how many licences to issue and whether to offer them in waves or in a single tranche. The issuing of new banking licences, proposed last year by finance minister Pranab Mukherjee, could serve a big political goal of greater financial inclusion among India's 1.2bn people, most of whom have no access to formal banking. It could also help in loosening the state's grip on the financial sector.

Alongside the RBI's deliberations, India's largely state-owned banking sector has a deadline of end-March to detail how it intends to make services available to more people. The RBI has directed

Exhibit 15.5 continued

that within five years the banking system must be extended to India's "villages", or centres with populations of more than 2,000 people.

A profitable business model for bringing banking to India's millions remains elusive, and potentially politically explosive.

Microfinance companies have hit hurdles in a country mistrustful of profiting off the poor. Proponents of "financial inclusion" are putting great store in technological advances expanding financial services, but regulators and bankers acknowledge there is no simple solution, in spite of India's expertise in IT and investment in technology.

The central bank is eyeing the ingenuity of India's most successful business leaders to tap the country's large savings pool.

Margins in financial services in India are high and competition gentle, leaving wide opportunity for competitive private provision – as show by ICICI Bank, India's biggest private bank with assets of $81bn

and a major provider of unsecured personal loans. Some new private sector banks have proved an overnight success, quickly gaining a reputation for innovation and eye-catching branding.

Yes Bank, launched just six years ago by former Rabo India head, Rana Kapoor, has a capitalisation of $12bn. But its success has been to target the corporate sector and wealthy individuals in advance of the wider, costlier retail deposit market. Its rise has fuelled wider corporate interest in banking licences, but is also causing a dilemma for the RBI. Regulators must ensure new entities fulfil a social mandate of providing services to the poorer market rather than mining the profits of niche markets.

The RBI is likely to attach social provisions to banking licences, something it did not do in the last round awarded. Given the financial rewards and value a banking licence brings, some companies have already expressed interest. Larsen

& Toubro, India's largest engineering and construction company, is eyeing a banking licence for subsidiary L&T Finance, which specialises in infrastructure finance.

Yet a concentration of financial resources among business houses risks unhealthy cross-subsidisation of financial and industrial operations, with a threat to transparency.

Wary of volatility, the RBI has already ruled out real estate companies diversifying into banking. Within 20 years, Indian officials expect the banking system to be much more dynamic. They foresee banks being able to offer low-income households credit and micro insurance in addition to simpler savings and remittances products, and the emergence of global Indian banks.

The guidelines will determine whether a new generation of tycoon-led banks is among them.

Source: Financial Times, 6 January 2011, p. 22. Reprinted with permission.

The regulatory obstacles to establishing a financial service firm are thought to be damaging the UK's international standing as well as reducing competition – *see* **Exhibit 15.6.**

Exhibit 15.6

FSA's delays for new businesses spark City fears

Sam Jones

The City watchdog is now taking three times as long to approve new financial businesses as it did before the crisis, raising new concerns over damage to London's standing as an international financial centre.

Entrepreneurs seeking to set up new financial services businesses such as banks, brokerages or hedge funds must now wait almost three months on average for a decision from the Financial Services Authority.

The steep rise in registration time – up from just seven weeks at the beginning of 2007 – comes in spite of a fall in the number of companies applying for permission to trade, down from a peak of nearly 2,200 in the 2006-07 financial year to just over 1,500 in the 12 months to April this year.

The FSA says that the extended registration process is a reflection of heightened diligence in response to the financial crisis, but critics

warn that it could become a drag on London's international position.

"These delays risk reducing competition and harming the City's international competitiveness," said Jonathan Davies, a partner at London law firm Reynolds Porter Chamberlain.

The FSA said the increased registration times were the result of changes implemented by the regulator to ensure a more thorough and rigorous vetting process.

Exhibit 15.6 continued

In particular, the watchdog had increased its scrutiny of individuals seeking to set up or run new businesses.

The FSA now interviews every individual – including directors, non-executive directors, executives and partners – who may exercise a "significant influence function" in a new business. According to people familiar with the process, those individuals are also now subject to detailed background checks, including checks for criminal records. An FSA insider described the approach as "intensive and intrusive supervision".

It is understood that a greater number of cases than ever before are being referred to a special internal tribunal set up by the regulator to vet and advise on the suitability of individuals to work in the financial services sector.

While stricter oversight of the City has been broadly welcomed in many quarters, including many large city institutions, smaller financial services businesses claim they are being unfairly penalised by the stricter regime.

"I understand the principle of it all, but it's misdirected," said one fund manager who has recently set up a new London-based hedge fund.

"It has taken us literally months to jump through various hoops and try and get off the ground – none of which is beneficial to our investors, who are the ones that really scrutinise us."

Hedge fund managers typically run on very tight margins to begin with and can struggle to afford costs such as full-time compliance officers or lawyers. Incidences of fraud or market abuse by London-based hedge funds have been few and far between, the industry points out.

The added regulator burden, they say, is one of a growing number of factors leading many to consider starting up new businesses abroad or redomiciling to locations such as Geneva or the Channel Islands.

Source: Financial Times, 11 October 2010, p. 3. Reprinted with permission.

Types of regulation

A key question, once you have accepted the need for regulation, is: who should carry out the task? We have three possibilities: the industry itself, government or a government agency.

By the industry itself

Self-regulation has a number of advantages. The people within the industry have a clear need to preserve its high reputation. If the public image of a sector of financial services is badly damaged then confidence can evaporate along with the desire to place money in the hands of those in that industry. Not only does it become embarrassing to admit that you are member of that tainted service sector at dinner parties (just ask investment bankers!) but jobs might be lost in their thousands.

A further advantage of self-regulation is that the people most knowledgeable about the industry are those working in it. They know all the tricks being played and can quickly adapt the rules to deal with any new tricks. They also know the most efficient ways of running a decent industry and so can avoid regulatory overkill, such as unreasonable high safety standards or excessive compliance costs. In other words, self-regulation is usually 'lighter' than regulation by a government-imposed body.

Even self-regulation requires the back-up of legislation to ensure, say, minimum standards to be able to join the industry and then to insist that participants abide by the rules. Without this insistence, free-riders will enter to enjoy the raised reputation of the industry with consumers, without having to pay the costs of compliance or suffer the constraints.

The arguments against self-regulation include the suspicion that the institutions will be continuously tempted to slacken the rules. Second, power to permit industry entry is put in the hands of the existing players, who might be tempted to put up barriers to discourage new firms from entering the industry. A third problem is that it is difficult to regulate a firm that has activities in many different financial service industries. For example, conglomerate banks also offer investment products and insurance services, pension funds and investment advice. Unless the self-regulatory body's remit is very widely defined, misdemeanours, bad practice and fraud can seep in through the cracks between the regulators.

Self-regulatory organisations are usually dependent on funding from the industry itself to function, which could encourage it to be more favourably disposed towards the producer rather than the consumer.

By the government

There are many cases where self-regulation is clearly not sufficient to maintain the integrity of the financial system and so governments are compelled to intervene by providing a regulatory structure. However, there is a danger here. Governments realise that they will be criticised if there is a financial scandal but will not receive much praise if a series of scandals is avoided. They can therefore have a tendency to err on the side of heavy regulation to reduce even small risks of failure. This will raise the cost to producers and consumers unreasonably. Also governments tend to be less agile than industry self-regulators in responding to new developments and tricks of the morally challenged.

By a government agency

This is designed to capture the best elements of the other two options. An organisation is established by the government, but the government does not control its day-to-day activities, nor intervene in its decisions. Instead of government bureaucrats the agency is run by a group of experts with longstanding industry experience. The government establishes the guiding principles and goals but then stands back to avoid being tempted to meddle because of some political motivation. The government may, however, provide legislative back-up to ensure that the agency has strong powers, e.g. the right to prosecute insider dealers in a criminal court or the right to fine firms caught disobeying the rules.

Using respected industry veterans to run the agency engenders greater practitioner respect for it than would be the case if government officers were in charge. This allows a lighter touch where the key focus is on following the spirit of the rules rather than the letter of the law. This approach requires subtlety that civil servants may lack. Also, poachers turned game-keepers are likely to be more alert and agile in keeping up with the latest tricks on the financial streets.

Even though former practitioners are in charge, they have a statutory framework that prevents them from slackening the rules, or unreasonably restricting entry of new firms to a financial service. Also, the regulator can be given the powers to examine a full range of financial services and markets and so can avoid the problem of some activities falling between the cracks of an industry by industry regulatory structure.

On the downside, the agency route can be a lot more expensive than self-regulation by the industry.

International competitiveness

Prior to the 2008 financial crisis there was much comment among those informed about financial matters concerning the problem of **competitive laxity** in regulation. That is, financial centres that try to impose strict rules find that financial institutions respond not by tightening their systems and raising probity, but by moving operations to a different jurisdiction, where the rules are looser. This sort of **regulatory arbitrage** is still very much on the minds of regulators and politicians today as they try to make the systems in their countries more robust. As soon as they announce that they will impose an extra rule to make things fairer and safer the cry goes up from the banks and others that they will lose out to overseas competitors who do not have to obey that rule. Furthermore, given that they will be at a competitive disadvantage, they, too, might have to move abroad. The danger is that the regulators and politicians around the globe each back down in turn in the face of this pressure.

One solution is to stand up to the banks, etc. and say, 'If you want to do very risky things or unfair things then we would prefer it if you did go somewhere else, so we are going to impose the rule ourselves even if no other country does the same' – this is termed the unilateral approach. A difficulty arises when the proposed curtailment is borderline in terms of fairness and risk – then you might lose thousands of jobs in financial services for little gain. Of course, the authorities would like to achieve international agreement (multilateral approach) so that all the financial centres impose the same rule to avoid regulatory arbitrage (as with Basel III), but this is difficult to attain.

Exhibit 15.7 describes the shift to de-emphasise the UK regulator's role as a champion of the City, and a greater emphasis on prudential regulation. **Exhibit 15.8** is a letter published in the *FT* from experienced practitioners who are fully aware of the importance of fair dealing and ethical behaviour to sustain a financial centre. **Exhibit 15.9** sums up the core elements of regulation. *See also* **Exhibits 15.10 – 15.12.**

Exhibit 15.7

Regulator to soften focus on keeping City's edge

By **Paul J Davies** and **Brooke Masters**

The City regulator will put less emphasis on maintaining London's competitiveness in relation to other financial centres, its head said yesterday, in a striking acknowledgement that the approach had undermined the stability of the financial system.

Lord Turner, chairman of the Financial Services Authority, said that prudential regulation of institutions and the financial system had suffered as regulators in many countries had in the past put too much focus on the attractiveness to the financial industry of their home markets.

"What we have just been through shows that getting it wrong in a prudential sense was so costly economically that you would have to believe the competitive advantage was extremely strong for it to have been worth it," Lord Turner said.

"We are interested in competitive markets rather than competitive*ness*."

The comments were made as Lord Turner answered questions after a speech at the biennial gathering of the Association of British Insurers in London.

The ABI has called on the regulator and government to strive to maintain the UK's competitiveness in its response to the financial crisis. "Over-regulation drives out capital, so consumers suffer high prices and, in the case of insurers, more risk falls on customers," it said in its recent response to the Turner Review of financial regulation.

Lord Turner did offer some succour to insurers, saying that while a regulatory revolution was needed in banking, insurance regulation faced no equivalent need.

But Lord Turner's remarks are sure to spark anxiety in the City, particularly in the banking and alternative investment sectors,

where many participants fear that new regulation will increase costs and cut into profits.

Several prominent UK hedge funds warned the Treasury last week that they were prepared to move to Switzerland unless a proposed European Union directive on alternative investments was radically changed.

George Osborne, shadow chancellor, speaking at the ABI earlier in the day, had called for the public authorities to ensure they did not "needlessly undermine London's competitive advantage" with "badly designed new regulation and uncompetitive tax rates".

Source: Financial Times, 10 June 2009, p. 2. Reprinted with permission.

Exhibit 15.8

Bringing back the City's rock-solid reputation

From **Sir John Craven**, **Mr Rupert Hambro** and others

Sir, The undersigned, among many others, were deeply involved in the creation of what is today the world's largest capital market: the Euromarket.

This market originated in the US, the Continent, and then in London in the late 1960s, where it became

firmly anchored – and now flourishes with volumes undreamt of at the time. There are many reasons why it concentrated in London: the City's history, law, language, skill sets and supporting services. But a major factor was the City's international reputation for fair dealing

and ethical behaviour. This was important because, at the time, the Euromarket was unregulated and over-the-counter, involving global counterparties, large and small. Trust was paramount.

It is difficult to deny that, in recent years, behaviour in the whole-

▶

Exhibit 15.8 continued

sale financial services industry has resulted in a severe loss of trust. There are many reasons for this: consolidation, different career aspirations and general cultural changes are but a few. Regulation has become more prescriptive in response to the explosion in City volumes in recent years, as a result of which the letter of the law has become paramount, while its spirit has been smothered almost to extinction.

This deterioration has an impact not only on the City's international standing, but on domestic perceptions as well. The legitimate discussion on compensation practices might be less heated if the City's reputation for ethical business conduct were rock solid.

The trend towards more complex regulation is irreversible. But the trend away from the highest standards of business practice need not be. The wholesale financial services industry still attracts new talent, if in smaller numbers in the present crisis. Those responsible for inducting and mentoring new recruits should remind them that the City's reputation for fair dealing played a critical role in attracting business to London, and can do so again, in a world where competition between financial centres is even greater than it was it was when we began.

Sir John Craven
Rupert Hambro
Lord Leach of Fairford
Charles S. McVeigh III
David Potter
Peter Spira
Stanislas Yassukovich
Minos Zombanakis

Source: Financial Times, 3 November 2009, p. 12. Reprinted with permission.

Regulation of UK financial services

Now that we have covered the basic principles lying behind regulation we will look at the example of the UK to illustrate the range of responsibilities typically given to regulators.

Interestingly, the UK regulatory system is going through something of an upheaval at the time of writing. For more than a decade the Financial Services Authority has dominated the scene. It is a 'super-regulator' with oversight of an amazing range of financial sectors. This is in contrast to some systems (e.g. the US) where there are a dozen or more regulators, each looking after one or a limited range of types of financial service.

In 2013 the FSA will split in two.[1] The main body, the Financial Conduct Authority[2] will still be a super-regulator covering a very wide range of financial services – *see* **Exhibit 15.13**. One important function, that of the individual regulation of the 2,200 biggest banks, insurers and brokers on the issue of safety and soundness (micro-prudential supervision), will be transferred to the new Prudential Regulatory Authority (PRA), a subsidiary of the Bank of England. It will be responsible for granting permission for their activities and approving their senior management. It will have the powers to impose additional capital requirements, limit leverage and change the risk weighting of assets in order to reduce the risk of failure. It is expected that it will be staffed by old FSA hands and will be headed by Hector Sants, the current FSA chief executive.

The Bank of England previously had the responsibility together with the FSA and the Treasury of ensuring the systemic safety of the banking system; that is, setting rules on capital and liquidity reserves for banks across the sector as a whole and imposing other rules to reduce contagion risk. Following the 2008 financial crisis it was thought wise to concentrate this macro-prudential regulation in the hands of one regulator together with the micro-prudential regulation of individual banks (and other finance businesses), rather than have the 'tripartite' approach where people in the Bank of England, Treasury and the FSA are not quite clear which of them should be taking charge when a systemic threat arises – as was the case up to 2008. The additional consideration is that these systemically important institutions might need access to central bank funding in an emergency and so it is best if they are regulated by the Bank.

---

[1] An informal division of the FSA took place in April 2011 so that 'road tests' could be carried out and the staff could be reassured about their future jobs.

[2] Until February 2011 this organisation was to be called the Consumer Protection and Markets Authority (CPMA).

Exhibit 15.9   The core elements of regulation

Licensing
Is a person fit and proper to manage a provider?
Only those who have met the standards required (integrity, honesty, capability) are allowed to provide a service in the industry. Training schemes and qualifications are encouraged by regulators to raise standards

Disclosure and monitoring
Disclosure of information about the operations of the financial firm and on-going monitoring may reveal whether a conflict of interest exists, whether risk management procedures are sound, whether the managers are competent and the institution is run with integrity.
This may involve off-site analysis of information provided and on-site inspections by the regulator

Prudential limits
Examples:
Capital and liquidity requirements of banks and insurance firms.
Pension funds to have sufficient funds to meet commitments.
Whether securities firms are in a sound financial condition

Fair trading on exchanges
A fair treatment of traders, particularly retail investors.
Prohibitions on insider dealing (using non-public information) – see Exhibit 15.10 for an example – and market manipulation or abuse (e.g. spreading false rumours) – see Exhibit 15.11.
Transparency of trading, e.g. open disclosure of price quotes by market makers.
Best execution provisions (see Chapter 8).
Prices of trades to be published.
Issuers of securities to provide prospectus and financial statements (see Chapter 9)

Exposure limits
e.g. no single borrower to account for more than 10% of a bank's loans

Penalties
In the event of non-compliance penalties may be imposed: e.g. fines, de-licensing, imprisonment, banning directors from the industry. For less serious offences a private warning or public censure may be sufficient

Mandatory information provisions and consumer education
Customers should obtain the right information at the right time to help them make a decision. Financial products/services to be clearly explained including risks, potential returns and costs such as charges. This must be presented in a consistent format to allow comparison. Regulators often accept a responsibility to educate and foster financial literacy. This is to reduce the need for more heavy handed regulation

Restricting activities
Prohibiting certain firms from a line of business or prohibiting a particular combination of financial services within the same organisation or a ban on anyone from engaging in the activity, e.g. no mortgage lending without proof of borrower's income.
Commercial companies are often not allowed to hold large equity stakes in a bank, and vice versa. Regulators may insist that financial service functions be separated. This may by splitting into in-house departments with Chinese Walls between them. Or insisting on separately capitalised group companies or splitting up the company.
Anti-monopoly provisions restrict activity/prices

Duty of care
Prescribing appropriate financial institution behaviour to avoid harm to customers.
No misrepresentation, fraud or mis-selling. Knowing the financial position, investment goals, knowledge and experience of the customer before providing advice or selling a service to ensure that it is suitable, e.g. not selling a high risk investment to someone needing a low risk portfolio.
Eliminating unfair terms in contracts.
A firm must protect client assets while it holds them on behalf of the client – e.g. ringfencing them – see Exhibit 15.12

Complaints handling and compensation
Put systems in place to assist consumers pursuing a complaint against a firm and to secure recompense.
Provide compensation if a firm is bust, e.g. bank deposit insurance

Exhibit 15.10

China starts crackdown on insider trading

Jamil Anderlini

Market participants say the market is reacting to what appears to be the government's most serious campaign in years aimed at tackling rampant insider trading and stock manipulation.

The slide has coincided with a nationwide campaign, announced last week by the State Council, China's cabinet, to crack down on the "grim situation" of insider trading.

Mainland China's markets are notoriously opaque and speculative. Everyone, from small retail investors to top fund managers, appears to trade on tips from contacts who claim to have "inside" information.

"If you ask any Chinese investor whether they think a chairman or executive of a company is trading in their own stock, nine out of 10 would expect that to be the case just as they would expect a government official to be taking bribes," says Fraser Howie, co-author of *Red Capitalism* and other books on China's stock markets.

Last week's announcement marked the first time the Chinese cabinet has publicly addressed the issue of insider trading and was

interpreted by investors as a signal of the government's determination to head off a new stock bubble.

Chinese investors and fund managers appear to be bracing themselves for the wave of prosecutions as the first casualties of this latest campaign begin to emerge.

Chinese media reports and market speculation claim that three top fund managers have already been investigated in the new crackdown.

All three individuals have denied they are the subject of any investigation, but two of them have resigned from their positions at leading Chinese investment funds.

Although, if true, this would be the most serious crackdown on insider trading in years, Beijing has a dismal record of catching people for a practice that everyone in the market says is rampant. In the past eight years, the China Securities Regulatory Commission (CSRC) has sent less than 90 cases of insider trading for criminal investigation and prosecution in Chinese courts.

And, in September this year, a real-estate company called Dragon

Wing Development became the first Chinese corporate entity convicted of insider trading since 1997.

Wu Jinglian, a Chinese government economist, recently described the country's stock market as being in the "age of robber barons" and pointed to insider trading by government officials as especially common.

In private, senior regulatory officials admit that government officials and their relatives are some of the worst offenders and the problem is serious even among those who are supposed to be policing the market.

Liu Jipeng, an economics professor at the China University of Political Science and Law, says that in China government officials have the power to influence even minor business decisions at listed companies, giving them enormous advantages over ordinary investors and a huge incentive to buy shares in anticipation of their own actions.

Source: Financial Times, 25 November 2010, p. 34. Reprinted with permission.

Exhibit 15.11

FSA sinks talons into Eagle with £2.8m fine

By Brooke Masters

The Financial Services Authority has fined Simon Eagle, chief executive of defunct stock-broking group SP Bell, £2.8m for share ramping – the largest financial penalty ever levied on an individual by the City regulator.

Mr Eagle was also banned from working in the financial services industry.

According to the FSA, Mr Eagle deliberately set out to push up the price of Fundamental-E Investments, an Aim-quoted

company. He instructed SP Bell to sell the company's shares to their clients and rolled the purchases from account to account to create the impression of rising demand.

The share price rose from $2^1/_2$p in May 2003 to $11^3/_4$p in July 2004,

Exhibit 5.11 continued

earning Mr Eagle £1.2m and enabling him to purchase 10 per cent of the company.

Mr Eagle, who represented himself and could not be reached for comment, paid disgorgement of £1.3m in profits and a penalty of £1.5m.

Margaret Cole, FSA enforcement director, said: "This scheme was rotten throughout and at the core was Simon Eagle. He showed a breathtaking disregard for his clients, for his duty as an approved person and chief executive, and for the effect of his scheme on markets... This tough action shows that

we are determined to keep dishonest cheats, like Simon Eagle, out of financial services."

Winterflood Securities, the marketmaker that put through Mr Eagle's manipulative trades, has already paid a £4m penalty. The FSA found, and the Court of Appeal agreed, that the firm, part of Close Brothers, and its traders has committed unintentional market abuse by failing to stop suspicious trades.

Mr Eagle's case dates back to 2004, so it predates the FSA's recent efforts to bring criminal charges in serous market abuse cases. People familiar with the process said that

if the investigation had started more recently, the regulator would probably have considered using its powers of prosecution.

Martyn Hopper, an attorney at Herbert Smith, called the fine a "significant result" for the FSA.

He said: "Market manipulation cases are much harder to prosecute than insider dealing because they are so complex. It's quite significant that the FSA has managed to get a result on one."

Source: Financial Times, 21 May 2010, p. 16. Reprinted with permission.

Exhibit 15.12

FSA fines two City brokers for not ringfencing clients' money

FT

By **Alistair Gray**

The City watchdog flexed its muscles again yesterday when it punished divisions of Astaire Group and Close Brothers for failing to segregate clients' money from their own.

The Financial Services Authority said Rowan Dartington and Close Investments put investors at risk in breaches during the financial crisis and fined them £511,000 and £98,000 respectively.

The penalties came days after the FSA fined JPMorgan's securities arm a record £33m for similar problems. They form part of the wider investigation into how banks and brokers protect client money.

Margaret Cole, the FSA's enforcement director, said: "Firms should be in no doubt that if they fail to get their house in order in this regard we will take action against them."

Shares in Astaire were suspended eight weeks ago after the City stockbroker said £1.4m went missing at Rowan Dartington, its wealth management arm.

The FSA said Rowan Dartington "could not rely on the accuracy of its internal books and records" after it failed to properly test and implement a new software system installed in May 2007.

Under FSA rules, banks, brokers and insurance companies are required to ringfence client money and keep it in separate accounts with trust status.

Of the £1.4m missing money, more thank £1m remains unrecovered, Astaire added.

Meanwhile, Close Investments was fined for similarly failing to properly protect client money in the two years to January 2010.

No clients lost money as a result of the errors, both Close and Astaire said.

Source: Financial Times, 8 June 2010, p. 22. Reprinted with permission.

Exhibit 15.13   UK financial services industry regulation

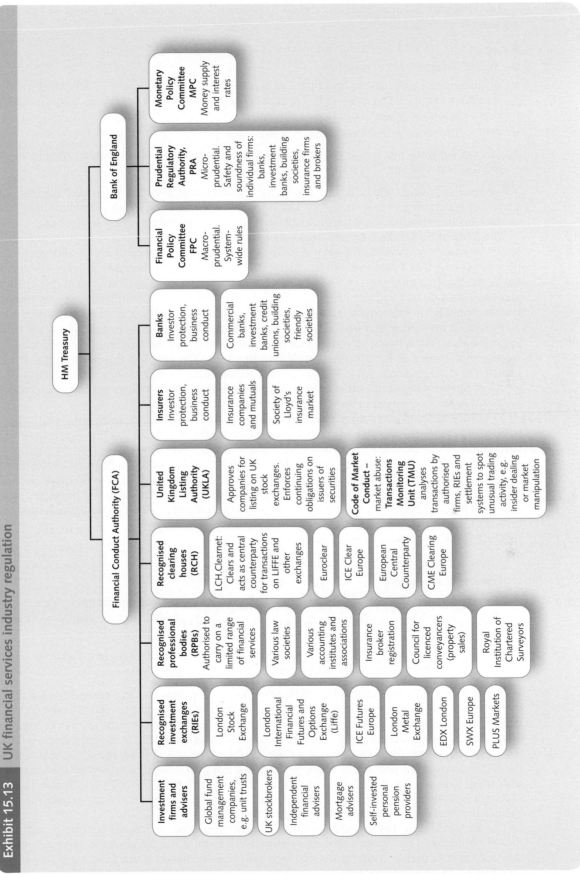

The Financial Conduct Authority retains responsibility for protecting consumers and preserving market integrity, covering:

- investor protection, including that for bank customers;
- market supervision and regulation;
- business conduct of banks and financial services, including approval of consumer-related managers and the supervision of investment managers and other firms whose failure would be non-systemic (they would not cause a contagion);
- civil and criminal enforcement of market abuse rules;
- UK Listing Authority – supervision of initial public offerings and subsequent monitoring of listed companies (*see* Chapter 9).

While most companies will be answerable to only one regulator, the PRA-supervised firms will be under the supervision of two regulators. The FCA will cover the good treatment of customers and general business conduct while the PRA will cover safety and soundness of the institution.

The Bank of England's **Financial Policy Committee,** making decisions that apply to the entire sector to ensure systemwide financial stability including the avoidance of credit and asset bubbles, meets only four times a year to set rules. It might, for example, increase capital requirements above the Basel III minimum in normal times to ensure safety, and then lower them in a crisis so that the banks do not withdraw lending when the economy is already suffering. It may impose system-wide higher risk weights against specific classes of bank assets in markets that appear too exuberant. It may insist that banks increase their forward-looking loss provisioning when lending is growing fast. It might set nationwide borrowing limits such as maximum amount of a loan relative to the value of the property backing up that loan. The FPC has also been set the task of identifying emerging threats to the system from the 'shadow banking sector' – this comprises a group of financial institutions that individually or collectively act like banks but are not as heavily regulated as banks. *See* later in the chapter for more on shadow banking.

The PRA division does the hard work of day-to-day handling of individual institutions to ensure firm level stability and soundness. Of course, the Bank also has the Monetary Policy Committee to set interest rates and adjust the money supply – *see* Chapter 7.

The FSA/FCA can be described as semi-detached from government: it is financed by the industries it regulates, but its powers come from legislation; it often consults the financial services companies before deciding on principles, rules and codes of conduct, but it has basic principles approved by the government and it is answerable to the Treasury, which appoints its board, and through them Parliament.

The FSA/FCA tries to achieve the following:

1   Maintaining confidence in the financial system.

2   Protecting consumers.

3   Reducing financial crime, such as money laundering, fraud and insider dealing.

4   Financial stability – contributing to the protection and enhancement of stability in the UK financial system.

5   Helping people to gain the knowledge, aptitude and skills to manage their financial affairs effectively by promoting public understanding of the financial system.

While pursuing these objectives the regulator makes it clear that it is not removing all risk for the investor. Investment risk is an inherent part of the system and those who take the benefits from an investment when everything goes right have to accept that from time to time investment losses will occur. Also, the complete absence of consequences for the client should a financial firm fail may encourage laziness in choosing a place for their money and other moral hazards, and so the FSA/FCA does not promise to rescue failed firms, nor guarantee all money deposited/invested with them (but see Financial Services Compensation Scheme later). The FSA/FCA also tries to maintain healthy competition by encouraging entry into the industry and trying to strike the right balance between the costs and benefits of tighter regulation.

The FSA/FCA also has powers over unregulated firms and persons regarding breaches of money laundering regulations and short selling. In addition, it has the power to prosecute unauthorised firms or persons carrying on regulated activities. Its market abuse powers are very strong – *see* **Exhibit 15.14** for an example.

Exhibit 15.14

Broker fined for 'market abuse' in FSA commodities crackdown

By **Javier Blas**

A commodities broker was fined for "market abuse" by the Financial Services Authority yesterday in the first such penalty and a sign that the regulator is starting to crack down on price manipulation in the London-based raw materials markets.

The FSA said it had fined Andrew Kerr, a former broker at Sucden Financial, £100,000 and banned him from working in the financial industry. Mr Kerr has agreed to settle the case.

The regulator said Mr Kerr "deliberately manipulated" the Liffe robusta coffee futures and options markets on August 15 2007 on behalf of a client, which it did not identify. It is unclear whether the FSA will take action against the client, but coffee market participants said it was likely to do so.

Mr Kerr organised a series of trades during a key period of the day, which serves to price options, to boost artificially the price of coffee futures, the FSA said. Mr Kerr moved the market to $1,752 a tonne, up from about $1,145. The "small size of the coffee futures market meant that it was particularly vulnerable to price manipulation," the FSA said.

"Mr Kerr's financial benefit from the market manipulation was limited to his commission," the regulator said. But it added he was "doubtless motivated" by a desire to attract further business. Brokers estimated the commission at as low as $100 and no more than $500.

Source: *Financial Times*, 3 June 2010, p. 17. Reprinted with permission.

The FSA/FCA has a budget of over £450 million per year and employs more than 3,000 well-paid staff. The amount each of the 29,000 regulated firms pays depends on its size and the type of business it undertakes. The minimum fee of £844 in 2011 was paid by 43 per cent of those businesses. The FSA/FCA also receives money from financial penalties imposed on errant firms (raising about 10–20 per cent of its budget). **Exhibit 15.15** describes the anger felt by many in the financial service sector about the high level of charges. **Solvency II** is a strengthening in the capital reserves and risk management standards for all EU medium and large-sized life insurance companies. It is designed to reduce the chance of consumer loss or market disruption in insurance due to the firm experiencing a large decline in asset values (e.g. the share market declining by 40 per cent or more, or a large rise in bond defaults), say because of another financial shock like that in 2008.

Exhibit 15.15

Insurance industry says watchdog's fees 'unjustified'

By **Paul J Davies**

The insurance industry has attacked the higher fees being demanded by the City watchdog as "unjustified" and expressed concerns about "the lack of effective oversight" of how it sets its budget requirements.

The Financial Services Authority said its annual funding needs would rise 9.9 per cent to £454.7m when it issued its business plan for 2010–11 in mid March. Today is the deadline for industry responses to the plan.

The regulator said the rise in fees, which are paid by all regulated financial companies, reflected a tougher approach to supervision and enforcement in the wake of the crisis and the cost of preparing for European capital rules – known as Solvency II – that are being drawn up in Europe.

The Association of British Insurers, however, claimed that the latest increase on top of a 36 per cent rise last year would mean many insurers will have seen their fees double over the past three years.

"It is difficult to see the justification for these increases as insurers and insurance regulation were proven to be both strong and

▶

Exhibit 15.15 continued

stable during the financial crisis" said Peter Vipond, director of regulation and tax at the ABI.

"We are concerned about the lack of effective oversight [by government and parliament] of the way in which the FSA sets its budget requirements and charges levies to firms."

The FSA said much of the increase in its funding needs stemmed from the costs of Solvency II, which alone would cost £100m–£150m by the time it was implemented in 2012. The regulator plans to take on 460 more staff, or an extra 14 per cent.

Source: Financial Times, 12 April 2010, p. 4. Reprinted with permission.

The introduction of a single super-regulator for a country was unusual when in 2001 the FSA was given powers over several areas of financial services (it was set up in 1997 with a more limited remit). However, the advantages of a unified approach are well recognised today and many countries (e.g. Japan, Germany and Sweden) have a super-regulator for their financial sectors. Increasingly, financial institutions provide a wide range of services and so a unified approach to regulation is needed. This allows greater insight into the firm's practices and avoidance of the problem of financial activities falling between the cracks of separate regulator's responsibilities. Also, there are economies of scale in investigation and monitoring (having six different regulators visiting a firm and asking similar questions is clearly inefficient for the regulated and the regulator).

Authorisation

All firms or individuals offering financial advice, products or services in the UK must be authorised by the FSA/FCA.[3] Engaging in a regulated activity without authorisation can result in a two-year prison sentence. The FSA insists on high standards when assessing for authorisation. These require competence, financial soundness and fair treatment of customers. Firms are authorised to carry out specific activities, e.g. giving financial advice only, or managing a client's money in a fund, or stockbroking.

Monitoring

Even after initial approval, firms cannot relax as the FSA/FCA continues to monitor adequacy of management, financial resources and internal systems and controls. It also insists that any information provided to investors is clear, fair and not misleading. If firms fail to meet these standards they can be fined or even stopped from doing business. The FSA/FCA also works closely with the criminal authorities and uses civil and criminal powers. The following are some of the rules it enforces:

- Independent financial advisers have to ensure the product sold to an investor is suited to their needs – this requires knowledge of the consumer's personal and financial situation.

- Insurance companies, especially those providing with-profits policies, endowments and other savings products, should have significantly more assets than they owe to customers under the policies they have sold them.

- Market 'abuse' is not allowed. For example, individuals are not allowed to trade on inside information or to manipulate share prices by, for example, providing misleading information to the market.

- There must be a clear separation of clients' money from the firms' money ('ring fencing').

The FSA/FCA cannot look in detail at each of the 29,000 companies it regulates on a routine basis because this would impose an excessive cost burden on the industry, so it uses a 'risk-based approach'. It has a process for categorising firms into risk classes based on the likely impact that

---

[3] Or have special exemption. A list of those registered as authorised by the FSA can be found at www.fsa.gov.uk.

a firm would have on consumers or the market if it was to breach the rules (e.g. number of consumers likely to be affected and the systemic threat) and on the probability of that particular problem occurring. Firms that pose little risk of operating against the objectives of the FSA/FCA, labelled 'low-impact firms', are allowed to submit basic information in regulatory reports twice a year. They do not have regular visits. This 'light touch' regulation applies to over 90 per cent of the firms under supervision. This allows the regulator to concentrate resources on activities and institutions that appear to pose the greatest risk to customers and markets.

For medium and high-impact firms a regular (on a cycle of 1–4 years) risk assessment is made. This is used to determine a risk mitigation programme proportionate to the risks identified. More work is put in by the regulator in investigating a firm if the firm is large or particularly risky. High-impact firms will be subject to 'close and continuous' work, resulting in a schedule of regular visits to senior managers and a detailed examination of the control functions the firm has in place.

Of course, any firm that seems to be operating outside the spirit of the rules will receive a lot more attention, even if it is normally classified as low-impact. As a first step it may be required to complete a questionnaire. It may then receive a number of visits, and ultimately be punished (or individuals punished) through, for example, being fined, losing authorisation to operate or being subject to legal action.

The FSA/FCA emphasises broad principles rather than its rules. The problem with a regulator sticking strictly to rules is that they can result in inflexibility – just 'ticking boxes' – rather than concentrating the minds of the regulated on the spirit underlying the rules. Also a rule-based approach can be less flexible when it comes to permitting innovation from existing or new firms. A principles-based approach has less prescription and allows the regulator to meet new situations (e.g. new tricks by those smart people in the City) by using some degree of judgement rather than being hidebound by rules. Lawyers will forever be finding loopholes in rules; they find that more difficult if the rules are set in a framework of general principles, when the principles have greater weight.

Following the financial crisis the FSA became much less 'light-touch' and much more intrusive – *see* **Exhibit 15.16**. There is a danger that London will lose the goodwill and openness that exists between the regulated and the regulator, and end up with a more antagonistic US-type of relationship where lawyers are to the fore.

Exhibit 15.16

FSA's new approach ruffles feathers

FT

Brooke Masters

City firms say the Financial Services Authority's new approach to regulation, which includes sitting in on bank board meetings and issuing bigger fines for misbehaviour, makes the agency more like the intrusive US Securities and Exchange Commission than the "light touch" policeman they had been used to.

Before the 2007 collapse of Nothern Rock, FSA supervisors were best known for a co-operative approach that, at least in the minds of those being supervised, emphasised box-ticking over deep understanding.

The relationship teams that interacted with banks would want proof that firms had policies in place to deal with common issues, such as handling customer complaints and keeping data private, but rarely delved into great detail.

If a firm called to report a compliance problem, in most cases the FSA's reaction would be to ask what the firm was doing internally to prevent a recurrence, rather than to open an investigation.

All that has changed. Hector Sants, FSA chief executive, has warned City executives that regulators will be "judging the judgments"

that board members make. The shift has come as something of a shock.

"No firm is 100 per cent compliant, but now when firms report problems, they are no longer saying 'thank you for telling us about it'. We are moving from a reporting system to one where the FSA looks into things and makes its own mind up," Says Tim Dolan, lawyer with Pinsent Masons.

Lawyers and bankers round the Square Mile are saying that the regulator appears to be moving towards an "enforcement-led" approach, in which the FSA uses fines and crimi-

Exhibit 15.16 continued

nal cases to deter misbehaviour rather than a quiet word.

"Five years ago, enforcement was the dog that didn't bark. Now it is very much on the top table," says a partner at one top City law firm.

In practical terms, the shift is clearly visible. City brokers and banks say that when supervisory visits uncover issues, the FSA is now requiring them to hire outside experts – usually from the big audit firms – to do what are known as section 166 investigations, after the section of the law that enables them.

The reports are funded by the firms but not controlled by them and go straight to the FSA. "It's £600,000 to £1m – and you've got [an accounting firm] hanging around the place for 10 weeks," fumes one chief executive.

Executives and board members are finding they can no longer tell the FSA that particular issues are being handled by the risk or compliance departments.

"If the FSA asks someone an question, it expects them to have a answer," says Jan Putnis, of lawyers Slaughter & May. "'The FSA has said: 'Why don't you know about that?'"

The regulators have also invited themselves to board meetings of at least half a dozen big banks and brokers. In some cases they have made presentations, but in others they have simply watched the proceedings and interviewed directors afterwards.

"Governance is important, so how else would you assess it?" says Lyndon Nelson, the FSA's head of risk.

The FSA is also making it harder for financial services firms from other European Union countries to exercise their right to "passport" into London.

They recently demanded detailed liquidity information from a French firm and are trying to impose conditions on how the London branch would be treated in a failure.

US banks, meanwhile, report that they are being required to keep more cash or highly liquid bonds in their UK branches to prevent a repeat of the Lehman Brothers failure, when it emerged that the US parent had swept most of the UK's cash across the Atlantic before its collapse.

Above all lawyers and bankers say, the FSA is poking its nose into new areas, asking to review client files, looking at particular contracts and generally asking for more data.

"They are looking more closely at contract terms for retail custom-ers and saying you need to change them. They have always had the power but they are using it in a more strategic way then we have seen before," says Michael Raffan, partner at law firm Freshfields.

Not surprisingly, many in the City are not pleased.

"Our clients feel it is a sledge-hammer to crack a nut," says Tom O'Riordan of the Paul Hasting law firm. "The regulators are invasively telling them that [certain synthetic financial] products are not appropriate for these markets. They will say, if you were to sell it, we would want x, y, z conditions."

Some observers wonder if the FSA is setting itself too hard a task.

"The FSA is creating very high expectations for its engagement with banks," says James Gardner, a partner at Linklaters. "Interviewing incoming management for licensing purposes is one thing – but if the FSA really is going to carry on monitoring whether executives properly understand their business model, this may stretch its resources very thin."

Source: Financial Times, 20 July 2009, p. 21. Reprinted with permission.

Consumer complaints

There are three steps a person with a grievance can take.

1 *Raise the issue with the financial service company* All firms should have a formal complaints procedure, and the complainant is encouraged by the FSA/FCA to start here, giving the firm a chance to right the wrong. After all, the firm is best placed to check its records and see what happened. Most regulated firms have **compliance officers** whose job it is to ensure the FSA/FCA rules are being followed. Roughly three out of four complainants dissatisfied with the response of the company choose not to pursue it further, believing it would be futile to do so. However, there are further positive steps a complainant could take.

2 *Independent complaints scheme* Most financial services firms belong to an independent complaints scheme – the FSA/FCA insists in most cases.[4] These are beneficial to the system because they increase the confidence of investors and other financial clients by responding to the fear of consumers that they lack knowledge (information asymmetry) to be able to stand up to the financial professionals. There are two types: arbitration schemes and ombudsman schemes. Under both the complaint will be investigated and, if found to be justified, the firm will be ordered to put matters right. Many of the schemes provide for a financial award, up to a maximum of £150,000. Under arbitration both the complainant and the firm agree in advance to

---

[4] The firm's literature should set out its regulatory body and scheme.

accept the arbitrator's decision. Importantly, in accepting this the complainant gives up the right to take the case to court. The advantage is that it is much quicker and cheaper than going to court. Under the **Financial Ombudsman Scheme**[5] **(FOS)** the independent and impartial ombudsman collects together the facts of the case and arrives at what seems to them a reasonable and fair settlement. The firm is then under an obligation to accept the decision,[6] but the complainant remains free to take the case to court. The service is free to consumers. The ombudsman's approach is less legalistic than arbitration and allows for more 'common-sense' factors of fairness. The FOS looks at complaints about most financial problems involving:

- banking;
- insurance;
- mortgages;
- credit cards and store cards;
- loans and credit;
- pensions;
- savings and investments;
- hire purchase and pawnbroking;
- money transfer;
- financial advice;
- stocks, shares, unit trusts and bonds.

If the FOS finds in the complainant's favour it can order a firm to pay compensation up to a maximum of £150,000. The FOS may even order the firm to pay compensation for distress and inconvenience on top of financial loss.

3   *Go to court* Litigation is often expensive, time-consuming and frustrating, and so should only be contemplated as a last resort. A relatively fast and informal service is provided by the small claims track or the small claims court (maximum claim in England £5,000, Northern Ireland £2,000 and Scotland £3,000). The complainant does not need a solicitor, and court fees are low. The complainant may not even have to attend the court as judges can make judgements on the paper evidence.

Compensation

The complaint steps described in the last section are all well and good if the firm that has behaved badly is still in existence. But what if it is defunct? The **Financial Services Compensation Scheme (FSCS)**[7] can compensate consumers (and small companies) if an *authorised* company is unable to pay money it owes. Note that if a consumer does business with a firm not authorised by the FSA/FCA, e.g. an offshore company,[8] they are not covered by FSCS or the complaints procedure.

The FSCS service is free for the consumer and small business. It covers investments (e.g. bad advice, bad investment management), money deposited in accounts (at banks, building societies and credit unions), insurance products (e.g. car insurance, life insurance), mortgage advice, pensions and endowments. For investments and home finance (mortgages) the maximum payout is £50,000 per person. For deposit claims (e.g. bank accounts) the scheme pays £85,000 per person (per bank). For insurance the scheme pays 90 per cent of the loss.

In order to compensate victims of mis-selling or other malpractice the FSCS raises money from the financial service firms via a regular annual levy supplemented by additional levies in years of high compensation payouts, and this can be very costly for them – *see* **Exhibit 15.17**. Examples of some of the charges for the Keydata compensation: Brewin Dolphin paid £6m, IG Group paid £4 million and Charles Stanley £2.6 million. No wonder they were upset! – but, at least the compensation helps maintain the image of fairness to customers.

---

[5] www.financial-ombudsman.org.uk or telephone 0845 080 1800.
[6] Although they can appeal through the courts.
[7] www.fscs.org.uk
[8] One based and regulated outside the UK, such as Bermuda or Jersey.

Exhibit 15.17

Fund managers to foot Keydata bill

By Alice Ross

Fund management groups are being forced to pay £236m towards the cost of compensating investors who lost money in the collapse of Keydata, the structured product provider, in a move that has angered the industry.

Some larger fund managers face unexpected bills totalling millions of pounds after the Financial Services Compensation Scheme said the fund management industry would have to take the hit for a mis-selling case that would normally have been paid for by financial advisers.

Nearly 30,000 investors lost money after buying "death bond" packages sold by Keydata, which was put into administration in 2009. Almost 20,000 are eligible to claim compensation from the FSCS, which this week said it would have to raise a special levy in order to make the payments.

The £326m levy was so large the FSCS had to pass most of the cost on to fund managers, even though they are in a separate group from financial advisers for compensation purposes.

Investments intermediaries are subject to a £100m limit on the amount they have to pay each year.

The FSCS said it was the first time it had demanded that one group pay for the errors of another.

In a sign of the impact that the stock market crash of 2008 and 2009 has had in exposing unsafe products sold to private investors, the FSCS said the need to raise the special levy was a result of the "sharply increasing costs of paying claims resulting from major investment failures".

Fund managers are privately furious that they are being expected to foot most of the bill – £236m out of the total of £326m – which will be shared among all the fund managers that sell products to retail investors.

The Investment Management Association, the trade body for fund managers, said the Keydata case related to the sale of unlisted bonds issued by a Luxembourg vehicle that owned US life assurance policies – and so had "nothing to do with fund management as conducted by its members".

Source: Financial Times, 23 January 2011, p. 34. Reprinted with permission.

Regulation of markets

Financial markets need high-quality regulation in order to induce investors to place their trust in them. There must be safeguards against unscrupulous and incompetent operators. There must be an orderly operation of the markets, fair dealing and integrity. However, the regulations should not be so restrictive as to stifle innovation and prevent the markets from being competitive internationally. London's financial markets have a unique blend of law, self-regulation and custom to regulate and supervise their members' activities.

The FSA/FCA supervises exchanges, clearing houses and settlement houses. It also conducts market surveillance and monitors transactions on seven **recognised investment exchanges (RIEs)** – *see* **Exhibit 15.13**. The RIEs work with the FSA/FCA to protect investors and maintain the integrity of markets. Much of the monitoring and enforcement is delegated to the RIEs. The London Stock Exchange, for example, vets new stockbrokers and tries to ensure compliance with LSE rules, aimed at making sure members (e.g. market makers and brokers) act with the highest standards of integrity, fairness, transparency and efficiency. It monitors market makers' quotations and the price of actual trades to ensure compliance with its dealing rules. It is constantly on the look-out for patterns of trading that deviate from the norm with the aim of catching those misusing information (e.g. insider dealing), creating a false or misleading impression to the disadvantage of other investors or some other market distorting action – *see* **Exhibit 15.18** for an example of a successful prosecution for insider dealing. Mr Littlewood received a prison sentence of over three years, Helmy Omar Sa'id got two years and faced deportation and Angie Littlewood receive a suspended prison sentence.

The LSE, in partnership with the FSA/FCA, also requires companies to disseminate all information that could significantly affect their share prices. It insists on timely and accurate director statements to the stock market so that there is not a false market in the company's shares – *see* **Exhibit 15.19**.

Exhibit 15.18

Insider dealers face sentence in long-running FSA case

Jane Croft and Brooke Masters

One of the most far-reaching probes carried out by the Financial Services Authority will reach a conclusion today as the investment banker Christian Littlewood, his wife Angie and her friend Helmy Omar Sa'id are sentenced to their part in a £2.15m insider trading scam.

The unravelling of the case began in August 2008 when a trading platform flagged a series of well-timed trades before a takeover of Highway Insurance plc.

The FSA found that four separate accounts all linked to Mr Sa'id, a Singaporean national, had collectively made £160,000 buying shares in the two weeks before the deal, according to FSA officials who worked on the case. When the FSA looked at Mr Sa'id's other trading records, they spotted suspicious trades around 21 merger announcements.

"Insider lists" of everyone known to have had advance warning of the deals revealed that Dresdner Kleinwort Wasserstein bankers had worked on 15 of them – but not on the Highway takeover.

Then the FSA investigators struck gold: records showed that Mr Littlewood, a senior Shore Capital corporate financier working on the Highway deal, had previously worked at DKW.

More than two years, four search warrants and 1,700 gigabytes of data later, Mr Littlewood, his wife Angie who traded under her maiden name of Siew-Yoon Lew, and her friend Mr Sa'id have pleaded guilty to eight counts of criminal insider trading from 2000 to 2009. They are scheduled to be sentenced this morning.

The case underlines the FSA's renewed determination to uncover and punish insider dealing by market professionals.

"This outcome is the result of a long, hard slog," said Margaret Cole, FSA managing director for enforcement. Faced with 10 years of banking and trading data that showed the trio had made £590,000 in profits on £2.15m in trades, Mr Littlewood's lawyer argued at the sentencing hearing that the other two participants were more culpable. Although the 37-year-old banker, who made as much as £350,000 a year, had repeatedly provided information to his wife, Lord Macdonald QC said his client was not aware of the "scale" of the trading.

Lord Macdonald said Mr Littlewood had told his wife to limit her trades to £20,000 rather than the hundreds of thousands she and

Mr Sa'id invested before takeovers in stocks such as RCO Holdings and Staffware.

"The level of trading is a strong pointer here, he was not aware of its scale," Lord Macdonald told the court, adding: "No sensible person could believe this trading would fail to be noticed... it was suicidal."

But Nicholas Dean QC, prosecuting, told the court that before Mr Littlewood met his wife, his then girlfriend – dubbed "Miss N" – had invested in shares linked to DKW clients, as suggested by Mr Littlewood.

"Miss N carried out all the trading and Christian Littlewood provided the capital but she added some savings," Mr Dean told the court, adding that the couple had made profits of £20,000. Soon afterwards, Mr Littlewood met his wife and they married in 2000. Within months, Mrs Littlewood and Mr Sa'id, an old friend of hers from Singapore, were buying thousands of pounds in shares before price-sensitive deals that caused the price to rise.

Source: *Financial Times*, 2 February 2011, p. 3. Reprinted with permission.

Exhibit 15.19

FSA to probe profit warnings

By Michael Peel, Jennifer Hughes and Stanley Pignal

Leading companies are being probed by the financial watchdog over possible failures to disclose key data to the stock market, in a wide-ranging crackdown that threatens fines and prosecutions.

Top City lawyers say they have seen a surge in inquiries by the Financial Services Authority about whether businesses – including Rentokil Initial, the support services company, and Rok, the building

group – kept investors properly informed ahead of profits warnings that sent shares tumbling.

Lawyers say the regulator's focus on disclosure could lead to disputes with companies over

▶

Exhibit 15.19 continued

what information should have been revealed and when, especially given the chaotic wider circumstances surrounding many decisions during the credit crisis.

The regulator's more frequent approaches to leading multinationals during the past few months shows it was "really hot on people updating the market promptly", said Sara George, a barrister at Allen & Overy and a former FSA prosecutor.

"The expectation is you drop everything else. You gather all your directors and advisers in one room and you start drafting, overnight if necessary, to make sure there is not a false market in your shares," she said.

Lawyers for big companies said they had seen a sharp rise in the numbers of letters sent by the FSA's supervisory arm to ask for background information about profits warnings, particularly when these resulted in share price falls of 10 per cent or more.

The FSA's inquiries have led to an increase in cases referred to its enforcement department for full investigation, people familiar with the matter say. The probes, which are still at an early stage, could lead to fines for companies for breaking listing rules or criminal prosecutions of executives for "market abuse".

Source: Financial Times, 5 January 2009, p. 1. Reprinted with permission.

Regulation of companies

If you invest in a company by buying its shares or bonds, you have a right to receive information about that company, and to expect that there are laws and other pressures to discourage the management from going astray and acting against your interests.

There are various checks and balances in the corporate world, the most important being the requirements under the Companies Acts. The Department for Business, Innovation and Skills enforces the law and is able to intrude into a company's affairs. Accountants and auditors also function, to some extent, as regulators, helping to ensure companies do not misrepresent their position. The Financial Reporting Council oversees corporate reporting. Furthermore, any member of the public may access the accounts of any company easily and cheaply at Companies House (*www.companieshouse.gov.uk*). In the case of mergers of listed or other public limited companies, the City Panel on Takeovers and Mergers acts to ensure fairness for all shareholders.

The Office of Fair Trading and the Competition Commission investigate, rule on and enforce remedies with regard to anti-competitive behaviour – *see* **Exhibit 15.20** for an example of their impact on financial services.

Exhibit 15.20

RBS fine sets cost on 'cosy and rotten practices'

FT

By **Michael Peel** and **Sharlene Goff**

The near-£30m fine on Royal Bank of Scotland for breaking competition rules is a small fraction of the cost of bailing out the company but a big reminder of official determination to tackle a long-neglected area of corporate law.

RBS's penalty for sharing loan-pricing data with Barclays employees dwarfs most Financial Services Authority sanctions and is almost as much as the punishment imposed this year on the arms dealer BAE Systems to settle a five-year criminal probe into suspected bribery.

The RBS fine is the latest in a series of cases brought by the Office of Fair Trading as it grapples with the cosy but illegal sharing of pricing information that it believes has become rooted in several big industries.

Ali Nikpay, the OFT's senior director of cartels and criminal enforcement, says: "What we are trying to do with cases like this is send a clear message that this kind of activity really does carry substantial penalties".

RBS is being fined because it admitted its staff "unilaterally"shared information with Barclays on the pricing of loans to large law, accountancy and property firms, the OFT says. The communication took place "on the

▶

Exhibit 15.20 continued

fringes of social, client or industry events or through telephone conversations".

The penalty is the culmination of a two-year investigation triggered when Barclays volunteered information on its role, a decision that meant the bank escaped penalties under OFT leniency rules aimed at encouraging informants.

The RBS fine came on the same day as Philip Collins, the OFT chairman, said the watchdog had begun to ask questions about whether City markets were competitive and offered good value to consumers and the wider economy.

Mr Nikpay says Mr Collins's comments were not co-ordinated with the RBS announcement and

not part of a wider OFT assault on the banking industry although he acknowledges the watchdog takes a "holistic look at these things"

Source: Financial Times, 31 March 2010, p. 3. Reprinted with permission.

A free press has a very important role in ferreting out and reporting foul play, poor service, incompetence and chicanery. The pensions regulator (discussed in Chapter 4) also has quite an impact on financial services – *see* **Exhibit 15.21** for an example.

Exhibit 15.21

Regulator sets sights on pension fund risks

By **Norma Cohen**

Pension funds will be prevented from investing in risky assets, including stocks, by the Pensions Regulator under plans to stop weaker companies with large pension shortfalls from making huge bets.

David Norgrove, chairman of the regulator, will outline his concerns that some schemes are taking risks that could leave a bigger hole in the industry funded Pension Protection Fund in a speech to funds today.

"We have to ensure that they are not putting all their money on the 2:30 at Newmarket and if it doesn't work out, they will fall back on the PPF," he said. "To some extent, we have seen some behaviour like that."

Some schemes were so underfunded their only hope of recovery lay in big bets. The regulator was also concerned about standards of governance, particularly for smaller schemes.

"We come across a fair degree of criminality at the smaller end of schemes," said Mr Norgrove.

Investment curbs would affect a few weak companies initially but as schemes close to new members and to future accruals trustees will need to insure that the investment strategy takes as few risks as possible. "Eventually it will move up the scale," he said. Companies will need to be well funded and have few or no investment risks.

Under those circumstances, defined benefit schemes might cease to be significant investors in equities and property.

Mr Norgrove said that despite cash injections from employers, defined benefit schemes today are not much better funded. "Contributions have had to run to keep up with rising longevity, falling discount rates and shortfalls in investment returns," he said. "We clearly can't have a situation where we move from recovery plan to recovery plan."

Source: Financial Times, 7 December 2010, p. 1. Reprinted with permission.

Fraud and money laundering

Fraud costs the UK economy an estimated £38 billion annually, equivalent to £765 for every adult member of the population.[9] The FSA/FCA is one of several UK organisations that investigates and responds to suspicions of fraud. The **City of London Police** is, however, the 'National Lead

---

[9] The National Fraud Authority figures for 2011 – *see* www.attorneygeneral.gov.uk/nfa/WhatAreWeSaying/ NewsRelease/Pages/fraud-costs-the-UK-over-38billion.aspx. Two-thirds is public sector fraud (e.g. benefit and tax fraud), but that still leaves a lot of financial sector fraud – estimated at £3.6 billion.

Force' for fraud with a remit to create a centre of excellence for fraud investigations and to use its expertise to help police forces across the UK. It has a large squad (178 personnel at the last count) focused solely on preventing and detecting fraud.[10] It is particularly concerned with organised crime groups and securing major convictions. It manages hundreds of fraud investigations each year. In 2010, for example, it identified 124 organised criminal gangs and had 154 defendants charged and awaiting prosecution at court.

Here are some examples of the frauds they stopped:

- In a boiler room investigation,* a Danish man was arrested by Spanish police and extradited to the UK in May 2009. This followed a joint investigation by the City of London and Dyfed-Powys Police. The fraudster was sentenced to nearly five years in prison after pleading guilty to running criminal operations that sold worthless or highly inflated shares to more than 500 investors, with a combined loss of more than £2 million.

- Operation Soundwave led to a national and international investigation into a £25 million boiler room fraud. Over Christmas 2009, Northumbria and Greater Manchester Police assisted 20 City officers in making 12 arrests in the north of England. At the same time detectives travelled to Sweden to arrest the main suspect and later had him extradited back to the UK.

- A man who attempted to steal more than $170 million was sentenced to nine years after an international investigation. The 32-year-old Edinburgh man's complex fraud involved taking over corporate accounts before he was stopped by City of London Police officers.

Source: The City of London Police Annual Report 2009–10

*In a **boiler room scam** the fraudsters harass potential investors through regular telephone calls or over the internet, eventually persuading them that they should invest in a 'great opportunity'. Needless to say, they are selling something of little or no value. Millions of pounds each year are taken from savers – particularly old people.

The **National Fraud Authority (NFA)**, operating a website **Action Fraud**, is the UK's national fraud reporting centre providing a central point of contact for information about fraud. People who are scammed, ripped off or conned can report a fraud, find help and support. The National Fraud Authority is an umbrella government organisation which co-ordinates and oversees the fight against fraud.

Insurance companies club together to pay for the **Insurance Fraud Bureau (IFB)** to combat bogus insurance claims. If this was not tackled all our insurance premiums would rise to pay for payouts to criminals lying about damage, theft, etc. Even when the bogus claims are kept under control by the IFB we are still paying far more for our insurance than would be the case if everyone was honest – estimated at an extra £44 p.a. by the IFB. The IFB concentrates on networks of fraudsters who repeat the crime, leaving most of the one-off frauds, such as deliberate damage to goods, to the insurance companies.

The **Serious Fraud Office (SFO)** investigates and prosecutes serious or complex fraud and corruption exceeding £1 million in value. It is a part of the criminal justice system – but remains an independent government department (with a high degree of autonomy from political control). It builds cases and brings criminals to justice and so helps maintain confidence in the UK's business and financial institutions.

If a suspected fraud is likely to give rise to widespread public concern, be complex and thus require specialist knowledge to investigate, or be international in scope, then the SFO is likely to be the organisation that tackles it. While much of its work is financial service related the majority is not, for example it investigated whether BAE Systems had been involved in corruption (bribes to Saudi officials) when selling arms to Saudi Arabia in the £43 billion Al Yamamah deal. **Exhibit 15.22** describes a successful SFO prosecution for fraud.

---

[10] The City of London Police deal with other financial crimes and the threat of terrorism in the Square Mile as well as normal community policing.

Exhibit 15.22

Two found guilty in Torex fraud case

By **Jane Croft** and **Philip Stafford**

Two former Torex Retail executives have been convicted of defrauding the shareholders of former Aim-quoted group.

Edwin Dayan and Christopher Ford were directors at the retail softwear company's subsidiary XN Checkout (XNC) and caused more than £1.65m in fictitious profits to be recognised within the company's published accounts.

The conviction draws a line under the case that was taken on by the Serious Fraud Office in 2007 after whistleblowers from Torex came to the prosecutor with information about alleged accounting irregularities at the company.

Mr Dayan was managing director of XNC and sat on Torex's main board as chief technology officer. Mr Ford was XNC's finance director.

The subsidiary had a contract to provide a depot repair service for equipment to Mitchells & Butlers, the pub and restaurant operator. After it lost the contract to IBM, it continued to provide the service as it was retained by IBM as subcontractor.

After 2003 IBM renegotiated the agreement with XNC so the amount it paid was reduced, which led to a shortfall in XNC's income.

The court heard that during the preparation of Torex's 2005 annual accounts, the two men created documents to make it look as if M&B had agreed to pay the shortfall and were liable to pay an extra sum to XNC for the service.

That was given to Torex's auditors BDO Stoy Hayward to justify an additional £756,000 in profit that was then entered into the accounting records of the parent Torex.

The two men continued the fabrication in Torex's 2006 accounts that were also bolstered by a further £900,000. In reality no money was owed by M&B and there was no agreement between the two companies about the shortfall.

Source: Financial Times, 20 January 2011, p. 20. Reprinted with permission.

Money laundering is concealing the source of illegally obtained money. It is the process of changing money obtained from crimes, such as drug trafficking, into a form that appears to be legitimate. The process often involves multiple international transactions across currencies and financial institutions in order to obscure the source. To combat money laundering the UK regulators require that any bank, share broker or other financial firm being asked to open an account for a person or company has to verify the customer's identity. Even solicitors carrying out house conveyancing are required to see purchasers' forms of identity, such as passports, driving licence and utility bills (even if they have known the client for years and asked for the same documents only months before for an earlier transaction!). Financial firms are also required to look out for suspicious transactions and report them. The FSA/FCA penalises firms that lack adequate systems and controls to detect and report money laundering. There are some people within the finance industry who help money launderers, using their contacts and knowledge about jurisdictions abroad where policing is lax. Criminal investigators are tasked with tracking them down. Suspected money laundering is reported to the **Serious Organised Crime Agency (SOCA)**, which is assisted by other investigating agencies such as the police. The City of London Police also have a major role here.

European Union regulation

As well as national financial service regulation we have another layer for the countries in the European Union. Only a brief overview can be provided here. We will concentrate on the basic principles that the EU legislators are applying and look at a few examples of the pan-European rules that have already been introduced.

The fundamental objective of the EU is to promote movement towards a single market in financial services regardless of national boundaries. It is thought movement toward such a goal will bring about improved welfare for consumers and faster economic growth. The **Financial Services Action Plan (FSAP)** is the process devised by the European Commission to provide momentum towards a single integrated market. It has three strategic objectives (not all are achieved):

1 Establishing a single market in wholesale financial services, including:

- the establishment of a common legal framework for securities and derivatives markets;
- providing the necessary legal certainty to underpin cross-border securities trading. This includes integrated securities settlement systems;
- the removal of the outstanding barriers to raising capital on an EU-wide basis.

  Many national rules hinder the offering of securities in other EU countries, making it costly. One action is to have common minimum rules on the contents of a prospectus when a company is raising money by selling securities (already, once a prospectus has been approved in one EU country it has a 'passport' to sell the securities in others);

- having a single set of rules for financial statements for listed companies. To a large extent this has been achieved because all EU countries have adopted International Financial Reporting Standards;
- a joined-up pension framework so that people can move to work in another country without fear of pension complications;
- rules on cross-border mergers of public limited companies, protecting minority shareholders.

2 Making retail[11] markets more open and secure. Creating a legal framework to allow financial institutions to offer their services throughout the EU by removing obstacles that hamper the cross-border purchasing or provision of these services (e.g. single bank account, mortgage credit). This includes:

- making sure that consumers are provided with clear and understandable information when they are investing some or all of their savings in another country;
- there are efficient and effective procedures for redress for incompetent, crooked or other malpractice in cross-border services;
- reducing the charges on low-value transfers of money between EU countries by encouraging more efficient, cheaper cross-border payments system, e.g. on credit card payments.

3 Strengthening the rules on prudential supervision. This covers areas such as capital and liquidity adequacy of banks and solvency margins for insurance companies.

The two key elements for achieving these objectives have been the principle of mutual recognition and the application of agreed minimum standards:

- ***Mutual recognition*** If a financial firm has been authorised to offer a service by one EU member state it is then free to operate in other member states selling its service there without requiring further authorisation from the host countries.
- ***Minimum standards*** Agreeing minimum standards for financial services. This ensures that if a firm is authorised by its home regulator it abides by reasonably tough rules that would protect clients throughout the EU – there is not a 'race to the bottom' by countries deliberately offering a lax regulatory environment to attract financial service firms to set up in their countries or to promote the growth of their domestic firms by lowering their costs or allowing doubtful activity.

Note that there is no attempt to create either full harmonisation in which the rules are identical in each country ('one size fits all'), or a common regulatory structure with a large centralised bureaucracy or a single European regulator in Brussels. The member states would not accept this level of interference in their economies. Politically, it is far easier for them to agree to adopt minimum standards and a 'passport' system, in which the granting of a licence in one EU country is sufficient for a financial firm to sell its services in all EU member states.

---

[11] Individuals rather than institutions.

Dozens of 'directives' have been published by the European Commission and then implemented by member countries. Some of the most significant directives:

- **Capital Liberalisation Directive, 1988** Money can be moved from one country to another without controls. This free movement was given a boost when the majority of EU states adopted the euro in 1999.

- **Capital Requirements Directive, 2006** Common minimum rules on bank and investment firm capital adequacy.[12] The directive links to the Basel rules – *see* Chapter 7.

- **First Banking Directive, 1977** Banks became free to open branches or establish subsidiaries in other member states. These were to operate under the supervisory rules of the host country. This limited the range of services to only those accepted by the host country's regulations. Thus a subsidiary of a French bank in Spain could only do what the Spanish regulators allowed local banks to do.

- **Second Banking Directive, 1989** A single banking licence allowed operations throughout the EU. This allowed a bank licensed in one EU country to sell its services in other EU countries regardless of whether the host country normally allows these services to be provided by its domestic banks. The activities permitted under this rule are those on an approved list and include securities business as well as banking services. As a safeguard the home and host country supervisors exchange information as they now have to share supervision. Home country regulators have the main responsibility, but host country regulators can impose monetary policy-related rules, e.g. liquidity reserves, and supervise consumer protection.

- **Markets in Financial Instruments Directive (Mifid), 2007** This is aimed at reducing the cost of trading securities and increase market competition in the investment services provided by stockbrokers, fund managers, derivative dealers and banks. Firms authorised in one member state to undertake specific services are able to perform the same ones in other EU countries. It also opened up stock exchanges to more competition by allowing trading to take place away from regulated exchanges. See Chapter 8 for more on Mifid, including a discussion of the 'best-execution' requirement for stockbrokers to obtain the best price, low cost of execution, speed and the likelihood of settlement of the trade going well.

- **Market Abuse Directive, 2003** A common EU legal framework for preventing and detecting market abuse and for ensuring a proper flow of information to the market. EU countries must reach the minimum standards in the directive. National regulators may pursue market abusers, including insider dealers, by either a civil case (requiring merely proof 'on the balance of probabilities') or a criminal case ('beyond reasonable doubt' – a much higher standard of proof). It also requires greater interchange of information between national regulators to better unearth wrong-doing.

- **Transparency Directive, 2004** All issuers of publicly-traded securities must provide annual financial reports within four months of their year-ends. The directive also sets the minimum content of annual, half-yearly and interim management statements. In addition there are minimum notification requirements for both issuers and investors in relation to the acquisition and disposal of the major holdings in companies, e.g. major shareholdings have to be publicly reported and any subsequent changes announced.[12]

In addition to agreeing to abide by directives, occasionally the EU states agree that they will all impose common rules on the financial sector – *see* **Exhibit 15.23** for an example on bankers' bonuses.

There is now a college of national supervisors – the **European System of Financial Supervisors.** Under this, three authorities, focused on different aspects of financial services, were created in 2011:

---

[12] The securities activities of banks require a capital reserve, separate to that for banking activities.

[13] The notification requirement is triggered when the size of holdings reaches, exceeds or moves below certain thresholds (5 per cent, 10 per cent, 15 per cent, 20 per cent, 25 per cent, 30 per cent, 50 per cent and 75 per cent). The shareholder will be required to inform the issuer. The issuer will then inform the market. These are minimum thresholds; the UK has adopted a tougher approach, with a lower limit of 3 per cent and then every 1% change to be announced.

Exhibit 15.23

EU sets new pay practices in stone

Brooke Masters, Megan Murphy and Nikki Tait

The European Union's new rules forcing banks to defer bonuses and limit cash payouts to employees would be among the strictest in the world.

The legislation sets in stone practices on pay that banks were forced to adopt after the crisis and introduces another layer of rules in an area which banks had hoped had moved out of the regulatory spotlight.

Under legislation agreed by the European Parliament and the council of member states, banks in the 27-nation bloc would have to defer 40 to 60 per cent of bonus payments for at least three years and at least half of the money would have to be paid in shares or other instruments linked to the banks' performance.

One effect, perhaps unanticipated by legislators, will be that lower-paid bankers are likely to be more affected in the short term than the high fliers in the public eye.

The biggest global institutions still generally determine the mix of cash and shares awarded on a sliding scale. Star traders allotted a $5m bonus will receive as little as 5 per cent of that in cash, while a relatively junior banker earmarked for $100,000 may still receive the total in cash at some banks.

That means the new EU rules would probably have the most impact on junior employees, rather than top rainmakers who already live with big deferrals.

Supporters of the EU bonus restrictions argue they will prevent banks from slipping back to the guaranteed bonuses and cash bonanzas that were common before the financial crisis.

"For too long, the incentives have been all wrong, encouraging excessive risk taking," argued Michel Barnier, EU internal market commissioner, who oversees financial regulation this week.

"These rules will help to put an end to the dangerous short-term behaviour we have seen," he claimed, adding that Brussels wants similar rules for the rest of the financial sector. But industry officials warn that inflexible legislation could undermine Europe's ability to attract and retain top talent. While the US and Asian nations in the Group of 20 have endorsed the principles of deferred bonuses and limiting cash payments, most have shield away from strict rules.

"If the G20 countries based outside of the EU fail to implement equivalent regimes these rules will have little impact in terms of eliminating risk-taking behaviour but will have a hugely detrimental impact upon our international competitiveness," said Stuart Fraser, policy chairman of the City of London.

In practice, the EU rules are not all that different from those set down in several European countries like the Netherlands and by the UK Financial Services Authority.

Source: Financial Times, 2 July 2010, p. 21. Reprinted with permission.

- **The European Banking Authority (EBA)** Headquartered in London, the EBA is concerned with ensuring EU-wide coordination on regulatory and supervisory standards with a focus on the stability of the financial system. It stress-tests European banks – examines and probes for weaknesses by imagining a set of adverse circumstances (e.g. a perfect storm combination of a rise in interest rates, high loan default rates and loss of bank access to money market funds). It will have much to say on the adoption of new capital and liquidity reserve standards over the next few years.

- **The European Insurance and Occupational Pensions Authority (EIOPA)** Based in Frankfurt, it focuses on EU coordination of rules for the protection of insurance policy holders, pension scheme members and beneficiaries. In the immediate future it will implement a new set of capital reserve rules for insurance companies (Solvency II), which results in more risk leading to more capital requirements.

- **The European Securities and Markets Authority (ESMA)** Located in Paris, it tries to improve the EU regulators' coordination on the functioning of markets and strengthen investor protection. It is charged with harmonising the regulation of issuance and trading of shares, bonds and other securities. It covers matters of corporate governance, auditing, financial reporting, takeover bids, clearing and settlement and derivative issues. It is currently working on a new directive on hedge funds and private equity and new rules on over-the-counter derivatives trading. It already has powers to fine credit rating agencies for breaching EU rules.

The committees of these three organisations, made up of the heads of national regulators, have the responsibility to try to achieve greater convergence of regulatory standards and practices across the EU. They will produce technical standards and plan for the adoption of EU regulatory law throughout the EU – some countries have been lax in adopting the EU-wide rules in the past and so need a little chivvying along.

Despite past attempts to gain greater cooperation at the EU level, regulation remains mostly a national affair, embedded in domestic regulation. However, these new bodies will have the power to override national authorities in 'emergency situations'. Also, the political mood seems to be to grant more powers to pan-EU regulatory bodies, and it is thought that their powers to override national regulators will be extended into a greater range of products and markets than those listed above.

In addition to these three, a new EU body, the **European Systemic Risk Board (ESRB),** was set up in 2011. It has whistle-blowing powers to prevent future crises. That is, it has powers to issue warnings and recommendations when it sees threats to economies or financial systems. The European Central Bank takes the lead role in the ESRB, but national central bankers dominate the board. We will have to wait and see if it is merely a talking shop fretting over, say, house prices in Spain and excess property lending in Ireland, but lacking teeth to do anything about a wayward economy.

Many people, particularly in the City of London, think that too much control over financial services and markets is being granted to pan-European regulators, who may not fully understand the needs of a financial centre like the City and who may have political agendas (e.g. to grab business from London) – *see* **Exhibit 15.24.**

Exhibit 15.24

Traders fear threat of political agendas   **FT**

Nikki Tait

Radical changes to Europe's system of supervising its banks, insurers and securities markets, taking effect this week, are central to plans by the European Union to bolster financial regulation and oversight in the 27-country bloc.

The creation of four new pan-European agencies is aimed at helping to prevent a repeat of the region's financial crisis. But the new supervisory bodies are being watched warily by traders and executives in the City of London, Europe's biggest financial centre.

London's fear is that the new entities' job of drawing up common, harmonised rules for the finance sector and protecting it from systemic problems will be overtaken by political agendas, and that the bodies will not appreciate sufficiently the need to keep Europe competitive with other global financial centres.

"It's an unsettling process. A single market [for financial services] is a good thing... But people need to be close to the markets they're regulating," says Barney Reynolds, head of the financial regulatory group at the law firm Shearman & Sterling in London.

The concern he adds is that the agencies may follow "a moralistic political agenda", rather than conduct a "dispassionate technical exercise".

On Tuesday, a European Commission spokesman hailed the creation of the new regulators as a "turning point in financial supervision in Europe", saying they would strengthen a system whose weaknesses had been laid bare by the financial crisis. In the process, they will also make Europe's financial sector more attractive to investors and more competitive, the spokesman said.

The four new agencies comprise three European supervisory authorities (ESAs) to oversee the banking, insurance and securities markets sectors, together with a broader European Systemic Risk Board (ESRB), which will warn about dangers building in the financial systems.

All three are being created from existing pan-European "committees" which are made up of national regulators from the 27 EU member states and function on a co-operative basis. By contrast, the new authorities will have more powers – including the ability to override national authorities in emergency situations – and greater resources, both in terms of staff and finance.

But the ESAs are expected to acquire about 150 staff in total in 2011 and cost about €40m ($53m) to run. That staffing should then double during the next four years – although it will remain a pale shadow of some national supervisors. The UK's Financial Services Authority, for example, employs more than 3,000.

The process of building up the ESAs' responsibilities is likely to accelerate through this year. ▶

Exhibit 15.24 continued

At least a dozen significant legislative proposals for the financial services sector are due to be released in 2011, and most will give specific rulemaking rights to the ESAs.

That means City institutions and their advisers will need to keep a close watch on Brussels, but also on Paris, Frankfurt and London, as they try to guard against excessive regulation.

"Unless you're keeping a hawk-eye, you blink and miss things," warns Mr Reynolds.

Source: Financial Times, 5 January 2011, p. 6. Reprinted with permission.

Global regulation

Following the financial crisis in 2008 there is much more enthusiasm within the policy-making classes for supra-national regulation, or, at least, coordination of regulatory rules. A good example of rules being set on a global scale (or at least for most of the world) is the Basel Committee's rules on bank capital reserves and liquidity rules – *see* Chapter 7.

To gain help from the International Monetary Fund, a country must open markets to overseas trade, flows of capital and liberate banks from stifling controls. The Financial Stability Board is charged with the task of developing supervisory and other policies to promote financial stability. It also coordinates with the IMF in sounding alarm bells about vulnerabilities in financial systems. For example, it is currently working on the too big to fail problem in banking.

There are a number of international organisations established by the relevant industry itself to promote higher standards of behaviour. For example, the International Swap and Derivatives Association (ISDA) is a global financial trade association for the world's major institutions that deal in privately negotiated derivatives.[14] Its purpose is to identify and reduce the sources of risk in the derivatives business. It sets standards for members, writes standardised contracts that members are encouraged to use, comments on netting and collateral arrangements, promotes sound risk management practices, and advances the understanding and treatment of derivatives and risk management.

Some gaps in the system?

One major problem is overcoming the political obstacles to effective international regulation. There is always a temptation for the country that would like to build up its financial service sector to race to the bottom, because footloose financial institutions are attracted by 'lightness of regulation' and will move. Thus regulatory arbitrage will always be with us, with some aspects of finance moving to the least regulated jurisdiction. Hence the need for robust international agreements on minimum standards. The problem is that each country examines a proposal for a tighter rule in the light of an assessment of the impact on its competitiveness. The intention of the national policy makers too often seems to be 'to find a regulatory regime that crimps competitors more than one's own companies'.[15] Hence the slowness in achieving worldwide (or G20) agreement on issues as diverse as bankers' bonuses (the new US rules are more flexible than the EU ones) or banning investment banks from proprietary trading (the US is strict, other countries less so, leaving loopholes).

On the other hand, the widespread recognition that under-regulation contributed to the 2008 financial crisis has reinforced the view that policy makers do not serve their people well if they allow too much slack. The tension between the desire for an easy-going light-touch regulated financial centre – egged on by bankers, etc. threatening to leave for more accommodating environments – and the need to protect consumers will always be with us. It will be interesting to see

---

[14] Its membership also includes many of the businesses, governmental entities and other end users that rely on over-the-counter derivatives.

[15] Joseph Stiglitz in *Financial Times*, 10 February 2010, p. 13.

how the politicians resolve the tension over the next few years (it does not help that such a high proportion of political party donations in the UK and US come from the finance sector).

Another major problem is that the regulators have paid little attention to the less obvious, but powerful, sectors within the financial system. I'm referring to the 'shadow banking system'. This is the collection of non-bank entities that move money and risk around the global financial system, bypassing the banks. The usual candidates to be included in this group include:

- *Hedge funds* Raising funds directly from wealthy individuals and institutional investors, they have a large and growing role in debt, equity and derivative markets. A failure of a large hedge fund could destabilise the markets and the banking system given that banks are often the counterparties in derivative and other deals, and they also lend to the funds.

- *Private equity funds* Originally set up to raise funds from long-term investors to invest in non-quoted companies, some have branched out into debt trading, and even have hedge fund arms. Failure of these ventures could pose a threat to banks and the wider system, as could a failure of a large leveraged buyout. Some funds have loan books larger than that of many banks. Much of that money was raised through bank borrowing, thus a failure to repay could imperil banks.

- *Money market funds* These bypass the banks by taking short-term money from investors to buy commercial paper and other securities. It was their abrupt withdrawal from lending via commercial paper, etc. following some defaults that caused corporates and banks to be unable to rollover their debt, leading many to failure in 2008. Many money market funds supplied cash for repayment over, say, 30 days. This was used to lend out on 25-year mortgages. Thus, non-banks (money market funds and special purpose vehicles issuing long-term bonds as securitised bonds) became conduits for maturity transformation, where short-term money is lent out into long-term securities. The expectation by those who borrowed from the money market funds was that they would always be there to supply more money, every 30 days. This was a silly assumption.

- *Securitisation* The securitisation of assets such as sub-prime mortgages greatly assisted the growth of the housing finance market. These securitised bonds were then repackaged (*see* Chapter 16) which created pockets of extreme risk in the financial system and as a result many banks failed.

- *Commodity funds* The banks are bypassed and money is placed at risk with large bets being taken on future movements of commodity prices using derivatives and borrowing. They might blow up resulting in huge losses, which might pose knock-on risks throughout the financial system, as banks might face bad debts.

- *Clearing houses* These processors of trading activity handle billions every day, asking for only a small margin in their role as central counterparties. They tend to have little capital in reserve, so in the event of a few defaults by traders the system might be in trouble. Contagious fear could spread if investors worry about the clearing house's promise to guarantee every deal. This could halt lending and other deals for a while.

- *Inter-dealer broker* If one of these organisations standing between traders and connecting them fails then billions could be lost.

Thus we face the problem that the regulators are busy constructing a strong Maginot Line,[16] such as raised Basel III capital and liquidity reserves, to protect banks, while the real danger may lie to the side. Risk can and has moved from the regulated and transparent elements in the system to the less regulated opaque sector. The shadow banks have become enormous sources of credit and may well fuel the next bubble, as they assisted with the Noughties one.

The Financial Stability Board has begun looking at shadow banking, and various governments and national regulators are starting to draw up lists of non-banks that might pose a systemic risk. But we are currently, 2011, only at the talking stage. The Federal Reserve Board has put together a chart showing the players in shadow banking – see www.ft.com/shadowbanks.

---

[16] Defensive fortifications along the French–German border which Hitler avoided by going through Belgium in 1940.

Concluding comments

It is a constant battle to maintain high levels of integrity and competence in the financial service sector. It is a battle that will never be completely won. Some people, even highly paid people (*viz.* investment bankers in 2007), will regularly come up with new ways of losing other people's money through stupidity, greed or chicanery. Despite this pessimistic conclusion we have to acknowledge that we have come a long way in making this vital economic sector reasonably safe for savers and businesses. The financial crisis showed that there are many issues that were not properly dealt with in the past. And so we are currently going through a period of toughening up the controls to avoid risks to consumers and the taxpayer. This is being done on an international scale with an unprecedented degree of cooperation and coordination between the national regulators, as they recognise the potential to miss malpractice in nationally focused systems. We certainly live in interesting times when it comes to regulation. Much will change over the next few years, and where the balance between light-touch and strict control will fall we cannot yet tell. But at least as you hear the debate on TV and read the newspapers over the next few years you will, having read this chapter, understand the core principles and issues around which it revolves.

Key points and concepts

- **Compliance costs:** putting in place systems and training to ensure that financial service staff behave according to the regulations.

- **Asymmetric information** occurs when one party in a negotiation or relationship is not in the same position as other parties, being ignorant of, or unable to observe, some information which is essential to the contracting and decision-making process. Managers and other employees of financial service companies have an information set that is often superior to that of the clients. This can lead to exploitation, for example, buyers of a financial product are unable to assess the true risk and return. Asymmetric information can lead to:

  - Reduced safety and soundness for the consumer or a financial market counterparty, e.g. insufficient surplus of assets over liabilities to be able to cover their obligations, concentration risk or bad management of client's stock broker accounts, pension funds and collective investment vehicles.
  - Producing conflicts of interest within financial service firms which can result in the misuse or concealment of information or its false or biased use.
  - Facilitating bad behaviour such as fraud.
  - Hiding and tolerating incompetence.

- **Contagion risk:** the failure of a company may lead to the failure of others leading to instability in the whole system. Regulation aims to ensure that individual banks have enough capital and liquid assets, that they write and continuously update 'living wills', insist that none is either too big to fail nor that it is too big to save.

- **Monopolistic/oligopolistic exploitation**: where one or a few firms exert undue market power over product pricing.

- **Dangers in a regulatory system**:

  - **Moral hazard:** the presence of a safety net encourages adverse behaviour.
  - **Agency capture:** when those that are supposed to be regulated take some control of the regulatory process and modify it to suit the interests of the producers rather than the consumers.
  - **Excessive compliance cost:** raised fees and lower returns for customers.
  - **Stifling innovation and growth:** the requirements to be licensed and costs of compliance impose such a bureaucratic load that few or no firms dare to enter the industry, thus inefficient monopolies/oligopolies are sustained.

▶

- **Types of regulation**:

    - **By the industry**. Positive points: a clear need to preserve high reputation; people most knowledgeable about the industry are those working in it. Negative points: temptation to slacken the rules; barriers to industry entry; difficult to regulate a firm that has activities in many different financial service industries; dependence on funding from the industry itself to function encourages softness on the producer.
    - **By the government**. Positive point: industry needs an externally imposed regulator. Negative points: heavy handed, less agile than practitioners.
    - **By government agency**. Positive points: legislative back-up to ensure that the agency has strong powers without political control; greater practitioner respect than would be the case if government officers were in charge; poachers turned game-keepers are likely to be more alert and agile in keeping up with the latest tricks; statutory framework that prevents a slackening of the rules or restricting entry of new firms; the regulator can be given the powers to examine a full range of financial services and markets. Negative point: can be expensive.

- **Competitive laxity/regulatory arbitrage:** financial centres that try to impose strict rules find that financial institutions respond not by tightening their systems and raising probity, but by moving operations to a different jurisdiction, where the rules are looser.

- **Core elements of regulation:**

    - licensing;
    - disclosure and monitoring;
    - mandatory information provisions and consumer education;
    - prudential limits;
    - restricting activities;
    - fair trading on exchanges;
    - duty of care;
    - exposure limits;
    - complaint handling and compensation;
    - penalties.

- The UK's **Financial Services Authority, FSA**, dominated the scene for over a decade. It is a 'super-regulator' with oversight of a wide range of financial sectors. In 2013 it will split in two. The main body, the **Financial Conduct Authority, FCA,** will be a super-regulator, retaining responsibility for protecting consumers and preserving market integrity. The **Prudential Regulatory Authority, PRA**, a subsidiary of the Bank of England, will handle individual regulation of the 2,200 biggest banks, insurers and brokers on the issue of safety and soundness (micro-prudential supervision).

- The Bank of England's **Financial Policy Committee, FPC,** makes decisions that apply to the entire sector to ensure system-wide financial stability, including the avoidance of credit and asset bubbles.

- **The FSA/FCA's objectives**:

    - maintaining confidence in the financial system;
    - protecting consumers;
    - reducing financial crime;
    - financial stability;
    - helping people to gain the knowledge, aptitude and skills to manage their financial affairs effectively by promoting public understanding of the financial system.

- **The FSA/FCA's tasks**:

    - authorisation of financial service firms;
    - monitoring of adequacy of management, financial resources, internal systems and controls, and ensuring that any information provided to investors is clear, fair and not misleading;
    - insisting on systems to deal with complaints;
    - through the Financial Services Compensation Scheme, compensating badly treated consumers;
    - regulation of markets for fair dealing and integrity. **Recognised investment exchanges (RIEs)** work with the FSA/FCA to protect investors and maintain the integrity of markets;
    - regulation of companies.

- Other constraints on bad behaviour: Companies Acts, accountants and auditors, the Financial Reporting Council, FRC, Companies House, City Panel on Takeovers and Mergers, Office of Fair Trading and the Competition Commission, a free press, the pensions regulator.

- **Fraud** investigation in the UK: FSA/FCA, City of London Police is the 'National Lead Force' for fraud, National Fraud Authority (NFA), the Insurance Fraud Bureau (IFB), Serious Fraud Office (SFO).

- **Money laundering** is concealing the source of illegally obtained money. It is the process of changing money obtained from crimes, such as drug trafficking, into a form that appears to be legitimate. Suspected money laundering is reported to the **Serious Organised Crime Agency, SOCA**.

- **European Union regulation** is motivated by movement towards a single market in financial services. The **Financial Services Action Plan (FSAP)** is the process devised by the European Commission to provide momentum towards a single integrated market. It has three strategic objectives:

  - establishing a single market in wholesale financial services;
  - making retail markets more open and secure;
  - strengthening the rules on prudential supervision.

- The two key elements for achieving the FSAP objectives have been the principle of **mutual recognition** and **the application of agreed minimum standards**. There is no attempt to create either full harmonisation in which the rules are identical in each country ('one size fits all'), or a common regulatory structure.

- Dozens of '**directives**' have been published by the European Commission and then implemented by member countries.

- **European System of Financial Supervisors** is a college of national supervisors. Under this, three authorities, focused on different aspects of financial services, were created in 2011:

  - **The European Banking Authority, EBA:** ensuring EU-wide coordination on regulatory and supervisory standards with a focus on the stability of the financial system.
  - **The European Insurance and Occupational Pensions Authority, EIOPA:** focuses on EU coordination of rules for protection of insurance policyholders, pension scheme members and beneficiaries.
  - **The European Securities and Markets Authority, ESMA**: tries to improve the EU regulators' coordination on the functioning of markets and strengthening of investor protection.

- **European Systemic Risk Board, ESRB:** has whistle-blowing powers to prevent future crises, powers to issue warnings and recommendations when it sees threats to economies or financial systems.

- **Global regulation:** the Bank for International Settlements (e.g. Basel III); the **International Monetary Fund** insisting that a country must open markets to overseas trade, flows of capital and liberate banks from stifling controls; the **Financial Stability Board, FSB**, is charged with the task of developing supervisory and other policies to promote financial stability and sounding alarm bells about vulnerabilities in the financial system; the **International Swap and Derivatives Association (ISDA)** is a global financial trade association for the world's major institutions that deal in privately negotiated derivatives.

- **Remaining gaps in regulation:**

  - political pressure to opt for national light-touch regulation;
  - the threat posed by the **shadow banking system:** a collection of non-bank entities that move money and risk around the global financial system, bypassing the banks. Includes hedge funds, private equity funds, money market funds, securitisation, commodity funds, clearing houses and inter-dealer brokers.

References and further reading

To keep up to date and reinforce knowledge gained by reading this chapter I can recommend the following publications: *Financial Times, The Economist*, and *The Bank of England Quarterly Bulletin (http://www.bankofengland.co.uk/publications/quarterlybulletin/index.htm)*.

Acharya, V. V., Cooley, T. F., Richardson, M. P. and Walter, I. (2010) *Regulating Wall Street: The Dodd–Frank Act and the New Architecture of Global Finance*. New York: New York University Stern School of Business.
    Discusses the regulatory environment and challenges in post-crisis America.

Dowd, K. (1996) 'The case for financial laissez-faire', *The Economic Journal*, Vol. 106, May, pp. 679–687.
    Argues that free-banking without regulations is stable.

Geneva Reports on the World Economy. Geneva and London: International Center for Monetary and Banking Studies and Centre for Policy Research (http://www.cepr.org/pubs/books/geneva/geneva.asp).
    Dozens of reports on the reform of the international financial system written by leading economists are available.

Mishkin, F. S. (2000) 'Prudential supervision: why is it important and what are the issues?' NBER Working Paper 7926.
    Describes the problem of asymmetric information for the financial system and thus the need for regulation.

Llewellyn, D. (1999) 'The economic rationale for financial regulation', FSA Occasional Paper 1, April, Financial Services Authority, London.
    Explains the welfare benefits of regulation of financial services.

Websites

Action Fraud www.actionfraud.org.uk
Bank of England www.bankofengland.co.uk
Centre for Policy Research www.cepr.org
City of London Police www.cityoflondon.police.uk
Companies House www.companieshouse.gov.uk
Department for Business, Innovation and Skills www.bis.gov.uk
European Banking Authority www.eba.europa.eu/
European Central Bank www.ecb.int
European Commission www.ec.europa.eu
European Insurance and Occupational Pensions Authority www.eiopa.europa.eu
European Securities and Markets Authority www.esma.europa.eu/
Federal Reserve www.federalreserve.gov
Financial Ombudsman www.financial-ombudsman.org.uk
Financial Stability Board www.financialstabilityboard.org
Financial Services Authority www.fsa.gov.uk
Insurance Fraud Bureau, IFB www.insurancefraudbureau.org
International Center for Monetary and Banking Studies www.icmb.ch
International Swap and Derivatives Association www.isda.org
National Fraud Intelligence Bureau (NFIB) www.nfib.police.uk
International Monetary Fund www.imf.org
Serious Fraud Office, SFO www.sfo.gov.uk
Serious Organised Crime Agency www.soca.gov.uk

Video presentations

Bank chief executives and other senior people describe and discuss aspects of their businesses, including the impact of regulation, in interviews, documentaries and webcasts at Cantos.com. (www.cantos.com) – these are free to view.

Case study recommendations

See www.pearsoned.co.uk/arnold for case study synopses.

Also see Harvard University: http://hbsp.harvard.edu/product/cases

- The Financial Reporting Environment: Adverse Selection and Moral Hazard Problems in Capital Markets (2001) Authors: Krishna Palepu, Paul Healy, Amy Hutton and Robert S. Kaplan. Harvard Business School.
- The Financial Crisis of 2007–2009: The Road to Systemic Risk (2009) Author: George (Yiorgos) Allayannis. Darden, University of Pennsylvania. Available on Harvard Case Study website.
- Regulation: A Transaction Cost Perspective (A Tribute to Oliver Williamson) (2010) Author: Pablo T. Spiller. *California Management Review*, winter Vol.52, No.2. Available on Harvard Case Study website.
- The 2007–2008 Financial Crisis: Causes, Impacts and the Need for New Regulations (2008) Authors: Danielle Cadieux and David Conklin. Richard Ivey School of Business. Available on Harvard Case Study website.
- The Weekend That Changed Wall Street (2009) Authors: Christopher Brandriff and George (Yiorgos) Allayannis. Darden, University of Pennsylvania. Available on Harvard Case Study website.
- Bear Stearns and the Seeds of its Demise (2008) Author: Susan Chaplinsky. Darden, University of Pennsylvania. Available on Harvard Case Study website.
- The Fall of Enron (2010) Authors: Paul Healy and Krishna Palepu. Harvard Business School.

Self-review questions

1 What are compliance costs?

2 What is concentration risk?

3 What is money laundering?

4 Illustrate moral hazard with reference to financial services.

5 Describe agency capture and provide an example.

6 Why might regulation stifle financial service industry innovation and growth?

7 What is competitive laxity?

8 What does the UK's Prudential Regulatory Authority do?

9 What does the UK's Financial Policy Committee do?

10 What is a recognised investment exchange?

11 List the FSA/FCA's objectives.

12 Use an illustration to help explain market abuse.

13 What does the Financial Ombudsman Scheme do?

14 How does the Financial Services Compensation Scheme help customers of financial service companies?

15 Explain and illustrate the anti-fraud role of the City of London Police and the Serious Fraud Office.

16 What are the roles of the European Banking Authority, the European Insurance and Occupational Pensions Authority, the European Securities and Markets Authority, European Systemic Risk Board?

Questions and problems

1 Write an essay constructing a case for and against regulation of financial services.

2 Describe, explain and illustrate the problems of asymmetric information, contagion and monopoly/oligopoly power, which can act against the interests of customers of financial services.

3 Describe and explain three examples of conflicts of interest faced by financial service firms, and recommend regulations to alleviate the problems.

4 Weigh up the arguments for and against financial sector regulation being conducted by the industry itself, the government or by a government agency.

5 Describe two types of financial fraud and briefly outline activities of the UK organisations that counter fraud.

6 Write an essay describing, explaining and illustrating the following key elements of regulation:

   ● licensing;
   ● disclosure and monitoring;
   ● mandatory information provisions and consumer education;
   ● prudential limits;
   ● restricting activities;
   ● fair trading on exchanges;
   ● duty of care;
   ● exposure limits;
   ● complaint handling and compensation;
   ● penalties.

7 Describe how UK financial services are regulated, including an explanation of the main agencies and their roles, their objectives and their methods of operation including authorisation, monitoring, complaint handling, compensation, market regulation and company regulation.

8 Describe and illustrate with examples the impact of European Union regulation on financial services. Include an explanation of the principles behind EU directives.

9 Explain the potential threats from the shadow banking system and make recommendations to alleviate the problem.

10 Do you think that there needs to be greater international cooperation in the regulation of financial services? Explain your reasoning and provide examples.

Assignments

1 If you are familiar with a financial service firm describe the regulatory structure that it has to comply with and report your estimates of the costs of compliance.

2 As a personal user of financial services (e.g. family bank account, house insurance, share owner, unit trust holder, paying into a pension fund) describe the concerns you have when you place trust in the managers of these providers. To what extent are you reassured by the regulatory system currently in place to protect you, and to what extent do you think there is room for improvement? Make recommendations.

Web-based exercises

1 Go to the website of the Financial Services Conduct Authority to obtain information on the different tasks that it has to carry out. Write a report explaining the areas of finance in which it intervenes and describe the nature of that intervention. Pay particular attention to the actions against financial crime and describe three recent successful prosecutions for breaches of the rules.

2 Go to the European Commission website (www.ec.europa.eu) and other websites to read about the current proposals to introduce new financial service industry directives or modifications of old directives. Describe and explain the motives for the proposed directives, the nature of the new rules and the impact you think they will have on financial service providers in your country.

3 Go to the Bank of England website (www.bankofengland.co.uk) to obtain information of the structure of the Bank with regard to financial industry regulation. Write a report describing the different sections of the bank, including illustrations of actions taken in the past two years to effect the Bank's objectives. Also describe the way in which the Bank cooperates with other central banks and finance regulators around the world to better regulate the financial system.

The financial crisis

LEARNING OUTCOMES

Understanding the financial crisis is important for us all, so that we learn the lessons from the mistakes of others. By the end of this chapter the reader should be able to:

■ explain, with examples, why it is wrong to rely simple-mindedly on complex mathematics and economic modelling when making financial decisions. Knowledge of history and knowledge of people are more important than algebra in finance;

■ describe and illustrate the concept of reflexivity which can lead markets to far-from-equilibrium states;

■ discuss the various complex derivative instruments that contributed to the crisis by obscuring from view the real risks individual banks were taking, and to which the whole system was exposed. These range from collateralised debt obligations to structured investment vehicles;

■ provide a description of the stages of the financial crisis itself and the way in which events in the markets driven by exuberance, greed, fear and panic overwhelmed the key players;

■ explain the key insights we ought to always remember about markets and institutions.

This is a difficult chapter to write. It would have been easy if all I had to do was give a run-down of the sequence of events that took place, or to lay blame at the door of 'greedy bankers', 'incompetent regulators' or 'inattentive governments'. But you already know about sub-prime mortgages, fancy derivatives and relaxed overseers. What I need to do is go behind the obvious and explore the underlying causes. These lie in the rather opaque and confused land of psychology, and in the area of the structure of organisations and systems.

While I will still provide the highlights of the crisis, so you will learn what happened to Lehman Brothers, Northern Rock, etc., they will be set in the much wider context of people factors. There are two aspects to this: (i) people behaving in irrational ways, and (ii) people behaving in entirely rational ways from their perspective, given their incentives, but which result in a stupid/irrational outcome for the system as a whole.

The autistic mathematicians and the autistic financial economists[1]

The financial centres of the world hire thousands of people every year who are great at maths and mathematical economics. Some have degrees in engineering or physics, others in pure mathematics, economics or even rocket science. They are highly respected, usually have PhDs and can bamboozle you with their mastery of algebraic formulae and mental gymnastics. The pity is that they are applying their skills to an area of intellectual endeavour, called finance, which is not fundamentally mathematical. As the great investors, such as Warren Buffett and Peter Lynch, both with decades of experience, tell us, all the mathematics you need was picked up at school by the time you were 14.[2] They may be exaggerating to make a point, but what the mathophiles are failing to appreciate is that finance is a multifaceted discipline, in which the largest contribution is from the study of human psychology: humans acting in rational and irrational ways as individuals, and humans acting in groups in rational and irrational ways.

So, the mathematicians turn up at the financial centres on large salaries and they impress their bosses, the leaders of the banks and other institutions, who fail to fully take on board the assumptions behind the algebra. But, by golly, they know an impressive formula when they see one – or at least they think they do. The self-confidence of the mathematician is further reinforced by the admiration and intellectual support of their closely related kin, the financial economists. These people have high algebraic skills, too, and like to practise them as often as possible. There are many opportunities to converse in algebra with fellow autistic financial economists. There are regular seminars in the economics departments of universities the world over, where old and young economists start a presentation to fellow economists by making a number of assumptions about the world.

They simplify. They model, you see, so that the problem they are dealing with is tractable. In too many cases, in reality what they are doing is rushing to the bit that they really want to do (the bit they can cope with), where everything is neat and tidy, without too many messy human factors – that is, to use algebra to show an encapsulating view of world. They love to show off modelling skill with algebra. So they spend one minute making assumptions about how humans behave. Usually these 'humans' are wonderfully rational, amazing calculating machines capable of absorbing infinite amounts of information and then ordering and processing it to make rational decisions – just as an economist would.

So, one minute for assumptions and then 49 minutes algebra, leaving 10 for questions. Ah great! Heaven. It does not matter that the assumptions might be a little unrealistic – look at the quality

---

[1] In the following I am not implying that all mathematicians and economists are autistic in the medical sense of being unable to understand the emotions of others and have difficulty in social interaction. Merely that they have a tendency to fail to properly include human emotions and other human traits such as cognitive and memory limitations in drawing conclusions about decision making and thus how financial markets work, while placing too much emphasis on cold hard maths assuming complete human rationality.

[2] See either Arnold, G. (2009) *The Financial Times Guide to Value Investing*, Financial Times Prentice Hall or Arnold, G. (2011) *The Great Investors: Lessons on Investing from the Master Traders*, Financial Times Prentice Hall.

of the 'analysis'. The room is full of fellow blinkered followers of models, except for a few, who sit at the back and, if they are feeling brave, timidly suggest that perhaps the Emperor does not have many clothes on. The assumptions do not fit their everyday experience, it just does not feel right. But those people are quickly silenced. Don't they understand that you have to model the world in a simplistic way, so that you can understand it? 'But,' the brave soul might say, 'if the assumptions and subsequent models leave out vital human factors, such as limited cognitive processing ability, the power of emotions to corrode rational decision making, and the all too apparent failings of individual and collective memory, will they reflect the way people actual behave in market places?' The rest of the room coughs and many have patronising thoughts about the inadequacy of the questioner's thinking. They will get it eventually – one day developing the ability to suspend disbelief.

What we have here is cognitive dissonance. The financial economists have a long-held view of the way people and the markets behave while many of the rest of us may see things differently. If we try to inject the thought of irrational actions into the economist's debate they suffer pain, anxiety, frustration as their deeply imbedded beliefs are challenged by clearly relevant facts. Many of the better ones have now taken on board the importance of human psychology and sociological studies, most have not. Furthermore, it is mathematical whizzes who tend to be hired in the financial centres.

Universities are not the only place for rational algebraic debate among financial economists. They have conferences all over the world where they gather and then mutually reinforce their belief in the rightness of their methodological approaches. They have journals into which the most 'sophisticated' papers, in terms of mathematical prowess, have greater chance of inclusion. Those that focus on the 'soft' disciplines, with few formulae, are relegated to the low-ranking journals.

The products of the algebra-loving factories, products in terms of both ideas and trained disciples, are now powerfully positioned throughout the world. Not only were the disciples hired by banks, but these kind of thinkers were also recruited by the very best central banks, regulatory agencies, credit rating agencies and think tanks. The brightest of them gradually learn to moderate the stances they were taught at their prestigious *alma mater*, and increasingly become more multi-faceted, multi-disciplinary. After all, they know from their own family life and simple observation on the street that people do not obey mathematical rules or the economist model. Or at least not consistently. Those trained as economists have a greater opportunity to become more disciplinary-inclusive than the mathematicians hired straight into the financial centres. These poor souls have less time than the economists to see the place of mathematics in a wider perspective.

Maths, it has to be acknowledged, is a useful tool, but only one tool among many. Charlie Munger, a great investor and a great thinker, says that we should beware of 'a man with a hammer' because such a man sees every problem as a nail. The rocket scientists hired by the banks and those that rely on them (supposedly overseeing them) should have more intellectual tools in the toolbox, ranging from the idea of the madness of crowds to the psychological effect of an incentive system.

Here I provide two brief examples of the over-reliance on simplistic models to make billion (or trillion) dollar decisions. You may detect a few more instances later in the chapter where models fail to capture the complex of human-driven decision making as I run through the events of 2007 and 2008.

Example 16.1   Modelling default rates on securitised loans and bonds

David Li wrote a paper that was published in the *Journal of Fixed Income* in 2000.[3] This was very influential because it provided a neat model for pricing CDOs. These are explained in much more detail later, but for now you need to know that they are a kind of securitised bond (*see* Chapter 6), with the security being provided by debts owed, usually mortgage debt. Thus the holders of mortgage-based CDOs ultimately receive a return from the repayment of monthly mortgage amounts and borrowers redeeming their mortgages. I say 'ultimately' because CDOs were often (mostly) constructed from other securitised bonds, which get their income from mortgage payers.

▶

---

[3] Li, David X. (2000) 'On default correlation: a copula function approach', *Journal of Fixed Income*, March, Vol. 9, pp. 43–55.

The right to receive this flow of income needed to be valued, so that the holders, which were generally banks as well as some other financial institutions, could value their assets and estimate profits made over a period. The value of debt owed to you depends on the likelihood of the borrowers defaulting. David Li provided a formula useful for estimating CDO value without having to establish the likelihood of repayment from each of the thousands of mortgage payers. His short cut was to use the market prices of credit default swaps, CDSs (*see* Chapter 11) and the prices of bonds, that relate to that CDO. Now that investment bankers had a quick and easy way of valuing CDOs they could really go to town selling them and holding them on their balance sheets. From virtually nothing in 2000 the market grew to issue over $550 billion of CDOs per year by 2006, and had more than $4,700 billion outstanding (for comparison, UK annual GDP is around $2,000 billion and the total balance sheet capital of any nation's banks are far less). The CDS market was also boosted from under $1,000 billion of outstanding CDSs in 2000 to over $62,000 billion in 2007 (more than the output of goods and services for the entire world for one year).

It was not just the investment banks that adopted the formula; bond investors took comfort from it when deciding how much to invest, as did commercial banks from around the world who piled into US CDOs to obtain the high yield they were offering. Even more worrying, the rating agencies and the financial regulators used the model.

The limitations of the formula were available for scrutiny, but few bothered to look as they excitedly booked 'profits' (and bonuses) from creating, dealing and holding CDOs. The problem was that these reported profits were largely illusory because they failed to take account of the true risk. The inputs to the formula relied on obtaining numbers for default rates and the correlation between two or more credit risks, such as between two or more asset-backed securitised bonds held by a CDO. The mathematicians naturally measured these default rates and correlations over recent years and *assumed* that these were the relevant numbers for future-orientated estimations. They assumed that correlation was constant rather than volatile, ignoring the warnings of leading statisticians and experienced derivative dealers that asset prices can switch from low correlation to being very highly correlated when prices are falling across the board. The problem was that the early and mid-2000s were unusually benign for mortgage holders. Interest rates were down to very low levels and house prices were on a rising trend, and so very few defaulted. There was also low correlation between defaults – it was rare for all the different housing markets in America to be down at the same time, or so they thought.

You cannot blame the mathematicians, they are not trained to have the wider, longer-history perspective. They do formulas and calculations, not the soft stuff. Even if the mathematicians had qualms about the model's limitations; they had bosses who wanted to hold more and more CDOs, CDSs, etc. because they *seemed* so profitable. The problem is the bosses did not understand the maths and how the model worked – a single correlation number came out of the end of a black-box computer calculation and that was enough for them to punt a billion or two of the company's money. Thus we had a position where the balance sheet values of trillions of dollars worth of financial instruments were dependent on the assumption of a continuing benign housing market. When house prices stopped rising and defaults increased the value of CDOs fell.

Why did the credit rating agencies rate CDOs at low default risk, despite the obvious dangers in the assumptions? Well, that is another story (one that will be addressed later in the chapter). Hint: they made a lot of money from rating CDOs. They also employed a lot of algebra lovers. For now here is a comment from Kai Gilkes, who worked for ten years at rating agencies: 'Everyone was pinning their hopes on house prices continuing to rise. When they stopped rising, pretty much everyone was caught on the wrong side, because the sensitivity to house prices was huge … Why didn't rating agencies build in some cushion for this sensitivity to a house-price-depreciation scenario? Because if they had, they would have never rated a single mortgage-backed CDO.'[4]

To be fair to David Li, he did try to warn people that it was false reassurance to assume that correlations on default were always going to remain the same as they had been in the benign conditions of the late 1990s and early 2000s: 'Very few people understand the essence of the model … The most dangerous part is when people believe everything coming out of it.'[5] As so often with these models the originators provide plenty of warnings and provisos, but somehow the bankers and other followers tend to ignore them or fail to understand the subtleties.

---

[4] Li quoted in Salmon (2009).
[5] Quoted in Salmon (2009).

Example 16.2	**Modelling daily value at risk**

Banks hold a very wide range of assets, from corporate loans to complicated derivatives, and they bear a number of obligations. Senior managers of banks can lose track as to the extent to which the firm as a whole is exposed to risk. One division might be building up large holdings of bonds while another is selling credit default swaps, and yet another is packaging up mortgage bonds and selling CDOs. Perhaps what one division is doing will offset the risk that another is taking on. On the other hand, it might be that risk is merely compounded by the combination of positions. Each day the mix of assets and liabilities changes and therefore the risk exposure changes.

Back in the 1990s some bankers[6] thought it would be a good idea to produce a single number that encapsulated the overall risk profile of the bank each evening. The senior managers could look at that and be reassured that they were not taking excessive risk. If the number started to look dangerously high then they could instruct a reweighting of assets and obligations until a safety margin was restored. The measure that they came up with is called value at risk, or VaR, which asks: 'If tomorrow is a bad day (e.g. different asset classes, such as shares and bonds, fall in market price significantly), what is the minimum that the bank will lose?' VaR is an estimate of the loss on a portfolio over a period of time (usually 24 hours is chosen) that will be *exceeded*[7] with a given frequency, e.g. a frequency of one day out of 100, or five days out of 100. Another way of looking at the frequency element is called the confidence level. Thus with a 99 per cent confidence level set the VaR might turn out to be $100 million. Therefore for 'one-day VaR' there is a 1 per cent chance that that the portfolio could lose more than $100 million in 24 hours. A 95 per cent confidence level means that there is a 95 per cent chance that the loss will be less than the derived figure of say $16 million for a day, and a 5 per cent chance that it will be greater than $16 million

So, how does a bank calculate VaR estimates? They need some numbers and some assumptions. One assumption often made is that returns on a security (share, derivative, bond, etc.) follow a particular distribution. The usual assumption is the normal distribution where there is a large clustering of probabilities of returns around the average expected return and then very small probabilities of the extremes ('thin tails'). Also, the distribution of possible outturns is symmetrical about the mean – there is the same chance of being, say, £3 million above the average expected return as being £3 million below it – *see* **Exhibit 16.1** for a normal distribution of probabilities, a bell-shaped symmetrical curve. The usual source of data, whether combined with a normal distribution assumption or not, is a long time series of an historical data set of daily return data for the securities – then the mathematicians assume that this represents the future distribution of returns. Another important source of information is the calculation of the extent to which asset returns move together. Then it is assumed that these correlations remain true for future estimations.

Exhibit 16.1 shows a possible output from using VaR. On the right-hand side the return numbers increase but the probability of earning those high returns decrease significantly the further we move away from the average expected return. The probabilities for returns below average are symmetrical with those above average in this case where we assume 'normality'. (If we used real past return data the distribution may not be quite normal and the maths for calculating the confidence level becomes more complicated, but it can still be handled. Skewed distribution just creates more fun for the mathematicians.) You can read off the 99 per cent chance of not losing more than the amount marked by the red line. If the red line is at $100 million then one day out of 100 we would lose more than $100m, in theory.

A key assumption is that the past data has a very close bearing on the future probabilities. Even using the normality method you need past data to estimate the size of the various probabilities. So, you might gather data from the previous three or five years. If unusual/infrequent events are not present in that dataset you might be missing some extreme positive or negative possibilities.

---

[6] J.P. Morgan led on this.

[7] Many books and articles get this wrong and say the VaR is a measure of the *maximum* amount of money at risk rather than a level that will be exceeded. In reality the loss can go much higher than the VaR figure. The VaR figure is better seen as a minimum loss on a bad day. Obviously, this misunderstanding and misrepresentation would have been read by many bankers and therefore contributed to their failure to understand the extent of their bank's risk exposure.

Exhibit 16.1 A VaR analysis assuming a normal distribution of the probabilities of return on an asset or collection of assets

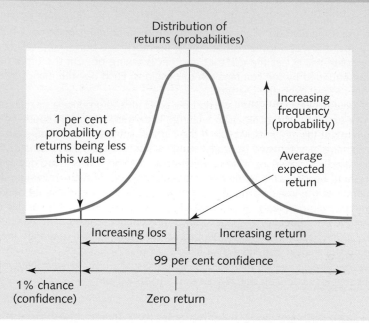

One of these events might have a massive impact on risk but might be missed if the data set is limited to a period of stability. Indeed it might be missed even if the dataset is extensive if the event is very rare. An influential writer on derivatives and market player, Nicolas Taleb,[8] was warning us long before the crisis that the mathematicians were not allowing for the possibility of extreme events (called black swans) – that the tails of the distribution are in fact much bigger, 'fatter', than generally supposed, because extreme things hit us more often then we anticipate. There are 'high-impact rare events', often caused by human reactions to apparently insignificant triggers; reactions such as exuberance, fear and panic. Asset returns and liabilities which appeared to be uncorrelated suddenly all move together to a much greater extent than short-memory players in financial markets expect. There are risks out there that we did not know existed, until it is too late. The more experienced old hands know that unexpected and unimaginable events shape the markets, leaving them with question marks concerning the extent to which they can trust historical data to be the only guide.

VaR led many senior bankers into a false sense of security prior to the crisis. They were thus emboldened to double and triple their bets on securities such as mortgage CDOs because they appeared to produce high profits without raising VaR much. Many regulators insisted on the disclosure of VaR. Indeed, under the Basel capital rules for banks VaR could be used as an argument for lowering capital requirements. Banks jumped at the chance of lowering capital buffers so as to increase return on equity (*see* Chapters 2 and 7) – they leveraged themselves up. They particularly liked to stock up on 'high-quality' mortgage-based CDOs because the model told them that they had trivial VaR and so they were required to hold only trivial capital reserves. Yes, the regulators have much to answer for, too. They placed far too much faith in these mathematical models. They even allowed banks to do their own calculations of risk exposure, and more or less accepted that for setting capital limits.

Prior to the summer of 2007 banks tended to use historical evidence going back between one and five years to estimate VaR. By then a large part of their exposure was to the mortgage market. In the mid-2000s this had been as placid as the sea was when the *Titanic* was crossing the Atlantic – no trouble encountered for day after day. It would seem that VaR gave little indication of real

---

[8] Taleb, N.N. (2001) *Fooled by randomness: the hidden role of chance in the markets and in life,* Texere. Taleb, N.N. (2008) *The Black Swan: The Impact of the Highly Improbable,* Penguin.

likely losses. For example, in the autumn of 2007 Bear Stearns reported an average VaR of $30m,[9] which is tiny for a bank with so many assets. It could withstand days and days of such losses and barely notice. So according to VaR it was hardly at risk at all. And yet within weeks it was bust, losing $8,000 million of value. As the complete failure of the bank approached, the VaR number did rise slightly to $60 million because it started to incorporate data for the more recent days when securities became more volatile as the market mayhem started – but it still had lots of older placid data pushing the number down. It turned out that 'highly unlikely events' such as a correlated fall in house prices all over the US, and the fall in market prices of derivatives and bonds can all happen at the same time. The average man on the street could have told them that, but these mathematicians and financial economists could not see past their complex algebra. The guys over at Merrill Lynch were perplexed: 'In the past these AAA CDO securities had never experienced a significant loss in value.'[10] But how long was that 'past' – if they could find a decade of data they would have been lucky, because these instruments were so young. As the crisis got under way most of the large banks experienced day after day losses that should only happen once in 1,000 years (according to their models). In their language these were six-sigma (standard deviation) events, which were virtually impossible from their faithful-to-the-algebra perspective. Indeed, in August 2007 the market experienced several 25-sigma events – these should happen only once every 14 billion years, that is, since the Big Bang! How confusing for them – the model let them down when it really mattered. Triana (2009) likens VaR to buying a car with an air bag which protects you 99 per cent of the time, that is when conditions are moderate, but if you have a serious crash it fails.

Bear Stearns understood the problems with VaR. Take this statement from their filing with the Securities and Exchange Commission on 29 February 2008:

> VaR has inherent limitations, including reliance on historical data, which may not accurately predict future market risk, and the quantitative risk information generated is limited by the parameters established in creating the models. There can be no assurance that actual losses occurring on any one day arising from changes in market conditions will not exceed the VaR amounts shown below or that such losses will not occur more than once in 20 trading days. VaR is not likely to accurately predict exposures in markets that exhibit sudden fundamental changes or shifts in market conditions or established trading relationships. Many of the Company's hedging strategies are structured around likely established trading relationships and, consequently, those hedges may not be effective and VaR models may not accurately predict actual results. Furthermore, VaR calculated for a one-day horizon does not fully capture the market risk of positions that cannot be liquidated in a one-day period.[11]

Despite this list of doubts they had used it because everyone else did (and the regulators allowed them to get away with it):

> However, the Company believes VaR models are an established methodology for the quantification of risk in the financial services industry despite these limitations. VaR is best used in conjunction with other financial disclosures in order to assess the Company's risk profile.'[12]

Being 'established' is not the same as being best suited to the task. They are basically saying: 'If all the other fellas are using it to leverage up profits and bonuses, why can't we?' This is not very scientific, no matter how much algebra you use to bamboozle.

Once faith in VaR had evaporated those lending to banks became afraid that the risk metrics they publicly announced under-reported their real exposure. They took the action that you or I would take when told that borrowers might default on what they owe: stop lending any more and try to call in old loans. The problem is the entire banking system was a complex web of loans to each other and once confidence had gone the whole system collapsed. Notice the key words here are not quantifiable – 'afraid', 'confidence' – these fuzzy things are just as important to understand about finance as the maths, if not more so.

---

[9] *Source*: Triana (2009).
[10] *Source*: Triana (2009).
[11] www.sec.gov/Archives/edgar/data/777001/000091412108000345/be12550652-10q.txt
[12] www.sec.gov/Archives/edgar/data/777001/000091412108000345/be12550652-10q.txt

Reflexivity

George Soros is the most famous and the most respected of the hedge fund managers, who made a fortune for himself and the backers of his Quantum Fund. However, his first love and abiding passion is economic philosophy. Indeed, it is his understanding of the importance of human thought on market prices that made him and his investors so much money. At the heart of his ideas is reflexivity in markets, in which the behaviour of market prices results from a two-way feedback mechanism with participants (e.g. investors) moving prices and fundamentals in response to their (faulty) perceptions, and their perceptions, in turn, formed by market movements and fundamentals. Knowledge of this human tendency can help identify bubbles and irrational downward spirals.

Early in life Soros developed his philosophy of how people in social structures operate as a group to occasionally lead the economic (or political or social) fundamentals away from a near-to-equilibrium state to a far-from-equilibrium state. His observations and anticipations of financial market movements are but a sub-set of manifestations of his theory of 'reflexivity'. The same philosophical base can be used to describe and analyse, for example, the movement of a society from an open, rule-of-law, democratic form to one increasingly closed and authoritarian. It can also be used to describe and explain individual human interactions such as love and hate, amongst a host of other applications.

In contrast to the 'rational man model' assumed by most economists Soros observed that decisions are based on people's perception or interpretation of the situation. Furthermore, their decisions can change the situation, alter the fundamentals (e.g. the price of houses in a country or the price of dot.com shares). Then changes in the fundamentals thus caused are liable to change the perceptions of individuals. And so on.

Soros was born in Hungary in 1930. Living under both Nazi and Communist regimes gave Soros a healthy respect for the objective aspect of reality. His experiences of living in the far-from-equilibrium conditions of first the German and then the Russian occupation of his country provided insight which played an important role in preparing him for a successful career as a hedge fund manager. He, more than most, became aware that stability is a commodity that comes and goes.

When admitted to the London School of Economics he chose to study economics but quickly found it a trial for two reasons: (i) he was poor at maths, and economics was increasingly becoming a mathematical discipline; and (ii) he was more interested in addressing the foundations of economics, such as the assumptions of perfect knowledge, while his teachers preferred algebraic constructs built on such time-honoured assumptions.

The bright spots in his university experience were his encounters with Professor Karl Popper, who supplied inspiring ideas and engaged with Soros seriously.

> Karl Popper ... maintained that reason is not capable of establishing the truth of generalisations beyond doubt. Even scientific laws cannot be verified because it is impossible to derive universally valid generalisations from individual observations, however numerous, by deductive logic. Scientific method works best by adopting an attitude of comprehensive scepticism: Scientific laws should be treated as hypotheses which are provisionally valid unless and until they are falsified ... He asserted that scientific laws cannot be verified ... One nonconforming instance may be sufficient to destroy the validity of the generalisation, but no amount of conforming instances are sufficient to verify a generalisation beyond any doubt.[13]

The economists' need to maintain the assumption of perfect knowledge on the part of economic actors directly contradicted Popper's contention that understanding by humans is inherently imperfect. Yet economists kept trying to create a discipline with generalisations comparable with those of Isaac Newton in physics, resulting in a discipline increasingly convoluted and mathematical.

In rejecting the standard economists' model and influenced by Popper, Soros started developing a framework of human behaviour in which misconceptions and misinterpretations play a major role in shaping the course of history. Market participants do not base their decisions on knowledge

---

[13] Soros, G. (2008) *The Crash of 2008 and What It Means*, New York: Public Affairs, pp. 35–36.

alone because biased perceptions have a powerful impact not only on market prices but also the fundamentals that those prices are supposed to reflect. Note for now the two influences of biased perceptions – many readers of Soros' work only take on board the first and thus glibly conclude that he is not saying anything particularly original – the original bit is the second element.

First element: influencing market prices.
Second element: influencing the fundamentals those prices are supposed to reflect.

Classical economics

The Enlightenment view of the world is that reality lies there, passively waiting to be discovered. Reason acts as a searchlight to illuminate that reality. Thus, there is a separation between, on the one hand, people's thoughts and understanding of the world and, on the other, the object. The thinking agents cannot influence the underlying reality. Thus in natural science we can explain and predict the course of events with reasonable certainty.

Economic and other social areas of 'study' – Soros does not permit the use of the word 'science' with social disciplines – tried to imitate Newtonian physics and develop 'laws' to describe the fundamental processes. To make their models work in a 'scientific' manner economists would simplify reality by making assumptions, for example, that market participants base their decisions on perfect knowledge, or that supply and demand curves could be taken as independently given (with supply not influencing demand, and demand not influencing supply, except through the classical interaction on the economist's diagram).

For the physical scientists it is obvious that to gain knowledge there must be a separation between thoughts and their objective. The facts must be independent of the statements made about them. So, the Earth will move around the Sun in a fairly predictable pattern regardless of what the observer thinks about the movement. Many economists follow a sequence of logic analogous to the physics model in trying to describe economic outcomes – *see* **Exhibit 16.2**.

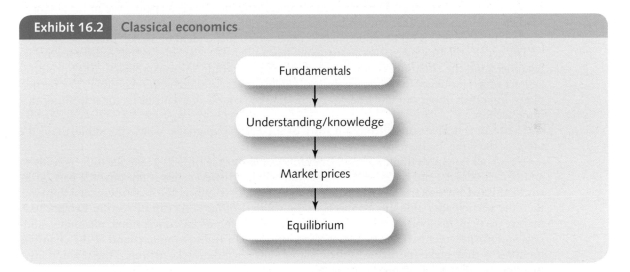

Exhibit 16.2   Classical economics

When we move away from the physical sciences we frequently encounter a problem. In social phenomena it is often difficult to separate fact from thoughts. The decision maker in trying to make sense of the world attempts to be a detached observer, but can never fully overcome the fact that they are part of the situation they seek to comprehend. For example, people and human organisations, such as lending institutions, try to understand the underlying facts about the housing market, but in doing so – and in taking action – they influence the reality of the house supply, demand and prices. Under the classical economics paradigm demand and supply curves are supposed to determine the market price. But it seems reasonable to suggest that in many cases these curves are themselves subject to market influences, in which case prices cease to be uniquely determined. We end up with fluctuating prices rather than equilibrium.

Another example: It is thought that the markets are on the look-out for a recession looming over the horizon, that they anticipate it. Soros takes a different viewpoint, believing that it is more correct to say that markets help to precipitate recessions; that:

1 Markets are always biased in one direction or another.
2 Markets can influence the events they anticipate.

For example, it would be difficult to argue that the *reaction* of the financial markets to news coming out of the US residential mortgage market in 2008 did *not* influence events to take us into recession.

Soros' paradigm

So, the widely held paradigm that financial markets tend toward equilibrium is both false and misleading. Soros contends that, first, financial markets never reflect underlying reality accurately and, second, occasionally, these distortions affect the fundamentals that market prices are supposed to reflect. These ideas provide profound insight into both the setting of prices and the movement of underlyings. Market participants' misconceptions, misunderstandings and misjudgments affect market prices and, more importantly, market prices affect the fundamentals.

The economists' classic model does allow for deviations from the theoretical equilibrium, but only in a random manner, and the deviations will be corrected in a fairly short time frame. Soros says that market prices do not reach the theoretical equilibrium point; they are in a continual state of change relative to the theoretical equilibrium.

The role of perceptions is key to understanding reflexivity. Participants in the financial markets have expectations about events. These expectations affect the shapes of both the supply and the demand curves. Decisions to buy or to sell an asset are based on expectations about future prices and future prices are, in turn, contingent on buy or sell decisions in the present.

The assets that are currently rising in price often attract buyers, whereas those that are falling encourage more sales – self-reinforcing trends. Anyone who has spent time in the financial markets becomes aware that reinforcing trends exist. Soros asks rhetorically: How could self-reinforcing trends persist if supply and demand curves were independent of market prices?

The act of thinking by market participants has a dual role. On the one hand, they are trying to understand the situation; on the other, their understanding (or misunderstanding) produces actions which influence the course of events. The two roles interfere with each other. The participants' imperfect understanding leads to actions and the course of events bears the imprint of that imperfection.

The term reflexive comes from a feature of the French language, where the subject and the object is the same. It also means reflection (not reflexes).

We are all taught to think in terms of events as a sequence of facts – one set of facts leads to another set of facts, and so on, in a never-ending chain. However, this is not how the part of the world affected by humans actually works. The facts are first subject to the participants' thinking, then the participants' thinking connects to the next set of facts. As can be seen in **Exhibit 16.3**, market participants look at the fundamentals through a fog of misconceptions, misunderstandings and misjudgments. They have biased perceptions. In trying to understand – 'the cognitive function' – they make mistakes. In their biased state they then take action – 'the manipulative function' – and this moves market prices.

So far, so conventional: standard economics allows for the less well-informed actors to make misinterpretations and poor decisions because markets are not perfect, and for them to do so as a herd. Soros' insight is that, rather than a return to theoretical equilibrium as the participants realise their errors (or the errors are merely part of a large set of off-setting random events), the distortions in market prices create distortions in the fundamentals – the 'prevailing trend' itself is altered – and simultaneously the perceptions of participants is altered in response to the fundamentals changing, resulting in an indeterminate outcome, as perceptions feed off the course of events and the course of events feeds off perceptions. We get indeterminacy in both the cognitive and manipulating functions because of the reflexive connection between them.

In most cases the reflexive interaction is relatively insignificant because there are forces at play that bring thinking and reality together, such as people learning from experience or new evidence

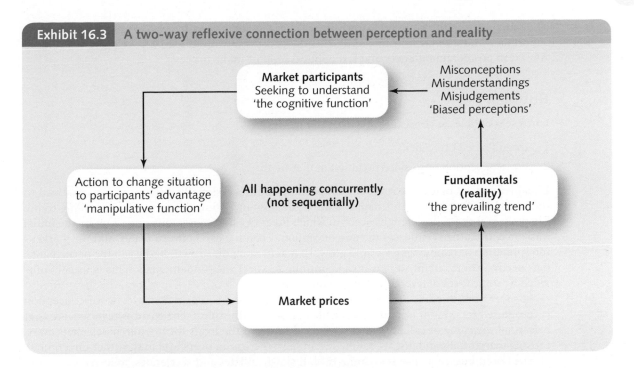

Exhibit 16.3   A two-way reflexive connection between perception and reality

coming to light. These are termed 'near-equilibrium conditions' and the impact of reflexivity can be disregarded. In these cases classical economic theory applies, and the divergence between perceptions and reality can be ignored as mere noise.

Occasionally, however, the reflexive interaction can lead to massive market distortions, with no tendency for them to come together – 'far-from-equilibrium conditions' – leading to boom/bust sequences. In this case the theories developed around the assumption of equilibrium become irrelevant. We are presented with a one-directional process in which changes in both perceptions and reality are irreversible (at least for a period). Just as mutation has a role in biology so misconceptions and mistakes play a role in human affairs.

When thinking about Exhibit 16.3 try to picture the stages presented following one another so quickly that the whole thing becomes a blur of concurrently occurring (and cross-impacting) cognitive function, manipulative function, market prices and fundamentals. People taking decisions make an impact on the situation (the manipulative function), which changes the situation, which is liable to change their perceptions (the cognitive function). 'The two functions operate concurrently, not sequentially. If the feedback were sequential, it would produce a uniquely determined sequence leading from facts to perceptions to new facts and then new perceptions, and so on. It is the fact that the two processes occur simultaneously that creates an indeterminacy in both the participants' perceptions and the actual course of events.'[14]

If we take the stock market, for example, we observe that people trade shares in anticipation of future prices, but those prices are contingent on the investors' expectations. We cannot assume that expectations in the market is a form of knowledge in the same way that a physical scientist can predict the motions of the stars – the movement of the stars is truly independent of the expectations of the scientist. In the absence of knowledge, participants bring in an element of judgement or bias into their decision making. Thus, outcomes diverge from expectations.

Soros uses 'equilibrium' as a figure of speech. He does not see a stable equilibrium from which deviates the occasional boom/bust process. Equilibrium should be seen as a moving target because market prices get buffeted by the fundamentals they are supposed to reflect.

Example of a reflexive statement outside of finance: 'You are my enemy.' Whether this is true or not depends on how you react to it. It is indeterminate.

Example of an act of the manipulative function that failed to achieve the outcome intended: 'President George W. Bush declared a War on Terror and used it to invade Iraq on false pretenses.

---

[14] Soros, G. (2008) p. 10.

The outcome was the exact opposite of what he intended: He wanted to demonstrate American supremacy and garner political support in the process; but he caused a precipitous decline in American power and influence and lost political support in the process.'[15]

Bubbles

Soros sees bubbles as consisting of two components:

1   a trend based on reality;

2   a misconception or misinterpretation of that trend.

Usually financial markets correct misconceptions, but, occasionally misconceptions can lead to the inflation of a bubble. This happens when the misconception reinforces the prevailing trend. Then a two-way feedback might occur in which the prevailing trend, now puffed up by the initial misconception, then reinforces the misconception. Then the gap between reality and the market's interpretation of reality can grow and grow. In maintaining the growth in the gap the participants' bias needs a short circuit so that it can continue to affect the fundamentals. This is usually provided by some form of leveraged debt or equity.

At some point the size of the gap becomes so large that it is unsustainable. The misconception is recognised for what it is, and participants become disillusioned. The trend is reversed. As asset prices fall the value of collateral that supported much of the loans for the purchases melts away, causing margin calls and distress selling. Eventually, there is an overshoot in the other direction.

The boom/bust sequence is asymmetrical. It slowly inflates and accelerates, followed by a more rapid reversal. Soros says that there are eight stages to the boom/bust sequence. We will take the example where the underlying trend is earnings per share ('the prevailing trend') and the participants' perceptions (cognitive function) are reflected in share prices through the manipulative function, i.e. they buy or sell shares pushing the prices up or down. In turn, the change in share prices may affect both the participants' bias and the underlying trend.

Thus, share prices are determined by two factors:

(a) the underlying trend – earnings per share, eps;

(b) the prevailing bias.

Both (a) and (b) are influenced by share prices, hence a feedback loop.

In **Exhibit 16.4** the divergence between the two curves is an indication of the underlying bias. (Soros said that the true relationship is more complex than we are representing here because the earnings curve includes, as well as the underlying trend, the influence of share prices on that trend. Thus the prevailing bias is expressed only partially by the divergence between the two curves – it is also partially already reflected in those curves.)

Stage 1 – no trend recognition

The underlying trend is gently sloping upwards, but is not yet recognised.

Stage 2 – recognising the trend and reinforcement

The trend is recognised by market participants. This changes perceptions about the underlying. The newly developing positive prevailing bias pushes shares along. At this stage the change in share prices may or may not affect the underlying trend, i.e. the level of earnings of companies. If it does not then the reflexive boom does not materialise – the correction in share prices leads to the loss of the underlying trend, i.e. eps do not continue to rise abnormally.

If the underlying trend is affected by the rise in share prices then we have the beginning of a self-reinforcing process, and we start to move into a far-from-equilibrium state. The underlying trend becomes increasingly dependent on the prevailing bias and the bias becomes increasingly exaggerated.

---

[15] Soros, G. (2008) p. 38.

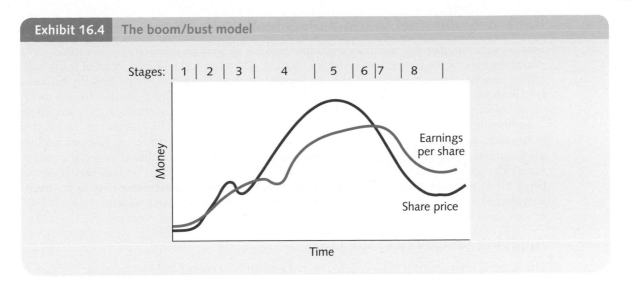

Exhibit 16.4   The boom/bust model

Stage 3 – testing

Both the prevailing bias and the trend are tested by external shocks – there may be several tests, but here we show only one. Prices suffer setbacks. If the test causes the bias and trend to fail to survive then the potential bubble dies.

Stage 4 – period of acceleration

Survival through the tests makes both the bias and the trend stronger. The underlying trend (eps) becomes increasingly influenced by share prices. Also the rise in share prices becomes increasingly dependent on the prevailing bias. Both the bias and the trend become seemingly unshakable. Conviction is so strong that share price rises are no longer affected by setbacks in the earning trend. Now far-from-equilibrium conditions become firmly established – the normal rules no longer apply.

Stage 5 – unsustainability

Exaggerated expectations reach such a peak that reality can no longer sustain them. This is 'the moment of truth'.

Stage 6 – twilight period

Participants realise that their prevailing bias is high and they lower their expectations. The trend may be sustained by inertia, but is no longer reinforced by belief, so it rises at a lower rate. This is the twilight period or period of stagnation – people no longer believe in the game, but continue to play.

Stage 7 – tipping point

The loss of belief eventually causes a reversal in the trend that had become ever more dependent on an ever stronger bias. When the trend reverses we have the crossover or tipping point.

Stage 8 – catastrophic downward acceleration

A downward trend reinforces the now negative prevailing bias – the gap between share price, as a reflection of expectations, and the eps levels is now negative. A crash occurs. Eventually the pessimism goes too far and the market stabilises.

Reflexivity does not follow a predetermined pattern

Soros emphasises that this is only one possible path resulting from the interplay of a trend and a prevailing bias. Some far-from-equilibrium reflexive situations follow this pattern of initial self-reinforcement, unsustainability of the gap between thinking and reality, followed by collapse, creating a historically significant event. But there are also reflexive interactions that correct themselves before they reach boom proportions, and thus do not become historically significant. There is nothing determinate or compulsory about the boom/bust pattern. The process may be aborted at any time. Also, there are many other processes going on at the same time, e.g. changes in other asset markets, changes in the regulatory environment, changes in the political or social environment. The various processes may interfere with one another leading to boom/bust sequences being hit by external shocks. There may be patterns that tend to repeat themselves in far-from-equilibrium situations, but the actual course of events is indeterminate and unique.

Applying reflexivity to the crisis

The housing bubble of the 2000s is a sub-part of a much larger super-bubble that stretches back to the early 1980s.

Housing bubble

The US housing bubble followed the course described by Soros' in his boom/bust model. Lax lending standards were supported by a prevailing misconception that the value of the collateral for the loans was not affected by the willingness to lend. Loans were packaged up into financial securities and sold on to unsuspecting investors around the world. Those securitised bonds issued in the early stages of the boom showed a low default rate on the underlying mortgages. Credit rating agencies based their estimates of future default rates on the recent benign past – another misconception. As house prices rose the rating agencies became even more relaxed as they rated collateralised debt obligations. In trying to perceive future risks and returns all participants failed to recognise the impact that they, themselves, made.

While Wall Street was creating all these weird and obscure financial instruments – and getting fat fees for arranging them – mortgage originators became increasingly aggressive in encouraging ordinary people to take on the responsibilities of a mortgage. The value of a loan as a proportion of the value of a house got higher and higher. Towards the end of the boom people who had no job and nothing to put down as a deposit on a house were being granted mortgages. The attraction of fee income lies at the heart of this. The mortgage arrangers received a fee for arranging the mortgage regardless of what happened to the house owner thereafter; the banks received fees for arranging securitised bonds, and yet more fees for CDOs, and yet more fees for even more complex instruments.

But all of this was okay if you believed that the value of homes and thus collateral for the loans, was growing and would continue to grow. This belief, for a while, created its own fulfilment: faith in the housing market led to more loans; the additional demand for housing stimulated by the availability of cheap mortgages led to house prices rising, providing more collateral; confidence in the housing market rose due to the additional collateral and low rates of default on mortgages because home owners could easily refinance in a rising market to avoid default; more loans were forthcoming; and so on.

People became dependent on double-digit house price rises to finance their lifestyles. As they withdrew housing 'equity' through remortgages the savings rate dropped below zero. When home owners became over-extended and house prices stopped rising they had to cut back on remortgaging. There was a reduction in demand from both people moving and from people staying put and remortgaging. The moment of truth came in the spring of 2007 when New Century Financial Corp. went into bankruptcy. People started to ask questions: perhaps the value of the collateral for mortgages was not destined to rise for ever and was artificially supported by the willingness of lenders to make fresh loans. If they stopped, perhaps much of the 'value' in houses would prove to be an illusion.

A twilight period followed when house prices were falling but participants continued to play the game – new mortgages were signed and securitisations created. In August 2007 there was a significant acceleration in downward price movements. Over the next year contagion spread from one segment of financial markets to another, until Lehman's collapse sparked a further downward lunge.

The super-bubble

The super-bubble also reached its tipping point in 2007–2008. This reflexive process evolved over a period of a quarter of a century. The main prevailing trend was ever more sophisticated methods of credit expansion, supported by the trend to globalisation and the trend towards the removal of regulations with increasing financial innovation.

The prevailing misconception was 'market fundamentalism', which promotes the notion that markets should be free to find their own level with very little intervention by regulators. Market fundamentalism became a guiding principle in the financial system in the early 1980s.

The long-term boom combined three major trends, each of which contained at least one defect.

Trend 1 – ever increasing credit expansion

The long-term credit expansion was manifest in rising consumer loan to value of asset (house) ratios and the expansion of credit as a percentage of GDP. This trend has been helped along by the authorities' response to any sign of economic downturn or threat to the banking system. Learning lessons from the Great Depression they were quick to stimulate the economy through counter-cyclical lower interest rates or loose fiscal policy, and if anything endangered the banks there would be bail-outs.

After a few years of intervention the participants started to think there was an asymmetry to the risk of credit expansion. If they expand credit (lower lending standards) and things go right, then the lenders are the winners. If they expand and things go wrong, then they will be bailed out by the authorities. This is an example of the moral hazard problem, in which the presence of a safety net encourages adverse behaviour.

High levels of leverage became normal. Indeed, banks, hedge funds and private equity firms thrived on it. Credit terms for car loans, credit card debt, commercial loans as well as mortgages all reached absurdly easy levels. Japan was another source of credit expansion. During its grindingly long recession it held interest rates near to zero. This encouraged the 'carry trade': international financial institutions borrow in yen and invest the borrowed funds elsewhere in the world at higher yields. The US was not alone. The love of leverage infected other economies from the UK to Spain.

Trend 2 – globalisation of financial markets

The process of globalisation of financial markets accelerated with the petro-dollar recycling[16] in the 1970s, but it got a significant boost with Thatcherism and Reaganism in the 1980s. They saw globalisation of financial markets as a useful development because freeing up financial capital to move around the world makes it difficult for any state to intervene, to tax capital or to regulate it because it can evade such moves by transferring somewhere else. Financial capital was promoted to a privileged position. Governments often have to put the aspirations of their people in second place behind the requirements of international capital – we saw this in 2010–2011 with the Eurozone financial crisis as governments desperate to impress the financial markets with their stewardship of the economy cut budget deficits. The market fundamentalists, who dominated political and financial thinking in the quarter century until the 2007 crisis, thought that taking our lead from the markets was a good thing.

According to the market fundamentalists, globalisation was to bring about a level playing field. In reality, the international financial system ended up in the hands of a consortium of financial authorities answerable to the developed countries. The whole system has favoured the US and the other developed countries at the centre of the financial system, while penalising the developing economies at the periphery. The 'Washington consensus' (IMF, World Bank, etc.) sought to impose strict market discipline on individual less developed countries if they ran into difficulties. But when the western financial system is threatened, the rules are bent.

---

[16] The oil-producing nations in OPEC put up the price of oil, producing massive inflows of cash which they then invested elsewhere in the world.

Furthermore, the US has the benefit of the dollar being the main international reserve currency, accepted by central banks around the world – these organisations, such as the central bank of China, would often invest current account surpluses in US government and agency bonds. This permitted the US to intervene in markets to counter its downturns and financial crises – inflating credit – while other countries were forced to live within their means. Also, it was safer to hold assets at the centre, and thus the US sucked up the savings of the world as US consumers went on a spending spree. Perversely capital flowed from the less developed world to the US.

Trend 3 – progressive removal of financial regulations and the accelerating pace of financial innovation

Between the end of the Second World War and the early 1980s banks and markets were strictly regulated. President Reagan, however, would refer to the 'magic of the marketplace', especially after market fundamentalism received a significant fillip from the manifest failures of communism and other forms of state intervention. An amazing array of new financial instruments was invented and many were widely adopted. The more complicated the financial system became, the less participants and regulators could understand what was going on.

Periodic financial crises over the quarter century (such as the Long Term Capital Asset Management crisis, the dot.com bubble crash, the 2001 terrorist attack) served as tests of the prevailing trend and the prevailing misconception. When these tests were passed, the trend and the misconception were reinforced. Progressively, in an atmosphere of *laissez-faire,* the authorities lost control of the financial system and the super-bubble developed.

The US housing bubble brought the super-bubble to a point of unsustainability – both the trends and the misconceptions became unsustainable; then a tipping point was reached for both bubbles, with the sub-prime crises acting merely as a trigger that released the unwinding of the super-bubble.

The flaw in the market fundamentalist view is that just because state intervention is subject to error does not mean that markets are perfect.

> The cardinal contention of the theory of reflexivity is that all human constructs are flawed. Financial markets do not necessarily tend towards equilibrium; left to their own devices they are liable to go to extremes of euphoria and despair. For that reason they are not left to their own devices; they have been put in the charge of financial authorities whose job it is to supervise them and regulate them … The belief that markets tend towards equilibrium is directly responsible for the current turmoil; it encouraged the regulators to abandon their responsibility and rely on the market mechanism to correct its own excesses.[17]

Some of the more proximate causes of the crisis

The decade leading up to 2008 was unprecedented in terms of innovation in the financial markets. But alongside some good innovations there was an out-of-control complexity, combined with ignorance and misaligned incentives.

Low interest rates

The September 2001 attack on the World Trade Center led to a loss of confidence which compounded the cautiousness of consumers and investors following the dot.com bust of 2000. Recession and deflation were a possibility and so interest rates were lowered in the West. In the US, short-term rates stayed around 1 per cent between 2002 and 2004. Deflation did not occur and the rate of interest was frequently less than the inflation rate. Interest rates were further lowered by the huge amount of Chinese savings being invested in US government Treasury bills and bonds.

---

[17] Soros, G. (2008) pp. 94–104.

Low interest rates encouraged a boom in house prices and in economic output. Low interest rates also led to a 'search for yield': investors and bankers, discontented with low returns on deposits and safe investments, became prepared to accept more risk to obtain higher rates of return.

Innovation in the mortgage market

In the US, two government-sponsored enterprises (GSEs), Fannie Mae and Freddie Mac, were at the centre of mortgage securitisation at the start of the 1990s. They bought bundles of mortgages from mortgage originators (e.g. banks) and then created and sold mortgage-backed securities (MBSs), a type of asset-backed security (ABS) (*see* Chapter 11). The GSEs guaranteed the interest and principle on these MBSs. And given that the government was likely to rescue its creations if they ran into trouble, a guarantee from the GSEs was taken to be as good as a guarantee from the US Treasury.

The GSEs would not take just any old mortgage. They usually insisted that the house owner owed no more than 80 per cent of the value of the house (loan-to-value ratio, LTV) and the maximum size of mortgage was $417,000. They also investigated the borrower's income, state of employment, history of bad debts (if any) and amounts of other assets. In other words, this system is pretty safe because only the most creditworthy enter it. It was for 'prime' mortgages only.

Now for some innovation. In the early 1990s new lenders emerged who were willing to lend to people who did not qualify as prime borrowers. They would often employ independent firms of mortgage brokers to persuade families to take out a mortgage. The brokers received a commission for each one sold. The number of sub-prime lenders grew significantly over the 12 years to 2005 and the proportion of mortgages that were sub-prime rose to over 20 per cent. The rise of this market attracted the interest of the big names on Wall Street (e.g. Goldman Sachs, Merrill Lynch, Lehman Brothers, Bear Sterns and Morgan Stanley), which bought up sub-prime lenders. These borrowers could be charged higher interest rates than prime borrowers. They could also be charged large fees for setting up the loan. The sub-prime market boomed. By 2005 the largest US mortgage provider was the sub-prime lender Countrywide Financial, which had grown fast from 1980s obscurity.

A key characteristic of the new lenders is that they lent at different interest rates to different groups of mortgagees classified on the basis of likelihood-of-default statistical models. These relied heavily on the borrower's **credit score**. These scores were calculated by examining a number of borrower characteristics, the most important of which became the absence (or low incidence) of missed or delayed payments on previous debts. The statisticians had discovered a high correlation between credit scores and defaults on mortgages in the 1990s and so it made sense to them to carry on with them in the 2000s. The problem is that the statisticians had not fully taken on board the extent to which mortgages in the 2000s were different to mortgages in the 1990s, particularly at the sub-prime end of the market.

Many of the 2000s mortgages required much less documentation than in the 1990s. People were often not even required to prove their level of income. They could just state their income. Nor was it necessary to pay for an independent valuation of the house; borrowers could just state the value of the house. Stated income loans were convenient for those without regular work, but anyone with common sense can see the potential temptation to overstating income to speculate on rising prices (they quickly became known as 'liar loans' on the street – a clue that the mathematicians could have picked up on if they had taken time to glance up from the algebra).

Another change was the help given with the deposit on the house. Whereas traditionally households would have to find 10 per cent or 20 per cent of the house value as a down-payment, in the new era brokers could offer a second mortgage (called a 'piggyback') which could be used as the deposit, so 100 per cent of the value of the house could be borrowed. Taking things a stage further, the UK's Northern Rock offered mortgages that were 125 per cent of the value of the house.

A further change was the increasing use of mortgages that had very low interest rates for the first two years ('teaser rates'), but after that they carried rates significantly higher than normal – 600 basis points above LIBOR was merely the average, many paid much more, i.e. well into double figures.

More rational players in this market allowed for the qualitative changes that had taken place in the housing markets in the noughties, rather than simplistically using a mathematical model developed in the 1990s for estimating default likelihood. Those wedded to quantified data in the statistical series had difficulties adjusting to the new reality.

Originate-and-hold to originate-and-distribute

Traditionally, if a bank grants a mortgage it keeps it on its books until it is repaid. This is called the **originate-and-hold model**. In this way banks have every incentive to ensure that the mortgagee can repay and can help those few who have temporary problems along the way. Fewer and fewer banks kept mortgages on the books in the 2000s. They preferred the **originate-and-distribute model**, selling them to other investors, usually through securitisations. Alongside this development was the movement of investment banks to use their own money to invest in securities rather than only provide (lower-risk) advice and other fee-based activities.

In the 1990s only around one-quarter of sub-prime mortgages were packaged up into securitisation vehicles and sold to bond investors; by the mid-2000s three-quarters were. In the good old days Freddie and Fannie dominated this market; in the boom of the mid-2000s the private firms overtook the GSEs and issued vast quantities of mortgage-based securities – more than $1,000 billion per year, cumulating to $11,000 billion by 2007. The leaders of this pack included the Wall Street investment banks as well as Countrywide and Washington Mutual.

Pressure was applied to the mortgage brokers to generate more mortgages which could then be repackaged so that the investment banks could generate fees and other profits from the transaction. The mortgage brokers were only too happy to oblige, so they ran after people to sign up for mortgages to receive commission. No job, no deposit, on welfare benefits? Don't worry, we have just the mortgage for you!

Despite losing their lead, the GSEs still participated. Apart from holding hundreds of billions of dollars worth of MBSs they had created, they also bought more than $1,000 billion of MBSs issued by the private firms. They felt safe because they had put in place 'safeguards'. First, if the loans were at more than 80 per cent of LTV they insisted on insurance being purchased from private insurance firms that pay out in the event of default. Second, the credit rating agencies had checked out the default likelihood on the private MBSs they bought and had concluded that they should be granted AAA status. What could go wrong?

Collateralised debt obligations (CDOs)

The financial markets were not only awash with freshly minted plain-vanilla securitised bonds, with mortgage income being paid into a trust (company or partnership), which then serviced the bond coupons. Something as simple as that was so 1990s. No, in the bright new era the innovators had to go one stage further, and then two and then three.

In straightforward securitisations (*see* Chapter 6) the bonds issued by the special purpose vehicle are all the same. Each bond holder has an equal share in the returns generated on the underlying loans and will suffer an equal loss in the event of a proportion of the borrowers defaulting. But, thought the innovators, there are bond investors who are willing to take the high risk of say the first 5 per cent of borrowers defaulting. They will do this for a high interest rate, say 25 per cent per year. They will then hope that only say 4 per cent actually default over the next ten years. Now that the first hit from defaulters has been accepted by the high-risk takers the other bonds that could be sold on that pool of loan obligations have a much lower chance of suffering a loss. If the underlying loans are mortgages then investors can see from the statistical data that it is rare that more than 4 per cent of mortgagees fail to repay. Thus, if the first 5 per cent of defaults is to be absorbed by the holders of the high-risk bonds – often called the '**equity tranche**' even though they are bonds – then there is hardly any chance of the low-risk bond holder suffering any loss through defaults.

A **collateralised debt obligation** is a bond issued by an SPV, set up by a deal structurer, usually an investment bank, where the SPV holds a pool of loans or a pool of debt securities.[18] The bonds are issued in a number of different classes or tranches, each with their own risk and return characteristics.

---

[18] The underlying assets could be commercial loans, credit card debt, property loans, corporate bonds or other debt.

Note that while the underlying securities might be mortgages, credit card debts, car loans debts, etc. from the first stage of securitisation, they can also be a collection of securitised bonds. Thus, many (most in 2005–2007) CDOs were actually securitisations of securitised bonds.

We will start with an example where the CDO holds a collection of mortgages, rather than ABSs. Imagine that Hubris and Grabbit, that well-known investment bank, has granted $1 billion of mortgages to families throughout America. These are all sub-prime and so have a relatively high chance of default, therefore it would be difficult to persuade bond investors, most of whom can only invest in AAA rated bonds, to purchase securitised bonds in a plain vanilla asset-backed securitisation. If the overall rate of interest charged to mortgagees is 9 per cent then Hubris and Grabbit could create a CDO vehicle as shown in **Exhibit 16.5**. It sells the rights to the mortgage income and principal to the SPV, which issues CDO bonds.

Exhibit 16.5	An example of a collateralised debt obligation

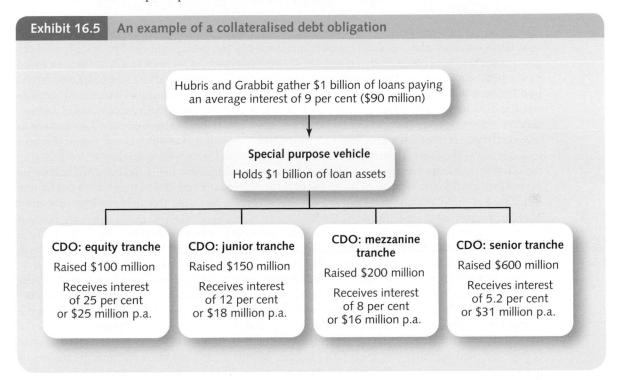

If it is accepted by potential CDO bond holders that there is a 4 per cent default rate then an equity tranche[19] of CDOs could be created raising $100 million for the SPV by selling bonds in it. If the estimates of default prove ovetime to be spot on, then of the original $1 billion, $40 million will be lost. The only tranche holders that will suffer will be the equity tranche, and they will still have $60 million left, plus the interest that has accumulated. To take this risk let us assume that these investors require 25 per cent per year interest. They might be lucky and only 2 per cent default in which case they accumulate a large sum. On the other hand if say 13 per cent of the mortgagees default it will wipe out their investments, as well as impact on the returns for the next tranche. This is the **junior tranche**. They have invested $150 million on a deal that gives them a fairly high rate of return at 12 per cent. But some of this will be forfeited if the default rate goes above 10 per cent. Because of the risk of experiencing a default these securitised bonds might be given a credit rating of around BBB– ('investment grade' but only just) and so could be bought by a range of financial institutions.

Tranche 3 is the **mezzanine tranche**, paying 8 per cent and will only suffer losses if the defaults amount to more than $250 million (the amounts absorbed by the equity and junior tranche holders). It might gain a single A credit rating. If Tranche 3 raised $200 million then the final tranche, '**senior tranche**', will comprise $600 million paying, say, 5.2 per cent per annum and will be granted an AAA rating. Thus Hubris and Grabbit have put in $1 billion of mortgage assets but sold CDOs (via the SPV) worth $1,050 million.

---

[19] Also known as the first-loss tranche or toxic waste.

If you think this is complicated enough, the innovators had hardly warmed up. Some CDOs were structured to have 17 or more different tranches. A **CDO squared (CDO²)** was made up of a package of other CDOs (which, in turn, might be made up of a variety of asset-backed bonds). Then there were **synthetic CDOs of ABS**: these take on credit risk using credit default swaps rather than holding ABSs or CDOs.

Banks were greatly encouraged to create CDOs by the capital reserve rules. If they held $1 billion of mortgages on their books they were required to hold, say, $40 million (4 per cent) of regulatory capital. If the bank sold 95 per cent of the loans in the form of CDOs, retaining 5 per cent in the form of the equity tranche, then it was required to hold much less equity capital.

Rating agencies

The credit rating agencies generally do not rate the equity tranche because of the high risk of loss. However, they play a pivotal role when it comes to the perception held by investors of the other tranches. We have already covered how these overseers of default risk became entranced by algebraic constructs such as David Li's (Gaussian copula) model with its emphasis on correlation between assets in a pool. On top of the default rates and correlations of defaults we need to add the difficulties for the rating agencies of (a) figuring out likely recovery rates should a mortgage or a mortgage-backed securitised bond default – will the organisers of the CDO be able to recover 70 per cent of what was lent to a mortgagee? Or will it be 40 per cent? This is difficult to judge (or is the correct word 'guess'?) and (b) the possibility of renegotiating or rescheduling the interest payments for a borrower that is running into difficulty. Being flexible with borrowers on conventional loans when they go through difficult times is relatively straightforward for the originate-and-hold lenders, but once the original mortgage has been through a couple of rounds of securitisation the connection with the mortgagee is greatly weakened and so specially tailored rescue reschedulings of payments become more difficult – which in itself increases the odds of total default. Thus, trying to measure the possible outcomes and likely future default rate/cash flow from owning a CDO is incredibly difficult.

Despite the difficulties and therefore the obvious need to err on the side of conservatism, the credit rating agencies were fully aware that they were in competition with each other. The customers for their services are the people trying to sell a bond or CDO. These customers need a rating from only one of the raters, thus they shopped around. To start with, Moody's developed a reputation for being fairly tough in granting investment grade status. The result was that Standard & Poor's picked up more fees from CDO issuers. Moody's later modified its cautious stance. Its mathematical models were altered and more asset-backed securities, ABSs and CDOs could be accepted as investment grade. This resulted in a booming fee income. You may think that they were persuaded to stray from the path of rigour, but I could not possibly comment.

But consider this: when it comes to rating corporate bonds there are thousands of potential customers, from BP to Unilever. It is fairly easy to be forceful in turning down a fee if one bond issuer out of a thousand is being too pushy in wanting an excessively favourable rating. The raters' long-term reputation can be preserved so that ratings on the thousands of other bonds rated are better trusted by bond holders. When it came to CDOs and other new-fangled securities such as SIVs (*see* below) the rating agencies were faced with a small group of banks that dominated the market. With the banks threatening to take their large fees to another rating agency you may think it far more difficult to resist the pressure to look at an issue favourably. They, quite naturally, did not want to offend the banks, especially given that towards the end of the boom half of their fee income could be from this 'structured finance' sector. The rating agencies worked very closely with the issuers of CDOs to advise on the cut-off points for the various tranches; they would help them structure them in such a way that the top AAA-rated element was as large as possible to maximise profit from selling the CDOs. To do this they did not investigate the underlying individual mortgages but relied on statistical databases: 'We aren't loan officers. Our expertise is as statisticians on an aggregate basis. We want to know, of 1,000 individuals, based on historical performance, what percentage will pay their loans?'[20] They used these statistical databases even when

---

[20] Claire Robinson, head of asset-backed finance for Moody's, quoted in Roger Lowenstein (2008) 'Triple-A Failure', *New York Times Magazine*, 27 April.

40–50 per cent of the mortgages going into a CDO SPV were stated income loans for people with chequered credit histories. To have such a high proportion of loans to high-risk mortgagees was a relatively new phenomenon – so what *reliable* data on default could they use?

To demonstrate the academic rigour of their models the rating agencies showed investors exactly how they worked. They even published them on the internet. This had a side effect: it presented an opportunity for the bankers to tweak any new complex financial engineering scheme they were contemplating, so that they could exploit loopholes in the agencies' models, and achieve that all-important triple A rating (this game is called 'ratings arbitrage').

Structured investment vehicles (SIVs)

Here is an idea: mortgage-backed securities, composed of long-term debt obligations, carry higher interest rates than can be obtained by borrowing short term through the money markets. So, thinks a bright banker, why not create billions and billions of dollars worth of MBS paying, say, 8 per cent per year and then put them into a special purpose vehicle that is financed by commercial paper, paying, say, 7 per cent per year. The extra 1 per cent can come to us, the bankers, less a few expenses, of course. The more MBSs we create, the more we can make on the difference between the short-term interest rate and the long-term interest rate. So what we need to do is put lots of pressure/incentive on mortgage brokers to generate more mortgages so that our bonus next year can be even greater than last year.[21]

In ancient financial history, that is the 1980s, when bankers were more cautious, these types of vehicles were known as **conduits**. In order for them to obtain the very high credit ratings needed to sell commercial paper they had to offer investors belt-and-braces security. The sponsoring organisation, usually an investment bank, would provide an equity buffer by placing money in the conduit, and would also guarantee a line of credit. In other words, if the pool of mortgages ran into trouble and/or the commercial paper buyers refused to purchase paper for the next three-month period or whatever, the bank would step in to provide money to repay the maturing asset-backed commercial paper, so that the legally separate SPV did not have sell its assets in a 'fire sale' to repay the short-term money market investors.

Over time, with statistical models saying that the 2000s were a much calmer and safer environment in which to lend on the security of mortgages and ABSs, the idea of the conduit grew into the **structured investment vehicle (SIV)**. These, too, needed high ratings to sell commercial paper, but this time the sponsoring bank's guarantee of a line of credit was smaller and outside investors (other than the bank) were brought in to take an equity stake in the SIV. The advantage of these changes was that the investment bank could keep SIVs off their balance sheets. So they had a nice profit earner without the need to hold much regulatory capital. This could lead to great improvements in bank return on equity. Under the Basel rules for capital requirements, because the SIVs raised a proportion of their money other than from the sponsoring bank and because the credit lines offered were less than a year in duration, the bank did not have to hold capital reserves for the exposure. The amount of equity capital held within an SIV was typically only 5 per cent or 10 per cent of the assets. Thus they were 10 or 20 times geared.

Of course, you can see the flawed thinking: however many mathematical models you build to calculate past default rates on mortgages, etc., and however many databases you look at to estimate the likelihood of the commercial paper market drying up, you cannot exclude the possibility that the people making decisions will suddenly change behaviour *en masse*. In particular, you need to remember that money market investors are looking for very safe investments. If there is even a hint of trouble in the SIVs they will all pull their money at the same time: not just from that SIV but from the entire sector. If dozens of SIVs are then forced to sell their assets to repay commercial paper as it falls due, these assets (ABSs, CDOs, corporate bonds, Treasury bills, etc.) fall in value, undermining the asset base of banks and other institutions further. SIVs are required to regularly announce the value of their assets – that is to mark-to-market – and so they could not hide and delay reporting losses; they were there for all to see.

---

[21] They also invested in other long-term assets such corporate bonds, Treasury bonds, ABSs and CDOs based on credit card receivables and student debt. Also they raised money from medium-term notes as well as commercial paper.

One of the remarkable features of this period was the lack of understanding by regulators, governments, credit agencies and the financial press[22] of what the banks were doing. CDOs and SIVs were explained to them and to us only after the crash. They had grown very big in a very short period of time.

The internationalisation of risk

The activities discussed above were not confined to the US. London became the world's leading packager of SIVs, for example. Spanish mortgages were popular for CDO creation, and German banks bought vast quantities of AAA-rated US CDOs that offered a rate of return higher than on normal AAA-rated bonds. (Perhaps the high return should have raised some questions in their minds.) Despite the doubt expressed by staff members, the Royal Bank of Scotland grew its CDO business very fast, holding large quantities. UBS of Switzerland had $50 billion of CDOs on its trading desk in 2007. 'We were just told by our risk people that these instruments are triple A, like Treasury bonds. People did not ask too many questions,' said Peter Kurer, a member of the board.[23] Ah, that all-too-human failing: trusting people who have complex models to show you, that you don't understand.

Charles Pardue, one of the team who helped create acceptance for CDOs and SIVs through the intellectual work at J.P. Morgan (which was taken to ridiculous extremes by others), made the comment:

> I don't think that we should kid ourselves that everything that is being sold is fair value. I have been to dealer events where bankers are selling this stuff and the simplicity of the explanation about how it works scares me .... there are people investing in stuff they don't understand, who really seem to believe the models, and when the models change it will be a very scary thing.[24]

Credit default swaps (CDSs)

CDSs (described in Chapter 11) were important contributors to the crisis because they could be used to speculate on defaults without the need to hold the underlying corporate bond, ABS, CDO or SIV. Thus, a seller of a CDS could sell credit protection on, say, $10 million of bonds and receive a premium of say $150,000. If a default does not occur, the seller makes a $150,000 profit. CDSs are bought and sold in a secondary market, with their prices rising if the default risk rises. It was not unusual to find that the amount of CDSs outstanding for a given bond, CDO, etc. was a multiple of the underlying collateral value. Thus, there might be $500 million bonds in issue and $5 billion of CDS contract outstanding on those bonds. If the bond defaulted then the maximum loss was $500m, but if the CDS sellers had to pay out they needed to find $5 billion. So you can see how liability exposure was multiplied by the use of these derivatives, especially when you consider that by mid-2007 the total notional amount of CDSs outstanding was more than $45,000 billion (the US mortgage market was 'only' $7,100 billion).

A key contributor to the crisis is that the payout on default under a CDS is merely a promise. So it is only as good as the financial strength of the seller. There was no central counterparty to back up that promise as there is with exchange-traded derivatives. Once the financial strengths of numerous CDS sellers was demolished, the insurance that purchasers of CDSs thought they had evaporated.

Monoline insurers

The story of the crisis would not be complete without discussing the monoline insurers. Many investors in ABSs, MBSs, CDOs and SIVs were naturally concerned that these securities might be

---

[22] With the exception of Gillian Tett at the *Financial Times* and a handful of others. Professor Nouriel Roubini of New York Stern School of Business was warning of the impending crisis in the mid-2000s. Practitioners ignored or dismissed his comments, and derogatorily called him 'Dr Doom'.
[23] Quoted in Tett (2009) p. 163.
[24] Quoted in Tett (2009) p. 118.

riskier than the promoter or the credit rating indicated. So, to provide extra reassurance the sellers of these instruments sought to take out insurance, similar to car insurance, with a premium up front and a payout if an event happened, such as non-payment of interest or principal. The **monoline insurance** firms started out as very low-risk organisations which offered insurance on bonds issued by US municipal authorities (states, towns, etc.). The buyers of the bonds would accept a lower yield (pay a higher price) if they came with an insurance guarantee.[25] The sellers were willing to pay the insurance premium because they could then sell the bonds at a raised price (because they were now rated AAA) to more than compensate for the insurance premium.

Insurance is only as good as the soundness of the company providing the guarantee. So in the 1970s, 1980s and 1990s monoline insurers had very conservative balance sheets, allowing them to raise money by selling triple-A rated bonds in themselves. Insuring US municipalities (that raise taxes) results in a completely different order of risk than insuring the new securities backed by mortgages. However, in the 2000s the monolines thought they could stretch their expertise to this arena. The mathematicians at the monolines followed the same models used by the banks, rating agencies and regulators and so concluded that these complex instruments were low risk and therefore only a small insurance premium was required. They also became greedy, with some of them insuring 150 times the amount of their equity buffer. The slightest wobble in the sub-prime housing market and they would be insolvent as they paid out on defaults. They would not be able to raise more money in the event of a rise in mortgage delinquencies because the rating agencies would quickly reduce their ratings from AAA.

Many buyers of the fancy new instruments came to rely on the reassurance provided by the monolines. When they failed to meet their obligations this led to great losses for some organisations, and when those organisations could not meet their obligations it led to losses for their creditors.

The crash

From 2002 the foreclosure rate (that is, the proportion of US mortgage holders for whom the bank has got fed up with missed payments and repossessed the house) actually *fell* to 1 per cent in the first quarter of 2005. Over the same period the proportion of loans that was delinquent (mortgagees had not stuck to the agreement, but not so badly as to qualify for repossession) *fell* to 4.31 per cent. This seemed odd because there had been a large rise in the proportion of mortgages classified as sub-prime (e.g. $800 billion were sub-prime in 2005, almost half the total). Rising house prices had helped, because those with short-term money worries could remortgage (take out an extra loan on the security of the house) or sell the house for a profit; Americans did this in great volumes as the richest people in the world borrowed to sustain consumption at higher levels than income (there was a negative savings rate). Low interest rates and low unemployment also helped. However, this was the calm before the storm.

Some early rumblings

In the spring of 2005 the credit rating on the debt of General Motors was downgraded to junk status. This was not unusual. Many issues of corporate debt are downgraded every month. The difference this time was that investors in credit default swaps and CDOs started to panic, causing their market prices to move wildly – so wildly that they were moving more than was assumed in the models. The market was showing signs of (a) nervousness and (b) failing to behave according to the models.

US foreclosures and delinquencies rose in 2006 and 2007. In the first quarter of 2007 foreclosures rose to a record level of over 2 per cent of outstanding mortgages. In February 2007, HSBC announced that its US subsidiary focused on sub-prime lending, Household Finance, had experienced sharply rising default levels. New Century Financial (second largest sub-prime lender) made a similar announcement. Now the cost of buying default protection against BBB-rated bonds of CDOs through credit default swaps rose significantly, but at least the market was

---

[25] Apart from charging a premium, the insurers could also 'insure' via CDSs.

still operating and CDS protection could be bought. Many bankers retained their optimism and wanted to stay in the leveraged loan game. They could not afford to reduce the next-quarter earnings by withdrawing from a large part of their business, even if they had qualms about the long-term safety of the transactions. Chuck Prince, CEO of Citigroup, famously told the *FT* in the summer that the party would end at some point but there was so much liquidity that it would not be disrupted by turmoil in the US sub-prime market, 'When the music stops, in terms of liquidity, things will get complicated. But as long as the music is playing, you've got to get up and dance. We're still dancing … At some point, the disruptive event will be so significant that instead of liquidity filling in, the liquidity will go the other way. I don't think we're at that point.'[26]

By the third quarter of 2007 foreclosures on sub-prime loans had reached almost 7 per cent. Analysts were starting to believe studies that estimated that about 20 per cent of sub-prime mortgages would end in foreclosure. Whereas in the old days the lenders could have negotiated extra time to sell the house to raise more for both the bank and the family, or to let the borrower stay in the house making reduced payments, now, with securitisation, there was little opportunity for negotiation and rescheduling.

Bear Stearns had established two hedge funds and retained close financial links with them. The hedge funds had borrowed heavily to buy CDOs and other high-credit rated issues (on less than $1 billion of capital they had $15 billion of CDOs). While the cost of borrowing remained less than the income from the CDOs they reported high profits (and paid large bonuses). In the summer of 2007 these sub-prime-focused funds reported difficulties – in one month alone the mark-to-market value of the CDOs, etc. fell by 19 per cent. Bear tried to sell some assets to repay the creditors now demanding their money back; If they were not repaid they were entitled to take possession of their collateral. Merrill Lynch, which was owed roughly $850m, and J.P. Morgan, which was owed $500m, took possession of their collateral. Disaster was averted by Bear Stearns taking on the responsibility of compensating many of the hedge funds' creditors. And so, although the market was shaken, it was not yet too frightened.

Deutsche Industriebank, IKB, a medium-sized German lender, had sought to make large profits by entering the SIV market. It sold its commercial paper to European pension funds and investment funds of US public-sector bodies, which trusted the triple-A or double-A ratings, to invest in mortgage-linked CDOs. When in July 2007 Moody's and Standard & Poor's reduced the ratings on some sub-prime mortgage bonds, and after the collapse of Bear Stearns' funds, the investors in IKB's SIV knew they had made a mistake. They bargained for very low risk, and now the reassurance of high credit ratings was being removed. They lacked the skills or the data to value the securities that the SIV had invested in – they relied on credit ratings only. So, in their fear, they stopped buying fresh commercial paper. The offshoot SIVs of IKB had $20 billion of assets compared with the bank's liquid assets of $16 billion. The parent could not find the money to put into the SIVs to prevent the commercial paper holders insisting on a fire sale of assets to repay them within days. Such a fire sale was impossible anyway, given the lack of liquidity in the CDO markets. In the end, the German government forced a group of banks to lend enough to IKB for it to survive. Disaster averted.

Meanwhile, over in Paris, BNP Paribas stopped investors in three of its funds from being able to redeem their investments. It said that it was impossible to value the funds because of high exposure to the US sub-prime market. This disturbed investors.

Aware of a growing sense of foreboding among investors, some of the large banks, such as HSBC and Citibank, brought the assets and liabilities of their SIVs onto their balance sheets so that nervous outside investors could be paid off. Many banks started to realise that their assets were shrinking while they faced a marketplace where it was difficult to raise short-term money – confidence was slipping fast. Some managed to obtain infusions of capital from sovereign wealth funds through the selling of a number of new shares; others could not persuade anybody to buy their shares to bolster their defences.

The MBS and CDO markets worsened to the point where it became difficult to sell even plain vanilla AAA MBSs. People realised that they just did not know what the fancy securities were worth in a falling housing market.

---

[26] Nakamoto, Michiyo and Wighton, David (2007) 'Bullish Citigroup is "still dancing" to the beat of the buy-out boom', *Financial Times*, 10 July.

In August 2007, American Home Mortgage Investment Corporation filed for bankruptcy due to losses on mortgage-related assets and the inability to sell commercial paper. Countrywide, which had operated an almost conveyor belt machine approach to generating mortgages to sell on in a securitised form, said it was starting to stockpile mortgages because of a scarcity of investors. Tension was starting to spread and bankers were told to stop lending to any other financial institution that looked at all risky. They were starting to hoard cash. This was a rational response from the individual banks' perspective but the result was that the interbank loan market, commercial paper and other markets experienced rising interest rates and difficulties in funding. By this stage much of the world economy was dependent on the assumption of reasonably priced money always available. When it became apparent that this was a false assumption, fear increased. It grew further when the default rates on sub-prime mortgages were announced in the autumn, now at 16 per cent. This perplexed some because the economy was still growing and unemployment was low. The answer lay in very bad financial decisions: people had become overstretched after being seduced by the offer of a loan to buy a house that they could never have repaid given their low income. The chickens were coming home to roost.

A UK trigger

Northern Rock had built itself up from a small former building society into the fifth largest UK lender by taking advantage of the securitisation craze. By 2007 most of the funding for its mortgages came from a process of originate-and-distribute. It had nothing to do with US sub-prime, but had built up its own sub-prime operation and more damagingly it had come to rely on a quick selling-on of its loans to the wholesale financial markets to generate a flow of cash to cover mortgages it had already granted. When the psychology of fear swept over the markets, taking the place of enthusiasm for mortgage-related structured securities, suddenly the message went out around the world to stop investing in anything mortgage related. Northern Rock found itself with thousands of mortgages that it had to refinance within days or it would run out of cash. It could not find that cash in the frozen wholesale market and the possibility of attracting deposits from individual savers was a non-starter given the amount the bank now needed to fund. So it turned to the Bank of England to ask for emergency support.

Once word got out that Northern Rock was short of cash, millions of savers panicked. They quickly withdrew money from their online accounts and they queued around the block outside its branches. For the first time since the nineteenth century the UK had a bank run. The government was forced into reassuring depositors by guaranteeing all deposits with the bank. The Bank of England provided funds to keep it operating. Northern Rock was so badly wounded that no private buyer would take it on. So in early 2008 it was nationalised.

The UK regulatory system was particularly badly prepared for overseeing the financial innovations of the Noughties. Regulation was split between the Financial Service Authority, the Bank of England and the Treasury. The FSA was given responsibility for judging bank strategies. From its limited perspective, what it saw was that banks were complying with its rules and so it did not intervene. It did not have a system-wide focus and did not appreciate the threat from CDOs and SIVs. That was left up to the Bank of England, which did make noises about the worryingly fast growth of the banks' balance sheets, but without the backing of the FSA and the Treasury, it lacked the power to intervene.

Following the Northern Rock fiasco, in April 2008, the Bank of England introduced the Special Liquidity Scheme which enabled banks to swap their mortgage-backed securities and other assets for Treasury bills. These could then be sold in the market to raise cash.

A major US trigger – Bear Stearns

By the winter of 2007/2008 analysts, particularly those at the rating agencies, were having considerable doubts about their model assumptions. For example, the recovery rate for foreclosed mortgages was assumed to be 70 per cent. But that was calculated before the massive rise of sub-prime and the growth of the worst forms of sub-prime. These were termed NINJAs – No Income, No Job or Assets. They were granted on the assumption that house price rises would pay off the mortgage when the family moved. When they knew they were to be repossessed these households would leave their property in a much worse state than those in the 1990s. And, of course, house prices were falling. So now the analysts estimated that only 40 per cent of the loan amount would be recovered on a foreclosure. What made things even worse was that in some areas, as house prices fell and repossessions rose, the neighbourhood became blighted – nobody wanted to live there. This, together with growing negative equity (house worth less than mortgage), created a reflexive feedback loop, a self-fulfilling view on the future of house prices in that area. This psychological problem was not allowed for in the mathematical models on default levels. By now even the mathematicians were becoming frightened.

Citigroup had been one of the most enthusiastic creators of CDOs, particularly in 2006 and 2007. Many of these would be held on its balance sheet until buyers could be found. By the end of 2007 the amounts reached the staggering level of $55 billion. On top of that it had made promises to repay within days $25 billion of commercial paper secured by CDOs. It had to announce potential write-offs of up to $11 billion. It was not alone: Merrill Lynch wrote off $20.2 billion and UBS $15 billion. Bank shares fell dramatically.

Prior to the crisis the bankers had managed to persuade the regulators that the complex instruments they were creating would disperse risk to those most able to bear it – hinting that it would be borne by non-bank institutions and funds. In reality, the CDOs etc. seemed to be piling up on bank's balance sheets as they swapped assets between themselves and held inventories of them until they could be sold. They had concentrated risk rather than dispersed it.

For the next few months the write-offs announced by Citi, Merrill and UBS grew larger as banks found themselves at the centre of a downward spiral. The more losses that were revealed, the less confidence investors had. The less confidence, the more assets had to be sold (or marked to market) in a declining market, leading to lower confidence and thus reduced values.

Bear Stearns had become increasingly dependent on the repo market (*see* Chapter 5) to raise short-term funds. Using repos means that a substantial proportion of funding has to be rolled over on a daily basis. It used mortgage-backed bonds as collateral. Once confidence in these instruments declined, Bear found difficulties in obtaining short-term loans. In March 2008, the regulators realised that Bear was in trouble and that if it defaulted on its current repos it would cause panic in the wholesale markets. To prevent that they negotiated for other financial institutions to buy it. Eventually J.P. Morgan agreed to do so, but at a price that left little value for the previous shareholders in Bear. The directors had destroyed shareholder value on a massive scale.

The rescue of Bear, with the regulators to the fore, and the subsequent slashing of US prime interest rates, reassured the markets for a few months as they reasoned that the government and the Fed would not allow a major bank failure and a crash. But this sanguine view had to contend with some disturbing facts: (1) The assets of the SIVs had grown to be worth several trillion dollars – these needed regular refunding in a depressed market; (2) The shadow banks (SIVs, hedge funds, money market funds, etc. – *see* Chapter 15), which are regulated much less than the banks, now had a complex web of trading obligations with the banks, including $60,000 billion of CDSs. The system was so interconnected and so opaque that no one could figure how it could unravel if more confidence was lost.

The Lehman trigger

Many of the US sub-prime mortgages granted in 2005 and 2006 offered low teaser rates for the first two years, so by 2008 when households faced much higher monthly payments, the analysts were anticipating an accelerated default rate. This would reduce confidence in mortgage-related instruments further. Some analysts in spring 2008 estimated the loss in the prices of CDOs would turn out to total $400 billion. By September, with US houses 20 per cent down from their peak prices, things had got so bad in the securitised market that the loss in value weakened Fannie Mae and Freddie Mac to the point where they were taken into conservatorship (nationalisation) by the Fed. They had both operated with relatively small capital bases on which was piled a great deal of debt. A number of writers of credit default swaps on Freddie and Fannie securities suffered losses, hitting sentiment hard.

Lehman Brothers, like Bear Stearns, had drawn a high proportion of its funding from the repo market and had enormous exposure to residential mortgage bond instruments and commercial property. Once the other financial institutions suspected that Lehmans was losing money to the point where it might default, they simply stopped lending to it. It was on the point of collapse when the Fed assembled the heads of the major banks to cajole them into rescuing it. The government or the Fed could not rescue another irresponsible financial institution. They were already receiving criticism for rescuing Bear and the GSEs. If the regulators go on like this, it was said, they will create moral hazard in which financial institutions take outlandish risks knowing that the authorities will step in to prevent failure and the loss of those highly paid jobs and all those bonuses for 'risk taking'.

'No more soft touch' was the message. An example had to be made to ram home the idea that financial organisations would suffer the consequences of their actions. Ideally, Lehman's operations, asset and liabilities would be taken over by another bank(s), with its shareholders' value being wiped out and senior management removed. However, no other bank wanted to take on Lehman's positions and it was made bankrupt on 15 September. Not only did writers of CDSs on Lehman's debt have to take a hit but on that day it was counterparty to roughly $800 billion of CDSs. Because of the intertwined financial obligations institutions around the world had with Lehman's investors, the failure of Lehmans to meet its obligation had a whole series of knock-on effects. They panicked.

Some examples of the knock-on effects included:

- London-based hedge funds with money held by Lehman's had their assets frozen, so they could not complete deals they had made.

- Managers and investors in money market funds had believed that the authorities would save Lehman's and therefore their holdings of Lehman's debt was safe. Now the perception changed. They swallowed losses on Lehman and nervously looked around for who might be next. Fear and caution led to sharp reduction of short-term money availability, and spiralling interest rates. The Reserve Primary Fund, a money market fund, 'broke the buck' (the net asset value dropped below the amount put in by investors) causing even greater aversion to supplying finance to the commercial paper market – the market size fell by $500 billion in one week.

- The largest writer of credit default swaps, AIG, the world's largest insurance company, was headed toward losses of over $180 billion. It had nowhere near this amount of money to make good on its promises. Ben Bernanke of the Fed said that he was very angry that AIG, a stable insurance company, had developed hedge fund-type derivative positions (CDOs) that completely overshadowed its normal business.

- Stock markets fell, wiping away billions of paper wealth, helping to create a sense of doom.

- Institutions refused to deal with one another as rumours flew around about which would be the next to collapse. Trust had evaporated. Those financial economists, mathematicians and heads of banks were made painfully aware that markets need human trust and confidence more than they need complex mathematics.

Now the dominoes fell fast. In September 2008 AIG was granted an $85 billion loan from the Fed in exchange for a 79.9 per cent equity stake in the business (effectively nationalisation). It was too big and too interconnected to be allowed to fail. In the same month Merrill Lynch was so desperate that it agreed to be taken over by Bank of America. A few days later one of the largest UK banks the ailing HBOS was bought by Lloyds, and Washington Mutual (sixth largest US bank) collapsed and was sold to J.P. Morgan for a fraction of its previous value. Then the UK government was forced into nationalising Bradford and Bingley.

Government actions

Bank rescues

In the days after the loss of Lehmans the US Treasury and the Fed were shocked at the extent of the knock-on effects, and knew they had to do something. They proposed the creation of a fund of $700 billion to buy 'troubled assets' from the banks.[27] However, this was quickly changed to a plan to inject money directly into banks rather than merely purchase assets from them. The bank

---

[27] Called the Troubled Asset Relief Program (TARP).

leaders were gathered together and told that they would have to accept the injection of government money for preferred share stakes or they would not be eligible for any future bailout. The government holding of shares in Citigroup was increased so that it was, in effect, nationalised. When Bank of America realised just how rotten the assets of Merrill Lynch were they needed a further government injection. The government also permitted Goldman Sachs and Morgan Stanley to change from being technically classified as brokers into banks, allowing them to benefit from government bailouts including access to the Fed funds discount window (the US lender of last resort function – *see* Chapter 7). Goldman was forced to ask for an infusion of cash by selling $5 billion of preferred stock offering a very high dividend to Berkshire Hathaway (chairman – Warren Buffett).

The US Treasury insured the $3,400 billion money market mutual fund industry (it would not allow shares in money market funds to fall below the $1 in value put in by savers) to encourage investors to retain their savings in the system. This was bailing out 30 million Americans and comprised one half of all deposits at domestic US banks. If this had not been done US savers would have become very wary. The cascade of fear might have caused a Depression.

Over in London the government and the Bank of England were dead set against bank bailouts because they did not want to encourage moral hazard. However, once they realised the full extent of leverage in the system and that the banks faced not just a liquidity problem (as with Northern Rock) but a solvency problem (*see* Chapter 7), they decided to act. Mervyn King at the BoE was shocked: 'When we started this crisis there was a widespread view that banks were well capitalised. But now we realise that the problem was that assets sitting on their balance sheets which were supposed to be risk-free, carried a lot of risk. Perceptions of the value of those assets and the risks changed radically.'[28] The BoE set about injecting £200 billion of cash into the money markets. The government guaranteed £250 billion of bonds issued by banks as well buying equity stakes in some leading banks. Royal Bank of Scotland received £20 billion in new equity and Lloyds which had avoided the lure of structured finance and was strong before it bought the less disciplined HBOS received £17 billion.

Dexia was rescued by the governments of Germany, Luxembourg and Belgium, while the Irish government stopped a run on their banks by guaranteeing all deposits (a move that was to later virtually bankrupt the government). Hypo Real Estate was saved by the German government and Fortis was nationalised by the Dutch. Iceland nationalised its banks which had liabilities many times the size of the economy of its 320,000 people, and was forced to seek financial help from the International Monetary Fund.

Economy rescues

Recession started in the US economy at the end of 2007 and grew worse through 2008 to become the worst since the 1930s. Similar downturns were experienced in Europe, and the leading developing countries suffered a slowing down in growth. To combat lowered confidence in the economic future and rising unemployment, western governments pumped demand up in the economy by dramatically increasing deficit spending – i.e. spending far more than is raised in taxes by borrowing the difference. The rapidly rising levels of government debts will have severe long-term consequences as we ask later generations to pay off the bill for this borrowing. They also have dramatic political consequences, with many governments being rejected by the electorate for not preventing, or failing to effectively deal with, the crisis.

Western central banks reduced interest rates to close to zero to encourage economic activity (*see* Chapter 7 for a discussion on monetary policy). Governments and central banks also purchased bonds from the private sector (usually banks) to lower interest rates at the medium and longer end of the yield curve as well as supplying money to the system. This quantitative easing is discussed in Chapter 7 as are a number of other regulatory responses such as living wills and tighter bank capital ratios (*see also* Chapter 15).

---

[28] Quoted in Tett (2009) p. 283.

Concluding comments

Following each crisis there is always a feeling that, as we rush around tightening that regulation, banning that type of security, or changing that incentive, we are merely preparing for the last war. Even now, so soon after the last bust, clever bankers with mastery of complex maths will be working on innovative securities that will be designed to get around this or that regulation (regulatory arbitrage); fool this or that credit rating agency; bemuse and impress impressionable trustees of other people's money from pension funds to insurance funds and hedge funds. Hopefully there is a greater proportion of mathematical model sceptics who, while accepting that the models have their uses, realise that they need to be moderated, supplemented and even overridden by human decision makers, who take into account a wide range of factors beyond those immediately quantifiable.

Golden rules:

1   If you cannot understand it, don't invest in it. Have an acute awareness of the perimeter of your circle of competence: do you know what you know and know what you don't know? Don't trust others peddling complexity because you fear looking foolish when everyone else is saying what wonderful clothes the Emperor has. Complexity, particularly mathematical complexity, is not the same as sophistication. Modification for regulators: if you don't understand it, why are you allowing it?

2   If it looks too good to be true, it probably is. How did anyone believe that a CDO of ABSs could hold a credit rating of AAA, the same as for a highly reputable corporation, and yet offer hundreds of basis points more in interest?

3   Be wary of the power of some innovations to grow a new market quickly and then destroy. 'Successful innovation by its very nature initially outstrips our ability to regulate it' said Robert Merton.[29] Paul Volcker, a former chairman of the Fed, has doubts about the value of increasing the complexity of financial instruments. As he reflected on the financial scene he put the complexity-merchants in their place by saying that over the past 30 years the most useful innovation was the automatic teller machine: 'I wish somebody would give me some shred of neutral evidence about the relationship between financial innovation recently and the growth of the economy.'[30]

4   Beware of collective delusion. The pressure from the crowd to believe in a bad idea is powerful. Think independently. Even those supposedly great authorities, the regulators and the credit rating agencies, were proved to have hopelessly inadequate methods and a weakness for believing the prevailing wisdom, so you need to think for yourself.

5   High leverage is dangerous. Warren Buffett says: 'It's kind of like alcohol. One drink is fine, but ten will get you in a lot of trouble. With leverage, people have a great propensity to use it because it's so much fun when it works. There should be some ways of controlling leverage.'[31] Bankers focus on return on equity in the short run. So, for a given return on assets, the greater the proportion of those assets financed by leverage, the higher the return on equity. They can become addicted to raising earnings per share each quarter or half year by increasing leverage. They can do this for many years before the risk becomes apparent. They need help in controlling their addiction, which is where the regulators come in.

6   Avoid situations of interdependence that result in confused entanglement, where no one knows who is really holding the risk.

[29] Speaking in 'Making the financial markets safe: an interview with Robert Merton' (2009) *Harvard Business Review*, October. Available on Harvard Case Study website.

[30] Quoted in Tom Braithwaite (2011) 'Greenspan hits at Dodd-Frank law', *Financial Times*, 30 March.

[31] Speaking in an interview with Guy Rolnik (2011) 'Warren Buffett: the US is moving toward plutocracy', TheMarker, http://english.themarker.com/warren-buffett-the-u-s-is-moving-toward-plutocracy-1.351236.

7 Do not have incentive systems where it's heads I win, tails the other guy loses. Many of the bankers working in ABSs, CDOs, CDSs and SIVs took home large bonuses in the good times (over $1 million each year) regardless of the impact on those they were dealing with. Even when things turned sour many retained highly paid positions.

8 When financial bubbles blow up remember Cinderella, who knew it could not last but could not see clocks on the wall to tell her when it would all turn to pumpkins and mice, and besides which she was having so much fun. Everyone thinks they will be able to get out five minutes before midnight.[32]

9 Recognise that banks are not very good at self-regulation. As well as the authorities insisting on robust capital and liquidity reserves, they must implement some form of separation of the 'casino' activities of investment banking trading and derivatives activities from the retail banking operations. This must be structured so that the former can be allowed to go bust taking shareholder and wholesale market creditor wealth with them, but the retail bank activities can carry on following a government bailout, preserving the value to society of the deposit taking, business lending and money transmission functions. They should also insist on detailed and regularly updated plans for the orderly recovery or liquidation of a bank if it should at some point in the future run into trouble.

10 Remember that banks are full of smart people who will exploit a gap or loophole created because national authorities do not create regulatory structures that work across borders.

There will be another crisis; in fact, there will be many. I don't know when or where or what form they will take, but I do know that structures created by humans are subject to emotional surges, cognitive failure, hubris born of neat modelling and the tendency to forget most of the golden rules and the lessons of history. The best that we can hope for is that it is not too soon.

Key points and concepts

- Finance is a multidisciplinary subject, and not primarily mathematical.

- The algebra lovers, with their complex, yet unsophisticated, modelling of the world of human constructs, such as markets, can lead us astray.

- **Value at risk**, or **VaR**, is an estimate of the loss on a portfolio over a period of time (usually 24 hours is chosen) that will be exceeded with a given frequency, e.g. a frequency of one day out of 100, or five days out of 100.

- Mathematicians were not allowing for the possibility of extreme events (called black swans) – that the tails of the distribution are in fact much bigger, 'fatter', than generally supposed, because extreme things hit us more often than we anticipate.

- VaR led many senior bankers into a false sense of security prior to the crisis. They were thus emboldened to double and triple their bets on securities such as mortgage CDOs because they appeared to produce high profits without raising VaR much. Under the Basel capital rules for banks VaR could be used as an argument for lowering capital requirements.

- **Reflexivity**: decisions are based on people's perception or interpretation of the situation. Furthermore, their decisions can change the situation, alter the fundamentals. Changes in the fundamentals thus caused are liable to change the perceptions of individuals.

- Occasionally the reflexive interaction can lead to massive market distortions – **'far-from-equilibrium conditions'** – leading to boom/bust sequences.

- The **super-bubble reflexive process** evolved over a period of a quarter of a century. The main prevailing trend was ever-more sophisticated methods of credit expansion, supported by the trend to globalisation and the trend of the removal of regulations with increasing financial innovation.

▶

---

[32] I'm grateful to Warren Buffett for this analogy.

- Some of the main elements:
  - Low interest rates in early 2000s.
  - Growth of asset-backed securitisation.
  - Growth of sub-prime mortgages in 2000s, with increasingly lax criteria.
  - Incentives for mortgage brokers to sell high volumes.
  - Credit score models used data from a time when the mortgage market was significantly different.
  - Movement from the **originate-and-hold model,** where banks retain the loan on their books and therefore have every incentive to ensure that the mortgagee can repay and can help those few who have temporary problems along the way, to the **originate-and-distribute model**, selling them to other investors, usually through securitisations.
  - Massive growth in **collateralised debt obligation market:** a bond issued by a special purpose vehicle, SPV, set up by a deal structurer, usually an investment bank, where the SPV holds a pool of loans or a pool of debt securities. The bonds are issued in a number of different classes or tranches, each with their own risk and return characteristics.
  - **Credit rating agencies** seemed to follow the same limited mathematical models as others.
  - **Structured investment vehicles, SIVs** buy assets such as mortgages or ABSs after raising finance mostly by selling commercial paper.
  - The amount of CDSs outstanding for a given bond, CDO, etc. was often a multiple of the underlying collateral value. And the promise to pay was only as good as the financial strength of the CDS seller.
  - The **monoline insurance** firms started out as very low risk organisations who offered insurance on bonds issued by US municipal authorities. In the 2000s the monolines thought they could stretch their expertise to the mortgage backed securities market. The mathematicians at the monolines followed the same models used by the banks, rating agencies and regulators, and so concluded that these complex instruments were low risk and therefore only a small insurance premium was required. They also became greedy with some of them insuring 150 times the amount of their equity buffer.

References and further reading

Akerlof, G.A. and Shiller, R.J. (2009) Animal Spirits: How human psychology drives the economy, and why it matters for global capitalism. Princeton University Press. An easy-to-read warning on the powerful psychological forces impacting markets, such as confidence, fear, bad faith, corruption, and concern for fairness. A call for more intervention by authorities to manage and channel these animal spirits.

Arnold, G. (2009) *The Financial Times Guide to Value Investing: How to become a disciplined investor.* Financial Times Prentice Hall. Combines the ideas of six investors with financial and corporate strategy theory to present an investment philosophy.

Arnold, G. (2011) *The Great Investors: Lessons on Investing from the Master Traders.* Financial Times Prentice Hall. Describes the issues regarded by very experienced and highly regarded financial market players – none uses complex maths.

Augar, P. (2009) *Chasing Alpha: How Reckless Growth and Unchecked Ambition Ruined the City's Golden Decade.* London: The Bodley Head.
> An accessible account of the crisis from someone who has great experience in the City.

Authers, J. (2010) *The Fearful Rise of Markets: A Short View of Global Bubbles and Synchronised Meltdowns.* London: Pearson Education Ltd.
> A highly readable account of the events which led to the crisis and some ideas on preventing future crises, set in the context of the practical world of finance. John Authers is a highly respected FT columnist.

Bootle, R. (2009) *The Trouble with Markets: Saving Capitalism from Itself.* London: Nicholas Brealey Publishing.
> An attack on the idea that markets are always right is all the more powerful when presented by a City economist with more than three decades of experience.

Brummer, A. (2009) *The Crunch: How Greed and Incompetence Sparked the Credit Crisis.* London: The Random House Group Ltd.
> A readily accessible account of the crisis.

Buffett, W. (various): Chairman's Letter accompanying the Berkshire Hathaway Annual Report.
 If you want to understand finance and investment, read these insightful, witty and accessible letters. Available on the internet.

Cable, V. (2009) *The Storm: The World Economic Crisis and What it Meant.* London: Atlantic Books.
 The UK government's minister for business with a great deal of experience of the City concentrates on how we get out of the mess and try to make a better system for the future.

Davies, H. and Green, D. (2010) *Banking On The Future: The Fall and Rise of Central Banking.* Princeton University Press.
 Presents ideas of improvement in central banking drawing on lessons from the crisis.

El-Erian, M. (2008) *When Markets Collide: Investment Strategies for the Age of Global Economic Change.* New York: McGraw-Hill.
 Valuable insight into the workings of modern financial markets, highlighting the dangers.

Fox, J. (2009) *The Myth of the Rational Market: A History of Risk, Reward, and Delusion on Wall Street.* New York: HarperCollins.
 Chronicles the rise of financial economists' ideas over the last century and how things worked out in a way more complex than they grasped.

Grant, J. (2008) *Mr Market Miscalculates: The Bubble Years and Beyond.* Mount Jackson, VA: Axios Press.
 A collection of articles tracing events in recent US financial history.

Kaufman, H. (2009) *The Road to Financial Reformation: Warnings, Consequences, Reforms.* Hoboken, NJ: John Wiley & Sons Inc.
 Draws on the history of financial innovation to provide underlying causes of the crisis.

Kaufman, M. T. (2002) *'Soros'.* New York: Vintage Books.
 A well-written biography of Soros as well as an exploration of his ideas.

Lewis, M. (2008) *Panic: The Story of Modern Financial Insanity.* London: Puffin Books.
 An account of the crisis focused on the main personalities.

Li, D. X. (2000) 'On default correlation: a copula function approach', *Journal of Fixed Income*, Vol. 9, pp. 43–55.
 An influential model presented.

Lynch, P. (1993*) 'Beating The Street'.* New York: Simon & Schuster.
 One of the greatest fund managers gives insight into real investing rather than mathematical investing.

Lynch, P. (1990) *'One Up On Wall Street'.* London: Penguin Books.
 One of the greatest fund managers gives insight into real investing rather than mathematical investing.

Mason, P. (2009) *Meltdown: The End of the Age of Greed.* London: Verso.
 A UK writer presents an easy-to-read account of the crisis.

McLean, B. and Nocera, J. (2010) *All The Devils Are Here: The Hidden History of the Financial Crisis.* London: Penguin Books Ltd.
 Explains the events and people very well – easy to follow.

Montier, J. (2003) *Behavioural Finance: Insights into Irrational Minds and Markets.* Chichester: John Wiley and Sons Ltd.
 A short book focusing on behavioural factors in markets.

Montier, J. (2007) *Behavioural Investing: A Practitioner's Guide to Applying Behavioural Finance.* Chichester: John Wiley and Sons Ltd.
 An important book presenting a number of articles explaining the influence of behavioural factors on markets.

Montier, J. (2009) *Value Investing: Tools and Techniques for Intelligent Investment.* Chichester: John Wiley & Sons Ltd.
 Moving away from financial economists' models to a more holistic approach to share investing.

Montier, J. (2010) *The Little Book of Behavioural Investing: How Not to Be Your Own Worst Enemy.* Chichester: John Wiley & Sons Ltd.
 A summary of James Montier's key ideas on the importance of taking account of behavioural influences on markets.

Morris, C. R. (2008) *The Two Trillion Dollar Meltdown: Easy Money, High Rollers, and the Great Credit Crash.* New York: Public Affairs.

Patterson, S. (2010) *The Quants: How a New Breed of Math Whizzes Conquered Wall Street and Nearly Destroyed it.* New York: Crown Business.
 An account of the key developments in mathematical financial models over the last 40 years which contributed to the financial crisis. Written somewhat like a movie script with personalities involved, but nevertheless contains great insights.

Peston, R. (2008) *Who Runs Britain? ... And Who's to Blame for the Economic Mess We're In.* London: Hodder & Stoughton.
 An account of the powerful financial players who seem to have too much power relative to our elected representatives in the UK. Written by the BBC news business editor.

Rajan, R. G. (2010) *Fault Lines: How Hidden Fractures Still Threaten the World Economy.* Princeton University Press.
 Flaws still exist in the key economies of the world and need to be fixed.

Reinhart, C. M. and Rogoff, K. S. (2009) *This Time is Different: Eight Centuries of Financial Folly.* Princeton University Press.
 A comprehensive and rigorous analysis of financial crises.

Robinson, L. and Young, P. L. (2010) *The Gathering Storm: How to Avoid the Next Crisis from the Minds that Predicted the Crunch*. Torun: Derivatives Vision.
A collection of writings on the crisis.

Salmon, F. (2009) 'Recipe for disaster: the formula that killed Wall Street', *Wired*, 23 February.
A critique of the use of David Li's Gausian copula formula.

Shiller, R. J. (2003) *The New Financial Order: Risk in the 21st Century*. Princeton University Press.
A call for ways of hedging risk.

Shiller, R. J. (2008) *The Subprime Solution: How Today's Global Financial Crisis Happened, and What To Do About It*. Princeton University Press.
The subprime crisis was caused by irrational exuberance and overextension of credit. This accessible book provides ideas for avoiding future bubbles and helping the economy out of the current mess.

Shleifer, A. (2000) *Inefficient Markets: An Introduction to Behavioural Finance*. Oxford University Press.
A forceful set of arguments is presented to counter the view that markets are rational pricing machines producing efficiently priced securities. They are influenced by behavioural factors.

Slater, R. (2009) '*Soros, The World's Most Influential Investor*'. New York: McGraw-Hill.
A biography and discussion of Soros' ideas.

Smithers, A. (2009) *Wall Street Revealed: Imperfect Markets and Inept Central Bankers*. Chichester: John Wiley and Sons Ltd.
A master of stock market history, financial valuation and clear thinking explains that markets are only imperfectly efficient, that they can rise too far as a result of exuberance and fall excessively due to over-pessimism.

Soros, G. (1995) '*Soros on Soros*'. New York: John Wiley & Sons, Inc.
A discussion of George Soros' ideas.

Soros, G. (2008) *The Crash of 2008 and What it Means*.

New York: Public Affairs.
An insightful account of the crash embedded in an economic philosophy.

Soros, G. (1994) *The Alchemy of Finance*. New York: John Wiley & Sons, Inc.
An early presentation of George Soros' ideas – not the easiest of reads.

Stiglitz, J. (2010) *Freefall: Free Markets and the Sinking of the Global Economy*. London: Penguin Books Ltd.
A call for radical reforms in response to the crisis including a new global financial architecture.

Taleb, N. N. (2001) *Fooled by Randomness: The Hidden Role of Chance in the Markets and in Life*. New York: Texere LLC.
Humans, particularly market players, generally underestimate randomness and the potential for extreme events to occur.

Taleb, N. N. (2008) *The Black Swan: The Impact of the Highly Improbable*. London: Penguin.
Insufficient probability is placed on the chance of high-impact rare events to occur.

Tett, G. (2009) *Fool's Gold: How Unrestrained Greed Corrupted a Dream, Shattered Global Markets and Unleashed a Catastrophe*. London: Little, Brown.
An excellent account of the personalities behind the innovations in finance, the instruments used and the sequence of events.

Triana, P. (2009) *Lecturing Birds on Flying: Can Mathematical Theories Destroy the Financial Markets?* Hoboken, NJ: John Wiley and Sons, Inc.
A former derivatives trader and now a professor takes a critical look at quantitative financial models. An entertaining and accessible read.

Wolf, M. (2009) *Fixing Global Finance: How to Curb Financial Crises in the 21st Century*. Yale University Press.
A leading columnist at the FT provides a view of the crisis and its consequences that is less USA-centric than many other books, with greater attention to the future of the international financial system.

Video presentations

Bank chief executives and other senior people describe and discuss the impact of the financial crisis and its current consequences, including the impact of regulation, in interviews, documentaries and webcasts at Cantos.com. (www.cantos.com) – these are free to view.

Case study recommendations

See www.pearsoned.co.uk/arnold for case study synopses.
Also see Harvard University: http://hbsp.harvard.edu/product/cases

- Subprime Meltdown: American Housing and Global Financial Turmoil (2008) Author: Julio Rotemberg. Harvard Business School.
- Bear Stearns and the Seeds of its Demise (2008) Author: Susan Chaplinsky. Darden, University of Pennsylvania. Available on Harvard Case Study website.
- The Financial Crisis of 2007–2009: The Road to Systemic Risk (2009) Author: George (Yiorgos) Allayannis. Darden, University of Pennsylvania. Available on Harvard Case Study website.
- Western Asset Arbitrage (CDOs at Lehman's) (2009) Authors: Rahul Prabhu and Elena Loutskina. Darden, University of Pennsylvania. Available on Harvard Case Study website.
- The Great Recession, 2007–2010: Causes and Consequences (2010) Authors: Danielle Cadieux and David Conklin. Richard Ivey School of Business, University of Western Ontario. Available on Harvard Case Study website.
- Lincoln Financial Meets the Financial Crisis (2010) Authors: Robert C. Pozen and Peter Spring. Harvard Business School.
- Geithner and Bernanke Amid the Global Financial Crisis (2009) Author: Frank Warnock. Darden, University of Pennsylvania. Available on Harvard Case Study website.
- Managing Risk in the New World (2009) Roundtable discussion with Robert S. Kaplan, Anette Mikes, Robert Simons, Peter Tufano, Michael Hofmann and David Champion. Harvard Business Review, October. Available on Harvard Case Study website.
- The Weekend that Changed Wall Street (2009) Authors: Christopher Brandriff and George (Yiorgos) Allayannis. Darden, University of Pennsylvania. Available on Harvard Case Study website.
- Making the Financial Markets Safe: An Interview with Robert Merton (2009). Interviewed by David Champion. *Harvard Business Review*, October. Available on Harvard Case Study website.
- Bank of America-Merrill Lynch (2010) Authors: Guhan Subramanian and Nithyasri Sharma. Harvard Business School.
- Goldman Sachs: A Bank for All Seasons (A) (2010) Authors: Lena Genello Goldberg and Tiffany Obenchain. Harvard Business School.

Self-review questions

1 What is a structured investment vehicle?

2 Describe a collateralised debt obligation.

3 What is value at risk?

4 What are the originate-and-hold and the originate-and-distribute models of banking?

5 What role is performed by the monoline insurers?

Questions and problems

1   Explain the role of collateralised debt obligations, structured investment vehicles and credit default swaps in the events leading to the financial crisis. Describe and illustrate the character of each of these instruments.

2   Describe and explain George Soros' theory of reflexivity. Use reflexivity to explain at least some of the causes of the 2008 crisis.

3   Describe, explain and illustrate the following:

   (a) value at risk;
   (b) collateralised debt obligation;
   (c) structured investment vehicles.

4   It has been argued that over-reliance on mathematical models is a perennial problem in the financial markets. What is your view on this given the events of the period 2000 to 2009. Include a description of two of the models used prior to the crisis which might have been contributory causes.

5   Outline the key financial crisis events in 2007 and 2008 and discuss whether you think the governments and regulatory agencies took the correct steps.

Appendices

I   Future value of £1 at compound interest

II   Present value of £1 at compound interest

III Present value of an annuity of £1 at compound interest

IV Future value of an annuity of £1 at compound interest

V   Answers to the mathematical tools exercises in Chapter 5, Appendix 5.2

VI Answers to end-of-chapter numerical questions

Interest rate

Periods	1	2	3	4	5	6	7	8	9	10	11	12	13	14	15
1	1.0100	1.0200	1.0300	1.0400	1.0500	1.0600	1.0700	1.0800	1.0900	1.1000	1.1100	1.1200	1.1300	1.1400	1.1500
2	1.0201	1.0404	1.0609	1.0816	1.1025	1.1236	1.1449	1.1664	1.1881	1.2100	1.2321	1.2544	1.2769	1.2996	1.3225
3	1.0303	1.0612	1.0927	1.1249	1.1576	1.1910	1.2250	1.2597	1.2950	1.3310	1.3676	1.4049	1.4429	1.4815	1.5209
4	1.0406	1.0824	1.1255	1.1699	1.2155	1.2625	1.3108	1.3605	1.4116	1.4641	1.5181	1.5735	1.6305	1.6890	1.7490
5	1.0510	1.1041	1.1593	1.2167	1.2763	1.3382	1.4026	1.4693	1.5386	1.6105	1.6851	1.7623	1.8424	1.9254	2.0114
6	1.0615	1.1262	1.1941	1.2653	1.3401	1.4185	1.5007	1.5869	1.6771	1.7716	1.8704	1.9738	2.0820	2.1950	2.3131
7	1.0721	1.1487	1.2299	1.3159	1.4071	1.5036	1.6058	1.7138	1.8280	1.9487	2.0762	2.2107	2.3526	2.5023	2.6600
8	1.0829	1.1717	1.2668	1.3686	1.4775	1.5938	1.7182	1.8509	1.9926	2.1436	2.3045	2.4760	2.6584	2.8526	3.0590
9	1.0937	1.1951	1.3048	1.4233	1.5513	1.6895	1.8385	1.9990	2.1719	2.3579	2.5580	2.7731	3.0040	3.2519	3.5179
10	1.1046	1.2190	1.3439	1.4802	1.6289	1.7908	1.9672	2.1589	2.3674	2.5937	2.8394	3.1058	3.3946	3.7072	4.0456
11	1.1157	1.2434	1.3842	1.5395	1.7103	1.8983	2.1049	2.3316	2.5804	2.8531	3.1518	3.4785	3.8359	4.2262	4.6524
12	1.1268	1.2682	1.4258	1.6010	1.7959	2.0122	2.2522	2.5182	2.8127	3.1384	3.4985	3.8960	4.3345	4.8179	5.3503
13	1.1381	1.2936	1.4685	1.6651	1.8856	2.1329	2.4098	2.7196	3.0658	3.4523	3.8833	4.3635	4.8980	5.4924	6.1528
14	1.1495	1.3195	1.5126	1.7317	1.9799	2.2609	2.5785	2.9372	3.3417	3.7975	4.3104	4.8871	5.5348	6.2613	7.0757
15	1.1610	1.3459	1.5580	1.8009	2.0789	2.3966	2.7590	3.1722	3.6425	4.1772	4.7846	5.4736	6.2543	7.1379	8.1371
16	1.1726	1.3728	1.6047	1.8730	2.1829	2.5404	2.9522	3.4259	3.9703	4.5950	5.3109	6.1304	7.0673	8.1372	9.3576
17	1.1843	1.4002	1.6528	1.9479	2.2920	2.6928	3.1588	3.7000	4.3276	5.0545	5.8951	6.8660	7.9861	9.2765	10.7613
18	1.1961	1.4282	1.7024	2.0258	2.4066	2.8543	3.3799	3.9960	4.7171	5.5599	6.5436	7.6900	9.0243	10.5752	12.3755
19	1.2081	1.4568	1.7535	2.1068	2.5270	3.0256	3.6165	4.3157	5.1417	6.1159	7.2633	8.6128	10.1974	12.0557	14.2318
20	1.2202	1.4859	1.8061	2.1911	2.6533	3.2071	3.8697	4.6610	5.6044	6.7275	8.0623	9.6463	11.5231	13.7435	16.3665
25	1.2824	1.6406	2.0938	2.6658	3.3864	4.2919	5.4274	6.8485	8.6231	10.8347	13.5855	17.0001	21.2305	26.4619	32.9190

Periods	16	17	18	19	20	21	22	23	24	25	26	27	28	29	30
1	1.1600	1.1700	1.1800	1.1900	1.2000	1.2100	1.2200	1.2300	1.2400	1.2500	1.2600	1.2700	1.2800	1.2900	1.3000
2	1.3456	1.3689	1.3924	1.4161	1.4400	1.4641	1.4884	1.5129	1.5376	1.5625	1.5876	1.6129	1.6384	1.6641	1.6900
3	1.5609	1.6016	1.6430	1.6852	1.7280	1.7716	1.8158	1.8609	1.9066	1.9531	2.0004	2.0484	2.0972	2.1467	2.1970
4	1.8106	1.8739	1.9388	2.0053	2.0736	2.1436	2.2153	2.2889	2.3642	2.4414	2.5205	2.6014	2.6844	2.7692	2.8561
5	2.1003	2.1924	2.2878	2.3864	2.4883	2.5937	2.7027	2.8153	2.9316	3.0518	3.1758	3.3038	3.4360	3.5723	3.7129
6	2.4364	2.5652	2.6996	2.8398	2.9860	3.1384	3.2973	3.4628	3.6352	3.8147	4.0015	4.1959	4.3980	4.6083	4.8268
7	2.8262	3.0012	3.1855	3.3793	3.5832	3.7975	4.0227	4.2593	4.5077	4.7684	5.0419	5.3288	5.6295	5.9447	6.2749
8	3.2784	3.5115	3.7589	4.0214	4.2998	4.5950	4.9077	5.2389	5.5895	5.9605	6.3528	6.7675	7.2058	7.6686	8.1573
9	3.8030	4.1084	4.4355	4.7854	5.1598	5.5599	5.9874	6.4439	6.9310	7.4506	8.0045	8.5948	9.2234	9.8925	10.6045
10	4.4114	4.8068	5.2338	5.6947	6.1917	6.7275	7.3046	7.9259	8.5944	9.3132	10.0857	10.9153	11.8059	12.7614	13.7858
11	5.1173	5.6240	6.1759	6.7767	7.4301	8.1403	8.9117	9.7489	10.6571	11.6415	12.7080	13.8625	15.1116	16.4622	17.9216
12	5.9360	6.5801	7.2876	8.0642	8.9161	9.8497	10.8722	11.9912	13.2148	14.5519	16.0120	17.6053	19.3428	21.2362	23.2981
13	6.8858	7.6987	8.5994	9.5964	10.6993	11.9182	13.2641	14.7491	16.3863	18.1899	20.1752	22.3588	24.7588	27.3947	30.2875
14	7.9875	9.0075	10.1472	11.4198	12.8392	14.4210	16.1822	18.1414	20.3191	22.7374	25.4207	28.3957	31.6913	35.3391	39.3738
15	9.2655	10.5387	11.9737	13.5895	15.4070	17.4494	19.7423	22.3140	25.1956	28.4217	32.0301	36.0625	40.5648	45.5875	51.1859
16	10.7480	12.3303	14.1290	16.1715	18.4884	21.1138	24.0856	27.4462	31.2426	35.5271	40.3579	45.7994	51.9230	58.8079	66.5417
17	12.4677	14.4265	16.6722	19.2441	22.1861	25.5477	29.3844	33.7588	38.7408	44.4089	50.8510	58.1652	66.4614	75.8621	86.5042
18	14.4625	16.8790	19.6733	22.9005	26.6233	30.9127	35.8490	41.5233	48.0386	55.5112	64.0722	73.8698	85.0706	97.8622	112.4554
19	16.7765	19.7484	23.2144	27.2516	31.9480	37.4043	43.7358	51.0737	59.5679	69.3889	80.7310	93.8147	108.8904	126.2422	146.1920
20	19.4608	23.1056	27.3930	32.4294	38.3376	45.2593	53.3576	62.8206	73.8641	86.7362	101.7211	119.1446	139.3797	162.8524	190.0496
25	40.8742	50.6578	62.6686	77.3881	95.3962	117.3909	144.2101	176.8593	216.5420	264.6978	323.0454	393.6344	478.9049	581.7585	705.6410

Interest rate

Periods	1	2	3	4	5	6	7	8	9	10	11	12	13	14	15
1	0.9901	0.9804	0.9709	0.9615	0.9524	0.9434	0.9346	0.9259	0.9174	0.9091	0.9009	0.8929	0.8850	0.8772	0.8696
2	0.9803	0.9612	0.9426	0.9246	0.9070	0.8900	0.8734	0.8573	0.8417	0.8264	0.8116	0.7972	0.7831	0.7695	0.7561
3	0.9706	0.9423	0.9151	0.8890	0.8638	0.8396	0.8163	0.7938	0.7722	0.7513	0.7312	0.7118	0.6931	0.6750	0.6575
4	0.9610	0.9238	0.8885	0.8548	0.8227	0.7921	0.7629	0.7350	0.7084	0.6830	0.6587	0.6355	0.6133	0.5921	0.5718
5	0.9515	0.9057	0.8626	0.8219	0.7835	0.7473	0.7130	0.6806	0.6499	0.6209	0.5935	0.5674	0.5428	0.5194	0.4972
6	0.9420	0.8880	0.8375	0.7903	0.7462	0.7050	0.6663	0.6302	0.5963	0.5645	0.5346	0.5066	0.4803	0.4556	0.4323
7	0.9327	0.8706	0.8131	0.7599	0.7107	0.6651	0.6227	0.5835	0.5470	0.5132	0.4817	0.4523	0.4251	0.3996	0.3759
8	0.9235	0.8535	0.7894	0.7307	0.6768	0.6274	0.5820	0.5403	0.5019	0.4665	0.4339	0.4039	0.3762	0.3506	0.3269
9	0.9143	0.8368	0.7664	0.7026	0.6446	0.5919	0.5439	0.5002	0.4604	0.4241	0.3909	0.3606	0.3329	0.3075	0.2843
10	0.9053	0.8203	0.7441	0.6756	0.6139	0.5584	0.5083	0.4632	0.4224	0.3855	0.3522	0.3220	0.2946	0.2697	0.2472
11	0.8963	0.8043	0.7224	0.6496	0.5847	0.5268	0.4751	0.4289	0.3875	0.3505	0.3173	0.2875	0.2607	0.2366	0.2149
12	0.8874	0.7885	0.7014	0.6246	0.5568	0.4970	0.4440	0.3971	0.3555	0.3186	0.2858	0.2567	0.2307	0.2076	0.1869
13	0.8787	0.7730	0.6810	0.6006	0.5303	0.4688	0.4150	0.3677	0.3262	0.2897	0.2575	0.2292	0.2042	0.1821	0.1625
14	0.8700	0.7579	0.6611	0.5775	0.5051	0.4423	0.3878	0.3405	0.2992	0.2633	0.2320	0.2046	0.1807	0.1597	0.1413
15	0.8613	0.7430	0.6419	0.5553	0.4810	0.4173	0.3624	0.3152	0.2745	0.2394	0.2090	0.1827	0.1599	0.1401	0.1229
16	0.8528	0.7284	0.6232	0.5339	0.4581	0.3936	0.3387	0.2919	0.2519	0.2176	0.1883	0.1631	0.1415	0.1229	0.1069
17	0.8444	0.7142	0.6050	0.5134	0.4363	0.3714	0.3166	0.2703	0.2311	0.1978	0.1696	0.1456	0.1252	0.1078	0.0929
18	0.8360	0.7002	0.5874	0.4936	0.4155	0.3503	0.2959	0.2502	0.2120	0.1799	0.1528	0.1300	0.1108	0.0946	0.0808
19	0.8277	0.6864	0.5703	0.4746	0.3957	0.3305	0.2765	0.2317	0.1945	0.1635	0.1377	0.1161	0.0981	0.0829	0.0703
20	0.8195	0.6730	0.5537	0.4564	0.3769	0.3118	0.2584	0.2145	0.1784	0.1486	0.1240	0.1037	0.0868	0.0728	0.0611
25	0.7798	0.6095	0.4776	0.3751	0.2953	0.2330	0.1842	0.1460	0.1160	0.0923	0.0736	0.0588	0.0471	0.0378	0.0304
30	0.7419	0.5521	0.4120	0.3083	0.2314	0.1741	0.1314	0.0994	0.0754	0.0573	0.0437	0.0334	0.0256	0.0196	0.0151
35	0.7059	0.5000	0.3554	0.2534	0.1813	0.1301	0.0937	0.0676	0.0490	0.0356	0.0259	0.0189	0.0139	0.0102	0.0075
40	0.6717	0.4529	0.3066	0.2083	0.1420	0.0972	0.0668	0.0460	0.0318	0.0221	0.0154	0.0107	0.0075	0.0053	0.0037
45	0.6391	0.4102	0.2644	0.1712	0.1113	0.0727	0.0476	0.0313	0.0207	0.0137	0.0091	0.0061	0.0041	0.0027	0.0019
50	0.6080	0.3715	0.2281	0.1407	0.0872	0.0543	0.0339	0.0213	0.0134	0.0085	0.0054	0.0035	0.0022	0.0014	0.0009

Periods	16	17	18	19	20	21	22	23	24	25	26	27	28	29	30
1	0.8621	0.8547	0.8475	0.8403	0.8333	0.8264	0.8197	0.8130	0.8065	0.8000	0.7937	0.7874	0.7812	0.7752	0.7692
2	0.7432	0.7305	0.7182	0.7062	0.6944	0.6830	0.6719	0.6610	0.6504	0.6400	0.6299	0.6200	0.6104	0.6009	0.5917
3	0.6407	0.6244	0.6086	0.5934	0.5787	0.5645	0.5507	0.5374	0.5245	0.5120	0.4999	0.4882	0.4768	0.4658	0.4552
4	0.5523	0.5337	0.5158	0.4987	0.4823	0.4665	0.4514	0.4369	0.4230	0.4096	0.3968	0.3844	0.3725	0.3611	0.3501
5	0.4761	0.4561	0.4371	0.4190	0.4019	0.3855	0.3700	0.3552	0.3411	0.3277	0.3149	0.3027	0.2910	0.2799	0.2693
6	0.4104	0.3898	0.3704	0.3521	0.3349	0.3186	0.3033	0.2888	0.2751	0.2621	0.2499	0.2383	0.2274	0.2170	0.2072
7	0.3538	0.3332	0.3139	0.2959	0.2791	0.2633	0.2486	0.2348	0.2218	0.2097	0.1983	0.1877	0.1776	0.1682	0.1594
8	0.3050	0.2848	0.2660	0.2487	0.2326	0.2176	0.2038	0.1909	0.1789	0.1678	0.1574	0.1478	0.1388	0.1304	0.1226
9	0.2630	0.2434	0.2255	0.2090	0.1938	0.1799	0.1670	0.1552	0.1443	0.1342	0.1249	0.1164	0.1084	0.1011	0.0943
10	0.2267	0.2080	0.1911	0.1756	0.1615	0.1486	0.1369	0.1262	0.1164	0.1074	0.0992	0.0916	0.0847	0.0784	0.0725
11	0.1954	0.1778	0.1619	0.1476	0.1346	0.1228	0.1122	0.1026	0.0938	0.0859	0.0787	0.0721	0.0662	0.0607	0.0558
12	0.1685	0.1520	0.1372	0.1240	0.1122	0.1015	0.0920	0.0834	0.0757	0.0687	0.0625	0.0568	0.0517	0.0471	0.0429
13	0.1452	0.1299	0.1163	0.1042	0.0935	0.0839	0.0754	0.0678	0.0610	0.0550	0.0496	0.0447	0.0404	0.0365	0.0330
14	0.1252	0.1110	0.0985	0.0876	0.0779	0.0693	0.0618	0.0551	0.0492	0.0440	0.0393	0.0352	0.0316	0.0283	0.0254
15	0.1079	0.0949	0.0835	0.0736	0.0649	0.0573	0.0507	0.0448	0.0397	0.0352	0.0312	0.0277	0.0247	0.0219	0.0195
16	0.0930	0.0811	0.0708	0.0618	0.0541	0.0474	0.0415	0.0364	0.0320	0.0281	0.0248	0.0218	0.0193	0.0170	0.0150
17	0.0802	0.0693	0.0600	0.0520	0.0451	0.0391	0.0340	0.0296	0.0258	0.0225	0.0197	0.0172	0.0150	0.0132	0.0116
18	0.0691	0.0592	0.0508	0.0437	0.0376	0.0323	0.0279	0.0241	0.0208	0.0180	0.0156	0.0135	0.0118	0.0102	0.0089
19	0.0596	0.0506	0.0431	0.0367	0.0313	0.0267	0.0229	0.0196	0.0168	0.0144	0.0124	0.0107	0.0092	0.0079	0.0068
20	0.0514	0.0433	0.0365	0.0308	0.0261	0.0221	0.0187	0.0159	0.0135	0.0115	0.0098	0.0084	0.0072	0.0061	0.0053
25	0.0245	0.0197	0.0160	0.0129	0.0105	0.0085	0.0069	0.0057	0.0046	0.0038	0.0031	0.0025	0.0021	0.0017	0.0014
30	0.0116	0.0090	0.0070	0.0054	0.0042	0.0033	0.0026	0.0020	0.0016	0.0012	0.0010	0.0008	0.0006	0.0005	0.0004
35	0.0055	0.0041	0.0030	0.0023	0.0017	0.0013	0.0009	0.0007	0.0005	0.0004	0.0003	0.0002	0.0002	0.0001	0.0001
40	0.0026	0.0019	0.0013	0.0010	0.0007	0.0005	0.0004	0.0003	0.0002	0.0001	0.0001	0.0001	0.0001	0.0000	0.0000
45	0.0013	0.0009	0.0006	0.0004	0.0003	0.0002	0.0001	0.0001	0.0001	0.0000	0.0000	0.0000	0.0000	0.0000	0.0000
50	0.0006	0.0004	0.0003	0.0002	0.0001	0.0001	0.0000	0.0000	0.0000	0.0000	0.0000	0.0000	0.0000	0.0000	0.0000

Appendix III

Present value of an annuity of £1 at compound interest $\dfrac{1 - 1/(1+i)^n}{i} \times A$

Interest rate

Periods	1	2	3	4	5	6	7	8	9	10	11	12	13	14	15
1	0.9901	0.9804	0.9709	0.9615	0.9524	0.9434	0.9346	0.9259	0.9174	0.9091	0.9009	0.8929	0.8850	0.8772	0.8696
2	1.9704	1.9416	1.9135	1.8861	1.8594	1.8334	1.8080	1.7833	1.7591	1.7355	1.7125	1.6901	1.6681	1.6467	1.6257
3	2.9410	2.8839	2.8286	2.7751	2.7232	2.6730	2.6243	2.5771	2.5313	2.4869	2.4437	2.4018	2.3612	2.3216	2.2832
4	3.9020	3.8077	3.7171	3.6299	3.5460	3.4651	3.3872	3.3121	3.2397	3.1699	3.1024	3.0373	2.9745	2.9137	2.8550
5	4.8534	4.7135	4.5797	4.4518	4.3295	4.2124	4.1002	3.9927	3.8897	3.7908	3.6959	3.6048	3.5172	3.4331	3.3522
6	5.7955	5.6014	5.4172	5.2421	5.0757	4.9173	4.7665	4.6229	4.4859	4.3553	4.2305	4.1114	3.9975	3.8887	3.7845
7	6.7282	6.4720	6.2303	6.0021	5.7864	5.5824	5.3893	5.2064	5.0330	4.8684	4.7122	4.5638	4.4226	4.2883	4.1604
8	7.6517	7.3255	7.0197	6.7327	6.4632	6.2098	5.9713	5.7466	5.5348	5.3349	5.1461	4.9676	4.7988	4.6389	4.4873
9	8.5660	8.1622	7.7861	7.4353	7.1078	6.8017	6.5152	6.2469	5.9952	5.7590	5.5370	5.3282	5.1317	4.9464	4.7716
10	9.4713	8.9826	8.5302	8.1109	7.7217	7.3601	7.0236	6.7101	6.4177	6.1446	5.8892	5.6502	5.4262	5.2161	5.0188
11	10.3676	9.7868	9.2526	8.7605	8.3064	7.8869	7.4987	7.1390	6.8052	6.4951	6.2065	5.9377	5.6869	5.4527	5.2337
12	11.2551	10.5753	9.9540	9.3851	8.8633	8.3838	7.9427	7.5361	7.1607	6.8137	6.4924	6.1944	5.9176	5.6603	5.4206
13	12.1337	11.3484	10.6350	9.9856	9.3936	8.8527	8.3577	7.9038	7.4869	7.1034	6.7499	6.4235	6.1218	5.8424	5.5831
14	13.0037	12.1062	11.2961	10.5631	9.8986	9.2950	8.7455	8.2442	7.7862	7.3667	6.9819	6.6282	6.3025	6.0021	5.7245
15	13.8651	12.8493	11.9379	11.1184	10.3797	9.7122	9.1079	8.5595	8.0607	7.6061	7.1909	6.8109	6.4624	6.1422	5.8474
16	14.7179	13.5777	12.5611	11.6523	10.8378	10.1059	9.4466	8.8514	8.3126	7.8237	7.3792	6.9740	6.6039	6.2651	5.9542
17	15.5623	14.2919	13.1661	12.1657	11.2741	10.4773	9.7632	9.1216	8.5436	8.0216	7.5488	7.1196	6.7291	6.3729	6.0472
18	16.3983	14.9920	13.7535	12.6593	11.6896	10.8276	10.0591	9.3719	8.7556	8.2014	7.7016	7.2497	6.8399	6.4674	6.1280
19	17.2260	15.6785	14.3238	13.1339	12.0853	11.1581	10.3356	9.6036	8.9501	8.3649	7.8393	7.3658	6.9380	6.5504	6.1982
20	18.0456	16.3514	14.8775	13.5903	12.4622	11.4699	10.5940	9.8181	9.1285	8.5136	7.9633	7.4694	7.0248	6.6231	6.2593
25	22.0232	19.5235	17.4131	15.6221	14.0939	12.7834	11.6536	10.6748	9.8226	9.0770	8.4217	7.8431	7.3300	6.8729	6.4641
30	25.8077	22.3965	19.6004	17.2920	15.3725	13.7648	12.4090	11.2578	10.2737	9.4269	8.6938	8.0552	7.4957	7.0027	6.5660
35	29.4086	24.9986	21.4872	18.6646	16.3742	14.4982	12.9477	11.6546	10.5668	9.6442	8.8552	8.1755	7.5856	7.0700	6.6166
40	32.8347	27.3555	23.1148	19.7928	17.1591	15.0463	13.3317	11.9246	10.7574	9.7791	8.9511	8.2438	7.6344	7.1050	6.6418
45	36.0945	29.4902	24.5187	20.7200	17.7741	15.4558	13.6055	12.1084	10.8812	9.8628	9.0079	8.2825	7.6609	7.1232	6.6543
50	39.1961	31.4236	25.7298	21.4822	18.2559	15.7619	13.8007	12.2335	10.9617	9.9148	9.0417	8.3045	7.6752	7.1327	6.6605

Periods	16	17	18	19	20	21	22	23	24	25	26	27	28	29	30
1	0.8621	0.8547	0.8475	0.8403	0.8333	0.8264	0.8197	0.8130	0.8065	0.8000	0.7937	0.7874	0.7812	0.7752	0.7692
2	1.6052	1.5852	1.5656	1.5465	1.5278	1.5095	1.4915	1.4740	1.4568	1.4400	1.4235	1.4074	1.3916	1.3761	1.3609
3	2.2459	2.2096	2.1743	2.1399	2.1065	2.0739	2.0422	2.0114	1.9813	1.9520	1.9234	1.8956	1.8684	1.8420	1.8161
4	2.7982	2.7432	2.6901	2.6386	2.5887	2.5404	2.4936	2.4483	2.4043	2.3616	2.3202	2.2800	2.2410	2.2031	2.1662
5	3.2743	3.1993	3.1272	3.0576	2.9906	2.9260	2.8636	2.8035	2.7454	2.6893	2.6351	2.5827	2.5320	2.4830	2.4356
6	3.6847	3.5892	3.4976	3.4098	3.3255	3.2446	3.1669	3.0923	3.0205	2.9514	2.8850	2.8210	2.7594	2.7000	2.6427
7	4.0386	3.9224	3.8115	3.7057	3.6046	3.5079	3.4155	3.3270	3.2423	3.1611	3.0833	3.0087	2.9370	2.8682	2.8021
8	4.3436	4.2072	4.0776	3.9544	3.8372	3.7256	3.6193	3.5179	3.4212	3.3289	3.2407	3.1564	3.0758	2.9986	2.9247
9	4.6065	4.4506	4.3030	4.1633	4.0310	3.9054	3.7863	3.6731	3.5655	3.4631	3.3657	3.2728	3.1842	3.0997	3.0190
10	4.8332	4.6586	4.4941	4.3389	4.1925	4.0541	3.9232	3.7993	3.6819	3.5705	3.4648	3.3644	3.2689	3.1781	3.0915
11	5.0286	4.8364	4.6560	4.4865	4.3271	4.1769	4.0354	3.9018	3.7757	3.6564	3.5435	3.4365	3.3351	3.2388	3.1473
12	5.1971	4.9884	4.7932	4.6105	4.4392	4.2784	4.1274	3.9852	3.8514	3.7251	3.6059	3.4933	3.3868	3.2859	3.1903
13	5.3423	5.1183	4.9095	4.7147	4.5327	4.3624	4.2028	4.0530	3.9124	3.7801	3.6555	3.5381	3.4272	3.3224	3.2233
14	5.4675	5.2293	5.0081	4.8023	4.6106	4.4317	4.2646	4.1082	3.9616	3.8241	3.6949	3.5733	3.4587	3.3507	3.2487
15	5.5755	5.3242	5.0916	4.8759	4.6755	4.4890	4.3152	4.1530	4.0013	3.8593	3.7261	3.6010	3.4834	3.3726	3.2682
16	5.6685	5.4053	5.1624	4.9377	4.7296	4.5364	4.3567	4.1894	4.0333	3.8874	3.7509	3.6228	3.5026	3.3896	3.2832
17	5.7487	5.4746	5.2223	4.9897	4.7746	4.5755	4.3908	4.2190	4.0591	3.9099	3.7705	3.6400	3.5177	3.4028	3.2948
18	5.8178	5.5339	5.2732	5.0333	4.8122	4.6079	4.4187	4.2431	4.0799	3.9279	3.7861	3.6536	3.5294	3.4130	3.3037
19	5.8775	5.5845	5.3162	5.0700	4.8435	4.6346	4.4415	4.2627	4.0967	3.9424	3.7985	3.6642	3.5386	3.4210	3.3105
20	5.9288	5.6278	5.3527	5.1009	4.8696	4.6567	4.4603	4.2786	4.1103	3.9539	3.8083	3.6726	3.5458	3.4271	3.3158
25	6.0971	5.7662	5.4669	5.1951	4.9476	4.7213	4.5139	4.3232	4.1474	3.9849	3.8342	3.6943	3.5640	3.4423	3.3286
30	6.1772	5.8294	5.5168	5.2347	4.9789	4.7463	4.5338	4.3391	4.1601	3.9950	3.8424	3.7009	3.5693	3.4466	3.3321
35	6.2153	5.8582	5.5386	5.2512	4.9915	4.7559	4.5411	4.3447	4.1644	3.9984	3.8450	3.7028	3.5708	3.4478	3.3330
40	6.2335	5.8713	5.5482	5.2582	4.9966	4.7596	4.5439	4.3467	4.1659	3.9995	3.8458	3.7034	3.5712	3.4481	3.3332
45	6.2421	5.8773	5.5523	5.2611	4.9986	4.7610	4.5449	4.3474	4.1664	3.9998	3.8460	3.7036	3.5714	3.4482	3.3333
50	6.2463	5.8801	5.5541	5.2623	4.9995	4.7616	4.5452	4.3477	4.1666	3.9999	3.8461	3.7037	3.5714	3.4483	3.3333

Interest rate

Periods	1	2	3	4	5	6	7	8	9	10	12	14	16	18	20	25	30	35	40	45	50
1	1.0000	1.0000	1.0000	1.0000	1.0000	1.0000	1.0000	1.0000	1.0000	1.0000	1.0000	1.0000	1.0000	1.0000	1.0000	1.0000	1.0000	1.0000	1.0000	1.0000	1.0000
2	2.0100	2.0200	2.0300	2.0400	2.0500	2.0600	2.0700	2.0800	2.0900	2.1000	2.1200	2.1400	2.1600	2.1800	2.2000	2.2500	2.3000	2.3500	2.400	2.4500	2.5000
3	3.0301	3.0604	3.0909	3.1216	3.1525	3.1836	3.2149	3.2464	3.2781	3.3100	3.3744	3.4396	3.5056	3.5724	3.6400	3.8125	3.9900	4.1725	4.3600	4.5525	4.7500
4	4.0604	4.1216	4.1836	4.2465	4.3101	4.3746	4.4399	4.5061	4.5731	4.6410	4.7793	4.9211	5.0665	5.2154	5.3680	5.7656	6.1870	6.6329	7.1040	7.6011	8.1250
5	5.1010	5.2040	5.3091	5.4163	5.5256	5.6371	5.7507	5.8666	5.9847	6.1051	6.3528	6.6101	6.8771	7.1542	7.4416	8.2070	9.0431	9.9544	10.9456	12.0216	13.1875
6	6.1520	6.3081	6.4684	6.6330	6.8019	6.9753	7.1533	7.3359	7.5233	7.7156	8.1152	8.5355	8.9775	9.4420	9.9299	11.2588	12.7560	14.4384	16.3238	18.4314	20.7813
7	7.2135	7.4343	7.6625	7.8983	8.1420	8.3938	8.6540	8.9228	9.2004	9.4872	10.0890	10.7305	11.4139	12.1415	12.9159	15.0735	17.5828	20.4919	23.8534	27.7255	32.1719
8	8.2857	8.5830	8.8923	9.2142	9.5491	9.8975	10.2598	10.6366	11.0285	11.4359	12.2997	13.2328	14.2401	15.3270	16.4991	19.8419	23.8577	28.6640	34.3947	41.2019	49.2578
9	9.3685	9.7546	10.1591	10.5828	11.0266	11.4913	11.9780	12.4876	13.0210	13.5795	14.7757	16.0853	17.5185	19.0859	20.7989	25.8023	32.0150	39.6964	49.1526	60.7428	74.8867
10	10.4622	10.9497	11.4639	12.0061	12.5779	13.1808	13.8164	14.4866	15.1929	15.9374	17.5487	19.3373	21.3215	23.5213	25.9587	33.2529	42.6195	54.5902	69.8137	89.0771	113.330
11	11.5668	12.1687	12.8078	13.4864	14.2068	14.9716	15.7836	16.6455	17.5603	18.5312	20.6546	23.0445	25.7329	28.7551	32.1504	42.5661	56.4053	74.6967	98.7391	130.162	170.995
12	12.6825	13.4121	14.1920	15.0258	15.9171	16.8699	17.8885	18.9771	20.1407	21.3843	24.1331	27.2707	30.8502	34.9311	39.5805	54.2077	74.3270	101.841	139.235	189.735	257.493
13	13.8093	14.6803	15.6178	16.6268	17.7130	18.8821	20.1406	21.4953	22.9534	24.5227	28.0291	32.0887	36.7862	42.2187	48.4966	68.7596	97.6250	138.485	195.929	276.115	387.239
14	14.9474	15.9739	17.0863	18.2919	19.5986	21.0151	22.5505	24.2149	26.0192	27.9750	32.3926	37.5811	43.6720	50.8180	59.1959	86.9495	127.913	187.954	275.300	401.367	581.859
15	16.0969	17.2934	18.5989	20.0236	21.5786	23.2760	25.1290	27.1521	29.3609	31.7725	37.2797	43.8424	51.6595	60.9653	72.0351	109.687	167.286	254.738	386.420	582.982	873.788
16	17.2579	18.6393	20.1569	21.8245	23.6575	25.6725	27.8881	30.3243	33.0034	35.9497	42.7533	50.9804	60.9250	72.9390	87.4421	138.109	218.472	344.897	541.988	846.324	1311.68
17	18.4304	20.0121	21.7616	23.6975	25.8404	28.2129	30.8402	33.7502	36.9737	40.5447	48.8837	59.1176	71.6730	87.0680	105.931	173.636	285.014	466.611	759.784	1228.17	1968.52
18	19.6147	21.4123	23.4144	25.6454	28.1324	30.9057	33.9990	37.4502	41.3013	45.5992	55.7497	68.3941	84.1407	103.740	128.117	218.045	371.518	630.925	1064.70	1781.85	2953.78
19	20.8109	22.8406	25.1169	27.6712	30.5390	33.7600	37.3790	41.4463	46.0185	51.1591	63.4397	78.9692	98.6032	123.414	154.740	273.556	483.973	852.748	1491.58	2584.68	4431.68
20	22.0190	24.2974	26.8704	29.7781	33.0660	36.7856	40.9955	45.7620	51.1601	57.2750	72.0524	91.0249	115.380	146.628	186.688	342.945	630.165	1152.21	2089.21	3748.78	6648.51
25	28.2432	32.0303	36.4593	41.6459	47.7271	54.8645	63.2490	73.1059	84.7009	98.3471	133.334	181.871	249.214	342.603	471.981	1054.79	2348.80	5176.50	11247.2	24040.7	50500.3
30	34.7849	40.5681	47.5754	56.0849	66.4388	79.0582	94.4608	113.283	136.308	164.494	241.333	356.787	530.312	790.948	1181.88	3227.17	8729.99	23221.6	60501.1	154107	383500
35	41.6603	49.9945	60.4621	73.6522	90.3203	111.435	138.237	172.317	215.711	271.024	431.663	693.573	1120.71	1816.65	2948.34	9856.76	32422.9	104136	325400	987794	2912217
40	48.8864	60.4020	75.4013	95.0255	120.800	154.762	199.635	259.057	337.882	442.593	767.091	1342.03	2360.76	4163.21	7343.86	30088.7	120393	466960	1750092	6331512	22114663
45	56.4811	71.8927	92.7199	121.029	159.700	212.744	285.749	386.506	525.859	718.905	1358.23	2590.56	4965.27	9531.58	18281.3	91831.5	447019	2093876	9412424	40583319	167933233
50	64.4632	84.5794	112.797	152.667	209.348	290.336	406.529	573.770	815.084	1163.91	2400.02	4994.52	10435.6	21813.1	45497.2	280256	1659761	9389020	50622288	260128295	1275242998

1 (a) £124   **(b)** £125.97

2 (a) £26,533   **(b)** £163,665

3 (a) 14.2 years   **(b)** 4.96 years

4 Present values of the four options:

   (a) £1,000,000
   (b) £1,104,883
   (c) £1,500,000
   (d) £1,283,540

Given the time value of money of 9 per cent per annum and certainty about the future (e.g. that you will live to enjoy the perpetuity), the official answer is c. You may like to question whether this is what you would really go for. If you prefer another option, try to explain what that option says about your time value of money.

5 6%

6 £675

7 14.93%

8 (a) £32.20   **(b)** £31.18

9 £4,731

10 £6,217, 8.24%

11 Present value of a ten-year £800 annuity = £4,711. Therefore you could invest £4,711 @ 11% and receive £800 per year for ten years. Reject Supersalesman's offer.

12 £6,468

Appendix VI
Answers to end-of-chapter numerical questions

Chapter 5

1 **(a)** $16,500.00 **(b)** $16,542.05

2 **(a)** 1.28592% **(b)** 1.29006%

3 $1999.41

4 **(a)** 3.04687% **(b)** 3.097205%

5 **(a)** 0.4417% **(b)** 0.094186%

6 $3.782 \times 365/360 = 3.7717\%$

7 $(6000000–5950000)/5950000) \times (365/176) \times 100$ The yield to maturity on the second CD is 1.74274%, which is less than the yield on the first, so the first CD is the better option.

8 $((5000000-4975000)/4975000) \times (365/60) \times 100 = 3.05695\%$

9 **(a)** $850000 +(850000 \times (2.61/100) \times (42/365)) = £852, 552.79$

(b) $850,000 +((850000 \times (2.61/100) \times (67/365)) = £854,072.32$

10 **(a)** $3,000,000 \times 0.0008 = \$2,400$

(b) $2,997,600

(c) $3,000,327.57

Chapter 6

1 **(a)** £95.20 **(b)** 8.06%

2 **(a)** €100 **(b)** 10.15% **(c)** €103.62

3 **(a)** $9 \times 6.2788 +100/(1.095)^{10}=£96.86$

(b) $9 \times 6.5613 +100/(1.085)^{10}=£103.28$

(c) 8.25%

(d) 8.57%

4 (a) £105.2966

(b) £63.7903

5 (a) $\dfrac{100}{(1.05)^5} = \$78.3526$

(b) $\dfrac{100}{(1.10)^5} = \$62.0921$

6 Bond 1: €96.3636   Bond 2: €101.8182

7 (a) Yield curve

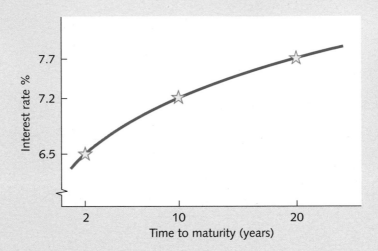

(b) Two-year bond

$$\dfrac{6}{1.065} + \dfrac{106}{(1.065)^2} = £99.0897$$

10-year bond

$$6 \times 6.9591 + 100/(1.072)^{10} = £91.6491$$

20-year bond

$$6 \times 10.0413 + 100/(1.077)^{20} = £82.9298$$

(c) Two-year bond

$$\dfrac{6}{1.085} + \dfrac{106}{(1.085)^2} = £95.5722$$

10-year bond

$$6 \times 6.3615 + 100/(1.092)^{10} = £79.6431$$

20-year bond

$$6 \times 8.6908 + 100/(1.097)^{20} = £67.8439$$

(d) Two-year bond

$$\frac{6}{1.045} + \frac{106}{(1.045)^2} = £102.809$$

Ten-year bond

$$6 \times 7.6473 + 100/(1.052)^{10} = £106.1178$$

20-year bond

$$6 \times 11.7546 + 100/(1.057)^{20} = £103.5264$$

(e) The longest dated bond is the most volatile.

10 16.08%

11 7.5%

14 (a) 100/40=£2.50

(b) (2.50 – 1.90)/1.90=31.6%

(c) £1.90 × 40=£76

Chapter 9

10 Mahogany:

(a) Three old shares @ £3   9
One new share @ £2   2
                              11

$$\frac{11}{4} = £2.75$$

(b) 30 million

(c) Discuss pre-emption rights and ability to sell rights. If Patrick sold his rights, he would receive: 75p × 3,000 = £2,250

(d) $\dfrac{£2.75 - £2.00}{3} = 25\text{p}$

12 Yellowhammer: £1.82, 8p

Chapter 10

1 (i) Sold @ 5,086 × £10 × 5   = 254,300
  Bought @ 5,500 × £10 × 5   = 275,000
  Loss   £20,700

(ii) Sold @ 5,086 × £10 × 5   254,300
  Bought @ 4,500 × £10 × 5   225,000
  Gain   £29,300

2 (a) In October, sell 30,000,000/(5020 × 10) = 598 March future contracts @5035. Then in March close the position by buying 598 March contracts.

(b) FTSE 100 Index @ 4000:

Loss on shares = (1020/5020) × 30,000,000 = £6,095,618

Gain on futures:

Able to buy @ 4000   598 × 10 × 4,000   = 23,920,000
Able to sell at @ 5035   598 × 10 × 5,035   = 30,109,300
                              £6,189,300

Overall gain: £6,189,125 – £6,095,618 = £93,682

FTSE 100 @ 6000:

Gain on shares (980/5020) × 30,000,000 = £5,856,574

Loss on futures:

Able to buy @ 6000   598 × 10 × 6000   = 35,880,000
Able to sell @ 5035   598 × 10 × 5035   = 30,109,300
Loss on futures   £5,770,700

Overall gain £5,856,574 – 5,770,700 = £85,874

(c)

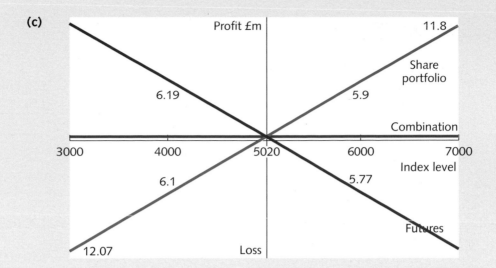

3 (a)

£000s								
Day	*1*	*2*	*3*	*4*	*5*	*6*	*7*	*8*
Value of future	390	410	370	450	420	400	360	410
Initial margin	20	–	–	–	–	–	–	–
Variation margin	–10	20	–40	+80	–30	–20	–40	50
Accumulated profit (loss)	–10	+10	–30	+50	+20	0	–40	+10

4 (a) FRA The treasurer agrees a 6 against 9 FRA whereby the counterparty will pay compensation to the company should interest rates fall below 8 per cent. These payments will exactly offset any loss of interest below 8 per cent. However, if interest rates rise above 8 per cent the company will pay compensation to the counterparty such that the company effectively receives 8 per cent return on deposited money. Certainty is achieved.

Interest rate future

Three-month sterling interest future contracts (September contracts) are bought at 92.00. Each contract is for a nominal £500,000; therefore 40 contracts are bought to hedge the full £20 million. If interest rates fall, the rise in the value of the future will offset the fall in interest on deposited money.

(b) FRA

Interest rates at 7%

The loss on the underlying:

$20,000,000 \times 0.01 \times 3/12$	= –£50,000
The counterparty pays compensation to equal this loss	= £50,000
Overall loss due to interest rate changes	0

Interest rates at 9%

Gain on the underlying:

$20,000,000 \times 0.01 \times {}^3/_{12}$ = £50,000
The counterparty receives compensation to equal this gain = –£50,000
Overall loss due to interest changes   0

Interest rate future

Interest rates at 7%

Loss on the underlying   = –£50,000
Futures sold at 93.00 in September
100 ticks $\times$ £12.50 $\times$ 40   = £50,000
Overall loss due to interest rate changes   0

Interest rates at 9%

Gain on the underlying   = £50,000
Futures position is closed by selling at 91.00 in September
Loss: 100 ticks $\times$ £12.5 $\times$ 40   = –£50,000
Overall loss due to interest rate changes   0

5 **(a)** Red Wheel could sell 30 three-month sterling interest rate futures dated for December at 91.70.

  (b) Rate of interest = 8.30%.

     Gain on derivative: 91.70 – 90.00 = 170 ticks.

     This exactly offsets the additional interest paid to the lender:

     Gain on derivative: 170 $\times$ 12.50 $\times$ 30 = £63,750.

     Loan interest above 8.3%:

     £15 million $\times$ 0.017 $\times$ ${}^3/_{12}$ = £63,750.

  (c) Rate of interest = 8.30%

     Loss on derivative: 91.70 – 93.00 = 130 ticks

     130 $\times$ 12.50 $\times$ 30 = –£48,750

     Gain from interest rate being lower than 8.3%:

     £15 million $\times$ 0.013 $\times$ ${}^3/_{12}$ = £48,750

7 **(a)** Sell 500 March futures in Akzo Nobel on 7th January @ €45.96

(b) Gain on underlying (€50 – €45.65) × 50,000 = €217,500

Loss on futures:

Sold @ €45.96	45.96 × 500 × 100	=	€2,298,000
Bought @ €50	50 × 500 × 100	=	€2,500,000
			€202,000

Overall gain = €217,500 – €202,000 = €15,500

c Loss on underlying (€40 – €45.65) × 50,000 = €282,500

Gain on futures:

Sold @ €45.96	45.96 × 500 × 100	=	€2,298,000
Bought @ €40	40 × 500 × 100	=	€2,000,000
			€298,000

Overall gain: €298,000 – €282,500 = €15,500

Chapter 11

1 A possible hedging strategy:

Purchase 20 June 450 put options and hold to expiry.

If share price falls to 400p:

Loss on shares	£1 × 20,000	20,000
Gain on options	50p × 20,000	10,000
Less Option premium		
19p × 1,000 × 20		3,800
		£6,200

Overall loss £13,800

If share price rises to 600p:

Gain on shares	£1 × 20,000	20,000
Less Option premium		3,800
Overall gain		£16,200

2   **(a)** £520 loss

   (b) £520 – £520 = 0

   (c) £800 – £520 = £280 profit

3

Option	Intrinsic value	Time value
700 call	32p	23.5p
750 call	0	28p
700 put	0	17.5p
750 put	18p	22p

In-the-money options: 700 call, 750 put.

Out-of-the-money options: 750 call, 700 put.

4

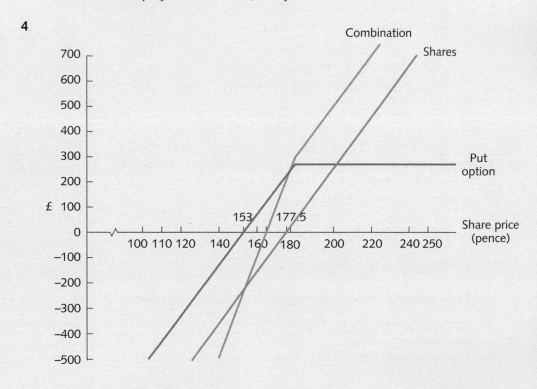

5 Black plc and White plc

(a)

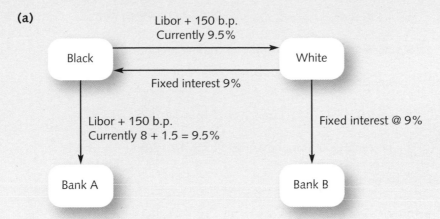

Libor + 150 b.p.
Currently 9.5%

Black → White

Fixed interest 9%

Libor + 150 b.p.
Currently 8 + 1.5 = 9.5%

Fixed interest @ 9%

Bank A

Bank B

(b)
- Future variable interest rates may fall below 9 per cent (i.e. Libor @ 7.5 per cent). This will impose an opportunity cost of entering the swap arrangements.
- Black must accept the possibility of counterparty default.
- Transaction costs (e.g. legally binding contracts) may be considerable.
- Black needs to consider its overall asset and liability profile.

(c) The cap seller compensates Black:

50,000,000 (0.10 − 0.085)	=	£750,000
Black pays interest @ 10 + 1.5	= 11.5% to Bank A:	
50,000,000 x 0.115	=	£5,750,000

The compensation from the cap seller means that Black will not pay more than £5 million (net) per annum

(d) Consult main text

10 (a) The student should fully describe these instruments. A possible numerical illustration:

Maximum exposure given the margin required is £120,000

£120,000/555 = 216

Spread bet: £216 per pence downward movement in the underlying from 555p

CFD: Sell 21,582 shares at a price of 556p (£120,000/£5.56 = 21,582 shares)

(b) At 640p–650p: Close position at 650p.

Loss 650 − 555 = 95   Loss = 95 × £216 = £20,520

As a percentage of initial notional trading margin: £20,520/£12,000 = 171%

(c) Close position at 490p

$$555 - 490 = 65 \qquad \text{Gain} \; = \; 65 \times £216 = £14,040$$

As a percentage of initial notional trading margin: £14,040/£12,000 = 117%

(d) Close position at 630p

$$556 - 630 = -74 \qquad \text{Loss} \; = \; 74p \times 21,582 = £15,971$$

As a percentage of initial margin: £15,971/£12,000 = 133%

(e) Close position at 485p

$$556 - 485 = 71 \qquad \text{Loss} \; = \; 71p \times 21,582 = £15,323$$

As a percentage of initial margin: £15,323/£12,000 = 128%

11

	Fixed	*Floating*
Attik	8%	LIBOR + 2.5%
Battik	7%	LIBOR + 1.2%

Battik has an absolute advantage in both but Attik has a comparative advantage in borrowing at fixed rate (100 bp difference compared with 130 bp difference)

A possible swap: Attik borrows fixed @ 8%
Battik borrows floating @ LIBOR + 1.2%
Attik agrees to pay Battik LIBOR + 2.35%
Battik agrees to pay Attik fixed @ 8%

Result for Attik: Pays and receives fixed @ 8%. Pays LIBOR + 2.35% an improvement of 15 basis points compared with borrowing in floating rate market.

Result for Battik: Pays LIBOR + 1.2%, receives LIBOR + 2.35%. Resulting a net payment of 115 bp. It pays 8% fixed but also benefits from the swap by 115 bp therefore the net fixed cost is 6.85%, a 15 bp improvement than if it had borrowed fixed @ 7%.

13 Euro swap: Swap five-year floating for the fixed rate. Your firm will pay 4.37 + 0.20 = 4.57% to swap market counterparty. Then your firm will pay LIBOR + 230 bp to original lender and receive floating rate @ LIBOR, effectively setting the overall interest rate at 230 bp + 457 bp = 687 bp fixed for five years. €400 million × 0.0687 = €27.48 million per year.

Sterling swap: Swap a four -year obligation to pay LIBOR in return for receiving 4.56 − 0.20% = 4.36%. Pay 620 bp and receive 436 bp. Net payment = 184bp + LIBOR

Chapter 12

1 (a) £5,287.34

   (b) ¥94,565,500

   (c) ¥188,869,000

   (d) £529.47

2 (a)

Expected income	A\$10m
Actual income $^{11}/_{1.2}$	A\$9.167m
Exchange rate loss	A\$0.8333m

(b)

	A\$10.0000m
A\$10 million $^{11}/_{1.05}$ =	A\$10.4762m
Exchange rate gain	A\$0.4762m

(c) Exporter agrees to deliver NZ\$11 million in six months to forward market counterparty. It will receive 11 million/1.09 = A\$10.09174 million regardless of spot exchange rates in six months' time.

(d) *See* Chapter 12.

4 (a) *Forward market hedge*

   Agree to buy R150 million of sterling three months forward

   $$\frac{150}{7.5} = £20 \text{ million}$$

   If spot rate in three months is R7.00/£ and the exchange was made at spot rate, then:

Sterling income 150/7	=	£21.429m
Income due to forward commitment	=	£20.000m
'Loss' due to inability to exchange at spot		£1.429m

   If the spot rate in three months is R8.00/£ and the exchange was made at spot rate, then:

Sterling income 150/8	=	£18.75m
Income due to forward commitment	=	£20.00m
'Gain' due to forward contract	=	£1.25m

Money market hedge

Borrow in rand now an amount which, with accumulated interest, will become R150 million in three months. Exchange this sum at the current spot rate for sterling. In three months pay lender with sum received from customer.

Amount borrowed $\dfrac{150m}{1+0.025}$ = R146.3415 million

Exchanged at spot for sterling $\dfrac{146.3415}{7.46}$ = £19.6168 million

(*Note*: Certainty about income from the export deal because sterling is received now.)

In three months:

Amount owed to lender 146.3415 million × 1.025 = R150m
Repay lender with amount received from customer = R150m

If exchange rates move to R7.00/£:

'Loss' due to lost opportunity to exchange at spot
£21.429 million – £19.6168 million = £1.8122m
(less interest on sterling for three months)

If exchange rates move to R8.00/£:

'Gain' due to money market hedge
£19.6168 million – £18.75 million = £0.8668m
(plus interest on sterling for three months)

Options

Buy rand put sterling call option.

In three months consider whether to exercise this in the light of knowledge of spot rates.

If spot rate R7.00/£:

Exchange R150 million at spot 150/7 = £21.429m
(let the option lapse)
Less the cost of option (premium)   £0.400m
                                                                       £21.029m

If spot rate R8.00/£:

Exercise option to exchange @R7.5/£ (150/7.5) = £20.000m
less cost of option (premium)   £0.400m
                                                                      £19.600m

This is better than having to exchange @ R8.00/£ which would have produced merely £18.75 million.

7 **(a)** $\dfrac{1+0.02}{1+0.04} \times 2 = \text{SFr}1.9615/\text{£}$

8 **(b)** $\dfrac{1+0.05}{1+0.07} \times 1.02 = \text{C\$}1.0009/\text{A\$}$

9 **Lozenge plc**

Numerical aspects only. (Students should also describe and explain instruments and methods used. They should consider the advantages and disadvantages of each – for more details of these consult the chapter.)

Forward market hedge

At the current time agree a forward contract whereby Lozenge plc will purchase $12 \times 50{,}000 = \text{M\$}600{,}000$ in three months. To do this it will need to provide $600{,}000/5.425 = \text{£}110{,}599$ to the counterparty in three months.

Then, if the Malaysian dollar rises against sterling in the intervening period, Lozenge will not have to pay more than £110,599. Say the exchange rate moved to M\$4.00/£: an unhedged Lozenge would pay $600{,}000/4.00 = \text{£}150{,}000$. Hedging has 'saved' the firm a sum of £150,000 – £110,599. On the other hand, the firm cannot take advantage of a favourable forex move.

If the Malaysian dollar had weakened to M\$7.00/£ and the firm was able to exchange at the spot rate, it would pay only $600{,}000/7 = \text{£}85{,}714$. Thus £110,599 – £85,714 = £24,885 foregone by entering into the forward contract.

Option hedge

An option permits the firm to benefit from a favourable exchange rate while hedging against an unfavourable movement. However, a premium has to be paid, which reduces net income.

Lozenge could purchase the right, but not the obligation, to sell sterling and buy Malaysian dollars at a cost of $600{,}000/5.425 = \text{£}110{,}599$ for a premium of $15{,}000/5.4165 = \text{£}2{,}769$.

If the Malaysian dollar strengthens to M\$4.00/£, then Lozenge will exercise the right to purchase at M\$5.425/£. This will 'save' £150,000 – £110,599 – £2,769 = £36,632 compared with a no hedge policy.

If the Malaysian dollar weakens against sterling to M\$7.00/£, then Lozenge will abandon the option and exchange at spot rate.

Cost of imports: $(600{,}000/7) + 2{,}769 = \text{£}88{,}483$.

This is cheaper than if a forward contract approach or money market approach were adopted, but more expensive (due to the option premium) than if a no hedge approach were adopted.

Money market hedge

Exchange sterling now for Malaysian dollars, so that there will be M$600,000 with accumulated interest in three months:

$$\frac{600,000}{1.03} = \text{M}\$582,524$$

$$\text{Sterling required} = \frac{582.524}{5.4165} = \pounds107,546$$

If the sterling is borrowed, then to be comparable with the alternative hedging approaches (which involve the handing over of sterling in three months), we need to increase by three months' interest:

$$\pounds107,546\ (1.03) = \pounds110,773$$

In three months:

Pay supplier with Malaysian dollars already purchased (including accumulated interest) M$600,000.

10 (a) $\frac{1.02}{1.05} \times 1.77 = \text{\euro}1.7194/\text{US}\$$

(b) $\frac{1.06}{1.09} \times 1.77 = \text{\euro}1.7213/\text{US}\$$

11 (a) Forward purchase of sterling

$$\frac{\text{Won }1,507\text{m}}{1,450} = \pounds1.03931\text{m}$$

(b) Borrow in won and exchange for sterling immediately.

$$\text{Amount borrowed: } \frac{1,507}{1.005} = \text{Won }1,499.5\text{m}$$

$$\text{Exchange: } \frac{1,499.5\text{m}}{1,507} = \pounds995,023$$

In one month the lender is paid with the won received from the customer.

9/11 Refers to the terrorist attack on the US World Trade Center on September 11 2001.

Abandon The choice made by a holder of a warrant or option to allow it to expire without exercise.

ABS *See* Asset-backed security.

Absolute return The actual percentage return made on an asset.

Accept a bill Agree to pay a bill. *See* Acceptance credit.

Acceptance credit (bank bill, banker's acceptance) An institution (e.g. bank) commits itself to the payment of a sum of money in the future as stated in the acceptance credit document. The borrower is given this document (which can be passed on to a supplier) in return for a promise to pay a sum on the maturity date to the institution. The acceptance credit can be sold in the discount market to obtain funds for the borrower (or to pass on to a supplier).

Accounting rate of return (ARR) A measure of profitability based on accounting numbers. Profit divided by assets devoted to the activity (e.g. project, entire business) as a percentage.

Accounts payable Short-term debts owed by a firm to its creditors for goods and services received. A term used more in the US – in the UK 'creditors' is usually used.

Accounts receivable Customer debts to a company. A term used more in the US – in the UK 'debtors' is usually used.

Accredited investors US class of investor where individuals must have a net worth > $1m and institutional investors > $5m.

Accumulation units Unit trusts (q.v.) that reinvest income.

Acquisition *See* Takeover.

Action Fraud The website operated by the National Fraud Authority.

Active management A manager makes use of a particular strategy in buying and selling shares to try to outperform an index, as opposed to passive management, where the manager simply tracks an index.

Activist strategy A hedge fund strategy where the hedge fund buys shares in a company and uses the share ownership to press for changes in management policy which will result in a profit on the shares.

Adverse selection problem When there is an opportunity or incentive for some firms/individuals to act to take advantage of their informational edge over others then the firms/individuals doing that activity will be disproportionately made up of those taking advantage rather than being truly representative of the population as a whole, e.g. the tendency for those presenting more-than-average risks to continue with insurance. This will raise the cost of insurance for the whole group, including those of less-than-average risk. This is caused by asymmetric information in which the poorer-than-average risk policy holder knows more about their risk level than the insurer does.

Affirmative covenants Loan agreement conditions that require positive action on the part of the borrower, e.g. a statement that a bond will pay regular dividends, or that the borrower will distribute information regularly.

Agence France Trésor (AFT) French government treasury.

Agency Acting for or in the place of another with their authority.

Agency capture Those that are supposed to be regulated take some control of the regulatory process.

Agency costs Costs of preventing agents (e.g. managers) pursuing their own interests at the expense of their principals (e.g. shareholders). Examples include contracting costs and costs of monitoring. In addition there is the agency cost of the loss of wealth caused by the extent to which prevention measures have not worked and managers continue to pursue non-shareholder wealth goals.

Agency office An office established by a bank in a foreign country to assist its domestic customers.

Agent A person who acts for or in the place of another with that other person's authority (the 'principal').

AGM *See* Annual general meeting.

Agreement costs The costs involved in setting up a financial agreement.

Agricultural commodities Raw unprocessed foodstuffs that can be transported in bulk.

AIM admission document The document needed for a company to be quoted on the Alternative Investment Market in the first instance. It is similar to a prospectus.

AIM *See* Alternative investment market.

Alfred Jones A US investment manager who in 1949 created the first hedge fund strategy.

Algorithm Computer program designed to aid fast trading by processing large volumes of information and making a decision based on the information.

Allfinanz German term for bancassurance (q.v.).

Allotment In a new issue of shares, if more shares are demanded at the price than are available, they may be apportioned (allotted) between the applicants.

Allow to lapse (option) Do not take up the right to exercise the option.

Alpha (Alpha coefficient, α) A measure of performance greater than or less than the market as a whole after allowing for beta in the capital asset pricing model (q.v.). That portion of a share's return that cannot be explained by its responsiveness to moves in the market as a whole. Sometimes called stock-specific return. It is often used as an indication of a fund manager's performance.

Alternative Investment Market (AIM) The more lightly regulated share market set up in 1995 and operated by the London Stock Exchange, focused particularly on smaller, less well-established companies.

American Depositary Receipts (ADRs) Depositary receipts issued in the US.

American Research and Development Corporation (ARD) The company founded by Georges Doriot (q.v.) which was the first to provide private equity investment to encourage business growth after the Second World War.

American-style option (American option) An option which can be exercised by the purchaser at any time up to the expiry date.

AMEX The American Stock Exchange which trades equities, options and exchange-traded funds. It is now part of the NYSE Euronext group (q.v.).

Amortisation (1) The repayment of a debt by a series of instalments. (2) The gradual writing off of the balance sheet value of intangible assets.

Analyst A researcher of companies' prospects and predictor of their share price performance. Also analyses other securities.

Angel network event Where entrepreneurs can make a pitch and try to get investment from business angels (q.v.).

Angel *See* Business angels.

Annual equivalent rate (AER) *See* Annual percentage rate.

Annual general meeting (AGM) A limited company must hold in each calendar year an annual general meeting. It is an opportunity for shareholders to meet and talk with each other and with those who run the company on their behalf. The managers give an account of their stewardship. All shareholders are entitled to attend and vote. Election of directors may take place.

Annual percentage rate (APR) The true annual interest rate charged by a lender. It takes full account of the timing of payments of interest and principal.

Annual results Annual company accounts. This term is often used for the preliminary results.

Annual yield *See* Yield.

Annuity (1) (General) An even stream of payments (the same amount each time) over a given period of time. (2) (Insurance) In return for either regular payments or a lump sum payment which is invested by the receiving company, the insured or their spouse will receive regular income payments either for a set time or until death.

Arbitrage The act of exploiting price differences on the same instrument or similar securities by simultaneously selling the over-priced security and buying the underpriced security.

ArcaEx An MTF (q.v.).

Archangel An experienced business angel, who coordinates angel groups.

Arrangement fee A fee for agreeing and setting up a financial transaction such as a bank loan.

Asset In the financial markets an asset is anything that can be traded as a security, e.g. share, option, commodity, bond.

Asset-backed security (ABS) A security which is backed by underlying assets such as loans, cash flows, receivables etc. in a securitisation. A security backed by mortgages is a mortgage-backed security in which the bonds issued as ABSs pay interest and capital from income received from mortgages.

Asset backing The value of the assets held in the business – often measured on a per share basis.

Asset class Asset types, e.g. bonds, shares.

Asset liquidity The extent to which assets can be converted to cash quickly and at a low transaction cost.

Asset management (1) (General) Managing assets (money, investments) in an efficient manner. (2) (Banking) Lending money with the expectation of an overall low risk of default, high diversification, adequate liquidity and good rates of return.

Asset stripping Taking over a company and selling off all or some of its assets.

Asset transformers Intermediaries who, by creating a completely new security – the intermediate security – mobilise savings and encourage investment. The primary security is issued by the ultimate borrower to the intermediary, who offers intermediate securities to the primary investors.

Asset-backed commercial paper Commercial paper secured on assets.

Asset-backed securities (ABS) Bonds secured by a group of assets. *See* Securitisation.

ASX Australian Securities Exchange.

Asymmetric information One party in a negotiation or relationship is not in the same position as other parties, being ignorant of, or unable to observe, some information which is essential to the contracting and decision-making process.

At-the-market Price determined by current supply and demand.

At-the-money option The current underlying price is equal to the option exercise price.

ATM Automated teller machine.

Audit The service carried out by an auditor (q.v.).

Auditor Auditors determine whether the company's financial statements are misleading and whether the accounts show a true and fair view.

Aunt Agathas City jargon for small investors.

Authorised corporate director (ACD) An OEIC (q.v.) manager.

Authorised share capital The maximum amount of share capital that a company can issue. The limit can be changed by a shareholder vote.

Back office That part of a financial institution which deals with the settlement of contracts, accounting, regulatory matters and management information processes.

Back-to-back loan Company A and Company B lend to each other the same amount with the same maturity but in different currencies. The purpose is to hedge against currency fluctuations.

BACS (Bankers' Automated Clearing System) UK automated clearing system.

Bad debts Debts that are unlikely to be paid.

Balance of payments A record of the payment made for goods and services obtained by a country and other transfers of currency abroad less the receipts for goods and services sold and other transfers of currency from abroad. The balance on the current account (visible trade and invisible trade) is the difference between national income and national expenditure in the specified period. The capital account is made up of such items as the inward and outward flow of money for investment and international grants and loans.

Balance sheet Provides a picture of what a company owns, what it owes and is owed on a particular day in the past. It summarises assets, liabilities and net worth (capital).

Balloon repayment on a loan The majority of the repayment of a loan is made at or near the maturity date, with the final payment being substantially larger than the earlier payments.

Baltic Exchange An organisation owned by its members which oversees and regulates aspects of the maritime and shipping industry. It provides independent daily shipping market information; maintains professional shipbroking standards, resolves disputes and ensures its members abide by its code of conduct.

Baltic Exchange Capesize Index (BCI) A shipping and freight index published by the Baltic Exchange (q.v.) based on ten daily Capesize vessel assessments including voyage and time charter rates.

Baltic Exchange Dry Index (BDI) The most important and influential shipping and freight index published by the Baltic Exchange (q.v.) the BDI is a daily index made up of 20 key dry bulk routes.

Baltic Exchange Handysize index (BHSI) A shipping and freight index published by the Baltic Exchange (q.v.) based on six daily time charter rates.

Baltic Exchange Panamax Index (BPI) A shipping and freight index published by the Baltic Exchange (q.v.) based on four daily panamax vessel assessments of time charter rates.

Baltic Exchange Supramax Index (BSI) A shipping and freight index published by the Baltic Exchange (q.v.) based on nine daily time charter rates.

Baltic Freight Index (BFI) This Baltic Exchange index was replaced by the Baltic Exchange Dry Index (q.v.).

Baltic Indices A series published by the Baltic Exchange (q.v.) of indices based on the cost of freight and shipping on specified routes and types of vessel.

Bancassurance Companies offering both banking and insurance.

Band(FX) A percentage of a fixed currency value within which countries have to keep.

Bank bill *See* Acceptance credit.

Bank covenants *See* Covenant.

Bank for International Settlements (BIS) Controlled by central banks, the BIS was established to assist international financial coordination. It promotes international monetary coordination, provides research and statistical data, co-ordination and trusteeship for intergovernmental loans and acts as a central bank for national central banks, accepting deposits and making loans.

Bank of England The central bank of the United Kingdom, responsible for monetary policy. It oversees the affairs of other financial institutions, issues banknotes and coins, manages the national debt and exchange rate, and is lender of last resort.

Bank rate The interest rate at which central banks make short-term loans to commercial banks.

Bank run Depositors fear that a bank may be in trouble and increasing numbers of them try to withdraw their money. The bank does not have enough vault cash to cover all the withdrawals.

Bank supervision Monitoring by the authorities to ensure that banks are run properly.

Banker's acceptance A negotiable financial instrument guaranteed by a bank used to facilitate trade. Also known as acceptance credit (q.v.).

Bankruptcy Commonly used to describe an individual or company that cannot meet its fixed commitments on borrowing which leads to legal action. However, technically, in the UK individuals become bankrupt whereas firms become insolvent.

Banque Populaire French mutual/cooperative bank

Barings Bank The UK's oldest bank, forced into collapse by Nick Leeson's (q.v.) disastrous speculative trading.

Barter system An economic system relying on the exchange of goods using no cash.

Base currency The first currency in a forex currency pair.

Base rate (1) The interest rate targeted by the Bank of England that forms the basis for interest rates on bank loans, overdrafts and deposit rates. (2) The standard variable rate (q.v.) charged by a bank.

Basel accords *See* Basel rules.

Basel committee A group of national bank regulators that meets regularly to agree risk management rules that affect all banks.

Basel II *See* Basel rules.

Basel III *See* Basel rules.

Basel rules A set of rules or accords set by the Basel committee (q.v.) to regulate banks and impose minimum solvency and liquidity standards.

Basis point (bp) One-hundredth of 1 per cent, usually applied to interest rates.

BATS, BATS Europe One of the MTFs (q.v.).

Bausparkassen German cooperative banks which provide mortgages and loans.

Bear An investor who takes the view that prices are likely to fall.

Bear fund Designed to do well when shares are falling in price.

Bear market A market of falling prices.

Bear Stearns A US investment bank that was bailed out by the Fed (q.v) in 2008 but still went bankrupt.

Bearer bond The ownership of a bond is not recorded on a register. Possession of the bond is sufficient to receive interest, etc.

Bells and whistles Additional features placed on derivatives or securities, such as bonds, that are designed to attract investors or reduce issue costs.

Benchmark A financial security or index of financial securities the returns or level of which is considered to be a suitable reference rate for other securities, e.g. the interest rate on a ten-year gilt is a reference benchmark for corporate bond interest.

Beta A measure of the systematic risk of a financial security. It is a measure of the sensitivity to market movements of a financial security's return, as measured by the covariance between returns on the asset and returns on the market portfolio divided by the variance of the market portfolio. In practice, a proxy (e.g. FTSE 100 index) is used for the market portfolio.

Bey *See* Bond equivalent yield.

Bid premium The additional amount an acquirer has to offer above the pre-bid share price in order to succeed in a takeover offer.

Bid price The price at which a market maker will buy shares or a dealer in other markets will buy a security or commodity.

Bid to cover ratio The ratio between an amount on offer and the amount investors bid to buy.

Bid yield The yield to maturity on a bond given the market price at which the market makers will buy from investors.

Bid–offer spread (bid–ask spread in the US) The difference between the market maker's buy and sell prices.

Big Bang 1986 deregulation and liberalisation of London Stock Market.

Bill A legal document with a promise to pay or a demand for payment.

Bill of exchange A document setting out a commitment to pay a sum of money at a specified point in time, e.g. an importer commits itself to paying a supplier. Bills of exchange may be discounted – sold before maturity for less than face value.

Bill of lading A document issued by a carrier to confirm that they have received the goods being shipped.

BIS *See* Bank for International Settlements.

Blue chip A company regarded as of the highest quality – little risk of a sharp decline in profits or market value.

Board of Directors People elected by shareholders to run a company.

BoE *See* Bank of England.

Bond A debt obligation with a long-term maturity (more than one year), usually issued by firms and governments.

Bond covenant *See* Covenant.

Bond equivalent yield (bey) Bond equivalent rate, coupon equivalent yield, equivalent bond yield, investment rate of return. The annual interest rate on a bond based on the purchase price.

Bond indenture *See* Trust deed.

Bond insurance Insurance that pays out if an issuer of a bond fails to fulfil its obligations.

Bond market Deals in debt securities with maturities of more than one year.

Bonus issue *See* Scrip issue.

Book building A book runner (lead manager) invites major institutional investors to suggest how many shares (or other financial securities) they would be interested in purchasing and at what price in a new issue or secondary issue of shares (or other financial securities). This helps to establish the price and allocate shares.

Book runner *See* Book building.

Borsa Italiana Italian stock market which merged with the LSE (q.v.) in 2007.

Bought deal An investment bank (the 'lead manager', perhaps together with co-managers of the issue), buys an entire security issue (e.g. shares) from a client corporation raising finance. The investment bank usually intends to then sell it out to institutional clients within hours.

Bourse Alternative name for a stock exchange. A French word, but used in other countries, particularly in Continental Europe.

Boutique bank, boutique investment bank A small investment bank usually specialising in offering advice for fees,

Branch Part of a bank acting on behalf of the bank.

Breaking of the buck When a US money market fund falls in value from the $1 per share put in by the investor.

Bretton Woods The New Hampshire (US) town where the 1944 Bretton Woods conference took place. The conference resulted in an exchange rate system whereby currencies were fixed to the US dollar which was fixed to gold at $35 per ounce of gold.

British Bankers Association (BBA) Trade association of British banks. Sets model contracts, publishes interest rates, e.g. interbank rates, advocates on behalf of banks.

British Private Equity & Venture Capital Association (BVCA) The UK body overseeing private equity and venture capital.

Broad money A multiple of the monetary base. It is narrow money (q.v.) plus money held in short term deposits and securities.

Broker Assists in the buying and selling of financial securities and/or insurance by acting as a 'go-between', helping to reduce search and information costs.

Broker-dealer An individual acting as agent for buyers and sellers, but who, at the same time, trades for his own account and may also be a market maker.

Brokerage A company offering broking services.

BTANS (Bons du Trésor à intérèts annuels) French medium-term government bonds.

Bubble An explosive upward movement in a financial security or other asset prices not based on fundamentally rational factors, followed by a crash.

Building society A UK financial institution, the primary role of which is the provision of mortgages. Building societies are non-profit-making mutual organisations. Funding is mostly through small deposits by individuals.

Bulge bracket A term used to describe leading investment banks.

Bulk carrier A large ship transporting unpackaged goods.

Bull An investor taking the view that prices will rise.

Bull market A market of rising prices.

Bulldog A foreign bond issued in the UK.

Bullet bond, bullet repayment All the capital is repaid at the end of the loan term.

Bundesanleihen (Bunds) 10- and 50-year German bonds.

Bundesbank The German central bank.

Bundesobligationen (Bobls) Five-year German bonds.

Bundesrepublik Deutschland Finanzagentur (BDF) German Financial Agency.

Bundesschatzanweisungen (Schatze) German two-year bonds.

Business angels (informal venture capitalists) Wealthy individuals prepared to invest in a start-up, early-stage or developing firm. They often have managerial and/or technical experience to offer the management team as well as equity and debt finance. They undertake medium- to long-term investment in high-risk situations.

Buy-back *See* Share buy-back.

Buy-side The investment institutions that advise on large purchases of securities.

Buyout The purchase of a controlling interest in or the whole of a company.

BVCA *See* British Private Equity & Venture Capital Association.

CAC 40 (Compagnie des Agents de Change 40 Index) A stock market index of French shares quoted in Paris.

Caisses d'Epargne French savings banks.

Caisses Régionales de Crédit Agricole Mutuel French cooperative banks.

Cajas de ahoro (cajas) Spanish local savings banks.

Call option This gives the purchaser the right, but not the obligation, to buy a fixed quantity of a commodity, financial instrument or some other underlying asset at a given price, at or before a specified date.

Call-back features The issuer of a bond has the right but not the obligation to buy the bond back on specified terms.

CAMELS System of bank inspection: C = capital adequacy (q.v.) A = asset quality M = management E = earnings L = liquidity S = sensitivity to market risk.

Cap (1) An interest rate cap is a contract that effectively gives the purchaser the right to set a maximum level for interest rates payable. Compensation is paid to the purchaser of a cap if interest rates rise above an agreed level. (2) (Derivatives) Any feature that sets a maximum return, payout or cost.

Capital (1) Funding for a business – can be equity only or equity plus debt. (2) Another term for net worth – total assets minus total liabilities.

Capital adequacy management A bank acquires and manages the amount of capital it needs to run efficiently and safely.

Capital Asset Pricing Model (CAPM) An asset (e.g. share) pricing theory which assumes that financial assets, in equilibrium, will be priced to produce rates of return which compensate investors for systematic risk as measured by the covariance of the assets' return with the market portfolio return (i.e. beta).

Capital gain A gain made when an asset has increased in value and is sold.

Capital gearing The extent to which the firm's total capital is in the form of debt.

Capital introduction (cap-intro) Prime brokers help hedge funds find investors.

Capital Liberalisation Directive, 1988 An EU directive permitting money to be transferred easily and freely throughout the EU.

Capital Requirements Directive, 2006 An EU directive establishing rules on capital adequacy for the financial services industry.

Capital reserves The amount of capital held by companies and banks to enable them to run efficiently and with a low risk of insolvency.

Capital transfer The buying and selling of assets (capital) which may have an effect on a country's balance of payments (q.v.).

Capitalisation (1) An item of expenditure is taken on to the balance sheet and capitalised as an asset rather than written off against profits. (2) Short for market capitalisation (q.v.).

Capitalisation issue *See* Scrip issue.

Capitalisation weighted In an index the shares are weighted by the market capitalisation of the company.

Capped bonds The interest cannot rise above a certain level.

Captives A private equity or venture capital organisation that raises its capital from one institution (or a small group of institutions).

Carbon trading Trading in carbon emissions.

Carried interest The accrued profit (capital gain) made in private equity funds.

Cartel A group of otherwise competing firms entering into an agreement to set mutually acceptable prices, output levels and market shares for their products.

Cash dividend A normal dividend by a company, paid in cash rather than a scrip dividend.

Cash settled In the derivatives market some contracts are physically settled at expiry date (e.g. coffee is delivered in return for cash under the derivative contract). However, many derivatives are not physically delivered; rather, a cash difference representing a gain or loss on the closed derivative position changes hands.

Cassa di Compensazione e Garanzia (CC&G) Italian clearing house.

Casualty insurance Insurance that covers most types of accident, illness or damage.

CBOE *See* Chicago Board Options Exchange.

CBOT *See* Chicago Board of Trade.

CCCL (Cheque and Credit Clearing Company) Manages the UK cheque clearing system.

CDS *See* Credit default swap.

Ceding commission Commission paid by reinsurer to original insurer.

Central bank A bankers' bank and lender of last resort, which controls the credit system of an economy, e.g. controls note issue, acts as the government's bank, controls interest rates and regulates the country's banking system.

Central clearing system A system such as BACS (q.v.) which transfers electronically all payments and deposits made.

Central Counter-party (CCP) clearing house *See* Clearing house.

Central Counterparty Clearing (CCC) US clearing house (q.v.).

Certificate of deposit (CD) A deposit is made at a bank. A certificate confirming that a deposit has been made is given by the bank to the lender. This is normally a bearer security. Most CDs can then be sold in the secondary market whenever the depositor (firm or investor) needs cash.

CFD *See* Contract for difference.

CHAPS (Clearing House Automated Payment System) The UK same-day interbank clearing system for sterling payments (computer based).

Charge cards These are similar to credit cards (q.v.) but the user is expected to pay off the full amount every month.

Cheque (US check) A means of paying for goods or services.

Chi-X An MTF (q.v.).

Chicago Board of Trade (CBOT) The world's oldest (established 1848) futures and options exchange in Chicago, USA. Now part of CME Group (q.v.).

Chicago Board Options Exchange (CBOE) The largest options exchange in the world, trading options on shares, indices and interest rates.

Chicago Mercantile Exchange *See* CME.

Chief executive officer (CEO) The manager/director in overall charge of the running of the business.

Chief financial officer (CFO) The manager/director in overall charge of the financial affairs of the business.

Chinese walls Barriers within a financial service company designed to prevent sensitive information being passed on to another branch of the organisation.

Chip card *See* smart cards.

CHIPS (Clearing House Interbank Payment System)The US system for settling US dollar payments the same day between banks.

City Code on Takeovers and Mergers Provides the main governing rules for UK-based companies engaged in merger activity. Self-regulated and administered by the Takeover Panel.

City of London A collective term for the financial institutions located in the financial district to the east of St Paul's Cathedral in London (also called the Square Mile). However, the term is also used to refer to all UK-based financial institutions, wherever they are located.

City of London police Lead the battle against financial fraud.

City Panel on Takeovers and Mergers Administers the code on takeovers and mergers and ensures fairness for shareholders.

City *See* City of London

Clawback (1) (shares) Existing shareholders often have the right to reclaim shares sold under a placing as though they were entitled to them under a rights issue (2) (fees) A portion of fees may be claimed back in the event of underperformance.

Clean price On a bond the prices are generally quoted 'clean', that is without taking account of the accrued interest since the last coupon payment.

Clearing a trade The stock exchange (or other market clearer) ensures that (1) all reports of a trade are reconciled to make sure all parties are in agreement as to the number of shares traded and the price; and (2) the buyer and seller have the cash and securities to do the deal.

Clearing bank Member of the London Bankers' Clearing House, which clears cheques, settling indebtedness between two parties.

Clearing house An institution which registers, monitors, matches and settles mutual indebtedness between a number of individuals or organisations. The clearing house may also act as a counterparty, that is it acts as buyer to every seller and seller to every buyer.

Clearing price The price at which the demand curve and the supply curve intersect.

Close (1) (private equity) When a target amount of investment has been reached and the fund has reached its required size. (2) The execution of a deal when all documentation has been satisfactorily completed.

Closed-end funds Collective investment vehicles (e.g. investment trusts) that do not create or redeem shares on a daily basis in response to increases and decreases in demand. They have a fixed number of shares for lengthy periods.

Closing out a futures position The taking of a second action in the futures market (say, selling the future) which is exactly opposite to the first action (say, buying the future). Also called reversing the trade.

CLS Bank A bank owned by member banks which carry out foreign exchange trading. It enables the simultaneous settlement of both sides of an FX contract, thereby avoiding Herstatt risk (q.v.).

CLS *See* Continuous linked settlement.

CME (Chicago Mercantile Exchange) An exchange which trades a wide range of currency futures and options, interest rate futures and options, commodity futures and options and share index futures and options.

CME ClearPort The clearing service offered by the CME Group (q.v.).

CME Group The trading group established by the Chicago Mercantile Exchange, comprising CME, CBOT, NYMEX and COMEX (qq.v.).

Co-investing (private equity) When an investor (limited partner) invests in both the private equity fund and a company in which the fund is investing.

Co-lead manager The title given to an underwriter (e.g. for a bond sale) who has joint lead manager status and may sometimes be engaged in structuring the transaction. Usually part of the selling group. Usually does not act as a bookrunner.

Cooperative bank A bank mutually owned by its members.

CoCos *See* Contingent convertible.

Collar A ceiling and floor interest rate placed on the variability of interest payable on a debt, often achieved by the simultaneous purchase of an interest rate cap and sale of an interest rate floor.

Collateral Property pledged by a borrower to protect the interests of the lender.

Collateralised debt obligation (CDO) A type of asset-backed security (q.v.) which promises to pay out cash flows to investors. A bond issued by an special purpose vehicle, SPV, set up by a deal structurer, usually an investment bank, where the SPV holds a pool of loans or a pool of debt securities. The bonds are issued in a number of different classes or tranches, each with their own risk and return characteristics.

Collective investment *See* Pooled funds.

COMEX Commodity Exchange dealing in metals now part of the CME Group (q.v.).

Commercial banking Carries out core and corporate (qq.v.) banking functions.

Commercial bill (bank bill or trade bill) A document expressing the commitment of a borrowing firm to repay a short-term debt at a fixed date in the future.

Commercial mortgage-backed security Bonds secured on commercial property. A form of securitised bond.

Commercial paper (CP) An unsecured note promising the holder (lender) a sum of money to be paid in a few days – average maturity of 40 days. If they are denominated in a foreign currency and placed outside the jurisdiction of the authorities of that currency then the notes are Eurocommercial paper.

Commercial paper programme *See* Revolving underwriting facility.

Commitment fee A fee payable in return for a commitment by a bank to lend money at some future date. In some cases the fee is only payable on the undrawn portion of the loan, in others the fee also applies to funds already drawn down under the arrangement.

Committed facility The lender is obliged to provide funds upon request if any agreed conditions are met.

Commodity bubble *See* Bubble.

Commodity index A weighted index based on the prices of groups of commodities.

Commodity Raw materials or food stuffs which can be stored, accurately measured and are fungible.

Commodity Trading Advisors (CTAs) *See* Managed futures.

Common stock The term used in the US to describe ordinary shares in a company.

Community bank A local bank operated by and for the local community.

Companies Acts The series of UK laws enacted by Parliament governing the establishment and conduct of incorporated business enterprises. The Companies Act 2006 consolidated the Acts that preceded it.

Companies House The place where records are kept of every UK company. These accounts, etc. are then made available to the general public.

Company registrar *See* Registrar.

Competition Commission The Commission may obtain any information needed to investigate possible monopoly anti-competitive situations referred to it. It may then block anti-competitive action.

Competitive laxity Financial centres that try to impose strict rules are subject to the threat of financial institutions taking their business to a different jurisdiction and so are more likely to be lax.

Compliance costs The costs involved in complying with regulations (q.v.).

Compliance Methods of ensuring that financial market operators meet any legal and supervisory requirements.

Compliance officer Responsible for ensuring regulations are being followed.

Compound interest Interest is paid on the sum which accumulates, whether or not that sum comes from the principal or from interest received at intermediate dates.

Compound return The income received on an investment is reinvested in the investment and future returns are gained on both the original capital and the ploughed-back income.

Concentration risk Risk occurring when investments or lending are focussed excessively on one sector.

Conflict of preference There is a conflict of preference between the primary investors wanting low-cost liquidity and low risk on invested funds, and the ultimate borrowers wanting long-term risk-bearing capital.

Conflicts of interest These arise when a person or institution has a number of objectives (interests) and is free to choose which receives the most emphasis, when one of them might have the potential to corrupt the motivation to act.

Consolidated accounts All the income, costs, assets and all the liabilities of all group companies, whether wholly or partially owned, are brought together in the consolidated accounts. Consolidation must take place if 50 per cent or more of a subsidiary's shares are held by the parent. If less than 50 per cent of the shares are held consolidation may still be required.

Consolidated tape A proposed electronic system that would potentially list all bid and offer prices for a group of financial securities from all exchanges that trade there.

Consolidation of shares The number of shares is reduced and the nominal value of each remaining share rises.

Consumer loan, personal loan Loan made to member of public.

Consumer Price Index *See* CPI.

Contagion risk In some financial sectors, say banking, the failure of one company may lead to the failure of others leading to instability in the whole system.

Contingent convertible, CoCos (1) (Bonds) Allow conversion only when a predetermined price is reached. (2) (Banks) Allow conversion if a bank's core capital falls below a predetermined level.

Continuing obligations Standards of behaviour and actions required of firms listed on the London Stock Exchange, enforced by the United Kingdom Listing Authority (q.v.).

Continuous Linked Settlement (CLS) A system designed to reduce the risk of failure of one counterparty to a foreign exchange transaction to fulfil an obligation.

Payment of the two sides of the currency deal is made simultaneously, organised by the CLS Bank (q.v.).

Continuous order book Throughout the trading day orders are automatically matched and executed against one another.

Contract for differences (CFD) Similar to spread betting, but there is no settlement date. The buyer and seller agree to pay, in cash, at the closing of the contract, the difference between the opening and closing price of the underlying securities, e.g. shares, multiplied by the number of shares in the contract.

Controlling shareholder Any shareholder able to control the composition of the board of directors and therefore the direction of the company. Strictly speaking this is 50 per cent, but even a 30 per cent shareholder can exercise this degree of power, and therefore 30 per cent is used as the cut-off point for some purposes.

Convergence The coming together of the futures price and the underlying share price as the final trading day of a futures contract approaches.

Conversion premium The difference between the current share price and the conversion price, expressed as a percentage of the current share price for convertible bonds.

Conversion price The share price at which convertible bonds may be converted.

Conversion ratio The nominal (par) value of a convertible bond divided by the conversion price. The number of shares available per bond.

Conversion value The value of a convertible bond if it were converted into ordinary shares at the current share price.

Convertible arbitrage A hedge fund strategy which takes advantage of the small price differentials in the price of convertible securities and shares in a company.

Convertible bonds, convertible loan stock Bonds which carry a rate of interest and give the owner the right to exchange the bonds at some stage in the future into ordinary shares according to a prearranged formula.

Convertible loan stocks *See* Convertible bonds.

Core banking The provision of basic banking functions, taking deposits, making loans and offering payment mechanisms.

Core Tier 1 Bank capital designated by Basel III as solely money put into the bank by shareholders and shareholders' retained earnings.

Corporate Adviser Required by PLUS-markets of all companies on their list to advise the company especially with regard to its responsibilities on PLUS.

Corporate banking Carries out core banking (q.v.) plus banking for corporations and other large organisations.

Corporate bond A bond issued by a company.

Corporate broker Stockbrokers that act on behalf of companies quoted on an exchange. For example, they may provide advice on market conditions or may represent the company to the market. Corporate brokers are knowledgeable about the share and other financial markets. They advise companies on fund raising (e.g. new issues). They try to generate interest among investors for the company's securities. They stand prepared to buy and sell companies' shares to assist share liquidity.

Corporate finance department of investment banks The department assisting firms in raising funds (e.g. rights issues, bond issues) and managing their finances.

Corporate Governance Code Guidelines of best practice for companies regarding the powers and responsibilities of directors, shareholders and senior managers.

Corporation of Lloyd's Oversees Lloyd's market, establishing standards and providing services to support its activities.

Corporation tax A tax levied on the profits of companies.

Correspondent bank A bank which carries out transactions on behalf of another (usually foreign) bank.

Cost-income ratio (C/I) Measures the ability to hold costs down relative to income. Calculated by dividing non-interest expenses by net interest income plus non-interest income.

Council of Lloyd's Responsible for the management and supervision of Lloyd's market.

Counter currency *See* Secondary currency.

Counter-cyclical regulatory capital Extra bank capital required by Basel III (q.v.) in boom times.

Counterparty risk The risk that a counterparty to a contract defaults and does not fulfil its obligations.

Counterparty The buyer for a seller or the seller for a buyer.

Country risk Risk to transactions overseas or assets held abroad due to political, legal, regulatory or settlement changes or difficulties, e.g. nationalisation or law forbidding repatriation of profits.

Coupons An attachment to bond or loan note documents which may be separated and serve as evidence of entitlement to interest. Nowadays it refers to the interest itself: the nominal annual rate of interest expressed as a percentage of the principal value.

Court of directors The management entity of the BoE (q.v.).

Covenant A solemn agreement.

Cover Offsetting one position in a financial security with an equal and opposite transaction in the same or linked (e.g. derivative) security.

Covered bonds Bonds that are asset-backed securities (q.v.), but if the bond issuer goes bankrupt, the investor has a claim on the assets of the securitisation. If the securitised assets decline in value, the bond holders have a claim on the issuer's assets.

Covered call option writing Writing a call option on an underlying when the writer owns at least the number of underlying securities included in the option.

Covered warrants The same as warrants except that financial institutions issue them, selling the right to buy or sell shares in industrial and commercial companies.

CPI (consumer price index) An index which measures the cost of a basket of retail goods and services.

Creation unit of ETF shares A bundle of securities e.g. shares tracking an index of say shares or other assets.

Creative accounting The drawing up of accounts which obey the letter of the law and accounting body rules but which involve the manipulation of accounts to show the most favourable profit and balance sheet.

Crédit Agricole France's biggest retail bank.

Credit card A credit card holder is able to purchase goods or services, and pay for them later, either the full amount or part.

Credit default swap Invented in the 1990s they are an insurance-like contract which allows, for a fee, the risk of a borrower defaulting to be passed on to financial market participants.

Credit derivative An instrument for which the payoff is linked to changes in the underlying's credit standing, e.g. if the credit rating changes on a bond issued by a company from BBB– to D the holder will receive a payout on a credit derivative (sold by a financial institution) which takes as its underlying that particular company's bond.

Credit facility or Credit line A short-term borrowing arrangement with a bank or other lender under which borrowing may fluctuate at the behest of the borrower up to a fixed total amount, e.g. overdraft, revolving facility.

Credit insurance (1) An insurance policy that pays out on trade debts held by the firm when customers fail to meet their obligations. (2) An insurance policy that pays out in the event of default on a debt instrument.

Credit multiplier effect The 'knock-on' effect of the creation of money in an economy that comes from an increase or decrease in the monetary base.

Crédit Mutuel French mutual/cooperative bank

Credit rating An estimate of the quality of a debt from the lender's viewpoint in terms of the likelihood of interest and capital not being paid and of the extent to which the lender is protected in the event of default.

Credit risk premium or credit spread The additional yield (over, say, reputable government bonds) on a debt instrument due to the borrower's additional perceived probablity of default.

Credit risk The risk that a counterparty to a financial transaction will fail to fulfil its obligation.

Credit union A non-profit organisation accepting deposits and making loans, operated as a cooperative.

Credit-rating agencies They assess a company's or security's credit rating, and are paid fees by companies, governments, etc. which, with a good credit rating, are more likely to attract lenders.

Creditor One to whom a debt is owed.

Crest or CREST An electronic means of settlement and registration of shares and other securities following a sale on the London Stock Exchange, operated by CRESTCo.

Cross-rate The exchange rate between two (usually thinly-traded) currencies expressed in terms of a third currency, usually the US dollar.

Cum-dividend (1) An investor buys a government bond (q.v.) when it is still designated cum-dividend or cum-coupon and is entitled to the accrued interest since the last coupon was paid. (2) A share (q.v.) designated cum-dividend indicates that the buyer will be entitled to a dividend recently announced by the company.

Cum-rights Shares bought on the stock market prior to the ex-rights day are designated cum-rights and carry to the new owner the right to subscribe for the new shares in the rights issue.

Cumulative If a payment (interest or dividend) on a bond or share (qq.v.) is missed in one period those securities are given priority when the next payment is made. These arrears must be cleared up before shareholders receive dividends.

Currency option A contract giving the right but not the obligation to buy or sell currency on specified terms.

Currency option hedge Negating FX risk by off-setting deals dealing in currency options.

Currency peg A currency is pegged (fixed) at a set exchange rate with another currency, often the US dollar.

Currency reserve control A reserve of gold and foreign currencies held by a central banks.

Currency swap *See* Swap.

Currency swaption Option to enter a currency swap (q.v.) contract.

Currenex A multibank dealing system (q.v.) for trading currencies.

Current account balance *See* Balance of payments.

Current account deficit A country imports more goods and services than it exports, affecting its balance of payments (q.v.).

Current account *See* Sight bank account.

Current yield *See* Yield.

Custodian Safeguards a company's or individual's financial assets. Usually a bank.

Customer direct trades FX trades where a customer approaches a bank directly, without using an intermediary.

Daily Official List (DOL) The daily record setting out the prices of all trades in securities conducted on the London Stock Exchange. *See also* SEDOL.

Dark pool Trading venue where large orders can be placed anonymously to reduce the effect of the trade on market prices.

DAX 30 (Deutsche AktienindeX) A stock market index of 30 German shares quoted on Deutsche Börse (q.v.).

Day count convention The number of months and/or days that are used in financial calculations. It varies.

Debentures Bonds issued with redemption dates a number of years into the future or irredeemable. Usually secured against specific assets (mortgage debentures) or through a floating charge on the firm's assets (floating debentures). In the US and Canada debenture means an unsecured debt with a fixed coupon.

Debit card A bank customer is able to make payments directly from their current account using an EFTPOS (q.v.) terminal, and also to check details of their bank account.

Debt An obligation to pay.

Debt capital Capital invested in a company in the form of loans or bonds.

Debt maturity The length of time left until the repayment or nominal value on a debt becomes due.

Debt rating A rating given by one of the credit rating agencies (q.v.) to bonds.

Debt restructuring Negotiating with lenders to vary the terms of the debt in time of difficulty.

Debtors Those who owe a debt.

Decentralisation (Fund Management) Delegating decision making to multiple managers.

Dedicated short bias A hedge fund strategy which takes predominantly short positions (q.v.) in anticipation of price declines.

Deep (financial markets) With many buyers and sellers and therefore a great deal of activity.

Deep discounted bonds Bonds sold well below par value, usually because they have little or no coupon.

Deep discounted rights issue A rights issue price is much less than the present market price of the old shares.

Default A failure to make agreed payments of interest or principal, or failure to comply with some other loan provision.

Defensive open market operation The central bank intervenes to offset market conditions that might affect the level of money in the economy thus targeting an interest rate.

Deferred preference shares Rank below ordinary shares for dividends.

Defined benefit A pension which pays out a fixed amount based on years worked and final salary or some average salary.

Defined contribution A pension into which fixed amounts are paid, but the pension paid out is linked to the return made by the pension fund.

Dematerialisation Traditionally the evidence of financial security ownership is by written statements on paper (e.g. share certificates). Increasingly such information is being placed on electronic records and paper evidence is being abandoned.

Demutualisation Mutual entities converting into companies with shareholders.

Deposit facility A facility offered by the ECB (q.v.) for member banks to deposit money at a prearranged rate.

Depository Person or firm, often a large bank, entrusted with safekeeping of funds, securities, or other valuable assets.

Depositary receipts Certificates, representing evidence of ownership of a company's shares (or other securities) held by a depository. Depositary receipts (DRs) are negotiable (can be traded) certificates which represent ownership of a given number of a company's shares which can be listed and traded independently from the underlying shares. There are a number of forms of DRs including American depositary receipts (ADRs), global depositary receipts (GDRs), euro depositary receipts (EDRs) and retail depositary receipts (RDRs).

Depository institutions, deposit-taking institutions (DTIs) Financial institutions which obtain funds mainly from the public by taking in deposits.

Derivative A financial asset (instrument), the performance of which is based on (derived from) the behaviour of the value of an underlying asset.

Deutsche Börse German stock exchange.

Development capital Second-stage finance (following seed finance – *see* Seedcorn capital or money and Early-stage capital) to permit business expansion.

Dilution The effect on the earnings and voting power per ordinary share from an increase in the number of shares issued without a corresponding increase in the firm's earnings.

Direct debit A bank facility used for recurring payments. The beneficiary is able to vary the amount.

Direct Edge An MTF (q.v.).

Direct foreign investment The cross-border purchase of commercial assets such as factories and industrial plant for productive purposes.

Directors' dealings The purchase or sale of shares in their own company. This is legal (except at certain times of the company's year). Some investors examine directors' dealings to decide whether to buy or sell.

Directors' report Information and commentary on company performance and other matters contained in a company's annual report and accounts.

Dirty float *See* Managed float.

Dirty price, full price, invoice price On a bond a buyer pays a total of the clean price and the accrued interest since the last coupon payment.

Discount (1) A deduction from the normal price or value, the opposite of premium. (2) The amount below face value at which a financial claim sells, e.g. bill of exchange or zero coupon bond. (3) The extent to which an investment trust's shares sell below the net asset value. (4) The amount by which a future value of a currency is less than its spot value. (5) The action of purchasing financial instruments, e.g. bills, at a discount. (6) The degree to which a security sells below its issue price in the secondary market. (7) The process of equating a cash flow at some future date with today's value using the time value of money.

Discount house An institution that purchases promissory notes and resells them or holds them until maturity.

Discount market deposit Originally it was money deposited with a London discount house. However, there is now a collection of UK institutions and dealers in money market instruments such as trade bills. These are normally repayable at call or very short term. Clearing banks are the usual depositors.

Discount rate (1) The rate of return used to discount cash flows received in future years. It is the opportunity cost of capital given the risk class of the future cash flows. (2) The rate of interest at which some central banks lend money to the banking system.

Discount to par A value less than the face value.

Discount window borrowing A bank borrowing extra reserves from the central bank to alleviate a short-term lack of reserves.

Discount yield, discount basis, discount rate, rate of discount The yield on a bond based on the face value.

Discounting The process of reducing future cash flows to a present value using an appropriate discount rate.

Disintermediation Borrowing firms bypassing financial institutions and obtaining finance directly from the market.

Distressed A company is suffering financial problems which could lead to bankruptcy.

Distressed debt Bonds which were issued by a company which is now in financial trouble and unable to meet its obligations.

Distressed securities investing Hedge fund managers buy shares or debt in companies which are in financial trouble, in the hope that they will recover.

Distribution units *See* Income units.

Diversification To invest in varied projects, enterprises, financial securities, products, markets, etc.

Divestiture (Divestment) The selling off of assets or subsidiary businesses by a company or individual.

Dividend cover The number of times net profits available for distribution exceed the dividend actually paid or declared. Earnings per share divided by gross dividend per share or total post-tax profits divided by total dividend payout.

Dividend payout ratio The percentage of a company's earnings paid out as dividends.

Dividend per share The total amount paid or due to be paid in dividends for the year (interim and final) divided by the number of shares in issue.

Dividend policy The determination of the proportion of profits paid out to shareholders over the longer term.

Dividend That part of a company's profit paid to ordinary shareholders, usually on a regular basis.

Dividend yield The amount of dividend paid on each share as a percentage of the share price.

DMO (Debt Management Office) Part of the UK Treasury. It is responsible for debt and cash management for the UK Government, lending to local authorities and managing public sector funds. It issues gilts (q.v.)

Documentary letter of credit Issued by financial institutions they authorise payment to an exporter once all documentation is present and correct.

DOL *See* Daily Official List.

Domestic bonds Bonds which are issued and traded in the country of their currency.

Domestic medium-term notes Medium-term notes (q.v.) denominated in the domestic currency.

Dot.com A company reliant on the internet for its activities.

Dow or Dow Jones Industrial Average (DJIA) The best-known and oldest index of movements in the price of US stocks and shares. There are 30 shares in the index.

Dragons' Den A BBC TV programme offering investment from business angels (q.v.).

Drawdown arrangement A loan facility is established and the borrower uses it (takes the money available) in stages as the funds are required.

Dual-class US shares which have different degrees of voting rights.

Due diligence When a transaction is contemplated, such as a merger or a loan, a detailed investigation of the company is carried out, usually by specialists, to ensure that its condition is suitable for the transaction.

Duration of a bond The weighted (by discounting the present payment values) average maturity of all cash returns (coupon and principal payment).

Dynamic open market operations The central bank intervenes to increase or decrease the level of money available in the economy and thereby moves the markets to a target interest rate.

E-money also known as electronic money, as e-currency, electronic cash, electronic currency, digital money, digital cash, digital currency, cyber currency. Money transferred by electronic means, such as using a smart card (q.v.)

E-trading Trading using electronic and internet services.

Earnings multiple Price–earnings ratio.

Earnings per share (EPS) Profit after tax and interest divided by number of shares in issue.

Earnings Profits, usually after deduction of tax.

Earnings yield Earnings per share divided by current market price of share.

EBA *See* European Banking Authority.

EBIT A company's Earnings (profits) Before Interest and Taxes are deducted.

EBITDA Earnings Before Interest, Taxation, Depreciation and Amortisation. Or as cynics have it: Earnings Before I Tricked The Dumb Auditor.

ECB European Central Bank The central bank responsible for conducting monetary policy for the euro area.

Economic and Monetary Union (EMU) The 17 EU members who have adopted the euro with a single central bank, the ECB (q.v.), having control over interest rates.

Economic exposure *See* Economic risk.

Economic risk The risk that a company's economic value may decline as a result of currency movements causing a loss in competitive strength.

Economies of scale Larger size of output by a company often leads to lower cost per unit of output.

EDX London An equity derivative exchange based in London owned by the London Stock Exchange and OM AM of Sweden.

Effective annual rate (EAR) *See* Annual percentage rate.

Efficient market hypothesis (EMH) The EMH implies that new information is incorporated into a share price (or other security) (1) rapidly and (2) rationally. *See also* Efficient stock market.

Efficient stock market Share prices rationally reflect available information. In an efficient market no trader will be presented with an opportunity for making an abnormal return, except by chance. *See also* Efficient market hypothesis.

EFTPOS (Electronic Funds Transfer at Point Of Sale) A computerised system allowing the automatic transfer of money from a buyer to a seller of goods or services at the time of sale.

EIOPA *See* European Insurance and Occupational Pensions Authority.

EIS, Enterprise Investment Scheme A UK government-backed scheme with tax advantages encouraging investment in smaller companies.

Electronic Communications Networks (ECNs) *See* Multilateral trading facilities.

Electronic platform A trading system matching buyers and sellers using computers, communication links and/or the internet.

Electronic purse *See* Smart cards.

Electronic settlement Transferring securities from sellers to buyers without certificates – it is a computer entry only.

Electronic trading system *See* Electronic platform.

Emerging market bonds Bonds issued by emerging markets.

Emerging markets Security markets in newly industrialising countries and/or capital markets at an early stage of development.

EMU *See* Economic and Monetary Union.

End-investors The ultimate buyers of securities, usually institutional investors.

Endowment A policy (savings scheme) in which a lump sum is payable, either at the end of the term of the policy or on death during the term of the policy.

Enterprise Investment Scheme *See* EIS.

Entrepreneur Defined by economists as the owner-manager of a firm. Usually supplies capital, organises production, decides on strategic direction and bears risk.

EONIA (Euro Overnight Index Average) Overnight interest rate of the euro in the eurozone.

Equity, equity capital An ownership share of a business, each equity share representing an equal stake in the business. Capital invested in a company in the form of shares. The capital is not automatically repaid, but share owners can sell their shares

Equity indices Baskets of shares indicating the movement of the equity market as a whole or sub-sets of the markets.

Equity kicker (sweetener) The attachment to a bond or other debt finance of some rights to participate in and benefit from a good performance (e.g. to exercise an option to purchase shares). Often used with mezzanine finance (q.v.) and high-yield bonds.

Equity long/short A hedge fund strategy taking both long and short positions (qq.v.) in shares or other securities.

Equity market neutral A hedge fund strategy aiming for a market neutral (q.v.) position – a profit is expected regardless of the movements in the market as a whole.

Equity option The right but not the obligation to buy or sell shares at a pre-agreed price in the future.

Equity shareholders' funds *See* Shareholders' funds.

Equity warrants A security issued by a company that gives to the owners the right but not the obligation to purchase shares in the company in the future at a fixed price during or at the end of a specified time period. It is the company itself that sells this right to purchase.

Equity-linked bonds *See* Convertible bonds.

ERM *See* Exchange Rate Mechanism.

ESCB *See* European System of Central Banks.

ESMA *See* European Securities and Markets Authority.

eSpeed A multibank dealing system (q.v.).

ESRB *See* European Systemic Risk Board.

ETC *See* Exchange Traded Commodities.

ETF *See* Exchange traded fund.

EU *See* European Union.

Eurex Derivative exchange based in Switzerland and Germany.

EURIBOR (Euro Interbank Offered Rate) Short-term interest rates in the interbank market (highly stable banks lending to each other) in the currency of euros.

Euro medium-term notes Medium-term notes (q.v.) issued outside the control or jurisdiction of the authorities of the country of the currency of issue.

Euro Swiss francs Swiss francs traded in the eurocurrency market.

Eurobanking Depositing and lending outside the jurisdiction of the country of the currency being used.

Eurobonds Bonds issued outside the jurisdiction of the authorities of the country of the currency of issue.

Eurocommercial paper *See* Commercial paper.

Eurocredit Medium- to long-term loans in the eurocurrency markets.

Eurocurrency banking Transactions in a currency outside the jurisdiction of the authorities of the country of the currency of issue. For example, transactions in Canadian dollars in London. No connection with the currency in the eurozone.

Eurocurrency Currency held outside its country of origin, for example, Australian dollars held outside Australia outside the jurisdiction of the authorities of the country of the currency of issue. Note: this market existed long before the creation of the currency in the eurozone. It has no connection with the euro.

Eurocurrency deposits Short-term wholesale money market deposits made in the eurocurrency market.

Eurodeposit account Short-term wholesale money market deposits are made into an account set up for that purpose made in the eurocurrency market.

Eurodollar A deposit or credit of dollars held outside the regulation of the US authorities, say in Tokyo, London or Paris.

Eurodollar bond A bond issued in dollars outside the US outside the jurisdiction of the authorities of the country of the currency of issue.

Euroeurobonds Bonds issued in euros outside the eurozone outside the jurisdiction of the authorities of the country of the currency of issue.

Euromarkets Informal (unregulated) markets in money held outside the jurisdiction of the country of origin, e.g. Swiss francs lending outside the control of the Swiss authorities – perhaps the francs are in London. No connection with the euro, the currency in use in the eurozone. Euromarkets began in the late 1950s and now encompass the eurocurrency, eurocredit and eurobond markets as well as over-the-counter derivatives and commodity markets.

Euronext The combined financial stock market comprising the French, Dutch, Belgian and Portuguese bourses. Now merged with NYSE.

Euronext.liffe Euronext, the organisation combining the French, Dutch, Belgian and Portuguese stock markets, bought LIFFE (q.v.) and renamed it Euronext.liffe. After merger with NYSE it is now called NYSE Liffe.

EURONIA (Euro Overnight Index Average) London overnight interest rate of the euro.

Euronotes A short-term debt security. These are normally issued at a discount to face value for periods of one, three and six months' maturity. They are tradable once issued and are bearer securities. They are issued outside the jurisdiction of the currency stated on the note. They are backed up by a revolving under-writing facility which ensures that the issuer will be able to raise funds.

European Banking Authority (EBA) Promotes coordination in regulatory and supervisory stand-ards of banks across the EU.

European Central Bank *See* ECB.

European Insurance and Occupational Pensions Authority (EIOPA) Promotes coordination of insurance regulation across the EU.

European Monetary Union *See* Economic and Monetary Union.

European Private Equity & Venture Capital Association (EVCA) The European body acting as a trade association for private equity and venture capital.

European Securities and Markets Authority (ESMA) Promotes coor-dination in financial markets and investor protection across the EU.

European System of Central Banks Comprises the ECB (q.v.) and the national central banks (NCBs) of all EU Member States whether they adopted the euro or not.

European System of Financial Supervisors A college for national supervisors.

European Systemic Risk Board (ESRB) Issues warnings and rec-ommendations about economic and/or financial threats.

European Union An economic and political union of 27 European countries originally established in 1951.

European-style options Options which can be exercised only by the purchaser on a predetermined future date.

Eurosecurities Financial securities such as bonds, commercial paper, convertibles, floating rate notes, medium-term notes, and prom-issory notes offered on or traded in markets outside the control of the authorities of the currency of denomination.

Eurosterling bond A bond issued in sterling outside the control of the authorities of the currency of denomination.

Eurosterling Sterling traded in the eurocurrency market outside the control of the authorities of the cur-rency of denomination.

Eurosystem The Eurosystem com-prises the ECB and the National and Central Banks of those coun-tries that have adopted the euro.

Euroyen Japanese yen traded in the eurocurrency market outside the control of the authorities of the cur-rency of denomination.

Eurozone Those countries (17 at present) that joined together in adopting the euro as their currency.

EVCA *See* European Private Equity & Venture Capital Association.

Event driven A hedge fund strategy which takes advantage of events which affect financial markets.

Event risk The risk that some future event may increase the risk on a financial investment, e.g. an earth-quake event affects returns on Japanese bonds.

Ex-coupon A bond sold without the right to the next interest payment.

Ex-dividend When a share or bond is designated ex-dividend a purchaser will not be entitled to a recently announced dividend or the accrued interest on the bond since the last coupon – the old owner will receive the dividend (coupon).

Ex-rights price of a share The theo-retical market price following a rights issue.

Ex-rights When a share goes 'ex-rights' any purchaser of a share after that date will not have a right to subscribe for new shares in the rights issue.

Excess An amount that must be paid by a policy holder to an insurance company in the event of a claim.

Excess reserves The extra cash reserves a bank might be required to hold beyond those held at the central bank.

Exchange controls The state controls the purchase and sale of currencies by its residents.

Exchange Rate Mechanism A system established in 1979 in which cur-rencies of participating European countries were kept within strict exchange limits.

Exchange rate The price of one cur-rency expressed in terms of another.

Exchange-traded commodities An exchange-traded fund (q.v.) that deals in commodities.

Exchange-traded fund (ETF) An open-ended fund that tracks the per-formance of an index or sector of the market. Its value fluctuates accord-ing to the value of its investments.

Exchange trading Trading of finan-cial instruments on regulated markets.

Exchangeable bond A bond that entitles the owner to choose at a later date whether to exchange the bond for shares in a company. The shares are in a company other than the one that issued the bond.

Execution-only brokers A stock-broker who will buy or sell shares cheaply but will not give advice or other services.

Executive directors Manage day-to-day activities of the firms as well as contributing to boardroom discus-sion of company-wide policy and strategic direction.

Exercise price (strike price) The price at which an underlying will be bought (call) or sold (put) under an option contract.

Exit (1) The term used to describe the point at which a private equity investor can recoup some or all of the investment made. (2) The closing of a position created by a transaction.

Exit charge The charge made to exit a fund.

Exotic A term used to describe an unusual financial transaction, e.g. exotic option, exotic currency (i.e. one with few trades).

Exotic currencies An FX term for currencies which are thinly traded and illiquid.

Expansion capital Capital needed by companies at a fast-development phase to increase production capac-ity or to increase working capital and capital for the further devel-opment of the product or market. Venture capital is often used.

Expansion, development or growth (private equity) Companies at this stage are on to a fast-growth track and need extra financial support.

Expectations hypothesis of the term structure of interest rates (yield curve) Long-term interest rates reflect the market consensus on the changes in short-term interest rates.

Expectations theory of foreign exchange The current forward exchange rate is an unbiased predic-tor of the spot rate at that point in the future.

Expiry date of an option The time when the rights to buy or sell the option cease.

Extendable commercial paper The life of the paper can be extended by putting back the redemption date.

Externality The cost or benefits of a transaction to third parties who are not directly involved in it.

Extraordinary items Unusual/infrequent events which produce an extraordinary gain or loss.

Face value *See* Par value.

Factoring To borrow from factors against the security of trade debtors. Factoring companies also provide additional services such as sales ledger administration and credit insurance.

Fair game In the context of a stock market this is where some investors and fund raisers are not able to benefit at the expense of other participants. The market is regulated to avoid abuse, negligence and fraud. It is cheap to carry out transactions and the market provides high liquidity.

Fallen angel Debt which used to rate as investment grade but which is now regarded as junk, mezzanine finance (q.v.) or high-yield finance.

Fannie Mae The nickname for the Federal National Mortgage Asssociation, FNMA.

Fat finger trade When an incorrect trade is made (e.g. billions instead of millions) by someone pressing an incorrect keyboard button.

FCA *See* Financial Conduct Authority.

Federal Deposit and Insurance Corporation US corporation which insures bank deposits.

Federal funds rate The rate at which US financial institutions will lend to each other overnight.

Federal Open Market Committee (FOMC) US monetary policy making committee.

Federal Reserve Bank (the Fed) US central bank which has 12 regional divisions.

Fedwire (Federal Reserve Wire Network) An RTGS (q.v.) US settlement system.

FEER The Fundamental Equilibrium Exchange Rate (FEER) is the exchange rate between two currencies that results in a sustainable current account balance. The exchange rate is expected to move (in theory) so as to achieve current-account balance.

FFA *See* Forward freight agreement.

Final close (private equity) The end of the capital-raising stage in a private equity fund.

Finance house A financial institution offering to supply finance in the form of hire purchase, leasing and other forms of instalment credit.

Finance lease (also called capital lease, financial lease or full payout lease) The lessor expects to recover the full cost (or almost the full cost) of the asset plus interest, over the period of the lease.

Financial Conduct Authority (FCA) The new name for the part of the FSA (q.v.) that regulates UK financial services.

Financial gearing (leverage) *See* Gearing.

Financial instrument A real or virtual document representing monetary value, e.g. bond, share, option, certificate of deposit, etc.

Financial intermediaries They put lenders and borrowers in touch with each other, or create intermediate securities.

Financial model A type of financial analysis using mathematical logic and a simplified version of the real world.

Financial Ombudsman Scheme (FOS) UK In cases of dispute or complaint between clients and firms involving financial matters, the impartial and independent FOS collects the relevant information and arrives at a decision which is binding on the firm but the complainant can take the matter to court. This service is free to consumers.

Financial Policy Committee (FPC) The Bank of England body which meets four times a year to decide UK macroprudential financial policy.

Financial Reporting Council (FRC) The UK's independent regulator responsible for ensuring high quality corporate reporting, accounts and governance.

Financial Services Action Plan (FSAP) An EU plan to work towards a single integrated market in Europe.

Financial Services Authority (FSA) The chief financial services regulator in the UK, now about to be split into the Financial Conduct Authority (FCA) and the Prudential Regulatory Authority (PRA) (q.v.).

Financial Services Compensation Scheme (FSCS) The FSCS is the UK's compensation fund for customers of authorised financial services firms which are unable to meet their obligations.

Financial Stability Board (FSB) A global body tasked with developing policies to promote financial stability.

Financing gap The gap in the provision of finance for medium-sized, fast-growing firms. Often these firms are too large or fast growing to ask the individual shareholders for more funds or to obtain sufficient bank finance. Also they are not ready to launch on the stock market.

First Banking Directive 1977 An EU directive permitting banks to open and operate branches in other EU countries.

First close (private equity) The point at which the required amount has been raised and a private equity fund comes into existence.

Fitch Ratings A credit rating agency (q.v.).

Fixed charge (e.g. fixed charged debenture or loan) A specific asset(s) assigned as collateral security for a debt.

Fixed exchange rate The national authorities act to ensure that the rate of exchange between two currencies is constant.

Fixed income arbitrage A hedge fund strategy which takes advantage of the small price differentials in the price of fixed-income securities.

Fixed interest (Fixed rate) Interest on a debt security is constant over its life.

Fixed-interest securities Strictly, the term applies to securities, such as bonds, on which the holder receives a predetermined interest pattern on the par value (e.g. gilts, corporate bonds, eurobonds). However, the term is also used for debt securities even when there is no regular interest, e.g. zero-coupon bonds (q.v.), and when the interest varies, as with floating rate notes (q.v.), for example.

Fixing system The system used to set the price of gold and silver.

Flat rate The rate of interest quoted by a hire purchase company (or other lender) to a hiree which fails to reflect properly the true interest rate being charged as measured by the annual percentage rate (APR) (q.v.).

Flat yield *See* Yield.

Float (1) The difference between the cash balance shown by a firm's cash book and the bank account. Caused by delays in the transfer of funds between bank accounts. (2) An exchange rate that is permitted to vary against other currencies. (3) An issuance of shares to the public by a company joining a stock market. (4) For insurance companies and pension funds it is the pool of money held in the firm in readiness to pay claims.

Floating charge The total assets of the company or an individual are used as collateral security for a debt. There is no specific asset assigned as collateral.

Floating exchange rate A rate of exchange which is not fixed by national authorities but fluctuates depending on demand for and supply of the currency.

Floating FX regime *See* Floating exchange rate.

Floating-rate borrowing (floating interest) The rate of interest on a loan varies with a standard reference rate, e.g. LIBOR or bank base rate.

Floating-rate notes (FRNs) Notes issued in which the coupon fluctuates according to a benchmark interest rate charge (e.g. LIBOR, q.v.). Issued in the euromarkets generally with maturities of 7–15 years. Reverse floaters – those on which the interest rate declines as LIBOR rises.

Floor (1) An agreement whereby, if interest rates fall below an agreed level, the seller (floor writer) makes compensatory payments to the floor buyer. (2) (Credit default swap) The minimum interest to be received.

Flotation The issue of shares in a company for the first time on a stock exchange.

Follow-on offering *See* Seasoned equity offerings.

FOMC *See* Federal Open market Committee.

Footsie Nickname for FTSE 100 index. Trademarked.

Foreign banking Transactions in a domestic currency with non-residents.

Foreign bonds Bonds issued in a domestic market and currency by a foreign entity.

Foreign exchange control Limits are placed by a government on the purchase and sale of foreign currency.

Foreign exchange markets (forex or FX) Markets that facilitate the exchange of one currency into another.

Foreign exchange risk The risk of suffering a loss due to foreign exchange shifts.

Foreign exchange swap, FX swap, forex swap A two part exchange of currencies: (1) a contract to exchange currencies on an agreed date usually for spot; (2) a contract to reverse the exchange at a more distant date at the FX forward rate.

Used by professional investors to balance their currency position.

Foreign exchange future Standardised contracts for the exchange of currency on an exchange at a future date.

Forex A contraction of 'foreign exchange'.

Forfaiting A bank (or other lender) purchases a number of sales invoices or promissory notes from an exporting company; usually the importer's bank guarantees the invoices.

Forward agreement *See* Forward.

Forward An OTC contract between two parties to undertake an exchange at an agreed future date at a price agreed now.

Forward Freight Agreement (FFA) Standardised contracts dealing in future freight rates (shipping contracts to transport a cargo).

Forward market A market for transactions which will take place some time in the future.

Forward market hedge A contract to exchange two currencies at a future date at an agreed rate of exchange which negates exchange rate risk.

Forward-rate agreement (FRA) An agreement about the future level of interest rates. Compensation is paid by one party to the other to the extent that market interest rates deviate from the 'agreed' rate.

FOS *See* Financial Ombudsman Scheme.

FPC *See* Financial Policy Committee.

Freddie Mac The nickname for the Federal Home Loan Mortgage Corporation, FHLMC.

Free float (Free capital) The proportion of a quoted company's shares not held by those closest (e.g. directors, founding families) to the company who may be unlikely to sell their shares.

Frictional unemployment Caused by the difficulty of matching workers with employers.

Front-end fee, facility fee Fees charged up front for providing and setting up a financial facility.

Front-end charge *See* Initial charge.

FSA *See* Financial Services Authority.

FSAP *See* Financial Services Action Plan.

FSB *See* Financial Stability Board.

FTSE 100 share index An index representing the UK's 100 largest listed companies' shares. An average weighted by market capitalisation.

FTSE 250 Share index based on the 250 companies next in size to the top 100.

FTSE 350 Combination of the FTSE 100 and FTSE 250.

FTSE Actuaries All-Share Index (the 'All-Share') The most representative index of UK shares, reflecting about 600 companies' shares.

FTSE AIM All-Share Index of most AIM (q.v.) companies.

FTSE Fledgling Index of Main Market listed companies too small to be in the FTSE All-Share.

FTSE SmallCap Companies An index of shares included in the FTSE All-Share but not in the top 350 companies.

Full price (bonds) *See* Dirty price.

Fund management Investment of and administering a quantity of money, e.g. pension fund, insurance fund, on behalf of the fund's owners.

Fund of funds A fund which invests in a group of other funds, enabling investors to be more diversified. The managers are supposed to have skills in selecting the best funds.

Fund of hedge funds A hedge fund which invests in a group of other hedge funds with the aim of lessening risk.

Fundamental Equilibrium Exchange Rate *See* FEER.

Fundamental value An investment fund strategy which invests in undervalued and unpopular companies.

Funded pension scheme Employees and/or employers make regular payments and the funds are invested to provide an income for pensioners.

Fungible Interchangeable items or securities; can be exchanged for each other on identical terms.

Future A standardised contract between two parties to undertake a transaction at an agreed price on a specified future date.

Future-based bet (spread betting) Betting on the price of shares on a quarter day in the future.

FX A contraction of 'foreign exchange'.

FXAll A multibank dealing system (q.v.) for currency trade.

FXConneect A multibank dealing system (q.v.) for currency trade.

G20 The group of 20 finance ministers and central bank governors established in 1999 to discuss key issues in the global economy.

Gate (hedge funds) A limit is placed on the amount that can be withdrawn by investors from the fund at any one time.

GDP (nominal, real) Gross domestic product, the sum of all output of goods and services produced by a nation. Nominal means including inflation, and real means with inflation removed.

Gearing (financial gearing) The proportion of debt capital in the overall capital structure. Also called leverage. High gearing can lead to exaggeratedly high returns if things go well or exaggerated losses if things do not go well.

GEMMS (Gilt-edged market makers) Firms recognised and approved by the DMO and the Bank of England which are primary dealers in gilts (q.v.). They are required to make a continuous market in gilts.

General inflation The process of steadily rising prices resulting in the diminishing purchasing power of a given nominal sum of money. Measured by an overall price index (RPI and CPI qq.v) which follows the price changes of a 'basket' of goods and services through time.

General insurance Insurance against specific contingencies, e.g. fire, theft and accident.

General obligation bonds Bonds that have a priority claim on the lender's revenue in case of default.

General partner (GP) The active manager of a private equity or venture capital fund.

George Soros A hedge fund manager famous for predicting the ERM (q.v.) crisis and profiting from it.

Georges Doriot A Frenchman who became a US citizen and began private equity investment.

Gilts (gilt-edged securities) Fixed-interest UK government securities (bonds) traded on the London Stock Exchange. A means for the UK government to raise finance from savers. They usually offer regular interest and a redemption amount paid years in the future.

Ginnie Mae The nickname for the General National Mortgage Asssociation, GNMA.

Giro A way for people without cheques to pay for goods and services over the counter at post offices.

Global banks Banks that are active in a number of countries.

Global custodian Looks after the large collections of investments made by institutions.

Global Depositary Receipts (GDRs) Non-American depositary receipts.

Global macro A hedge fund strategy which takes advantage of perceived misalignments in currencies, interest rates or other macroeconomic variables.

Globalink A multilateral dealing system (q.v.).

Globalisation The increasing internationalisation of trade, particularly financial product transactions. The integration of economic and capital markets throughout the world.

Goal independence The central bank decides the goals of monetary policy rather than government.

Going concern A judgement as to whether a company has sufficient financial strength to continue for at least one year. Accounts are usually drawn up on the assumption that the business is a going concern.

Going long Buying a financial security (e.g. a share) in the hope that its price will rise.

Going public Market jargon used when a company becomes quoted on a stock exchange (the company may have been a public limited company, plc, for years before this).

Going short See Short selling.

Gold standard An exchange rate where a currency is fixed at a set price in gold, discontinued in recent times due to the difficulty of sourcing the requisite amount of gold.

Golden shares Shares with extraordinary powers, such as being able to block a takeover.

Governing Council The body of the ECB (q.v.) which determines monetary policy.

Government bonds Bonds issued by governments in the domestic currency.

Grace period A lender grants the borrower a delay in the repayment of interest and/or principal at the outset of a lending agreement.

Great Depression A severe worldwide economic depression that began in 1929 and continued through the 1930s.

Gross (finance) Before tax is deducted.

Gross dividend yield Dividend per share before deduction of tax/share price $\times$ 100

Gross domestic product See GDP.

Gross margin See Gross profit margin.

Gross present value The total present value of all the cash flows, excluding the initial investment.

Gross profit margin (gross margin) Profit defined as sales minus cost of sales expressed as a percentage of sales.

Gross profit Turnover less cost of sales.

Gross redemption yield (Gross yield to redemption) A calculation of the redemption yield (see Yield) for a bond before deduction of tax. See Yield to maturity.

Gross yield Yield before tax deduction.

Guaranteed loan stock (bond) An organisation other than the borrower guarantees to the lender the repayment of the principal plus the interest payment.

Haircut (1) A margin imposed on the collateral of a repurchase agreement (q.v.) to protect the buyer from fluctuations. (2) A loss of value on a debt instrument due to some form of default.

Hallmark (precious metals) To be hall-marked means to be stamped with an official mark guaranteeing quality and purity.

Hang Seng Index Main index for Hong Kong shares.

Hard commodity Generally refers to commodities which are mined or extracted, e.g. metals, rubber, rather than grown or reared.

Hard currency A currency traded in a foreign exchange market for which demand is persistently high. It is unlikely to depreciate by large percentages. The major currencies (e.g. US dollar, euro and sterling) are considered hard currencies.

Hedge or Hedging Reducing or eliminating risk by undertaking a countervailing transaction.

Hedge fund A collective investment vehicle that operates relatively free from regulation allowing it to take steps in managing a portfolio that other fund managers are unable to take, e.g. borrowing to invest, shorting the market.

Hedge fund index An index which tracks the performance of a hedge fund.

Her Majesty's Revenue and Customs See HMRC.

Herstatt risk In 1974 the German bank Herstatt was closed by the Bundesbank. It had entered into forex transactions and received deutschmarks from counterparties in European time, but had not made the corresponding transfer of US dollars to its counterparties in New York time. It is the risk that arises when forex transactions are settled in different time zones.

HIBOR Hong Kong Interbank Offered Rate.

High Frequency Trading (HFT) Ultra fast internet trading using computer algorithms (q.v.).

High powered money Describes the monetary base (q.v.).

High water mark (hedge funds) A manager whose fund's performance has fallen does not receive a performance fee until the fund has reached a previously attained level.

High yield bonds *See* Junk bonds and Mezzanine finance.

Hire purchase (HP) The user (hiree) of goods pays regular instalments of interest and principal to the hire-purchase company over a period of months. Full ownership passes to the hiree at the end of the period (the hiree is able to use the goods from the outset).

HMRC (Her Majesty's Revenue and Customs) The prinicipal tax collecting authority in the UK.

Hurdle rate The required rate of return. The opportunity cost of the finance provider's money. The minimum return required from a position, making an investment or undertaking a project. (Hedge funds) A performance target which must be achieved before a performance fee is paid.

Hybrid finance A debt issue or security that combines the features of two or more instruments, e.g. a convertible bond is a package of a bond with an option to convert. Also used to indicate that a form of finance has both debt risk/return features (e.g. regular interest and a right to receive principal at a fixed date) and equity risk/return features (e.g. the returns depend to a large extent on the profitability of the firm).

ICE, Intercontinental Exchange Operates leading regulated exchanges, trading platforms and clearing houses. Deals in futures and derivatives.

IFB *See* Insurance Fraud Bureau.

Ijara Islamic leasing transaction.

IMF The International Monetary Fund created at the Bretton Woods conference (q.v.), an organisation of 187 countries, promotes global financial stability.

Impact day The day during the launch of a new issue of shares when the price is announced, the prospectus published and offers to purchase solicited.

Impatience to consume An individual would prefer to have cash to use now than in the future.

Imperfect hedge The hedge position will partly, but not exactly, mirror the change in price of the underlying.

In-the-money option An option with intrinsic value. For a call option (q.v.) the current underlying price is more than the option exercise price. For a put option (q.v.) the current price of the underlying is below the exercise price.

Income units Unit trusts (q.v.) that pay out income. Also known as distribution units.

Income yield *See* Yield.

Incubators Organisations established to assist fast-growing young firms. They may provide finance, accounting services, legal services, offices, etc.

Independent A private equity or venture capital organisation that raises its capital from the financial markets – it is not owned by one institution.

Index funds (trackers) Collective passively-managed investment funds (e.g. unit trusts) which try to replicate a stock market index rather than to pick winners in an actively managed fund.

Index *See* Market index.

Index-linked gilts (stocks) The redemption value and the coupons rise with inflation over the life of the UK government bond.

Indices *See* Market index.

Inflation risk The risk that the nominal returns on an investment will be insufficient to offset the decline in the value of money due to inflation.

Inflation The process of prices rising resulting in the fall of the purchasing power of currency units.

Inflation-linked Usually refers to investment securities. The returns go up equivalent to the rise in inflation.

Informal venture capitalist *See* Business angel.

Information asymmetry One party to a transaction (e.g. loan agreement) has more information on risk and return relating to the transaction than the other party.

Information costs The cost of gathering and analysing information, e.g. in the context of deciding whether to lend money to a firm.

Informed investors Those that are highly knowledgeable about financial securities and the fundamental evaluation of their worth.

Initial charge A charge made when buying securities to cover administration costs. Also called sales charge or front-end charge.

Initial margin An amount that a derivative contractor has to provide to the clearing house when first entering upon a derivative contract.

Initial public offering (IPO) (new issue) The offering of shares in the equity of a company to the public for the first time.

Insolvency The position of being insolvent, unable to pay debts. Liabilities exceed assets.

Instalment credit A form of finance to pay for goods or services over a period through the payment of principal and interest in regular instalments.

Institutional Shareholder Committee A coming together of investment funds to set standards of behaviour expected from institutional shareholders (pension and insurance funds, investment trusts etc.) and to lobby for improvement in companies and investment.

Institutionalisation The increasing tendency for organisational investing, as opposed to individuals investing money in securities (e.g. pension funds and investment trusts collect the savings of individuals to invest in shares).

Instrument (finance) A general term for all types of financial documents, such as shares, bonds, commercial paper, etc.

Instrument independence The central bank is free to use monetary instruments without political interference.

Insurable risk Risk that can be transferred through the payment of premiums to insurance companies.

Insurance Fraud Bureau The insurance industry's body combating fraud and bogus insurance claims.

Insurance premium An amount paid out to insure against a risk, such as a house fire or car accident.

Insurance underwriting The process of assessing, calculating, selecting and committing to an insurance risk

Inter-dealer direct trades FX trades between banks.

Inter-office trading 24-hour telephone trading on the LME (q.v.).

Interbank brokers Brokers in the forex markets who act as intermediaries between buyers and sellers. They provide anonymity to each side.

Interbank lending Lending carried out in the interbank market.

Interbank market The wholesale market in short-term money and foreign exchange in which banks borrow and lend among themselves. It is now extended to include large companies and other organisations.

Intercontinental Exchange *See* ICE.

Interest cover The number of times the income (profit or cash flow) of a business exceeds the interest payments made to service its loan capital.

Interest rate cap *See* Cap.

Interest rate parity (IRP) of exchange rate determination The interest rate parity theory holds true when the difference between spot and forward exchange rates is equal to the differential between interest rates available in the two currencies.

Interest rate risk The risk that changes in interest rates will have an adverse impact.

Interest rate swap A contract for one stream of future interest payments to be exchanged for another based on a specified principal amount, usually exchanging fixed rate for floating rate interest.

Interest yield *See* Yield.

Interest-withholding tax Tax is deducted before the investor receives interest.

Interim dividend A dividend related to the first half-year's (or quarter's) trading.

Interim profit reports A statement giving unaudited profit figures for the first half of the financial year, shortly after the end of the first half-year.

Intermediaries offer A method of selling shares in the new issue market. Shares are offered to financial institutions such as stockbrokers. Clients of these intermediaries can then apply to buy shares from them.

Intermediate debt *See* Mezzanine finance or Junk bonds.

Intermediate security To help solve the conflict of preference between savers (investors) in society and the ultimate borrowers, intermediaries (e.g. banks) create intermediate securities (e.g. bank accounts) offering the characteristics attractive to investors, i.e. high liquidity, low risk and the ability to deal in small amounts.

Internal rate of return (IRR) The discount rate that makes the present value of a future stream of cash flows equal to the initial investment(s).

International banking Banking transactions outside the jurisdiction of the authorities of the currency in which the transaction takes place.

International bonds Some people use the term to mean the same as eurobonds, others extend the definition to encompass foreign bonds as well.

International Capital Market Association (ICMA) A self-regulatory organisation designed to promote orderly trading and the general development of the euromarkets.

International Monetary Fund *See* IMF.

Internet banking Banking carried out using a computer and the internet.

Interpolation Estimating intermediate data points on a set of data where observed points are at intervals.

Intraday (literally within the day) *See* Spot.

Intrinsic value (1) (company) The discounted value of the cash that can be taken out of a business during its remaining life. (2) (options) The payoff that would be received if the underlying is at its current level when the option expires.

Introduction A company with shares already quoted on another stock exchange, or where there is already a wide spread of shareholders, may be introduced to the market. This allows a secondary market in the shares even though no new shares are issued.

Inventory *See* Stock.

Investbx Birmingham stock exchange.

Investment bank or merchant bank Banks that carry out a variety of financial services, usually excluding high street banking. Their services are usually fee based, e.g. fees for merger advice to companies.

Investment grade debt Debt with a sufficiently high credit rating (BBB– or Baa and above) to be regarded as safe enough for institutional investors that are restricted to holding only safe debt.

Investment return *See* Yield.

Investment trusts (investment companies) Collective investment vehicles set up as companies selling shares. The money raised is invested in specific assets such as shares, gilts, corporate bonds and property.

Invoice An itemised list of goods shipped, usually specifying the terms of sale and price.

Invoice discounting Invoices sent to trade debtors are pledged to a finance house in return for an immediate payment of up to 80 per cent of the face value.

Invoice finance A method of receiving finance secured by receivables (trade debtors). A finance house advances funds to a firm. When a customer pays on the invoice the company pays the finance house with interest.

Invoice price (bonds) *See* Dirty price.

IOU A colloquialism intended to mean 'I owe you'. The acknowledgement of a debt.

IRP *See* Interest rate parity.

IRR See Internal rate of return.

Irredeemable, perpetual Financial securities with no fixed maturity date at which the principal is repaid.

ISA Individual Savings Account

ISDA *See* International Swap and Derivatives Association.

Islamic bonds Bonds which comply with Islamic law.

Issuer ratings Ratings given by one of the credit rating agencies (q.v.) to the whole entity, not just its bonds.

Issuing house *See* Sponsor.

IUA (International Underwriting Association of London) World's largest organisation for large-scale insurance and reinsurance companies.

JGBs Japanese government bonds.

John Maynard Keynes A renowned UK economist who was instrumental in founding the World Bank and the IMF (q.v.).

John Paulson A US hedge fund manager famous for predicting the sub-prime mortgage crisis and profiting from it.

Joint stock enterprise The ownership (share) capital is divided into small units, permitting a number of investors to contribute varying amounts to the total. Profits are divided between stockholders in proportion to the number of shares they own.

Joint venture A business operation (usually a separate company) is jointly owned by two or more parent firms. It also applies to strategic alliances between companies where they collaborate on, for example, research.

Jonathan's Coffee-house The home of the club which eventually became the London Stock Exchange.

Junior debt *See* Subordinated debt.

Junk bonds Low-quality, low credit-rated company bonds. Rated below investment grade (less than BBB– or Baa). Risky and with a high yield.

Kangaroo A foreign bond issued in the Australian market.

KfW bank The German bank which made a large loss trading with Lehman Brothers.

Kicker *See* Equity kicker.

Laissez-faire The principle of the non-intervention of government in economic affairs.

Landesbanken German mutual regional banks, prone to various inefficiencies.

landMARK Groups of companies from particular UK regions which are on the London Stock Exchange Official List.

LBMA *See* London Bullion Market Association.

LCH Clearnet (LCH) Settles mutual indebtedness between a number of organisations. It settles ('clears') trades for equity traders, derivative traders, bond traders and energy traders, and guarantees all contracts, acting as counterparty to all trades on an exchange.

Lead manager In a new issue of securities (e.g. shares, bonds, syndicated loans) the lead manager controls and organises the issue. There may be joint lead managers, co-managers and regional lead managers.

Lead underwriter *See* Book building.

Leasing The owner of an asset (lessor) grants the use of the asset to another party (lessee) for a specified period in return for regular rental payments. The asset does not become the property of the lessee at the end of the specified period. *See also* Finance lease and Operating lease.

Lender of last resort This is usually the central bank, which provides a group of financial institutions with funds if they cannot otherwise obtain them.

Lessee The user of an asset under a lease.

Lessor The provider of an asset under a lease.

Letter of credit Obliges a bank to pay an exporter after the goods have been shipped to the importer.

Leverage Borrowing. *See* Gearing.

Leveraged buyout (LBO) The acquisition of an existing company, subsidiary or unit by another, financed mainly by borrowings. The capital raised is usually between 60 and 90 per cent debt finance.

Leveraged recapitalisation The financial structure of the firm is altered in such a way that it becomes highly geared.

Liability An obligation to pay a debt.

Liability insurance Insurance that covers against third-party claims.

Liability management A bank must source the appropriate mixture of low-cost funds and manage its customers' deposits efficiently.

LIBID (London Interbank Bid rate) The average rate which London banks would offer on deposits.

LIBOR (London Interbank Offered Rate) The rate of interest offered on loans to highly rated (low-risk) banks in the London interbank market for a specific period (e.g. three months). Used as a reference rate for other loans.

Life insurance or life assurance Insurance under which the beneficiaries receive payment upon death of the policyholder or other person named in the policy. Endowment policies offer a savings vehicle as well as cover against death.

LIFFE (London International Financial Futures and Options Exchange) The main derivatives exchange in London – now called NYSE Liffe and owned by NYSE-Euronext (q.v.).

LIFFE CONNECT NYSE Liffe's (q.v.) global derivatives trading system.

Limit bid In a book-building exercise a potential institutional investor states that it will buy a given number of shares at a particular price.

Limit prices An order to a broker to buy a specified quantity of a security at or below a specified price, or to sell it at or above a specified price.

Limited companies (Ltd) Private companies with no minimum amount of share capital, but with restrictions on the range of investors who can be offered shares. Limited liability for the debts of the firm is granted to the shareholders. They cannot be quoted on the London Stock Exchange.

Limited liability The owners of shares in a business have a limit on their loss, set as the amount they have committed to invest in shares.

Limited partner (LP) An investor in a private equity or venture capital fund not taking part in the management of the fund.

Line of credit *See* Credit facility.

Liquid Able to be turned into cash easily, quickly and without loss of value.

Liquid reserves (banking) Vault cash (q.v.) plus assets that can easily and quickly be turned into cash to meet outflows.

Liquidate Turn into cash.

Liquidation analysis Bankers explore their position in the event of the failure of a business to which they lent money.

Liquidation of a company The winding-up of the affairs of a company when it ceases business. This could be enforced by an inability to make payment when due or it could be voluntary when shareholders choose to end the company. Assets are sold, liabilities paid (if sufficient funds) and the surplus (if any) is distributed to shareholders.

Liquidation value The value of a company on liquidation.

Liquidity coverage ratio Basel III (q.v.) insists that banks have sufficient liquidity to maintain them during a financial crisis, a ratio of liquid assets to net cash outflows for a 30-day period under a stress scenario.

Liquidity management Ensuring that a company's cash resources are utilised to their maximum advantage and that a bank has enough ready cash to satisfy customers' needs.

Liquidity risk The risk that an organisation may not have, or may not be able to raise, cash funds when needed.

Liquidity The degree to which an asset can be sold quickly and easily without loss in value.

Liquidity-preference hypothesis (liquidity premium theory) of the term structure of interest rates The yield curve is predominately upward sloping because investors require an extra return for lending on a long-term basis.

Listed companies Those on the Official List (q.v.) of the UK Listing Authority.

Listed funds (hedge funds) Hedge funds which are listed on a stock market.

Listed Private Equity (LPEQ) Private equity funds which are listed on a stock market.

Listing agreement The UK Listing Authority (q.v.) insists that a company signs a listing agreement committing the directors to certain standards of behaviour and levels of reporting to shareholders.

Listing fees The admission and annual fees charged by stock markets for admitting a company to its lists.

Listing particulars *See* Prospectus.

Listing Rules The regulations concerning the initial flotation of a company on the London Stock Exchange and the continuing requirements the company must meet.

Living will (finance) A proposal detailing how to wind down a bank should it get into difficulty. It would also include a plan of action to revive the bank. Frequently updated.

Lloyd's Insurance Market A collection of insurance business in London founded over two centuries ago. 'Names' supply the capital to back insurance policies. Names can now be limited liability companies rather than individuals with unlimited liability to pay up on an insurance policy.

Lloyd's of London *See* Lloyd's insurance market.

Lloyd's Register Founded by Edward Lloyd, who also founded Lloyd's of London, but unconnected to Lloyd's of London. It provides a comprehensive list of world shipping, shipowners, wrecks, etc.

LME *See* London Metal Exchange.

LMEselect The electronic trading system of the London Metal Exchange (q.v.).

Loan covenants Restrictions on managerial action during the lifetime of the loan.

Loan stock A fixed-interest debt financial security. May be unsecured.

Loan to deposit ratio The amount of loans issued by a bank divided by the amount of deposits attracted.

Local authority bills/deposits Lending money to a UK local government authority by purchasing their bonds.

Local authority bond A long-term debt investment issued by a local authority such as a county or city.

Lock-up (hedge funds) Funds may not be withdrawn from the fund during the duration of the lock-up, usually one to two years.

London Bullion Market Association (LBMA) Market that trades in precious metals.

London Metal Exchange (LME) Trades metals (e.g. lead, zinc, tin, aluminium and nickel) in spot, forward and option markets.

London Stock Exchange (LSE) The London market in which securities are bought and sold.

Long bond Often defined as bonds with a time to maturity greater than 15 years, but there is some flexibility in this, so a 10-year bond is often described as being long.

Long position A positive exposure to a quantity – if the price rises the position improves. Owning a security or commodity; the opposite of a short position (selling).

Long-form report A report by accountants for the sponsor of a company being prepared for flotation. The report is detailed and confidential. It helps to reassure the sponsors when putting their name to the issue and provides the basis for the short-form report included in the prospectus.

Long-Term Capital Management A hedge fund which failed spectacularly in 1998 and had to be bailed out by a group of banks.

Long-term insurance *See* Life insurance.

Long/short strategy An investment strategy which takes both long and short positions (qq.v.).

Loss carryforward provision *See* High water mark.

Lot or piece The unit value of bonds.

Low-grade debt *See* Mezzanine finance or Junk bonds.

LPEQ *See* Listed private equity.

LSE *See* London Stock Exchange.

LTCM *See* Long-Term Capital Management.

Ltd Private limited company.

M & A *See* Mergers and acquisitions.

Maastricht Treaty The 1992 agreement that established the EU (European Union), the successor to the EC (European Community).

Macro-prudential regulation Focused on preventing systemic risks (q.v.) to the entire financial system.

Main Market The Official List of the London Stock Exchange, as opposed to the Alternative Investment Market (q.v.).

Main refinancing operations (MRO) *See* Open market operations.

Maintenance margin (futures) The level of margin that must be maintained on a futures account (usually at a clearing house). Daily marking to market of the position may reveal the need to put more money into the account to top up to the maintenance margin.

Making a book Market makers offering two prices: the price at which they are willing to buy (bid price) and the price they are willing to sell (offer price).

Managed float A floating FX system in which the government or central bank intervenes to change the value of its currency.

Managed futures A hedge fund strategy taking advantage of the changes in commodity or financial futures prices.

Management buy-in (MBI) A new team of managers makes an offer to a company to buy the whole company, a subsidiary or a section of the company, with the intention of taking over the running of it themselves. Venture capital often provides the major part of the finance.

Management buyout (MBO) A team of managers makes an offer to its employers to buy a whole business, a subsidiary or a section so that the managers own and run it themselves. Venture capital is often used to finance the majority of the purchase price.

Managing Director (MD) An executive responsible for running a business.

Maple A foreign bond issued in the Canadian market.

Marché à Terme d'Instruments Financiers (MATIF) The French futures and options exchange, merged with Euronext, and now part of the NYSE Euronext group.

Margin (futures) Money placed aside to back a futures purchase or sale. This is used to reassure the counterparty (effectively the clearing house in most cases) to the future that money will be available should the purchaser/seller renege on the deal.

Margin call A demand to top up the margin (q.v.).

Marginal lending rate Discount window borrowing (q.v.) from the European Central Bank.

Marine insurance The insurance of ships' hulls and cargoes. Lloyd's of London (q.v.) is a leading marine insurer.

Market Abuse Directive, 2003 An EU directive for preventing and detecting market abuse, such as price manipulation or insider dealing.

Market capitalisation The total value at market prices of the shares in issue for a company (or a stock market, or a sector of the stock market).

Market equilibrium When the forces of supply and demand are evenly balanced.

Market in managerial control Teams of managers compete for control of corporate assets, e.g. through merger activity.

Market index A sample of shares is used to represent a share (or other) market's level and movements.

Market maker A person or organisation that stands ready to buy and sell shares from investors on their own behalf (at the centre of quote-driven system of share trading). Also known as dealer.

Market neutral An investment strategy that seeks to make a positive return regardless of overall market movements by combining short and long positions.

Market segmentation hypothesis of the term structure of interest rates The yield curve is created (or at least influenced) by the supply and demand conditions in a number of sub-markets defined by maturity range.

Markets in Financial Instruments Directive *See* Mifid.

Marking to market The losses or gains on a derivative contract or other financial assets are assessed daily in reference to the value of the underlying price.

Matador A foreign bond issued in the Spanish domestic market.

Matched-bargain system *See* Order-driven trading.

Matching principle The maturity structure of debt matches the maturity of projects or assets held by the firm. Short-term assets are financed by short-term debt and long-term assets are financed by long-term debt.

Matching The company matches the inflows and outflows in different currencies, so that it is necessary to deal on the currency markets only for the unmatched portion of the total transactions.

Maturity transformation Intermediaries offer securities with liquid characteristics to induce primary investors to purchase or deposit funds. The money raised is made available to the ultimate borrowers on a long-term, illiquid basis.

Maturity, Maturity date or Final maturity (Redemption date) The time when a financial security (e.g. a bond) is due to be redeemed and the par value is paid to the lender.

Means of exchange Currency used for buying and selling goods.

Medium-term note (MTN) A document setting out a promise from a borrower to pay the holders a specified sum on the maturity date and, in many cases, a coupon interest in the meantime. Maturity can range from nine months to 30 years (usually one to five years).

Medium-term note programme Issuance under one set of legal documents of numerous MTNs over a period of time.

Merchant bank *See* Investment bank.

Merger arbitrage An event-driven hedge fund strategy which takes a long position in the target company and a short position in the acquiring company, in the expectation that the target's shares will rise relative to the acquirer's.

Merger The combining of two business entities under common ownership.

Mergers and acquisitions (M&A) The buying, selling and combining of companies.

Metric Method of measurement.

Mezzanine finance Unsecured debt or preference shares offering a high return with a high risk. Ranked behind secured debt but ahead of equity. It may carry an equity kicker (q.v.).

Micro-prudential regulation Focused on supervising individual banks to guard against a raised probability of bank failure.

Microfinance Taking small deposits and making small loans for the benefit of people on low incomes.

Middleman *See* Financial intermediary.

Mifid An EU directive designed to increase competition in share dealing and consumer protection.

MM Main Market (q.v.).

Mobilisation of savings The flow of savings primarily from the household sector to the ultimate borrowers to invest in real assets. This process is encouraged by financial intermediaries.

Model Code for Directors' Dealings London Stock Exchange rules for directors dealing in shares of their own company.

Monetary base Currency in circulation plus bank reserves.

Monetary Policy Committee (MPC) The BoE (q.v.) committee responsible for setting monetary policy.

Monetary policy The deliberate control of the money supply and/or rates of interest by the central bank.

Money laundering Concealing the source of illegally obtained money.

Money market fund A fund placing investors' money in the money market, i.e. short-term, securities.

Money market hedge Negating FX risk by dealing on the money market.

Money markets Wholesale financial markets (i.e. those dealing with large amounts) in which lending and borrowing on a short-term basis takes place (< 1 year). Examples of instruments: banker's acceptances, certificates of deposit, commercial paper, Treasury bills.

Monoline insurance Started out as very low risk organisations who offered insurance on bonds issued by US municipal authorities. In the 2000s the monolines thought they could stretch their expertise to the mortgage backed securities market and so insured CDOs and SIVs.

Monopoly One producer in an industry. However, for Competition Commission purposes a monopoly is often defined as a market share of 25 per cent.

Moodys A leading credit rating agency (q.v.).

Moral hazard The presence of a safety net (e.g. an insurance policy) encourages adverse behaviour (e.g. carelessness). An incentive to take extraordinary risks (risks that tend to fall on others) aimed at rectifying a desperate position. The risk that a party to a transaction is not acting in good faith by providing misleading or inadequate information.

Moratorium A period of delay agreed on by a creditor and a debtor for recovery of a debt.

Mortgage bank A former building society that has converted to being a bank.

Mortgage bond In the US a secured bond.

Mortgage debentures Bonds secured using property as collateral.

Mortgage-backed securities Securitised bonds backed by a collection of mortgage payments. *See* Securitisation.

Mortgage-style repayment schedule A regular monthly amount is paid to a lender which covers both interest and some capital repayment. At first most of the monthly payment goes towards interest. As the outstanding debt is reduced, the monthly payment pays off a larger and larger amount of the capital.

MPC *See* Monetary Policy Committee.

MTF, Multilateral Trading Facility Electronic trading system matching buyers and sellers using computers.

MTNs *See* Medium-term note.

Multi-currency programme A commercial paper programme (q.v.) which uses a range of currencies.

Multi strategy The use of a number of different investment strategies.

Multi-lateral netting Settlement of the net amount of all FX trades.

Multibank dealing system An electronic dealing system managed by a group of banks.

Multilateral Trading Facilities *See* MTF.

Municipal debt Debt (e.g. bonds) issued by a municipality.

Mutual bank A bank owned by its members.

Mutual funds A collective investment vehicle the shares or units of which are sold to investors – a very important method of investing in shares in the US.

Mutually owned organisations Organisations run for the benefit of the members (usually the same as the consumers of the organisation's output) and not for shareholders. Examples include some insurance organisations, building societies and the cooperative societies.

Naked (or uncovered) Long or short positioning in a derivative without an offsetting position in the underlying. *See also* Uncovered call option writing.

Naked CDS A credit default swap where the buyer or seller do not own debt in the reference entity.

Named peril policy An insurance policy that covers named risks.

Names Members of Lloyd's of London.

Narrow money The monetary base, money defined in a very narrow way, currency in circulation plus banks' deposits with the central bank.

NASDAQ (National Association of Securities Dealers Automated Quotation system) OMX A series of computer-based information services and an order execution system for the US over-the-counter securities (e.g. share) market plus Scandinavian and Baltic shares.

National debt The cumulative outstanding borrowings of a government.

National Fraud Authority (NFA) Coordinates and oversees the fight against fraud in the UK.

National Savings Lending to the UK government through the purchase of bonds, and placing money into savings accounts.

National Venture Capital Association (NVCA) The US body overseeing private equity and venture capital.

Natural rate of unemployment, non-accelerating inflation rate of unemployment (NAIRU) The rate of unemployment that does not cause rising inflation. Equilibrium between the labour market and the economy.

NCB National central banks of EU countries.

Near-cash (near-money, quasi-money) Highly liquid financial assets but which are generally not usable for transactions and therefore cannot be fully regarded as cash, e.g. Treasury bills.

Negative covenants Loan agreements conditions that restrict the actions and rights of the borrower until the debt has been repaid in full.

Negotiability (1) Transferable to another – free to be traded in financial markets. (2) Capable of being settled by agreement between the parties involved in a transaction.

NEST (National Employment Savings Trust) A low-cost pension scheme introduced by the UK government for companies and individuals who are new to pension schemes.

Net assets (Net worth), Net asset value (NAV) Total assets minus all the liabilities. Fixed assets, plus stocks, debtors, cash and other liquid assets, minus long- and short-term creditors.

Net current assets The difference between current assets and current liabilities (q.v.).

Net Interest Income (NII) A bank's interest income less its interest expense.

Net interest yield Gross yield less tax.

Net profit (Net income) Profit after interest, tax and extraordinary charges and receipts.

Net stable funding rule A Basel III rule to reduce banks' dependence on short-term funding.

Net worth A company's or individual's total assets minus total liabilities.

Netting When subsidiaries in different countries settle intra-organisational currency debts for the net amount owed in a currency rather than the gross amount.

Neuer Markt German stock exchange for smaller young companies. Now closed due to financial scandals and loss of confidence among investors.

New issue The sale of securities, e.g. debentures or shares, to raise additional finance or to float existing securities of a company on a stock exchange for the first time.

Newcits The name given to funds, especially relevant to hedge funds, established to comply with UCITS III.

NFA *See* National Fraud Authority.

Nikkei index or Nikkei 225 Stock Average A share index based on the prices of 225 shares quoted on the Tokyo Stock Exchange.

Nil paid rights Shareholders may sell the rights to purchase shares in a rights issue without having paid anything for these rights.

NIM (1) (new issue market) A market for selling and buying newly-issued securities (2) (Net Interest Margin) A method of judging a bank's performance. Calculated by dividing the interest income less the interest expense by assets.

Nomad *See* Nominated adviser.

Nominal return (or interest rate) The return on an investment including inflation. If the return necessary to compensate for the decline in the purchasing power of money (inflation) is deducted from the nominal return we have the real rate of return.

Nominal value *See* Par value.

Nominated adviser (Nomad) Each company on the AIM (q.v.) has to retain a nomad. They act as quality controllers, confirming to the London Stock Exchange that the company has complied with the rules. They also act as consultants to the company.

Nominated brokers Each company on the AIM (q.v.) has to retain a nominated broker, who advises the company, helps to bring buyers and sellers together and comments on the firm's prospects.

Nominee accounts An official holder of an asset is not the beneficial owner but merely holds the asset in a nominee account for the beneficiary. In the stock market, the most common use of nominee accounts is where execution-only brokers act as nominees for their clients. The shares are registered in the name of the broker, but the client has beneficial ownership of them.

Nominee company Operates nominee accounts (q.v.).

Non-life insurance *See* General insurance.

Non-proportional reinsurance *See* Reinsurance.

Non-recourse A lending arrangement, say in project finance, where the lenders have no right to insist that the parent company(s) pay the due interest and capital should the project company be unable to do so.

Non-voting shares A company may issue two or more classes of ordinary shares, one of which may be of shares that do not carry any votes.

Northern Rock A UK bank which suffered a bank run (q.v.) in 2007, and had to be rescued by the BoE (q.v.). In 2008 it was nationalised by the UK government.

Note (promissory note) A financial security with the promise to pay a specific sum of money.

Note issuance facility (Note purchase facility) A medium-term arrangement allowing borrowers to issue a series of short-term promissory notes (usually 3–6-month maturity). A group of banks guarantees the availability of funds by agreeing to purchase any unsold notes at each issue date while the facility is in place.

Notional trading requirement *See* Margin.

International Swap and Derivatives Association (ISDA) Global financial trade association for institutions dealing in derivatives.

NVCA *See* National Venture Capital Association.

NYBOT, New York Board of Trade Leading commodity trading centre, part of ICE (q.v.).

NYMEX New York Mercantile Exchange Derivatives exchange now part of the CME Group (q.v.).

NYSE Liffe *See* Euronext Liffe and LIFFE.

NYSE The New York Stock Exchange.

NYSE-Euronext The organisation that controls and integrates the stock exchanges in New York, Paris, Brussels, Amsterdam and Lisbon as well as owning Liffe.

OATS (obligations assimilables du Trésor) French long-term government bonds.

Obligation A debt that you are obliged to pay.

Obligation acceleration When an obligation becomes due and payable before its expiry date, usually triggered by default on the part of the reference entity (q.v.).

OECD Organisation for Economic Co-operation and Development.

Ofex Original name of PLUS (q.v.).

Off-balance-sheet finance Assets are acquired in such a way that liabilities do not appear on the balance sheet, e.g. some lease agreements permit the exclusion of the liability in the accounts.

Offer document (1) A formal document sent by a company attempting to buy all the shares in a target firm to all the shareholders of the target setting out the offer. (2) The legal document for an offer for sale in a new issue.

Offer for sale A method of selling shares in a new issue. The company sponsor offers shares to the public by inviting subscriptions from investors. (1) Offer for sale by fixed price – the sponsor fixes the price prior to the offer. (2) Offer for sale by tender – investors state the price they are willing to pay. A strike price is established by the sponsors after receiving all the bids. All investors pay the strike price.

Offer for subscription A method of selling shares in a new issue. The issue is aborted if the offer does not raise sufficient interest from investors.

Offer price (1) The price at which a market maker in shares will sell a share, or a dealer in other markets will sell a security or asset. (2) The price of a new issue of securities, e.g. a new issue of shares.

Office of Fair Trading (OFT) The UK Director-General of Fair Trading has wide powers to monitor and investigate trading activities, and take action against anti-competitive behaviour. He can also refer monopoly situations to the Competition Commission (q.v.).

Official List (OL), Main Market The daily list of securities admitted for trading on highly regulated UK markets such as the London Stock Exchange. It does not include securities traded on the Alternative Investment Market (AIM) (q.v.).

Offshore Outside home country jurisdiction and financial regulation, usually in tax havens such as Bermuda or the Cayman Islands.

Oligopoly A small number of producers in an industry.

Ombudsman An independent UK service for settling disputes between individuals or businesses providing financial services and their customers.

OMX Scandanavian and Baltic group of stock exchanges merged in 2007 with NASDAQ.

ONS Office for National Statistics in the UK.

Onshore fund A fund authorised and regulated by the regulator in a country.

Open account trading Goods are shipped, and payment is requested on delivery or at a set time in the future, usually in 30, 60 or 90 days.

Open market operations A central bank buying and selling securities in the market to achieve a target interest rate and quantity of money in the economy.

Open offer New shares are sold to a wide range of external investors (not existing shareholders). However, under clawback provisions, existing shareholders can buy the shares at the offer price if they wish.

Open outcry Where trading is through oral calling of buy and sell offers and hand signals by market members.

Open policy An insurance policy that covers all loss or damage not specifically excluded.

Open repo A repurchase agreement (q.v.) with no end date.

Open-ended funds The size of the fund and the number of units depends on the amount investors wish to put into the fund e.g. a unit trust. The manager adds to or liquidates part of the assets of the fund depending on the level of purchases or sales of the units in the fund.

Open-ended investment companies (OEICs) Share-issuing collective investment vehicles with one price for investors. OEICs are able to issue more shares if demand increases from investors, unlike investment trusts. OEICs invest the finance raised in securities, primarily shares.

Open-ended investment vehicles (OEIVs) Collective funds with no restrictions on the amount of share or units issued.

Operating gearing *See* Gearing.

Operating lease The lease period is significantly less than the expected useful life of the asset and the agreed lease payments do not amount to a present value of more than 90 per cent of the value of the asset.

Operational deposits *See* Required reserves.

Opportunity cost of capital The return that is sacrificed by investing funds in one way rather than investing in an alternative of the same risk class, e.g. a financial security.

Option A contract giving one party the right, but not the obligation, to buy or sell a financial instrument, commodity or some other underlying asset at a given price, at or before a specified date.

Option premium The amount paid by an option purchaser (holder) to obtain the rights under an option contract.

Order book system *See* Order-driven trading system.

Order-driven trading system Buy and sell orders for securities are entered on a central computer system, and investors are automatically matched according to the price and volume they entered (also called matched bargain systems) – SETS is an example (q.v.).

Ordinary shares The equity capital of the firm. The holders of ordinary shares are the owners and are therefore entitled to all distributed profits after the holders of preference shares, debentures and other debt have had their claims met. They are also entitled to control the direction of the company through the power of their votes – usually one vote per share.

Originate-and-distribute model Banks make loans, then sell them to other investors, usually through securitisations.

Originate-and-hold model Where banks retain the loan on their books and therefore have every incentive to ensure that the mortgagee can repay and can help those few who have temporary problems along the way.

OTC *See* Over-the-counter trade.

Other early-stage (private equity) A form of venture capital, funds are provided for initial commercial manufacturing and sales.

Out-of-the-money option An option with no intrinsic value. For a call option (q.v.) the current price of the underlying is less than the exercise price. For a put option (q.v.) the current price of the underlying (q.v.) is more than the exercise price.

Over-subscription In a new issue of securities investors offer to buy more securities (e.g. shares) than are made available.

Overdraft A permit to overdraw on an account (e.g. a bank account) up to a stated limit; to take more out of a bank account than it contains. This arrangement is usually offered for a period, say six months or one year, but most banks retain the right to call in the loan (demand repayment) at any time.

Overnight Lending or borrowing of cash or securities in the financial markets which is repaid within 24 hours.

Over-the-counter (OTC) trade Securities trading carried on outside regulated exchanges. These bilateral deals allow tailor-made transactions to be put together.

Panamax A ship which will fit through the Panama canal.

Panda A foreign bond isssued in the Chinese domestic market.

Paper A term for some securities, e.g. certificates of deposit, commercial paper.

Par value (nominal, principal, stated book or face value) A stated and fixed value of a share or bond. Not market value, which fluctuates.

Participating (preference share) May receive extra dividend if company profits are high.

Partnership An unincorporated business formed by the association of two or more persons who share the risk and profits.

Passive fund *See* Tracker fund.

Passive management Where a fund mirrors an index with no managerial share/bond selection input, as opposed to active management, where the manager actively trades to make profits.

Payment mechanism A means of transferring funds from suppliers to users and from payers to payees

Payment versus payment The simultaneous settlement of the two sides trading promoted by CLS Bank (q.v.).

PEIT *See* Private equity investment trust.

Pension deficit When the amount of assets in a pension fund is not sufficient to pay out the projected pensions.

Pension Funds Directive An EU directive regulating the running of pension schemes.

Pension funds These manage money on behalf of members to provide a pension upon the member's retirement. Most funds invest heavily in shares.

Pension holiday When a pension fund does not need additional contributions for a time, it may grant the contributors, e.g. companies and/or members, a break from making payments.

Pension Protection Fund (UK) Compensates pensioners of defined benefit schemes should there be insufficient funds to pay pensions.

Pension scheme A scheme under which retirement benefits accrue and are distributed to the beneficiary employees.

Pensions Regulator (UK) Supervises the pension industry and employers who administer pension schemes.

Perfect hedge Eliminates risk because the movements in the value of the hedge (q.v.) instrument are exactly contrary to the change in the value of the underlying (q.v.).

Performance fee A fee paid to some fund managers (especially hedge fund managers) dependent on the returns achieved.

Permanent capital Capital, such as through the purchase of shares in a company which cannot be withdrawn.

Perpetual *See* Irredeemable.

Perpetuity A regular sum of money received at intervals for ever.

Personal guarantee An individual associated with a company, e.g. director, personally guarantees that a debt will be repaid.

Personal/private pension A pension scheme set up for an individual by that individual but through a financial institution. Contributions to the fund are subject to tax relief in the UK.

Pfandbriefe German covered bond (q.v.).

Physical delivery Settlement of a futures contract by delivery of the underlying (q.v.) rather than cash settlement based on price movement during the holding of the open position.

Physical settlement *See* Physical delivery.

Piece *See* Lot.

Pip The smallest FX trading variation equal to one ten-thousandth of one unit of currency.

Placing, place or placement A method of selling shares and other financial securities in the primary market. Securities are offered to the sponsors' or brokers' private clients and/ or a narrow group of institutions.

Plain vanilla A bond that lacks any special features such as a call or put provision.

Platform Software that allows investors and traders to deal electronically.

Plc Public limited company.

PLUS-Markets Group plc This is a provider of primary and secondary equity market services independent of the London Stock Exchange. It operates and regulates the PLUS service.

Political risk Changes in government or government policies impacting on trade, returns and volatility of returns.

Pool (1) (insurance) See float. (2) (investment) (a) A bundle of securities joined together and offered for sale to investors (b) The combined investment of a group of people.

Pooled funds Organisations (e.g. unit trusts) that gather together numerous small quantities of money from investors and then invest in a wide range of financial securities.

Portfolio investment (1) Investment in a variety of instruments. (2) (in national accounting) Investment made by firms and individuals in bonds and shares issued in another country. An alternative form of foreign investment is direct investment, buying commercial assets such as factory premises and industrial plant.

PPP See Purchasing power parity.

PRA See Prudential Regulatory Authority.

Pre-emption rights The strong right of shareholders to have first refusal to subscribe for further issues of shares. See Rights issue.

Precious metal Gold, silver and other metals which are rare and have a high economic value.

Preference share These normally entitle the holder to a fixed rate of dividend but this is not guaranteed. Holders of preference shares precede the holders of ordinary shares, but follow bond holders and other lenders, in payment of dividends and return of principal. Participating preference share: share in residual profits. Cumulative preference share: share carries forward the right to preferential dividends. Redeemable preference share: a preference share with a finite life. Convertible preference share: may be converted into ordinary shares.

Preferred ordinary shares Rank higher than deferred ordinary shares for an agreed rate of dividend or share of profits. They carry votes. Not the same as preference shares.

Preliminary annual results (Preliminary profit announcements, prelims) After the year-end and before the full reports and accounts are published, a statement on the profit for the year and other information is provided by companies quoted on the London Stock Exchange.

Premium (1) (On an option) The amount paid to an option writer to obtain the right to buy or sell the underlying. (2) (Foreign exchange) The forward rate of exchange stands at a higher level than the current spot rate. (3) (Investment trusts) By how much the share price exceeds the net asset value per share. (4) (Insurance) An amount paid (usually annually) to insure against risk.

Prepayment, payment in advance, payment on shipment Goods are paid for when they are shipped rather than when received by an overseas buyer.

Present value The current worth of future cash flows when discounted.

Price discovery The process of forming prices through the interaction of numerous buy and sell orders in an exchange.

Price formation The mechanisms leading to a price for an asset, e.g. many buyers and sellers in a company's shares through their buy or sell actions (e.g. via market makers or on a computerised system) arrive at a price to carry out transactions.

Price limit The maximum price an investor will buy at or the minimum price an investor will sell for.

Price-earnings ratio (PER, Price-earnings multiple, PE multiple, PE ratio, P/E ratio) Historic: share price divided by most recently reported annual earnings per share. Forward (prospective): share price divided by anticipated annual earnings per share.

Price-sensitive information That which may influence the share price or trading in the shares.

Primary dealer A firm approved by governments to deal in government securities. In the UK they are known as GEMMS (q.v.).

Primary investors The household sector contains the savers in society who are the main providers of funds used for investment in the business sector.

Primary market A market in which securities are initially issued to investors rather than a secondary market in which investors buy and sell to each other.

Prime broker An investment bank which offers trading service (securities lending, custody, etc.) to hedge funds and professional investors.

Prime grade See Investment grade.

Principal (1) The capital amount of a debt, excluding any interest. (2) A person acting for their own purposes accepting risk in financial transactions, rather than someone acting as an agent for another. (3) The amount invested.

Private banking Banking services provided to high net worth individuals. Also known as wealth management.

Private equity fund A fund set up to attract investors which invests equity in unquoted companies.

Private limited company (Ltd) A company which is unable to offer its shares to the wider public.

Private-client representative An investment bank employee who deals with clients individually.

Privatisation The sale to private investors of government-owned equity (shares) in state-owned industries or other commercial enterprises.

Professional securities market Depositary receipts are traded on this market on the London Stock Exchange.

Project finance Finance assembled for a specific project. The loan and equity returns are tied to the cash flows and fortunes of the project rather than being dependent on the parent company/companies.

Promissory note A debtor promises to pay at a fixed date or a date to be determined by circumstances. A note is created stating this obligation.

Proportional reinsurance See Reinsurance.

Proprietary platform An electronic dealing system set up by a single bank for its customers.

Proprietary transactions (Proprietary trading) A financial institution, as well as acting as an agent for a client, may trade on the financial markets with a view to generating profits for itself, e.g. speculation on forex (q.v.).

Prospectus A document containing information about a company (or unit trust/OEIC – q.v.), to assist with a new issue (initial public offering) by supplying details about the company and how it operates.

Protection & Indemnity (P&I) Clubs Give insurance on third-party liabilities relating to shipping.

Provision (1) Sum set aside in accounts for anticipated loss or expenditure. (2) A clause or stipulation in a legal agreement giving one party a right.

Prudential Regulatory Authority (PRA) A subsidiary of the Bank of England, it supervises and regulates financial institutions, banks, insurers, brokers, etc. for macro-prudential risk.

Prudential supervision Monitoring by the authorities to ensure that banks are run properly to avoid excessive risk to solvency and liquidity.

Public limited company (Plc) A company which may have an unlimited number of shareholders and offers its shares to the wider public (unlike a limited company – q.v.). Must have a minimum share value of £50,000. Some Plcs are listed on the London Stock Exchange.

Public pension A state-funded pension.

Public-to-private (PTP) The management of a company currently quoted on a stock exchange may return it to unquoted status with the assistance of private equity finance.

Pull to par, pull to maturity, pull to redemption The convergence of a bond price to its nominal value as it approaches maturity.

Purchasing power parity (PPP) theory of exchange rate determination Exchange rates will be in equilibrium when their domestic purchasing powers at that rate of exchange are equivalent. Movements in exchange rates will be a function of the differential in the two currencies' inflation rates.

Put features *See* Put options.

Put option This gives the purchaser the right, but not the obligation, to sell a financial instrument, commodity or some other underlying asset at a given price, at or before a specified date.

PvP *See* Payment versus payment.

Qualified purchasers US class of investor where individuals must have a net worth > $5m and institutional investors > $25m.

Qualitative analysis Relying on subjective elements to take a view, e.g. valuing shares by judging quality of management and strategic position.

Quantitative analysis Using statistics and complex mathematical models to measure financial performance.

Quantitative easing A way to boost the economy. More money is created by the central bank buying assets from the financial markets. This raises the amount of money that can be lent.

Quasi-money *See* Near-cash.

Quaternary buyout A company is sold on for a fourth time. *See* Buyout.

Quote currency *See* Secondary currency.

Quote-driven trading system Market makers post bid and offer prices on a computerised system.

Quoted Those shares with a price quoted on a recognised investment exchange (RIE) (e.g. the Official List of the London Stock Exchange (q.v.)).

Rabobank Nederland Netherlands organisation that acts for independent cooperatives.

Random walk theory The movements in prices are independent of one another; one day's price change cannot be predicted by looking at the previous day's price change.

Ranking (debt) Order of precedence for payment of obligations. Senior debt receives annual interest and redemption payments ahead of junior (or subordinated) debt. So, if the company has insufficient resources to pay its obligations the junior debt holders may receive little or nothing.

Rating *See* Credit rating.

Real rate of return The rate that would be required (obtained) in the absence of inflation. The nominal return minus inflation.

Realised gain A gain made when a deal has been completed and money released.

Receivable (Accounts receivable) A sum due from a customer for goods delivered: trade credit.

Receiver A receiver takes control of a business if a creditor successfully files a bankruptcy petition. The receiver may then sell the company's assets and distribute the proceeds among the creditors.

Recognised investment exchange (RIE) A body authorised to regulate securities trading in the UK, e.g. the London Stock Exchange.

Recourse finance The lender has the possibility to call on the guarantor for payment.

Recourse If a financial asset is sold (such as a trade debt), the purchaser could return to the vendor for payment in the event of non-payment by the borrower.

Recoverability of debt The extent to which the lender is protected in the event of default (q.v.) by the amount of cash that can be raised from the defaulted asset, e.g. a bond.

Redemption fee The charge made for withdrawing money from a fund.

Redemption The payment of the principal amount, or the par value, of a security (e.g. bond) at the maturity date resulting in the retirement and cancellation on the bond.

Redemption yield *See* Yield to maturity.

Reduced voting shares Shares which do not have full voting rights.

Reference entity The company issuing the underlying in a credit default swap upon which the buyer and seller are speculating.

Reference obligation The specific underlying (e.g. a particular bond issued) in a credit default swap.

Registrar An organisation that maintains a record of share (and other securities) ownership for a company. It also communicates with shareholders on behalf of the company.

Regulation The process of rule making and legislation creating the supervisory system.

Regulatory arbitrage A form of financial engineering where banks take advantage of differences in regulatory systems to gain greater freedom to act as they wish, e.g. by operating in a country with lax regulation.

Regulatory News Service (RNS) A system for distributing important company announcements and other price-sensitive financial news run by the London Stock Exchange.

Reinsurance An insurance company insures part or all of an insurance risk with another insurance company. It can be proportional (part of one risk or all risks) or non-proportional (insures a set amount).

Reflexivity Decisions are based on people's perception or interpretation of the situation. Furthermore, their decisions can change the situation, alter the fundamentals. Then changes in the fundamentals thus caused are liable to change the perceptions of individuals. Occasionally the reflexive interaction can lead to massive market

distortions – 'far-from-equilibrium conditions' – leading to boom/bust sequences.

Relationship banking A long-term, intimate and relatively open relationship is established between a corporation and its banks. Banks often supply a range of tailor-made services.

Relationship manager A manager in a corporate finance bank who liaises with key executives in a company.

Relative return A return made on an asset relative to the performance of an index.

Relative value *See* Long/short strategy.

Rembrandt A foreign bond issued in the Netherlands.

Renminbi sovereign bonds Chinese government bonds.

Repayment holiday *See* Grace period.

Repo *See* Repurchase agreement.

Reporting accountant A company planning to float on the London Stock Exchange employs a reporting accountant to prepare a detailed report on the firm's financial controls, track record, financing and forecasts.

Representative office A small office established by a bank in a foreign country to assist its domestic customers.

Repudiation A refusal to pay or acknowledge a debt or similar contract.

Repurchase of share A company has prospered and buys back its own shares.

Repurchase agreement, repo An agreement to buy back sold securities on agreed terms at a later date in order to borrow money for a few days or weeks.

Required reserves ratio The ratio of required reserves to deposits that banks must hold.

Required reserves The amount of reserves (a fraction of deposits received) that a bank must hold by order of the central bank or other regulatory authority.

Required return The minimum rate of return given the opportunity cost of capital.

Rescheduling, restructuring finance Rearranging the payments made by a borrower to a lender – usually as a result of financial stress.

Reserves Unallocated cash. Can be used for contingencies. (banking) Required reserves plus vault cash (qq.v.).

Restrictive covenants *See* Negative covenants.

Restructuring costs The costs associated with a reorganisation of the business, e.g. closing factories, redundancies.

Retail banking Banking for individual customers or small firms, normally for small amounts. High-volume, low-value banking. Also known as personal banking.

Retail financial markets Markets dealing with individual investors.

Retail Price Index (RPI) An index which measures the cost of a basket of retail goods and services, and is used to measure inflation.

Retrocession A reinsurance company reinsuring a risk accepted by a reinsurance firm.

Return on assets (ROA) Judges how profitable a firm is relative to its total assets. Calculated by dividing net profit after tax by total assets.

Return on capital employed (ROCE); return on investment (ROI) Measures of profitability. Profit return divided by the volume of resources devoted to the activity. Resources usually includes shareholders' funds, net debt and provisions. Cumulative goodwill, previously written off, may be added back to the resources total. See also Accounting rate of return.

Return on equity (ROE) Profit attributable to shareholders as a percentage of equity shareholders' funds. Calculated by dividing the net profit after rax by the equity capital.

Revenue bonds Bonds which receive interest and repayment from a particular project.

Reverse floater Floating-rate notes on which the interest rate declines as LIBOR rises.

Reverse floating-rate notes *See* Reverse floater.

Reverse repo A repurchase agreement (q.v.) to firstly buy securities (and thereby lend money) with an agreement in place to sell them back at a later date.

Reverse takeover The acquiring company is smaller than the target in terms of market capitalisation and offers newly created shares in itself as consideration for the purchase of the shares in the acquirer. So many new shares are created that the former shareholders in the target become the dominant shareholders in the combined entity.

Reversing the trade *See* Closing out a futures position.

Revolving credit, revolving credit facility (RCF) An arrangement whereby a borrower can draw down short-term loans as the need arises, to a maximum over a period of years.

Revolving underwriting facility (RUF) A bank(s) underwrites the borrower's access to funds at a specified rate in the short-term financial markets (e.g. by issuing euronotes) throughout an agreed period. If the notes are not bought in the market the underwriter(s) is obliged to purchase them.

Riba The Islamic word for interest.

RIE *See* Recognised investment exchange.

Right to exchange Holders of convertible securities have the right to convert them into shares on prearranged terms.

Rights issue An invitation to existing shareholders to purchase additional shares in the company in proportion to their existing holdings.

Ring (commodities) Trading on the LME (q.v.) is carried out in a ring.

Ring fencing Keeping company's money separate from clients' money.

Ringgit Malaysian currency.

Risk arbitrage Taking a position (purchase or sale) in a security, commodity, etc., because it is judged to be mispriced relative to other securities with similar characteristics. The comparator securities are not identical (e.g. shares in Unilever and in Procter & Gamble) and therefore there is an element of risk that the valuation gap will widen rather than contract. An extreme form of risk arbitrage is to take a position hoping to make a profit if an event occurs (e.g. a take-over). If the event does not occur there may be a loss. The word 'arbitrage' has been stretched beyond breaking point, as true arbitrage should be risk free.

Risk averter Someone who prefers a more certain return to an alternative with an equal expected return but which is more risky.

Risk lover (seeker) Someone who prefers a more uncertain alternative to an alternative with an equal but less risky outcome.

Risk management The selection of those risks a business should take and those which should be avoided or mitigated, followed by action to avoid or reduce risk.

Risk premium The extra return, above the risk-free rate, for accepting risk.

Risk spreader A financial institution which allows small savers to spread (reduce) risk by investing in a large diversified portfolio.

Risk The measurable likelihood of loss or less-than-expected returns. A future return has a variety of possible values. Sometimes measured by standard deviation (q.v.).

Risk transformation Intermediaries offer low-risk securities to primary investors to attract funds, which are then used to purchase higher-risk securities issued by the ultimate borrowers.

Risk-free rate of return (RFR) The rate earned on riskless investment, denoted r_f. A reasonable proxy is short-term lending to a reputable government.

Roadshow Companies and their advisers make a series of presentations to potential investors, usually to entice them into buying a new issue of securities.

Roll over To extend finance by reissuing on expiry of a loan.

Rolled-over overdraft Short-term loan facilities are perpetuated into the medium and long term by the renewal of the overdraft facility.

Rolling cash spread betting, rolling daily bets An investor's position is rolled over to the next day.

Rolling settlement Shares and cash are exchanged after a deal has been struck a fixed number of days later – usually after three days – rather than on a specific account day.

RPI *See* Retail price index.

RTGS (Real Time Gross Settlement) A system where payments are settled individually and continuously.

Running yield *See* Yield.

S&P 500 Standard & Poor's index of 500 leading US shares.

S&P GSCI A commodity index established by Standard & Poor's.

Safe haven Investing in a safe investment in time of trouble, such as major financial turmoil. UK or US government bonds and Treasury bills, for example, are usually regarded as safe havens.

Sale and leaseback Assets (e.g. land and buildings) are sold to another firm (e.g. bank, insurance company) with a simultaneous agreement for the vendor to lease the asset back for a stated period under specific terms.

Sale and repurchase agreement *See* Repurchase agreement.

Sales charge *See* Initial charge.

Sales ledger administration The management of trade debtors: recording credit sales, checking customer creditworthiness, sending invoices and chasing late payers.

Samurai A foreign bond, yen-denominated, issued by a non-Japanese entity in the domestic Japanese market.

Sarbanes-Oxley A US government Act of 2002 which set standards for corporate behaviour.

Savings and loans bank A US bank mutually owned by its members for the purpose of lending for the purchase of real estate and houses.

Savings bank (US) A bank established to help poor people save.

Scrip dividends Shareholders are offered the alternative of additional shares rather than a cash dividend.

Scrip issue The issue of more shares to existing shareholders according to their current holdings. Shareholders do not pay for these new shares. Company reserves are converted into issued capital.

SDR *See* Special drawing rights.

SEAQ (Stock Exchange Automated Quotation System) A real-time computer screen-based quotation system for securities where market makers on the London Stock Exchange report bid-offer prices and trading volumes, and brokers can observe prices and trades.

Search costs The cost of finding another person or organisation with which to transact business/investment.

Seasoned equity offerings (SEOs) Companies that have been on a stock exchange for some time selling new shares, e.g. via a rights issue.

SEC *See* Securities and Exchange Commission.

Second Banking Directive, 1989 An EU directive expanding on the First Banking Directive. A single banking licence allows operations throughout the EU. Supervision and regulatory responsibility are shared between the home and the host countries.

Second-tier markets Trading markets other than those provided for the leading (biggest company) shares and other securities.

Secondary buyout A company is sold on again to private equity buyers. *See* Buyout.

Secondary market (Secondary market trading facility) A system to allow current holders of shares or other securities to trade between themselves.

Secondary purchase A private equity-backed company is sold to another private equity fund.

Securities and Exchange Commission (SEC) The US federal body responsible for the regulation of securities markets (exchanges, brokers, investment advisers, etc.).

Securities house This may mean simply an issuing house. However, the term is sometimes used more broadly for an institution concerned with buying and selling securities or acting as agent in the buying and selling of securities.

Securitisation Financial assets (e.g. a claim to a number of mortgage payments, called a mortgage-backed security) which are not tradable can be repackaged into other securities (e.g. bonds) and then sold. These are called asset-backed securities.

Security (1) A financial asset, e.g. a share or bond. (2) Asset pledged to be surrendered in the event of a loan default.

Security market line (SML) A linear (straight) line showing the relationship between systematic risk and expected rates of return for individual assets (securities). According to the capital asset pricing model (q.v.) the return above the risk-free rate of return (q.v.) for a risky asset is equal to the risk premium for the market portfolio multiplied by the beta coefficient.

SEDOL Stock Exchange Daily Official List A journal published daily giving prices and deals for shares on London's Official List. Companies are given SEDOL numbers to identify them.

Seedcorn (private equity) A form of venture capital. It is financing to allow the development of a business concept.

Self-invested personal pension (SIPP) A pension scheme which allows the contributor control over the type and amount of investments made by the fund. It has tax advantages in the UK.

Self-amortising A reduction in the amount outstanding on a loan by regular payments to the lender.

Self-regulation Industry participants regulate themselves within a light-touch legislated framework.

Sell-side The brokers/brokerage companies who give advice and in a trade are actively selling securities.

Selling the rights nil paid In a rights issue those entitled to new shares (existing shareholders) are entitled to sell the rights to the new shares without the need to purchase the new shares.

Semi-annual Twice a year at regular intervals.

Semi-captives A private equity or venture capital organisation that raises its capital from the financial markets, but is dominated by the participation of an organising institution.

Semi-sovereign bonds *See* Sub-sovereign bonds.

Semi-strong efficiency Share prices fully reflect all the relevant, publicly available information.

Senior debt *See* Subordinated debt.

Separate legal person A company is a legal entity under the law. It is entitled to make contracts and be sued, for example, separately from the owners of the company.

Serious Fraud Office (SFO) Investigates and prosecutes crimes of serious fraud in the UK.

Serious Organised Crime Agency (SOCA) Handles serious crime in the UK, especially financial crime.

SETS (Stock Exchange Electronic Trading System) An electronic order book-based trading system for the London Stock Exchange. Brokers input buy and sell orders directly into the system. Buyers and sellers are matched and the trade executed automatically.

SETSsq A share trading system run by the London Stock Exchange with a focus on lightly traded shares (few trades per day).

Settlement price The price calculated by a derivatives exchange at the end of each trading session as the closing price that will be used in determining profits and losses for the marking-to-market process for margin accounts.

Settlement The completion of a transaction, e.g. upon the sale of a share in the secondary market cash is transferred as payment, in return ownership is transferred.

Shadow banking system Powerful non-bank bodies that move money and risk without involving banks, e.g. hedge funds.

Share buy-back, share repurchase The company buys back some or all of its own shares from shareholders.

Share certificate A document showing ownership of part of the share capital of a company.

Share Companies divide the ownership of the company into ordinary shares. An owner of a share usually has the same rights to vote and receive dividends as another owner of a share. Also called equity and stock (q.v.).

Share markets Institutions which facilitate the regulated sale and purchase of shares; includes the primary and secondary markets.

Share option scheme Employees are offered the right to buy shares in their company at a modest price some time in the future.

Share split (stock split) Shareholders receive additional shares from the company without payment. The nominal (par) value of each share is reduced in proportion to the increase in the number of shares, so the total book value of shares remains the same.

Shareholder A person who has invested capital into a business in return for a share of the equity.

Shareholder wealth maximisation The maximising of shareholders' purchasing power. In a pricing efficient market, it is the maximisation of the current share price.

Shareholders' funds (equity) The net assets of the business (after deduction of all short- and long-term liabilities and minority interests) shown in the balance sheet.

Sharia, Shari'ah law Islamic law governing, amongst other things, financial dealings.

Shell company A company with a stockmarket quotation but with very little in the way of real economic activity. It may have cash but no production.

Shipping finance Mainly carried out in US dollars by large global commercial or investment banks.

Short position In a derivative contract the counterparty in a short position is the one that has agreed to deliver the underlying (q.v.).

Short selling The selling of financial securities (e.g. shares) not yet owned, in the anticipation of being able to buy at a later date at a lower price.

Short term Less than one year for financial instruments.

Short-term interest rate future The three-month interest rate future contract traded on LIFFE (q.v.). Notional fixed-term deposits for three-month periods starting at a specified time in the future.

Short-term interest rate products, STIR Money market securities with a maturity of less than one year such as Treasury bills or commercial paper.

Short-term sterling interest rate future (colloquially known as short sterling) The three-month sterling interest rate future contract traded on LIFFE (q.v.). Notional fixed-term deposits for three-month periods starting at a specified time in the future.

Short-termism A charge levelled at the financial institutions in their expectations of the companies to which they provide finance. It is argued that long-term benefits are lost because of pressure for short-term performance.

Shorting Same as short selling.

Shorts UK government bonds (gilts) with less than five years to maturity.

SIBOR Singapore Interbank Offered Rate.

SICOM Singapore Commodity Exchange.

Side pocket (hedge funds) Illiquid investments may be put into a side pocket. This prevents their value being withdrawn until they are liquidated.

Sifi (Systemically important financial institutions) Banks that are 'too big to fail' or 'too big to save' and could cause systemic risk (q.v.).

Sight bank account (current account, cheque/check account) One where deposits can be withdrawn without notice.

Sight drafts A bill payable on demand.

Silicon Valley A part of north California where there is a huge concentration of internet-based businesses.

Simple interest Interest is paid on the original principal; no interest is paid on the accumulated interest payments.

Simple yield *See* Yield.

Single stock futures Derivatives which have a single stock as their underlying.

Sinking fund Money is accumulated in a fund through regular payments in order eventually to repay a debt.

SIS x-clear SIS x-clear Ltd is part of SIX Group, the integrated Swiss financial market infrastructure provider. As Central Counterparty (CCP) Swiss x-clear offers clearing and risk management services for SIX Swiss Exchange and the London Stock Exchange.

Small claims court A fast and informal way to deal with complaints and claims e.g. for financial loss.

Smart cards, electronic purses, chip cards Money is preloaded onto these cards, and the customer is able to purchase goods valued up to the amount on the card.

Smart order routing Electronically routing a buy or sell order to the location/trading venue where the best price is available.

SOCA *See* Serious Organised Crime Agency.

Soft commodity Generally refers to commodities which are grown or reared, e.g. sugar, cocoa, beef, etc.

Solvency II An EU directive which will take effect in 2013. It will set out new, strengthened EU-wide requirements on capital adequacy and risk management for insurers.

Solvency The ability to pay legal debts.

SONIA (Sterling Overnight Interbank Average) Overnight interest rate for loans in sterling.

Sovereign Wealth Fund A collective fund set up and managed by a government.

Sparkasse German mutual-type bank acting for the local community.

Special dividend An exceptionally large dividend paid on a one-off basis.

Special drawing rights (SDRs) A composite currency designed by the International Monetary Fund (IMF). Each IMF member country is allocated SDRs in proportion to its quota.

Special Liquidity Scheme A BoE (q.v.) scheme to swap less liquid assets for more liquid assets to encourage lending and so boost the economy.

Special purpose vehicle or entity (SPV, SPE) Companies set these up as separate organisations (companies) for a particular purpose. They are designed so that their accounts are not consolidated with those of the rest of the group.

Special resolution A company's shareholders vote at an AGM or EGM with a majority of 75 per cent of those voting. Normally special resolutions are reserved for important changes in the constitution of the company. Other matters are dealt with by way of an ordinary resolution (50 per cent or more of the votes required).

Specialist funds Investment funds such as hedge funds, private equity funds, etc. aimed at experienced investors.

Speculate To take a position in financial instruments and other assets with a view to obtaining a profit on changes in their value.

Speculative bubble *See* Bubble.

Speculative grade Bonds with a credit rating below investment grade.

Speculative motive for holding cash This means holding cash so that unexpected opportunities can be taken immediately.

Spinning Allocating shares from an IPO to preferred executives in return for future business.

Spiraling When a reinsurance company unknowingly reinsures itself.

Sponsor Lends its reputation to a new issue of securities, advises the client company (along with the issuing broker) and coordinates the new issue process. Sponsors are usually investment banks or stockbrokers. Also called an issuing house.

Spot market A market for immediate (within two business days) transactions (e.g. spot forex market, spot interest market), as opposed to an agreement to make a transaction some time in the future (e.g. forward, option, future).

Spot rate of interest *See* Spot market.

Spot trading Trading in the spot market q.v.

Spread betting Betting on the movement between the buying (offer) and selling (bid) prices of a security. A margin is required up front.

Spread The difference between the price to buy and the price to sell a financial security. Market makers quote a bid–offer spread for shares. The lower price (bid) is the price an investor receives if selling to the market maker. The higher (offer) price is the price if the investor wishes to buy from the market maker.

Square Mile The mediaeval boundary of the City of London, enclosing roughly a square mile.

Stakeholder A party with an interest (financial or otherwise) in an organisation, e.g. employees, customers, suppliers, the local community.

Stakeholder pension A tax efficient pension with low costs.

Stamp duty A tax imposed by a government on certain legal documents such as some shares and securities.

Standard & Poor's 500 An index of leading (largest) 500 US shares

listed in the New York Stock Exchange. Companies are weighted by market capitalisation on the NYSE.

Standard & Poor's A leading credit rating agency (q.v.).

Standard deviation A statistical measure of the dispersion around an average. A measure of volatility. The standard deviation is the square root of the variance. A fund or a share return can be expected to fall within one standard deviation of its average two-thirds of the time if the future is like the past.

Standard variable rate The base or standard rate of interest charged by a bank.

Standardisation (commodities) Commodities must adhere to strict quality and quantity guidelines.

Standing facilities Discount window borrowing (q.v.) from the Bank of England.

Standing order A bank facility used for recurring payments. Only the account holder is able to vary the amount.

Start-up capital Finance for young companies which have not yet sold their product commercially. High risk; usually provided by venture capitalists, entrepreneurs or business angels.

Statutory Established, regulated or imposed by or in conformity with laws passed by a legislative body, e.g. Parliament.

Sterling bonds Corporate bonds which pay interest and principal in sterling.

Sterling (1) (Pound sterling) The currency of the UK. (2) A grade of silver.

STIR *See* Short-term interest rate products.

Stock (1) Another term for inventory of raw materials, work-in-progress and finished items. (2) US term for share.

Stock exchange A market in which securities are bought and sold. In continental Europe the term bourse may be used.

Stock Exchange Automated Quotations *See* SEAQ.

Stock Exchange Electronic Trading System *See* SETS.

Stock market *See* Stock exchange.

Stock split *See* Share split.

Stockbroker A regulated professional who arranges the buying and selling of shares and other securities for investors.

Stockholders *See* Shareholder.

Stocks and shares There is some lack of clarity in the distinction between stocks and shares. Shares are equities in companies. Stocks are financial instruments that pay interest, e.g. bonds. However, in the US shares are also called 'common stocks' and the shareholders are sometimes referred to as the stockholders. So when some people use the term stocks they could be referring to either bonds or shares.

Stop-loss order An instruction to sell a security when it reaches a particular price. Designed to prevent excess loss for the investor.

Store cards Allow customers to purchase goods and pay later. *See also* Credit cards.

Store of value (finance) Money or other items of value used as currency or savings.

Straddle A combination of call and put options (q.v.).

Straight bond One with a regular fixed rate of interest and without the right of conversion (to, say, shares) or any other unusual rights.

Strategic position A firm's competitive position within an industry and the attractiveness of the industry.

Strategic review A review of a company's direction and purpose. It may involve discussion of whether to sell the business.

Strike bid In a book-building exercise a potential institutional investor states that it will buy a given number of shares within the initial price range.

Strike price (1) In the offer for sale by a tender it is the price selected that will sell the required quantity of shares given the offers made. (2) The price paid by the holder of an option when/if the option is exercised. *See* Exercise price.

Strips (Separate Trading of Registered Interest and Principal of Securities) bonds Bonds which can be broken down into their constituent parts, e.g. individual coupons, and these are then traded separately.

Strong form efficiency All relevant information, including that which is privately held, is reflected in the security (e.g. share) price.

Structural unemployment Caused by the mismatch of workers' skills and the available employment.

Structured investment vehicle, SIV Buys assets such as mortgages or ABSs after raising finance mostly by selling commercial paper.

Sub-sovereign bonds Another term for local authority and municipal bonds (q.v.).

Subordinated debt, junior debt A debt which ranks below another liability in order of priority for payment of interest or principal. Senior debt ranks above junior (subordinated) debt for payment.

Sub-prime mortgage A mortgage designed for people with a low credit rating charged at an interest rate above prime.

Subscription rights A right to subscribe for some shares.

Subsidiary A company is a subsidiary of another company if the parent company holds the majority of the voting rights (more than 50%), or has a minority of the shares but has the right to appoint or remove directors holding a majority of the voting rights at meetings of the board on all, or substantially all, matters or it has the right to exercise a dominant influence.

Sukuk A form of Islamic bond.

Summary financial statement Companies often send small investors a summary of the financial statements rather than the full report and accounts. This suits many investors and saves the company some money. However, an investor is entitled to receive a full annual report and accounts. It may be necessary to make a request for this.

Supertanker A very large ship up to 550,000 tonnes in weight.

Supervision Monitoring the position and behaviour of individual firms, and enforcing the regulations if required.

Supply curve Shows the volume of goods/services on offer at various prices.

SVR *See* Standard variable rate.

Swap An exchange of cash payment obligations. An interest rate swap is where one company arranges with a counterparty to exchange interest-rate payments. In a currency swap the two parties exchange interest obligations (receipts) for an agreed period between two different currencies.

Swaption or swap-option An option to have a swap at a later date.

Sweep facility Automatic transfer of funds from one account to another account.

Sweetener *See* Equity kicker.

SWIFT (Society for Worldwide Interbank Financial Telecommunication) A messaging service that sends payment orders between banks and financial institutions. They then arrange settlement.

Syndicate Typically, a group of firms that jointly undertake a financial transaction.

Syndicated loan A loan made by a number of banks to one borrower.

Systematic (Undiversifiable or market or residual) risk That element of return variability from an asset which cannot be eliminated through diversification (q.v.). Measured by beta (q.v.). It comprises the risk factors common to all firms.

Systemic risk The risk of failure within the financial system causing a domino-type effect bringing down large parts of the system.

T + 3 *See* Three-day rolling settlement.

Takeover (acquisition) Many people use these terms interchangeably with merger. However, some differentiate takeover as meaning a purchase of one firm by another with the concomitant implication of financial and managerial domination. Usually applied to hostile (without target management approval) mergers.

Takeover Panel The committee responsible for supervising compliance with the (UK) City Code on Takeovers and Mergers (q.v.).

Tangible assets Those that have a physical presence.

TARGET (Trans-European Automated Real-time Gross Settlement Express Transfer System), now TARGET 2 Real-time cross-border EU settlement system for payments.

Target financing rate The short-term interest rate set by the ECB (q.v.).

Tariff Taxes imposed on imports.

Tax allowance An amount of income or capital gain that is not taxed.

Tax avoidance Steps taken to reduce tax that are permitted under the law.

Tax evasion Deliberately giving a false statement or omitting a relevant fact. Illegal.

Tax haven A country or place with low rates of tax and less or flexible regulations.

Tax shield The benefit for a company that comes from having some of its capital in debt form, the interest on which is tax deductible, resulting in a lower outflow from the company to the tax authorities.

Taxable profit That element of profit subject to taxation. This frequently differs from reported profit.

techMARK The London Stock Exchange launched techMARK in 1999. It is a subsection of the shares within the LSE's Official List (q.v.). It is a grouping of technology companies. It imposes different rules on companies seeking a flotation from those that apply to the other companies on the Official List (e.g. only one year's accounts are required).

Technical analysis Analysis of share price movements and trading volume to forecast future movements from past movements.

Telephone banking Banking carried out 24 hours per day via landlines or mobile telephones.

Tender offer A public offer to purchase securities.

TER *See* Total expense ratio.

Term assurance Life assurance taken out for less than the whole life – the insured sum is paid only in the event of the insured person dying within the term.

Term loan A loan of a fixed amount for an agreed time and on specified terms, usually with regular periodic payments. Most frequently provided by banks.

Term securities Securities that have a set length of maturity, with a penalty for early withdrawal.

Term structure of interest rates The patterns of interest rates on bonds with differing lengths of time to maturity but with the same risk. Strictly it is the zero coupon implied interest rate for different lengths of time. *See also* Yield curve.

Terminal value The forecast future value of sums of money compounded to the end of a time horizon.

Tertiary buyout A company is sold on for a third time to a private equity firm. *See* Buyout.

The Baltic Exchange A company dealing in all aspects of shipping and trade routes, including sales, chartering, insurance, shipbroking, etc.

The Royal Mint The UK company responsible for producing UK coins.

TheCityUK A London-based body which promotes the competitiveness of UK financial services and publishes a range of trade and financial reports.

Three-day rolling settlement (T+3) After a share transaction in the stock exchange investors pay for shares three working days later.

Thrift bank A bank usually owned by its members.

TIBOR Tokyo Interbank Offered Rate.

Tick The minimum price movement of a security or derivative contract.

Tier 1 capital That part of a bank's capital defined as shareholders' equity.

Time charter A vessel is hired for a specified length of time

Time deposit, term deposit, fixed deposit, savings account Money deposited for a set time or for which a lengthly notice to withdraw must be given. Money cannot be withdrawn on demand.

Time value of money A pound received in the future is worth less than a pound received today – the present value of a sum of money depends on the date of its receipt.

Time value That part of an option's value that represents the value of the option expiring in the future rather than now. The longer the period to expiry, the greater the chance that the option will become in-the-money before the expiry date. The amount by which the option premium exceeds the intrinsic value.

Total (or market) capitalisation *See* Market capitalisation.

Total Expense Ratio (TER) Fund management costs compared with either annual income or capital.

Total shareholder return (TSR) or Total return The total return earned on a share over a period of time: dividends per share plus capital gain divided by initial share price.

Touch prices *See* Yellow strip.

Tracker fund An investment fund which is intended to replicate the return of a market index. Also called an index fund or passive fund.

Trade Buy and/or sell financial instruments.

Trade credit Where goods and services are delivered to a firm for use in its production and are not paid for immediately.

Trade debtor A customer of a firm who has not yet paid for goods and services delivered.

Trade execution The actual completion of the buying and/or selling securities.

Trade receivables Amounts owed to companies but not yet paid by customers.

Trade sale A company buys another company in the same line of business.

Traded option An option tradable on a market separate from the underlying (q.v.).

Trading floor A place where traders in a market (or their representatives) can meet to agree transactions face to face. However, investment banks, fund managers and other financial institutions often have 'trading floors' where they 'meet' counterparties via the telephone or compute to conduct transactions.

Trading income Income attained from trading on the markets.

Trail commission Paid by investment companies to financial advisers.

Transaction risk The risk that transactions already entered into, or for which the firm is likely to have a commitment in a foreign currency, will have a variable value in the home currency because of exchange rate movements.

Transactional banking Banks compete with each other to offer services at the lowest cost to corporations, on a service-by-service basis.

Translation risk This risk arises because financial data concerning profits and balance sheets denominated in one currency are then expressed in terms of another currency.

Transparency Directive, 2004 An EU directive requiring financial reports within four months of a year end.

Treasury bill A short-term money market instrument issued (sold) by the government, mainly in the UK and the US, usually to supply the government's short-term financing needs.

Treasury bond Long-term (maturity > 10 years) government bonds.

Treasury department Department in a company responsible for financial and economic policy.

Treasury Inflation-Protected Securities (TIPS) Index-linked bonds linked to the CPI (q.v.).

Treasury management To plan, organise and control cash and borrowings so as to optimise interest and currency flows, and minimise the cost of funds. Also to plan and execute communications programmes to enhance investors' confidence in the firm.

Treasury note A medium-term (maturity longer than one year) instrument issued (sold) by the central bank, mainly in the UK and the USA, usually to supply the government's financing needs.

Troy ounce A measurement equal to 31.103 grams used for measuring precious metals.

Trust deed A document specifying the regulation of the management of assets on behalf of beneficiaries of the trust.

Trustees Those that are charged with the responsibility for ensuring funds and trusts are administered correctly.

TSE Tokyo Stock Exchange.

Tulipmania A seventeenth-century Dutch bubble, when investors in bulbs paid absurdly high prices. See Bubble.

Turnover (revenue or sales) (1) Money received or to be received by the company from goods and services sold during the year. (2) In portfolio management, the amount of trading relative to the value of the portfolio.

Turquoise An MTF (q.v.).

UCITS (Undertakings for Collective Investment in Transferable Securities) A series of EU regulations aimed at promoting a free inter-country market for collective investments. UCITS III allowed derivative trading which encouraged hedge funds to join a regulated market.

UK Payments Council Oversees and controls all the various payment services.

UKLA, UK Listing Authority Maintains list of all companies listed on the LSE. This organisation is part of the Financial Services Authority (q.v.) and rigorously enforces a set of demanding rules on companies at the time when they join the stock market and in subsequent years.

Ultimate borrowers Firms investing in real assets need finance which ultimately comes from the primary investors.

Umbrella structure One fund containing a number of sub-funds.

Uncommitted facility An agreement such as an overdraft, between a bank and a company with no commitment on the part of the bank to continue to lend a set amount.

Uncommitted line of credit An agreement that a bank will lend an amount for a short time. It can be revoked at any time.

Uncovered (naked) call option writing Writing a call option (q.v.) on an underlying (q.v.) when the writer does not own the underlying securities included in the option.

Underlying The asset (e.g. share, commodity) that is the subject of a derivative contract.

Undertakings for Collective Investment in Transferable Securities directives See UCITS.

Underwriters (1) These (usually large financial institutions) guarantee to buy the proportion of a new issue of securities (e.g. shares) not taken up by the market, in return for a fee. (2) They assess insurance risks and set the amount and terms of the premium.

Unfunded pension scheme (pay-as-you-go, PAYG) A public scheme where current contributions to the scheme pay current pensioners. There are no accumulated funds.

Uninformed investors Those that have no/little knowledge about financial securities and the fundamental evaluation of their worth.

Unit of account Currency representing a fixed value.

Unit trust An investment organisation that attracts funds from individual investors by issuing units to invest in a range of securities, e.g. shares or bonds. It is open ended, the number of units expanding to meet demand.

United Nations Conference on Trade and Development (UNCTAD) A UN organisation which promotes the integration of developing countries into the world economy.

Universal banks Financial institutions involved in many different aspects of finance including retail banking and wholesale banking.

Unlisted Shares and other securities not on the Main Market of the London Stock Exchange (q.v.) are described as unlisted.

Unquoted firms Those shares with a price not quoted on a recognised investment exchange, RIE (e.g. the Official List or AIM of the London Stock Exchange – q.v.).

Unrealised gain One part of a deal has taken place, but the second part has not. There is a 'paper' gain.

Unsecured A financial claim with no collateral or any charge over the assets of the borrower.

Valuation risk (price risk) The possibility that, when a financial instrument matures or is sold in the market, the amount received is less than anticipated by the lender.

Value at risk, or **VaR** An estimate of the loss on a portfolio over a period of time (usually 24 hours is chosen) that will be exceeded with a given frequency, e.g. a frequency of one day out of 100, or five days out of 100.

Vanilla bond See Straight bond.

Variable rate The interest rate payable varies with short-term rates (e.g. six month LIBOR).

Variation margin The amount of money paid after the payment of the initial margin required to secure an option or futures position, after it has been revalued by the exchange or clearing house. Variation margin payments may be required daily to top the account up to the maintenance margin level.

Vault cash The actual cash (notes etc.) on the premises of a bank.

Vendor placing Shares issued to a company to pay for assets, or issued to shareholders to pay for an entire company in a takeover are placed with investors keen on holding the shares in return for cash. The vendors can then receive the cash.

Venture capital (VC) Finance provided to unquoted firms by specialised financial institutions. This may be backing for an entrepreneur, financing a start-up or developing business, or assisting a management buyout or buy-in. Usually it is provided by a mixture of equity, loans and mezzanine finance. It is used for medium-term to long-term investment in high-risk situations.

Venture capital fund A fund set up to attract investors which invests in the equity in unlisted companies.

Venture capital trusts (VCTs) A UK government-backed scheme with important tax advantages which encourages investors to invest in VCTs which invest in small and fast-growing companies.

Voice broker trades FX trades done by brokers over the telephone.

Volume transformation Intermediaries gather small quantities of money from numerous savers and repackage these sums into larger bundles for investment in the business sector or elsewhere.

Vulture capitalist A term used to describe private equity or venture capital funds which take over a company and oust the founders.

Warrant A financial instrument which gives the holder the right to subscribe for a specified number of shares, bonds or another asset at a fixed price at some time in the future.

Warren Buffett A world-famous US investor.

Weak-form efficiency Share prices fully reflect all information contained in past price movements.

Wealth management *See* Private banking.

Weighted by share price In an index higher-priced shares are given more weight.

Whole-of-life policies Life assurance that pays out to beneficiaries when the insured dies (not limited to, say, the next ten years).

Wholesale bank One that lends, arranges lending or supplies services on a large scale to corporations and within the interbank market. As opposed to retail banks which deal in relatively small sums for depositors and borrowers.

Wholesale financial markets Markets available only to those dealing in large quantities. Dominated by interbank transactions.

Windfall An unexpected return.

Winding-up The process of ending a company, selling its assets, paying its creditors and distributing the remaining cash among shareholders.

Winner's curse In winning a merger battle, the acquirer suffers a loss in value because it overpays.

Working capital The difference between current assets and current liabilities – net current assets or net current liabilities (q.v.).

World Bank A bank owned by 187 member countries which provides financial and technical assistance to developing countries.

World Trade Center A large complex of buildings providing offices which was the object of a terrorist attack in 2001.

Writer of an option The seller of an option contract, granting the right but not the obligation to the purchaser.

Xetra DAX *See* DAX 30.

Yankees A foreign bond, US dollar-denominated, issued by a non-US entity in the domestic US market.

Yellow strip The yellow band on a SEAQ or SETS screen which displays the highest bid and the lowest offered prices that competing market makers or other investors are offering in a security. They are known colloquially as the 'touch' or 'yellow strip' prices.

Yield curve A graph showing the relationship between the length of time to the maturity of bonds and the interest rate.

Yield The flat yield (interest yield, running yield, simple yield, current yield and income yield) on a fixed interest security is the gross interest amount, divided by the current market price, expressed as a percentage.

Yield to maturity (YTM), redemption yield, gross redemption yield he yield to maturity of a bond is the discount rate such that the present value of all cash inflows from the bond (interest plus principal) is equal to the bond's current market price.

YTM *See* Yield to maturity.

Zero coupon bond (or zero coupon preference share) A bond that does not pay regular interest (dividend) but instead is issued at a discount (i.e. below par value) and is redeemable at par, thus offering a capital gain.

Page entries in **bold** denote glossary entries.

3i 579
9/11 301, 660, **G:1**

abandon **G:1**
Abate, Joseph 195
Abbey/Abbey National 48, 100, 103, 250, 306
ABN Amro/ABN Amro Hoare Govett 39, 87, 579
ABS *see* asset-backed security
absolute return 561, **G:1**
Abu Dhabi Investment Authority (ADIA) 157
accept a bill 83, **G:1**
acceptance credit (bank bill, banker's acceptance) 49, 197, 198–200, 526–7, **G:1**
accountants, as regulators 628
accounting, flotation process 379
accounting rate of return (ARR) **G:1**
accounts payable **G:1**
accounts receivable **G:1**
accredited investors 562, **G:1**
accumulation units 147, **G:1**
ACE Tempest Reinsurance Ltd 123
Ackerrmann, Josef 80
acquisition *see* takeover
Action Fraud 630, **G:1**
active management **G:1**
activist strategy 577, **G:1**
Admati, Anat R. 316
Adnams 389
ADRs *see* American depositary receipts
adverse selection problem 119, **G:1**
advertising, flotation process 380
affirmative covenants 233, **G:1**
Afghanistan 63
African Barrick Gold 393
Agarwal, Anil 394
Agence France Trésor (AFT) 231, **G:1**
agency **G:1**
agency capture 610, **G:1**

agency costs **G:1**
agency offices 98, **G:1**
agent **G:1**
aging populations 131, 132
AGM *see* annual general meeting
Agnew, James 368
agreement costs 15, **G:1**
Agricultural Bank of China 24
agricultural commodities 544–7, **G:1**
Ahrendts, Angela 496
AIA 11, 84
AIG 11, 84, 608, 671
AIM *see* Alternative Investment Market
AIM admission document 388, **G:1**
Aima 557
Airbus 107
Albertini, Gabriele 465
Albourne Partners 568
Algo Technologies 350
algorithm 349–50, **G:1**
Allfinanz 54, **G:1**
Allfirst Bank 484
Alliance & Leicester 103, 250
Alliance of Independent Advisors to Financial Markets 346, 347
Allied Irish Banks (AIB) 484
allotment **G:1**
allow to lapse (option) 442, **G:1**
alpha (alpha coefficient, α) 564, 567, 575, **G:1**
Alsea 238
alternative equity markets 387
Alternative Investment Fund Managers (AIFM) Directive 557, 570
Alternative Investment Market (AIM) 357, 358, 359, 387–9, **G:1**
  introductions 380
  listing fees 379
  PLUS 390
  SETSqx 364
  venture capital trusts 590
Amaranth 29

Amazon 245
Ambac 247
Ambea 593
American depositary receipts (ADRs) 356, **G:1**
American Express 46
American Home Mortgage Investment Corporation 669
American option *see* American-style option
American Research and Development Corporation (ARD) 579, **G:2**
American Stock Exchange 337
American-style option (American option) 443, **G:2**
AMEX **G:2**
amortisation **G:2**
Amsterdam 11
Amundi 130
analyst **G:2**
Anderson, Ruth 383
angel network events 584, **G:2**
angels *see* business angels
Anglo Irish Bank 304
annual charges, unit trusts 145
annual equivalent rate (AER) *see* annual percentage rate
annual general meeting (AGM) **G:2**
annual percentage rate (APR) 214, **G:2**
annual reports, Alternative Investment Market 388
annual results **G:2**
annual yield *see* yield
annuity 121, 211–12, **G:2**
AOL 245
Apollo Management 593
Apple 589
arbitrage 149, 433, 575, **G:2**
arbitrageurs 433
arbitration schemes, consumer complaints 624–5
ArcaEx342, **G:2**
archangel 584, **G:2**
Ardagh Glass 242
Argentina 534

ARM plc 340
Armstrong, Patrick 351
arrangement fees 42, **G:2**
arranging banks 52
Arsenal 247
Asaria, Iqbal 108
ask rate, swaps 462
asset 55, **G:2**
asset-backed commercial paper
    (ABCP) 188–9, 190, **G:2**
asset-backed security (ABS) 246–8,
    250, **G:2**
asset-backed *sukuk* 258
asset backing 55, **G:2**
asset-based *sukuk* 258
asset class **G:2**
asset disposal 45, 233
asset liquidity **G:2**
asset management 12, 314, 57, 61,
    96, **G:2**
asset securitisation 247
asset stripping **G:2**
asset transformers 16–18, **G:2**
Association of British Insurers
    (ABI) 78, 142, 399, 403, 614,
    621–2
Association of Investment
    Companies 142
Astaire Group 618
AstraZeneca 443, 444–7
ASX (Australian Securities
    Exchange) 536, **G:2**
asymmetric information 44, 119,
    603–8, **G:2**
at-the-market 425, **G:2**
at-the-money option 444, 466, **G:2**
ATMs (automated teller machines)
    46, **G:2**
audit 387, **G:2**
auditors 628, **G:2**
Aunt Agathas 453, **G:2**
Australia 60, 138, 483, 498, 544,
    546–7
Australian Securities Exchange
    (ASX) 536, **G:2**
Australian Stock Market 337
Austria 46, 100, 180, 303
authorisation in financial sector,
    UK 622
authorised corporate directors
    (ACDs) 148, **G:2**
authorised share capital **G:2**
autistic mathematicians and
    financial economists 646–51
Autostrade 252, 256–7
Avenues 346, 347

average reserve ratio 293
Aviva 607–8

BAA 80, 93, 334
Babcock 134
back office **G:2**
back-to-back loan **G:2**
backfill bias, hedge fund indices
    573
BACS (Bankers' Automated
    Clearing System) 18, 47, **G:2**
bad debts **G:2**
BAE Systems 334, 628, 630
Bain Capital 579
Baker, Andrew 557
balance of payments **G:2**
balance sheet 85, **G:2**
balance sheet effect, translation
    risk 497
balloon repayment on a loan 43,
    44, **G:2**
Baltic Exchange 529–30, **G:2–3**,
    G:31
Baltic Exchange Capesize Index
    (BCI) 530, **G:3**
Baltic Exchange Dry Index (BDI)
    530, 531, 532, **G:3**
Baltic Exchange Handysize index
    (BHSI) 530, **G:3**
Baltic Exchange Panamax Index
    (BPI) 530, **G:3**
Baltic Exchange Supramax Index
    (BSI) 530, **G:3**
Baltic Freight Index (BFI) 530,
    531, **G:3**
Baltic indices 530, **G:3**
bancassurance 54, **G:3**
BancoEspírito Santo 334
band (FX) 493, **G:3**
Banesto 251
bank bill *see* acceptance credit
bank bonuses 12, 76, 77, 634
bank covenant *see* covenant
Bank for International Settlements
    (BIS) 309, 318, **G:3**
bank notes, issue and replacement
    of 317–18
Bank of America/Bank of America
    Merrill Lynch 26
    commercial paper 189
    corporate broking 88
    FICC operations 94
    government funds 608
    Lloyds rights issue 401
    mergers and acquisitions 84,
    87

multilateral trading facilities
    344
private equity 579
takeover of Merrill Lynch 671,
    672
universal banking 39
Bank of China 549
Bank of England 187, 318–19, **G:3**
    bank supervision 307
    base rate 42
    financial crisis 669, 672
    Financial Policy Committee
    620
    independence 297
    inflation target 295, 296, 297,
    319
    interest rates 6
    Monetary Policy Committee
    620
    pension scheme 156
    quantitative easing 299
    regulation 615, 620
    Special Liquidity Scheme 302
Bank of Italy 465
Bank of New York Mellon 194
Bank of Nova Scotia-Scotia
    Mocatta 550
Bank of Scotland 250
bank rate **G:3**
bank run 301, **G:3**
bank supervision 604–5, **G:3**
    agency capture 610
    bonuses 634
    contagion risk 608–9
    EU 633, 634
    India 610–11
    monopoly/oligopoly 609
banker's acceptance *see* acceptance
    credit
BankhausHerstatt 491
banking 7, 25–7, 36–74
    asset and liability management
    61
    asset transformation 16, 18
    capital adequacy 61–4, 307–16
    cash management 53
    clearing systems 47–9
    commercial banking services
    54–5
    committed facilities 49–52
    core 39–40
    corporate 49–52
    deposits 39–40
    development 14
    economies of scale 18
    FX risk management and
    interest rate management 53

FX trading 484–6
guarantees 53
important financial centres 12
lending 40–6
liabilities 39–40
liquidity management and
    reserves 57–60, 307–16
nature of 37–8
operation 55–7
overseas trade 53
payment mechanisms 46–9
regulation *see* bank
    supervision
shipping finance 532
supervision 306–7, 308
uncommitted facilities 49
universal 37, 39
bankruptcy **G:3**
BanquePopulaire 103, **G:3**
BarCap 79, 87–8
Barclays/Barclays Capital 22, 26, 78
Basel III rules 313
capital position 312
Eurobonds 257
failed takeover of ABN Amro
    39
FICC operations 94
FX trading 485
gold 550
incompetence 607–8
investment banking 82
junk bonds 242
loan-pricing data shared with
    RBS 628–9
mergers and acquisitions 84
Mexican hedging 451
Ocado flotation 383
pensions 133
systemic importance 305
Turner proposals 306
Barden, Stefan 415
Barings Bank 413, 418, 433, **G:3**
Barnier, Michel 424, 634
Barr, Michael 239
barter system 13, 172, **G:3**
base currency 486, **G:3**
base rate 7, 8, 42, 187, **G:3**
    see also bank rate
Basel accords *see* Basel rules
Basel committee 60, 79, 309, 636,
    G:3
Basel II/Basel III *see* Basel rules
Basel rules 309–16, 610, 613, 637,
    650, 665, **G:3**
basis points (bps) 42, 169, **G:3**
Basra, David 250

BATS, BATS Europe 342, 343–4,
    346, 347, 353, 354, **G:3**
Baupost 559
bausparkassen101, **G:3**
Bava, Zeinal 335
BayernLB 101
Bayley, Nick 389
BBC 133
BBVA 251
BC Partners 593
BDO Stoy Hayward 631
bear **G:3**
bear fund **G:3**
bear market **G:3**
Bear Sterns 79, 195, 302, 608, 668,
    669–70, 671, **G:3**
    sub-prime mortgages 661
    VaR 651
bearer bond 252, **G:3**
Beattie, Niki 348
Beaumont Cornish 390
Beijing 10
Belgium 316, 672
bells and whistles 254, **G:3**
benchmark 174, 231, **G:3**
Benetton family 257
Berkshire Hathaway 122, 123, 672
Bermuda 118, 564
Bernanke, Ben 296, 299–300, 320,
    671
beta **G:3**
Bettonte, Luca 256
bey *see* bond equivalent yield
Bharti 610
BHP Billington 87, 399, 545
biased information 606–7
bid–offer spread 89, 90, 145, 487,
    G:3
bid premium **G:3**
bid price 88–9, 145, 453, **G:3**
bid rate 462, 486–7
bid to cover ratio 182, **G:3**
bid yield 261, **G:3**
Bien, Melanie 459
Big bang 21, 54, 355, **G:3**
Big Mac Index 509–10
bill **G:3**
bill of exchange 83, 197–8, 526–7,
    G:3
bill of lading 526, **G:4**
Bioventix 390
BIS *see* Bank for International
    Settlements
Black and Scholes' option pricing
    model (BSOPM) 474
Blackabyplc 259–60

Blackrock 139, 151, 543, 544
Blackstone Group 84
Bloomberg 226
Bloomer, Jonathan 134
blue chip 392, **G:4**
Blue Oar 389
Bluebay Asset Management 242
Bluebird plc 260–2
BlueCrest Capital 571
BNP Paribas 668
Board of Directors **G:4**
BOC Group 80
BoE *see* Bank of England
Boeing 102, 107, 499
boiler room fraud 630
bond covenant *see* covenant
bond equivalent yield (bey) 181,
    182, 186, **G:4**
bond indenture *see* trust deed
bond insurance 243, **G:4**
bond market 2–3, 219–82, **G:4**
bonds 2–3, 221–2, **G:4**
    convertible 243–5
    corporate 232–3
    covered 250–1
    credit rating 234–40
    demand and supply curves
        268–70
    duration 265–8
    and equity, comparison
        between 221
    Eurobonds (international
        bonds) 252–5
    foreign 251–2
    government 222–31
    high-yield (junk) 240–2
    investment banks 83
    Islamic 257–8
    local authority/municipal 243
    medium-term notes 255–7
    repayments 233–4
    securitisation 246–50
    strips 245–6
    term structure of interest rates
        271–4
    valuing 258–65
    variety 221–2
    volatility of returns 264–5
    warrants 405
Bondscape 226
Bonham Carter, Edward 384
bonus issue *see* scrip issue
book building (book runners) 51,
    255, 381–2, 383, **G:4**
book runner *see* book building
boom/bust cycle 656–8

BorsaItaliana 337, **G:4**
Boshiwa 11
Boston 12
Boston Scientific 606
bought deal 403, **G:4**
Boulger, Ray 459
Bourlot, Jean 544
Bourse 335, **G:4**
boutique bank, boutique
    investment bank 82, **G:4**
Bowie, David 247
BP 133, 238
Bradford and Bingley 671
branches of banks 98–100, **G:4**
Brazil
    Big Mac Index 509
    bonds 238
    commodities 534, 535, 545
    credit rating 229
    depositary receipts 356, 357
    financial crisis (1999) 184
    FX market 509, 510
    local authority bills 195
breaking of the buck 171, **G:4**
Brennan, Michael 390
Bretton Woods 492–3, **G:4**
Brevan Howard 558, 559, 567, 569
Brewin Dolphin 625
Bridgewater Pure Alpha 559
Brin, Sergey 333
Britannia 103
British Airways 86, 141, 393–4
British Bankers Association (BBA)
    60, 174–5, 177, **G:4**
British Gas 86
British Private Equity & Venture
    Capital Association (BVCA)
    580, 581, 587, **G:4**
British Virgin Islands 564
Broad, Andrew 498
broad money 286, **G:4**
broker-dealer **G:4**
brokerage **G:4**
brokers 16, 86, 87–8, **G:4**
    see also corporate brokers;
        nominated brokers
Brown Brothers Harriman 420
BT 133, 138–40, 141, 566
BTANS (Bons du Trésor à
    intérètsannuels) 231, **G:4**
bubble 544, 545–6, 656–7, **G:4**
Buchan, Hamish 156
Buffett, Warren 122, 126, 569, 594,
    646, 672, 673, **G:33**
building societies 18, 21, 27,
    102–3, **G:4**

bulge bracket 81, **G:4**
bulk carrier **G:4**
bull **G:4**
bull market **G:4**
Bulldog 251, **G:4**
bullet bond, bullet repayment 43,
    44, 232, **G:4**
Bundesanleihen (Bunds) 231, **G:4**
Bundesbank 231, **G:4**
Bundesobligationen (Bobls) 231,
    G:4
Bundesrepublik Deutschland
    Finanzagentur (BDF) 231,
    G:4
Bundesschatzanweisungen
    (Schatze) 231, **G:4**
Bunge 419
Burberry 382, 496
business angels 583–4, 586, **G:4**
business lending 41–6
BusinessBecause.com 584
Büsst, Russell 130
Butler, Jason 48
buy-back see share buy-back
buy-side 97, **G:4**
buyout **G:4**
    see also leveraged buyout;
        management buyout;
        quaternary buyout;
        secondary buyout; tertiary
        buyout
BVCA see British Private Equity &
    Venture Capital Association

C. Hoare and Co. 97
Cable and Wireless 134
CAC 40 (Compagnie des Agents de
    Change 40 Index) 451, **G:4**
Cadbury 93, 133, 134, 368
Caisse de Dépôt et Placement du
    Quebec 545
Caissesd'Epargne 103, **G:4**
CaissesRégionales de
    CréditAgricoleMutuel 103,
    G:4
Caja Madrid 251
cajas de ahoro (cajas) 101, **G:4**
Calcot 419
Calderini, Pablo 93
call-back features 254–5, **G:4**
call option 443–7, 450, 504, **G:4**
call option holder (call option
    buyer) 443–6
call option writer 446–7
CalPERS (Califonia Public
    Employees' Retirement
    System) 139, 239, 566

CAMELS 307, 308, **G:4**
Canada 28, 180, 195, 233, 246, 251,
    337
Canadian Pacific Corporation 221
Candover 588
cap 457–9, **G:4**
cap-and-trade 548
capital 55, **G:4–5**
capital adequacy management 57,
    61–4, 307–16, **G:5**
capital allocation 340
    Capital Asset Pricing Model
        (CAPM) **G:5**
capital gain **G:5**
capital gearing **G:5**
capital introduction (cap-intro)
    97, **G:5**
Capital Liberalisation Directive
    (1988) 633, **G:5**
Capital Requirements Directive
    (2006) 633, **G:5**
capital reserves **G:5**
Capital Structure 242
capital-to-assets ratio 63–4
capital transfer 513–14, **G:5**
capitalisation 392, **G:5**
    see also market capitalisation
capitalisation issue see scrip issue
capitalisation weighted **G:5**
capped bonds 254, **G:5**
captives 591, **G:5**
carbon trading 548, **G:5**
Carlyle Group 588, 593
Carr, Roger 92–3
Carret, Phillip 432–3
carried interest 579, **G:5**
carry trade 511–12, 659
Carstens, Agustin 450, 451
cartel **G:5**
Cartwright, Stacey 496
Carville, James 274–5
cash 18
cash dividend **G:5**
cash holdings, banks 40, 56
cash management, banks 53
cash settled 421, 451, 469, **G:5**
casino banking 92
Cassa di Compensazione e
    Garanzia (CC&G) 362, **G:5**
Castaing, John 330
casualty insurance 121, **G:5**
Catholic church 101
Caylon 257
Cayman Islands 564, 565
CBOE see Chicago Board Options
    Exchange

CBOT *see* Chicago Board of Trade
CCCL (Cheque and Credit
    Clearing Company) 47, **G:5**
CDC 134
CDO squared 664
CDS *see* credit default swap
ceding commission 123, **G:5**
Centerparks 594
central banks 283–327, **G:5**
    bank lending 58
    bank rescues 63
    bank reserves 64
    base rate 42
    cash deposits 40
    clearing systems 47
    coordination between central
        banks and with international
        bodies 318
    currency issue 317–18
    currency reserve control 318
    financial crisis 672
    government banker 316–17
    independence 297–9
    lender of last resort 58, 301–6
    monetary policy 285–300
    money markets 187
    national debt management
        316–17
    payments system, smooth
        functioning of the 318
    safety and soundness of the
        financial system 300–16
    see also specific central banks
central clearing system **G:5**
Central Counter-party (CCP)
    clearing house *see* clearing
    house
Central Counterparty Clearing
    (CCC) 361, 362, **G:5**
Central Securities Depository
    (CSO) **G:5**
Centre for the Study of Financial
    Innovation (CSFI) 587, 588
Centrica 92, 93
Cerberus 133, 134, 588, 593
certificate of deposit (CD) 195–6,
    G:5
Cestar, Matthew 242
CFD *see* contract for differences
CHAPS (Clearing House
    Automated Payment
    System) 18, 47, **G:5**
Charcol, John 459
charge cards 46, **G:5**
Charles Stanley 625
Chase 39

Cheltenham and Gloucester 103
cheques (US checks) 18, 46, **G:5**
Cheveley, George 545, 546
Chi-X 342, 343, 344, 345, 362, **G:5**
    dark pools 353, 354
Chicago 12
Chicago Board of Trade (CBOT)
    414, 535, 536, **G:5**
Chicago Board Options Exchange
    (CBOE) **G:5**
Chicago Mercantile Exchange *see*
    CME
chief executive officer (CEO) **G:5**
chief financial officer (CFO) **G:5**
Chile 238
Chin, David 11
China
    bank reserves 64
    Big Mac Index 509
    Burberry 496
    central banking 293
    clothing industry 49, 496
    commodities 534, 543, 545
    cooperatives 103
    criticism of Goldman Sachs 95
    equity markets 335, 336–7,
        357
    FX regime 493–4
    gold 548–9
    government bonds 231
    hedging 451
    IMF report on Chinese
        economy 510
    listings in Hong Kong 11
    regulation of financial sector
        617
    state-owned banks 54
    US Treasury bills and bonds 5,
        514, 660
China Medical System 11
China Meihya 390
China Securities Regulatory
    Commission (CSRC) 337,
    617
Chinalco 399
Chinese walls 92, 93, 607, **G:5**
chip cards *see* smart cards
CHIPS (Clearing House Interbank
    Payment System) 49, **G:5**
Chongqing Machinery & Electric
    579
Cifuentes, Arturo 239
Cinven 588
Citibank 668
Citic Pacific 484
Citicorp 39

Citigroup 11, 26
    Abu Dhabi Investment
        Authority 157
    commercial paper 189
    corporate broking 88
    EMI 588
    financial crisis 670, 672
    FX trading 485
    government funds 608, 672
    mergers and acquisitions 84,
        87
    multilateral trading facilities
        344
    proprietary trading 93
    systemic importance 305
    Terra Firma's acquisition of
        EMI 80
    toxic assets 79
    universal banking 39
City *see* City of London **G:5**
City Code on Takeovers and
    Mergers **G:5**
City of London **G:5**
    Eurobonds 253, 256
    FX market 481, 482, 484
    growth of financial services
        20–1
    hedge funds 30, 565
    history 354
    importance as financial centre
        10, 11, 12, 20–1
    international banking 26, 98
    Islamic banking 108
    regulation 611–12, 614–15, 635
    reinsurance 118, 124–30
    shipping 533
City of London Police 629–30, 631,
    G:5
City Panel on Takeovers and
    Mergers 628, **G:5**
Clake, Anthony 572
classical economics 653–4
clawback **G:5**
    fees 565, 566, 567
    shares 403
clean price 226, **G:5**
clearing 47, 539, 547
clearing a trade 47–9, 361–4, **G:6**
clearing banks 25, 47, **G:6**
clearing house 361–3, **G:6**
    exchange-traded derivatives
        423
    futures 415, 416–17
    over-the-counter derivatives
        424
    shadow banking system 637

clearing price 89, **G:6**
Clearnet 362
Clements, Kenneth 510
Climate Human Capital 390
Clinton, Bill 274–5
close **G:6**
Close Brothers 618
Close Investments 618
closed-end funds 29, 153, **G:6**
closing out a futures position
    420–1, **G:6**
CLS *see* Continuous Linked
    Settlement
CLS Bank 491, **G:6**
CME (Chicago Mercantile
    Exchange) 485, 491, 502,
    536, **G:6**
CME ClearPort491, **G:6**
CME Group 422, 536, 541, 547,
    G:6
CNPC 238
co-investing 591, **G:6**
co-lead manager **G:6**
CoCos *see* contingent convertible
cognitive dissonance 647
Cohen, Steven 559
coins, issue of 317
Cole, Margaret 385–6, 606, 608,
    618, 627
collar 458, **G:6**
collateral 44–5, **G:6**
collateralised debt obligations
    (CDOs) 96, 662–5, 666, 668,
    670, **G:6**
    housing bubble 658
    pricing 647–8
    VaR 650
collective investment *see* pooled
    funds
Collins, Phillip 629
Collins Stewart 88
Colstonplc 465–7
COMEX **G:6**
commercial banking **G:6**
commercial bill (bank bill or trade
    bill) **G:6**
commercial mortgage-backed
    security 248, **G:6**
commercial paper (CP) 51–2, 83,
    169, 187–90, **G:6**
commercial paper programme
    see revolving underwriting
    facility
commitment fee 50, 257, **G:6**
committed facility 49–52, **G:6**
Committee of European Securities
    Regulators (CESR) 344–5

commodity 523–4, 533–48, 550–5,
    G:6
    agricultural 544–7
    carbon trading 548
    clearing 547
    derivative trading in 539, 541
    exchange traded funds 542–4
    exchanges 534–6
    funds, in shadow banking
        system 637
    indices 541–2, 543
    London Metal Exchange
        538–9
    NYSE Liffe 539, 540
    speculative bubbles 544, 545–6
    standardisation 536–8
commodity bubble *see* bubble
Commodity Futures Trading
    Commission 350, 351
commodity index 541–2, 543, **G:6**
Commodity Trading Advisors
    (CTAs) *see* managed futures
common stock 331, **G:6**
community bank **G:6**
Companies Acts (UK) 386, 628,
    G:6
Companies House 628, **G:6**
company registrar *see* registrar
company regulation 628–9
compensation 616, 625–6
Competition Commission 628, **G:6**
competitive laxity 613, **G:6**
complaints handling 616, 624–5
compliance **G:6**
compliance costs 603, 610, **G:6**
compliance officer 624, **G:6**
compound interest 207, 208–9, **G:6**
compound return **G:6–7**
concealment of information 607
concentration risk 310, 605, **G:7**
conduits 189, 190, 665
conflict of preference 15–16, **G:7**
conflicts of interest 80–1, 605–7,
    G:7
consolidated accounts **G:7**
consolidated tape 344–5, **G:7**
consolidation of shares 404, **G:7**
consultants, pension funds 136
consumer education 616
consumer loan (personal loan) 41,
    G:7
Consumer Price Index *see* CPI
Consumer Protection and Markets
    Authority (CPMA) 615
contagion risk 608–9, **G:7**
contingent convertible (CoCo)
    313, **G:7**
continuing obligations 385–7, **G:7**

continuous compounding 214
Continuous Linked Settlement
    (CLS) 491, **G:7**
continuous order book **G:7**
contract for differences (CFD) 457,
    G:7
contract hire 106
controlling shareholder 583, **G:7**
convergence **G:7**
conversion gilts 224
conversion premium 243, 244, **G:7**
conversion price 243–4, **G:7**
conversion ratio 243, 244, **G:7**
conversion value 244, **G:7**
Conversus Capital 590
convertible arbitrage **G:7**
convertible bond arbitrage, hedge
    funds 577
convertible bonds (convertible
    loan stocks) 243–5, 246, 254,
    G:7
convertible preference shares 333
Co-operative Bank 48, 103
cooperative banks 27, 54, 101, 103,
    G:6
core banking 39–40, **G:7**
Core Tier I 311, **G:7**
corn 534
Corporate Advisers 389–90, **G:7**
corporate assistance 82–6
corporate banking 49–55, 67–74,
    G:7
corporate behaviour 341
corporate bonds 3, 232–3, 235,
    238, **G:7**
corporate brokers 87–8, 378, **G:7**
corporate finance department of
    investment banks 84, **G:7**
Corporate Governance Code
    386–7, **G:7**
corporate restructuring 84–5
Corporation of Lloyd's 126, 127,
    128, **G:7**
corporation tax **G:7**
correspondent banks 98, **G:7**
cost–income ratio (C/I) 67, **G:7**
Council of Lloyd's 126, **G:7**
counter currency *see* secondary
    currency
counter-cyclical regulatory capital
    314, **G:7**
counterparty **G:7**
    exchange-traded derivatives
        423
    futures 415, 416–17
    over-the-counter derivatives
        422, 423
    swaps 461

counterparty risk 169, 423, **G:7**
country risk **G:8**
Countrywide Financial 661, 662, 669
coupon equivalent rate *see* bond equivalent yield
coupons 224, **G:8**
Court of Directors 318, **G:8**
covenant 233, **G:8**
cover **G:8**
covered bonds 250–1, **G:8**
covered call option writing 447, **G:8**
covered warrants 356, **G:8**
CPI (Consumer Price Index) **G:8**
Crandall, Lou 195
creation unit of ETF shares 149, **G:8**
creative accounting **G:8**
CréditAgricole78, 103, 313, **G:8**
credit cards 18, 46, **G:8**
credit default swap (CDS) 467–71, 666, 671, **G:8**
credit derivative **G:8**
credit events 469–71
credit expansion 659
credit facility (credit line) **G:8**
credit insurance 105, **G:8**
credit line *see* credit facility
credit multiplier effect 287, 288, 292, **G:8**
CréditMutuel 103, **G:8**
credit rating 190–2, **G:8**
    bonds 228, 234–40, 250, 255
    commercial paper 188
    world 229
credit-rating agencies 190, 234, 239, **G:8**
    CDOs 648
    conflicts of interest 606
    financial crisis 658, 664–5
    syndicate lending 51
credit risk **G:8**
credit risk premium (credit spread) **G:8**
credit scores, mortgages 661
credit spread *see* credit risk premium
Credit Suisse 26, 79, 82
    Basel III rules 313
    capital and liquidity adequacy 313
    corporate banking 88
    exchange-traded funds 544
    Federal Reserve Primary Dealer Credit Facility 302
    financial crisis 86

FX trading 485
hedge funds 566, 574
junk bonds 242
mergers and acquisitions 84
multilateral trading facilities 344
pensions 133
Pignatellis, Sean 606
credit unions (CUs) 102, 103, **G:8**
creditors **G:8**
creditworthiness 46
CREST 342, 363–4, **G:8**
Creswell, Robin 130
Criminal Justice Act (1993, UK) 386
cross-rate 491–2, **G:8**
cum-dividend 226, **G:8**
cum-rights 401, **G:8**
cumulative **G:8**
cumulative preference shares 332
Cura 577
currency in circulation 286
currency issue, by central banks 317–18
currency option hedge 482, 503–6, **G:8**
currency peg 493, **G:8**
currency reserve control 318, **G:8**
currency swap *see* swap
currency swaption 482, **G:8**
Currenex485, **G:8**
current account *see* sight bank account
current account balance *see* balance of payments
current account deficit 513–14, **G:8**
current yield *see* yield
custodian 54, 156–8, **G:8**
customer direct trades 485, 486, **G:8**

Daily Official List (DOL) **G:8**
Daiwa Securities 82
Dalio, Ray 559
Daniels, Eric 401
dark pool 342, 344, 345, 347, 351–4, **G:8–9**
Dartington, Rowan 618
dated gilts 224
Davies, Jonathan 611
Dawson, Guy 82
Dax 30 (Deutsche AktienindeX) 451, **G:9**
day count convention 180, **G:9**
Dayan, Edwin 631
de Klerk, Peter 535

dealer's spread 226, 228
Dealogic 52
Dean, Nicholas, QC 627
Debenhams 382
debentures 232–3, **G:9**
debit cards 18, 46, **G:9**
debt 331, **G:9**
debt capital 23, **G:9**
Debt Management Office *see* DMO
debt maturity **G:9**
debt rating 234–5, **G:9**
debt restructuring 470, **G:9**
debtors 103–5, **G:9**
decentralisation 136, 137, **G:9**
dedicated short bias 575, **G:9**
deep (financial markets) **G:9**
deep discounted bonds 234, **G:9**
deep discounted rights issue 402, **G:9**
default 232, 234–5,238–40, **G:9**
defensive open market operation 290, **G:9**
deferred preference shares 333, **G:9**
defined benefit 132–4, 139, 142, **G:9**
defined contribution 135, 142, **G:9**
Degorce, Patrick 566
Delaware, USA 564
delinquent mortgages 667
Dell, Michael 566
demand curves for bonds 268–70
dematerialisation 187, **G:9**
demutualisation 103, **G:9**
Denmark 41, 248
Department for Business, Innovation and Skills (UK) 628
Department of Labor (USA) 141
Depfa 464, 465
deposit facility 319, **G:9**
depositary receipts (DRs) 356–7, **G:9**
depositor insurance 301, 302
depository **G:9**
depository institutions (deposit-taking institutions, DTIs) 37, **G:9**
Depository Trust & Clearing Corporation 363
derivatives 413–14, **G:9**
    commodities 539, 541
    exchange-traded funds 151
    exchanges 424
    innovations 21
    investment banking 95
    market's impact on our lives 7
    OTC market 24
    users 431–3

Deutsche Bahn (DB) 243
Deutsche Bank/Deutsche Bank
    Citigroup 26, 78, 79, 82, 101
    Agricultural Bank of China
        IPO 24
    corporate banking 88
    FICC operations 94
    FX trading 484, 4875
    gold and silver 550
    hedge funds 571
    Linde's takeover of BOC 80
    Liquid Commodities Indices
        542
    mergers and acquisitions 84
    Mexican hedging 451
    privatisation 86
    proprietary trading 93
    swaps 464, 465
Deutsche Borse312, 337, 343, 352,
    363, **G:9**
Deutsche Bundespost 195
Deutsche Industriebank (IBK) 668
Deutsche Telekom 88
development capital **G:9**
development of money and
    financial institutions 12–19
Dexia 672
Diageo 220, 232, 257
Dichev, Ilia 560
dilution **G:9**
Diment, Brett 238
Diners Club 46
direct debit 46, **G:9**
Direct Edge 342, 347, **G:9**
direct foreign investment **G:9**
directors 386–7
directors' dealings 386, **G:9**
directors' report **G:9**
dirty float *see* managed float
dirty price (full price, invasive
    price) 226, **G:9**
disclosure of information 616
discount **G:9**
    bonds 258
    FX 488
    rights issues 402
discount basis *see* discount yield
discount house **G:9**
discount market deposit **G:9**
discount pricing 168–9
discount rate 291–2, **G:9–10**
discount to par 180, **G:10**
discount window borrowing
    291–2, **G:10**
discount yield (discount basis,
    discount rate) **G:10**
    commercial paper 189

Treasury bills 181, 183, 186
discounting 213–14, **G:10**
disintermediation 23, **G:10**
distressed **G:10**
distressed debt **G:10**
distressed securities investing 577,
    G:10
distribution units *see* income units
Divanna, Jo 108
diversification **G:10**
divestiture (divestment) 85, **G:10**
dividend 4, **G:10**
    loan covenants 45
    negative covenants 233
    ordinary shares 331
    preference shares 332
dividend cover **G:10**
dividend payout ratio **G:10**
dividend per share **G:10**
dividend policy **G:10**
dividend yield **G:10**
DMO (Debt Management Office)
    180, 182, 224, 226, 246, 316,
    G:10
documentary letter of credit
    524–5, **G:10**
Dodd-Frank financial reform act
    (USA) 305, 558
DOL *see* Daily Official List
Dolan, Tim 623
domestic bonds 94, **G:10**
domestic medium-term notes
    255–7, **G:10**
Domino's 248
Donald, Charles 88
Doriot, Georges 579, **G:15**
dot.com 245, 581, 660, **G:10**
Douglas, Nathan 171
Dow/Dow Jones Industrial
    Average (DJIA) 392, 393,
    541, 542, **G:10**
Dowley, Justin 82
Dragon Wing Development 617
Dragons' Den 584, **G:10**
drawdown arrangement 43, **G:10**
Dresdner Kleinwort Wasserstein
    627
Drexel Burnham Lambert 241
DSW 348
dual-class 333, 334, **G:10**
dual track, investment banking
    80–1
Dubai Islamic Bank 258
Dublin 11
due diligence **G:10**
Dufey Group 356
Dunkin Donuts 248

duration of a bond **G:10**
"Dutch disease" 157
Dutch East India Company 329–
    30, 529
duty of care 616
dynamic open market operations
    290, **G:10**

e-cash 47
e-money 47, **G:10**
e-trading 348–51, **G:10**
Eagle, Simon 617–18
earnings **G:10**
earnings multiple **G:10**
earnings per share (EPS) **G:10**
earnings yield **G:10**
East India Company 529
easyJet 382
EBA *see* European Banking
    Authority
eBay 584
EBIT **G:10**
EBITDA **G:10**
ECB (European Central Bank) 187,
    319–20, **G:10**
    depositor insurance 301
    enhanced credit support
        303–4
    EONIA 178
    funding, addiction to 303–4
    government debt markets 317
    independence 297, 298–9
    inflation target 295, 296
    Irish financial crisis 301
    lender of last resort 302
    marginal lending facility 291
    regulation 635
Economic and Monetary Union
    (EMU) 319, 493, **G:10**
Economic Crime Agency (ECA)
    630
economic exposure *see* economic
    risk
economic growthand monetary
    policy 295
economic risk 497–9, 507, **G:10**
economies of scale **G:10**
    business loans 42
    financial intermediaries 18
    investment banking 82
    money market funds 170
    monopoly/oligopoly 609
    regulation of financial services
        622
    universal banking 37, 39
Economist, The 509
Edmond de Rothschild group 558

education of consumers 616
EDX London **G:10**
Efama 557, 558
effective annual rate (EAR) *see* annual percentage rate
efficient market hypothesis (EMH) **G:10**
efficient stock market **G:10**
EFTPOS (Electronic Funds Transfer at Point Of Sale) 46, **G:10**
Egg 47
Egypt 399
EIOPA *see* European Insurance and Occupational Pensions Authority
EIS (Enterprise Investment Scheme) 590, **G:10**
Electricité de France (EdF) 243
Electronic Communications Networks (ECNs) *see* MTF
electronic platform 485–6, **G:11**
electronic purse *see* smart cards
electronic settlement **G:11**
electronic trading system *see* electronic platform
Elson, Charles 334
emerging market bonds 83, 235, 237, 238, **G:11**
emerging markets 184, 356, **G:11**
EMI 80, 588
Employee Benefits Security Administration (EBSA) 141
Employee Retirement Income Security Act (1974, USA, ERISA) 141
employment and monetary policy 295
Empora.com 584
EMU *see* Economic and Monetary Union
end-investors 97, **G:11**
end-of-life reporting bias, hedge fund indices 572–3
endowment 28, 120, **G:11**
enhanced money market funds 171
Enterprise Inns 606
Enterprise Investment Scheme *see* EIS
Entertainment Rights 386
entrepreneurs **G:11**
Eon 80
EONIA (Euro Overnight Index Average) 178, **G:11**
Epstein, Daniel 399
Equitas 126
equity, equity capital 23, **G:11**

and bonds, comparison between 221
and debt finance, comparison between 331
equity index futures 421–2
equity indices **G:11**
equity kicker (sweetener) 240, **G:11**
equity-linked bonds *see* convertible bonds
equity long/short 575, **G:11**
equity market neutral **G:11**
equity markets 328–74
equity option **G:11**
equity-related Eurobonds 254
equity shareholders' funds *see* shareholders' funds
equity tranche 662, 663, 664
equity warrants **G:11**
equivalent bond yield *see* bond equivalent yield
ERM *see* Exchange Rate Mechanism
Ermotti, Sergio 79
ESCB *see* European System of Central Banks
ESMA *see* European Securities and Markets Authority
eSpeed 485, **G:11**
ESRB *see* European Systemic Risk Board
Essar Energy 393
ETC *see* Exchange Traded Commodities
ETF *see* exchange traded fund
ETF Securities 543–4
EU *see* European Union
Eurasian Natural Resources 377
Eurekahedge 570
Eurex 363, 422, **G:11**
EURIBOR (Euro Interbank Offered Rate) 178, **G:11**
euro 231, 253, 493
euro bonds 252
Euro medium-term notes 255–7, **G:11**
euro Swiss francs **G:11**
euro to UK pounds exchange rate (2001–11) 6
eurobanking **G:11**
Eurobonds 251, 252–5, 256–7, **G:11**
Euroclear UK & Ireland 363
Eurocommercial paper *see* commercial paper
Eurocredit 179, **G:11**
Eurocurrency 178, 427, **G:11**

Eurocurrency banking 26, 98, **G:11**
Eurocurrency certificates of deposit 196
Eurocurrency deposits 196, **G:11**
Eurodeposit account 179, **G:11**
Eurodollar 178, 179, **G:11**
Eurodollar bond 252, **G:11**
Eurodollar certificates of deposit 196
Euroeurobonds 94, 252, **G:11**
euromarkets **G:11**
Euronext 337, 425, **G:11**
Euronext Amsterdam 347
Euronext.liffe 536, 539, 540, 547, **G:11**
EURONIA (Euro Overnight Index Average) 178, **G:11**
euronotes **G:11–12**
European Banking Authority (EBA) 634, **G:12**
European Central Bank *see* ECB
European Commission
  equity markets 334, 344, 346, 347, 348, 363
  Financial Services Action Plan 631
  hedge funds and private equity 557
  mutuals 101
  over-the-counter derivatives 424
  regulatory directives 633
European Court of Justice 334–5
European Federation of Investors (EFI) 348
European Insurance and Occupational Pensions Authority (EIOPA) 634, **G:12**
European Investment Bank (EIB) 253, 464
European Monetary Union *see* Economic and Monetary Union
European Parliament 634
European Private Equity & Venture Capital Association (EVCA) 580, 581, **G:12**
European Securities and Markets Authority (ESMA) 557, 634, **G:12**
European-style options 443, **G:12**
European System of Central Banks (ESCB) 319, **G:12**
European System of Financial Supervisors 633, **G:12**
European Systemic Risk Board (ESRB) 635, **G:12**

European Union (EU) **G:12**
  book-building 381
  clearing systems 47, 49
  covered bonds 250, 251
  equity markets 334, 338, 342, 344–5, 352, 353, 362–3
  hedge funds 557–8, 564, 569, 570
  insurance 123
  junk bonds 241–2
  Kyoto treaty 548
  money markets 171
  over-the-counter derivatives 424
  Pension Funds Directive 142
  private equity 557–8, 580, 581
  regulation of financial sector 604, 624, 631–6
  rights issues 399
  unit of account 172
Eurosecurities179, **G:12**
Eurostar 334
Eurosterling **G:12**
Eurosterling bond 252, **G:12**
Euroswissfrancs 178
Eurosystem 319, **G:12**
Eurotunnel 377
Euroyen 178, **G:12**
eurozone **G:12**
  bond markets 3, 271
  central banking 289
    see also ECB
  certificates of deposit 196
  interbank market 178
EVCA *see* European Private Equity & Venture Capital Association
event driven 577, **G:12**
event risk **G:12**
Everest Re Group Ltd 123
Evolution Group 88
ex-coupon **G:12**
ex-dividend 226, **G:12**
ex-rights **G:12**
ex-rights price of a share 400, 401, 402, **G:12**
excess 119, **G:12**
excess reserves 56, 286, **G:12**
exchange controls **G:12**
exchange rate 486–92, **G:12**
  central banking 294–5
  determination 507–10
  regimes 492–4
  risk 497–507
Exchange Rate Mechanism (ERM) 493, 578, **G:12**

Exchange Traded Commodities (ETC) 151, 543, 547, **G:12**
exchange-traded derivatives 422–4
exchange traded fund (ETF) 149–51, 542–4, 571–2, **G:12**
exchange trading 24, **G:12**
exchangeable bond 245, 246, **G:12**
execution-only brokers **G:12**
executive directors 386, **G:12**
exercise price (strike price) 443, 444, 446, 447, **G:12**
exercising an option 442
exit 591–3, **G:12**
exit charge 145, **G:12**
exotic **G:12**
exotic currencies 488, **G:12**
expansion capital 585–6, **G:12**
expansion, development or growth (private equity) **G:12**
expectations hypothesis of the term structure of interesting rates (yield curve) 272–3, **G:12**
expectations theory of foreign exchange 513, **G:12**
expiry date of an option **G:12**
exports 524–7
exposure limits 616
extendable commercial paper 188, **G:12**
externality **G:12**
extraordinary items 65, **G:12**

face value *see* par value
Facebook 334
factoring 27, 55, 103–5, 527, **G:13**
failure to pay 470
Faiman, Jonathan 382
fair game 338, **G:13**
fair trading on exchanges 616
Fairfield Energy 383
Fairfield Greenwich 568–9
fallen angel 240, **G:13**
false dissemination 605–6
Fannie Mae 248, 661, 662, 670, **G:13**
far-from-equilibrium conditions 655, 656–7, 658
Farallon Capital Management 559
fat finger trade 350, **G:13**
FCA *see* Financial Conduct Authority
Federal Deposit and Insurance Corporation 301, **G:13**
federal funds rate 178, 187, 289, 320, **G:13**

Federal Home Loan Mortgage Corporation (FHLMC) *see* Freddie Mac
Federal National Mortgage Association (FNMA) *see* Fannie Mae
Federal Open Market Committee (FOMC) 320, **G:13**
Federal Reserve Bank (the Fed) 320–1, **G:13**
  commercial paper 190
  federal funds rate 178, 187, 289, 320
  financial crisis 302, 670, 671, 672
  independence 297
  inflation target 296
  lender of last resort 301, 302
  Long-Term Capital Management 413, 574
  Primary Dealer Credit Facility 302
  quantitative easing 299–300, 304
  regulation of financial sector 608–9
  repos 195
  shadow banking system 637
  World Trade Center attack 301
Fedwire (Federal Reserve Wire Network) 49, **G:13**
FEER (Fundamental Equilibrium Exchange Rate) 513, **G:13**
Fell, Patrick 60
Feltes, Richard 534
Ferguson, Sir Alex 92
Ferrari, Bruno 534
Ferrovial 80
FFA *see* Forward Freight Agreement
Fiat 242
Fidelity Investment Trust 384, 433
Figic 247
final close (private equity) 591, **G:13**
finance houses 27, 103–7, **G:13**
finance lease (capital lease, financial lease, full payout lease) 107, **G:13**
financial advisers, flotation process 378–80
financial centres 9–12
Financial Conduct Authority (FCA) 615, 620–1, **G:13**
  authorisation 622

consumer complaints 624
fraud 629
markets 626
money laundering 631
monitoring 622–3
see also Financial Services
Authority
financial crisis 645–79
Basel rules 310–11, 312
central banks 298–9, 300
contagion 608–9
credit rating agencies 192
derivatives 413
lender of last resort 304
private equity 581
regulation 636, 660
securitisation 247
Turner proposals for
international banks 306
US current account deficit 514
financial economists 646–51
financial gearing **G:13**
Financial Industry Regulatory
Authority 347
financial institutions 24–30
financial instrument **G:13**
financial intermediaries 14–19, **G:13**
financial market activity 12, 13
financial model **G:13**
Financial Ombudsman Scheme
(FOS) 625, **G:13**
Financial Policy Committee (FPC)
620, **G:13**
financial ratios 45, 233
Financial Reporting Council
(FRC) 386, 628, **G:13**
Financial Services Action Plan
(FSAP) 631–2, **G:13**
Financial Services Authority (FSA)
G:13
bank supervision 307
employees 635
financial crisis 669
hedge funds 565, 572
insurance 123
liquidity rule change 59–60
post-listing obligations 386
price-sensitive information,
disclosure of 385–6
regulation of financial sector
609, 615, 617–18, 620–2
asymmetric information
606, 607–8
authorisation 622
companies 628
consumer complaints 624
dangers 611–12

fees 621–2
fraud 629
markets 626–8
money laundering 631
monitoring 622–4
Turner proposals for
international banks 306
UKLA 342, 376
unit trusts 144, 145, 147
see also Financial Conduct
Authority
Financial Services Compensation
Scheme (FSCS) 147, 301,
625, 626, **G:13**
Financial Stability Board (FSB)
636, 637, **G:13**
financial supermarkets 22, 54
financial system
safety and soundness of the
300–16
stability, monetary policy's
impact on 295
Financial Times (*FT*)
bonds 226, 227, 230, 235,
236–7, 261
call options 443
exchange rates 488, 489
exchange-traded funds 150
investment trusts 154, 155
LIFFE share options 447, 448
market indices 396, 397–8
money market interest rates
200, 201
share price information 390,
391
unit trusts 146, 147, 148
financing advice, investment banks
82–4
financing gap 582, **G:13**
Finland 100
Finsider 257
First Banking Directive (1977) 633,
G:13
first close (private equity) 591, **G:13**
First Direct 47
first-loss tranche *see* equity tranche
Firth Rixson 588
Fitch Ratings 190, 191, 239, **G:13**
bonds 226, 235, 236–7, 240
fixed charge collateral **G:13**
collateral 45
debentures 232, 233
fixed exchange rate 492–3, **G:13**
fixed income arbitrage 576–7, **G:13**
fixed income, currencies and
commodities trading (FICC)
94

fixed interest 179, **G:13**
fixed-interest securities 221, 356,
G:13
fixing system 549–50, **G:13**
flat rate **G:13**
flat yield *see* yield
float 118, 122, 136, **G:13**
floating charge **G:13–14**
collateral 45
debentures 232–3
floating exchange rate 493–4, **G:14**
floating FX regime *see* floating
exchange rate
floating-rate bonds 232
floating-rate borrowing (floating
interest) 179, **G:14**
floating-rate notes (FRNs) 234,
254, **G:14**
floor 458, **G:14**
floor writers 458
flotation 24, **G:14**
follow-on offering *see* seasoned
equity offerings
FOMC *see* Federal Open Market
Committee
food inflation 534
Footsie **G:14**
see also FTSE 100 share index
Ford, Christopher 631
Ford Motor Company 103, 189,
333
foreclosure, US mortgages 667,
668, 670
foreign assets and liabilities,
valuation of 496
foreign banking 26, **G:14**
foreign bonds 94, 251–2, **G:14**
foreign currency futures contract
501–3
foreign exchange 480–522
banks 55
daily turnover *v* UK GDP 22,
23
forwards 414
risk management 53
foreign exchange control **G:14**
foreign exchange future 482, **G:14**
foreign exchange markets (forex,
FX) 7, 480–522, **G:14**
central banks 318
current account deficit and
capital flows, influence of
513–14
efficiency 514
exchange rate 486–92
determination 507–10
regimes 492–4

foreign exchange markets
        (*continued*)
    risk 497–507
    expectations theory 513
    impact on our lives 6–7
    interest rate parity theory
        510–12
    mistakes 484
    monetary policy's impact on
        295
    purchasing power parity
        507–10
    trading 484–6
    volatility and its effects 494–7
foreign exchange risk 527, **G:14**
foreign exchange swap (FX swap,
        forex swap) 482, **G:14**
forex **G:14**
    see also foreign exchange entries
forfaiting 53, 527, **G:14**
Fortis 305, 672
forward (forward agreement)
        414–15, **G:14**
    comparison with options,
        futures and FRAs 454
    FX 481, 482, 488, 490
Forward Freight Agreement (FFA)
        530–1, **G:14**
forward market 7, **G:14**
forward market hedge 501, **G:14**
forward-rate agreement (FRA)
        430–1, 454, 465–7, **G:14**
FOS *see* Financial Ombudsman
        Scheme
FPC *see* Financial Policy
        Committee
France
    bancassurance 54
    bonds 231, 243, 250
    collective investments 143
    financial market activity 12, 13
    hedge funds 570
    household and business
        lending 41
    index options 451
    insurance 122
    investment banking 78
    local authority bills 195
    mutuals 100, 103
    overdrafts 42
    SICAVs 54
    Treasury bills 180
    universal banks 37
France Telecom 246
Francois-Poncet, Andre 593
Frankfurt 11
Fraser, Stuart 634

fraud 569, 607, 629–31
Frawley, Mike 543
Freddie Mac 248, 661, 662, 670,
        G:14
free float (free capital) 364, 377,
        G:14
Freeman Consulting 84
Fresnillo 393
frictional unemployment 295, **G:14**
front-end charge *see* initial charge
front end fee (facility fee) 50, **G:14**
front-running 347
FSA *see* Financial Services
        Authority
FSAP *see* Financial Services Action
        Plan
FSB *see* Financial Stability Board
FTSE 100 share index 4, 392–5,
        G:14
    futures 422
    index options 451, 452
FTSE 250 share index 396, **G:14**
FTSE 350 share index 396, **G:14**
FTSE Actuaries All-Share Index
        (the All-Share) 392, 396,
        G:14
FTSE AIM All-Share 396, **G:14**
FTSE All-Small 396
FTSE Fledgling Index 396, **G:14**
FTSE indices 396, 397–8
FTSE SmallCap Companies 396,
        G:14
Fuhr, Deborah 151
full price (bonds) *see* dirty price
fund management **G:14**
fund of funds **G:14**
fund of hedge funds 568–9, **G:14**
fund supermarkets 145
Fundamental-E Investments 617
Fundamental Equilibrium
        Exchange Rate *see* FEER
fundamental growth 578
fundamental value 578, **G:14**
funded pension scheme 132–3,
        G:14
fungible **G:14**
Futuragene 381
future-based bet 456, **G:14**
futures 7, 415–30, 454, **G:14**
    FX 482
futures commission merchants 425
futures hedge 501–3
futures price of cocoa (2009–11) 8
FX **G:14**
    see also foreign exchange entries
FXAll485, **G:14**
FXConnect 485, **G:14**

G20 318, 424, 634, **G:14**
Gala Coral 588, 593
Gallagher, Claudine 357
Gandover 593
Gardner, James 624
Gardner, Sir Roy 92
Garvety, Padhraic 303–4
gate (hedge funds) 562–3, **G:14**
Gayne, Alisdair 87
GDP (nominal, real) **G:14–15**
gearing (financial gearing) **G:15**
Geberit 242
GEMMS 226, **G:15**
General Atlantic 593
General Electric (GE) 103, 188,
        189, 258, 392
general inflation **G:15**
general insurance 27, 120, 121,
        122, **G:15**
General Motors 103, 189, 667
General National Mortgage
        Association (GNMA) *see*
        Ginnie Mae
general obligation bonds 243, **G:15**
general partner (GP) 579–80, 585,
        591, **G:15**
Geneva 11, 12
Gensler, Gary 351
George, Sara 628
Germany
    Allfinanz 54
    bonds 231, 243, 250
    European Central Bank 305
    exchange-traded derivatives
        422
    financial crisis 666, 672
    financial market activity 12, 13
    giro payments 46
    hedge funds 570
    household and business
        lending 41
    index options 451
    insurance 122
    local authority bills 195
    mutuals 100, 101
    NeuerMarkt 387
    overdrafts 42
    payment mechanisms 18
    regulation of financial sector
        622
    settlement cycle 363
    shipping 532
    stockbroking by banks 54
    swaps 464
    Treasury bills 180
    universal banks 37
Getco 344

Gilkes, Kai 648
gilts (gilt-edged securities) 3, 223–8, **G:15**
Ginnie Mae 248, **G:15**
giro 46, **G:15**
Gissing, Jason 382, 383
Glass, Paul 606
Glass–Steagall Act (1933, USA) 81
Glazer, Malcolm 92
Glencore 419, 420, 544
global banks 81–2, **G:15**
Global Brands Licensing 390
global custodian 54, **G:15**
Global Depositary Receipts (GDRs) 356, **G:15**
Global Financial Centres report 9
global macro 578, **G:15**
global regulation of financial sector 636
Globalink 485, **G:15**
globalisation 22, 659–60, **G:15**
goal independence 297, **G:15**
going concern 45, **G:15**
going long 366, **G:15**
going public 376, 592, **G:15**
going short *see* short selling
gold 523–4, 548–55
gold standard 492, **G:15**
golden shares 334–5, **G:15**
Goldman Sachs 26, 79
    Agricultural Bank of China IPO 24
    BAA 80
    bulge bracket 81
    corporate banking 88
    criticism in China 95
    employee compensation 77
    Eurobonds 257
    exchange traded funds 544
    FICC operations 94
    financial crisis 661, 672
    FX trading 485
    government funds 608
    hedge funds 558
    Hepalink investment 337
    mergers and acquisitions 84
    Mexican hedging 451
    Ocado flotation 383
    pensions 134
    private equity 579
    proprietary trading 91, 92–3
    return on equity 78
    systemic importance 305
Google 331, 333, 334, 589, 594
Governing Council, ECB 319, **G:15**
government agencies, regulation by 613

government assistance, investment banks 82–6
government banker, central bank as 316–17
government bonds 222–3, 228, **G:15**
    central banks 316–17
    China 231
    credit rating 235
    France 231
    Germany 231
    Japan 231
    UK 223–8
    USA 228–31
Government of Singapore Investment Corporation 368
Government Pension Fund Global (Norway) 157
government regulation 613
Gower, Christopher 606
grace period 43, **G:15**
Grade, Michael 383
Graham, Paul 571
Granite master trust 249
Great Depression **G:15**
Greece
    European Central Bank 298, 303
    Exchange Rate Mechanism 493
    government debt 3
    interbank loan market 59
    interest rates 202
    naked credit default swaps 470
    risk-free return 173
    speculators 433
Greenspan, Alan 514
Greer, Bob 545–6
Grigson, David 383
gross (finance) **G:15**
gross dividend yield **G:15**
gross domestic product *see* GDP
gross margin *see* gross profit margin
gross present value **G:15**
gross profit **G:15**
gross profit margin (gross margin) **G:15**
gross redemption yield (gross yield to redemption) 225, **G:15**
    see also yield to maturity
gross yield **G:15**
growth in the financial services sector 20–3
    stifling of, through regulation 610–12
Grundfest, Joseph 239

guaranteed loan stock (bond) 233, **G:15**
guarantees
    bank 53
    exports 527
Gulf African Bank 108

haircut 193–4, **G:15**
Haldane, Andy 315
Halfords 382
Halifax 48, 103
hallmark **G:15**
Hand in Hand 118
Hang Seng Index **G:15**
Hanover Re Group 123
hard commodity **G:15**
hard currency **G:15**
Harley, John 593
Hartford Growth (Trading) Fund 381
Hayes, Angela 606
Haynes, Alasdair 343, 344
HBOS (Halifax Bank of Scotland) 48, 59, 671, 672
hedge (hedging) 29, 431, **G:15**
    commodities 534, 535
    index options 451–3
    share options 449–51
    short-term interest rate futures 428–30
hedge fund 29–30, 556–78, 594–601, **G:15**
    fund managers 564–8
    fund of hedge funds 568–9
    gates and lock-ups 562–3
    indices 572–3
    innovations 23
    investors 561–2
    leverage 573–4
    listed 569
    pension funds invested in 139
    prime brokerage 578
    registration 564
    shadow banking system 637
    side pocket 563–4
    strategies 574–8
    UCITS 569–72
hedge fund index 572–3, **G:15**
Hedge Fund Research 573, 574, 577
hedgers 431
Hedman, Eric 248
Helgason, Ari 584
Henry Bath 544
Hepalink 337
Her Majesty's Revenue and Customs *see* HMRC

Hermes BPK 566
Herstatt risk 491, **G:15**
Hester, Stephen 66
Hewitt Associates 139
HIBOR (Hong Kong Interbank
     Offered Rate) 178, **G:15**
high-frequency trading (HFT)
     348–51, 352, 353, 354, **G:16**
high-net-worth individuals 97
high powered money 288, **G:16**
high water mark (hedge funds)
     565, **G:16**
high yield bonds *see* junk bonds;
     mezzanine finance
Highways Insurance 627
hire purchase (HP) 27, 55, 105–6,
     G:16
Hirsch, Stanley 381
HMRC (Her Majesty's Revenue
     and Customs)158, **G:16**
Hobbs, David 393, 394
Hollingworth, David 459
Hong Kong
     central banking 293
     Chinese government bonds
        231
     equity markets 352, 357
     financial market activity 12, 13
     FX market 483, 484
     gold 549
     importance as financial centre
        10, 11, 12
     interbank lending 178
     proprietary trading 92
     taxi driver loans 247
Hong Kong Monetary Authority
     293
Hopper, Martyn 618
Horner, Simon 557
Horowitz, Keith 91
Horta-Osorio, Antonio 306
Household Finance 667
household lending 41
housing bubble 658–9
Howie, Fraser 617
HSBC
     Basel III rules 313
     capital position 312
     custodianship 156
     depositary receipts 357
     financial crisis 667, 668
     FX trading 485
     gold and silver 550
     interest rates 202
     investment banking 79, 84
     Invoice Finance 104
     Islamic mortgages 108

Ocado flotation 383
     Turner proposals 306
     universal banking 39
Hudson Bay Company 529
Hunt, Brad 363
hurdle rate 567, **G:16**
Hutchison Whampoa 246
hybrid finance **G:16**
Hypo Real Estate 672
Hyva 579

Iberia 394
IBK 668
IBM 133, 221, 631
ICE (Intercontinental Exchange)
     425, 502, 536, **G:16**
Iceland 180, 305, 306, 313, 604,
     672
ICICI Bank 611
IFB *see* Insurance Fraud Bureau
IG Group 625
*ijara*107, **G:16**
illiquidity 61–2
IMF (International Monetary
     Fund) **G:16**
     Bretton Woods conference
        493
     central banks 318
     Iceland 672
     Irish financial crisis 301, 318
     purchasing power parity
        509–10
     regulation 636
     special drawing rights 200, 488
     Washington consensus 659
impact day 382, 383, **G:16**
impact of financial markets on our
     lives 2–7
impatience to consume 172–3,
     G:16
imperfect hedge **G:16**
imports 524, 525
In House Group 390
in-the-money option 444, **G:16**
income statements 65–7
income units 147, **G:16**
income yield *see* yield
incompetence 607–8
incubators **G:16**
independent non-executive
     directors 386–7
independents 590–1, **G:16**
index *see* market index
index funds (trackers) **G:16**
index-linked gilts (stocks) 228,
     G:16
index options 451–3

India
     commodities 534, 535, 545
     cooperatives 103
     depository receipts 356
     gold 549
     outsourced operations 23
     public float 377
     reform of financial services
        sector 30–1
     regulation of banks 610–11
indices *see* market index
Indonesia 252
inflation **G:16**
     bonds 225–6, 228, 269, 270
     central banking 285, 293, 297,
        298, 319
        monetary policy's impact
        on the economy 294–5, 296,
        299–300
     commodities 534
     and interest rates 202
     purchasing power parity 508,
        512
     time value of money 173, 174
inflation-linked **G:16**
inflation risk **G:16**
Infonavit 238
informal venture capitalist 583–4,
     G:16
information asymmetry 44, 119,
     603–8, **G:16**
information costs **G:16**
information provision, mandatory
     616
informed investors **G:16**
initial charge 145, **G:16**
initial margin 416, 417, 420, **G:16**
initial public offering (IPO) 10, 11,
     24, 83, **G:16**
     see also new issue
innovation in financial services
     sector 21–3
     financial crisis 660, 661–2
     stifling of, through regulation
        610–12
insider trading 617, 626, 627
insolvency 57, 61, 305–6, 470, **G:16**
instalment arrangements 43
instalment credit **G:16**
Institutional Money Market Funds
     Association 171
Institutional Shareholder
     Committee 142, **G:16**
institutionalisation **G:16**
instrument (finance) **G:16**
instrument independence 297,
     G:16

insurable risk **G:16**
insurance 116–30, 158–66
   asymmetric information 119
   banks 54–5
   and credit default swaps,
     difference between 468
   exports 527
   firms 118
   funds 27–8
   history 118
   junk bonds 242
   London market 124–30
   marine 531
   monoline insurers 666–7
   need for 118
   premiums 121–3
   process 119
   regulation 605, 630
   reinsurance 123–4
   types 120–1
   UK share market 366
   underwriting 119
Insurance Fraud Bureau (IFB) 630,
   G:16
insurance premium **G:16**
insurance underwriting **G:16**
inter-dealer broker 637
inter-dealer direct trades 485, 486,
   G:16
inter-office trading 539, **G:16**
interbank brokers **G:16**
interbank lending 40, 59, **G:16**
interbank market 174–8, **G:16–17**
Intercontinental Exchange *see* ICE
interest cover 45, **G:17**
interest only repayment
   arrangement 44
interest rate cap *see under* cap
interest rate parity (IRP) theory of
   exchange rate determination
   510–12, **G:17**
interest rate risk 264, 268, **G:17**
interest rate swap 459–63, 466–7,
   G:17
interest rates
   banking 7, 42, 43, 46, 49, 50,
     61
   bonds 221–2, 228, 230, 240,
     258, 271–4
   central banking 285, 289–90,
     291–2, 299
     monetary policy's impact on
       the economy 294, 295, 296
   commercial paper 188
   conversions
     from 365-day to 360-day
       basis 207

     from monthly and daily
       rates to annual rates 214
   determining 210–11
   Eurocurrency 179
   financial crisis 660–1
   forward rate agreements 430,
     465–7
   interbank market 174–8
   money market 168–9, 200–3
   pure 172–3
   short-term interest rate futures
     427–30
   time value of money 174
   Treasury bills 187
interest risk management 53
interest-withholding tax 252, **G:17**
interest yield *see* yield
interim dividend **G:17**
interim profit reports 386, 388,
   G:17
intermediaries offer 381, **G:17**
intermediate debt *see* junk bonds;
   mezzanine finance
intermediate security 16, **G:17**
internal rate of return (IRR) 260,
   587, 588, **G:17**
International Bank for
   Reconstruction and
   Development (IBRD) *see*
   World Bank
international banking 26, 97–100,
   306, **G:17**
international bonds 94, 252–4,
   G:17
International Capital Market
   Association (ICMA) 252,
   G:17
international competitiveness
   613–15
International Financial Reporting
   Standards 632
International Monetary Fund *see*
   IMF
International Organisation of
   Securities Commissions
   (IOSCO) 352–3
International Swap and Derivatives
   Association (ISDA) 305,
   636, **G:22**
international trade problem 197
internationalisation of risk 666
internet 22, 47, 581
internet banking 47, 48, **G:17**
interpolation **G:17**
intraday *see spot entries*
intraday bets 456
intrinsic value 442, 443, **G:17**

introduction 380, **G:17**
inventory *see* stock
InvercaixaValores 257
Investbx354, **G:17**
investment, effects of FX volatility
   on 496
investment advice 96–7
investment bank (merchant bank)
   25–6, 76–97, 108–15, **G:17**
Investment Company Act (1940,
   USA) 152
investment grade debt 191, 235,
   236, **G:17**
investment grade syndicated loans
   51, 52
Investment Management
   Association 142, 626
investment period 211
investment return *see* yield
investment risk 620
investment trusts (investment
   companies) 29, 153–6, 590,
   G:17
Investors Chronicle 380
invoice **G:17**
invoice discounting 105, **G:17**
invoice finance **G:17**
   see also factoring
invoice price (bonds) *see* dirty
   price
IOU 187, 221, **G:17**
Ireland, Republic of
   collective investments 143
   credit rating 229
   CREST 363
   ECB funding, addiction to 303
   Exchange Rate Mechanism
     493
   financial crisis 301, 318, 672
   hedge funds 564
   household and business
     lending 41
   investment rates 202
   risk-free return 173
Iron Maiden 247
IRP *see* interest rate parity (IRP) of
   exchange rate determination
IRR *see* internal rate of return
irredeemable (perpetual) 234, 333,
   G:17
ISA (Individual Savings Account)
   G:17
ISDA *see* International Swap and
   Derivatives Association
Islamic banking 107–8
Islamic bonds 257–8, **G:17**
Islamic Development Bank 258

issuer ratings 235, **G:17**
issuing house *see* sponsor
It's a Wonderful Life 301
Italy
    banking restrictions 81
    Exchange Rate Mechanism 493
    household and business lending 41
    interest rate derivatives 95
    local authority bills 195
    national debt 316
    speculators 433
    swaps 464–5
ITV 93
IUA (International Underwriting Association of London) 124, **G:17**

J.C. Bamford (JCB) 376
Jakob, Olivier 451
James, Simon 545
Japan
    banking restrictions 81
    bonds 231, 243, 251–2, 271
    central banking 299, 300
    certificates of deposit 196
    cooperatives 103
    equity markets 342–3, 357
    financial crisis 659
    financial market activity 12, 13
    FX market 483
    giro payments 46
    insurance market 117, 122
    interbank lending 178
    investment banking 78
    national debt 316
    pensions 138
    post office 46
    regulation of financial sector 622
    rights issues 399
    universal banks 37
    US Treasury bills and bonds 514
Japan Bank for International Cooperation (JBIC) 251–2
Jefferies 383
Jenkins, J. P. 389
JGBs (Japanese government bonds) 231, **G:17**
Jieng, Liu 617
Jillings, Kate 584
Jimmy Choo 593
Jinglian, Wu 617
John Lewis 383
joint stock enterprise 335, **G:17**
joint venture **G:17**

Jonathan's Coffee-house 330, **G:17**
Jones, Alfred Winslow 559–61, 574, 575, **G:1**
Jones, Chris 569
JPMorgan/JPMorgan Cazenove/ JPMorgan Chase 11, 22, 26, 30, 79
    American Depositary Receipts 356
    Basel III rules 313
    Centrica 92
    corporate broking 88
    employee compensation 77
    exchange traded funds 543, 544
    FICC operations 94
    financial crisis 668, 670, 671
    FSA fine 618
    FX trading 485
    gilts 226
    hedge funds 565
    Manchester United 92
    mergers and acquisitions 39, 84, 87
    Ocado flotation 383
    Pardue, Charles 666
    pensions 133
    repos 194
    swaps 464, 465
    Unitas Capital 579
    universal banking 39
    VaR 649
junior debt *see* subordinated debt
junior tranche 663
junk bonds 191, 235, 237, 240–2, **G:17**
Jupiter Fund Management 384–5
JWM Partners 574, 576

Kabul Bank 63
kangaroo 251, **G:18**
Kanjorski, Paul 351
Kaplan, Steven 587
Kappor, Rana 611
Karzai, Hamid 63
Kawabani, Nagi 558–9
Kazakhmys 393
Keele University 247
Kelleher, Colm 79
Kennedy, John F. 257
Kenya 47
Kerr, Andrew 621
Kershaw, Dagmar Kent 242
Kerviel, Jéróme 92
Ketchum, Rick 347
Key Asset Management 569
Keydata 625–6

Keynes, John Maynard 493, **G:17**
KfW bank 484, **G:18**
kicker *see* equity kicker
Kienle, Markus 348
King, Mervyn 296, 319, 672
Kingsman 535
Kingsman, Jonathan 535
Klarman, Seth 559
Klein, Robin 584
Kohlberg Kravis Roberts (KKR) 593
Konigbauer, Peter 545
Kraft 368
Krämer, Jörg 298
Kurer, Peter 666
Kyoto treaty 548

L&T Finance 611
L'Occitaine 11
laissez-faire **G:18**
Lambert, Richard 394
Lan, Yihui 510
landesbanken 101, **G:18**
landMARK **G:18**
Larsen & Toubro 611
Lazard 26, 82, 84
LBMA *see* London Bullion Market Association
LCH Clearnet (LCH) 362, 539, 547, **G:18**
LCH Investments 558, 559
lead manager 51, 255, 257, **G:18**
lead underwriter *see* book building
leasing 27, 55, 106–7, **G:18**
Leeson, Nick 418, 433
Legal & General 133
Legal &General Investment Management (LGIM) 139, 399
legal expenses, flotation process 379
legal requirements, flotation process 379
Legoland 593
Lehman Brothers 79
    Basel rules 310, 313
    breaking of the buck 171
    central banking 298, 302, 303, 305
    collapse 134, 177, 190, 194, 670–1
    contagion 608
    counterparty risk 363
    European Central Bank 298, 303
    Federal Reserve 302
    KfW 484

side pockets 563
systemic risk 304
Turner proposals for international banks 306
UK reserves 624
corporate broking 87
credit default swaps 469
FICC operations 94
and Nomura 82
sub-prime mortgages 661
swaps 464
Leiman, Ricardo 420
lender of last resort 58, 301–6, **G:18**
lenders' strikes 81
lending 40–6, 85
Lescure, Roland 545
lessee 106, **G:18**
lessor 106, **G:18**
letter of credit 53, **G:18**
leverage 573–4, 575, **G:18**
    see also gearing
leveraged buyout (LBO) 586, 589, **G:18**
leveraged loans (syndicated loans) 51, 52
leveraged recapitalisation 240–1, **G:18**
Levin, Garry 88
Lewis, John 579
Li, David 647–8, 664
liability 55, **G:18**
liability insurance 121, **G:18**
liability management 57, 61, 314, **G:18**
liar loans 661
liberalisation, and stock market growth 335
LIBID (London Interbank Bid Rate) **G:18**
LIBOR (London Interbank Offered Rate) 23, 174–7, **G:18**
    business loans 42
    caps 458
    floating-rate notes 234
    foreign bonds 251, 252
    forward rate agreements 430, 465–7
    medium-term notes 255
    swaps 459, 460–3, 466–7
licensing 616
life insurance/assurance 28, 117–18, 120–1, 122, **G:18**
LIFFE (London International Financial Futures and Options Exchange) 21, **G:18**
    call options 447

exchange-traded derivatives 422
futures 416, 422, 425, 426, 429
put options 447
share options 442–3, 447, 448
LIFFE CONNECT 425, **G:18**
LIMEAN 177
limit bid **G:18**
limit prices **G:18**
limited companies (Ltd) **G:18**
limited liability 4, 331, **G:18**
limited liability partnership (LLP) 591
limited partner (LP) 579–80, 585, **G:18**
Linde 80
line of credit *see* credit facility
Lion Capital 593
liquid **G:18**
liquid reserves (banking) 40, 56, **G:18**
liquidate 233, 592, **G:18**
liquidation analysis 45, **G:18**
liquidation of a company **G:18**
liquidation value **G:18**
liquidity **G:18**
    adequacy, banks 307–16
    and market makers 88
    secondary markets in money market instruments 168
liquidity coverage ratio 314, **G:18**
liquidity management 57–60, **G:18**
liquidity-preference hypothesis (liquidity premium theory) of the term structure of interest rates 274, **G:18**
liquidity risk 55, 307, 310, 314–16, **G:18**
listed companies **G:18**
listed funds (hedge funds) 569, **G:18**
Listed Private Equity (LPEQ) 589–90, **G:18**
listing agreement 376, **G:18**
listing fees 379, **G:18**
listing particulars *see* prospectus
Listing Rules **G:19**
lit pools 352
Littlewood, Christian and Angie 626, 627
living will (finance) 304–6, 608, **G:19**
Lloyd, Edward 532
Lloyd's insurance market 123, 124, 125–30, 531, **G:19**
Lloyd's of London *see* Lloyd's insurance market

Lloyd's Register 532, 533, **G:19**
Lloyds Banking Group 37
    capital position 312
    Cheltenham and Gloucester 103
    corporate broking 87
    factoring 104
    financial crisis 48, 671, 672
    Halifax 103
    Islamic mortgages 108
    loan-to-deposit ratio 66
    net interest margin 66
    Ocado flotation 383
    privatisation 86
    rescue by UK government 63, 86
    rights issue 401
    securitisation 249
    taxpayer-owned shares 304
LME *see* London Metal Exchange
LMEselect538, **G:19**
loan covenants 45, **G:19**
loan stock 233, **G:19**
loan to deposit ratio 65, 66, **G:19**
loans *see* lending
local authority bills/deposits 195, **G:19**
local authority bond 243, **G:19**
lock-up (hedge funds) 562–3, **G:19**
Locke, Paul 156
London *see* City of London
London Bullion Market Association (LBMA) 549, **G:19**
London Clearing House 362
London Eye 593
London Interbank Offered Rate *see* LIBOR
London Metal Exchange (LME) 414, 536, 538–9, 547, **G:19**
London Silver Fixing 550
London Stock Exchange (LSE) 337, 342, **G:19**
    average order size 352
    clearing and settlement 362, 363
    corporate bonds 232
    deregulation 21
    FTSE All Share Index 392
    history 354–5
    investment trusts 153
    mergers 337
    multilateral trading facilities 342, 344, 346
    primary market 357–9
    regulation 345, 626
    rights issues 396
    SEAQ 364–5

London Stock Exchange
    (*continued*)
    secondary markets 359
    SETS 360–1
    SETSqx 364
    share capital, raising 376–89
    trading speed 348–9
    variety of securities traded
        355–7
    warrants 405
London Traded Options Market
    442
long bond 221, **G:19**
long-form report 379, **G:19**
long position **G:19**
    contracts for difference 457
    futures 414, 425
    hedge funds 559, 560, 561,
        575–6
long/short strategy 575–6, **G:19**
Long-Term Capital Management
    (LTCM) 413, 573–4, 576,
    660, **G:19**
long-term insurance *see* life
    insurance/assurance
long-term savings institutions 27–8
longevity 133–4
longevity swaps 133, 134
loss carryforward provision *see*
    high water mark
lot (piece) 232, **G:19**
Louis Dreyfus 420
Loveday, Damien 139
LPEQ *see* Listed Private Equity
LSE *see* London Stock Exchange
LTCM *see* Long-Term Capital
    Management
Ltd **G:19**
Lucida 134
Luxembourg 143, 564, 672
Lynch, Peter 646

M0 286
M&As *see* mergers and acquisitions
M&G Asset Management 139, 144
Maastricht Treaty 297, 493, **G:19**
Macaulay, Frederick 265
Macdonald, Lord, QC 627
Mackay, Graham 394
macro-prudential regulation 314,
    G:19
Madame Tussauds 247, 383, 593
Madoff, Bernard 557, 566, 568–9
Main Market (MM) 357–9, **G:19**
    floating on the 376–85
    pre-emption rights, waiving of
        403

SETSqx 364
UK Corporate Governance
    Code 386
main refinancing operations
    (MRO) *see* open market
    operations
maintenance margin (futures)
    415–16, 417, **G:19**
Major, John 210
making a book **G:19**
Malaysia 108, 258
managed float 493–4, **G:19**
managed futures **G:19**
management buy-in (MBI) 586,
    589, **G:19**
management buyout (MBO) 586,
    589, **G:19**
management fees 257
managers
    investment trusts 153
    pension funds 136–7
Managing Director (MD) **G:19**
Manchester United 92
mandated lead arranger (MLA) 51
mandatory information provision
    616
Mandelson, Lord 78
Manium, Bharat 542
Mannesmann 84
Mantega, Guido 509
Maple 251, **G:19**
Marché à Termed'Instruments
    Financiers (MATIF) **G:19**
margin (futures) 416–20, **G:19**
margin account, futures 415–16
margin call 416, 419–20, 425, 457,
    G:19
marginal lending facility 291
marginal lending rate 291, **G:19**
marine insurance 531, **G:19**
Marine Protection & Indemnity
    Clubs *see* Protection &
    Indemnity (P&I) Clubs
Market Abuse Directive (2003)
    633, **G:19**
market capitalisation **G:19**
market equilibrium **G:19**
market fundamentalism 659, 660
market in managerial control 341,
    G:19
market index 392–6, **G:19**
market maker **G:20**
    exchange-traded funds 149–50
    gilt-edged 226
    index options 451
    investment banks 86, 88–90
    money markets 169

quote-driven trading 365
SETSqx 364
trading systems 360–1
market neutral 561, 576, **G:20**
market regulation 626–8
market risk 310
market segmentation hypothesis of
    the term structure of interest
    rates 274, **G:20**
Market Structure Practice 348
Marketguard 459
Markets in Financial Instruments
    Directive *see* Mifid
marking to market 90, 417–20,
    G:20
Marks & Spencer 22, 89, 393
Marshall Wace 572
master trusts 249–50
Mastercard 46
Matador 251, **G:20**
matched-bargain system *see* order-
    driven trading system
matching 500, **G:20**
matching principle **G:20**
mathematical tools for finance
    207–14
mathematicians 646–51
Matthews, Nick 303
maturity (maturity date, final
    maturity, redemption date)
    169, **G:20**
maturity transformation 18, **G:20**
Maughan, Simon 60
Mauri, Mauro 465
Maxwell, Robert 136
MBIA 247
McGrath, Rob 354
McKinsey 314
McNamara, Paul 607
McPhee, John 498
McRae, Tim 498
means of exchange 13, 172, **G:20**
Mearns, Alexander 570
Meat & Livestock Australia 498
Mediobanca 257
medium-dated bonds 221
medium-term note programme
    257, **G:20**
medium-term notes (MTNs) 51,
    83, 255–7, **G:20**
Melas, Dimitris 542
MEMC Electronics 588
merchant bank *see* investment
    bank
Merchant Navy Officers pension
    fund 134
merger arbitrage 577, **G:20**

mergers 341, 628, **G:20**
mergers and acquistions (M&As)
    G:20
    investment banking 79, 84–5
    syndicate lending 51, 52
Meridian 130
Meriwether, John 576–7
Merlin Entertainment 593
Merrill Lynch 302, 651, 661, 668,
    670, 671, 672
Merton, Robert 673
metric **G:20**
Metrick, Andrew 588
Metro 544
Metro-Goldwyn-Mayer 469
Mexico 184, 229, 238, 450–1, 534
Meyer-Witting, Kirsten 348
mezzanine finance 591, **G:20**
mezzanine tranche 663
MF Global 606
micro-prudential regulation 314,
    G:20
microfinance 101, **G:20**
middlemen *see* financial
    intermediaries
Mifid 342, 343, 344, 346, 347–8,
    363, 633, **G:20**
Milan 464–5
Milken, Michael 241
minimum standards 632
Mirror pension fund 136
misuse of information 605
Mitchell, Katy 390
Mitchells & Butlers 92, 631
Mizuko 78
MKP 577
MM *see* Main Market
mobile phone banking 47
mobilisation of savings **G:20**
Model Code for Directors'
    Dealings 386, **G:20**
Moec, Gilles 304, 317
monetary base 286, 288, **G:20**
monetary policy 285–300, **G:20**
Monetary Policy Committee
    (MPC) 318–19, 620, **G:20**
money 13–14, 15, 171–4
money laundering 631, **G:20**
Money Management 148
money market fund 637, **G:20**
money market hedge 501, 502, **G:20**
money markets 167–218, **G:20**
    banker's acceptances 197,
        198–200
    bills of exchange 197–8
    central banks 187
    certificates of deposit 195–6

commercial paper 187–90
credit ratings 190–2
Eurocurrency 178–80
funds 170–1
impact on our lives 5–6
interbank market 174–8
interest rates 168–9, 200–3
local authority/municipal bills
    195
repos 192–5
short-term money 169–70
Treasury bills 180–7
money supply 285, 286, 288–93
Mongolian Mining Corporation 11
monitoring of financial sector 616,
    622–4
Monk, Andrew 389
monoline insurance 666–7, **G:20**
monopoly 609, **G:20**
Moody's 190, 191, 239, 252, **G:20**
    bonds 226, 235, 236–7
    financial crisis 664, 668
moral hazard 609, **G:20**
    financial crisis 671, 672
    insurance 119
    lender of last resort 304, 305
moratorium 470, **G:20**
Morgan Stanley 26, 79
    Agricultural Bank of China
        IPO 24
    Basel III rules 313
    bulge bracket 81
    commercial paper 189
    corporate broking 88
    Federal Reserve Primary
        Dealer Credit Facility 302
    financial crisis 661, 672
    FX trading 485
    government funds 608
    mergers and acquisitions 84
    Mexican hedging 451
    multilateral trading facilities
        344
    proprietary trading 91
Moro, Anthony 356–7
Morparia, Kalpana 30
Morris, Peter 587–8
Morrison, Hank 499
mortgage-backed securities 248,
    249, 661, 662, 668, **G:20**
mortgage bank 103, **G:20**
mortgage bond 233, 248, **G:20**
mortgage companies,
    securitisation 246–7, 248
mortgage debentures 232, **G:20**
mortgage-style repayment
    schedule 43, 44, **G:20**

mortgages 41
    derivatives 413
    endowment 28, 120
    financial crisis 658, 661–2,
        667–70
    sub-prime *see* sub-prime
        mortgage
    swaps 463
    tracker 458–9
Moscow stock exchange 335
MPC *see* Monetary Policy
    Committee
MSCI Commodity Producers
    Indices 542
MSD Capital 566
MTF (multilateral trading facility)
    342–8, **G:20**
Mukherjee, Pranab 610
multibank dealing system 485, **G:21**
multi-currency programme188,
    G:20
multilateral approach to regulation
    613
multilateral netting 491, **G:21**
multilateral trading facility *see* MTF
Multiplan 593
multi-strategy 578, **G:21**
Munger, Charlie 647
Munich Re Group 123
municipal bills 195
municipal bonds 243
municipal debt **G:21**
murabaha 107
musharakah 107
mutual bank **G:21**
mutual funds 28, 152, **G:21**
mutual recognition 632
mutually owned organisations 27,
    100–3, 118, **G:21**
Myners, Lord 77, 78, 399

naked (uncovered) **G:21**
naked CDS 470–1, **G:21**
named peril policy 121, **G:21**
Names (Lloyd's of London) 126,
    127, 128–9, **G:21**
narrow money 286, **G:21**
NASDAQ (National Association
    of Securities Dealers
    Automated Quotation
    system) OMX 337, **G:21**
    average order size 352
    Chi-X 343
    collapse 581
    multilateral trading facilities
        342, 347
    smart order routing 346

National Air Traffic Control 334
National Association of Pension Funds 142, 368
national debt 316–17, **G:21**
National Fraud Authority (NFA) 630, **G:21**
National Savings **G:21**
National Venture Capital Association (NVCA) 581, **G:21**
National Welfare Fund (Russia) 157
Nationwide 65–6, 103, 249
Natixis 78
natural liquidity, money market funds 171
natural rate of unemployment (non-accelerating inflation rate of unemployment, NAIRU)295, **G:21**
Navy Federal Credit Union 102
NCB **G:21**
near-cash (near-money, quasi-money) 56, 170, **G:21**
near-equilibrium conditions 655
negative covenants 233, **G:21**
negotiability **G:21**
   certificates of deposit 195, 196
   money market instruments 168
Nelson, Lyndon 624
NEST (National Employment Savings Trust) 132, **G:21**
net assets (net worth, net asset value, NAV) **G:21**
   exchange-traded fund 149–50
   investment trusts 153–4
   mutual funds 152
   OEICs 149
   OEIVs 144
net current assets **G:21**
Net Interest Income (NII) 67, **G:21**
net interest margin (NIM) 65–6, **G:21**
net interest yield **G:21**
net profit (net income) **G:21**
net stable funding rule 314, **G:21**
net worth **G:21**
Netherlands
   credit rating 252
   financial crisis 672
   giro payments 46
   household and business lending 41
   insurance 122
   mutuals 100, 103
   pensions 138

netting 500, **G:21**
network effects 609
Network Rail 133, 256
NeuerMarkt 387, **G:21**
New Century Financial 658, 667
new issue 376, **G:21**
new issue market (NIM) 24, **G:21**
New Look 383
New York 30, 118, 484, 565
   importance as financial centre 10, 11, 12, 20
New York Board of Trade *see* NYBOT
New York Mercantile Exchange *see* NYMEX
newcits 152, 570, **G:21**
Newedge 194, 543
NFA *see* National Fraud Authority
Ng, Kester 11
Nikkei index/Nikkei 25 Stock Average 413, 418, 433, **G:21**
Nikpay, Ali 628, 629
nil paid rights **G:21**
NIM *see* net interest margin; new issue market
NINJA mortgages 669–70
Nixon, Richard 493
Noble 420
Noel family (Fairfield Greenwich) 568
Nomad *see* nominated adviser
nominal rate of interest 174
nominal return (or interest rate) **G:21**
nominal value *see* par value
nominated adviser (nomad) 388, 389, **G:21**
nominated brokers 388, **G:21**
nominee accounts **G:21**
nominee company 364, **G:21**
Nomura 78, 79, 82
   corporate broking 88
   mergers and acquisitions 84
   private equity 579
   Stewart, Rod 247
   takeover of Tricorn 82
non-executive directors 386–7
non-life insurance *see* general insurance
non-negotiable securities 174, 195, 196
non-proportional insurance *see* reinsurance
non-recourse **G:22**
non-voting shares 333, **G:22**
Nordic Capital 579
Norgrove, David 141, 629

Nortel 141
Northern Foods 415
Northern Rock 25, 57, 61, 314, **G:22**
   financial crisis 301, 304, 623, 661, 669, 672
   securitisation 247, 249, 250
Norway 157, 368, 532
note (promissory note) 233, **G:22**
note issuance facility (NIF, note purchase facility) 51–2, **G:22**
notional amount, forward rate agreements 465
notional trading requirement 455
   see also margin (futures)
Numis 383
NVCA *see* National Venture Capital Association
NYBOT (New York Board of Trade) 502, 536, **G:22**
NYMEX (New York Mercantile Exchange) 536, **G:22**
NYSE (New York Stock Exchange) **G:22**
   average order size 352
   exchange-traded funds 149
   multilateral trading facilities 342, 347
   open outcry trading 359
NYSE Euronext 337, 347, 350, **G:22**
NYSE Liffe *see* Euronext.liffe; LIFFE

O'Neill, Jim 92
O'Riordan, Tom 624
OATS (obligations assimilables du Tresor) 231, **G:22**
Obama, Barack 91–2
obligation **G:22**
obligation acceleration 470, **G:22**
Ocado 382–4
OECD (Organisation for Economic Co-operation and Development) 310, 509, **G:22**
Ofex **G:22**
off-balance-sheet finance 50–1, **G:22**
offer document **G:22**
offer for sale 380, 381, **G:22**
offer for subscription **G:22**
offer price **G:22**
   market makers 88–9
   spread betting 453
   unit trusts 145
offer rate 486–7

Office of Fair Trading (OFT) 78, 628–9, 630, **G:22**
Official List (OL), Main Market 377, 378, 388, **G:22**
offshore **G:22**
oil 450–1
Oil Stabilisation Fund (Russia) 157
oligopoly 609, **G:22**
ombudsman 147, 624–5, **G:22**
OMX 337, **G:22**
one share, one vote principle 333
Ongoing 334
ONS (Office for National Statistics) 366, 368, **G:22**
onshore fund **G:22**
open account trading 526, **G:22**
open-ended funds 28, **G:22**
open-ended investment companies (OEICs) 28, 29, 146, 148–9, **G:22**
open-ended investment vehicles (OEIVs) 144, **G:22**
open insurance policies 121
open market operations 187, 288–9, 290, 292, 319, **G:22**
open offer 403, **G:22**
open outcry 359, 360, 538, **G:22**
open policy **G:22**
open repo **G:22**
operating gearing see gearing
operating lease 106–7, **G:22**
operational deposits see required reserves
operational risk 310
opportunity cost of capital 168, **G:22**
option 7, 441–53, 471–9, **G:23**
 call option holder 443–6
 call option writers 446–7
 comparison with futures, forwards and FRAs 453, 454
 index options 451–3
 LIFFE share options 447, 448
 pricing 473–4
 put options 447–9
 share options 442–3, 449–51
option premium 442, **G:23**
 call options 443, 444, 446, 447
 put options 447
Orange 246
order book system see order-driven trading system
order-driven trading system 360, **G:23**
ordinary shares 330–1, **G:23**
 deferred 333
originate-and-distribute model 662, 669, **G:23**

originate-and-hold model 662, **G:23**
Osaka 413, 414, 418, 433
Osborne, David 130
Osborne, George 319, 614
OTC see over-the-counter (OTC) trade
other early-stage (private equity) 585, **G:23**
out-of-the-money option 444, **G:23**
over-subscription **G:23**
over-the-counter (OTC) trade 24, **G:23**
 commodities 547
 corporate bonds 232
 derivatives 414, 422–4
 Eurobonds 255
 forwards 414
 FX 481
overdraft 42–3, 49, **G:23**
overnight 171, **G:23**
overseas trade 53

Pacific Life Re 133
Page, Larry 333
Panama canal 529
panamax **G:23**
Panda 251, **G:23**
Pantheon 588
paper **G:23**
par value (nominal, principal, stated book or face value) **G:23**
 bonds 224, 258
 money markets 168
 shares 404
 Treasury bills 180
Pardue, Charles 666
Paris 11
Paris Expori 461–3
participating (preference share) 332, **G:23**
Partner Re Ltd 123, 133
partnership **G:23**
pass-throughs 249
passive fund see tracker fund
passive management **G:23**
Paulson, Hank 80, 93
Paulson, John 557, 559, 568, 574, 594, **G:17**
Paulson & Co 558, 568, 574
pay-as-you-go (PAYG) pension schemes 131–2, 136
Payden&Rygel Global 130
payment in advance 526
payment mechanism 318, **G:23**

payment on shipment 526
payment versus payment (PvP) 491, **G:23**
PEIT see private equity investment trust
Peloton Partners 574
Pemex 238
penalties 616
Pension Act (2008, UK) 132
pension deficit 132–3, **G:23**
pension fund asset holdings 138–40
pension funds 27, **G:23**
 commodities 545
 junk bonds 242
 regulation 629
 trustees, consultants and managers 136–7
 UK share market 366
Pension Funds Directive 142, **G:23**
pension holiday **G:23**
Pension Insurance Corporation (PIC) 133, 134
Pension Protection Fund (PPF, UK) 141, 142, 629, **G:23**
pension scheme 55, 116–17, 131–42, 158–66, **G:23**
Pensions Institute 137
Pensions Regulator (UK) 140–1, 629, **G:23**
People's Bank of China 64, 293
perfect hedge 452, 503, **G:23**
Perform xvi–xvii
performance fee 565–8, **G:23**
permanent capital 55, **G:23**
Permira 579, 588
perpetual see irredeemable
perpetuity 213, **G:23**
personal guarantee 45, **G:23**
personal loan see consumer loan
personal pension (private pension) 135, **G:23**
Peter Hamro Mining 393
petro-dollar recycling 659
Petropavlosk 393
Pets at Home 593
Pfandbriefe 250, **G:23**
Pfeffer, John 593
Philippines 251–2
Photo-Me International 385–6
physical delivery (physical settlement) 469, **G:23**
Picard Surglés 593
Pictet&Cie 97
piece see lot
Pierce, Jonathan 60, 66
piggyback mortgages 661

Pignatellis, Sean 606
Pioneer 545
pip 486, **G:23**
placing, place or placement 381,
    383, 403, **G:23**
plain vanilla 232, **G:23**
plant hire 107
platform **G:23**
Platinum Grove 574
Plc *see* public limited company
PLUS-Markets Group plc 377,
    389–90, 590, **G:24**
political risk 51, 527, **G:24**
Ponzi schemes 557, 568–9
pool **G:24**
pooled funds 116–17, 142–66,
    G:24
Popper, Karl 652
Porta, Giorgio 465
portfolio investment **G:24**
portfolio manager 152
Portugal 173, 202, 298, 303, 334–5
Portugal Teleco 334–5
post offices 16, 46
PotashCorp 87
PPP *see* purchasing power parity
    (PPP) theory of exchange
    rate determination
PRA *see* Prudential Regulatory
    Authority
Prache, Guillaume 348
Prada 11
pre-emption rights 396–401, **G:24**
    waiving of 403
precious metal **G:24**
preference share 332–3, **G:24**
preferred ordinary shares **G:24**
preliminary annual results
    (preliminary profit
    announcements, prelims)
    386, **G:24**
premium **G:24**
    bonds 258
    caps 458
    foreign exchange 488
    insurance 118, 120, 121–3
    investment trusts
    options 442
        call options 443, 444, 446,
        447
        put options 447
prepayment (payment in advance,
    payment on shipment) 526,
    G:24
present value 209, **G:24**
price discovery 341, **G:24**

price–earnings ratio (PER, price–
    earnings multiple, PE
    multiple, PE ratio, P/E ratio)
    G:24
price formation 341, **G:24**
price limit 425, **G:24**
price-sensitive information 385–6,
    388, **G:24**
Primark 495
primary dealer **G:24**
primary financial market 20, 24
primary investors 14, **G:24**
primary market 357–9, **G:24**
primary security 16
prime broker 97, 578, **G:24**
prime grade *see* investment grade
    debt
Prince, Chuck 668
principal **G:24**
Pritchard, Mark 381
private banking 12, 97, **G:24**
private-client representative 96,
    G:24
private equity fund 23, 29, 637,
    G:24
private equity investment 97,
    556–8, 578–601
private equity investment trust
    (PEIT) 590
private limited company (Ltd)
    G:24
private pension *see* personal
    pension
private placement 558
private–public partnerships (PPPs)
    86
privatisation 86, 335, **G:24**
Procter & Gamble 52, 382, 413
professional securities market 357,
    G:24
professional services 12
profit and loss account effect,
    translation risk 497
profit warnings 627–8
project finance 50–1, **G:24**
promissory note 187, **G:24**
property insurance 121
proportional reinsurance *see*
    reinsurance
proprietary platform 485, **G:24**
proprietary transactions
    (proprietary trading) 87,
    90–3, 484, 558, **G:24**
prospectus 380, **G:24**
Protection & Indemnity (P&I)
    Clubs 124, 125, **G:24**

Protégé Partners 569
provision **G:25**
Prudential 84, 133, 134
prudential limits 616
Prudential Regulatory Authority
    (PRA) 59, 615, 620, **G:25**
prudential supervision 306–7, **G:25**
public limited company (Plc) **G:25**
public pension 136, **G:25**
public relations, flotation process
    380
public-to-private (PTP) 586, **G:25**
publicity issues, quoted firms 341
pull to par (pull to maturity, pull
    to redemption) 258, **G:25**
Punch Taverns 606
purchasing power parity (PPP)
    theory of exchange rate
    determination 507–10, 512,
    G:25
pure rate of interest 172–3
put features *see* put options
put options 447–9, **G:25**
    currency option hedge 504
    Eurobonds 255
    hedging 449–50, 451, 453
Putnis, Jan 624
PvP *see* payment versus payment

Qatar Financial Centre Authority 9
Quakers 108
qualified purchasers **G:25**
qualitative analysis **G:25**
quantitative analysis **G:25**
quantitative easing 299–300, **G:25**
Quantum Fund 559, 578, 652
quasi-money *see* near-cash
quaternary buyout 592, 593, **G:25**
Queen, Michael 579
quote currency *see* secondary
    currency
quote-driven trading system 88–9,
    360, 364–5, **G:25**
quoted **G:25**

Rabobank Nederland 103, 252,
    G:25
Raffan, Michael 624
Ralfe, John 141
random walk theory **G:25**
ranking (debt) **G:25**
rate of return 263–4
rating *see* credit rating
ratings arbitrage 665
Rausing, Jörn 382
RBS Hoare Govett 88

RCO Holdings 627
Readers Digest International 141
Reagan, Ronald/Reaganism 659, 660
real rate of interest 174
real rate of return **G:25**
real-time gross settlement (RTGS) system 47
realised gain 90, **G:25**
receivable (accounts receivable) **G:25**
receiver 232, **G:25**
recognised investment exchange (RIE) 626, **G:25**
recourse **G:25**
recourse finance 50, 198, **G:25**
recoverability of debt 235, **G:25**
redeemable bonds 259
redeemable preference shares 332
redemption 182, **G:25**
redemption date 224
redemption fee **G:25**
redemption yield *see* yield to maturity
reduced voting shares 333, **G:25**
reference entity 468, **G:25**
reference obligation 468, **G:25**
reflexivity 652–60, **G:25**
registrar 379, **G:25**
regulation 602–44, **G:25**
    financial crisis 636, 660, 669
Regulation Q of the US Banking Act (1933) 179
regulatory arbitrage 310, 613, **G:25**
Regulatory News Service (RNS) 342, **G:25**
Reid, Robert 498
reinsurance 118, 123–4, **G:25**
relationship banking 44, **G:25–6**
relationship manager 85, **G:26**
relative return 561, **G:26**
relative value *see* long/short strategy
Relative Value Fixed Income Convertible Arbitrage Index 576–7
Relative Value Opportunity II 576–7
Reliance Industries 610
Rembrandt 251, **G:26**
Renaissance Technologies 559
Renminbi sovereign bonds **G:26**
Rentokil Initial 627
repayment holiday *see* grace period
repo *see* repurchase agreement **G:26**

reporting accountant 379, **G:26**
representative office 98, **G:26**
repudiation 470, **G:26**
repurchase agreement (repo) 192–5, 289, 670, **G:26**
repurchase of share 592, **G:26**
required reserves 55–6, 285, **G:26**
required reserves ratio 286, 292–3, **G:26**
required return 173
rescheduling (restructuring) finance 45, **G:26**
Reserve Bank of India (RBI) 610–11
Reserve Primary Fund 171, 671
reserves 55–60, **G:26**
    safe level 307–9
    supply and demand 289–90
resolution regime 304
restrictions on activities 616
restrictive covenants *see* negative covenants
restructuring costs **G:26**
restructuring of business loans 45
retail banking 25, 40–9, 67–74, **G:26**
retail financial markets **G:26**
Retail Price Index (RPI) 228, **G:26**
retirement age 131, 136
retrocession 124, **G:26**
return on assets (ROA) 63, **G:26**
return on capital employed (ROCE) **G:26**
return on equity (ROE) 64, 78, **G:26**
return on investment (ROI) **G:26**
Reuters-Jefferies CRB index 545
revenue bonds 243, **G:26**
reverse floater (reverse floating-rate notes) 254, **G:26**
reverse repo 192–3, 289, **G:26**
reverse takeover 381, **G:26**
reversing the trade *see* closing out a futures position
revolving credit, revolving credit facility (RCF) 49–50, 188, **G:26**
revolving underwriting facility (RUF) 51–2, 188, **G:26**
Reynolds, Barney 635, 636
Riba **G:26**
Richard, Dough 584
RIE *see* recognised investment exchange
right to exchange 243, **G:26**
rights issue 24, 396–402, 403, **G:26**
ring (commodities) 538, **G:26**

ring fencing 622, **G:26**
ringgit **G:26**
Rio Tinto 399
risk 173, 413, **G:27**
risk arbitrage **G:26**
risk averter **G:26**
risk-free rate of return (RFR) 173, **G:27**
risk lover (seeker) **G:26**
risk management 85, **G:26**
risk premium 173–4, **G:26**
risk spreader 28–9, **G:26–7**
risk taker 29–30
risk transfer 50
risk transformation 16, **G:27**
risk-weighted assets (RWAs) 309, 313–14
roadshow **G:27**
Robledo, Alfredo 464, 465
Rogers index 542
Rok 627
Rolet, Xavier 345, 362
roll over 188, **G:27**
rolled-over overdraft 49, **G:27**
rolling cash spread betting, rolling daily bets 456, **G:27**
rolling settlement **G:27**
Rolls-Royce 86, 334, 344
Roman, Emmanuel 570
Ross, Donald 239
Ross, Thomas 470
Rothschild 82
Rothschild, N.M. 86
Roubini, Nouriel 666
Royal Bank of Scotland (RBS) 37
    capital position 312
    central banking 305
    Corporate Banking 104
    financial crisis 63, 86, 666, 672
    fine 628–9
    FX trading 485
    net interest margin 65, 66
    takeover of ABN Amro 84
    taxpayer-owned shares 304
    toxic assets 79, 86
Royal Dutch Shell 425, 426
Royal Exchange Assurance 118
Royal Mail Group 334
Royal Mint 317, **G:31**
RPI *see* Retail Price Index
RSA 134
RTGS (real time gross settlement) **G:27**
running yield *see* yield
Rusnak, John 484
Russia 157, 180, 184, 229, 357

S&P 500 (Standard & Poor's 500)
4, 392, 451, **G:27**, **G:29**
S&P GSCI 542, 543, **G:27**
Sa'id, Helmy Omar 626, 627
SABMiller 394
SAC Capital 559
safe haven **G:27**
safety deposits 54
safety of financial institutions/
products 604–5
Sainsbury's 22
Saintfiet, Guy 139
sale and leaseback **G:27**
sale and repurchase agreement *see*
repurchase agreement
sales charge *see* initial charge
sales ledger administration 105,
G:27
Saluzzi, Joe 354
Sampdoria 232
Samurai bonds 251–2, **G:27**
San Francisco 12
Sands, Peter 312
Santander 100, 103, 306, 312
Sants, Hector 615, 623
Sarbanes–Oxley Act (2002, USA)
387, **G:27**
Sarnver brothers 584
Saudi Arabia 108
Saunders, Neil 495
Savage, Luke 130
Savills Private Finance 459
savings and loan bank 27, 102,
G:27
savings bank (US) 27, 102, **G:27**
Schack, Justin 351
Schäuble, Wolfgang 300
Schema Ventotto 257
Schoar, Antoinette 587
Scila 347
SCOR 123
Scott, Andrew 512
Scott, Bob 141
scrip dividends 404, **G:27**
scrip issue 404, **G:27**
SdK 348
SDRs *see* special drawing rights
Seah, Shi Pei 510
SEAQ (Stock Exchange Automated
Quotations) 364–5, **G:27**
search costs 15, **G:27**
seasoned equity offerings (SEOs)
83, **G:27**
Seat 246
SEC *see* Securities and Exchange
Commission
Second Banking Directive (1989)
633, **G:27**

second-tier markets 387, **G:27**
secondary buyout 592, 593, **G:27**
see also buyout
secondary currency 486
secondary market 20, 24, **G:27**
bonds 224, 228, 231, 232, 255,
258
London Stock Exchange 359
money market instruments
168, 180, 188, 198
Treasury securities 289
warrants 405
secondary market trading facility
G:27
secondary purchase 586, **G:27**
Securities and Exchange
Commission (SEC) **G:27**
commercial paper 189
credit-rating agencies 239
e-trading 350
financial crisis 651
flash crash 350, 351
hedge funds 561–2
mutual funds 152
regulation of financial sector
606, 608, 623
securities house **G:27**
securitisation 95–6, 246–50, 637,
G:27
security **G:27**
Security First Network Bank 47
security market line (SML) **G:27**
SEDOL (Stock Exchange Daily
Official List) **G:27**
seedcorn (private equity) 585,
G:27
self-amortising 43, **G:27**
self invested personal pension
(SIPP) 135, **G:27**
self-managed investment trusts
153
self-regulation 612, **G:27**
self-selection bias, hedge fund
indices 572
sell-side 97, **G:27**
selling the rights nil paid **G:28**
semi-annual 262, **G:28**
semi-captives 591, **G:28**
semi-sovereign bonds *see* sub-
sovereign bonds
semi-strong efficiency 514, **G:28**
Sen, Amrita 545
senior debt *see* subordinated debt
senior tranche 663
separate legal person **G:28**
Serious Fraud Office (SFO) 630–1,
G:28

Serious Organised Crime Agency
(SOCA) 630, 631, **G:28**
SETS (Stock Exchange Electronic
Trading System) 360–1, 364,
G:28
SETSqx364, 365, **G:28**
settlement 341, 361-4, 420–2,
469–71, 491, **G:28**
settlement price 422, **G:28**
SG Warburg 257
shadow banking system 620, 637,
670, **G:28**
Shafir, Rob 78–9
Shah, Mitesh 470
Shanghai 10, 11, 335, 336, 357
Shapiro, Mary 239
share 4, 331, **G:28**
borrowing, lending and
shorting 366
development 14
ordinary 330–1
ownership (UK) 366–8
preference 332–3
unusual types of 333–5
see also equity markets
share buy-back (share repurchase)
331, 404–5, **G:28**
share call options 443
share capital, raising 375–411
Alternative Investment Market
387–9
financial pages, understanding
the 390–6, 397–8
Main Market 376–87
placings, open offers and
clawback 403
PLUS 389–90
rights issues 396–402
scrip issues, scrip dividends,
splits and consolidation 404
share buy-backs and special
dividends 404–5
warrants 405
share certificate **G:28**
share dealing by directors 386
share markets 4–5, 94, **G:28**
share option scheme **G:28**
share options 442–3, 449–51
share split (stock split) 404, **G:28**
shareholder 331, 340, **G:28**
shareholder wealth maximisation
G:28
shareholders' funds (equity) **G:28**
Sharia, Shari'ah law 107–8, 257–8,
G:28
shell company **G:28**
Shenzhen 10, 11, 335, 336–7

shipping 523–4, 528–33, 550–5
shipping finance 532–3, **G:28**
Shore Capital 627
short position **G:28**
    futures 414, 425
    hedge funds 559, 560, 575–6
short selling 29, 366, **G:28**
short term 169–70, **G:28**
short-term interest rate future 427–30, **G:28**
short-term interest rate (STIR) products 169, **G:28**
short-term sterling interest rate future (short sterling) **G:28**
short-termism **G:28**
shorting 366, **G:28**
    see also short selling
shorts 221, **G:28**
    bonds 221
SIBOR (Singapore Interbank Offered Rate) 178, **G:28**
SICOM (Singapore Commodity Exchange) 536, **G:28**
side pocket (hedge funds) 563–4, **G:28**
Sifi (systemically important financial institutions) 304, 305, **G:28**
sight bank account (current account, cheque/check account) 40, **G:28**
sight drafts 198, **G:28**
Sihuan Pharmaceutical Holdings 11
Silicon Valley **G:28**
silver 549, 550
Silver Lake Partners 593
Silverstone master trust 249
Simmons 593
simple interest 207, **G:28**
simple yield *see* yield
Singapore
    depositary receipts 356, 357
    derivatives exchange 413, 418, 433
    financial market activity 12, 13
    FX market 483, 484
    importance as financial centre 10, 12
    interbank lending 178
    proprietary trading 92
    sovereign wealth funds 157
    stock exchange 337
Singh, Manmohan 30, 31
single stock futures 425–6, **G:28**
sinking fund 234, **G:28**
Sinochem 87

SIS x-clear **G:28**
Sketch, Nick 156
skimmed milk powder futures contract 540
Skype 340, 584, 594
Skyrm, Scott 194
small claims court 625, **G:29**
smart cards (electronic purses, chip cards) 47, **G:29**
smart order routing 345, 346, **G:29**
SNCF 195, 243
SOCA *see* Serious Organised Crime Agency
SociétéGénérale 92, 242, 313, 413, 550
Sócrates, José 334
Sofia stock exchange 335
soft commodity **G:29**
Solca, Luca 495
solvency **G:29**
Solvency II 123, 621–2, 634, **G:29**
solvency risk 307
SONIA (Sterling Overnight Interbank Average) 178, **G:29**
Soros, George 559, 578, 594, 652–3, 654–8, 660, **G:15**
soundness of financial institutions/ products 604–5
South Korea 238
sovereign bonds 94, 222
Sovereign Wealth Fund 156, 157, **G:29**
SP Bell 617
Spain
    asset-backed securities 248
    covered bonds 250
    European Central Bank 298, 303
    Exchange Rate Mechanism 493
    financial crisis 659, 666
    household and business lending 41
    mutuals 101–2
    Super Fondos 54
Spajic, Luke 470, 471
Sparkassen 101, **G:29**
special dividend 405, **G:29**
special drawing rights (SDRs) 200, 488, **G:29**
Special Liquidity Scheme 669, **G:29**
special purpose vehicle/entity (SPV/SPE) 50, **G:29**
    collateralised debt obligations 662–3
    commercial paper 189
    investment banking 95

securitisation 247–8
sukuk 257, 258
special resolution 403, **G:29**
specialist funds 357, **G:29**
speculate 431–3, 511–12, **G:29**
speculative bubble *see* bubble
speculative grade **G:29**
speculative motive for holding cash **G:29**
spinning 605, **G:29**
spiraling 124, **G:29**
sponsor 378, 383, **G:29**
spot market 7, 272–3, **G:29**
spot rate of interest *see* spot market
spot trading 95, **G:29**
spot transactions, FX 481, 482, 488
spread **G:29**
    bonds 235
    exchange-traded funds 150
    FX 486–7
    spread betting 453, 455
    unit trusts 145
spread betting 453–6, **G:29**
Square Mile 354, 355, **G:29**
Squires, Gary 141
Staffware 627
Stagg, Nick 389
stakeholder **G:29**
stakeholder pension 135, **G:29**
stamp duty **G:29**
Standard & Poor's 189, 190, 191, 239, 252, **G:29**
    bonds 226, 235, 236–7
    financial crisis 664, 668
Standard & Poor's 500 *see* S&P 500
Standard Chartered 312–13, 356, 357, 579
standard deviation **G:29**
Standard Life 250
standard variable rate (SVR) **G:29**
standardisation (commodities) 536–8, **G:29**
standing facilities 291, **G:29**
standing order 46, **G:29**
Starbucks 589
start-up capital 585, **G:29**
state-owned banks 54
status issues, quoted firms 341
statutory **G:29**
Steiner, Tim 382, 383
sterling **G:29**
sterling bonds **G:29**
Stewart, Rod 247
STIR *see* short-term interest rate products
stock 331, **G:29**
    see also gilts; share

stock exchange 4, **G:29**
    comparison of major markets
       337–8, 339
    growth 335–7
    importance of 337, 338–42
    nature of 335
    tasks 341–2
Stock Exchange Automated
    Quotations *see* SEAQ
Stock Exchange Electronic Trading
    System *see* SETS
stock market *see* stock exchange
stock split *see* share split
stockbrokers 54, **G:29**
    see also brokers
stockholder *see* shareholder
stocks and shares **G:30**
Stonehenge 463
stop-loss order 455–6, 457, **G:30**
store cards 46, **G:30**
store of value (finance) 172, **G:30**
straddle 418, **G:30**
straight bond 232, **G:30**
straight fixed-rate Eurobonds 254
strategic position **G:30**
strategic review **G:30**
Straub, Alexander 584
Strauss-Kahn, Dominique 510
strike bid **G:30**
strike price 380, 444, **G:30**
    options *see* exercise price
strips (Separate Trading of
    Registered Interest and
    Principal of Securities)
    bonds 245–6, **G:30**
strong form efficiency 514, **G:30**
structural unemployment 295,
    G:30
structured investment vehicle
    (SIV) 189, 190, **G:30**
    financial crisis 664, 665–6, 668
Studzinski, John 79
subordinated debt (junior debt)
    45, 233, 235, 240, **G:30**
sub-prime mortgage 302, 661, 667,
    668, 669–70, **G:30**
sub-sovereign bonds **G:30**
subscription rights **G:30**
subsidiary 100, **G:30**
Sucden Financial 621
Suez canal 529
sugar 535
sukuk 257–8, **G:30**
summary financial statements
    G:30
Sun Fire Office 118
Sun Microsystems 589

super angels 584
super-bubble 659, 660
supermarket banking services 22
supertanker **G:30**
supervision 603, **G:30**
    see also regulation
supply curve 268–70, **G:30**
survivorship bias, hedge fund
    indices 572, 573
SVR *see* standard variable rate
swap 441–2, 459–72, 474–9, 482,
    G:30
swaption (swap-option) 464, 482,
    G:30
Sweden 41, 622
sweep facility 170, **G:30**
sweetener *see* equity kicker
SWIFT (Society for Worldwide
    Interbank Financial
    Telecommunication) 47,
    G:30
Swiss Re Group 123, 133
Switzerland 54, 289, 313, 422, 483
syndicate **G:30**
syndicated loan 51, 52, **G:30**
synthetic CDOs of ABS 664
systematic (undiversifiable/
    market/residual) risk 90,
    G:30
systemic risk 304, **G:30**
Syyrila, Jarkko 557, 558

T+3 *see* three-day rolling
    settlement
Taiwan 357
takeover (acquisition) **G:30**
Takeover Panel **G:30**
Taleb, Nicolas 650
tangible assets **G:30**
TARGET/TARGET 2 (Trans-
    European Automated
    Real-time Gross Settlement
    Express Transfer System)
    47, **G:30**
target financing rate 319, **G:30**
tariff **G:30**
Tata Group 610
tax allowance **G:30**
tax avoidance **G:30**
tax evasion **G:30**
tax haven 118, **G:30**
tax shield **G:30**
taxable profit **G:30**
taxation, preference shares 332,
    333
Taylor, Brian 347
TechMARK357, 377, **G:31**

technical analysis **G:31**
technological innovations 22–3
Telecom Italia/Telecom Italia
    Mobile 246, 256
Telefónica 334, 356
telephone banking 47, **G:31**
Temasek (Singapore) 157
tender offer **G:31**
Tennessee Valley Authority (TVA)
    464
TER *see* total expense ratio
term assurance 28, 120, **G:31**
term loan 43–4, 49, **G:31**
term securities 196, **G:31**
term structure of interest rates
    271–4, **G:31**
terminal value **G:31**
Terra Firma 80, 588
tertiary buyout 592, 593, **G:31**
Tesco 22, 258
Tett, Gillian 666
Thatcher, Margaret/Thatcherism
    86, 659
TheCityUK **G:31**
Theleme Partners 566
Themis Trading 354
Thomas Cook 393
Thomson Reuters 84
Thomson Reuters/Jefferies
    Commodities Research
    Bureau Index 542
Threadneedle 242
three-day rolling settlement (T+3)
    363, **G:31**
thrift bank 102, **G:31**
Thwaites 389
TIBOR (Tokyo Interbank Offered
    Rate) 178, **G:31**
tick 429, **G:31**
tier 1 capital 309–10, 311, **G:31**
time charter **G:31**
time deposit (term deposit, fixed
    deposit, savings account) 40,
    195, **G:31**
time value 443, **G:31**
time value of money 172–4, **G:31**
TMX 337
TNK-BP 238
Tokyo 484
Tokyo Stock Exchange *see* TSE
Tolckmitt, Jens 250, 251
Tomlinson, Lindsay 78
too big to fail problem 304–6
Tookey, Tim 66
Torex Retail 631
Toronto 12
Tory, Michael 82

total capitalisation *see* market
capitalisation
total expense ratio (TER) 154,
G:31
total shareholder return (TSR,
total return) **G:31**
totalitarian directed economy 340
touch prices *see* yellow strip
Towerbrooke 593
toxic waste *see* equity tranche
Toyota 258
TPG 588
tracker fund 145, **G:31**
trade 523–8, 550–5, **G:31**
    exports, payment for 524–7
    FX risk 528
    growth of 524, 525, 529
trade acceptance 526
trade bill *see* bill of exchange
trade credit **G:31**
trade debtor **G:31**
trade execution 97, **G:31**
trade receivables **G:31**
    see also debtors
trade sale 592, **G:31**
traded option **G:31**
trading floor 360, **G:31**
trading income 90, **G:31**
trading speed 348–51
Trafigura 420
trail commission 145, **G:31**
transaction risk 497, 499–506,
    G:31
transactional banking 44, **G:31**
Transatlantic Holdings Inc. 123
translation risk 497, 506–7, **G:31**
Transparency Directive (2004)
    633, **G:31**
Transport for London 243
Travelers 39
traveller's cheques 55
Treasury bill 5–6, 40, 180–7, **G:31**
Treasury bond 231, 300, **G:31**
Treasury department 184–5, **G:31**
    UK 615, 669
    USA 671, 672
Treasury Direct 184
Treasury Inflation-Protected
    Securities (TIPS) 231, **G:31**
Treasury management **G:31**
Treasury note 228–31, **G:31**
Treasury securities 289
Tremont Capital 569
Trethowan, Ross 498
Trew, Pat 574
Trichet, Jean-Claude 298, 299, 303,
    304, 317

Tricorn Partners 82
triple-A money market funds 171
triple play, investment banking 80
Trippitt, Mike 65, 66
Troubled Asset Relief Program
    (TARP) 671
Troy ounce **G:31**
Truell, Edmund 133
trust deed 233, **G:32**
trustees **G:32**
    bond sinking funds 234
    pension funds 136
    trust deeds 233
    unit trusts 147
TSE (Tokyo Stock Exchange) 231,
    337, 342–3, **G:32**
Tudor Investment Corporation 567
tulipmania 544, **G:32**
Tüngler, Marco 348
Turkey 238
Turner, Lord 306, 614
turnover (revenue or sales) **G:32**
Turquoise 342, 344, 349, 353, **G:32**
Tussauds 247, 383, 593

UBM 257
UBS (Union Bank of Switzerland)
    11, 26, 82
    capital and liquidity adequacy
    313
    corporate broking 88
    financial crisis 666, 670
    FX trading 485
    Lloyds rights issue 401
    mergers and acquisitions 84
    Ocado flotation 383
    privatisation 86
    SG Warburg 257
    swaps 464, 465
    toxic assets 79
UCITS (Undertakings for
    Collective Investment in
    Transferable Securities) 152,
    562, 569–72, **G:32**
UK Financial Investments (UKFI)
    86
UK Payments Council 47, **G:32**
UK pounds to euro exchange rate
    (2001–11) 6
UKLA (UK Listing Authority) 342,
    G:32
    Main Market, floating on the
    376, 377–8, 379, 380, 383
    post-listing obligations 385–7
Ukraine 229
ultimate borrowers 15, **G:32**
umbrella structure **G:32**

uncommitted facility 49, **G:32**
uncommitted line of credit 49,
    G:32
uncovered (naked) call option
    writing 447, **G:32**
undated gilts 224
underlying 413, 417–18, 420, **G:32**
Undertakings for Collective
    Investment in Transferable
    Securities *see* UCITS
underwriters **G:32**
    commercial banks 23
    flotation process 378
    insurance 119
    investment banks 83
    origins of term 118
unemploymentand monetary
    policy 295, 296, 299, 300
unfunded pension scheme (pay-as-
    you-go, PAYG) 131–2, **G:32**
Unica 535
Unicredit 79
unilateral approach to regulation
    613
uninformed investors **G:32**
Union BancairePrivée 569
unit of account 172, **G:32**
unit trust 18, 28, 144–8, **G:32**
Unitas Capita 579
United Kingdom
    bank base rate (2001–11) 7, 8
    bank liquidity rule change
    59–60
    banking 37, 48, 65–6, 78
    bonds 3
        debentures 232
        Eurobonds 253, 257
        gilts 223–8
        local authority 243
        strips 246
        term structure of interest
        rates 271
    building societies 100, 102–3
    card v. cheque transactions 46
    central banking
        Basel III rules 313
        depositor insurance 301
        inflation 295, 296
        quantitative easing 299
        reserves, supply and demand
        of 289
        standing facilities 291
        see also Bank of England
    clearing systems 47
    coins, issue of 317
    collective investments 143,
        144, 147, 148, 153

United Kingdom (*continued*)
  corporate broking 87
  credit rating 229
  custodians 158
  endowment mortgages 28
  equity markets
    average order size 352
    clearing and settlement
      363–4
    golden shares 334
    history 330, 354
    multilateral trading facilities
      342
    reduced voting shares 333
    share ownership 366–8
  Exchange Rate Mechanism 578
  exports, finance's importance
    in 30
  factoring 104
  financial crisis 301, 302, 669,
    671
    Basel III rules 313
    credit expansion 659
    government actions 672
    internationalisation of risk
      666
  financial market activity 13
  FTSE indices 392–6
  FX market 482, 483, 493, 495
  funeral fees 247
  GDP 22, 23, 222
  government rescue of Royal
    Bank of Scotland and Lloyds
    63
  growth of financial services
    20–1
  hedge funds 565
  hire purchase 106
  household and business
    lending 41
  index options 451
  insurance 117, 121, 122–3
  interest rates (1981–2011) 202
  international banks, Turner
    proposals 306
  investment trusts 29
  Islamic banking 108
  life assurance companies 28
  money markets 174–7, 180–5,
    196
  national debt 316
  overdrafts 42
  payment mechanisms 18
  pensions 27, 131–2, 135, 136,
    137, 138–41, 142
  political party donations 637

  Post Office 16
  private equity funds 29, 579–
    80, 581, 583, 587, 589
  project finance 50
  proprietary trading 92, 93
  public spending (2010) 492
  regulation of financial sector
    606, 609, 611–12, 614–31
  rights issues 396, 399, 400,
    401, 403
  securitisation 248–50
  share capital, raising 376–90
  share market price movements
    (1990–2011) 4
  shipping 528–9, 532
  speculators 433
  stockbroking 54
  super tax on bank bonuses 12,
    91
  Treasury bills 5–6
  unit of account 172
  unit trusts 28
  see also City of London
United Nations Conference on
  Trade and Development
  (UNCTAD) **G:32**
United States of America
  bank liquidity rule change 60
  banking 37, 39, 48, 97–8
    investment 79, 81–2, 87,
      91–2, 93, 96–7
  bonds 238, 275
    covered 250–1
    debentures 233
    Eurobonds 253, 257
    junk 240, 241–2
    mortgage bonds 233
    municipal 243
    notes 233
    strips 246
    term structure of interest
      rates 271
    Treasury notes and bonds
      228–31
  book-building 381
  central banking 289, 296,
    299–300, 301
    see also Federal Reserve
    Bank
  clearing systems 47, 49
  collective investments 143
  corn crop 534
  corporate broking 87
  credit rating agencies 239
  Dodd-Frank financial reform
    act 305

  equity markets 338, 342, 347,
    349, 350, 352, 353
    clearing and settlement 361,
      362, 363
  exchange traded funds 149,
    543
  financial crisis 302, 666
    Basel III rules 313
    Bear Stearns 669–70
    crash 667, 669–71
    credit expansion 659
    globalisation of financial
      markets 659, 660
    government actions 671–2
    housing bubble 658–9
    interest rates 660–1
    mortgage market 661, 667,
      668, 669–70
  financial market activity 12, 13
  futures, buying and selling 425
  FX market 482, 483, 493, 514
  hedge funds 561–2, 564, 570
  index options 451
  insurance 117, 122
  interest rates (1981–2011) 203
  Kyoto treaty 548
  market indices 392
  merchant banking 81
  money markets 171
    certificates of deposit 196
    commercial paper 188–9
    Eurocurrency 179
    interbank market 178
    local authority bills 195
    repos 194–5
    Treasury bills 5, 184–6
  mutuals 28, 102, 152
  over-the-counter derivatives
    424
  pensions 131, 138, 139, 141
  political party donations 637
  private equity 581, 582, 589
  proprietary trading 91–2, 93
  regulation of financial sector
    604, 606, 608–9, 623, 624
  rights issues 399, 403
  Sarbanes–Oxley regulations
    387
  securitisation 247, 248
  share market price movements
    (1990–2011) 4
  sub-prime mortgages 247
  underwriting 83
universal banks 37, 39, **G:32**
University Superannuation
  Scheme (USS) 27, 133, 139

unlisted 24, **G:32**
unquoted *see* unlisted
unquoted firms 578, **G:32**
unrealised gain 90, **G:32**
unsecured 41, **G:32**
US dollar, in FX market 483, 491, 492–3

Vale 238
valuation risk (price risk) **G:32**
value at risk (VaR) 649–51, **G:32**
value of the financial system 1–35
vanilla bond *see* straight bond
Vantage Capital 385
variable rate 232, 333, **G:32**
variation margin 417, 419, **G:32**
vault cash 56, 286, 289, **G:32**
Vedanta Resources 393, 394
Velentza, Maria 347
Vellucci, Michael 420
vendor placing 403, **G:32**
venture capital (VC) 97, 340, 578, 585, 589, **G:32**
   see also private equity
venture capital fund **G:32**
venture capital trusts (VCTs) 153, 590, **G:32**
Venture Production 243–4
Verdict 495
VereinigteOostindischeCompagnie (VOC) 329–30
Vietnam 335
Vicary-Smith, Peter 608
Vipond, Peter 622
Virgin Money 22
Visa 46
Viterra 80
Vivo 334–5
Vodafone 84, 170, 246
voice broker trades 485, 486, **G:32**
Volcker, Paul 91, 673
Volcker rule 91
volume transformation 18, **G:32**
vulture capitalist **G:32**
VW 334

Wace, Ian 572
Waddell & Reed 351
Waitrose 382
Walker, Simon 588
Walt Disney 221
Warburg, Siegmund 257
Warner Chilcott 52
warrant 254, 356, 405, **G:32**
warrant arbitrage 577
Warsaw stock exchange 335
Washington consensus 659
Washington Mutual 662, 671
Watson Wyatt 567
weak-form efficiency 514, **G:33**
wealth management *see* private banking
Weaver, David 79
Weber, Axel 298, 317
weighted by share price 392, **G:33**
West China Cement 11
WestLB 101
WH Ireland 390
wheat 544, 546–7
whole-of-life policies 28, 120, **G:33**
wholesale bank 25, **G:33**
wholesale financial markets 5, 168, **G:33**
Wilhelmsson, Mats 347
Willebois, Joost van der Does de 347
William Hill 382
Wind 242
windfall **G:33**
winding-up **G:33**
winner's curse **G:33**
Winterflood Securities 618
Wipro 377
with profits endowment policies 120
without profits endowment policies 120
WolfsonMicroselectronics 386
wool 538
Woolland, John 87
Woolworths 386

working capital **G:33**
World Bank (International Bank for Reconstruction and Development) 253, 493, 549, 659, **G:33**
World on a Hanger 584
World Trade Centre 301, 660, **G:33**
writer of an option 443, 446–7, **G:33**

Xetra DAX *see* DAX 30
XN Checkout (XNC) 631

Yale University 588
yankees 251, **G:33**
Yarbrough, Ted 247
Yearsley, Ben 48
yellow strip 360, 365, **G:33**
Yes Bank 611
yield **G:33**
   bonds 255–6, 261–2, 271–4
   money markets 168, 180, 182, 183, 189
yield curve **G:33**
yield to market 196
yield to maturity (YTM, gross redemption yield, redemption yield) 225, 231, 261–2, 263–4, 266–7, 268, **G:33**
Yu, Gwen 560
Yusado, Ayako 588

Z/Yen Group 9
zero coupon bond (zero coupon preference share) **G:33**
   bonds 235, 245, 254, 265–6
   Treasury bills 184
Zimbabwe 297
Zuckerberg, Mark 334
Zurich 11